Freedom in the World

The findings of the *Comparative Survey of Freedom* and the Map of Freedom include events up to January 1, 2001.

Freedom in the World

The Annual Survey of Political Rights & Civil Liberties
2000-2001

Adrian Karatnycky
General Editor
and the Freedom House Survey Team

transaction

FOUNDED 1941

ISSN: 0732-6610
ISBN: 0-7658-0101-9(cloth);0-7658-0884-6(paper)
Printed in the United States of America

The Library of Congress has catalogued this serial title as follows:

Freedom in the world / —1978-
New York : Freedom House, 1978-
v. : map; 25 cm.—(Freedom House Book)
Annual.
ISSN 0732-6610=Freedom in the World.
1. Civil rights—Periodicals. I. R. Adrian Karatnycky, et al. I. Series.
JC571.F66   323.4'05-dc 19   82-642048
AACR 2   MARC-S
Library of Congress   [84101]

Contents

Foreword 1

The Survey Team 3

Freedom in the World 2000-2001 Adrian Karatnycky 5

Globalism Nightmare or Global Civil Society? Benjamin R. Barber 17

The Human Rights Agenda versus National Sovereignty Jeremy Robkin 26

Introduction 37

Country Reports 39

Related and Disputed Territories Reports 598

Survey Methodology 648

Tables and Ratings
Table of Independent Countries 655
Table of Related Territories 657
Table of Disputed Territories 657
Table of Social and Economic Indicators 658
Combined Average Ratings, Independent Countries 660
Combined Average Ratings, Related and Disputed Territories 661
Table of Electoral Democracies 662

Sources 664

The Map of Freedom—2000 667

Foreword

Freedom in the World is an institutional effort by Freedom House to monitor the progress and decline of political rights and civil liberties in 192 nations and 17 related and disputed territories. These year-end reviews of freedom began in 1955, when they were called the Balance Sheet of Freedom and, still later, the Annual Survey of the Progress of Freedom. This program was expanded in the early 1970s, and has appeared in a more developed context as a yearbook since 1978.

Since 1989, the survey project has been a year-long effort produced by our regional experts, consultants, and human rights specialists. The survey derives its information from a wide range of sources. Most valued of these are the many human rights activists, journalists, editors, and political figures around the world who keep us informed of the human rights situation in their countries

The survey team is grateful to the considerable advice and input of our *Freedom in the World* advisory board, consisting of Prof. David Becker, Prof. Daniel Brumberg, Dr. Larry Diamond, Prof. Charles Gati, Prof. Jeane J. Kirkpatrick, Thomas Lansner, Dr. Seymour Martin Lipset, Prof. Alexander Motyl, Dr. Joshua Muravchik, Dr. Daniel Pipes, and Prof. Arthur Waldron.

Throughout the year, Freedom House personnel regularly conduct fact-finding missions to gain more in-depth knowledge of the vast political transformations affecting our world. During these investigations, we make every effort to meet a cross section of political parties and associations, human rights monitors, religious figures, representatives of both the private sector and trade union movement, academics, and journalists.

During the past year, Freedom House staff and survey team members traveled to Argentina, Albania, Algeria, Bosnia-Herzegovina, Botswana, China, Croatia, Czech Republic, Canada, Costa Rica, Cuba, East Timor, Ecuador, Bulgaria, Egypt, France, Hungary, India, Israel, Jordan, Latvia, Lithuania, Mexico, Peru, Poland, Romania, Russia, Sierre Leone, Ukraine, Venezuela, and Yugoslavia. The Survey project team also consults a vast array of published source materials, ranging from the reports of other human rights organizations to often rare, regional newspapers and magazines.

Among those responsible for the production of *Freedom in the World* are Linda Stern, editor; Mark Wolkenfeld, production coordinator; and Trish Fox, proofreader. The cover was designed by Anne Green.

Principal support for *Freedom in the World* has been generously provided by the Lynde and Harry Bradley Foundation and the Smith Richardson Foundation.

The Survey Team

Martin Edwin "Mick" Andersen has worked as a correspondent for *Newsweek* and *The Washington Post* in Argentina. He has also served on the staff of the Senate Foreign Relations Committee and as a senior adviser for policy planning with the criminal division of the U.S. Justice Department. He has written for *Foreign Policy,* the *SAIS Review*, the *Los Angeles Times*, and *The Washington Times*. He recently edited a U.S. government-funded study on possible democratic transitions in post-Castro Cuba. He is the author of *Dossier Secreto: Argentina's Desaparecidos and the Myth of the "Dirty War,"* and a forthcoming history of Argentine law enforcement written in Spanish.

Gordon N. Bardos is a program officer and Balkans specialist at the Harriman Institute, Columbia University. He has written articles for *The Harriman Review*, *Cambridge Review of International Affairs*, and the *RFE/RL Research Report*.

Michael Goldfarb is press officer and a researcher at Freedom House. He has worked as a reporter in Israel for United Press International and as a writer for Time Online.

Charles Graybow is a former research coordinator of *Freedom in the World*. Since 1991, he has served as the Asia specialist for the survey. He has participated in human rights missions to several South Asian and West African countries.

Kristen Guida is a senior researcher at Freedom House and Middle East analyst for *Freedom in the World*, and has recently studied and traveled in the region. She coordinates research for the annual *Survey of Press Freedom* published by Freedom House.

Adrian Karatnycky is president of Freedom House and coauthor of several books on East European politics.

Edward R. McMahon is research assistant professor of Political Science and the director of the Center on Democratic Performance at the State University of New York at Binghamton. He recently served as senior advisor for democracy and governance at the Bureau for Policy and Program Coordination, U.S. Agency for International Development. From 1989 to 1998, he was senior program officer and regional director for West, East, and Central Africa at the National Democratic Institute for International Affairs.

Aili Piano is a senior researcher at Freedom House and the coordinator of *Freedom in the World*, and has written for Freedom House's *Nations in Transit* survey since its inception in 1994. She is a specialist on the former Soviet Union and has worked as a diplomatic attaché at the Estonian Mission to the United Nations.

Arch Puddington is vice president for research at Freedom House. He has written widely on American foreign policy, race relations, organized labor, and the history of the cold war. He is the author of *Broadcasting Freedom: The Cold War Triumph of Radio Free Europe and Radio Liberty* and is currently writing a biography of the late trade union leader, Lane Kirkland.

Amanda Schnetzer is a senior researcher at Freedom House and the coordinator of *Nations in Transit*, a survey of political and economic conditions in the post-Communist world. Previously, she was a foreign policy researcher at the American Enterprise Institute.

Cindy Shiner has worked as a freelance journalist for the past ten years, spending much of her time in Africa. She has written for *The Washington Post*, done broadcasts for National Public Radio, and served as a consultant on Africa issues for Human Rights Watch.

Leonard R. Sussman is senior scholar in international communications at Freedom House and director of Freedom House's annual *Survey of Press Freedom*. He has written extensively on press freedom and global journalism.

Anny Wong is a policy analyst for the RAND Corporation. She has written books and articles on Japanese foreign policy, international environmental issues, and international relations in the Asia-Pacific region. She has lived and worked in Asia-Pacific countries, and received her doctorate from the University of Hawaii at Manoa.

Kendra Zaharescu is assistant to the president of Freedom House. She assisted with the coordination of the World Forum on Democracy, which was held in June 2000 and cosponsored by Freedom House and the Stefan Batory Foundation. From 1997 to 1999, she worked as a Peace Corps volunteer in Romania.

ACADEMIC ADVISERS

David Becker is associate professor of government at Dartmouth College.

Daniel Brumberg is assistant professor of government at Georgetown University.

Larry Diamond is senior research fellow at the Hoover Institution and coeditor of the *Journal of Democracy*.

Charles Gati is fellow and senior adjunct professor in European studies at the Foreign Policy Institute, School for Advanced International Studies, Johns Hopkins University.

Jeane J. Kirkpatrick, the former U.S. ambassador to the United Nations, is senior fellow at the American Enterprise Institute.

Thomas Lansner is assistant dean of student affairs and adjunct assistant professor of international affairs at the School of International and Public Affairs, Columbia University.

Seymour Martin Lipset is professor of public policy at the School of Public Policy, George Mason University.

Alexander J. Motyl is associate professor of political science and deputy director of the Center for Global Change and Governance, Rutgers University, Newark, New Jersey.

Joshua Muravchik is resident scholar at the American Enterprise Institute.

Daniel Pipes is director of the Middle East Forum and editor of *Middle East Quarterly*.

Arthur Waldron is professor of international relations at the University of Pennsylvania.

INTERNS
Alexandra Chopivsky
Kathleen Kim

Linda Stern, *General Editor*
Mark Wolkenfeld, *Production Coordinator*
Cover design by Anne Green

The 2000-2001 Freedom House Survey of Freedom

Adrian Karatnycky

As a new president assumes office, the United States has an opportunity to shape its foreign policy in an environment of democratic states that share America's commitment to democracy, the rule of law, and economic freedom rooted in property rights. This emerging environment should enhance the prospects of broad international cooperation on behalf of the expansion of freedom, prosperity, and stability.

In particular, the new administration will inherit a world in which there is forward momentum toward greater freedom. As the year 2000 draws to a close, Freedom House's year-end Survey of Freedom in the World shows no letup in the world's two-decade-long march toward increased political rights and civil liberties.

The State of Freedom: 2000

As the year draws to close, there are 86 Free countries (2,465.2 billion people; 40.69 percent of the world population) in which a broad range of political rights are respected; 58 Partly Free countries (1,435.8 billion people; 23.70 percent of the world's population) in which there is a mixed record with more limited political rights and civil liberties, often accompanied by corruption, weak rule of law, and the inordinate political dominance of a ruling party, in some cases characterized by ethnic or religious strife. There are 48 countries rated Not Free (2,157.5 billion people; representing 35.61 percent of the globe's population), in which basic political rights and civil liberties are denied.

In all, the Survey shows that in the year 2000, there has been significant progress toward freedom in 25 countries and significant setbacks for freedom in 18 countries. Moreover, 40.69 percent of people living under freedom is the highest in the history of the Survey.

The Decade's Trend

Today, there are ten more Free countries than five years ago. In the same period, there has been a decline in the number of Not Free countries by five, and there are four fewer Partly Free countries. The trend is even more dramatic when compared to the state of affairs a decade ago. Since 1990, there has been an overall increase of 21 in the number of Free countries, an increase of 8 in the number of Partly Free states, and a drop of 2 in the number of Not Free states. These figures reflect an increase of 27 sovereign countries during the decade, largely due to the disintegration and separation of multinational states.

These gains have been registered during a period when many believed that the world was spinning out of control because of a series of bloody and widely reported civil wars and interethnic conflicts. In fact, the Survey evidence shows clear gains for freedom in each of the last seven years. Moreover, Survey evidence indicates that the impression of a growing number of ethnic conflicts is considerably exaggerated. In fact,

Freedom in the World—2000-2001

The population of the world as estimated in mid-2000 is 6,058.5 million persons, who reside in 192 sovereign states. The level of political rights and civil liberties as shown comparatively by the Freedom House Survey is:

Free: 2,465.2 million (40.69 percent of the world's population) live in 86 of the states.

Partly Free: 1,435.8 million (23.70 percent of the world's population) live in 58 of the states.

Not Free: 2,157.5 million (35.61 percent of the world's population) live in 48 of the states.

A Record of the Survey
(population in millions)

SURVEY DATE	FREE	PARTLY FREE	NOT FREE	WORLD POPULATION
January '81	1,613.0 (35.90%)	970.9 (21.60%)	1,911.9 (42.50%)	4,495.8
January '83	1,665.4 (36.32%)	918.8 (20.04%)	2,000.2 (43.64%)	4,584.1
January '85	1,671.4 (34.85%)	1,117.4 (23.30%)	2,007.0 (41.85%)	4,795.8
January '87	1,842.5 (37.10%)	1,171.5 (23.60%)	1,949.9 (39.30%)	4,963.9
January '89	1,992.8 (38.86%)	1,027.9 (20.05%)	2,107.3 (41.09%)	5,128.0
January '90	2,034.4 (38.87%)	1,143.7 (21.85%)	2,055.9 (39.28%)	5,234.0
January '91	2,088.2 (39.23%)	1,485.7 (27.91%)	1,748.7 (32.86%)	5,322.6
January '92 (a)	1,359.3 (25.29%)	2,306.6 (42.92%)	1,708.2 (31.79%)	5,374.2
January '93	1,352.2 (24.83%)	2,403.3 (44.11%)	1,690.4 (31.06%)	5,446.0
January '94	1,046.2 (19.00%)	2,224.4 (40.41%)	2,234.6 (40.59%)	5,505.2
January '95	1,119.7 (19.97%)	2,243.4 (40.01%)	2,243.9 (40.02%)	5,607.0
January '96	1,114.5 (19.55%)	2,365.8 (41.49%)	2,221.2 (38.96%)	5,701.5
January '97	1,250.3 (21.67%)	2,260.1 (39.16%)	2,260.6 (39.17%)	5,771.0
January '98	1,266.0 (21.71%)	2,281.9 (39.12%)	2,284.6 (39.17%)	5,832.5
January '99 (b)	2,354.0 (39.84%)	1,570.6 (26.59%)	1,984.1 (33.58%)	5,908.7
January 2000	2,324.9 (38.90%)	1,529.0 (25.58%)	2,122.4 (35.51%)	5,976.3
January 2001	2,465.2 (40.69%)	1,435.8 (23.70%)	2,157.5 (35.61%)	6,058.5

(a) The large shift in the population figure between 1991 and 1992 is due to India's change from Free to Partly Free.

(b) The large shift in the population figure between 1998 and 1999 is due to India's change from Partly Free to Free.

the last few years have seen an overall decline in the number of major civil wars and interstate conflicts that claim more than 1,000 lives per annum.

Country Trends

Four countries entered the ranks of the Free: Mexico, Croatia, Ghana, and Suriname. Mexico held a successful free and fair presidential election that marked the end of the uninterrupted reign of the country's former dominant party—the Institutional Revolutionary Party (PRI)—and the election of Vicente Fox, candidate of the opposition National Action Party (PAN). The successful election of a president from outside the PRI, which had governed Mexico since 1929, was accompanied by continuing diversification in the media and an increasingly vibrant civil society.

Croatia, which saw the election of a reform-oriented government, registered significant progress in the deepening of the rule of law, the emergence of greater press freedom and more independent media, and an increasing vibrancy within civil society. In addition, the coming to power of a new political coalition resulted in significant improvements in the areas of governance, accountability, and transparency.

Suriname advanced from Partly Free to the ranks of Free countries as a result of a free and fair election process that signaled an end to the military's significant influence on the country's political life. As importantly, civil liberties made gains because of diligent efforts by the government to hold former officials accountable for past human rights violations.

Ghana held free and fair parliamentary and presidential elections in December 2000, and saw an opposition party emerge as the country's new leading political force.

One country, Congo (Brazzaville), moved forward from Not Free to Partly Free as a result of the resolution of the country's civil war through the consolidation of a peace process and an easing of repression stemming from the peace agreement that was signed in late 1999.

Three countries—Fiji, the Solomon Islands, and Ecuador—were dropped from Free to Partly Free designations.

Fiji experienced a coup organized by rebels from the indigenous island population. Although the military eventually stepped in and restored order, the legitimately elected leadership was not reinstalled. Instead, the military imposed an interim civilian government in contravention of the country's constitution.

The Global Trend			
	Free	Partly Free	Not Free
1990-1991	65	50	50
1995-1996	76	62	53
2000-2001	86	58	48

Tracking Democracy	
Number of Democracies	
1995-1996	117
2000-2001	120

The Solomon Islands saw its rating decline because of an 18-month reign of ethnic violence that brought about a practical collapse of all government institutions. While a peace agreement was signed in October between the two warring factions, peace remains tenuous.

Ecuador also exited the ranks of the Free as a result of a partially successful military coup in January that brought about the overthrow of the elected president, who was subsequently replaced by the country's vice president.

Two countries—the Kyrgyz Republic and Haiti— moved from the ranks of the Partly Free to the Not Free. The Kyrgyz Republic experienced the further consolidation of power by the country's president and a presidential and parliamentary election process that was neither free nor fair. Haiti underwent a series of elections deemed to be neither free nor fair by international observers.

Twenty countries registered significant progress in political rights and civil liberties—though not enough to warrant a category shift. They are Antigua and Barbuda, Argentina, Benin, Bosnia and Herzegovina, Brazil, Djibouti, Dominican Republic, East Timor, Indonesia, Mali, Niger, Oman, Pakistan, Peru, Senegal, Somalia, Taiwan, Uruguay, Vietnam, and Yugoslavia.

Among the most significant of the countries registering gains in freedom was Peru, where the broadcast of a videotape showing the country's security chief bribing a parliamentarian precipitated a political crisis that eventually ended in the resignation of the authoritarian president, Alberto Fujimori. Fujimori's resignation led to the installation of a respected caretaker president and a government headed by former United Nations Secretary-General Javier Perez de Cuellar. New elections are scheduled for April 2001. In addition, post-Fujimori Peru has seen the expansion of media freedoms.

Free and fair presidential elections and the orderly transfer of power in Taiwan further improved the country's level of political freedom. Progress was also observable in the prosecution of government officials linked to allegations involving defense contracts.

Despite worrying signs of ethnic strife, significant steps toward political freedom and human rights also were taken in Indonesia, where, despite interethnic tensions, the young democratic government began to make efforts to examine and punish former high-ranking leaders from the Suharto era for corruption. Political rights advanced as a more dynamic and pluralistic system saw the strengthened role of political parties.

In Oman, gains in civil liberties resulted from the expansion of opportunity for women, particularly in the economic and business spheres.

There were 13 countries that declined in freedom without changing categories: Azerbaijan, Côte d'Ivoire, Georgia, Guinea-Bissau, Israel, Liberia, Mace–donia, Nigeria, Russia, Sierra Leone, Trinidad and Tobago, Uganda, and Ukraine.

The 11 Worst-Rated Countries

Afghanistan
Burma
Cuba
Equatorial Guinea
Iraq
North Korea
Libya
Saudi Arabia
Sudan
Syria
Turkmenistan

The 2 Worst-Rated Disputed Territories

Chechnya (Russia)
Tibet (China)

Among the countries that saw significant erosion of freedom was Azerbaijan, where a rigged election in November was not only marred by electoral violations and voter fraud, but was accompanied by severe pressure on independent civic groups, worker organizations, and media that are not sympathetic to the ruling regime. Freedom of association was also circumscribed through police pressures against protesters.

In Russia, political rights eroded as a result of serious irregularities in the country's March presidential election, particularly heavy government pressures on the press, and the absence of equal access by presidential candidates to the broadcast media.

In Ukraine, an end-of-year scandal involving the disappearance of an eminent journalist refocused attention on extensive government harassment of independent media through tax inspections, confiscation of print runs, and extensive use of libel law.

Most Repressive

Today, there are 48 states that systematically deny a broad range of freedoms and violate basic political rights and civil liberties. Among these, 11 countries have been given the Survey's lowest rating of 7 for political rights and 7 for civil liberties. The 11 worst-rated countries represent a narrow range of systems and cultures. Two—Cuba and North Korea—are one-party Marxist-Leninist regimes and 7 are majority-Islamic countries (Afghanistan, Iraq, Libya, Saudi Arabia, Sudan, Syria, and Turkmenistan). Of these, Turkmenistan is a post-Communist society; Iraq, Libya, and Syria are led by secular Baathist, or socialist, parties. Afghanistan is a fundamentalist Islamic theocracy; Sudan is led by a government that also embraces fundamentalist Islamic rhetoric; and Saudi Arabia has made important concessions to its conservative Islamic clerical leadership. The remaining worst-rated countries are Burma, a tightly controlled military dictatorship, and Equatorial Guinea. There are also two worst-rated territories: Tibet (under Chinese jurisdiction) and Chechnya, a region where a large segment of the indigenous population has been engaged in a protracted struggle for independence from Russia.

Electoral Democracy

For the seventh consecutive year, freedom has registered incremental gains, both in terms of enhanced political rights and in increased civil rights and liberties. Progress towards freer civic institutions, a vibrant and diverse press, and a strengthened rule of law has coincided with the growth of electoral democracy.

Electoral democracy, while a crucial element of freedom, is not by itself the equivalent of freedom. Electoral democracies are characterized by a range of competing political parties with alternative programs, the ability of these parties to raise and use resources in open political campaigns, and a free and fair election process. Electoral democracies require a diffusion of power among different branches of government and a regular cycle of elections in an environment in which an orderly change of the political elite among competing groups is possible.

Electoral democracies may differ from Free countries in that they may still suffer serious defects in interethnic relations, discrimination against minorities and social groups, and a weak rule of law.

Today, there are 120 electoral democracies. That number has remained relatively steady in the last four years. These democracies represent 63 percent of the world's states. Three significant entrants into the ranks of electoral democracies were Mexico, which held its first fully free and fair presidential elections after what were widely regarded as free and fair parliamentary and state elections in 1997 and 1998; Senegal, where free and fair presidential elections led to a peaceful transfer of power to an opposition leader; and Yugoslavia, where a democratic election for president took place despite attempted fraud in the initial vote count, and the results of a parliamentary election were unchallenged by the competing political parties.

Fiji, the Kyrgyz Republic, and Haiti have exited the ranks of electoral democracies. Fiji lost its status as a democracy after a coup that, though largely unsuccessful, led to the overthrow of a democratically constituted government and its replacement by a government imposed by the military. The Kyrgyz Republic saw tainted elections that were neither free nor fair at the parliamentary and presidential levels. Haiti's elections for both president and parliament were deemed seriously flawed by the international community.

There are reasons to believe that next year will offer further momentum for new transitions toward democracy. One major candidate for movement towards freedom is Peru, where the authoritarian president, Alberto Fujimori, resigned and presidential elections were scheduled for April 2001. East Timor, too, is in the middle of a democratic transition that may lead to democratic elections.

Freedom and Prosperity

This year's Survey findings on political and civic freedoms have been compared with levels of economic prosperity in all countries. The Survey finds that higher levels of political freedom tend to correlate with higher levels of economic prosperity. Thus, the median per capita gross domestic product (GDP) for the most Free countries (those with a combined average of 1) is $20,847. The median GDP per capita for Free countries rated 1.5 is $9,094. Free countries with a combined average of 2 have a median GDP of $5,123, while Free countries with an average rating of 2.5 have a median GDP of $3,796. Countries on the cusp between Free and Partly Free (combined average rating of 3) have a median GDP of $2,718.

At the same time, Partly Free countries with a combined average rating of 3.5 have a median GDP of $2,006. Partly Free states with a rating of 4 have a median GDP of $1,940, while Partly Free states with a freedom rating of 4.5 have a median GDP of $3,194. States with a 5 rating—countries in which there are severe problems with rights abuses—have a median GDP of $1,398. More repressive states, with a 5.5 rating, have a median GDP of $2,317. Not Free states with a rating of 6 have a median GDP of $1,637. Highly repressive Not Free states with a combined score of 6.5 have a median GDP of $1,689, while the most repressive states have a median GDP of $2,892.

Significantly, while the freest countries are also the most prosperous and have the highest median and average per capita GDP, there is no similar absolute correlation between the most repressive states and the least prosperity. Indeed, the findings suggest that many impoverished countries preserve a higher degree of political rights and civil liberties than some prosperous states.

Among countries with a per capita GDP of more than $15,000, there were 24 rated Free; 2, Partly Free; and 3, Not Free. Of the countries with per capita GDP between $5,000 and $15,000, there were 32 rated Free; 9, Partly Free; and 7, Not Free. Among countries with a per capita GDP of between $2,500 and $5,000, there were 11 rated Free; 14, Partly Free; and 11, Not Free. Of countries with per capita GDP of $1,000 to $2,500, there were 6 rated Free; 16, Partly Free; and 17, Not Free. Among the poorest countries, those with a per capita GDP below $1,000, there were 2 rated Free; 12, Partly Free; and 7, Not Free. (Updated comparative figures were unavailable for 11 Free countries, 5 Partly Free countries, and 3 Not Free countries).

In the countries with the highest level of freedom (that is, those with a combined average rating from 1 to 2), we find a significant number of poorer countries such as Belize (per capita GDP: $4,566); Benin (per capita GDP: $867); Bolivia (per capita GDP: $2,269); Cape Verde (per capita GDP: $3,233); Jamaica (per capita GDP: $3,389), and São Tomé and Príncipe (per capita GDP: $1,469).

At the same time, among the countries with the greatest number of political and civil rights violations and a high degree of repression (combined average rating of 6-7), we find a handful of more prosperous states: Bahrain (per capita GDP: $13,111); Brunei (per capita GDP: $16,765); and Libya (per capita GDP: $6,697).

Thus, it is possible to conclude that significant national wealth does not automatically lead to increased levels of political, civic, and personal freedom. Nevertheless, the correlations between prosperity at the upper reaches of freedom and poverty at the lowest reaches of freedom are striking. Indeed, at the highest level of freedom, the median per capita GDP is nearly seven times greater than that recorded by the world's most repressive states.

Freedom and Economic Growth

While the Survey findings already suggest that high levels of respect for political rights and civil liberties are attainable by poorer countries, it is nevertheless important to examine whether the large number of prosperous countries in the Free category suggest that freedom is a consequence of prosperity and development or whether prosperity is a consequence of basic political and civic freedoms.

To attempt to answer the question, we looked at all countries with a population of one million or more and examined their records of average annual economic growth over a ten-year period. The data revealed that among all such Free countries, the average annual GDP growth rate was 2.56 percent, compared with 1.81 percent for Partly Free countries and 1.36 percent for Not Free countries. However, such data might reflect the dynamism of the advanced industrial countries, which are almost universally free and democratic.

The differences in the growth indicators of poorer countries were even more dramatic. Our survey found that for all Free countries with a per capita GDP of less than $5,000, the average ten-year annual growth rate was 3.23 percent. This was more than double the 1.47 average ten-year annual growth rates of Partly Free poorer countries (with a per capita GDP of less than $5,000). Finally, among the less-developed Not Free countries, average per capita GDP growth over a ten-year period stood at 1.41 percent, again less than half that of Free poorer countries. Less-developed Free countries that achieved average annual growth rates above four percent over a ten-year period included Benin, Bolivia, the Dominican Republic, El Salvador, India, and Papua New Guinea.

From these data, it appears that repressive countries with high sustained economic growth rates, such as China, are the exception rather than the rule. Indeed, it is possible to conclude that as a general principle, economic growth is accelerated in an environment of political freedom. Thus, the Survey findings support the position of such economists as Nobel laureate Amartya Sen, who views "development as freedom."

From these findings, it is possible to consider some of the reasons why economic development is promoted by greater levels of political freedom. A primary factor is the evidence that political freedom tends to reinforce economic freedom and a vibrant private sector based on property rights. Indeed, there is a high and statistically significant correlation between the level of political freedom as measured by Freedom House and economic freedom as measured by the Wall Street Journal/Heritage Foundation survey.

A second important reason is that open and free societies benefit from an active and engaged citizenry and lively, investigative news media that expose and help combat corruption. Moreover, the natural rotation of alternative political elites reduces the opportunities for cronyism and for incestuous relations between politicians and the business community. Additionally, free societies are characterized by a neutral and independent judiciary, which is essential in the enforcement of contracts and the honest adjudication of differences among parties. It also can be argued—as the Harvard scholar Dani Rodrik has shown—that free societies that protect the right to association and collective action create an environment conducive to a more balanced distribution of wealth and income. This, in turn, improves social stability and serves as an internal economic engine for prosperity by creating a vibrant, working middle class.

Regional Variations

At the dawn of the new millennium, democracy and freedom are the dominant trends in Western and East-Central Europe, in the Americas, and increasingly in the Asia-Pacific region. In the former Soviet Union the picture remains mixed, with progress toward freedom stalled and a number of countries consolidating into dictatorships. In Africa, too, Free societies and electoral democracies remain a distinct minority. While there are no true democracies or Free countries within the Arab world, and a low proportion of Free and democratic Muslim states, 1999 was a year of democratic ferment in the Islamic world. However, 2000 was marked by political stagnation, with a few modest gains offset by setbacks in Iran and Egypt, and an upsurge of violence between Israelis and Palestinians.

Of the 53 countries in Africa, 9 are Free (17 percent), 25 are Partly Free (47 percent), and 19 are Not Free (36 percent). Only 21 African countries (40 percent) are electoral democracies. Generally, the region continued to be the most dynamic part of the world, but there was little evidence of forward momentum toward greater openness. One small sign of hope this year was that eight African states registered gains for freedom while only six suffered significant setbacks.

In Asia, 18 of the region's 39 countries are Free (46 percent), 10 are Partly Free (26 percent), and 11 are Not Free (28 percent). Despite the looming presence of Communist China and the rhetoric of "Asian values," 23 (59 percent) of the region's polities are electoral democracies.

In East-Central Europe and the former U.S.S.R., there is now evidence of a deepening chasm. In Central Europe and parts of Eastern Europe, including the Baltic states, democracy and freedom prevail; in the Commonwealth of Independent States (CIS), however, progress toward the emergence of open societies has stalled or failed. Overall, 19 of the 27 post-Communist countries of East-Central Europe and the CIS are electoral democracies (70 percent). In addition, 11 of the region's states are Free (41 percent), 10 are Partly Free (37 percent), and 6 are Not Free (22 percent). Of the 12 non-Baltic former Soviet republics, 6 countries are Partly Free, 6 are Not Free, and none are Free. Stagnation and reversals for freedom characterized virtually all the non-Baltic Soviet states.

Western Europe remains the preserve of Free countries and democracies, with all 24 states both free and democratic.

Among the 35 countries in the Americas, 31 are electoral democracies (89 percent). In addition, 23 states are rated as Free (66 percent), 10 are Partly Free (28 percent), and 2—Cuba and Haiti—are Not Free (6 percent).

In the 14 Middle Eastern countries (excluding those in North Africa), the roots of democracy and freedom are weakest. In this region there is only one Free country, Israel (7 percent); there are three Partly Free states—Jordan, Kuwait, and Turkey (21 percent)—and ten countries that are Not Free (71 percent). Israel and Turkey are the region's only electoral democracies (14 percent).

Freedom and Ethnicity

Just as there are important regional variations in basic freedoms and political systems, there are also noteworthy distinctions between mono-ethnic and multiethnic countries with regard to freedom and democracy. Indeed, democracy is, as a rule, significantly more successful in mono-ethnic societies (that is, societies in which there is a single dominant majority ethnic group representing more than two-thirds of the population) than in ethnically divided and multiethnic societies.

When this year's Survey data are examined through the prism of ethnic composition, they offer some revealing findings. For example, of Free countries, 64 (74 percent) have a dominant ethnic majority representing more than two-thirds of the population, while 22 (26 percent) do not. Among Partly Free countries, 24 (41 percent) are mono-ethnic, while 34 (59 percent) are multiethnic or ethnically divided. And among the Not Free states, there are 26 (54 percent) that are mono-ethnic, while 22 (46 percent) are not. In short, a state with a dominant ethnic group is some three times more likely to be Free than a multiethnic state.

Similar patterns can be found among the democracies. Of the world's 120 electoral democracies, 79 (66 percent) have a dominant ethnic group and 41 (34 percent) do not. Of the 72 countries that do not have a democratic government, 35 (49 percent) are mono-ethnic and 37 (51 percent) are not.

One reason for this outcome is that in ethnically divided and multiethnic societies, political parties tend to form around ethnic allegiances. This is particularly the case in multiethnic states where ethnic groups are not heterogeneously dispersed throughout the country, but live in specific geographic regions. Many African states fall into this pattern. At the same time, as a rule, in societies where there is a single dominant ethnic group, political mobilization along primarily ethnic lines is less likely and politics tend to divide along the lines of economic and class-based interests. This is the record of the nation-states in much of Western and Central Europe and in most countries in the Americas.

At the same time, it must be said that there are numerous examples of successful multiethnic societies, many of which have a strong tradition of decentralized power, federalism, and protection of ethnic and minority rights, and a strong and vibrant market system open to the participation of a broad range of religious and ethnic communities.

Major Events:
The Five Major Gains for Freedom and the Five Major Setbacks for Freedom in 2000

Each year, Freedom House points to five key events that have advanced freedom around the world and five key events that have constituted setbacks for liberty.

Five Major Gains for Freedom

1. Mexico: The election of President Vicente Fox brought democracy to Mexico after more than 70 years of virtual one-party government by the Institutional Revolutionary Party. Early signs suggest that Fox intends to reform and democratize Mexico's political and judicial structures.

2. Yugoslavia: With the election of President Vojislav Kostunica, the bloody rule of Slobodan Milosevic has come to an end, a development that gives rise to hope for genuine peace in the Balkans and the emergence of the rule of law in Belgrade.

3. New Asian Values: In the Philippines, impeachment procedures were brought against an allegedly corrupt president; in Indonesia, charges of corruption and abuse of power were advanced against military officers and the son of the former dictator; and in Taiwan, the justice minister launched a crackdown on corruption. All represent crucial gains for the rule of law in formerly authoritarian states and set a new model for democratic "Asian values."

4. Peru: The resignation of President Alberto Fujimori has been followed by important gains for political freedom, human rights, the rule of law, and the prospect of free and fair elections in April 2001.

5. The Community of Democracies: The convening in June 2000 of a conference of the world's democratic states creates the possibility of a new era of cooperation and concerted policy towards the spread of freedom.

Five Major Setbacks for Freedom

1. Israel and Palestine: The upsurge of violence represents a serious setback for peace and stability in the Middle East.

2. Erosion of political liberties in Russia and Ukraine: Both countries have suffered from growing authoritarianism and continuing rampant corruption.

3. Venezuela: Despite the holding of free and fair elections, President Hugo Chavez has expanded his attempt to centralize control from the state sector to civil society, including a naked power grab aimed at the country's independent trade unions.

4. Iran: Prospects for reform waned as conservative clerics led a backlash against the press, students, and moderate political figures.

5. War in Africa: Civil war, ethnic conflict, and war between states engulfed much of Africa, with little relief in sight. Most disturbing is the prospect of a widening of Sierra Leone's civil strife into Guinea and neighboring states.

Policy Implications

For the new team that will shape U.S. foreign policy and for the new U.S. Congress, the Survey's findings offer some important signposts. First, they show that the U.S. commitment to the promotion of democracy initiated in the Reagan administration, continued under President Bush, and expanded under President Clinton, has borne fruit. U.S. moral and material support for civic movements, independent media, property rights, and the rule of law in transitional and closed societies, coupled with diplomatic pressures, has helped advance democracy's tide.

The advance of fundamental freedoms around the world creates new opportunities for international cooperation on behalf of security, freedom, and economic growth.

Both major U.S. political parties appear to understand the importance of this trend. In its 2000 platform, the Republican Party called for the creation of a Global Fellowship of Freedom. The Democratic Clinton administration, through U.S. Secretary of State Madeleine Albright, played a key role in promoting cooperation through the Community of Democracies.

As this bipartisan consensus has taken shape, a sharp debate has unfolded over how to promote global respect for human rights. On one side are strong proponents of U.S. sovereignty, who are skeptical of the efficacy, reliability, and jurisdiction of a growing body of "international law" that is not subject to the regulation and modification of democratically constituted legislative authority. On the other are those who argue for permanent institutions to enforce international law, including the emerging International Criminal Court.

A middle ground on which both sides could agree rests in the fostering of systematic cooperation among the countries that adhere to the rule of law and democratic practice, and increased cooperation among the democracies in exerting pressure against regimes that violate basic rights and support terrorism.

In this regard, the limited progress made in the last year toward the creation of the Community of Democracies creates important new possibilities. The Community of Democracies—a ministerial-level meeting of 107 countries—adopted a wide-ranging declaration in Warsaw in June 2000. The declaration pledged states to work together in coordinated fashion in assisting transitional societies. It also pledged the Community to create democracy caucuses in global and regional organizations. However, the credibility of the Community was undermined by the participation of several states in which democratic practices are routinely violated. The evolution of the Community of Democracies should, therefore, proceed on the basis of rigorous conditions of membership and should unite only established democratic states and transitional societies in which free and fair multiparty elections have occurred.

Significantly, the Community of Democracies initiative has been followed up at the United Nations, where for the first time a caucus of the democracies has been established and has begun to meet. This precedent deserves to be replicated at other international bodies and can become an important force for the reform of ineffective international organizations.

No one expects cooperation among free and open societies to produce unanimity of views. Still, on issues such as coordinated responses to threats against emerging democracies, cooperation against rogue and genocidal regimes, and commitments to strengthening civil society and the private sector, consensus can be shaped with proper U.S. leadership.

As the Survey's findings indicate, the promotion of political freedom is not exclusively a matter of values or morality. The Survey's findings make clear that political rights and civil liberties can also reinforce economic development. This in turn suggests that efforts to help strengthen property rights, market systems, and the rule of law should be part of the effort to assist less-developed countries.

If the leaders of the new administration and the Congress reaffirm and deepen their commitment to the promotion of democracy around the world, they can play a key role in shaping a more prosperous, more open, and—over time—more secure world.

Adrian Karatnycky is president of Freedom House.

Democracy and Globalism

The following two essays take up the question of the relationship between globalism, human rights, democracy, and national sovereignty. Globalism, of course, can come in various forms. To most, the concept of globalism is directly related to the spread of a world economy, free trade, and open markets. There are, however, other aspects to globalism, in particular the relatively recent movement to expand the scope of international law in ways that would supercede national sovereignty in such areas as human rights and the environment.

In *Freedom in the World: 2000-2001*, two authorities on the globalist phenomenon set forth their views on the strengths, and, especially, the dangers of these new trends. Benjamin R. Barber focuses his attention on the potential impact on democracy and individual autonomy inherent in the rise of megacorporations and a world regime where multinational corporations become ever more powerful. Unlike some critics of globalism, Barber recognizes both the inevitability of a world economy as well as its potential benefits. Moreover, he sees the rise of transnational movements for citizen participation, human rights, and social justice as an important and altogether positive part of the globalist equation.

Jeremy Rabkin, by contrast, issues a warning against the ambitions and institutions of the global human rights movement. Rabkin's specific concern is the erosion of national sovereignty inherent in such organizations as the International Criminal Court, and in the efforts to place foreign nationals on trial for human rights offenses, as Spain tried to do in the case of former Chilean President Augusto Pinochet. Rabkin believes that human rights might well be undermined by a human rights regime that becomes overly intrusive and treats with disdain the right of emerging democratic states to forge their own path to peace and justice without the intervention of the "world community."

Globalism Nightmare or Global Civil Society?

Benjamin R. Barber

William Jefferson Clinton's two terms are over, and George W. Bush's first term has just begun. Despite the many differences, the two men share one premise: a belief in the inevitability and deep importance of globalization. We live in a global world, where interdependence in economics, ecology, technology, and entertainment means that no nation can any longer survive as an island. Not North Korea, not Cuba, not Afghanistan, not even Texas. At the same time that globalization's influence is becoming an ineluctable presence, the character of globalization is becoming ever more skewed. Economic concerns increasingly are dominating politics. While we are hardly living in the twilight of sovereignty that writers like Walter Wriston have prophesied, sovereignty—once the traditional mark of the nation-state—has been passing to market institutions such as the multinational corporation and the international bank. If Clinton really did build a bridge to the twenty-first century, it is the bridge of globalization—not actually his creation, but an edifice constructed from dollars, yen, and euros as well as labor, capital, and goods—which spans the once large chasm between nation-states and some indeterminate global society.

In principle, there is no reason why globalization should not mean political and civic integration as well as economic and financial internationalization, but in practice the last 20 years have witnessed a radical asymmetry in its primary tendencies—an asymmetry that privileges the economic and market sectors and marginalizes the political sector and makes the idea of global civil society look more like a pipe dream than a reality. Global markets prefer the private to the public, the commercial to the civic, and the consumerist to the social. They associate liberty with the corporate sector, however monopolistic it may be, while associating coercion and dependency with the government sector, however democratic it may be. They treat crucial democratic values as so many relics of a previrtual civilization. Finally, they point to fundamental changes in the relationship between capitalism and democracy brought about by the new information economy—changes that have remained too much on the periphery of the debate.

The Radical Asymmetries of Globalization

The asymmetry of the new globalism is evident in mergers like those of Disney and ABC; Viacom and CBS; MCI, WorldCom, and Sprint; and now AOL, Time Warner, and EMI. It is manifest in the new global reach of effective software monopolies such as Microsoft. The elephantine entities created by mergers present a challenge not just to economic competition in the domain of goods, labor, and capital, but to democracy and its defining virtues: free and autonomous information (which can only be guaranteed by the independent existence of plural, discretely owned media); social and political diversity (which can only be guaranteed by genuine pluralism in society); and full participation by citizens in deciding public policies and securing public goods (which can only be guaranteed by a robust public domain in which public goods and the nature of the society in which we live are democratically chosen). When Congress passed the 1996 Telecommunications Bill—the first major piece of legislation dealing with new media since the Federal Communications Act of 1934 (which had treated radio transmissions as a public utility worthy of government protection)—it effectively ceded the modern information economy to the private sector, and hence to the forces that control global markets. In doing so, it legitimized the continuing globalization of our economic vices in the absence of any globalization of our civic virtues.

There is nothing intrinsic in globalization that affords vice an advantage, but when globalization is skewed towards private relationships and values and eludes public regulation and mores, it fosters global vices and restrains global virtues. Hence, we appear to have more successfully globalized crime, drugs, and terrorism than law enforcement, medicine, and conflict resolution; we have made more progress in markets for exploitation, servitude, and pornography than in institutions guaranteeing equity, fairness, and literacy; we've speculated in capital rather than creativity and amassed private capital at the expense of humanity, rather than securing social capital in humanity's name. Consequently, civil society, citizenship, and civic virtue have remained properties of the democratic nation-state, untenable in the anarchy of global markets. Ironically, national boundaries have become too porous to hold the economy in, without becoming flexible enough to let democracy out.

The difficulty nation-states have with globalization comes not just from the force of what is happening in the international arena but from ideological developments within nation-states. For the market anarchy of the global economy is, to a degree, being replicated within nations by the still-powerful ideology of privatization. When President Clinton proclaimed the "end of the era of big government" in his 1996 State of the Union address, he in effect certified the privatization of power on the center left. Not decentralization—the devolution of power down the democratic public ladder to states, municipalities, and neighborhoods—but privatization, the shifting of concentrated power at the highest levels from public to private hands, without any devolution but with a pronounced de-democratization. Power shifted from authorities that were hierarchical, but were also public, transparent, and accountable, to authorities that were equally hierarchical but private, opaque, and undemocratic. This is not decentralization but de-democratization. It seems likely to continue in the new corporatist cabinet being assembled by George W. Bush, for whom privatization appears to remain a primary goal (although President Bush has also acknowledged the importance of citizenship and community in his inaugural speech, so a fair assessment cannot yet be made). President Bush's Justice Department's announced philosophy of deemphasizing antitrust and antimerger activity is likely to encourage accelerating merger mania in (what in *Jihad vs. McWorld* I have called) the "infotainment telesector," further concentrating private power over the information economy and effectively destroying the autonomy, diversity, and integrity of the sector most essential to democracy. The new monopolies are particularly insidious because while monopolies of the nineteenth century were in durable goods and natural resources, and exercised control over the goods of the body, new information age monopolies of the twenty-first century are over news, entertainment, and knowledge, and exercise control over the goods of the mind and spirit. Privatization ideology seems to blinker us, making coercion and control from below invisible: when governments control information and news, we call it totalitarianism, but when monopolistic corporations control them, we call it virtual integration and free-market synergy.

Some argue that the impact on diversity is not critical, because hardware and information delivery "pipes" appear to be multiplying (satellites, cable, fiber optic networks). Yet a business section background article on the AOL takeover of Time Warner in *The New York Times* carried the headline "Takeover May Increase U.S. Cultural Dominance of the Web on the Continent." An invisible twin headline might have read "Takeover May Increase Cultural Dominance of the World's Largest Media Company Over American Audiences." Analysts argue AOL and Time Warner cover different consumer bases, and the new partners, Steve Case of AOL and Gerald Levin of Time Warner, both promise to pursue "open access" on cable so that the owners of the pipes that carry content do not become monopoly gatekeepers of the content their pipes carry. However, it is hardly clear between AOL and Time Warner who actually represents the pipes and who the content. That is the whole point of vertical integration. AOL controls online content, but as a Web server is also a monolithic Web portal. Time Warner wanted the deal to get its content on the Web. Time Warner is a content provider but, via its control of cable installations, also controls pipes. AOL wanted the deal to get its Net services on fast, hard-wired cable (it currently depends on snail-speed telephone lines). To suggest there is no real overlap, to suggest there is other than *one* audience and *one* information market, is to badly misunderstand the technology and to muddy the real issues of monopoly and globalization in the new information society. As the *New York Times* media columnist Denise Caruso has written, in the aftermath of the AOL/Time Warner deal, there is good reason to be urgently concerned with "the future of broadband and how best to ensure that no single company abuses its control of the Internet's infrastructure" (January 31, 2000). Europeans already view the Web with alarm as one more stalking-horse for America's content monopolies.

They have a point. The object of "convergence" is to eliminate the features that separate hardware and software, the carriers and the content, until there is a seamless stream of information and entertainment entering your home at maximum speed, with maximum interactivity, and maximum viewing ease. One medium, one content, one audience. Telephones, computers, televisions, VCRs, DVDs, video stores, and content companies are the segmented way of the past. The new "push-technology" media company in Hollywood, for example, must control them all; in an economy that demands integration and convergence, this means they must control (own) one another.

Under such circumstances, monopoly is hardly an accidental outcome but rather a necessary condition for doing business in this new world. Vertical integration is not an economic strategy but a condition of synergy. When, in response to the government's hard questions about Microsoft's monopoly, Bill Gates insists his integration of an Internet portal into his Windows computer operating system is a "natural" extension of his original product, he is being truthful. However, the truth he tells is that convergence means monopoly, and that synergy means vertical integration, and that a capitalism still defined by real diversity, genuine competition, plural markets, and multiple firms is an anachronism—that the practices of the industrial past have no place in the postindustrial, information-economy future, above all in the global economy, where information technology behemoths bestride the world like a colossus.

To a degree, such development represents nothing more than a new and powerful logic of the information economy, one that has to dictate its own imperatives. The challenge is that, in the global arena, we have not figured out the impact of this new economic logic in which monopoly is a public good on the older traditional logic of the democratic society which holds that monopoly is a public bad. There were good reasons for thinking that many broadsides and newspapers and magazines were better than a few when the Founding Fathers wrote the First Amendment. There were good reasons for thinking that broadcast media were public utilities over which the public had special claims when legislators wrote the Federal Communications Act in 1934. There were good reasons for thinking that diversity of content and pluralism of culture were integral virtues of a democratic society when America made multiculturalism an educational goal of the 1980s and 1990s. Does an "advance" in private technological and economic logic mean that the public logic of democracy must accommodate itself uncomplainingly to that change? Or is it technology and the information economy that need to be reassessed and revised to meet our public goals and common good as a democratic people? Should private logic dominate public logic in a democracy? How about on the world stage, where governments are no longer the prime-time players? Are Steve Case, Gerald Levin, and Ted Turner appropriate unelected representatives to shape not only America's, but the world's, destiny as an information society? Shelley called poets the "unacknowledged legislators of the world," but it appears that the captains of computing are today's global lawmakers. Will their decisions become de facto legislation for peoples to whom they have no accountability? These troublesome questions cannot be answered in the context of national politics. Nor can we answer them in a global setting where anarchy is the civic rule and market Darwinism the operating principle. How do we address the erosion of democracy in the asymmetrical setting of global markets, where such civic and political tools as are available to us within nations have gone missing altogether?

The outlook is not sanguine, but neither is it quite so pessimistic as the diagnosis suggests. For there is an emerging international alternative to global markets in new transnational civic organizations and social movements that in the last few years have finally gained a foothold. While demonstrators in Seattle, Prague, and London protested the dehumanizing anarchy of global institutions that seemed to have abdicated responsibility for the fiscal and labor arenas for which their creators had given them responsibility—the International Monetary Fund (IMF), the World Trade Organization (WTO), and the World Bank—practical women and men in nongovernmental organizations (NGOs), nonprofits, and existing international organizations were working hard to forge new tools. At the same time, groups both liberal and conservative within nation-states were marking the limits of the privatization strategy, and looking for ways to secure traditional values, pluralist choices, and genuine cultural and civic diversity. This in turn creates a perspective that can help nation-states reassert control over the global economy and its telecommunication technologies through traditional concert-of-nations approaches. After all, the IMF and the WTO are not supranational organizations but the tools of groups of powerful nations. They will bend to the will of the Group of 8, if G-8 governments can once again represent the public interests of their sovereign peoples and can find ways to cooperate with one another around those public interests. Likewise, international institutions of the kind that have proliferated in the umbra of the United Nations still offer ample opportunities for cooperation around civic ends as long as they can be separated from partisan political programs. Let me offer a brief portrait of both the transnational civic approach and the traditional concert-of-nations approach. Between the two of them, progressive critics of global market anarchy have a real chance to become relevant. This is especially true in light of the attention being paid to issues of global civil society both by grant-making foundations like Ford, Rockefeller, and the Carnegie Corporation, and by operating foundations such as Freedom House and George Soros's Open Society Institute.

The Transnational Civil Society Approach

Supporters of market approaches to social interaction often forget that the marketplace functions effectively within nation-states because it is only one of three sectors. The private business sector is not only legally constituted and regulated by the public government sector (the corporation is a legal construction), but the two are, in turn, mediated by a civil society that, like government, is public and composed of communities and other collective associations, but like the market is voluntary and free. Within nation-states, it is not the market alone, but this stable tripod of governmental, civic, and private institutions that generates liberty and produces the pluralistic goods of a free society. Rip the market from its nesting place in nation-states, however, and you have wild capitalism—wild not in itself (the market is supposed to be aggressively competitive), but by globalizing its ambitions, it slips the civilizing embrace of its nation-state hosts.

The reaction to the global market's anarchy has often been frustration and reactionary nationalism. Protectionism, isolationism, America-firstism, and the kind of go-it-alone bravado we saw in the last Congress betray a deep insecurity in the face of a world out of control. The "resistance groups" that took to the streets in Seattle, Washington, D.C., and Prague, and will presumably orchestrate protests around future WTO and IMF meetings, cannot, however, really claim to speak for the world. As Egypt's economy minister Youssef Boutros-Ghali said, "The world is not represented on the streets of Seattle. The truth is, most of the world's population was inside the conference in Seattle, not outside" (the *New York Times,* A21, February 1, 2000). In fact, there is (in former Mexican President Ernesto Zedillo's critical phrase), an element of "globophobia" in America's fear of a world out of control—a world in which American soldiers serve under foreign command, Islamic fundamentalists conspire to wage terror in the American heartland, jobs hemorrhage abroad, immigrants inundate the nation and rend its fragile unity. This can look like an American version of Austrian ultra-nationalist Jorg Haider's politics of fear.

The politics of fear is not the only stance possible, however. The world is out of control because the instruments of control—democratic governing institutions and their civil society supports—simply do not exist in the international setting where markets in currency, labor, and goods run like engines without governors. Nonetheless, there are signs of an emerging internationalism, around transnational civic institutions, global social movement, and a world "public opinion" yoked to the human rights movement, that promise a degree of countervailing power in the international arena and that serve as an alternative to the reactionary politics of Pat Buchanan or Jorg Haider. For a long time, when protesters would cry "no globalization without representation," one would look in vain for a global "we the people" to be represented. That is now changing. There is another internationalism out there today, a forming crystal around which a more extensive global "we the people" can accrete. Protests will not roll back market globalization—which is ineluctable and irreversible—but people who care about the public good can work to create on a global scale the civic balance found within nations. Five years ago there were NGOs and UN institutions, but little in the way of a global civic movement. Today that has changed. Look at these examples drawn from the last half dozen years:

· Freedom House, the Batory Foundation (in Poland), the U.S. State Department, and the government of Poland collaborate in convening an international meeting of "the democracies" in Warsaw, in which parallel meetings of foreign ministers and NGOs are held, featuring significant interaction among them (Warsaw, June 2000).

· The market-friendly, stealth Multilateral Agreement on Investment that would further erode national attempts to regulate foreign investment is subjected to broad citizen scrutiny and indefinitely deferred.

· The Clinton administration, in a final act, approves the creation of the new International Criminal Tribunal, long opposed by the U.S. Congress (congressional approval will eventually be required, but the president's concurrence is a breakthrough).

· A young woman named Jody Williams, with celebrity help from a princess (sadly, deceased), creates a worldwide civic movement for a ban on land mines that actually enacts a treaty to which a majority of the world's nations (not including the United States) subscribe.

· A Bangladeshi visionary develops an idea for microfinancing that makes mini-loans to women in third world societies that at once jump-starts enterprise and liberates women from traditional servitude; the idea becomes a tool of UNCTAD, the World Bank, and many other international institutions.

· Striking fear into retired tyrants everywhere, European public opinion and spirited English law lords make possible the arrest of a Chilean former dictator who may actually be tried in Spain, where he has been charged for his crimes; ill-health gets Pinochet off the hook (he is back in Chile as of 2001), but the tocsin has sounded. Dictators are no longer safe in their retirement havens.

· Women's groups from around the world meet in Beijing in a demonstration of international solidarity that asks nothing of national governments and everything of civic institutions that are powerfully reinforced by their action.

· Citizen groups use "Good Housekeeping Seal" methods to underwrite safe fisheries ("Dolphin-safe Tuna") and rug manufacturing without child labor ("Rugmark"), while students at Duke University lead a movement to assure that campus sports apparel is not manufactured in child-exploiting sweatshops; the Clinton administration pushes for a voluntary partnership of apparel manufacturers aimed at curbing abuses.

· Hundreds of NGOs gather regularly in new international organizations like Civicus, the World Forum on Democracy, the National Endowment for Democracy, and Transparency International, beginning to establish the infrastructure and civic networking across nations that corporations have enjoyed for decades courtesy of the World Economic Forum at Davos, Switzerland.

· Global Internet communication among groups facilitated by organizations like Peter Armstrong's OneWorld.org and Globalvision's new Media Channel.org supersite are diverting the new telecommunications from pure commerce to the public interests of global civil society.

· President Clinton offers the corporate leaders at Davos a "wake-up call" in 2000 reminding them that there are "new forces seeking to be heard in the global dialogue," progressive forces that want to democratize rather than withdraw from the new world order, while the new Bush administration continues the new focus on global economics as a crucial dimension of American foreign policy.

· "Europe" reacts as "Europe" to coalition talks between Austria's traditional parties and Jorg Haider's reactionary Freedom Party, again signaling the potency of an emerging transnational public opinion operating across state boundaries.

These civic efforts—the work of citizens rather than governments, or of governments reacting to citizens (and not just their own)—embody a global public opinion in the making, a global civic engagement that can alone give the abstraction of international rights political weight, a natural outreach of citizens and civic groups that make entities like "Europe" more than a mere function of economic and security concerns. Coteries of NGOs, the shifting voice of global public opinion, and the unsteady hand of the international rights movement may not be the equal of multinational corporations or international banks, but they represent a significant starting place for countervailing power. They put flesh on the bare bones of legalistic doctrines of universal rights. James Madison noted that a declaration of rights is a paper fortress from which it is impossible to defend real rights. Rights depend on engaged citizens and a civic space where their activities are possible. These new transnational civic spaces offer possibilities for transnational citizenship and hence an anchor for global rights.

De-Privatizing the State (The Concert-of-Nations Approach)

These emerging transnational civic realities cannot allow us to fool ourselves into thinking that the Open Society Institute can compete with Soros's own investment funds, that Amnesty International or Medecins Sans Frontiéres is the equivalent in clout of AOL/Time Warner or the IMF. International markets spin out of control not just because the economy has been internationalized, but because nation by nation by nation we have conspired in the transfer of sovereignty from popular hands that are transparent and accountable to private hands that are neither. We remain bemused by privatization on the Thatcher-Reagan-Blair-Clinton model and so are unable to avail ourselves of the many potential control mechanisms already in place. We bemoan the absence of international regulation over and governance of free markets, but in truth the international institutions most often vilified are ultimately instruments of sovereign nations acting in concert. Their subservience to multinational corporations and powerful banking and financial interests reflects not the erosion of sovereignty but the sellout of sovereign peoples to the myths of privatization. Technically, like the UN, the WTO is itself a creature of nation-states and, like the IMF and many other market institutions, could be regarded as the exoskeleton of an international governance organism. However, privatization—globalization's nasty twin—has robbed the nations that nominally control it of their democratic will, and they appear to be servants rather than masters of the new global corporate sovereigns. With the animals running the zoo, those who seek such public good as environmental protection, transparency, accountability, labor safety, and the protection of children—or even an adequate legal framework that can secure fair competition and capitalist growth—look in vain for keepers, and finally settle for theatrics, raising a ruckus rather than effecting a change. This is not a partisan issue of right versus left. Social conservatives, mercantilist advocates of government regulation of competition in the name of fairness and diversity, and those who care about the traditional public goods (service, citizenship, social responsibility) from the so-called right side of the political spectrum, can join social progressives, democratic advocates of government regulation, and those who care about progressive public good (welfare, safety nets, equity) in opposing a raw laissez-faire approach to markets. Ecology is in truth a conservationist, and hence a conservative, approach to interacting with our environment (let's conserve our planetary heritage!).

By remaining vigilant (critics say stubborn) in confronting the pressures of privatization, France has in fact held open the possibility of exerting political control over the international arena through international institutions and it has done this in part because Gaullist "conservatives" have shown an interest in the public good no less robust than social democrats. Paris has generally been governed by Gaullists and remains one of the world's great cities in which the public good is passionately protected. Because, unlike the UN, most global trade organizations can be controlled by small numbers of powerful states, the attitudes of the French and Japanese and Americans to their own domestic "public sectors" will be a crucial determinant of how successfully global markets are regulated and managed. Were they to agree on policy, the G-8 nations could probably work their will at the IMF and the WTO. Ironically, although global markets erode national sovereignty, a reassertion of national sovereignty as a consequence of domestic political campaigns aimed at challenging privatization could go a long way towards controlling global markets.

Currently, the WTO treats national boycotts of imported goods, even when they are motivated by safety or environmental or child labor concerns, as illegal. Its members can change these provisions. Currently, third world nations worry with reason that first world environmental and safety and minimum wage concerns are a way of putting a human face on protectionism. Currently, critics of NGOs are quite right to notice that with respect to transparency, accountability, and representativeness, most NGOs are even less "democratic" than the international institutions like the IMF and the World Bank of which they are so critical. The danger is that in deploying a rhetoric of environmentalism and safety standards and labor fairness, the United States ends up imposing impossible-to-meet standards, which allows it to take back the jobs it has lost to developing nations—in the name of protecting their people. Underpaid third world child-laborers should not be banned from the manufacturing workplace if their alternative is not education but prostitution. A fair wage in Mexico or Ghana cannot be measured by a fair wage in Chicago or Dijon. If first world governments want third world reform, they must adopt cost-sharing in which North-South transfers are integral to that reform. All of this can happen through multilateral institutions like the WTO and the IMF, if member nations will it.

National sovereignty may be a dying concept, but it is a long way from dead. Ironically, this is good news for global civil society. For sovereign nations remain the only true countervailing powers capable of opposing, subduing, and civilizing the anarchic forces of the global economy and putting onto the bare bones of an emerging global civil society the muscles it needs to act as a countervailing force to global markets. The emerging global alternative to world markets, international civil society, needs the active support of sovereign states for its fragile new institutions to have even a modest impact. Working together, however, progressive and conservationist forces within traditional nation-states—those who embrace the rule of law and regulation, whether from the right or the left—can make league with civic forces already active in the international arena. Between them, they can guarantee that democracy and civil society will have a voice in how the world is organized and governed, and that global markets will serve not only customers but citizens, not only the private desires of wealthy consumers but the public interests of the world's peoples. Global civil society is not yet a firm reality then, but with the continuation of present international civic trends and the active support of national governments, it can become much more than a pipe dream.

Benjamin R. Barber is the Walt Whitman Professor of Political Science and directs the Walt Whitman Center for the Culture and Politics of Democracy at Rutgers University. He is the author of Jihad vs. McWorld *and of the forthcoming* The Truth of Power: Intellectuals in the White House.

The Human Rights Agenda versus National Sovereignty

Jeremy Rabkin

In today's world, "human rights" is a powerful slogan, evoking a powerful idea. The same, of course, can be said of other weighty phrases: "liberty and equality," "democracy and justice," even the "will of God." What, precisely, should these abstract terms mean in practice? On this, there is no agreement. Nor is there agreement on the related question of who is empowered to define these concepts.

A compelling answer appears in the founding document of the United States, the Declaration of Independence. The validity of human rights, it proclaims, is a "self-evident" truth: "all men . . . are endowed by their Creator with certain unalienable Rights" and "to secure these rights, Governments are instituted among Men, deriving their just powers from the consent of the governed." Human rights have a higher source than any government, but in practice, they can only be made "secure" by governments. The "just powers" of government rest, in turn, on a system of consent—some version of constitutional democracy. Nearly half the complaints against British authority listed in the body of the Declaration deal with depredations against the authority of local legislatures and local courts.

For more than 50 years, the United Nations has tried, in one way or another, to serve the goal announced in its Charter of "promoting and encouraging respect for human rights." Yet "promoting and encouraging" are not the same as securing or enforcing rights. Until quite recently, international authority could hardly be described as a serious alternative, let alone a serious threat, to America's founding vision. True, the UN has sponsored a series of international treaties that set forth human rights standards in lengthy lists. These treaties do not include any serious enforcement provisions, however. They do not compel signatories to accept the interpretations of the committees that the UN has appointed to monitor their effectiveness. Nor do they allow the UN to give one state the authority to enforce human rights in another sovereign state. Given the lack of enforcement mechanisms, these treaties have posed no serious threat to any sovereign state, which is why many of the core human rights agreements have been signed by some of the most brutal and repressive regimes in the world.

In recent years, however, the world has begun to move toward arming international human rights advocates with much stronger legal powers. It is much less clear, in this setting, that international human rights norms are compatible with the classic American understanding of human rights. It is even more unclear that the world is ready for the alternative. We may be heading not for a new era of international respect for human rights, but for an exacerbation of conflicts in which the very credibility of human rights is one of the victims.

New Trends

The end of the cold war, the collapse of communism and disintegration of the Soviet Empire, the expansion of international trade—all generated much optimism in the 1990s about prospects for international cooperation to advance such worthy aims as the protection of human rights. In this context, many people saw the NATO air war against Serbia in the spring of 1999 as a crucial turning point in world affairs. Czech president Vaclav Havel, for example, described the war as a "precedent" for an international law of human rights—"a law that ranks higher than the law which protects the sovereignty of states."

The notable fact about the NATO campaign, however, is that it was launched by NATO on its own initiative and only afterwards approved, to some degree, by the UN Security Council. Even if the Security Council becomes more receptive to the idea of launching wars on behalf of human rights, no one expects that NATO will put its own armies and air forces at the UN's disposal. Nor does anyone expect that the UN will develop independent war-fighting capacities. Real military force is likely to remain the exclusive possession of sovereign states, to be exercised in accordance with complex calculations of national self-interest.

In some ways, the most important innovation occurred earlier, during the conflict over Bosnia. For years, outside powers had deplored the communal violence and "ethnic cleansing" campaigns that followed the breakup of Yugoslavia, especially in Bosnia. Several NATO countries sent troops, under UN sponsorship, but these forces, fearing involvement in direct combat, did little to protect civilians. In Srbrenica, Dutch troops stood by as Bosnian Muslims were massacred in what the UN itself had proclaimed an internationally protected safe zone. In 1994, the United States and other Western powers responded to such horrors, not by mobilizing more forceful military intervention, but by getting the Security Council to establish a special war crimes tribunal for the former Yugoslavia, with power to indict and try perpetrators of atrocities on its own initiative.

This may not have been a very useful response to the problems on the ground—withholding bombers and sending in lawyers. Nevertheless, the tribunal did mark a genuine change in international human rights policy. This war crimes tribunal, based in The Hague, has often been compared to the Nuremberg Tribunal that tried top Nazi leaders for crimes against humanity. The Nuremberg trials, however, were organized by the four occupying powers in Germany, after the Nazi government's unconditional surrender. The Allied powers exercised all governing power in Germany, so any courts in Germany would have had to be Allied courts. The Yugoslav tribunal, by contrast, was imposed by the Security Council at a time when the UN did not claim and certainly did not exercise governing power in Yugoslavia. Moreover, it was imposed despite the objections of governments in the region that were still accepted as the lawful representatives of member states in the UN.

As no great power objected to the new tribunal, however, the Security Council plan went forward. A year later, the Security Council responded in a similar way to the massacre of nearly a million Tutsi civilians by the Hutu government of Rwanda. The UN again did nothing to stop the genocide. Indeed, most UN forces in the region were actually withdrawn when the massacres began—to protect European troops from harm. When a Tutsi army ended the carnage by overthrowing the Hutu government, however, the UN again stepped forward—with lawyers. A tribunal was established to try perpetrators of genocide in Rwanda, this time with the full agreement of the new Tutsi government.

Impatience with such ad hoc interventions helped to revive interest in old discussions about a permanent international criminal court. The idea was initially broached in the late 1940s, in connection with the UN's convention on the punishment of genocide (which otherwise leaves the punishment to states where such crimes occur). The project did not seem very practical during the cold war. In the wake of communism's collapse, though, the idea of a permanent international court was taken more seriously by many of the world's governments. In 1998, a detailed plan for an international criminal court was drafted at a UN-sponsored conference in Rome. It was supported by well over 100 countries at the conference. The plan called for the establishment of a permanent, independent prosecutor, able to launch investigations and seek indictments on his own initiative and then proceed to trial before a permanent court of judges—again with no direct approval from any national government or any other international body.

Meanwhile, national governments began to get into the act of human rights enforcement. Shortly after the conclusion of the Rome conference, British authorities arrested former Chilean president Augusto Pinochet while he was recovering from back surgery in London. Pinochet was sought by a Spanish magistrate who was determined to try him for crimes committed against Chileans and other nationals during his 17 years as military dictator of Chile. British courts wrangled about the legality of extraditing Pinochet for more than a year before the House of Lords determined that Britain could indeed extradite Pinochet because it could (as British extradition law required) try him for such offenses in Britain. As the Lords saw it, torture had become a universal crime under the 1989 UN Convention Against Torture. The House of Lords held that the traditional immunity to heads of states for their official acts—previously acknowledged by British, American, and most other national courts—had been implicitly overruled by the torture convention. The convention nowhere says that it overrides traditional immunities however, (and nothing in the formal drafting memoranda says this either), so Chile had had no reason to believe that it was opening itself to such foreign prosecutions when it signed the convention (under Pinochet's own government).

The Pinochet affair was widely heralded as a step toward making good on universal justice. The European Union (EU) parliament applauded Pinochet's arrest, and several other European governments offered to host trials of their own, if Spain decided not to proceed. In the end, British authorities decided that Pinochet should be allowed to return to Chile, ostensibly because he was too sick to stand trial. Still, the precedent now exists, and human rights advocates have urged more such ventures in international justice.

The United States did not endorse the Pinochet trial, but it has offered its own characteristic approach to international justice—the unleashing of tort lawyers. The 1993 Torture Victims Protection Act allows victims to seek civil damages in U.S. courts, even for acts committed by foreign governments, against foreign victims, on foreign soil. Since only individual perpetrators are liable and they can easily shield their assets by removing them from the United States, recovery is quite difficult. Nevertheless, a number of suits have already been advanced (most recently against former Salvadoran army officers now living in Florida), and as precedents accumulate, we may see more ambitious efforts in U.S. courts.

Just over the horizon are proposals to integrate human rights standards into trade agreements, so that countries which commit human rights abuses can be made subject to trade sanctions. Such sanctions are not new, but they have previously been imposed at the discretion of national states. The trade agreements for the World Trade Organization (WTO) do not now allow for such sanctions. Making provision for them would also make such sanctions subject to formal adjudication before the dispute-settling panels and appellate authority of the WTO—which would mean that international adjudication could establish, definitively, which countries should and which should not be considered human rights violators. This would mark a major change in itself.

Taken together, these trends might suggest that the world really is moving toward the establishment of an international legal order in which human rights take a prominent place. This new human rights order faces many obstacles, including some obstacles, however, it *ought* to face.

American Resistance

The first and most obvious obstacle is the unwillingness of the United States to submit to constraints on its sovereignty. America has always behaved with considerable ambivalence toward international norms that would determine the relations between American citizens and their own government. In the early 1950s, prominent legal advocates, including the president of the American Bar Association, insisted that U.S. participation in international human rights conventions would violate limitations implied in the U.S. Constitution. For decades, the Senate refused to ratify any of these conventions. The previous Bush administration managed to secure ratification to four international human rights treaties (on the punishment of genocide, on race discrimination, on torture, and on civil and political rights), but the Senate attached an encompassing set of reservations and understandings in each case, to assure that treaty ratifications would have no direct effect on domestic law.

This situation may now be changing. The Clinton administration took the lead in championing the UN Security Council resolutions establishing the war crimes tribunal for Yugoslavia. Several years later, Clinton's defense secretary, William Cohen, expressed outrage when the tribunal's prosecutor insisted on interviewing top NATO commanders to determine whether NATO had committed war crimes by targeting civilian sites in its bombing war against Serbia. Yet the Clinton administration had already agreed to such questioning in principle, as the tribunal was given jurisdiction extends to all war crimes in that territory, without regard to nationality. The Clinton administration went even further when it helped to initiate negotiations for a permanent international criminal court. The United States then found itself at odds with most other countries when the treaty made no provision to exempt American military personnel from prosecution by the new court. In one of his last acts as president, Clinton signed the treaty establishing the International Criminal Court (ICC), even as he recommended that the Senate delay ratification pending major changes in the court's charter.

For many human rights activists, there is a simple answer to the problem of American exceptionalism: the United States must change its policies to keep in step with world opinion. Otherwise, it is said, America will forfeit its position of leadership.

Some advocates—even in the United States—go a step further: they contend that America must change or else the world will force it to change. The very respectable and mainstream journal *Foreign Affairs* recently published an article by a Hofstra University law professor, Peter Spiro, that seeks to rebut arguments by those who call for greater safeguards of U.S. sovereignty: "Indeed, the [U.S.] Constitution will have to adapt to global requirements sooner or later.... During the twentieth century, the United States was able to defy various international norms only because other countries were unwilling to bear the costs of sanctioning America for its sins; at the same time, international organizations had little power to wield on their own.... But economic globalization will inevitably bring the United States into line." He predicts that other countries will organize boycotts of U.S. products to enforce American compliance with international human rights standards.

It is extremely unlikely that a two-thirds majority of the U.S. Senate will be cowed by such threats. It is far more likely that any serious effort to implement such threats will provoke outrage among most Americans. Most members of Congress would demand that the president respond accordingly. An organized global threat to American independence would seem to justify rather extreme American responses.

In fact, such responses are already being considered. Last spring, Republican leaders in the Senate cosponsored a bill that would have immediately ended all foreign and military aid to any country participating in the new ICC. In the event that any American were held for trial by the court, the bill authorized the president to respond with all means, including force.

If this response seems a bit extreme, the fact is that the ICC "statute" (as the treaty is called) makes it very hard for the United States to sit on the sidelines. The statute not only extends jurisdiction to perpetrators who are nationals of states that ratify the court's charter. It also extends jurisdiction to alleged criminals whose victims belong to ratifying states. Then it goes further and allows nonsignatory states to associate themselves with the ICC for the purpose of offering up a particular accusation, without subjecting themselves to the general oversight of the court in other matters.

This means that U.S. military personnel, whether serving in UN peacekeeping missions or in separate American military efforts, may be subject to the oversight of an international prosecutor. It is true, as advocates of the ICC emphasize, that every country is given the opportunity to undertake its own trials before the ICC would intervene. The statute holds that the ICC is to have the last call, however, so that an American decision not to prosecute, and even an American trial that results in acquittal or conviction on some lesser charge, could be overridden by an international official in The Hague. There has been talk about securing exemptions for American participants in UN peacekeeping ventures. The ICC statute makes no such provision, however: the court is designed to be immune to great power pressures. (The statute allows the Security Council to "suspend" a prosecution for a year at a time, but even such action is subject to great power veto; so Russia or France could stop the United States from invoking this limited safeguard.) If the ICC goes into effect, then the United States might well become more reluctant to participate in UN-sponsored peacekeeping efforts.

Even if the prosecutors of the ICC can be relied upon to exercise restraint toward Americans, the existence of the ICC will almost certainly serve to encourage human rights prosecutions by national courts. The statute, as now written, is not an alternative to, but rather a reinforcement of, Pinochet-style prosecutions. The preamble actually speaks of "the duty of every State to exercise its criminal jurisdiction over those responsible for international crimes"—without in any way limiting this "duty" to a state's own nationals or even to crimes committed against its own nationals.

So the United States faces the prospect of a world in which Americans are prey to any foreign government that wants to settle a grievance or score propaganda points by seizing an American and putting him on trial. It need not even be for an offense against the nation conducting the trial. It could simply be for alleged human rights abuses in the United States.

In this regard, the behavior of the EU is far from reassuring. The EU has repeatedly invoked international human rights norms to criticize the United States for its domestic conduct. The EU Commission has particularly condemned the American practice of capital punishment as contrary to international norms. The fact that the United States has not ratified these norms matters not at all (in the European view), since a UN committee has held that these norms have now become obligatory on all states. Germany has now launched a suit in the International Court of Justice, protesting that Arizona has wrongfully executed two Americans for murders committed in that state (the perpetrators were born in Germany but moved to the United States as young children). None of these gestures can force America to change its own laws, but they signal a readiness to see the United States held to international norms when an American does fall into foreign custody.

Many human rights advocates argue that the United States would not only strengthen international standards by cooperating but would be better off for such cooperation. This argument is not likely to convince the American people, who will find it hard to understand why the United States, the world's oldest democracy, cannot be trusted to make decisions for itself without the oversight of countries that—in living memory—were responsible for mass murder and now claim to be special champions of human rights.

Meanwhile, nations friendly to the United States will be subject to the political whims of international opinion. Israel, in particular, will be vulnerable to international prosecutions seeking to make good on European criticism that Israel is overreacting to Palestinian violence. The United States can exercise a veto against one-sided condemnations in the Security Council. It will be unable, however, to prevent the ICC or some bystander state from prosecuting Israeli leaders.

So, if international legal standards are pressed forward, they are likely to trigger sustained American opposition. Will that be good for the cause of international human rights?

A situation where the United States is ranged against the majority of the world's established democracies is not a promising prospect. It is far from the only problem, however. The world's newest democracies present even greater challenges.

Resistance in the Less Developed World

For many people, the main appeal of an international human rights regime is its potential for preventing the widespread violation of basic rights in developing countries. It is certainly true that human rights advocates in developing countries often appeal to the moral authority of international norms. Governments that seek to reassure their own people—or the international community—about their commitment to liberalization have often sought to register their good intentions by ratifying international rights treaties. Even China ratified the Covenant on Civil and Political Rights for this reason.

Expressing good intentions, however, is something different from submitting to international authority. The UN has been able to secure at least rhetorical commitment to human rights norms from some of the world's most repressive regimes—at the price of avoiding any threat of serious enforcement. Whether or not that is a sound bargain, it is certainly frustrating to human rights advocacy groups. So now we are moving to more aggressive measures.

The ICC is remarkably aggressive in removing fundamental decisions from national to international hands. Take the case of pardons and amnesties. Every country that has made a transition to democracy has extended some form of amnesty to officials of the old government. With few exceptions, in fact, amnesties have been quite comprehensive and sweeping. Is that wrong? Plainly, advocates of the Pinochet prosecution thought the democratic government in Chile was wrong to uphold the amnesty of Pinochet. The ICC would institutionalize the Pinochet model, as the ICC statute makes no provision at all for respecting amnesties.

The inability to offer amnesty to a previous regime will create serious problems for a developing country trying to recover from a new round of rebellion and repression (or repression followed by successful rebellion). The United States granted general amnesty to Confederate rebels after the Civil War—even to those threatened with capital punishment during the war for massacring black troops. In the 1970s, Spain and Portugal made their transitions from decades of fascist repression without prosecuting those responsible for past abuses, as France and other countries that collaborated with the Nazis had earlier turned a blind eye to most atrocities committed by their own governments during World War II. Why should less developed countries be held to a higher standard?

A reasonable concern is that an outside prosecution will look like the imposition of an outside power; in other words, a return to Western imperialism. This is a serious concern because human rights enforcement is increasingly taking on the character of a new form of imperial rule.

Part of the problem is that the energy for international human rights enforcement is provided not by governments but rather by nongovernmental organizations, and the priorities of NGOs tend to be the priorities of Western activists. Chile's Pinochet was not the bloodiest of dictators, but he received special attention from a Spanish magistrate because the Chilean military government allowed leftist opponents to leave Chile and organize opposition networks in other countries—where they worked to organize exactly the sort of prosecution that was finally launched in Spain.

A larger and more enduring source of energy comes from feminist organizations. They were highly active in UN conferences on population in 1994 and on women's rights in 1995, and provoked much controversy by pressing for international recognition of abortion rights and sexual autonomy rights (especially for homosexual activity). Western countries, urged on by feminist advocacy groups, tended to support these aims. Most developing countries, especially Islamic countries, rejected them. Yet United Nations human rights committees continue to pursue the feminist agenda. The monitoring committee for the Convention on the Elimination of Discrimination Against Women (CEDAW), for example, chided Belarus for instituting a national mother's day (which the committee saw as leading to dangerous sex stereotyping), told the government of Libya to reinterpret the Koran so that its requirements would be "permissible under CEDAW," told the Kyrgyz Republic that it must legalize lesbianism, told China that it must legalize prostitution, and so on.

These admonitions can now be shrugged off as so much unwanted advice from Western busybodies. If the international human rights movement is going to be armed with legal enforcement machinery, however, it is certain to provoke much more opposition. Its feminist priorities will make an easy target for those who denounce human rights as Western impositions.

Developing countries might be more vulnerable to trade sanctions than a major power like the United States. Nevertheless, trade sanctions do not have an impressive record of success. Would WTO–approved trade sanctions actually help to blunt the charge that human rights standards are a Western imposition? Would such sanctions not be more likely to convert the WTO into a target of nationalist resentments? Meanwhile, if globalized trade does help to nurture new constituencies for human rights, is it sensible to make global trade hostage to the demands of advocacy groups?

Constitutional Flaws

In the end, the American problem and the problem with less developed countries are simply the most obvious illustrations of a general problem. The idea of a world law of human rights implies there is a structure of international authority—a world state of some sort—to enforce this law. Of course, there is nothing of the sort. Rather, we have the odd spectacle of international institutions claiming the authority to lay down the law—without the power to see it through.

Even a domestic court, it is true, depends on executive authorities to enforce its rulings on the ground. In countries where there is some respect for law, executive officials do feel obligated to uphold court rulings. After all, courts are part of the same government and the reputation of the government as a whole is at stake when its courts are defied.

When it comes to international courts, however, no national government has quite the same stake in upholding the court's authority. NATO forces in the Balkans have been notoriously sluggish about apprehending war criminals sought by the special tribunal in The Hague. Had a NATO commander or soldier been indicted, it is extremely unlikely that the United States or any other NATO country would have allowed him to be tried by the tribunal. If the ICC comes into existence and proceeds to issue arrest warrants, how many governments will stir themselves to catch their own nationals or even nationals of states with which they want to stay on good terms?

Ineffectual human rights programs are nothing new in the world. The problem may be more serious when enforcement does "work." Sometimes, as in the Pinochet case, a bystander government may be quite willing to apprehend another country's culprit. What if a prosecution then goes forward against the wishes of the home state?

Even in a domestic setting, there are times when executive authorities feel they cannot leave matters to criminal courts. Almost every country vests a pardoning authority in the executive to deal with cases where prosecution might stir dangerous protest or be viewed by most citizens as unjust. In extreme circumstances, executive authorities may direct police or military forces to disregard contrary court rulings (as President Lincoln did, during the Civil War).

Such measures have the potential to throw a country into turmoil or into lawless military dictatorship. In a democracy, however, there is an ultimate appeal to the people. How much injustice or illegality will a people tolerate to save their country in an hour of emergency or to heal the wounds of former strife? Perhaps it is too facile to suggest such problems can all be settled by plebiscite—though that is, in fact, what happened in a number of Latin American countries in the 1980s, where amnesties for brutal military suppression of left-wing terrorism were approved by popular referenda.

The fact remains that people who inhabit the same country must somehow learn to live together. In new democracies, people have sometimes shown heroic patience and forbearance in accepting former oppressors or violent foes back into their society, as in South Africa and the Baltic states. With all the imperfections of democracy, shouldn't this matter be left to local determination?

What happens, after all, if an outside intervention triggers a new round of civil strife and rebellion? No international court commands its own army. Third-party states that undertake a trial do not commit themselves to fixing the consequences. They seek to render judgment from a distance—without any responsibility for the consequences.

This is, perhaps, the deepest problem. When street crime begins to rise or financial swindles proliferate, citizens in a democracy may demand that police and prosecutors step up their responses. Most of the time, though, governments set enforcement priorities without much notice, because the assumption is that the law applies to all and will be generally enforced. This would be an absurd assumption, however, for international human rights standards. No one thinks such standards could be enforced against China or Russia as readily as they might be against Chile or Estonia. No one thinks the scale of human rights abuses is the same in Western Europe as in sub-Saharan Africa.

How, then, does the world set enforcement priorities for human rights? There is no world democracy that can register citizen protest—and then balance that with contending views and competing concerns. At best, we have a chorus of self-selected NGOs, whose priorities may be much influenced by their own ideological fixations or fundraising opportunities.

So we will have some interventions driven by the agitation of NGOs and then a vast amount of inattention. The idea that an international law of human rights is operating in the background can be a highly effective soporific. To speak of "law" at all in this context suggests that the process is operating on its own. International authorities will take care of the problem. Isn't that why we have them? So national governments, which might make a difference, are off the hook. Problem in Rwanda? The UN has sent in lawyers to clean up the mess. On to the next challenge. After a series of feckless international mediation efforts failed to disarm Fouday Sanko's terrorist forces in Sierre Leone—notorious for amputating the limbs of civilians, including women and children— the United Nations established a third special-war-crimes tribunal in the fall of 2000. The international community was happy to provide lawyers, but not the long term military protection the country required.

The temptation to fall back on symbolic gestures is particularly great when human rights challenges are framed as the general concern of all nations. During the cold war, the United States was eager to call attention to Soviet repression and the fate of peoples in "captive nations." In the 1980s, the United States took active steps to pressure Latin American dictatorships into moving toward democracy—among other reasons, because the U.S. government wanted to remove the taint of military repression from its anti-Communist coalition.

If we make international institutions the arbiters of respectable government, we pretend that all states are on the same level. The most brutal and repressive are given equal status to the most orderly and democratic. It will be hard to rally respectable states against the brutal ones when we have already determined that the most brutal get an equal say or are, in some ways, full partners in the task of ensuring human rights. Here we have a recipe for neglect on one side and politicized interventions on the other.

This takes us back to the problem that there is not, in functional terms, a world community living under a world law.

In the past, advocacy groups have had to rely on the strength of outside governments. Nevertheless, when outside governments acted—whether with diplomatic gestures, economic sanctions, or military threats—they acted as governments. Everyone understood that governments had to weigh a whole series of concerns before deciding how and when to act and how far to press their agendas. If there is "international justice" for human rights offenses, then advocacy groups can go directly to international forums, skipping over the complex calculations of national governments.

Governments may be quite happy to sit on the sidelines—or pretend that they do. Even in the Pinochet case, the Spanish magistrate who launched the case was prodded into action by advocacy groups. The British and Spanish governments then treated the matter as if it were entirely a matter for courts to decide and had no bearing on state-to-state relations between Chile and various European countries. This was, of course, never the case, as the British home secretary ultimately demonstrated by ordering Pinochet returned to Chile based on medical reports that were never submitted to judicial inspection (let alone to challenge by advocacy groups).

No one pretends that governments that act in public and in their own name will always act from disinterested motives. On the contrary, precisely as a matter of self-interest, governments have strong incentives—especially when they do act openly and in their own names—to weigh ends and means, priorities and consequences, in their dealings with other states. Clearly, democratic governments are more accountable to their own people than a private advocacy group can be. Governments are also more accountable to other states, since they have permanent, ongoing relations to protect. Advocacy groups can flit from one "hot" issue to the next, change their focus, even change their names, when things go badly.

Advocacy groups can certainly play a useful role in highlighting injustice, publicizing abuses, inspiring and assisting local protests in other countries. When governments allow advocacy groups to trigger legal mechanisms, however, they abdicate their own responsibilities to these private groups—which have no responsibility for the consequences of their actions. The chaos this can breed is hardly propitious for human rights. In particulr, it may make it harder to develop stable institutions in turbulent regions. If the traditional American view is correct, human rights are best secured by stable, constitutional arrangements. Nations can develop such arrangements for themselves. The world as a whole cannot.

It is, of course, frustrating for human rights advocates to work with a world divided into so many separate sovereign states. Yet this is as it should be. Few people would want to live in a world where a handful of diplomats or lawyers could lay down the law for billions of people, divided into so many different cultures, with such very different circumstances and challenges.

The legalization of human rights standards appeals to many activists who seem to regard it as an international analog to the assertions of judicial authority in the heyday of the U.S. Supreme Court under Chief Justice Earl Warren. Many of those who helped organize Human Rights Watch and other human rights advocacy groups in the past two decades were, in fact, veterans of the American Civil Liberties Union and similar domestic litigation groups. Yet judicial activism was effective in the United States—to the extent that it was—because most Americans, including most government officials, had great respect for their own Constitution and great reserves of loyalty to Court rulings, even if they did not agree with them. It is hard to see how we teach respect for constitutional democracy by establishing a system of free-floating international appeals, hovering above every actual constitutional state.

In particular circumstances, international institutions may help to bring improvements in local situations. Yet they also risk encouraging the sense that national elections and national constitutions are simply formal spectacles, while the world is really run by shadowy networks of well-connected advocacy groups. Such notions can be highly poisonous in new democracies. They may be hard to put down, however, if present trends continue.

Jeremy Rabkin is associate professor of government at Cornell University and the author of Why Sovereignty Matters.

Introduction to Country and Related Territory Reports

The *Freedom in the World 2000-2001* survey contains 192 country and 17 related and disputed territory reports. Each report begins with a section containing basic political, economic, and social data arranged in the following categories: **polity, economy, population, purchasing power parities (PPP), life expectancy, ethnic groups, capital, political rights** [numerical rating], **civil liberties** [numerical rating], and **status** [Free, Partly Free, or Not Free].

The **polity** category contains an encapsulated description of the dominant centers of freely chosen or unelected political power in each country or territory. The following polity descriptions were used in this year's survey: *presidential* – the president enjoys predominant power beyond ceremonial functions, while the legislature, if there is one, enjoys limited or no independence from the executive; *parliamentary* – the government (i.e., prime minister, cabinet) is approved by the legislature, and the head of state, if there is one, enjoys a largely ceremonial role; *presidential-parliamentary*—the president enjoys predominant power beyond ceremonial functions, and the government is approved by the legislature; *traditional chiefs* – traditional chiefs wield significant political power; *traditional monarchy*—the country's monarch enjoys predominant power through hereditary rule (as opposed to a constitutional monarchy); *principality*—the country's monarch is a prince who may enjoy either predominant power or a largely ceremonial role (constitutional monarchy); *dominant party* – the ruling mass-based party or front dominates the government, while allowing other parties to organize and compete short of taking control of the government; *one party* – absolute rule is enjoyed by the one legal party in the country; *military*—the military enjoys predominant power, despite the possible existence of a head of state or legislature; *international protectorate*—an international governing body, such as the United Nations, administers the country. In addition, the term "democracy" may be added to those polities in which the most recent national elections met minimum standards for free and fair elections as judged by international observers.

Polities may be modified by one or more of the following descriptions: insurgency, military-dominated, military-influenced, clergy-dominated, dominant party, federal, transitional, postconflict. While the preceding list of polities may be applied to most countries, exceptions do occur. In those rare cases where the polities listed above do not adequately reflect the current situation in a particular country, other polity descriptions have been used.

The reports contain a brief description of the **economy** of each country or territory. Non-industrial economies are called *traditional* or *pre-industrial*. Developed market economies and developing countries with a modern market sector have the designation *capitalist*. *Mixed capitalist* countries combine predominantly private enterprise with substantial government involvement in the economy for social welfare purposes. *Capitalist-statist* economies have both large market sectors and government-owned productive enterprises. *Mixed capitalist-statist* economies have the characteristics of capitalist-statist economies, as well as major social welfare programs.

Statist economies place virtually the entire economy under direct or indirect government control. *Mixed statist* economies are primarily government controlled, but also have significant private enterprise. Economies in transition between statist and capitalist forms may have the word "transitional" included in their economy description.

The **population** and **life expectancy** figures were obtained from the *2000 World Population Data Sheet* of the Population Reference Bureau.

The **purchasing power parities (PPP)** show per capita gross domestic product (GDP) in terms of international dollars in order to account for real buying power. These figures were obtained from the *2000 United Nations Development Program Human Development Report*. However, for some countries, especially tiny island-countries, this information was not available.

Information about the **ethnic groups** in a country or territory is provided in order to assist with the understanding of certain issues, including minority rights, addressed by the survey. Sources used to obtain this information included *The World Almanac and Book of Facts, 2000* and the CIA *2000 World Factbook*.

The **political rights** and **civil liberties** categories contain numerical ratings between 1 and 7 for each country or territory rated, with 1 representing the most free and 7 the least free. The **status** designation of Free, Partly Free, or Not Free, which is determined by the combination of the political rights and civil liberties ratings, indicates the general state of freedom in a country or territory. The ratings of countries or territories which have improved or declined since the previous survey are indicated by asterisks next to the ratings. Positive or negative trends which do not warrant a ratings change since the previous year may be indicated by upward or downward trend arrows, which are located next to the name of the country or territory. A brief explanation of ratings changes or trend arrows is provided for each country or territory as required. For a full description of the methods used to determine the survey's ratings, please see the chapter on methodology.

Following the section on political, economic, and social data, each country report is divided into two parts: an **overview** and an analysis of **political rights and civil liberties**. The overview provides a brief historical background and a description of major current events. The political rights and civil liberties section summarizes each country or territory's degree of respect for the rights and liberties which Freedom House uses to evaluate freedom in the world.

Reports on related and disputed territories follow the country reports. In most cases, these reports are comparatively brief and contain fewer categories of information than do the country essays. In this year's survey, reports are included for 16 related and disputed territories.

Afghanistan

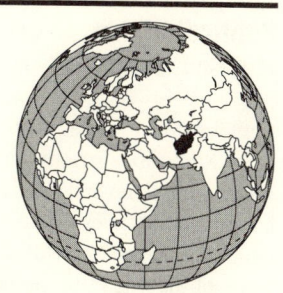

Polity: Fundamentalist
theocracy (civil conflict)
Economy: Mixed-statist
Population: 26,700,000
PPP: na
Life Expectancy: 46
Ethnic Groups: Pashtun (38 percent), Tajik (25 percent),
Hazara (19 percent), Uzbek (6 percent), other (12 percent)
Capital: Kabul

Political Rights: 7
Civil Liberties: 7
Status: Not Free

Overview:

Civil conflict, drought, sanctions imposed by the United Nations, and the ruling Taliban's harsh social code continued to cause severe hardship for ordinary Afghans in 2000. The Taliban overran a string of opposition-held towns in northeastern Afghanistan in August and September, and by year's end controlled roughly 95 percent of the country. As with a 1999 Taliban offensive that captured part of the Shomali plains north of Kabul, the latest fighting caused tens of thousands of civilians to flee their homes.

Following a nineteenth-century Anglo-Russian contest for influence in Afghanistan, Britain recognized the country as an independent monarchy in 1921. King Zahir Shah ruled from 1933 until being deposed in a 1973 coup. Afghanistan has been in continuous civil conflict since 1978, when a Communist coup set out to transform this highly traditional society. The Soviet Union invaded in December 1979 and installed a pro-Moscow Communist faction. More than 100,000 Soviet troops faced fierce resistance from United States-backed *mujahideen* (guerrilla fighters) before finally withdrawing in 1989.

The ethnic-based mujahideen overthrew the Communist government in 1992, and then battled for control of Kabul, killing more than 25,000 civilians in the capital by 1995. The main forces were the Pashtun-based *Hizb-i-Islami* (Islamic Party) and the Tajik-dominated *Jamiat-i-Islami* (Islamic Association). The fighting has intensified the ethnic cleavage between the rural-based Pashtuns, who form a near majority and have ruled for most of the past 250 years, and the large Tajik minority.

Initially organized around theology students, the ethnic-Pashtun Taliban militia ousted in 1996 a nominal government in Kabul headed by the Jamiat's Burhanuddin Rabbani. Defeating or buying off mujahideen commanders, the Taliban soon controlled most of the country except for parts of northern and central Afghanistan that remained in the hands of a self-styled Northern Alliance of ethnic Tajik, Uzbek, and Hazara Shiite forces. The Taliban captured the key northern city of Mazar-i-Sharif and several northern provinces from the Uzbek warlord Rashid Dostam in August 1998, and in September 1998 overtook central Bamian province, the Hazara Shiite stronghold.

The onset of winter in November 2000 led to a lull in the latest fighting. However, an estimated 60,000 people in northern Afghanistan remained internally displaced. Winter also brought increased hardship to the 4 million people in south and central Afghanistan whom the World Food Program said were severely affected by the country's worst drought in decades.

Political Rights and Civil Liberties: There are no democratic processes or institutions at any level in Afghanistan. The Taliban rule by decree through an inner circle of Kandahar-based clerics, led by former mujahideen fighter Mullah Mohammed Omar. Appointed local *shura* (councils) also rule by decree. Authorities strictly enforce these decrees, which regulate nearly all aspects of social affairs. Several civilian-based opposition parties function clandestinely but face harassment. Amnesty International reported in March 1999 that the Taliban had detained and severely tortured up to 200 Afghan political figures in the past year on account of their peaceful political activity.

The Taliban rely on the UN and foreign nongovernmental organizations (NGOs) to provide basic services, food-for-work programs, mine clearance, and refugee repatriation. Only three foreign governments recognize the Taliban state, even though it controls 95 percent of the country. The last major territory outside Taliban control is the northern Panjshir Valley, the stronghold of the Tajik-based forces of Ahmad Shah Masood, a Rabbani loyalist and fabled anti-Soviet military commander. Regional states reportedly help arm the various factions. The UN imposed aviation and financial sanctions in November 1999 after the Taliban refused to extradite the Saudi-born militant Osama bin Laden, who allegedly plotted the 1998 bombings of two U.S. embassies in East Africa. In late December, the UN Security Council gave the Taliban one month to surrender bin Laden and close alleged terrorist training camps or else face an arms embargo.

In recent years, armed factions in Afghanistan's civil conflict have committed torture, killings, and other abuses against civilians, and have carried out several massacres of civilians and soldiers during military operations. Since coming to power, the Taliban have arbitrarily detained and tortured thousands of men from ethnic minority groups, some of whom were killed or disappeared. Rockets and mortar fire continued to cause some civilian deaths in 2000, although far fewer than in the mid-1990s. Taliban fighters reportedly often looted and burned homes in areas they conquered.

The judiciary consists of tribunals in which clerics with little legal training hand down rulings based on Pashtun customs and the Taliban's interpretation of the *Sharia* (Islamic law). Proceedings are brief, defendants lack the right to legal counsel, there are no due process safeguards, and there is no right of appeal. In a society where families of murder victims have the option of either carrying out court-imposed death sentences or granting clemency, victims' relatives have killed convicted murderers on several occasions. Authorities have also bulldozed alleged sodomizers beneath walls, stoned adulterers to death, and amputated the hands of thieves. Prison conditions are inhumane.

The Taliban's social code and its interpretation of the Sharia have created severe hardships for women. Religious police from the Department for the Promotion of Virtue and Prevention of Vice regularly flogged, beat, and otherwise punished women in detention centers and public places for violating Taliban dress codes, which include wearing the *burqa*, a one-piece garment covering the entire body. The *Financial Times* reported in February that Taliban enforcers had become less active in Kabul.

Authorities continued to enforce the rural Islamic custom of *purdah* even in urban areas. Purdah requires families to isolate women from men who are not relatives. The Taliban have also generally enforced the custom of *mehrem*, requiring women to be accompanied by a male relative when they leave their homes. However, the *Financial Times* reported in March that women in Kabul are increasingly traveling in groups of two or three without a male relative.

The Taliban also continued to ban most women from working. This has created severe hardship for many women, particularly some 28,000 war widows in Kabul. The Taliban permitted female doctors and nurses to return to work in early 2000 following reports that numerous women had died after being unable to obtain medical assistance in the country's gender-segregated hospitals. However, in early July, the Taliban prohibited women in Kabul from working for international aid groups outside of the health sector.

The Taliban continued to formally ban girls from going to school, although officials did allow some privately funded, underground "home schools" for girls to function despite their being banned in 1998. In addition, authorities reportedly ran a few primary schools for girls in Kabul. Only about one-quarter of boys attend school, largely because 80 percent of teachers are women and they can no longer work. The *Financial Times* reported in February that relief workers estimate that impoverished children make up at least half of the country's population, and that there are an estimated 40,000 street children in Kabul out of a population of one million.

The Taliban sharply restrict freedom of expression and of association, and run a tightly controlled broadcast outlet, Radio Voice of Sharia. The Taliban banned televisions, videocassette recorders, videos, and satellite dishes in 1998, and destroyed such stock found in shops. By some accounts authorities in Kabul have slightly relaxed enforcement of the ban. There are few, if any, civic groups and no known trade unions.

The Taliban continued to restrict religious freedom by forcing Afghans to adopt their ultraconservative Islamic practices. Roughly 85 percent of the population is Sunni Muslim. The Taliban and other factions have committed widespread abuses against the Hazara Shiite minority. Outside areas of Taliban control, the rule of law is similarly nonexistent. Local authorities and strongmen administer justice arbitrarily according to the Sharia and traditional customs. Rival groups carry out torture and extrajudicial killings against opponents and suspected sympathizers. Northern-based opposition groups publish propaganda newspapers, operate radio stations, and run the only television station in Afghanistan from Faizabad. The opposition also operates schools for both boys and girls.

The UN estimates that Afghanistan is the most heavily mined country in the world despite more than a decade of internationally assisted mine clearance. Fighting has left tens of thousands of Afghans internally displaced, and there are some 2.6 million Afghan refugees in Iran and Pakistan. Despite some efforts by the Taliban to curb production, Afghanistan continued to be the world's largest producer of opium, the raw material for heroin. The UN-imposed sanctions worsened economic conditions in a country already ravaged by two decades of war.

↟Albania

Polity: Presidential-
parliamentary democracy
Economy: Mixed statist
(transitional)
Population: 3,400,000
PPP: $2,804
Life Expectancy: 73

Political Rights: 4
Civil Liberties: 5
Status: Partly Free

Ethnic Groups: Albanian (95 percent), Greeks (3 percent), others, including Roma, Serbs, and Bulgarians (2 percent)
Capital: Tirana
Trend Arrow: Albania received an upward trend arrow because municipal elections in October were the most violence free the country has enjoyed in the post-Communist period; however, widespread illegality in many parts of the country continues to inhibit governmental and social stability.

Overview: Albania's attempt to build a democratic polity made some progress in 2000, as local elections in October took place without the widespread violence characteristic of earlier elections. Still, the main opposition party questioned the results of the elections, casting a shadow over the proceedings, and continued lawlessness in many parts of the country hampered more dramatic improvements in the country's development.

From World War II until 1990, a xenophobic Communist regime ruled Albania and turned it into the most isolated country in Europe. In 1990, however, the Communist regime collapsed, and in March 1992, multiparty elections brought the Democratic Party (DP), under the leadership of Dr. Sali Berisha, to power. Berisha's government, however, was plagued by corruption, and Berisha himself quickly assumed autocratic ways of dealing with criticism. The collapse of several pyramid investment schemes in early 1997 caused much of the Albanian population to lose their life savings and led to a near civil war in the country. In the subsequent years the central government has been unable to reimpose meaningful control over much of northern Albania. In late 1997, the Socialist Party (SP), led by former Prime Minister Fatos Nano and several younger colleagues, came to power and has controlled the government in Tirana ever since.

Albania has been plagued by instability throughout its post-Communist history. In 2000, one of the major political-constitutional problems Albania faced involved the adoption of a new electoral code, which contained provisions for recounting votes and determining the validity of elections, as well as more efficient voter registration provisions. The Albanian parliament (*Kuvend Popullore*) adopted the new provisions despite an opposition boycott in May. Nevertheless, the passage of the new code, drafted with significant help from international experts, was seen as a step forward in institutionalizing Albania's electoral system. Another sign of increasing stability was Albania's admission into the World Trade Organization on July 17.

Despite these developments, however, Albania's domestic political scene remains extremely volatile. Former President Sali Berisha has remained a vociferous opponent of the ruling SP, led by Nano. Berisha has frequently accused the SP of criminal corruption and ties to Albanian organized crime. Berisha also frequently criticized the work of foreign election monitors in the country, claiming they were biased in favor of the Socialists. Another problem confronting Albania has been governmental instability. The current prime minister, Ilir Meta, has reshuffled his cabinet several times since coming to office in October 1999, most recently in July 2000, when personnel in the Ministries of Defense, Justice, and Public Works were fired or rotated.

Contrary to many pre-election forecasts, Berisha's DP did relatively poorly in the 2000 municipal elections, held on October 1. Although international monitors reported serious problems in the organization of the second round of municipal elections (which the DP boycotted), the overall election process marked progress.

One of the spillover effects of the Kosovo conflict is the problem it has raised for a resolution of both the Albanian national question and the Albanian state question; in fact, the Albanian national question dominated much of the public debate in the 2000 municipal elections. Since the anarchy of 1997, restoring viable state institutions in the country has been a slow process. Since Kosovo, Albanians in Albania proper are now dealing with the question of whether the "solution" to the Albanian state question should be found within the country along a north-south Tirana-Vlore axis, or whether it will be found outside the country, along a Tirana-Pristina (i.e., Kosovo) axis.

Political Rights and Civil Liberties:

The Albanian constitution guarantees citizens freedom of expression and of the press, as well as freedom of association. These rights are generally respected. Several political parties exist and compete for power, although the rhetoric employed by competing politicians is inflammatory by European standards. In the 2000 municipal election campaign, however, rival candidates for the mayoral race in Tirana met in a televised public debate and managed to avoid such heated rhetoric, an event hailed as offering a more civilized example for Albanian public life. Albania also has several active trade unions, the most prominent of which are the Confederation of Trade Unions of Albanian, with some 280,000 members, and the Confederation of Unions, which is affiliated with the SP. The are no significant reports of governmental harassment of either foreign or domestic nongovernmental organizations (NGOs), although several foreign NGOs have refused to operate in northern Albania because of the lack of security in the region.

Albania's small Greek minority (approximately 3 percent of the population, concentrated in southern Albania) has intermittently been subjected to various forms of discrimination. During the 2000 municipal elections campaign, despite the bitter rivalry between the SP and the DP, both parties agreed to join forces to prevent a party representing ethnic Greeks in the town of Himara, the Union for Human Rights, from gaining seats in the municipal assembly.

The Albanian constitution provides for freedom of religion and religious practice. Although much of Albanian society became secularized during the Communist period, approximately 70 percent of the population is nominally Muslim, 20 percent is Roman Catholic, and 10 percent Orthodox Christian. There were no major complaints about freedom of worship in the country in 2000, although there have been several reported incidents of vandalism against Greek Orthodox places of worship in southern Albania. The government still has not fully resolved the issue of restitution of church properties confiscated during the Communist period.

Freedom of the press is also generally respected, and there are few direct attacks on the media. The level of adherence to U.S.- or European-style journalistic ethics, however, remains low, as Albanian media are considered to be prone to excessive sensationalism and irresponsibility. Also, most media outlets are directly linked to certain political or business groups, which compromises their reporting. The state television and radio network, Radio Televize Shqiptare (RTSH), and the official state news agency, the Albanian Telegraphic Agency (ATA), are both considered to be excessively pro-government.

The position of women in Albanian society continues to pose significant problems. Many segments of Albanian society, particularly in the mountains of northeastern Albania, still abide by a medieval moral code in which women are considered chattel property and may be treated as such. The kidnapping of young women to serve as brides is frequently reported in these areas. According to the Albanian constitution, however, there are no legal impediments to women's role in politics and society, although women are vastly underrepresented in most governmental institutions. The Albanian labor code mandates that women are entitled to equal pay for equal work, but data is lacking on whether this is respected in practice. The trafficking of women and girls for the purposes of prostitution remains a significant problem.

Albania continues to be plagued by widespread lawlessness. Since 1997, more than 100 policemen have been killed in a country with a population half the size of New York City. In August, Arben Zylyftari, widely considered to be Albania's best police officer, was killed in a shootout with a murder suspect in the northern town of Shkoder. Another northern town, Tropoje, has gone through five police chiefs since the summer of 1999. Northern Albania is especially unstable owing to a variety of factors, including the fact that it is Berisha's home base, and that the Kosovo Liberation Army has a strong presence in the region, effectively preventing legitimate state institutions from establishing authority there. Another problem facing Albania is the persistence of blood feuds between different families and clans. The weakness of state institutions has also provided space for international criminal syndicates to operate more freely in Albania, and international law enforcement officials claim that Albania has become an increasingly important transshipment point for drug smugglers moving opiates, hashish, and cannabis from southwest Asia to Western Europe and the United States. In November, the Organization for Security and Cooperation in Europe spokesperson in Albania was forced to leave the country after receiving death threats.

Algeria

Polity: Dominant party (military-influenced)
Political Rights: 6
Civil Liberties: 5
Status: Not Free
Economy: Statist
Population: 31,500,000
PPP: $4,792
Life Expectancy: 69
Ethnic Groups: Arab Berber (99 percent), European (1percent)
Capital: Algiers

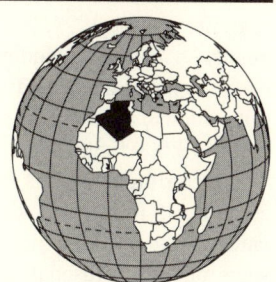

Overview:

Algerians suffered a ninth year of violent conflict despite President Abdelaziz Bouteflika's efforts to end the fighting between radical Islamists and government forces. His year-old "civil reconciliation plan" has yielded few tangible results as he struggles with the politically dominant army, public apathy, and international criticism of Algeria's human rights record.

After a violent liberation struggle convinced France to abandon 130 years of colonial rule, Algeria achieved independence in 1962. The National Liberation Front (FLN) ruled as a virtual one-party regime until the political system was reformed in 1989. Antigovernment sentiment stemming from corruption, housing shortages, unemployment, and other severe economic and social problems boosted the opposition Islamic Salvation Front (FIS) despite the party's avowed commitment to theocratic rule under *Sharia* (Islamic law). In 1992, the army canceled a second round of legislative elections in which the FIS had achieved a commanding lead and banned the party, setting off a civil conflict marked by often random violence that has claimed more than 100,000 lives.

Accurate information about the conflict is difficult to obtain because of heavy official censorship and an Islamist campaign that has killed approximately 70 journalists and forced many into exile. While radical Islamists are primarily responsible for the massacres of men, women, and children that have characterized the conflict, government-backed militias have also apparently committed some mass killings. Human rights groups have charged government forces with thousands of disappearances, torture, and other excesses against alleged militants and their suspected supporters.

Bouteflika, a former foreign minister, was elected president in April 1999. Although the military approved seven presidential candidates, the ruling generals openly favored Bouteflika, which made him the guaranteed winner well before the polls opened. His six opponents withdrew from the race on the eve of elections, charging vote rigging and electoral fraud.

Weeks after taking office, Bouteflika began an aggressive campaign to shore up his legitimacy and to win the support of a public weary of conflict, high unemployment, and rampant corruption. He introduced his reconciliation plan, the cornerstone of which was a peace agreement between the government and the Islamic Salvation Army (AIS), the armed wing of the outlawed FIS. When the AIS offered a formal ceasefire in June 1999, Bouteflika announced an amnesty for Islamist rebels who renounced violence, excluding those convicted of rape or murder. The peace plan won wide support in a referendum in September. After further negotiations, the AIS won a full pardon just prior to the amnesty deadline of January 13, 2000. Numbering between 800 and 3,000 fighters, the AIS formally disbanded.

According to reports from various sources, between 1,700 and 5,500 rebels, including AIS fighters, took advantage of the amnesty. However, the radical Armed Islamic Group (GIA), which has been blamed for most of the killings of the past eight years, publicly refused the amnesty and vowed to continue its attacks. As the amnesty expired, Bouteflika promised a merciless campaign to eradicate remaining guerrilla factions. The first seven months of 2000 saw a marked escalation of violence, with at least 200 people killed each month in attacks attributed to Islamists and military operations against rebel strongholds. At year's end, almost daily reports of killings in clashes between the army and guerrillas continued. The Muslim holy month of Ramadan, which occurred in December, saw at least 300 killed in an upsurge of violence.

Despite promises to reform the judiciary, privatize state-owned industries, and fight corruption, Bouteflika has achieved little in these areas. The army continues to dominate politics, limiting his authority. Changes in official policy reflect shifts in the balance of power among infighting military factions whose vested interests could be threatened by political and economic reform. Yet Bouteflika has moved to consolidate his power. In August, he dismissed 13 high-ranking local officials and replaced several members of his cabinet, including the prime minister, with supporters from the FLN.

With little success and widespread public apathy at home, Bouteflika turned his attention to international diplomacy. He participated in shuttle diplomacy between Ethiopia and Eritrea, and became the first Algerian leader since 1982 to visit France. His warm reception in Paris in June suggested a breakthrough in relations, but Bouteflika failed to receive an official apology for French occupation of Algeria, a guarantee of economic aid, or an agreement to purchase advanced weapons from France. Furthermore, he was confronted by protesters, including human rights groups and families of missing Algerians, who demanded investigations into human rights abuses during the past eight years.

Political Rights and Civil Liberties: Algerians' right to choose their government freely in democratic elections has never been honored. The country has effectively been under martial law since the cancellation of the 1992 polls. April 1999 presidential elections were restricted to seven military-approved candidates. Reports of irregularities included official intimidation of contenders' supporters, media favoritism of the military-backed candidate, padding of election rolls, and distribution of preprinted ballots. Upon withdrawing from the race, Bouteflika's opponents called the electoral process a "charade." June 1997 legislative polls excluded the main Islamic opposition groups and were conducted under severe restrictions of free expression and association. The 1996 constitution expanded presidential powers and banned Islamic-based parties. The continuing state of emergency and an antiterrorism decree give the regime almost unlimited power.

Both sides in the conflict commit serious human rights abuses, and the rule of law is seldom respected. In October 1999, Bouteflika publicly denounced the judiciary, saying that it "has not been able to protect the citizens against serious abuses. In fact, most of the time it supports the views of the powerful." Around the same time, the president announced the formation of a national commission to reform the judiciary, but as yet no specific reforms have been announced.

The 1992 Antiterrorist Law suspends many due process safeguards. Security forces and pro-government militias are responsible for extrajudicial executions, torture, arbitrary arrests, detention without trial, and disappearances. Despite government claims that security forces are routinely brought to justice for human rights abuses, the authorities have not made such cases public. No independent investigation into the fate of up to 4,600 people who disappeared since 1993, after having been abducted by security forces and state-armed militias, has been initiated. Armed Islamist rebels continue to abduct and brutally murder men, women, and children, although government soldiers and pro-government militias are primary targets.

In a change of policy, Bouteflika in March invited four international human rights organizations to visit Algeria during May and June. Amnesty International (AI) delegates met with officials and human rights activists and reported that although the human rights situation in Algeria is improving, the need for a full, independent investigation into human rights abuses by government and antigovernment forces remains. AI also expressed concern that the amnesty offered under the civil reconciliation plan will hinder investigations into abuses committed by militants who have surrendered. AI visited again in November, and reported that authorities refused to meet with the delegation to discuss human rights abuses committed in the past eight years. The Paris-based Federation of Human Rights Leagues accused security forces and militia of summarily executing suspected Muslim rebels in various parts of the country.

Press freedom is limited by governmental pressure, legal constraints, and the Islamist insurgency. Although violence against journalists has abated in recent years, some 70 journalists have been killed by Islamists and hundreds have fled the country. According to Reporters Sans Frontieres, of five journalists "disappeared" between 1994 and 1997, two were kidnapped by armed Islamists and three were evidently taken by security forces. The government controls broadcast media. Foreign journalists are rarely granted visas to work in Algeria, and few foreign titles have permission to appear on Algerian newsstands. The state of emergency restricts press freedom and punishes undefined threats to the state or to public order. A 1990 law requires speech to respect "individual dignity, the imperatives of foreign policy, and the national defense." "Reading committees" used to censor the private press were abolished in 1998, but the state monopoly on paper, printing, and advertising leaves private media vulnerable to financial pressure. In February, two journalists were ordered to pay symbolic fines in a defamation suit filed by a retired military general. A visit by a delegation of Algerian journalists to Israel in June was called "treasonous" by Bouteflika, members of the ruling coalition, and Islamists, which prompted concern in the international press freedom community for their safety.

Freedom of assembly is sharply limited. Official permission is required for public meetings, with the exception of legal opposition party meetings. However, public assemblies that do not support the government are rarely permitted. Emergency legislation restricts freedom of association. Nongovernmental organizations must have licenses, and the interior ministry may deny a license to or dissolve any group regarded as a threat to public order. Membership in the FIS is illegal, and despite the 1999 peace agreement between the government and the FIS, the government has given no indication that the FIS will be allowed to return to political life.

Islam is the state religion, and the law limits the practice of other faiths. However, small Christian and Jewish communities practice without government interference. Radical Muslims have killed and issued public threats against perceived "infidels," though extremists do not differentiate between religious and political killings.

Berbers, who live mainly in the northeastern Kabylie region, have been targeted by radical Islamists for their liberal interpretation of Islam. The largest ethnic minority, Berbers have sought to maintain their cultural and linguistic identity in the face of the government's Arabization program. A 1998 law made Arabic the official language of Algeria and marginalized Tamazight, the native Berber language. The law requires that all official business, national broadcast media, communications equipment, and medical prescriptions use Arabic.

The 1984 Family Code, based on Sharia, discriminates against women in matters of marriage, divorce, inheritance, and child custody. In August, the government announced plans to appoint five women as ambassadors to foreign capitals.

Workers have the right to establish trade unions and to strike. About two-thirds of the labor force is unionized.

Andorra

Polity: Parliamentary democracy
Economy: Capitalist
Population: 100,000
PPP: na
Life Expectancy: na
Ethnic Groups: Spanish (61 percent), Andorran (30 percent), French (6 percent), other (3 percent)
Capital: Andorra la Vella

Political Rights: 1
Civil Liberties: 1
Status: Free

Overview:

After being ruled jointly since 1278 by the French state and the Spanish bishops of Seo de Urgel, Andorra acquired independence and adopted its first constitution in 1993. The constitution defines Andorra as a "parliamentary co-principality" in which the president of France and the bishop of Seo de Urgel serve as co-princes, heads of state with limited and largely symbolic power. Sovereignty rests with Andorra's citizens.

Politics is dominated by five major parties. Four of them governed in coalition until early 1997, when the Liberal Union party won 18 of the 28 Consell General (parliament) seats. Marc Forne Molne of the Liberal Union currently serves as head of the cabinet of ministers.

Andorra has no national currency, but circulates Spanish pesetas and French francs. By virtue of its association with Spain and France, it has also adopted the euro despite not being a member of the European Monetary Union. In 1991, Andorra established a customs union with the European Union (EU) that permits free movement of industrial goods. Andorra became a member of the United Nations in 1993 and a member of the Council of Europe in 1994.

With the creation of the EU internal market, Andorra has lost its privileged duty-free status and is recovering from an economic recession. Tourism, the mainstay of Andorra's economy, accounts for about 80 percent of gross domestic product. Because of banking secrecy laws and Andorra's tax haven status, the financial services sector is of growing importance to the economy.

Political Rights and Civil Liberties:

Andorrans can change their government democratically. Elections were held in 1997 to choose members of the Consell General, which selects the head of government. Popular elections to the 28-member Consell are held every four years, with 14 members chosen by the national constituency and 14 chosen to represent the seven parishes, or administrative divisions.

The judiciary is independent and efficient, and citizens enjoy full due process rights, including the right to free counsel for the indigent. Freedom of speech and the press is guaranteed in law and in practice. The domestic press consists of two daily and several weekly newspapers. Andorra has two radio stations, one state owned and one privately owned, and six television stations. Several French and Spanish stations can be accessed in Andorra.

There are no limitations on domestic or foreign travel, emigration, or repatriation. Andorra does not expel persons with valid claims to refugee status and cooperates with the UN High Commissioner for Refugees and other humanitarian organizations in assisting refugees.

Women enjoy the same legal, political, social, and professional rights as men, although they are underrepresented in government. Of 11 government ministers, only 2 are women, and there is only one female member of the Consell. The Association of Andorran Women actively promotes women's issues through education and outreach. It has reported that many women have been dismissed from employment because of pregnancy.

Workers may form trade unions, bargain collectively, and strike. A police trade union was registered during 1999. It is the first such association to exist in Andorra.

↑Angola

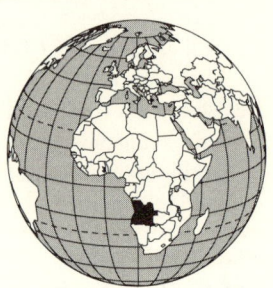

Polity: Presidential-parliamentary (insurgency)
Economy: Statist
Population: 12,900,000
PPP: $1,821
Life Expectancy: 47
Ethnic Groups: Ovimbundu (37 percent), Kimbundu (25 percent), Bakongo (13 percent), mestizo (2 percent), European (1 percent), other (22 percent)
Capital: Luanda
Trend Arrow: Angola received an upward trend arrow due to greater freedom exercised by civil society and opposition political parties.

Political Rights: 6
Civil Liberties: 6
Status: Not Free

Overview:

Confident from gains on the battlefield, President José Eduardo dos Santos extended a pardon offer to his adversary of 25 years, Jonas Savimbi, if the guerrilla leader publicly expressed regret for the war. Savimbi rejected the offer. Efforts to end the war that had resumed in 1998 were stepped up through the more active involvement of the Roman Catholic Church. Thousands of people participated in a peace march in the capital, Luanda, in June.

Angola has been at war since shortly after independence from Portugal in 1975. During the cold war, the United States and South Africa backed UNITA while the former Soviet Union and Cuba supported the Marxist Dos Santos government. The conflict has claimed at least half a million lives.

The United Nations Security Council voted in February 1999 to end the UN peace-keeping mission in Angola following the collapse of the peace process and the shooting down of two UN planes. However, the UN maintains an office in the country. Neither the MPLA nor UNITA has ever fully complied with the 1994 Lusaka peace accords. UN secretary general Kofi Annan warned in October that he feared Angola's conflict could spread across the borders into Zambia and Namibia and threaten peace and security in the southern Africa region. In Namibia, both Namibian and Angolan forces, as well as UNITA, have been accused of rights abuses, including extrajudicial executions and torture. There have been raids by UNITA across the Zambian border, and attacks by Angolan government forces.

A Catholic Church-sponsored Congress for Peace was held in Luanda in September 2000, bringing together civil society groups, a wide cross section of church members, opposition politicians, and officials from the ruling party. The ruling Popular Movement for the Liberation of Angola (MPLA) and the rebel National Union for the Total Independence of Angola (UNITA) have traditionally dominated peace discussions, excluding other Angolans.

Despite greater freedom allowed in discussing the civil war, repression of the press continued with a number of arrests and trials that human rights groups say have been unfair. Journalists denounced plans for a new "gag law," which incorporates articles included in a state security law and would make it nearly impossible to cover any matter relating to the country's political life without risking incarceration.

Petroleum accounts for 90 percent of government revenue, but state corruption and a lack of transparency have prevented the average Angolan from benefiting from the wealth. In May 2000, the government signed on to an International Monetary Fund program for transparency and accountability in the oil industry in an effort to unblock Western donor budgetary financing. Angola has been mortgaging its oil earnings to raise commercial loans and has also used its oil revenue to procure weapons. Angola accounts for about ten percent of annual global production of diamonds, which UNITA has used to fund its weapons purchases. International sanctions have been placed against UNITA, but there are numerous reports of sanctions busting.

Political Rights and Civil Liberties:

Angolans freely elected their representatives for the only time in the September 1992 UN-supervised presidential and legislative elections. The vote was described by international observers as generally free and fair despite many irregularities. But Savimbi rejected his defeat to Dos Santos in the first round of presidential voting and resumed the war.

The MPLA dominates the 220-member national assembly, although 70 UNITA members continue to sit in parliament. New elections were provisionally scheduled for 2001, but the government says they will be held "only if conditions permit." Opposition parties met in September 2000 to define a strategy for their participation in future elections and decided that they should contribute to resolve the country's problems together. More than 100 political parties exist in Angola, and so far they have seemed to take no real steps towards cohesion. Twelve opposition parties hold seats in parliament.

Religious freedom is generally respected, and the Roman Catholic Church has taken on an increasingly prominent role in trying to bring about peace. Serious human rights abuses, including torture, abduction, rape, sexual slavery, and extrajudicial execution, by both government and rebel security forces, have been widespread. Both sides conduct forced recruitment of civilians, including minors. Local courts rule on civil matters and petty crime in some areas, but an overall lack of training and infrastructure inhibit judicial proceedings, which are also heavily influenced by the government. Many prisoners were detained for long periods in life-threatening conditions while awaiting trial.

Despite constitutional guarantees of freedom of expression, the media have suffered a serious clampdown characterized by severe and sometimes violent measures. A new draft press law has been described as a "gag law." It includes 81 articles, one of which guarantees presidential immunity to criticism and possible prison terms of up to eight years. The draft law also gives authorities the right to decide who can be a journalist, and the power to seize or ban publications at their discretion. Journalists who are arrested may be held for 30 days until charges are filed, and journalists can be prosecuted within a two-year period from the date of publication. Public debate on the bill ended in October 2000.

In March 2000, Rafael Marques, a freelance journalist who had written an article criticizing Dos Santos, was sentenced to six-months imprisonment and a heavy fine for defamation. He was unlawfully detained and denied legal counsel of his choice during the trial. The sentence was later suspended. André Mussamo, a radio journalist, was accused of divulging state secrets in an article which he had drafted but not published. He was detained for more than three months.

Despite legal protections, de facto societal discrimination against women remains strong, particularly in rural areas. There is a high incidence of spousal abuse. Women are most likely to become victims of land mines because they are usually the ones who forage for food and firewood.

Labor rights are guaranteed by the constitution, but only a few independent unions are functioning and those exist in the cities. The government dominates the labor movement and restricts worker rights, although there has been some improvement. The vast majority of rural agricultural workers remain outside the modern economic sector, and their livelihood has been further jeopardized by the war.

Antigua and Barbuda

Polity: Dominant party
Economy: Capitalist-statist
Population: 100,000
PPP: $9,277
Life Expectancy: 76
Ethnic Groups: Black (89 percent), other including British, Portuguese, Lebanese, and Syrian (11 percent)
Capital: St. John's

Political Rights: 4
Civil Liberties: 2*
Status: Partly Free

Ratings Change: Antigua and Barbuda's civil liberties rating changed from 3 to 2 largely due to increased accountability of its prison system and some improvement in the regulation of its crime-susceptible offshore financial sector.

Overview: Efforts to improve the regulation of Antigua and Barbuda's offshore financial sector won qualified praise from the international community, as the long-reigning Bird family dynasty, currently headed by Prime Minister Lester Bird, sought to respond to international pressure to fight money laundering. In 1999 Bird received a strong vote of confidence in elections for policies that have made the two-island nation one of the region's most prosperous. However, in recent years it has become increasingly apparent that Antigua's democratic institutions have been threatened by individuals who infiltrated government bodies as a means of weakening fledgling money laundering and offshore business controls. Meanwhile, Antiguan business leaders threatened forceful protests if the government institutes a first-ever tax on corporate income.

Antigua and Barbuda is a member of the Commonwealth. The British monarchy is represented by a governor-general. The islands gained independence in 1981. Under the 1981 constitution, the political system is a parliamentary democracy, with a bicameral parliament consisting of a 17-member house of representatives elected for five years and an appointed senate. In the house, there are 16 seats for Antigua and 1 for Barbuda. Eleven senators are appointed by the prime minister, four by the parliamentary opposition leader, one by the Barbuda Council, and one by the governor-general.

Dominated by the Bird family and the Antigua Labour Party (ALP), rule has been based more on power and the abuse of authority than on law. The constitution has been consistently disregarded. The Bird tenure has also been marked by scandals ranging from Antigua's role as a transshipment center for South American cocaine destined for the United States and Europe, to its involvement in arms smuggling for the Colombian cartels, to its importance as a money-laundering center.

In 1994 Vere Bird, patriarch of the most prominent family, stepped down as prime minister in favor of his son Lester. In the run-up to the 1994 election, three opposition parties united to form the United Progressive Party (UPP). The UPP campaigned on a social-democratic platform emphasizing rule of law and good governance. In the election, the ALP won 11 of 17 parliamentary seats, down from 15 in 1989, while the UPP won 5, up from 1.

After taking office as prime minister, Lester Bird promised cleaner, more efficient government. But his administration continued to be dogged by scandals. In 1995 Bird's brother, Ivor, was convicted of smuggling cocaine into the country, but received only a fine.

The country's thriving offshore-banking industry has repeatedly been the target of international concern about inadequate regulation and vetting that led to a surge in questionable banking operations, a number with alleged links to Russian organized crime. In 1998, Antigua and Barbuda's offshore industry, serviced by some 50 loosely regulated banks, was rocked by public disclosure of what the U.S. Customs Service called the biggest non-narcotics money-laundering racket it had ever uncovered. A crackdown in 1999 on Russian-owned banks (six were closed down in 1998) has been offset by renewed efforts to ensure even greater banking secrecy and a reluctance to cooperate with foreign law enforcement.

The March 1999 elections resulted in the ALP winning 12 of the 17 parliamentary seats; the UPP, 4; and the Barbuda People's Movement retaining its single seat. In 2000, Antigua appeared poised to move to rein in its offshore financial industry, following pressure for greater international cooperation from the Financial Action Task Force (FATF) based in Paris. Plans to institute a corporate income tax in Antigua and Barbuda, which enjoys the lowest tax rate of the eight countries of the Organization of Eastern Caribbean States, do not include additional levies on the lucrative offshore industry.

Political Rights and Civil Liberties:

Constitutionally, citizens are able to change their government by democratic means. However, the ruling party's long-standing monopoly on patronage and its power to provide access to economic opportunities make it difficult for opposition parties to attract membership and financial support. Political parties, labor unions, and civic organizations are free to organize. In 1999, an international observer group noted that the national voter registry included 52,348 names, out of a total population of some 69,000 people, a number that appeared inflated given that an estimated 40 percent of the population is below voting age. This anomaly was even more glaring given that the country's week-long registration period for new voters is restrictive and appears to disenfranchise potential participants in elections.

The judiciary, which is part of the eastern Caribbean legal system, is nominally independent, but subject to manipulation by the ruling party; it has been nearly powerless to address corruption in the executive branch. There is an intra-island court of appeals for Antigua and five other former British colonies in the Lesser Antilles.

The islands' security forces are composed of the police and the small Antigua and

Barbuda Defence Forces. The police, which are organized, trained, and supervised according to British law-enforcement practices, generally respect human rights; basic police reporting statistics, however, are confidential. Conditions at the country's eighteenth-century prison, which was recently privatized, are primitive and the institution has been criticized for abusing its inmates. These credible reports have been met with a government willingness to both investigate the charges and take administrative action. The government does permit visits to the prison by independent human rights groups.

The ALP government and the Bird family control the country's television, cable, and radio outlets. Opposition parties claim that they receive limited coverage from, and have little opportunity to express their views on, the government-controlled electronic media. Freedom of religion is respected. Social discrimination and violence against women is a problem; the governmental Directorate of Women's Affairs has sought to increase awareness about women's rights under the law.

The Industrial Court mediates labor disputes, but public sector unions tend to be under the sway of the ruling party. Demonstrators are occasionally subject to harassment by the police, who are politically tied to the ruling party.

Argentina

Polity: Presidential-parliamentary democracy (federal)
Economy: Capitalist
Population: 37,000,000
PPP: $12,013
Life Expectancy: 73
Ethnic Groups: European [mostly Spanish and Italian] (85 percent), other, including mestizo, Indian (15 percent)
Capital: Buenos Aires

Political Rights: 1*
Civil Liberties: 2*
Status: Free

Ratings Change: Argentina's political rights rating changed from 2 to 1 due to efforts to curb opportunities for congressional and executive branch corruption, particularly by changing laws and regulations governing the conduct of elections and in promoting ethical behavior of elected representatives. Its civil liberties rating changed from 3 to 2 due to improvements in the treatment of the media, in attention to issues of public corruption, and, to a lesser extent, in the operation of the judiciary.

Overview:
In office for its first year, the multiparty government of President Fernando de la Rua found itself confronted by a minefield of public corruption and economic sluggishness bequeathed by his predecessor, Carlos S. Menem. Faced with a senate and a judiciary packed with Menem supporters, De la Rua lost a crucial ally—his vice president—who resigned in protest of the official handling of a congressional bribery scandal that appeared similar to tactics used during the Menem government. The scandal threatened to wreck De la Rua's center-left coalition and squander the clean-government political capital it had

won while in the opposition. By year's end, the government's tentative efforts to confront spiraling violent crime and the growing impoverishment of parts of the middle class led to growing disaffection with the government as well. The fight against crime has been complicated by Menem's legacy of security forces and intelligence agencies seasoned with former death squad activists and former members of a lethal military regime, whose presence has exacerbated a troublesome and long-standing problem of excessive violence and corruption on the part of the police.

The Argentine Republic was established after independence from Spain in 1816. Democratic rule was often interrupted by military coups. The end of Juan Peron's authoritarian rule in 1955 led to a series of right-wing military dictatorships as well as left-wing and nationalist violence. Argentina returned to elected civilian rule in 1983, after seven years of repression of suspected leftist guerrillas and other dissidents.

As amended in 1994, the 1853 constitution provides for a president elected for four years with the option of reelection to one term. Presidential candidates must win 45 percent of the vote to avoid a runoff. The legislature consists of a 257-member chamber of deputies elected for six years, with half the seats renewable every three years, and a 72-member senate nominated by elected provincial legislatures for nine-year terms, with one-third of the seats renewable every three years. Two senators are directly elected in the newly autonomous Buenos Aires federal district.

As provincial governor, Menem, running an orthodox Peronist platform of nationalism and state intervention in the economy, won a six-year presidential term in 1989, amidst hyperinflation and food riots. Once inaugurated, Menem discarded statist Peronist traditions by implementing, mostly by decree, an economic liberalization program.

Rampant corruption and unemployment headed voters' concerns when in October 1997 they handed Menem's Peronists their first nationwide defeat. The Alliance, composed of the centrist Radical Party and the center-left Front for a Country in Solidarity beat Menem's party, 46 percent to 36 percent. On November 29, 1998, Buenos Aires mayor and Radical Party leader Fernando de la Rua won a contested primary to become the Alliance candidate in the 1999 presidential elections. In anticipation of his party's eventual defeat, Menem orchestrated the packing of the Argentine senate with two members of his ruling party in an attempt to stave off corruption inquiries until at least 2001.

At the end of 1999, Transparency International ranked Argentina 72 out of 99 nations rated for public corruption. Menem's feud with the Peronist Party presidential nominee, Buenos Aires governor Eduardo Duhalde, sealed the latter's fate as Duhalde was beaten by De la Rua 48.5 percent to 38 percent in national elections held on October 24, 1999. The Peronists retained control of the senate, with 35 of 67 seats, and they hold the governorships in 18 of 23 provinces. Upon taking office, De la Rua sought to put the government's accounts in order, cut spending, raise taxes, and push forward with unpopular labor reforms. He also made a series of appointments and issued sweeping rules and regulations designed to rein in public corruption. A reform-minded serving police officer was appointed head of the corruption-riddled Federal Police, and there also appeared to be a greater willingness by some judges to investigate cases of official corruption, including vote-buying scandals in both houses of congress. In April, De la Rua dismissed a nine-member military tribunal after they claimed military rather than civilian courts had jurisdiction over cases in which military personnel had been accused of kidnapping, and in some cases killing, hundreds of babies born to detained women during the so-called dirty war of the 1970s and 1980s.

De la Rua's government also moved to confront a problem of mostly narcotics-related money laundering that had ballooned under Menem. In May, the Alliance received a boost when its candidate, Anibal Ibarra, won the Buenos Aires mayoralty vacated by De la Rua when he assumed the presidency in December. In October 2000 De la Rua twice reshuffled his cabinet, the second time after Vice President Carlos Alvarez's stunning decision to resign. Alvarez stepped down after the president's determination appeared to waiver on uncovering the truth about the reported buying of congressional votes in order to pass labor legislation. Possible government involvement, including members of De la Rua's inner circle, was suspected in the vote buying. In December, a judge who himself was under investigation for "illegal enrichment," dropped the charges against the 11 senators named in the scandal, saying he lacked sufficient evidence to proceed.

Political Rights and Civil Liberties:

Citizens can change their government through elections. Constitutional guarantees regarding freedom of religion and the right to organize political parties, civic organizations, and labor unions are generally respected. The 1999 elections were generally free and fair, with serious complaints of voter fraud in only one province. More worrisome was the trend towards campaigning through the mass media, a costly process financed by money from largely undisclosed sources. Scandals uncovered in 2000 lent credence to reports throughout the Menem administration of congressional vote buying. Several senators resigned their seats in order to face possible criminal charges after an investigation was launched by a judge.

The situation of human rights groups and journalists, the latter of which had been subjected to more than 1,000 beatings, kidnappings, and death threats during Menem's rule, improved notably under De la Rua. In 2000, several people, including Buenos Aires police officers, were sentenced in connection with their role in the murder three years earlier of a photojournalist, reportedly at the instigation of a key Menem associate and business leader. In 2000, journalist Eduardo Kimel was sentenced to a one-year suspended sentence and fined $20,000 for publishing, in a book about the 1976 massacre of five religious workers during the military regime, that the judge in the case did not properly investigate the still-unsolved crime.

Labor is dominated by Peronist unions. Union influence, however, has diminished because of corruption scandals, internal divisions, and restrictions on public sector strikes decreed by Menem to pave the way for his privatization program. In 1998, a deadlocked congress approved a government-sponsored labor flexibility initiative after a congressional deputy who was allegedly filmed by state intelligence agents in a gay bordello operated by the agents changed positions on the measure and voted for it.

Menem's authoritarian ways and manipulation of the judiciary resulted in undermining the country's separation of powers and the rule of law. In 1990, Menem pushed a bill through the Peronist-controlled senate that allowed him to stack the supreme court with an additional four members and to fill the judiciary with politically loyal judges. He used the supreme court to uphold decrees removing the comptroller general and other officials mandated to probe government wrongdoing. Overall, the judicial system is politicized, inefficient, and riddled with the corruption endemic to all branches of government. The politization of the judiciary and the tenure of scores of incompetent and—it is widely believed—corrupt judges remain grave problems.

Public safety is a primary concern for Argentinians who just a generation ago enjoyed a country with one of the world's lowest rates of violent common crime. Within a decade, crime in Argentina has doubled and, in Buenos Aires, tripled, a reflection of high unemployment levels and a widening gap between rich and poor. Criminal court judges are frequent targets of anonymous threats. Police misconduct, during the Menem administration often seemingly promoted by senior government officials—including the president himself—resulted in a number of allegedly extrajudicial executions by law enforcement officers. The Buenos Aires provincial police, in particular, have been heavily involved in drug trafficking, extortion, vice, and, at least until 2000, the collecting of political funds for the ruling Peronist Party. Arbitrary arrests and ill-treatment by police are rarely punished in civil courts owing to intimidation of witnesses and judges, particularly in the Buenos Aires province. There the newly elected governor, Carlos Ruckauf, has pursued ironhanded anticrime policies, exhorting a police force, already heavily criticized for excessive force, to shoot at criminals' arms and legs without prior warning, "pumping them full of bullets." Ruckauf named to top provincial justice posts a former military coup leader and a former policeman accused of systematic torture in detention camps during a previous armed forces dictatorship. In August 2000, the provincial supreme court declared its "deep preoccupation" with the abuse, including torture, meted out by the police to adolescents, saying that the "recurring problem" had been "consistently" brought to Ruckauf's attention. The Center for Legal and Social Studies noted in early 2000 that in the previous two years the number of civilians killed by the police had risen in the greater Buenos Aires area by 78 percent, from 113 to 202. In October 2000 the reformist stewardship of Federal Police chief Ruben Jorge Santos was tarnished somewhat when 11 officers, including two senior officials, were charged in connection with a prison escape the month before in which two men held for the 1999 assassination of the Paraguayan vice president escaped.

Prison conditions are generally substandard. In 2000, it was revealed that prisoners in a federal jail ran a workshop to strip stolen cars and paid wardens who smuggled drugs into the prison for them. Witnesses at a trial told how mutineers in a recent prison riot killed seven fellow inmates, cooked their bodies, and fed them to their hostages.

The investigation of a 1994 car bombing of a Jewish organization, in which more than 80 people died, has languished because of sloppy police work at the crime scene and alleged complicity by members of the security forces with the terrorists. Six policemen believed to have served as accomplices in the crime are scheduled for trial in 2001. The Roman Catholic majority enjoys freedom of religious expression. The 250,000-strong Jewish community is a frequent target of anti-Semitic vandalism. Neo-Nazi organizations and other anti-Semitic groups, frequently tied to remnants of the old-line security services, some of whom retain their posts, remain active.

A study released by the United Nations Children's Fund in 2000 showed that child prostitution was a serious problem, exacerbated by the growing number of hungry children.

Armenia

Polity: Presidential-parliamentary democracy
Economy: Mixed statist (transitional)
Population: 3,800,000
PPP: $2,072
Life Expectancy: 71
Ethnic Groups: Armenian (93 percent), Russian (2 percent), other, including Kurdish (5 percent)
Capital: Yerevan

Political Rights: 4
Civil Liberties: 4
Status: Partly Free

Overview:

The fallout from the October 1999 assassinations of Prime Minister Vazgen Sarkisian and Parliamentary Speaker Karen Demirchian continued to dominate the political scene in the year 2000. The crisis created an initial power vacuum in the country's leadership that paralyzed domestic and international policy initiatives and ignited a power struggle between President Kocharian and the slain prime minister's allies. In January 2000, investigators alleged that several members of President Robert Kocharian's inner circle may have been behind the October 27 shootings, prompting some opposition figures to call for Kocharian's resignation. However, Kocharian gradually consolidated his power throughout the year to emerge as the most powerful figure in the country's leadership.

This landlocked, predominantly Christian region was ruled at various times by Macedonians, Romans, Persians, Mongols, Turks, and others. Following a brief period of independence from 1918 to 1920, the Russian region came under Communist control and was designated a Soviet republic in 1922, while western Armenia was returned to Turkey. Armenia declared its independence from the Soviet Union in September 1991.

Nine political parties were banned prior to the 1995 parliamentary elections, thereby ensuring the victory of the Republican bloc led by the ruling Armenian National Movement (ANM). In the 1996 presidential election, the ANM's Levon Ter Petrosian defeated former Prime Minister Vazgen Manukian, who ran on a pro-market, anticorruption platform. Petrosian resigned in February 1998 following mass defections from the ANM and the resignation of key officials in protest over his gradualist approach in negotiations over control of Nagorno-Karabakh, the disputed Armenian enclave in Azerbaijan. In March, Prime Minister Kocharian, who earlier had served as president of Nagorno-Karabakh, was elected president over former Soviet Armenian leader Karen Demirchian. In April, Kocharian appointed former Finance and Economy Minister Armen Darbinian as prime minister.

Parliamentary elections on May 30, 1999, resulted in an overwhelming victory for the Unity bloc, a new alliance of Defense Minister Vazgen Sarkisian's Republican Party and Karen Demirchian's People's Party. The Unity bloc, which campaigned on a populist platform of greater state involvement in the economy and increased social spending, received 56 seats, while the Communist Party came in a distant second with 10 seats. International observers reported some improvements over previous elections, including the adoption of a new electoral code in February containing some recommendations of the international community, more balanced media coverage before and during the vote, and the return to the political arena of previously banned parties. However, they also cited significant inaccuracies of voter lists, the presence of unauthorized persons in polling stations, and the lack of effective and impartial electoral commissions. In June, Prime Minister Armen Darbinian resigned and was replaced by Sarkisian, while Demirchian was named speaker of parliament.

The relationship between Sarkisian and Demirchian, on the one hand, and the politically weaker President Kocharian, on the other, was marked by power struggles and policy differences. However, the two sides managed to achieve a relatively calm and functioning, although brief, balance of power. Just five months after parliamentary elections, the country was plunged into a political crisis when five gunmen stormed the parliament building on October 27 and assassinated Sarkisian, Demirchian, and several other senior government officials. The gunmen, who claimed they had acted alone and were trying to save Armenia from government corruption, surrendered to police 18 hours later.

On November 3, President Kocharian appointed Aram Sarkisian, Vazgen Sarkisian's younger brother and the director of a cement factory, as the new prime minister. Armen Khachatrian, a parliamentary deputy and head of the Foreign Affairs Commission, was chosen as the new speaker of parliament. In contrast to their experienced and powerful predecessors, both men were regarded as relatively weak and unknown. However, Aram Sarkisian soon proved to be a strong opponent of Kocharian's policies, and a period of growing tensions between the president and prime minister resulted.

During the first few months after the assassinations, a number of senior-level Kocharian supporters were arrested for their alleged connection with the attacks, including the presidential advisor Aleksan Harutiunian and the deputy director of the pro-Kocharian Armenian National Television, Harutiun Harutiunian. The arrests, as well as a claim by chief prosecutor Gagik Jahangirian that the killings were part of a larger coup d'etat plan, prompted some political figures to call for Kocharian's resignation. Meanwhile, Jahangirian's close ties with Aram Sarkisian and his Unity bloc called into question the independence and impartiality of the investigation.

While Kocharian's authority was initially diminished following the parliamentary shootings and implications of complicity by his inner circle, he gradually began to increase his power in the spring of 2000. In March, he enacted a sweeping reshuffle of the army command dominated by supporters of Unity. On April 15, presidential aide Aleksan Harutiunian was released from pretrial detention; he was eventually cleared of all charges in June, while Harutiun Harutiunian was released the same month. Kocharian's dismissals of Prime Minister Sarkisian and Defense Minister Vagharshak Harutiunian in May and the subsequent formation of a new government, in which the Unity bloc agreed to cooperate with Kocharian, was generally regarded as a tactical victory for the president. Andranik Margarian, a Soviet-era dissident and head of the Republican Party, was named the new prime minister on May 12. Presidential advisor and former security minister Serge Sarkisian, who had been an early suspect in connection with the October shootings, was appointed to the important post of defense minister.

By the end of 2000, Jahangirian was unable to substantiate his main theory that the five gunmen who had been arrested for the October 1999 assassinations had acted on the orders of influential backers to overthrow the government. His failure to find evidence establishing a link between the killers and Kocharian and his associates also effectively cleared the president of a connection with the crime. However, various theories about who may have orchestrated the murders remained the subject of considerable speculation at year's end.

Already-strained relations between Turkey and Armenia worsened after some European parliaments adopted resolutions labeling as "genocide" the mass killings of Armenians by the Ottoman Turks in 1915. In late October, the U.S. House of Representatives cancelled a vote on a similar nonbinding resolution after the administration expressed concern that it would seriously damage relations with its NATO ally Turkey. Turkey maintains that the killings were not genocide but the result of general partisan fighting during World War I in which all parties suffered.

Armenia took another step toward institutional integration with Europe when in November it was given an invitation to join the Council of Europe in 2001. Along with Azerbaijan, Armenia was the last of the eligible former Soviet countries to be approved for membership, largely because of concerns over human rights practices and the ongoing conflict with Azerbaijan over the disputed territory of Nagorno-Karabakh. Little progress was made during 2000 in internationally led peace negotiations over Nagorno-Karabakh's status, as political infighting following the October 1999 assassinations of the Armenian prime minister significantly hindered initially promising discussions.

Political Rights and Civil Liberties: Armenians can change their government democratically, although the 1995 and 1999 parliamentary and 1996 and 1998 presidential elections were characterized by serious irregularities. In 1995, voters approved the government-backed constitution, which provides for a weak legislature and a strong presidency. The directly elected president appoints the prime minister, who can be removed by the legislature in a no-confidence vote. Most political parties in Armenia are dominated by specific government officials or other powerful figures, espouse similar political platforms, or are weak and ineffective.

Self-censorship among journalists is common, particularly in reporting on Nagorno-Karabakh, national security, or corruption. A new civil code adopted in 1999 replaced punishments for libel, including publication of a retraction or compensation for damages, with harsher sentences of up to three years in prison. Armenian National Television Deputy Director Harutiun Harutiunian, who had been arrested for complicity in the October 1999 killings in parliament, alleged that he had been subjected to physical and verbal abuse during his five months in detention. In June 2000, journalist Vaghan Ghukasian was interrogated and beaten at the offices of the Interior Ministry, an attack he believed was in retaliation for an article that criticized the investigation of the parliamentary shootings. A new television and radio law, which was adopted in October, was criticized by various media experts for granting the state greater control over the country's broadcast media. According to the law, all licensing issues will be decided by two regulatory bodies to be appointed by the president. While most newspapers are privately owned, the majority operate with very limited resources and consequently are dependent on economic and political interest groups for their survival. In addition to two state television channels, a number of private television stations broadcast throughout the country, and most radio stations are privately owned.

Freedom of religion is somewhat restricted in this overwhelmingly Christian country. The Armenian Apostolic Church, to which 90 percent of Armenians formally belong, has been granted official status as the national church and is not subject to certain restrictions imposed on other religious groups, including having to register with the State Council on Religious Affairs. Provisions in a law on religious organizations forbid proselytizing except by the Armenian Apostolic Church and require religious organizations to have at least 200 members to register.

The government generally respects freedom of assembly and association, although the registration requirements are cumbersome and time consuming. In late October 2000, close to 10,000 people took part in a mass protest demanding the resignation of President Kocharian for his failure to improve the country's economy. Seventeen participants were arrested and sentenced to one to two weeks in prison. A second, separate rally in early November demanding that Kocharian step down attracted up to 5,000 protesters. While the constitution enshrines the right to form and join trade unions, labor organizations are weak and relatively inactive.

The judiciary, which is subject to political pressure from the executive branch, is characterized by widespread violations of due process and corruption. Under a criminal procedure code which went into effect in early 1999, witnesses do not have the right to legal counsel while being questioned in police custody, and detainees may not file a complaint in court before trial regarding abuses suffered during criminal investigations. Police frequently make arbitrary arrests without warrants, beat detainees during arrest and interrogations, and use torture to extract confessions.

The government places some restrictions on travel, particularly for those possessing state secrets or subject to military service. Equality of opportunity is hindered by unfair business competition and the concentration of key industries in the hands of oligarchs and influential clans who received preferential treatment in the early stages of privatization. Traditional customs limit professional opportunities for women, and trafficking in women and girls for the purpose of prostitution is believed to be a serious problem.

Australia

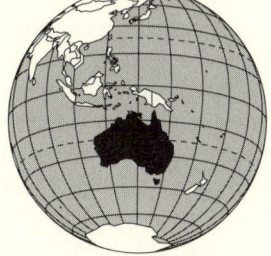

Polity: Parliamentary democracy (federal)
Economy: Capitalist
Population: 19,200,000
PPP: $22,452
Life Expectancy: 78
Ethnic Groups: White (92 percent), Asian (7 percent), other, including Aboriginal (1 percent)
Capital: Canberra

Political Rights: 1
Civil Liberties: 1
Status: Free

Overview: Following through on its central promise from the 1998 election campaign, John Howard's center-right coalition government introduced a controversial goods and services tax (GST) in July 2000. Howard's government also staked out conservative positions on Aboriginal rights and other social issues ahead of elections due by October 2001.

Claimed by the British in 1770, Australia gained independence in January 1901 as a commonwealth of six states. The government adopted the Northern Territory and the capital territory of Canberra as territorial units in 1911. In the post-World War II era, political power has alternated between the center-left Labor Party and the conservative coalition of the Liberal Party and the smaller, rural-based National Party. Under Bob Hawke and later Paul Keating, Labor governments in the 1980s and early 1990s began cutting tariffs; deregulating financial markets; privatizing transport, telecommunications, and utilities; and reorienting Australia's trade and diplomatic priorities toward Asia.

The Liberal-National coalition took power under Howard after winning the 1996 elections amid a high unemployment rate and an economic slowdown. In its first term, Howard's government aggressively promoted small- and medium-sized business interests, tried to curb the influence of trade unions, and backed the interests of farmers and miners over Aboriginal land claimants. In a defining act, the government supported a stevedoring company's dismissal in 1998 of some 1,400 dock workers in one of Australia's largest labor disputes in decades. A court ultimately ordered the workers reinstated. The government also satisfied demands of farmers and miners by winning parliamentary approval in 1998 for controversial legislation restricting Aboriginal claims to pastoral lands.

Seeking a fresh mandate before the regional crisis that began in 1997 could undermine Australia's economy, Howard led the coalition to victory in elections on October 3, 1998. The Liberal and National parties won 80 lower house seats (64 and 16, respectively); Labor, 66; and independents, 2. The government had campaigned on its handling of the economy, a pledge to introduce the GST while cutting income taxes, and plans to further privatize the state-owned Telstra telecommunications company, despite concerns of rural voters that unprofitable but needed services would be cut. Labor leader Kim Beazley criticized the proposed GST for taxing food and promised a jobs-creation program. The far-right One Nation party won a senate seat with its campaign against Aboriginal land rights and Asian immigration.

Howard's policies toward Australia's Aboriginal minority have continued to be a key issue in the coalition's second term. Despite pressure from activists and many ordinary Australians, Howard said in May 2000 that the government would not apologize formally for past injustices toward Aborigines. The prime minister argued that one generation should not have to apologize for the wrongdoings of another, and downplayed the forced removal of some 100,000 Aboriginal children from their parents in an official assimilation policy between 1910 and the early 1970s. Several marginal parliamentary seats are located in rural areas, where many white voters are considered to be indifferent to Aboriginal issues.

Howard had made a concession on Aboriginal rights in April, when he bowed to pressure from within his own government and ordered the Northern Territory to exclude juveniles from a 1997 mandatory sentencing law. The move came after a 15-year-old Aboriginal boy committed suicide in February while serving a 28-day mandatory sentence for petty theft. Critics said that mandatory sentencing laws in the Northern Territory and Western Australia disproportionately affect Aborigines. However, the federal government can change the law only in the Northern Territory, which is not a state.

In introducing the GST in July, the government risked alienating its supporters among small business owners, who complained about the tax's administrative burden. The senate had narrowly approved the GST in 1999 after the government agreed to an exemption for food.

Political Rights and Civil Liberties: Australians can change their government through elections. The 1900 constitution established a directly elected bicameral parliament that currently consists of a 76-member senate and a 148-member house of representatives. Lower house elections are held under an alternative vote system in single-member districts. In a November 1999 referendum, voters rejected a plan to replace the queen of England as head of state with a president elected by parliament. Polls showed that a majority of Australians favored a republic, but with a directly elected president.

Fundamental freedoms are respected in practice and safeguarded by an independent judiciary. Australia's primary human rights concerns involve its Aboriginal minority. The 399,000 Aborigines and Torres Strait Islanders frequently face discrimination and mistreatment by police; are 15 times more likely to be incarcerated than whites (down from 29 times more likely in the early 1990s), often because they cannot afford a fine or are denied bail for minor offenses; and die in custody at far higher rates than whites. The United Nations Committee on the Elimination of Racial Discrimination (CERD) said in March that the mandatory sentencing law in the Northern Territory and a less draconian one in Western Australia "appear to target offenses that are committed disproportionately by indigenous Australians." According to the Law Council of Australia, Aborigines constitute roughly 75 percent of the prisoners but only 24 percent of the general population in the Northern Territory.

Separately, CERD had criticized in 1999 what it called Australia's "racially discriminatory" policies under 1998 amendments to the 1993 Native Title Act that restrict Aboriginal claims to state-owned pastoral land. The government countered that under the amended law, 79 percent of Australian land is still subject to native-title claims. The government had enacted the amendments at the behest of rural interests, who feared losing land rights after a court ruled in 1996 that under the Act, native title could coexist with farming and mining leases on pastoral land. The then-Labor government had passed the act after the high court formally recognized that from a legal standpoint, Aborigines inhabited Australia prior to the British arrival in 1770. Aboriginal groups could therefore claim native title where they had maintained a connection to the land. The act requires the government to compensate Aboriginal groups with valid claims to state land.

Aborigines and Torres Strait Islanders have a life expectancy that is 20 years lower than, and an infant mortality rate that is nearly twice as high as, corresponding figures for white Australians. Aborigines also face societal discrimination and inferior educational opportunities. The government is generally responsive to these concerns and has undertaken numerous initiatives in health care and education.

In another controversial issue, the official Australian Human Rights Commission has criticized the government's practice of detaining asylum seekers pending resolution of their claims, which can take up to five years. The UN Human Rights Committee said in July that the mandatory immigration detention law "raises questions of compliance" with Australia's international commitments.

Australian trade unions are independent and active, although recent legislation has curbed their power and contributed to a decline in union rolls. The 1994 Industrial Relations Reform Act encouraged the use of workplace contracts linked to productivity rather than industry-wide collective bargaining. The 1997 Workplace Relations Act restricted the right to strike to the periods when contracts are being negotiated, abolished closed shops, and limited redress for unfair dismissal. The International Labor Organization (ILO) ruled in 1998 that the Workplace Relations Act breaches ILO conventions for failing to promote collective bargaining. The ILO called on the government in March to amend provisions to the act that link strike action to interference in trade, and to amend provisions of the Trade Practices Act that make secondary strikes illegal.

Austria

Polity: Parliamentary democracy (federal)
Economy: Mixed capitalist
Population: 8,100,000
PPP: $23,166
Life Expectancy: 77
Ethnic Groups: German (99 percent), other, including Slovene, Croatian (1 percent)
Capital: Vienna

Political Rights: 1
Civil Liberties: 1
Status: Free

Overview: Extensive diplomatic sanctions imposed by the European Union (EU) greeted Austria at the dawn of the new millennium, after Jorg Haider's nationalist Freedom Party joined the ruling coalition, led by center-right chancellor Wolfgang Schussel. The government faced public demonstrations at the end of the year over the government's budget cuts. A dispute developed during the year between Austria and the Czech Republic, over the latter country's decision to begin operating a Soviet-designed nuclear power plant close to the Austrian border. The issue was defused by the end of the year when the Czech government agreed to Austrian demands for international monitoring at the plant.

The Republic of Austria was established in 1918, after the collapse of the Austro-Hungarian Empire, and was reborn in 1945, seven years after its annexation by Nazi Germany. Occupation by Western allies and the Soviet Union ended in 1955 under the Austrian State Treaty, which guaranteed Austrian neutrality and restored national sovereignty.

Past pro-Nazi remarks by Haider, along with populist, xenophobic denunciations of immigrants, prompted the EU to impose sanctions against Austria at the beginning of 2000. In March 1999, Haider, the son of a former minor Nazi Party official, espousing an anti-immigrant platform, was elected governor of the southern province of Carinthia. By then his party already held 40 out of 183 national council seats. In national elections held later in the year, Haider's party captured 26.9 percent of the popular vote, shunting the government's junior coalition partner, the Christian Democratic Austrian People's Party (OVP), into third place and chipping away substantially at the dominance of the ruling Social Democrat Party's (SPO). Analysts had speculated at the time that the Freedom Party's strong electoral finish was due in part to public displeasure with coalition politics, high taxes, and an austerity budget.

Despite Haider's resignation as Freedom Party leader in February 2000, the EU maintained sanctions against Austria, claiming the Freedom Party platform had not changed. Susanne Riess-Passer assumed the party leadership. Haider, who does not hide his ambition to one day become Austrian chancellor, remains governor of Carinthia. As early as April, however, consensus among EU member-states on the sanctions began to crumble. Finland, a Union member, was the first to break ranks and urge fellow EU members to end their boycott of Austria, claiming the sanctions were hampering EU policy planning.

As pressure continued to mount within the EU, France, which held the EU presidency at the time, requested a human rights report on Austria, the results of which would determine whether sanctions could be lifted. A report filed in September by an EU panel concluded that Austria had not adopted any extreme right-wing policies and sufficiently respected the rights of minorities, refugees, and immigrants. But the report did criticize the Freedom Party as a "right-wing populist party with radical elements," and stated the EU's intention of maintaining a "particular vigilance" over developments in Austria. By the end of September, the sanctions were lifted. In October the Freedom Party suffered setbacks in elections in Styria, Austria's largest province. It captured only 12 percent of the vote compared with 29 percent in general elections in 1999.

Political Rights and Civil Liberties:

Austrians can change their government democratically. The country's provinces possess considerable latitude in local administration and can check federal power by electing members of the upper house of parliament. Voting is compulsory in some provinces. The independent judiciary is headed by a supreme court and includes both constitutional and administrative courts.

A 1955 treaty prohibits Nazis from exercising freedom of assembly and association. Nazi organizations are illegal, but Nazis are welcomed in the Freedom Party. In 1992, public denial of the Holocaust and justification of approval of Nazi crimes against humanity were outlawed. In general, Austrian police enforce these anti-Nazi statutes more enthusiastically when extremists attract international attention. However, Austria was called to task during the year for its Nazi-era behavior.

In March, the World Jewish Congress accused Austria of holding art stolen from Jews during World War II. The next month, several lawsuits were filed in American courts seeking $18 billion in Holocaust-era damages. The suits were filed against the Austrian state and industries on behalf of former slave workers and Jews whose property was seized by the state.

Austrian media are free. Legal restrictions on press freedom on the grounds of public morality or national security are rarely invoked. The Austrian Broadcasting Company, which controls radio and television, is state owned, but is protected from political interference by a broadcasting law.

Women hold approximately 10 percent of federal assembly seats and approximately 20 percent of provincial seats. They are prohibited by law from working at night in most occupations. Nurses, taxi drivers, and a few other workers are exempted from this ban. Women generally earn 20 percent less than men and are not allowed to serve in the military. The ruling SPO has pledged to begin to address gender biases by ensuring that women occupy 40 percent of all party and government posts by 2003.

During the year, Austria streamlined the process under which family members may join immigrants already in the country. Police, however, faced charges of brutality and racism against nonwhite, and, ostensibly, foreign immigrants, by Amnesty International. An Amnesty International country report documented cases of nonwhite detainees beaten, kicked, punched and sprayed with pepper gas by police. The report accused the police of not conforming to European human rights conventions and standards.

Under Austria's informal *proporz* system, many state and private sector appointments—including those of senior teachers in state schools—are made on the basis of affiliation with the two main political parties.

Trade unions retain an important independent voice in Austria's political, social, and economic life. Fifty-two percent of workers are organized in 14 national unions, all of which belong to the Austrian Trade Union Federation and which are managed by supporters of the country's traditional political parties. Although not explicitly guaranteed in the constitution or in national legislation, the right to strike is universally recognized.

Austria's Trade Union Federation organized a demonstration outside the parliament building in Vienna in December to protest the government's budget cuts. The government seeks to eliminate the budget deficit in two years, in part by cutting unemployment benefits, higher charges for medical prescriptions and the introduction of tuition fees for university students.

Azerbaijan

Polity: Presidential (dominant party)
Economy: Mixed statist (transitional)
Population: 7,700,000
PPP: $2,175
Life Expectancy: 70
Ethnic Groups: Azeri (90 percent), Dagestan peoples (3 percent), Russian (3 percent), Armenian (2 percent), other (2 percent)
Capital: Baku

Political Rights: 6
Civil Liberties: 5*
Status: Partly Free

Ratings Change: Azerbaijan's civil liberties rating changed from 4 to 5 due to increased harassment of the media and opposition political groups leading up to the November parliamentary elections.

Overview: Azerbaijan's November parliamentary elections, in which President Heydar Aliev's Yeni Azerbaijan ruling party won an overwhelming victory, were marred by widespread electoral fraud. International election monitors cited numerous serious irregularities, while political opposition parties refused to recognize the legitimacy of the new legislature and convened mass rallies to protest the results. Despite the widespread condemnation of the vote, Azerbaijan was accepted as a member of the Council of Europe only days after the poll.

Controlled by the Ottoman Empire since the 17th century, Azerbaijan entered the Soviet Union in 1922 as part of the Transcaucasian Soviet Federal Republic, becoming a separate Soviet republic in 1936. Following a referendum in 1991, Azerbaiajn declared independence from the disintegrating Soviet Union.

In June 1992, Abulfaz Elchibey, leader of the nationalist opposition Azerbaijan Popular Front, was elected president in a generally free and fair vote. A military coup one year later ousted him from power and installed the former first secretary of the Azerbaijan Communist Party, Heydar Aliev, in his place. In October 1993 presidential elections, Aliev reportedly received almost 99 percent of the vote. Azerbaijan's first post-Soviet parliamentary elections, held in November 1995, saw five leading opposition parties and some 600 independent candidates barred from the vote in which President Aliev's Yeni Azerbaijan party won the most seats. A new constitution adopted that year further strengthened Aliev's already sweeping powers.

In October 1998, Aliev was chosen president with more than 70 percent of the vote in an election characterized by serious irregularities, including election law violations and a lack of transparency in the vote-counting process. Six months later, Aliev underwent heart bypass surgery in the United States, returning to Azerbaijan after almost two months of recuperation in Turkey. His illness focused attention on his eventual successor, with most suspecting that Aliev's son Ilham, who is vice president of the state oil company SOCAR, was being groomed to be the country's next president. On August 22, Abulfaz Elchibey died of prostate cancer in Turkey, with tens of thousands of mourners attending his funeral service in Baku.

More than half a year before the November 5, 2000, parliamentary election, several thousand people attended an April 29 demonstration in Baku, which was organized by the opposition Azerbaijan Popular Front to protest a draft electoral law. Clashes between the protesters and riot police left over 50 injured while dozens were arrested. Opposition parties criticized the law, which was eventually adopted in July, for providing them with insufficient representation in the country's Central Election Commission (CEC). In September, the CEC ruled to disqualify most opposition parties, including Musavat and the Democratic Party of Azerbaijan, from competing in the upcoming parliamentary poll for allegedly failing to collect the required number of signatures to appear on the ballot. After considerable international pressure, President Aliev ordered the CEC to reverse its decision in early October. Nevertheless, according to Human Rights Watch, the government continued to use means to prevent opposition candidates from contesting the poll, including intimidating those gathering signatures for candidates' registration, arbitrarily declaring signature lists invalid, and using delaying tactics to prevent candidates from completing the registration process in time.

In a widely expected victory, the ruling Yeni Azerbaijan Party captured 62.5 percent of the vote for the 25 seats distributed by proportional representation, according to the CEC. The Azerbaijan Popular Front received 11 percent of the vote, followed by the Communist Party with 7 percent and the Civil Solidarity Party with 6 percent. While Yeni Azerbaijan also received a majority of the 100 seats awarded in single-mandate constituencies, the CEC ordered new elections for nearly a dozen to be held on January 7. International monitors, including representatives from the Organization for Security and Cooperation in Europe (OSCE) and Council of Europe, cited serious irregularities during the elections, including the stuffing of ballot boxes, a flawed counting process, falsified election results, a strong pro-government bias in state-run media, intimidation of voters by local officials, and denial to international observers of access to polling stations. According to the OSCE, the actual voter turnout was far below the 70 percent claimed by the CEC.

Despite widespread criticism of the elections, the Council of Europe approved Azerbaijan's application for membership just days after the vote. International human rights groups criticized the decision, which would allow Azerbaijan to join the organization in January 2001, because of the country's lack of progress on human rights and serious irregularities in the parliamentary poll.

On November 14, opposition parties announced their refusal to recognize the election results, declared their intention not to participate in the new parliament, and called for the holding of new elections. Four days later, they convened rallies in several cities to protest the election and demand the resignation of Azerbaijan's leadership; nearly 15,000 demonstrators gathered in Baku alone. Although election results were overturned in 11 voting districts, in which new votes were scheduled for January 2001, the results in the remaining districts were officially declared valid.

In May 2000, parliament ratified agreements for the construction of the proposed Baku-Ceyhan oil pipeline. However, the U.S.-backed project, which is projected to begin operating in 2004 or 2005, would still require an assured supply of oil and financial backing to be commercially viable. The pipeline, which would bypass Russian territory, is widely regarded as a means of reducing Moscow's influence in the region.

The most recent international mediation efforts over control of the disputed territory of Nagorno-Karabakh, which call for the enclave and Azerbaijan to form a common state, remained inconclusive at year's end. While Armenia has largely accepted the plan, Azerbaijan has pushed for clearer guarantees of sovereignty over the territory. At the same time, Azerbaijan continued to lobby for the repeal of Section 907 of the Freedom Support Act, which blocks U.S. aid to Azerbaijan. The sanctions, which were enacted in 1992 during the height of the Nagorno-Karabakh conflict, represent the only ones of their kind against a former Soviet state.

Political Rights and Civil Liberties:

Citizens of Azerbaijan cannot change their government democratically. President Aliev, who in 1999 celebrated 30 years of almost uninterrupted rule since becoming Azerbaijan's Communist Party leader in 1969, has imposed an authoritarian rule while building a cult of personality. The 1995 constitution gives the president control over the government, legislature, and judiciary. The 1993 and 1998 presidential and 1995 and 2000 parliamentary elections were considered neither free nor fair by international observers. Opposition political party members face frequent harassment and arrest by the authorities.

Although the constitution guarantees freedom of speech and the press, journalists who publish articles critical of the president or other prominent state officials are routinely prosecuted, and self-censorship is common. Many newspapers struggle financially in the face of heavy fines or imprisonment of their editors and staff. A new media law adopted by parliament in December 1999 and signed into law by President Aliev in February 2000 empowers an agency of the executive branch to distribute broadcast licenses and shut down broadcasters charged with violating broadcast regulations, while broadcasters do not have the right to appeal through the court system.

The government stepped up its campaign against the country's independent media in 2000, particularly during the pre-election period. The journal *Monitor Weekly*, which had been critical of the government, was forced to suspend publication in May, while the independent Azerbaijan Broadcasting Agency (ABA) was shut down without warning for ten days in October. Physical attacks against journalists during the year included an April 29 police beating of 17 journalists covering an opposition rally in Baku and an assault by police officers against two newspaper reporters from the daily *Bu Gun* on May 27. Rauf Arifoglu, the editor of the country's largest opposition newspaper, *Yeni Musavat*, was arrested in August and charged with several serious crimes. Human rights groups insisted that the charges were a politically motivated attempt by the government to intimidate Arifoglu prior to the November parliamentary elections, in which he planned to run. Although he was released after six weeks of pretrial detention, the charges against him remained at year's end.

Following President Aliev's November 1999 public statement of his commitment to religious freedom, a number of groups with long-standing registration applications, including the Jehovah's Witnesses, were registered, while abuses against foreigners and converts to nontraditional faiths decreased. Nevertheless, the government continues to restrict some religious activities of foreigners and Azerbaijanis who are members of nontraditional religious groups through burdensome registration requirements and interference in the dissemination of printed materials. Muslims, Russian Orthodox Christians, and Jews are considered members of "traditional" religions and can worship freely.

The government frequently restricts freedom of assembly and association, particularly for political parties critical of the government. In October, police prevented members of the Civil Unity Party from holding a demonstration in Baku to protest the government's refusal to register their party. According to Human Rights Watch, several members were beaten and injured. In June, President Aliev signed a law on NGOs that prevents domestic organizations from monitoring elections if they receive a certain amount of funding from foreign sources. Most trade unions belong to the state-run Azerbaijani Labor Federation, and there is no effective collective bargaining system.

The judiciary, which does not function independently of the executive branch, is inefficient and corrupt. Detainees are often held for long periods before trials, and their access to evidence and lawyers is restricted. Police abuse of suspects during arrest and interrogation reportedly remains commonplace, with torture often used to extract confessions. Despite presidential decrees in June and October granting amnesty to dozens of political prisoners, opposition and human rights groups insist that hundreds remain in custody.

The more than 750,000 refugees who fled the war in Nagorno-Karabakh remain in Azerbaijan, often living in appalling conditions. Most are unable or unwilling to return to their homes because of fears for their safety and concerns over dismal economic prospects in the breakaway territory.

Significant parts of the economy remain in the hands of a corrupt nomenklatura, which severely limits equality of opportunity. Most women work in the low-paying public sector, and traditional norms perpetuate discrimination and violence against women.

Bahamas

Polity: Parliamentary democracy
Economy: Capitalist-statist
Population: 300,000
PPP: $14,614
Life Expectancy: 74

Political Rights: 1
Civil Liberties: 1
Status: Free

Ethnic Groups: Black (85 percent), white (12 percent), Asian and Hispanic (3 percent)
Capital: Nassau

Overview: The government of the Bahamas announced in October 2000 that it was creating a new intelligence unit to investigate suspicious financial activity in the island chain as part of an effort to remove the country from an international money-laundering "blacklist." The measure followed the release of a report in June by the Financial Action Task Force (FATF)—a coordinating body set up a decade ago by the Group of 7 (G-7) economic powers to coordinate international efforts against money laundering)—that cited the Bahamas for not doing enough to fight illegal flows of cash. The finding was made just four months after the United States called for the Bahamas to improve its judicial system, win convictions against narcotics kingpins, and speed up extraditions. In August 2000, the country mourned the death of former Prime Minister Lynden Pindling, the "Black Moses," his country's independence hero and leader of the Bahamas for 25 years.

The Bahamas, a 700-island nation in the Caribbean, is a member of the Commonwealth. It was granted independence in 1973. The British monarchy is represented by a governor-general.

Under the 1973 constitution, a bicameral parliament consisted of a 49-member house of assembly directly elected for five years and a 16-member senate with 9 members appointed by the prime minister, 4 by the leader of the parliament opposition, and 3 by the governor-general. The number of seats in the assembly has been reduced by 9, to 40, in keeping with a campaign promise by the Free National Movement (FNM) party. The prime minister is the leader of the party that commands a majority in the house.

Pindling's Progressive Liberal Party (PLP), dogged by years of allegations of corruption and high official involvement in narcotics trafficking, was ousted after two and a half decades rule by Ingraham and the FNM in the 1992 elections. Hubert Ingraham, a lawyer and former cabinet official, had been expelled by the PLP in 1986 for his outspoken attacks on corruption and became leader of the FNM in 1990.

Ingraham vowed to bring honesty, efficiency, and accountability to government. Pindling, at the time the western hemisphere's longest-serving head of government, relied on his image as the father of the nation's independence. With 90 percent of the electorate voting, the FNM won 32 seats in the house of assembly to the PLP's 17. Pindling held his own seat and became the official opposition leader.

Upon taking office as prime minister, Ingraham appointed a Commission of Inquiry to investigate the Pindling government. In 1995 the commission detailed widespread mismanagement and malpractice in the national telephone and airline companies. In the 1997 election, Ingraham claimed credit for revitalizing the economy by attracting foreign investment. Voters handed his FNM a 34 to 6 majority in parliament, rebuking Pindling and the PLP for a second time. In April 1997, Pindling resigned as opposition leader and was replaced by Perry Christie, who had served in the PLP cabinet until he denounced government corruption in the wake of a drug probe.

In the last few years, a spiraling crime rate linked to illegal narcotics and gunrunning has left Bahamians questioning whether the islands were returning to the ways of the last decade, when the Bahamas earned the nickname "a nation for sale." In March 2000, the U.S. State Department praised the Bahamas for giving "high priority" to combating the transshipment of drugs and for cooperation on regional antinarcotics efforts. In addition to setting up the new antidrug intelligence unit, the Ingraham government also announced sweeping plans to bring the country's financial sector into full compliance with international standards and practices. In June, amendments to the Money Laundering (Proceeds of Crime) Act strengthened requirements for financial institutions to report suspicious and unusual transactions. Among the initiatives undertaken in October were the mandating of cooperation of bank supervisors with international authorities and the granting of permission to home-country banking regulators to conduct inspections to ensure that Bahamas-licensed affiliates of foreign banks comply with international standards. That same month the U.S. Internal Revenue Service went to court to seek records of U.S. taxpayers with credit card accounts in the Bahamas and two other offshore havens.

Political Rights and Civil Liberties:

Citizens can change their government democratically. Constitutional guarantees regarding the right to organize political parties, civic organizations, and labor unions are generally respected, as is the free exercise of religion. Human rights organizations have broad access to institutions and individuals.

The judicial system is headed by a supreme court and a court of appeals, with the right of appeal under certain circumstances to the Privy Council in London. There are local courts, and on the outer islands the local commissioners have magisterial powers. Despite antidrug legislation and a 1987 agreement with the United States to suppress the drug trade, there is evidence of drug-related corruption and money laundering, although less than during the Pindling years.

Violent crime is a growing concern, particularly in Nassau, and has been a focus of the Ingraham government. Nongovernmental organizations have documented the increase in recent years of violent crime, as well as the occasional beating of prisoners and other abuses by police, including arbitrary arrests and lengthy pretrial detention. No independent agency exists to investigate reports of police abuse.

Rights groups also criticize the inhumane conditions and overcrowding at the Fox Hill prison, the country's only penal facility. Fox Hill remains filled to more than twice its intended capacity. In 1996 Ingraham reinstated the death penalty for murder. In 1998, he commuted the death sentences of 17 prisoners who had spent more than five years on death row, in keeping with the limit set by the Privy Council in London. However, that September he announced that his government would limit the right of appeal in capital cases. Ingraham also initiated the hiring of 200 more police officers in an effort to crack down on violent crime. In 1998, 30 people sat on death row. Two people were executed.

There are three daily and several weekly newspapers, all privately owned, and they express a variety of views on public issues, as do the government-run radio station and four privately owned radio broadcasters. Opposition politicians claim, however, that the state-run television service, Broadcasting Corporation of the Bahamas (ZNS), does not accord them the same coverage as that given to the ruling party. Full freedom of expression is constrained by strict libel laws. Unlike its predecessor, the Ingraham government has not made use of these laws against independent newspapers. It has amended media laws to allow for private ownership of broadcasting outlets.

Labor, business, and professional organizations are generally free. Unions have the right to strike, and collective bargaining is prevalent. Discrimination against the disabled and persons of Haitian descent persists. Between 25,000 and 40,000 Haitians reside illegally in the Bahamas. Tight citizenship laws and a strict work permit system leave Haitians with few rights. The influx has created social tension because of the strain on government services. Violence against women is a serious, widespread problem. In 1999, the government and private women's organizations began a public awareness campaign highlighting the problems of abuse and domestic violence. In 2000, the Department of Social Services created two shelters for battered women.

Bahrain

Polity: Traditional monarchy
Economy: Capitalist-statist
Population: 700,000
PPP: $13,111
Life Expectancy: 73
Ethnic Groups: Bahraini (63 percent), Asian (13 percent), other Arab (10 percent), Iranian (8 percent), other (6 percent)
Capital: Manama

Political Rights: 7
Civil Liberties: 6
Status: Not Free

Overview:

More than a year after the accession of Sheikh Hamad ibn Isa al-Khalifa as emir, Bahrain has seen limited progress toward democratic reform. Members and suspected members of Shiite-led opposition groups campaigning for the restoration of parliament continued to face summary arrest, torture, and forcible deportation in 2000.

Bahrain has been ruled by the al-Khalifa family since 1782. The country was a British protectorate from 1861 to 1971, when British forces withdrew after years of Arab nationalist disturbances. The emir retained a virtual monopoly on power until the adoption of a constitution, which provided for a partially elected national assembly, in 1973. Describing Bahrain's new legislative body as "obstructionist," the emir ordered its dissolution in 1975.

With the Iranian revolution in 1979 and the accompanying spread of Islamic fundamentalism, resentment among Bahrain's majority Shiite population against its Sunni rulers intensified. The government faced an opposition which had grown to include not only leftist and secular elements, but religious ones as well. Religious and secular opposition activists were arrested and exiled in large numbers during the 1980s and 1990s.

Sheikh Isa ibn Salman al-Khalifa, who ruled from 1961 until his death in 1999, responded to international calls for political liberalization by appointing a consultative council of 30 prominent business and religious leaders in 1993. The council, or *Shura*, was expanded to 40 members in 1996. It has no legislative power.

The arrest of a Shiite cleric and several Sunni former parliamentarians in 1994 for petitioning for the reinstatement of parliament and the release of political detainees sparked civil unrest that has killed more than 40 people. According to international human rights monitors, the Bahraini government has arrested thousands of people, sentenced hundreds to prison, and expelled more than 500 people. Security forces routinely raid homes and beat and arrest families for suspected opposition activities. The government flatly rejects criticism of its rights record and blames Iran for inciting unrest. Political analysts and private sector businessmen, however, blame the government's failure to resolve widespread social and economic disparities, particularly unemployment, which stands at about 30 percent in the Shiite community.

Under pressure from the opposition and from international human rights groups, Sheikh Hamad allowed Amnesty International to visit Bahrain in 1999 for the first time in 12 years. He has also released a number of political detainees, including Sheikh Adbul Ameer al-Jamri, a former parliamentarian and leading Shiite activist who had been held without trial for three years. In September 2000, Sheikh Khalifa ibn Salman al-Khalifa, Bahrain's prime minister, appointed four women, one of whom is Christian; a Jewish businessman; and another businessman of Indian descent to the Shura. This was the first time non-Muslims and women were allowed to sit on the council. In November, the government set up a 46-member committee to draw up a national charter. In late December, Sheikh Hamad announced that the charter, which provides for a partly-elected parliament, would go to a referendum. The proposed parliament's responsibilities and powers are still unclear.

Opposition figures continued to campaign for the restoration of an elected parliament with full legislative power. Many observers believe that true political reform is unlikely as long as neighboring Saudi Arabia opposes the spread of democracy in the region. Moreover, Sheikh Hamad has retained his late father's prime minister, who apparently authored the hardline position that the government has taken toward the opposition since 1994. According to exiled reformers, prospects for reconciliation remain weak and the political atmosphere remains volatile.

Political Rights and Civil Liberties:

Bahrainis cannot change their government democratically. Political parties are prohibited, and most opposition leaders are currently either imprisoned or exiled. The emir rules by decree and appoints all government officials, including the 15-member cabinet, the 40-member Shura, the urban municipal councils, and the rural *mukhtars* (local councils). Citizens may submit petitions to the government and appeal to the emir and officials at regularly scheduled audiences.

The interior ministry maintains informal control over most activities through informant networks. Agents may search homes without warrants and have used this authority frequently against Shia. Despite the decreasing frequency of violent antigovernment protests, the London-based Bahrain Freedom Movement (BFM) reported dozens of cases in which security forces arrested and severely beat men, women, and children in early morning raids during 2000.

The 1974 State Security Act allows authorities to detain individuals suspected of "antigovernment activity," which includes participation in peaceful demonstrations and membership in outlawed organizations, for up to three years without trial. Detainees are subject to torture, forced confessions, incommunicado detention, and inadequate prison conditions. Their lawyers have also been targeted by police. Authorities do not release information about the numbers detained or the identities of detainees, but it is believed that more than 1,000 people remain in prison for political reasons. In March 2000, authorities released Abdelwahab Hussein, a Shiite opposition leader detained in 1996, only to arrest him again the following day without explanation. On July 3, 2000, the government officially announced the retirement of Ian Henderson, a British national who had served as chief of the intelligence service since 1966. In January, British police had launched an investigation into Henderson's alleged role in the torture of pro-democracy Bahraini activists.

The Bahraini government continued to deport people considered to be security threats. According to the U.S. State Department, those who accept foreign citizenship or passports or who engage in "antigovernment activities" abroad forfeit their Bahraini citizenship. The BFM reported numerous forcible deportations in 2000.

The judiciary is not independent. Members of the al-Khalifa family serve as judges in courts at all levels. Courts are also staffed by judges brought from other countries, such as Egypt, on renewable contracts. Security trials are held secretly, the right to an attorney is limited, and verdicts are not subject to appeal. A 1999 decree requires that those convicted in state security courts pay compensation for damages or face extended jail terms. The four Shiite civil judges may not handle cases deemed politically sensitive.

Freedom of speech and of the press is sharply limited. Privately owned newspapers refrain from criticizing the ruling family, while radio and television are government owned and broadcast only official views. Despite an official ban, an estimated six percent of Bahraini homes had access to satellite broadcasting in 1999. Human Rights Watch reported that Internet access has been easily obtainable since 1995, and according to the BBC, there were some 37,500 Internet subscribers (about six percent of the population) in Bahrain at the beginning of 2000. No authorization is required to launch a Web site, although authorities have blocked sites and reportedly monitor Internet use. A small number of Bahrainis have been detained or questioned on suspicion of using the Internet to transmit information to opposition groups outside the country. One journalist from *The Economist* was imprisoned in November with no official explanation. He was released after nine days.

Political parties and organizations are prohibited. Some professional societies and social or sports clubs may serve as forums for political discussion, but they may not engage in political activity. The bar association, the only association exempt from the ban on political activity, was dissolved in 1998. Bahrainis are not permitted to demonstrate, and even peaceful protests are met with intimidation by security officials. Human rights monitors, including the UN Rapporteur on Torture, are regularly denied entry into Bahrain by the government.

Bahraini women may own and inherit property, represent themselves in public and legal matters, obtain passports and leave the country without permission of a male relative, work outside the home, drive without escorts, and wear clothing of their choice.

A non-Bahraini woman will automatically lose custody of her children if she divorces their Bahraini father. Labor law does not discriminate against women, but there is discrimination in the workplace, including wage disparity and denial of opportunity for advancement. The government appointed its first woman ambassador in late 1999 and also appointed four women to the Shura in September 2000.

Islam is the state religion, and Bahrainis are overwhelmingly Muslim. The state controls all official religious institutions through monitoring and funding. Non-Muslims, including Jews, Christians, Hindus, and Bahais, are free to practice, maintain places of worship, and display religious symbols. Sunni Muslims enjoy favored status with the government, while Shia generally receive inferior educational, social, and municipal services. Beginning in 1999, Shia were permitted to work in the defense forces and the interior ministry, though only in subordinate positions.

Independent labor unions and collective bargaining are nonexistent. The law restricts strikes deemed damaging to worker-employer relations or the national interest. According to a report issued in October 2000 by the International Confederation of Free Trade Unions, Bahrain has failed to ratify key International Labor Organization conventions on the right to organize, collective bargaining, and workplace discrimination, and thousands of Bahrainis have been imprisoned for attempting to organize. In March, a Bahraini court ruled that 200 Gulf Air workers who were arbitrarily dismissed without prior consultation or representation were ineligible for compensation. Foreigners who come to Bahrain to work as domestics are frequently mistreated and denied pay. Bahraini law does not protect these workers.

Bangladesh

Polity: Parliamentary democracy
Economy: Capitalist-statist
Population: 125,810,000
PPP: $1,361
Life Expectancy: 59
Ethnic Groups: Bengali (98 percent), Bihari, others (2 percent)
Capital: Dhaka

Political Rights: 3
Civil Liberties: 4
Status: Partly Free

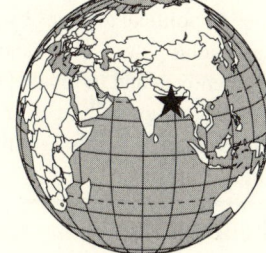

Overview:

The political gridlock that has undermined Bangladesh's economy since the mid-1990s continued in 2000, as the opposition Bangladesh Nationalist Party (BNP) and three allies boycotted parliament and organized several nationwide strikes. Accusing the Awami League government of corruption and abuse of power, the opposition called on Prime Minister Sheikh Hasina Wajed to hold elections before they are due in mid-2001.

Bangladesh won independence in December 1971 after Indian troops helped defeat occupying West Pakistani forces in a nine-month war. The 1975 assassination of Prime Minister Sheikh Mujibur Rahman by soldiers precipitated 15 years of often turbulent military rule and continues to polarize Bangladeshi politics. The country's democratic transition began with the resignation in 1990 of the last military ruler, General H.M. Ershad, after weeks of pro-democracy demonstrations. Elections in 1991 brought the BNP to power under Khaleda Zia.

The political strikes and parliamentary boycotts began in 1994, when Hasina's center-left Awami League began boycotting parliament to protest alleged corruption in Zia's BNP government and a rigged by-election. The Awami League and the BNP differ relatively little on domestic policy. Many disputes reflect the personal animosity between Hasina, the daughter of independence leader Sheikh Mujibar Rahman, and Zia, the widow of a former military ruler allegedly complicit in Sheikh Mujibar's 1975 assassination.

The Awami League boycotted the February 1996 elections, which the BNP won, but forced Zia's resignation in March. At the June 1996 elections, held with a 73 percent turnout, the Awami League won 146 of 300 parliamentary seats (30 additional seats are reserved for women); the BNP, 113; the Jatiya Party of former dictator Ershad, 33; and smaller parties, independents, and vacant seats, 8.

Under Hasina, the government signed a 1996 Ganges River water-sharing accord with India and a 1997 accord ending a low-grade insurgency in the Chittigong Hill Tracts. Hasina's government also has allowed foreign companies to invest in offshore natural gas exploration, though it has refused to permit gas to be exported until Bangladesh accumulates a 50-year reserve. By some estimates, Bangladesh also achieved near self-sufficiency in food production over the past four years. An October World Bank report praised Bangladesh's fiscal year 2000 growth of 5.2 percent, but noted that each one-day nationwide strike costs the economy $60 million. There were 28 days of political strikes in 1999, the latest year for which figures are available.

Hasina's government denied the opposition's charges of wrongdoing, but contributed to political tensions by passing a controversial public order law in January that it said would improve law and order. The opposition said the law could be used against its members and to break general strikes. Further raising tensions, an anti-corruption bureau laid graft charges in September against BNP leader Zia and nine other former government officials over the 1995 purchase of two passenger aircraft when Zia was prime minister.

Political Rights and Civil Liberties: Bangladeshis can change their government through elections. The June 1996 vote was the first under a constitutional amendment requiring a caretaker government to conduct elections; it was Bangladesh's freest election despite some violence and irregularities. Lower house elections are held in single-member districts under simple-plurality rule. A September 1991 referendum transformed the powerful presidency into a largely ceremonial head-of-state position in a parliamentary system.

Both the Awami League and the BNP have undermined the legislative process through lengthy parliamentary boycotts while in opposition. In recent years, political violence during demonstrations and general strikes has killed dozens of people in major cities. Awami League activists continued in 2000 to forcibly break up some opposition rallies, and police continued to use excessive force against opposition protesters. The opposition forcibly disrupted some pro-government rallies and used violence to enforce general strikes. Student wings of political parties continued to be embroiled in violent campus conflicts.

The high court is independent, but according to the United States Department of State's country report for 1999, "lower level courts are more susceptible to pressure from the executive branch." Lower courts are also rife with corruption and are severely backlogged, and pretrial detention is lengthy. Many defendants lack counsel, and poor people in general have limited recourse through the courts. Amnesty International said in November that successive governments since independence have tolerated "widespread and persistent" torture. It said the majority of cases involve torturing criminal suspects to get them to confess to crimes they didn't commit, although police also tortured political dissidents and innocent bystanders. Police also routinely rape suspects and prisoners. Prison conditions are extremely poor.

Authorities continued to occasionally arbitrarily detain political opponents and ordinary citizens, and to detain citizens without charge under the 1974 Special Powers Act. The government generally detains political opponents for short periods, and many of these detentions appear to be politically motivated. The broadly drawn Public Safety Act that came into effect in February provides for jail terms of between 2 to 14 years for hijacking, committing extortion, damaging property, obstructing traffic, "causing panic," and other offenses. Human rights advocates have sharply criticized the practice under which authorities place some female victims of rape, kidnapping, prostitution, and trafficking in "safe custody" in prison, where they are vulnerable to rape and other abuses.

The print media are diverse and often critical of the government. However, journalists frequently face pressure from organized crime groups, political parties, the government, and Islamic fundamentalists, and practice some self-censorship. The Paris-based Reporters Sans Frontieres (RSF) said that a reporter who was murdered in July in Jessore had been exposing the illegal activities of a local organized crime ring, and was the third journalist to be murdered in western Bangladesh since August 1998. In an effort to cover up their abuses against protesters, police occasionally beat journalists covering demonstrations. RSF expressed concern in March at "the increasing number of criminal charges brought against opposition journalists by ministers and members of parliament of the ruling party." That month, authorities also arrested a journalist under the Public Safety Act for allegedly inciting students at a Koranic school to attack the police. Political considerations influence the distribution of government advertising revenue and subsidized newsprint, upon which most publications are dependent. The state-owned Bangladesh Radio and Television owns most broadcast media, whose coverage favors the ruling party.

Rape, dowry-related assaults, acid throwing, and other violence against women occur relatively frequently. A September United Nations report said that 47 percent of all Bangladeshi women are subjected to violence by their male partners. A law requiring rape victims to file police reports and obtain medical certificates within 24 hours of the crime in order to press charges prevents most rape cases from reaching the courts. Police also accept bribes not to register rape cases and rarely enforce existing laws protecting women. In rural areas religious leaders occasionally arbitrarily impose floggings and other punishments on women accused of violating strict moral codes. Women also face discrimination in health care, education, and employment, and are underrepresented in politics and government. Under customary laws of the minority Hindu community, women have no legal rights to divorce or inheritance. Muslim women, in theory, enjoy greater legal protection in family matters, but these laws are routinely flouted.

The Bangladesh National Women Lawyers Association said in a 1999 report that organized groups traffick nearly 25,000 Bangladeshi women and children each year into Middle Eastern and other South Asian countries for the purpose of prostitution and low-paid labor. Law enforcement officials rarely investigate trafficking, and human rights groups say the police are often engaged in these and other crimes.

Islam is the official religion. Hindus, Christians, and other minorities worship freely but face societal discrimination. There are occasional reports of violence against members of the Ahmadiya religious minority. The Garos and other tribal minorities have little input in land issues affecting them, and minority rights groups say that Bengalis have cheated many tribal people out of their land. A 1997 accord between the government and the Chittigong Hill Tracts (CHT) People's Solidarity Association ended a 24-year insurgency in the CHT that sought autonomy for the Chakmas and 12 other indigenous tribes and killed 8,500 soldiers, rebels, and civilians. A February Amnesty International report said the government had not fully implemented some of the accord's main provisions, including the rehabilitation of refugees, return of land confiscated from tribal people, and withdrawal of nonpermanent army camps.

Roughly 260,000 Rohingya refugees fleeing forced labor, discrimination, and other abuses in Burma entered Bangladesh in 1991 and 1992; some 20,000 Rohingya refugees and 100,000 other Rohingyas not documented as refugees remain in Bangladesh. In recent years, authorities have turned back many arrivals at the border. Bangladesh also hosts some 300,000 Urdu-speaking Biharis, who were rendered stateless at independence in 1971 and seek repatriation to Pakistan.

According to the U.S. State Department, nongovernmental human rights organizations report that they face some harassment by government intelligence agents, ruling party activists, and Muslim religious leaders. Trade union formation is hampered by a 30 percent employee approval requirement and restrictions on organizing by unregistered unions. Employers can legally fire or transfer workers suspected of union activities. Unions are largely prohibited in the two export-processing zones. The law prohibits many civil servants from joining unions; these workers can form associations that are prohibited from bargaining collectively. The Bangladesh Independent Garment Workers Union is one of the few diligent, nonpartisan unions. The estimated 1.5 million women working in the garment industry continued to face dangerous working conditions, sexual harassment, and anti-union discrimination. Garment exports earned $4 billion in the year ending in June 1999. UNICEF reported in 1999 that at least 6.3 million children under age 14 are working in Bangladesh, mostly as maids, servants, farm workers, or rickshaw pullers.

Aid donors frequently blame corruption, a weak rule of law, limited bureaucratic transparency, and political polarization for undermining economic development. Moreover, heavy flooding in September 2000 displaced tens of thousands of people from their homes.

Barbados

Polity: Parliamentary democracy
Economy: Capitalist
Population: 300,000
PPP: $12,001
Life Expectancy: 77
Ethnic Groups: Black (80 percent), white (4 percent), other (16 percent)
Capital: Bridgetown

Political Rights: 1
Civil Liberties: 1
Status: Free

Overview:

In 2000, the three main political parties offered support for a plan to turn Barbados, known as "Little England" for its many colonial trappings, into a republic and replace the Queen of England as head of state with a president who shares the island's majority African roots. Economic performance continued to be strong, a reflection of government efforts to diversify the economy by creating financial and computer services industries.

A member of the Commonwealth, Barbados achieved independence in 1966. The British monarchy is represented by a governor-general. The government is a parliamentary democracy with a bicameral legislature and a party system based on universal adult suffrage. The senate comprises 21 members, all appointed by the governor-general: 12 on the advice of the prime minister, 2 on the advice of the leader of the opposition, and the remaining 7 at the discretion of the governor-general. A 28-member house of assembly is elected for a five-year term. Executive authority is vested in the prime minister, who is the leader of the political party commanding a majority in the house.

Since independence, power has alternated between two centrist parties—the Democratic Labor Party (DLP), under Errol Barrow, and the Barbados Labor Party (BLP), under Tom Adams. Adams led the BLP from 1976 until his death in 1985. Adams was succeeded by Bernard St. John, but the BLP was defeated and Barrow returned to power in 1986. Barrow died in 1987 and was succeeded by Erskine Sandiford, who led the DLP to victory in the 1991 elections.

Under Sandiford, Barbados suffered a prolonged economic recession as revenues from sugar and tourism declined. By 1994, the economy appeared to be improving, but unemployment was still at nearly 25 percent. Sandiford's popularity suffered, and he was increasingly criticized for his authoritarian style of government. He lost a no-confidence vote in parliament when nine BLP legislators were joined by four DLP backbenchers and one independent legislator who had quit the DLP. David Thompson, the young finance minister, replaced Sandiford.

In the 1994 election campaign, Owen Arthur, an economist elected in 1993 to head the BLP, promised to build "a modern, technologically dynamic economy," create jobs, and restore investor confidence. The BLP won 19 seats; the DLP, 8; and the New Democratic Party (NDP), a disaffected offshoot of the DLP formed in 1989, won 1 seat.

Arthur combined a technocratic approach to revitalizing the economy with savvy politics. He appointed a number of promising young cabinet members and, in the run-up to the 1999 election, was able to boast that in five years, unemployment had been halved, to 12 percent. The BLP retained power in 1999 by winning 26 of 28 parliamentary seats, a rout that left Prime Minister Owen Arthur firmly in control of his country's political fortunes for the foreseeable future. The results of the election gave Arthur the mandate he needed to declare Barbados a republic. The feeble showing by Thompson's DLP in the elections created worries that the parliamentary opposition was in danger of withering away.

Since returning to office, Arthur has devoted considerable attention to new crime-fighting strategies in the face of increases in the number of armed robberies and burglaries. The proposal to renounce allegiance to the queen is part of a two-year constitutional review under consideration by parliament. Among the reforms under consideration are changes in the legislative process and a proposal to allow women the same right that men have to share their citizenship with foreign spouses.

Political Rights and Civil Liberties: Citizens can change their government through democratic elections, and the January 1999 elections were free and fair. Constitutional guarantees regarding freedom of religion and the right to organize political parties, labor unions, and civic organizations are respected. Apart from the parties holding parliamentary seats, other political organizations abound, including the small, left-wing Workers' Party of Barbados.

The judicial system is independent and includes a supreme court that encompasses a high court and a court of appeals. Lower-court officials are appointed on the advice of the Judicial and Legal Service Commission. The government provides free legal aid to the indigent. In 1992 the court of appeals outlawed the practice of public flogging of criminals. The prison system is antiquated and overcrowded, with more than 800 inmates held in a building built for 350.

Human rights organizations operate freely, and the government allows private groups to visit prisons to ascertain conditions. The high crime rate, fueled by an increase in drug abuse and narcotics trafficking (there has been some decrease in drug-related crime recently), has given rise to human rights concerns. There are numerous complaints of excessive force used by the Royal Barbados Police Force to extract confessions and there are occasional reports that police do not always seek warrants before searching homes. A counternarcotics agreement signed between the United States and Barbados in late 1996 provides funding for the Barbados police force, the coast guard, customs, and other ministries, for a broad array of programs to combat drug-related crimes. Barbados also entered into an updated extradition treaty with the United States, as well as, in May 1997, a maritime law enforcement agreement.

Freedom of expression is fully respected. Public opinion expressed through the news media, which are free of censorship and government control, has a powerful influence on policy. Newspapers are privately owned, and there are two major dailies. Private and government radio stations operate. The single television station, operated by the government-owned Caribbean Broadcasting Corporation (CBC), presents a wide range of political viewpoints.

In 1992, a domestic violence law was passed to give police and judges greater power to protect women, although violence and abuse continue to be major social problems. Also, women are represented at all levels of government and politics.

Part of the country's move to break with the British Crown has been a government effort to exalt Bajan heros at the expense of English ones, such as Admiral Lord Horatio Nelson, whose statue stands in Trafalgar Square, Bridgetown. The effort has created resentment among the whites who make up about seven percent of the country's 265,000 people. In response, Arthur appointed a 13-member National Reconciliation Committee to foster greater understanding between the majority black and the minority Anglo communities.

There are two major labor unions and various smaller ones that are politically active. Women make up roughly half of the workforce. Some 12,000 Barbadians—8.5 percent of the economically active population—earn less than the minimum wage of U.S.$85 a week.

Belarus

Polity: Presidential   **Political Rights:** 6
Economy: Statist   **Civil Liberties:** 6
Population: 10,000,000   **Status:** Not Free
PPP: $6,319
Life Expectancy: 68
Ethnic Groups: Belarusian (78 percent), Russian (13 percent), Polish (4 percent), Ukrainian (3 percent), other (2 percent)
Capital: Minsk

Overview:

In 2000 the Belarusian government continued its assault on basic political rights and civil liberties. Using his influence over security forces, the legislature, and courts, President Aleksandr Lukashenko presided over undemocratic parliamentary elections, government disruptions of protests and rallies, harassment of opposition groups and the media, and politically motivated arrests and trials.

When Belarus declared independence in 1991, it ended centuries of foreign ascendancy by Lithuania, Poland, Russia, and ultimately the Soviet Union. Stanislaw Shushkevich, a reform-minded leader, served as head of state from 1991 to 1994. That year voters made Aleksandr Lukashenko the country's first post-Soviet president. He has pursued a close union with Russia, subordinated the government and courts to his political whims, denied citizens basics rights and liberties, and ruled by decree ever since.

In a 1996 referendum, Belarusian citizens favored constitutional amendments that extended Lukashenko's presidential term by two years, broadened presidential powers, and created a new bicameral parliament. Lukashenko ignored a court ruling that the referendum was nonbinding, and Prime Minister Mikhail Chyhir resigned in protest. Since July 1999, when the president's original mandate expired, most Western nations have refused to recognize him as the legitimate head of state. Likewise, they recognize the pre-1996 Supreme Soviet led by Syamyon Sharetsky as the country's legitimate legislative body.

Opposition parties agreed to participate in October 2000 parliamentary elections if the government (1) passed a more democratic and transparent electoral code, (2) guaranteed equal access of candidates to state media, (3) ceased its harassment and imprisonment of opposition figures, and (4) granted parliament more substantial duties. When the government failed to meet these demands, seven opposition parties boycotted the election. While some opposition candidates participated in the election, only three received a mandate. The election commission reported voter turnout at 60 percent, but the opposition accused the commission of falsifying the number and declared the election invalid.

Lukashenko employed a variety of tactics to suppress his opponents in 2000. These included police raids on the headquarters of the Belarusian Popular Front and the Social Democratic Party; the detention of journalists, representatives of nongovernmental organizations, and other participants in a rally celebrating the important—if fleeting—1918 declaration of independence; and the disqualification of numerous opposition candidates from the October election. In two high-profile cases, the Minsk city court convicted Mikalay Statkevich for organizing the unauthorized 1999 freedom march and former Prime Minister Mikhail Chyhir for corruption. By law, the convictions barred Statkevich and Chyhir from running in the October parliamentary election, but eventually they were allowed to register.

Suppression of the media continued apace in 2000. Government authorities seized copies of the independent newspaper *Rabochy* and charged the printer with "propagandizing . . . the boycott" of the October election. Tax inspectors seized equipment from the same printing house, Magic, which provides services to many independent newspapers. Dmitry Zavadsky, a Belarusian cameraman for Russian Public Television, disappeared in Minsk and is presumed dead. Sources for the Committee to Protect Journalists believe Zavadsky was abducted for possessing film footage that shows "Belarusian security agents fighting against Russian forces in Chechnya." In November, the independent news agency Belapan received an anonymous letter claiming that nine suspects—seven of whom are associated with the state security service—had been arrested. Investigators have refused to comment fully on the case and the letter.

Political Rights and Civil Liberties: Despite a constitutional guarantee of universal, equal, and direct suffrage, citizens of Belarus cannot change their government democratically. President Lukashenko has promised a presidential election in 2001, and opposition groups are preparing to nominate a challenger.

In October 2000, Belarus held elections to the Chamber of Representatives, parliament's lower house. During the campaign, the Council of Europe and the Organization for Security and Cooperation in Europe noted numerous violations of the January 2000 electoral code and refused to send official election-day observers. State media coverage of the campaign was limited and biased, and approximately half of all opposition candidates were denied registration. State security forces threatened legal action against any opposition leader who called for a boycott. On polling day, thousands of observers from Belarusian NGOs reported irregularities such as ballot box stuffing and tampering with voter registration lists. Most Western governments refused to recognize the results. In November, delegates of local councils elected 56 senators to the 64-seat Council of the Republic, parliament's upper house. Lukashenko controls appointments to the eight remaining seats.

Russia holds extraordinary sway over Belarusian politics. The two countries have signed several treaties calling for a single currency, uniform tax laws, a shared securities market, and a common defense policy. They also plan to create a supreme council, a cabinet of ministers, a parliament, and a court. In November 2000, President Lukashenko acknowledged that he receives regular reports from Russia's secret service, even though information sharing of this kind is forbidden by Russian law.

The Lukashenko regime systematically curtails press freedoms. State media are subordinated to the president whose administration controls decisions on content and the appointment of senior editors. Harassment and censorship of independent print media are routine. Independent electronic media do not exist. The Law on Press and Other Media prohibits media coverage of any association not registered with the state and severely limits the media's ability to criticize public officials. The State Press Committee can issue warnings to publishers for unauthorized activities such as changing a publication's title or distributing copies abroad. It also can arbitrarily shut down publications without court orders.

The constitution states that all religious faiths are equal before the law and that individuals have the right to profess and practice their faith. In reality, government decrees and registration requirements limit the activities of many religious groups. The government openly favors the Belarusian Orthodox Church.

The government rigorously limits freedom of assembly and association. Protests and rallies require authorization from local authorities who can arbitrarily withhold or revoke permission. A January 1999 presidential decree called for all associations to re-register with the state. To date, many groups either have been denied registration or simply have refused to re-register. In May 2000, the Belarusian Congress of Democratic Trade Unions appealed to the International Labor Organization about infringements on workers' rights to organize. Lukashenko retaliated by freezing the group's bank account. Late in the year, approximately 168,000 teachers signed an appeal demanding better wages.

Belarus has a three-tiered judiciary and a constitutional court. The constitution calls for judicial independence, but courts are subject to weighty government influence. Opposition members, independent journalists, and other persons who oppose government policies experience arbitrary arrest and imprisonment. The right to a fair trial is not always respected.

The constitution outlines a range of personal liberties and freedoms, but the government honors them selectively. Wiretaps by state security agencies limit the right to privacy; arbitrary search and seizure compromises the inviolability of the home; and the internal passport system controls freedom of movement and choice of residence. Belarus retains its Soviet-era economic model, and living standards are in decline. The International Monetary Fund, which suspended lending to Belarus in 1996, refuses to consider new lending until the country undertakes serious market reforms. Lukashenko, however, openly resists reform—even despite pressure from Russia. The government can confiscate private property from companies and individuals that have "caused damage to the state."

Belgium

Polity: Parliamentary democracy (federal)
Economy: Capitalist
Population: 10,200,000
PPP: $23,223
Life Expectancy: 77
Ethnic Groups: Fleming (55 percent), Walloon (33 percent), mixed and others, including Moroccan and Turkish (12 percent)
Capital: Brussels

Political Rights: 1
Civil Liberties: 2
Status: Free

Overview:

Having recovered from a disastrous 1999, defined by scandals surrounding poisoned poultry, child predators, political skullduggery, and incompetent policing, Belgium worked to recast its image in 2000, with Foreign Minister Louis Michel promoting his country as a guiding light of European integration, one characterized as tolerant and antinationalist. But by October, Belgium's resurgent right-wing party, the Vlaams Blok, firmly entrenched itself as a major political player, scoring big gains in municipal elections and raising the specter of ascendant anti-immigrant and extreme nationalist sentiments in Belgium, traditionally thought to have been kept in check.

Modern Belgium dates from 1830, when the territory broke away from the Netherlands and formed a constitutional monarchy. Today, the largely ceremonial monarchy symbolizes the weakness of Belgian unity. Ethnic and linguistic antagonism during the 1960s prompted a series of constitutional amendments, in the period 1970-1971 and in 1993, that devolved power to regional councils at the expense of the central government in Brussels. A 1993 amendment formally transformed the country into a federation of Flanders, Wallonia, and bilingual Brussels, with the German-speaking area accorded cultural autonomy. Also in 1993, parliament adopted an amendment establishing three directly elected regional assemblies with primary responsibility for housing, transportation, public works, education, culture, and the environment. The weak central government continues to oversee foreign policy, defense, justice, monetary policy, taxation, and the management of the budget deficit, although Prime Minister Guy Verhofstadt, as part of his program of devolving some federal powers, did grant the regions more power over agricultural policy during the year. The Federal Ministry is scheduled to be abolished altogether next year.

Belgium's current coalition government, formed in July 1999, is composed of Greens, Liberals, and Socialists. The October 2000 municipal elections saw impressive gains by the Vlaams Blok in Flanders, the Dutch-speaking northern portion of Belgium. Claiming Belgium was facing rising crime and illegal immigration, the Blok made its most impressive gains in Antwerp, the Flemish capital, where it captured more than one-third of the votes, or 20 of the 55 seats in the city's municipal council. The party captured one-fifth of the votes cast throughout the rest of Flanders, a five-percentage-point increase since Belgium's previous municipal elections, held in 1994. The party seeks to separate Flanders from the French-speaking southern part of the country and declare the area an independent state. The party also supports the deportation of all non-European foreigners back to their home countries.

Mindful of Austria's experience with its far-right Freedom Party, which was incorporated into the country's ruling coalition earlier in the year, Antwerp's political leaders—part of a "rainbow coalition" of liberals, socialists, and ecologists—vowed to defang the newly empowered right-wing by blocking its participation in the local government. Nonetheless, the country continues to face increased ethnic and linguistic tensions between its French-speaking Walloons, who worry that they are losing their identity, and the Flemings, many of whom call for a confederated or separate state.

Belgium's political parties are split along linguistic lines, with both Walloon and Flemish parties ranging across the political spectrum. Numerous small ethnic parties and special interest groups have emerged, leading to a decline in the dominance of the three major parties: the Social Democrats, Christian Democrats, and Liberals.

Political Rights and Civil Liberties:

Belgians can change their government democratically. Non-voters are subject to fines. Political parties generally organize themselves along ethnic lines, with different factions of the leading parties subscribing to a common platform for general elections. Each ethnic group has autonomy in its region, but constitutional disputes arise when members of one group elected to office in a different territory refuse to take competency tests in the dominant language of that region. The country's judiciary is independent but has continued to experience criticism as a result of the country's ongoing political and criminal scandals.

While freedom of speech and the press is guaranteed, Belgian law prohibits some forms of pornography as well as incitements to violence. Libel laws have some minor restraining effects on the press, and restrictions on the right of civil servants to criticize the government may constitute a slight reduction of the right to civil speech. Autonomous public boards govern the state television and radio networks and ensure that public broadcasting is linguistically pluralistic. The state has permitted and licensed independent radio stations since 1985.

In August, Belgian courts issued an emergency injunction to prevent *The Investigator* magazine from publishing a list of names of 50 suspected pedophiles living in Belgium, on the grounds of honoring the presumption of innocence and protecting human rights. Belgium is still reeling from the high-profile murder case of Marc Dutroux, a convicted child-rapist who is yet to be tried for the kidnapping, sexual abuse and murders of four young girls, and who briefly escaped from police custody in 1998.

Belgians enjoy freedom of religion and association. Christian, Jewish, and Muslim institutions are state subsidized in this overwhelmingly Roman Catholic country, and other faiths are not restricted. Immigrants and linguistic minorities argue that linguistic zoning limits opportunity. Belgium has enacted measures to promote sexual equality, including the prohibition of sexual harassment. Legislation mandates that, in the next general parliamentary election, 33 percent of the candidates be women. Approximately 60 percent of the workforce holds membership in labor unions, which have the right to strike—one that they frequently exercise—even in "essential" services.

Belize

Polity: Parliamentary democracy
Economy: Capitalist
Population: 300,000
PPP: $4,566
Life Expectancy: 75
Ethnic Groups: Mestizo (44 percent), Creole (30 percent), Maya (11 percent), Garifuna (7 percent), other (8 percent)
Capital: Belmopan

Political Rights: 1
Civil Liberties: 1
Status: Free

Overview: In October 2000, Belize's 21,000 Maya Indians finally succeeded in getting indigenous rights on the national agenda as Prime Minister Said Musa's government signed an agreement recognizing for the first time "that the Maya people have rights to lands and resources in southern Belize based on their long-standing use and occupancy." However, the Maya are still treated under Belizean law as squatters on their own ancestral lands. It remained uncertain whether the change in the government's Indian policy will be followed by reforms in discriminatory laws affecting indigenous peoples.

Belize is a member of the Commonwealth, and the British monarchy is represented by a governor-general. Formerly British Honduras, the name was changed to Belize in 1973. Independence was granted in 1981.

Since independence, the government has changed hands three times, alternating between the center-right United Democratic Party (UDP) and the center-left People's United Party (PUP). In the 1993 elections, the UDP and National Alliance for Belizean Rights (NABR) formed a coalition, winning 16 of the 29 seats in the house of representatives.

The August 1998 elections proved to be a referendum on Prime Minister Manuel Esquivel's largely unfulfilled pledge that his UDP would create jobs. Esquivel was successful in resisting a regional trend toward currency devaluation. Tired of a long-stagnant economy, voters carried opposition leader and former Attorney General Musa to power, giving his PUP 26 out of 29 seats in parliament. Musa, who ran on an antitax, pro-jobs platform, pledged to make Belize a party to international treaties on indigenous and women's rights. Among Musa's early initiatives were the creation of a national health service and a pruning back of the power of cabinet ministers.

The government has approved logging and oil concessions on more than 700,000 acres of forests and coastal areas that surround Maya lands and that the Indians depend on for subsistence activities. In 1999, efforts by Indian groups to assure their land rights before the Inter-American Commission on Human Rights were effectively blocked by the Musa government. In August 2000, even as discussions were taking place over Maya rights, the government announced that a U.S.-based oil company registered in the Virgin Islands would begin widespread exploratory drilling in the southern region that includes Maya lands. In response the Inter-American Commission asked that the government suspend all permits, licenses, and concessions for logging and oil exploration until it can rule on a case brought before it by the Toledo Maya Cultural Council on whether the government has violated Indian rights by permitting development on their ancestral lands.

Political Rights and Civil Liberties:

Citizens can change their government democratically in peaceful, fair, and open elections. The 29-seat house of representatives is elected for a five-year term. Members of the senate are appointed: 5 by the governor-general on the advice of the prime minister; 2 by the leader of the parliamentary opposition; and 1 by the Belize Advisory Council. Since independence from Great Britain, each election in racially diverse Belize has resulted in the incumbent party's being ousted. In the 1998 elections there was a 78 percent turnout of a population that has swelled in recent years because of immigration from other Central American countries. There are no restrictions on the right to organize political parties, and there are mestizo, Creole, Maya, and Garifuna in parliament. Civil society is well established, with a large number of nongovernmental organizations working in social, economic, and environmental areas.

In general, the judiciary is independent and nondiscriminatory, and the rule of law is respected. However, judges and the director of public prosecutions must negotiate the renewal of their employment contracts, which renders them vulnerable to political influence. Lengthy backlogs of trials are in part the result of the low pay received by judges, which results in high turnover rates. Narcotics cases often go on for years while defendants are free on bail. Occasional reports of police misconduct and brutality can be investigated either by the police department's internal affairs office or by a recently created ombudsman's office.

Prison conditions do not meet minimum standards. The government opened a new facility in 1993 to alleviate overcrowding. However, this new prison, which houses death row inmates, provides in some cases one bed for six inmates, nonworking toilets, and inadequate protection from the weather.

Belizeans have suffered from an increase in violent crime, much of it related to drug trafficking and gang conflict. In February 1996 the U.S. government added Belize to its list of major drug-transit countries despite the anticrime measures undertaken in 1995, including the adoption of a quick trial plan, and the country remained on the list in 1997.

The Belize Human Rights Commission is independent and effective. Human rights concerns include the plight of migrant workers and refugees from neighboring Central American countries and charges of labor abuses by Belizean employers. Most of the estimated 40,000 Spanish speakers who have immigrated to the largely English-speaking country since the 1980s do not have legal status. Some have registered under an amnesty program implemented in cooperation with the United Nations High Commissioner for Refugees. Reports continue of mistreatment of migrant workers, however.

There are judicial restrictions on freedom of the press. Belize has six privately owned newspapers, three of which are subsidized by major political parties; there is, however, no daily press. The mostly English-language press is free to publish a variety of political viewpoints, including those critical of the government, and there are Spanish-language media. Belize has a literacy rate of more than 90 percent. Radio and television are saturated with political advertising during elections. Fourteen private television stations operate, including four cable systems. There is an independent board to oversee operations of the government-owned outlets.

There is freedom of religion, and the government actively discourages racial and ethnic discrimination. More than half of the 21,000 Belizean Maya live in the Toledo district, where they form nearly two-thirds of the population. Despite their claim to be the original inhabitants of Belize, they have no secure title to their ancestral lands, which have been targeted by foreign, mostly Malaysian, investors. This land, for thousands of years, has provided Maya Indians with food, medicinal plants, building materials, and hunting grounds. In 1996 the Maya organized demonstrations and took legal steps to block government-negotiated logging contracts. They also opposed the paving of a major road that would afford businesses access to the area. Land claims continue to be fought out in the courts.

Labor unions are independent and well organized and have the right to strike, but the percentage of the workforce that is organized has declined to 11 percent. Unionized workers earn two to three times as much as their neighbors. Disputes are adjudicated by official boards of inquiry, and businesses are penalized for failing to abide by the labor code. Violence against women is a problem.

Benin

Polity: Presidential-parliamentary democracy
Economy: Mixed statist
Population: 6,400,000
PPP: $867
Life Expectancy: 54
Ethnic Groups: African [42 ethnic groups, including Fon, Adja, Bariba, Yoruba] (99 percent)
Capital: Porto-Novo

Political Rights: 2
Civil Liberties: 2*
Status: Free

Ratings Change: Benin's civil liberties rating changed from 3 to 2 due to an easing of restrictions on the press.

Overview:

Benin was rattled in January when President Mathieu Kérékou appeared on television accusing militias "of certain parties" of being involved in plotting to overthrow him. Opposition parties demanded proof. The coup rumors were linked to grumbling for field allowances by Beninese soldiers who had served as peacekeepers in Liberia. Such demands had led to a coup in nearby Côte d'Ivoire in December 1999, and it appeared as though Benin's leader feared the same.

Benin was once the center of the ancient kingdom of Dahomey, the name by which the country was known until 1975, when Kérékou renamed it. Six decades of French colonial rule had ended in 1960, and Kérékou took power 12 years later, ending successive coups and countercoups. He imposed a one-party state under the Benin People's Revolutionary Party. But by 1990, economic hardships and rising internal unrest forced him to agree to a transition to democracy that culminated in his defeat by Nicéphore Soglo in the March 1991 presidential elections. The country's human rights record subsequently improved. Kérékou made a comeback in 1996.

Benin held legislative elections in March 1999 that further consolidated the democratic transition the country began a decade ago. It was the third such election held since a national conference in 1990 ushered in democracy after nearly 20 years of single-party rule under Kérékou, who pursued Marxist-Leninist policies.

An alliance of about ten opposition parties formed early in 2000, led in part by former President Nicéphore Soglo. The country has up to 100 political parties, and it is unclear how many might present candidates for presidential elections to be held in early 2001.

Historically, Benin has been divided between northern and southern ethnic groups, which are the main roots of current political parties. Northern ethnic groups enlisted during Kérékou's early years in power still dominate the military. The armed forces continue to play an apolitical role in government affairs despite concerns about morale within their ranks and ethnic imbalance. The south has enjoyed more advanced development.

Benin is a poor country whose economy is based largely on subsistence agriculture. The government received debt relief in July worth $460 million under the Heavily Indebted Poor Countries Initiative, which is sponsored by the World Bank and International Monetary Fund, for its efforts to implement economic reforms. A code of ethics aimed at curbing graft in the allocation of government contracts was launched in July 1999.

Political Rights and Civil Liberties:

Benin held its first genuine multiparty elections in 1991. The president may serve two five-year terms, while national assembly members may serve an unlimited number of four-year terms. Under the guidance of Benin's Independent National Electoral Commission, the legislative polls proceeded smoothly and were judged free and fair by international observers. In the March 1999 election, 56 political parties put up candidates for the 83 parliamentary seats that had been allocated on the basis of proportional representation. It was the first year that an electoral commission in Benin had taken an oath of moral responsibility. The penalty for violation was a stiff fine and five years in prison stripped of all civil and political rights.

The opposition Democratic Renewal Party won 11 of the 83 seats. It maintains cordial relations with Soglo's Renaissance Party, which won 27 seats. The two parties and several others in the opposition have a combined total of 42 parliamentary seats against 41 by pro-Kérékou candidates. There are 19 political parties represented in the National Assembly.

Harsh libel laws have been used against journalists, but constitutional guarantees of freedom of expression are largely respected in practice. Most broadcast media are state owned, but they allow opposition and other reports critical of the government. Independent radio and television stations began operating in 1997 under a liberalized broadcasting law. An independent and pluralistic press publishes articles highly critical of both government and opposition leaders and policies. Press repression that occurred in 1999 eased in 2000.

The judiciary is generally considered to be independent but is inefficient and susceptible to corruption at some levels. The judicial system is based on French civil law and local customary law. An African judicial training center for lawyers was set up in Benin in August 2000. Its aim, as a nongovernmental organization (NGO), is to protect free expression and other rights.

Freedom of assembly is respected in Benin, and requirements for permits and registration are often ignored. Religious freedom is respected. Numerous NGOs and human rights groups operate without governmental hindrance. The Benin League for the Defense of Human Rights was a key investigator into claims that hundreds of people were extrajudicially executed in neighboring Togo after the disputed 1998 presidential election there. Human rights are largely respected in Benin, although concern has been raised over the operation of anticrime vigilante groups in the southwest. Mob justice appeared to have decreased somewhat in 2000. Prison conditions are harsh.

The right to organize and join unions is constitutionally guaranteed and respected in practice. Strikes are legal, and collective bargaining is common. A new labor code went into effect in 1999 after long discussions between unions, the government, and the national assembly. Several labor federations are affiliated with political parties and international labor groups. Approximately 75 percent of wage earners belong to labor unions. Laws prohibit employer retaliation against strikers, and the government enforces them effectively.

Although the constitution provides for equality for women, they enjoy fewer educational and employment opportunities than men, particularly in rural areas. Women hold positions in the cabinet and national assembly. In family matters, in which traditional practices prevail, their legal rights are often ignored. They have equal inheritance and property rights, but local custom in some areas prevents them from inheriting real property. Active women's rights groups have been effective in drafting a family code that would improve the status of women and children under the law.

Smuggling children into neighboring Nigeria for domestic service and meager compensation is reportedly widespread. In July 2000, the Child Labor News Service reported that 49,000 rural Beninese children (eight percent of the rural child population) were working abroad. Most were working on plantations in Côte d'Ivoire or as domestic servants in Gabon.

Bhutan

Polity: Traditional monarchy
Economy: Pre-industrial
Population: 900,000
PPP: $1,536
Life Expectancy: 61
Ethnic Groups: Bhote, Nepalese, Sarchops, indigenous or migrant tribes
Capital: Thimphu

Political Rights: 7
Civil Liberties: 6
Status: Not Free

Overview:

Signaling modest movement on a long-standing dispute, Bhutan and Nepal agreed in December 2000 on a procedure for verifying the citizenship of the 94,000 Nepali-speaking Bhutanese refugees living in Nepal since the early 1990s. However, the two sides put off negotiations over actually repatriating the refugees until after the lengthy verification process is completed.

Britain began guiding this Himalayan land's affairs in 1865 and installed the ruling Wangchuk dynasty in 1907. London's role ended with a 1949 Indo-Bhutan treaty that gave India control over Bhutan's foreign affairs. Since then, New Delhi has supported the Wangchuk family's continued rule as an absolute monarchy. The current monarch, Jigme Singye Wangchuk, succeeded his father to the throne in 1972.

The government began in 1987 requiring all citizens to adopt the dress and customs of the ruling, northern-based Ngalong Drukpa-ethnic group. Authorities said they feared for the survival of Drukpa culture due to the large numbers of Nepali-speakers, also known as Southern Bhutanese, in the south. The situation for the Southern Bhutanese worsened in 1988, when authorities began applying a discriminatory 1985 Citizenship Act to arbitrarily strip thousands of Nepali speakers of their citizenship after a census showed Southern Bhutanese to be in the majority in five southern districts. The act confirmed the primary basis for citizenship to be residence in Bhutan in 1958, the year the kingdom extended citizenship to most Southern Bhutanese. But to prove citizenship, Southern Bhutanese now had to show a 1958 land-tax receipt, which had been of little importance when issued three decades earlier. The act also tightened requirements for transmitting citizenship to persons born after 1958.

Southern Bhutanese groups organized pro-democracy demonstrations in 1990, although hardline groups reportedly carried out arson attacks and committed some political killings and other anti-government violence. In the early 1990s, soldiers reportedly raped and beat many Southern Bhutanese villagers and detained thousands as "anti-nationals." Tens of thousands of Southern Bhutanese fled to India and then into Nepal.

Under the December 2000 agreement, a 10-person, bilateral team will begin verifying documents and interviewing family heads in 2001. The team will place refugees into one of four categories first agreed to in 1993: bona fide Bhutanese whom authorities forcibly evicted; former Bhutanese who emigrated and therefore lost their citizenship rights under Bhutanese law; non-Bhutanese; and Bhutanese who have committed criminal acts. Many refugee activists fear that they will be placed wrongly into one of the latter three categories.

Moreover, since Bhutanese soldiers reportedly made many Southern Bhutanese sign "voluntary migration forms" before forcibly expelling them in the early 1990s, ordinary villagers potentially could be placed into the category of former Bhutanese who lost their citizenship by emigrating. The Bhutanese government maintains that most of the refugees either left voluntarily or were illegal immigrants. Refugee leaders say the vast majority of those in the camps are genuine Bhutanese nationals.

The government recently has faced pressure for political reform from members of the country's third-major ethnic group, the Sarchops in eastern Bhutan, who in 1994 launched the Druk National Congress (DNC) party in exile. Since then, the DNC has organized demonstrations, wall postering, and other peaceful pro-democracy activities, mainly in eastern Bhutan. In 1997 and 1998 authorities arrested scores of suspected DNC members and sympathizers, including monks, religious teachers, and children and other relatives of DNC members.

Political Rights and Civil Liberties: Bhutanese lack the democratic means to change their government. King Wangchuk and a small circle of Ngalong Drukpa elites wield absolute power and make key decisions. In June 1998, King Wangchuk dissolved the council of ministers, or cabinet, removed himself as its chairman, and gave parliament the power, in theory, to remove the king through a two-thirds vote. The king also allowed the legislature to elect a majority of the cabinet, although the king will still assign portfolios. The diplomat Jigme Thinley became head of the council of ministers. It is unclear what effect these changes have had in practice.

The 150-member national assembly meets irregularly and in practice has little independent power. Every three years village headmen choose 100 national assembly members, while the king appoints 40 seats and religious groups choose 10 seats. The national assembly is often a forum for diatribes against the Southern Bhutanese, who hold a disproportionately small number of seats. In practice, authorities prohibit political parties, and none legally exist.

In the early 1990s the army and police committed grave human rights violations against Southern Bhutanese, including arbitrary arrests, beatings, rapes, destruction of homes, and robberies. Authorities have punished few, if any, of those responsible, which has resulted in a continued climate of impunity. The rudimentary judiciary is not independent. The king appoints and can dismiss judges, most of whom have little legal training. Several detainees and prisoners have reportedly died in custody in recent years as a result of poor conditions. The government released 40 political prisoners in December 1999. They included South Asia's best-known political prisoner, Tek Nath Rizal, whom authorities sentenced in November 1993 to life imprisonment under a broadly drawn National Security Act legislated three years after his imprisonment.

Authorities restrict freedom of expression and prohibit criticism of the king, except indirectly during national assembly discussions. The state-owned weekly *Kuensel* is Bhutan's sole regular publication and offers only pro-regime views. The state-controlled Bhutan Broadcasting Service's multilingual radio broadcasts and television service similarly do not offer opposition viewpoints. Authorities began operating a public-access Internet server in 1999, although the cost may make access prohibitive for most Bhutanese. Satellite television reception is illegal, although in practice it is generally tolerated.

Freedom of assembly is nonexistent. In recent years security forces have arrested participants in peaceful pro-democracy demonstrations in eastern Bhutan, as well as Bhutanese refugees living in Nepal who entered and demonstrated inside Bhutan. Authorities sharply restrict freedom of association for political purposes but permit some business and civic organizations to function.

The sixth Five Year Plan (1987-1992) introduced the program "One Nation, One People," which promoted *driglam namzha*, the national dress and customs of the ruling Drukpas. A 1989 royal decree made driglam namzha mandatory for all Bhutanese, although enforcement is sporadic. The government continued to ban the Nepali language as a subject of instruction in schools.

The government reportedly continued to require Southern Bhutanese to obtain official no-objection certificates (NOC) to enter schools, take government jobs, and sell farm products. According to an April article in the *Bangkok Post* and other accounts, Bhutanese refugees say that authorities do not permit Nepali-speaking children in southern Bhutan to attend school, although it is difficult to confirm the extent to which this is true. In recent years, authorities have reportedly denied NOCs for schooling to children of Sarchop pro-democracy activists. In 1998, the government fired 219 mostly Southern Bhutanese civil servants, many of whom were related to pro-democracy activists.

The Drukpa Kagyu sect of Mahayana Buddhism is the official state religion. Buddhist *lamas* (priests) wield fairly strong political influence. During a 1997 crackdown on Sarchop pro-democracy activists, authorities reportedly closed 13 monasteries of the Nyingmpa school of Buddhism that is practiced by most Sarchops.

Independent trade unions and strikes are de facto illegal. Officials often force villagers to contribute "voluntary" labor for infrastructure projects. Property rights are limited. In recent years the Bhutanese government has resettled some northern Bhutanese on land belonging to Southern Bhutanese refugees.

In recent years, New Delhi has urged Thimpu to evict hundreds of Assamese and Bodo militants from the Indian state of Assam living in jungle camps in southern Bhutan. According to Indian press reports, Bhutanese officials say they are trying to persuade the guerrillas to peacefully vacate the bases. However, some Indian officials accuse Thimpu of sheltering the militants.

Bolivia

Polity: Presidential-parliamentary democracy
Economy: Capitalist
Population: 8,300,000
PPP: $2,269
Life Expectancy: 62
Ethnic Groups: Quechua (30 percent), Aymara (25 percent), mestizo (25-30 percent), European (5-15 percent)
Capital: La Paz (administrative), Sucre (judicial)

Political Rights: 1
Civil Liberties: 3
Status: Free

Overview:

In 2000, President Hugo Banzer Suarez, a dictator turned democrat elected in 1997, found himself facing a devastating political and economic crisis caused by his government's success in eradicating the production of coca leaf, the essential ingredient for making cocaine. Banzer won high praise in Washington for eliminating more than 90 percent of the illegal coca crop in a nation that had been the world's second largest producer of cocaine. However, South America's poorest country dropped even deeper into poverty as Bolivia lost as much as $700 million in illegal drug income in two years, leaving 35,000 peasant families without income. Bloody street protests paralyzed the country for several weeks, causing more than a dozen deaths and $200 million in economic losses.

After achieving independence from Spain in 1825, the Republic of Bolivia endured recurrent instability and military rule. However, the armed forces, responsible for more than 180 coups in 157 years, have stayed in their barracks since 1982.

As a result of recent reforms, presidential terms run five years and congress consists of a 130-member house of representatives and a 27-member senate. The principal parties are Banzer's conservative National Democratic Action (ADN); its governing coalition partner, the social-democratic Movement of the Revolutionary Left (MIR); and the center-right Revolutionary Nationalist Movement (MNR). Banzer had come in first in elections in 1985, but a parliamentary coalition instead selected the octogenarian former president, Victor Paz Estenssoro, the founder of the MNR. In 1989 the MIR's Jaime Paz Zamora, who had run third in the polls, became president through an alliance with the ADN.

In 1993, the MIR-ADN candidate was retired General Banzer, who came in second to the MNR's Gonzalo Sanchez de Losada, a planning minister in Paz Estenssoro's 1985-1989 administration. Sanchez de Losada oversaw the massive privatization of Bolivia's state-owned enterprises and, under U.S. pressure, stepped up coca eradication. A series of labor strikes and mass protests in early 1995 was followed by the imposition by Sanchez de Losada of a six-month state of siege.

Throughout 1996, the government privatization program brought regular street protests. As Sanchez de Losada's term ended, a government otherwise hailed for initiatives such as improved access to the courts, efforts to reform a corrupt, inefficient judiciary, and broad decentralization was mired in increasingly bitter labor disputes. In nationwide municipal elections held in December 1999, conducted using the electoral code and political party legislation recently approved by congress, the ruling coalition made a strong showing, although the opposition MNR won the largest number of council seats and votes as a single party.

Throughout 2000 Banzer's opponents sought to hold him accountable for his alleged involvement as Bolivia's military ruler in Operation Condor, a 1970s plan by regional military regimes to eliminate leftists. In October, coca leaf farmers agreed to temporarily halt actions in which a coalition of teachers, peasants, and coca producers paralyzed traffic for a month along the country's main highways and generated violent confrontations in several regions. The truce came after the government agreed to halt construction of three military bases in the prime coca-growing region and to set up a committee to determine the use of $80 million in U.S. aid designed to promote alternative crop development. Banzer vowed to press on with his government's fight against cocaine trafficking. Official corruption, much of it drug related, continued to be a significant problem.

Political Rights and Civil Liberties: Citizens can change their government through elections. In 1997, congressional elections were held under new legislation in which in half of the 130 lower house contests were elected individually and directly, rather than from party lists, with the top vote getter representing a single constituency. The national elections held that year were free and fair.

The judiciary, headed by the supreme court, remains the weakest branch of government and is corrupt, inefficient, and the object of intimidation by drug traffickers, as are Bolivia's mayoral, customs, and revenue offices. Both the Sanchez de Losada and Banzer governments have made serious efforts to improve the administration of justice, including making it more accessible. Banzer has implemented previously agreed-upon innovations such as the creation of an independent council in charge of judicial appointments, a public ombudsman, and a constitutional tribunal chosen by congress. The judicial council has suspended dozens of judges and fined or placed on probation hundreds more because of incompetence or unlawful delays of the legal process. These generally positive developments, however, appeared to hit a roadblock of sorts when in February 2000, an Italian communications consultant regarded by the U.S. government as a narcotics chieftain and money launderer was acquitted by a local court on the grounds of insufficient evidence. The release of the man, who is married to Banzer's niece and who had wiretapped U.S. embassy offices and antidrug agencies, resulted in the resignations of both the justice and information ministers.

Government-sponsored as well as independent human rights organizations exist, and they frequently report of security force brutality. The congressional Human Rights Commission is active and frequently criticizes the government. However, rights activists and their families are subject to intimidation. Prison conditions are harsh, with some 5,500 prisoners held in facilities designed to hold half that number, and nearly three-quarters of prisoners are held without formal sentences. In mid-1999, the government announced that the Bolivian military will backstop law-enforcement efforts in violent, crime-plagued sections of major urban areas.

Evidence abounds that drug money has been used to finance political campaigns and buy the favor of government officials, including police and military personnel. Critics say that Law 1008, the Law to Regulate Coca and Controlled Substances, passed in 1988, is excessively harsh, restricts suspects' constitutional rights, and violates international norms and standards of due process. Government forces, particularly the troops of the Mobile Rural Patrol Unit (UMOPAR), have in past years committed serious human rights abuses, including murder, arbitrary detention, and the suppression of peaceful demonstrations during coca-eradication efforts in the tropical lowland region of Chapare. Police officers have also been killed in the line of duty fighting the peasant coca producers. Military troops, as well as police, have been used to suppress internal disturbances, adding to the propensity for violence.

The constitution guarantees free expression, freedom of religion, and the right to organize political parties, civic groups, and labor unions. However, freedom of speech is subject to some limitations. Unions have the right to strike.

The languages of the indigenous population are officially recognized, but the 40 percent Spanish-speaking minority still dominates the political process. More than 520 indigenous communities have been granted legal recognition under the 1994 Popular Participation law, which guarantees respect for the integrity of native peoples. Indian territories are often neither legally defined nor protected, and coca growers and timber thieves exploit Indian lands illegally. Some Indians are kept as virtual slaves by rural employers through the use of debt peonage, with employers charging workers more for room and board than they earn. The observance of customary law by indigenous peoples is common in rural areas; in the remotest areas, the death penalty, forbidden by the constitution, is reportedly sometimes used against those who violate traditional laws or rules.

The press, radio, and television are mostly private. Journalists covering corruption stories are occasionally subject to verbal intimidation by government officials, arbitrary detention by police, and violent attack.

Violence against women is pervasive. In 1999, there was increasing cooperation between Bolivian and Argentine authorities to clamp down on the illegal exploitation of Bolivian children who are lured to work in sweatshops in Argentina.

Bosnia-Herzegovina

Polity: International Protectorate
Economy: Mixed statist (transitional)
Population: 3,800,000
PPP: na
Life Expectancy: 73
Ethnic Groups: Serbian (31 percent), Muslim (44 percent), Croatian (17 percent), other (8 percent)
Capital: Sarajevo

Political Rights: 5
Civil Liberties: 4*
Status: Partly Free

Ratings Change: Bosnia-Herzegovina's civil liberties rating changed from 5 to 4 because of a modest improvement in the situation for religious minorities and small increases in refugee returns.

Overview:

The year 2000 was one of elections in Bosnia-Herzegovina. In April, local municipal elections were held for the second time in the postwar period, and in November, statewide elections for various institutions were held for the third time since the Dayton Peace Accords (DPA) were signed in 1995. In general, although the more vehemently nationalist parties seemed to be losing some ground, the elections held in 2000 showed that nationalism is still far from a spent force in the country.

Immediately upon being recognized as an independent state in April 1992, Bosnia-Herzegovina was plunged into a 43-month-long civil war. In November 1995, the DPA, an internationally sponsored peace agreement, brought an end to the fighting by creating a loosely knit state composed of the Bosniac-Croat "Federation of Bosnia-Herzegovina" and the Republika Srpska (RS). The DPA also gave the international community a very powerful role in running post-Dayton Bosnia-Herzegovina. This included the deployment of a NATO-led peacekeeping force, and a leading role for international civilian agencies such as the Office of the High Representative (OHR) and the Organization for Security and Cooperation in Europe (OSCE). In 1997, the International High Representative in Bosnia-Herzegovina was given the authority to impose laws on the country, and to dismiss publicly elected officials from office. Despite the efforts of the international community, however, most aspects of political, social, and economic life in postwar Bosnia-Herzegovina are still divided along ethnic lines.

Bosnia's April municipal elections produced mixed results. On one hand, international officials claim that before the elections, nationalist parties controlled 124 out of 146 municipalities in the country. After the elections, this number fell to 76. The number of votes gained by non-nationalist parties such as the Social-Democratic Party of Bosnia-Herzegovina (SDP) increased from 187,000 in 1997 to 280,000 in 2000. These figures, however, have to be measured against the fact that the 2000 municipal elections also witnessed a dramatic decline in the number of refugees and displaced persons registering to vote in their prewar homes. By one estimate, the number of Bosniac voters choosing to vote in the RS fell by half between the 1997 and 2000 elections.

This suggests that the vast majority of people driven from their homes during the war have given up hope of ever returning.

In the statewide elections held on November 11, nationalist parties did unexpectedly well, especially among Croat and Serb voters. Nevertheless, in the Bosnia wide House of Representatives (one house in the two-chamber Parliamentary Assembly), the three main nationalist parties that had dominated Bosnian politics since 1990—the Bosniac Party of Democratic Action (SDA), the Croatian Democratic Community (HDZ), and the Serbian Democratic Party (SDS)—saw their total of 27 seats in the 42-member chamber fall to 19 seats. The SDA and HDZ also lost their majority in the Bosniac-Croat Federation parliament. In the RS, the SDS candidate won the race for the presidency, defeating the international community's favored candidate, RS Prime Minister Milorad Dodik, and the SDS became the strongest single party in the RS National Assembly.

On the same day that the November elections were held, the HDZ organized an unofficial referendum for Croat voters, essentially asking them if they supported the creation of a third entity in Bosnia. The measure passed by an overwhelming margin, showing that large segments of Bosnia's population remain unhappy with the DPA. To further stress this point, in the wake of the referendum's passing, HDZ President Ante Jelavic declared that as far as the Croats in Bosnia-Herzegovina were concerned, the mission of the OHR and the OSCE had come to an end.

In October, long-time Bosniac leader Alija Izetbegovic retired from public office. Thus, by the end of 2000, the three politicians (Izetbegovic, Croatia's Tudjman, and Serbia's Milosevic) who had led their peoples to war, had signed the DPA, and had in so many ways obstructed the implementation of the peace process, were no longer on the scene. Despite the improvement in Bosnia's international environment, however, at the end of 2000 it remained unclear whether the country enjoyed the internal domestic consensus needed to make the DPA a success.

Political Rights and Civil Liberties: The DPA authorized the OSCE to organize and monitor elections at all levels of government in Bosnia-Herzegovina. Elections throughout the postwar period have regularly been certified "free and fair," although the parties that held power from 1990 to 1998 enjoyed many advantages in terms of access to state-owned media and the ability to divert government funds into their electoral coffers. Over the past several years, international officials have been trying to level the electoral playing field. On February 18, 2000, the OSCE adopted a rule prohibiting officials from serving in both governmental positions and public enterprises. By May, 136 officials had resigned their positions in public enterprises, while 7 officials chose to resign their elective office. Electoral reforms introduced in 2000 specified new rules on campaign financing (including spending ceilings per voter per electoral campaign), regulations forcing parties to reveal their financial records, and the introduction of a preferential voting system in the RS in an effort to bring more moderate politicians to power.

In general, voters are allowed to freely elect their representatives and are allowed to form political parties insofar as the programs of those parties are not deemed to be at odds with the DPA. The International High Representative, however, has the authority to remove publicly elected officials from office. From January to November 2000, the current High Representative used these powers to remove more than 30 officials. Similarly, the inability of Bosniacs, Croats, and Serbs to agree to anything of substance required the High Representative to impose laws and regulations on the country regarding a wide variety of issues, ranging from judicial reform, passports, and the national anthem, to a law on metrology.

The situation for the press in Bosnia showed some minimal improvements in 2000. Most notably, independent media appeared for the first time in Croat-populated areas (the so-called Herceg-Bosna), where previously the media scene was dominated by pro-HDZ publications and/or publications from Croatia proper. Nevertheless, the press still remains subject to various forms of harassment. A survey of journalists carried out in 2000 showed that 62 percent of those surveyed had personally experienced intimidation and interference with their work. In June, Federation financial police raided the offices of the Sarajevo daily newspaper *Dnevni Avaz*. Although *Dnevni Avaz* had previously been considered a pro-SDA newspaper, it adopted a more independent editorial position during the first half of the year, and high-ranking SDA officials blamed the paper for the SDA's poor showing in the April municipal elections.

Freedom of religion in Bosnia showed some improvement in 2000. Individuals living in areas dominated by members of their own ethnic group do not experience any limitations on their religious rights; however, the same does not hold true for individuals who are members of a local ethnic minority. In this sense, religious intolerance is often a reflection of the prevailing atmosphere of intolerance for ethnic minorities in various parts of the country, rather than religious persecution per se. All three major religious organizations in the country—Islamic, Catholic, and Orthodox—have claims against the government for property confiscated during the Communist period. In October 2000, the first mosque to be built in the RS in the postwar period was dedicated outside of Prijedor, and in November, Banja Luka authorities granted permission for the historic Ferhadija mosque (destroyed in 1993) to be rebuilt.

Citizens enjoy the right to freedom of assembly, and demonstrations and other forms of public discussion are frequent occurrences. Free trade unions exist and are very active. The judiciary in Bosnia is considered to be under the influence of the nationalist parties who had exclusive control over the various ethnic and regional governments in the country from 1990-97. In 1997, the OHR and the OSCE began a major judicial reform campaign aimed at improving the professionalism and independence of the judiciary.

Freedom of movement and the return of refugees and displaced persons to their homes continued to show very modest improvements in 2000. A hopeful development was the beginning of returns to areas in the eastern RS where some of the worst instances of forced expulsions had occurred, such as around the town of Foca/Srbinje. Overall, so-called minority returns, that is, those in which the returnee goes to an area in which she or he is not a member of the local ethnic majority, rose to 32,000 from January to September 2000, triple the number during the same period in 1999. At this rate, however, it would take some 20 years for all of the country's refugees and displaced persons to return to their homes. Further complicating the return of refugees and displaced persons is a complex system of property rights legislation, which often makes it difficult for individuals to reclaim the property they owned or had rights to before 1992. Local officials have been notably reluctant to engage in meaningful reforms in this area, forcing the High Representative to impose, annul, or amend numerous pieces of property legislation over the course of the year.

Legally, women are entitled to full equality with men. In practical terms, however, women are significantly underrepresented in politics and government. To compensate for the absence of women in public life, the OSCE has instituted a regulation forcing political parties to list 3 women among the top 10 names on the candidate's lists. In the postwar period, women have often been discriminated against in the workplace in favor of demobilized soldiers.

Botswana

Polity: Parliamentary democracy and traditional chiefs
Political Rights: 2
Civil Liberties: 2
Status: Free
Economy: Capitalist
Population: 1,600,000
PPP: $6,103
Life Expectancy: 46
Ethnic Groups: Batswana (95 percent), Kalanga, Basarwa and Kgagaladi (4 percent), white (1 percent)
Capital: Gaborone

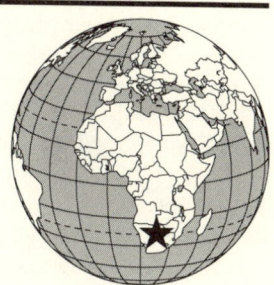

Overview:

The biggest challenge facing Botswana in 2000 was AIDS, and the disease threatens to roll back outstanding progress the country has made in the areas of economic and social development. The economy has been growing at an average rate of 8.5 percent since the late 1960s, but growth this year is expected to drop drastically for the first time, largely due to the AIDS epidemic.

Botswana has an outstanding record in Africa for human rights, although there are occasional reports of police misconduct and poor treatment of indigenous Basarwa. Botswana is Africa's longest continuous multiparty democracy; elected governments have ruled the country since it gained independence from Britain in 1966. In October 1999 Botswana held its seventh general elections since independence. President Mogae, a former central bank chief, succeeded Ketumile Masire as president in April 1998. Mogae was confirmed as the country's leader in October 1999. A referendum on whether the president should be directly elected was withdrawn shortly before a scheduled vote in late 1997.

Botswana has one of the highest AIDS prevalence rates in the world. The HIV infection rate rose from 4.4 percent in 1992 to 17 percent in 1998. The government of President Festus Mogae announced in August 2000 that an HIV-disclosure law would be introduced, which would compel HIV-positive people to disclose their status to sexual partners. Not doing so would be considered a criminal offense.

On the political front, the Balopi Commission, which includes former parliamentarians, continued to hold meetings around the country to examine the efficacy of three articles in the constitution that created a "house of chiefs," or consultative body to parliament, in 1966. The commission seeks to determine whether the house of chiefs still serves the body politic, needs to be changed, should be abolished, or should be left as is. The commission includes representatives of eight tribes and four ad hoc positions.

Hundreds of Namibians early in the year sought refuge in Botswana after fleeing insecurity in Namibia, where the government has been struggling against Caprivi secessionists. Extradition warrants for 14 Caprivi secessionists who fled to Botswana in 1998 were nullified on technical grounds in September, and a new hearing was scheduled for November. They are wanted in Namibia on charges of treason, murder, and illegal possession of arms and ammunition.

Economic progress has been built on sound fiscal management and low rates of corruption. Unemployment and crime are rising problems. The government is making efforts to diversify its economy from overreliance on the beef and diamond sectors.

Political Rights and Civil Liberties: Citizens of Botswana can change their government democratically. The Independent Election Commission created in 1996 has helped consolidate Botswana's reputation for fairness in voting. Botswana uses a constituency system in which the candidate who polls the highest number of votes in a constituency becomes the member of parliament.

The ruling Botswana Democratic Party (BDP), which has held power since independence, won by a wide majority in legislative and local elections in October 1999, soundly defeating a fractured opposition. The BDP scored a significant breakthrough by winning the Gaborone Central constituency. It is the first time the BDP has held a seat in Gaborone in 15 years. A major change in voting patterns was the election of six women, all from the ruling BDP, to parliament. There were only two women in the previous parliament. Voter apathy was high. Only 57 percent of 800,000 eligible voters registered, despite the passing of a new law that lowered the voting age from 21 to 18.

In the October 1999 election the BDP swept 33 of 40 national assembly seats. The opposition had gone into the election holding 13 seats. The historical opposition party, the Botswana National Front (BNF), won 6 seats, while the breakaway Botswana Congress Party (BCP) was reduced to a single seat, a reflection of voter dissatisfaction with the split in 1998. Despite its poor showing, the BCP said it would regroup and stand behind its leader, Michael Dingake, and would never rejoin the BNF.

Botswana's national assembly, elected for five years, chooses the president to serve a concurrent five-year term. The assembly's choice is confirmed by the courts when the winning party receives more than half the seats in the parliament.

There is a free and vigorous press in cities and towns, and political debate is open and lively. The opposition and government critics, however, receive little access to the government-controlled broadcast media. Botswana's first state-owned television went on the air in August 2000. The country had been depending on the South African Broadcasting Corporation and a satellite television channel. The only other station is the private Gaborone Broadcasting Corporation Television, which has a limited reach. There are a number of private radio stations in Gaborone.

Botswana's courts are generally considered to be fair and free of direct political interference. Trials are usually public, and those accused of the most serious violent crimes are provided public defenders. The University of Botswana Legal Assistance Center and the Botswana Center for Human Rights offer free legal services, but are limited by a lack of resources. Treatment of the indigenous Basarwa (Bushmen, or "red people") has drawn local and international concern because of government relocation schemes, including forcible evictions from traditional lands to make way for game parks and cattle ranching. Only a few thousand Basarwa are permitted to practice traditional nomadic lifestyles in the central Kalahari Desert. Almost 50,000 others have been resettled in villages or as laborers on farms. Some Basarwa, however, returned to their traditional areas in 1999 after the government acquiesced to demands.

Concentration of economic power has hindered labor organization. While independent unions are permitted, workers' rights to strike and to bargain for wages are restricted.

Progress in improving the rights of women has been slow, although analysts say this could begin to change with the election of more women to parliament. Three women serve in the cabinet. Domestic violence is reportedly rampant, and there is little movement to stem it through police action or education, especially in rural areas. The government has delayed admitting women into the military.

Brazil

Polity: Presidential-parliamentary democracy (federal)
Political Rights: 3
Civil Liberties: 3*
Status: Partly Free

Economy: Capitalist-statist
Population: 170,100,000
PPP: $6,625
Life Expectancy: 67
Ethnic Groups: White (55 percent), mixed (38 percent), black (6 percent), other (1 percent)
Capital: Brasilia
Ratings Change: Brazil's civil liberties rating changed from 4 to 3 due to improvements in tackling corruption and organized crime.

Overview:
Corruption and violent lawlessness dominated the news in Brazil in 2000, as the government of President Fernando Henrique Cardoso came in for congressional scrutiny in a public works bribery scandal, and violent urban crime continued to spiral upward. In June, a live television broadcast of a hostage drama in Rio de Janeiro, in which a young woman was killed, caused Cardoso to announce a wide-ranging national crackdown on crime, including a $1.7 billion national public safety program. In August, Cardoso unveiled a wide-ranging anticorruption package designed to stem the accusations of illegality dogging a government that has shown greater resolve in solving the problem than any other Brazilian government.

After gaining independence from Portugal in 1822, Brazil retained a monarchial system until a republic was established in 1889. Democratic rule has been interrupted by long periods of authoritarian rule, most recently under military regimes from 1964 to 1985, when elected civilian rule was reestablished. A new constitution, which went into effect in 1988, provides for a president to be elected for four years and a bicameral congress consisting of an 81-member senate elected for eight years and a 503-member chamber of deputies elected for four years.

Civilian rule has been marked by corruption scandals. The scandal having the greatest political impact led to the impeachment by congress of President Fernando Collor de Mello (1989-1992). Collor resigned and was replaced by a weak, ineffectual government led by his vice president, Itamar Franco.

In early 1994, Cardoso, Franco's finance minister and a market-oriented centrist, forged a three-party, center-right coalition around his own Social Democratic Party (PSDB). As his anti-inflation plan appeared to work dramatically, Cardoso, a former Marxist backed by big media and big business, jumped into the lead. In October 1994 Cardoso won the presidency with 54 percent of the vote, against 27 percent for Luis Ignacio "Lula" de Silva, the leader of the leftist Worker's Party (PT) and an early front-runner. The senate was divided among 11 parties, and the chamber of deputies among 18. Cardoso's coalition did not have a majority in either house.

Cardoso spent 1995 cajoling opponents and bargaining for the congressional votes needed to carry out his economic liberalization program. That fall, his government was rocked by a bribery and phone-tapping scandal. In April 1996, Cardoso indicated that he favored a constitutional amendment to drop the one-term limit, which would allow him to run for reelection in 1998, and in 1997 he was able to secure congressional approval for such a measure.

In 1996, land issues were high on the political agenda. In January, Cardoso announced presidential decree 1775, which allows states, municipalities, and non-Indians to challenge, at the federal level, proposed demarcation of Indian lands. Following the decree, miners and loggers increased their encroachments on Indian land. In another development, a radicalized movement representing landless peasants continued to occupy mostly fallow land in rural areas to pressure the government to settle rural families. The activism contributed to scores of violent conflicts between peasants on the one hand and, on the other hand, the military, the police, and private security forces, which act with virtual impunity.

In 1998, Cardoso's first-ballot victory (nearly 52 percent of the votes cast) over Lula, his nearest rival, was tempered somewhat by a less convincing win at the congressional and gubernatorial levels. His win was also overshadowed when published accounts of secretly recorded conversations seemed to indicate that two top officials were steering a bid to privatize part of the state-run telephone holding company to a consortium of personal friends, who ended up losing the auction.

The revelation in 1999 of a vast criminal conspiracy centered in the jungle state of Acre highlighted the lawlessness of Brazil's remote areas and moved Cardoso to take firm measures to combat organized crime. In June, Cardoso's choice for chief of the federal police was forced to resign after holding office just three days when he was alleged to have participated in the torture of political prisoners during the military regime. At the same time, a power struggle between the state intelligence service (*Abin*) and the federal police, in which the wiretapping of top political figures, including Cardoso himself, was revealed, contributed to the scandal over the privatization of the national telecommunications system.

In 2000, the Brazilian senate removed for the first time ever one of its members, accused of corruption. Public safety issues appeared to increasingly determine how people spent both their money and their time. Bulletproof-vehicle sales are booming in Brazil; some 50 percent of big-city residents say that they avoid leaving their homes after dark for fear of attack; and the private security market is one of the country's fastest-growing industries—30 percent a year.

In September, a congressional committee probing organized crime and drug trafficking released an explosive report implicating nearly 200 officials in 17 of Brazil's 27 states—including at least 10 state and federal congressmen and a host of police officers, judges, mayors, and other local officials. Cardoso used the opportunity to warn that what he called a barrage of unfounded accusations was eroding faith in Brazilian democracy. In October, mayoral candidates of the moderately left, anti-corruption PT swept to victory in a number of the country's most important cities, including São Paulo—Brazil's financial and economic nerve center—giving a boost to the party's chances in the 2002 presidential elections.

Political Rights and Civil Liberties: Citizens can change their government through elections. Recent efforts to modernize elections procedures were considered highly successful in the November 2000 municipal elections, with state-of-the-art electronic voting allowing results from even the most remote areas to be tabulated in 12 hours. The new system dramatically diminished the incidence of blank or annulled ballots, which in the past have often come from illiterate voters unable to discharge their civic duty. The speed with which the votes were tabulated also appeared to reduce the possibility for chaotic, fraud-ridden elections. However, a 1999 study showed that nepotism is rife in the congress, where one-third of all deputies have placed their wives, children, and relatives on the official government payroll.

The constitution guarantees freedom of religion, freedom of expression, and the right to organize political and civic organizations. Cardoso is credited with initiating a marked change in attitudes concerning international criticism on rights issues, from aggressive, nationalistic rejection to dialogue and openness. He created a ministerial-rank secretariat charged with defending human rights. The crime of torture was upgraded from a misdemeanor to a serious crime punishable by up to 16 years in prison.

In the past decade, the murder rate in Brazil has doubled, with 45,000 deaths due to gunshot wounds in 1999 and 2,495 people murdered by vigilante death squads over the past three years. The state capital of São Paulo has a death rate—50 deaths per 100,000 people—comparable in the western hemisphere only to that of Colombia's war-torn cities. The climate of lawlessness is reinforced by a weak judiciary, although recently some improvements have been made. Brazil's supreme court is granted substantial autonomy by the constitution. However, the judicial system is overwhelmed (with only 7,000 judges for a population of more than 150 million) and vulnerable to chronic corruption. With a few exceptions, it has been virtually powerless in the face of organized crime. A national breakdown in police discipline and escalating criminal violence, fueled by a burgeoning drug trade and increasing ties to Italian and other foreign criminal organizations, have added to a climate of lawlessness and insecurity. Human rights, particularly those of socially marginalized groups, are violated with impunity on a massive scale.

In a positive development, federal government prosecutors have begun to act as public interest advocates on issues ranging from the environment and consumer and Indian rights to monitoring police behavior. Recent legal reforms have given itinerant "traveling judges" broad special powers to decide on legal matters in makeshift courtrooms, enabling the system to clear thousands of backlogged criminal and civil cases and allowing the rural poor a greater possibility to have their issues addressed by law.

The 124-point national public safety plan, initiated in 2000 by Cardoso, included recruiting 2,000 more federal police, an implicit recognition that cash-strapped state governments have not been able to forge from their undisciplined and demoralized local police effective crime-deterring units. The plan also included a provision to set up a national registry of police officers with criminal records, in order to ensure they do not receive later employment in Brazil's burgeoning private security firms. There are some 1.3 million private security guards in Brazil, more than twice the number of police serving in the country's 27 states.

Brazil's police are among the world's most violent and corrupt, with local media claiming that some 15,000 officers have been accused of torture but that none has been sentenced. (In August 2000, the United Nations special rapporteur on torture traveled to Brazil, where he noted that he visited those countries where the number of torture accusations suggested the practice was commonplace and needed to be investigated.) Police are often grossly underpaid in the lower ranks, and working conditions are poor. Extrajudicial killings are usually disguised as shootouts with dangerous criminals. Military policemen in São Paulo and Rio de Janeiro have secretly been caught on videotape attacking people on the street, extorting money, and opening fire on—and killing—motorists during routine operations. In many cities "death squads," often composed of off-duty state police, terrorize shantytown dwellers and intimidate human rights activists attempting to investigate abuses.

Since 1994, the federal government has deployed the army to quell police strikes and bring order to Rio de Janeiro's 400 slums, most of which are ruled by gangs in league, or in competition, with corrupt police and local politicians. Public distrust of the judiciary has resulted in poor citizens taking the law into their own hands, with hundreds of reported lynchings and mob executions. In response to U.S. pressure, the Brazilian military is playing an increasing role in antinarcotics efforts.

The prison system in Brazil is anarchic, overcrowded, and largely unfit for human habitation, and human rights groups charge that the torture and other inhumane treatment common to most of the country's detention centers turns petty thieves into hardened criminals. In 2000, a parliamentary report charged the prisons were a "reinvention of hell" and singled out a jail in São Paulo as a "medieval dungeon" where guards used a special machine to deliver electric shocks to prisoners' genitalia. The 2000 public safety plan calls for new prisons to be built in order to relieve chronic overcrowding.

The press is privately owned. There are dozens of daily newspapers and numerous other publications throughout the country. The print media have played a central role in exposing official corruption. In recent years TV Globo's near monopoly on the broadcast media has been challenged by its rival, Sistema Brasiliero de Televisão (STB). In a negative development, on December 27, 2000, Cardoso promulgated a controversial law that aimed to shield public officials from slander by means of firing and fining public prosecutors who make charges that they cannot prove in court.

Large landowners control nearly 60 percent of arable land, while the poorest 30 percent of landowners share less than two percent. In rural areas, violence linked to land disputes is declining, but courts have increasingly supported the eviction of landless farmers. Thousands of workers are forced by ranchers in rural areas to work against their will and have no recourse to police or courts. Although casualties of rural violence appeared to decrease in the period 1998-2000, a total of 1,186 people—four times the number of casualties during a 1964-1985 military dictatorship—were killed between the return of democratic rule in 1985 and June 2000.

Violence against women and children is a common problem. Protective laws are rarely enforced. In 1991 the supreme court ruled that a man could no longer kill his wife and win acquittal on the ground of "legitimate defense of honor," but juries tend to ignore the ruling. Forced prostitution of children is widespread. Child labor is prevalent, and laws against it are rarely enforced. A recent UNICEF study reported that 53 percent of the 17.5 million children and young people forced to work in Latin America are in Brazil, and of these one million are younger than ten years old. A Roman Catholic Church pastoral land commission said in December 2000 that slavery persists on farms, with a total of 1,080 rural slaves having been freed the previous year.

Violence against Brazil's 250,000 Indians continues. In May 1998, the coordinator of the Organization of Indigenous Peoples was murdered by unidentified gunmen. The 1988 constitution guarantees indigenous peoples land rights covering some 11 percent of the country, and by law outsiders can enter Indian reserves only with permission. However, the government has completed the demarcation and registration of only 187 of the 559 eligible Indian reservations. Court and administrative rulings have eroded indigenous land claims, putting a third of the promised territory in legal limbo. Decree 1775 has opened Indian land to greater pressure from predatory miners and loggers. In some remote areas, Colombian drug traffickers have been using Indians to transport narcotics. In April 2000, police used excessive force in breaking up a peaceful demonstration by 2000 Indians protesting, with Cardoso's explicit support, the 500th anniversary of Portugal's arrival in Brazil. In August, 50 Caiapo tribe members kidnapped 16 Brazilian tourists in protest against the government's suspension, in 1990, of the demarcation of 1.85 million hectares of tribal lands.

Industrial labor unions are well organized and politically connected; many are corrupt. The right to strike is recognized, and there are special labor courts. Hundreds of strikes have taken place in recent years against attempts to privatize state industries.

Brunei

Polity: Traditional monarchy **Political Rights:** 7
Economy: Capitalist-statist **Civil Liberties:** 5
Population: 300,000 **Status:** Not Free
PPP: $16,765
Life Expectancy: 76
Ethnic Groups: Malay (64 percent), Chinese (20 percent), other (16 percent)
Capital: Bandar Seri Begawan

Overview: The year 2000 showed several signs that important changes are afoot in this small kingdom, suggesting some degree of openness heretofore unknown. In July 2000, Brunei's Sultan Hassanal Bolkiah announced plans to turn his kingdom into an international offshore financial center. New laws covering international banking, business companies, trusts and limited partnerships, and registered agents and trustee licensing were introduced. Other new laws on insurance licensing and regulation, securities, and mutual funds will follow within a year. In fact, Brunei hopes to fill a niche market in the rapidly growing world of Islamic financing. There are also plans to build business and industrial centers in border areas it shares with Malaysia and Indonesia.

Brunei, a hereditary sultanate, consists of two noncontiguous enclaves on the northern coast of Borneo. It became a British protectorate in 1888. The country's first written constitution was adopted in 1959 and provided for five advisory councils: the Privy Council, the Religious Council, the Council of Succession, the Council of Ministers, and the Legislative Council. In 1962, the leftist Brunei People's Party (PRB), which sought to remove the sultan from power, won all 10 elected seats in the 21-member Legislative Council. The results were annulled, and a rebellion ensued. Occupying British troops crushed a PRB-backed rebellion seeking an independent state encompassing nearby British territories. The sultan assumed constitutionally authorized emergency powers for a stipulated two-year period. These powers have since been renewed every two years, and elections have not been held since 1965. Sultan Haji Hassanal Bolkiah Mu'izzaddin Waddaulah ascended the throne in October 1967.

Brunei achieved full independence from Great Britain in 1984. In 1985, the government recognized the moderate Brunei National Democratic Party (PKDB) and, a year later, the offshoot Brunei National Solidarity Party (PPKB). In 1998, the sultan dissolved the PKDB and detained two of its leaders for two years, reportedly after the party called for elections. In 1995, the authorities permitted a PPKB general assembly. Abdul Latif Chuchu, one of the two former PKDB leaders detained from 1988 to 1990, was elected party president. Chuchu later resigned under government pressure, and since then, the PPKB has been inactive. In August 1998, the sultan announced that his son, Prince Billah, would be heir to the sultanate.

For years, the kingdom's population refrained from criticizing the sultan's lifestyle as they benefited from oil sales revenues. Quiet public dissatisfaction against corruption and abuse of power has grown in recent years as the economy suffers from the Asian financial crisis and a 40 percent drop in world oil prices. Adding to the pressure has been the exposure of corruption and gross mismanagement of Brunei's largest private firm, Amedeo Development Corporation, which collapsed two years ago. The firm, managed by the sultan's brother, Prince Jefri, lost an estimated $16 billion to $18 billion. Prince Jefri's extravagant lifestyle in the midst of economic concerns further scarred the image of the royal family. The sultan subsequently appointed prince Mohamed to replaced Prince Jefri as chief of the Brunei Investment Agency, which manages the royal family's worldwide assets of more than $60 billion. The sultan also allowed the government to file a $15 billion lawsuit against Prince Jefri for financial misconduct. The lawsuit was eventually settled out of court and Prince Jefri was granted $500,000 per month as living stipend.

Oil and gas accounts for more than half of Brunei's economic activity and about 80 percent of its exports, but this natural wealth is rapidly depleting. With income behind economic growth, a chronic budget deficit, rising unemployment, and a weak private sector, the government recognizes that it has to find new ways to support the economy in the long run. At present, the government employs more than 75 percent of the labor force and the economy needs to grow at twice its current rate to keep up with population growth. The problem is serious enough that the sultan said an income tax would be considered. To boost the private sector, the government created a $200 million start-up fund to aid entrepreneurs and the year 2001 was declared "Visit Brunei Year."

Although the government now supports a more diversified economy, political control has tightened in some areas. For example, an Islamic scholar was appointed vice chancellor of the University of Brunei Darussalam in 1999 and conservatives have sidelined more liberal members within the civil service.

Political Rights and Civil Liberties: Citizens of Brunei lack the democratic means to change their government. The sultan serves as prime minister (as well as finance and defense minister), rules by decree, and, along with an inner circle of relatives, holds absolute power. The Legislative Council has been fully appointed and the constitution partially suspended since 1970. Currently, only the Council of Ministers, composed largely of the sultan's relatives, and the Legislative Council convene. Since 1992, village chiefs have been chosen for life terms through local elections in which all candidates must have knowledge of Islam (although they may be non-Muslims) and cannot have past or current links with a political party. The chiefs communicate with the government through a village consultative council, and the sultan appoints the council's advisors. Citizens may petition the sultan. No public political party activity has occurred since 1995. Some members of non-Malay ethnic groups, including ethnic Chinese and others born in Brunei, are not automatically accorded citizenship, and Brunei's colonial-era nationalization laws are generally considered to be in need of reform.

There are privately owned newspapers, but they are either owned or controlled by the sultan's family, and they practice self-censorship on political and religious issues. The government-controlled Radio Television Brunei operates the only local broadcast media. A cable network offers international programming. Foreign journals with articles critical of the royal family or government are not allowed into the kingdom.

Islam is the official religion. Non-Muslims face bans or restrictions on building and repairing places of worship and import of religious books and educational materials. Religious education in non-Muslim schools is also prohibited. Since 1991, the sultan has promoted local culture and the primacy of the monarchy as the defender of Islam through a conservative Malay Muslim Monarchy (*Malayu Islam Beraja*, or MIB) ideology, apparently to ward off any incipient calls for democratization. Islamic studies and the study of MIB are required in all schools. Activities deemed offensive to Islam are actively curtailed, such as police confiscation of Christian and Buddhist icons as well as alcohol and foodstuffs that do not conform to Islamic dietary laws.

The government constrains the activities of international service organizations, including Rotary and Lions Clubs. There are three independent trade unions. All are in the oil sector but are largely inactive and their membership comprises less than five percent of the oil industry's workforce. Legislation does not explicitly recognize or deny the right to strike, but in practice, strikes do not occur.

The judiciary is independent. A 1996 appellate-level decision formally established the courts' power to discharge a defendant even if not requested to do so by the prosecution. Defendants enjoy adequate procedural safeguards, and in civil cases there is a right of appeal to the Privy Council in London. Although *Sharia* (Islamic law) supersedes civil law in some areas, it is applied only to Muslims. The police force is under civilian control. Police have broad powers to arrest without warrants, but in practice they generally obtain a warrant from a magistrate. The Internal Security Act (ISA) allows the government to detain suspects without a trial for renewable two-year periods. The ISA has occasionally been used to detain political dissidents.

Although the law permits government intrusion into the privacy of individuals, families, or homes, this rarely happens. Citizens can travel freely within the country and abroad. Under Sharia, Muslim women face some discrimination in divorce, inheritance, and child custody matters. There are occasional reports of physical abuse and ill treatment of female domestic servants and foreign workers.

Bulgaria

Polity: Parliamentary democracy
Economy: Mixed capitalist
Population: 8,200,000
PPP: $4,809
Life Expectancy: 71
Ethnic Groups: Bulgarian (85 percent), Turkish (9 percent), Macedonian (3 percent), Gypsy (3 percent)
Capital: Sofia

Political Rights: 2
Civil Liberties: 3
Status: Free

Overview:
In 2000, public support for Bulgaria's center-right government dropped considerably as a result of high unemployment, low salaries, poor living standards, and allegations of corruption among some of the highest political officials.

In May, the Bulgarian government survived a no-confidence vote after there were allegations in April that Prime Minister Ivan Kostov had been covering up intelligence reports, accusing ministers of corruption. The motion from the Bulgarian Socialist Party (BSP) was voted down 133 to 67 with 16 abstentions. Prime Minister Kostov was being blamed for high unemployment, which in April stood at 19 percent, and deteriorating living standards. The Bulgarian parliament passed a law declaring the former Communist regime from 1944 to 1989 criminal. The government also approved a law that would publicize the income, expenses, and property of senior state officials.

Occupied by the Ottoman Empire from 1396 to 1878, Bulgaria achieved full independence in 1908. Long-standing territorial ambitions led to Bulgaria's alliance with Germany in both world wars before the Soviet invasion in 1944 and subsequent establishment of a Communist-led government. From 1954 until 1989, the country was ruled by Communist Party leader Todor Zhivkov, who resigned in the wake of a mass prodemocracy rally in Sofia and the political changes that were sweeping across Eastern Europe. In the October 1996 presidential election, Petar Stoyanov of the Union of Democratic Forces (UDF), defeated BSP candidate Ivan Marazov in two rounds of voting. With the exception of a short-lived, UDF-led government elected in 1991, Bulgaria's parliament continued to be dominated by former Communists until 1997.

Sparked by a deepening economic crisis and growing crime and corruption, a week of mass street demonstrations in November 1996 succeeded in forcing the ruling BSP to agree to early parliamentary elections the following year. One month later, Zhan Videnov, prime minister and BSP leader, resigned. In the April 1997 vote for the national assembly, the UDF and its allied factions won 52 percent of the vote and 137 of 240 seats. The BSP captured 58 seats; the Alliance for National Salvation, 19; the Euroleft coalition, 14; and the Bulgarian Business Bloc, 12. UDF leader Ivan Kostov was named prime minister.

Bulgaria continued to make economic reforms, including stabilizing its national currency, privatizing state-owned businesses, and continuing negotiations with the European Union (EU) for membership. The EU issued a report in November, which praised Bulgaria for its privatization process, especially within the banking, health, and pension systems. By December, the EU agreed to lift visa restrictions for Bulgaria.

The World Bank approved a $50 million loan to help Bulgaria meet environmental standards set by the EU as well as a $63.3 million loan for a program that will revamp the health sector. The sale of Bulbank, the largest state-owned bank, for 360 million euros, represents Bulgaria's largest privatization operation. In August, under pressure from the EU, Bulgaria agreed to shut down four reactors at the Kozlodui nuclear plant, considered to be one of Europe's most dangerous installations, as yet another condition for membership.

After last year's war in Kosovo, which destroyed many of Bulgaria's trade routes to central and western Europe, Bulgaria agreed to finance and construct a $120 million bridge over the Danube River. After opposing NATO's request last year to use Bulgaria's airspace during its bombing campaign against Yugoslavia, the Bulgarian Socialist Party (BSP) announced a change of policy, supporting Bulgaria's push for NATO membership.

In March, Bulgaria was accused of violating the 1993 United Nations sanctions against Angola by selling arms to UNITA, the rebellion forces in Angola as well as Sierra Leone in exchange for diamonds. The UN does, however, recognize that Bulgaria has taken steps to tighten control over illegal arms sales. The sale of arms could, however, seriously jeopardize Bulgaria's membership negotiations with the EU.

Six Bulgarian medical workers accused of infecting 398 children in a Libyan hospital with the HIV virus are awaiting trial in Libya. The punishment is the death penalty.

Political Rights and Civil Liberties: Bulgarians can change their government democratically. The president is elected for a five-year term, and the unicameral national assembly, composed of 240 members, is elected every four years. The 1996 presidential, 1997 parliamentary, and 1999 local elections were regarded as free and fair by international election observers.

The constitution guarantees freedom of the press. There were no reports of harassment against journalists in 2000. Some positive reforms included the launching of a nationwide program in the Turkish language by the Bulgarian state television; a proposal by the government to establish a Balkan Media Academy in Sofia to train journalists to work for independent media in the Balkan region; and the establishment of the first private-broadcast TV operator, Rupert Murdoch's Balkan News Corporation, with nationwide coverage. In January, the Parliament approved a reform on its press law, which eliminated jail sentences for libel.

The constitution permits the formation of trade unions, and the 1992 Labor Code recognizes the right to strike and bargain collectively. Bulgaria's two largest unions are the Confederation of Independent Trade Unions (CITUB), a successor to the Communist-era union, and Podkrepa, an independent federation established in 1989. Estimates of the country's unionized workforce range from 30 to 50 percent, although this number is decreasing as large enterprises lay off workers and many new positions are created in smaller, non-union businesses. The constitution does, however, forbid the formation of political parties along religious, ethnic, or racial lines. In February, the constitutional court declared the United Macedonians Organization (Ilinden-PIRIN) party unconstitutional, violating their members' right to associate.

While freedom of worship is generally respected, the government restricts this right for some non-Orthodox religious groups. Organizations whose activities have a religious element are required by law to register with the council of ministers. Some groups, such as Jehovah's Witnesses, have endured harassment and interference in their activities before, or in the absence of, registration. In January, six Turkish nationals were extradited from Bulgaria, accused of having conducted illegal clerical activity. In an effort to comply with NATO standards, parliament reduced the length of mandatory military service to a six-month period. In 1998, the government passed an alternative civilian service law; however, conscientious objectors are required to commit double the time required for military service.

The judiciary is legally guaranteed independence and equal status with the executive and legislative branches of government. However, corruption, inadequate staffing, and low salaries continue to hamper the system. The EU report issued in November stated that there have been no improvements in the judicial system and it still remains weak. Pretrial detention facilities continue to be inhumane, overcrowded, and without adequate medical services. Excessive physical force and discrimination by law enforcement officials towards the Roma (Gypsy) population remains a serious problem.

Freedom of movement within the country and emigration rights are generally respected. Private property rights are formally protected, although corruption, organized crime, and government control of significant sectors of the economy impede competition and equality of opportunity.

Women are underrepresented in government and politics; fewer than 11 percent hold seats in parliament, although several do hold elective or appointive offices at high levels. According to a survey conducted by the Noema polling agency in June, one-quarter of the women in Bulgaria are victims of domestic violence and two-thirds of those never seek help. Trafficking of women for prostitution remains a serious problem.

↑Burkina Faso

Polity: Presidential-
parliamentary
(dominant party)
Economy: Mixed statist
Population: 11,900,000
PPP: $870
Life Expectancy: 45
Ethnic Groups: Mossi, Gurunsi, Senufo, Lobi, Bobo,
Mande, Fulani
Capital: Ouagadougou

Political Rights: 4
Civil Liberties: 4
Status: Partly Free

Trend Arrow: Burkina Faso received an upward trend arrow for taking a step toward ending impunity for security forces.

Overview:

Authorities in Burkina Faso made what appeared to be a step toward ending impunity for the country's security forces.

Three presidential guards were sentenced in August 2000 to between 10 and 20 years of imprisonment for the 1998 torture death of a former chauffeur of François Compaoré, the brother of President Blaise Compaoré. A coalition of pressure groups, calling itself the Collective of Political Parties, Labor Unions, and Nongovernmental Organizations Against Impunity, said it was happy about the ruling, but not satisfied. They want the president's brother, who was implicated in the crime, to be brought to justice as well.

Four of the five presidential guards initially charged in the killing of the driver, David Ouedraogo, have also been implicated in the death of well-known journalist Norbert Zongo, who was investigating Ouedraogo's murder. The deaths have galvanized Burkina Faso's civil society to speak out against impunity. A three-day strike in April considerably slowed activity in the capital, Ouagadougou. Thirty people were detained in connection with the protest, including the country's most prominent human rights leader, but they were soon released.

After gaining independence from France in 1960 as Upper Volta, Burkina Faso suffered a succession of army coups. In 1983, Compaoré installed himself as president in a violent coup against members of a junta that had seized power four years earlier and had pursued a watered-down Marxist-Leninist ideology. The populist, charismatic president Thomas Sankara and 13 of his closest associates were murdered. More Sankara supporters were executed two years later.

Parliament in April 2000 adopted a law governing the role of opposition parties in the country's democratic process. It remains to be seen whether interpretations of the law will be manipulated by the state, and whether the greater freedoms the law provides for will be allowed in practice.

Burkina Faso is one of the world's poorest countries. More than 80 percent of its 11 million people rely on subsistence agriculture. Concern has grown that political upheaval in neighboring Côte d'Ivoire will trigger the return of millions of Burkinabé who have been working there.

Burkina Faso has come under widespread criticism from both within West Africa and abroad for allegedly allowing its territory to be used for illegal arms shipments destined for Sierra Leone, Liberia, and Angola.

Political Rights and Civil Liberties: Burkina Faso's 1991 constitution guarantees its people the right to elect their government freely through periodic multiparty elections. In practice, this right has not been realized. Presidential polls in December 1991 were marred by widespread violence and an opposition boycott. Opposition parties and independent observers charged that 1997 legislative elections for five-year national assembly terms were marred by fraud. Opposition disunity and electoral rules sharply combined to reduce the opposition's representation in the legislature to well below the 31 percent of the popular vote that opposition parties had received. The ruling Congress for Democracy and Progress (CDP) took 101 of 111 national assembly seats.

The Independent National Electoral Commission established in May 1998 did not have control over important parts of the electoral process, particularly electoral rolls and voter cards. Compaoré was returned to office for a second seven-year term in November 1998 with nearly 88 percent of the vote. The polls were marked by heavy use of state patronage, resources, and media.

Municipal elections were held in September 2000 after being postponed twice because of protest activity. Several opposition parties boycotted the polls, saying that conditions for fair elections did not exist in the country and that further steps needed to be taken for ending impunity. Voter turnout was low. The ruling CDP won about 70 percent of seats available.

Burkina Faso has a vibrant free press, and freedom of speech is protected by the constitution and generally respected in practice. There is some self-censorship. At least 50 private radio stations, a private television station, and numerous independent newspapers and magazines function with little governmental interference. The media, which are often highly critical of the government, play an important role in public debate. The government forced a radio station off the air briefly in 2000. Broadcasting soon resumed, but without the call-in show that was criticized.

The Burkinabé judiciary is subject to executive interference in political cases, but is more independent in civil and criminal cases. National security laws permit surveillance and arrests without warrants. Police routinely ignore proscribed limits on detention, search, and seizure. Prison conditions are harsh, with overcrowding, poor diets, and minimal medical attention.

Burkina Faso is a secular state, and religious freedom is respected. Freedom of assembly is constitutionally protected and generally respected, with required permits usually issued routinely. Many nongovernmental organizations operate openly and freely, including human rights groups, which have reported detailed accounts of abuses by security forces. There have been some reports of harassment.

Labor unions and their rights are provided for in the constitution. They are a strong force in society and have staged strikes about wages, human rights abuses, and the impunity of security forces. Several labor confederations and independent unions bargain with employers.

Customary law sanctions discrimination against women and is used by traditional courts to resolve civil and family disputes, especially in rural areas. Constitutional and legal protections for women's rights are nonexistent or poorly enforced. Women's educational and employment opportunities are scarce in the countryside. A ministry of women's affairs was created in 1997, but women hold few senior government posts or parliamentary seats. Female genital mutilation is still widely practiced, even though it is illegal and a government campaign has been initiated against it.

Burma (Myanmar)

Polity: Military
Economy: Statist
Population: 48,900,000
PPP: $1,199
Life Expectancy: 61
Ethnic Groups: Burman (68 percent), Shan (9 percent), Karen (7 percent), Rakhine (4 percent), Chinese (3 percent), Mon (2 percent), Indian (2 percent), other (5 percent)
Capital: Rangoon

Political Rights: 7
Civil Liberties: 7
Status: Not Free

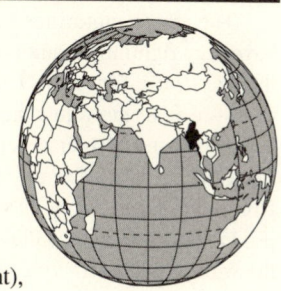

Overview:

Ten years after it nullified a landslide opposition victory in free elections, Burma's ruling junta continued in 2000 to crack down on and marginalize the democratic opposition, flout international human rights norms, and sanction the large-scale production and trafficking of illicit narcotics.

Burma achieved independence from Great Britain in 1948, following the Japanese occupation in World War II. The army overthrew an elected government in 1962 amid an economic crisis and several ethnic-based insurgencies. During the next 26 years General Ne Win's military rule helped impoverish what had been one of Southeast Asia's richest countries.

The present junta has been in power since the summer of 1988, when the army opened fire on peaceful, student-led pro-democracy demonstrations, killing an estimated 3,000 people. After suppressing the protests, army commanders General Saw Maung and Brigadier General Khin Nyunt created the State Law and Order Restoration Council (SLORC) to rule the country. In 1990, the opposition National League for Democracy (NLD) won 392 of the 485 parliamentary seats in Burma's first free elections in three decades. The SLORC refused to cede power and jailed hundreds of NLD members.

The SLORC reconstituted itself as the State Peace and Development Council in November 1997. The relatively young generals who took charge sidelined more senior officers and removed some of the more blatantly corrupt cabinet ministers. The junta appeared to be trying to improve its international image, attract foreign investment, and encourage an end to United States-led sanctions. Since then, the regime has sentenced hundreds of peaceful pro-democracy activists to lengthy jail terms, forced thousands of NLD members to resign from the party, and periodically detained dozens of NLD activists, particularly in advance of planned demonstrations.

In one of the largest single crackdowns in 2000, authorities arrested more than 100 NLD members and at least two dozen monks in the weeks leading to the tenth anniversary of the 1990 elections. The government also twice prevented NLD leader Aung San Suu Kyi and other party members from traveling outside Rangoon, and in late September placed Suu Kyi and nine other senior NLD members under effective house arrest. The regime had held Suu Kyi under house arrest between 1989 and 1995, and it continues to reject the 1992 Nobel laureate's call for a dialogue on democratic reform.

The ethnic minorities that constitute more than one-third of Burma's population have been fighting for autonomy from the Burman-dominated central government since the late 1940s. Since 1989, the regime has co-opted some 17 ethnic rebel armies with ceasefire deals that allow them to maintain their weapons and territory. With the junta's support, many former rebel groups have become major heroin traffickers. The *Far Eastern Economic Review* reported in April that one of these former rebel groups, the United Wa State Army, has 20,000 to 30,000 soldiers and controls most of the drug-producing areas in the Golden Triangle. Rangoon has angered Bangkok by tolerating the widespread trafficking of illicit methamphetamines from Burma to Thailand.

Early in the year, the army and troops from the pro-regime Democratic Karen Buddhist Army carried out what has become an annual dry-season offensive against the Karen National Union, the largest of three active insurgency groups. Several thousand Karen refugees fled to Thailand.

Political Rights and Civil Liberties: Burma continued to be ruled by one of the world's most repressive regimes. The junta controls the judiciary, and the rule of law is nonexistent. Authorities have imprisoned or driven into exile most vocal dissidents; severely restrict fundamental rights; and use a tightly controlled mass movement, the Union Solidarity Development Association, to monitor forced labor quotas, report on citizens, and intimidate opponents. General Than Shwe is nominally the junta leader and head of state. However, observers say that the real strongmen are Lieutenant General Khin Nyunt, the intelligence chief, and his rival, the more hardline General Maung Aye, the army commander. Former dictator Ne Win, 89, also wields influence. A state-controlled constitutional convention began drafting a new constitution in 1993 that would grant the military 25 percent of seats in a future parliament and formalize the army's leading role in politics. However, the convention has not met since 1996.

The United Nations Human Rights Commission adopted a resolution in April condemning torture, disappearances, and other "systematic and increasingly severe" human rights abuses in Burma. The UN Special Rapporteur for Burma similarly noted in October the "continuing deterioration of the human rights situation" in the country. Some of the regime's worst human rights abuses occur in Burma's seven ethnic-minority-dominated states in the context of the army's counterinsurgency operations against ethnic-based guerrilla movements. The *tatmadaw*, or Burmese armed forces, are responsible for extrajudicial killings, beatings, and arbitrary detentions of civilians, sometimes for refusing to provide food, money, or labor to military units. Soldiers also force civilians to work without pay as porters or human minesweepers and frequently press-gang children and other recruits into the services. Soldiers also occasionally arrest civilians as alleged insurgents or insurgent sympathizers and reportedly commit widespread incidents of rape.

Tens of thousands of civilians in Shan, Karenni, Karen, and Mon states and in

Tenasserim division remained in designated relocation sites. The army forcibly relocated them in the 1990s as part of its counterinsurgency strategy. The relocation centers generally lacked adequate food, water, health care, and sanitation facilities, and soldiers subjected the villagers to looting and other abuses. Thailand also continued to host some 120,000 mainly Karen, Karenni, Shan, and Mon refugees. Amnesty International released in 1999 reports documenting widespread abuses against civilians in the context of forced relocation programs, but also noted that armed opposition groups from the Shan, Karen, and other communities committed some killings and other abuses against ethnic Burman civilians in these states. Some ethnic-minority insurgencies reportedly also recruit child soldiers.

The International Labor Organization (ILO) called in November for its members to impose sanctions on Burma after an ILO monitoring team that visited in October found that while the regime had made progress in changing its laws to end forced labor, it had done little to put the changes into practice. The ILO had adopted in 1999 a resolution calling the regime's use of forced labor "a contemporary form of slavery" and suspended Burma from most of the organization's activities. In addition, an ILO Commission of Enquiry had reported in 1998 that the regime used forced labor in a "widespread and systematic manner." Forced labor appeared to be most prevalent in ethnic-minority-dominated states, where soldiers force civilians to work without pay under harsh conditions, generally on infrastructure projects or military-backed commercial ventures. While the use of forced labor appears to be down somewhat from the peak years between 1993 and 1996, the ILO estimates that there may be as many as 800,000 forced laborers in Burma.

Some 250,000 Muslim Rohingya refugees fled to camps in Bangladesh in 1991 and 1992 to escape extrajudicial executions, rape, forced labor, and other abuses in northern Arakan state. By mid-1997, all but 22,000 had returned to Burma. However, Rohingya continued to flee forced labor, arbitrary confiscation of property, and other abuses, and by mid-2000 an additional 100,000 Rohingya lived in Bangladesh outside the existing refugee camps. The refugee situation occurs in the context of the 1982 Burma Citizenship Law, which effectively denied most Rohingya citizenship. Consequently, Burmese authorities subjected Rohingya to restrictions on their freedom of movement and barred them from secondary education and civil service jobs.

While releasing several high-profile political prisoners during the year, the junta continued to arrest opponents for participating in peaceful political activities. Amnesty International said in November that authorities were currently holding 1,700 political prisoners. Agence France-Presse reported in April that officials of the International Committee of the Red Cross said that 1,450 of some 30,000 prisoners it had visited over the past year in Burmese jails are held for "security" reasons. Burmese authorities acknowledged in 1999 that 107 NLD members of parliament elected in 1990 were imprisoned or detained, although the actual number is believed to be far higher. The regime imprisons opposition activists and supporters under numerous broadly drawn laws that criminalize peaceful activities, including distributing pamphlets and distributing, viewing, or smuggling out of Burma videotapes of Suu Kyi's public addresses. The frequently used Decree 5/96 of 1996 authorizes jail terms of 5 to 25 years for aiding activities "which adversely affect the national interest." The decree also authorizes the home ministry to ban any organization violating a separate law against public gatherings of five or more people.

Prison conditions are abysmal. Amnesty International said in December that "torture has become an institution" in the country and that victims include political activists, criminals. and members of ethnic minorities. Dissidents say that more than 40 political prisoners have died in Rangoon's Insein prison since 1988.

The junta continued to control tightly all publications and broadcast services. The Paris-based Reporters Sans Frontieres (RSF) reported in January that authorities had released a journalist who had been held since 1996 after participating in an opposition rally, but that the regime continued to jail 12 other journalists. The 1996 Computer Law requires Internet users to obtain official authorization and provides for lengthy jail terms for unauthorized use. According to RSF, the regime amended the 1996 law in January to also prohibit citizens from using electronic mail to spread political information, and closed in December 1999 two private Internet service providers. The state owned the sole remaining Internet service provider.

The Directorate of Defense Services Intelligence continued to arbitrarily search homes, intercept mail, and monitor telephone conversations. The regime's high-tech information warfare center in Rangoon reportedly can intercept telephone, fax, e-mail, and radio communications.

The government reopened in July many of Burma's universities, which it had closed in the wake of student-led demonstrations in 1996. However, authorities made students pledge loyalty to the government, barred political activity on campuses, and shortened the academic term at many universities. Authorities also continued to closely monitor monasteries, interfere in Buddhist religious affairs, and hold many of the 300 monks arrested during a violent 1990 crackdown on monasteries.

Criminal gangs have trafficked thousands of Burmese women and girls, many from ethnic minority groups, to Thailand for prostitution. Independent trade unions, collective bargaining, and strikes are illegal. Several labor activists continued to serve long terms for their political and labor activities.

The junta's economic mismanagement continued to contribute to persistently high inflation rates, stagnant economic growth, and a hugely overvalued currency. Official corruption is reportedly rampant. The European Union and the United States maintained sanctions on Burma because of its human rights record and prevented it from receiving some multilateral aid.

Burundi

Polity: Civilian-military
Economy: Mixed statist
Population: 6,100,000
PPP: $570
Life Expectancy: 43
Ethnic Groups: Hutu [Bantu] (85 percent),
Tutsi (14 percent), Twa [Pygmy] (1 percent)
Capital: Bujumbura

Political Rights: 6
Civil Liberties: 6
Status: Not Free

Overview:

In 2000 Burundi continued to teeter between continuing violence and political instability on the one hand, and the prospect that successful multi-party negotiations would offer a framework for resolution of the country's long-standing crisis of governance on the other. Long-running negotiations in Arusha, Tanzania, mediated by Nelson Mandela, and assisted at one stage by President Bill Clinton, resulted in agreement on a future democratic political system by most, but not all, parties to the conflict pitting the Tutsi minority against a Hutu majority. Militant Hutu extremist groups have refused to fully accept the Arusha agreements, and have continued to stage intermittent guerilla attacks inside Burundi. Continued instability within the region further complicates efforts at reconciliation.

With the exception of a brief period following democratic elections in 1993, the minority Tutsi ethnic group has governed the country since independence in 1962. The military, judiciary, educational system, business sector, and news media have also been dominated by the Tutsi. Violence between the country's two main ethnic groups has occurred repeatedly since independence, but the assassination of the newly elected Hutu president Melchoir Ndadaye in 1993 resulted in sustained and widespread violence. Since 1993 an estimated 200,000 Burundi citizens, out of a population of 5.5 million, are estimated to have lost their lives.

Ndadaye's murder fatally weakened the hold on power of the Hutu-backed political party, FRODEBU. Negotiations on power sharing took place over the succeeding months, as ethnically backed violence continued to wrack the country. Cyprien Ntaryamira, Ndadaye's successor, was killed along with Rwanda president Juvenal Habyarimana in 1994 when their plane was apparently shot down while approaching Kigali airport in Rwanda. The event intensified killings in Burundi.

Under a 1994 power-sharing arrangement between the main political parties, Hutu politician Sylvestre Ntibantunganya served as Burundi's new president until his ouster by former President Pierre Buyoya in a 1996 military coup, which Buyoya claimed to have carried out to prevent further human rights violations and violence. Peace and political stability within the country continued to be elusive as armed insurgents sporadically staged attacks and the government security forces pursued an often ruthless campaign of intimidation. The search for peace eventually led to an agreement to allow a measure of political space for the parliament, which has a FRODEBU majority, and the beginning of negotiations in Arusha in 1998.

The Arusha negotiations on ending the civil war continued throughout 2000. After lengthy negotiations a peace agreement was concluded. Nineteen organized groups from across the political spectrum agreed to recommendations from committees on the nature of the conflict, reforms in the nation's governing institutions, security issues, and economic restructuring and development. The form of the political institutions through which power would be shared and the reform of the military proved to be especially sensitive and difficult issues. Even after the signing of the accord by the last of the 19 parties in September, questions about its implementation remained. There was lack of agreement on specifics, for example, regarding the 30-month transitional period until new national elections are held. Two key Hutu guerrila groups refused to sign the agreement. An upsurge in guerilla activity in the wake of the accord claimed hundreds of lives.

Political Rights and Civil Liberties: Citizens of Burundi cannot change their government democratically. Political and civil liberties within Burundi continue to be circumscribed, although parties and civic organizations do function. President Buyoya is an unelected chief of state. The constitution was suspended when he took power, as was the legitimately elected parliament. In June 1998 a transitional constitution was put into place; it reinstituted and enlarged the parliament through the appointment of additional members and created two vice presidents. The parliament's powers remain limited in practice, although it provides an outlet for political expression and remains an important player in determining the nation's future. Until a final Arusha agreement enters into force, it is not clear when the next presidential and parliamentary elections will be held, or under what conditions.

There are more than a dozen active political parties, ranging from those that champion extremist Tutsi positions to those that hold extremist Hutu positions. Most are small in terms of membership. FRODEBU and the Tutsi-dominated Unity for National Progress (UPRONA) remain the leading political parties.

Burundians continue to be subjected to arbitrary violence, whether from the government or from guerilla groups. Although detailed, specific figures on the number of dead or injured are difficult to obtain, widespread violence continued in parts of Burundi in 2000. This has been documented by respected independent organizations inside and outside Burundi, including Amnesty International, Human Rights Watch, and the ITEKA Human Rights League. Amnesty International issued several appeals during the year, for example, for investigations into human rights abuses allegedly conducted by both guerila and government forces. In addition to operations of the government security forces, there has been intense activity by armed opposition groups, particularly in the province of Rural Bujumbura.

Reprisals by the armed forces have often been brutal and indiscriminate, and have resulted in hundreds of extrajudicial executions, mainly of members of the Hutu ethnic group. Much of this violence has been committed in zones where the local civilian and military authorities ordered the civilian population to leave the area because of counterinsurgency operations. The continued impunity of the armed forces and the weakness of the Burundian judicial system are important contributing factors to the violence.

Citizens have also been subjected to arbitrary displacement from their homes. In September 1999, after a major relocation exercise near the capital, Bujumbura, the United Nations estimated there were more than 800,000 people—12 percent of the population—in these sites. The government began to close some of the controversial resettlement camps in 2000.

Some different viewpoints are expressed in the media, although they operate under significant self-censorship and the opposition press functions sporadically. The government-operated radio station allows a measure of diversity. The European Union has funded a radio station. The Hutu extremist radio broadcasts sporadically and has a limited listening range.

Constitutional protections for unionization are in place, and the right to strike is protected by the labor code. The Organization of Free Unions of Burundi is the sole labor confederation and has been independent since the rise of the multiparty system in 1992. Most union members are civil servants and have bargained collectively with the government. Freedom of religion is generally observed.

Women have limited opportunities for advancement in the economic and political spheres, especially in the rural areas. Approximately 80 percent of Burundi's population is engaged in subsistence agriculture, with few links to the modern economy.

Cambodia

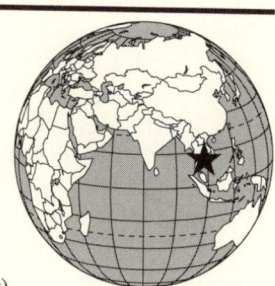

Polity: Dominant party (military-influenced)
Economy: Statist
Population: 12,100,000
PPP: $1,257
Life Expectancy: 54
Ethnic Groups: Khmer (90 percent), Vietnamese (5 percent), Chinese (1 percent), other (4 percent)
Capital: Phnom Penh

Political Rights: 6
Civil Liberties: 6
Status: Not Free

Overview:

Following a November 2000 attack by gunmen on government buildings in Phnom Penh, Cambodian authorities began a crackdown that human rights groups called a cover for arresting political opponents. During the year, the government also took tentative steps to bring to justice members of the murderous Khmer Rouge movement that ruled Cambodia in the late 1970s.

Cambodia won independence from France in 1953, and was ruled in succession by King Norodom Sihanouk, the United States-backed Lon Nol regime in the early 1970s, and the Maoist Khmer Rouge between 1975 and 1979. Under the Khmer Rouge, at least 1.7 million of Cambodia's 7 million people died by execution, disease, overwork, and starvation. Vietnam invaded in December 1978 and installed a government under the Khmer Peoples' Revolutionary Party (KPRP). During the 1980s, the KPRP government fought the allied armies of Sihanouk, the Khmer Rouge, and a former premier, Son Sann. An internationally brokered agreement signed in 1991 nominally ended the fighting, but the Khmer Rouge continued to wage a low-grade insurgency. The 1991 accord authorized the United Nations to temporarily control many key institutions, yet the KPRP government, headed by Hun Sen, a Khmer Rouge defector, maintained control of 80 percent of the army, most key ministries, and provincial and local authorities.

In Cambodia's first free parliamentary elections in 1993, the royalist United Front for an Independent, Neutral, and Free Cambodia (FUNCINPEC), headed by Prince Norodom Ranariddh, a Sihanouk son, defeated Hun Sen's Cambodian People's Party (CPP), the successor to the KPRP. Hun Sen used his control over the army to force his way into a uneasy coalition government. Having consolidated near total power by 1996, Hun Sen seized full power in a violent coup on July 5-6, 1997, following efforts by both Hun Sen and Ranariddh to attract allies from the now-disintegrating Khmer Rouge.

With the end of the Khmer Rouge insurgency, Cambodia has experienced generally stable authoritarian rule under Hun Sen amid corruption, poverty, and a weak rule of law. Hun Sen's CPP won a flawed election on June 26, 1998, that appeared to be little more than an effort to persuade international donors to resume aid that was suspended after the 1997 coup. Held under a reported turnout of more than 90 percent, the CPP won 64 seats; FUNCINPEC, 43; and the Sam Rainsy Party (SRP), led by Cambodia's leading dissident, 15. Hun Sen brought FUNCINPEC into a coalition government as a junior partner in November 1998. Having resumed lending to Cambodia in 1999, multilateral institutions and some bilateral donors urged the government in 2000 to fight corruption, improve fiscal management, reduce the size of the military and civil service, and curb illegal logging.

The most notable exception to this relative stability was the November 24 pre-dawn attack, which killed at least eight people. Conflicting figures issued by authorities suggested they had arrested at least 66 people and charged at least 47 of them. The New York-based Human Rights Watch accused Cambodia of arresting more than 200 people. Many were members or supporters of Cambodia's sole opposition party, the SRP, or of FUNCINPEC. An obscure, California-based anti-government group claimed responsibility for the attack.

Following years of international pressure, Cambodia reached a tentative agreement with the United Nations in July 2000 to establish a locally based tribunal with international participation to try former Khmer Rouge leaders on charges of genocide, crimes against humanity, and war crimes. By year's end parliament was considering enabling legislation for a court with a majority of Cambodian judges and a minority of foreign judges. The government is holding several former Khmer Rouge leaders who presumably would be brought to trial. However, it was not clear whether the tribunal would indict Ieng Sary and several other former Khmer Rouge leaders who have defected to the government and rule a semiautonomous zone in western Cambodia.

Political Rights and Civil Liberties: Cambodia's 1998 elections were neither free nor fair. The campaign was held in a climate of violence amid continued political killings. Authorities denied opposition parties access to broadcast media, disrupted some opposition rallies, and banned political demonstrations in Phnom Penh. Meanwhile, Hun Sen wielded his control over the civil service, local administration, military police, and Khmer-language media to a decisive advantage, particularly in the provinces. Hun Sen supporters held 10 of 11 seats on the National Election Commission, which changed the electoral formula, as workers counted ballots, to give the CPP a parliamentary majority.

The judiciary is politically controlled, operates with limited human and financial resources, and is reportedly rife with corruption. Cambodia's 1999 report on its implementation of the International Convention on Civil and Political Rights conceded that other branches of government undermine judicial independence. In addition, a UN experts group reported in 1999 that Cambodia's judiciary lacked the independence and capacity to try Khmer Rouge leaders for crimes against humanity and genocide in the 1970s, a finding that underscored the need for international participation in any Khmer Rouge trials. The Supreme Council of Magistry, a constitutional body that can take disciplinary actions against judges and prosecutors, reportedly took disciplinary action against several judges and a prosecutor in 2000.

Courts frequently ignore due process safeguards. In a case that underscored many of the judiciary's problems, Hun Sen ordered the rearrest in December 1999 of more than 60 people who allegedly had bribed their way out of prison. Their cases were handled without any due process rights, and by the end of 2000 many of them remained in jail. Pre-trial detention is lengthy. The Cambodian League for the Promotion and Defense of Human Rights (Licadho) said in June that police continued to commit torture with impunity, generally in order to extract confessions. Prisons are dangerously overcrowded and unsanitary, and authorities routinely abuse inmates. Mobs committed several vigilante-style killings of alleged criminals during the year. In the countryside, soldiers continued to commit rape, extortion, banditry, and extrajudicial killings with impunity.

Opposition parties have come under considerable pressure. There were 41 killings of FUNCINPEC officials and others following the 1997 coup and at least 21 political killings, mainly of FUNCINPEC supporters, in the two months prior to the 1998 elections. The New York-based Human Rights Watch reported in October 2000 that in recent months there had been numerous incidents of violence and harassment of members of the Sam Rainsy Party ahead of commune-level elections that may be held in 2001. During the year at least two SRP members and one FUNCINPEC member were killed for what appeared to be politically motivated reasons. The government made arrests in the cases and said the killings were personal disputes. Mobs attacked the SRP headquarters in Phnom Penh in May.

Cambodia has more than two dozen nongovernmental organizations (NGOs). Security forces routinely harassed and intimidated human rights activists, and authorities threatened to prosecute several human rights NGOs and workers.

Journalists continued to be harassed and threatened, although apparently less frequently than in previous years. There have been no convictions in the cases of six journalists murdered in the course of their work between 1994 and 1997. The broadly drawn 1995 press law permits the information ministry to suspend a newspaper for up to 30 days without a court order and subjects the press to criminal statutes. The Information Ministry suspended at least two publications in 2000, one of them twice, for 30-day periods for allegedly defaming the king and undermining national security. Despite these constraints, the private press continued to be vigorous, although the Paris-based Reporters Sans Frontieres (RSF) noted in May that only ten newspapers and magazines publish regularly. RSF also reported that members of the government or close associates own almost all of the six Khmer-language television stations and 14 Khmer-language radio stations. The information ministry has denied repeated requests from opposition leader Sam Rainsy for a license to operate a radio station.

The constitution refers only to the rights of the ethnic-Khmer majority, which raises questions about the legal status of the estimated 200,000 to 500,000 Vietnamese residents. In practice, ethnic Vietnamese face both official and unofficial harassment and discrimination. Traditional norms relegate women to an inferior status, and domestic violence is reportedly common. Brothel owners frequently abuse prostitutes and hold them in conditions of bonded servitude. There are several thousand street children in Phnom Penh, and child prostitution is a significant problem.

Cambodia has several independent trade unions. The *Financial Times* noted in April that most garment factories hire thugs to prevent the enforcement of court orders relating to labor rights and enlist police to harass strikers. In March, the labor ministry banned strikes outside factory or enterprise grounds and required workers to give at least seven days advance notice of a strike. Nevertheless, workers in the 120,000-strong garment sector frequently held strikes and demonstrations in Phnom Penh to protest against low wages, failure of employers to pay the minimum wage, poor and dangerous working conditions, forced overtime, and dismissal of pro-union staff. Washington increased Cambodia's garment export quota by 9 percent in 2000. However, it said that the U.S. would not increase the quota by the full 14 percent permitted under a 1998 agreement linking the quota to labor rights until Cambodia had met all of its commitments to comply with core international labor standards and enforced Cambodian law.

Property rights are tenuous. Licadho and other Cambodian human rights NGOs say that military and civilian authorities have in recent years forcibly evicted several thousand families from their land. Official corruption is widespread. Government officials, soldiers, and police tolerate and at times participate in money laundering, gun running, drug trafficking, and the activities of mainland Chinese prostitution rings, although the government has made some headway in reducing illegal logging. Despite these underground activities, gross domestic product was expected to grow 5.5 percent in 2000, according to the finance ministry.

Cameroon

Polity: Presidential (dominant party)
Economy: Capitalist
Population: 15,400,000
PPP: $1,474
Life Expectancy: 55
Ethnic Groups: Cameroon Highlander (31 percent), Equatorial Bantu (19 percent), Kirdi (11 percent), Fulani (10 percent), Northwestern Bantu (8 percent), Eastern Nigritic (7 percent), other African and non-African (14 percent)
Capital: Yaounde

Political Rights: 7
Civil Liberties: 6
Status: Not Free

Overview:
President Paul Biya and his ruling Cameroon People's Democratic Movement (CPDM) took some steps toward prison reform and tackling corruption in 2000, but it is not clear whether the measures are anything more than lip service from one of Africa's most enduring and repressive regimes. A United Nations human rights expert in March warned

of widespread and systematic torture, but said the administration appeared to be trying to address the problem.

The country was seized during World War I, in 1916, and divided between Britain and France after having been a German colony since 1884. Distinct Anglophone and Francophone areas were reunited as an independent country in 1961. Approximately one-fourth of Cameroonians are Anglophone. For more than three decades after independence, Cameroon was ruled under a repressive one-party system. In 1992 and 1997 President Biya held fraudulent multiparty elections, which he won after a boycott by the opposition Social Democratic Front (SDF), led by John Fru Ndi.

Cameroon's population comprises nearly 200 ethnic groups. Members of Biya's Beti ethnic group continue to occupy a disproportionate number of positions in the ruling party and military, although the cabinet has a more diverse ethnic mix. The administration remains largely Francophone, and the country's main opposition is from Anglophone Cameroonians. The linguistic distinction constitutes the country's most potent political division. Security forces in April 2000 arrested about 100 alleged Anglophone secessionists. The Roman Catholic bishop of Douala complained in June of hundreds of extrajudicial executions carried out by a paramilitary group formed in 1999 to fight crime.

Privatization has progressed, but graft and the absence of independent courts inhibit business development. The government in May 2000 set up an anticorruption body, including representatives from business, the judiciary, human rights groups, government ministries, and the security forces. It is unlikely that any serious reform will take place until changes are made in the government and judiciary. Under pressure from international lenders, the administration changed its procurement system, allowing for international consultants to conduct audits of major government contracts and annual spot audits for smaller ones.

There are hopes that construction of a pipeline running from Chad through Cameroon will help bring in jobs, and civil society has been active in trying to assure that the needs of the local population are met.

Political Rights and Civil Liberties:

Although Cameroon's constitution provides for a multiparty republic, citizens have not been allowed to choose their government and local leaders democratically. Presidential elections have been devalued by rampant intimidation, manipulation, and fraud. President Biya's reelection in 1997 with 93 percent of the vote was marred by serious procedural flaws, as well as by a boycott by the three major opposition parties, because the government dismissed demands for an independent election commission.

Legislative elections have also been fraudulent. The ruling CPDM won 116 seats and the SDF won 43 in polling in 1997 overseen by regime loyalists in the ministry of territorial administration. Municipal elections are scheduled for 2001 and legislative polls in 2002. During the last municipal elections, in 1996, the opposition won a number of important mayoral seats. But the government changed the constitution and appointed its own officials as city mayors, effectively nullifying the election results through an administrative maneuver.

The constitution provides for freedom of the press, but serious restrictions inhibit open political exchange. Criminal libel law is regularly used to silence regime critics. There was an easing of press repression in 2000, but abuses still occurred. A criminal court in April convicted journalist Michel Eclador Pekoua, of the private weekly *Ouest Echos,* on defamation charges and sentenced him to six months in prison. Three journalists with the biweekly publication *Dikalo* received similar sentences on charges of criminal defamation. Two were condemned in absentia.

Constitutional amendments in 1995 gave even more power to the presidency and only nominally strengthened a pliant judiciary. Cameroon's courts remain highly subject to political influence and corruption. The executive controls the judiciary and appoints provincial and local administrators. Military tribunals may exercise jurisdiction over civilians in cases involving civil unrest or organized armed violence. A group of alleged Anglophone secessionists, known as "the forgotten five," have been awaiting trial since 1995.

In the north, powerful traditional chiefs known as *lamibée* run their own private militias, courts, and prisons, which are used against the regime's political opponents. Torture and ill-treatment of prisoners and detainees are routine in Cameroon, despite legislation passed in January 1997 that prohibits torture. Indefinite pretrial detention under extremely harsh conditions is permitted after a warrant is issued or to "combat banditry." Prison conditions are harsh, and inmates routinely die. The International Committee of the Red Cross was granted access to Cameroon's detention facilities in 1999.

Various intelligence agencies operate with impunity, and opposition activists are often held without charges. Security forces routinely impede domestic travel. The cardinal of Douala wrote a letter in June to the local governor complaining of the "Operational Command" that was set up in 1999 to deal with crime. Reported violations were declining toward the end of 2000, but the cardinal said that up to 500 summary executions had been carried out. Independent sources could not verify the number but said it was plausible that at least 200 people had been summarily executed over the past year.

Numerous nongovernmental organizations operate in the country. Freedom of religion is generally respected, but there have been some reports of discrimination. Slavery reportedly persists in parts of the north, and discrimination exists against indigenous Pygmies.

In 1990 the national assembly passed a potentially significant bill calling for liberalizing the audio and visual media, but Biya has yet to sign the decree that would bring the bill into force. A handful of private radio stations broadcast religious or music programs. International radio stations can be heard on shortwave radios.

Trade union formation is permitted under the 1992 labor code, but some of the code's provisions have not been implemented and many government workers are not covered. Workers have the right to strike, but only after arbitration, the decisions of which the government can overturn. The Confederation of Cameroonian Trade Unions is technically independent, but is still influenced or intimidated by the ruling party. In 1996, the regime launched the Union of Free Trade Unions of Cameroon to further undermine union autonomy.

Violence against women is reportedly widespread. Women are often denied inheritance and landownership rights even when these are codified, and many other laws contain unequal gender-based provisions and penalties. Female genital mutilation is practiced in some parts of the country.

Canada

Polity: Parliamentary democracy (federal)
Economy: Capitalist
Population: 30,800,000
PPP: $23,582
Life Expectancy: 79
Ethnic Groups: British (40 percent), French (27 percent), other European (20 percent), Indian and Inuit (1.5 percent), other, mostly Asian (11.5 percent)
Capital: Ottawa

Political Rights: 1
Civil Liberties: 1
Status: Free

Overview:

In an impressive triumph, the Liberal Party, under the leadership of Prime Minister Jean Chretien, increased its control of Parliament in national elections held in November. The triumph made Chretien the first Canadian prime minister to win three consecutive terms in the post-World War II period. With U.S. president Bill Clinton leaving office, Chretien becomes the longest serving leader of a democratic country in the western hemisphere.

The results gave the Liberals a commanding 172 seats in the 301-seat house of commons, a gain of 17 seats from the last election in 1997. The Canadian Alliance, the principal conservative party, won 66 seats, a gain of 6. But other conservative parties lost strength, with the Progressive Conservatives winning only 12 seats. The election also represented a serious setback for the Bloc Quebecois, a separatist party, which saw its parliamentary representation decline from 44 to 38 seats, and for the New Democratic Party, a social democratic party, whose representation shrank from 21 to 13.

Colonized by French and British settlers in the seventeenth and eighteenth centuries, Canada came under the control of the British Crown under the terms of the Treaty of Paris in 1763. After granting home rule in 1867, Britain retained a theoretical right to overrule the Canadian Parliament until 1982, when Canadians established complete control over their own constitution. The country is governed by a prime minister, a cabinet, and the parliament. The parliament consists of an elected 301-member house of commons and an appointed 104-member senate. The British monarch remains nominal head of state, represented by a ceremonial governor-general appointed by the prime minister.

Political Rights and Civil Liberties:

Canadians can change their government democratically, and as a result of government canvassing, Canada has nearly 100 percent effective voter registration. Prisoners have the right to vote in federal elections, as do citizens who have lived abroad for fewer than five years.

In 1995, a federal law prohibiting the broadcasting of public opinion poll results two days prior to and during federal elections was upheld. A 1988 act to limit all forms of cigarette advertisement, however, was struck down as a violation of free speech. After passage in the house of commons, a modified, less comprehensive bill was passed by the senate in 1997.

The judiciary is independent. Limitations on freedom of expression range from unevenly enforced "hate laws" and restrictions on pornography to rules on reporting. Recently, there have been complaints that the judiciary has become overly activist and has issued decisions that have the effect of usurping the powers of the legislature.

The media are generally free, although they exercise self-censorship in areas such as violence on television.

Civil liberties have been protected since 1982 by the federal Charter of Rights and Freedoms, but have been limited by the constitutional "notwithstanding" clause, which permits provincial governments to exempt themselves by applying individual provisions within their jurisdictions. Quebec has used the clause to retain its provincial language law, which restricts the use of English on signs. The provincial governments, with their own constitutions and legislative assemblies, exercise significant autonomy. Each province has its own judicial system as well, with the right of appeal to the supreme court of Canada.

Canada's criminal law is based on British common law and is uniform throughout the country. Its civil law is also based on the British system, except in Quebec, where it is based on the French civil code.

The status of Quebec became a contentious issue in Canadian politics. Five years after Canada's divisive 1995 referendum on independence for Quebec, separatism for the province remained a primary political issue. Quebec premier Lucien Bouchard again threatened to hold another referendum on the province's status.

In 1996, parliament amended the constitution to outlaw discrimination based on "sexual orientation" by adding this term to a 1977 Human Rights Act list that includes age, sex, race, religion, and disability. Canada has also taken important steps to protect the rights of native groups. In April 1999, Canada created a new territory, Nunavut, consisting of regions in the country's vast north. The new territory is largely populated by Inuits, an indigenous group. During the past year, clashes, occasionally violent, broke out over competing claims about fishing rights involving native groups and commercial fishermen. There is also a major contorversy over native land claims in the western province of British Columbia.

Canada boasts a generous welfare system that supplements the largely open, competitive economy. There have recently been calls to make changes in the national health system, though any serious move towards privatization will probably be defeated due to the poor showing in national elections of the Canadian Alliance.

Trade unions and business associations enjoy high levels of membership and are free and well organized.

Religious expression is free and diverse, but religious education has been the subject of controversy in recent years. Many provinces have state-supported religious school systems that do not represent all denominations. In 2000, a major scandal was triggered by a series of legal actions taken by members of native groups who had been educated in schools operated by religious denominations under federal charter. The cases involved widespread allegations of physical and sexual abuse by teachers and administrators in incidents that went back several decades. The financial viability of several of the country's major Christian denominations, including the Roman Catholic and Anglican, has been threatened by huge settlements in civil suits.

Despite restrictions announced in 1994, the flow of immigrants into the country remains strong. Concern has been expressed about the possibility of terrorists taking advantage of the country's liberal immigration policies. In August 1999, there were demands for a crackdown on illegal immigrants after several boatloads of undocumented Chinese landed on Canada's western coast. In 2000, legislation was introduced that would allot more immigration slots for family reunification purposes while making it easier for the government to deport those who "abuse the system."

Cape Verde

Polity: Presidential-parliamentary democracy
Economy: Mixed statist
Population: 400,000
PPP: $3,233
Life Expectancy: 69
Ethnic Groups: Creole [mulatto] (71 percent), African (28 percent), European (1 percent)
Capital: Praia

Political Rights: 1
Civil Liberties: 2
Status: Free

Overview:

There was an uncharacteristic shake-up in Cape Verde's administration in 2000 when the prime minister, Carlos Alberto Wahnon de Carvalho Veiga, "suspended" his mandate in July to contest presidential elections in February 2001. Veiga's move, which was followed by his resignation in September, sent tremors through the country's political class, which is accustomed to little out of the ordinary. Vice Prime Minister Gualberto do Rosário, president of the ruling Movement for Democracy (MPD) party, was named to take over as prime minister, but not until October, and was charged with forming a new government barely four months ahead of the presidential polls. Veiga said he decided to resign to preserve calm and avoid "political games" played by some in the country. Analysts consider Veiga a favorite to win the election. Other candidates include former Minister David Hopfer Almada and Jorge Carlos Fonseca, as well as former Prime Minister Pedro Pires. President António Mascarenhas Monteiro is barred from running for a third term.

After achieving independence from Portugal in 1975, Cape Verde was governed under Marxist, one-party rule by the African Party for the Independence of Cape Verde for 16 years. The MPD won a landslide 1991 victory in the first democratic elections after Cape Verde became the first former Portuguese colony in Africa to abandon Marxist political and economic systems. In December 1995, the MPD was returned to power with 59 percent of the vote.

The West African archipelago appears to have made a firm transition to multiparty democracy, but extreme poverty has so far allowed no party to offer much material incentive for supporting constitutional rule. The government's austerity program is unpopular, but has drawn increased donor assistance. Very low voter turnout marked President Monteiro's 1996 reelection to a second five-year term. His free market policies are also supported by the prime minister and the MPD, which holds 50 of 72 seats in parliament.

The country's stagnant economy has been bolstered somewhat by increased exports and tourism, but infrastructure improvements are still needed to assist in private sector development. Cape Verde is one of Africa's smallest and poorest lands. It has few exploitable natural resources and relies heavily on imported food. Foreign aid and remittances by Cape Verdean expatriates provide a large portion of national income. The government is pursuing privatization and seeking international investment from business and from the country's large diaspora. Cape Verde has enthusiastically joined Portugal's efforts to create a Lusophone commonwealth.

Political Rights and Civil Liberties: The president and members of the national people's assembly, including six representatives chosen by citizens living abroad, are elected through universal suffrage in free and fair elections. Since the country's 1991 transition to multiparty democracy, Cape Verdeans have changed their government twice by democratic means. The 1992 constitution circumscribed the powers of the presidency, which was left with little authority beyond the ability to delay ratification of legislation, propose amendments, and dissolve parliament after a vote of no confidence. Referenda are permitted in some circumstances, but they may not challenge civil liberties or the rights of opposition parties. Legislative elections are scheduled for January 2001, and presidential polls are set for January.

Freedom of expression and of the press is guaranteed and generally respected in practice. No authorization is needed to publish newspapers and other publications. Broadcasts are largely state controlled, but there is a growing independent press. Criticism of the government is limited by self-censorship resulting from citizens' fear of demotion or dismissal.

Human rights groups, including the National Commission of the Rights of Man and the Ze Moniz Association, operate freely. There are no reported political prisoners, but abuses by police, including beatings, remain a problem. Police officers accused of abuses are usually not held accountable.

Reforms to strengthen an overburdened judiciary were implemented in 1998. Composed of a supreme court and regional courts that generally adjudicate criminal and civil cases fairly, the judiciary is independent, although cases are frequently delayed. Free legal counsel is provided to indigents, defendants are presumed innocent until proven guilty, and trials are public. Judges must bring charges within 24 hours of arrests. The police, which were controlled by the military until 1994, are now answerable to civilian authority.

The freedom of peaceful assembly and association is guaranteed and respected. The constitution requires the separation of church and state, and religious rights are respected in practice. There have, however, been an increasing number of desecrations of Roman Catholic churches over the years. The vast majority of Cape Verdeans belong to the Roman Catholic Church.

The constitution protects the right to unionize, and workers may form and join unions without restriction. Two confederations, the Council of Free Labor Unions and the National Union of Cape Verde Workers, include 25 unions with approximately 30,000 members.

Discrimination against women persists despite legal prohibitions against gender discrimination, as well as provisions for social and economic equality. Many women either do not know their rights or do not possess means to seek redress, especially in rural areas. Women receive less pay for equal work and are excluded from traditionally male professions. They are also subject to allegedly common, but seldom reported, domestic violence. Serious concerns about child abuse and the prevalence of child labor persist. Campaigns to promote women's civil and human rights and awareness of child abuse have been mounted by local nongovernmental organizations with international assistance.

Central African Republic

Polity: Presidential-parliamentary democracy
Economy: Capitalist-statist
Population: 3,500,000
PPP: $1,118
Life Expectancy: 45
Ethnic Groups: Baya (34 percent), Banda (27 percent), Mandjia (21 percent), Sara (10 percent), Mboum (4 percent), M'Baka (4 percent)
Capital: Bangui

Political Rights: 3
Civil Liberties: 4
Status: Partly Free

Overview:

The Central African Republic (CAR) was becoming increasingly unstable toward the end of the year. Fuel shortages and resultant high prices, caused by the war in the neighboring Democratic Republic of Congo, was exacerbating an economic crisis. Thousands of people marched through the streets of the capital, Bangui, in November against salary arrears. Calls were escalating for a no-confidence vote to be passed against Prime Minister Anicet Georges Dologuélé, whom critics accuse of taking advantage of his position and failing to relieve economic hardship.

The CAR, a sparsely populated country, gained independence from France in 1960 after a period of particularly brutal colonial exploitation. Colonel Jean-Bedel Bokassa seized power in 1967 and, as self-declared emperor, imposed an increasingly bizarre personal dictatorship on the renamed Central African Empire. After Bokassa began to murder schoolchildren, French forces finally ousted him in 1979. A French-installed successor was deposed by General Kolingba in 1981. Kolingba accepted a transition to a multiparty system that led to democratic elections in 1993, which Patassé won.

Profound divisions linger within the security forces that could reverse steps made toward peace. President Ange-Félix Patassé's former presidential guard, the Special Forces for the Defense of Democratic Institutions, has technically been dismantled, but the troops have not yet been integrated into the armed forces. They were largely drawn from Patassé's base in the north. The southern-dominated military traditionally has been loyal to former military ruler André Kolingba.

The National Program for Demobilization and Reintegration has been put on "technical hold." The government blames international donors for failing to provide the necessary funds, while the donors accuse the government of moving too slowly on reforms. Rumors abound of military subversion, and there are growing fears of social unrest.

A United Nations peacekeeping mission to CAR ended its mandate in February after helping create conditions necessary for elections in 1999. The UN mission was established in April 1998 following mutinies in 1996 and 1997 that wracked Bangui. The UN troops replaced African peacekeepers who were brought in to help maintain security following vigorous French military intervention.

Most of the country's people are subsistence farmers. The World Bank and International Monetary Fund have accused the government of executive interference in the country's privatization program, which is proceeding slowly.

Political Rights and Civil Liberties: Presidential and legislative elections were held in 1993 in line with the 1986 constitution, giving the CAR's people their first opportunity to choose their leaders in an open and democratic manner. President Patassé, leader of the Movement for the Liberation of the Central African People, was reelected in September 1999 for another six-year term, defeating André Kolingba. The incumbent narrowly won the first round, eliminating the need for a runoff. UN peacekeepers watched over the voting, and international observers judged the vote to be free, although there were reports of irregularities such as ballot shortages in some areas with a strong opposition following. Kolingba and other candidates claimed fraud. President Patassé's triumph was not matched by his party in the December 1998 national assembly elections, which produced a nearly even split between his supporters and his opponents.

Corruption, political interference, and lack of training hinder the efficiency and impartiality of judicial institutions. Limitations on searches and detention are often ignored. Conditions for prisoners, including many long-term pretrial detainees, are extremely difficult and sometimes life threatening. Police brutality is also a serious problem, and security forces act with impunity. Extrajudicial executions of criminal suspects are reported, and robbery and other abuses by various military factions have become a serious problem in the capital. A special anticrime police unit was less active in 2000, although it still had popular support and carried out extrajudicial executions of suspected criminals.

The UN-sponsored Radio Minurca provides nonpartisan civic and voter educational programming. Other broadcast media are dominated by the state and offer little coverage of opposition activities. The only licensed private radio stations are music- or religion-oriented. Legislation enacted in 1998 rescinded the government's authority to censor the press, but authorities have occasionally been restrictive and have used draconian criminal libel laws to prosecute journalists. In December 1999, President Patassé warned that action would be taken against media that have "a tendency to incite rebellion." At least three journalists were arrested in 2000.

Open public discussion is permitted, but constitutionally guaranteed freedom of assembly is not always honored by authorities. Discrimination against indigenous Pygmies exists. Several human rights and other nongovernmental organizations operate unhindered. Broad prohibitions against "fundamentalism" are widely considered to be aimed at Islamist tendencies and could provide scope for official restrictions on worship. Religious groups must register with the government, although religious freedom is generally respected in practice.

The CAR's largest single employer is the government, and government employee trade unions are especially active. Worker rights to form or join unions are legally protected. Two of five labor federations are independent. For strikes to be legal, a conciliation process is required. Wage guidelines are set by the government in consultation with employers and unions, but unions sometimes reach agreements with employers through collective bargaining. There were a number of strikes in 2000 over salary arrears

Societal discrimination in many areas relegates women to second-class citizenship, especially in rural areas, and constitutional guarantees for women's rights are generally not enforced. Women's access to education and jobs has been limited. However, women have made some gains in the political sphere; 80 women contested the national assembly elections in 1998. Eight won seats. Female genital mutilation is still practiced, but is reportedly diminishing.

Chad

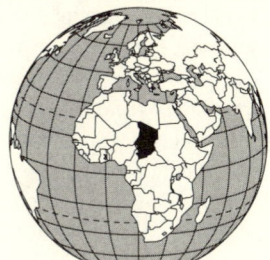

Polity: Presidential-parliamentary (military-dominated)
Economy: Capitalist
Population: 8,000,000
PPP: $856
Life Expectancy: 48
Ethnic Groups: Sara (28 percent), Sudan and Arab (12 percent), many others
Capital: N'Djamena

Political Rights: 6
Civil Liberties: 5
Status: Not Free

Overview: Intermittent fighting with rebels from the Movement for Democracy and Justice in Chad (MDJT), headed by former Defense Minister Youssouf Togoïmi, continued in 2000. Rebels claimed to have gained control of the Bardai district in the north, but the government subsequently transported reporters to the region to show that it was in government hands. There are indications that the rebels have expanded their ethnic base and its numbers, after beginning as a mainly Toubou force.

Judicial proceedings against former dictator Hissein Habre were dropped in Senegal. Habre had been arrested on charges of violating human rights, but the case was dismissed on the grounds that Senegal did not have jurisdiction. The case appeared to have been influenced by political considerations; for example, Habre's lawyer was an advisor to newly elected Senegalese president Abdoulaye Wade.

Chad has been in a state of almost constant war since achieving its independence from France in 1960. President Idriss Déby gained power by overthrowing Hissein Habré in 1990. Turmoil exacerbated by ethnic and religious differences is also fanned by clan rivalries and external interference. The country is divided between Nilotic and Bantu Christian farmers who inhabit the country's south and Arab and Saharan peoples who occupy arid deserts in the north.

Chad was a militarily dominated one-party state until Déby lifted the ban on political parties in 1993. A national conference that included a broad array of civic and political groups then created a transitional parliament, which was controlled by Déby's Patriotic Salvation Movement (MPS). Scores of political parties are registered.

Chad's army and political life are dominated by members of the small Zaghawa and Bideyat groups from President Déby's northeastern region. This is a source of ongoing resentment among the more than 200 other ethnic groups in the country. The formal exercise of deeply flawed elections and democratic processes has produced some opening of Chadian society, but real power remains with President Déby.

France, which remains highly influential in Chad, maintains a 1,000-member garrison in the country and serves as Déby's main political and commercial supporter. Brutality by Chadian soldiers and rebels marked insurgencies in the vast countryside, but the large-scale abuses of the past have abated somewhat.

An economically crucial and environmentally sensitive oil pipeline project moved ahead in 2000 after the World Bank agreed to support it. In an effort to minimize potential environmental and social problems, the World Bank had imposed several prerequisites for approving loans requested by Chad and Cameroon for the $3 billion pipeline. Hundreds of national and international nongovernmental organizations had petitioned the World Bank to put the project on hold for two years, citing the need to inform and educate the local population, minimize threats to the environment, and address human rights issues. These efforts have helped strengthen civil society in the country. The pipeline could bring Chad, one of the world's poorest countries, billions of dollars in new revenue, but serious questions remain about the government's ability to manage these revenues in a transparent and accountable fashion. These fears were reinforced by an announcement in November 2000 that an initial payment of approximately $4 million had been diverted for use by the Defense Ministry.

Political Rights and Civil Liberties: Citizens of Chad cannot change their government democratically. Chad has never experienced a peaceful, fair, and orderly transference of political power, and both presidential and legislative elections have been marred by serious irregularities and indications of outright fraud. President Déby's 1996 victory in Chad's first multiparty election was strongly endorsed by France, despite opposition and independent criticism. It is impossible to ascertain if President Déby's second-round victory with 69 percent of the vote was credible. Déby's most potent challengers were disqualified, opposition activists were intimidated, and the vote count was manipulated. Allegations of fraud also devalued the 1997 legislative elections. The current coalition government is dominated by the MPS with 65 seats, but also includes the Union for Renewal and Democracy, which has 29 of the 125 seats. The cabinet was reshuffled on August 30, 2000.

The president's term of office is five years. The legislature is unicameral. The sole chamber, the national assembly, has 125 members, directly elected for a four-year term. In a referendum held in March 1996, voters approved a new constitution based on the French model and providing for a unified and presidential state. Preparations began for presidential and legislative elections in 2001. An ostensibly independent election commission law was passed in 2000, despite significant opposition. It gives the predominance of seats to government representatives and those of parties in the ruling coalition. Intimidation and harassment by the National Security Agency hinder opposition efforts to organize.

In 2000, killings and torture with impunity by Chadian security forces and rebel groups reportedly continued. A number of members of the ruling party resigned in protest at military violence. Tens of thousands of Chadians have fled their country to escape the violence. Several of the 20 or more armed factions have reached peace pacts, but many of these agreements have failed. Chad's long and porous borders are virtually unpoliced. Trade in weapons among nomadic Sahelian peoples is rife, and banditry adds to the pervasive insecurity.

The rule of law and the judicial system remain weak, with courts heavily influenced by the executive. Security forces routinely ignore constitutional protections regarding search, seizure, and detention. Overcrowding, disease, and malnutrition make prison conditions life threatening, and many inmates spend years in prison without charges.

State control of broadcast media allows little exposure for dissenting views. Newspapers critical of the government circulate freely in N'Djamena, but have little impact among the largely rural and illiterate population.

Despite harassment and occasional physical intimidation, the Chadian Human Rights League, Chad Nonviolence, and several other human rights groups operate openly and publish findings critical of the government. Although religion is a source of division in society, Chad is a secular state and freedom of religion is generally respected. Women's rights are protected neither by traditional law nor the penal code, and few educational opportunities are available. Female genital mutilation is commonplace.

Workers' right to organize and to strike is generally respected, but the formal economy is small. Union membership is low. Most Chadians are subsistence farmers.

Chile

Polity: Presidential-parliamentary democracy
Economy: Capitalist
Population: 15,200,000
PPP: $8,787
Life Expectancy: 75
Ethnic Groups: European and European-Indian (95 percent), Indian (3 percent), other (2 percent)
Capital: Santiago

Political Rights: 2
Civil Liberties: 2
Status: Free

Overview:

In January 2000, Ricardo Lagos, 61, a moderate socialist and the leader of the Chile's Concertación coalition, won the presidency in a tight runoff race. Although former military dictator Augusto Pinochet escaped extradition to Spain to face human rights charges, returning to Chile in March following 503 days of house arrest in Great Britain, in April a court opened deliberations on whether he could face trial despite being a senator-for-life with immunity from prosecution. In August he was stripped of his immunity and a judge ordered the 84-year-old Pinochet to undergo mental and neurological tests before deciding to try him on some or all of the 177 criminal complaints lodged against him, a process that dragged on past year's end due to legal challenges. In December 2000, a judge stunned Chileans by indicting Pinochet on homicide and kidnapping charges.

Throughout the year, the judiciary expanded human rights protections by ruling that allegations of crimes against humanity, including torture, kidnapping, and genocide, fall within its purview and are not subject to amnesty decrees. The rights held out the possibility of cooperation with Lagos in pursuing necessary constitutional reforms only if he cooperated in getting Pinochet and other senior officials, such as the former secret police chief and a former army commander from Pinochet's regime, out of harm's way in the courts. In November two Chilean generals, one on active duty, were indicted for allegedly covering up a 1982 political assassination. The "Pinochet effect" appeared to be strengthening resolve in several neighboring countries to investigate their own once all-powerful military forces and to hold them accountable for acts those forces committed while presiding over de facto regimes.

The Republic of Chile was founded after independence from Spain in 1818. Democratic rule predominated in the twentieth century until the 1973 overthrow of Salvador Allende by the military under Pinochet. More than 3,000 people were killed or "disappeared" during his regime; some of them were pitched from aircraft into the Pacific Ocean or pushed out of helicopters over the Andes. The 1980 constitution provided for a plebiscite in which voters could reject another presidential term for Pinochet. In 1988, 55 percent of voters said no to eight more years of military rule, and competitive presidential and legislative elections were scheduled for 1989.

In 1989, Christian Democrat Patricio Aylwin, the candidate of the center-left Concertación for Democracy, was elected president over two right-wing candidates, and the Concertación won a majority in the chamber of deputies. But with eight senators appointed by the outgoing military government, the coalition fell short of a senate majority. Aylwin's government was unsuccessful in its efforts to reform the constitution and was stymied by a right-wing senate bloc in its efforts to prevent Pinochet and other military chiefs from remaining at their posts until 1997.

Eduardo Frei, a businessman and the son of a former president, was the Concertación candidate in the December 1993 elections, and he won handily over right-wing candidate Arturo Alessandri. Frei promised to establish full civilian control over the military but did not have the votes in congress. In 1995, the military defiance of a supreme court ruling that Pinochet's secret-police chief be jailed for the 1976 murder of an exiled opposition leader in Washington, D.C., finally ceased, and the army general was imprisoned. However, Frei had to retreat from demanding full accountability for rights violations that occurred under military rule.

The senate has 48 seats, including a senator-for-life position for Pinochet and 9 designated senators mandated by the 1980 constitution. In October 1997 Frei selected the army chief of staff as Pinochet's replacement from a list of names Pinochet submitted. In December, the ruling coalition won a convincing victory in an election in which all 120 lower house and 20 of 49 senate seats were open. However, the binomial electoral system, which allows a party receiving only 33 percent of the votes to share power in two-seat constituencies with a party receiving as much as 66 percent, resulted in pro-Pinochet forces retaining their veto on constitutional reforms.

Pinochet's detention produced a strong political polarization in Chile and resulted in several emergency meetings called by the new leadership of the armed forces, as well as a reunion of the National Security Council. The country, said one top general, was "in a critical situation." However, as the months of imprisonment lengthened for Pinochet in 1999, tempers subsided somewhat. A number of the general's cronies were called to account by the courts for their own repressive roles, while the current armed forces sought a dialogue with rights groups and relatives of the missing.

On December 12, 1999, Lagos faced right-wing Alliance for Chile candidate Joaquin Lavin, the mayor of a Santiago suburb and a former advisor to Pinochet, winning 47.96 percent to Lavin's 47.52 percent. Both candidates, however, fell short of the 50 percent majority needed to win outright in a first round, whose results showed a strong polarization between right and left. Lavin's strong showing—historically the right never received more than 40 percent of the votes—was fueled by an 11 percent unemployment rate and concerns about crime.

Lagos won the January 16, 2000, runoff election, taking a 2.6 percent lead over Lavin. However, he was initially hampered by the fact that his congressional opposition, bolstered by a group of designated senators left over from the Pinochet period, was in a position to block both labor and constitutional reforms. Although the Concertación coalition had 70 seats to the opposition's 50 in the lower house, it held just 20 seats in the senate to 18 held by the opposition. A bloc of 11 others were either senators-for-life or had been designated under Pinochet's rules. Lagos's strong early performance appeared, by late 2000, to be threatened by economic woes and transparency issues. The return to the front pages of the Pinochet case, and Lagos's firm position that the courts would have the final say, helped end the honeymoon period with the right and created new tensions in the military high command.

Although they found Lagos highly popular personally, Chileans faulted Lagos's government for Chile's soaring unemployment, price increases, and charges of government corruption. In October municipal elections, Lavin won 61 percent of the votes against 29 percent for Marta Larraechea, Frei's wife, in the contest for the Santiago mayoralty, one of 300 that were up for grabs. Although the ruling coalition won 51.2 percent of the votes nationwide, the opposition—capitalizing on the government's inability to bring down a 10.7 percent unemployment rate—raised its number of mayoral seats to 163 from 126, out of a total of 341, and garnered 40.9 percent of the vote. Both the army and navy threatened that Pinochet's trial would jeopardize the initiative to determine the fate of the "disappeared." In late December 2000, the Chilean top court dropped homicide and kidnapping charges against Pinochet, but appeared open to the possibility of trying the former dictator for responsibility in the 1973 "Caravan of Death," in which 73 political prisoners were executed.

Political Rights and Civil Liberties: Citizens can change their government democratically. The 2000 and 1999 elections were considered free and fair, although low registration rates among young voters are a cause for concern. The Pinochet extradition crisis showed that Chile's democratic transition requires constitutional reforms to ensure civilian control of the military. Failure to eliminate some of the most egregious features—such as nine appointed senators, four named by the military—of the 1980 constitution imposed by the Pinochet dictatorship heightened the sense of emergency sparked by the retired general's October 1998 detention in London.

In 1990, a Truth and Reconciliation Commission was formed to investigate rights violations committed under military rule. Its report implicated the military and secret police leadership in the deaths or forcible disappearances of 2,279 people between September 1973 and March 1990. However, in 1978, the Pinochet regime had issued an amnesty for all political crimes, and the supreme court, packed by Pinochet before leaving office, had before 2000 blocked all government efforts to lift the amnesty.

Chile's civilian governments have investigated hundreds of human rights cases involving incidents occurring after 1978 brought to civilian courts. The investigations have resulted in a handful of convictions. In June 1999, a civilian judge decided that five senior military officers—members of the so-called Caravan of Death that summarily executed 73 political prisoners in several cities—should be tried for the crimes committed in 1973. In 1999, the army commander, General Ricardo Izurieta, began a dialogue with human rights groups not only to clarify the fates of many disappeared political activists, but also to identify those military officers who had ordered their torture and death. In September 1999, the supreme court ratified a lower court ruling that the amnesty declared by Pinochet's regime was not applicable to cases in which people disappeared, because the absence of the victims' bodies meant the crimes committed were kidnappings, not murders. Thus, the crimes continued beyond the 1978 deadline established by the regime and could be prosecuted.

In Chile, freedom of expression is compromised by a variety of factors, most important of which are constraints on access to sources of information, although scores of publications present all points of view. Radio is both public and private. The national television network is state run, but open to all political voices. Self-censorship regarding Chile's recent political history is common, although less so than in earlier years. Judges may withhold information on cases being tried before them. Military courts can bring charges against civilians for sedition, which is defined as any comment that may affect the morale of the armed forces or police. As the offended party is the armed forces, the military tribunal plays the role of victim, prosecutor, and judge. In 1999, a Chilean judge ordered the immediate confiscation of all copies of *The Black Book of Chilean Justice,* a well-researched exposé of corruption in the judiciary. Its journalist author was forced to flee to the United States. In 2000, an alternative press law was rejected by the Chilean lower house.

The Carabineros, uniformed national police, have primary responsibility for public order, safety, and border security. The civilian Investigations Police are responsible for criminal investigations and immigration control. Although they are formally under the jurisdiction of the Ministry of Defense, which prepares their budgets, both organizations are under operational control of the Interior Ministry. The police are often the targets of complaints about brutality, and the due process rights of detainees are not always respected.

Chile has a strong trade union movement comprising 10 percent of the workforce, but one that has been hamstrung by a Pinochet-era labor code that restricts forming unions, prohibits collective bargaining at the multicompany level, and allows companies to hire replacement workers during a strike. Anti-union practices, such as layoffs, threats and surveillance by private security forces, are subject to weak sanctions that are rarely enforced. In 2000, Lagos promised to strengthen collective bargaining for union workers and to bring local legislation in line with International Labor Organization conventions establishing the right of workers to organize and to engage in collective bargaining.

Government corruption is comparatively minor when compared to corruption in other governments in the region, although military graft has been allowed to remain largely uninvestigated. A scandal in May involving compensation payments to government officials helped Lavin win the Santiago mayoralty.

Chile has around one million indigenous people, nearly all of them Mapuches. A 1993 indigenous rights law guaranteed that Indian lands could not be embargoed, sold, expropriated, or taxed. New development projects, promoted by the government, continue to threaten Mapuche lands in the south of Chile, where highly charged land disputes have resulted in the region's being dubbed the country's "little Chiapas," in allusion to Mexico's trouble southern state. At the end of the 1990s, Indian rights groups, which have few ties to traditional political parties, became increasingly radicalized in the face of government inaction.

In March 2000, one of Frei's last acts in office was to persuade the comptroller's department to overturn its own previous finding and authorize construction of the Ralco hydroelectric complex on the Bio-Bio River, a move bitterly opposed by indigenous communities. Upon taking office, Lagos began to make good on a campaign promise that the "Indian question" would receive priority attention. In May, he announced the creation of a "historical truth and new deal commission" to consider the needs of Mapuche communities. He also announced that the Mapuche will be given 370,000 acres of government-owned land, one-third of it before the end of 2001. There was evidence that some of the acts of violence alleged to have been committed by Indian activists were actually the work of agents provocateurs in the pay of the rapidly expanding logging companies.

In 2000, Lagos appointed five women to his 16-person cabinet. Violence and discrimination against women and violence against children remain problems.

China

Polity: One party   **Political Rights:** 7
Economy: Mixed statist   **Civil Liberties:** 6
Population: 1,264,500,000 **Status:** Not Free
PPP: $3,105
Life Expectancy: 70
Ethnic Groups: Han Chinese (92 percent), other, including
Tibetan, Mongol, Korean, Manchu, and Uighur (8 percent)
Capital: Beijing

Overview: Worker and farmer protests, popular anger over corruption, and the economic and social impact of China's impending entry into the World Trade Organization (WTO) were among the pressing issues facing the country's leadership in 2000. Continuing a policy set down in the early 1990s, Beijing responded by cracking down severely on dissidents while cautiously liberalizing the economy.

Chinese Communist Party (CCP) chairman Mao Zedong proclaimed the People's Republic of China on October 1, 1949, following victory over the Nationalist

Kuomintang. Mao's death in 1976 largely ended the brutal, mass ideological campaigns that had politicized nearly every aspect of public life and had resulted in millions of deaths. Deng Xiaoping emerged as paramount leader and initiated in December 1978 China's gradual transition from central planning to a market economy.

Following the April 1989 death of Hu Yaobang, whom CCP conservatives had removed as party-secretary-general in 1986 for tolerating student demonstrations, students began weeks of pro-democracy protests in Beijing and other cities that ended in the bloody army crackdown around Tiananmen Square on June 3-4, 1989. Hardliner Jiang Zemin, the Shanghai mayor and party boss, replaced the relatively moderate Zhao Ziyang as CCP secretary-general. Jiang became president in 1993, although Deng remained China's paramount leader until his death in 1997. Under Jiang, the government has continued implementing moderate free market reforms while tightly restricting dissent. The CCP hopes that economic development will stave off broad calls for political reform, but it fears that liberalizing the economy too fast will create social unrest at the same time that citizens are increasingly being exposed to foreign news and ideas about freedom and democracy.

At the CCP's Fifteenth Congress in September 1997, Jiang consolidated his authority by ousting several potential rivals from top posts and forcing several military figures out of politics. At the 1998 annual session of the rubber-stamp National People's Congress (NPC), Zhu Rongji, the architect of the economic reform process since the mid-1990s, replaced Li Peng as prime minister. Hu Jintao, the youngest member of the CCP politburo's seven-member standing committee, became politburo president.

In recent years the government has faced challenges from intellectuals, religious sects, and blue-collar Chinese. Authorities moved quickly to detain and jail members of the opposition China Democracy Party (CDP) after it emerged in 1998. However, they have had far less success in suppressing the Falun Gong mystical sect, which stunned the Chinese leadership in April 1999 when it organized the biggest demonstration in the capital since 1989 to demand official recognition. Following revelations that many party members and senior military officers belonged to the group, authorities banned Falun Gong in July 1999 and began detaining thousands of followers. Nevertheless, Falun Gong members have continued to hold periodic demonstrations in Beijing.

Chinese authorities have also faced worker protests over job losses and unpaid pensions and other benefits. The often violent protests have occurred amid Beijing's efforts to shut down or privatize most small- and medium-sized state-owned enterprises by the middle of the decade. China's expected entry into the WTO within a few years will require further reforms that could increase unemployment even more. However, officials have made limited progress in developing an effective and sustainable system of pensions, unemployment benefits, and health insurance for laid-off and retired state enterprise workers.

Beijing also faces serious social problems in rural areas, where farmers have frequently rioted, demonstrated, or otherwise protested against high and often arbitrary government fees and taxes. In one of the largest incidents in recent years, up to 20,000 farmers rioted for five days in August in southern Jiangxi province.

In yet another source of friction, leaders of the 7 million Turkic-speaking Uighurs and other, smaller Turkic groups in the northwestern Xinjiang region harbor long-standing grievances against Beijing for allegedly exploiting the region's rich mineral resources, controlling religious affairs, and altering the region's demographic balance by encouraging an influx of Han Chinese through job opportunities and other incentives. In recent years, authorities have committed widespread abuses while cracking down on both peaceful dissent and on armed Uighur groups that have carried out several bombings and assassinations. Amnesty International recorded 190 executions in Xinjiang between 1997 and mid-1999, mostly of Uighurs convicted of "subversion" or "terrorism" in unfair trials.

Reflecting the hope that economic development will weaken separatist tendencies, Beijing initiated a campaign in January 2000 to increase bank lending to Xinjiang and other impoverished, landlocked areas of western China. However, authorities maintained investment and regional protectionist policies that favor Guangdong and other wealthier southern and eastern provinces and have contributed to pronounced regional disparities in income and economic growth.

Official corruption also continued to be a serious problem. According to the *Far Eastern Economic Review*, China's auditor-general revealed in January that corrupt officials had stolen $15 billion in state money in 1999. In November, courts sentenced 14 people to death for their roles in a $6.6 billion smuggling racket in the port of Xiamin, although some analysts noted that senior officials had avoided prosecution during this first round of trials. Separately, authorities executed in September the former vice chairman of the NPC's Standing Committee for corruption, the highest ranking official executed since the founding of the People's Republic.

Political Rights and Civil Liberties:

Chinese citizens lack the democratic means to change their government. China continued to be a de facto single-party state in which the CCP controlled the judiciary and restricted sharply freedom of expression, association, assembly, and religion. Beijing signed the International Covenant on Civil and Political Rights in 1998 but has not ratified it, and compliance continued to be limited.

Under the 1982 constitution, the NPC is the highest organ of state authority. In practice, parliament has little independent power. However, in recent years delegates have registered protest votes over the government's handling of rising crime rates and other issues. While eight small, pro-government parties exist alongside the CCP, authorities have cracked down on members of the CDP, who made in 1998 the first attempt to register an opposition party since the founding of the People's Republic. Courts have sentenced more than 30 CDP members to prison terms of up to 13 years, mainly on subversion charges.

Under the 1987 Village Committees Organic Law, voters elect some 60 percent of China's 928,000 village councils. However, authorities permit only prescreened CCP candidates and some independents to compete. Moreover, nonelected CCP secretaries have far greater powers than the elected leaders, and in any case, county governments rather than village bodies hold key administrative powers. Independents have won seats in many villages, but throughout the country, balloting is characterized by irregularities and unfair procedures.

The CCP controls the judiciary through local party bodies called political-legal committees, and directs verdicts and sentencing in sensitive cases. Judges are poorly trained and are generally retired military officers selected on the basis of party loyalty. Bribery of judges is rampant, and local governments frequently intervene in ordinary cases.

Nevertheless, in recent years the government has made some efforts to strengthen the rule of law, improve training for judges and lawyers, and make the legal system less arbitrary in nonpolitical cases. The government revised the Criminal Procedure Law (CPL) in 1997 to grant defense lawyers a greater role and increase their access to defendants; end the presumption of guilt (although without establishing a presumption of innocence); and bar judges from ordering quick trial, and executions, for crimes that allegedly "seriously endanger public order." However, judicial authorities appeared to honor these provisions mainly in the breach, and suspects still do not have the right to a lawyer the first time they are interrogated, which is apparently when most pretrial torture occurs. Moreover, the 1997 revisions introduced new summary trial procedures in certain cases. The judiciary opened many trials to the public in 1999, although politically sensitive cases remained closed.

Ordinary citizens continued to sue township governments, employers, state enterprises, and local police, something that would have been impossible only a few years earlier. Claimants have won out of court settlements or outright victories in some cases. The courts generally accept only lawsuits that dovetail with central government policies and priorities, such as finding an orderly means to handle labor grievances, or that are useful in curbing arbitrary action by increasingly autonomous local officials. At the same time, judges are often reluctant to rule against local governments, which provide their salary and appointments. Local authorities have harassed plaintiffs and refused to comply with unfavorable judgments.

The 1997 CPL revisions eliminated the category of "counterrevolutionary" crimes that courts had used to imprison thousands of dissidents. However, authorities continued to apply broadly drawn laws against "endangering state security" and "leaking state secrets" to a wide range of political and nonpolitical activities. Authorities also continued to arbitrarily imprison dissidents and ordinary criminal suspects through administrative detention procedures for up to three years without charge or trial. The revised CPL also included a separate article aimed at pro-independence and autonomy movements in Xinjiang, Inner Mongolia, and Tibet. (A separate report on Tibet appears in the Disputed Territories section.)

The government continued to hold what may be upwards of several thousand political prisoners, although the exact number is difficult to determine. Authorities held many of these political prisoners, along with an unknown number of ordinary criminal suspects, without trial in *laogai*, or "reform through labor" camps. Amnesty International announced in May that it knew of 213 people who were still imprisoned or on medical parole relating to the 1989 pro-democracy protests. Unrelenting police harassment continued to prevent many dissidents from holding jobs or otherwise leading normal lives.

Amnesty International said in a May report that torture of political detainees and ordinary criminal suspects and prisoners is "widespread" in police stations, detention centers, prisons, "re-education through labor" camps, and repatriation centers throughout China. In recent years, authorities have sentenced some persons convicted of torture to heavy prison sentences, although most perpetrators go unpunished. Nearly 70 crimes are punishable by the death penalty. In addition to executing people convicted of violent crimes, in recent years China has executed numerous people for nonviolent offenses including hooliganism, theft of farm animals or rice, or corruption.

The government continued to permit private media to report on local government inefficiency, official corruption, and other problems that Beijing itself seeks to alleviate. However, the CCP maintained tight control over political content and prohibited media from directly criticizing the CCP's monopoly on power or top leaders. At least a dozen journalists remained in jail over their reporting. In recent years, the State Press and Publishing Bureau and the CCP's Department of Propaganda occasionally have warned, suspended, or banned liberal magazines, newspapers, and book publishers for breaching limits on freedom of the press. Authorities have also dismissed several journalists and editors for publishing books or articles with liberal views.

Authorities continued to regulate Internet access and content for China's 17to 20 million Internet users. The government announced in January regulations that provide for lengthy jail terms for the unauthorized release on the Internet of broadly-defined "state secrets." In October, authorities limited foreign ownership in Chinese Internet companies and made Web sites responsible for censoring illegal content including pornography and political topics.

According to the New York-based Human Rights Watch, more than 200,000 social groups are officially registered with the Ministry of Civil Affairs. Many work in nominally nonpolitical fields including the environment and the provision of social services for women and migrant workers. Authorities maintained a complex vetting process to deny licenses to politically oriented groups, based in part on State Council Order 43 of 1989. The order banned "identical or similar social organizations...within the same administrative area," thereby outlawing independent labor organizations or other nongovernmental organizations (NGOs) that serve a function ostensibly covered by an existing government-controlled organization. Authorities generally enforced regulations requiring NGOs to report to specific government departments, and maintained the right to shut down arbitrarily any NGO. Freedom of assembly is limited. Authorities permitted numerous public protests concerning labor and housing grievances and other ostensibly local issues, but dispersed many others.

Beijing maintained its tight controls over organized religious practice. Authorities continued to pressure Roman Catholic and Protestant churches to register with either the official Catholic Patriotic Association or its Protestant counterpart. In return for an easing of harassment, official churches must accept Beijing's power to appoint clergy; monitor religious membership, funding, and activities; and regulate the publication and distribution of religious books and other materials. Other regulations required students at state-approved seminaries to pass exams on political knowledge. Beijing also continued to deny official Catholic churches the right to maintain loyalty to the Vatican.

Many unregistered Protestant churches and openly pro-Vatican Catholic groups continued to function. However, in recent years authorities have raided, closed, or demolished scores of churches and detained hundreds of bishops, priests, and ordinary Protestant and Catholic worshippers for months and, in some cases, years. Agence France-Presse (AFP) reported in December that authorities in eastern Zhejiang province had destroyed or closed up to 1,200 Taoist, Buddhist, Catholic, and Protestant temples and churches during a year-long crackdown on allegedly illegal religious activities. In Xinjiang, authorities continued to maintain sharp restrictions on construction of mosques and on Islamic publishing and education, ban religious practice by those under 18, and enforce closure orders on dozens of mosques and Koranic schools. The government officially recognizes only five religions, and all others are prima facie illegal.

Amnesty International said in December that at least 77 Falun Gong followers are reported to have died either in custody or shortly after their release, apparently because of torture or other abuse, since September 1999. The same month, AFP reported that authorities had sentenced since mid-1999 some 450 Falun Gong members to prison sentences of up to 18 years, sent more than 600 to mental hospitals, put 10,000 in labor camps, and placed another 20,000 in detention centers, according to the Hong Kong-based Information Center for Human Rights and Democracy. While these figures could not be verified, they corresponded with those in a March Amnesty report, which said that authorities had arbitrarily detained tens of thousands of practitioners, some repeatedly for short periods, since the government banned the Falun Gong movement in July 1999. Amnesty estimated that authorities were still holding "thousands" of Falun Gong practitioners and had sentenced hundreds more to prison terms after unfair trials or to forced labor camps without trial. Authorities have also extended the crackdown to other Qi Gong groups that, like the Falun Gong, combine spirituality and meditation.

China's strict family planning policy continued to limit urban couples to one child, while in rural areas parents of a girl could petition authorities for permission to try to have a son. Couples adhering to the policy received preferential education, food, and medical benefits, while those failing to comply faced a loss of jobs and benefits, fines, or even forced abortion and sterilization. As in past years, authorities sometimes punished couples failing to pay the fines by seizing livestock and other goods and destroying homes. In recent years, anecdotal evidence has suggested that authorities are enforcing the policy somewhat less rigidly, although this varies by region.

Chinese women continued to face social and economic discrimination and sexual harassment in the workplace, and tended to be far likelier than men to be laid off in state enterprise restructuring. In rural areas, women continued to be abducted or otherwise sold into prostitution or marriage at fairly high rates.

By law all unions must belong to the CCP-controlled All-China Federation of Trade Unions, and independent trade unions are illegal. Private factories reportedly frequently paid workers below-minimum wages, forced them to work overtime, and arbitrarily dismissed employees. Authorities occasionally permitted workers to hold strikes to protest against dangerous conditions, low wages, and unpaid wages and benefits. The government continued to require most prisoners to work for little or no compensation.

In the 1980s and 1990s, tens of millions of Chinese entered the private sector in the Special Economic Zones in southern cities or other urban areas, or found work in the semiprivate, small-scale township and village enterprises in the countryside. This released them from dependence on the *danwei*, or state work unit. However, for many urban dwellers the danwei continued to control everything from the right to change residence to permission to have a child. The economic reforms initiated since the late 1970s have also given workers more flexibility to relocate to areas of fast economic growth, which, combined with a shortage of jobs in rural areas, has contributed to a "floating population" of 80 million to 100 million migrants seeking work in the cities.

Colombia

Polity: Presidential-
parliamentary democracy
(insurgencies)
Economy: Capitalist-
statist
Population: 40,000,000
PPP: $6,006
Life Expectancy: 71
Ethnic Groups: Mestizo (58 percent), white (20 percent), mulatto (14 percent), black
(4 percent), other, including Indian (4 percent)
Capital: Bogota

Political Rights: 4
Civil Liberties: 4
Status: Partly Free

Overview:

Government control appeared to be eroding through much of
Colombia in 2000, as the Revolutionary Armed Forces of
Colombia (FARC), the country's main guerrilla group, went
through the motions of seeking a settlement of a civil war whose main casualty continued to be a conflict-weary public. Plan Colombia, the government's $7.5 billion pro-
gram to destroy coca (cocaine) and poppy (heroin) crops, which in turn would dry up
resources for illegal armed groups, appeared an uncertain bet to achieve either goal.
President Andrés Pastrana did achieve some success in severing notorious ties between
the armed forces and paramilitary death squads, whose members several times were
reported to have danced and drank as they executed their victims. However, the breadth
of collaboration seemed to suggest the greatest work at tie cutting yet lay ahead.

The guerrillas, who by some accounts now control more than half the national territory, kept up their armed offensives despite the ongoing talks and despite the growing
number of civilian casualties their actions have created. Colombia's most notorious
death squad leader admitted what has long been an open secret—not only do the
paramilitaries make big money from the drug trade (as do the guerrillas), but they are
also financed by local and foreign private enterprise. In a two-year period—1998 to
2000—the paramilitary forces have nearly doubled their numbers, even as the government has taken some steps to curb their might. One big loser in 2000 was the country's
national police force, whose personnel is highly exposed to guerrilla violence as a result of their being deployed around the country in undermanned and underprotected
commissaries. In March, a multimillion-dollar graft scandal in congress resulted in the
resignation of the speaker of the house and served to underscore the venality of much
of Colombia's traditional ruling elite. Meanwhile, Colombia's neighbors continued to
be alarmed at the spillover effects—assassinations, armed incursions and a flood of
refugees—of the worsening civil war.

Following independence from Spain in 1819, and after a long period of federal
government with what are now Venezuela, Ecuador, and Panama, the Republic of
Colombia was established in 1886. Politics have since been dominated by the Liberal
and Conservative parties, whose leadership has largely been drawn from the traditional
elite. Under President César Gaviria (1990-1994) of the Liberal Party, a new constitution was approved; it limits presidents to a single four-year term and provides for an

elected bicameral congress, with a 102-member senate and a 161-member chamber of representatives.

Modern Colombia has been marked by the corrupt machine politics of the Liberals and Conservatives; left-wing guerrilla insurgencies; right-wing paramilitary violence, the emergence of vicious drug cartels; and gross human rights violations committed by all sides.

In the 1994 legislative elections, the Liberals retained a majority in both houses of congress. Ernesto Samper, a former economic development minister, won the Liberal presidential nomination. The Conservative candidate was Pastrana, a former mayor of Bogotá and the son of a former Colombian president. Both candidates pledged to continue Gaviria's free-market reforms.

Samper won in a June 1994 runoff election, with 50.4 percent, besting Pastrana by 1.8 percent. With strong U.S. encouragement, Samper presided over the dismantling of the Cali drug cartel, most of whose leaders were captured in 1995. The arrests, however, netted persuasive evidence that the cartel had given $6 million to the president's campaign, with Samper's approval. In February 1996 the country's prosecutor-general formally charged Samper with illegal enrichment, fraud, falsifying documents, and covering up his campaign financing. In June the house, dominated by Samper's Liberals, voted 111 to 43 to clear Samper on grounds of insufficient evidence.

The murder of journalists and human rights workers, repeated humiliation of the military by leftist insurgents, a continued upswing in paramilitary violence linked to the military, and army claims of the subversive intent of unarmed groups dominated much of the news from Colombia in 1997. In the June 21, 1998, election, Pastrana won the presidency of Latin America's third most populous country in an impressive victory over the Liberal Party candidate, Interior Minister Horacio Serpa. In an effort to consolidate the peace process, in November Pastrana oversaw the regrouping by FARC guerrillas in, and the withdrawal by a dispirited military from, a so-called demilitarized zone of five southern districts. The move, strongly resisted by the military, gave the guerrillas de facto control over a territory the size of Switzerland.

In 1999, talks with the FARC sputtered along, burdened by the sweeping political, social, and economic reforms being demanded by the rebels, and by the government's inability to reign in the paramilitaries. They were also hampered by military reluctance to grant the FARC concessions beyond the de facto partitioning of the country. (Guerrilla groups now control some 40 percent of the national territory.) The governments of neighboring Panama, Ecuador, Venezuela, and Brazil also expressed concern about the deadly violence spilling over into their countries. Colombia resumed extradition of its nationals after a nine-year hiatus, handing over two top drug suspects to U.S. authorities.

In 2000, the FARC guerrillas appeared to be trying to consolidate their control of as much as 40 percent of the country, issuing laws and setting up judicial institutions, in a clear bid to negotiate with the government from a position of strength. In March, Standard & Poor's downgraded once-prosperous Colombia, making it more expensive for the government to raise foreign and domestic capital. In July police seized more than 3,270 pounds of pure cocaine with a street value of $53 million that was meant to bankroll the activities of top paramilitary chieftain Carlos Castaño. That same month, the attorney general charged four generals and a colonel—three of whom were still on active duty—with aiding paramilitaries who massacred 18 people in May 1998. A month later, after Colombia's chief prosecutor said he had a list of businessmen who financed the paramilitaries, Castaño acknowledged private enterprise support.

In August, President Bill Clinton traveled to Cartegena to show support for the beleaguered Pastrana, whose government was to receive $1.3 billion in aid approved by the U.S. Congress the month before. In the run-up to October municipal elections, critical of the government's antidrug and antiviolence strategies, both guerrillas and paramilitaries prevented citizens from registering to vote. Election Day turnout, however, was strong, with Independents winning mayoral races in four of Colombia's five largest cities—including Bogotá, the capital—in what was seen as a challenge to the dominance of the traditional Liberal and Conservative parties. In October, although under battlefield pressure from the guerrillas, the military purged 89 mostly lower-ranking officers and 299 rank-and-file soldiers, after Pastrana granted the armed forces the right to fire members for misconduct. In November, Castano admitted eight members of congress had been kidnapped as a way of protesting the government's "gradual handover" of the country to the guerrillas.

Political Rights and Civil Liberties:

Citizens can change their government through elections. The 1991 constitution provides for broader participation in the system, including two reserved seats in the congress for the country's small Indian minority. Political violence, and a generalized belief that corruption renders elections meaningless, have helped to limit voter participation, although an impressive 60 percent voted in the 1998 presidential contest. In 1998, Pastrana proposed a broad reform of the political system designed to combat corruption and promote greater public participation in decision making. He also offered the guerrillas a presidential pardon and guarantees for their post-peace participation in legal political activities. In 2000, hundreds of candidates for municipal office, a keystone to carrying out Colombia's antidrug program, were pressured for allegiance by contending armed groups, with 21 mayoral candidates murdered in the run-up to the vote. On the day of the vote, however, voter turnout was heavy amid peaceful conditions. In the period 1997 to 2000, 34 mayors have been assassinated and 100 others—10 percent of the total—were kidnapped.

According to the U.S. Central Intelligence Agency, Colombia produced 520 tons of cocaine in 1999, with illegal drug plantations increasing by 20 percent. The country has been ranked by Transparency International as one of the 20 most corrupt nations in the world. The March 2000 congressional graft scandal, which included $49,119 for a new toilet and $50,000 for toilet paper and soap, dealt a body blow to Pastrana's claim that his ruling coalition would clean up a hotbed of corruption that Colombians see as reflective of their country's moral decay.

The justice system remains slow and compromised by corruption and extortion. The civilian-led Ministry of Defense is responsible for internal security and oversees both the armed forces and the national police; civilian management of the armed forces, however, is limited. The country's national police force, once a focal point of official corruption, has been reorganized and is now Colombia's most respected security institution. In 2000 the FARC began to routinely execute policemen it captured after attacking police outposts; human rights monitors point out that many officers are not involved in the government's anti-guerrilla operations. In mid-July General Rosso José Serrano, the highly respected director of the national police who oversaw the sacking of 8,000 corrupt cops, stepped down from his post, saying that he could not face going to more policemen's funerals. Colombia's 165 prisons, which were built for 32,000 people but hold more than 47,000, are frequent sites of murders and riots.

Constitutional rights regarding free expression and the freedom to organize political parties, civic groups, and labor unions are severely restricted by political and drug-related violence and the government's inability to guarantee the security of its citizens. Colombia is one of the most violent countries in the world. In 1999 alone there were nearly 3,000 kidnappings—eight per day for political and nonpolitical purposes—as well as 25,000 murders that were unrelated to the rebel insurgency; in 2000, the number of those reported kidnapped rose seven percent, to 3,162. Political violence in Colombia continues to take more lives than in any other country in the western hemisphere, and civilians are prime victims. In the past decade an estimated 35,000 have died and about 1.5 million have been displaced from their homes, 308,000 in 1998 alone. More than 90 percent of violent crimes go unsolved. The paramilitaries, who in March 2000 began a "charm offensive" designed to make them appear respectable, are believed to have committed about 61 percent of all rights violations during the period September 1998 to March 2000. In November 2000, paramilitary forces massacred 37 fisherman in a village in northern Colombia. During the year, dozens of children have been killed by the guerrillas, the paramilitaries, or the army.

Human rights violations have soared to unprecedented highs, with atrocities being committed by all sides in the conflict. Human rights workers in Colombia are frequently murdered by an underfunded military often lacking in personal and tactical discipline, and by rightist paramilitary forces. The growth of the paramilitary groups, in the pay of narcotics traffickers and large landowners and protected by a military which shares a common enemy—the guerrillas—is out of control. Athough since taking office Pastrana has sacked four generals accused of paramilitary ties, government efforts to sever ties to the right-wing militia remain tepid, and these groups operate freely at the local level. In May 1999, police shut down a huge paramilitary drug laboratory. Left-wing guerrillas, some of whom also protect narcotics production facilities and drug traffickers, also systematically violate human rights, with victims including Sunday churchgoers and airline passengers. The FARC guerrillas also regularly extort payments from hundreds of businessmen throughout the country. In March 2000 seven top military commanders were cashiered for collaborating with rightist paramilitary groups, and more than a dozen paramilitaries have been killed by government forces. However, in 2000 Human Rights Watch has credibly reported that in half of Colombia's 18 army brigades, the military shared intelligence with the paramilitary forces, while providing them with weapons and coordinating with them on a daily basis. All sides operate with a high degree of impunity.

Journalists are frequently the victims of political and revenge violence. In 2000, 11 reporters were killed; in 1999, 6 were murdered and at least 13 fled the country after receiving death threats. More than 120 journalists have been murdered in the past decade, and many were killed for reporting on drug trafficking and corruption. Another category of killings is known as "social cleansing"—the elimination of drug addicts, street children, and other marginal citizens by vigilante groups often linked to police.

There are approximately 80 distinct ethnic groups among Colombia's 800,000-plus indigenous inhabitants. These Native Americans are frequently the targets of violence despite their seeking to remain neutral in the armed conflict. In 1999, FARC guerrillas kidnapped three U.S. Native American-rights activists and killed them. Indian claims to land and resources are under challenge from government ministries and multinational corporations. In 2000, members of the U'wa tribe were violently repressed by the police as they protested a U.S. oil company's plans to drill on lands the tribe considered sacred. In September, heavily armed gunmen—believed to be paramilitaries—murdered four members of the Embera-Katio indigenous communities. The attack came after an April 2000 agreement that the government would grant the Embera lands to replace those flooded by a dam project, as well as protect them from paramilitary violence.

The murder of trade union activists continued, as Colombia remained the most dangerous country in the world for organized labor. More than 2,500 trade union activists and leaders have been killed in little more than a decade. Labor leaders are targets of attacks by paramilitary groups, guerrillas, narcotics traffickers, and other union rivals. According to the United Nations, some 948,000 Colombian children under the age of 14 work in "unacceptable" conditions.

↓ Comoros

Polity: Presidential (military-dominated)
Economy: Capitalist
Population: 600,000
PPP: $1,398
Life Expectancy: 59
Ethnic Groups: Antalote, Cafre, Makoa, Oimatsaha, Sakalava
Capital: Moroni

Political Rights: 6
Civil Liberties: 4
Status: Partly Free

Trend Arrow: Comoros received a downward trend arrow because of the failure of the regime on Grande Comore to restore democratic rule and guarantees of human rights after seizing power in 1999, and persistent repression on the island of Anjouan.

Overview: A reconciliation deal was signed in August 2000 between the military government of Colonel Azali Assoumani, on the main island of Grande Comore, and separatists on the island of Anjouan. The Organization of African Unity (OAU) and the Comorian opposition rejected the "Fomboni Declaration" as a gimmick by both military regimes to retain power and said the deal would undermine the unity and territorial integrity of the Comoros. Neither regime has international recognition.

Two mercenary invasions and at least 18 other coups and attempted coups have shaken Comoros since independence in 1975. In 1990, in the country's first contested elections, Supreme Court Justice Said Mohamed Djohara won a six-year term as president. A September 1995 attempted coup by elements of the Comoros security forces, who were aided by foreign mercenaries, was reversed by French soldiers. An interim government ruled for five months until President Mohamed Taki Abdoulkarim was elected in 1996 in internationally monitored elections that were considered free and fair. Tadjidine Ben Said Massonde became the interim ruler when Taki died suddenly in November 1998. Azali seized power in April the following year.

Comoros comprises three islands – Grande Comore, Anjouan, and Mohéli. Anjouan voted for self-determination in a 1997 referendum, repulsed an attempted invasion by the government, and then dissolved into violence as rival separatist groups took up arms against each other. Separatists on Mohéli have also declared independence, but appear more willing to compromise. Mayotte Island, the fourth island of the Comorian archipelago, voted to remain a French overseas territory in a 1974 referendum and today enjoys a far higher, French-subsidized standard of living.

The OAU stands by the April 1999 Antananarivo agreement, which gives greater autonomy to the islands of Anjouan and Mohéli, and provides for a rotating presidency. The Azali regime in August adopted a transitional charter in a meeting that was boycotted by the opposition. The charter would restore constitutional rule and give separate power to the presidency, the judiciary, and parliament. There was no provision for the holding of free and fair elections. Azali had pledged to leave power by April 2000.

The human rights situation in Comoros has not improved since Azali seized power in 1999. Christians and some opposition figures were subjected to threats and harassment. Security forces in the capital, Moroni, broke up a demonstration in October against military rule, and raided homes and mosques. About 20 people were arrested. Political repression on Anjouan remained severe.

Political Rights and Civil Liberties: Comorians are no longer constitutionally guaranteed the right to change their government. The head of state has legislative power, organized through ordinances, and executive power, exercised through decrees.

Comorians exercised their constitutional right to change their government democratically in open elections for the first time in the 1996 parliamentary and presidential elections. Taki won the presidency in a runoff election with more than 60 percent of the vote. The conservative Islamic main opposition party held several seats in the national assembly. Anjouan held its own legislative elections in August 1999. Secessionists won an overwhelming majority in voting that was marked by some intimidation and a low turnout.

Freedoms of expression and association are not guaranteed. The semiofficial weekly *Al-Watwan* and several private newspapers sharply critical of the government are published in the capital, but they appear only sporadically because of limited resources. All are believed to exercise extensive self-censorship. A few private television and radio stations, such as Radio Tropique, operate without overt governmental interference. Transmissions from French-controlled Mayotte are easily received, and some people have access to satellite and other international broadcasting. Foreign publications are readily available.

The Comorian legal system is based on *Sharia* (Islamic law) and remnants of the French legal code and is subject to influence by the executive and other elites. The largely independent judiciary is headed by a supreme court. Most minor disputes are settled by village elders or a civilian court of first instance.

There were reports arbitrary arrest and detention in 2000. Rights abuses on Anjouan escalated in 2000 with the arrest in September of up to 100 opposition supporters who protested the Fomboni agreement. Harsh prison conditions are marked by severe overcrowding and the lack of adequate sanitation facilities, medical attention, and proper diet.

Islam is the official state religion. Non-Muslims are legally permitted to practice, but there were reports of restrictions and detentions. Detainees are sometimes subjected to attempts to convert them to Islam. Christians are not allowed to proselytize.

Unions have the right to bargain and strike, but collective bargaining is rare in the country's small formal sector. Comorians are among the world's poorest people, and the ongoing secessionist crisis has further damaged an already tenuous, agriculture-based economy. Remittances from the large overseas Comorian community sustain many families. The country relies heavily on foreign aid and earns a small amount through exports of vanilla, ylang-ylang, and cloves.

Women possess constitutional protections despite the influence of Islamic law. In practice, however, they enjoy little political or economic power and have far fewer opportunities for education or salaried employment. One woman holds a cabinet position. Economic hardship has forced more and more young girls, known as *mpambe*, into domestic servitude. They receive room and board, but little or no pay. The regime has taken no action to protect or promote child welfare.

Congo, Republic of (Brazzaville)

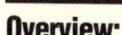

Polity: Military (post-conflict)
Economy: Mixed statist
Population: 2,800,000
PPP: $995
Life Expectancy: 49
Ethnic Groups: Kongo (48 percent), Sangha (20 percent), Teke (17 percent), M'Bochi (12 percent), others (3 percent)
Capital: Brazzaville

Political Rights: 6
Civil Liberties: 4*
Status: Partly Free

Ratings Change: Congo-Brazzaville's civil liberties rating changed from 5 to 4, and its status from Not Free to Partly Free, as a result of further consolidation of peace and an easing of repression since peace agreements were signed at the end of 1999.

Overview:

Military ruler Denis Sassou-Nguesso called for an "all-embracing dialogue" on the country's future and said election dates would be announced in March 2001. Gabonese President Omar Bongo, who is acting as mediator, said such a dialogue could include the country's main exiled political leaders: former President Pascal Lissouba and Prime Minister Bernard Kolelas. Kolelas said he was encouraged by the proposal, but the lack of a venue for such a dialogue, and the government's ambivalent commitment to it, remain stumbling blocks.

A decade after its independence from France, a 1970 coup established a Marxist state in Congo. In 1979, General Sassou-Nguesso seized power and maintained one-party rule as head of the Congolese Workers' Party. Domestic and international pressure forced his acceptance of a national conference leading to open, multiparty elections in 1992. Lissouba, of the Pan-African Union for Social Democracy, won a clear victory over Kolelas, of the Congolese Party for Genuine Democracy and Development, in a second-round presidential runoff that excluded Sassou-Nguesso, who had run third in the first round.

Disputes over 1993 legislative polls led to armed conflict. The fighting subsided but flared once again among ethnic-based militias in 1997. Sassou-Nguesso had built a private army in his native northern Congo and forcibly retook the presidency in October that year. Peace agreements signed in late 1999 between Sassou-Nguesso and a number of senior rebel leaders were seen by many observers as a stopgap approach to ending the war because the accords did not include Lissouba and Kolelas. The peace led to a halt in the fighting and included an amnesty for combatants who voluntarily disarmed. Sassou-Nguesso has had military support from Angola and political backing from France. Civil wars in the neighboring Democratic Republic of Congo and nearby Angola made large numbers of weapons and fighters available to fuel the conflict.

Mistrust lingers and a number of fighters remain armed. Security, however, has improved markedly throughout the country. About 600,000 of 810,000 internally displaced persons have returned to their homes. There were fewer reports of human rights abuses in 2000 than in previous years, although arbitrary arrests continued. Steps were made toward further liberalization of the press.

The country's economically important train linking Brazzaville with the southern oil city of Point-Noire became operational again in August 2000. The International Monetary Fund in November approved a credit worth U.S.$14 million for postconflict reconstruction. Economic growth has been forecast.

Political Rights and Civil Liberties: Congolese have not had the right to change their leaders through elections since civil war broke out in 1997. They elected their president and national assembly deputies to five-year terms of office through competitive multiparty elections for the first time in 1992 and 1993, respectively. Lissouba's 1992 victory at the polls was widely considered to be free and fair. Presidential polls set for July 1997 were preempted by the war that returned Sassou-Nguesso to power. Sassou-Nguesso, who received only 17 percent of the vote in the 1992 presidential elections, has promised to conduct open, multiparty elections in 2001. But sharp ethnic divisions among the country's nearly three million people can be expected to produce electoral results similar to those in 1992, when voting along ethnic lines gave Sassou-Nguesso little support outside his minority ethnic base in the north.

Legislative elections in 1992 produced no clear majority. After an anti-Lissouba coalition formed, the president dissolved the assembly and called for fresh polls. Legislative polls in 1993 produced a presidential majority, but were marred by numerous irregularities. Several parties boycotted the second round.

Sassou-Nguesso appointed a 75-member transitional assembly, the National Transition Council, in 1997, but it does not have a broad political base and exercises no real power. Sassou-Nguesso replaced the 1992 constitution with the Fundamental Act, which established a highly centralized presidential system of government. A new constitution has been drafted and is expected to be put to referendum in 2001. Most of the country's dozens of political parties are formed along ethnic lines.

The government generally respects press freedom, but continues to monopolize the broadcast media. However, broadcasts from neighboring countries are widely heard. The government, in 2000, approved a freedom-of-information bill, which confirmed the abolition of censorship and sharply reduced penalties for defamation. A 1996 law that imposed registration requirements and severe penalties for slander and defamation, however, remains in effect. About 10 private newspapers appear weekly in Brazzaville, and these sometimes print articles or letters that are unflattering to the government.

Freedom of assembly and association is constitutionally guaranteed, and this right is generally respected in practice. Fear of abuses by security forces prevents public demonstrations. Members of security forces or other armed groups manning checkpoints or roadblocks commonly extort bribes from travelers, and rights abuses such as beatings and rapes are reported.

There have been numerous and persistent reports of atrocities against civilians committed by both sides in the conflict. Victims described persecution by soldiers and militia members who have not disarmed. Violations included arbitrary detentions, beatings, and rapes. A United Nations report in November 1999 said that tens of thousands of women had been raped during the war and a whole generation of youth had resorted to a life of plunder and extortion. Most of the president's soldiers are from northern ethnic groups, which exacerbates tensions between northerners and southerners.

Scarce resources and understaffing create a backlog of court cases and long periods of pretrial detention. The judiciary is subject to corruption and political influence. The three-tier formal court system of local courts, courts of appeals, and the supreme court was generally considered to be politically independent until the civil war. In rural areas, traditional courts retain broad jurisdiction, especially in civil matters. In September 1999, authorities set up two military tribunals to try soldiers accused of committing atrocities.

Prison conditions are life threatening, with reports of beatings, overcrowding, and other ill-treatment. Local human rights groups, however, as well as the ICRC, have been allowed access. Nongovernmental organizations (NGOs) generally operate freely. Religious freedom is respected in law and practice. Pygmy groups suffer discrimination, and many are effectively held in lifetime servitude through customary ties to Bantu "patrons."

Workers' rights to join trade unions and to strike are legally protected. Collective bargaining is practiced freely. Unions are legally required to accept nonbinding arbitration before striking, but many strikes have proceeded without adherence to this process. Most workers in the formal (wage) sector are union members, and unions have made efforts to organize informal sectors such as those of agricultural and retail trade.

There is extensive legal and societal discrimination against women despite constitutional protections. Access to education and employment opportunities, especially in the countryside, are limited, and civil codes regarding family and marriage formalize women's inferior status. Polygyny is legal, while polyandry is not. Violence against women reportedly is widespread. NGOs have drawn attention to this issue and provided counseling and assistance to victims.

Congo, Democratic Republic of (Kinshasa)

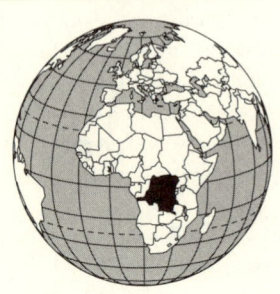

Polity: Presidential (military-dominated) (insurgencies)
Economy: Capitalist- statist
Population: 52,000,000
PPP: $822
Life Expectancy: 51
Ethnic Groups: More than 200 ethnicities, mostly Bantu
Capital: Kinshasa

Political Rights: 7
Civil Liberties: 6
Status: Not Free

Overview:

Little real progress has been made on the ground in implementing the Lusaka peace agreement that was signed in August 1999 to end the civil war in the Democratic Republic of Congo. In August, President Laurent Kabila closed the Kinshasa office of former Botswanan President Ketumile Masire, the chief peace negotiator, and said he wanted the whole Lusaka agreement renegotiated. Kabila appeared no more flexible in negotiating peace towards the end of the year despite a number of military setbacks. The United Nations has authorized the deployment of 5,000 peacekeepers in addition to the 500 UN civilian and military personnel who remain on standby. The Lusaka accord provides for a UN-monitored ceasefire, which both sides have violated, and a dialogue that would bring together community and national leaders to decide the country's future. Kabila installed a new parliament in August, calling it a true representation of the people, but it is no more representative than any of the other assemblies before it.

As the Belgian Congo, the vast area of central Africa that is today the Democratic Republic of Congo, was exploited with a brutality that was notable even by colonial standards. The country was a center for cold-war rivalries from Belgium's withdrawal in 1960 until well after Colonel Joseph Désiré Mobutu came to power with Central Intelligence Agency backing in 1964. The pro-Western Mobutu was forgiven for the severe repression and financial excesses that made him one of the world's richest men and his countrymen among the world's poorest people. Domestic agitation for democratization forced Mobutu to open up the political process in 1990. In 1992, his Popular Revolutionary Movement, the sole legal party after 1965, and the Sacred Union of the Radical Opposition and Allied Civil Society, a coalition of 200 groups, joined scores of others in a national conference to establish a High Council of the Republic to oversee a democratic transition. Mobutu manipulated and delayed the transition, but civil society grew stronger and the press became freer. Kabila has begun to reverse these advances.

A longtime guerrilla fighter, Kabila came to power in May 1997 after a seven-month advance backed by Rwanda and Uganda across the country, which was then known as Zaire. He easily tapped into popular hatred for Mobutu, who fled to Morocco and died of cancer shortly after Kabila's takeover. Many of Mobutu's former supporters are now allied with the rebels. The new war erupted in late 1998 after Kabila fell out with the Rwandan and Zairian Tutsi who helped him to seize power. Kabila now mainly relies on a narrow base of backers who share his Katangan ethnicity.

Serious human rights abuses against civilians continue to be perpetrated by both government and rebel forces. Opposition supporters, journalists, and human rights workers are routinely arrested and harassed, and public demonstrations are forbidden. Arbitrary detentions, unfair trials by a military court, rapes, and extrajudicial executions are also reported.

The war has drawn forces from at least eight countries into the fighting, including Zimbabwe, Angola, Namibia, Chad, and Sudan on the side of Kabila, and Uganda, Rwanda, and Burundi on the part of the rebels. (Neither Sudan nor Burundi has admitted its involvement.) Former Rwandan militia, former Rwandan armed forces members, and Mai-Mai guerrillas have also joined in repelling the rebel attack.

There are three main rebel groups seeking to oust Kabila: the Movement for the Liberation of Congo and two factions of the Congolese Rally for Democracy (RCD). Splits in the rebel ranks and disagreements between their backers, Uganda and Rwanda, have hindered both peace efforts and their military endeavor. Fighting between Ugandan and Rwandan forces in the northern city of Kisangani in June claimed the lives of more than 700 civilians.

Bartering and the black market have largely replaced the formal economy. Most of the country's approximately 48 million people live marginal lives as subsistence farmers despite vast resources of timber, diamonds, copper, and other minerals. A UN-appointed panel is investigating illegal extraction of the country's resources. Kabila has lost some of his access to diamonds because rebels control much of the country's eastern resource-rich areas.

Political Rights and Civil Liberties:

The people of the Democratic Republic of Congo have never been permitted to choose or change their government through democratic and peaceful means. President Kabila rules by decree. There are no elected representatives in the entire country, despite Kabila's promise to hold polls by April 1999. He replaced his own Alliance of the Democratic Forces for the Liberation of Congo with Libyan-inspired Popular People's Committees. In theory, they are supposed to be elected by local residents and exercise local government powers throughout the country, but in practice they monitor the activities of the Congolese. Mobutu's successive unopposed presidential victories and legislative polls were little more than political theater. Infrastructure and institutions to support a free and fair election are almost entirely absent.

At least 400 political parties registered after their 1990 legalization, but they were later banned under Kabila when he took power. Although he eased restrictions with a new law in January 1999, political activity remains harshly suppressed and opposition members are routinely harassed and detained. The 1999 law gives broad powers to the ministry of the interior to suspend or disband parties "in the event of violation of the law and emergency or the risk of serious public disorder." Rebel groups in the east tolerated no level of nonviolent political opposition, using intimidation, detention, and travel restriction.

A decree provides for independence of the judiciary, but in practice it is subject to corruption and manipulation. The president may dismiss magistrates at will. Courts are grossly ineffective in protecting constitutional rights, and security forces and government officials generally act with impunity. The civil judiciary is largely dysfunctional. A Court of Military Order, which was initially created in 1997 to restore military discipline, increasingly delivers harsh sentences to civilians on questionable security and political convictions. Kabila appoints the country's judges. Defendants have no automatic right of appeal to a higher court, and many lack counsel. The military court ordered the execution of 250 people in the first two years of its existence. Human Rights Watch in February accused Congo of violating its promise to the UN not to carry out the death penalty on convicted criminals. Long periods of pretrial detention are common in prisons in which poor diet and medical care can be life threatening.

Serious human rights abuses by Kabila's armed forces and rebel soldiers continue unabated. Violations include extrajudicial executions, torture, rapes, beatings, and arbitrary detentions. Ethnic killings by both government and rebel forces have been reported. Numerous nongovernmental organizations (NGOs), including human rights groups, operate despite intimidation and arrest. At least 13 representatives of NGOs were detained in South Kivu in October. Almost all of them were tortured before they were released the same day.

The government uses the war as a pretext for repression. Amnesty International in May said both sides in the conflict had unlawfully killed thousands of unarmed civilians and subjected many others to torture, rape, and other forms of cruel, inhuman, and degrading treatment. It also said many people have "disappeared." Several hundred thousand civilians have fled to neighboring countries or have become internally displaced. Amnesty also said in December that 50 suspected political opponents of the Kabila government were being held incommunicado in government-controlled areas of the country. The rights group said the detainees, most of whom were from the Kivu regions, would likely face the death penalty.

Freedom of expression and freedom of assembly are sharply limited by decree. Statutes provide for freedom of the press, but the government continued to sharply restrict the work of journalists. Church radio networks are growing, but the state-controlled broadcasting network reaches the largest numbers of citizens.

A number of independent newspapers are published in Kinshasa, but they are not widely circulated beyond the city. Independent journalists are frequently threatened, arrested, or attacked, which prompts self-censorship. Common accusations include "relaying intelligence to the enemy," "discouraging the population of soldiers," and "divulging state secrets or defense secrets." When a targeted journalist cannot be found, editors, other journalists, visitors to the newspaper offices, or family members can be taken hostage.

Human Rights Watch in September called on the government to immediately release five jailed journalists and to reverse a ban on ten private and church-owned radio and television stations imposed earlier in the month. The Court of Military Order found four of the journalists guilty of "high treason" and "publication of articles hostile to the government." Another journalist, Freddy Loseke Lisumbu la Yayenga, editor of *La Libre Afrique*, is reported to be seriously ill and requires immediate medical attention. He was sentenced in May 2000 to three years' imprisonment. The communications ministry in October replaced the management of four of the ten banned private radio and television stations with former associates of the communications minister and broadcasts resumed.

Human Rights Watch also called on the rebel RCD in the east to release a freelance photographer, who was detained in August, and reopen a radio station, Radio Mandaeleo, owned and operated by civil society organizations. The Kinshasa-based Journalists in

Danger said in October that more than 100 journalists had been detained for long periods since Kabila came to power in 1997. It said "the press has practically ceased to exist" in rebel-held areas of the country.

Freedom of religion is respected in practice, although religious groups must register with the government to be recognized. Despite constitutional protections, women face de facto discrimination, especially in rural areas. They also enjoy fewer employment and educational opportunities and often do not receive equal pay for equal work. Violence against women has soared since the onset of armed conflict in 1996.

More than 100 new independent unions registered after the end of one-party rule in 1990. Previously, all unions had to affiliate themselves with a confederation that was part of the ruling party. There is little union activity, owing to the breakdown of the country's formal economy. Civil servants who work in public institutions that have largely ceased to function are often owed months of salary arrears.

Costa Rica

Polity: Presidential-parliamentary democracy
Political Rights: 1
Civil Liberties: 2
Economy: Capitalist-statist
Status: Free
Population: 3,600,000
PPP: $5,987
Life Expectancy: 76
Ethnic Groups: White and mestizo (96 percent), black (2 percent), Indian (1 percent), Chinese (1 percent)
Capital: San José

Overview: Costa Rica's constitutional court rejected Nobel laureate and former President Oscar Arias Sánchez's attempt to run for the office again in February 2002 by refusing in September of 2000 to declare unconstitutional the country's prohibition on additional presidential terms. The move put to an end Arias's attempt to reassume the office he held when he was awarded. Previously Arias had won 88 percent of the vote in a nonbonding, privately organized and financed poll in which Costa Ricans were asked if they would support ending a ban on second terms for presidents. The court decision left Arias supporters scrambling to find a figure who could push forward free-market reforms they say are necessary for Costa Rica to compete in a globalized economy.

The Republic of Costa Rica achieved independence from Spain in 1821 and became a republic in 1848. Democratic government was instituted in 1899 and briefly interrupted in 1917 and again in 1948, when the country was torn by a brief but brutal civil war. The 1949 constitution, which bans the formation of a national army, has proved to be the most durable in Latin America.

The social democratic National Liberation Party (PLN), was the dominant party for nearly three decades. In the 1994 elections, José Maria Figueres narrowly defeated Rodriguez, a conservative congressman and respected economist, of the Social Christian Party (PUSC), the country's other principal political organization. Figueres, son of the legendary former president José "Pepe" Figueres, campaigned against the neoliberal economic policies of the outgoing president, Rafael A. Calderon, Jr., of the PUSC. Miguel Angel Rodriguez proposed to deepen structural reforms.

The country's economic woes result in part from a vast reduction in levels of foreign aid and international lending from governments that had been eager to keep Communists at bay. Despite his earlier campaign pledges, Figueres's last two years in office were characterized by some of the free-market policies championed by his opponent in the presidential elections.

In the February 1, 1998, presidential contest, Rodriguez returned as the PSUC's standard-bearer and bested, with 47 percent of the vote, the anticorruption maverick crusader José Miguel Corrales of the PLN, a former congressman and soccer star. The PSUC, however, failed to win a working majority in the unicameral national assembly and was forced to make an alliance with smaller parties to sustain its legislative program.

Despite a booming economy, Rodriguez appears to have had problems winning public approval for his government. Public safety remains a primary concern of the residents of the capital, San José. A much-touted 1999 reform of the Costa Rican legislature ended up creating more controversy than real change. Support for the 58-year-old Arias's potential candidacy signaled the degree to which Costa Ricans, who have a tradition of participation in electoral politics, are growing dissatisfied with the two traditional parties.

Political Rights and Civil Liberties: Costa Ricans can change their government democratically. The 1998 victory of presidential candidate Rodriguez reflected the fact that the PLN and PSUC dominate the political landscape, although numerous other parties exist. Allegations about drug-tainted campaign contributions continue to dog both major parties. New campaign laws have been instituted to make party financing more transparent.

The 1949 constitution provided for three independent branches of government and abolished the military. The president and the 57-member legislative assembly are elected for four years and are prohibited from seeking a second term. The assembly has power equal to that of the president, including the ability to override presidential vetoes.

The judicial branch is independent, its members elected by the legislature. A supreme court with power to rule on the constitutionality of laws is in operation, as are four courts of appeals and a network of district courts. An independent national election commission is chosen by the supreme court. Delays in the justice system, particularly the slow pace in processing criminal cases, in part due to budget cuts, have created volatile situations in overcrowded, violence-prone prisons. There are some 5,300 prisoners in Costa Rica jammed into facilities designed to hold less than half that number. Illegal narcotics are widely available in the prisons, and drug abuse there is common.

The police have a tradition of being highly politicized, with a large portion owing their appointments to political sponsors. However, the Rodriguez administration moved forward with implementation of a 1994 police code designed to depoliticize and professionalize the force in order to create a permanent career path within the institution. Numerous charges of human rights violations by the heavily armed police are still made. Independent Costa Rican human rights monitors report increases in allegations of arbitrary arrest and brutality.

A rise in violent crime and clashes in rural areas between squatters and landowners are blamed on a large immigrant population. An estimated 420,000 Nicaraguans—15 percent of Costa Rica's total population—live in the country, more than half illegally. In the aftermath of Hurricane Mitch in 1998, Costa Rica declared a temporary amnesty for these and other illegal Central American immigrants, and some 160,000 Nicaraguans took advantage of the opportunity to legalize their situation. In 1999, the legislative assembly passed legislation allowing for U.S. antidrug patrols to operate in Costa Rican waters. The measure was approved a year after Costa Rica instituted a tough anti-money-laundering law.

An official ombudsman provides recourse for citizens or foreigners with human rights complaints. The ombudsman has the authority to issue recommendations for rectification, including sanctions against government bodies, for failure to respect rights. The press, radio, and television are generally free. Six major privately owned dailies serve a society that is 90 percent literate. Television and radio stations are both public and commercial, with at least six private television stations providing an influential forum for public debate. However, restrictive libel laws continue to dampen full exercise of press freedoms.

Constitutional guarantees regarding freedom of religion and the right to organize political parties and civic organizations are respected. In recent years, however, a reluctance to address restrictions on labor rights has been noticeable.

Solidarity, an employer-employee organization that private business uses as an instrument to prevent independent unions from organizing, remains strong and has generally been tolerated by successive governments. Solidarity remains entrenched in Costa Rica's free-trade zones, where labor abuses by multinational corporations are rife. Minimum wage and social security laws are often ignored, and fines for noncompliance are minuscule. In 1999, the Costa Rican affiliate of the International Confederation of Free Trade Unions brought a complaint before the International Labor Organization concerning an attack and death threats against a banana workers' leader. Woman workers are often sexually harassed, made to work overtime without pay, and fired when they become pregnant.

Costa Rica's Indian population, numbering 64,000, or two percent of the national total, have demanded the right to self-government and ownership of their traditional lands.

In 1999, the legislative assembly passed a law criminalizing sex with minors, in an attempt to crack down on the country's growing sex-tourism industry. Violence against women and children is a problem, although the government has shown concrete support for programs and policies to combat it.

Côte D'Ivoire

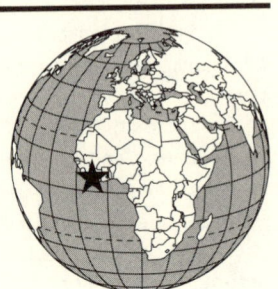

Polity: Presidential-parliamentary
Economy: Capitalist
Population: 16,000,000
PPP: $1,598
Life Expectancy: 47
Ethnic Groups: Baoule (23 percent), Bete (18 percent), Senoufou (15 percent), Malinke (11 percent), Agni, foreign Africans, non-Africans (33 percent)
Capital: Yamoussoukro (official); Abidjan (de facto)

Political Rights: 6
Civil Liberties: 5*
Status: Partly Free

Ratings Change: Cote d'Ivoire's civil liberties rating changed from 4 to 5 because of a crack-down on political opposition members after military ruler General Robert Gueï was swept from power after trying to annul the results of October elections which he had manipulated. Another crackdown on the opposition preceded parliamentary elections in December.

Overview: Political violence wracked Côte d'Ivoire following presidential elections in October and preceding legislative elections in December. General Robert Gueï, who had seized power from President Henri Konan Bédié in December 1999, pledged he would step down if he lost the election in October. However, when initial results showed he was losing, he sacked the electoral commission, detained its officers, and declared himself the winner. Tens of thousands of people took to the streets in a popular uprising that toppled him from power.

Côte d'Ivoire gained independence from France in 1960, and President Félix Houphouët-Boigny ruled until his death in 1993. Bédié assumed power and won fraudulent elections in 1995. Tension had been escalating in the lead-up to the presidential polls in October 2000, and General Gueï took the opportunity to seize power after days of army rioting in the commercial capital of Abidjan in December 1999. Côte d'Ivoire retains strong political, economic, and military backing from France, which maintains a military garrison near Abidjan, and French military advisors serve with many units of Côte d'Ivoire's 14,000-strong armed forces.

During the Houphouët-Boigny period, Côte d'Ivoire became an African model for economic growth and political stability. Increasing political and social unrest is a threat to further investment. Also hurting the economy has been a plunge in the world price of cocoa, Côte d'Ivoire's chief export.

Clashes erupted between supporters of Alassane Ouattara of the Republican Rally (RDR) and Laurent Gbagbo of the Ivorian Popular Front (FPI) in 2000. The supreme court had excluded Ouattara from the presidential poll, saying he could not sufficiently prove that he was genuinely Ivorian. His supporters denounced the election and called for a new vote. Gbagbo, supported by the national police, or gendarmes, refused to call for new polls. More than 150 people were killed in the violence, which mainly claimed the lives of Ouattara supporters, most of whom are northern Muslims or from the Diola ethnic group. Similar clashes broke out preceding the legislative election in December, which Ouattara was also barred from contesting. Divisions along political, ethnic, and religious lines have deepened and could lead to further violence. The military is divided, and Gueï, who still commands the loyalty of some troops, remains a potential threat.

Political Rights and Civil Liberties:

The people of Côte d'Ivoire have only partially been able to carry out their constitutional right to freely and fairly elect their leaders. President Bédié was declared president with 95 percent of the vote in a 1995 presidential election that was neither free nor fair. Alassane Ouattara, the opposition's most formidable candidate, was barred from the contest. The 1995 presidential poll was boycotted by all of the major opposition parties. Demonstrations were banned, and the media were intimidated. Voting in the October 2000 presidential election appeared to be carried out fairly, but only 5 of 19 potential candidates were allowed to contest the vote. Gbagbo was eventually declared the winner with 59.4 percent, compared with 32.7 percent for Gueï.

Gbagbo's FPI won 96 of the 196 seats in the December 2000 legislative elections, while 77 went to the Democratic Party of Côte d'Ivoire (PDCI). Independents won 16 seats, and four parties shared the remaining 7. Only 33 percent of the electorate voted. The PDCI, which ruled the country from independence until the December 1999 coup, had held 147 of the 175 seats in the previous parliament, whose membership was increased in 2000 from 175 to 225. The FPI had 13 seats. The RDR boycotted the polls. Elections were not held in most constituencies in the north because of unrest that followed the supreme court's ruling that also barred Ouattara from the legislative election. Voting was to take place in January 2001 in those constituencies.

Côte d'Ivoire does not have an independent judiciary. Judges are political appointees without tenure and are highly susceptible to external interference. In many rural areas, traditional courts still prevail, especially in the handling of minor matters and family law. Many deaths from diseases aggravated by poor diets and inadequate or nonexistent medical attention have been reported in the country's prisons. A large portion of inmates are pretrial detainees who sometimes wait for years for a court date.

Respect for human rights in Côte d'Ivoire deteriorated considerably during the year. Human Rights Watch reported that more than 150 people were killed in post-election violence and hundreds of others were wounded, detained, or tortured, or disappeared. The violations were carried out by members of the local police and gendarmes, as well as civilians. In one incident, the bodies of 57 people were discovered in a field outside Abidjan. The Gbagbo government allowed international investigators to probe reports of rights violations.

State-owned newspapers and a state-run broadcasting system are usually unreservedly pro-government. Several private radio stations and a cable television service operate, but only the state broadcasting system reaches a national audience. Press freedom suffered considerably during the year, with the harassment, beating, and detention of journalists. In February, soldiers raided the offices of the independent *Le Jeune Democrate* and *Le National*. Soldiers raided *Le National* again in March and threatened some journalists with death. In April, Jules Toualy, a reporter with *Le Jeune Democrate*, was detained by soldiers and tortured, according the international Committee to Protect Journalists. Soldiers detained and beat Joachim Beugré of the private daily *Le Jour* in September. He and his publisher were reportedly interrogated by Gueï, who pressed them to reveal their sources for an article about his parentage.

Côte d'Ivoire's economy has long attracted workers from neighboring countries. Immigrants constitute up to 40 percent of the total population, and resentment towards them exploded into violence following the October presidential election. Members of the northern Diola ethnic group were targeted along with foreigners. Thousands of migrants from Burkina Faso, Mali, and other countries fled Côte d'Ivoire in the lead-up to the voting. Clashes between indigenous groups and migrants from Burkina Faso over land in the southwest have claimed several lives in recent years.

Religious freedom is guaranteed but is not respected in practice. Muslims and mosques were targeted in the October violence. Churches were attacked in retaliation. Muslims, who are predominantly from the north, were seen as siding with foreign migrants and the opposition RDR. The country's Muslim community itself is divided.

Women suffer widespread discrimination, despite official encouragement for respect for constitutional rights. Women were reportedly beaten and sexually humiliated by the local police and gendarmes in post-election violence. Equal pay for equal work is offered in the small formal sector, but women have few chances to obtain, or advance in, wage employment. In rural areas that rely on subsistence agriculture, education and job opportunities for women are even scarcer. Female genital mutilation is still practiced, although a law that made it a crime was adopted in 1998. Violence against women is reportedly common.

Authorities have sometimes taken harsh action against strikers, although union formation and membership are legally protected. The Federation of Autonomous Trade Unions of Côte d'Ivoire represents several independent unions formed since 1991. Notification and conciliation requirements must be met before legal strikes can be conducted. Collective bargaining agreements are often reached with the participation of government negotiators who influence wage settlements.

Croatia

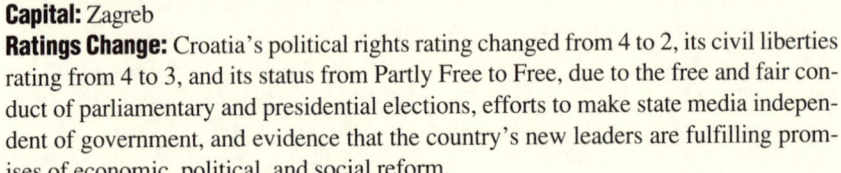

Polity: Parliamentary democracy
Economy: Mixed capitalist
Population: 4,600,000
PPP: $6,749
Life Expectancy: 73
Ethnic Groups: Croatian (78 percent), Serbian (12 percent), Muslim (1 percent), other (9 percent)
Capital: Zagreb

Political Rights: 2*
Civil Liberties: 3*
Status: Free

Ratings Change: Croatia's political rights rating changed from 4 to 2, its civil liberties rating from 4 to 3, and its status from Partly Free to Free, due to the free and fair conduct of parliamentary and presidential elections, efforts to make state media independent of government, and evidence that the country's new leaders are fulfilling promises of economic, political, and social reform.

Overview: The ruling Croatian Democratic Union (HDZ) suffered defeat in parliamentary and presidential elections early in 2000.

Opposition candidates in both races had campaigned against the HDZ's abuses of power under the late President Franjo Tudjman and had promised to rebuild Croatia's credibility as a Western democratic nation. A coalition of center-left opposition parties formed a new parliamentary majority, and Ivica Racan, the head of the Social Democratic Party (SDP), became prime minister. Voters elected Stjepan Mesic of the Croatian People's Party (HNS) as president. Since the elections, Croatia has been invited to join the World Trade Organization and NATO's Partnership for Peace, and the European Union has agreed to open talks on a stabilization and association agreement.

In May 1990, Croatia, a republic of the Socialist Federal Republic of Yugoslavia, elected Franjo Tudjman president. When Croatia declared independence in 1991, civil conflict erupted in Serb enclaves of the country and the Yugoslav army invaded. One-third of Croatia remained under Serb control until 1995, when Tudjman launched an offensive to reclaim the territory. Ethnic Serbs fled Croatia in masses. Despite plans with Slobodan Milosevic to partition Bosnia and Herzegovina, Tudjman was prominent in the 1995 Dayton peace process that ended the Bosnian war.

Throughout the 1991–1995 period, Tudjman used Croat nationalism to build a strong base of support. He also began to plunder state coffers, suppress the media, and subordinate the government and the judiciary to his personal and political whims. The HDZ was victorious in free (but not fair) parliamentary elections in 1995 and 1997. Tudjman was reelected in an unfair election in 1997.

In January 2000, a total of 282 candidates participated in democratic elections to the lower house of parliament. A center-left coalition of the SDP and the Croatian Social Liberal Party (HSLS) won 71 seats with nearly 49 percent of the vote. A coalition of the Croatian Peasant Party (HSS), the Liberal Party (LS), the HNS, and the Istrian Democratic Party (IDS) took 24 seats with 16.44 percent of the vote. Together, these two coalitions wrested control from the HDZ, which won only 46 seats, or 31.5 percent of the vote. A right-wing coalition of the Croatian Christian Democratic Union and the Croatian Party of Rights also won 5 seats with 3.52 percent of the vote. Voter turnout in Croatia was 75 percent; it was much lower at polling stations in Serbia and Bosnia. SDP leader Ivica Racan became prime minister.

Croatia's constitution calls for extraordinary elections within 60 days of a president's death. President Tudjman died on December 11, 1999, and the first round of voting took place January 24, 2000. Thirteen candidates successfully registered. The leading contenders were Mate Granic of Tudjman's HDZ, Stjepan Mesic of the HNS, and Drazen Budisa of the HSLS. In the first round Mesic received 41.11 percent of the vote; Budisa, 27.71 percent; and Mate Granic, 22.47 percent. Only Mesic and Budisa advanced to the second round, which Mesic won with 56 percent of the vote. Voter turnout was 63 percent in round one and 61 percent in round two.

In February, Croatia's new parliament agreed to support a four-year reform program aimed at building a market economy, honoring civil liberties and minority rights, tackling corruption, and restoring the country's international credibility. The program designated 2000 a year of economic austerity, and labor unions agreed to a limited truce. The government also slated the country's 11 largest companies for privatization and announced a major tax incentive for foreign investors.

Croatia's new leaders linked the restoration of civil liberties with reductions in presidential power. To that end, parliament approved groundbreaking constitutional amendments that transformed the country's semipresidential system into a parliamentary one. Likewise, the new leadership has taken steps to restore press freedoms, honor privacy rights, ensure equality before the law, and address the specific needs of minority populations.

President Mesic discovered more than 830 cassettes and 14,000 transcripts that are rife with evidence of corruption. Tudjman, it seems, secretly taped every conversation in his office. Already, powerful business executives, sporting officials, and members of Tudjman's family have been arrested or are under investigation for bribery or embezzlement. At least 70 army officers have been accused of faking injuries to get better pensions, and 100 corrupt police officials have been fired.

In 2000, Croatia agreed to fulfill its obligations to Bosnia under the 1995 Dayton Accord. It also pledged to cooperate with the international tribunal at the Hague in its investigation of war crimes committed in Croatia and Bosnia between 1991 and 1995. In September, when 12 top generals publicly opposed the arrest of dozens of suspected war criminals, President Mesic summarily fired seven of them. In December, the government refused to allow General Petar Stipetic, the nation's highest-ranking military official, to testify until the tribunal clarified whether Stipetic was a witness or a suspect.

Political Rights and Civil Liberties: Croatian voters can change their government democratically. The 1990 constitution guarantees citizens age 18 or older the right to universal and equal suffrage. The parliamentary and presidential elections in 2000 were peaceful, free, and fair. In both cases, opposition parties and candidates proved victorious. Multiple factors contributed to the elections' success, including adherence to election laws, the provision of equal access for candidates to free airtime on state media, fair polling, and the honest tabulation of ballots. Parliament adopted a new parliamentary election law in November 1999. The 1992 law on presidential elections remains in force.

The Organization for Security and Cooperation in Europe has repeatedly criticized Croatia's Law on Citizenship for favoring ethnic Croats over minorities. For example, unlike Croats in Bosnia, Serbs in exile have had difficulty proving their Croatian citizenship and, therefore, exercising their right to vote. The new parliamentary election law guarantees five seats for ethnic minorities.

Despite constitutional guarantees of freedom of expression, President Tudjman suppressed and intimidated independent media and put state media completely under his control. For the 2000 parliamentary elections, however, the lower house required Croatian Radio and Television (HRT), the state broadcaster, to give equal coverage to all candidates. HRT voluntarily adopted the same guidelines for the presidential election. Croatia's new leadership has removed Tudjman loyalists from senior positions at HRT and has vowed to foster an environment in which independent media can flourish. Legislation to transform HRT into an independent public service corporation was pending before parliament at year's end.

Freedom of religion is generally respected. In May 2000, the government established a commission to study the adoption of a law on religious minorities. Rights of association, assembly, and protest are also respected, although the former regime was known to restrict assembly rights arbitrarily. All associations must register their activities.

The constitution guarantees equality before the law. Under the Tudjman regime, persons could be denied the right to a fair trial, judicial appointments were politically motivated, and the security services served the president's needs. In 2000, though, Croatian courts started hearing economic corruption and war crimes cases, and parliament supported changes to the Law on Internal Affairs aimed at ending the use of wiretapping as a political tool.

The constitution also secures the right to move and travel freely, although registration in one's place of residence is required. After years of indifference, Croatia has agreed to work actively to repatriate thousands of ethnic Serbs who fled the country in 1995. Croatia is also home to thousands of internally displaced persons.

While the constitution states that "entrepreneurial and market freedom are the basis of the economic system," Croatian citizens have often found these freedoms difficult to exercise. President Tudjman, in particular, fostered an environment in which bribery and embezzlement were commonplace, privatization programs lacked transparency, and individuals were frequently deprived of salaries and pensions. Even though Croatia's new leadership has launched an aggressive economic reform program, it still became the target of strong criticism in 2000 when unemployment reached 20 percent.

Cuba

Polity: One party
Economy: Statist
Population: 11,100,000
PPP: $3,967
Life Expectancy: 76
Ethnic Groups: Mulatto (51 percent), white (37 percent), black (11 percent), Chinese (1 percent)
Capital: Havana

Political Rights: 7
Civil Liberties: 7
Status: Not Free

Overview:

U.S.-Cuban relations took some unexpected turns in 2000, against a backdrop of unprecedented media coverage of the story of child shipwreck survivor Elián Gonzalez, who was ordered returned to his father after a lengthy legal battle with émigré relatives in Florida. In response to pressure from U.S. farmers and businessmen who pushed for a relaxation of economic sanctions against Fidel Castro's island dictatorship, in October the United States eased the 38-year-old embargo on food and medicine to Cuba. However, the aging caudillo's grip on the island was anything but relaxed. Repression of the independent media and other civil society dissidents continued unabated, and Cuba's tightening of emigration policy increased the likelihood of high-risk escapes by boat from the island. Cuba is also the western hemisphere's per capita leader in the practice of capital punishment, surpassed in the world only by Iran and the Democratic Republic of the Congo.

Cuba achieved independence from Spain in 1898 as a result of the Spanish-American War. The Republic of Cuba was established in 1902, but was under U.S. tutelage under the Platt Amendment until 1934. In 1959 Castro's July 26th Movement—named after an earlier, failed insurrection—overthrew the dictatorship of Fulgencio Batista, who had ruled for 18 of the previous 25 years.

Since then, Fidel Castro has dominated the Cuban political system, transforming it into a one-party state. Communist structures were institutionalized by the 1976 constitution installed at the first congress of the Cuban Communist Party (PCC). The constitution provides for a national assembly which, in theory, designates a Council of State, which in turn appoints a Council of Ministers in consultation with its president, who serves as head of state and chief of government.

In reality, Castro is responsible for every appointment. As president of the Council of Ministers, chairman of the Council of State, commander-in-chief of the Revolutionary Armed Forces (FAR), and first secretary of the PCC, Castro controls every lever of power in Cuba. The PCC is the only authorized political party, and it controls all governmental entities from the national to the municipal level.

Since the 1991 collapse of the Soviet Union, which had subsidized the Cuban economy, Castro has sought Western foreign investment. Most investment has come from Europe and Latin America, but those funds have not made up for the $5 billion in annual Soviet subsidies. The government claims the economy has rebounded in the past three years, but the "special period" austerity program, involving drastic cutbacks in energy consumption and tight rationing of food and consumer items, remains in place.

The legalization of the U.S. dollar since 1993 has heightened social tensions, as the minority with access to dollars from abroad or through the tourist industry has emerged as a new moneyed class and the desperation of the majority without has increased. State salaries have shrunk to $4 or less a month.

The cycles of repression Castro has unleashed with increasing frequency against opponents, meant to keep at bay social forces set into motion by his economic reforms, continued throughout 1997. Stepped-up actions against peaceful dissidents preceded the Fifth Congress of the PCC held in October 1997, as well as elections the same month to the National Assembly of Popular Power. Two small bomb explosions at hotels in Havana on July 13, 1997, also provided a pretext for action against peaceful opposition groups, which Cuban authorities tried to link to terrorist activities.

Neither the Fifth Congress, where one-party rule was reaffirmed, nor the one-party national elections, provided any surprises. Castro proudly pointed to a reported 95 percent turnout at the polls; critics noted that nonparticipation could be construed by authorities as dissent and many people were afraid of the consequences of being so identified.

In the aftermath of the visit of Pope John Paul II, January 21-25, 1998, the number of dissidents confirmed to be imprisoned dropped from 1,320, in 1996, to 381 in mid-June 1998. Part of the decline was due to the release of 140 of 300 prisoners held for political activities or common crimes whose freedom was sought by the pontiff.

In February 1999, the government introduced tough legislation against sedition, with a maximum prison sentence of 20 years. It included penalties against unauthorized contact with the United States and the import or supply of "subversive" materials, including texts on democracy, by news agencies and journalists. A month later, a court used the new law in sentencing four well-known dissidents to prison terms of up to five years. Castro used the occasion of the Ibero-American summit, which was boycotted by several Latin American leaders, to lash out at Cuba's small band of vocal dissidents and members of the independent press.

Throughout 2000, Cuban authorities intimidated and imprisoned independent journalists, with more than 15 questioned by state security agents or placed under arrest and 19 others forced into exile. In May the government freed from jail on conditional liberty three well-known antigovernment activists, who together with Vladimir Roca are known as the Group of Four. In July two dissidents were sentenced to five or more years in prison, an action Amnesty International said overshadowed the release of nine other prisoners of conscience during the year. In October more than 100 people were detained around the island for questioning.

Political Rights and Civil Liberties:

Cubans cannot change their government through democratic means. On January 11, 1998, members of the national assembly were elected in a process in which a reported 98.35 percent of 7.8 million registered voters turned out. There were only 601 candidates for an equal number of seats; opposition or dissident groups were forbidden to present their own candidates. Although the national assembly is vested with the right of legislative power, when it is not in session this faculty is delegated to the 31-member Council of State elected by the assembly and chaired by Castro.

All political and civic organization outside the PCC is illegal. Political dissent, spoken or written, is a punishable offense, and those so punished frequently receive years of imprisonment for seemingly minor infractions. There has been a slight relaxation of strictures on cultural life; nevertheless, the educational system, the judicial system, labor unions, professional organizations, and all media remain state controlled. A small group of human rights activists and dissident journalists, together with a still-shackled Roman Catholic Church, provide the only glimmer of an independent civil society.

In Cuba the executive branch controls the judiciary. The 1976 constitution is remarkable for its concentration of power in the hands of one individual—Castro, president of the Council of State. In practice, the council serves as a de facto judiciary and controls both the courts and the judicial process as a whole. In 1999, the Cuban government showed some willingness to enhance antinarcotics cooperation between the island republic and the United States. In 1999, Cuba executed at least 21 prisoners by firing squad, and in 2000 held another 24 on death row, awaiting a final decision on their execution sentence by the Council of State. Two of those on death row are Salvadoran nationals who were convicted of terrorism after confessing to a 1997 bombing campaign against hotels in Cuba that killed an Italian citizen.

Cuba under Castro has one of the highest per capita rates of imprisonment for political offenses of any country in the world. There are several hundred political prisoners, most held in cells with common criminals and many convicted on vague charges such as "disseminating enemy propaganda" or "dangerousness." There are credible reports of torture of dissidents in prison and in psychiatric institutions, where a number of those arrested in recent years are held. Since 1991, the United Nations has voted annually to assign a special investigator on human rights to Cuba, but the Cuban government has refused to cooperate. In 1993 vandalism was decreed to be a form of sabotage, punishable by eight years in prison. Groups that exist apart from the state are labeled "counterrevolutionary criminals" and are subject to systematic repression, including arrests, beatings while in custody, confiscations, and intimidation by uniformed or plainclothes state security.

The press in Cuba is the object of a targeted campaign of intimidation by the government. Independent journalists, particularly those associated with five small news agencies they established, have been subjected to continued repression, including jail terms at hard labor and assaults while in prison by state security agents. At a time when their potential audiences are increasing, as a result of the Internet, about 100 independent journalists have been branded "counterrevolutionaries" by the authorities. Foreign news agencies must hire local reporters only through government offices, which limits employment opportunities for independent journalists. In 1999, in the run-up to the November summit of Ibero-American leaders, Castro singled out 17 independent journalists by name and said they were "counterrevolutionary" conspirators paid by the United States.

Freedom of movement and the right to choose one's residence, education, or job is severely restricted. Attempting to leave the island without permission is a punishable offense. In August 2000, the U.S. State Department charged that Cuba was not abiding by a 1994 agreement seeking to establish ground rules for the orderly migration of 20,000 Cubans plus their family members to the United States. Noting that more than 100 Cubans to whom the United States had granted visas were denied exit permits by the Cuban government in a 75-day period, it said that the island's policy was encouraging Cubans "denied the means to migrate in a safe, orderly and legal fashion to risk their lives in desperate sea voyages."

Cuban authorities have failed to carry out an adequate investigation into the July 1994 sinking of a tugboat carrying at least 66 people, of whom only 31 survived, as it sought to flee Cuba. Several survivors alleged that the craft sank as it was being pursued and assaulted by three other Cuban vessels acting under official orders, and that the fleeing boat was not allowed to surrender. The government denied any responsibility, claiming the tragedy was an accident caused by irresponsible actions of those on board. Citing what it calls compelling evidence, including eyewitness testimony, in 1999 Amnesty International concluded that the force employed by the Cuban government was "disproportionate" to the nature of the crime. It noted that "if events occurred in the way described by several of the survivors, those who died as a result of the incident were victims of extrajudicial execution." Those in Cuba commemorating the dead, or who have peacefully protested the sinking, have faced harassment and intimidation.

In 1991 Roman Catholics and other believers were granted permission to join the Communist Party, and the constitutional reference to official atheism was dropped the following year. Religious freedom has made small gains. Afro-Cuban religious groups are now carefully courted by Cuban officials. In preparation for the papal visit in 1998, Catholic pastoral work and religious education activities were allowed to take place at previously unheard-of levels, and Christmas was celebrated for the first time in 28 years. In 1999, it was revealed that a year earlier Castro had agreed to a secret deal to allow 400 Jews, part of a small religious community numbering around 1,500 people, to emigrate to Israel.

In the post-Soviet era, the rights of Cubans to own private property and to participate in joint ventures with foreigners have been recognized. Non-Cuban businesses have also been allowed. In practice, there are few rights for those who do not belong to the PCC. Party membership is still required for good jobs, serviceable housing, and real access to social services, including medical care and educational opportunities.

Many blacks have benefited from access to basic education and medical care since the Castro revolution, and much of the police force and army enlisted personnel is black. However, credible reports say the forced evictions of squatters and residents lacking official permission to reside in Havana is primarily targeted against individuals and families from the eastern provinces, which are traditionally areas of black or mixed-race populations.

About 40 percent of all women work, and they are well represented in the professions. However, violence against women is a problem, as is child prostitution.

Cyprus (Greek)

Polity: Presidential- **Political Rights:** 1
parliamentary democracy **Civil Liberties:** 1
Economy: Capitalist **Status:** Free
Population: 900,000
PPP: $17,482
Life Expectancy: 78
Ethnic Groups: Greek (78 percent), Turkish (18 percent),
other (4 percent)
Capital: Nicosia

Overview:

Resolution of the conflict that has kept Cyprus divided since 1974 continued to prove elusive throughout the year. United Nations-sponsored "proximity" talks, so-called because the two Cypriot leaders refuse to meet face-to-face and only in proximity to one another through intermediaries, took place in New York in September with no substantive results. Talks resumed in November in Europe but quickly collapsed.

Annexed to Britain in 1914, Cyprus gained independence in 1960 after a ten-year guerrilla campaign to demand union with Greece. In July 1974, Greek Cypriot national guard members, backed by the military junta in power in Greece, staged an unsuccessful coup aimed at unification. Five days later, Turkey invaded, seized control of 37 percent of the island, and expelled 200,000 Greeks from the north. Currently, the entire Turkish Cypriot community resides in the north, and property claims arising from the division and population exchange remain unsettled.

A buffer zone called the "Green Line" has divided Cyprus since 1974. The capital, Nicosia, is the world's last divided city. The division of Cyprus has been a major point of contention in the long-standing rivalry between Greece and Turkey in the Aegean. Tensions and intermittent violence between the two populations have plagued the island since independence. UN resolutions stipulate that Cyprus is a single country of which the northern third is illegally occupied. In 1982, Turkish-controlled Cyprus made a unilateral declaration of independence that was condemned by the UN and that remains unrecognized by every country except Turkey. [See Turkish Cyprus under Related Territories.]

Cypriot president Glafcos Clerides attended negotiations in New York in September 2000 which were organized to lay the groundwork for meaningful negotiations toward a comprehensive settlement of the conflict. These negotiations marked the fourth round of proximity talks which began in December 1999 under UN auspices. UN mediators, hoping the round of talks would address the core issues—and historic deal-breakers—of territorial allotment and reunification, insisted that each party to the conflict treat the other as political equals. Taking this to mean that Turkish Cyprus had a claim to independent statehood in its own right, Clerides balked, objecting to what he perceived as a slight to his status as president of all of Cyprus. Negotiations resumed in November but ended abruptly, with the two sides unable to narrow their differences. The collapse of the talks further imperiled Turkey's chances of ascension to the European Union.

Peace in Cyprus remains fragile. Propaganda in schools and in the media has sustained hostility among Cypriot youth. Blatant economic disparity exists between the prosperous south and the stagnating north. Cyprus ranks among the most heavily militarized countries in the world.

Political Rights and Civil Liberties: Greek Cypriots can change their government democratically. Suffrage is universal and compulsory, and elections are free and fair. The 1960 constitution established an ethnically representative system designed to protect the interests of both Greek and Turkish Cypriots. The independent judiciary operates according to the British tradition, upholding the presumption of innocence and the right to due process. Trial before a judge is standard, although requests for trial by jury are regularly granted.

Freedom of speech is respected, and a vibrant independent press frequently criticizes authorities. Several private television and radio stations in the Greek Cypriot community compete effectively with government-controlled stations. In addition, the government also publishes a Cyprus Internet home page, which features information regarding efforts to resolve the island's protracted dispute as well as current developments and policy statements by Cypriot leaders.

Cypriot authorities moved to counter the influence of alleged religious cults operating on the island, some of which use religion to mask illegal activities such as drug trafficking. While necessitating close monitoring of suspect religious groups, and not ruling out potential crackdowns, authorities assured citizens during the year that they would act within the guidelines of the Universal Declaration of Human Rights and its provisions protecting religious freedom.

Czech Republic

Polity: Parliamentary democracy
Economy: Mixed capitalist
Population: 10,300,000
PPP: $12,362
Life Expectancy: 74
Ethnic Groups: Czech (94 percent), Slovak (3 percent), other, including Polish (3 percent)
Capital: Prague

Political Rights: 1
Civil Liberties: 2
Status: Free

Overview: In the year 2000 the Czech and Slovak Republics celebrated the end of their "velvet divorce." Prague proudly hosted its first International Monetary Fund (IMF) meeting, but antiglobalization protesters turned rallies violent. A scandal in the ruling Czech Social Democratic Party (CSSD), efforts to meet European Union (EU) accession requirements, and a power struggle between Havel and the CSSD-Civic Democratic Party (ODS) alliance also marked the year.

In December 1989, an anti-Communist opposition led by Vaclav Havel and the Civic Forum brought down the Czechoslovak government. The country held its first post-Communist elections in 1990; adopted a new constitution and a charter of freedoms in 1992; and dissolved the state into the Czech and Slovak Republics in 1993. Havel became president of the new Czech Republic in 1993.

In 1992, under Finance Minister Vaclav Klaus, the country began an aggressive program of political and economic reforms. Klaus, a member of the ruling center-right ODS, became prime minister the same year. He resigned in 1997 amid allegations of corruption in the ODS and in the midst of an economic recession. In 1998 the ODS ceded control of the government to the CSSD after close parliamentary elections but negotiated control of key government positions. In 1999 the Czech Republic joined NATO and ratified the EU social charter.

In 2000 Prague hosted the annual IMF meeting. When demonstrations turned violent, police detained several hundred protesters and brought criminal charges against a few. While some activists cried police brutality, most observers agreed that, in general, the police had responded appropriately and had acted with restraint.

Petra Buzkova, the deputy chair of parliament's lower house, accused fellow CSSD-party members of plotting to discredit her and filed slander charges in court. The government ordered the arrest of two *Mlada Fronta Dnes* journalists who had implicated a government official in the plot but had refused to reveal their source. Havel pardoned the journalists, but they vowed to force a court decision on their right to protect sources. This incident and others underscored the tense relationship between journalists and the Zeman government.

In 2000, the government reformed the commercial code and announced plans to privatize remaining state assets, but it hit two potential stumbling blocks to EU accession: Austria's strong opposition to the new Temelin nuclear power plant and the Chamber of Deputies' rejection of important judicial reforms. In its annual assessment of Czech accession progress, the European Commission (EC) called for the continuation of economic restructuring and the immediate acceleration of administrative reform, judicial reform, and the fight against corruption and economic crime.

The Quad Coalition, a grouping of liberal opposition parties, trounced the CSSD and the ODS in November elections for one-third of the senate. The coalition now holds 39 seats in the 81-member body. The failure of the CSSD and the ODS to secure a decisive senate majority effectively quashed their plans to limit President Havel's powers through constitutional reform. The power struggle remained alive at year's end, though, in cases pending before the constitutional court. Havel has challenged amendments to the law on political parties that would make it difficult for small parties to gain representation in parliament. Zeman, meanwhile, has contested Havel's appointment of a new Czech National Bank head without his approval.

Political Rights and Civil Liberties:

Czech citizens age 18 or older can change their government democratically under a system of universal, equal, and direct suffrage. Voters elect members of the senate and the Chamber of Deputies, the upper and lower houses of parliament, respectively. Parliament chooses the president, who appoints judges, the prime minister, and other cabinet members.

The Czech Republic has a solid record of free and fair elections. In May 2000, parliament introduced a first-past-the-post system for electing members of the Chamber of Deputies and raised the threshold for securing seats. Fearing the creation of a de facto two-party system, Havel has challenged the changes in court. Elections for one-third of the senate and for the country's new regional assemblies took place in November 2000. Both elections were marked by low voter turnout.

The Charter of Fundamental Rights and Freedoms gives minorities the right to help resolve matters pertaining to their group. A 1999 law restored citizenship to many residents—especially Roma (Gypsies). In August 2000, the head of the International Romany Union, a Czech lawyer, called for the recognition of Roma as a stateless nation. Likewise, the United Nations called on the country to end discrimination against Roma in housing, education, and employment. In November parliament approved the creation of a governmental Council for Ethnic Minorities.

Freedom of expression is honored, although the Charter prohibits threats against individual rights, state and public security, public health, and morality. Print and electronic media are largely in private hands. In 2000, the Law on Free Access to Information took effect, parliament amended broadcasting laws to meet EU standards, and several legal cases raised important questions about freedom of speech. In one case, Michal Zitko, the publisher of a controversial Czech edition of Hitler's *Mein Kampf*, was found guilty of promoting fascism—a movement that suppresses civil rights and freedoms. Zitko has appealed the case. In December, journalists at Czech Television (CT) protested the appointment of Jiri Hodac to head the state-run broadcaster. The journalists, who accused Hodac of maintaining close ties to the center-right Civic Democrats, took over the CT newsroom, broadcast their own programs, and cast the appointment as a politically motivated challenge to their independence. Hodac responded by firing 20 staffers and blacking out all broadcasts. The conflict remained unresolved at year's end.

The government respects freedom of religious conviction. A 1991 law requires religious groups to register in order to receive state financial support. In March 2000, the government and the Prague Jewish community settled a dispute over a thirteenth-century Jewish cemetery discovered at a Prague construction site.

Czech citizens may assemble peacefully, form associations, and petition the government. Trade unions and professional associations are free. There are more than 40,000 registered nongovernmental organizations, and approximately 40 percent of the workforce belongs to a trade union. Judges, prosecutors, and members of the armed forces and police may not strike.

The independent judiciary consists of a supreme court, a supreme administrative court, and high, regional, and district courts. There is also a constitutional court. Accession to the EU requires judicial reform, but efforts to pass legislation have been unsuccessful. While the supreme court has claimed some success in reducing trial delays, the European Court for Human Rights ruled in 2000 that Czech courts had violated the rights of a German businessman by denying him a speedy trial. The European Roma Rights Center has presented a case before the same court charging racial discrimination in Czech schools. Also in 2000, thousands of inmates rioted to protest prison conditions.

The Charter specifies "fundamental human rights and freedoms" including privacy, property ownership, sanctity of the home, and choice of residence. The Charter also guarantees the right to education, fair wages, and protection of one's health. Citizens generally enjoy all of these rights, although Czech Roma continue to experience discrimination. In August 2000, the government approved an affirmative action plan for women.

Denmark

Polity: Parliamentary democracy
Economy: Mixed capitalist
Population: 5,300,000
PPP: $24,218
Life Expectancy: 76
Ethnic Groups: Mostly Danish, some German, Inuit
Capital: Copenhagen

Political Rights: 1
Civil Liberties: 1
Status: Free

Overview:

Prime Minister Poul Nyrup Rasmussen suffered a setback when Danes voted by a wide margin against adopting the euro in a September referendum. The outcome of the referendum reflected popular concerns about preserving democracy, national sovereignty, and Denmark's generous welfare state. It also gave a boost to Pia Kjaersgaard's ultranationalist Danish People's Party (DPP), which has seen its popularity nearly double since the 1998 general election.

Denmark is the oldest monarchy in Europe. Queen Margrethe II, whose reign began in 1972, performs mostly ceremonial functions, such as appointing the prime minister and cabinet ministers after they have been chosen by parliamentary leaders. The 1953 constitution established a unicameral parliament, or Folketing, in which 135 of the 179 members are elected in 17 mainland districts. Two representatives from each of the semiautonomous regions of the Faeroe Islands and Greenland are also elected. The remaining seats are allocated on a proportional basis to parties receiving more than two percent of the vote. An extensive system of local representation includes both regional and local councils. Prime Minister Rasmussen heads a minority coalition government comprising his Social Democrats and the Radical Liberals.

In voting against the euro, Danes defied the government, main opposition parties, big business, major trade unions, and economists, all of whom support monetary union. But some opponents of the euro say that monetary union will weaken Denmark's welfare system. Others cite European sanctions against Austria following the electoral success of Jorg Haider's Freedom Party as proof of the EU's undemocratic tendencies. And nationalists like Kjaersgaard oppose European integration along with immigration as a threat to national identity. Foreign minister Niels Helveg Petersen resigned in December in disagreement over Danes' decision to opt out of participation in the euro and European defense.

The DPP's anti-Europe, anti-immigrant platform has gained significant support among Danes. Seven percent voted for the party in the 1998 election, and 12 percent of people polled in late 2000 said that they would vote for the DPP in the next election. However, DPP participation in government in the near future appears unlikely, as most major and minor parties refuse to align themselves with a party that they consider to be xenophobic. Rasmussen's government appeared to be stable at year's end. A general election is due by March 2002.

Political Rights and Civil Liberties: Danes can change their government democratically. Representatives are elected to the Folketing at least once every four years in a modified system of proportional representation. The autonomous territory of Greenland held a general election in 1999 for its 31-seat parliament. Prime Minister Jonathan Motzfeldt's social-democratic Siumut Party has dominated politics on the island for more than 20 years. The Danish monarchy, whose role is largely ceremonial, still enjoys vast support among Danes.

The judiciary is independent, and citizens enjoy full due process rights. The court system consists of 100 local courts, two high courts, and a 15-member supreme court with judges appointed by the queen on recommendation of the government.

Danish media reflect a wide variety of political opinions and are frequently critical of the government. The state finances radio and television broadcasting, but state-owned television companies have independent editorial boards. Independent radio stations are permitted but tightly regulated.

The rights of racial, ethnic, and religious minorities are widely respected. However, the DPP has tapped into public fears about crime and national identity to rally opinion against immigrants. In January 2000, the DPP placed an ad in a national newspaper mocking a campaign by a group that assists jobless immigrants in finding work. The ad drew heavy criticism from rights activists and politicians, one of whom compared Pia Kjaersgaard to Hitler. But anti-immigrant sentiment has risen, and in 2000 the government responded with legislation barring immigrants under age 25 from bringing foreign spouses to Denmark. Another measure makes learning Danish a requirement for receiving some forms of welfare.

Denmark is among the countries most tolerant of homosexuals. In 1989, Denmark became the first country to grant legal recognition to same-sex partnerships. In May 2000, Denmark passed legislation granting gays and lesbians in registered partnerships the right to adopt each other's children.

Freedom of worship is guaranteed to all. More than 90 percent of the population belongs to the state-supported Evangelical Lutheran Church. The Evangelical Lutheran faith is taught in public schools, although students are not required to attend religious classes.

Women constitute approximately 45 percent of the Danish labor force. According to the Swiss-based Inter-Parliamentary Union, Denmark ranks behind only Sweden in its percentage of women in parliament; more than 30 percent of Danish parliamentarians are women.

Workers are free to organize, bargain collectively, and strike. The vast majority of wage earners belong to trade unions and their umbrella organization, the Danish Federation of Trade Unions.

Djibouti

Polity: Presidential-
parliamentary democracy
(dominant party)
Economy: Capitalist
Population: 600,000
PPP: $1,266
Life Expectancy: 51

Political Rights: 4
Civil Liberties: 5*
Status: Partly Free

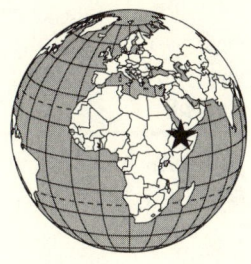

Ethnic Groups: Somali (60 percent), Afar (35 percent),
other (5 percent)
Capital: Djibouti
Ratings Change: Djibouti's civil liberties rating changed from 6 to 5 due to the signing
of a peace accord between the government and the radical wing of the Front for the
Restoration of Unity and Democracy (FRUD).

Overview: Djibouti appeared in the international spotlight by hosting talks
on peace in Somalia. The talks eventually led to the election
in August 2000 of a Somalian president and national assem-
bly after Somalia had spent nearly a decade without any form of central authority. For
its own part, Djibouti was engaged in a more private peace process. It reached an accord in February with the radical wing of the Front for the Restoration of Unity and
Democracy (FRUD). The agreement between President Ismael Omar Guelleh and
FRUD's Dini Ahmed Dini ended the Afar insurgency in the north.

Djibouti was known as the French Territory of the Afar and Issa before receiving
independence from France in 1977. President Hassad Gouled Aptidon controlled a one-
party system until 1992, when a new constitution adopted by referendum authorized
four political parties. In 1993, he was declared winner of a fourth six-year term in
Djibouti's first contested presidential elections. Both the opposition and international
observers considered the poll fraudulent.

Afar rebels of FRUD had launched a three-year guerrilla war against Issa "tribal
dictatorship" in 1991 with demands for an installation of a democratic, multiparty system. The largest FRUD faction agreed in 1994 to end its insurgency in exchange for inclusion
in the government and electoral reforms. Djibouti's people are deeply divided along ethnic
and clan lines. The majority Issa (Somali) and minority Afar peoples hold most political
power. Legislative elections in 1997 returned the ruling party to power, thereby rein-
forcing the long dominance of the Mamassan clan of the majority Issa ethnic group.

President Aptidon stepped down in April 1999 after 22 years in power, opening
the way for the country's first free presidential election since independence. Guelleh,
of the ruling Popular Rally for Progress (RPP) party, defeated opposition leader Moussa
Ahmed Idriss, of the Unified Djiboutian Opposition (ODU). Guelleh, who is Aptidon's
nephew and a former head of state security, had long been considered the de facto
head of government and president's heir apparent.

Approximately 2,700 French troops are among 10,000 French residents of Djibouti.
French advisors and technicians effectively run much of the country, though this is
slowly changing.

Djibouti has little industry, few natural resources, and high unemployment. Services provide most of the national income. Efforts to curb rampant corruption have met with little success. However, in July the International Monetary Fund praised Djibouti's efforts at privatization, especially management of its Red Sea port.

Political Rights and Civil Liberties: The trappings of representative government and formal administration have had little relevance to the real distribution and exercise of power in Djibouti. The April 1999 presidential poll was marked by low turnout among the fewer than 200,000 eligible voters. Guelleh won the poll with 74 percent of the vote, compared to 26 percent for Moussa Ahmed Idriss. For the first time since elections began in 1992, no group boycotted the vote. Although international observers declared the poll generally fair, the ruling party had the advantage of state resources to conduct its campaign.

The 1997 legislative elections were marginally more credible than the plainly fraudulent 1992 polls, but easily reinstalled the ruling RPP, which, in coalition with the legalized arm of FRUD at the time, won all 65 national assembly seats. Aptidon had sought the appearance of ethnic balance in government by appointing Afars as prime ministers. FRUD leaders joined the cabinet as part of the 1994 peace pact.

Constraints on political activities eased in the 1990s. Five political parties exist. Freedom of assembly and association is nominally protected under the constitution, but the government has little tolerance for political protest. The judiciary is not independent, owing to routine governmental interference. A position was established in 2000 for a mediator for Djiboutians to seek redress in disputes with the government.

Despite constitutional protection, freedom of speech is not guaranteed. The government closely controls all electronic media. There is one official newspaper. Independent newspapers, most of which are in the form of newsletters, are generally allowed to circulate freely, but journalists exercise self-censorship. Islam is the official state religion, but freedom of worship is respected.

Security forces arrest dissidents without proper authority, despite constitutional requirements that arrests may not occur without a decree presented by a judicial magistrate. Prison conditions are harsh with reports of beatings and torture, and rapes of female inmates. There are complaints of harassment of political opponents and union leaders.

The formal sector in the largely rural agricultural and nomadic subsistence economy is small. Workers may join unions and strike, but the government routinely obstructs the free operation of unions. The state body, the General Union of Djiboutian Workers, and the Union of Djiboutian Workers formed a confederation in 1995 and have gained increasing support despite government harassment. About 70 percent of formal workers are members of the confederation.

Despite equality under civil law, women suffer serious discrimination under customary practices in inheritance and other property matters, divorce, and the right to travel. Women have few opportunities for education or within the formal economic sector. Female genital mutilation is almost universal among Djibouti's women, and legislation forbidding mutilation of young girls is not enforced. The government has made efforts at increasing the enrollment of girls in school.

Dominica

Polity: Parliamentary democracy
Economy: Capitalist
Population: 100,000
PPP: $5,102
Life Expectancy: 76
Ethnic Groups: Mostly black and mulatto, Carib Indian
Capital: Roseau

Political Rights: 1
Civil Liberties: 1
Status: Free

Overview:

The centrist opposition Dominica Labour Party (DLP) swept to victory for the first time in 20 years in the January 30, 2000, elections, winning 10 of 21 parliamentary seats and forging a coalition with the right-wing Dominica Freedom Party (DFP). DLP leader and former left-wing activist Rosie Douglas came to power after charging that the incumbent United Workers Party (UWP), headed by Prime Minister Edison James, had sold hundreds of passports to wealthy foreigners who, according to the United States, included Russian gangsters and Chinese immigrant smugglers. Douglas, who maintains close links to Cuba, promised a business development that minimized environmental damage, and the former Marxist quickly moved to assure the business sector that his years as a black-power firebrand were behind him.

Dominica has been an independent republic within the Commonwealth since 1978. Internally self-governing since 1967, Dominica is a parliamentary democracy headed by a prime minister and a house of assembly with 21 members elected to five-year terms. Nine senators are appointed—five by the prime minister and four by the opposition leader. The president is elected by the house for a five-year term.

In 1993 Prime Minister Eugenia Charles of the DFP announced her intention to retire in 1995 after 15 years in power. External Affairs Minister Brian Alleyne defeated three other candidates in a vote of DFP delegates to become the new party leader.

In June 1995, the UWP won a narrow majority, 11 of 21 seats, in parliamentary elections. James, a former head of the Banana Growers' Association, became prime minister. The UWP victory marked a significant shift of power from the traditional establishment to a new and younger business class. The DFP and the DLP won five seats each. The DFP's Alleyne and the DLP's Douglas reached an agreement to share the official opposition post by alternating each year. Alleyne assumed the post first. A high court, however, ruled that one of the winning DFP candidates was not qualified to sit in parliament since he still held a public service position. The ruling reduced the DFP's representation in parliament to four seats. Special elections, held in 1996, resulted in an additional seat for the UWP, raising its share to 12 of 21 seats. Douglas became the opposition leader. In early 1996 Alleyne resigned as head of the DFP and was replaced by former diplomat Charles Savarin.

Dominica's offshore business sector includes some 4,600 international companies, five offshore banks, and five Internet gambling companies. Offshore banking interests, in particular, have raised concerns about penetration by international organized crime, particularly Russian organizations. In March 1999, the U.S. State Department noted the rapid expansion of offshore businesses and expressed concern that "between 200 and 300 Russians have reportedly purchased citizenship." James' decision to call snap elections for January 2000 caught some observers off guard, and during the campaign the prime minister touted the island's 3.5 percent economic growth in 1999 as well as his government's record of building homes, schools, and water pipelines. James denied the DLP's charge that some of the estimated 1,000 foreigners who received passports were criminals. After the January 2000 election, Douglas announced that Dominica's program of raising money by selling passports and "economic citizenship" would end.

Political Rights and Civil Liberties:

Citizens are able to change their government through free and fair elections, as was the case with the January 2000 vote in which 60,000 people were registered to participate. There are no restrictions on political, civic, or labor organizations. Several civic groups emerged during the James administration to call for more accountability and transparency in government.

The press is free, varied, and critical. Television and radio, both public and private, are open to a variety of views. Since 1990, television has been used as an effective campaign tool by all parties. The government respects academic freedom and labor rights.

Freedom of religion is recognized. However, the small Rastafarian community has charged in the past that its religious rights are violated by a policy of cutting off the dreadlocks of those who are imprisoned, and that Rastafarian women are harassed by immigration officials who single them out for drug searches.

There is an independent judiciary, and the rule of law is enhanced by the court's subordination to the inter-island Eastern Caribbean Supreme Court. But the judicial system is understaffed, which has led to a large backlog of cases. The only prison on Dominica is plagued by overcrowding and sanitation problems.

The Dominica Defense Force was disbanded in 1981 after being implicated in attempts by supporters of former Prime Minister Patrick John to overthrow the government. John was convicted in 1986 for his role and given a 12-year prison sentence. He was released by executive order in 1990, became active in the trade union movement, and lost as a DLP candidate in the 1995 election. The Dominica police are the only security force. Occasional instances of excessive use of force by police are one of the few human rights complaints heard. In 1997 the commissioner and deputy commissioner of the police were forced to retire as a result of recommendations by a commission of inquiry that investigated allegations of mismanagement, corruption, and police brutality. Under new leadership, the police created an Internal Affairs Department late that year to investigate public complaints against the police and to provide officers with counseling.

Workers have the right to organize, strike, and bargain collectively. Though unions are independent of the government and laws prohibit anti-union discrimination by employers, fewer than 10 percent of the workforce are union members.

There are 3,000 indigenous Carib Indians, many of whom live on a 3,783-acre reservation on the northeast coast created in 1903 and expanded in 1997. The reservation is governed by the 1978 Carib constitution.

Inheritance laws do not fully recognize women's rights. When a husband dies without a will, the wife cannot inherit the property, though she may continue to inhabit their home. There are no laws mandating equal pay for equal work for men and women in private sector jobs. Government welfare officials have expressed concern over the growing number of cases of child abuse.

Dominican Republic

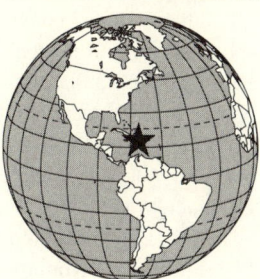

Polity: Presidential-parliamentary democracy
Economy: Capitalist-statist
Population: 8,400,000
PPP: $4,598
Life Expectancy: 71
Ethnic Groups: Mixed (73 percent), white (16 percent), black (11 percent)
Capital: Santo Domingo

Political Rights: 2
Civil Liberties: 2*
Status: Partly Free

Ratings change: The Dominican Republic's civil liberties rating changed from 3 to 2 due to its willingness to successfully prosecute a former senior military officer and to make improvements in the criminal justice system.

Overview: Hipolito Mejia, the center-left candidate of the Dominican Revolutionary Party (PRD), swept to power in the May 16, 2000, presidential elections. He crowned his party's virtual lock on power at all levels of government by promising to use the Dominican Republic's seven percent annual economic growth rate to promote more social spending, and to review the privatizations undertaken by his predecessor, Lionel Fernandez, of the Dominican Liberation Party (PLD). Mejia came within a hairsbreadth of the 50 percent of the votes plus one needed to win an absolute majority in the first round of the presidential contest. The second- and third-place contenders surprised the country by announcing, after a bitterly fought contest, to not force a runoff vote.

After achieving independence from Spain in 1821 and from Haiti in 1844, the Dominican Republic endured recurrent domestic conflict. The assassination of General Rafael Trujillo in 1961 ended 30 years of dictatorship, but a 1963 military coup led to civil war and U.S. intervention. In 1966, under a new constitution, civilian rule was restored with the election of the conservative Joaquin Balaguer.

The constitution provides for a president and a congress elected for four-year terms. The congress consists of a 30-member senate and, as a result of a recent census, a house that in 1998 went from 120 members to 149. Balaguer was reelected in 1970 and 1974, but was defeated in 1978 by Silvestre Antonio Guzman of the social-democratic PRD. The PRD was triumphant again in 1982 with the election of Salvador Jorge Blanco, but Balaguer, heading the right-wing Social Christian Reformist Party (PRSC), returned to power in 1986 and was reelected in 1990 in a vote marred by fraud.

In the May 1994 election, the main contenders were Balaguer, fellow-octogenarian Juan Bosch of the PLD, and the PRD's José Francisco Peña Gomez. The Balaguer machine attacked front-runner Peña Gomez, who is black, as a Haitian who secretly planned to unite the neighboring countries. Balaguer was declared the winner by a few thousand votes in an election rife with fraud. Amid street protests and international pressure, Balaguer agreed to hold new presidential elections in 18 months. The legislative results stood. The PRD and its allies took 57 seats in the house and 15 in the senate; the PRSC, 50 and 14; and the PLD, 13 and 1.

When congress convened, the PLD backed the PRSC's plan to lengthen Balaguer's shortened term from 18 months to two years, with elections in May 1996. In exchange, Balaguer made a PLD legislator president of the house. The PRD protested, but tacitly conceded by announcing that Peña Gomez would again be its standard-bearer in 1996. Vice President Jacinto Peynado won the PRSC primary in 1995. The PLD's lavish spending campaign tended to confirm the view that the money was coming from Balaguer, who wanted to stop Peña Gomez, and thus avoid any future corruption investigation. In promoting its candidate, Leonel Fernandez, a U.S.-trained lawyer, the PLD took a page from the race-baiting book of the PRSC. In May 1996, Peña Gomez won 45.9 percent of the vote; Fernandez, 38.9 percent; and Peynado, 15 percent. Fernandez won 51.3 percent, and the presidency, in a May 16, 1996, runoff.

The May 1998 legislative and municipal elections were held for the first time since Balaguer was forced to cut short his term. The campaign was violent; more than a dozen people were killed, mostly in clashes between PRD and PRSC groups. Peña Gomez died of natural causes on election eve. Because of the resulting sympathy vote, the PRD made a clean sweep of the legislative contest, although the ruling PLD actually increased its parliamentary strength and maintained enough votes to uphold presidential vetoes.

Fernandez's program of economic liberalization spurred the fastest-growing economy in Latin America. His government also won plaudits for efforts to reach out beyond his party to create consensus around social issues and to improve the administration of justice. However, critics charged that a wave of foreign investments were mishandled.

In the May 2000 presidential elections, Mejia, a former agriculture minister and a PRD outsider, struck a chord among those who felt left out by the economic prosperity, particularly the 20 percent who live below the poverty level. Mejia won 49.87 percent of the vote, compared to 24.9 percent for ruling party candidate Danilo Medina and 24.6 percent for Balaguer, who was running for his eighth term in office. He named a cabinet containing both long-term PRD stalwarts and young reformers, and promised to make good on his pledges to fight graft, create jobs and invest in housing and other public works projects.

Political Rights and Civil Liberties: Citizens of the Dominican Republic can change their government through elections. Although the country has a history of fraudulent elections, and the run-up to the May 2000 presidential elections was marked by heightened tension and outbreaks of interparty violence, the balloting was considered by international observers to have been free and fair. Constitutional guarantees regarding free expression, freedom of religion, and the right to organize political parties and civic groups are generally respected. Civil society organizations in the Dominican Republic are some of the most well organized and effective in Latin America. However, the violent political campaigns, the frequent government-labor clashes, and repressive measures taken by police and the military mean that free expression is somewhat circumscribed.

The media are mostly private. Newspapers are independent and diverse but subject to government pressure through denial of advertising revenues and imposition of taxes on imported newsprint. Dozens of radio stations and at least six commercial television stations broadcast. In 1997 the National Commission on Public Events and Radio Broadcasting shut down dozens of programs with religious-magical content.

The judiciary, headed by a supreme court, is politicized and riddled with corruption, although significantly less so in recent years. The courts offer little recourse to those without money or influence, although reforms implemented of late show some promise in increasing citizen access to the courts. Prisons, in which nine out of ten inmates have not been convicted of a crime, are grossly overcrowded, with poor health and sanitary conditions, and violence is routine. Torture and arbitrary arrest lead the complaints against the security forces, which are militarized and sometimes operate outside the civilian chain of command. Extrajudicial executions of common criminals are a problem which remain largely unaddressed, in part because the government, the media, and others appear concerned that attention to the issue will negatively affect the tourism industry. In one case, a Dominican related to a high-ranking police officer fled back to the island after being accused of murder in New York City; he remained in hiding and, it is believed, may enjoy some official protection. On a positive note, in August 2000 a retired general and three accomplices were sentenced to long jail terms for the murder in 1975 of an opposition journalist, a move that dented the aura of impunity for human rights violators from the Balaguer period.

In September 1997 Fernandez moved to clean up the country's antinarcotics forces and to restructure the supreme court in an effort to root out corruption and to reduce growing complaints of human rights abuses by the police. He led the effort in his role as chairman of the National Judicial Council, which oversees judicial appointments. Responsibility for appointing judges was in the past held by the senate, which tended to increase politicization and de-emphasize professional criteria. The supreme court has now assumed this role.

Labor unions are well organized. Although legally permitted to strike, they are often subject to government crackdowns. Peasant unions are occasionally targeted by armed groups working for large landowners.

Haitians, including children, work in appalling conditions on state-run sugar plantations, and their movement is restricted by the Dominican government. A 1992 labor code recognizes sugar workers' right to organize, but abuses continue. Dominican officials say as many as 400,000 Haitians work as illegal aliens, primarily on the plantations and in agriculture, out of a total of between 1 million and 1.5 million living in the Dominican Republic. The children of Haitian immigrants born in the Dominican Republic are refused legal residency by authorities in an application of what the Inter-American Commission on Human Rights of the Organization of American States called a "restrictive interpretation" of the Dominican constitution. The denial of residency affects more than 250,000 children.

Violence and discrimination against women is a serious problem, as are trafficking in women and girls, child prostitution, and child abuse.

East Timor

Polity: International
protectorate
Economy: Capitalist-statist
Population: 800,000
PPP: na
Life Expectancy: 46
Ethnic Groups: Timorese, Javanese, others
Capital: Dili

Political Rights: 6
Civil Liberties: 3*
Status: Partly Free

Ratings Change: East Timor's civil liberties rating changed from 4 to 3 due to an improved security situation that permitted independent media and nongovernmental organizations to function freely.

Overview:
Following widespread violence and looting that devastated East Timor in 1999, an interim United Nations administration helped rebuild the former Indonesian territory in 2000 and prepare it for independence. However, neither the UN nor local East Timorese leaders made much progress in preparing the country for elections, building political institutions, or setting a comprehensive timetable for independence.

The Portuguese arrived on Timor around 1520, and in the nineteenth and early twentieth centuries took formal control of the eastern part of the island. Following the overthrow of the Caetano regime in Portugal, Lisbon agreed in 1974 to hold a referendum on self-determination in East Timor. However, Portugal abandoned its colony in early 1975, and two Timorese groups—the leftist Revolutionary Front for an Independent East Timor (Fretilin) and the right-wing Timorese Democratic Union—began fighting for control of the territory. Indonesia invaded in December 1975 and formally annexed East Timor as its 27th province in 1976. The Indonesian army forcibly repressed dissent and waged counterinsurgency operations against Fretilin's armed wing, the East Timorese National Liberation Army (Falintil). By 1979, civil conflict and famine had killed up to 200,000 Timorese. For the next two decades, the poorly equipped armed resistance waged a low-grade insurgency from the rugged interior.

In an incident that drew international condemnation, Indonesian soldiers killed dozens of civilians holding a peaceful pro-independence march in the territorial capital of Dili in November 1991. The 1996 award of the Nobel Peace Prize to Carlos Felipe Ximenes Belo, the East Timor Roman Catholic bishop, and Jose Ramos Jorta, the leading East Timorese independence activist, brought renewed international attention to Indonesian abuses in the territory.

Reversing former President Suharto's hardline policies toward the territory, Indonesian President B. J. Habibie announced in January 1999 that he favored granting East Timorese their independence if they rejected autonomy in a referendum. Yet Habibie had limited control over the Indonesian military, which armed pro-integration militia that began attacking pro-independence activists and suspected supporters. As the violence continued, Indonesia and Portugal, which the UN still recognized as the administering powers in East Timor, agreed on May 5 to a UN-run referendum on self-determination in the territory.

Soldiers and militia forced some 40,000 to 60,000 villagers to flee their homes and continued to commit rights violations with impunity in the weeks leading up to the August 30, 1999 referendum, in which 78.5 percent of participating voters chose independence over autonomy. The turnout was 98.5 percent. In early September, soldiers and pro-Indonesian militia drove more than 250,000 people into West Timor, killed up to 1,000 civilians, and destroyed much of East Timor's infrastructure. An Australian-led multi-national force entered East Timor under UN auspices on September 20 and began restoring order. In October, Indonesia transferred authority over East Timor to the UN, and Falintil leader Jose "Xanana" Gusmao returned to the territory following seven years in prison in Jakarta. Gusmao was widely viewed as the country's likely post-independence leader.

After relieving the interim force in early 2000, a UN peacekeeping force maintained adequate security throughout most of the territory. However, in the summer a series of clashes between peacekeepers and militia fighters near the border with Indonesia's West Timor killed at least three peacekeepers. The militia operated out of East Timorese refugee camps in West Timor, where they harassed refugees and, in early September, led a mob attack that killed four UN staffers at a refugee office in Atambua. The attack forced international relief agencies to halt the repatriation process and vacate the West Timor refugee camps, where between 85,000 and 120,000 refugees remained as of early September, according to UN estimates. More than 167,000 refugees had returned to East Timor. The UN administrator for the territory warned in October that pro-Jakarta militia had been infiltrating deeper into East Timor in recent weeks.

During the year, political leaders made little progress in establishing a framework for an independent government. The Timorese National Council of Resistance (CNRT), an umbrella group of 21 East Timorese factions, led by Gusmao, held the territory's first multiparty congress in August. However, it achieved few concrete agreements on institutions for self-rule.

Political Rights and Civil Liberties: East Timor is a non-self-governing territory under an interim UN administration, the UN Transitional Administration in East Timor (UNTAET), headed by a senior UN official, Sergio Viera de Mello. Formal independence is unlikely before the end of 2001. The CNRT plans to hold elections in August 2001 for a constituent assembly that will decide the country's political structure and draft a constitution. However, UNTAET and East Timorese leaders have made few preparations for elections and relatively little progress in building political institutions. Although UNTAET brought the CNRT into a de facto coalition government in June, several local leaders have criticized UNTAET for not including more East Timorese in the interim administration.

While the UN peacekeeping troops provided largely adequate protection for civilians, Reuters reported in September that pro-integration militia were harassing some villagers near the border with West Timor. In addition, Human Rights Watch reported that local CNRT officials and Falintil members abused many East Timorese returning from West Timor because of alleged links to pro-Jakarta militia. Several returnees were killed. Similarly, Amnesty International said in August that vigilante groups had harassed, intimidated, beaten, tortured, and arbitrarily detained some suspected supporters of integration with Indonesia and ethnic and religious minorities.

Although its civilian police force carried out some investigations, UNTAET's efforts to bring to justice suspects in the 1999 violence were hampered by the fact that most of the suspects were in Indonesia. The 1999 violence began following Jakarta's decision that January to hold a referendum on self-determination in East Timor. Backed by the Indonesian military, militia committed extrajudicial killings, disappearances, rape, arbitrary detention, torture, destruction of homes, and other abuses against CNRT members and other pro-independence activists and alleged supporters, as well as human rights monitors, journalists, humanitarian workers, and, later, UN staff.

Beginning on September 4, 1999, when the UN announced the referendum results, militia and soldiers began a systematic campaign of extrajudicial executions, rape, disappearances, and other attacks against civilians that forced hundreds of thousands of people into the mountains or into West Timor and other parts of Indonesia. Militia subsequently seized control of most camps in West Timor and used intimidation, harassment, and, in some cases, extrajudicial killings, abductions, rape, and forcible recruitment to effectively prevent many refugees from returning to East Timor.

The UN set up a new judiciary in East Timor and introduced a provisional criminal procedure code in 2000. With the help of foreign donors, numerous nongovernmental organizations began functioning during the year. At year's end, the territory also had two daily newspapers.

UNTAET's efforts to prepare the country for independence were hampered by an extremely high unemployment rate, a high rate of inflation, and the September 1999 destruction by militia and soldiers of up to 70 percent of East Timor's infrastructure, according to World Bank estimates. Many donors slowed reconstruction activities by falling behind in disbursing aid that had been pledged. Moreover, the international presence in the territory created distortions in the local economy, as many Timorese left farms and other work to provide services to foreign humanitarian workers. Damage to processing plants limited exports of arabica coffee, the dominant source of foreign exchange. Oil and gas are also potential revenue earners. The CNRT is reportedly seeking a treaty with Canberra that would place most of the petroleum-rich Timor Gap under Dili's control. Australia prefers maintaining the 1989 Timor Gap Treaty between Canberra and Jakarta, which evenly divides petroleum revenue, when an independent East Timor assumes Indonesia's former treaty obligation, which Jakarta has ceded to UNTAET.

Ecuador

Polity: Presidential-   **Political Rights:** 3*
parliamentary democracy   **Civil Liberties:** 3
Economy: Capitalist-statist   **Status:** Partly Free
Population: 12,600,000
PPP: $3,003
Life Expectancy: 70
Ethnic Groups: Mestizo (55 percent), Indian (25 percent),
Spanish (10 percent), black (10 percent)
Capital: Quito
Ratings Change: Ecuador's political rights rating changed from 2 to 3, and its status
from Free to Partly Free, due to a partially successful military coup in January 2000
that succeeded in overthrowing the elected president, who then was replaced by the
country's vice president .

Overview:
In January 2000, a cadre of young military officers, supported
by several indigenous groups, forced ailing President Jamil
Mahuad from power and proclaimed a "parliament of the
people" to fight corruption and poverty, before being forced to cede control to Gustavo
Noboa, Mahuad's elected vice president. The return to civilian rule came after the armed
forces chief, who initially supported the rebels and became a member of a transitory
civilian-military junta, backed down in the face of strong condemnation of the "proto-
coup" from the U.S. State Department and at least 20 regional commanders under his
command. In February, Noboa, Ecuador's fifth president in three years, decorated the
putschist general, Carlos Mendoza, for "professional excellence," in an apparent attempt to heal the schisms opened within the armed forces by the partially successful
action against civilian rule. Throughout 2000, the alleged causes of the rebellion, carried out during the worst economic crisis in seven decades, continued to be fiercely
debated by contending political and social forces, while fears rose about the spillover
effects of violence in neighboring Colombia. Noboa's economic program largely mirrored that of his predecessor, Mahuad, including a plan to phase out the local currency
and replace it with the U.S. dollar by the end of 2000.

Established in 1830 after achieving independence from Spain in 1822, the Republic of Ecuador has endured many interrupted presidencies and military governments.
The last military regime gave way to civilian rule when a new constitution was approved
by referendum in 1978.

The constitution provides for a president elected for four years, with a runoff between two front-runners if no candidate wins a majority in the first round. The 77-
member unicameral National Chamber of Deputies is composed of 65 members elected
on a provincial basis every two years and 12 elected nationally every four years.

The 1992 national elections were won overwhelming by Sixto Durán Ballen, whose
Republican Union Party nonetheless garnered only 13 of 77 legislative seats. Durán
Ballen's term was marked by general strikes against his economic austerity measures,
allegations of corruption, indigenous protests against business-backed land reform, and
the impeachment of cabinet ministers by an opposition-controlled congress.

In 1996 elections, Abdala Bucarám Ortiz, the flamboyant former mayor of Guayaquil known as "El Loco" (the Crazy Man), won 54 percent of the vote in runoff elections, carrying 20 of Ecuador's 21 provinces. Once in office, Bucarám, who had previously fled the country twice under threat of prosecution for corruption, applied a stringent, market-oriented austerity program. The authoritarian flavor and frenetic corruption of his government sparked mass protests.

In February 1997, a 48-hour general strike led by Indians and students prompted congress to depose Bucarám on grounds of "mental incapacity." Congressional speaker Fabian Alarcón was selected as his replacement after the military high command jettisoned its support for Bucarám's vice president and constitutionally mandated successor, Rosalía Arteaga.

In July 1997 Alarcón, himself accused of employing more than 1,000 no-show employees while speaker, dismissed the supreme court, ostensibly to carry out the "depoliticization" of the justice system mandated by the referendum, but in effect removing the chief judge, who was pressing to have the interim president investigated. Despite Alarcón's efforts to be allowed to finish out Bucarám's four-year term, he was met by strong political and civic opposition.

In May 1998, Jamil Mahuad, the mayor of Quito, posted a first-place finish in presidential elections in which the runner-up was Alvaro Noboa, who, despite being the candidate of Bucarám's Partido Roldosista Ecuatoriano (PRE), promised that neither the party nor the former president would play any part in his campaign. Mahuad, a Harvard-educated lawyer, bested Noboa, a banana tycoon, 51 to 49 percent in the July 12 runoff election.

In 1999, the economic challenges facing Mahuad appeared daunting, as the country faced its worst crisis in decades. The government was torn by savage infighting and fallout from regional tensions, and often faced violent protests from students, transport workers, and rural Indians. After partially defaulting on its foreign debt in September, the government sought to restructure its external and internal debt through talks with creditors. In November the army high command denounced what it called irresponsible conduct by "certain leaders" that, it said, was threatening the existence of the country's democratic institutions. Citing jurisdictional issues, Mahuad refused to testify on charges that he and various aides kept $3.1 million in campaign contributions for themselves.

Young military officers, many of Native American ancestry, concerned that Mahuad's government was spending ever more money bailing out local banks while it reduced the armed forces budget, made common cause with indigenous leaders representing as many as four million of some of the country's poorest inhabitants in the effort to overthrow Mahuad. Political divisions continued for most of 2000 even after the hapless president was forcibly removed from office. For most of August, the Ecuadoran congress split into two separate entities in a dispute over the privatization of 18 electricity companies and the state-owned oil company. The adoption of the U.S. dollar as the local currency, which was officially declared in April, was the object of continued protests by Indian and leftist-led labor unions throughout 2000, who say it will hurt the poor by causing prices to rise to international levels, while eliminating critical subsidies for basic food and services. Proponents of the plan say the currency change will help eliminate Latin America's highest inflation rate, stabilize the economy, and promote business investment. In September 2000 Transparency International ranked Ecuador as Latin America's most corrupt nation. In late 2000, the Ecuadoran government sought to cope with tens of thousands of Colombian refugees seeking refuge from escalating warfare between guerrilla, paramilitary, and army forces in their own country.

Political Rights and Civil Liberties:

Citizens can change their government through elections, although the January 2000 coup attempt represented a clear reversal of democratic trends in Ecuador. The 1998 campaign had seemed to mark a return to electoral means as a way of resolving political differences. Mahuad's victory came after Alvaro Noboa ran what is believed to be the most expensive national campaign in Ecuadoran history. In 1998, the national constituent assembly decided to retain Ecuador's presidential system. It also mandated that in the year 2002, a presidential candidate will need to win 40 percent of valid votes in first-round balloting and exceed by 10 percent those received by the nearest rival in order to avoid a runoff.

Constitutional guarantees regarding freedom of expression, freedom of religion, and the right to organize political parties are generally respected. However, for several years Ecuador appeared to be virtually ungovernable as a result of near-constant gridlock among the executive, legislative, and judicial branches, particularly through the use, by congress, of easy and sometimes frivolous votes of censure and impeachment in order to block executive initiatives.

The judiciary, generally undermined by the corruption afflicting the entire political system, is headed by a supreme court that, until 1997, was appointed by the legislature and thus subject to political influence. In reforms approved by referendum in May 1997, power to appoint judges was given over to the supreme court, with congress given a final chance to choose that 31-member body based on recommendations made by a special selection commission.

Evidence suggests that drug traffickers have penetrated the political system through campaign financing, and sectors of the police and military through bribery. Ecuador is a transshipment point for cocaine passing from neighboring Colombia to the United States and a money-laundering haven. In 1999, incursions from both Colombian guerrilla groups and their paramilitary enemies into Ecuadoran territory added to regional concern about the extent to which the neighboring country's civil war would affect public safety and the survival of democratic institutions. The 1999 murder of Jaime Hurtado González, a congressman and former presidential candidate, at the hands of right-wing paramilitaries in broad daylight in downtown Quito, sent shock waves through Ecuador's political establishment.

Violent crime has undermined public faith in the police to maintain order. In 1999 a sharp increase was reported in the number of handgun licenses issued by the military. Ecuador has numerous human rights organizations, and despite occasional acts of intimidation, they report on arbitrary arrests and instances of police brutality. The military is responsible for a significant percentage of abuses, particularly when deployed in states of emergency. Abuses, including torture, are committed with relative impunity, with police and military personnel tried in military rather than civilian courts.

Indians, who make up between a third and nearly half of the country's population and who have been in the forefront of protests against the country's endemic poverty and political corruption, are the frequent victims of abuse by military officers working in league with large landowners during disputes over land. A consequence of the continuing lack of access of Native Americans to effective systems of justice emerged in 1998, when Ecuadoran Indians held several U.S. oil company employees against their will, in support of a demand that the firm pay royalties to, and contribute to, health care, education, and housing for Indians. Vigilante acts committed in Native American communities also appear to be on the upswing in recent years.

The media are mostly private and outspoken. The government controls radio frequencies. Labor unions are well organized and have the right to strike, although the labor code limits public sector strikes. Workers in the country's booming flower industry are routinely exposed to harmful pesticides.

Violence against women is common in Ecuador, and frequently occurs on holidays in which alcohol is consumed in large quantities. The problem is particularly acute in Indian areas, where women frequently do not report abuse to the authorities, in part because they are afraid of harming their community's reputation. Homosexuals are also often the victims of police brutality and harassment.

Egypt

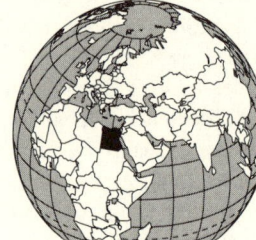

Polity: Dominant party (military-influenced)
Political Rights: 6
Civil Liberties: 5
Economy: Mixed statist
Status: Not Free
Population: 68,300,000
PPP: $3,041
Life Expectancy: 67
Ethnic Groups: Egyptian, Bedouin, Berber (99 percent), other (1 percent)
Capital: Cairo

Overview:
The government of President Hosni Mubarak resisted intensified pressure for democratic and economic reform in 2000. Despite the effective neutralization of Islamic insurgents and a sharp reduction in militant violence, the government in February extended for three years the emergency law that allows it to suppress political dissent in the name of protecting national security. The legislation was used regularly throughout the year to crack down on the opposition, particularly in the run-up to parliamentary elections in October and November.

Egypt gained formal independence from Great Britain in 1922, though the latter continued to exercise gradually dwindling control until its surrender of the Suez Canal Zone in 1956. Colonel Gamel Abdel Nasser became head of state in 1954 after leading a coup that overthrew the monarchy, and ruled until his death in 1970. A constitution adopted in 1971 under Nasser's successor, Anwar al-Sadat, grants full executive powers to the president, who is nominated by the 454-member People's Assembly and elected to a six-year term in a national referendum. Sadat was assassinated by Islamic militants in 1981 for making peace with Israel. Under Mubarak, the ruling National Democratic Party (NDP) continues to dominate a tightly controlled political system.

In the early 1990s, the radical *Gamaat Islamiya* (Islamic Group) tapped into popular discontent with official corruption, high unemployment, and widespread poverty. In a campaign to establish an Islamic republic by force, it escalated attacks on police, Coptic Christians, and tourists. The government's response has been the brutal repression of all forms of political dissent. Thousands of suspected militants have been tried and jailed without due process, and more than 70 political prisoners have been executed under special military courts set up to handle terrorist offenses. The nonviolent Muslim Brotherhood, a fundamentalist movement dating from the 1920s that is officially outlawed but generally tolerated, has been a particular target because of its popularity.

Years of repression and a relentless military campaign have largely eradicated the threat of Islamist violence. In addition, ideological rifts and policy disputes within the two major extremist groups, Gamaat Islamiya and Jihad, have left both groups divided and ineffective. Popular support for militants has eroded as a result of their greater emphasis on violence than on alternative policy. The Gamaat announced a ceasefire in March 1999, and the government has since followed a policy of gradually releasing jailed suspected militants who renounce extremist ideology. Some Jihad leaders began to call for peace in early 2000, but the government, as yet, questions the credibility of such announcements. Authorities continue to reject the idea of dialogue with any Islamist group.

With legislative elections due at year's end, opposition party members and NGOs began an intensive campaign promoting constitutional reforms to ensure an election fairer than the 1995 poll, which was fraught with irregularity, violence, and vote rigging. Although the government rejected calls for significant reform, a constitutional court ruling in July effectively invalidated the 1990 and 1995 legislatures on the grounds that elections were supervised by police rather than judges and were therefore unconstitutional. The ruling forced the government to guarantee full judicial supervision of 2000 elections, a move welcomed by opposition groups.

The NDP won 170 seats outright, but more than 200 candidates who ran as independents switched over to the NDP after winning seats. Muslim Brotherhood candidates won 17 seats, making the outlawed party the largest opposition faction in parliament. The Wafd party won 7 seats; Tagammu, 6; the Nasserist Party, 2; and the Liberal Party 1. Despite improvements in procedure, observers called the 2000 election only marginally fairer than past contests. Unlike the NDP, opposition parties were subject to limits on their media coverage. By September, a reported 1,000 Muslim Brothers were behind bars as the result of a government campaign to avoid any significant opposition. In a notable case, Saad Eddin Ibrahim, the director of the Ibn Khaldoun Center for Development, an independent research institute that intended to monitor the elections, was arrested in June along with ten associates. He was charged with harming Egypt's image and accused of spying for the U.S. In September, he faced further charges of illegal foreign funding and bribery. One election observer sent by Amnesty International was assaulted at a Cairo polling station, and there were credible reports that police used intimidation and roadblocks to prevent people from voting. Eleven people died in election-related unrest.

Ambiguity in the government's economic policies caused concern among investors during the year. The Egyptian economy has recently withstood poor oil revenues, a reduction in tourism due to terrorism, and lower investor confidence in emerging markets, while a program of liberalization has achieved growth rates of about five percent. However, the government balked at the scheduled privatization in 2000 of a state cement company and one of the four major state banks, reportedly because of hostile public opinion. It has also delayed signing a partnership agreement with the European Union that would open its market to European imports. In July, Standard & Poors downgraded its outlook on Egypt from stable to negative, citing an increasing fiscal deficit and questionable commitment to privatization.

Egypt continued to play the role of regional mediator in the Middle East peace process throughout 2000, and in late October hosted an emergency summit of the 22-member Arab League in response to the outbreak of hostilities between Palestinians and Israeli forces. In convening the summit, leaders sought to promote a unified Arab response to the crisis and to prove their commitment to the Palestinian cause in the face of widespread anti-Israel street demonstrations throughout the Arab world. In November, Egypt recalled its ambassador to Israel, citing "Israeli aggression" against Palestinians.

Political Rights and Civil Liberties: Egyptians cannot change their government democratically. The constitution does not allow for a presidential election. Instead, the elected People's Assembly nominates one candidate to be confirmed in a national referendum. The assembly has limited influence in economic, security, and foreign policy; almost all legislation is initiated by the executive. The 1995 parliamentary elections were characterized by widespread fraud and irregularity. In July 2000, the constitutional court effectively invalidated the parliament elected in 1995 by ruling that the traditional system of interior ministry supervision of elections was unconstitutional, and that elections should be supervised by the judiciary. Consequently, elections were held in three rounds during October and November so that a relatively small number of judges could supervise all polling stations. Despite this measure, the elections were regarded as neither free nor fair.

The 264-member *Shura*, or upper house of parliament, has no legislative authority; its role is restricted to issuing opinions and reports on topics of its choosing. The NDP dominates the People's Assembly, the Shura, and local government. Political opposition remains weak and ineffective. Requests to form political parties are routinely denied by the NDP-controlled Political Parties Committee (PPC), usually because their platforms are "unoriginal." The PPC has allowed the legal establishment of two political parties in the last 20 years, bringing the total to 16. The NDP uses the political parties law and other restrictions to impede opposition activities and access to media. The popular Muslim Brotherhood may not compete in elections because of a ban on religion-based parties, but its members may run as independents. Thousands of Muslim Brothers were rounded up and arrested prior to the 2000 legislative elections.

Emergency law has been in effect since Sadat's assassination in 1981 and is up for renewal every three years. Its provisions allow for the arrest without charge of suspected opponents of the regime, as well as their families and acquaintances. Torture, poor prison conditions, and lack of adequate food and medical care are pervasive in custody. However, the interior ministry in September announced that it would ban flogging and caning as punishments. Another positive development came in November, when two policemen were jailed for the torture of two detainees, one of whom died in custody.

The judiciary operates with limited independence. The president appoints both the general prosecutor and the head of the court of cassation, Egypt's highest court. Under Law 25/1996, the president may refer civilian cases to military courts. Since 1992, suspected Gamaat Islamiya and Muslim Brotherhood activists have been tried in military courts, where due process rights are severely curtailed. There is no appellate process for verdicts by military courts; instead, verdicts are subject to review by other military judges and confirmed by the president. While Gamaat convicts are frequently executed, no Muslim Brothers have ever been sentenced to death. Fifteen Brotherhood members were sentenced to between three- and five- years' imprisonment in November for membership in an illegal organization and "infiltrating" professional syndicates, universities, and trade unions.

The Egyptian courts have recently demonstrated a greater degree of independence, and have thus established themselves as the only serious challenge to state authority. In addition to the July ruling on electoral procedures, the constitutional court ruled in June that a restrictive NGO law passed in 1999 was unconstitutional on the grounds that it was not subjected to the proper parliamentary debate procedures. In June, the supreme state security court handed down the maximum penalty against 31 businessmen, including four members of parliament, in the first corruption case to target politicians. In July, an administrative court ruled against government interference in bar association elections. Also in July, an administrative court overturned the PPC's suspension of the opposition Labor Party and its newspaper. Each of these rulings has possible far-reaching implications for government openness and accountability.

The Press Law, the Publications Law, the Penal Code, and libel laws restrict press freedom. Criticism of the president, the government, and foreign heads of state may result in fines or imprisonment. The government owns stock in the three major daily newspapers, and the president appoints their editors in chief. The government also monopolizes printing and distribution of newspapers. Opposition parties publish newspapers with government subsidies. The information ministry owns and operates all broadcast media. The government announced in January that it would allow the establishment of private joint stock companies for satellite broadcasting, and reserve the right to censor content. Three journalists from the opposition *Al-Shaab* and five from *Al-Ahrar* were sentenced to prison in April for libel. *Al-Shaab* was closed for four months by the PPC because of alleged divisions within the leadership of the paper's parent Labor Party. A satirist was charged in July with threatening national security for writing a public service announcement urging Egyptians to vote. Egypt has some 250,000 Internet users in a population of 66 million, of which nearly half are illiterate.

In September, Amnesty International denounced systematic harassment of opposition politicians and civil society institutions in the run-up to legislative elections. The PPC temporarily closed the Islamist Labor Party in July, citing a party leadership struggle. In February, the secretary-general of the Egyptian Organization for Human Rights (EOHR) was charged with illegally receiving money from foreign sources. The case was dropped a month later with no official explanation. The EOHR's registration as an official NGO was delayed indefinitely for "security reasons" in July. In April, the bar association was placed under judicial supervision for three years in an attempt by the government to limit participation by the Muslim Brotherhood. The government denied legal recognition to a union of women's NGOs established in 1999, and instead set up its own umbrella organization. The interior ministry may withhold approval for public demonstrations under emergency law. The ministry of social affairs has broad powers to merge and dissolve NGOs. A new law on associations that expanded these powers was declared unconstitutional in June.

Women face discrimination in many legal and social matters. Foreign-born husbands and children of Egyptian women are denied Egyptian citizenship, and a woman must have permission from a male relative to travel abroad. A ban on female genital mutilation took effect in 1997, though it is not widely enforced. In 1999, the government repealed a law allowing a rapist to avoid punishment by marrying his victim. In a society that links family honor to the chastity of its women, a rape victim may consent to marry her attacker in order to avoid disgracing, and perhaps being murdered by, her family. "Honor killings" occur in both Muslim and Christian communities. A personal status law passed in January makes it easier for a woman to obtain a divorce and allows her to call upon the state to garnishee her husband's wages to help support her. A new marriage contract issued in August provides a space for mutually agreed-upon conditions, such as a wife's right to work or to travel abroad, so long as the conditions comply with Islamic law.

The government portrays itself as a staunch supporter of Islam, the state religion, as it cracks down on fundamentalist influences in academia, mosques, and other institutions. The *imams* (spiritual leaders) of licensed mosques are chosen and paid by the government, which also monitors sermons. Most Egyptians are Sunni Muslim. Orthodox and other Coptic Christians constitute about ten percent of the population. The Jewish community reportedly numbers about 200, and there are small numbers of Shiite Muslims and Bahais. Any perceived illegitimate interpretation of Islam is grounds for heresy and sedition charges. Security officials arrested 48 people in March for membership in an alleged Muslim cult that believes the government is heretical.

Muslims have murdered, kidnapped, raped, and forcibly converted scores of Copts in recent years, and burned or vandalized Copt homes, shops, and churches. The government has seized Coptic Church-owned land, has closed churches, and frequently uses an Ottoman Empire-era law to deny permission to build or repair churches. No official has been held accountable for the arrest and reported torture of some 1,200 Copts in late 1998 in connection with sectarian violence resulting from the murder of two Copts in August 1998. Courts in Sohag and Dar al-Salam began trying 135 defendants in June in connection with sectarian unrest that killed at least 21 Copts and one Muslim in December 1999 and January 2000. Twenty defendants received prison sentences ranging from six months to ten years in Dar al-Salam, while 19 were acquitted. In December, a Sohag court released 58 Muslims and 31 Copts pending the outcome of the trial.

The 1976 law on labor unions sets numerous restrictions on the formation and operation of unions and the conduct of their elections. The government-backed Egyptian Trade Union Federation is the only legal labor federation. Article 124 of the penal code prohibits labor strikes.

Child labor is a serious problem. By law, children under 14 are not permitted to work, except in agriculture, where they may take seasonal jobs at age 12 as long as they do not miss school. The law is routinely ignored, however. A recent Egyptian study found that 64 percent of children work before age 14. With poverty and unemployment pervasive in Egypt, many children forego school to earn money for their families. They find informal sector jobs in agriculture or manufacturing that do not guarantee standard working hours, safety regulations, or stable wages.

El Salvador

Polity: Presidential-par-
liamentary democracy
Economy: Capitalist
Population: 6,300,000
PPP: $4,036
Life Expectancy: 69
Ethnic Groups: Mestizo (94 percent),
Indian and white (6 percent)
Capital: San Salvador

Political Rights: 2
Civil Liberties: 3
Status: Free

Overview:

Former guerrillas of the *Frente Farabundo Marti* (FMLN) continued in 2000 to consolidate their electoral gains by becoming the leading party in the Salvadoran legislature, after winning 31 seats in the national assembly in March 12 legislative elections. Although the ruling *Alianza Republicana Nacionalista* (ARENA) remained dominant in the municipal contests, taking 124 mayoralties, the FMLN also improved its showing, winning 78 races, 24 more than it had in 1997. In October, memories of the vicious civil war that wracked the country for more than a decade were stirred as two retired generals faced a wrongful-death lawsuit in Florida for their alleged responsibility in the 1980 murders of four American churchwomen before being acquitted.

Independence from the Captaincy General of Guatemala was declared in 1841, and the Republic of El Salvador was established in 1859. More than a century of civil strife and military rule followed.

Elected civilian rule was established in 1984. The 1983 constitution, and subsequent reforms, provide for a president elected for a five-year term and an 84-member, unicameral national assembly elected for three years. More than a decade of civil war (which left more than 70,000 dead) ended with the United Nations-mediated peace accords signed in 1992 by the FMLN and the conservative government of President Alfredo Cristiani.

The FMLN participated in the 1994 elections, backing its former ally Ruben Zamora of the Democratic Convergence (CD) for president and running a slate of legislative candidates. The incumbent party, ARENA, nominated San Salvador mayor Armando Calderon Sol. The Christian Democrats (PDC) nominated Fidel Chávez Mena. The PDC had previously held power under President José Napoleon Duarte (1984-1989). The well-oiled ARENA political machine sounded populist themes and attacked the FMLN as Communists and terrorists. The FMLN-CD coalition offered a progressive but moderate platform and called for compliance with the peace accords. Calderon Sol won just under 50 percent, setting up a runoff against Zamora, who had come in second with 25 percent. In the runoff, Calderon Sol defeated Zamora, 68 percent to 32 percent.

In the March 16, 1997, elections ARENA won 28 congressional seats, 11 fewer than in 1994, to the FMLN's 27, with other parties splitting the difference. The FMLN also dramatically improved its municipal presence, winning 2 of the 3 largest cities (in coalition with other parties), 6 of 14 departmental capitals, and 10 of the 19 municipalities in San Salvador department. At the same time, ARENA suffered significant reversals, reflected in its having won 35 percent of the vote, as compared with 45 percent in previous polls.

In 1998, the FMLN's electoral chances in the following year's elections appeared to dim, as the party split into hardline Marxist and reformist camps. Although social democratic leader Facundo Guardado, himself a former guerrilla leader and a leading reformist, emerged as the party's presidential nominee, business and social sectors worried that the FMLN was still committed to social revolution.

Francisco Flores, the presidential candidate of the long-ruling, rightist ARENA, swept to victory in the March 1999 elections, in the aftermath of which the major opposition party, FMLN, dominated by former guerrillas, fell back into crisis. Crime and public safety remain grave challenges in one of the most violent countries in the Americas. ARENA nominee Flores, a 39-year-old philosopher and the former president of the legislature, beat Guardado in the first round of voting, 51.4 to 28.9 percent, in contrast to the near-tie voting two years earlier. After his inauguration, Flores promised that public security would be a priority issue in this small country where, on average, 17 murders are committed each day.

In 2000, a more hardline faction headed by Shafick Handal regained leadership of the FMLN, whose electoral luster was enhanced by the performance of the mayor of San Salvador, Hector Silva. Meanwhile Flores has had to pay the costs of public weariness with ARENA's decade-long rule, and in his first year in office he faced stiff protests against his government's free-market policies, particularly the privatization of some of the country's health services. In a West Palm Beach court, General José Guillermo Garcia and General Carlos Eugenio Vides Casanova, defense minister and director of the National Guard in 1980, respectively, were tried for one of the most heinous atrocities of the civil war. They were accused of bearing ultimate responsibility for the killings of three nuns and a lay worker and for covering up the role of senior officers. Former U.S. ambassador Robert White, who served in El Salvador at the time of the murders, testified that he long believed that there was a cover-up of the killings by both the Salvadoran and the U.S. governments.

Political Rights and Civil Liberties: Citizens can change their government democratically. The 1999 elections were free and fair, although there were charges that hurricane relief funds were used by ARENA to elect Flores, and abstentions reached a new high. The 2000 legislative and local elections, which the FMLN turned into something of a referendum on ARENA's performance, actually drew a higher turnout than the 1999 vote.

The constitution guarantees free expression, freedom of religion, and the right to organize political parties, civic groups, and labor unions. Random killings, kidnappings, and other crimes—particularly in rural areas—have reinforced the country's reputation as one of the most violent in Latin America. The 1992 peace accords have led to a significant reduction in human rights violations; nevertheless, political expression and civil liberties are still circumscribed by sporadic political violence, repressive police measures, a mounting crime wave, and right-wing death squads, including "social cleansing" vigilante groups. The crime wave has also been fed by the deportation of hundreds of Salvadorans with criminal records from the United States. In 1999, the national assembly approved a law that allows civilians to possess war weapons, such as AK-47s and M-16s, for their own defense. In 2000 the national assembly approved a constitutional amendment that allows the government to negotiate with the United States an extradition treaty, which would give El Salvador the ability to return Salvadoran nationals who committed crimes to the United States to stand trial. It is estimated that more than 100 Salvadorans accused of murder in the United States have taken refuge in El Salvador.

The judicial system remains ineffectual and corrupt, and a climate of impunity is pervasive. A first step toward judicial reform came in 1994 with the naming by the new legislature of a more politically representative 15-member supreme court, which controls the entire Salvadoran judiciary. Poor training and a lack of sustained disciplinary action for judges, as well as continued corruption, a lack of professionalism, and a painfully slow system of processing cases, greatly undermine public confidence in the justice system.

Although El Salvador is one of the few Latin American countries to restrict military involvement in internal security, the army occasionally joins the police in patrolling San Salvador and some rural districts in crackdowns on gang violence. The National Civilian Police (PNC), which incorporated some former FMLN guerrillas into its ranks, has been unable to curb the country's rampant crime while protecting human rights. Complaints of police brutality and corruption are widespread; scores of policemen have been imprisoned on rights charges. In June 2000 Flores announced that 24 senior- and middle-ranking PNC officers were being cashiered because of their involvement with organized crime. Prisons are overcrowded, conditions are wretched, and up to three-quarters of the prisoners are waiting to be charged and tried. Dozens of inmates have been killed during prison riots.

The media are privately owned. Left-wing journalists and publications are occasionally targets of intimidation. Although the country is overwhelmingly Roman Catholic, evangelical Protestantism has made substantial inroads, leading to friction.

Labor, peasant, and university groups are well organized. The archaic labor code was reformed in 1994, but the new code lacks the approval of most unions because it significantly limits the right to organize in some areas, including the export-processing zones known as *maquiladoras*. Unions that strike are subject to intimidation and violent police crackdowns. Child labor is a problem, as is violence against women.

Equatorial Guinea

Polity: Presidential (military-dominated)
Economy: Capitalist-statist
Population: 500,000
PPP: $1,817
Life Expectancy: 50
Ethnic Groups: Fang (83 percent), Bubi (10 percent), other (7 percent)
Capital: Malabo

Political Rights: 7
Civil Liberties: 7
Status: Not Free

Overview:

The pursuit of oil by U.S. companies off the shores of Equatorial Guinea has given the country a higher profile on the world economic stage and appears to have forced President Teodoro Obiang Nguema Mbasogo to at least take a shallow look inward. The country continues to be ruled by one of Africa's most repressive regimes, but there are indications that Obiang feels some sort of international pressure to at least appear as though he's making reforms.

Equatorial Guinea achieved independence in 1968 following 190 years of Spanish rule. It has since been one of the world's most tightly closed and repressive societies. President Obiang seized power in 1979 by deposing and murdering his uncle, Francisco Macias Nguema. Pressure from donor countries demanding democratic reforms prompted Obiang to proclaim a new "era of pluralism" in January 1992. Political parties were legalized, and multiparty elections announced, but in practice Obiang and his clique wield all power. The right of people to freely elect the country's leaders does not exist.

While municipal elections held in April 2000 were no more credible than previous polls, observers from opposition parties were positioned at some voting stations. Obiang in October reportedly urged Prime Minister Angel Serafin Seriche Dougan to resign for doing too little about corruption. Any serious attempt to combat corruption would probably bring Obiang under pressure from the ruling elite that has benefited from Equatorial Guinea's income from oil wealth.

Talks are under way to reform the country's labor laws, and the International Committee of the Red Cross (ICRC) has been granted access to Equatorial Guinea's prisons, which have a reputation for torture and other ill-treatment. The justice minister and a relative, the son of the country's first president, were reportedly detained on conspiracy charges under murky circumstances in August and September, but were later freed.

Thanks to oil, Equatorial Guinea boasts one of the highest figures for per capita gross domestic product in Africa, but few of the benefits have yet to be felt by the average person. The start of offshore oil production in 1995 helped replace subsistence farming and timber as the economic linchpins. U.S. companies dominate the oil sector. The country is to benefit from a $173 million loan by the U.S. Overseas Private Investment Corporation (OPIC) for construction and operation of a methanol plant. It is OPIC's largest-ever loan to a project in sub-Saharan Africa.

Political Rights and Civil Liberties: Equatorial Guinea's citizens are unable to change their government through peaceful, democratic means. The February 1996 presidential election was neither free nor fair, and was marred by official intimidation, a near total boycott by the political opposition, and very low voter turnout.

The March 1999 parliamentary elections were also marred by intimidation and fraud and were neither free nor fair. Many opposition candidates were arrested or confined to their villages prior to the polls. The ruling Democratic Party of Equatorial Guinea (PDGE) won 75 of 80 seats. Led by the Convergence for Social Democracy and the Popular Union, seven opposition parties claimed massive fraud, demanding an annulment, and those that won parliamentary seats refused to take them up. Amnesty International said at least 90 opposition party activists were detained for short periods in 1999. The November 1998 legislative elections for the 85-member House of People's Representatives were also manipulated by the regime.

Opposition parties were widely believed to have won overwhelmingly in September 1995 municipal elections. The regime's official results, released 11 days after balloting, reported an unconvincing but unsurprising landslide victory by the PDGE. Municipal elections held in April 2000 produced similar results. The government announced a turnout of 91 percent and that the ruling party had won 98 percent of the vote. The mechanics of the poll, however, were slightly better than in previous years. Opposition representatives were reportedly present at some polling stations as observers.

President Obiang wields broad decree-making powers and effectively bars public participation in the policymaking process. The November 1991 constitution prohibits the impeachment of the head of state. Opposition parties, while legal, may not be organized on an ethnic, regional, or provincial basis.

With partial exception for members of legalized political parties, freedom of association and assembly is not allowed. Opposition demonstrations without prior authorization were banned in 1993. Authorization must be obtained for any gathering of ten or more people for purposes the government deems political. Freedom of movement is also restricted, as citizens and residents must obtain permission for travel both within the country and abroad.

The judiciary is not independent, and laws on search and seizure, as well as detention, are routinely ignored by security forces, who act with impunity. Civil cases rarely go to trial. A military tribunal handles cases tied to national security. International aid money has been provided for codifying the country's legal provisions. No published gazette of laws exists.

Opposition parties are continually harassed and intimidated, especially outside the capital, Malabo. Amnesty International reported in June that hundreds of political activists had been arrested and held without charge or trial in recent years "for exercising their rights to freedom of expression and assembly." Unlawful arrests, beatings, and torture remain commonplace. There are persistent reports of torture by soldiers and police to extract confessions. Prisons conditions are extremely harsh. The ICRC was eventually granted access to prisoners in December 1999 after repeated attempts.

There are no effective human rights organizations in the country, and the few international nongovernmental organizations operating in Equatorial Guinea are subject to restrictions. The aid agency Medecins Sans Frontiéres (Doctors Without Borders) suspended its operations in the country in January 2000, saying the government denied it access to people the agency said were suffering from the direct consequences of corruption.

Press freedom is constitutionally guaranteed, but the government restricts those rights in practice. Nearly all print and broadcast media are state run and tightly controlled. A few small independent newspapers publish occasionally but exercise self-censorship, and all journalists must be registered. Mild criticism of infrastructure and public institutions is allowed, but nothing disparaging about the president or security forces is tolerated. Some underground pamphlets appear irregularly. Few foreign publications are available.

Five people detained in November and December 1999 were sentenced by a military court to up to three years in prison for possessing a two-year-old Amnesty International appeal document, photocopying a Spanish newspaper article, and possessing an opposition newspaper. The court said the material was "of dubious provenance." Authorities in November seized hundreds of copies of the independent weekly, *La Opinion,* before they were distributed.

About 80 percent of the population is Roman Catholic. Freedom of individual religious practice is generally respected, although President Obiang has warned the clergy against interfering in political affairs. The majority Fang ethnic group actively discriminates against the Bubi and other ethnic minorities. Monopoly political power by the president's Mongomo clan of the Fang ethnic group persists. Differences between the Fang and the Bubi are a major source of political tension that has often erupted into violence. Fang vigilante groups have been allowed to abuse Bubi citizens with impunity.

Unions are permitted by the constitution, but no law enabling their formation has been enacted. Strikes are barred. No labor unions exist, and there is no law on the right to bargain collectively.

Constitutional and legal protections of equality for women are largely ignored. Traditional practices discriminate against women, and few have educational opportunities or participate in the formal economy or government. Violence against women is reportedly widespread. There is no child rights policy.

Eritrea

Polity: One-party (transitional)
Economy: Mixed statist
Population: 4,100,000
PPP: $833
Life Expectancy: 51
Ethnic Groups: Tigrinya (50 percent), Tigre and Kunama (40 percent), Afar (4 percent), Saho (3 percent), other (3 percent)
Capital: Asmara

Political Rights: 7
Civil Liberties: 5
Status: Not Free

Overview:
Hostilities with Ethiopia ended, at least temporarily, with the signature of a cease-fire in June after an Ethiopian advance succeeded in making significant territorial gains. The agree-

ment provided for a United Nations-led buffer force to be installed along the Eritrean side of the contested border and further negotiations to determine the final boundary line. The war dominated the country's political and economic agenda and reflected deeper issues of nationalism and political mobilization by governments that have long used the presence of real or perceived enemies to generate popular support and unity.

In 1950, after years of Italian occupation, Eritrea was incorporated into Ethiopia. Eritrea's independence struggle began in 1962 as a nationalist and Marxist guerrilla war against the Ethiopian government of Emperor Haile Selassie. The seizure of power by a Marxist junta in Ethiopia in 1974 removed the ideological basis of the conflict, and by the time Eritrea finally defeated Ethiopia's northern armies in 1991, the Eritrean People's Liberation Front (EPLF) had discarded Marxism. Internationally recognized independence was achieved in May 1993 after a referendum supervised by the UN produced a landslide vote for statehood.

Since 1993, Eritrea has engaged in hostilities with Sudan, Yemen, and in 1998, Ethiopia. It has also had strained relations with Djibouti. A constitution was adopted in May 1997, but many of its provisions have yet to be implemented. For example, national elections have yet to take place. Eritrea's proclivity to settle disputes by the force of arms and continued tight government control over the country's political life have dashed hopes raised by President Isaias Afwerki's membership in a group of "new African leaders" who promised more open governance and a break with Africa's recent tradition of autocratic rule.

The war with Ethiopia began in 1998. In May 2000, an Ethiopian military offensive succeeded in making significant territorial gains. Eritrea signed a truce with Ethiopia in June which stipulated that international peacekeepers be deployed in a security zone while negotiations continued on resolving ongoing disputes between the two countries about the border.

The war with Ethiopia has impeded Eritrea's progress in developing a de facto and de jure pluralist political system. The challenge now faced by the government is to follow through on long-delayed promises to institute a pluralist political system. By the end of 2000, some initial moves had been made in establishing a timetable for this change.

Externally based opposition groups, some of which are backed by Eritrea's foes in Ethiopia and Sudan, have begun to function. In 2000 there were also some reports of growing political disaffection with the government. For example, there were reports that a de facto curfew was declared around the capital of Asmara, and that students who protested against the war were evacuated to military camps outside of Asmara.

Political Rights and Civil Liberties:

Eritreans cannot change their government democratically. Created in February 1994 as a successor to the EPLF, the Popular Front for Democracy and Justice (PFDJ) maintains dominance over the country's political and economic life that is unlikely to change in the near- to medium-term future. The PFDJ has had broad public support, although in 2000, the existence of exiled opposition groups and some reports of internal disaffection with the war suggested that its rule is not monolithic.

In 1994 a 50-member constitutional commission was established. In 1997 a new constitution authorizing "conditional" political pluralism with provisions for a multiparty system was adopted. The constitution provides for the election of the president from among the members of the national assembly by a vote of the majority of its members. The term of office is five years, for a maximum of two terms. The appointed national assembly comprises 75 members of the PFDJ central committee, 60 members of the former Constituent Assembly, and 15 representatives of Eritreans residing abroad.

In reality, Eritrea has yet to institutionalize a democratic political system. In October the national assembly decided that the first elections should be held in December 2001, and appointed a committee that will draft regulations governing political parties. Until this, no timetable had ever been drafted and adopted concerning implementing legislation and statutes regarding political parties and elections. Polls were supposed to have been held in 1998, but were postponed indefinitely following the outbreak of hostilities with Ethiopia. Independent political parties authorized by the constitution are not yet registered. The war with Ethiopia provided a useful rationale for the government to continue to keep this issue unresolved.

Eritrea's political culture places priority on group interests over those of the individual. This view has been forged in part by years of struggle against outside occupiers and austere attachment to Marxist principles. Eritrea's aggressive foreign policy has contributed significantly to regional instability and to a sense of victimization among Eritreans, which in turn afford a rationale for continued strong central government control.

The rights of citizens to select their leadership and to freely associate remain seriously limited. Many inside and outside the government argue that in the current context emphasis must be placed on maintaining domestic unity and consensus. Parties based on ethnicity or religion are to be barred.

The new constitution's guarantees of civil and political liberties are unrealized as pluralistic media and rights to political organization continue to be absent. A judiciary was formed by decree in 1993 and has yet to adopt positions that are significantly at variance with government perspectives. Low levels of training and resources limit the courts' efficiency. Constitutional guarantees are often ignored in cases relating to state security. While free discussion in public fora may be tolerated, the dissemination of dissenting views is not. Government control over all broadcasting, and pressures against the independent print media, have constrained public debate. A 1997 press law allows only qualified freedom of expression, subject to the official interpretation of "the objective reality of Eritrea."

The government has maintained a hostile attitude towards civil society and has refused international assistance designed to support the development of pluralism in society. The government controls most elements of civil life, either directly or through affiliated organizations. The absence of energetic independent media and nongovernmental human rights organizations in turn has a dissuasive effect upon the potential development of other civil society groups.

Official government policy is supportive of free enterprise, and citizens generally have the freedom to choose their employment, establish private businesses, and function relatively free of government harassment. Until recently, at least, government officials have enjoyed a reputation for relative probity.

The government finally adhered to the Geneva Convention in July 2000, permitting some independent monitoring of conditions in detention facilities and granting representatives of the International Committee for the Red Cross (ICRC) broad access to prisoners and detainees. Arbitrary arrest and detention are problems. The provision of speedy trials is limited by a lack of trained personnel, inadequate funding, and poor infrastructure, and the use of a special court system limits due process.

Women played important roles in the guerilla movement, and the government has worked in favor of improving the status of women. In an effort to encourage broader participation by women in politics, the PFDJ named three women to the party's executive council and 12 women to the central committee in 1997. Women participated in the constitutional commission (filling almost half of the positions on the 50-person committee) and hold senior government positions, including the positions of minister of justice and minister of labor.

Equal educational opportunity, equal pay for equal work, and penalties for domestic violence have been codified, yet traditional societal discrimination persists against women in the largely rural and agricultural country. Jehovah's Witnesses face some societal discrimination.

Estonia

Polity: Parliamentary democracy
Economy: Mixed capitalist
Population: 1,400,000
PPP: $7,682
Life Expectancy: 69
Ethnic Groups: Estonian (65 percent), Russian (28 percent), other (7 percent)
Capital: Tallinn

Political Rights: 1
Civil Liberties: 2
Status: Free

Overview:

After enduring a recession during much of 1999 caused by the August 1998 Russian financial crisis, Estonia's economy showed signs of significant growth throughout the year 2000. The country's economic recovery served to improve government efforts to harmonize Estonian legislation and practices with requirements for eventual European Union (EU) membership, for which Estonia remains a front-runner among Eastern European and former Soviet states.

Dominated by Sweden in the sixteenth and seventeenth centuries and annexed by Russia in 1704, Estonia became independent in 1918. Soviet troops occupied the country during World War II, following a secret protocol in the 1939 Hitler-Stalin pact which forcibly incorporated Estonia, Latvia, and Lithuania into the U.S.S.R. Under Soviet rule, approximately one-tenth of Estonia's population was deported, executed, or forced to escape to the West. Subsequent Russian immigration substantially altered the country's ethnic composition, with ethnic Estonians constituting 88 percent before World War II and just over 61 percent in 1989. Estonia regained its independence following the disintegration of the Soviet Union in 1991.

Estonia's second post-independence parliamentary elections in March 1995 saw a shift to the center-left Coalition Party/Rural Union (KMU) over the right-of-center Pro

Patria/Estonian National Independence Party coalition. The results reflected popular dissatisfaction among the elderly and rural electorate, who were hardest hit by the previous government's market reforms. The KMU subsequently formed a majority coalition government with the leftist Center Party, which held until October 1995, when the Center Party left the coalition and was replaced by the right-of-center Reform Party. In February 1997, Prime Minister Tiit Vahi resigned following allegations of corruption and Mart Siiman of the Coalition Party was named as the new prime minister.

In March 1999 parliamentary elections, the leftist Center Party won the largest percentage of votes, with 23.4 percent, capturing 28 of 101 seats. However, the Reform Party, Pro Patria, and the Moderates, who together took 53 seats, subsequently formed a center-right majority coalition government. The Center Party and its leader, Edgar Savisaar, with whom various political forces expressed reluctance to cooperate, was effectively forced into the opposition. The other three parties that secured enough votes to enter parliament were the centrist Coalition Party and the left-of-center Country People's Party, each of which took seven seats, and the United People's Party, representing some of the country's large ethnic Russian population, which captured six seats. Local elections held in October saw the three members of the national governing coalition enjoy victories in two-thirds of the country's local councils. In Tallinn, the Center Party secured the single largest number of seats. However, the "triple alliance" again managed to exclude the Center Party from its majority ruling coalition, which it formed with parties including those representing the country's Russian-speakers.

In February 1999, parliament adopted amendments to the language law requiring those working in the service sector, including businesspeople, public servants, and local government workers, to use Estonian when working with the public. The law was criticized by political parties representing Russian-speakers and by representatives of some international organizations as violating the principle of free movement of labor and services. In June 2000, the law was further amended to no longer require the unconditional use of Estonian in the private sector, but only in certain areas where it would be in the public interest, such as those involving health or safety.

Estonia's economy, which had suffered from the effects of Russia's 1998 financial crisis, enjoyed considerable growth throughout 2000. After having experienced 1.4 percent growth in gross domestic product (GDP) for 1999, GDP grew by seven percent in the third quarter of 2000 year-on-year. Privatization of the last major infrastructure and energy firms, which has been plagued by political and financial concerns, proceeded slowly during the year.

EU membership remained high on the country's political and economic agenda throughout 2000. Despite the commitment of successive governments to harmonize Estonian legislation and practices with EU directives, the effects of membership on Estonia's economy ultimately remain unclear. Recent opinion polls have indicated a decline in public support for EU membership, particularly in connection with fears of increases in the prices of consumer goods.

Political Rights and Civil Liberties: Estonians can change their government democratically. However, the country's citizenship law has been criticized for disenfranchising many Russian-speakers who arrived in Estonia during the Soviet era and are regarded as immigrants who must apply for citizenship. Although noncitizens may not participate in national elections, they can vote, but not serve as candidates, in local elections. The 1992 constitution established a 101-member unicameral legislature elected for four-year terms, with a prime minister serving as head of government and a president as head of state. After the first president was chosen by popular vote in 1992, subsequent presidential elections reverted to parliamentary ballot. According to international observers, the 1995 and 1999 parliamentary elections were free and fair.

The government respects freedom of speech and the press. There are three national private television stations that broadcast both Estonian- and Russian-language programs. More than 30 radio stations are privately operated, and dozens of independent national and regional newspapers offer diverse viewpoints. Religious freedom is respected in law and practice in this predominantly Lutheran country.

The constitution guarantees freedom of assembly, and the government respects this provision in practice. Political parties are allowed to organize freely, although only citizens may be members. Workers have the right to organize freely, to strike, and to bargain collectively, and the main trade unions operate independently of the state.

While the judiciary is independent and generally free from government interference, low salaries and heavy workloads continue to deter many lawyers from choosing a career in the judiciary. There have been credible reports that some police officers physically or verbally abuse suspects. Despite ongoing improvements in the country's prison system, including recently announced plans to build a new detention center, overcrowding, a lack of financial resources, and inadequately trained staff remain problems.

Of Estonia's population of just under 1.5 million, more than 1 million are Estonian citizens, of which more than 112,000 have been naturalized since 1992. Although the exact number of illegal aliens is unknown, an estimated 30,000 to 80,000 individuals in Estonia are without proper documentation, including temporary or permanent residence permits.

Although women enjoy the same legal rights as men, they continue to be underrepresented in senior-level business positions and the government.

Ethiopia

Polity: Dominant party **Political Rights:** 5
Economy: Mixed statist **Civil Liberties:** 5
Population: 64,100,000 **Status:** Partly Free
PPP: $574
Life Expectancy: 43
Ethnic Groups: Oromo (40 percent), Amhara and Tigrean (32 percent), Sidamo (9 percent), other (19 percent)
Capital: Addis Ababa

Overview:
Two major events in Ethiopia in 2000 were legislative and local elections in May, and the cessation of hostilities with Eritrea in June. Ethiopia was also badly affected by drought and famine conditions, although the situation improved in the latter part of the year.

Ethiopia's long tradition of imperial rule ended in 1974, when Emperor Haile Selassie was overthrown in a Marxist military coup. Colonel Mengistu Haile Mariam subsequently became the leader of a brutal dictatorship that lasted until it was overthrown by a coalition of guerilla groups in 1991. These groups were spearheaded by the Ethiopian People's Revolutionary Democratic Front (EPRDF), itself an alliance of five parties.

The EPRDF government instituted a transition period that resulted in the establishment of formal democratic institutions. A constitution adopted in 1994 established a federal system of government, with power vested in a directly elected 548-member body, the Council of People's Representatives. A second chamber of parliament, the 117-member Federal Council, represents ethnic minorities and professional groups. Ethiopia is made up of nine federal regions. The first official multiparty elections to the council in 1995 were boycotted by the opposition.

There are currently more than 60 legally recognized political parties active in Ethiopia, although the political scene continues to be dominated by the EPRDF. Opposition parties claim that their ability to function is seriously impeded by government harassment, although observers note that these parties are often reluctant to participate in the political process. There is a small but growing civil society, which has been subjected to some restrictions by the government.

As expected, the ruling Ethiopian People's Revolutionary Democratic Front (EPRDF) gained a landslide victory against a weak and divided opposition in the 2000 legislative balloting, winning 472 seats. A handful of opposition candidates were elected, but the parliament reelected Prime Minister Meles Zenawi to another five-year term in October.

An Ethiopian offensive in the spring resulted in significant territorial gains; negotiations with Eritrea subsequently resulted in a ceasefire. Ethiopia continued to be criticized for expelling, usually on short notice, thousands of Eritreans resident in Ethiopia, many of whom had lived there for generations.

Ethiopia is a country with a highly conflictual political environment. The war with Eritrea had proved an effective tool of political mobilization for the government of Prime Minister Meles, since opposition to policies pursued by the government could be equated with a lack of patriotism, or even treason. This growth of nationalist sentiment had resulted in fewer overt instances of jailing or other forms of political intimidation than in previous years, and although productive dialogue remained elusive, opposition parties did participate in the May local elections.

Political Rights and Civil Liberties: In principle, the 1995 constitution is an extremely progressive document. The government has devolved some power to regional and local governments and courts. The constitution provides for a broad range of democratic institutions and political activity, including the right of secession. As with many elements of the Ethiopian political system, however, the reality differs. The EPRDF today controls all of the elected regional councils either directly or with coalition partners. It is highly unlikely that any region would, in fact, be allowed to secede.

Executive power is vested in a prime minister, who is selected by the Council of People's Representatives. Opposition parties and some observers criticized the government's conduct of the May 2000 legislative elections. They state that the polls were subject to government interference, that the opposition was denied some access to the media, and that opposition supporters were subject to harassment and detention. The Ethiopian government continues to selectively harass opposition parties, and impede their ability to participate in the political process. However, the opposition was able to engage in some criticism of the government in the media during the official election campaign, and a series of unprecendented public debates was broadcast over state-run radio and television during the electoral campaign.

Opposition parties also bear some responsibility for limiting in practice the right of Ethiopian people to express their political preferences. Until the 2000 elections, many parties refused to participate openly in the nation's political life. One key party, the All Amhara People's Organization (AAPO), made clear that it was only taking part because it would lose its legally constituted status if it failed to take part in two consecutive elections. Some parties have supported, either directly or indirectly, armed resistance to the government. A rebellion in the south by the banned Oromo Liberation Front (OLF) and the Islamic Front for the Liberation of Oromia, for example, continues at a low level. Oromos constitute 40 percent of Ethiopia's population of nearly 65 million. OLF supporters have been imprisoned or detained without trial.

Amnesty International reported that thousands of Eritreans living in Ethiopia have been rounded up and forcibly deported. The organization said 52,000 Eritreans have been deported from Ethiopia since the war began. One international human rights organization charged that the deportations in Ethiopia have developed into a "systematic, country-wide operation to arrest and deport anyone of full or part Eritrean descent." The Ethiopian government claims that even Eritreans with Ethiopian citizenship pose a threat to national security, given the fighting between the two countries. Amnesty International said it could find no evidence to support Ethiopia's charges that 40,000 of its citizens have been seriously ill-treated and forcibly deported from Eritrea since May 1990.

A 1992 law guarantees freedom of the press. However, it also forbids publishing articles that are defamatory, threaten the safety of the state, agitate for war, or incite ethnic conflict. Journalists also can be jailed for publishing secret court records. Broadcast media remain under close scrutiny by the government. Harassment and intimidation of the independent print media have led to significant self-censorship.

Prior to the war with Eritrea, much of the independent press did criticize Ethiopia's friendly relations with its neighbor. Harassment of the independent press lessened considerably as the war with Eritrea heated up, and the government policy toward Eritrea shifted. By April 2000, according to Reporters Sans Frontieres, for example, the number of reporters in jail had dropped to eight from a high of about two dozen at the end of 1998, although the press continues to be faced with direct and indirect government intimidation.

Ethiopia is the third most populous country in Africa, with a mixed ethnic makeup reflecting its imperial heritage. The Ethiopian Coptic Church is influential, particularly in the north. There is a large Muslim community in the south, made up mainly of Arabs, Somalis, and Oromos. Christians and Muslims each account for approximately 40 percent of the population, with the remainder largely animists.

The judiciary is officially independent, although there are no significant examples of decisions at variance with government policy. Trade union freedom to bargain and strike has not yet been fully tested. Religious freedom is generally respected. Privatization programs are proceeding, and the government has undertaken a major financial liberalization reform program to attract foreign investment.

Women traditionally have few land or property rights and, especially in rural areas, few opportunities for employment beyond agricultural labor. Violence against women and social discrimination are reportedly common despite legal protections.

Fiji

Polity: Military-installed civilian
Economy: Capitalist
Population: 800,000
PPP: $4,231
Life Expectancy: 73
Ethnic Groups: Fijian [Melanesian-Polynesian] (49 percent), Indian (46 percent), other (5 percent)
Capital: Suva

Political Rights: 6*
Civil Liberties: 3
Status: Partly Free

Ratings Change: Fiji's political rights rating changed from 2 to 6, and its status from Free to Partly Free, after rebels tried to depose an elected government and the military installed an interim civilian government.

Overview: Efforts to establish a multiracial democracy in Fiji were in tatters at year's end, several months after an attempted coup in May by ethnic-Fijian hardliners led to the ouster of an elected civilian government headed by a prime minister of Indian descent. Installed by the military following the putsch, an interim administration headed by Laisenia Qarase began drafting a new constitution that would largely exclude Indo-Fijians from political power.

Fiji's paramount chiefs ceded sovereignty over these South Pacific islands to the British in 1874. The British began bringing Indian laborers to work on plantations in 1879. At independence in 1970, the indigenous-Fijian and Indo-Fijian communities were roughly equal in population.

Following 17 years of rule by the indigenous-Fijian Alliance Party, the 1987 elections brought to power the country's first government largely composed of Indo-Fijians. Backed by indigenous-Fijian hardliners alarmed at the emerging political influence of the economically successful Indo-Fijian community, Lieutenant Colonel Sitiveni Rabuka, an indigenous Fijian, seized power in coups in May and September 1987.

An appointed civilian government introduced a constitution in 1990 that guaranteed that indigenous Fijians would always have a majority in parliament. It granted them 37 of the 70 seats in the lower house, and also required the prime minister to be an indigenous Fijian. Elections in 1992 and 1994 led to coalition governments headed by coup leader Rabuka.

Amid a continuing exodus of skilled Indo-Fijian workers, parliament amended the constitution in 1997 to end the indigenous-Fijians' guaranteed parliamentary majority and permit an Indo-Fijian prime minister. The amendments created a 71-seat house with 25 seats open to all races; 23 reserved for indigenous Fijians; 19 for Indo-Fijians; 3 for "general electors" (mainly whites and East Asians); and 1 for Rotuma Island. The amendments also required the largest party in parliament to invite all parties gaining more than ten percent of the parliamentary vote into the government. In a nod to ethnic Fijians, the constitution also empowered the unelected Great Council of Chiefs to appoint the largely ceremonial president, and the president to appoint the 32-member senate.

Held in March 1999, the first elections under the new constitution brought to power a multiracial coalition government under Mahendra Chaudhry, who became the country's first Indo-Fijian prime minister. Final results gave Chaudhry's Indo-Fijian-based Labor Party all 19 Indo-Fijian constituencies and 18 of the 25 open constituencies; the ethnic-Fijian Fijian Association Party, 10 seats; Rabuka's Fijian Political Party, 8; four smaller parties, 11; and independents, 5.

Chaudhry was immediately confronted with sensitive issues involving land and logging. The prime minister angered indigenous-Fijian landowners by pressuring them to renew expiring 30-year leases held by Indo-Fijian tenant farmers. Indigenous Fijians own roughly 83 percent of the land, while Indo-Fijian tenant farmers are the main producers of sugar and other commodities. While many landowners favored putting their land to development use, Indo-Fijians complained about the lack of secure land tenure. The Chaudhry government also angered some indigenous-Fijian landowners by giving a contract to harvest government-owned mahogany plantations on their land to a British company, rather than to an American concern that had offered a more lucrative bid.

Amid a series of anti-government demonstrations, businessman George Speight and an armed gang that included some members of the army's Counter Revolutionary Warfare (CRW) unit seized Chaudhry and other officials in the parliament building on May 19, 2000. A key supporter of the American-backed mahogany bid that Chaudhry had rejected, Speight held the hostages until July 13 while wresting concessions from the mainly ethnic-Fijian military, which agreed to scrap the 1997 constitution, replace President Ratu Kamisese Mara, install a government that excluded Indo-Fijians, and grant amnesty to the rebels.

Having defused the crisis, the military installed an interim government, headed by Qarase, a banker, and appointed Ratu Josefa Iloilo as president. After Speight demanded a more hardline government, authorities arrested the putsch leader and more than 300 of his supporters in late July for failing to surrender their weapons as required under the amnesty agreement. A court formally charged Speight and 14 of his supporters with treason in August for having allegedly threatened the president over the composition of the government.

The ousted government won a small victory on November 15, when the high court ruled that the Qarase government was unconstitutional and ordered the Chaudhry administration reinstated. Having installed the Qarase government, the military said it respected the decision but did not indicate what it would do if the ruling is upheld on appeal. In a sign of rifts in the army in the aftermath of the coup, members of the CRW attempted a mutiny on November 2 that left eight soldiers dead and 22 civilians wounded.

Political Rights and Civil Liberties: Fiji is headed by a military-appointed, interim civilian government, which said in November that it would hold elections by March 2002. At year's end a government committee was drawing up guidelines for a new constitution that reportedly would exclude Indo-Fijians from power. As amended in 1997, the now-defunct constitution had ended the indigenous-Fijians' guaranteed parliamentary majority. However, it had placed some voting along ethnic lines by reserving 46 of the 71 lower house seats for the various ethnic communities. The constitution also had explicitly stated that ethnic-Fijian interests have primacy over those of other ethnic communities, though it also contained a fairly comprehensive bill of rights.

While authorities generally respect individual rights, some media and nongovernmental organizations have criticized the potential restrictions on civil liberties contained in the 1998 Emergency Powers Act. The act authorizes the president to declare a state of emergency, under which parliament can impose broad press and communications censorship, seize private property, conduct searches without warrants, and ban public meetings.

The judiciary is independent. After beginning operations in early 2000, an official Human Rights Commission received some 50 complaints by May. Most complaints alleged employment discrimination on the grounds of race, gender, religion, language, or age. Another continuing problem is police abuse of detainees and prisoners, although the government has punished some offending officers.

Immediately after the rebels seized parliament in May, indigenous Fijians looted and burned some shops in downtown Suva owned by Indo-Fijians. In June and July, gangs of indigenous Fijians looted and burned numerous Indo-Fijian shops and homes on the two largest islands, Viti Levu and Vanua Levu, forcing hundreds of Indo-Fijians to flee their homes.

Fiji's private media vigorously report on alleged official corruption and ethical violations, although journalists practice some self-censorship. Both the Rabuka and Chaudhry governments had criticized the political coverage in the country's newspapers, generally without providing any factual grounds for the criticism. Shortly after taking office in 1999, the Chaudhry government ordered official advertising to be placed only in the *Daily Post*, on the grounds that the government was the paper's largest shareholder. The move disadvantaged the *Fiji Times*, whose news coverage the government had repeatedly criticized. The government also refused to renew the work permit of the *Fiji Times'* editor in chief, a foreign national, on the grounds that there were Fijian citizens capable of filling the job. In addition, the Chaudhry government also began several court proceedings against journalists. In a positive development, a high-court judge dismissed in April a defamation action by an assistant minister against Fiji One, the lone noncable television station, and three of its journalists.

No government has used the Press Correction Act, which authorizes officials to arrest anyone who publishes "malicious" material, or to order a publication to publish a "correcting statement" to an article. However, both the Rabuka and Chaudhry governments initiated actions against newspapers over their coverage of parliament under the Parliamentary Privileges and Powers Act. While the act authorizes jail terms of up to two years for breaches of parliamentary privilege, no actual disciplinary measures were taken.

Radio is a key source of information on the outer islands, and there are both publicly and privately held stations. The provincial governments hold a majority stake in Fiji One, which generally provides balanced news coverage.

Rape and domestic violence are serious problems. In some rape cases, the practice of *bulubulu* (traditional reconciliation) allows the offender to apologize to a victim's relatives to avoid a felony charge. In addition, courts frequently impose lenient sentences for rape. Women are underrepresented in government and politics, although they have made significant inroads in the civil service and professions. Indo-Fijians are underrepresented in the senior civil service and the military leadership.

Trade unions are independent and vigorous. Factory conditions are often poor, particularly in the garment and canning industries. The country's tourism industry said in July that the May coup attempt had already cost operators $93 million in lost business and forced them to lay off 20,000 staffers. Tourism contributes about 20 percent of Fiji's gross domestic product and is the top foreign exchange earner.

Finland

Polity: Parliamentary democracy
Economy: Mixed capitalist
Population: 5,200,000
PPP: $20,847
Life Expectancy: 77
Ethnic Groups: Finn (93 percent), Swede (6 percent), other, including Lapp [Saami] (1 percent)
Capital: Helsinki

Political Rights: 1
Civil Liberties: 1
Status: Free

Overview:

In February, Finns, for the first time in their nation's history, elected a woman president. Tarja Halonen, a left-leaning member of the Social Democratic Party (SDP), won after two rounds of voting, edging out four other female candidates—from a total field of seven—from across the political spectrum. The election marked only the second direct popular vote for president in Finland, where presidents are elected to six-year terms.

The achievement of Finnish independence followed some eight centuries of foreign domination, first by Sweden (until 1809) and subsequently as a Grand Duchy within the pre-revolutionary Russian Empire.

Finland's current constitution, issued in July 1919, was amended in February 1999 and came into force in 2000. The amended constitution diminishes the power of the president (which was unusually broad under the former constitution) while increasing the power of the parliament. The parliament now has greater sway over calling elections, and can appoint national representatives to international gatherings, including European Union (EU) meetings. Finland joined the European Monetary Union in 1999 and was an active and outspoken EU member in 2000. Finland was the first EU country to call for the lifting of diplomatic sanctions against Austria, imposed in February after the far-right Freedom Party became junior partner in Austria's coalition government. Finland still remains outside of NATO.

Halonen's victory followed the reelection one year earlier of Finland's fragile coalition government, led by Paavo Lipponen of the SDP. Although the SDP lost 12 of the 63 seats it had held since the 1995 elections, the coalition (including the SDP, the National Coalition Party, the Left Alliance, the Greens, and the Swedish People's Party) won more than half the seats in Finland's 200-seat unicameral parliament, the Eduskunta.

Political Rights and Civil Liberties:

Finns can change their government by democratic means. The Aland Islands, populated mainly by Swedes, have their own provincial parliament. The local Liberal Party won the elections that took place in mid-October 1999. The result seems to have been something of a blow to earlier demands for even greater autonomous powers in Aland, as the Liberals do not share the Free Conservative and Center Party beliefs that the current system is inadequate.

Finland has a large variety of newspapers and magazines and is ranked among the highest in terms of Internet users per capita in the world. Newspapers are privately owned, some by political parties or their affiliates; many others are either controlled by or support a particular party.

The rights of ethnic and religious minorities are protected. The Saamis (or Lapps), who make up less than one percent of the population, are guaranteed cultural autonomy by the constitution.

Both Finnish and Swedish are official languages of the country. In recent years, concern has risen about increasing instances of racist and xenophobic behavior. Finland receives on average 700 to 900 asylum seekers per year. To facilitate their absorption, the government has revised Finland's Aliens Law and adopted a new law promoting the integration of immigrants into Finnish society. Both laws took effect on May 1, 1999. Further reforms took place in 2000, allowing for more rapid processing of asylum claims filed by refugees from the so-called safe countries of Poland, Slovakia, the Czech Republic, and Bulgaria.

Finns enjoy freedom of religion, and both the predominant Lutheran Church and the smaller Orthodox Church are financed through a special tax from which citizens may exempt themselves. The archbishop and the bishops of the Lutheran Church are appointed by the president.

Finnish workers have the right to organize, bargain, and strike, and an overwhelming majority belong to trade unions. The 1.1 million-member Central Organization of Finnish Trade Unions, which is linked to the SDP, dominates the labor movement.

The constitution provides for an independent judiciary, consisting of the supreme court, the supreme administrative court, and the lower courts. The president appoints supreme court justices, who in turn appoint the lower court judges.

Gender-based equality is guaranteed by law. In 1906, Finland became the first country in Europe to give women full political entitlement, including the rights to vote and hold office. Women hold an exceptionally high proportion of parliamentary seats.

⬆France

Polity: Presidential-par- **Political Rights:** 1
liamentary democracy   **Civil Liberties:** 2
Economy: Mixed   **Status:** Free
capitalist
Population: 59,400,000
PPP: $21,175
Life Expectancy: 78
Ethnic Groups: French, regional minorities (Corsican,
Alsatian, Basque, Breton), various Arab and African immigrant groups
Capital: Paris
Trend Arrow: France received an upward trend arrow for the introduction of a plan to devolve greater autonomy to Corsica.

Overview:
France recast its national, political, and social identities during the year, challenging the concept of a unified, strong, and indivisible Fifth Republic in the process. A devolution plan was drafted for the French island of Corsica that would establish sweeping powers of autonomy for its inhabitants, many of whom harbor separatist leanings. The controversial autonomy proposal led to the resignation of France's interior minister, who protested the plan fearing it would inspire other separatist elements within the country. French voters approved a shorter presidential term during the year, and authorities faced widespread civil protests over high gasoline taxes that ground most commercial activity and transportation to a halt. Political scandals continued to dominate much of French political life throughout 2000, tainting President Jacques Chirac and Paris mayor Jean Tiberi. A series of violent attacks against Jews and Jewish establishments, including synagogues, took place in the fall, a spillover from the violence raging in the Middle East. A cabinet reshuffle in the fall left Prime Minister Lionel Jospin with the possibility of fresh challenges to his already controversial policy of a shorter workweek. Fears over mad cow disease, or BSE, increased among French citizens during the year, with five times as many head of cattle (153 cases) testing positive for the disease than in 1999. The disease can spread to humans.

After World War II, France established a parliamentary Fourth Republic, which was governed by coalitions and ultimately failed because of the Algerian war. The Fifth Republic began in 1958 under Prime Minister (and later President) Charles de Gaulle. Election of the president by popular suffrage began in 1965. In 1992, French citizens narrowly approved European political and economic union under the Maastricht Treaty. Prime Minister Jospin began a government of "cohabitation" with President Chirac, a conservative, after winning an upset election in 1997. In October 2000, French voters went to the polls approving a referendum to cut short the presidential term from seven years to five, marking the most radical change to the French constitution in 40 years. The shorter term now puts parliamentary and presidential elections on the same schedule, reducing or potentially eliminating the awkward cohabitation arrangement, which often features a president and a prime minister from different parties, often at odds over policy planning.

In March, the Gaullist Rally for the Republic (RPR), President Chirac's political party, suspended Paris mayor Jean Tiberi as head of the Paris branch of the party after the discovery of more than 1,000 ineligible names on party voter logs. All but 60 were dead or had moved out of Paris. By May, the scandal surrounding Tiberi had grown, with 15 more officials coming under investigation. The suspension followed a judicial probe last year into the 1995 Paris mayoral elections, which turned up evidence of fraud in two Paris districts, both traditional strongholds of Mayor Tiberi. Hundreds of pro-Tiberi ballots had been turned in from voters allegedly not living in the districts. In October 1999, President Chirac and Mayor Tiberi were named in the press in association with an electoral fraud scandal emanating from the 1989 Paris city elections, when Chirac was mayor and Tiberi his deputy. According to reports, Chirac's RPR plotted to ensure victory by registering hundreds of fake voters.

In September 2000, the president was implicated in a kickback scandal. A former official and member of the RPR, Jean-Claude Mery, who died in 1998, alleged in videotaped statements made in the 1990s that construction companies had made secret donations to the RPR in return for contracts to develop public housing. He said Chirac knew about the kickbacks and approved them. The scandal deepened when it was later revealed that former Finance Minister Dominique Strauss-Kahn acquired the videotape from an attorney in return for a tax break for one of the lawyer's clients, rumored to be the well-known fashion designer Karl Lagerfeld. Strauss-Kahn, who served in the cabinet of Prime Minister Jospin, the socialist political rival to Chirac, resigned from the cabinet in 1999 over a fraud scandal.

In October, Prime Minister Jospin suffered a political setback with the resignation from the cabinet of Minister of Employment Martine Aubry, who stepped down to run for mayor of Lille. Aubry was the chief architect of the 35-hour workweek, instituted last year to the chagrin of many employers. Speculation spread quickly that Jospin would be facing an uphill battle in negotiations with labor unions and employer federations in instituting the new workweek schedule more widely.

Despite the political scandals, the French economy performed robustly during the year. Tax cuts amounting to 40 billion francs (U.S.$6 billion) were announced in March. The unemployment rate finally fell below ten percent. The government did, however, face vociferous public protest over the cost of gasoline. In September, nationwide protests and blockades of major French highways, seaports, borders, and rail links prompted the government to reduce gasoline taxes. France faced intense criticism from fellow European countries for caving in under the pressure of protests, which quickly spread across the continent in the wake of the French tax cut.

In recent years, the National Front, a far-right party led by the racist Jean-Marie Le Pen, has exerted a strong influence in regional politics, but it suffered a series of setbacks in 1998. Most notable was the banning of Le Pen from politics for one year. In January 1999, the party split in two after Bruno Megret, leader of a rebel faction, claimed leadership of the National Front. The move touched off a series of legal proceedings to decide which faction had rights to the party name and symbol. In April 2000, Le Pen was prohibited from sitting on the European Parliament in the wake of a French court conviction of assault, which barred him from holding public office.

Political Rights and Civil Liberties: French citizens can change their government democratically by directly electing the president and national assembly. The constitution grants the president significant emergency powers, including rule by decree under certain circumstances. The president may call referenda and dissolve parliament, but may not veto its acts or routinely issue decrees. Decentralization has given mayors significant power over housing, transportation, schools, culture, welfare, and law enforcement. The judiciary is independent.

In March 1999, the parliament passed a legal reform bill setting maximum limits on detention of suspects during a criminal investigation. Also included in the bill was the formation of "detention judges" to rule on the justification of incarceration. Additionally, those being held for interrogation must have immediate access to an attorney. Supporters of the reform bill, concerned over possible abuses of power by judges, had contended that old laws allowed for excessive detention periods during inquiries and had unfairly presumed guilt over innocence.

France has drawn criticism for its treatment of immigrants and asylum seekers. Despite legal provisions authorizing refuge seekers to cross the border without visas or identity papers, border guards have occasionally used excessive force to discourage crossings.

The status of foreigners in France is confused by a succession of sometimes contradictory immigration laws. The National Front and other far-right groups have gained popularity by blaming immigrants for high unemployment. In fact, the jobless rate of immigrants is generally much higher than that of the native French.

Soon after taking office, Prime Minister Jospin eased the country's residency rules by giving illegal immigrants a one-year period to apply for legal residency. Approximately 150,000 of the country's estimated 1 million illegal residents applied for papers. Government officials stated that approximately two-thirds of the applicants would be allowed to remain in France. The government further eased residency requirements by allowing foreigners to remain in France legally if they are seriously ill, if they are joining family members who are legally present, or if they are single, financially self-sufficient, long-term residents.

During the fall, a wave of anti-Semitic violence swept the country. Synagogues were vandalized, including the Paris Great Synagogue, which was shot at by snipers during High Holy Day services. Others, located throughout France, were burned down and many others torched. Stones were thrown at Jews in several incidents, among other acts of harassment. The violence, mostly carried out by Muslims, took place during violent clashes between Israelis and Palestinians in the West Bank, Gaza Strip, and Israel.

The press in France is free, although the government's financial support of journalism and the registration of journalists have raised concerns about media independence. Publication of opinion polls results is prohibited in the week preceding any election. In May, a new press law banning photographs showing suspects in handcuffs or scenes that may jeopardize a victim's dignity was introduced. The move prompted many complaints from French media outlets. Earlier in the year, in accordance with French anti-hate laws, the government banned Internet auctions of Nazi memorabilia. Also in May, Prime Minister Jospin issued a call for greater Internet controls to combat computer crime and online sabotage.

Amid continuing violence on the French island of Corsica—there were approximately 100 terrorist attacks in the first half of the year according to the interior ministry—Jospin unveiled a devolution plan for the island, addressing, in concrete terms for the first time, Corsican autonomy. During a transition period to last through 2002, the

Corsican Regional Assembly would be granted limited self-government in the areas of education, culture, and the environment. A second phase, to take place throughout 2003 and 2004, would allow for the Corsican Assembly to pass its own laws for the more widespread teaching of the Corsican language, and for the limited right to adapt some French laws. Implementation of the second phase, dependent on the success of the first and the total absence of violence, would necessitate reform of the French constitution.

Interior Minister Jean-Pierre Chevenement resigned in protest over the devolution plan. Opposed to conceding French sovereignty over the island, he warned against setting what he called a dangerous precedent that would embolden other separatist elements within France, specifically those in the Basque and Breton regions. In May, Breton separatists were investigated for the April bombing of a McDonald's restaurant that left one person dead.

Labor rights in France are respected in practice, and strikes are widely and effectively used to protest government economic policy. The government acted to further entrench the shortened workweek during the year, originally adopted in October 1999. French employers, claiming the law cuts efficiency and raises costs, continued to object and to lobby the government for a revision of the law. Women enjoy equal rights in France.

Gabon

Polity: Dominant party
Economy: Capitalist
Population: 1,200,000
PPP: $6,353
Life Expectancy: 52
Ethnic Groups: Bantu, other Africans, Europeans
Capital: Libreville

Political Rights: 5
Civil Liberties: 4
Status: Partly Free

Overview:

Apparently aware that he does have critics after 33 years of rule, the last ten of which have been a facade of democracy, President Omar Bongo was granted judicial immunity by the country's parliament in October 2000. The constitutional immunity lasts until beyond the expiration of the presidential term. Bongo was elected in 1998 to his second seven-year term since opening Gabon to multiparty politics in 1990. Opposition parties have begun jostling for position and funding ahead of parliamentary elections scheduled for the end of 2001, but fragmentation in the past has prevented them from being a serious threat to Bongo's ruling Gabonese Democratic Party (PDG). Additionally, elections have been unfair and marred with irregularities.

Straddling the equator on central Africa's west coast, Gabon gained independence from France in 1960. Bongo, whom France raised from soldier to president in 1967, completed his predecessor's consolidation of power by officially outlawing the opposition. France, which maintains marines in Gabon, has intervened twice to preserve Bongo's regime. In 1990, protests prompted by economic duress forced Bongo to accept a conference that opposition leaders hoped would promote a peaceful democratic transition. But Bongo retained power in rigged 1993 elections that sparked violent protests, which were repressed by his presidential guard.

The 1994 Paris accords claimed to institute true democratic reforms. Municipal elections in 1996 saw major opposition gains, including the election of Paul Mba Abbesole, the leader of the largest opposition party, as mayor of Libreville. Legislative polls delayed by decree until December 1996 were again beset by fraud as Bongo's PDG won an overwhelming, but unconvincing, victory.

Gabon's human rights record has been better than that of some of its neighbors, but arbitrary arrest, poor prison conditions, and forced expulsion of African immigrants continue to be problems. Press repression eased somewhat in 2000.

Gabon's capital, Libreville, ranks among the most expensive cities in the world. Little of the country's oil wealth trickles down to the average Gabonese, most of whom are subsistence farmers, while three decades of autocratic and corrupt rule have made Bongo among the world's richest men. State institutions are influenced or controlled by Bongo and a small elite, with strong backing by both the army and France. The highly profitable French Elf Aquitaine oil company plays a dominant role in the country's economic and political life.

Political Rights and Civil Liberties:

Gabon's citizens have never been able to exercise their constitutional right to change their government democratically despite a gradual political opening since 1990. There are numerous political parties, but the PDG has ruled since Bongo created it in 1968. His electoral victory in 1998, with 61 percent of the vote, followed a campaign that made profligate use of state resources and state media. The polling, which was partially boycotted by the opposition, was marked by serious irregularities. The nominally independent National Election Commission, which was created under the new constitution approved by referendum in 1995, proved neither autonomous nor competent. Legislative elections in 1993 and 1996 have also been seriously flawed.

The judiciary suffers from political interference. Rights to legal counsel and public criminal trials are generally respected, but the law presumes guilt. Judges may deliver summary verdicts, and torture remains a standard route to producing confessions. Prison conditions are marked by beatings and insufficient food, water, and medical care. Arbitrary arrest and long periods of pretrial detention are common. The right of assembly and association is constitutionally guaranteed, but permits required for public gatherings are sometimes refused. Freedom to form and join political parties is generally respected, but civil servants may face harassment based on their associations. Nongovernmental organizations operate openly, but no independent local human rights groups exist to investigate reports of violations.

A government daily and at least one dozen private weeklies, which are primarily controlled by opposition parties, are published. At least six private radio and television broadcasters have been licensed and operate. The state is authorized to criminalize civil libel suits. Officials have suspended licenses for independent newspapers and private broadcasters in the past, imprisoned journalists, and imposed fines.

A draft communications code that would have further restricted press freedom by expanding the scope of criminal libel laws passed the national assembly in 2000, but it died in the senate. Observers considered this a victory for press freedom because the bill was not rubber-stamped, as usually happens. Authorities, in May, pardoned two journalists with criminal libel suits pending against them. One returned to the country and opened a newspaper. By the end of October, the judiciary had no pending libel suits against journalists.

While no legal restrictions on travel exist, harassment on political and ethnic bases has been reported. Discrimination against African immigrants is also reported, including harassment by security forces, arbitrary detention, and expulsion. Most indigenous Pygmies live in the forest and are largely independent of the formal government. Religious freedom is constitutionally guaranteed and respected. An official ban on the Jehovah's Witnesses is not enforced.

Legal protections for women include equal-access laws for education, business, and investment. In addition to owning property and businesses, women constitute more than 50 percent of the salaried workforce in the health and trade sectors. Women continue to face legal and cultural discrimination, particularly in rural areas, and are reportedly subject to widespread domestic violence.

The constitution recognizes the right to form unions, and virtually the entire formal private sector workforce is unionized. Strikes are legal if they are held after an eight-day notice advising that outside arbitration has failed. Collective bargaining is allowed by industry, not by firm. Public sector employees may unionize, but their right to strike is limited if a strike could jeopardize public safety. Despite legal protections, the government has taken action against strikers and unions and used force to suppress illegal demonstrations.

The Gambia

Polity: Dominant party (military-dominated)
Economy: Capitalist
Population: 1,300,000
PPP: $1,453
Life Expectancy: 47
Ethnic Groups: Mandinka (42 percent), Fula (18 percent), Wolof (16 percent), Jola (10 percent), Serahuli (9 percent), other (5 percent)
Capital: Banjul

Political Rights: 7
Civil Liberties: 5
Status: Not Free

Overview:

Several key events contributed to a charged political atmosphere by year's end in The Gambia in the lead-up to presidential elections scheduled for October 2001. There was an alleged coup attempt against President Yahya A. J. J. Jammeh in January. In April, security forces killed 16 people in clashes with student demonstrators who had been protesting the earlier killing of a student. Two months later, authorities charged the leader of the opposition United Democratic Party, Ousainou Darboe, and 24 others with murder after a clash with ruling party members. One person died. Charges against all but Darboe and four others were dropped. An opposition leader, in late October, called on all politicians to resume activities and warned that a "people's power" revolution such as the one that toppled Côte d'Ivoire's military ruler could unfold in The Gambia if elections were not free and fair.

After receiving independence from Britain in 1965, The Gambia functioned as an electoral democracy under President Sir Dawda K. Jawara and his People's Progressive Party for almost 30 years. A 1981 coup by leftist soldiers was reversed by intervention from Senegal, which borders The Gambia on three sides. The two countries formed the Confederation of Senegambia a year later, but it was dissolved in 1989. Senegal declined to rescue the Jawara government again when Jammeh struck in 1994. The leaders of the 1994 coup denounced the ousted government's alleged corruption, promising transparency, accountability, and early elections. Instead, they quickly imposed draconian decrees curtailing civil and political rights and the free media.

Local government elections that were originally scheduled to be held in 1997 were to take place in November 2000. They have been postponed until January 2001, but there is doubt as to whether they will be held at all before the October presidential polls. In December, Jammeh sacked the head of the Independent Electoral Commission after the supreme court had ruled in its favor. The commission was pursing legal action against the government over its refusal to organize local elections under existing laws. The government is wary of defeat in local elections because the decentralization of power will probably make it more difficult for the ruling Alliance for Patriotic Reorientation and Construction to win the presidential vote and win it fairly. The 1996 presidential poll was marred by intimidation, irregularities, and fraud. Legislative elections in January 1997 produced a sweeping victory for the ruling party, but were deeply flawed.

The Gambia is a poor, tiny country of approximately one million people, most of whom are subsistence farmers.

Political Rights and Civil Liberties: The Gambia's citizens are denied their right to choose or change their government by peaceful means. The country's 1996 presidential and 1997 legislative elections were neither free nor fair, and President Jammeh and his parliamentary majority cannot be considered democratically elected. The 1996 presidential contest barred the most formidable opposition candidates and was marked by military intimidation of the opposition and heavy use of state resources and the media to promote Jammeh's candidacy. A new constitution, adopted by a closely controlled 1996 referendum, allowed Jammeh to transform his military dictatorship to a nominally civilian administration.

The constitution provides for an independent judiciary. While lower courts are sometimes subject to executive influence, the judiciary in general has demonstrated its independence on several occasions, at times in significant cases. There are a number of judges from Nigeria, Ghana, and other African countries, who tend to operate fairly and vigorously. Local chiefs preside over courts at the village level. The judicial system recognizes customary law, or *Sharia* (Islamic law), primarily in marriage matters.

Performance of the courts is being tested through a lawsuit brought by popular opposition figure Omar Jallow. He has taken the government to court over Decree 89, which prohibits any former ministers from participating in political activity or taking up a government post until 2024. The severe penalties for challenging the decree, including large fines and life imprisonment, have prevented anyone from challenging it. Jallow is currently working abroad.

The Jammeh regime has awarded itself extensive repressive powers. A 1995 decree allows the National Intelligence Agency to cite "state security" to "search, arrest, or detain any person, or seize, impound, or search any vessel, equipment, plant, or property without a warrant." In such cases, the right to seek a writ of habeas corpus is suspended. Torture in jails and barracks has been reported. The International Committee of the Red Cross and human rights groups have been allowed to visit prisons, where life-threatening conditions prevail. Human rights groups and other nongovernmental organizations operate relatively freely.

Freedom of assembly is restricted. Free expression and the independent press have been constant targets of Jammeh's repression. There are vibrant, independent print media, but harassment and self-censorship inhibit free expression. The draft National Media Commission Bill would make annual registration compulsory for all media houses and journalists, as well as give extra powers to the minister of information, allowing him to revoke registration licenses.

State-run Radio Gambia broadcasts only tightly controlled news that is also relayed by private radio stations. A single government-run television station now operates. There was an attempt to burn down the independent Radio 1-FM during the year. Citizen FM, which the government closed in February 1998, began broadcasting again in late 2000 following a court judgment in its favor. Citizen FM broadcasts in a number of indigenous languages.

Freedom of religion is guaranteed, and the government respects this right. Religious and traditional obstacles to the advancement of women are being addressed by both the government and women's organizations. The vice president is a woman. However, higher education and wage employment opportunities for women are still far fewer than those for men, especially in rural areas. Sharia provisions regarding family law and inheritance restrict women's rights. Marriages often are arranged. Female genital mutilation is widely practiced, but women's groups are working to eliminate the practice.

All workers except civil servants and security forces may unionize under the 1990 Labor Act, which also provides the right to strike. Activities of the country's two labor federations are limited by broader restrictions on political rights and civil liberties.

Georgia

Polity: Presidential-parliamentary democracy
Economy: Mixed capitalist (transitional)
Population: 5,400,000
PPP: $1,960
Life Expectancy: 73

Political Rights: 4*
Civil Liberties: 4
Status: Partly Free

Ethnic Groups: Georgian (70 percent), Armenian (8 percent), Russian (6 percent), Azeri (6 percent), Ossetian (3 percent), Abkhaz (2 percent), other (5 percent)
Capital: Tbilisi
Ratings Change: Georgia's political rights rating changed from 3 to 4 due to significant electoral fraud in the April presidential election.

Overview:

In an election whose outcome was widely seen as a foregone conclusion, the heavily favored incumbent, Eduard Shevardnadze, was chosen for a third term in office in the April 2000 presidential vote. However, his win and the country's efforts at democratization were tarnished by accusations of serious electoral fraud, with most observers citing his overwhelming margin of victory and inflated voter turnout figures as indications that the official election results were not credible.

Absorbed by Russia in the early nineteenth century, Georgia gained its independence in 1918, but was overrun by the Red Army three years later. In 1922, it entered the U.S.S.R. as a component of the Transcaucasian Federated Soviet Republic, becoming a separate union republic in 1936. An attempt by the region of South Ossetia in 1990 to declare independence from Georgia and join Russia's North Ossetia sparked a war with Georgian forces. Although a ceasefire was signed in June 1992, the territory's final political status remains unresolved.

Following a national referendum in April 1991, Georgia declared its independence from the Soviet Union. Nationalist leader and former dissident Zviad Gamsakhurdia was elected president on May 26, but his authoritarian and erratic behavior resulted in his overthrow in January 1992 by opposition forces, led by Mkhedrioni paramilitary group leader Dzhaba Ioseliani and National Guard commander Tengiz Kitovani. In early 1992, former Georgian Communist Party head and Soviet foreign minister Eduard Shevardnadze was invited by Ioseliani to return from Moscow to serve as acting head of state; on October 11, Shevardnadze was elected president with 95 percent of the vote. A concurrent parliamentary election resulted in more than 30 parties and blocs gaining seats, although none secured a clear majority.

In 1993, Georgia experienced the violent secession of the long-simmering Abkhazia region and armed insurrection by Gamsakhurdia loyalists. Although Shevardnadze blamed Russia for arming and encouraging Abkhazian separatists, he legalized the presence of 19,000 Russian troops in Georgia in exchange for Russian support against Gamsakhurdia, who was defeated and reportedly committed suicide. In early 1994, Georgia and Abkhazia signed an agreement in Moscow that called for a ceasefire, the stationing of Commonwealth of Independent States troops under Russian command along the Abkhazian border, and the return of refugees under United Nations supervision. Parliamentary elections in November and December 1995 resulted in the Shevardnadze-founded Citizens' Union of Georgia (SMK), winning the most seats, while a concurrent presidential poll saw Shevardnadze secure victory with 77 percent of the vote.

The parliamentary elections of October 1999 were largely regarded as an informal referendum on Shevardnadze's seven-year presidency. Shevardnadze's ruling SMK was pitted against the opposition Revival Party led by his archrival Aslan Abashidze, the leader of the autonomous republic of Ajaria. The electoral campaign was dominated by mutual recriminations, with Shevardnadze accusing his opponent of being financed from abroad (a clear reference to Russia) and Abashidze accusing the president of vote rigging and ordering his assassination. The SMK won 132 seats in the 235-seat parliament, while the Revival Party came in second with 58 seats. Election observers from the Organization for Security and Cooperation in Europe (OSCE) concluded that despite a number of irregularities, including the intimidation of precinct election commission members and the presence of unauthorized personnel in polling stations, the vote was generally fair.

In the April 9, 2000, presidential elections, Shevardnadze easily won a second five-year term with a reported 81 percent of the vote. His closest challenger, former first secretary of the Communist Party Central Committee and current leader of the parliament minority, Dzhumber Patiashvili, received only 17 percent of the vote; four other candidates secured less than one percent each. Aslan Abashidze withdrew his candidacy from the race only one day before the vote. Shortly after the election, Georgia amended its constitution to officially transform Ajaria into the Ajarian Republic, leading to speculation that Shevardnadze had granted formal autonomy to the territory in exchange for Abashidze's withdrawal from the poll.

While Shevardnadze's win was largely anticipated, the large margin of his victory led to accusations of electoral fraud. Given the country's widespread voter apathy, most analysts believe that the official voter turnout figure of 76 percent was seriously exaggerated. A Commission on Security and Cooperation in Europe report concluded that "the election marked regression" even compared with the flawed 1999 parliamentary vote, and cited the "flagrant boosting of turnout totals and [Shevardnadze's] figures" as damaging to the country's efforts at democratization. Other monitoring organizations noted numerous irregularities, including the stuffing of ballot boxes, the presence of police in polling stations, a lack of transparency in the vote tabulation process, and a strong pro-Shevardnadze bias in the state media.

Georgia's already tense relations with Russia were further strained after Moscow accused Tbilisi of being lax in patrolling its border with Chechnya and of harboring Chechen rebels in its territory, and expressed its opposition to Georgia's growing cooperation with NATO. In early December, Moscow introduced a visa regime for Georgians traveling to Russia, although the move does not apply to residents of Abkhazia or South Ossetia. While the decision was ostensibly aimed at impeding the movement of Chechen rebels and weapons across the border, it also represented an attempt to pressure Tbilisi to decrease its pro-Western orientation. During a November 1999 OSCE meeting in Istanbul, Moscow agreed to close two of its four military bases in Georgia by mid-2001. While Russia began its withdrawal from the Vaziani and Gudauta bases in 2000, the fate of the other two bases remained inconclusive at year's end.

Long-standing demands of greater local autonomy continued unresolved throughout the year. Eight years of peace talks between South Ossetia and Georgia have failed to find a solution to the territorial status of the region, which has maintained de facto independence from Tbilisi since 1992. In the southwestern region of Ajaria, Aslan Abashidze exercises almost complete control over the territory, which has retained considerable autonomy since 1991. A final agreement to the protracted conflict in Abkhazia remains elusive, as Tbilisi and Sukhumi continued to disagree on key issues, including the territory's final political status.

Political Rights and Civil Liberties:

While Georgians can formally elect their government democratically, the most recent presidential election in April 2000 was marred by examples of serious electoral fraud, including inflated voter turnout figures and an unrealistically wide margin of victory for Shevardnadze. The 1999 parliamentary vote was deemed to be generally fair, although observers cited numerous irregularities, including ballot box stuffing and intimidation of precinct election commission members. Widespread fraud was noted in the autonomous republic of Ajaria, while no voting took place in the separatist territories of Abkhazia and South Ossetia, which remained largely outside central government control.

While the country's independent press often publishes discerning and critical political analyses, economic difficulties limit the circulation of most newspapers, particularly outside the capital. Independent newspapers and television stations face harassment by the authorities, while journalists in government-controlled media frequently practice self-censorship. Akaki Gogichaishvili, host of the television program Sixty Minutes on the independent Rustavi-2 station, claimed that he had received a death threat on May 18 from Georgia's deputy prosecutor-general after a report on corruption in the state-funded Georgian Writers' Union.

Although freedom of religion is respected for the country's largely Greek Orthodox population, members of "nontraditional" religions and foreign missionaries face harassment and intimidation by police and certain Greek Orthodox practitioners. According to Human Rights Watch, the ultranationalist Guldani Orthodox Diocese, led by defrocked Georgian Orthodox priest Father Basili, has been responsible for numerous attacks against Jehovah's Witnesses and members of other faiths. In most cases, police failed to punish those responsible and even actively participated in some of the attacks. There are no laws requiring registration of religious groups, although the Greek Orthodox Church enjoys a tax-exempt status not accorded to other faiths.

National and local governments often restrict freedom of assembly, particularly concerning supporters of the late President Gamsakhurdia. On October 28, police used force to disperse some 200 Gamsakhurdia supporters in Tbilisi who were demonstrating for the current government to resign and for the restoration of the late president's leadership group. Thousands of people took to the streets in Tbilisi in late 2000 to protest chronic shortages of electricity.

The judiciary is not fully independent, with courts influenced by pressure from the executive branch. The payment of bribes to judges, whose salaries remain inadequate, is reportedly common, while strong clan-based traditions encourage the granting of personal favors. Police frequently beat prisoners and detainees to extract confessions and fabricate or plant evidence on suspects. Prison conditions, which continue to be abysmal, suffer from overcrowding and inadequate sanitation, food, and medical care. The constitution and Law on Trade Unions allow workers to organize and bargain collectively and prohibit anti-union discrimination, and these rights are generally respected. The Amalgamated Trade Unions of Georgia, the successor to the official Soviet-era union, is the country's main trade union confederation and has no official affiliation with the government.

Ethnic conflicts in Abkhazia and South Ossetia, as well as an influx of thousands of refugees from neighboring Chechnya, have created a serious refugee problem and repatriation efforts have proceeded slowly. In December, President Shevardnadze declared a state of emergency in the eastern region of Kakheti, which he said was prompted by growing crime in the area. The region includes the Pankisi gorge that is home to several thousand Chechen refugee and where a number of hostage takings occurred during the year.

The government initiated a high-profile campaign to eliminate corruption, which remains endemic throughout all levels of Georgian society, by establishing an anti-corruption agency in September headed by respected intellectuals. Most women work in low-paying occupations and continue to be underrepresented in parliament and other government organs. Social taboos limit the reporting and punishment of rape and other spousal abuses.

Germany

Polity: Parliamentary democracy (federal)
Economy: Mixed capitalist
Population: 82,100,000
PPP: $22,169
Life Expectancy: 77
Ethnic Groups: German (92 percent), Turkish (2 percent), other (6 percent)
Capital: Berlin

Political Rights: 1
Civil Liberties: 2
Status: Free

Overview:

In 2000 the opposition center-right Christian Democratic Union (CDU) reeled from damaging revelations about questionable campaign financing during Helmut Kohl's 16 years as chancellor. As the CDU's new leadership worked to restore the party's image, the government, led by the Social Democratic Party (SPD) of Gerhard Schroder, scored important political and economic successes.

Germany was divided into Soviet, U.S., British, and French occupation zones after World War II. Four years later, the Allies helped to establish a democratic Federal Republic of Germany, while the Soviets oversaw the formation of the Communist German Democratic Republic (GDR). The division of Berlin was reinforced by the 1961 construction of the Berlin Wall. After the collapse of Erich Honecker's hardline GDR regime in 1989 and the destruction of the wall in 1990, citizens voted in the GDR's first free parliamentary election, in which parties supporting rapid reunification prevailed. In the spring of 1999, the German military participated in NATO air strikes in Kosovo, its first combat mission since World War II.

Schroder's SPD defeated Kohl's CDU in September 1998, ending Kohl's 16-year rule. The SPD formed a coalition with the Green Party, which was given the foreign ministry and two other ministerial-level positions in the new government. Despite criticism of his economic policies and defeats in several state elections in 1999, Schroder successfully pushed a major tax reform bill through the opposition-controlled *Bundesrat*, or upper house of parliament, in July 2000. Favored by economists, big business, trade union leaders, and foreign investors, the bill contains Germany's most radical tax reform since World War II. The SPD also won major state elections in North Rhine-Westphalia in May and Schleswig-Holstein in February. Prior to the campaign finance scandal, the CDU had been favored to win in both states.

A parliamentary committee investigating unreported political contributions to the CDU under Kohl's administration has encountered resistance from the former chancellor, who has admitted receiving more than $1 million in unreported donations but refuses to name the donors. He has also vowed to block the release of files from the former East German secret service, the *Stasi*, which reportedly contain recorded telephone conversations in which CDU officials refer to secret party funds. Kohl's refusal to cooperate with investigators has drawn criticism from within the CDU, which has forced him to resign as honorary chair of the party. He retains his seat in parliament, however, and therefore his immunity from prosecution. In February, CDU leader Wolfgang Schaeuble resigned over criticism of his handling of the scandal.

In March, CDU secretary-general Angela Merkel became the first woman and first former East German elected to lead the party. Her political credentials and her criticism of Kohl early in the finance scandal earned her the confidence of the party and its supporters. However, by year's end she was beset by party infighting and criticized for being weak and indecisive, and for lacking coherent policy ideas. In July, the lower house of parliament, or *Bundestag*, fined the CDU some $3 million over the financial scandal, leaving the party in dire financial condition. A CDU state official in Hesse resigned in September over allegedly covering up embezzlement of party funds in the early 1990s. CDU general secretary Ruprecht Polenz was apparently forced to resign in October in an effort by Merkel to reassert control over the party. Polenz had been criticized for not doing enough to divert attention from the party's internal problems. A policy paper on immigration published by the CDU in November only deepened divisions between party right-wingers and centrists. It also drew sharp attacks from immigrant advocates and other politicians for its references to a *Leitkultur*, or "guiding culture," to which immigrants must conform. Opinion polls in September put Merkel 20 points behind Schroder.

Political Rights and Civil Liberties: Germans can change their government democratically. The federal system provides for considerable self-government in the 16 states. The country's judiciary is independent.

The German press and broadcast media are free and independent, offering pluralistic views. However, Nazi propaganda and statements endorsing Nazism are illegal. Germany has exceeded other countries' practices in its attempts to police the Internet by blocking access to obscene, violent, or "dangerous" material. The government has brought charges against service providers and individual users. After a series of racist attacks during the summer of 2000, state and federal officials agreed to crack down on neo-Nazi Internet sites. German NDR Radio reported in August that some 90 right-wing groups had transferred their sites to U.S.-based service providers to avoid the crackdown. In December, the German supreme court ruled that individuals outside Germany who post Nazi propaganda aimed at Internet users inside Germany could be prosecuted under German law. However, it is unlikely that the ruling can be enforced in practice.

Freedom of assembly and association is guaranteed. Public rallies and marches require official permits, which are occasionally denied to right-wing radicals. A Berlin court in August banned a march planned to mark the anniversary of the death of Nazi-era deputy leader Rudolf Hess. In September, the government banned the German branch of Blood and Honor, an international skinhead group. Individuals are free to form political parties and to receive federal funding as long as the parties are democratic in nature. Beginning in October, the government, the Bundestag, and the Bundesrat all voted to ban the far-right National Democratic Party (NPD). A fringe party with some 6,000 members, the NPD advocates pro-German policies and opposes immigration, and its members have been blamed for inciting violence against foreigners. The ban was before the constitutional court at year's end, and a final ruling could take years.

Freedom of religion is guaranteed by the Basic Law (constitution). State governments subsidize church-affiliated schools and provide religious instruction in schools and universities for those of the Protestant, Roman Catholic, and Jewish faiths. Scientologists, who claim 30,000 adherents in Germany, have been at the center of a heated debate over the group's legal status. Major political parties exclude Scientologists from membership, claiming that the group does not constitute a religion, but rather a for-profit organization based on antidemocratic principles. Officials accuse the group of financially exploiting followers and exerting psychological pressure on those who attempt to leave it.

The Basic Law gives ethnic Germans entering the country unrestricted citizenship and legal residence immediately upon application. Parliament passed a law in 1999 granting automatic citizenship to children born in Germany to foreign immigrants. The law also allows dual citizenship for the first time in German history, although only until age 23, when dual citizens must choose between their parents' or German nationality. Foreign adults can now receive citizenship after living in Germany for eight years. In August, the government launched an initiative to grant 20,000 new work permits to foreigners with excellent skills in computer technology. The move was aimed at rectifying acute domestic skills shortages. In December, the government relaxed a three-year-old ban on the employment of asylum seekers.

Germany has no antidiscrimination law to protect immigrants, and even ethnic German immigrants face hostility from citizens, particularly in the east, who attribute the country's social and economic woes to immigration. The interior ministry recorded some 600 attacks by neo-Nazis or far-right-wingers against immigrants, Jews, and the homeless each month from January to July 2000, and at least 1,100 attacks in August alone. Three people, including a Mozambican immigrant, were killed in such attacks. What appeared to be a rising tide of racist violence led the government to announce measures to crack down on neo-Nazis, including the allocation of new funds for an educational effort to fight racism and for victims of violence. Schroder toured the country during the summer appealing for tolerance and announced the government's intention to ban the far-right NPD.

In the wake of lawsuits filed by Holocaust survivors against German companies, Germany established a fund in 1999 to compensate Nazi-era slave laborers who were forced to work for German manufacturers. In May 2000, the upper house of parliament approved a bill paving the way for compensation worth ten billion German *marks* (U.S.$4.6 billion). Half of the money is to come from German industry, the other half from the government. In August, Germany's Roman Catholic Church announced that it would pay some $5 million in compensation for its role in forced labor during the Nazi era.

Trafficking in women is a serious problem, according to reports by the U.S. State Department. Estimates of the number of women trafficked through and to Germany per year are variable, ranging between 2,000 and 20,000. Some 80 percent of these come from Eastern Europe and the former U.S.S.R. Laws against trafficking have been modified to address the problem more effectively, and currently provide penalties of up to ten years in prison. In October, the Bundestag voted to allow women to serve combat duty in the military. In December, the Bundesrat began debating proposals to give legal recognition to same-sex relationships.

Labor, business, and farming groups are free, highly organized, and influential. Trade union federation membership has dropped sharply in recent years, however, as a result of the collapse of industry in the east and layoffs in the west.

Ghana

Polity: Presidential-parliamentary democracy
Economy: Capitalist-statist
Population: 19,500,000
PPP: $1,735
Life Expectancy: 60
Ethnic Groups: Akan (44 percent), Moshi-Dagomba (16 percent), Ewe (13 percent), Ga (8 percent), other (19 percent)
Capital: Accra

Political Rights: 2*
Civil Liberties: 3
Status: Free

Ratings Change: Ghana's political rights rating changed from 3 to 2, and its status from Partly Free to Free, because of free and fair elections that led to a peaceful transfer of power to an opposition candidate after two decades under the leadership of Jerry Rawlings.

Overview:

Ghana made history in 2000 with a peaceful transfer of power that occurred when an opposition candidate defeated an incumbent in free and fair presidential elections. The election was hailed in Africa and abroad as a successful test of Ghana's democracy, despite isolated incidents of violence. John Kufuor, a businessman, replaced President Jerry Rawlings, a former fighter pilot who was in power for two decades. Kufuor soundly secured a victory with 56.7 percent of the vote in the second round of polling, compared with 43.3 percent for his opponent, Vice President John Atta Mills. The government continued to make efforts to improve human rights in the country during the year, but intimidation of the media continued.

Once a major slaving center and long known as the Gold Coast, the former British possession became black Africa's first colony to achieve independence. After the 1966 overthrow of its charismatic independence leader, Kwame Nkrumah, the country was wracked by a series of military coups for 15 years. Successive military and civilian governments vied with each other in both incompetence and mendacity.

In 1979, Flight Lieutenant Rawlings led a coup against the ruling military junta and, as promised, returned power to a civilian government after a purge of corrupt senior army officers. However, the new civilian administration did not live up to Rawlings's expectations, and he seized power again in December 1981 and set up the Provisional National Defense Council (PNDC). The PNDC junta was radically socialist, populist, and brutally repressive, banning political parties and free expression. Facing a crumbling economy, Rawlings, in the late 1980s, transformed Ghana into an early model for the structural adjustment programs urged by international lenders. A new constitution adopted in April 1992 legalized political parties, and Rawlings was declared president after elections that were neither free nor fair.

Ghana's economy has suffered in recent years as the result of a fall in the world prices for cocoa and gold, which are among the country's main foreign exchange earners. The country has also been battered by a sharp drop in the value of its currency, the *cedi*. Ghanaians are likely to be scrutinizing the new government's efforts at revitalizing the economy.

Political Rights and Civil Liberties: The December 1996 presidential and parliamentary elections under Ghana's 1992 constitution allowed Ghanaians their first opportunity since independence to choose their representatives in genuine elections. A broad civic education campaign and international assistance with registration and other electoral procedures preceded voting. However, the elections were also marked by the ruling party's extensive use of state media and patronage to support incumbents. Rawlings's five percent reelection victory, which extended his 16-year rule, was also assured by opposition disunity.

About 200 international observers monitored voting in the 2000 presidential and parliamentary elections and hailed the process as free and fair. The opposition, led by Kufuor, of the National Patriotic Party (NPP), alleged intimidation and other irregularities as the second round of voting in the presidential polls began, but those claims dissipated as the polling proceeded and his looming victory became apparent. Kufuor had led the seven candidates in the first round of voting in December with 48.4 percent, followed by Mills, of the National Democratic Congress (NDC), with 44.8 percent. The opposition also broke the NDC's stranglehold on parliament, with the NPP winning 99 of the 200 seats available, compared with 92 for the NDC, which had previously held 133 seats.

Ghanaian courts have acted with increased autonomy under the 1992 constitution, but are still occasionally subject to executive influence. Traditional courts often handle minor cases according to local customs that fail to meet constitutional standards. Scarce judicial resources compromise the judicial process, leading to long periods of pretrial detention under harsh conditions.

Ghana continued in 2000 to improve its respect for human rights, but abuses by security forces, including arbitrary detention and beatings, continued. Amnesty International expressed concern in August over the detention of a middle-aged couple whose son had been involved with a daughter of President Rawlings. The son said he was detained and beaten before finally fleeing to Britain. When his parents sought his whereabouts, they were accused of assaulting a police officer and were themselves detained.

The right to peaceful assembly and association is constitutionally guaranteed, and permits are not required for meetings or demonstrations. Numerous nongovernmental organizations (NGOs) operate openly and freely. Religious freedom is respected, but there is occasional tension between Christians and Muslims and within the Muslim community itself.

Freedom of expression is constitutionally guaranteed and generally respected. Despite the licensing of several independent radio and television stations, however, the Rawlings government allowed little expression of opposition views over the national radio and television networks as well as in the two daily newspapers it controls. Ghanaians enjoy open political debate, reflected in a number of robust private print media. Financial problems and government pressure, however, constrain the independent press. The government uses criminal libel laws, that make reporting false information a felony, in order to intimidate the media. Other obscure and rarely used laws have been invoked to intimidate the media.

In November 2000, the publisher and editor of the private *Ghanaian Chronicle*, Nana Kofi Coomson, was arrested for allegedly having diskettes that authorities said were stolen from the headquarters of the NDC. He was later released on bail. A media critic on state-run Ghana Television was arrested in November for allegedly making libelous statements against President Rawlings. Chris FM, a rural private radio station, was temporarily closed in November following allegations that a parliamentary candidate had used the station to broadcast inflammatory statements against political rivals of the NDC. Violence between supporters of the NDC and NPP erupted after the broadcast, leaving more than a dozen people injured. In September, the news editor of *The Crusading Guide*, Sedi Bansah, was arrested by the deputy minister of defense and faced pressure to disclose the identity of a source of information.

Ghanaian women suffer societal discrimination that is particularly serious in rural areas, where opportunities for education and wage employment are limited, despite their equal rights under the law. Women's enrollment in universities, however, is increasing. Domestic violence against women is said to be common, but often remains unreported. Legislation in 1998 doubled the prison sentence for rape. Women protested in Accra in December against what they said was police inaction regarding an alleged serial killer who has killed at least 30 women in the past three years. NGOs and the national human rights commissioner are campaigning against the *tro-kosi* system, in which young girls are forced into indefinite servitude to traditional priests.

The government has not interfered with the right of workers to associate in labor unions and has encouraged pluralism in labor organizations, but civil servants may not join unions. The Industrial Relations Act demands arbitration before strikes are authorized. The Ghana Federation of Labor was inaugurated in 1998 and is intended to serve as an umbrella organization for several other labor unions. The right to strike is guaranteed, but there have been no legal strikes since independence.

Greece

Polity: Parliamentary democracy
Economy: Mixed capitalist
Population: 10,600,000
PPP: $13,943
Life Expectancy: 78
Ethnic Groups: Greek (98 percent), other, including Macedonian and Turk (2 percent)
Capital: Athens

Political Rights: 1
Civil Liberties: 3
Status: Free

Overview:

Greece's ruling socialists were narrowly reelected on April 9, 2000. The Panhellenic Socialist Movement (PASOK) has ruled Greece since 1981, except from 1990 to 1993, when the conservative New Democracy Party (ND) held power.

Costas Simitis took over as prime minister four years ago and in that time has pushed forward pro-market policies, bringing the economy into line with the European Union. Simitis and his party, PASOK, defeated Costas Karamanlis of New Democracy with 43.83 percent of the votes while Karamanlis received 42.77 percent. Of the 300 seats in the unicameral parliament, PASOK won 158 seats; New Democracy, 125; the Communist Party of Greece, 11; the Coalition of the Left and Progress, 6.

Greece gained independence from the Ottoman Empire in 1830. The ensuing century brought continued struggle between royalist and republican forces. Occupation by the Axis powers in 1941 was followed by civil war between non-Communist and Communist forces that lasted until 1949. A military junta came to power as the result of a coup in 1967 and ruled until 1973, when naval officers failed to oust the junta and restore the monarchy. The failed 1973 coup led, however, to the formal deposition of the monarch and the proclamation of a republic. The current constitution, adopted in 1975, provides for a parliamentary system with a largely ceremonial president.

In June 2000, Greece was formally declared a member of the European Monetary Union and will adopt the euro in January 2001. Greek-Turkish relations continued to improve in early 2000 after Greece endorsed Turkey's bid for the European Union (EU) in December 1999. The countries signed low-level accords in January for tourism, the environment, the protection of investments, and for fighting terrorism and organized crime. However, relations diminished during NATO exercises at the end of this year after Greece pulled out over a dispute with Turkey regarding military boundaries.

Terrorism remains a serious problem. A top British defense minister was shot dead in June by the November 17 urban guerilla group, which has killed at least 23 Greeks, Americans, and Turks since 1975. The United States issued a report in June, which stated that Greece, by failing to arrest or convict any terrorists, was not cooperating fully in the fight against terrorism. In an effort to combat terrorism, the Greek government has considered tough new measures, including setting up telephone hot-lines for the public to give information about terrorism, a witness protection program, and the establishment of nonjury trials for terrorist suspects.

Political Rights and Civil Liberties: Greeks can change their government democratically. The Greek parliament has 300 members, elected for a four-year term by a system of proportional representation. Voting is compulsory for citizens between the ages of 18 and 70. The president is elected for a five-year term by parliament.

Among democratic countries, Greece is considered one of the worst with respect to freedom of expression. There continue to be frequent criminal charges in cases of libel and defamation. The public prosecutor may press charges against publishers and can seize publications deemed offensive to the president or to religious beliefs. A controversial law bans "unwarranted" publicity for terrorists from the media, including terrorists' proclamations following explosions. In 2000, there were reports of Turkish journalists being arrested, and Macedonian journalists were denied entrance at the borders of Greece. Another journalist was verbally and physically harassed after participating in an antiracist group movement with a local Roma (Gypsy) community.

Ninety-eight percent of the population belongs nominally to the state-sponsored Greek Orthodox Church. Orthodox bishops have the privilege of granting or denying permission to other faiths to build houses of worship in their jurisdictions. Members of non-Orthodox communities have been barred from entering occupations such as primary school teaching, the military, and the police. In June, the government announced that it would issue new identity cards that do not indicate the cardholder's religion. This is part of an effort by the Greek government to separate church and state and bring Greece in line with other EU members.

The government formally recognizes only the "Muslim minority" specified in the 1923 Treaty of Lausanne, applying the term to several different ethnic communities. Most of the Muslim community (officially estimated at 120,000 persons) is ethnically Turkish and objects to its classification as a merely "Muslim" minority. The country's Pomaks, the ethnically Slavic Muslim minority, make similar objections. Muslim Roma encounter large-scale discrimination in receiving education and other social benefits. Police brutality against the Roma remains a serious problem. The United Nations issued a report on the Roma in August, which included the raids on Roma slum settlements outside Athens to clear space for the 2004 Olympic Games. There were several other reports that some municipal councils unanimously decided to evict their Roma populations, holding them responsible for the increase in crime rates. These decisions were never condemned by the state. The Muslims object to the Greek government's prerogative to appoint its *Muftis*, or Muslim community leaders.

Greeks enjoy freedom of association, and all workers except military personnel and the police have the right to form and join unions, which are usually linked to political parties. A general strike paralyzed Greece in the beginning of October and again in December. The Greek unions were demonstrating against the government's unpopular labor reforms to combat high unemployment in preparation for Greece's entry into the EU's single-currency group in 2001.

The judiciary is independent. The constitution provides for public trials, and trial court sessions are usually open to the public. In 2000, Greek courts continued to ignore international norms and case law for minority rights, and Greece has been convicted three times by the European Court of Human Rights on Turkish minority cases.

Greece has a long history of jailing conscientious objectors to military service. In 1997, however, the government passed a new law to allow objectors to perform alternative, civilian service. The measure requires objectors to serve twice as long as military conscripts and was therefore criticized by Amnesty International as "punitive."

Women's groups have continued to organize to seek more equitable child custody and divorce laws and the creation of a family court.

Grenada

Polity: Parliamentary democracy
Economy: Capitalist-statist
Population: 100,000
PPP: $5,838
Life Expectancy: 72
Ethnic Groups: Mostly black, some European and South Asian
Capital: St. George's

Political Rights: 1
Civil Liberties: 2
Status: Free

Overview: Prime Minister Keith Mitchell announced in February 2000 a "zero tolerance" anticrime crackdown in the wake of growing concerns over an upswing of violent, often drug-related, delinquency. In keeping with several other Caribbean leaders, Mitchell said he was thinking of reintroducing the death penalty, subject to referendum, in a country that has not seen hangings since 1978. In August, the First International Bank of Grenada collapsed, leaving thousands of depositors—mostly U.S. citizens—facing the loss of millions of dollars. What happened to the bank, whose founder was a formerly bankrupt American who changed his identity when he applied for Grenadian "economic citizenship," offered a hard lesson in a region with growing dependency on the lucrative licensing fees that it earns from offshore financial institutions.

Grenada, a member of the Commonwealth, is a parliamentary democracy. The British monarchy is represented by a governor-general. Grenada, which gained independence in 1974, includes the islands of Carriacou and Petite Martinique. The bicameral parliament consists of a 15-seat house of representatives and a 13-seat senate, to which the prime minister appoints 10 senators and the opposition leader, 3.

Maurice Bishop's Marxist New Jewel Movement seized power in 1979. In 1983 Bishop was murdered by New Jewel hardliners Bernard Coard and Hudson Austin, who took control of the country. A joint U.S.-Caribbean military intervention removed Coard and Austin, who along with two others were originally sentenced to death, only to have their sentences commuted to life imprisonment. In the 1984 elections, the New National Party (NNP), a coalition of three parties, won the majority of seats. Herbert Blaize became prime minister until his death in 1989, when Deputy Prime Minister Ben Jones replaced him.

In the 1990 elections the NNP coalition unraveled, and there were five principal contenders: The National Party (TNP), headed by Jones; the centrist National Democratic Congress (NDC), led by Nicholas Braithwaite, head of the 1983-1984 interim government; the NNP, headed by Keith Mitchell; the leftist Maurice Bishop Patriotic

Movement (MBPM), led by Terry Marryshow; and Eric Gairy's rightist Grenada United Labour Party (GULP).

The NDC won 7 seats and took in a defector from the GULP, and Braithwaite became prime minister with a one-seat majority. After implementing unpopular economic reforms, the aging Braithwaite stepped down in early 1995 in favor of Agricultural Minister George Brizan.

The 1995 campaign was a raucous affair. Brizan sought to retain power by pointing to the improved economy. The other candidates accused the ruling NDC of corruption and harped on high unemployment.

The NNP startled local observers by winning 8 of 15 seats. The NDC won 5 seats and the GULP, 2. Mitchell became prime minister. Afterwards, NDC deputy leader Francis Alexis split off to form the Democratic Labour Party (DLP), in a move that underscores the fractious nature of Grenadian politics.

In his first months in office, Mitchell was accused by opposition leader Brizan and others of censoring news unfavorable to the government in state-run television and radio broadcasts, and of purging civil servants appointed during the NDC administration. Mitchell denied the allegations. In 1996 Mitchell's reorganization of the state-owned Grenada Broadcasting Corporation (GBC) was viewed by some as another attempt to fill political positions with NNP supporters and to control the dissemination of information at GBC. In 1997 the NDC charged the government with granting a casino license to a foreign company it alleged has gangster connections.

In May 1998, former Deputy Prime Minister Herbert Preudhomme was elected leader of the bitterly divided GULP, a year after Gairy died. The ruling NNP was plunged into crisis over the resignation of its foreign minister, whose loss left it with only 7 of 15 parliamentary seats. Grenada's parliament was dissolved in December 1998, paving the way for elections in 90 days. In 1999, the NNP made a sweep of all but 1 of 15 seats in parliament. Opposition complaints of alleged corruption seemed to miss the mark, as the NNP entered into the electoral fray boasting an enviable economic record; in four years, unemployment plummeted from 25 percent to 14 percent, and the economy posted a strong performance. Mitchell was also aided by a divided political opposition which, after the crushing defeat, seemed in danger of disappearing altogether.

In mid-August 2000, Mitchell reshuffled his cabinet, a move the lone opposition deputy blasted as an attempt to deflect attention from the First International scandal, as the bank admitted contributing thousands of dollars to the NNP's 1999 election campaign. The crisis created by the government takeover of First International came after a local auditor warned that the bank, which increased its assets from $110,000 to $14 billion in one year, was "in complete violation" of Grenadian offshore laws. However, Mitchell had been warned as much as 17 months earlier that the bank was in serious difficulty. Grenada's strict bank secrecy regulation and offers of citizenship, complete with passports, issued together with a new name, created worries of "one-stop-shopping" for international criminals. The relatively few protests about the bank's failure heard from depositors in the United States and Canada very likely reflected their wish not to advertise themselves as tax evaders in their own countries.

Political Rights and Civil Liberties: Citizens are able to change their government through democratic elections, and the 1999 elections were considered free and fair, although in light of the 2000 banking scandal, credibility was added to complaints of questionable contributions to the NNP. Many political parties exist, and few obstacles face those establishing new parties. But there has been a decline in turnout, as young people, in particular, appear to have lost confidence in a system riddled with fragmented politics and allegations of corruption. Following the crushing defeat suffered by Grenada's opposition parties, their role as alternatives in future elections was seriously in doubt.

The independent, prestigious judiciary has authority generally respected by the 750-member Royal Grenada Police Force. There are no military or political courts. In 1991 Grenada rejoined the Organization of Eastern Caribbean States court system, with the right of appeal to the Privy Council in London. Detainees and defendants are guaranteed a range of legal rights that the government respects in practice. Like many Caribbean island-nations, Grenada has suffered from a rise in violent, drug-related crime, particularly among increasingly disaffected youth. Prison conditions are poor, though they meet minimum international standards and the government allows human rights monitors to visit.

Newspapers, including four weeklies, are independent and freely criticize the government. Television is both private and public, and the main radio station is part of the GBC, a statutory body not directly controlled by the government. Since the 1995 elections, a number of new radio and television stations, not one of which is aligned with the NNP, were issued licenses to operate. In October 1999, the arrest of two journalists critical of the government caused an uproar among the opposition and human rights groups.

Constitutional guarantees regarding the right to organize political, labor, or civic groups are respected. The free exercise of religion and the right of free expression are generally respected.

Numerous independent labor unions include an estimated 20 to 25 percent of the workforce. A 1993 law gives the government the right to establish tribunals empowered to make "binding and final" rulings when a labor dispute is considered of vital interest to the state. The national trade union federation claimed the law was an infringement on the right to strike. Workers have the right to organize and to bargain collectively.

Women are represented in the government, though in greater numbers in the ministries than in parliament. No official discrimination takes place, but women generally earn less than men for equal work. Domestic violence against women is common. Police say that most instances of abuse are not reported, and others are settled out of court.

⬇ Guatemala

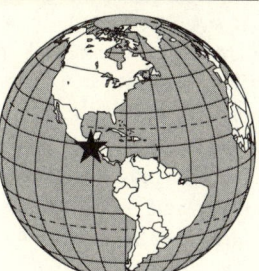

Polity: Presidential-
parliamentaty democracy
Economy: Capitalist-
statist
Population: 12,700,000
PPP: $3,505
Life Expectancy: 64

Political Rights: 3
Civil Liberties: 4
Status: Partly Free

Ethnic Groups: Mestizo (56 percent), Indian (44 percent)
Capital: Guatemala City
Trend Arrow: Guatemala received a downward trend arrow due to general worsening of the rule of law throughout the country and extreme government indifference to corruption.

Overview:

A still semiautonomous military, a badly reformed police force engaged in acts of brutality and corruption, and a legal system too weak to make a difference made for a short honeymoon for President Alfonso Portillo in his first year in office. A United Nations report issued in August blamed the government for dozens of politically motivated slayings; death threats against judges, journalists, and lawmakers; and hundreds of wrongful arrests. Vigilante killings in rural areas where residents are mostly Indian were also partly blamed on the government, with the new National Civil Police (PNC) singled out as responsible for some of the most serious cases of extrajudicial execution and torture. On a postive note, retired General Efraín Ríos Montt, Portillo's father-in-law and a man accused of genocide during his own 1982-1983 presidency, and who in 1999 was elected to a congressional seat and then as president of the congress, was brought up on corruption charges.

The Republic of Guatemala was established in 1839, 18 years after independence from Spain. The nation has endured a history of dictatorship, coups, and guerrilla insurgency, with only intermittent democratic government. A 36-year civil war formally ended with the signing of a peace agreement in 1996. The country has had elected civilian rule since 1985. Amended in 1994, the 1985 constitution provides for a four-year presidential term and prohibits reelection. An 80-member unicameral congress is elected for four years.

A right-wing businessman, Jorge Serrano, became president in 1991 after winning a runoff election. In 1993 Serrano attempted to dissolve the legislature. After initially supporting him, the military changed course as a result of mass protests and international pressure, and Serrano was sent into exile. The congress chose as his replacement Ramiro de León Carpio, the government's human rights ombudsman.

De León Carpio was practically powerless to halt human rights violations by the military or to curb its power as final arbiter in national affairs. After United Nations-mediated talks were launched between the government and the Guatemalan National Revolutionary Unity (URNG) left-wing guerrillas, the latter called a unilateral truce for the 1995 election and backed the left-wing New Guatemala Democratic Front (FDNG). The top presidential contenders were former Guatemala City mayor Alvaro

Arzú, of the National Advancement Party (PAN), and Alfonso Portillo Cabrera of the hard-right Guatemalan Republic Front (FRG). FRG founder and military dictator Efraín Ríos Montt was constitutionally barred from running. Arzú won with 36.6 percent of the vote; Portillo Cabrera had 22 percent. In the January 7, 1996, runoff, Arzú defeated Portillo, 51.2 percent to 48.8 percent.

Soon after taking office, Arzú reshuffled the military, forcing the early retirement of generals linked to drug trafficking, car-theft rings, and human rights abuses. The purge had the backing of a small but influential group of reformist officers who dominated the military high command. After a brief suspension of peace talks in October 1996 because of a rebel kidnapping, subsequent agreement on the return of rebel forces to civilian life and a permanent ceasefire led to the December 1996 peace accords.

Arzú's government won plaudits for important advances in carrying out the peace process. These included the successful demobilization of the URNG guerrillas and their political legalization; the retirement of more than 40 senior military officers on corruption and narcotics charges; and the reduction of the army's strength by one-third. A UN-sponsored truth commission mandated by the peace accords began receiving tens of thousands of complaints of rights violations committed during the 36-year internal conflict.

By 1999, however, it was clear that the government would not move further to implement those reforms meant to correct the social and economic inequalities that had led to the conflict. These included ending the military's political tutelage and impunity, recognizing the rights of the Maya Indians, and reforming taxation to pay for health, education, and housing programs for the poor. In February the truth commission said that state security forces had been responsible for 93 percent of human rights abuses committed during the civil war, which claimed as many as 200,000 lives, and that high-ranking officials had overseen 626 massacres in Indian villages.

In 1999, Guatemala held its first presidential elections since the end of the country's 36-year civil war. The elections were held at a time of growing concern over the failure of the government to implement key reforms it had agreed to as part of the UN-brokered peace settlement. In a May 1999 referendum, voters rejected a package of 50 amendments to the constitution, approved by congress a year earlier, which had been prepared in accordance with the UN-brokered peace plan, in an election that was characterized by a high degree of abstentions. The presidential election saw former Marxist guerrillas participate openly for the first time as part of a left-wing coalition.

Before the first-round voting in November, Portillo, who campaigned on a human rights and development platform, admitted to have killed two men in Mexico 17 years earlier, in self-defense, he said. As a candidate, the FRG standard bearer successfully dodged the accusation that he was merely a surrogate candidate for Ríos Montt, and was able to moderate the party's hard line ideology. He went on to beat the PAN candidate, former Guatemala City mayor Oscar Berger, 48 to 30 percent. Alvaro Colom, of the New Nation Alliance (ANN), which included the former guerrillas, drew 12 percent. In the December 26 runoff, Portillo, who campaigned on a populist platform of fighting crime, reducing unemployment, and aiding the poor, overwhelmed Berger, 68 to 32 percent.

In 2000, Portillo began his presidency with an unprecedented shakeup of the military high command, claiming for himself the lead role in restructuring and modernizing the armed forces. However, throughout the year the army continued a pattern of interference with civilian institutions, particularly the police. Faced with opinion polls that showed his popularity, as well as his reputation for leadership, plummeting as a result in large part to worries over crime, Portillo replaced his internal security minister with an FRG deputy and retired army major with a controversial rights record. In August Ríos Montt was accused by opposition lawmakers of altering an alcohol tax after its approval by congress and before its publication, at the urgings of powerful liquor interests. In October, a long-awaited presidential report on the 1998 slaying of human rights activist, Bishop Juan Gerardi, offered no new information and was deemed useless by those pressing for a more thorough investigation of the case. Two days before his death, Bishop Gerardi had released a report blaming the military for 90 percent of the rights abuses committed during the civil war. On a positive note, in August Portillo promised to compensate victims of rights abuses during the long-running civil war, and to prosecute those responsible for such violations.

Political Rights and Civil Liberties:

Citizens can change their governments through elections. In the run-up to the November elections, which were largely free and fair, the Supreme Electoral Tribunal conducted an energetic voter turnout campaign among the country's 4.4 million registered voters. The constitution guarantees religious freedom and the right to organize political parties, civic organizations, and labor unions. However, despite increasing freedoms, Guatemala has yet to end a tradition of military dominance; recommendations by the truth commission for the purging of senior military commanders involved in atrocities have been largely ignored. The rule of law is undermined by the systemic corruption that afflicts all public institutions, particularly the legislature and the courts.

Despite penal code reforms in 1994, the judicial system remains ineffectual for most legal and human rights complaints. In general, it suffers from chronic problems of corruption, intimidation, insufficient personnel, lack of training opportunities, and a lack of transparency and accountability. Drug trafficking is a serious problem, and Guatemala remains a warehousing and transit point for South American drugs going to the United States. In 1999, the U.S. State Department reported that Guatemalan traffickers, frequently tied to the military, moved between 200 and 300 metric tons of cocaine into northern markets, up from 50 tons earlier in the decade. In April 1999, a constitutional court judge, Epaminondas González Dubon, who had ordered the extradition to the United States of a military officer accused of drug trafficking, was murdered.

Human rights organizations are the targets of death threats and the victims of frequent acts of violence, suggesting that a parallel power structure still operates with impunity in Guatemala. In September two respected human rights organizations were raided by heavily armed men, and their staff beaten and threatened with death. In December members of the Mutual Support Group (GAM), another prominent rights organization, were threatened and intimidated, and armed men stole a vehicle belonging to the group.

Native Americans are largely shut out from the national justice system. Although indigenous languages are now being used in courtrooms around the country, traditional justice systems receive only lip service from Guatemalan authorities. Similarly, cursory recruitment efforts have resulted in only a handful of Native American recruits for the new civilian police. In July 2000, the general director and an aide of the Regional Coordination of Integrated Cooperatives, involved in settling land disputed in rural Indian communities, were killed by heavily armed assailants. In September, Indian villages stormed a police station and took two chiefs hostage in reprisal for what they say was police mistreatment of Maya peoples.

Guatemala remains one of the most violent countries in Latin America. The closing of military barracks throughout the country—the armed forces were the one Guatemalan institution that enjoyed a truly national presence—while the PNC was being created and deployed created a noticeable vacuum in which criminal interests were free to operate. One result was an upsurge of vigilantism and lynchings. In July 2000, eight men accused of running drugs and guns were burned to death in a largely Indian vicinity in the western highlands. The vigilantes were egged on by a paramilitary squadron. In September, Indian villagers stoned and beat to death three alleged rapists in an isolated central highlands area. In Guatemala City, neighborhood patrols—some armed with automatic weapons—have sprung up in a desperate attempt to arrest the spiraling crime wave; paramilitary units are said to be reorganizing; and throughout the country private security guards far outnumber the PNC. In June 2000, Portillo called out 4,000 army troops to assist the PNC in patrolling urban areas.

In 1998 the first convictions on war crimes charges were handed down in November, when three pro-government paramilitary force members were sentenced to death for their roles in a 1982 massacre of Indian peasants. In August 1999, 12 soldiers, including one officer, were given five-year sentences, with the possibility of parole, for the killing of 11 returned indigenous refugees, including two children, in 1995.

The press and most of the broadcast media are privately owned, with several independent newspapers and dozens of radio stations, most of them commercial. Five of the six television stations are commercially operated. However, journalists remain at great risk. In recent years, more than a dozen Guatemalan journalists have been forced into exile. The 1993 murder of newspaper publisher Jorge Carpio Nicolle, a former presidential candidate, remains unsolved. In a positive development, in 1999 two men were convicted and sentenced to 30 years in prison for killing a newspaper editor two years earlier. In April 2000, a photographer for the Guatemala City daily *Prensa Libre* and two colleagues were wounded by private security guards as they covered a street demonstration. Just two weeks earlier the Organization of American States special rapporteur for freedom of expression visited the country to urge greater respect for press freedom.

Some 32 percent of the population are illiterate; this rate of illiteracy is the highest in the Americas after Haiti. Eighty percent live below poverty levels, and infant mortality among the Maya—some 60 percent of the population—is among the highest on the continent.

The Runejel Junam Council of Ethnic Communities (CERJ) represents the interests of the country's Indians, a majority of the population who have faced severe repression and violence by the army and allied paramilitary organizations, as well as being used by the URNG guerrillas. In 1996, Indians showed signs of flexing some political muscle. Indian candidates won control of an estimated 40 urban areas, including Guatemala's second largest city, and ten percent of congressional seats. Under a new law, Maya descendants are allowed to seek office as independents, and not as representatives of the national political parties that have ignored their needs.

Workers are frequently denied the right to organize and are subjected to mass firings and blacklisting, particularly in export-processing zones, where the majority of workers are women. Existing unions are targets of systematic intimidation, physical attacks, and assassination, particularly in rural areas during land disputes. According to a United Nations report issued in December 2000, Guatemala has the highest rate of child labor in the Americas, with one-third of school-age children forced to work on farms or in factories. Use of Guatemala as a transit point for illegal aliens, particularly from Asia, frequently leads to abuses, including death.

↓ Guinea

Polity: Dominant party   **Political Rights:** 6
(military-influenced)   **Civil Liberties:** 5
Economy: Capitalist   **Status:** Not Free
Population: 7,500,000
PPP: $1,782
Life Expectancy: 47
Ethnic Groups: Peuhl (40 percent), Malinke (30 percent), Soussou (20 percent), other (10 percent)
Capital: Conakry
Trend Arrow: Guinea received a downward trend arrow for repression of immigrants from Liberia and Sierra Leone, following cross-border raids by armed men based in both of those countries.

Overview: Tens of thousands of refugees from Liberia and Sierra Leone, as well as Guinean civilians, were on the move in southern Guinea at the end of the year, following several cross-border attacks by fighters based in Liberia and Sierra Leone. The attacks, which began in earnest in September, have claimed hundreds of lives. Guinean security forces, backed by vigilante groups, detained about 5,000 nationals from Liberia and Sierra Leone in September and put them through rigorous identity checks, searching for suspected insurgents. Human Rights Watch documented beatings and rapes. The detainees were released days later, but the intimidation prompted the return home of thousands of economic immigrants from the two neighboring countries.

The violence has exacerbated tension among the Mano River Union countries: Guinea, Liberia, and Sierra Leone. Both Liberia and Guinea have accused the other of harboring dissidents seeking to overthrow their governments. The Economic Community of West African States decided in December to send some 1,500 military observers to patrol the border regions to prevent an escalation of the fighting and in order to help protect the nearly 500,000 refugees from Liberia and Sierra Leone living in Guinea.

Under Ahmed Sékou Touré, Guinea declared independence from France in 1958. Alone among France's many African colonies, it rejected the domination of continued close ties with France. Paris retaliated quickly, removing or destroying all "colonial property" and enforcing an unofficial but devastating economic boycott. Sékou Touré's one-party rule became high repressive, and Guinea was increasingly impoverished under his Soviet-style economic policies. Lansana Conté seized power in a 1984 coup, and was nearly toppled by a 1996 army mutiny. Amidst general looting in Conakry, he rallied loyal troops and reestablished his rule. Conté defends his tight rule by saying it is necessary to avoid ethnic conflict.

Former opposition presidential candidate Alpha Condé, who leads the Guinean People's Rally, was sentenced to five years in prison for sedition in a trial that international observers said was unfair. Condé and a number of his supporters were detained after the December 1998 presidential elections, which were not considered fair, and charged with attempted subversion.

Guinea's economy has been suffering from a world drop in the price of bauxite. The country is the world's second largest producer of the mineral and is also rich in gold, diamonds, and iron ore.

Political Rights and Civil Liberties: The Guinean people's constitutional right to freely elect their government is not yet respected in practice. Guinean politics and parties are largely defined along ethnic lines. Conté was returned to office in a December 1998 presidential election that lacked credible opposition, as state patronage and media strongly backed the incumbent. His reelection to another five-year term, with 54.1 percent of about 2.7 million votes reported, was unconvincing, although broad manipulation of the electoral process and opposition disunity probably made more blatant forms of vote rigging unnecessary. The Higher Council on Electoral Affairs was neither autonomous nor powerful enough to level the electoral landscape, although the polls were an improvement over past elections. Hundreds of people, however, were arrested after the election, including the official third-place finisher, Alpha Condé.

Electoral manipulation and fraud in the 1993 presidential polls made a mockery of the vote. The June 1995 national assembly elections were more open. A total of eight opposition parties won just enough seats to deny the ruling Progress and Unity Party the two-thirds majority required to enact constitutional changes; but the ruling party's share of seats in the 114-member assembly was probably fraudulently inflated far above the proportion of votes it received. The president retains decree power that could eviscerate the parliamentary process. Despite cumbersome requirements for official recognition of political parties, about 50 are recognized.

There was a low turnout in June 2000 municipal elections. The opposition claimed fraud, and protests followed. Legislative elections scheduled for November 2000 were postponed indefinitely. The government attributed the delay to insecurity in the country.

While nominally independent, the judicial system remains infected by corruption, nepotism, ethnic bias, and political interference, and lacks resources and training. Minor civil cases are often handled by traditional ethnic-based courts. Arbitrary arrests and detention are common, and persistent maltreatment and torture of detainees is reported. Prison conditions are harsh and sometimes life threatening.

Several statutes restrict freedom of association and assembly in apparent contravention of constitutional guarantees. The government may ban any gathering that "threatens national unity." Several human rights groups and many nongovernmental groups operate openly. Constitutionally protected religious rights are respected in practice, although the main body representing the country's Muslims, who constitute more than 80 percent of the population, is government controlled.

The government has wide powers to bar any communications that insult the president or disturb the peace. All broadcasting, as well as the country's largest and only daily newspaper, are state controlled, and offer little coverage of the opposition and scant criticism of government policy. The print media have little impact in rural areas, where incomes are low and illiteracy is high. Several weekly newspapers in Conakry offer sharp criticism of the government despite frequent harassment. A restrictive press law allows the government to censor or shutter publications on broad and ill-defined bases. Defamation and slander are considered criminal offenses. Officials in July 2000 suspended accreditation for three local correspondents working for international media on the grounds that they had tarnished the image of Guinea.

Women have far fewer educational and employment opportunities than men, and many societal customs discriminate against women. Constitutionally protected women's rights are often unrealized. Spousal abuse and other violence against women are said to be prevalent. Female genital mutilation is illegal and women's groups are working to eradicate the practice, but is still widely carried out.

The constitution provides for the right to form and join unions. However, about 80 percent of Guinea's seven million people are subsistence farmers. Only a very small formal sector exists, and about five percent of the workforce is unionized. Several labor confederations compete in this small market and have the right to bargain collectively.

Guinea-Bissau

Polity: Presidential-parliamentary democracy
Economy: Mixed statist
Population: 1,200,000
PPP: $616
Life Expectancy: 45
Ethnic Groups: Balanta (30 percent), Fula (20 percent), Manjaca (14 percent), Mandinga (13 percent), Papel (7 percent), other (16 percent)
Capital: Bissau

Political Rights: 4*
Civil Liberties: 5
Status: Partly Free

Ratings Change: Guinea-Bissau's political rights rating changed from 3 to 4 following an uprising by the former army chief of staff and his subsequent killing, and the detention of several opposition leaders.

Overview:

Populist Kumba Yala won the second round of presidential elections in January 2000. The ballot was seen by many as a last hope for peace in the country following the toppling of President João Bernardo Vieira in May 1999 after a year-long rebellion that pitted forces loyal to him against those backing the former army chief, General Ansumane Mané.

Guinea-Bissau won independence from Portugal in 1973 after a 12-year guerrilla war. The African Party for the Independence of Guinea-Bissau and Cape Verde (PAIGC) held power for the next 13 years. Luís Cabral became president in 1974 and made Vieira his prime minister, but Vieira toppled Cabral in 1980. Constitutional revisions in 1991 ended the PAIGC's repressive one-party state. Vieira won the country's first free and fair presidential election in 1994, but he eventually came to be seen as the leader of a corrupt ruling class.

The June 1998 army mutiny broke out when Vieira sacked General Ansumane Mané, accusing him of smuggling arms to rebels in the southern Casamance region of neighboring Senegal, which for years complained that Guinea-Bissau was backing the rebels. Encouraged by France, about 3,000 troops from Senegal and Guinea intervened on behalf of Vieira. They were replaced by fewer than 600 unarmed West African peacekeepers, which made Vieira vulnerable to his overthrow in May 1999.

Guinea-Bissau's new military leaders moved swiftly to hold legislative and presidential elections in November 1999, in line with an agreement that had been worked out under the auspices of the Economic Community of West African States. International observers declared the voting free and fair.

President Yala and General Mané met in May 2000 to discuss improving relations between the government and the military, but by November Mané had declared himself the head of the armed forces and revoked military promotions that Yala had made. Fighting erupted between supporters of the president and those allied with Mané, who fled into the countryside and was killed. More than 100 suspected government opponents, including several military officers and political opposition leaders, were detained on suspicion of backing what the government was calling an attempted coup. Deep divisions remain in Guinea-Bissau. Thousands of people turned out for the funeral of Mané, who was considered a hero in the country's independence struggle.

The vast majority of Guinea-Bissau's one million citizens survive on subsistence farming. Cashew nuts are a key export. There are hopes for substantial oil reserves offshore, where drilling began in 1989.

Political Rights and Civil Liberties: The people of Guinea-Bissau were able to choose their government freely for the first time in 1994, and both direct presidential polls and legislative elections were judged free and fair by international observers. The PAIGC retained the presidency and a parliamentary majority, but five opposition parties were represented in the national assembly. Voting in the November 1999 legislative and presidential elections was declared free and fair by international observers despite widespread delays, isolated cases of violence, and other voting irregularities. The January 2000 runoff pitted Yala, of the Social Renewal Party (PRS), against Malam Bacai Sanha, of the PAIGC. In legislative voting, the opposition PRS obtained 38 of the 102 seats, followed by the Resistance of Guinea with 29, and the PAIGC with 24. The 11 remaining seats went to five of the ten other parties that fielded candidates. The president is elected for a five-year term, while parliamentarians serve for four years.

Freedom of speech and the press is constitutionally guaranteed, but journalists practice self-censorship. Several private radio stations and community radio stations have begun broadcasting since the end of the war. Few private newspapers publish, and the lack of vibrant independent media may be due more to financial constraints than to government interference. Amnesty International in May said two state television journalists and a politician, Fernando Gomes, were arbitrarily detained and held in harsh conditions after state television aired statements by Gomes, who is also a prominent human rights defender. Gomes had criticized the political situation in the country and accused the prime minister of corruption. He and the journalists were released two days later.

Freedom of assembly and freedom of expression are constitutionally guaranteed and generally respected. The judiciary enjoys some autonomy, but is largely controlled by the executive branch. In March, the president fired the attorney general following the state's failure to obtain a conviction in the first trial of a senior member of the deposed regime. Judicial performance is often unpredictable owing to political interference, poor training, and scant resources. Traditional law usually prevails in rural areas. A UN peace-building office has helped the supreme court, which has been especially vulnerable to political pressure, train 37 new judges and is also monitoring trials.

Police routinely ignore rights of privacy and protections against search and seizure. Severe mistreatment of detainees is reported. The UN has expressed concern over the continued detention of military and political prisoners under harsh conditions and has appealed to authorities to speed up the judicial process. At least 100 people who were detained on Vieira's ouster are still in jail. More than 100 others were arrested following Mané's uprising in November.

Most people follow traditional religions, but proselytizing is permitted and there is a significant Muslim population, as well as a small Christian minority. While official registration is required, no religious group has been denied registration since 1982, and religious freedom is respected.

Eleven labor unions operate, and workers have the right to organize and to strike with prior notice. Most people, however, work in subsistence agriculture. Most wages are established in bilateral negotiations between workers and employers.

Women face some legal and significant traditional and societal discrimination, although it is prohibited by law. They generally do not receive equal pay for equal work and have fewer opportunities for education and jobs in the small formal sector. Domestic violence against women is common, and female genital mutilation is widespread. The government has formed a national committee to discourage the practice.

Guyana

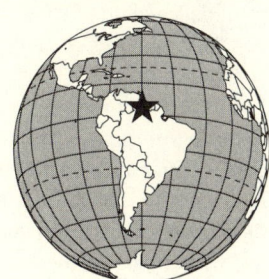

Polity: Parliamentary democracy
Economy: Mixed statist
Population: 700,000
PPP: $3,403
Life Expectancy: 65
Ethnic Groups: East Indian (49 percent), black (32 percent), mixed (12 percent), Indian (6 percent), white and Chinese (1 percent)
Capital: Georgetown

Political Rights: 2
Civil Liberties: 2
Status: Free

Overview:

In 2000, President Bharrat Jagdeo paved the way for general elections to be held in January 2001. Jagdeo, who took office the year before when President Janet Jagan stepped down, also urged action to implement the recommendations for reform of the 1980 constitution that were submitted to parliament by a constitution reform commission. The protection of Guyana's small indigenous populations continued to be one of the most important human rights issues yet to be faced by the country's ruling elite.

Guyana is a member of the Commonwealth. Indo-Guyanese outnumber Afro-Guyanese, 52 percent to 36 percent. From independence in 1966 until 1992, Guyana was ruled by the autocratic, predominantly Afro-Guyanese, People's National Congress (PNC). The 1980 constitution provides for a strong president and a 65-seat national assembly elected every five years. Twelve seats are occupied by elected local officials. The leader of the party winning the plurality of parliamentary seats becomes president for a five-year term. The president appoints the prime minister and cabinet.

The first free and fair elections were held in 1992, and 80 percent of the eligible population voted. The PNC lost to an alliance of the predominantly Indo-Guyanese People's Progressive Party (PPP) and the Civic party. PPP leader Cheddi Jagan, having moderated his Marxism since the collapse of communism, became president with 52 percent of the vote; PNC leader Desmond Hoyte took 41 percent. A third candidate from the Working People's Alliance (WPA), the only mixed-race party in the country, won less than 2 percent. In the legislature, the PPP won 36 of 65 seats; the PNC, 26; the WPA, which campaigned on a platform of multiracial cooperation, won 2 seats, and the centrist United Force took 1.

Fear and distrust of the Indo-Guyanese ruling party continued among Afro-Guyanese, despite Jagan's record of governing in a relatively evenhanded manner. He was slow to move on promised constitutional and electoral reforms, but in 1995 got to work with an eye towards the next elections, due in 1997.

Jagan's work was cut short by his death in March 1997. He was replaced by Samuel Hinds, a member of Civic, the PPP's coalition partner. Hinds called elections for December 15, 1997. Cheddi Jagan's widow, Janet, beat the PNC's Hoyte by a 5 to 4 margin, or roughly 60,000 votes. The vote was bitterly disputed as rigged. The army was called upon to help quell civil disturbances, even after a special commission sent by the Caribbean Community (Caricom), the regional multilateral group, found no evidence of election fraud. In 1998, progress was made on constitutional reform as parliament began the process of setting up a broad-based committee to oversee changes in the 1980 constitution.

Ill health forced Janet Jagan to resign in August 1999, and she was replaced by Finance Minister Jagdeo, who promised to heal racial and political divides and to welcome foreign investment. In 2000, indigenous-rights issues continued to be a primary human rights concern, as only 6,000 out of 24,000 square miles recommended for titling, or demarcation as indigenous-owned, land by a 1969 government commission had actually been titled to Native Americans by the end of the century. Indigenous lands, titled and untitled, are frequently allocated to mining and logging interests or set aside as protected areas, mostly without any attempt to inform the affected communities or to seek their participation or consent.

Political Rights and Civil Liberties: Citizens can change their government through direct, multiparty elections. Claims by the opposition PNC concerning vote rigging and mismanagement in the 1997 elections were judged by a Caricom-selected investigative commission to be largely without merit, although numerous administrative shortcomings were detected. In 1997, an effort was made to reduce the possibility of the fraud and impersonation that had marred previous contests by requiring voters to have identification cards bearing their photographs when they went to the polls.

Under the 1980 constitution, the president has wide powers and immunities. Because the constitution lacks explicit guarantees, political rights and civil liberties rest more on government tolerance than institutional protection. The rights of free expression, freedom of religion, and freedom to organize political parties, civic organizations, and labor unions are generally respected.

Several independent newspapers operate freely, including the daily *Stabroek News*. Only two radio stations operate; both are government owned. The government owns one television station. Seventeen privately owned television stations freely criticize the government.

The judicial system is independent; however, due process is undermined by the shortage of staff and funds. Prisons are overcrowded, and conditions poor. Guyana is the only Caribbean country to have cut all ties to the British Privy Council, the court of last resort for other former colonies in the region. Guyanese officials have complained that U.S. efforts to deport Guyanese from the United States to Guyana caused an upsurge in violent crimes such as carjackings and shootouts with police. Indigenous peoples are routinely denied the right to a fair trial and due process of law, in particular the failures to provide translation services during trials for indigenous defendants and the absence of defense counsel.

The Guyana Defence Force and the Guyana Police Force are under civilian control, with the latter invested with the authority to make arrests and maintain law and order throughout the country. The Guyana Human Rights Association, an autonomous, effective group backed by independent civic and religious groupings, has charged the police with frequent recurrence to excessive force, sometimes causing death. Although authorities have taken some steps to investigate extrajudicial killings, and charges against some officers have been brought, abuses are still committed with impunity. The police are also prone to corruption, particularly so given the penetration by the hemispheric drug trade. Popular disaffection with the police could be seen when, in February 2000, Guyana's most-wanted criminal was killed after an 11-hour gun and grenade battle with police. A week later, he was given a hero's funeral attended by thousands of people.

Labor unions are well organized. In 1995 the government sought to dilute the right to strike among some public sector unions. Companies are not obligated to recognize unions in former state enterprises sold off by the government.

Racial clashes have diminished since the 1992 election, but long-standing animosity between Afro- and Indo-Guyanese remains a concern. The government has formed a multiparty race relations committee to promote tolerance.

There are nine indigenous peoples in Guyana, numbering approximately 80,000 people, or ten percent of the population. Human rights violations against them are widespread and pervasive, particularly concerning the failure of the state to adequately respect indigenous land and resource rights. Logging and mining concessions, which cover vast areas of Guyana, often cause substantial environmental degradation, which in turn causes a decline in indigenous subsistence resources and health. As indigenous land and resource rights are fundamentally related to cultural rights, the latter are also curtailed when the former are violated. Indigenous attempts to seek redress through the courts have been met with unwarranted delays by the judiciary. Legislation pertaining to indigenous peoples is outdated and discriminatory, vesting in government ministers arbitrary and far-reaching powers that do not apply to other Guyanese citizens. Intergovernmental oversight bodies have criticized this legislation and recommended its revision on a number of occasions, to no avail. There is widespread discrimination with regard to the provision of education and health services in indigenous communities, and disregard for their customary laws and institutions of governance.

Domestic violence against women is troubling, as is the government's reluctance to address the issue.

Haiti

Polity: Presidential-parliamentary
Economy: Capitalist-statist
Population: 6,400,000
PPP: $1,383
Life Expectancy: 54
Ethnic Groups: Black (95 percent), mulatto, and white (5 percent)
Capital: Port-au-Prince

Political Rights: 6*
Civil Liberties: 5
Status: Not Free

Ratings Change: Haiti's political rights rating changed from 5 to 6 and its status from Partly Free to Not Free, due to a series of sham elections, conducted under a heavy threat of intimidation, that resulted in former President Jean-Bertrand Aristide and his Lavalas Family sweeping to power in largely uncontested polls.

Overview:
Former President Jean-Bertrand Aristide, revered by some as a defender of the powerless, and Haiti's first democratically elected president, swept to victory in a November 2000 presidential contest boycotted by all major opposition parties and held against a backdrop of widespread civil unrest and voter intimidation. Aristide ran on a populist platform of economic reactivation, but opponents claimed he was bent on establishing a one-party state. Aristide's nearly 92 percent of the vote in the presidential election was mirrored in contests for nine senate seats—all won by his Lavalas Family party—giving his new government all but one seat in the upper house. In elections, held in three stages in May, June and July, which opponents claimed were rigged, the Lavalas Family also won 80 percent of the seats in the lower house.

According to U.S. intelligence sources, at least seven of the senators elected on Aristide's slate are in the pay of Colombian drug cartels, a worrisome development that reflects the penetration of the foreign drug lords throughout Haitian society, including its U.S.-trained police force. Money laundering and the narcotics trade have also become growth industries in Haiti's failing economy. In August 2000, the U.S. Justice Department announced that it was ending a long-running, scandal-ridden police and prosecutorial training effort in Haiti, without giving a reason for its decision.

Since gaining independence from France in 1804 following a slave revolt, the Republic of Haiti has endured a history of poverty, violence, instability, and dictatorship.

A 1986 military coup ended 29 years of rule by the Duvalier family, and the army ruled for most of the next eight years. Under international pressure, the military permitted the implementation of a French-style constitution in 1987. It provides for a president elected for five years, an elected parliament composed of a 27-member senate and an 83-member house of representatives, and a presidentially appointed prime minister.

In the 1990 elections, Aristide, a charismatic left-wing priest, won in a landslide over conservative Marc Bazin. Aristide sought to establish civilian authority over the military; he also railed against corruption. Haiti's elite and the military then conspired to overthrow him. In response, he overstepped the constitution by calling on supporters to defend the government by violent means.

Aristide was overthrown in September 1991. Haiti came under the ruthless control of the military triumvirate of General Raoul Cedras, General Philippe Biamby, and Colonel Michel François. Tens of thousands of paramilitary thugs terrorized the populace, and the regime was steeped in narcotics trafficking. The United States and the United Nations imposed a trade and oil embargo.

In September 1994, facing an imminent U.S. invasion, Cedras and Biamby agreed to step down. U.S. troops took control of the country, and Aristide was reinstated. His security, as well as that of average Haitians, now depended on U.S. and UN forces. Aristide dismantled the military before the June 1995 parliamentary elections got underway. International observers questioned the legitimacy of the June election and Aristide's supporters fell out among themselves. The more militant Lavalas movement remained firmly behind him. But the National Front for Change and Democracy (FNCD), a leftist coalition that had backed him in 1990, claimed fraud and boycotted the runoff elections. In the end, Lavalas won an overwhelming parliamentary majority.

In the fall Lavalas nominated René Preval, Aristide's prime minister in 1991, as its presidential candidate. With Aristide backing him and the FNCD and most other major opposition parties boycotting, the result of the December 17, 1995, election, which opposition politicians claimed was marred by serious irregularities and fraud, was a forgone conclusion. Preval won about 89 percent of a turnout of less than one-third of those eligible.

Preval took office February 7, 1996. The UN had planned to withdraw its troops by the end of the month. The new U.S.-trained Haitian National Police, however, clearly lacked the competence to fill the void. At Preval's urging, the UN extended its stay, but by June cut its presence to 1,300. The final U.S. combat force had withdrawn two months earlier.

In September 1996, Preval purged much of his security force, which, according to U.S. officials, was involved in the murders a month earlier of two politicians from the right-wing Mobilization for National Development (MDN) party, which counted on heavy support from former soldiers. Senate elections held in April 1997 were fraught with irregularities, and the resulting ongoing election dispute meant that parliament would not approve a new prime minister to replace Rosny Smarth, who resigned in June 1997 following growing criticism of the government's economic policies. In September, Aristide announced an alliance with other congressional groups to oppose Preval's economic reform plans.

In March 1999, Senator Yvon Toussaint, of the Organization of People in Struggle (OPL), was murdered by unidentified gunmen, and several parliamentary OPL deputies facing death threats later fled into exile. In June, Port-au-Prince police chief Jean

Coles Rameau, who had been arrested in the Dominican Republic, was extradited to Haiti following the killing of 11 detainees a week earlier in the Haitian capital. In October, the secretary of state for public security was forced to resign, after months of pressure from Aristide's forces.

In May 2000, ten police officers hijacked at gunpoint a ferry with more than 100 people on board in an unsuccessful attempt to win political asylum in the United States. In July, Leon Manus, the head of the elections commission, who had ruled that a Lavalas Family victory in May congressional elections was based on fraud, went into exile after he received death threats for refusing to certify "the false final results," and as the Haitian police hunted for him. In October six policemen accused of plotting to assassinate Haiti's top leaders, including Aristide, and stage a coup were arrested as they tried to flee the country. Food prices skyrocketed throughout the year, reflecting a broad inflationary spiral. Narcotics trafficking through Haiti now accounts for at least 13 percent of all the cocaine reaching the United States, up fourfold from just a decade ago. A senior U.S. Justice Department official said that Haiti's poverty, weak criminal justice system, and continuing political crisis made it "an ideal target and staging area for the large and sophisticated international drug trafficking syndicates." In December, opposition political parties said that they would work to create an alternative government before Aristide was sworn in on February 7, 2001. Meanwhile, Aristide promised outgoing President Bill Clinton that he would undertake a broad range of political and economic changes that the White House said, if implemented, could usher in "a new beginning for Haiti's democratic future."

Political Rights and Civil Liberties: Alleged irregularities in the May 2000 parliamentary elections caused Haiti's opposition parties to boycott the November presidential contest. The credibility of the charges raised against Aristide's Lavalas Family party machine were such that the United States, Canada, and the European Union—all of which provided significant financial and technical support to Aristide's government after he was returned to power in 1994—refused to send observers to the sham November elections. According to the Aristide-dominated Provisional Electoral Council, the former president won 92 percent of 2.87 million votes cast, or 61 percent of eligible voters. However, most independent observers say the turnout was significantly lower. Opposition politicians claimed that ballot boxes had been stuffed and tally sheets tampered with in order to inflate the turnout figures.

The constitution guarantees a full range of political rights and civil liberties. The protection of such rights in 2000, however, remained precarious, as the rule of law was tenuous at best and the situation was aggravated by a yawning security vacuum. Ongoing subterranean political warfare involving the former military, Aristide supporters, and others continued to claim lives. In 2000 the Lavalas Family itself appeared to be falling victim to open strife between warring factions.

The judicial system remains corrupt, inefficient, and essentially dysfunctional, particularly in rural areas, and U.S. reform efforts, tainted by allegations of corruption involving U.S. Agency for International Development (USAID), Justice Department contractors, and others, were abruptly brought to a halt in mid-2000. The legal system is also hampered by a large case backlog, an outdated legal code, poor facilities, and the fact that business is conducted in French, rather than Creole, Haiti's majority language.

Prison conditions are grim, and a severe backlog of cases means hundreds suffer lengthy pretrial detention periods. A positive development occurred in November 2000, when 16 Haitian soldiers were convicted for their role in the 1994 massacre of more than a dozen slum dwellers.

The new 5,200-member Haitian National Police force is inexperienced and lacking in resources. Human rights groups say the police frequently use excessive force and mistreat detainees, pointing to the fact that in 1999 police killed 66 people, twice the number as the year before. Accusations of corruption have also grown more frequent. In 1998 the UN mission in Haiti said that an increasing number of police were involved in drug smuggling. The police have been increasingly called upon to put down protests against the government's economic austerity program. At least 500 officers have been cashiered from the 6,000-member force for rights abuses, corruption, or drug trafficking within the past few years. In 2000, opposition politicians accused Aristide of using the police force to further his own political ambitions, and there were credible reports of ballot box stuffing, in favor of his Lavalas Family, by uniformed officers. In a positive development, in September 2000 the former chief of police and three other officers were convicted of killing 11 people—the first time members of the new force has gone to trial. The 11 dead, who the police said were gang members killed in a shootout in May 1999, were reportedly unarmed, and several were lying face down on the ground before they were killed.

Mob violence and armed gangs posed severe security threats in urban areas. Former soldiers and others linked to the former military regime, as well as common criminals, were responsible for much of the violence, including political assassinations. Break-ins and armed robberies, rare a few years ago, are now commonplace, and many observers tie the growing violence directly to increases in the drug trade and in local narcotics consumption. Haitian officials also say that the rise in crime is due to the repatriation of convicted criminals from other countries, particularly the United States. Turf wars between rival drug gangs have resulted in the killing of scores of people, including several policemen. Private security forces that carry out extralegal search and seizure are flourishing.

A number of independent newspapers and radio stations exist. Outlets critical of the government remain targets of official intimidation, including mob attacks. Television is state run and strongly biased toward the government. In October 1998, a former Haitian judge was arrested in connection with the 1982 murder of a well-known journalist.

Labor rights, as with all other legally sanctioned guarantees, are essentially unenforced. Unions are generally too weak to engage in collective bargaining, and their organizing efforts are undermined by the high unemployment rate.

Honduras

Polity: Presidential-par-liamentary democracy
Economy: Capitalist-statist
Population: 6,100,000
PPP: $2,433
Life Expectancy: 70
Ethnic Groups: Mestizo (90 percent), Indian (7 percent), black (2 percent), white (1 percent)
Capital: Tegucigalpa

Political Rights: 3
Civil Liberties: 3
Status: Partly Free

Overview:

Official corruption and the lingering power of Honduras's once-omnipotent military dominated the headlines during much of 2000, as the country prepared for presidential elections to be held in 2001. In January, the country's most important human rights group complained that senior government officials, police officers, and businessmen both financed and protected death squads operating on the Atlantic coast and in the country's central region, their targets mostly consisting of youth gang leaders and homeless children. Sweeping changes made in the military high command in February 2000, and the cashiering of 26 active-duty officers in May, formed part of an ongoing effort by President Carlos Flores to assert his authority over military institutions unhappy with civilian challenges to their economic power and legal impunity. The frustrated efforts of a respected former international civil servant to depoliticize and clean up the Honduran Social Investment Fund (FIS) pointed to a continuing problem, albeit one the Flores government has moved to confront—that of official corruption. Transparency International has called Honduras one of the most corrupt countries in the world.

The Republic of Honduras was established in 1839, 18 years after independence from Spain. It has endured decades of military rule and intermittent elected government. The last military regime gave way to elected civilian rule in 1982. The constitution provides for a president and a 130-member, unicameral congress elected for four years.

The two main parties are the center-left Liberal Party (PL) and the conservative National Party (PN). In the 1993, the PN nominated Oswaldo Ramos Soto, an outspoken right-winger. The PL, which held power during most of the 1980s, nominated Roberto Reina, a 67-year-old progressive and a former president of the Inter-American Court of Human Rights. Reina won with 52 percent of the vote. The PL won 70 seats in congress, the PN, 56. Two small left-wing parties took the remaining 4.

Reina promised a "moral revolution" and greater civilian control over the military. His administration had a positive, if mixed, record. The size of the military was reduced greatly, although its spending remained secret, and officers suspected of rights offenses were protected. The process of separating the police from the military was undertaken following the December 1996 approval by congress of a constitutional amendment to place the police under civilian control.

However, a virulent crime wave, believed to be in part the work of former and serving military and intelligence officers, continued unabated. Several leaders of Indian and Garifuna minority groups attempting to defend their land from encroachments by non-Indian landowners were murdered.

On November 30, 1997, PL presidential candidate Flores, a U.S.-trained engineer and newspaper owner, won a resounding, 54 to 41 percent victory over PN candidate Nora Melgar. The ruling party won 67 congressional seats and retained control over 180 of Honduras's 297 municipal districts. Flores immediately announced that civilian control of the armed forces would be strengthened by the creation of a functional defense ministry and the newly civilianized police would enjoy an increased budget. He also appointed five women to high-level posts, including that of minister of security, the portfolio in charge of the new civilian national police. In September 1998, congress voted to end more than 30 years of military autonomy by suppressing the post of commander in chief of the armed forces, a move that created unrest in the barracks.

In May 1999 a civilian judge ordered the arrest for abuse of authority of the general who had retired at the end of the previous year as commander in chief of the armed forces. A July 1999 crisis within the army, which brought a drastic reorganization of the military high command, was apparently the result of efforts by the civilian defense minister to audit the military's lucrative pension fund and holding company. The crisis was resolved only after Flores granted concessions to the rebellious officers in secret negotiations. In August 2000, in a move many hailed as a blow to military impunity, the former chief of the armed forces and nine other retired officers, including two generals, were accused in civilian court of embezzling $349,000. In late August, the security minister was fired after several police officers implicated in narcotics trafficking were arrested and a deputy police commander was reportedly under investigation by the Drug Enforcement Agency. On a positive note, that same month the Honduran congress ratified an antidrug accord signed four months earlier with the United States which provides for joint air, sea, and land patrols and allows U.S. Coast Guard vessels to board "in exceptional circumstances" suspect ships in Honduran waters.

Political Rights and Civil Liberties: Citizens are able to change their government through elections. The 1997 presidential contest was considered generally free and fair. Constitutional guarantees regarding free expression, freedom of religion, and the right to form political parties and civic organizations are generally respected. But repressive measures coming in the face of peaceful protests and mounting crime have limited political rights and civil liberties.

The judicial system, headed by the supreme court, is weak and corruption prone. In 1998 the new court was packed with lawyers close to both the military and to officials accused of corruption. Death threats and violent attacks face judges who assert themselves in human rights cases. Although 90 percent of the 10,000 people incarcerated are awaiting trial, they share deplorable prison conditions with convicted inmates. Drug-related corruption is rampant, and in August 2000, Guatama Fonseca, Honduras's new security minister, charged that "venal" judges were protecting drug smugglers.

In 1997 the government moved to place the police under civilian control, a task made easier by the emergence of a cadre of police professionals at the top reaches of a force controlled by the military since 1963. However, Reina frequently used the military for internal security tasks, putting down labor unrest, quelling street protests, and seeking to control street crime, a pattern continued by Flores in March 1999 when, in response to demands from business organizations, he sent 12,000 troops into the streets. Arbitrary detention and torture by the police still occur. A crime wave throughout Honduras has been fueled by the presence of some 120 youth gangs whose main activities include murder, kidnapping, and robbery. Where crime rings have been effectively broken up, good police work, rather than troops in the streets, has made the difference. The need to strengthen and professionalize the poorly equipped civilian police is hampered by a lack of public confidence in them. In August 2000, Fonseca, the newly appointed security minister, promised to target members of the police suspected of working in concert with drug traffickers.

The military exerts considerable, if waning, influence over the government. By naming a civilian instead of a general to head the armed forces in January 1999, Flores said he hoped to strengthen government control over the military. The oversight offensive also included civilian control of the armed forces budget and the independent auditing of military business ventures—both sources of much high-level corruption. A constellation of military-owned businesses makes the armed forces one of Honduras' ten largest for-profit enterprises. In December 2000 the United Nations announced that it will finance the audit of firms owned by the military, including a bank, brokerages, radio stations, a security firm, and a public relations agency. Most criminal cases against the military remained in military court jurisdiction, and the charges were usually dismissed. However, beginning in 1999, military personnel are no longer immune from prosecution in civilian courts.

In 1998, army officers were implicated in drug trafficking, including taking sides in cartel turf wars and protecting drug shipments in transit through Honduras. The military remains the country's principal human rights violator, and the institution protects members connected to both political repression and street crime, often linked to narcotics. In February 1998, the human rights leader Ernesto Sandoval was murdered in a "death-squad" style assassination. The death squads are now also reportedly involved in the "social cleansing" murders of youth gang members in San Pedro Sula, the country's second largest city.

Labor unions are well organized and can strike, although labor actions often result in clashes with security forces. Labor leaders, religious groups, and indigenous-based peasant unions pressing for land rights remain vulnerable to repression. On December 31, 1999, José Cosme Reyes, the local secretary of the National Lenca Indigenous Organization, was strangled to death by unknown assailants. His death brought to 54 the number of indigenous leaders killed in a nine-year period. In May 1999, prosecutors asked courts to issue arrest warrants for ten landowners in connection with the killing of at least 42 of the Indians in land disputes. On a positive note, in September 2000, the government reached an agreement with indigenous and black peoples in Honduras that gave their concerns a more prominent place in the public agenda.

Some 85,000 workers, mostly women, are employed in the low-wage *maquiladora* (assembly plant) export sector. Child labor is a problem in rural areas and in the informal economy. UNICEF has estimated that, in the aftermath of the devastating Hurricane Mitch in 1998, more than 42,000 children joined an estimated 1.3 million between the ages of 10 and 17 who left school to work in the country's streets, factories, and fields. In August 2000, the Latin American branch of the U.S. organization Covenant House, a group that protects the rights of minors, said that Honduran death squads had killed 338 children and young people in extrajudicial executions since the beginning of 1998.

Hungary

Polity: Parliamentary democracy
Economy: Mixed capitalist
Population: 10,000,000
PPP: $10,232,000
Life Expectancy: 71
Ethnic Groups: Hungarian (90 percent), Roma (4 percent), German (3 percent), other (3 percent)
Capital: Budapest

Political Rights: 1
Civil Liberties: 2
Status: Free

Overview: In the year 2000, Hungary celebrated a millennium of statehood, and Prime Minister Viktor Orban declared the country's economic and political transition from communism a success. Efforts to meet European Union (EU) accession requirements, the retirement of two-term President Arpad Goncz, and allegations of high-level corruption also marked the year.

King Stephen I, who ruled from 1001 to 1038, is credited with founding the Hungarian state. In the centuries that followed, however, Hungarian lands passed through Turkish, Polish, and Austrian hands. In the mid-nineteenth century, Hungary established a liberal, constitutional monarchy under the Austrian Hapsburgs, but two world wars and a Communist dictatorship in the twentieth century forestalled true independence.

By the late 1980s, Hungary's economy was in decline, and the Hungarian Socialist Worker's Party came under intense pressure to accept reforms. Ultimately, the party congress dissolved itself, and Hungary held its first free, multiparty parliamentary election in 1990. The new parliament made Jozsef Antall, a member of the conservative Hungarian Democratic Forum, the new head of state. Since then, government control has passed freely and fairly between left- and right-leaning parties, and the country has followed an aggressive reform path. Hungary joined NATO in 1999.

In 2000, Prime Minister Orban declared the end of Hungary's post-Communist transition when output and real wages reached 1989 levels. The United Nations Committee on Trade and Development called Hungary's economy "the most open" in the region, and the European Commission (EC) praised Hungary's progress in fulfilling EU accession criteria. The EC still urged the country to reduce the backlog of cases before the supreme court, renew anti-corruption efforts, address overcrowding in prisons, and sustain improvements in the treatment of Roma (Gypsies).

President Goncz completed his second and final term in August. In a third round of voting, parliament elected Ference Madl, a professor of international law and a member of the Hungarian Academy of Sciences, to this largely ceremonial post. Madl served as minister of education and culture after Hungary's first democratic elections in 1990.

Fallout from an illegal oil-import scheme in the early 1990s continued. In March 2000, parliament launched an investigation into the role played by state police. In June, former police Lieutenant Istvan Sandor testified that the current interior minister and several members of parliament had been involved, but he was unable to offer solid evidence. The incident highlighted long-standing concerns about corruption in Hungary and other post-Communist countries in the region.

Political Rights and Civil Liberties: Hungary is a multiparty, parliamentary democracy that comprises legislative, executive, and judicial branches of governments. Citizens age 18 and older enjoy universal suffrage and can change their government democratically. They elect 386 deputies to the unicameral national assembly under a mixed system of proportional and direct representation. Parliament elects both the president and the prime minister.

Post-Communist elections in Hungary have been free and fair. In June 2000, parliament elected Ference Madl president in a third round of voting. President Goncz had completed the maximum two terms in office. After parliamentary elections in 1998, the Organization for Security and Cooperation in Europe praised Hungary's "strong electoral process" and the media's balanced coverage. Twenty-six parties registered for the first round of elections; six received a mandate.

The 1998 election resulted in a change of government when the opposition Hungarian Civic Party (FIDESZ) formed a center-right coalition government with the Independent Smallholders' Party (FKGP) and the Hungarian Democratic Forum (MDF). Together they control 213 out of 386 seats in the national assembly. The ruling Hungarian Socialist Party (MSZP) captured only 134 seats. The new parliament elected Victor Orban, of FIDESZ, prime minister. The next parliamentary elections are scheduled for 2002.

The constitution guarantees national and ethnic minorities the right to form self-governing bodies, and all 13 recognized minorities have exercised this right. In July 2000 more than 40 Roma filed a complaint against Hungary with the European Court of Human Rights. In September the government announced a two-year, $8.2 million program to provide vocational training and other programs for Roma youth. The Interior Ministry has pledged to deal with police violence against Roma by providing special training and hiring more Romany police officers.

Independent media thrive in Hungary, but oversight of state television and radio remains a controversial issue. A 1996 media law requires ruling and opposition parties to share appointments to the boards overseeing state television and radio. But critics charge that the current government has manipulated the law by approving boards composed solely of its supporters and has thereby gained undue influence over hiring and reporting. The issue was highlighted in 2000, when opposition parties failed to make new appointments to two boards. The government prompted criticism from Western ambassadors and press freedom advocates when it again confirmed boards composed of only its supporters. Parliament extended the lustration law to the media in 2000, and the constitutional court ruled on three freedom of speech cases. The court upheld a ban on displaying authoritarian symbols such as swastikas and the hammer and sickle, ruled in favor of a prohibition against the desecration of national symbols, and struck down a ban on speech that could incite public panic.

The constitution guarantees religious freedom and provides for the separation of church and state. There are approximately 100 registered religious groups—primarily Roman Catholics, Lutherans, Calvinists, and Jews—to which the state provides financial support for worship, parochial schools, and the reconstruction of property. A

1991 law requires the state to provide restitution for church properties that were seized under communism. In 2000, the constitutional court deemed that a law on compensating Holocaust victims was discriminatory because the amount of recompense was significantly less than that awarded to victims of the 1956 anti-Communist uprising.

The government respects citizens' rights to form associations, strike, and petition public authorities. Railway employees, farmers, and health care workers all went on strike in 2000 to demand better wages. Likewise, 50 civic organizations picketed parliament to demand better wages and benefits for the poor, and 5,000 representatives of the country's six trade union confederations protested amendments to the labor code. Trade unions now account for less than 30 percent of the workforce. There are more than 60,000 registered nongovernmental organizations.

Hungary has a three-tiered independent judiciary and a constitutional court. The constitution guarantees equality before the law, and courts are generally fair. In an effort to improve judicial efficiency, more than 90 new judges were appointed in 2000. Legislation designed to reduce the length of civil court procedures also came into effect. In 1999 the national police agency set up an internal affairs division to deal with corruption in its ranks.

The government respects personal autonomy and privacy. It also honors the institutions of family and marriage and recognizes the equality of women and men. In 2000, a two-year investigation ended when Prosecutor-General Peter Polt confirmed that in 1996 the socialist-led government hired a private detective to spy on the FIDESZ parliamentary group.

The constitution states that the Hungarian economy is a market economy in which private property, free enterprise, and competition are respected. The country boasts one of the fastest-growing and freest economies in the region, and approximately 80 percent of state-owned enterprises have been privatized. In its 2000 progress report, the European Commission urged Hungary to reduce "significant regional differences" in unemployment and to "increase the flexibility and mobility of labour."

Iceland

Polity: Parliamentary democracy
Economy: Capitalist
Population: 300,000
PPP: $25,110
Life Expectancy: 79
Ethnic Groups: Icelander
Capital: Reykjavik

Political Rights: 1
Civil Liberties: 1
Status: Free

Overview:

In parliamentary elections in May 1999, Prime Minister David Oddsson's conservative Independence Party and the centrist Progressive Party led by Foreign Minister Halldor Asgrimsson held on to a majority of seats in the *Althingi* (parliament) as voters responded to their promises of continued stability and prosperity. Oddsson, who has been in power for nine years, is now Europe's longest-sitting prime minister. Under his leadership, the country has continued its economic upswing, with the unemployment rate remaining below 2 percent in 2000, among the lowest rates in the world.

Iceland achieved full independence in 1944. Multiparty governments have been in power since then. On August 1, 1996, the former finance minister and former leader of the leftist People's Alliance, Dr. Olafur Ragnar Grimsson, was sworn in as Iceland's fifth president.

During the year, the government continued with a deregulation and privatization program affecting a few industries such as telecommunications. Although Iceland has strong historical, cultural, and economic ties with Europe, Icelanders are hesitant to join the European Union (EU), primarily because of its Common Fisheries Policy, which Icelanders believe would threaten their marine industry. Fishing accounts for 80 percent of Iceland's exports and half of its export revenues.

President Oddsson continues to rule out joining the European Monetary Union. Meanwhile, the opposition is divided into two camps, with the Social Democratic faction of the United Left bloc in favor of submitting an application to the EU, and the Green-Left Alliance opposing Union membership.

Iceland handed over its citizens' genetic data to a private, U.S.-backed, medical research company in 2000, raising some fears over privacy issues. Iceland, the most genetically homogenous nation on earth, went ahead with the plan on the grounds that the data could provide scientists with vital clues into the origin of diseases, thus increasing the chances of discovering cures. While a law was passed requiring doctors to hand over patient information, the government did contain a provision that allows citizens to opt out of providing genetic data. Only five percent of Icelanders reportedly decided not to participate in the program.

Political Rights and Civil Liberties: Icelanders can change their government democratically. Iceland's constitution, adopted by referendum in 1944, vests power in a president (whose functions are mainly ceremonial), a prime minister, a legislature, and a judiciary. The president is directly elected for a four-year term. The unicameral legislature is also elected for four years (subject to dissolution). The prime minister, who performs most executive functions, is appointed by the president but is responsible to the legislature.

The constitution provides for freedom of speech, freedom of peaceful assembly and association, and freedom of the press. A wide range of publications includes both independent and party-affiliated newspapers. An autonomous board of directors oversees the Icelandic State Broadcasting Service, which operates a number of transmitting and relay stations. There are both private and public television stations. Iceland has the highest Internet penetration rate in the world, with more than 80 percent of the population accessing the Internet from home.

In recent years Iceland has not received a substantial number of refugees or asylum seekers. During the Kosovo crisis, Iceland accepted a few dozen refugees. Although there is no national refugee legislation, a draft refugee law is under preparation. Legislation adopted in 1996 permits homosexuals to live together in a formal relationship with the same legal rights as in marriage, minus the rights to adopt children or to be artificially inseminated.

Virtually everyone in the country holds at least nominal membership in the state-supported Lutheran Church. Freedom of worship is respected, and discrimination on the basis of race, language, social class, or sex is outlawed. About 76 percent of all eligible workers belong to free trade unions, and all enjoy the right to strike. Disabled persons enjoy extensive rights in employment and education.

The country's judiciary is independent. The law does not provide for trial by jury, but many trials and appeals use panels consisting of several judges. All judges, at all levels, serve for life. Gender-based equality is guaranteed by law. There remains about a 20 percent gap in earnings between men and women in comparable jobs. In 1995, women held 17 out of the 63 seats in parliament. After the 1999 elections, the number rose to 22. The Women's Alliance, an Icelandic feminist movement founded in 1983, is registered as a political party and has its own parliamentary faction.

India

Polity: Parliamentary democracy
Economy: Capitalist-statist
Population: 1,002,000,000
PPP: $2,077
Life Expectancy: 63
Ethnic Groups: Indo-Aryan (72 percent), Dravidian (25 percent), other (3 percent)
Capital: New Delhi

Political Rights: 2
Civil Liberties: 3
Status: Free

Overview:

Prime Minister Atal Bihari Vajpayee's right-wing coalition pushed ahead with free-market measures in 2000, including a 28 percent fuel price increase in October and plans to privatize and reduce the size of the power, banking, and insurance sectors. Yet the Indian public seemed far from reaching a consensus over the scope and pace of economic liberalization. Some opposition parties, and even members of Vajpayee's coalition, criticized the measures, which could cost millions of state workers their jobs and cause farmers and other influential groups to lose subsidies.

India achieved independence in 1947 with the partition of British India into a predominantly Hindu India, under Prime Minister Jawaharlal Nehru, and a Muslim Pakistan. The centrist, secular Congress Party ruled continuously for the first five decades of independence, except for periods of opposition from 1977 through 1980 and from 1989 through 1991. During the campaign for the 1991 elections, a suspected Sri Lankan Tamil separatist assassinated former Prime Minister Rajiv Gandhi, heir to the political dynasty of Congress standard-bearers Nehru and Indira Gandhi. After Congress won the elections, the incoming prime minister, P. V. Narasimha Rao, responded to a balance-of-payments crisis by initiating gradual reforms of the autarkic, control-bound economy.

Even as the crisis receded, Congress lost eleven state elections in the mid-1990s. The party's traditional electoral base of poor, low-caste, and Muslim voters appeared disillusioned with the economic liberalization and the government's failure to prevent communal violence. In December 1992 and January 1993, northern India and the city of Bombay had experienced some of the worst communal violence since independence after Hindu fundamentalists destroyed a sixteenth-century mosque in the northern town of Ayodhya. The rioting killed some 2,000 people, mainly Muslims. In the state elections, regional parties made gains in southern India, and low-caste parties and the BJP gained in the northern Hindi-speaking belt.

These trends continued at the national level in the April-May 1996 parliamentary elections. The BJP captured 161 seats, versus 140 for Congress. However, in May a BJP-led minority government resigned after 13 days in office after failing to attract secular allies. A minority United Front (UF) government, dominated by leftist and regional parties, took office but subsequently collapsed in November 1997. It fell when Congress withdrew its support after an official commission linked a tiny, Tamil Nadu-based UF party to Sri Lankan guerrillas implicated in Rajiv Gandhi's assassination.

The turmoil among centrist and leftist parties provided an opening for the BJP to form a government under Vajpayee after winning the early elections held in February and March 1998. Final results gave the BJP (178 seats) and its allies 245 seats, while Congress (140) and its allies won 166. One of the government's first major acts was to carry out a series of underground nuclear tests in May 1998. Archrival Pakistan responded with its own atomic tests.

Holding only a minority of seats, the BJP government faced frequent threats and demands from small but pivotal coalition members. The government fell after a Tamil Nadu-based party defected, but won reelection in voting held in September and October 1999. Final results gave the BJP-led, 22-party National Democratic Alliance 295 seats (182 for the BJP), against 112 seats for Congress. The BJP's share of the popular vote held at 25 percent, while Congress's share rose from 26 to 29 percent. Among smaller parties, the election confirmed the continued decline of leftist parties and the growing importance of regional and caste-based parties. The BJP had campaigned on Vajpayee's handling of a summer crisis in which Indian troops repelled an incursion into Kashmir by Pakistani-backed forces, and on suggestions that Italian-born Sonia Gandhi, the Congress leader and widow of Rajiv Gandhi, was unsuitable to lead an Indian government because of her foreign origins. Polls showed most voters were concerned primarily with local economic issues.

Vajpayee spent much of 2000 trying to build support for the government's free-market policies. While Congress mainly favored the liberalization process, it was opposed by some coalition members as well as by the National Volunteer Service, a far-right Hindu organization that exerts considerable influence on the Vajpayee government but which favors economic self-reliance and protectionism. Both Congress and some coalition members heavily criticized Vajpayee's backing in December of calls for a Hindu temple to be built in Ayodhya on the site of the mosque that Hindu fanatics razed in 1992.

Political Rights and Civil Liberties: Indian citizens can change their government through elections. However, democratic rule continued to be undermined by pervasive criminality in politics, decrepit state institutions, a weak rule of law, and widespread corruption. A survey commissioned by the Central Vigilance Commission, released in November, showed that almost 50 percent of Indians using government services in five major cities end up paying bribes. The Berlin-based Transparency International's 2000 Corruption Perceptions Index ranked India in a tie for 69th place out of 90 countries with a score of 2.8 on a 0 to 10 scale. The top-ranked, least corrupt country, Finland, received a score of 10.

The 1950 constitution provides for a lower, 543-seat *Lok Sabha* (House of the People), directly elected for a five-year term (plus 2 appointed seats for Indians of European descent), and an upper *Rajya Sabha* (Council of States). Executive power is vested in a prime minister and cabinet.

Recent elections have generally been free although not entirely fair. Violence and irregularities have marred balloting in many districts. The Associated Press reported in February that violence during state elections in the impoverished northern state of Bihar killed 43 people. In the 1999 national elections, guerrilla attacks in Bihar, northeast India, and interparty clashes in several states killed some 130 people.

Moreover, criminality has penetrated the electoral process. The chief vigilance commissioner, N. Vittal, told a November seminar on corruption in New Delhi that India's "political process and the system of election depend on black money" that is obtained illegally through tax evasion and other means, according to Agence France-Presse (AFP). In 1998, *The New York Times* cited studies showing that more than one-third of state legislators in Uttar Pradesh, India's most populous state, had criminal records. Also that year, the London-based *Financial Times* cited Indian press allegations that it took three kidnappings to pay for a poll campaign in Uttar Pradesh. In neighboring Bihar, many legislators reportedly lead criminal gangs, and political killings are routine. The Election Commission estimated in 1997 that 40 members of parliament and 700 state assembly representatives nationwide faced charges for, or had been convicted of, offenses ranging from extortion to murder.

The judiciary is independent. In recent years judges have exercised unprecedented activism in response to public interest litigation over official corruption, environmental issues, and other matters. However, corruption is reportedly rife among lower-level judges, poor people cannot generally afford to take cases to court, and there is a backlog of more than 30 million cases. As a result, cases take an average of 20 years to dispose, according to AFP. Amnesty International said in 1999 that "many people await trial for longer than their ultimate sentence."

Police continued to routinely torture suspects to extract confessions and to abuse ordinary prisoners, particularly low-caste members. Rape of female detainees by police continued to be a problem.

Police, army, and paramilitary forces continued to be implicated in "disappearances," extrajudicial killings, rape, torture, arbitrary detention, and the destruction of homes, particularly in the context of insurgencies in Kashmir and in Assam and other northeastern states. (A separate report on Kashmir appears in the Related Territories section.) While the National Human Rights Commission continued to monitor custodial deaths and other abuses, it had few enforcement powers. This is partly because the criminal procedure code requires central or state government approval, which is rarely granted, to prosecute security force members. Security forces continued to detain suspects under the broadly drawn 1980 National Security Act, which authorizes detention without charge for up to one year (two in Punjab). During the year, the government considered introducing into parliament a tough draft security law, the Prevention of Terrorism Bill. Amnesty International said in June that the bill did not provide adequate safeguards to prevent human rights violations by authorities.

In India's seven northeastern states, more than 40 mainly tribal-based insurgent groups sporadically attacked security forces and engaged in intertribal and internecine violence. The rebel groups have also been implicated in numerous killings, abductions, and rapes of civilians. Many of them raised money through extortion of tea plantations. The militants ostensibly seek either greater autonomy or independence for their ethnic or tribal groups. During counter-insurgency operations the army has committed atrocities with impunity in Assam, Manipur, and other northeastern states. The 1958 Armed Forces (Special Powers) Act grants security forces broad powers to use lethal force and detention in Assam and four nearby states, and provides near immunity from prosecution to security forces acting under it.

Left-wing guerrillas called Naxalites control some rural areas in Andhra Pradesh, Madhya Pradesh, Bihar, and Orissa, and kill dozens of police, politicians, landlords, and villagers in these states each year. The Naxalites also run parallel courts in parts of Bihar. Naxalites and the Ranvir Sena, a technically illegal private army backed by middle-caste politicians and upper-caste landlords, continued to engage in tit-for-tat atrocities in Bihar that killed scores of people during the year. The New York-based Human Rights Watch/Asia reported in 1999 that in the past four years, Naxalites had killed more than 1,100 landowners, while the Ranvir Sena had killed more than 400 low-caste peasants.

India's private press continued to be vigorous, although journalists face numerous constraints. In recent years, the government has occasionally censored articles critical of its policies by using its power under the Official Secrets Act to censor security-related articles. The Paris-based Reporters Sans Frontieres said in April that in the previous three years authorities had detained 15 journalists in Manipur on charges of supporting militant groups. Radio is both public and private. However, the state-owned All India Radio enjoys a dominant position, and its news coverage favors the government. The government maintains a monopoly on domestic television broadcasting, although foreign satellite broadcasts are available.

There are some restrictions on freedom of assembly and association. Section 144 of the criminal procedure code empowers state-level authorities to declare a state of emergency, restrict free assembly, and impose curfews. In recent years, officials have occasionally used Section 144 to prevent demonstrations. Human rights groups say that in recent years police and hired thugs have occasionally beaten, arbitrarily detained, or otherwise harassed villagers and members of nongovernmental organizations who were protesting forced relocations from the sites of development projects. The organizations alleged that the government had awarded the projects with little local consultation and had provided inadequate compensation to those affected. Human rights organizations generally operated freely. However, Amnesty International reported in April that authorities occasionally carried out or tolerated abuses against human rights activists, including "threats, harassment, false criminal cases and in some cases torture, ill-treatment, 'disappearances' and even political killings."

Each year, several thousand women are burned to death, driven to suicide, or otherwise killed, and countless others are harassed, beaten, or deserted by husbands, in the context of dowry disputes. Although dowry is illegal, convictions in dowry deaths continued to be rare. Rape and other violence against women also continued to be serious problems. Anecdotal evidence suggested that brothel owners continued to hold many women and teenage girls in conditions of debt servitude and subjected them to rape, beating, and other torture. Local officials continued to be complicit or to tolerate these abuses. By many accounts, families often deny inheritances to Hindu women. Tribal land systems, particularly in Bihar, often deny tribal women the right to own land. Under *Sharia* (Islamic law), Muslim women face discrimination in inheritance rights.

The constitution bars discrimination based on caste, and laws set aside quotas in education and jobs for lower castes. However, evidence suggested that members of so-called scheduled castes and scheduled tribes, as well as religious and ethnic minorities, continued to routinely face unofficial discrimination. The worst abuse is faced by the 160 million *dalits*, or untouchables, who are often denied access to land, abused by landlords and police, and forced to work in miserable conditions. Religious freedom continued to be generally respected, but violence against religious minorities remained a problem. Attacks on Christians have increased since the BJP came to power in 1998. The Delhi-based United Christian Forum for Human Rights gave evidence in June of at least 35 anti-Christian incidents since the beginning of the year, including recent bomb attacks on four churches in three states and the murder of a Roman Catholic priest. Local media and some members of the *sangh parivar*, an umbrella organization of Hindu nationalist groups including the BJP, promote anti-Christian propaganda. Human Rights Watch said in March that the BJP and its allies have mandated Hindu prayers in certain state-sponsored schools and the revision of history books to include negative portrayals of Muslims and Christians.

Major cities each have thousands of street children, many of whom work in the informal sector. UNICEF estimates that overall there are up to 60 million child laborers in India. Many work in hazardous conditions, and several million are bonded laborers. According to the *Far Eastern Economic Review*, only about 16 million of India's 340 million workers are unionized. However, unionized workers wield disproportionate political and economic influence because they are concentrated in key industries including power, banking, and railways. Workers regularly exercised their rights to bargain collectively and strike. However, authorities forcibly broke up a major strike in Uttar Pradesh in January.

In the fall, the worst flooding in 22 years in West Bengal killed at least 1,000 people. Residents of the eastern state of Orissa continued to deal with the aftereffects of a powerful cyclone and subsequent flooding in 1999 that had left millions homeless and killed more than 10,000 people.

Economic reforms continue to devolve power to the states. However, there has been a widening gap in per capita income between the few states like Andhra Pradesh that have significantly liberalized their economies and attracted investment, and poorer and more protectionist states including Bihar and Uttar Pradesh, which together hold roughly one-quarter of India's population.

Indonesia

Polity: Presidential-
parliamentary democracy
(military-influenced)
Economy: Capitalist-statist
Population: 212,000,000
PPP: $2,651
Life Expectancy: 66

Political Rights: 3*
Civil Liberties: 4
Status: Partly Free

Ethnic Groups: Javanese (45 percent), Sundanese (14 percent),
Madurese (8 percent), Malay (8 percent), other (25 percent)
Capital: Jakarta
Ratings change: Indonesia's political rights rating changed from 4 to 3 due to growing
efforts by parliament to transform itself into a check on presidential power.

Overview: Just months after taking office, Indonesian President
Abdurahman Wahid began facing calls from opposition politicians in mid-2000 to resign or be impeached for alleged cor-
ruption and for failing to deal with violent separatist conflicts, sectarian violence, weaknesses in the military chain of command, and economic malaise. Wahid's parliamentary supporters accused opposition legislators of misusing their authority, and were
pledging late in 2000 to keep the president in office.

Following a four-year, intermittent war against the Dutch colonial rulers, Indonesia achieved full independence in 1949. After a series of parliament-led governments
collapsed, the republic's first president, Sukarno, concentrated power in the presidency
in 1957 under a so-called "Guided Democracy." Amid continued political turbulence
and economic decline, the Army Strategic Reserve, headed by General Suharto, crushed
a coup attempt in 1965 that it blamed on the Communist Party of Indonesia (PKI). The
army reportedly participated in a massacre of some 500,000 suspected PKI members,
many of them ethnic-Chinese between 1965 and 1967.

Suharto's autocratic "New Order" regime forcibly depoliticized society and gave control of key companies and trading monopolies to the president's family members and cronies, while launching development programs that helped lift millions of Indonesians
out of poverty. Suharto allowed only three political parties: the ruling Golkar; the nationalist Indonesian Democratic Party (PDI); and the Islam-oriented United Development Party (PPP). However, neither the PDI nor the PPP worked as a true opposition,
and the 500-seat parliament had little independent power. Every five years the 1,000-mem-
ber People's Consultative Assembly (MPR), which consisted of the parliament plus
500 appointed members, formally approved Suharto's decision to hold another term.

The regional financial crisis that began in July 1997 contributed to a sharp fall in the
value of the *rupiah*, as highly leveraged companies sold the currency to cover dollar-
denominated debts. By January 1998, the rupiah's slide had sent food prices soaring.
Following months of unprecedented anti-government demonstrations, the deaths of four
student protesters on May 12, and three days of urban riots in mid-May, Suharto resigned on May 21. Vice President B. J. Habibie, a long-time crony, became president.

While 48 parties contested Indonesia's freest elections in decades on June 7, 1999, the three Suharto-era parties and two parties linked to long-standing Muslim groups won the most seats. Final results for the 462 contested parliamentary seats (38 seats are reserved for the military) gave the Indonesian Democratic Party-Struggle (PDI-P), the successor to the PDI and led by Megawati Sukarnoputri, the daughter of the first president, 154 seats; Golkar, 120; PPP, 58; the National Awakening Party, led by Wahid, the leader of Indonesia's largest Muslim social group, 51; the National Mandate Party (PAN), led by Amien Rais, the former leader of a 28-million-member Islamic social organization, 35; and 16 other parties, 44.

Meeting to choose a president from among competing candidates for the first time, the MPR elected Wahid president and Megawati vice president in October 1999. The vote came after Habibie withdrew his candidacy amid controversy surrounding a bank scandal, his decision to drop a corruption probe into charities controlled by Suharto, and his policies which culminated in East Timor's independence in September.

Seeking to assert control over the military, in February 2000, Wahid suspended from the cabinet the last armed forces commander under Suharto, General Wiranto. The move came one month after an independent commission called for the attorney general to investigate Wiranto and 32 other officials over the military's alleged backing of militias that committed widespread abuses in East Timor in 1999.

By the spring, opposition legislators increasingly criticized Wahid over his seemingly aloof leadership style; scandals involving his private masseur and the rice distribution agency; and the controversial arrest in June of the central bank governor on corruption charges. Opponents also denounced Wahid for failing to curb separatist violence in Aceh and West Papua and violence along religious lines in the Moluccas, where the Associated Press estimated in mid-June that clashes between Christians and Muslims had killed more than 3,000 people since January 1999. Sectarian violence also flared in Sulawesi and Lombok.

By midyear, investors had sold the rupiah at 16-month lows on fears that the government would fail to meet its commitments to the International Monetary Fund to privatize debt-laden state companies, reform the largely insolvent banking system, and restructure private sector debt. During the August MPR session, Wahid responded to growing calls among lawmakers for his resignation by reshuffling his cabinet and ostensibly handing day-to-day management of the administration to Megawati. The vice-president's PDI-P pledged in November to support Wahid until his term expires in 2004, but a group of MPs led by Rais, the PAN leader and current MPR speaker, continued to call for Wahid's removal.

Political Rights and Civil Liberties:

While Indonesians can elect their legislators through elections, much of the Suharto-era political system remains in place. The president holds key executive powers but is indirectly elected, and the military holds seats in parliament. However, the MPR voted in August to scrap the military's 38 seats in 2009, and the parliament is becoming a forum for debate and a check on presidential authority.

The 1999 parliamentary elections were reasonably free although not entirely fair. Several domestic groups said that Golkar supporters illegally used welfare funds for campaigning and had tried to bribe voters. The election laws continued to require parties to accept the consensus-oriented Pancasila philosophy that Sukarno and Suharto had used to limit political mobilization. The law also hampered the formation of regional parties by requiring parties to show support in one-third of Indonesia's provinces in order to contest elections.

While the rule of law is weak throughout the country, the most serious human rights violations occurred in West Papua (see separate report in the Disputed Territories section), and to an even greater extent in Aceh, a resource-rich province of 4.6 million people in northern Sumatra. There, the army continued to be implicated in extrajudicial killings, disappearances, tortures, rapes, and other abuses against suspected members or sympathizers of the separatist *Aceh Merdeka* (Free Aceh) insurgency. The guerrillas reportedly carried out extrajudicial killings of soldiers and of civilians who allegedly assisted the army, while intimidating the population and raising money through extortion. In November 1999, Aceh Merdeka leaders rejected Wahid's offer of a referendum on autonomy for the province.

The government and Aceh Merdeka secured a ceasefire in May and extended it in September until January 2001. However, Amnesty International said in September that despite the ceasefire, by some estimates 120 people had been killed since June, mainly civilians, and "abductions, torture, and unlawful killings are taking place on a daily basis throughout Aceh." Aceh Merdeka pulled out of scheduled peace talks in mid-November after 38 people were killed as police tried to block access to a pro-independence rally that drew some 400,000 people in Banda Aceh, the provincial capital.

Another area of concern was West Timor, where the United Nations Security Council and Western governments criticized Indonesia's failure to disarm the pro-Jakarta militia, which used violence and intimidation to obstruct repatriation of East Timorese refugees. Some 250,000 refugees had fled to West Timor in early September 1999 to escape attacks by pro-Indonesian militia after East Timor voted for independence from Jakarta in an August 1999 referendum. After militia killed three UN workers in Atambua, West Timor, on September 6, 2000, the UN pulled its staff from the camps and suspended its voluntary repatriation program. By year's end, some 100,000 refugees remained in West Timor.

During the year, international human rights organizations called for investigations and trials into crimes against humanity and other crimes committed in East Timor in 1999, and into thousands of unresolved cases of extrajudicial killings, "disappearances," torture, and other abuses throughout Indonesia during the Suharto era. Authorities named 23 suspects in the East Timor violence and began some investigations, but no one had been charged by year's end. Elsewhere, the few prosecutions for human rights violations by security forces have tended to focus on junior officers and generally resulted in light sentences. In May, a court sentenced 24 soldiers and one civilian to between eight and a half to ten years in prison for shooting to death 57 students and teachers in Aceh in July 1999. While the sentences were some of the heaviest punishments ever given to Indonesian soldiers, critics said they were too light and that authorities had failed to punish the commanding officers.

Parliament approved a bill in November authorizing tribunals to try past human rights abuses including crimes against humanity. Both the president and parliament would have to approve any such ad hoc tribunal. However, Indonesia currently does not have laws on crimes against humanity or torture, and it was unclear how the new law would be interpreted in light of a July constitutional amendment passed by the MPR affirming that criminal laws cannot be applied retroactively.

The moves to hold security forces accountable for past abuses occur as political leaders try to redefine civil-military relations. While the military still has parliamentary seats, legislators have created the legal basis for civilian control over the military. This replaced the longstanding doctrine of *dwifungsi* (dual function), which gave the military a formal role in both defense and politics. Wahid appointed a civilian defense minister in 1999 but at times appeared unable to control the armed forces, which are poorly supplied, lack effective leadership, and are prone to breakdowns in the chain of command. Some human rights groups accused security forces of fomenting violence in the Moluccas by supporting rival factions.

Another unresolved issue from the Suharto era concerned the huge fortunes amassed by the former president and his family. Following lengthy preliminary proceedings, Jakarta's district court said on September 28 that it was dropping all corruption charges against Suharto on health grounds. A September 13 explosion at the Jakarta Stock Exchange that killed 15 people was the latest and deadliest in a series of bombings that coincided with major developments in the corruption case against Suharto.

Wahid has made some efforts to reform the judiciary, including naming new judges to replace Suharto cronies and creating an ombudsman's office to investigate judicial misconduct. However, the judiciary continued to have limited capacity and resources, and corruption remained a problem. Anecdotal evidence suggested that security officers continued to torture suspects to secure confessions and to abuse prisoners. Prison conditions continued to be poor.

The government generally respected freedom of expression and tolerated opposing political views. The private print media reported relatively freely on all aspects of politics. Radio and television are both public and private.

Student organizations, trade unions, and other groups regularly held peaceful demonstrations. Legal aid, human rights, and environmental nongovernmental organizations operated fairly freely, although numerous activists and humanitarian workers have reportedly disappeared or been killed in Aceh. The official National Commission on Human Rights continued to criticize abuses by the armed forces, and in January implicated senior military officers in the violence in East Timor in 1999.

Violent attacks against the ethnic-Chinese minority continued, although there were far fewer attacks than in Suharto's last years in office. The government maintained some cultural, educational, and employment restrictions on ethnic-Chinese citizens, although authorities permitted the community to celebrate publicly the Lunar New Year for the first time since 1967. Women continued to face unofficial discrimination in education and employment opportunities. Anecdotal evidence suggested that in the Muslim community female genital mutilation continued to be practiced widely.

Workers can join independent unions, bargain collectively, and hold strikes. However, employers frequently ignored minimum wage laws, dismissed labor activists and strike leaders, and occasionally physically abused workers.

In the Berlin-based Transparency International's 2000 Corruption Perceptions Index, Indonesia tied for 85th place out of 90 countries with a score of 1.2 on a 0 to 10 scale. The top-ranked and least-corrupt country, Finland, received a 10. In the absence of adequate judicial and administrative enforcement, property rights remained fairly weak.

⬇ Iran

Polity: Presidential-
parliamentary
(clergy-dominated)
Economy: Capitalist-statist
Population: 67,400,000
PPP: $5,121
Life Expectancy: 70

Political Rights: 6
Civil Liberties: 6
Status: Not Free

Ethnic Groups: Persian (51 percent), Azeri (24 percent), Gilaki
and Mazandarani (8 percent), Kurd (7 percent), Arab (3 percent), other (7 percent)
Capital: Teheran
Trend Arrow: Iran received a downward trend arrow because of an intensified campaign by hardliners against opposition journalists and political figures.

Overview:

Despite having won a decisive victory in February's *Majlis*
(parliamentary) elections, moderate allies of President
Mohammad Khatami were unable to translate their political
gains into policy to address national demands for reform and modernization. Instead, a
hardline backlash following the first round of elections led to a reversal of minor open-
ings achieved since Khatami's election in 1997, and highlighted the absolute supremacy
of the right-wing political establishment led by Ayatollah Ali Khamenei.

Reformists clearly swept the majority of the 290-seat Majlis in the first round of
direct voting on February 18, taking about 170 of 224 seats. In runoffs for the remaining 66 seats, reformists took 52. Conservatives won about 40 seats. Five seats are reserved for religious minorities, and others went to independent candidates. In Tehran,
reformists took 26 of 30 seats. About 70 percent of reformist seats reportedly went to
the moderate pro-Khatami Islamic Iran Participation Front (IIPF), while nearly 30
percent went to the technocratic-reformist Executives of Construction. However, exact results were difficult to determine because of the annulment of several results and
delays in the necessary government endorsement of many others.

In January 1979, Shah Mohammad Reza Pahlavi, the hereditary monarch whose
decades-long authoritarian regime was marked by widespread corruption, fled Iran amid
mounting religious and political unrest. A month later, the exiled Ayatollah Ruhollah
Khomeini returned to lead the formation of the world's first Islamic republic. The 1979
constitution provides for a directly elected president and a 12-member Council of
Guardians. The council approves all presidential and parliamentary candidates and
certifies that all bills passed by the Majlis are in accord with *Sharia* (Islamic law).
Khomeini was named supreme religious leader for life and invested with control over
the security and intelligence services, armed forces, and judiciary. He was also given
the power to dismiss the president following a legislative request or supreme court ruling, as well as the final word in all areas of foreign and domestic policy.

Following Khomeini's death in June 1989, Ayatollah Ali Khamenei assumed the
role of supreme religious leader and chief of state. That August, Ali Akbar Hashemi
Rafsanjani, a cleric, ran unopposed for the presidency and won with nearly 95 percent
of the vote.

By the time of 1997 presidential elections, soaring inflation and unemployment, a marked decrease in per capita income due to declining oil revenues, a demographic trend toward a younger population, and restrictions on personal freedom had created a popular desire for change. Of four candidates selected by the Council of Guardians to succeed Rafsanjani, parliamentary speaker Ali Akbar Nateq-Nouri, the favorite of Khamenei and the majority conservatives in the Majlis, was expected to claim an easy victory. But Khatami, a former culture minister who was forced to resign in 1992 for being too liberal, ran on a platform of economic reform, rule of law, civil society, and improved foreign relations. He won the support of intellectuals, women, youth, and business groups seeking greater social freedom and an end to state interference in the economy. Ninety percent of the electorate turned out to vote, and 70 percent voted for Khatami.

Under the constraints of a highly restrictive political system, Khatami holds little real power. He is accountable to the Majlis and bound by the absolute authority of Khamenei. But his popularity has helped him advance a more moderate agenda. During his administration, Iran has seen a marked improvement in press freedom, with the emergence of numerous newspapers that have become immensely popular because of their diversity of views. Although political parties are still technically banned, informal groupings like the IIPF and the Executives of Construction have become increasingly active. Government accountability has improved slightly, as demonstrated by an official admission of intelligence ministry involvement in the 1998 murders of several dissidents. And there has been less severe enforcement of strict Islamic dress codes for women, laws banning satellite dishes, and restrictions on social interaction between men and women. Khatami won an important vote of confidence in February 1999, when reformist candidates won an estimated 80 percent of the seats in Iran's first nationwide municipal elections.

These improvements, however, have not been institutionalized, and conservatives have used the courts and the mosques to limit liberalization. Newspapers have been routinely shut down (and reopened under new titles) and journalists prosecuted. Pro-reform politicians and clerics have been jailed. Violence by pro-regime Islamist vigilantes has increased, as in the case of the brutal raid on a Tehran University dormitory in July 1999 following student protests over the closure of a newspaper. And the arrest of 13 Jews last year on charges of spying for the United States and Israel was seen by many as an attempt by hardliners to derail a nascent rapprochement between Iran and the West.

Hopes that the new parliament could achieve institutional changes such as an independent judiciary, government transparency, rule of law, and separation of powers were dimmed by a hardline backlash that began following the first round of Majlis elections in February. The Council of Guardians annulled several reformist victories and failed for months to ratify numerous others. The new Majlis opened on May 27 with 249 seats filled; the empty seats represented districts where results were either voided or unconfirmed. In March, Saeed Hajjarian, a close aide of Khatami, was shot in an assassination attempt by suspected members of the security forces. A major crackdown on the independent press led to the closure of nearly every reformist newspaper and the detention of three leading journalists by the end of April. Culture Minister Ataollah Mohajerani resigned in December under mounting pressure from conservatives, who blamed him for undermining moral standards. In August, Khamenei blocked an attempt by the Majlis to amend Iran's harsh press law. The proposed amendments were widely seen as a test of reformists' ability to deliver on their electoral promises. In an unprecedented display of frustration, Khatami addressed a special commission set up to monitor compliance with the constitution by saying, "After three and a half years as president, I don't have sufficient powers to implement the constitution, which is my biggest responsibility."

Khatami's government has succeeded in following a more pragmatic approach to international affairs. One of Iran's most pressing problems is its economic disarray. The country suffers from at least 20 percent unemployment, heavy reliance on volatile oil prices, state interference, rampant corruption and inflation, and a U.S. trade embargo. Poor living conditions and bleak job prospects have led to social unrest and an outflow of immigrants. The need for foreign investment has led to ongoing efforts to improve relations with the West and neighboring Arab countries. Following February's Majlis elections, U.S. secretary of state Madeleine Albright announced an easing of sanctions on Iranian consumer goods, and expressed regret over America's role in the 1953 overthrow of Iranian prime minister Mohammad Mossadegh. Official visits to England and Germany aimed to mend fences and promote understanding. Iranian and Turkish leaders agreed in August to cooperate on issues of terrorism and regional security. In March, Iran reached an agreement with Bahrain to ease travel between the two countries. Iranian officials also participated in rare high-level contacts with Egypt and Iraq.

Political Rights and Civil Liberties:

Iranians cannot change their government democratically. Ayatollah Khamenei has the final word on all matters of state and controls broadcast media, the judiciary, and the military. Political parties are technically illegal, although some political groupings have won legal recognition since 1997. All presidential and legislative candidates must support the ruling theocracy and demonstrate allegiance to Islamic principles. About 10 percent of candidates for February's Majlis elections were disqualified by the Council of Guardians for "lack of commitment" to the Islamic system. In the 1996 elections, this number was about 44 percent. No international observers were permitted to oversee polling or ballot counting, and there were reports of violence in several towns where reformist candidates were disqualified and incumbent conservatives won seats. Turnout was reportedly over 75 percent. At least three conservative MPs who gained seats because the Council overturned reformist appointments were later removed by the Majlis.

The state continues to maintain control through terror: arbitrary detention, torture, disappearance, summary trial, and execution are commonplace. Security forces enter homes and offices, open mail, and monitor telephone conversations without court authorization. Hardline vigilante groups commit extrajudicial killings with the tacit consent of the government. A UN investigator for human rights in Iran called upon the government in March to investigate some 50 suspicious deaths of intellectuals and dissidents in recent years. Although the government has investigated murder and other misconduct by hardliners and security officials, information about their cases is not made available, and the officials are rarely punished. The murders of several opposition figures and intellectuals in late 1998 was blamed on "rogue elements" in the intelligence service. Eight suspects were released in May 2000 because of a lack of evidence, while the prime suspect allegedly committed suicide in prison last year. Another 17 people went on trial for the killings in late December. Five people were sentenced to up to 15 years in prison for the March shooting of Saeed Hajjarian. The suspects admitted to being members of a right-wing vigilante group and to acting independently. However, witnesses identified the motorcycle on which the shooter fled as being of a type available only to the security forces.

The judiciary is not independent. Judges must meet strict political and religious qualifications. Bribery is common. Civil courts provide some procedural safeguards, though judges may serve simultaneously as prosecutors during trials. Revolutionary courts try political and religious cases, and are often assigned cases that normally fall under civil court jurisdiction. Charges are often vague, detainees are denied access to legal counsel, and due process rights are ignored. These courts are used frequently to prosecute critics of the Islamic system or the principle of Khamenei's supreme authority. The Special Court for Clergy is widely used to prosecute reformist clerics like Hassan Yousefi-Eshkevari, who was charged in October with apostasy and sedition after publicly advocating the separation of state and religion. The penal code is based on Sharia (Islamic law) and provides for stoning, amputation, and the death penalty for a range of social and political misconduct.

In a case that has received much international attention, ten Jews and two Muslims were convicted of spying for the U.S. and Israel by a Revolutionary Court in July. Their sentences of prison terms ranging from 2 to 13 years were reduced in September by up to 6 years. Three other Jews and two Muslims were found not guilty, and the case remains open against four Muslims and one Jew, who has fled Iran. Human rights groups denounced the unfairness of the trial, which was held in closed sessions with no jury, limited access to counsel, and a judge who also served as prosecutor. The ten convicted Jews lodged appeals with the prosecutor-general in October.

The reformist press played an active role in society after 1997 with political commentary, advocacy of a free and independent civil society, and investigative journalism. After the overwhelming victory of reform candidates in February's elections, however, hardliners launched a campaign against the press, shutting down some 30 papers and arresting journalists, editors, and cartoonists. Among those was Mohammad-Reza Khatami, brother of the Iranian president, who was charged with libel and defamation by a special press court for articles appearing in *Mosharekat*, the newspaper he edits. In April, the outgoing Majlis passed amendments to the press law banning criticism of the constitution and foreign funding for publications, and extending responsibility for press violations to writers as well as editors and publishers. In July, editors were ordered by the government to refrain from publishing cartoons that might harm the dignity of important politicians.

Broadcast media are owned and controlled by the government, although a ban on satellite dishes is not strictly enforced. Many viewers look to foreign television for entertainment and news. Authorities jammed transmissions of the BBC, Voice of America, and Radio Free Europe during February. In April, the supreme court ruled that the possession of videos or music that "corrupt public ethics" is permissible as long as the material is for personal use only. The government blocks Internet sites considered offensive, and service providers practice self-censorship. There are reportedly some 100,000 Internet users in Iran.

The constitution permits public assembly that does not "violate the principles of Islam." Election rallies held by opposition groups were broken up, sometimes violently, by conservative militia, with the consent of security forces. Eight people were killed when police fired on demonstrators protesting alleged ballot rigging in two southwestern towns in February, and demonstrations against the annulment of reformist election victories escalated into violent clashes. Right-wing militants prevented two leading opposition figures from addressing a student group in August, setting off days of clashes in the western city of Khorramabad in which a policeman was killed and several students injured. Reformists accused hardliners of provoking violence in order to create crises that would prove the moderates' inability to govern. Seventeen prominent reformists went on trial before a Revolutionary Court in November on charges of threatening Iran's security. The charges stem from the defendants' attending a seminar in Berlin on democratic reform in Iran.

Women face discrimination in legal and professional matters. They may be fined, imprisoned, or lashed for violating Islamic dress codes, though enforcement has slackened in recent years. Unlike women in Saudi Arabia and the Persian Gulf states, Iranian women may vote, stand for public office, and drive. A woman must have permission from a male relative to obtain a passport. One hundred women graduated from police training in October 2000, becoming the first women allowed to serve as police officers since the Islamic Revolution. In July, a religious decree lifted a ban on women leading prayers. They may now lead congregations of female worshippers. Ten women were elected to the Majlis in February, and one became the first woman on the nine-member Majlis presiding board. A government official named Farah Khosravi declared her intention to stand in presidential elections in 2001.

Religious freedom is limited. The constitution recognizes Zoroastrians, Jews, and Christians as religious minorities, and generally allows them to worship without interference. Iran is approximately 99 percent Muslim, with 89 percent Shiite and 10 percent Sunni. Religious minorities are barred from election to representative bodies (except for seats in the Majlis reserved for them) and from holding senior government or military positions, and they face restrictions in employment, education, and property ownership. Minorities may conduct religious education and establish community centers and certain cultural, social, sports, or charitable associations. Jewish families may not travel abroad together.

The Bahai faith is not recognized. Iran's largest non-Muslim religious minority, the more than 300,000 Bahais face official discrimination, a complete lack of property rights, arbitrary arrest, a ban on university admission, employment restrictions, and prohibitions on teaching their faith and practicing communally. Their marriages are not recognized by the government, leaving women open to charges of prostitution and their children regarded as illegitimate and lacking inheritance rights. Hundreds of Bahais have been executed since 1979.

There are no independent trade unions. The government-controlled Worker's House is the only legal federation. Collective bargaining is nonexistent.

Iraq

Polity: One-party   **Political Rights:** 7
(presidential dictatorship) **Civil Liberties:** 7
Economy: Statist   **Status:** Not Free
Population: 23,100,000
PPP: $3,197
Life Expectancy: 64
Ethnic Groups: Arab (75-80 percent), Kurd (15-20 percent),
other (5 percent)
Capital: Baghdad

Overview:

Thanks to higher oil prices, illicit oil trade, erosion of the United Nations-imposed air embargo, and international concern over the devastating effects of sanctions on Iraqi citizens, Iraqi president Saddam Hussein appears more firmly entrenched than at any time since the 1991 Persian Gulf War. Despite intermittent bombing by the United States and Britain and ten years of sanctions that have created a humanitarian crisis of epic proportions, he continues to refuse entry to UN weapons inspectors. Instead, he has waged a successful public relations campaign, gaining sympathy and support from the international community for the lifting of sanctions.

Iraq gained formal independence in 1932, though the British maintained influence over the Hashemite monarchy. The monarchy was overthrown in a military coup in 1958. A 1968 coup established a government under the Arab *Baath* (Renaissance) Socialist Party, which has remained in power since. The frequently amended 1968 provisional constitution designated the Revolutionary Command Council (RCC) as the country's highest power, and granted it virtually unlimited and unchecked authority. In 1979, Saddam Hussein, long considered the strongman of the regime, formally assumed the titles of state president and RCC chairman.

Iraq attacked Iran in 1980, touching off an eight-year war of attrition during which Iraq's economy suffered extensively and at least 150,000 Iraqis died. In August 1990, Iraq invaded Kuwait. At least 100,000 Iraqi troops were killed in the Persian Gulf War before a 22-nation coalition liberated Kuwait in February 1991. In April, the UN Security Council passed Resolution 687, which called on Iraq to destroy its weapons of mass destruction, to accept long-term monitoring of its weapons facilities, and to recognize Kuwait's sovereignty. The UN also imposed an oil embargo on Iraq, which may be lifted when the government complies with the terms of Resolution 687. In 1996, the UN initiated an oil-for-food program that allows Iraq to sell a limited amount of oil to pay for food and medicine.

An April 1998 progress report by UN Special Commission (UNSCOM) weapons inspector Richard Butler stated that Iraq had largely complied with Resolution 687 on nuclear and chemical weapons programs, but was less forthcoming about biological weapons. Saddam maintained that Iraq was in compliance with the resolution and demanded an end to sanctions. The June 1998 discovery of traces of a nerve agent in an Iraqi weapons dump prompted a protracted standoff. The UN Security Council voted to suspend sanctions reviews, and by October, Iraq had ended all cooperation with

UNSCOM. The U.S. and Britain began bombing military and potential weapons production sites in December.

In December 1999, after a year of air strikes and continuing political deadlock, the UN Security Council passed Resolution 1284, which would suspend sanctions for renewable 120-day periods, provided Baghdad cooperates with a new UN arms control body, called the UN Monitoring, Verification, and Inspection Commission (UNMOVIC). The resolution also lifted the ceiling on oil exports, but kept the revenues under strict UN control. Saddam rejected the resolution, pledging to refuse access to weapons inspectors without an unconditional lifting of sanctions. Hans Blix, a Swedish former foreign minister and director general of the International Atomic Energy Agency, was chosen in January 2000 to head UNMOVIC. Blix assembled a staff of politically neutral arms experts and technical personnel in order to encourage Iraqi cooperation, but Iraq refused to comply with the commission.

Sanctions have taken a massive toll on the Iraqi population. According to UNICEF, some 500,000 children under age five died between 1991 and 1998. Reportedly, only about 41 percent of the population has regular access to clean water. Contaminated water, deteriorating sewage treatment facilities, and sharp declines in health care services have increased the spread and mortality rate of curable disease. The UN Human Development Index, which ranks countries based on quality of life as measured by various social indicators such as education, health care, and material wealth, rated Iraq 55th in 1990. In 2000, Iraq dropped to 126th of 174 countries. The oil-for-food program was designed to improve conditions for Iraqis, but dilapidated oil production infrastructure and delays in receiving replacement parts have hindered the program's effectiveness. Two chief UN relief officials resigned in February in protest over the humanitarian situation in Iraq. One blamed the U.S. and Britain for using their veto power to hold up contracts, while the other blamed Iraqi officials for failure to distribute humanitarian aid. In 2000, the U.S. agreed to increase its imports of oil industry spare parts and lifted holds on more than $100 million in supply contracts. The UN also approved a list of goods, such as food, soap, and educational materials, that will no longer require committee review for import by Iraq.

Saddam has skillfully exploited divisions among Security Council members over sanctions. While the U.S. and Britain take a hardline approach, China, France, and Russia have pushed for lifting the sanctions in order to restore economic ties with Iraq. Sidestepping a ban on commercial flights to Iraq, both Russia and France began sending relief flights after Iraq reopened its international airport in August. By the end of the year, private flights carrying humanitarian aid and delegations interested in trade links were coming regularly from Europe, Africa, and Arab states. Iraqi officials met with foreign counterparts to discuss economic and political cooperation. Talks with Iran produced agreement to work toward normalization, while Saudi Arabia agreed to open its border with Iraq to facilitate Iraqi exports, and an oil pipeline between Iraq and Syria reopened in November after 18 years. A Baghdad trade fair in November drew 14 ministers and senior officials from Arab countries, as well as representatives from eight non-Arab countries.

As sanctions erode, illicit trade is rife. Iraq continues to smuggle oil through Turkey and the Persian Gulf. Observers estimate that for every legitimate load exported through Turkey, some 200 go illegally. With oil prices high in 2000, clandestine trade is extremely lucrative, even if most Iraqis do not reap the benefits. Considering that

Iraq has been able to break free of international isolation and enjoy economic benefits without cooperating with the UN, it seems unlikely that Saddam will allow weapons inspectors to return. In fact, his defiance of the West has only increased; he sent domestic flights to violate no-fly zones in November, and halted oil exports temporarily in December in a dispute with the UN over pricing.

The succession issue in Iraq was highlighted in September when several media outlets reported that Saddam was suffering from lymph cancer. Saddam's younger son, Qusay, has consolidated his role as likely successor by taking control of the state military and security apparatus after an assassination attempt against his older brother, Uday, in 1996. However, Uday made a comeback in 2000, winning a parliamentary seat for Baghdad in the March elections. While some saw his election as a move toward regaining a more prominent political role, others suggested that Saddam allowed him a minor role in politics to appease him. Uday has been called an embarrassment to his family because of his reputed brutality and other excesses, and his role in feuds that have undermined Saddam's power base. However, rumors of Saddam's ill health have circulated for years without verification, so any power struggle between his sons may take years to surface.

Political Rights and Civil Liberties:

Iraqis cannot change their government democratically. Saddam holds supreme power, and relatives and friends from his hometown of Tikrit hold most key positions. Opposition parties are illegal, and the 250-seat National Council (parliament) has no power. Members of the council serve four-year terms. Elections were held on March 27, 2000, for 220 of the seats; 30 seats reserved for Kurds are appointed by presidential decree. All candidates are vetted to ensure their support for the regime, and all are either Baathists or nominal independents loyal to the Baath party. High turnout is typical of Iraqi elections, as failure to vote may be seen as opposition to the government and thus may result in harassment, arrest, torture, or execution.

State control is maintained through the extensive use of intimidation through arrest, torture, and summary execution. Amnesty International reported that people suspected of involvement in opposition activities "can expect to be arrested without a warrant, held in secret detention, without access to family and lawyers, be brutally tortured—including, in one case, having their eyes gouged out—and finally, could face execution." The UN Commission on Human Rights in April adopted a resolution criticizing "all-pervasive repression and oppression sustained by broad-based discrimination and widespread terror." Exiled opposition groups reported the executions of dozens of political prisoners and army officers in 2000 for alleged conspiracy against the regime.

Some safeguards exist in civil cases, but political and "economic" cases are tried in separate security courts with no due process considerations. Theft, corruption, desertion from the army, and currency speculation are punishable by amputation, branding, or execution. Doctors have been executed for refusing to carry out punishments and for attempting reconstructive surgery.

Criticism of local officials and investigation into official corruption are occasionally tolerated, as long as they do not extend to Saddam or to major policy issues. The government makes little effort to block the signal of Radio Free Iraq, which began broadcasting in October 1998. Nonetheless, the government carefully controls most information available to Iraqis. Restricted access to satellite broadcasting was allowed beginning in 1999, but as of November 2000, access to foreign channels had not been made available. Uday Saddam Hussein, the elder son of the president, is head of the 702-member Iraqi Journalists' Union, chairman of several weekly newspapers, publisher of the *Babel* daily, and director of television and radio stations. Iraq set up its first Internet café in July.

Freedom of assembly and association is restricted to pro-Baath gatherings. During the campaign prior to parliamentary elections in March, all rallies were organized by the party. All active opposition groups are in exile, and regime opponents outside Iraq are subject to retaliation by the Iraqi regime. There have been several credible reports of Iraqi defectors receiving videotapes of their female relatives being raped in attempts to coerce them to abandon the opposition. In early 2000, the RCC passed Societies Law 13, which specifies that "the goals, programs, and activities of societies should not conflict with the principles and objectives of the great 17-30 July revolution, the independence of the country, its national unity, and its republican system." The law also prohibits the establishment or funding of any society without government permission.

Islam is the state religion. Shiite Muslims, who constitute more than 60 percent of the population, face severe persecution. For Shia, communal Friday prayer, the loaning of books by mosque libraries, broadcasting, book publishing, and funeral processions and observances are banned. The army has arrested thousands of Shia and executed an undetermined number of these detainees. Security forces have desecrated Shiite mosques and holy sites. The army has indiscriminately targeted civilian Shiite villages, razed homes, and drained southern Amara and Hammar marshes in order to flush out Shiite guerrillas. A Shiite prayer leader was executed in Baghdad in May on charges of inciting unrest in connection with clashes that broke out in several cities after the 1999 assassination of Iraq's top Shiite cleric.

Forced displacement of ethnic Kurds, Turkomans, and other non-Arab minorities continued in 2000. Five Kurdish political parties reported to the UN in June of the ongoing destruction of Kurd villages, expulsions to southern Iraq, and the renaming of schools, streets, and districts in the Baghdad-controlled Kirkuk region in northern Iraq as part of a government policy of "Arabization." Meanwhile, the government moved in early 2000 to grant some 60,000 Palestinians living in Iraq the right to limited home ownership.

Although laws exist to protect women from discrimination in employment and education, to include women in security and police forces, to require education for girls, and to grant women rights in family matters such as divorce and property ownership, it is difficult to determine whether these rights are respected in practice. Men are granted immunity for killing female relatives suspected of "immoral deeds." In May, the government announced that thousands of Iraqi schoolboys aged 12 to 17 would undergo military training during summer holidays as part of efforts to "prepare to back up the armed forces in case the need arises."

Independent trade unions do not exist; the state-backed General Federation of Trade Unions is the only legal labor federation. The law does not recognize the right to collective bargaining and places restrictions on the right to strike.

Ireland

Polity: Parliamentary democracy
Economy: Capitalist
Population: 3,800,000
PPP: $21,482
Life Expectancy: 77
Ethnic Groups: Celtic, English minority
Capital: Dublin

Political Rights: 1
Civil Liberties: 1
Status: Free

Overview:

A major financial scandal involving a former Irish prime minister and current Prime Minister Bertie Ahern continued to dominate headlines in 2000. However, Ireland's surging economy, in many ways exceeding European Union (EU) performance averages, helped deflect criticism of the prime minister and his ruling *Fianna Fail* party. Ireland has become a magnet for foreign labor and a key investment center for high technology and Internet companies. As a result, Ireland moved to both loosen its immigration laws and tighten its asylum application rules. Ireland faced numerous one-day strikes throughout the year as organized labor demonstrated against what it called insufficient wage hikes. The International Monetary Fund (IMF) warned Ireland that its economy was overheating.

Ireland's struggle to maintain identity and independence dates from the beginning of its conquest by England in the early Middle Ages. Ruled as a separate kingdom under the British Crown and, after 1800, as an integral part of the United Kingdom, Ireland received a measure of independence in 1921 when Great Britain granted dominion status to the 26 counties of southern Ireland. Six Protestant-majority counties chose to remain within the United Kingdom. The partition has long been regarded as provisional by the Irish republic, which until recently remained formally committed to incorporation of the northern counties into a unified Irish nation. Ireland's association with the Commonwealth was gradually attenuated and finally terminated in 1949. Since 1949, governmental responsibility has tended to alternate between the Fianna Fail and *Fine Gael* parties.

Prime Minister Ahern's involvement in an ongoing investigation into alleged improprieties by former Prime Minister Charles Haughey continued in 2000. Haughey allegedly siphoned funds intended for his Fianna Fail party for personal use. Ahern, a one-time protégé of Haughey's, signed several blank checks for Haughey while acting as Fianna Fail chief whip in the late 1970s.

Mary Harney, the leader of the small, conservative Progressive Democrats party and deputy prime minister, has threatened to withdraw from the government and bring down the coalition if more damaging disclosures are made during the investigation.

In spite of recriminations, Bertie Ahern's sometimes frail coalition continued to stay in power throughout 2000, at least partly as a result of the country's unprecedented economic prosperity: Ireland is Europe's fastest-growing economy, and, at seven percent per year, the Irish economy has grown twice as fast as the U.S. economy over the last five years. The Irish economy has also grown faster than that of any other EU state for each of the last three years. Ireland joined the European Monetary Union in 1999.

Ireland achieved "full employment" in 2000 with the unemployment rate remaining below five percent. With labor in short supply, the country continued to experience an immigration reversal, with more people, including many expatriates, moving into Ireland than leaving. Because of its skilled workforce and favorable corporate tax policies, Ireland has also become an investment haven, especially for U.S. high-technology and Internet companies. Ireland currently attracts one-third of all U.S. electronics investment in Europe.

In August, the IMF urged the government to halt further tax cuts in order to ward off what it termed "pronounced" signs of economic overheating. Indeed, Ireland's economic success has come with a price: the country's infrastructure has been unable to keep up with the economic surge and creeping inflation. Hospitals are overcrowded, roads are jammed, and housing is in short supply. While Ireland maintains a policy of neutrality, it is a member of the NATO-led Partnership for Peace program.

Political Rights and Civil Liberties: Irish citizens can change their government democratically. The Irish constitution, adopted in 1937, was theoretically applicable to the whole of Ireland; thus residents of Northern Ireland were considered citizens and could run for office in the South. As part of the peace accord signed in Northern Ireland in 1999, Ireland amended its constitution by formally revoking Articles Two and Three, which laid claim to the six counties of the North. The constitution provides for direct election of the president for a seven-year term and for a bicameral legislature consisting of a directly elected lower house (*Dail*) and an indirectly chosen upper house (*Seanad*) with power to delay, but not veto, legislation. The cabinet, which is responsible to the Dail, is headed by a prime minister, who is the leader of the majority party or coalition and is appointed by the president for a five-year term on the recommendation of the Dail. Suffrage in universal; citizens over 18 can vote.

Although free expression is constitutionally guaranteed, the five-member Censorship of Publications Board under the jurisdiction of the Ministry of Justice is empowered to halt publication of books. The board was established under the Censorship of Publications Act of 1946 and is frequently criticized as an anachronism by civil libertarians.

The constitution provides for freedom of religion, and the government does not hamper the teaching or practice of any faith. Even though Ireland is overwhelmingly Roman Catholic, there is no state religion. However, most primary and secondary schools are denominational, and their boards of management are partially controlled by the Catholic Church. Although religious instruction is an integral part of the curriculum, parents may exempt their children from such instruction. There is no discrimination against nontraditional religious groups, despite growing concern over the rapid growth in popularity of such groups as the Jehovah's Witnesses, the Church of Scientology, the Church of Christ, The Solar Temple, Avatar, and others.

The rights of ethnic and racial minorities are generally respected, although isolated racial incidents occur regularly. There are some 25,000 nomadic persons who regard themselves as a distinct ethnic group called Travellers, roughly analogous to the Roma (Gypsies) of continental Europe. Travellers are regularly denied access to premises, goods, facilities, and services; many employers do not hire them. The Employment

Equality Act of 1998 that came into force in October 1999 extends protection against discrimination in the workplace to include family status, religious belief, age, race, sexual orientation, disability, and membership in the Travellers community.

While Ireland moved to loosen its immigration laws in 2000 because of its economic boom and need for foreign labor, it drew criticism from Amnesty International and the Irish Refugee Council for passing tougher restrictions against asylum seekers. Ireland has become an attractive destination for asylum seekers from Africa and Eastern Europe. The new laws allow for longer detention periods of asylum seekers and reduces the amount of time applicants can prepare for judicial review from three months to 14 days. Critics of the new laws complained that those with legitimate claims would not have enough time to prepare their cases. A corollary policy of dispersing asylum seekers throughout the country was criticized for putting many refugee claimants at an unfair disadvantage, since they could ostensibly be denied fair access to quality legal representation. The police were also given new powers to detain and deport unsuccessful asylum seekers. Those caught trafficking in illegal immigrants can now face a ten-year prison sentence.

Ireland has an independent judicial system that includes a district court with 23 districts, a circuit court with eight circuits, the high court, the court of criminal appeals, and the supreme court. The president appoints judges on the advice of the government.

Discrimination against women in the workplace is unlawful, but inequalities persist regarding pay and promotions in both the public and private sectors. However, with the current labor shortage, the government is considering ways to increase female participation in the workforce. Only about 12 percent of the members of parliament are women. Women's reproductive rights are limited: abortion is legal only when a woman's life is in danger.

Labor unions are free to organize and bargain collectively. About 55 percent of workers in the public and private sectors are union members. Police and military personnel are prohibited from striking, but they may form associations to represent themselves in matters of pay and working conditions. The Irish Congress of Trade Unions organized nationwide one-day strikes throughout 2000, often bringing rail service to a standstill and closing schools. The unions within the umbrella group demanded pay increases commensurate with inflation, which in 2000 reached seven percent. The unions seek an overhaul of an agreement signed with the government that guarantees an annual five percent wage hike for three years. By year's end, the government had refused to renegotiate terms of the agreement, known as the Program for Prosperity and Fairness.

Israel

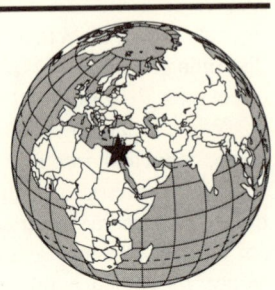

Polity: Parliamentary democracy
Economy: Mixed capitalist
Population: 6,200,000
PPP: $17,301
Life Expectancy: 78

Political Rights: 1
Civil Liberties: 3*
Status: Free

Ethnic Groups: Jewish (82 percent), non-Jewish [mostly Arab] (18 percent)
Capital: Jerusalem
Ratings Change: Israel's civil liberties rating changed from 2 to 3 because of the October shooting deaths of 13 Arab citizens of Israel at the hands of Israeli soldiers; the unarmed Arab-Israelis were demonstrating in support of widespread and violent Palestinian protests in the West Bank and Gaza.

Overview:

After withdrawing its troops from southern Lebanon and nearly completing a final-status peace accord with the Palestinians at Camp David in July 2000, Israel faced a renewed Palestinian uprising in the fall. This time Palestinians supplemented stones with guns, as militias and Palestinian security forces carried out attacks against Israelis. By year's end Israel was plunged into a severe political crisis, as the continuing violence claimed hundreds of Palestinian lives, and tens of Israeli lives, including Arab citizens of Israel shot by Israeli troops. Toward the end of the year, with the West Bank and Gaza Strip still percolating with violence, Prime Minister Ehud Barak's once-strong majority government was suddenly in the minority. His popularity plummeting, Barak, in a tactical move, resigned late in December. By pre-empting the dissolution of parliament, which would have brought full elections, Barak was able to remain caretaker prime minister and prevent his archrival, Likud Party member and former Prime Minister Benjamin Netanyahu, from running in snap elections called for February 2001. However, public opinion polls showed Barak losing by a landslide to Likud leader Ariel Sharon, a hawkish former general. Decimated in general elections in May 1999, the right-wing Likud Party enjoyed huge popularity gains as the Palestinian uprising wore on. Israeli president Ezer Weizman resigned from his post after becoming the subject of a corruption probe.

Israel was formed in 1948 from less than one-fifth of the original British Palestine Mandate. Its neighbors, rejecting a United Nations partition plan that would have also created a Palestinian state, attacked immediately following independence in the first of several Arab-Israeli conflicts. Israel has functioned as a parliamentary democracy since independence. Since 1977, the conservative Likud and the center-left Labor Party have shared or alternated power.

Following June 1992 *Knesset* (parliament) elections, Yitzhak Rabin's Labor-led coalition government secured a breakthrough agreement with the Palestinian Liberation Organization (PLO) in 1993. The Declaration of Principles, negotiated secretly between Israeli and Palestinian delegations in Oslo, Norway, provides for a phased Israeli withdrawal from the Israeli-occupied West Bank and Gaza Strip, and for limited Palestinian autonomy in those areas. Negotiations on the status of Jerusalem, Jewish settlements, refugees, and Israel's borders began in November 1999.

On November 4, 1995, a right-wing Jewish extremist, opposed to the peace process on the grounds that it would lead to a Palestinian state in the West Bank, assassinated Rabin in Tel Aviv. Foreign Minister Shimon Peres became acting prime minister and served until the 1996 elections, when, after a wave of suicide bombings carried out in Israel by Islamic radicals, Netanyahu, the right-wing Likud Party leader, was elected.

After winning a landslide election in 1999 on an ambitious peace-making platform, Prime Minister Ehud Barak saw his majority Labor Party-led coalition government turn to ruins by the middle of 2000. Central to Barak's political misfortunes was the loss of confidence in the government by key coalition members as the prime minister engaged the Palestinian leadership in the most far-reaching negotiations ever, at Camp David in July. Israelis for the first time seriously considered substantive compromise proposals on Jerusalem and the future status of Palestinian refugees that had previously been considered taboo. On the eve of the talks, Barak's multiparty coalition had all but fallen apart; it was down from 75 to 40 seats in the 120-member Knesset. Foreign Minister David Levy resigned in protest. Barak's determination to address all the final-status issues with the Palestinians at once, rather than in incremental steps, as proscribed by the Oslo process, was seen as dangerous by some members of his own cabinet. A former general and chief of staff, Barak's proclivity to strategize and make decisions in a solitary fashion rankled many in the Labor party leadership, who felt cut out of the process. Much of the public also became disillusioned with the prime minister, feeling he was insufficiently informing them about the compromise solutions he was proposing.

Part of the coalition's undoing was also the result of pure politics; the left-wing Meretz party pulled out of the government in protest against its ultra-orthodox, right-wing fellow coalition member, the Shas Party. The two parties had fought all year over an order by the Meretz leader, Education Minister Yossi Sarid, to close several parochial schools operated by Shas because of the schools' deep indebtedness. Sarid's order led to denunciatory attacks by Israeli chief Sephardic rabbi and Shas spiritual leader Ovadia Yosef, who called for Sarid to be "extirpated from earth." An investigation was ordered—and later dropped—to determine whether Yosef should be charged with incitement. Shas Party leader Aryeh Deri began serving a three-year prison term during the year after being convicted of accepting bribes in exchange for directing state funds to religious schools while he ran the interior ministry. His case further pitted the largely disenfranchised Sephardic community against Israel's Ashkenazic establishment.

In April, President Ezer Weizman became the target of a corruption probe, when he was accused of not declaring hundreds of thousands of dollars allegedly given to him by a French businessman. While the inquiry resulted in no charges, Weizman stepped down from his post in July. In his place, the Knesset elected Likud party member Moshe Katzav, dealing a political blow to Prime Minister Barak and his peace policies. Labor Party member and former Prime Minister Shimon Peres seemed certain to capture the presidency. In September, corruption charges were dropped against former Prime Minister Netanyahu. The attorney general claimed lack of evidence in a case alleging that Netanyahu had accepted free services from a contractor and kept official gifts after leaving office. His exoneration set the stage for a political comeback.

Intensive peace negotiations between Israel and Syria broke down in January over disagreements concerning final borders around the Golan Heights. A March summit between U.S. president Bill Clinton and Syrian president Hafez al-Assad, designed to sound out the Syrian leader on his peace terms and jump-start negotiations with Israel, failed to produce any forward momentum. The key sticking point centered on which country should control a strip of shoreline along the eastern edge of the Sea of Galilee, located below the western slopes of the Golan. The sea serves as Israel's primary fresh water source. Israel has agreed in principle to a return of all of the Golan in return for security guarantees. Prior to losing the Golan in 1967, Syria had used the territory to shell northern Israeli towns. With the June death of Assad, and the ascension to power of his relatively inexperienced son Bashar, the prospect of further talks appeared, at best, remote.

In June, Israel withdrew from its self-declared "security zone" in southern Lebanon, after occupying the area for 18 years to protect its northern region from attacks by Hezbollah, a radical Shi'ite Muslim group active in Lebanon. Hezbollah guerrillas kidnapped three Israeli soldiers after infiltrating the border in a surprise raid in October.

At Camp David in July, Israel and the Palestinians, with President Clinton mediating, spent over two weeks negotiating the key final-status issues of Jerusalem, the size of a Palestinian state, and the fate of Palestinian refugees. For the first time, Israel offered compromise solutions on Jerusalem, agreeing to some form of Palestinian control and quasi-sovereignty over East Jerusalem, which contains Islamic holy sites. Israel also offered 95 percent of the West Bank to the Palestinians. The Palestinians rejected the Israeli offers, and no agreement was reached.

At the end of September, perhaps in protest to the government's expressed willingness to compromise on Jerusalem, right-wing Likud leader Ariel Sharon visited the Temple Mount in Jerusalem's Old City, the site of the Al Aqsa Mosque. A widespread Palestinian uprising erupted, ultimately taking on a life of its own and lasting through the end of year. As the violence intensified, Prime Minister Barak found his political future in jeopardy. Despite attempts to reach ceasefires and restart the peace talks, violence confined largely to the West Bank and Gaza Strip persisted, claiming more than 300 Palestinian lives. The radical Islamic group Hamas claimed responsibility for separate car- and bus-bomb attacks in Israel that claimed the lives of four people. Nearly 50 Israeli soldiers and civilians were killed by December 31. In one case in October, two Israeli reserve soldiers were dragged from a Palestinian police station in Ramallah and lynched by a mob.

Seemingly unable to contain the violence, Prime Minister Barak resigned in December, calling for snap elections for February 2001. By submitting a formal resignation and scheduling early elections, Barak was able to remain caretaker prime minister. According to Israeli law, only sitting members of parliament may contest the premiership. Barak's move was widely seen as a tactical maneuver to outflank the Likud Party and its resurgent former leader, Benjamin Netanyahu, who was unable to challenge Barak since he was no longer a member of the Knesset. By the end of the year, however, public opinion polls showed the prime minister trailing significantly behind Ariel Sharon.

Political Rights and Civil Liberties: Israeli citizens can change their government democratically. Although Israel has no formal constitution, a series of Basic Laws has the force of constitutional principles. In August, Prime Minister Barak called for the drafting of a constitution; he proposed a "civil revolution" that would undermine the power of the Orthodox Jewish establishment over most aspects of Jewish Israeli life, such as marriage. Barak also proposed a national service program to end army exemptions of Orthodox Jewish males who can claim that Torah study prevents them from mandatory military service.

The judiciary is independent, and procedural safeguards are generally respected. Security trials, however, may be closed to the public on limited grounds. The Emergency Powers (Detention) Law of 1979 provides for indefinite administrative detention without trial. The policy stems from emergency laws in place since the creation of Israel. Most administrative detainees are Palestinian, but there are currently two Lebanese detainees being held on national security grounds. Members of Lebanese Shi'ite Muslim groups, they are believed to have the most direct knowledge of Israeli airman Ron Arad, believed to be held in Lebanon since his plane was shot down in 1986. In July 1999, Justice Minister Yossi Beilin announced a plan to cancel the legal basis for holding Lebanese detainees for indefinite periods without formal charges. He also announced the eventual canceling of the emergency laws, seen as increasingly irrelevant in an overall climate of peace. In the spring of 2000 Israel did release 13 Lebanese detainees who had been held, some for several years, as "bargaining chips." They were to be used in prisoner exchanges to secure the release of Israeli servicemen.

Freedoms of assembly and association are respected. Newspaper and magazine articles on security matters are subject to a military censor, though the scope of permissible reporting is expanding. Editors may appeal a censorship decision to a three-member tribunal that includes two civilians. Arabic-language publications are censored more frequently than are Hebrew-language ones. Newspapers are privately owned and freely criticize government policy.

Publishing the praise of violence is prohibited under the Counter-terrorism Ordinance. In November, the Israeli supreme court lowered the standard by which public speech or publications can be deemed inciteful and harmful to the "values of public order," including "social cohesion." Previously, only public statements found to be threatening to the foundations of democratic rule were considered tantamount to sedition and subject to punishment. This ruling followed the passage of legislation in early 1999, which legalized pirate radio stations run by settlers and religious activists who in the past had been accused of inciting hatred through anti-peace broadcasts.

In August, the World Association of Newspapers (WAN) criticized Israel for the wounding of two journalists covering demonstrations at Lebanon's border with Israel. Israeli troops shot them while responding to rock throwing at a border fence. In October, Reporters Sans Frontières criticized Israel for not adequately protecting journalists, several of whom had been caught in the crossfire during Palestinian-Israeli clashes in the West Bank and Gaza Strip.

Freedom of religion is respected. Each community has jurisdiction over its own members in matters of marriage, burial, and divorce. In the Jewish community, the Orthodox establishment handles these matters. A heated debate has erupted in recent years over the Orthodox monopoly on conversions, which denies certain rights, such as citizenship and marriage, to Reform and Conservative converts. However, a 1999 lower court ruling rejected the Orthodox hold on conversions, clearing the way for the participation of the Reform and Conservative branches of Judaism. This ruling, combined with supreme court decisions early in 1999 that exemption from military service for students in religious schools was illegal, touched off significant religious protests. In May 2000, the supreme court overruled a ban on women wearing prayer shawls and praying audibly at the Western Wall in the Jewish Quarter of Jerusalem's Old City. The ultra-Orthodox establishment condemned the ruling.

Some one million Arab citizens receive inferior education, housing, and social services, relative to the Jewish population. Housing restrictions were eased somewhat in March when the Israeli supreme court overturned a 52-year-old policy banning the sale of public land to non-Jews. The court ruled the old law was discriminatory to Israeli's Arab population, and perpetuated inequality among the country's citizens. In November, Chief Justice Aharon Barak publicly called for full equality of Arab citizens, saying there can be no true democracy in Israel without it. Israeli Arabs are not subject to the military draft, though they may serve voluntarily. Those who do not join the army do not enjoy the financial benefits available to Israelis who have served, including scholarships and housing loans.

In October, 13 Israeli Arabs were killed by Israeli troops during demonstrations initially in response to the Palestinian uprising taking place in the West Bank and Gaza. The protests ultimately gave voice to long-held frustrations among Israel's Arab citizens, who have often felt like second-class citizens and who were counting on Prime Minister Barak to fulfill a campaign pledge to improve their lot. The violence gave way to some of the worst civil strife in Israel in decades, with riots sweeping many Arab villages and Jewish towns. Prime Minister Barak, succumbing to growing criticism that his initial launching of an inquiry into the shooting deaths was insufficient, eventually appointed a state commission with wider judicial powers to investigate the killings. He also outlined a $1 billion plan to address road, sewage, housing, and education shortfalls in Arab-Israeli communities.

Women are underrepresented in public affairs; only nine women were elected to the 120-seat Knesset in 1996. In the May 1999 election, an Arab woman, Husaina Jabara, was elected to the Knesset for the first time. However, women continue to face discrimination in many areas, including in military service, where they are barred from combat units, and in religious institutions. In May 2000, Amnesty International criticized Israel for not protecting the rights of foreign women smuggled into the country to work as prostitutes. According to an Amnesty International report, hundreds of women are smuggled in each year with the promise of well-paying jobs, only to be sold into prostitution, raped, and at times tortured.

Most Bedouin housing settlements are not recognized by the government and are not provided with basic infrastructure and essential services. In September, residents of four recognized Bedouin villages in the Negev desert elected their own representatives to local governments for the first time. The interior ministry usually appoints representatives.

Workers may join unions of their choice and enjoy the right to strike and to bargain collectively. Three-quarters of the workforce either belong to unions affiliated with *Histadrut* (General Federation of Labor) or are covered under its social programs and collective bargaining agreements.

Italy

Polity: Parliamentary democracy
Economy: Capitalist-statist
Population: 57,800,000
PPP: $20,585
Life Expectancy: 78
Ethnic Groups: Italian, small minorities of German, French, Slovene, and Albanian
Capital: Rome

Political Rights: 1
Civil Liberties: 2
Status: Free

Overview:

The sweeping defeat of center-left parties in Italy's first direct regional assembly elections in April led to the resignation of Prime Minister Massimo D'Alema and the end of the 57th Italian government since World War II. With a view to a May referendum on electoral reform, President Carlo Ciampi avoided dissolving parliament by appointing Giuliano Amato prime minister. A former prime minister and renowned financial expert, Amato won a vote of confidence for his new center-left government on April 28.

Italy's fractious and unstable governments have failed during the past several years to implement the reforms necessary to tackle the country's myriad political problems. Such reforms include overhauling current electoral laws, which engender political instability by allowing dozens of small parties to wield disproportionate influence in parliament; creating a framework for devolution in order to neutralize secessionist sentiment among northern Italians; and developing measures to prevent conflicts of interest. The May referendum, in which voters overwhelmingly approved proposals related to electoral reform and judicial restructuring, failed to pass because of low voter turnout. Observers believe that the chances of any serious electoral reform before the next general election in April 2001 are slim, and thus it is likely that the next government will suffer the same instability as previous ones.

Modern Italian history dates from the nineteenth-century movement for national unification. Most of Italy had merged into one kingdom by 1870. Italy sided with Germany and Austria-Hungary at the outset of World War I, but switched to side with the Allied powers during the war. From 1922 to 1943, the country was a Fascist dictatorship under Benito Mussolini, who sided with the Axis powers during World War II. A referendum in 1946 replaced the monarchy with a republican constitution, which provides for a president whose role is largely ceremonial. He is elected to a seven-year term by an assembly of parliamentarians and delegates from the regional councils. The president chooses the prime minister, who is often, but not always, a member of the largest party in the chamber of deputies, the lower house of parliament. Members of the upper house, the senate, are elected on a regional basis.

The center-left has held power since the 1996 general elections, which followed the collapse of a center-right coalition led by prime minister and media mogul Silvio Berlusconi in 1994. Despite the infighting that has led to four government changes since 1996, the center-left presided over economic austerity measures that brought Italy into line with Maastricht Treaty criteria for the European Monetary Union. However, by the end of 2000, disunity and low poll ratings suggested that the 2001 elections will go to Berlusconi's center-right coalition, which includes his own *Forza Italia* (Go, Italy), the post-Fascist National Alliance, and the northern-nationalist Northern League. While the left appears wanting for new policy ideas, Berlusconi promotes policies to tackle crime, overhaul the tax system, privatize pensions, modernize infrastructure, provide technical training to young people, and encourage tourism in the south. He received 59 percent approval ratings in opinion polls at year's end, despite a string of convictions for bribery and accounting irregularities.

Yet victory by the right is by no means certain. Xenophobic attacks against gays, Muslims, and foreigners by Northern League head Umberto Bossi in October drew harsh criticism from political opponents and rights advocates. The National Alliance leader of the regional council of Lazio, which includes Rome, announced his intention to set up a commission to review school history books. He explained that the books glorify World War II anti-Fascists without giving sufficient attention to the murders of Italians by Yugoslav Communists in the north. Such moves, aside from embarrassing coalition partners, may affect the center-right's popularity before April 2001.

On the economic front, Italy continues to see the slowest growth of the major European countries. A general suspicion of free market forces, coupled with the belief that privatization is unpopular with voters, has kept the process of privatizing state industries incomplete. Moreover, the process has been fraught by mismanagement. In addition, Italy's leading trade association reported late in the year that some 20 percent of all Italian businesses (accounting for about 15 percent of GNP) are controlled by organized crime. On the positive side, the Italian Antitrust Authority has stepped up its efforts and become increasingly effective in the past two years against anticompetitive practices in the private sector. During the summer, it fined insurance companies $350 million and oil companies $320 million for price fixing. Although the authority is understaffed, it has been praised by the Organization for Economic Cooperation and Development for the transparency and speed with which it functions.

Political Rights and Civil Liberties: Italians can change their government democratically. Citizens are free to form political organizations, with the exception of the constitutionally forbidden prewar Fascist Party. The postwar constitution, designed to prevent another Mussolini-style dictatorship, sharply restricts the powers of the executive in favor of the legislative and judicial branches of government. The result has been unstable governing coalitions, political deadlock, and heavy reliance on the referendum as a political tool.

The judiciary is independent but notoriously slow and inefficient. A 1995 law allows for preventive detention as a last resort, or in cases where there is convincing evidence of a serious offense, such as illegal activity involving organized crime or related to drugs, arms, or subversion. A maximum of two years is permitted for preliminary investigation. About half of some 52,000 inmates are waiting to be tried. The average waiting period for a trial is about 18 months, but can exceed two years. A decree issued in November 2000 extends the time limit on pretrial incarceration of suspects charged with either pedophilia or prostitution of minors. It would also give judges greater discretion in extending pretrial detention up to a six-year limit. Other provisions include abolishing the plea bargain for suspects facing life imprisonment and increasing surveillance of suspects under house arrest. In Italy, a defendant is given two chances to appeal a guilty verdict, during which he is presumed innocent and not jailed. The average civil trial lasts between three and five years. In 1999, Italy decriminalized minor offenses such as defaming the flag, insulting the dead, and public drunkenness in an effort to streamline the penal system. Under the new provisions, a number of transgressions were downgraded from criminal to civil offenses, and judges may impose curfews or sentences of community service on minors.

In July 2000, the government announced plans to reform Italy's prison system. The plans include building new prisons, renovating existing facilities, recruiting new prison officers, and deporting prisoners from outside the European Union sentenced to less than three years. Prison conditions and overcrowding have drawn criticism from domestic and international observers; Italy's prisons are holding about 9,000 more prisoners than they were designed to accommodate. Unrest reportedly occurred in some 52 prisons in the first half of July alone.

The Italian press is free and competitive. Most of approximately 80 daily newspapers are independently owned. The main state-owned television network and the three main channels of *Radio Audizioni Italiane* (RAI) provide Italians with most of their news. Their boards of directors are parliament-appointed. A February 2000 law on political advertising requires broadcasters to give political adversaries equal time, bans paid political ads on national television, and requires public broadcasters to give all parties free television time at certain hours. Private broadcasters must also provide equal time to opposing parties if they choose to run political ads. One journalist from *Il Messagero* was assaulted by police while covering a demonstration against the visit of Austrian far-right politician Jorg Haider to Rome in December. A television anchor and two assistant news directors at RAI resigned in September after the station broadcast graphic images in a report on child pornography. The broadcast created a political uproar as Italian prosecutors launched a massive crackdown on video, print, and Internet child pornography.

Freedom of assembly and association is guaranteed by the constitution, with the exception of Fascist and racist groups. Religious freedom is protected, and the government subsidizes several religions through tax revenues. In March, the government formally recognized Buddhists and Jehovah's Witnesses as official religions for the first time. Official recognition allows religions to establish their own schools and to benefit from a system in which taxpayers can donate a percentage of their income tax payment to the faith of their choice. Roman Catholics, Seventh-day Adventists, Waldensians, Baptists, Lutherans, Jews, and members of the Assembly of God already enjoy this right. Observers have raised concern over what appears to be an increase of xenophobia and anti-Semitism, particularly in the north. In one of several cases, a Catholic of Jewish descent was brutally attacked by three individuals who shouted anti-Semitic epithets at him. Umberto Bossi's public statements against Muslims, gays, and foreigners appear to resonate with Italians who fear that an influx of foreigners threatens the national identity.

There are no restrictions on women's participation in government and politics. However, few women hold elective office; they constitute 11 percent of the chamber of deputies and 8 percent of the senate. Women enjoy legal equality in marriage, property, and inheritance rights. Foreign women are particular victims of human trafficking. Tens of thousands have been smuggled in, primarily by Albanian organized crime rings, to work as prostitutes. Often their passports are destroyed and they are abused in an effort to frighten them into submission. The justice department has made efforts to end the practice, but many victims lack the courage to cooperate.

Workers may strike and bargain collectively. Some 40 percent of the workforce is unionized. The law prohibits discrimination by employers against union members and organizers.

↓ Jamaica

Polity: Parliamentary democracy
Economy: Capitalist
Population: 2,600,000
PPP: $3,389
Life Expectancy: 75
Ethnic Groups: Black (76 percent), Creole (15 percent), European, Chinese, East Indian (9 percent)
Capital: Kingston

Political Rights: 2
Civil Liberties: 2
Status: Free

Trend Arrow: Jamaica received a downward trend arrow due to the government's continued inability to effectively confront high levels of violence and insecurity.

Overview:

Prime Minister Percival J. Patterson promised in 2000 to stanch Jamaica's "rampant criminality" by introducing new efforts to control guns, creating a new police anti-organized-crime strike force, and reintroducing the death penalty. The get-tough promises came after key leaders of the vital tourism industry joined a crescendo of complaints from Jamaicans of all walks of life to put an end to a more than two-decades-long spiral of mostly drug-related street crime. The fierce crime wave has crippled local businesses and created an exodus of middle-class Jamaicans overseas. The decision on the death penalty was immediately condemned by international human rights organizations, and Jamaican lawmakers lashed out at what it called U.S. reluctance to provide real help in stemming the flow of illegal guns to the island and its Caribbean neighbors.

Jamaica, a member of the Commonwealth, achieved independence from Great Britain in 1962. It is a parliamentary democracy, with the British monarchy represented by a governor-general. The bicameral parliament consists of a 60-member house of representatives elected for five years, and a 21-member senate, with 13 senators appointed by the prime minister and 8 by the leader of the parliamentary opposition. Executive authority is vested in the prime minister, who leads the political party commanding a majority in the house.

Since independence, power has alternated between the social-democratic People's National Party (PNP) and the conservative Jamaica Labor Party (JLP). The PNP's Michael Manley, who died in 1997, was prime minister from 1972 to 1980, and again from 1989 until his resignation for health reasons in 1992. JLP leader Edward Seaga held the post from 1980 until 1989. During the 1970s the two parties helped to organize and arm slum dwellers, creating rival armed gangs to intimidate voters.

In 1992 the PNP elected Patterson to replace Manley as party leader and prime minister. In the 1993 elections, the PNP won 52 parliamentary seats, and the JLP 8. The parties differed little on continuing the structural adjustment begun in the 1980s, but the JLP was hurt by long-standing internal rifts. Irregularities and violence marred the vote. The PNP agreed to address subsequent JLP demands for electoral reform. Meanwhile, the Patterson government continued to confront labor unrest and an unrelenting crime wave.

In October 1995, Bruce Golding, a well-respected economist, businessman, and the former chairman of the JLP, left the party to launch the National Democratic Movement (NDM), one of the most significant political developments since independence. Golding brought with him a number of key JLP figures, including one other member of parliament, cutting the JLP's seats to six.

Politically motivated fighting between supporters of the JLP and the NDM claimed at least ten lives during 1996. In December 1997, the PNP won a third successive victory in parliamentary elections, taking 50 seats in the lower house to the JLP's 10. Confidence in Patterson's unprecedented second full term was reaffirmed in local elections held in September 1998, as the ruling PNP gained 75 percent of the vote and took possession of the capital and all 13 rural parishes. The 1997 and 1998 votes were characterized by unusually low levels of political violence, and were judged generally free and fair, despite a creaky electoral administration.

In April 1999, sweeping tax changes proposed by Patterson sparked a riot that left nine people dead, most killed by the police. In July, Vivian Blake, the alleged leader of a gang known as the Shower Posse, was extradited to the United States to face charges in a Miami court for participation in hundreds of murders, mostly drug related, in the United States in the 1980s.

The Private Sector Organization of Jamaica, made up of manufacturers, distributors, and exporters, has said that the island's four-year economic decline, marked by a 20 percent unemployment rate, is the result of three decades of crime. The increase in violent crime is largely the work of former politically organized gangs that now operate a lucrative drug trade that is only loosely tied to local party bosses. By early 2000, it became clear that Colombian drug traffickers had wrested away from Jamaican middlemen the direct control of local distribution of cocaine and its export to the United States. The Colombian takeover was the latest development in a three-year boom in hard-drug traffic that came in the wake of a crackdown on the drug trade in Puerto Rico, the Dominican Republic, and Mexico's Pacific coast. In September Seaga accused the government of running extortion rackets and the PNP of arming "activists"—gangsters— with licensed guns, charges denied by the government. In October Patterson dismissed the head of the police Civilian Intelligence Unit, after the elite group was accused of engaging in illegal wiretapping of leading politicians, including the prime minister and senior police officials.

Political Rights and Civil Liberties:

Citizens are able to change their government through elections. However, voter apathy in the 1998 local elections resulted in one of the lowest turnout rates—31 percent—in Jamaican history. Although the violence associated with the 1997 preelectoral period was significantly less than in previous years, it was nonetheless marked by thuggery on both sides, police intimidation, and large-scale confusion. Progress on electoral reform has been slow, and the municipal elections has been postponed for five years in order for electoral rolls to be updated and the voting system reformed. International concern has been expressed about candidate access to so-called garrison communities—armed political fiefdoms in 9 of the 60 parliamentary districts. Seaga's JLP controls only one, Tivoli Gardens, while the PNP controls seven, and the NDM one.

Constitutional guarantees regarding the right to free expression, freedom of religion, and the right to organize political parties, civic organizations, and labor unions are generally respected.

The judicial system is headed by a supreme court and includes several magistrate courts and a court of appeals, with final recourse to the Privy Council in London, which is drawn from members of Britain's House of Lords. The justice system is slow and inefficient, particularly in addressing police abuses and the violent conditions in prisons. Despite government efforts to improve penal conditions, a mounting backlog of cases and a shortage of court staff at all levels continues to undermine the judicial system. In February 1997 Jamaica signed on to the hemispheric antidrug strategy formulated by the Organization of American States (OAS). A September 2000 ruling by the Privy Council, that may save hundreds of convicted murderers on death row on Carribean islands, prompted Patterson, a proponent of executions, to declare that it was "another compelling reason" to create a much-touted Caribbean court to replace the Privy Council.

Violence is now the major cause of death in Jamaica, and the murder rate is one of the highest in the world. Much of the violence is the result of warfare between drug gangs known as posses. Criminal deportees from the United States and a growing illegal weapons trade are major causes of the violence. Mobs have been responsible for numerous vigilante killings of suspected criminals. Inmates frequently die as a result of prison riots. Jamaican officials complained that the United States was flagrantly applying a double standard by demanding a full effort by them to help stop the flow of drugs into the United States, but at the same time failing to stem the flow of drugs to Jamaica.

Human rights groups say that there are continuing concerns over criminal justice practices in Jamaica. These include the imposition of death sentences following trials of questionable fairness; killings by police in disputed circumstances and deaths in custody; corporal punishment and alleged ill-treatment by police and prison wardens; appalling detention centers and prisons; and laws punishing consensual sexual acts in private between adult men. The June 2000 ruling by the Privy Council in London, which commuted the death penalty for six Jamaican inmates, said that inmates should be allowed lawyers when appealing before Jamaica's privy council, which advises on mercy pleas. It objected to a Jamaican law that gives death-row inmates only six months to have their cases heard by international human rights commissions. It also reaffirmed an earlier ruling that mandated, because of concerns about cruel and inhumane punishment, a lapse of no more than five years between sentencing and execution.

A mounting crime rate led the government to take the controversial steps of restoring capital punishment and restoring flogging. Rights groups protested both measures. Critics charge that flogging is unconstitutional because it can be characterized as "inhuman or degrading punishment," which the constitution prohibits. In 1998, a six-month limit on death-row appeals to international bodies was adopted. Jamaica has also announced its intention to withdraw from an agreement with the Inter-American Human Rights Commission of the OAS that gives prisoners the right to appeal to the commission in order to remove barriers to executions. There are 600 prisoners on death row.

There are an estimated 1.9 million radios in Jamaica—the highest per capita ratio in the Caribbean—but only 330,000 television sets, and there is generally low newspaper readership. Newspapers are independent and free of government control. Journalists are occasionally intimidated during election campaigns. Broadcast media are largely public but are open to pluralistic points of view. Public opinion polls play a key role in the political process, and election campaigns feature debates on state-run television.

In 1998, a woman was for the first time elected as speaker of parliament. Labor unions are politically influential and have the right to strike. The Industrial Disputes Tribunal mediates labor conflicts.

Japan

Polity: Parliamentary democracy
Economy: Capitalist
Population: 126,900,000
PPP: $23,257
Life Expectancy: 80
Ethnic Groups: Japanese (99 percent), other (1 percent)
Capital: Tokyo

Political Rights: 1
Civil Liberties: 2
Status: Free

Overview:

As the Japanese economy continued to stagnate amid rising levels of government debt and a debt-laden banking system, the Liberal Democratic Party (LDP) and its coalition partners won the June 2000 parliamentary elections behind a deeply unpopular prime minister, on promises to continue injecting money into the economy to keep it afloat.

Following its defeat in World War II, Japan adopted a United States-drafted constitution in 1947 that vested executive authority in a prime minister and cabinet, created the two-house Diet (parliament), and ended the emperor's divine status. In 1955, the two main conservative parties merged to form the governing LDP, and the two wings of the opposition Japan Socialist Party (JSP) united. This "1955 system" remained in place throughout the cold war, as the LDP won successive elections, presided over what became the world's second largest economy, and maintained close security ties to the U.S. The system rested on an "iron triangle" of politicians, business, and the bureaucracy. The bureaucracy set policy and imposed costly economic regulations that protected businesses, while the LDP spent heavily on public works projects to benefit its rural stronghold as well as its corporate backers, who funneled both legal and illegal contributions back to the ruling party.

Following a string of corruption scandals involving LDP politicians in the 1980s and the end of cold war security tensions, the ruling party lost power for the first time in the 1993 elections. However, the LDP returned to power in a coalition government in 1994. By the mid-1990s, two new parties had emerged as credible challengers to the LDP. Headed by maverick Ichiro Ozawa, the conservative New Frontier Party (NFP) promised economic deregulation and a more assertive foreign policy, while Naoto Kan's

Democratic Party promoted good governance. Yet, despite continued scandals, the LDP under Ryutaro Hashimoto won 239 out of 500 lower house seats in the early elections in October 1996 and formed a minority government.

Hashimoto's government was the first to confront economic problems that had been mounting since the collapse of Japan's "bubble economy," with its inflated asset prices in the early 1990s. When the regional financial crisis began in 1997, Japanese banks already had at least $600 billion in bad debt. As the crisis hit, consumer spending stalled as wages stagnated and companies laid off tens of thousands of workers. Further depressing consumption was a sales tax introduced in 1997 and growing fear that rising levels of public debt would erode the pension system's capacity to provide for Japan's aging population. Hashimoto proposed bureaucratic reforms and economic deregulation measures, but had trouble overcoming opposition from the party's own entrenched interests. He resigned after the LDP lost seats in the July 1998 upper house elections, and was succeeded by Foreign Minister Keizo Obuchi.

In fall 1998, Obuchi got parliament to approve more than $500 billion to restructure debt-ridden banks and to fund the first of several large fiscal stimulus packages. Obuchi also gave the government a lower house majority by forming a coalition in October 1999 with the lay-Buddhist New Komeito party and the Liberal Party, the successor to the NFP.

In a sudden development, Obuchi was incapacitated by a stroke on April 2, 2000, and died in May. Under his successor, Yoshiro Mori, the party secretary-general, the LDP won the most seats in an early election on June 25. Mori had called the election after his popularity slid following several verbal gaffes. Under a 62.4 percent turnout, final results for a smaller, 480-seat parliament gave the LDP 233 seats; the Democratic Party, which had merged with several smaller parties since the last election, 127; New Komeito, 31; the Liberal Party, 22; the Communist Party, 20; the Social Democratic Party (the successor to the JSP), 19; the New Conservative Party (NCP), a Liberal Party splinter, 7; and other parties and independents, 21. The main opposition Democratic Party had campaigned on a platform of deregulation and fiscal tightening. With the economy having grown by only 0.5 percent during the year until March 31, the LDP had pledged to continue spending heavily on public works until the economy recovered. After the election, the LDP formed a coalition government with New Komeito and the NCP.

Dogged by accusations of scandals and incompetence, the government survived a no-confidence motion on November 22, but only after the leader of the LDP's second largest faction and liberal wing, Koichi Kato, backed down from his threat to support the opposition. Several surveys by leading newspapers in November put support for the Mori government at between 15 and 18 percent.

Political Rights and Civil Liberties: The Japanese can change their government through elections. The lower house has 300 single-member, simple plurality districts, and 180 party-list, proportional representation seats. The upper house has 152 single-seat districts and 100 seats chosen by proportional representation. The districts favor the LDP's rural stronghold. The bureaucracy continued to function with limited transparency, and official corruption remained a problem. The Berlin-based Transparency International's 2000 Corruption Perceptions Index ranked Japan in a tie for 23rd place out of 90 countries with a score of 6.4 on a 1-to-10 scale, with Finland, the top-ranked and least corrupt country, receiving a 10.

The 650,000-strong ethnic-Korean community continued to face unofficial discrimination in housing, education, and employment opportunities. Koreans and other ethnic minorities born in Japan are not automatically considered Japanese citizens. Instead, those seeking citizenship must apply for naturalization and submit to an extensive background check. Authorities reportedly frequently deny applications. The three million Burakumin, who are descendants of feudal-era outcasts, and the tiny, indigenous Ainu minority continued to face unofficial discrimination and social ostracism.

The judiciary is independent. The criminal procedure code allows authorities to restrict a suspect's right to counsel during an investigation and bars counsel during interrogations; human rights groups say that in practice, access to counsel is limited. Rights organizations also say that the frequent practice of holding suspects in police cells from arrest to sentencing encourages abuse of detainees, which police sometimes commit to extract confessions. Penal authorities continued to subject prisoners to severe regimentation and dehumanizing punishments. Amnesty International said in August that at Narita Airport, people who are denied entry to Japan are sent to a special, privately run facility, where they are often subjected to torture and ill-treatment.

The press is independent, but is not always outspoken. Exclusive private press clubs provide major media outlets with access to top politicians and bureaucrats. In return, journalists often practice self-censorship regarding the financial condition of troubled companies and banks and other sensitive issues. The press also rarely covers organized crime. The education ministry routinely censors, or orders revisions to, passages in history textbooks describing Japan's World War II atrocities. The supreme court affirmed in 1997 the government's right of censorship, but for the first time ruled that the education ministry had exceeded its authority by censoring references to well-documented Japanese germ warfare experiments in China in the 1940s.

Women face unofficial employment discrimination and are frequently tracked into clerical careers. In recent years, the Ministry of Labor and the Japanese Trade Union Confederation have issued reports suggesting that sexual harassment in the workplace is widespread. A 1997 law banned workplace discrimination and sexual harassment against women and lifted restrictions on women's working hours. However, sanctions for corporate violators are weak. Organized groups continued to traffick women to Japan for purposes of prostitution. Teenage prostitution and child pornography continued to be fairly widespread, despite a 1999 law intended to crack down on both of these problems.

There is full freedom of religion; Buddhism and Shintoism have the most followers. In the wake of the 1995 terrorist attacks in the Tokyo subway by the Aum Shinrikyo cult, the government amended the Religious Corporation Law to give authorities greater oversight of "religious corporations"—religious groups that voluntarily register in order to receive tax benefits and other advantages.

Trade unions are independent and active. Members of the armed forces, police, and firefighters are not allowed to form unions or to strike. Civil servants cannot strike, and they face restrictions on bargaining collectively.

Jordan

Polity: Traditional monarchy and limited parliament
Economy: Mixed capitalist
Population: 5,100,000
PPP: $3,347
Life Expectancy: 70
Ethnic Groups: Arab (98 percent), other (2 percent)
Capital: Amman

Political Rights: 4
Civil Liberties: 4
Status: Partly Free

Overview:
Jordan made strides in 2000 with regard to the economy, foreign relations, and women's rights. However, analysts noted continuing stagnation in the country's democratic development, as promised political reforms went unrealized.

Great Britain installed the Hashemite monarchy in 1921 and granted the country full independence in 1946. King Hussein ascended the throne in 1952. His turbulent reign saw the loss of all territory west of the Jordan River in the 1967 Arab-Israeli War, assassination and coup attempts by Arab nationalists, and sporadic efforts to make peace with Israel. Under the 1952 constitution, executive power rests with the king, who appoints the prime minister and may dissolve the national assembly. The assembly currently consists of a 40-member upper house appointed by the king and an 80-member, directly elected lower house.

In 1989, Hussein responded to riots over fuel price increases by easing restrictions on freedom of expression and ending a 32-year-old ban on political party activity. The Muslim Brotherhood's political wing, the Islamic Action Front (IAF), took 22 seats in general elections that year. The electoral law was amended to prevent such a strong showing in 1993 elections, in which Islamists won 16 seats. Jordan signed a peace treaty with Israel in 1994, formally ending a 46-year state of war. In 1997, nine opposition and Islamist parties, led by the IAF, boycotted parliamentary elections to protest normalization of relations with Israel, restrictions on public freedom, ineffective economic policy, and the electoral law, which left Islamists at a disadvantage with regard to tribal leaders who support the king.

In January 1999, an ailing Hussein dismissed his long-standing heir, his brother Hassan, and named his son Abdullah crown prince in a surprise decision. Abdullah assumed power upon the death of King Hussein in February. Although the late king's motives for naming Abdullah were unclear, the new king's credentials as former commander of the elite internal security force and his marriage to a Palestinian woman help ensure the crucial support of the military and of Palestinians, who constitute about 60 percent of Jordan's population.

Unlike his father, who dedicated most of his energy to Arab-Israeli politics, Abdullah has made Jordan's economy his priority. He inherited a kingdom beset by 20 to 30 percent unemployment, rampant poverty, and an inefficient bureaucracy perceived by most to be widely corrupt. The economic "peace dividend" expected as a result of normalization with Israel has failed to materialize, while sanctions against Iraq and Israeli security measures in the West Bank have blocked Jordanian exports. Since his accession, the government has initiated new intellectual property laws and tax reforms, decreased import duties, privatized state-run freight railway and telecoms systems, and obtained membership in the World Trade Organization, as well as a trade pact with the United States. Signed in October 2000, the agreement makes Jordan the first Arab country to enjoy special access to U.S. markets.

Despite these improvements, both political and economic liberalization have been hampered by the government's need to balance its foreign policy with domestic interests. Increasingly vocal opposition to normalization with Israel by Islamist- and nationalist-led political, professional, and academic associations leads to official crackdowns on their activities. And while Abdullah has improved government relations with the Muslim Brotherhood, Jordan's political system is still carefully controlled to limit Islamist influence. The precarious balance between Jordan's Israel policy and public opinion was highlighted when fighting broke out in late September between Palestinians and Israelis in the West Bank and Gaza. Jordanian authorities banned public demonstrations after massive anti-Israel protests in and around Amman led to violent clashes with police.

A steep decline in popularity due to allegations of corruption, complaints about a lack of political accountability, the 1999 crackdown on the Islamic Resistance Movement (Hamas), and the slow pace of political and economic reform led to the resignation of the government in June. Former Industry and Trade Minister Ali Abul Ragheb was appointed prime minister and assembled a broad-based cabinet that includes Palestinians, Islamists, and nationalists. Despite hopes that the new cabinet would lead Jordan to economic prosperity, analysts noted that all recent governments have been charged by the royal palace with the goals of accountability and economic dynamism, but have failed because they operated within a political system in need of dramatic reform. One political commentator noted that accountability will not exist as long as changes in government are initiated by the monarchy and not by the parliament.

King Abdullah's foreign policy reflects his commitment to economic development and his desire to maintain the support of Islamists and Arab nationalists. While participating in diplomatic efforts to forward the Middle East peace process, Abdullah remained relatively disengaged from Israel. His first official visit there came late, in April 2000, and was described by observers as "lukewarm," involving only superficial discussions of regional issues. As violence flared late in the year in the West Bank and Gaza, Jordan struggled to maintain its relations with Israel as most Arab states froze their existing ties. Tensions increased when two Israeli diplomats were wounded in separate shooting attacks in Amman at the end of the year. Abdullah looked to promote economic cooperation with fellow Arab states, and, most notably, led efforts to end the trade embargo on Iraq by sending the first Arab humanitarian aid flight to Baghdad in September. Prime Minister Abul Ragheb made a landmark visit to Iraq in November, and the two countries agreed to set up an Iraqi-Jordanian oil pipeline. In December, Jordan directly violated sanctions by sending a commercial flight to Iraq. Although the consequences of this move regarding relations with the West are as yet unclear, such a display of support for the Iraqi people undoubtedly boosts the government's image among Arabs at home and abroad.

Political Rights and Civil Liberties: Jordanians cannot change their government democratically. The king holds broad executive powers and may dissolve parliament or dismiss the prime minister or cabinet at his discretion. Parliament may approve, reject, or amend legislation proposed by the cabinet, but is restricted in its ability to initiate legislation. The electoral law and the distribution of parliamentary seats favor pro-Hashemite strongholds. Amendments designed to ensure more equitable participation have yet to materialize.

Security forces arbitrarily arrest and detain citizens, particularly Islamists, and abuse detainees in order to intimidate or extract confessions from them. Suspects in cases involving state security enjoy few procedural safeguards. Lawyers for 28 defendants charged with planning to commit acts of terrorism against Westerners during millennium celebrations accused authorities in May of illegally detaining, beating, and torturing 15 of the suspects who were in custody in Jordan. The other 13 defendants were tried in absentia. The judiciary is subject to executive influence through the justice ministry and a committee whose members are appointed by the king. In August, King Abdullah ordered Prime Minister Abul Ragheb to review Jordan's legal system and report back with recommendations for reform.

The penal code, the State Security Law, the Law for Protecting State Secrets and Documents, and the Contempt of Court law all contain provisions that may be used to restrict freedom of expression and the press. All journalists are required by law to be members of the Jordan Press Association (JPA). Journalists may be expelled from the JPA for breaching its governing code, which prohibits journalists from holding additional jobs outside the profession and from receiving funding from foreign sources. Nidal Mansour, the chief editor of *Al-Hadath* and head of the Center for Defending Freedom of Journalists, was expelled from the JPA in September 2000 for violating both of these provisions, but a court ruling in December froze the JPA decision pending a final court order. *Al-Hadath* was then banned from publication by the information ministry until it appointed a new editor. Broadcasting is state owned and operated, as is Petra, the Jordanian news agency. However, the government began talks with media representatives in June about privatizing the sector. The government owns large shares of the popular *Al-Ra'i* and *Al-Dustour* newspapers. More affluent Jordanians have access to foreign broadcasting via satellite. Prior censorship of foreign publications was lifted in 1999. Jordan inaugurated its first Internet-based community radio station, AmmanNet, in October. Jordan reportedly has some 20,000 Internet subscribers.

The government grants permits for demonstrations, though it may refuse to do so on national security grounds. Police used tear gas and water cannons in April to disperse students protesting a decision by the University of Jordan to appoint half the members of the university's student council, and allow voting only for the other half. The decision was seen as an attempt to limit Islamist influence in the council. Four students were arrested in the demonstrations. Authorities banned public demonstrations in October after police clashed with protesters expressing solidarity with Palestinians during violence in the West Bank and Gaza. Several anti-Israel rallies took place despite the ban, however.

Political parties and other associations are licensed by the government. Jordan currently has some 40 nongovernmental organizations (NGOs), which handle numerous political and social issues, including human rights. While the government may restrict NGO activities, Islamists call upon the authorities to crack down on foreign financing of associations, which is seen as an attempt by the West and Israel to control the country. Hardline professional associations and unions issued a blacklist in November of Jordanian journalists, academics, artists, companies, and schools that have advocated cross cultural and economic ties with Israel. The apparent intention was to punish people who have dealt with Israel and to discourage others from doing so. Some unions revoke membership, and therefore the opportunity to work, for members who associate with Israel.

At least 20 women were reportedly killed by male relatives in 2000 for alleged sexual misconduct. In February, King Abdullah's brother Prince Ali led some 5,000 people in a march to protest laws granting impunity to men who commit honor killings. Although increasing attention to these killings, and activism by Jordanian and international women's groups have raised public interest in the issue, the laws remain on the books. Women may drive, vote, stand in elections, and pursue careers in many professions. However, they constitute only 14 percent of the workforce and hold no seats in the elected legislature. Aside from legal discrimination in matters of divorce, inheritance, pension and social benefits, and travel, women face social pressures that discourage their political and professional participation.

Islam is the state religion; more than 90 percent of the population is Sunni Muslim. Christianity and Judaism are recognized faiths, and the government does not interfere with worship. Although not recognized as a religious minority, Bahais may practice their faith. However, they face legal and social discrimination, and their personal status matters are heard in Islamic Sharia courts. The Palestinian majority faces systematic discrimination in government and military employment and university admission.

More than 30 percent of workers belong to trade unions. All unions belong to the sole trade federation, the General Federation of Jordanian Trade Unions, though membership is not mandatory. Workers have the right to bargain collectively and may strike with government permission. Jordanian labor laws do not protect domestic servants, most of whom are South Asian nationals. Abuse of these workers, including beatings, rape, long work hours, and inadequate food, is reportedly pervasive. Many domestic workers fail to report abuse for fear of deportation.

↓ Kazakhstan

Polity: Presidential (dominant party)
Economy: Mixed statist (transitional)
Population: 14,900,000
PPP: $4,378
Life Expectancy: 68
Ethnic Groups: Kazakh (51 percent), Russian (30 percent), Ukrainian (3 percent), Uzbek (2 percent), Tatar (1 percent), other (13 percent)
Capital: Astana

Political Rights: 6
Civil Liberties: 5
Status: Not Free

Trend Arrow: Kazakhstan received a downward trend arrow due to further expansion of President Nazarbayev's powers and an increasing crackdown on the country's media.

Overview:

As part of a growing trend towards authoritarianism throughout Central Asia, Kazakhstan's parliament overwhelmingly voted to grant President Nursultan Nazarbayev lifelong powers and privileges in June 2000. The legislation, which would increase Nazarbayev's already extensive executive powers, would provide the president with access to key government officials, influence over domestic and foreign policy, and immunity from criminal prosecution. Critics of the move charge that the decision may be a first step towards Nazarbayev's formally being named president-for-life.

This sparsely populated, multiethnic land stretching from the Caspian Sea to the Chinese border was gradually conquered by Russia from the 1730s to the 1840s. The abolition of serfdom in Russia encouraged the migration of large numbers of peasants to Kazakhstan during the second half of the nineteenth century. After a brief attempt at independence in 1917 in the wake of the Russian Revolution, Kazakhstan became an autonomous Soviet republic in 1920 and a union republic in 1936.

Former first secretary of the Communist Party Nursultan Nazarbayev was elected president on December 1, 1991, just two weeks before Kazakhstan declared independence from the U.S.S.R. The country's first national legislative elections, in March 1994, were invalidated by the constitutional court a year later because of numerous irregularities. Nazarbayev subsequently dissolved parliament and called for a referendum on April 29, 1995, in which a reported 95 percent of voters supported the extension of his term until December 2000. An additional referendum in August, which was boycotted by the main opposition parties, approved a new constitution strengthening the powers of the presidency. In December 1995 elections to a new bicameral parliament, Nazarbayev's People's Union of Kazakhstan Unity and its supporters captured most of the seats in the legislature. In December 1997, the country's capital was moved from Almaty to Astana, which had been known as Aqmola until May 1998.

In October 1998, parliament approved Nazarbayev's call for presidential elections to be held in January 1999, almost two years before their scheduled date, as well as an amendment to the constitution extending the presidential term of office from five to seven years. The key challenger, former Prime Minister Akezhan Kazhegeldin, was banned from competing on a legal technicality, while two other candidates were known as supporters of the incumbent. Nazarbayev was reelected over his three challengers with a reported 80 percent of the vote. The Organization for Security and Cooperation in Europe (OSCE), which monitored the elections, refused to recognize the results which it said fell "far short" of being democratic. Nazarbayev's challengers complained of harassment by local authorities, not having equal access to the media, and burdensome registration procedures.

In the September and October 1999 parliamentary vote, which was the first multiparty election in Kazakhstan's history, 33 candidates competed for the 16 seats becoming vacant in the 39-seat upper house (senate), while more than 500 candidates from ten parties vied for the 77 seats of the parliament's lower house (*Majlis*). As expected, Otan, the newly formed party loyal to Nazarbayev, won the single largest number of seats in the Majlis. Despite some improvement since the controversial presidential ballot in January, the parliamentary poll remained deeply flawed. The OSCE noted the obstruction and intimidation of opposition candidates, as well as the lack of independent election commissions.

On June 27, 2000, Kazakhstan's parliament overwhelmingly approved a law giving President Nazarbayev lifetime privileges after the end of his second term in office in 2006. Proposed by the pro-Nazarbayev Civilian Party, which includes some of the country's most influential industrialists, the law provides Nazarbayev with formal access to key government officials to advise them on domestic and foreign policy matters, as well as a permanent place on the Security Council. While some analysts have concluded that the law may lead to Nazarbayev's formally becoming president-for-life, others speculate that he would be content to continue running state affairs behind the scenes after he officially steps down from office.

In July, the multinational Offshore Kazakhstan International Operating Company (OKIOC) announced that test drilling conducted off the Caspian shelf had confirmed the discovery of oil in the East Kashagan field. While Nazarbayev claimed that the deposit would prove to be one of the world's largest, Western oil companies and industry experts remained more cautious in their assessment, concluding only that they were encouraged by initial results. A significant discovery of oil would be critical to the eventual success of the proposed Baku-Ceyhan pipeline, which is backed by Western governments and investors. However, early optimism is tempered by ongoing questions regarding the feasibility of various export route options, concerns about the impact of energy development on the environment, and recent allegations that Western oil firms bribed senior Kazakhstan government officials.

Political Rights and Civil Liberties:

Citizens of Kazakhstan cannot change their government democratically. The constitution grants the president considerable control over the bicameral legislature, the judiciary, and local governments. President Nazarbayev continues to enjoy sweeping executive powers and rules virtually unchallenged. Opposition parties have complained of harassment, surveillance, denial of access to the state-run media, and arbitrary banning from registering candidates. In March 2000, unknown assailants walled in the apartments of three opposition activists in advance of a protest meeting in which they were scheduled to take part.

While the constitution provides for freedom of the press, the government has repeatedly harassed or shut down many independent media outlets. The press is not permitted to criticize the president and his family, and self-censorship on other issues is widespread. The government controls or otherwise influences most newspapers and printing, distribution, and broadcast transmission facilities. Nazarbayev's eldest daughter, Dariga, controls several of the country's television companies, radio stations, and newspapers. Under a November 1999 government decision, all Internet service providers must route their lines through a new state registration system, allowing the state to establish control over the country's access to the Internet. During 2000, several newspapers were forced to close or had politically motivated libel charges brought against them. In May, the Committee to Protect Journalists named Nazarbayev to its annual ten worst enemies of the press list.

The constitution guarantees freedom of worship, although the government sometimes harasses certain non-traditional Islamic and Christian groups. Religious organizations must register with the ministry of justice to receive legal status, without which they cannot engage in legal transactions, including buying or renting property or hiring employees. Religious organizations that have encountered difficulties during registration include Jehovah's Witnesses and some Protestant sects, as well as certain Muslim and Orthodox groups.

The government continued to discriminate in favor of ethnic-Kazakhs in government employment, where Kazakhs predominate, as well as in education and housing. The 1999 Kazakhstani census revealed that, for the first time in decades, recent emigration by Russians had resulted in ethnic-Kazakhs constituting more than half of the country's population. In November 1999, a group of 22 people, including 12 Russian citizens, was arrested in the East Kazakhstan capital of Ust-Kamenogorsk on suspicion of preparing a separatist uprising with the aim of establishing an independent Russian republic in the northeastern part of Kazakhstan. Fourteen members of the group were found guilty in June 2000 and sentenced to up to 18 years in prison, although their terms were reduced the following month.

Freedom of association is hindered by complicated requirements that restrict the right to hold political gatherings. The government has cited minor infractions of the law to arrest and detain government opponents arbitrarily. Although the law gives workers the right to form and join trade unions, it does not provide independent union members with legal recourse from threats and harassment by enterprise management or state-run unions. Members of independent unions have been dismissed, transferred to lower-paying jobs, and threatened.

The constitution significantly constrains the independence of the judiciary, which is subservient to the executive branch. Judges are subject to bribery and political bias, and corruption is evident throughout the judicial system. Police frequently abuse detainees during arrest and interrogation. During 2000, inmates in three separate prisons engaged in mass self-mutilations to protest appalling conditions, including severe overcrowding and inadequate food and medical care.

While the rights of entrepreneurship and private property are legally protected, bureaucratic hurdles, and the control of large segments of the economy by clan elites and government officials loyal to Nazarbayev, limit equality of opportunity and fair competition. Traditional cultural practices and the country's economic problems limit professional opportunities for women, who are severely underrepresented in higher positions in government and in the leadership of state enterprises.

⬇ Kenya

Polity: Dominant party **Political Rights:** 6
Economy: Capitalist **Civil Liberties:** 5
Population: 30,300,000 **Status:** Not Free
PPP: $980
Life Expectancy: 51
Ethnic Groups: Kikuyu (22 percent), Luhya (14 percent),
Luo (13 percent), Kalenjin (12 percent), Kamba (11 percent),
Kisii (6 percent), Meru (6 percent), other African (15 percent), Asian,
European, and Arab (1 percent)
Capital: Nairobi
Trend Arrow: Kenya received a downward trend arrow due to lack of progress on constitutional reform and episodic political violence.

Overview:

Kenya failed to make progress in promoting political rights and civil liberties in 2000. An inconclusive and controversial constitutional reform process made little headway. President Daniel arap Moi signaled his intention to keep power firmly in hand, despite widespread calls for meaningful change. National elections are scheduled to take place no later than 2002, and Kenyan African National Union (KANU) members began to float trial balloons about the possibility of revising the constitution to allow Moi to run again.

Britain conquered Kenya in the late eighteenth century in order to open a route to control the Nile River headwaters in Uganda. In 1963 Kenya achieved its independence. The nationalist leader Jomo Kenyatta was president until his death in 1978, when he was succeeded by Moi. Moi's ascent to the presidency kept KANU in power, but gradually diminished the power of the previously dominant Kikuyu ethnic group.

In 1992, after a lengthy period as, effectively, a one-party state, multiparty elections were held as a result of domestic unrest and pressure from international aid donors. Moi was reelected president in controversial polling. In December 1997 presidential and parliamentary elections were held, and Moi again secured victory over a divided opposition, gaining 40.1 percent of the vote; KANU won 107 of the 220 seats in the newly expanded national assembly. An additional 12 seats were appointed by the government, which in effect gave KANU a majority. Moi's reelection was ensured by massive use of state patronage and the official media to promote his candidacy and by harassment of the divided opposition. Today, there is no clear successor to the longtime president; it is not even clear whether KANU will seek to change the constitution to permit Moi to seek reelection after his current term expires in 2003.

Kenya's politics are divided along ethnic lines. KANU has maintained power through the support of the president's own minority ethnic grouping, the Kalenjin, while combining an alliance of other minority groups and playing the two largest ethnic groups, the Kikuyu and the Luo, off against each other. The country is divided into seven provinces run by provincial commissioners appointed by the president.

In November 1997 the government instituted a number of constitutional changes. These allowed the formation of a coalition government, the review of the constitution by an independent commission (disbanded in 1999), and an increase in the number of directly elected seats in the parliament from 188 to 210. While President Moi initially tried to derail the review process that had been in effect forced on him, in 1998 he changed tack and accepted most opposition demands. However, by mid-1999 Moi changed tack once again and announced that any constitutional review would take place within the government-dominated parliament and would not involve public consultation, promoting suspicions that little will change. This provoked controversy within parliament and prompted public demonstrations in Nairobi.

The 1999 appointment of Richard Leakey, a respected opposition leader and man of unquestioned honesty, as head of the corruption-plagued civil service, and the adoption of an economic reform policy, did result in temporarily improved relations with the IMF and World Bank. It is not clear, however, whether the economic reform program will move ahead, given the political implications of the need to reduce the size of the government bureaucracy, enact anticorruption legislation, and reduce or eliminate extra-budgetary expenditures. In December, the high court declared the Kenya Anti-Corruption Authority (KACA) unconstitutional and therefore illegal, emasculating a body that had been in the process of prosecuting several influential people for graft. Kenya was rated 82nd out of 90 countries in Transparency International's 2000 Corruption Perception Index.

Despite Kenya's history of authoritarian rule, many necessary elements for the development of a democratic political system exist. Opposition parties are active and vocal. The parliament is the setting for much of the nation's political discourse. A varied and energetic civil society plays an important role in public policy debates. The printed press at times adopts independent and probing stances. These elements, however, do not often succeed in translating into actual policy change.

Political Rights and Civil Liberties:

Kenyans have been unable to exercise their right to choose their leaders in genuinely open and competitive elections. Moi's election victories have been achieved through political repression, media control, and dubious electoral procedures. His shrewd ability to play upon divisions within the opposition and to use the form, but not the spirit, of democratic institutions to advance his own interests, and those of KANU, are legendary. Physical violence, a usually docile judiciary, police powers, and executive decrees have been used against political opponents and in efforts to undermine the wider civil society. Power is heavily concentrated in the executive branch of government. In July 2000, Kenyan ministers called for changes to the constitution to allow arap Moi to stay in office after 2002.

The right of citizens to effectively participate in the political life of the country is limited. Legislation that had established the constitutional review process with the participation of a wide range of civic and associational groups was revised in 1999, and the process was channeled through the KANU-controlled parliament. The review proceeded very slowly in 2000, and a competing, unofficial commission, sponsored by the religious community, was organized. These activities took place against the backdrop of national elections, which must be held by 2002. It is unclear whether meaningful reforms can be enacted by then and, if not, whether the opposition would boycott these elections.

Meanwhile, ten opposition MPs scheduled to address a July rally against the government review process were attacked and held hostage in parliament by ruling party youths who also damaged their cars in the presence of police, who did nothing to stop the mayhem. The violent gangs also sealed off the venue of the meeting, which the police then cancelled, citing security reasons.

In 2000 the Kenyan parliament published a "list of shame" identifying by name a number of high-ranking government officials who were implicated in corruption. These included Vice President George Saitoti, Trade and Tourism Minister Nicholas Biwott, a son of Moi and nearly a dozen cabinet members. Under government pressure the report was subsequently revised and the names deleted.

Security forces regularly violate constitutional guarantees regarding detention, privacy, search and seizure. An American priest who was a longtime human rights campaigner was killed, allegedly by pro-KANU assassins. Groups such as the Kenyan Human Rights Commission and the National Council of Churches of Kenya have publicized abuses and demanded respect for civil and political liberties. The government's attitude towards civil society, however, is generally hostile and suspicious. In 1999, for example, a senior government minister warned that if nongovernmental organizations "meddle in politics" they risked deregistration, although such an action would be of questionable legality.

A number of judicial reforms have been announced in recent years. A report on judicial corruption was issued in 1999. Courts, however, are still heavily influenced by the executive and cannot be relied on to protect constitutional rights or to offer fair trials. Local chiefs still exercise sometimes arbitrary and violent power. Prison conditions are harsh and often life threatening.

Freedom of expression is severely limited by lack of access to the dominant state broadcast media and continued repression of the private press. The country's few private radio and television stations are either pro-Moi or carefully apolitical. Private print media remain vibrant, but under serious threat. Journalists have been charged with criminal libel, and independent publications are subject to harassment in their business operations. Moi has decreed that it is a crime to "insult" him, and sedition laws have been employed in efforts to silence any criticism.

Trade unions generally follow government policy on key issues. For example, the general-secretary of Central Organisations of Trade Unions (COTU) instructed members not to support calls by opposition parties and civil society groups for demonstrations over constitutional reform. Unions have occasionally defied a 1993 ministry of labor decree that forbids all strikes, despite constitutional guarantees to the contrary. Civil servants and university academic staff may join only government-designated unions. Approximately one-fifth of the country's 1.5 million industrial workforce is unionized.

Ethnically based tension continues in parts of Kenya. Competing land claims often provide the spark. In August, for example, three people were killed in ongoing tribal clashes between the Masai and Kipsigis communities in central Kenya. Pro-KANU elements have been accused of instigating ethnic cleansing for political purposes. A Judicial Commission on Tribal Clashes has been appointed, but it has had little effect.

Kenya's economy and infrastructure continued to deteriorate significantly. Most of Kenya's 29 million people are poor and survive through subsistence agriculture. Nepotism and fraud inhibit economic opportunity and discourage greater foreign investment. Excessive government regulation concerning economic activity breeds corruption.

In general, there is freedom of religion, although uneasy relations between Muslims and other faiths at times result in violence. For example, a mosque erected by newly converted Muslims in the Rift Valley, the scene of considerable ethnic conflict, was burned, allegedly by police officers. In early 2000, rioting between Catholics and Moslems occurred in central Kenya.

Women in Kenya continue to face serious obstacles in the exercise of their freedoms. A draft gender-equity bill created considerable public controversy, with some Muslims protesting that it was too sweeping in scope. Some evidence suggests that violence against women in increasing. A survey carried out by a women's rights group states that more than 49 women were murdered by their spouses in 1998 alone, a 79 percent increase in cases since 1995. Many of the cases have gone unpunished, despite repeated complaints by women's groups that Kenyan laws remain too lenient in sentencing offenders in cases of violence against women.

Women are also seriously underrepresented in Kenya's politics and government. With only 7 women legislators in a 222-member parliament, Kenya ranks last among the 15 eastern and southern African countries in its number of women legislators.

Kiribati

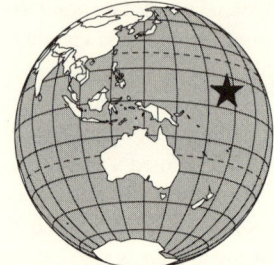

Polity: Presidential parliamentary democracy
Economy: Capitalist-statist
Population: 100,000
PPP: na
Life Expectancy: 62
Ethnic Groups: Micronesian (84 percent), Polynesian (14 percent), other (2 percent)
Capital: Tarawa

Political Rights: 1
Civil Liberties: 1
Status: Free

Overview:

For many years, Kiribati has marketed its location along the equator as a site for monitoring satellite launches and operations for foreign countries. In May, an agreement was signed with Japan's National Space Development Agency to begin a multimillion-dollar spaceport project on Christmas Island. This agreement gives Japan seven-year lease-free access, allowing unmanned space shuttles, launched from Japan, to land on the island. Negotiations are also under way with an American consortium.

The Republic of Kiribati consists of 33 inhabited islands of the Gilbert, Line, and Phoenix groups scattered over two million square miles of the central Pacific Ocean, as well as Banaba Island in the west. The country, with a Micronesian majority and a Polynesian minority, achieved independence from Great Britain in 1979.

The first post-independence legislative elections were held in March 1982. In July 1991, President Ieremia Tabai, the republic's first president, served out his third and final term. Tetao Teannaki, who received Tabai's backing, defeated Roniti Teiwaki in the presidential race. In May 1994, however, Teannaki was forced to resign after his government lost a vote of no-confidence introduced by the parliamentary opposition, which accused his administration of financial irregularities. In accordance with the constitution, a three-member caretaker Council of State, consisting of the speaker of parliament, the chief justice, and the chairman of the Public Service Commission (PSC), took over government authority until new elections were held. A brief constitutional crisis ensued after acting head of state Tekira Tameura was removed forcibly, on the grounds that his tenure as chairman of the PSC had expired three days earlier. In September 1994, the parliament elected Teburoro Tito as president with 51 percent of the votes. Tito was elected to a second term in November 1998. In 1999, Kiribati became a full member of the United Nations.

Like many other Pacific Island countries at low elevation, Kiribati is increasingly concerned about the impact of global climate change on surrounding sea levels. A new, independent newspaper, *The New Star*, was launched in May 2000 by former President Ieremia Tabai and former government publications manager Ngauea Uatioa. In September, the government decided to bar a New Zealand-based reporter from entering Kiribati to cover the Pacific Islands Forum, the annual summit meeting for leaders in the region. The reporter attributes this ban to his writings condemning pollution in the country and a Chinese satellite-monitoring base in South Tarawa. The Kiribati government said the ban is for the journalist's personal safety, as locals have been offended by his writing.

Political Rights and Civil Liberties: Citizens of Kiribati can change their government democratically. The 1979 constitution established a unicameral legislature, the Maneba ni Maungatabu, with 40 members directly elected for a four-year term, one appointed member, and one ex-officio member. The president, serving as both head of state and head of the government, is chosen in a nationwide ballot from among three or four candidates selected by parliament, and is limited to three terms. Local island councils serve all inhabited islands. Several parties exist, but most lack true platforms and are organized around specific issues or in support of particular individuals. Subsequent to the 1994 constitutional crisis, a five-member committee was established to review the 1979 constitution.

Freedom of speech and of the press is generally respected. The government-run radio station and newspaper offer diverse views, and Protestant and Catholic churches publish newsletters and other periodicals. The *New Star*, the new, independent newspaper, launched by Tabai and Uatioa in May 2000, now competes against the government's *Te Uekera*. Tabai and Uatioa have also tried unsuccessfully to establish an FM radio station in Kiribati. In 1999, they were fined for importing broadcasting equipment for the proposed radio station without a proper license.

While Christianity is the predominant religion, there is no state religion and freedom of worship is respected. The constitution provides for freedom of assembly and association, and these rights are respected in practice. More than 90 percent of the workforce is involved in fishing and subsistence farming. The Kiribati Trade Union Congress represents the small wage sector and has approximately 2,500 members. The law provides for the right to strike. The last strike occurred in 1980.

The judiciary is independent and free of government interference. The judicial system is modeled on English common law and provides adequate due process rights. The police force of about 250 is under civilian control. Traditional customs permit corporal punishment, and island councils on some outer islands occasionally order such punishment for petty theft and other minor offenses.

Citizens are free to travel domestically and abroad. The law prohibits interference in personal or family matters, and the government respects these provisions in practice. Women enjoy full rights to own and inherit property. Although gender discrimination persists in many areas, employment opportunities for women in this traditionally male-dominated society are slowly improving. In May 2000, trade unions launched a nationwide campaign to urge government and private employers to support comprehensive standards of maternity protection for working women.

Korea, North

Polity: One-party
Economy: Statist
Population: 21,700,000
PPP: na
Life Expectancy: 70
Ethnic Groups: Korean
Capital: Pyongyang

Political Rights: 7
Civil Liberties: 7
Status: Not Free

Overview:

North Korea undertook a string of surprising diplomatic initiatives. The most important was the historic three-day summit between the leaders of North and South Korea on June 13 in Pyongyang. The two sides agreed to promote economic cooperation and work towards reconciliation and reunification, with some kind of confederation, or "one country, two systems," as the preferred outcome. In early 2001, Kim is expected to make a reciprocal visit to Seoul in early 2001.

However, these diplomatic moves by Pyongyang were not matched by positive changes domestically. In fact, there were no improvements in political rights and civil liberties. Mass starvation is also never far away. The regime spends on arms, buying weapons from Russia and other countries and building missiles, using the lives of its people and its military arsenal as bargaining chips in international negotiations. A food crisis is expected in 2001. Some 2.4 million North Koreans are believed to have died from starvation in recent years. United Nations agencies are appealing for nearly $400 million in food aid, more than three times their request for 2000.

The Democratic Republic of Korea (DPRK) was established on September 9, 1948, following the end of World War II and the partition of the Korean peninsula by the Soviet-led Communist forces and U.S.-led Western democracies. With assistance from Moscow, Kim Il-Sung, a former Soviet army officer, became head of the North Korean government. In June 1950, Kim, with Soviet military support, invaded South Korea in an attempt to reunify the peninsula under Communist rule. The three-year Korean War ended in a truce after intervention by U.S. and Chinese troops, and left the two Koreas bitterly divided.

Throughout the cold war, Kim Il-Sung solidified his power base in the north through an extensive personality cult and the development of *Juche* (self-reliance), a homegrown ideology said to be an application of Marxism-Leninism specific to North Korea. In practice, it became an ideological justification for Communist leadership under

Kim's rule and for the pervasive Stalinist control of the economy and all aspects of public and private life.

By the 1990s, the North Korean economy was in negative growth annually. Disintegration of the Soviet Union in 1991 meant the loss of Pyongyang's cold war patrons in Moscow, and increasing isolation for North Korea. Kim Il-Sung died suddenly of a heart attack in 1994. His son and appointed successor Kim Jong-Il assumed power. This was the first known Communist dynastic succession. The young Kim delayed formally assuming positions of power, becoming general secretary of the Korean Workers' Party only in 1997. In 1998, the Korean legislature revised the socialist constitution and renamed it as the "Kim Jong-Il Constitution," thus marking the beginning of the Kim Jong-Il era. The legislature also abolished the post of president. This made the National Defense Commission (NDC) the highest organ of power in the North Korean government, and its chairman the de facto head of state. Kim was elected to head the NDC. He also heads the ruling party and is the supreme military commander.

Government mismanagement, natural disasters, and the end of food subsidies from former Communist allies have brought massive famine in recent years. The government accepts food aid from overseas, but reports allege that food aid is often diverted to military and government officials. Since Kim Jong-Il consolidated power in 1998, North Korea has tried to bring in foreign investment, while simultaneously asserting its independence and power in regional affairs. Hyundai, a top conglomerate in South Korea, agreed to transfer $906 million over six years to develop a tourist facility in the North and to organize tours for South Koreans. The first group of South Koreans visited Diamond Mountain in the North in November 1998 under heavily restricted conditions. Pyongyang has also opened free-economic zones, such as in Rajin-Sonbong and the Nampo-Wonson area south of the capital, as a way to revive the economy without undertaking serious reform. North Korean border crossings to trade in China have increased, and Pyongyang has not curbed these exchanges.

In recent years, Pyongyang has played a high-risk game of missile and nuclear threats to extract aid from the United States and Japan. In August 1998, North Korea launched a missile which flew over the northern Japanese island of Hokkaido and crashed into the Pacific Ocean. Pyongyang claimed that the launch was part of an effort to put a satellite into space. Both the United States and Japan reacted with tightened sanctions against North Korea. In September 1999, North Korea and the United States agreed in Berlin that North Korea would suspend long-range missile testing in exchange for easing of comprehensive sanctions imposed by the United States. The next day, North Korea made an unusual call for inter-Korean dialogues at all levels of government and society. In December 1999, Japan lifted the remaining sanctions: a freeze on talks to normalize bilateral relations and suspension of food aid.

North Korea is also suspected of building nuclear weapons. Pyongyang sought $300 million in cash and food aid from the United States in exchange for rights to inspect a site north of Pyongyang. U.S. rejection of this demand threatened to undermine the 1994 Framework Agreement under which North Korea agreed to give up its nuclear program in exchange for light-water reactors, which could not easily be used to make weapons. A breakthrough occurred on March 16, 1999, when Pyongyang agreed to open the facility in question to a U.S. team in May 1999, May 2000, and thereafter, in exchange for a U.S. pledge to launch an agriculture project in North Korea and to provide 100,000 tons of food aid. In December 1999, an agreement to build two of the light-water reactors was signed.

The series of diplomatic surprises in 2000 began with the opening of relations with Italy. Following the summit in June, Foreign Minister Paek Nam Sun attended the Association of Southeast Asian Nations (ASEAN) Regional Forum in Bangkok, in July, to use the opportunity to improve bilateral ties with the United States, China, Australia, Russia, Japan and Canada. In the same month, the two Koreas agreed to reopen border liaison offices at Panmunjom and to reconnect a rail link between the two sides. The first family reunions, which brought together 100 families from each side, was held in August. About 7.6 million South Koreans are believed to have relatives in the North.

In September, the two Koreas marched under one banner at the Summer Olympic Games in Australia. In the same month, defense chiefs from the two sides discussed plans to clear mines in the demarcation area to aid the reopening of land transport links. In October, senior North Korea military commander and vice chairman of the National Defense Commission (NDC), Jo Myong Rok, met U.S. president Bill Clinton in Washington, D.C. U.S. secretary of state Madeline Albright visited Pyongyang on October 22 for talks with Kim Jong-Il to clarify North Korea's position on its missile program and its view on the future of U.S. troops in South Korea. Kim Jong-Il was reported to favor the continued presence of U.S. forces to check Russian, Chinese and Japanese influence, and was reported to consider giving up North Korea's missile program, which earns the country about $500 million in overseas sales, in exchange for international assistance to launch civilian satellites. Albright was the highest level U.S. official to visit North Korea. In November, Pyongyang accepted a United Nations proposal to build a railway linking the two Koreas. A second round of North-South government talks followed in December. The North wanted economic aid but the South was eager to expand joint humanitarian projects.

Whether it is brinkmanship politics or diplomacy, it is clear that North Korea and its leadership need outside help to survive. And Pyongyang has been very successful. In food aid alone, North Korea obtained 200,000 tons of fertilizers—valued at $60 million—from South Korea before the summit, and another 100,000 tons after the meeting. In October, Seoul sent 500,000 tons of food aid. Since 1994, the share of North Korea's food imports obtained on concession terms has grown from zero to more than 80 percent.

Political Rights and Civil Liberties:

North Korea is arguably the most tightly controlled country in the world. Its citizens cannot change their government democratically. Elections are held regularly, but all candidates are state-sponsored and belong either to the ruling Workers' Party or to smaller, state-organized parties. The Supreme People's Assembly, nominally the highest organized state power, provides little more than a veneer of legitimacy to government decisions. Opposition parties are illegal, and there is little organized dissent as a result of the regime's repression, widespread internal surveillance, and isolationist policies. Even the most basic elements of a civil society do not exist in North Korea.

The judicial system consists of the Central Court, under which there are various municipal courts. The SPA has the power to elect and recall the president of the Central Court. The criminal law subjects citizens to arbitrary arrest, detention, and execution for "counterrevolutionary crimes" and other broadly defined political offenses. In practice, these can include nonviolent acts such as attempted defection, criticism of the leadership, and listening to foreign broadcasts. Defense lawyers persuade defendants to plead guilty rather than advocating for them. The rule of law is nonexistent.

Prison conditions are characterized by severe mistreatment of prisoners and, by some accounts, frequent summary executions. The regime operates "reeducation through labor" camps that reportedly hold tens of thousands of political prisoners and their families. Defectors say some political prisoners are "reeducated" and released after a few years, while others are held indefinitely.

Authorities implement arbitrary checks of residences, use electronic surveillance, and maintain a network of informants to monitor the population. At school, children are encouraged to report on their parents. The government assigns a security rating to each individual that, to a somewhat lesser extent than in the past, still determines access to education, employment, and health services. North Koreans face a steady onslaught of propaganda from radios and televisions that are pretuned to government stations.

Travel within the country generally requires a permit, which is normally granted only for state business, weddings, or funerals, although some reports suggest that internal travel restrictions have been slightly eased. Travel into the capital is heavily restricted, with permission usually granted only for government business. The government reportedly forcibly resettles politically suspect citizens. Chinese authorities return some refugees and defectors at the border, many of whom are reportedly summarily executed. Chinese sources say many North Koreans are, in fact, captured by North Korean agents operating across the border. Only a handful of foreign journalists are accredited in North Korea, and entry for foreign visitors is highly restricted.

The General Federation of Trade Unions is the sole legal trade union federation, and its affiliates are used to monitor workers. The regime does not permit strikes, collective bargaining, or other core labor activity. Religious practice is restricted to state-sponsored Buddhist and Christian services. Private property ownership is prohibited. Women are given equal status under the law, but they continue to battle gender discrimination at home and at work.

Korea, South

Polity: Presidential-parliamentary democracy
Economy: Capitalist-statist
Population: 47,300,000
PPP: $13,478
Life Expectancy: 73
Ethnic Groups: Korean
Capital: Seoul

Political Rights: 2
Civil Liberties: 2
Status: Free

Overview:

Midway through his five-year term, South Korean president Kim Dae Jung pushed forward with plans to shut down, privatize, or restructure heavily indebted firms despite strong opposition from labor unions, which had helped elect him in 1997. Although Kim argued that painful measures were needed to avoid a repeat of the financial crisis that wracked the economy in 1997, union leaders said that workers faced tens of thousands of layoffs and were being forced to shoulder the brunt of the restructuring costs.

The Republic of Korea was formally established in 1948, three years after the United States and the Soviet Union divided the Korean Peninsula. In the next four decades, authoritarian rulers directed an industrialization drive that transformed a poor, agrarian country into the eleventh-largest economy in the world.

South Korea's democratic transition began in 1987, when strongman Chun Doo Hwan and his chosen successor, Roh Tae Woo, conceded to direct presidential elections amid widespread student protests. Roh beat South Korea's best-known dissidents, Kim Young Sam and Kim Dae Jung, in presidential elections in December 1987.

Kim Young Sam merged his party with the ruling party in 1990 to form the conservative Democratic Liberal Party (DLP), and won the 1992 presidential election to become the first civilian president since 1961. Kim curbed the powers of the domestic security services, sacked hardline military officers, prosecuted former Presidents Chun and Roh for corruption and treason, and launched an anticorruption campaign. However, Kim's popularity waned as the reforms slowed. His DLP, renamed the New Korea Party, won only a plurality with 139 seats, a loss of 10, in parliamentary elections in April 1996.

By early 1997, an economic slowdown had forced eight highly indebted *chaebols* (business conglomerates) into bankruptcy and exposed serious weaknesses in the heavily indebted private sector. With the country perhaps weeks away from a private sector debt default, the government agreed in early December to a $57 billion International Monetary Fund-led bailout, in return for commitments to restructure companies and end lifetime labor guarantees. Amid the country's worst economic crisis in decades, on December 18, Kim Dae Jung became the first opposition candidate to win a presidential election. Backed by organized labor and his core support base in the southwestern Cholla region, Kim won 40.4 percent of the vote and defeated two conservative candidates, Lee Hoi Chang of the ruling party, renamed the Grand National Party (GNP), and Rhee In Je, a ruling party defector.

The Kim administration quickly persuaded foreign creditors to restructure some $150 billion in private sector debt and signed laws ending a tradition of lifetime employment. While gross domestic product contracted 5.8 percent in 1998, it grew by 10.7 percent in 1999. Yet Kim's ambitious plans to inject cash into struggling banks, to allow them to shut down or restructure indebted companies, faced strong opposition from trade unions, which argued that workers were being forced to accept widespread layoffs while the chaebols had made few changes to their business practices.

Despite losing some support among workers, Kim's Millennium Democratic Party (MDP) reduced the GNP's plurality in parliamentary elections on April 13, 2000. Under a record-low 57 percent turnout, final results for the 273 parliamentary seats gave the GNP 133 seats; the MDP, 115; the conservative United Liberal Democrats, 17; the conservative Democratic People's Party, 2; and independents, 6. During the campaign, the GNP had criticized the administration's restructuring plans as well as the speed of Kim's rapprochement with hardline North Korea, which led to the first-ever summit meeting between leaders of the two countries in June. The government ran on its record of returning economic growth to double-digit levels. However, the unemployment rate, though relatively low at 5 percent, remained above pre-crisis levels, and wages for most workers remained lower than before the crisis.

Although several unions held rallies late in the year to protest impending layoffs, the administration's corporate restructuring plans received a boost in November, when a group of creditors said they would force 52 firms to be liquidated, placed under receivership, sold, or merged. Separately, unions at Daewoo Motor, the country's second-largest carmaker, agreed to layoffs.

Political Rights and Civil Liberties:

South Koreans can change their government through elections. The 1988 constitution vested executive powers in a president who is directly elected for a five-year term, but imposed a one-term limit on the president and took away his power to dissolve the national assembly, which is directly elected for a four-year term. The national assembly has 227 members elected in single-member, simple-plurality districts and 46 elected via proportional representation. The prime minister is responsible to the president.

The judiciary is independent. However, according to the United States State Department's country report for 1999, "several recent scandals involving alleged illegal influence peddling and cronyism have damaged the image of prosecutors and judges." Moreover, the opposition continued to accuse the government of selectively prosecuting political opponents and other critics on tax evasion and other charges. In recent years, human rights organizations have reported that while police continue to abuse detainees to extract confessions, the number of such cases has declined.

A former dissident, President Kim has released dozens of long-term political prisoners held under the National Security Law (NSL), which broadly defines espionage and permits authorities to detain and arrest suspects for allegedly pro-North Korean acts. However, since coming to office, the administration has also used the NSL to arrest hundreds of students, labor leaders, and political activists. While authorities arrested some suspects on espionage charges, they arrested many others for what appeared to be peaceful expression or activity, including traveling to North Korea or distributing pro-Pyongyang literature. Courts handed down suspended sentences or short prison terms to most of those arrested, but long prison sentences to others. Officials justified the continued use of the NSL by citing the omnipresent North Korean security threat. The U.S. State Department estimated in its 1999 country report that the number of political prisoners appeared to be "under 200."

In recent years, some opposition politicians have claimed that they were being illegally wiretapped. These claims are somewhat plausible but difficult to verify.

The print media, which are privately owned, operate under several constraints. They include the government's arrest and jailing of several journalists in recent years under criminal libel laws. Press groups say that politicians and businesses use the libel laws to punish journalists for articles that are critical but factually accurate. In addition, the New York-based Committee to Protect Journalists said in 1999 that newspaper owners often urge journalists to avoid critical coverage of economic and business affairs. Most broadcast media are subsidized by the state, but they offer diverse views.

Civic groups continued to be highly active in promoting social and political reform. In January, a nonpartisan alliance of some 470 nongovernmental organizations, called Citizens' Solidarity, published the names of 114 members of the national assembly and candidates for the upcoming parliamentary elections that it said were unfit to hold office, because of alleged tax evasion, corruption, and other wrong doing.

Religious freedom is respected. Women face unofficial societal and employment discrimination and are frequently the first to be laid off during corporate restructuring. Rape, domestic violence, and sexual harassment continued to be serious problems. The government has generally been responsive to these issues. Members of the small ethnic-Chinese community cannot obtain citizenship or become civil servants and face some societal discrimination.

In recent years, authorities have prevented some demonstrations under a law that permits them to prohibit assemblies on public order grounds. However, students and workers continued to hold numerous demonstrations with minimal government interference.

The two largest trade unions are vigorous even though they have a combined membership of only 1.6 million workers. The 1998 Trade Union Labor Relations Adjustment Act will permit multiple unions at the company level beginning in 2002. The law prohibits defense and white-collar government workers from forming unions, although the latter can form more limited workplace councils. It also prohibits strikes in government agencies, state-run enterprises, and defense industries. The Kim administration has prosecuted some workers for allegedly instigating violent strikes or organizing strikes deemed illegal. Riot police broke up at least two major strike actions in 2000. Authorities rarely prosecute employers for labor violations, including illegally firing workers or physically abusing and forcing foreign workers to work longer hours and for less pay than initially promised.

While the Kim administration has introduced various anticorruption measures, including investigations into tax evasion, anecdotal reports continued to suggest that bribery, extortion by officials, and influence peddling are pervasive in politics, business, and daily life. The London-based *Economist* reported in April that some observers expected candidates for the legislative elections to spend, on average, ten times the legal campaign spending limit. The Berlin-based Transparency International's 2000 Corruption Perception Index ranked South Korea 48th out of 90 countries with a score of 4.0 on a 1 to 10 scale. The top-ranked and least-corrupt country, Finland, received a score of 10.

Kuwait

Polity: Traditional monarchy and limited parliament
Economy: Capitalist-statist
Population: 2,200,000
PPP: $25,314
Life Expectancy: 76
Ethnic Groups: Kuwaiti (45 percent), other Arab (35 percent), South Asian (9 percent), Iranian (4 percent), other (7 percent)
Capital: Kuwait City

Political Rights: 4
Civil Liberties: 5
Status: Partly Free

Overview:

An ongoing struggle between the government and parliament continued to hinder legislative progress, particularly on badly needed economic reforms. Meanwhile, Kuwaiti women took their fight for political rights to their country's highest court in 2000.

The al-Sabah family has ruled Kuwait since 1756. Under a special treaty, Kuwait ceded control of its foreign affairs and defense to Britain in 1899. The emirate gained full independence in 1961, and the 1962 constitution assigns broad executive powers to the emir, currently Sheikh Jaber al-Ahmad al-Jaber al-Sabah, who rules through an appointed prime minister and cabinet. The government shares power with the parliament, or national assembly, which is subject to dissolution or suspension by decree.

The legislative process has been paralyzed in recent years by a struggle between the government, which wants to reform the economic and financial sectors to offset dependence on oil revenues, and largely Islamist opposition parliamentarians, who oppose any perceived "Westernization," or measures that would endanger social spending. Sheikh Jaber dissolved parliament in May 1999 following a crisis that ensued when members of parliament threatened a no-confidence vote against the Islamic affairs minister over 120,000 misprinted copies of the Koran. Kuwaitis elected a new parliament in July. Another crisis erupted in February 2000 when the emir cancelled government penalties against two newspapers for publishing a "fabricated" emiri decree. MPs accused the cabinet of abusing its power, asserting that only the courts have the right to sanction newspapers. In December, the housing affairs minister was subject to a no-confidence vote over government measures to cut benefits that offer Kuwaitis homes under very generous loan terms.

Analysts have recently noted a conservative Islamist backlash in Kuwait characterized by attempts to impose stricter religious codes and limit foreign social influences. More women are covering themselves with the *hijab*, or traditional veil, while hardliners try to ban social events such as public concerts. In June, parliament voted to allow the establishment of private universities, but required that they be segregated by sex. In October, mounting criticism from Islamists over the government's "liberal" media policy led to the resignation of the information minister. In rare instances, attacks have occurred against video shops, newspapers, and expatriate workers. A woman was brutally beaten in April for not wearing the hijab, leading some liberal MPs and journalists to warn of "Algerian-style violence." However, Islamist groups in Kuwait are traditionally peaceful, and most condemned the incident.

A 1999 emiri decree granting women the right to vote was narrowly defeated by parliament last November. Currently, the electorate includes only Kuwaiti men over age 21 and those who have been naturalized for at least 20 years. In March 2000, several women's rights activists sued the interior ministry, demanding full political rights. While most of the cases were thrown out of administrative court, one was referred to the constitutional court in May. A decision is expected in January 2001.

Economists routinely express concern about the sustainability of Kuwait's cradle-to-grave welfare state. Some 95 percent of working Kuwaitis draw monthly tax-free salaries from the state, while an estimated 55 percent of the workforce is "underemployed," or placed in menial state jobs for the sake of employment statistics. A surge in oil prices in 2000 boosted the country's financial situation but provided little incentive to reform. Opposed to austerity measures that would place an economic burden on citizens, MPs sometimes launch investigations into alleged mismanagement and corruption by ministers in order to block government initiatives to cut the fiscal deficit, privatize state-run industries, and promote foreign investment.

In January, Alaa Hussein, the Kuwaiti appointed by Iraq to head Kuwait's interim government after the 1990 Iraqi invasion, was arrested upon his arrival in the country after ten years in exile. He had been sentenced to death in absentia for treason by a special state security court in 1993. A criminal court upheld the death sentence in May, as did an appeals court in July. Hussein has a final appeal to the court of cassation pending. In September, the United Nations Security Council awarded Kuwait $15.9 billion in compensation for lost oil production during the seven-month Iraqi occupation.

Political Rights and Civil Liberties:

Kuwaitis cannot change their government democratically. Political parties are illegal, although de facto groupings are tolerated. Under the 1962 constitution, the national assembly has limited power to approve the emir's choice of crown prince. The emir holds executive authority and rules through an appointed prime minister (usually the crown prince) and an appointed council of ministers. Legislative authority is shared by the emir and the national assembly, which is subject to dissolution by decree. Women, citizens naturalized for fewer than 20 years, members of the armed forces, the police, and other interior ministry personnel may not vote or seek election to the national assembly. In 1999, several national assembly candidates were prosecuted for defamation of government officials during an election campaign marked by widespread verbal attacks against the government for alleged corruption. About 30 tribal leaders were also prosecuted for holding illegal primary elections.

Parliament has waged an aggressive campaign against government corruption in recent years. In May, the assembly demanded that the government provide reports three times a year about several high-profile graft cases that have emerged in the past ten years, involving hundreds of millions of dollars and a number of senior officials. The demand is not binding on the government, which enjoys immunity from prosecution, and it is unclear as yet whether ministers will comply.

The emir appoints all judges, and renewal of many judicial appointments is subject to government approval. One court system tries both civil and criminal cases. *Sharia* (Islamic law) courts for Sunnis and Shia handle family law cases. Defendants have the right to appeal verdicts and to be represented by legal counsel, which the courts provide in criminal cases. Suspects may be detained for four days before being brought before an investigating official. People convicted of collaboration with Iraq during the 1990-1991 occupation remain incarcerated. Most of those tried in the Martial Law Court in 1991 and the Special State Security Court, which was abolished in 1995, did not receive fair trials. The UN Human Rights Committee issued a report in July expressing concern over the large number of offenses for which Kuwaiti courts can impose the death penalty, including vaguely defined offenses related to national security and also drug-related crimes.

The Printing and Publications Law and the penal code may both be used to restrict freedom of expression, and although prepublication censorship was abolished in 1992, journalists practice self-censorship. Direct criticism of the emir or of relations with other states, material deemed offensive to religion, incitement to violence, hatred, or dissent, and news that "affects the value of the national currency" are punishable by imprisonment and/or fines. The government announced plans in September to amend press laws to reduce penalties against journalists and to make it more difficult for authorities to shut down newspapers. Enforcement of restrictions is arbitrary. Newspapers are privately owned and frequently criticize government policies and officials. Two women were sentenced to prison in January for using "indecent language" and ridiculing religion in books they authored, but their sentences were converted to fines by an appeals court in March. Broadcasting is completely state owned. Citizens have access to foreign programs through satellite dishes, which are widely available.

Public gatherings require government approval. Informal, family-based, almost exclusively male social gatherings called *diwaniyas* provide a forum for political discussion. The law gives the government full authority to regulate, ban, or license any society and prohibits clubs and associations from engaging in political activities. The government denies formal recognition to human rights nongovernmental organizations and restricts their ability to organize publicly. However, some informal gatherings by human rights activists are tolerated. The parliamentary human rights committee has complained of government interference with their visits to prisons.

Women face discrimination in legal and social matters. Sharia courts give a woman's testimony lesser weight than that of a man; women must have permission of a male relative to obtain a passport; and only men are able to confer citizenship on children. Women are also legally disadvantaged in matters of marriage, divorce, and inheritance. The penal code provides relative impunity for men who commit violent crimes against women. Seven men were acquitted in June of attacking a female student for not wearing the hijab. An appeals court later sentenced four of them to a year in prison. An apparent increase in conservative Islamic sentiment may mean greater restrictions for women. Kuwait University announced plans in November to impose stricter dress codes on women. Women are prohibited from certain professions, such as the judiciary, but the field of possibility is widening. In December, the interior ministry announced that it would begin training women as police officers. At year's end, the constitutional court was considering an amendment to the election law that would grant women the right to vote.

Islam is the state religion, and both Sunnis and Shia worship freely. The government recognizes the Christian community of more than 150,000, including Roman and Greek Catholics, National Evangelicals (Protestants), Greek and Armenian Orthodox,

Coptic Orthodox, and Maronites. Leaders of these churches describe the government as tolerant. Hindus, Sikhs, Bahais, and Buddhists may not build places of worship, but may worship privately without interference. They number more than 60,000. A ban on organized, non-Muslim religious education is not widely enforced. In April, a gunman, presumably a Sunni extremist, opened fire on a Shiite religious center.

Some 120,000 *bidoon*, or stateless people, are considered illegal residents and denied citizenship and civil rights, including the right to travel, to register births, deaths, and marriages, and to confer Kuwaiti citizenship on their children. An estimated 240,000 live outside Kuwait because the state does not permit them to return. In October 1999, the interior ministry initiated a nine-month program during which bidoon who renounced Kuwaiti nationality could apply for five-year residency permits and other benefits. Almost immediately following the June 27, 2000 deadline, deportation procedures began against people deemed in violation of nationality and alien residence laws. A committee was established in July to handle cases of bidoon ordered deported. Some 37,000 bidoon reportedly became eligible for citizenship under amendments to the nationality law in May. In October, the government provisionally agreed to grant citizenship to 1,000 bidoon and their families.

The government maintains financial control over unions through subsidies that account for 90 percent of some union budgets. Only one union is permitted per industry or profession, and only one labor federation, the pro-government Kuwaiti Trade Union Federation, exists. Workers may strike, but no law protects them from resulting legal or administrative action. Roughly 100,000 foreigners who work as domestic servants are not protected under labor law and are vulnerable to physical and sexual abuse by employers. In March, India announced that because of such abuses, it would no longer issue immigration clearances to Indian nationals seeking domestic employment in Kuwait.

Kyrgyz Republic

Polity: Presidential
Economy: Mixed statist (transitional)
Population: 4,900,000
PPP: $2,317
Life Expectancy: 68
Ethnic Groups: Kyrgyz (52 percent), Russian (18 percent), Uzbek (13 percent), Ukrainian (3 percent), other (14 percent)
Capital: Bishkek

Political Rights: 6*
Civil Liberties: 5
Status: Not Free

Ratings Change: The Kyrgyz Republic's political rights rating changed from 5 to 6, and its status from Partly Free to Not Free, due to the holding of parliamentary and presidential elections that were neither free nor fair, and the further consolidation of power by the country's president.

Overview: Once regarded as Central Asia's greatest hope for democracy, the Kyrgyz Republic saw its reputation increasingly tarnished by seriously flawed February parliamentary and October presidential polls. President Askar Akayev's government stepped up its efforts to silence critics of the regime by barring opposition candidates and parties from competing in both elections, and by bringing politically motivated criminal charges against the most influential opposition figures. In an widely anticipated victory, President Akayev was overwhelmingly reelected to another five-year term in what international observers and opposition groups condemned as an undemocratic election marred by widespread irregularities.

Populated by nomadic herders and ruled by tribal leaders for centuries, the Kyrgyz Republic was conquered by Russia in the mid-1800s and incorporated into the Soviet Union in 1924. Following a declaration of independence from the U.S.S.R. in August 1991, Askar Akayev, a respected physicist, was elected president two months later in the country's first direct presidential vote. While Akayev introduced multiparty elections and pursued economic reforms in conjunction with International Monetary Fund (IMF) requirements, he faced strong resistance from a Communist-dominated parliament elected in 1990.

The 1995 parliamentary elections, which were contested by more than 1,000 candidates representing 12 political parties, saw voting occur largely along ethnic and clan lines. No single party won a clear majority, with a mix of governing officials, intellectuals, and clan leaders capturing 82 out of 105 seats. Later that year, Akayev was reelected president in early elections, with more than 70 percent of the vote. In a February 1996 referendum, 94 percent of voters endorsed constitutional amendments that substantially increased the powers of the presidency.

A series of constitutional amendments proposed by Akayev, including restructuring the parliament and providing for private ownership of land, were adopted by public referendum in October 1998. In December, the entire cabinet resigned after Akayev accused its members of mishandling the country's growing economic difficulties. Zhumabek Ibraimov, the former head of the property fund responsible for privatization, was subsequently appointed the new prime minister.

After just three months in office, Ibraimov died of cancer in April 1999, and was replaced by Armangeldi Muraliyev, a former governor of the southern region of Osh. Later that month, Felix Kulov, the mayor of Bishkek and an outspoken critic of Akayev, resigned in protest over supposed allegations that he was part of a plot to overthrow the government.

In August, armed Islamic militants entered the southern region of the Kyrgyz Republic twice from bases in neighboring Tajikistan, seizing several villages and holding their inhabitants hostage. Most of the rebels appeared to be members of the Islamic Movement of Uzbekistan (IMU), a radical group claiming to seek the overthrow of the secular government of Uzbekistan and replace it with an Islamic state. Among their proclaimed goals for the August incursions were the release of their supporters from Uzbek prisons and passage into Uzbekistan. However, many analysts believe that the IMU's primary aim is to expand its lucrative drug trafficking route north into Uzbekistan. After weeks of negotiations with, and military attacks against, the rebels, many of whom escaped back to Tajikistan, the last of the hostages was released in October.

In the highly flawed February 2000 parliamentary poll, opposition parties, including the Democratic Movement of Kyrgyzstan (PDMK), *El Bei-Bechora* (The People's Party), and *Ar-Namys* (Dignity), were barred from the vote over minor legal technicalities widely regarded as politically motivated charges. The El Bei-Bechora leader,

Danier Usenov, was banned from running in a single-mandate constituency in the March 12 second-round runoff for allegedly failing to accurately declare his personal assets. Ar-Namys chairman Felix Kulov, who ran as an independent candidate, lost in the runoff by a suspiciously large margin despite having enjoyed a secure lead in the first round. According to official election results, the Communist Party received the largest percentage of votes, 27 percent; followed by the pro-government Union of Democratic Forces with 19 percent; the Democratic Party of Women, 13 percent; the Party of War Veterans, 8 percent; the Fatherland Socialist Party (*Ata-Meken*), 6 percent; and the Party of My Country, 5 percent. International election observers, including representatives from the Organization for Security and Cooperation in Europe (OSCE), noted numerous serious irregularities such as interference by state officials in the electoral process, attempts to bribe voters, the stuffing of ballot boxes, violations in tabulating the votes, the forging of ballots, and an overt bias in state media in favor of pro-government parties.

Shortly after the second-round runoff, Kulov was arrested on charges of embezzlement and abuse of power allegedly committed while national security minister in the mid-1990s. Most analysts regarded Kulov's arrest as an attempt to prevent him from running against Akayev in the October presidential election. Following more than four months in detention and a closed military trial, Kulov was acquitted in August and immediately declared his candidacy for president.

For the second successive year, armed militants believed to be members of the IMU crossed from Tajikistan into the southern Batken province of the Kyrgyz Republic in mid-August. After several months of intense battles between the rebels and Uzbek and Kyrgyz troops, the fighting appeared to have ceased with the onset of winter.

The October 29 presidential election was contested by six candidates, including the heavily favored incumbent, Akayev, who received nearly 75 percent of the vote. Omurbek Tekebayev, deputy speaker of parliament and leader of the opposition Ata-Meken party, came in a distant second with 14 percent, while industrialist Almazbek Atambayev received 6 percent. The other three candidates received less than two percent each. Akayev's main rival, Kulov, had been denied registration as a candidate for refusing to take a mandatory Kyrgyz-language exam. Kulov, who acknowledged that Russian was his first language, and other critics of the test requirement, maintained that it violated election laws and the constitution, had been introduced that year to eliminate certain candidates from the race and ensure Akayev's reelection, and included arbitrary methods for evaluating language proficiency. As with the parliamentary elections, international monitors and opposition figures cited widespread irregularities, including the exclusion of candidates for political purposes, the stuffing of ballot boxes, and biased media coverage.

Political Rights and Civil Liberties: Citizens of the Kyrgyz Republic cannot change their government democratically. International election observers described the 2000 parliamentary and presidential elections as neither free nor fair. The 1996 constitution codifies strong presidential rule and a weak parliament, and the post of prime minister is largely ceremonial. The bicameral legislature is composed of a 45-member upper chamber, which meets only occasionally to approve the budget and confirm presidential appointees, and a 60-seat lower chamber. The constitution limits the president to only two terms in office. However, President

Akayev was allowed to run in 2000 after the constitutional court ruled that his first term began in 1995, rather than in 1991, when he ran effectively unopposed.

The government increased its crackdown against critics of the regime in 2000, including its conviction of opposition leader Danier Usenov on assault charges and its trial of Felix Kulov on charges of abuse of power and embezzlement. In August, the head of the Guild of Prisoners of Conscience, Topchubek Turgunaliyev, was sentenced to 16 years in prison on politically motivated charges of attempting to assassinate President Akayev.

While there is some degree of press freedom in the Kyrgyz Republic, state and private media are vulnerable to government pressure, which causes many journalists to practice self-censorship. All media are required to register with the ministry of justice, and an article in the criminal code regarding libel is used to prosecute journalists who criticize government officials. The Kyrgyz authorities increased their repression of the media leading up to the 2000 parliamentary and presidential elections. In January, the independent newspaper *Res Publica* was fined several thousand dollars for an article alleged to have violated the honor and dignity of a government official. In June, independent journalist Moldosali Ibrahimov was fined and sentenced to two years in prison for libel over a report that a judge had engaged in bribery. After having spent five weeks in jail, Ibrahimov was released and had his fine reduced following an appeals hearing. In August, three staff members of the independent weekly paper *Delo No* reportedly were harshly treated during interrogation over an article printed about the closed trial of Felix Kulov, which authorities claimed divulged state secrets.

Freedom of religion is generally respected in this largely Muslim country, although at times the government has infringed upon these rights. All religious organizations must register with the State Commission on Religious Affairs and the ministry of justice to obtain status as a legal entity. In 2000, the government increased its repression of the Hizb-ut-Tahrir Islamic movement, which it claims to be a dangerous group of religious extremists, convicting dozens of its members on charges of inciting religious and ethnic hatred.

Freedom of assembly and association is respected inconsistently, with local authorities sometimes using registration requirements for demonstrations to inhibit this right. Immediately following the second round of the 2000 parliamentary poll, dozens of protesters took to the streets in weeks of public demonstrations to condemn the flawed elections and the subsequent arrest of Felix Kulov and other opposition figures on politically motivated charges. Police reportedly responded by arresting and beating many of the participants. Most of the approximately two dozen political parties in the country are small and weak, and many were prohibited from fielding candidates in the last parliamentary election.

While some nongovernmental organizations operate with little or no state interference, the Kyrgyz Committee for Human Rights (KCHR), which has defended independent media and publicized government pressure on the judiciary, has faced ongoing harassment by the authorities. In July, police sealed the offices of the KCHR and issued an arrest warrant for its director, Ramazan Dyryldayev, who had fled abroad.

A 1992 law permits the formation of trade unions and the right to bargain collectively. Most workers belong to the Federation of Independent Trade Unions of Kyrgyzstan, the successor to the Soviet-era labor organization.

Despite various legislative reforms in the court system, the judiciary is not independent and remains dominated by the executive branch. Corruption among judges is reportedly widespread, and courts of elders continue to operate in remote regions of the country. Police frequently use violence against suspects during arrest and interrogation. Conditions in the country's prisons, which suffer from overcrowding, food shortages, and a lack of other basic necessities, remain very poor.

Personal connections, corruption, and organized crime limit business competition and equality of opportunity. In December, parliament voted to allow Kyrgyz citizens to own land for agricultural use. Women are active in the workforce and educational institutions, although they are underrepresented in government and politics. Domestic violence, rape, and trafficking of women and girls into forced prostitution abroad are serious problems.

⬇ Laos

Polity: One party
Economy: Statist
Population: 5,200,000
PPP: $1,734
Life Expectancy: 54
Ethnic Groups: Lao Loum (68 percent), Lao Theung (22 percent), Lao Soung [includes Hmong and Yao] (9 percent), Vietnamese, Chinese (1 percent)
Capital: Vientiane

Political Rights: 7
Civil Liberties: 6
Status: Not Free

Trend Arrow: Laos received a downward trend arrow due to a series of bombings that rocked the capital and hampered economic recovery and development efforts. According to some observers, the bombings reflected a deeper power struggle among the country's top leaders, while the government blamed anti-government elements.

Overview:

The economy continues to struggle, and rivalries between pro-Vietnam and pro-China forces within the ruling elite have spilled into society. A series of bombings rocked the capital and nearby areas since March. The government alleged that antigovernment rebels are responsible, using terrorism to hurt the country's fledging tourism industry. Observers also suggested that the bombings could be a form of public protest since there is no legal way to voice dissent and dissatisfaction with the government.

Laos, a landlocked, mountainous Southeast Asian country, became a French protectorate in 1893 and was occupied by Japan during World War II. In October 1953, the Communist Pathet Lao (Land of Lao) won independence from the French. Civil warfare broke out among Royalist, Communist, and conservative factions in 1964. In May 1975, the Pathet Lao took the capital from a Royalist government and seven months later established a one-party state under Prime Minister Kaysone Phomvihane's Lao People's Revolutionary Party (LPRP).

In theory, the 85-member national assembly is elected for a five-year term and names the president. In reality, the parliamentary elections are tightly controlled, and the LPRP leadership picks the president. The government is dominated by the military, and currently seven of nine members of the Lao Politburo are generals. The 1991 constitution codified the leading political role of the LPRP and transition to a limited market economy. Kaysone subsequently took over as president, and veteran revolutionary Khamtay Siphandon succeeded him as prime minister. The constitution also expanded the powers of the president, who heads the armed forces and can remove the prime minister. Kaysone died in 1992. Assembly speaker Nouhak Phoumsavan and Prime Minister Khamtay Siphandon became president and LPRP chairman, respectively. The government permitted preapproved independents to compete for the first time in the December 1992 parliamentary elections. Four independents won seats.

Generational shift in leadership continued in the sixth LPRP congress in March 1996, but the military's political role was strengthened. Several hardliners, who feared that privatization and other economic reforms could erode the LPRP's authority, were also promoted. At the December 1997 parliamentary elections, old-guard conservatives were chosen over technocrats supportive of market reforms. In February 1998, the national assembly chose Khamtay to replace Nouhak as president, and Vice President Sisavath Keobounphan became prime minister.

The LPRP introduced market reforms in 1986 to revive the Laotian economy. The government privatized farms and some state-owned enterprises, removed price controls, and encouraged foreign investment. Thailand became the biggest source of direct foreign investment, injecting $3 billion over the last ten years. The military entered into business, including logging; it also involved a casino in the north that is part of a joint venture with Malaysian companies. Fears of Thai economic hegemony, continued poverty, and international isolation led the government's push for membership in the Association of Southeast Asian Nations (ASEAN) in 1997.

Laotian leaders marked the 25th anniversary of the revolution in December 1999. However, Laos is among the world's ten poorest nations. President Khamtay appears to lack the will and strength needed to activate reform. The most visible government action was the dismissal of two key economic officials, Deputy Prime Minister and Foreign Minister Kamphoui Keoboualapha and Central Bank governor Cheuang Sombounknam, in August 1999, for their alleged mismanagement of fiscal and banking policy.

Political contest between pro-China and pro-Vietnam forces reached new heights in 2000. Observers believe the bombings since March were tied to this power contest. The first blast in Vientiane injured nine people at a restaurant, most of them foreign tourists. Bombs were also found in the international airport and the Vietnamese embassy. In July and August, former president and now senior adviser Nouhak held several crisis meetings with government officials. He warned that the country risks disintegration if rival factions within the government do not come to terms with each other. He was also reported to suggest that Laos might have to consider a radical reform of its rigid political system to reflect today's economic and political realities.

The government continues to maintain tight control of its population in the face of growing public dissatisfaction and international pressure. A six-member National Internet Committee was set up in April to advise the government on a strategy to regulate Internet use, although access is very limited. A group of 200 workers and students staged a demonstration in Champassak Province in early November. Government troops quickly quelled the protest and arrested 15 protesters. The United Nations Development Fund decided to make small grants to Laos to support nongovernmental organizations, community-based organizations, and other local community programs. Drug trafficking and use continue to worsen. Meetings were held with China, Thailand and Vietnam on border issues to address drug trafficking.

Prince Soulivong Savang and the exiled Lao royal family have become slightly more visible, but there are yet no real signs of a political movement to support a return of the monarchy. Most Laotians associate royal reverence with the mystical, not with abstract concepts of democracy or freedom.

Political Rights and Civil Liberties:

Laos is a one-party state controlled by the LPRP, and citizens cannot change their government democratically. Opposition parties are not expressly banned, but in practice they are not tolerated by the government.

Some elements of state control, including the widespread monitoring of citizens by police, have relaxed in recent years. Domestic and international travel restrictions were eased in 1994. However, the security service still searches homes without warrants, monitors some personal communications, and maintains neighborhood and workplace committees that inform on the population.

The judiciary is not independent of the government, and trials lack adequate procedural safeguards. Prison conditions are harsh. In February 1998, one of three former government officials imprisoned in 1990 for advocating peaceful reform died because he was denied medical treatment for diabetes. Most of the tens of thousands of people who were sent to "re-education" camps following the Communist victory in 1975 have been released, but unconfirmed reports suggest that the regime may still be holding several hundred political prisoners.

The constitution allows for freedom of speech and expression, but this freedom is extremely limited in practice. The government owns all newspapers and electronic media. Western movies and magazines are officially banned. The LPRP controls all associations and political assemblies, and prohibits nearly all except those approved by the government. In a rare instance, a protest by Hmong tribal people in front of the U.S. embassy in Vientiane in February 1998 over land policy won the Hmong some concessions from the government. In October 1999, 31 people were allegedly arrested for protesting in the capital against the government's failure to tackle mounting economic problems, and for demanding free elections, release of political prisoners, and dialogue with opposition groups.

There are no known convicted religious prisoners, but authorities frequently arrest and detain persons temporarily because of their religious beliefs. In June 1999, the government released eight Christians who were jailed for more than a year for their participation in a Bible class. Six Christian leaders were arrested along with 100 prodemocracy activists in November the same year for planning to stage a public demonstration. Tolerance of religion varies by region. The country's 30,000 to 40,000 Roman Catholics face greater repression in the north than in the central and southern provinces. The central government also appears unable to control or mitigate harsh treatment by some local or provincial authorities. All religious groups and gatherings have to obtain state approval. Foreigners cannot proselytize, and proselytizing by Laotians is strictly circumscribed in practice.

A ministerial decree in 1990 permits the formation of independent trade unions in private companies, but they must operate within the framework of the party-controlled

Federation of Lao Trade Unions. There is no legal right to bargain collectively. The right to strike exists, but bans on "subversive or destabilizing activities" prevent strikes from occurring.

Women and members of minority groups are represented in the national assembly, although not proportionately to their overall presence in the population. There are no women and only a few minorities in the Politburo and Council of Ministers. The Hmong, the largest of several hill tribes, have conducted a small-scale insurgency since the Communist takeover, but they have become less active in recent years. Both the Hmong guerrillas and the armed forces have been accused of occasional human rights violations in the context of the insurgency, including extrajudicial killings.

Latvia

Polity: Parliamentary democracy
Economy: Mixed capitalist
Population: 2,400,000
PPP: $5,728
Life Expectancy: 69
Ethnic Groups: Latvian (57 percent), Russian (30 percent), Belorussian (4 percent), Ukrainian (3 percent), Polish (3 percent), other (3 percent)
Capital: Riga

Political Rights: 1
Civil Liberties: 2
Status: Free

Overview:
The collapse of the ruling coalition in April following the resignation of Prime Minister Andris Skele over disagreements within the government on privatization policies ushered in Latvia's ninth government since independence in 1991. Former Riga mayor Andris Berzins was chosen to lead the new 69-seat majority coalition consisting of the same center-right political forces joined by the small New Party. In the midst of the government crisis, Latvia was rocked by a sensational pedophilia scandal involving accusations of involvement of several high-level government officials.

After having been ruled for centuries by Germany, Poland, Sweden, and Russia, Latvia gained its independence in 1918, but was annexed by the U.S.S.R. during World War II. More than 50 years of Soviet occupation saw a massive influx of Russians and the deportation, execution, and emigration of tens of thousands of ethnic Latvians. In 1991, Latvia regained its independence in the wake of the disintegration of the Soviet Union.

Following the October 1995 parliamentary elections, nonparty businessman and former Agriculture Minister Andris Skele was chosen to lead a tenuous six-party coalition government in December. The year 1997 was marked by continual government instability, with Skele surrendering the premiership to Guntars Krasts of the right-wing nationalist Fatherland and Freedom Party in July-August.

In the October 1998 parliamentary elections, Skele's newly created People's Party received the most votes, capturing 24 seats. However, Skele remained unpopular among many political forces for his authoritarian and abrasive style. The People's Party and Vilis Kristopans' Latvia's Way, although similar in political orientation, found their leadership at odds over personality conflicts and various business interests. After nearly two months of negotiations, parliament finally approved a new 46-seat minority government led by Kristopans and consisting of the center-right Latvia's Way, Fatherland and Freedom, and the center-left New Party, along with the tacit support of the leftwing Alliance of Social Democrats. The People's Party was excluded from the ruling coalition, which most observers predicted would not survive for long because of the ideological diversity of its members and its minority status in parliament.

On June 17, 1999, Latvian-Canadian academic and virtual political unknown Vaira Vike-Freiberga was elected by parliament as the country's first female president. Vike-Freiberga had no formal party affiliation but was supported by the People's Party, Fatherland and Freedom, and the Social Democrats. Incumbent President Guntis Ulmanis, who had served as head of state since 1993, was prevented by law from seeking a third term.

After only nine months in office, Prime Minister Kristopans stepped down on July 5, 1999, precipitating the collapse of his minority coalition government. His resignation followed the signing of a cooperation agreement two days earlier between coalition partner Fatherland and Freedom and the People's Party. Kristopan's brief term had been plagued by various policy defeats and political crises, culminating in the virtual isolation of the prime minister's party in its opposition to Vike-Freiberga's candidacy for president. Latvia's Way, the People's Party, and Fatherland and Freedom put aside enough of their differences to agree to form a new 62-seat majority coalition to be led by Kristopan's rival, Andris Skele, as prime minister.

A political firestorm erupted in February 2000 when Social Democrat member of parliament Janis Adamsons, the head of a parliamentary commission investigating a pedophilia case, announced that Prime Minister Skele, Justice Minister Valdis Birkavs, and State Revenue Service Director Andrejs Sonciks were linked to the scandal. The three officials, all of whom vigorously denied any involvement, were cleared of charges in August after prosecutors found no evidence to support the accusations.

Following months of growing strains within the ruling coalition over privatization issues and personality conflicts, Prime Minister Skele stepped down on April 12 after the collapse of his government. In early April, Economics Minister Vladmirs Makarovs, a member of Fatherland and Freedom, revoked the signatory rights of privatization agency head and Latvia's Way member Janis Naglis; the two had clashed over matters including the setting of sale prices for state firms to be privatized. Skele responded by firing Makarovs and reappointing his long-time ally Naglis as head of the privatization agency, prompting Fatherland and Freedom to withdraw its support of Skele's leadership. The following day, Latvia's Way also pulled out of the coalition, citing the inability of the government to continue under its current leadership. On May 5, Riga mayor Andris Berzins of Latvia's Way was chosen prime minister. While the new government, which included the previous coalition's three parties along with the small New Party, increased its majority in parliament from 61 to 70 seats, the future stability of the ruling coalition remains in question.

Russian-Latvian relations remained tense during the year, with Moscow continuing to accuse Riga of discriminating against the country's nearly 700,000 Russian-speakers. The Russian government criticized the war crimes trials of former Soviet partisan leader Vasily Kononov and former Soviet security official Yevgeny Savenko as persecution of opponents of Fascism.

In late 2000, the government approved new regulations to the country's often controversial language law stipulating the level of Latvian required for employees in certain private sector jobs. Among the professions covered under one of the regulation's six language categories are lawyers, certain medical personnel, telephone operators, and taxi drivers. Some human rights campaigners and politicians expressed concern over the selection of language categories for certain professions and the potential for problems in enforcement by state language inspectors.

Latvia's economy, which fell into recession throughout most of 1999 after the 1998 Russian financial crisis, showed increasing signs of recovery in 2000. However, the privatization of the few remaining large state enterprises, including Latvian Shipping Company and the oil shipping firm Ventspils Nafta, continued to be delayed as politicians sought to protect their vested interests in certain sectors of the economy. In August, parliament approved a bill removing the power utility Latvenergo from the country's privatization list. The decision came after more than 300,000 voter signatures were collected in support of state control of the energy company.

Political Rights and Civil Liberties:

Latvians can change their government democratically. However, Latvia's citizenship laws have been criticized for disenfranchising those who immigrated to Latvia during the Soviet period and who must now apply for citizenship. The constitution provides for a unicameral, 100-seat parliament (*Saeima*), whose members are elected for four-year terms by proportional representation, and who in turn select the country's president. According to international observers, the most recent national legislative elections in 1998 were free and fair.

The government respects freedom of speech and the press. Private television and radio stations broadcast programs in both Latvian and Russian, and newspapers publish a wide range of political viewpoints. However, many media outlets routinely report rumors and accusations as fact without benefit of hard evidence. Freedom of worship is generally respected in this country in which the three largest denominations are Roman Catholicism, Lutheranism, and Orthodoxy.

Freedom of assembly and association is protected by law, and gatherings occur without government interference. Communist, Nazi, and other organizations whose activities would contravene the constitution are banned. Workers have the right to establish trade unions, strike, and engage in collective bargaining. However, some private sector employees fear dismissal if they strike, as the government is limited in its ability to protect their rights.

Although the government generally respects constitutional provisions for an independent judiciary, reform of the courts has been slow and judges continue to be inadequately trained and prone to corruption. The legal system has been criticized for being slow to charge accused Nazi war criminals, including Konrads Kalejs and Karlis Ozols, against whom criminal investigations were launched in 2000. In mid-December, Kalejs was arrested in his adopted home of Australia after a request for his extradition was made by Latvia's prosecutor-general. Severe backlogs in the court system have led to lengthy delays in reviewing cases and to large numbers of persons being held in pretrial detention. In one prominent case, former banker Alexander Lavent, who was arrested in connection with the 1994 collapse of Banka Baltija, has been held in detention for more than five years without a conviction. Lavent's lengthy incarceration, which former Justice Minister Valdis Birkavs called a violation of human rights, has attracted widespread local and international criticism. There have been credible reports of police using excessive force against suspects and detainees, and prison facilities remain severely overcrowded.

Amendments adopted in 1998 to the Law on Citizenship, which were designed to ease and accelerate the naturalization process, came into effect in 1999. The amendments eliminate the so-called "naturalization windows," or specific periods during which noncitizens may apply for citizenship, and offer citizenship to noncitizens' children born after August 21, 1991, at their parents' request and without a Latvian language test. In March 2000, parliament adopted amendments to a law governing the legal status of Latvia's stateless population, which represents about 25 percent of the population. The amendments reaffirmed the rights of noncitizens to preserve their language and culture, and to enjoy the basic human rights guaranteed by the constitution.

Women possess the same legal rights as men, although they frequently face hiring and pay discrimination. While women are underrepresented in senior-level business and government positions, Vaira Vike-Freiberga became Latvia's first female head of state in June 1999.

Lebanon

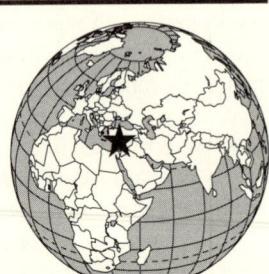

Polity: Presidential-parliamentary (military-and foreign-influenced, partly foreign-occupied)
Economy: Mixed statist
Population: 4,200,000
PPP: $4,326
Life Expectancy: 70
Ethnic Groups: Arab (95 percent), Armenian (4 percent), other (1 percent)
Capital: Beirut

Political Rights: 6
Civil Liberties: 5
Status: Not Free

Overview:
Lebanon experienced major political changes in 2000: Israel withdrew from its self-declared "security zone" in the country's south after a 15-year occupation, leaving the area largely in the hands of the radical Islamist group Hezbollah, and opposition candidates swept to victory in parliamentary elections, reinstalling the controversial Rafik al-Hariri as prime minister. Many critics alleged widespread irregularities in election campaigning and balloting. While Syria maintained its de facto occupation of Lebanon and exercised significant influence over the election outcome, the Lebanese registered uncommonly open criticism of Syria's overbearing role in Lebanon's internal affairs. After Israel's withdraw from the south, many found the continuing Syrian presence unjustified. As Israel withdrew, several thousand former Israeli-allied South Lebanese Army (SLA) militiamen fled into Israel. Many of those remaining faced charges of conspiracy

and were sentenced to prison terms. Lebanon continued to face serious economic difficulties in 2000; the withdrawal of Israeli forces from the south revealed a region beset by economic underdevelopment and in need of major rehabilitation.

Lebanon gained full sovereignty from France in 1946. An unwritten National Pact in 1943 gave Christians political dominance over the Muslim population through a mandatory six to five ratio of parliamentary seats. After three decades during which non-Christians tried to end this system, a civil war erupted among Muslim, Christian, and Druze militias in 1975, claiming more than 150,000 lives before it ended in 1990. Complicating the situation was the presence of the Palestine Liberation Organization (PLO), which, after having been expelled from Jordan in 1971, used Lebanon as a base for attacks against Israel and constituted an occupying force. Syria sent troops into Lebanon to support the government in 1976. Syrians, who consider Lebanon part of Greater Syria, continue to occupy the country today.

The Lebanese assembly ratified a peace plan put forward by the Arab League on November 5, 1989, in Taif, Saudi Arabia. The Taif Accord maintained the tradition of a Maronite Christian president indirectly elected to a six-year term, but it transferred most executive power to the prime minister, a Sunni Muslim, by agreement. Parliament is evenly split between Muslims and Christians.

After Israel withdrew its forces from a 440-square-mile security zone in the south, in June, the Shiite, pro-Iranian Hezbollah militia moved in to fill the power vacuum. Despite international and United Nations pressure to mobilize its army along the Israeli border, Lebanon had by year's end only apportioned some police and army personnel to towns and villages within the former security zone, but not at the actual border. Lebanon publicly refuses to protect Israel's border in the absence of a peace agreement with its southern neighbor. Israel's withdrawal was certified as complete by the UN and in full compliance with UN resolution 425 which stipulated the terms of the withdrawal. In October, Hezbollah guerillas kidnapped three Israeli soldiers in a cross-border raid, signaling a willingness to exercise its authority in the south and its desire to display its relevancy in Arab-Israeli affairs.

The Lebanese government is not sovereign in its own country. With some 35,000 to 40,000 troops in Lebanon, Syria dominates the country politically and militarily. The 128-member parliament, elected in September 2000, follows the Syrian line on internal and regional affairs.

Despite huge electoral gains by opposition candidates—who claimed 92 out of the 128 parliamentary seats—the elections generated pronounced criticism over alleged irregularities and Syria's overbearing influence in Lebanon's electoral process. Rafik al-Hariri, disgraced in 1998 as prime minister, mounted a stunning comeback, displacing Prime Minister Salim al-Hoss, who, along with President Emile Lahoud, had been handpicked to lead Lebanon by Syrian president Bashar al-Assad. Assad selected the two while in charge of Lebanon for his father, the late Hafez al-Assad. Prime Minister Hariri, while considered an opposition candidate, nonetheless maintains strong ties to the Syrian political establishment. A multibillionaire land developer, he has initiated massive construction projects in Syria.

Interior Minister Michel Murr, a staunch Syrian ally who ran as a candidate, faced serious doubts that he was running an open and honest campaign, as his government post puts him in control of police and internal security forces and the granting of licenses. Indeed, some candidates with no ties to Syria were harassed; campaign posters were torn down, cars vandalized, and shots were fired at the home of a former parliament speaker and opponent of Syria. Nassib Lahoud, a sitting member of parliament who during the election called for an examination of Lebanon's relationship with Syria, was banned from displaying campaign posters. In some areas, his posters were replaced with those promoting the candidacy of a Syrian-supported list led by Interior Minister Murr.

According to the Lebanese Association for Democratic Elections (LADE) and other independent observers, the elections were deemed "unfree and unfair" as a result, primarily, of Syrian meddling. LADE reported the illegal presence of security forces at polling stations, which served to intimidate voters. The organization criticized state-supported candidates who distributed voter registration cards to their own supporters after the official deadline. "Many of these cards were issued to people who didn't even have a voter registration card in the first place," said LADE in a statement. Many observers doubted that the election results—in spite of the large opposition gains—would translate into significant political change as long as Syria maintains its presence in Lebanon.

Lebanon's economy worsened in 2000, presenting Prime Minister Hariri with the enormous task of reforming a severely depressed economy in order to attract much-needed foreign investment. The Israeli withdrawal from the south revealed a region severely underdeveloped. Lebanese and other nongovernmental organizations estimated the cost of rebuilding the south at $1.3 billion, citing infrastructural, agricultural, educational, and health projects, along with removal of land mines, as major priorities. Lebanon's deficit stood at $22 billion, or 140 percent of gross domestic product. Lebanon suffers from a brain drain, as hundreds of thousands of educated Lebanese have left in recent years. Based on the prime minister's proclivity for ambitious public spending, which drew past accusations of driving up the nation's debt in his previous term as premier, many critics expressed doubt over his ability to improve the economy.

Political Rights and Civil Liberties: Shortcomings in the electoral system limit the right of Lebanese citizens to change their government. The parliamentary elections held in 2000 were neither prepared for nor carried out impartially. According to the constitution, a president is to be elected by parliament every six years. In fact, Syria's choice of president is simply ratified by parliament. Just prior to the election of Emile Lahoud as president in October 1998, parliament amended a constitutional requirement that senior government officials resign their posts at least two years before running for office.

The judiciary is influenced by Syrian political pressure, which affects the appointments of key prosecutors and the investigation of magistrates. The judicial system comprises civilian courts, a military court, and a judicial council. International standards of criminal procedure are not observed in the military court, which consists largely of military officers with no legal training. The average case is tried in minutes. Extragovernmental groups, such as Palestinian factions and Hezbollah, detain suspects and administer justice in areas under their control, generally without due process safeguards.

Arbitrary arrest and detention are commonplace. Security forces use torture to extract confessions. Prison conditions do not meet international standards. After the Israeli withdrawal from the country's south, roughly 2,000 militiamen of the now-defunct SLA remained in Lebanon rather than seek refuge in Israel. Collaboration trials began in June for the remaining SLA members. Many were sentenced in batches and without adequate representation. The courts refused to hear cases on an individual basis, and one lawyer reportedly handled 700 cases by himself. By the end of September, more than 1,000 former militiamen were sentenced to prison terms ranging from three weeks to 15 years.

While Lebanon enjoys greater press freedoms than its patron Syria, the government has not abated its crackdown on independent broadcasting, which flourished during the civil war. Some candidates in the parliamentary elections were denied television coverage. In 1998, a government decree banned two of the country's four satellite television stations from broadcasting news or political programming. Since the crackdown began in 1996, the government has licensed only 5 television stations, 3 of which are owned by government figures; it has also licensed 6 radio stations that may carry news and 20 stations that may carry only entertainment. Fifty-two television stations and 124 radio stations have been closed. The appropriation of frequencies is a slow and highly politicized process.

Print media are independent of the government, though their content often reflects the opinions of the various local and foreign groups that finance them. Insulting the dignity of the head of state or foreign leaders is prohibited. All foreign print media are subject to government approval. In June, Reporters Sans Frontières filed a complaint with Lebanon's interior ministry over the banning of major foreign newspapers, including the French dailies *Liberation* and *Le Monde* and the *International Herald Tribune*, during the days immediately following Syrian president Hafez al-Assad's death. All three papers carried articles critical of Assad's legacy. Following the ban, a military court sentenced Salah Noureddine, a Lebanese man, to one year in jail for publicly criticizing the late Syrian ruler.

Rates of Internet access in Lebanon are substantial. In 1999 there were an estimated 50,000 users, with more than 25 Lebanese Internet service providers. Many cybercafés can be found in Beirut. Internet access does not appear to be closely monitored or controlled by the state.

While the government generally tolerates public demonstrations, those protesting Syria are dealt with swiftly. In April, Lebanon moved to suppress several peaceful anti-Syria protests. Army and security forces broke up demonstrations by university students calling for the withdrawal of Syrian troops from Lebanon, injuring several demonstrators. Eight people were arrested and sentenced to prison terms ranging from ten days to six weeks. Human Rights Watch criticized the prosecution of civilians in the country's military court.

Citizens may travel abroad freely, though internal travel is restricted in certain areas. Syrian troops maintain checkpoints in areas under their control. The government does not extend legal rights to some 180,000 stateless persons who live mainly in disputed border areas. In January 1999 the government announced a plan to lift travel restrictions imposed on Lebanon's Palestinian population. Palestinian travel documents are to be treated the same as passports. After 1995, Lebanon had required Palestinians once living in Lebanon to obtain visas to return.

Some 350,000 to 500,000 Palestinian refugees live without adequate electricity and water; they face restrictions on work, on building homes, and on purchasing property. Palestinians are denied citizenship rights. Lebanon insists that Israel repatriate all Palestinian refugees in Lebanon. Lebanese authorities are loath to absorb the refugees into regular society for fear of upsetting the country's delicate sectarian balance. Palestinian refugee camps are noted breeding grounds of radical anti-Israel sentiment, and large segments of their residents are heavily armed. Lebanese authorities warily avoid the often-violent camps.

Women suffer legal and social discrimination. Although women commonly work in fields such as medicine, law, journalism, and banking, they are severely underrepresented in politics. Women constitute only two percent of parliament. Lebanon has ratified the United Nations Convention for the Eradication of all forms of Discrimination Against Women (CEDAW), but has not applied all its recommended laws. Women continue to receive smaller social security payouts than men, and female government employees often do not receive the same benefits as their male counterparts. Men convicted of so-called honor crimes—usually the murder of women deemed to have violated their families' honor—are often not severely punished.

All workers except those in government may establish unions, strike, and bargain collectively. Foreign domestic workers are routinely abused by employers, who pay them little or nothing and confiscate their passports to prevent them from leaving. Women are most vulnerable to brutality or sexual abuse. Lebanon has no written code to arbitrate domestic-worker disputes.

⬇ Lesotho

Polity: Parliamentary and traditional chiefs (transitional)
Economy: Capitalist
Population: 2,100,000
PPP: $1,626
Life Expectancy: 55
Ethnic Groups: Sotho (99.7 percent), other, including European and Asian (0.3 percent)
Capital: Maseru

Political Rights: 4
Civil Liberties: 4
Status: Partly Free

Trend Arrow: Lesotho received a downward trend arrow due to repeated manipulations and delays in creating conditions for holding general elections.

Overview: General elections that were to be held in April 2000 are unlikely to take place before March 2001 because of repeated infighting within the Interim Political Authority (IPA). The 24-member body, which was set up following postelection violence in September 1998 to oversee preparations for the polls, includes two representatives from each of the country's 12 main political parties. The South African Development Community (SADC), the United Nations, and the Commonwealth have repeatedly stepped in to mediate. An independent electoral commission that was created in 1999 resigned in January 2000, following pressure from opposition parties that questioned its impartiality. It resumed work after the addition of international experts.

Lesotho's status as a British protectorate saved it from incorporation into South Africa. King Moshoeshoe II reigned from independence in 1966 until the installation of his son as King Letsie III in a 1990 military coup. Democratic elections in 1993 did not lead to stability. After violent military infighting, assassinations, and a suspension of constitutional rule in 1994, King Letsie III abdicated to allow his father's reinstatement. He resumed the throne following the accidental death of his father in January 1996.

Troops from South Africa and Botswana were sent to the mountain kingdom at the request of Prime Minster Pakalitha Mosisili, under the mandate of the 14-country SADC in September 1998, to quell army-backed violence and a potential overthrow of the government. The violence was touched off by the results of national assembly elections the previous May. Although international observers described the voting as free and fair, demonstrators rejected the results that gave the ruling Lesotho Congress for Democracy (LCD) 79 of 80 national assembly seats. At least 100 people were reportedly killed before order was restored.

An agreement, drafted by the Commonwealth in 1998, allows the elected but highly unpopular government to retain power, but stipulates that new elections be supervised by an independent election commission. The agreement also calls for the formation of a security liaison committee with representatives from all political parties and the Lesotho army, as well as a joint committee on the public media to ensure equitable air time for campaigning.

Entirely surrounded by South Africa, Lesotho is highly dependent on its powerful neighbor. Its economy is sustained by remittances from its many citizens who work in South African mines. But a world slump in gold prices has led to job losses and decreased earnings. Some reports said that more than 10,000 Lesotho miners employed in South African gold mines lost their jobs in 2000.

Political Rights and Civil Liberties: The people of Lesotho are guaranteed the right to change their leaders through free and fair elections, but mistrust and delays have marred the process. Legislative elections in May 1998 were determined to be generally free and fair, but the LCD's 60 percent vote translated into an almost total exclusion of opposition parties such as the Basotho National Party (BNP). The appearance of irregularities and the virtual elimination of opposition voices from government fueled protests against the results.

A new Mixed Member Parliament electoral model, which will expand the number of seats in parliament by 50, to 130, to give the opposition more representation, has been developed by the IPA. The additional seats will be elected by proportional representation, while the others will continue to be chosen by the "first-past-the-post" system of awarding seats to whomever gets the most votes. In subsequent elections, the number of constituency seats and proportional representation seats is to be equal.

The senate, the upper house of the bicameral legislature, includes royal appointees and Lesotho's 22 principal traditional chiefs, who still wield considerable authority in rural areas. Any elected government's exercise of its constitutional authority remains limited by the autonomy of the military, the royal family, and traditional clan structures.

Courts are nominally independent, but higher courts are especially subject to outside influence. The large case backlog often leads to lengthy delays in trials. Freedom of assembly, freedom of expression, and freedom of religion are generally respected. Mistreatment of civilians by security forces reportedly continues. Several nongovernmental organizations operate openly. In December, a court martial sentenced 33 members of the Lesotho Defense Force to prison terms of up to 13 years for mutiny during the 1998 unrest. Prison conditions are poor, but not life threatening.

The government generally respects freedom of speech and the press, but journalists have suffered occasional harassment and attacks. There are several independent newspapers that routinely criticize the government. The press suffered badly during the 1998 rioting, when the offices of most independent publications were pillaged. All have resumed publishing. There are four private radio stations, and extensive South African radio and television broadcasts reach Lesotho.

The 1993 constitution bars gender-based discrimination, but customary practice and law still restrict women's rights in several areas, including property rights and inheritance. A woman is considered a legal minor while her husband is alive. Domestic violence is reportedly widespread. Women's rights organizations have highlighted the importance of women participating in the democratic process as part of a broader effort to educate women about their rights under both customary and common law.

Labor rights are constitutionally guaranteed, but the labor and trade union movement is weak and fragmented. Approximately ten percent of the country's labor force, which is mostly engaged in subsistence agriculture or employment in South Africa, is unionized. Collective bargaining rights and the right to strike are recognized by law, but are sometimes denied by government negotiators. Security forces have violently suppressed some wildcat strikes. There were threats of violence against workers who failed to heed a strike call in May. The opposition BNP has called for strikes to press the government to agree to early elections.

Liberia

Polity: Presidential-parliamentary democracy
Economy: Capitalist
Population: 3,200,000
PPP: na
Life Expectancy: 50
Ethnic Groups: Indigenous tribes (95 percent), Americo-Liberians (5 percent)
Capital: Monrovia

Political Rights: 5*
Civil Liberties: 6*
Status: Partly Free

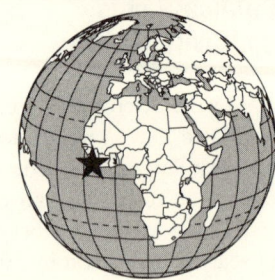

Ratings Change: Liberia's political rights rating changed from 4 to 5, and its civil liberties from 5 to 6, because of increasingly restrictive freedom of the political opposition, due to attacks on human rights activists and repression of the media.

Overview: The government of President Charles Taylor found itself increasingly isolated from the international community following reports of continued human rights abuses and allegations of arms smuggling to neighboring Sierra Leone. A United Nations report in December accused Taylor of providing weapons and training to Revolutionary United Front fighters in exchange for diamonds, with the help of international arms dealers. Taylor denied the charges. The persistent allegations of arms smuggling prompted the United States in October to impose visa restrictions on Liberian officials. Taylor has called for an international arms embargo imposed on Liberia in 1992 to be lifted, while accusing Guinea of harboring dissidents who are reportedly attacking Liberia's northern counties. Liberia's diplomatic relations with Guinea had deteriorated significantly by the end of the year.

Liberia was settled by freed American slaves in 1821 and became an independent republic in 1847. Americo-Liberians, descendants of the freed slaves, dominated the country until 1980, when Sgt. Samuel Doe led a violent coup that led to the killing of President William Tolbert. Doe's regime concentrated power among members of his Krahn ethnic group and suppressed others.

Forces led by Taylor, a former government minister, and backed by Gio and Mano ethnic groups, which had been subject to severe repression, launched a guerrilla war from neighboring Côte d'Ivoire against the Doe regime on Christmas Eve, 1989. In 1990, Nigeria, under the aegis of the Economic Community of West African States, led an armed intervention force that prevented Taylor from seizing the capital but failed to protect Doe from being captured and tortured to death by a splinter rebel group. Taylor and his National Patriotic Party (NPP) won elections in 1997; their victory was generally considered to be a vote for peace. The last remaining peacekeepers left Liberia in October 1999.

Liberia's economy has yet to recover from the war, and it could suffer further if international sanctions are imposed against the Taylor government. Per capita incomes are only a fraction of their prewar level.

Security forces continued to commit abuses with impunity, including arbitrary detention, torture, and extrajudicial killings. Human rights defenders, journalists, and political activists are increasingly under threat in Liberia. The U.S.-based Carter Center, which has been promoting political and human rights in Liberia for several years, closed its Monrovia office in November, saying the atmosphere was no longer conducive to carrying out its work.

Political Rights and Civil Liberties:

Charles Taylor and his National Patriotic Party (NPP) assumed power after 1997 elections that constituted Liberia's most genuine electoral exercise in decades. The votes for the presidency and national assembly on the basis of proportional representation were held under provisions of the 1986 constitution, but were conducted in an atmosphere of intimidation. Taylor's landslide victory reflected more of a vote for peace than for a particular personality, as many people believed he would go back to war if he lost. Taylor's NPP won three-quarters of the seats in the legislature. The president appoints the governors of the country's 13 counties.

Liberia's judiciary is only nominally independent and is vulnerable to corruption, influence by government officials, a lack of resources, and intimidation by security forces. Human rights groups say security forces often ignore summonses to appear in court to explain disappearances. Clan chieftains in some rural areas administer criminal justice through the traditional practice of trial-by-ordeal, or torture. There are lengthy pretrial detentions, often in life-threatening conditions. Human rights groups have complained about the treatment of prisoners, although the International Committee of the Red Cross has been able to visit a number of prisons.

Liberia has a poor human rights record. Security forces, which are divided into a number of different units, commit abuses with impunity, including arbitrary detentions, torture, extrajudicial killings, and disappearances. They often act independently of government authority, particularly in rural areas. Numerous civil society groups, including human rights organizations such as the Catholic Justice and Peace Commission and the Center for Democratic Empowerment (CEDE), operate in the country. Their employees are subject to repeated harassment by security forces. In November, about 100 men armed with knives and other weapons attacked the CEDE offices and beat former President Amos Sawyer and CEDE Executive Director Conmany Wesseh, a vocal rights-activist and proponent of arms control. Wesseh was also attacked in 1999, and subsequently sent his family to live abroad.

Liberia's independent media have survived despite years of war, assaults, and harassment at the cost of extensive self-censorship. Some members of the print media have received death threats and are under persistent surveillance, but independent newspapers continue to publish articles critical of the government, at their own risk. The government dominates the broadcast media, and most independent stations offer religious programming. In March 2000, authorities closed both the privately owned Star Radio and Radio Veritas, which is run by the Roman Catholic Church. Star Radio, which was run by the Swiss Hirondelle Foundation, had not reopened by the end of the year, while Radio Veritas had resumed broadcasting news. The Liberian government in August came under harsh international criticism for its treatment of four international journalists from Britain's Channel Four television who were in Liberia filming a documentary. They were detained and charged with espionage after authorities searched their hotel rooms and discovered a prepared script, which the journalists had said was used to raise funds to report their story. They were released after a week, following the intervention of Western diplomats.

The constitution provides for the right of peaceful assembly and association, and the government generally respects these rights in practice. However, many Liberians will not openly criticize the government, fearing either harassment by security forces or detention.

Religious freedom is respected in practice, but Muslims have been targeted because many Mandingos follow Islam. Mandingos, from the northern regions of the country, are blamed for backing Taylor's opponents. Ethnic tension has declined since the war ended, but it occasionally flares into conflict in land disputes or clashes linked to insecurity along the border regions.

Treatment of women varies by ethnic group, religion, and social status. Many women continue to suffer from physical abuse and traditional societal discrimination, despite constitutionally guaranteed equality. Women married under traditional law are considered the property of their husbands and are denied rights of inheritance and child custody if their husbands die. Several women's groups are working to treat abused women and raise awareness of their human rights. The Association of Female Lawyers in Liberia persuaded the Justice Ministry in August 2000 to allow its attorneys to prosecute rape cases. Liberian law allows only the state to prosecute criminal cases.

Union activity and the right to strike are permitted by law. Unions proliferated during the war, although their power was extremely limited. Their activity has also been curtailed by lack of economic movement. Unions are prohibited from engaging in partisan political activity and government interference was common before and during the war.

Libya

Polity: One party **Political Rights:** 7
(presidential dictatorship) **Civil Liberties:** 7
Economy: Mixed statist **Status:** Not Free
Population: 5,100,000
PPP: $6,697
Life Expectancy: 70
Ethnic Groups: Arab-Berber (97 percent), other, including
Greek, Italian, Egyptian, Pakistani, Turkish, Indian (3 percent)
Capital: Tripoli

Overview: Colonel Mu'ammar al-Qadhafi continued a diplomatic offensive aimed at ending Libya's international isolation during 2000. His bid for respectability abroad began in 1999 with the surrender of two Libyan nationals suspected in the 1988 bombing of PanAm Flight 103 over Lockerbie, Scotland. The two suspects went to trial in May 2000, under Scottish law, in the Netherlands. Regionally, Qadhafi continued to promote a pan-African policy with the aim of creating a unified African state with himself as leader. However, clashes between Libyans and African expatriates late in the year proved an embarrassing setback for Qadhafi's pan-Africanism, while a British announcement of its seizure of an illicit weapons shipment to Libya threatened to slow the progress of diplomatic relations with the West. Diplomatic successes notwithstanding, Libyans continued to suffer from rampant corruption, mismanagement, and severe restrictions on their political and civic freedom.

After centuries of Ottoman rule, Libya was conquered by Italy in 1912, and occupied by British and French forces during World War II. In accordance with agreements made by Britain and the UN, Libya gained independence under the staunchly pro-Western King Idris I in 1951. Qadhafi seized power in 1969 amid growing anti-Western sentiment regarding foreign-controlled oil companies and military bases on Libyan soil.

Qadhafi's hostility toward the West and his sponsorship of terrorism have earned Libya pariah status. Clashes with regional neighbors, including Chad over the Aozou strip and Egypt over their common border, have led to costly military failures. Suspected Libyan involvement in the bombing of PanAm Flight 103 prompted the UN to impose sanctions including embargoes on air traffic and the import of arms and oil production equipment in 1992. The United States has maintained unilateral sanctions against Libya since 1981 because of the latter's sponsorship of terrorism.

In a turnaround attributed by some observers to maturity, Qadhafi made several constructive changes to his foreign policy beginning in 1999. In addition to surrendering the two Lockerbie suspects, he agreed to pay compensation to the families of 170 people killed in the 1989 bombing of a French airliner in Niger. He also accepted responsibility for the 1984 killing of British police officer Yvonne Fletcher by shots fired from the Libyan embassy in London, and expelled the Abu Nidal organization, a militant Palestinian group responsible for numerous terrorist attacks, from Libya. The U.S. State Department praised this move as a "strong signal of support" for the Middle East peace process.

The UN suspended sanctions in 1999, but stopped short of lifting them permanently because Libya has not explicitly renounced terrorism. The United States eased some restrictions to allow American companies to sell food, medicine, and medical equipment to Libya, but in November 2000 renewed its travel ban for one year. Britain restored diplomatic ties with Libya for the first time since 1986. The European Union (EU) lifted sanctions but maintained an arms embargo. Business and political delegations streamed into Libya throughout 2000 from Europe, Asia, and the Middle East, as potential investors set their sights on Libya's lucrative oil industry.

However, Qadhafi's quest for respectability hit a snag when Britain announced in January 2000 that it had intercepted an illicit shipment of missile parts bound for Libya, in breach of the EU arms embargo and international ballistic missile treaties. The announcement may have contributed to a subsequent decision by the EU to postpone inviting Qadhafi to Brussels for talks under the Barcelona Declaration, which regulates relations between the EU and 12 southern-Mediterranean countries. The EU decided that Libya was not ready to meet the terms of the declaration, which stipulates respect for human rights, free trade, democracy, and support for the Middle East peace process.

Qadhafi has in recent years sought to ease Libya's isolation through vigorous diplomacy focused on sub-Saharan Africa. Resentful of the lack of Arab support for Libya in the wake of Lockerbie, he turned away from his vision of pan-Arabism and began promoting a united Africa. Presenting himself as a peace broker, he has undertaken several peacemaking missions on the continent. The numerous conflicts there present an opportunity for Qadhafi to further Libyan strategic and economic interests across Africa. He sponsored efforts throughout the year to mediate disputes in Sudan, Chad, Somalia, and the Democratic Republic of Congo.

Despite his improved international stature, Qadhafi has become increasingly isolated domestically, even within his own Qadhadhifa clan. Ethnic rivalries among senior junta officials have been reported, while corruption, mismanagement, and unemployment have eroded support for the regime. Disaffected Libyans see little of some $10 billion per year in oil revenue, and have yet to reap the benefits of suspended UN sanctions. Economists stress the need to deregulate and privatize the state-dominated economy and to diversify away from dependence on oil. However, laws this year increased restrictions on private enterprise, mandating a minimum of 500 shareholders and at least $550,000 in capital, and disallowing more than five percent ownership by any single shareholder. These restrictions will reportedly be applied retroactively.

Political Rights and Civil Liberties: Libyans cannot change their government democratically. Qadhafi rules by decree, with almost no accountability or transparency. Libya has no formal constitution; a mixture of Islamic belief, nationalism, and socialist theory in Qadhafi's *Green Book* provides principles and structures of governance, but the document lacks legal status. Libya is officially known as a *jamahiriyah*, or state of the masses, conceived as a system of direct government through popular organs at all levels of society. In reality, an elaborate structure of revolutionary committees and people's committees serves as a tool of repression. Real power rests with Qadhafi and a small group of close associates that appoints civil and military officials at every level. In March, Qadhafi dissolved 14 ministries, or General People's Committees, and transferred their power to municipal councils, leaving five intact. While some praised this apparent decentralization of power, others speculated that the move was a power grab in response to rifts between Qadhafi and several ministers.

The judiciary is not independent. It includes summary courts for petty offenses, courts of first instance for more serious offenses, courts of appeal, and a supreme court. Revolutionary courts were established in 1980 to try political offenses, but were replaced in 1988 by a people's court after reportedly assuming responsibility for up to 90 percent of prosecutions. Political trials are held in secret, with no due process considerations. Arbitrary arrest and torture are reportedly commonplace. Amnesty International estimates that there are at least 1,000 political prisoners in Libya. In September AI also reported allegations of torture and pretrial irregularities, including denial of access to counsel, in the cases of 16 health professionals, including a Palestinian and six Bulgarians. The accused are suspected of infecting nearly 400 children with HIV. The death penalty applies to a number of political offenses and "economic" crimes, including currency speculation and drug- or alcohol-related crimes. Libya actively abducts and kills political dissidents in exile.

Limited public debate occurs within government bodies, but free expression and free media do not exist in Libya. The state owns and controls all media and thus controls reporting of domestic and international issues. Foreign programming is censored, but satellite television is widely available in Tripoli. Members of the international press reported fewer restrictions on their movement and less interference from officials in the past year. However, in August, international journalists, covering the release negotiated by Libya of European hostages taken by Muslim militants in the Philippines, were barred from the handover ceremony.

Independent political parties and civic associations are illegal; only associations affiliated with the regime are tolerated. Political activity considered treasonous is punishable by death. Public assembly must support and be approved by the government. Instances of public unrest are rare.

About 98 percent of Libyans are Sunni Muslim. Islamic groups whose beliefs and practices differ from the state-approved teaching of Islam are banned. According to the U.S. State Department, small communities of Christians worship openly. The largely Berber and Tuareg minorities face discrimination, and Qadhafi reportedly manipulates, bribes, and incites fighting among tribes in order to maintain power.

Qadhafi's pan-African policy has led to an influx of African immigrants in recent years. Poor domestic economic conditions have contributed to resentment of these immigrants, who are often blamed for increases in crime, drug use, and the incidence of AIDS. In late September, clashes between Libyans and African nationals reportedly resulted in the deaths of some 50 people, though exact numbers were unavailable. The fighting was allegedly the result of a trivial dispute. By year's end, thousands of African immigrants were moved to military camps, and thousands more had been repatriated to Sudan, Ghana, and Nigeria. Qadhafi blamed "hidden forces" for trying to derail his united-Africa policy, and security measures were taken, including restrictions on the hiring of foreigners in the private sector.

Women's access to education and employment have improved under the current regime. However, tradition dictates discrimination in family and civil matters. A woman must have her husband's permission to travel abroad.

Independent trade unions and professional associations do not exist. The only federation is the government-controlled National Trade Unions Federation. There is no collective bargaining, and workers have no legal right to strike.

Liechtenstein

Polity: Principality and parliamentary democracy
Economy: Capitalist-statist
Population: 30,000
PPP: na
Life Expectancy: 72
Ethnic Groups: Alemannic (88 percent), other, including Italian and Turkish (12 percent)
Capital: Vaduz

Political Rights: 1
Civil Liberties: 1
Status: Free

Overview:
Liechtenstein faced serious money-laundering allegations during the year. While an investigation largely exonerated the country's banking system, the principality nonetheless took steps to make its notoriously opaque banks more transparent. The political standoff between Prince Hans Adam II and the government continued in 2000, with the prince threatening to leave the country for Austria.

Liechtenstein was established in its present form in 1719 after being purchased by Austria's Liechtenstein family. Native residents of the state are primarily descendants of the Germanic Alemani tribe, and the local language is a German dialect.

From 1938 until 1997, the principality was governed by an FBPL-VU coalition. The FBPL was the senior partner for most of this period. Liechtenstein's constitution, adopted in 1921, has been amended several times.

One of the world's most secretive tax havens, Liechtenstein came under intense criticism that it was a money-laundering haven. In April, France called the country the most dangerous tax and judiciary haven in Europe, alleging Liechtenstein's banks were replete with foreign political slush funds, organized-crime-syndicate accounts, and funds deposited by international terrorists. The Paris-based Financial Action Task Force, an international anti-laundering group, listed the country as "non-cooperative." In June the Organization for Economic Cooperation and Development (OECD) classified Liechtenstein as a "harmful" tax haven.

In September an Austrian prosecutor was called in to investigate allegations by the German secret service that the country's banks and several prominent lawyers had been involved in large-scale money laundering of funds belonging to Russian organized-crime figures and Colombian drug cartels. The investigator found that the country did not exceed other states in terms of white-collar crime and stated that most laundered money in Liechtenstein had been "prewashed" in other countries. However, the principality still heeded western pressure and abandoned its policy of permitting anonymous accounts.

On the political front, Prince Hans Adam II and the government remained in dispute over the degree of the royal family's powers. The prince, one of the only European monarchs whose powers are not largely ceremonial, pledged to devolve more powers to the citizenry. Prime Minister Mario Frick claimed that the prince in fact desires to centralize more authority in his own hands. The prince has threatened to arrange for a referendum on constitutional reform, saying he will relocate to Austria should he lose the vote. Such a move would raise the question of how Liechtenstein would be governed.

Prince Hans Adam II faced a reprimand by the European Court of Human Rights in 1999 for abusing his subjects' freedom of speech. The court fined the prince for refusing to reappoint a judge he had dismissed for suggesting that the supreme court, and not the prince, should have the last word in constitutional matters. The prince, who has ruled the principality since 1989, has ignored the legislature on several occasions, most notably when he had the country join the European Economic Area (EEA), despite deputies' doubts.

Since 1997, the Patriotic Union (VU) led by Prime Minister Frick has held 13 seats in the 25-seat unicameral *Landtag* (legislature). The Progressive Citizens' Party (FBPL), which later voted to end its long-standing coalition with the VU, holds 10 parliamentary seats, and the Free Voters' List holds 2 seats.

Liechtenstein's economy is closely intertwined with Switzerland's. Its official currency is the Swiss franc. To reduce the country's economic dependence on Switzerland, Prince Hans Adam II led the principality into membership not only in the EEA but also in the United Nations, the European Free Trade Association, the World Trade Organization, and the General Agreement on Tariffs and Trade.

Political Rights and Civil Liberties:

Liechtensteiners can change their government democratically. The prince exercises legislative powers jointly with the Landtag. He appoints the prime minister from the Landtag's majority party or coalition, and the deputy chief of the five-member government from the minority. Parties with at least eight percent of the vote receive representation in the parliament, which is directly elected for four years on the basis of proportional representation. The sovereign possesses power to veto legislation and to dissolve the Landtag. Participation in elections and referenda is compulsory.

The government respects freedom of speech. Two daily newspapers are published, each representing the interests of one of the two major political parties, as is one weekly newsmagazine. There are two television stations, one owned by the state and one private. While there is only one private radio station, residents regularly receive radio and television broadcasts from neighboring countries.

In 1998 and 1999, Liechtenstein received a high number of asylum seekers who were given temporary protection. The number of asylum seekers reaches almost two percent of the total population of Liechtenstein. A strict policy prevents significant numbers of second- and third-generation residents from acquiring citizenship.

Although Roman Catholicism is the state religion, other faiths are practiced freely. Roman Catholic or Protestant religious education is compulsory in all schools, but exemptions are routinely granted.

Liechtensteiners enjoy freedom of association. The principality has one small trade union. Workers have the right to strike, but have not done so in more than 25 years. The prosperous economy includes private and state enterprises. Citizens enjoy a very high standard of living.

The independent judiciary, subject to the prince's appointment power, is headed by a supreme court that includes civil and criminal courts, as well as an administrative court of appeals, and a state court to address questions of constitutionality.

Although only narrowly endorsed by male voters, the electoral enfranchisement of women at the national level was unanimously approved in the legislature in 1984 after defeats in referenda in 1971 and 1973. By 1986, universal adult suffrage at the local level had passed in all 11 communities. In the 1989 general elections, a woman won a Landtag seat for the first time. Three years later, a constitutional amendment guaranteed legal equality.

Lithuania

Polity: Parliamentary democracy
Economy: Mixed capitalist
Population: 3,700,000
PPP: $6,436
Life Expectancy: 70
Ethnic Groups: Lithuanian (80 percent), Russian (9 percent), Polish (7 percent), Belorussian (2 percent), other (2 percent)
Capital: Vilnius

Political Rights: 1
Civil Liberties: 2
Status: Free

Overview:

Faced with the public's dissatisfaction over its economic austerity policies, the ruling Homeland Union/Lithuanian Conservatives (HU/LC) experienced a resounding defeat in both the March local elections and the October parliamentary vote. The center-left New Alliance (Social Liberals) secured the most seats in the municipal poll, while the left-wing Social Democratic Coalition, led by former president and Communist leader Algirdas Brazauskas, captured the most seats in the national legislature. However, an ideologically diverse grouping of four parties secured enough support to form a new centrist government with Rolandas Paksas as prime minister.

Lithuania merged with Poland in the sixteenth century and was subsequently absorbed by Russia in the eighteenth century. After gaining its independence at the end of World War I, Lithuania was annexed by the Soviet Union in 1940 under a secret protocol of the 1939 Hitler-Stalin pact. The country regained its independence with the collapse of the U.S.S.R. in 1991.

In 1992 parliamentary elections, the Lithuanian Democratic Labor Party (LDDP), the successor to the Communist Party, won 79 of 141 seats. Algirdas Brazauskas, a former head of the Communist Party, became the country's first directly elected president, in 1993. With two LDDP-led governments tainted by financial scandal in the wake of a banking crisis, the HU/LC secured the most votes in parliamentary elections in 1996, followed by the Christian Democrats. The two parties formed a center-right coalition government, and Gediminas Vagnorius of the HU/LC was named prime minister.

In January 1998, Lithuanian-American and independent candidate Valdas Adamkus was narrowly elected president over former prosecutor-general Arturas Paulauskas.

Prime Minister Vagnorius of the HU/LC, a party with which Adamkus agreed on a number of issues, was chosen to serve a second term.

Following months of growing tensions between Adamkus and Vagnorius over political, economic, and personal issues, Adamkus called on Vagnorius in mid-April 1999 to resign. Vagnorius, who stepped down on May 3, was succeeded by Vilnius mayor and HU/LC member Rolandas Paksas on May 18. However, Paksas' term in office lasted less than six months, when he resigned on October 27 in protest over the controversial sale of part of the state-owned Mazeikiu Oil complex to the U.S. energy company Williams International. On October 29, President Adamkus nominated HU/LC member and parliamentary First Deputy Chairman Andrius Kubilius as prime minister, the same day on which the Williams deal was formally concluded. On November 2, parliament approved Kubilius by a vote of 82 to 20.

In the March 2000 local election, the ruling HU/LC captured only 199 of 1,667 seats on various municipal councils, a considerable decrease from the 483 seats secured in the previous vote in 1997. Widespread dissatisfaction with the government's austerity policies and the country's economic difficulties had eroded much of the party's popularity during the year. The newly created center-left New Allliance (Social Liberals), led by Arturas Paulauskas, won the single largest number of seats, at 270, while the Farmers' Party/Christian Democratic Union coalition came in second overall with 224 seats. Both forces managed to capitalize on the public's discontent not only with the HU/LC, but also with the four other major established political parties of both the right and the left: the Christian Democrats, Center Union, Social Democrats, and the LDDP.

The results of the local election foreshadowed another loss in the October 8 parliamentary vote for the HU/LC, which came in a distant fourth with only nine seats. The left-wing Social Democratic Coalition, which united four leftist parties including the LDDP and was led by former President Algirdas Brazauskas, secured the most number of seats at 51. Popular discontent with persistent economic hardships was one of the factors in the victory of the coalition, which had campaigned on a platform of greater attention to social issues and increased support for the country's agricultural sector. However, the informal New Policy electoral bloc, which was composed of the ideologically diverse Liberal Union (34 seats), New Alliance (29 seats), Center Union (3 seats), and Modern Christian Democratic Union (1 seat) parties, bypassed the Social Democratic Coalition to form the new government. The bloc obtained a bare parliamentary majority by also securing the support of two smaller parties that had won a total of six seats. In late October, parliament confirmed Rolandas Paksas as the new prime minister, returning him to the post one year after the end of his previous tenure in that position. The New Alliance's Arturas Paulauskas was named parliamentary chairman.

Under a November 1999 lustration law, all former KGB collaborators were required to register with a special state commission during a six-month period from February 1 to August 5, 2000. With the exception of certain government officials, those who came forward would have their names kept in a confidential database, while those who did not would risk having their identities disclosed to the public and being banned from certain professions. By the end of the registration process, some 1,500 Lithuanians had registered themselves with the commission.

While the economic recession of 1999, which resulted largely from the August

1998 Russian crisis, lasted longer in Lithuania than in its two Baltic neighbors of Estonia and Latvia, the economy began to recover slowly during the year 2000. In December, Lithuania became the last European Union candidate state to be formally accepted as a member of the World Trade Organization.

Political Rights and Civil Liberties: Lithuanians can change their government democratically. The 1992 constitution established a 141-member parliament (*Seimas*), in which 71 seats are selected in single-mandate constituencies and 70 seats are chosen by proportional representation, all for four-year terms. A July 2000 amendment to the electoral law changed the single-mandate district contests from majority (more than 50 percent of the vote) to plurality, or first-past-the-post races. The president is directly elected for a five-year term. The 1996 and 2000 national legislative elections and the 1997-1998 presidential vote were conducted freely and fairly.

The government generally respects freedom of speech and the press. There is a wide variety of privately owned newspapers, and several independent, as well as state-run, television and radio stations broadcast throughout the country. In December 1999, parliament approved new amendments to the law on media eliminating the compensation ceiling for libel and slander. Critics of the law argue that it could increase the number of frivolous lawsuits and jeopardize press freedom and investigative reporting. Freedom of religion is guaranteed by law, and enjoyed in practice, in this largely Roman Catholic country. The extremist Freedom Union, known for its anti-Semitic remarks, garnered a surprise victory in the 2000 local elections in the second city of Kaunas, including the mayoral post.

Freedom of assembly and association is generally respected. Although the Communist Party of Lithuania continues to be banned, the LDDP was formed in 1990 as its successor. Workers have the right to form and join trade unions, to strike, and to engage in collective bargaining. However, ongoing problems include inadequate or employer-biased legislation, management discrimination against union members, and the court system's lack of expertise in labor-related issues.

While the judiciary is largely independent from the executive branch, there is a severe lack of qualified judges, who consequently suffer from excessive workloads. In July 2000, parliament adopted the country's first post-Soviet civil code, which was drafted in accordance with European Union norms. Accused Nazi war criminal Aleksandras Lileikis, whose trial had been repeatedly delayed for more than two years because of his poor health, died in September before a final court verdict could be passed. Various Jewish groups had criticized the numerous delays of the trial, which was the first Nazi-war-crimes proceeding in Lithuania. There have been credible reports of police abuse of suspects and detainees, and overcrowding in prisons and pretrial detention facilities remains a serious problem.

The rights of the country's ethnic minorities are protected in practice. In 1992, Lithuania extended citizenship to all those born within its borders, and more than 90 percent of nonethnic Lithuanians, mostly Russians and Poles, became citizens. Women face discrimination in educational institutions and the workplace, including underrepresentation in upper-level management positions and lower average wages compared to men.

Luxembourg

Polity: Parliamentary democracy
Economy: Capitalist
Population: 400,000
PPP: $33,505
Life Expectancy: 77
Ethnic Groups: Luxembourger (70 percent), other European (30 percent)
Capital: Luxembourg

Political Rights: 1
Civil Liberties: 1
Status: Free

Overview:

Luxembourg's Grand Duke Jean abdicated his 36-year reign as constitutional monarch in September 2000, handing over power to his son, Prince Henri. One year after winning re-election to another five-year term, Prime Minister Jean-Claude Juncker and his Christian Social Party (PCS) continued to enjoy popular support and sought to solidify Luxembourg's growing role in the European Union (EU). Juncker lobbied for the retention of smaller states' rights within the EU during the year, stating that countries such as Luxembourg can play key mediating roles among larger member states.

After centuries of domination and occupation by foreign powers, the small landlocked Grand Duchy of Luxembourg was recognized as an autonomous, neutral state in 1867. After occupation by Germany in both world wars, Luxembourg abandoned its neutrality and became a vocal proponent of European integration. Luxembourg joined NATO in 1949, the Benelux Economic Union (with Belgium and the Netherlands) in 1948, the European Economic Community (later the European Union) in 1957, and the European Monetary Union in 1999.

Prime Minister Juncker voiced concern during 2000 that the economy may be growing at an unsustainable level. With more jobs being created than can be filled with Luxembourg's existing labor pool, the country has been forced to import foreign workers. The prime minister expressed worry over future social security outlays, since eventually many payments will have to be exported abroad. Luxembourg enjoys the lowest unemployment rate in the EU (2.7 percent), with incomes almost two times the EU average.

Luxembourg's multiparty electoral system is based on proportional representation. Executive authority is exercised by the prime minister and the cabinet on behalf of the Grand Duke of Luxembourg. While the grand duke's role is largely ceremonial, all bills must be signed by him before becoming law, and he maintains the power to dissolve parliament. The government is appointed by the sovereign, but is responsible to the legislature. Luxembourg's current constitution, adopted in 1868, has been revised several times.

Political Rights and Civil Liberties:

Luxembourgers can change their government democratically. Voting is compulsory for citizens, and foreigners may register to vote after five years of residence. The prime minister is the leader of the dominant party in the 60-member, unicameral chamber of deputies (parliament), for which popular elections are held every five years. The grand duke appoints the 21 members of the council of state, which serves as an advisory body to the chamber.

The constitution provides for freedom of speech and of the press. Print media are privately owned, and all media are free of censorship. The government issues licenses to private radio stations. Radio and television broadcasts from neighboring countries are freely available.

Although foreigners constitute nearly 35 percent of the population, antiforeigner incidents are infrequent. Luxembourg's population grew 12 percent in the 1990s, and it is expected to nearly double by 2025. EU citizens who reside in Luxembourg enjoy the right to vote and to run in municipal elections. Minimum residency requirements are 6 years for voters and 12 years for candidates.

The constitution provides for freedom of religion in this predominantly Roman Catholic country. There is no state religion, but the state pays the salaries of Roman Catholic, Protestant, and Jewish clergy, and several local governments subsidize sectarian religious facilities.

All workers have the right to associate freely and to choose their representatives. About 65 percent of the labor force is unionized. Unions operate free of government interference. The two largest labor federations are linked to, but organized independently of, the Socialist Workers' and Christian Social parties. The right to strike is constitutionally guaranteed. The law mandates a maximum workweek of 40 hours. All workers receive at least five weeks of paid vacation yearly, in addition to paid holidays.

The independent judiciary is headed by the supreme court, whose members are appointed for life by the grand duke. Defendants are presumed innocent. They have the right to public trials and are free to cross-examine witnesses and to present evidence in court.

Luxembourg's education system is coming under strain as more and more foreign students enroll in the country's schools. Almost half the school population is foreign, many of whom do not speak German or Luxembourgish, the primary languages of instruction.

Women constitute 38 percent of the workforce. The law mandates equal pay for equal work and encourages equal treatment of women. According to the International Confederation of Trade Unions, Luxembourg, with the highest per capita income in the EU, has one of the widest gender pay gaps in the EU. The differences are least in the highest-paid professions and more substantial at lower salary levels. To date, there have been no work-related discrimination lawsuits in the courts.

Macedonia

Polity: Parliamentary democracy
Economy: Mixed statist (transitional)
Population: 2,000,000
PPP: $4,254
Life Expectancy: 73

Political Rights: 4*
Civil Liberties: 3
Status: Partly Free

Ethnic Groups: Macedonian (65 percent), Albanian (22 percent), Turkish (4 percent), Roma (3 percent), Serb (2 percent), other (4 percent)
Capital: Skopje
Ratings Change: Macedonia's political rights rating changed from 3 to 4 because of politically motivated violence against several members of parliament, and municipal elections in September which resulted in several incidents of violence and vote fraud.

Overview:

The year 2000 was another difficult one in Macedonia as relations between the two main ethnic groups in the country, Slavic Macedonians and ethnic-Albanians, continued to deteriorate. Nor was significant progress made in improving Macedonia's dire economic situation.

Macedonia was recognized as one of the independent successor state of the former Yugoslavia in 1991. Internally, the country suffers from a growing social and political polarization between its two primary ethnic groups, Macedonian Slavs and ethnic-Albanians, and from a very poor economy. Externally, Macedonia suffers from a variety of disputes with its neighbors. Greece asserts that use of the name Macedonia connotes a territorial claim to the adjacent Greek province of Macedonia (which is why in international bodies Macedonia must go by the name "The Former Yugoslav Republic of Macedonia"). Bulgaria denies the existence of a Macedonian language, claiming it is just a local variant of Bulgarian, and Macedonia still has unresolved territorial issues with its northern neighbor, the Federal Republic of Yugoslavia, along with unresolved financial and property issues resulting from disputes over succession rights to their former common state.

Despite this difficult situation, however, since gaining independence Macedonia has defied expectations by avoiding either a breakup of the country or civil war. Three sets of multiparty parliamentary elections have been held in the country since 1991, and postindependence governments have always been careful to include Albanian parties in the ruling coalition. Parliamentary elections in 1998 resulted in the first transfer of power from the left-of-center governmental coalition that had ruled Macedonia since independence to a grouping of opposition parties.

Economically, Macedonia has been in desperate straits for most of the past decade. Unemployment stands at 35 percent according to official statistics. In eight years of independence, Macedonia has received less than $300 million in direct foreign investment. From 1991 to 1995, Greece imposed an economic embargo on Macedonia; however, the economic sanctions against Yugoslavia (Macedonia's main economic partner) also did significant damage to the country's economy. The Kosovo conflict in 1999 did even further damage by cutting off the country's trade routes to European Union countries and by causing a flood of Albanian refugees that crossed the Macedonian border in search of refuge during the crisis.

For most of 2000, Macedonia's center-right ruling governmental coalition consisted of Ljubco Georgievski's Internal Macedonian Revolutionary Party—Democratic Party for Macedonian National Unity (VMRO-DPMNE), Vasil Tupurkovski's Democratic Alternative (DA), and the ethnic-Albanian Party of Democratic Prosperity (PDP). The mainly left-of-center opposition consists of the Social Democratic League of Macedonia (SDSM), together with a collection of smaller parties. In August, six members of VMRO-DPMNE quit the party and joined the SDSM-led coalition. Mobs allegedly recruited by Georgievski's ruling coalition stoned the houses of the six members of parliament, and shots were fired in several of these incidents. The municipal election results, however, did not result in a significant shift in the balance of political power within the country. In November, Tupurkovski's DA left the coalition. Although Georgievski was able to avert having to call for new elections by bringing representatives of minor parties into his coalition, the DA's defection significantly weakened his position in the run-up to parliamentary elections due in 2001.

Macedonian-Albanian relations have deteriorated since the war in Kosovo in 1999. In January, three Macedonian policemen were killed in the mainly ethnic-Albanian village of Aracinovo. Over the summer, there were reports that a so-called Albanian National Army was operating in parts of northwestern Albania bordering Kosovo, an area that has also become an important part of the transit route for drug and weapons smugglers in the region.

More positive news regarding relations between the two groups came on July 25, when the Macedonian parliament passed a law designed by international experts, setting up a private, internationally funded Albanian-language university in the country. In previous years, the issue of an Albanian-language university in the town of Tetovo had been the focus of considerable political conflict. It is unclear, however, to what extent either Albanians or Macedonians will be satisfied with this solution.

Political Rights and Civil Liberties: Macedonia's municipal elections, which required up to three rounds in some areas in September and October, were flawed in many respects. Among the most frequently cited irregularities was the so-called multiple vote, in which the head of a family would vote for several members of the household. In several towns in western Macedonia, the first round of voting had to be annulled because of violence or fraud. In Ohrid, during the second round of elections, gangs allegedly recruited by rival political parties provoked a large-scale street fight in which several people were shot. The Organization for Security and Cooperation in Europe (OSCE) preliminary report on the municipal elections claimed that they did not fully meet the country's OSCE commitment to conduct elections free from violence and intimidation, and to safeguard the secrecy of the ballot.

An important constitutional problem Macedonia faces is satisfying the demands of its Albanian minority for a more privileged status within the country. Albanians want the constitution rewritten so as to make them a constituent people within the country and to turn Macedonia into a federal state, with significant authority devolved to local governments. Macedonians are afraid such moves would only be a prelude to the possible secession of Albanian-populated areas in the country. Albanians are also demanding that Albanian be named the second official language of the country.

The Macedonian constitution guarantees freedom of religious belief and practice. Sixty-six percent of the population is Orthodox Christian, and 30 percent is Muslim, while the remaining 4 percent belongs to a variety of different religious groups. While there is no discrimination by the government against various religious organizations, there are occasional tensions that result from the fact that religious affiliations often overlap with ethnic identities; for example, problems between Macedonian Slavs and ethnic-Albanians can sometimes assume undertones of being problems between Orthodox Christians and Muslims. Religious groups have to register with the government, and foreign religious organizations have reported some delays in getting their applications processed. The restitution of church-owned property nationalized by the Communists from 1945 to 1990 is pending resolution following an April 14 decision by the Macedonian parliament to denationalize such properties.

On the whole, the government does not repress the media. In May, however, an Albanian vice director of the country's most important television station, Macedonia Television (MTV), resigned because of the station's alleged anti-Albanian politics. International officials have also criticized MTV for giving the ruling coalition considerably more airtime than opposition parties. In July, the staff of an Albanian-language newspaper critical of the ruling coalition claimed that government pressure was forcing a local publishing company to stop printing the paper. Experts on Macedonia's media believe that one of the major problems facing the media is the lack of professionalism and proper journalistic training.

Over the course of the year, there were repeated claims by trade and labor unions that employers were not honoring Macedonia's Law on Working Relations, which prevents the exploitation of workers and sets a minimum wage.

Women in Macedonia are entitled to the same legal rights as men, although lingering patriarchal social attitudes limit women's participation in nontraditional social roles in both the economy and in government. Domestic violence and trafficking in women, particularly from countries such as Moldova, Ukraine, and neighboring Kosovo, remains a problem. In Muslim areas, many women are effectively disenfranchised because proxy voting by male relatives is widespread.

Madagascar

Polity: Presidential-par-
liamentary democracy
Economy: Mixed statist
Population: 14,900,000
PPP: $756
Life Expectancy: 58
Ethnic Groups: Malayo-Indonesian tribes, Arab, African,
Indian, French
Capital: Antananarivo

Political Rights: 2
Civil Liberties: 4
Status: Partly Free

Overview: Madagascar in 2000 continued its hesitant process of consolidating democratic institutions. Provincial council elections,
part of a policy to extend democratic governance at the re-
gional levels, finally occurred. Public-policy debates about constitutional reform took
place. A weak party system complicates efforts at governance.

Madagascar, the world's fourth largest island, lies 220 miles off Africa's southeastern coast. After 70 years of French colonial rule and episodes of severe repression,
Madagascar gained independence in 1960. A leftist military junta seized power from
President Philbert Tsiranana in 1972. A member of the junta, Admiral Didier Ratsiraka,
emerged as leader in 1975 and maintained power until his increasingly authoritarian
regime bowed to social unrest and nonviolent mass demonstrations in 1991. Under a
new 1992 constitution, opposition leader Albert Zafy won the presidency with more
than 65 percent of the vote.

President Zafy failed to win reelection after being impeached by the supreme court
in 1996. Ratsiraka won a narrow victory in a December 1996 presidential runoff election that was deemed mostly free and fair by international observers. His campaign
pledges of commitment to the democratic rule of law have been honored indiffer-
ently.

The development of a number of institutions mandated by the new, democratic
constitution has been slow, and political influence appears to have undermined the independence of the supreme court. A decentralization plan was narrowly approved in a
1998 referendum that was boycotted by the country's increasingly fractious opposition. A long history of irregular financial dealings continued as the International Monetary Fund (IMF) refused to release scheduled aid.

Legislative elections in May 1998 were viewed as more problematic than preceding polls since Madagascar's transition to multiparty politics in 1992. The Christian
Churches Council and several political groups, for example, noted that the elections
were marred by fraud and other abuses. Ratsiraka's party, the Association for
Madagascar's Renaissance (AREMA) won 63 of 150 parliamentary seats and emerged
as the leading force in a coalition government. A new party led by Norbert Ratsirahonana,
a former prime minister, fared well in and around the capital of Antananarivo.

Race and ethnicity are important factors in Madagascar's politics. Its mostly very
poor population is divided between highland Merina people of Malay origin and coastal
peoples mostly of black-African origin. A referendum on a new constitution held in

1998 resulted in a narrow victory for the changes proposed by President Ratsiraka, which increased the power of the presidency.

Political Rights and Civil Liberties: Citizens have the right to change their government democratically. The president is directly elected by universal adult suffrage. The legislature is to be bicameral, but the upper house has not yet been created. Legislative power is vested in the 150-member national assembly, elected for four years by proportional representation. A constitutional referendum gave the president the power to appoint or dismiss the prime minister; formerly the national assembly had this power.

Elections were held in December 2000 for provincial councils, as part of the government's decentralization policy. In November 1999 municipal polls resulted in overall success for independents who did not have close identification with particular party affiliations. Approximately 150 parties are registered amid a welter of shifting political alliances. Opposition parties exist and are active. They tend to suffer from internal divisions (as does AREMA) and a lack of resources.

Political and civic organizations exercise their right to effect the public policy process. In 1999, for example, opposition leaders and the Madagascar Council of Christian Churches undertook a public information campaign to revise the constitution to limit the powers of the president.

Although the government was accused of seeking to influence the election of the head of the Malagasy journalists' association in March, 2000, in general the press enjoys considerable freedom. Several daily and weekly newspapers publish material sharply critical of the government and other parties and politicians. The state monopoly of radio and television has been abolished. In addition to state radio and television, at least ten private radio stations are now broadcasting, and rebroadcasts of Radio France International are available throughout the country.

The judiciary is, in general, demonstrating increasing autonomy, despite the supreme court's clearly unconstitutional decision to allow the postponement of elections in 1997. Lack of training, resources, and personnel hampers the courts' effectiveness. Case backlogs are prodigious. Most of the 20,000 people held in the country's prisons are pretrial detainees who suffer extremely harsh conditions. In many rural areas, customary law courts that follow neither due process nor standardized judicial procedure often issue summary and severe punishments.

The right to free association is respected, and hundreds of nongovernmental organizations, including lawyers' and human rights groups, are active. The government does not interfere with religious rights. More than half of the population adhere to traditional Malagasy religions and coexist with Christians and Muslims. In 1997, the Rally for Madagascar's Muslim Democrats was registered as the country's first Islamic political party.

More than 70 percent of the population live in poverty. The agricultural sector dominates the economy. It contributed 41 percent to the gross national product in 1996 and employed 75 percent of the working population. The government has undertaken a modestly successful economic reform program; GDP was estimated to have increased by 4.5 percent in 1999. The IMF and the World Bank approved major loans in 1999, and Madagascar may benefit from assistance under the Heavily Indebted Poor Countries (HIPC) initiative as early as 2001.

Workers' rights to join unions and to strike are exercised frequently. Some of the country's free labor organizations are affiliated with political groups. More than four-fifths of the labor force is employed in agriculture, fishing, and forestry at subsistence wages.

Approximately 45 percent of the workforce is female. Malagasy women hold significantly more governmental and managerial positions than women in continental African countries. At the same time, they still face societal discrimination and enjoy fewer opportunities than men in higher education and official employment.

Malawi

Polity: Presidential-parliamentary democracy
Economy: Capitalist
Population: 10,400,000
PPP: $523
Life Expectancy: 40
Ethnic Groups: Chewa, Nyanja, Lomwe, Ngonde, Tumbuku, Yao, Sena, Tonga, Ngoni, Asian, European
Capital: Lilongwe

Political Rights: 3
Civil Liberties: 3
Status: Partly Free

Overview: President Bakili Muluzi threatened in October to arrest opposition leaders if they continued their call for a national strike and civil disobedience to force him to act on the reports of high-level corruption in his government. But by November he had given in to the local and international pressure and sacked his cabinet after receiving a report by the Anti-Corruption Bureau on graft involving government ministers. Widespread corruption has been threatening to undermine Malawi's democracy and further damage an ailing economy. The supreme court in October 2000 upheld the results of the June 1999 presidential election, ending a 16-month dispute over the vote's outcome.

President (later President-for-Life) Hastings Kamuzu Banda ruled Malawi for nearly three decades after the country gained independence from Britain in 1963. Banda exercised dictatorial and often eccentric rule through the Malawi Congress Party (MCP) and its paramilitary youth wing, the Malawi Young Pioneers. Facing a domestic economic crisis and strong international pressure, he accepted a referendum approving multiparty rule in 1993. Muluzi won the presidency in an election in 1994 beset by irregularities, but seen as largely free and fair. The army's violent December 1993 dispersal of the Young Pioneers helped clear the way for the polls.

Violence erupted in opposition strongholds of northern Malawi after presidential and parliamentary election results from the June 1999 elections indicated wins for the ruling United Democratic Front (UDF). Angry supporters of the opposition coalition of the MCP and the Alliance for Democracy (MCP-AFORD) attacked mosques, shops, and homes of suspected UDF supporters.

Malawi had been running without local authorities since Muluzi first came to power in 1994. He had fired all local authorities, saying they were loyalists of former President Banda. The government in October 2000 bowed to public pressure and withdrew a contentious local government bill designed to give Muluzi the sole authority to appoint city and other municipal or district mayors. The ruling UDF scored a landslide victory in November's local polls in voting that was marked by low turnout.

Malawi's economy is dependent on tobacco, but the crop registered a 14 percent drop in earnings in 2000.

Political Rights and Civil Liberties:

The citizens of Malawi are guaranteed the right to choose their leaders. In May 1994, the president and members of the national assembly won five-year terms in Malawi's first generally free and fair multiparty elections. However, there was limited opposition access to media as well as problems with voter registration. The opposition appealed the result to the courts. The results of the June 1999 presidential poll went to the courts as well. Three presidential contenders sued the electoral commission for allegedly illegally declaring Muluzi the winner. They contended Muluzi failed to win enough votes. Muluzi won 51 percent, compared to 44 percent for leading opposition candidate Gwanda Chakuamba, of the MCP-AFORD alliance. The supreme court in October 2000 upheld the results of the election.

In polls for the national assembly in 1999, the ruling party managed to retain a narrow majority, winning 99 seats compared with 94 for MCP-AFORD. There are no clear-cut ideological differences between the three parties.

The judiciary has demonstrated broad independence in its decisions, but due process is not always respected by an overburdened court system that lacks resources and training. A legal resource center has been established under the Law Society of Malawi, with assistance from the British government.

Rights of free expression and free assembly are generally respected. Many human rights and other nongovernmental organizations operate openly and without interference. The constitutionally mandated Human Rights Commission met for the first time in 1999. Religious freedom is usually respected, but Muslims were targeted in postelection violence in 1999 in protest against the ruling party. President Muluzi is a Muslim. Malawi is 75 percent Christian and about 20 percent Muslim.

There are no reported political prisoners in Malawi. Police brutality is still said to be common, and extrajudicial killings have been reported, either while detainees were in custody or just after they were released. Arbitrary arrest and detention are common. The government has sought community involvement in its reform of the police. Appalling prison conditions lead to many deaths, including suffocation from overcrowding. The Community Service Act, passed in 1999, permits some offenders to provide community service instead of suffering imprisonment.

Freedom of speech and the press is guaranteed. It is generally respected in practice, although journalists still practice some self-censorship. The government has used libel and other laws to harass journalists. A broad spectrum of opinion is presented in the country's two dozen newspapers. The state-owned Malawi Broadcasting Corporation controls television and most radio service, which reaches a larger audience than print media do. There are four private radio stations.

About 60 percent of Malawi's ten million people have no access to land, and the issue is a potential breeding ground for social unrest. The government said in August 2000 that it planned to ask donors for U.S.$25 million to purchase land for a resettlement program for 21,000 landless peasants. Despite equal protection of the law under the 1995 constitution, customary practices maintain de facto discrimination against women in education, employment, and business. Traditional rural structures deny women inheritance and property rights, and violence against women is reportedly routine.

The right to organize and to strike is legally protected, with notice and mediation requirements for workers in essential services. Unions are active but face harassment and occasional violence during strikes, and there have been reports of union employees being fired for their political views. Collective bargaining is widely practiced, but not specifically protected by law. The International Labor Organization and the Malawi Congress of Trade Unions said in October 2000 that the owners of some tobacco and tea estates were using child labor and that the country could therefore face international trade sanctions.

Malaysia

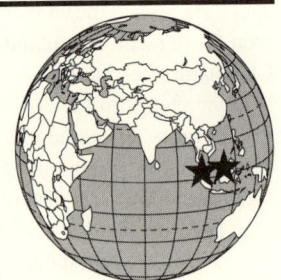

Polity: Dominant party
Economy: Capitalist
Population: 23,300,000
PPP: $8,137
Life Expectancy: 72
Ethnic Groups: Malay and other indigenous (58 percent), Chinese (26 percent), Indian (7 percent), other (9 percent)
Capital: Kuala Lumpur

Political Rights: 5
Civil Liberties: 5
Status: Partly Free

Overview: After winning an election in 1999 that saw a large swing in support to the Islamic fundamentalist *Parti Islam se-Malaysia* (Pas), the ruling National Front coalition tried to appeal to conservative Muslims in 2000 while pursuing criminal charges against five opposition figures.

Malaysia was established in 1963 through a merger of independent, ex-British Malaya with the British colonies of Sarawak, Sabah, and Singapore (Singapore withdrew in 1965). The 14-party, ruling National Front has captured at least a two-thirds lower house majority in ten straight general elections since 1957. The Front consists of several race-based parties, led by the conservative, Malay-based United Malays National Organization (UMNO). Since taking office as prime minister in 1981, Mahathir Mohamad has promoted economic development and racial harmony while restricting political dissent. Until recently, his greatest political challenge came in the late 1980s, when a breakaway UMNO faction formed *Semangat '46* (Spirit of '46, the year UMNO was founded in Malaya) and joined the country's first Malay-led opposition coalition. However, the opposition foundered in the 1990 elections and Semangat '46 rejoined the Front in 1996.

Mahathir's policies helped Malaysia achieve nearly a decade of 8 percent economic growth by the time the regional financial crisis began in 1997, but also contributed to excessive corporate borrowing and a high current account deficit. In addition, critics accused the government of tolerating crony capitalism and accumulating a large public debt. By spring 1998 the economy was heading into recession, and Mahathir's calls for expansionary fiscal and monetary policies drew open criticism from Anwar Ibrahim, the deputy prime minister and Mahathir's presumed successor. In September, Mahathir fired Anwar and had him jailed on corruption and sodomy charges. In the following months, police forcibly dispersed unprecedented antigovernment demonstrations in Kuala Lumpur and several towns that drew thousands of students and other youths who called for *reformasi* (reform).

Following a seven-month trial that drew international and domestic criticism, a court convicted Anwar of abuse of power in April 1999. Anwar's wife, Wan Azizah Ismail, responded by founding *Keadilan* (the National Justice Party), which entered into a new, opposition Alternative Front coalition with Pas, the main Malay-based opposition party; the ethnic-Chinese-based Democratic Action Party (DAP); and the Tamil-based Malaysian People's Party. At the November 29, 1999 elections, held under a 72 percent turnout, the National Front won 148 seats, led by UMNO with 72; the Alternative Front, 42 (Pas, 27; DAP, 10; Keadilan, 5); and Parti Bersatu Sabah, an opposition party based in Sabah state, 3. While Keadilan had presented itself as a secular, Malay-based alternative to UMNO, which lost 16 seats, the biggest swing, of 20 seats, went to the Islamic-oriented Pas, which apparently gained the support of many conservative Malays angered by Mahathir's treatment of Anwar. Strong support from the Chinese and Indian minorities helped the Front retain its two-thirds majority, but its share of the popular vote fell to 56 percent from 65 percent in 1995. The Alternative Front named Pas president Fadzil Noor as parliamentary opposition leader on December 8.

Shortly after the election, Mahathir announced that he was beginning what would be his last term. On May 11, 2000, UMNO returned Mahathir as party president and Deputy Prime Minister Abdulah Ahmad Badawi, his likely successor, as deputy president after party leaders successfully discouraged challenges for the top posts.

Political Rights and Civil Liberties:

Malaysians have a limited ability to change their government through elections. While elections are generally free, they are not fair because of the government's partisan use of state-run media and other resources and its use of numerous security laws to restrict freedoms of expression, assembly, and association. Nevertheless, in the 1999 elections, the opposition Pas retained control of Kelantan state and captured oil-rich Terengganu for the first time.

The constitution provides for a house of representatives (193 seats in the 1999 elections), which is directly elected for a five-year term, and a 58-member senate. Executive power is vested in a prime minister and cabinet. The king serves as a largely ceremonial head of state, but can delay legislation for 30 days.

The opposition alleged that Mahathir timed the 1999 elections to prevent the participation of some 650,000 new voters, who had registered in spring 1999 amid unprecedented antigovernment demonstrations. The law did not allow voters who signed up during the spring registration period to cast ballots until January 2000. Following the vote, the Bangkok-based Asian Network for Free Elections said its election monitors had found evidence of irregularities in the voter registration process and of ineligible voters casting ballots. A local monitoring group, Permantau, also reported irregularities. Following UMNO's victory in the March 1999 Sabah state elections, the opposition Parti Bersatu Sabah and human rights groups had accused the Front of bribing and intimidating voters, charges the Front denied.

While these accusations of irregularities are plausible, an arguably greater problem is the government's use of the law and state resources to undermine the opposition. The government said in September that rather than continue paying oil royalties due to Terengganu directly to the state administration, it would disburse the money through a federal agency that would choose projects for funding. Critics charged the government with trying to undermine Terengganu's opposition administration. In March, Malacca withdrew some state business from banks and professionals suspected of supporting the opposition during the 1999 general elections.

In its country report for 1999, the United States State Department noted, "A number of high-profile cases continued to cast doubt on judicial impartiality and independence, and to raise questions of arbitrary verdicts, selective prosecution, and preferential treatment of some litigants and lawyers." In August, the Geneva-based International Commission of Jurists condemned as "politically motivated" a court's sentencing of Anwar that month to nine years in jail for sodomy, to be served following his six-year jail term for abuse of power. In ordinary cases, defendants enjoy most due process rights. However, in some circumstances police can deny detainees access to legal counsel, and there are restrictions on the right to appeal.

The government can detain suspects without judicial review or formal charges under the 1960 Internal Security Act (ISA), the 1969 Emergency Ordinance, and the 1985 Dangerous Drugs Act (DDA). Both the ISA and the Emergency Ordinance permit authorities to detain suspects for up to two years. Enacted at a time when Malaysia faced a Communist insurgency, the ISA has, in recent years, been used by authorities for long-term detention of suspected Communist activists, ordinary suspects, and "religious extremists," and occasionally to detain non-Communist political opponents for less than 60 days. According to the U.S. State Department's country report for 1999, the Home Ministry said in late 1998 that authorities were detaining 223 persons under the ISA, nearly all of them for document forgery or illegal-alien smuggling. While there were no figures available for detentions under the Emergency Ordinance, the State Department report said that police had detained 1,375 suspected drug traffickers under the DDA in 1999.

To curb political dissent , the government more frequently has used the Official Secrets Act, criminal defamation laws, the 1984 Printing Presses and Publications Act (PPPA), which bars the publication of "malicious" news, and the colonial-era Sedition Act, which restricts public discussion on issues defined as sensitive, including certain racial and religious topics. In January, authorities charged two opposition leaders with sedition and a third under the Official Secrets Act. During the year, the social activist Irene Fernandez continued to stand trial after being accused in 1996 of "malicious publication of false news" over a 1995 report by her organization, Tenaganita, which detailed alleged abuse and torture of migrant workers at detention camps. The DAP deputy leader, Lim Guan Eng, spent 12 months in jail in 1998 and 1999 under the Sedition Act and the PPPA for having publicly criticized the government's handling of statutory rape allegations against a former state chief minister in 1994.

The media face numerous constraints, and journalists practice self-censorship. In May, a court convicted and fined the printer of *Harakah*, the Pas newspaper, after he pleaded guilty to sedition over an article in which the jailed Anwar accused Mahathir of conspiracy. Having pleaded not guilty in the same case, *Harakah's* editor was on trial for sedition at year's end. In March, authorities used the PPPA to withdraw the publishing license of the pro-opposition *Detik* magazine, ostensibly on technical grounds, and to restrict *Harakah* to two editions per month from twice weekly. The PPPA permits the government to ban or restrict allegedly "subversive" publications, requires newspapers to renew their licenses annually, and prohibits publications from challenging such actions in court. Previously, the government had closed three newspapers under the PPPA in 1987.

Most major newspapers are owned by individuals and companies close to the ruling National Front, and their coverage favors the government. State-run Radio Television Malaysia is the major broadcaster and mainly offers pro-government views. Prior to the 1999 elections, government officials openly said the state broadcast media would not cover the opposition.

In recent years, authorities have permitted the opposition somewhat greater campaigning opportunities by relaxing a 1969 ban on political rallies during campaigns. The government had permitted only indoor "discussion sessions." Since the reformasi movement began in September 1998, police have permitted some antigovernment demonstrations but have forcibly dispersed others and arrested hundreds of demonstrators, including peaceful protesters. Many of those arrested were acquitted, although some were convicted. The 1967 Police Act requires permits for all public assemblies except for workers on picket lines. The government tightened its policy in March, when it banned public rallies in Kuala Lumpur.

The newly formed official National Human Rights Commission began receiving complaints in April, mainly of police abuse. However, the commission lacks enforcement powers. The U.S. State Department and Amnesty International have reported in recent years that police have abused some protesters during and after antigovernment demonstrations, and have also occasionally tortured or otherwise abused ordinary detainees.

Under the 1966 Societies Act, authorities have refused to register some organizations and have deregistered some political opposition groups. The act requires any association (including political parties) of more than six members to register with the government. Nongovernmental organizations operate openly but face some harassment.

While Islam is the official religion, non-Muslims worship freely in this secular country. Authorities restrict and monitor some "deviant" Islamic sects including the Shias, periodically detain members of deviant sects under the ISA, and restrict the content of sermons at government-affiliated mosques. The government blamed Islamic fundamentalists for an armed hostage crisis in early July that killed three people, and cited the incident as evidence of the need to maintain these restrictions.

Sharia (Islamic law) courts have authority over family and property matters in the Muslim community. In each of the nine states with traditional sultans, the sultan is at the apex of the Islamic religious establishment. The king, who is elected by and from among the nine sultans, supervises Islamic affairs in the four remaining states. In recent years, Mahathir has angered religious leaders by advocating a progressive practice of Islam, criticizing the *ulama* (religious scholars) who head the Sharia courts for discrimination against women, and proposing to unify the state Islamic laws under a federal system. Pas-controlled administrations in Kelantan and Terengganu have imposed some religious-based dress, dietary, and cultural restrictions on Muslims.

The government has taken numerous measures to promote women's equality and is generally responsive to the problems of sexual harassment in the workplace and violence against women, including domestic violence and rape. The 1999 U.S. State Department report noted, "Malaysia is a source, transit point, and destination country for trafficking in women and girls for sexual exploitation."

Ethnic-Malays enjoy quotas in education, the civil service, and business affairs. The government established the quotas in 1971 in response to anti-Chinese riots in 1969. The riots occurred in the context of mounting Malay frustration over the economic success of the ethnic-Chinese minority. In peninsular Malaysia, indigenous people have limited opportunity to own land on an individual basis, despite recent legal changes permitting them to do so. Indigenous people in eastern Malaysia allege that logging and plantation companies encroach on their land.

Most workers have the right to join trade unions and bargain collectively. The law allows a union to represent only workers in single, or similar, trades or industries. The government continued to discourage the formation of national unions in the export-oriented electronics industry. The law restricts the right to strike.

Mahathir has frequently denounced corruption within UMNO, and there is also evidence of corruption in business affairs. The Berlin-based Transparency International's 2000 Corruption Perceptions Index ranked Malaysia 36 out of 90 countries with a score of 4.8 on a 0 to 10 scale, with Finland, the top-ranked and least-corrupt country, receiving a 10.

Maldives

Polity: Presidential
Economy: Capitalist
Population: 300,000
PPP: $4,083
Life Expectancy: 65
Ethnic Groups: Sinhalese, Dravidian, Arab
Capital: Male

Political Rights: 6
Civil Liberties: 5
Status: Not Free

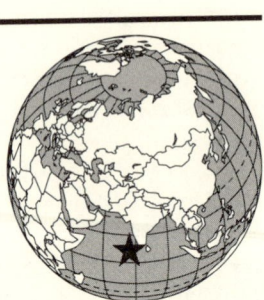

Overview:

A 500-mile-long string of 26 atolls in the Indian Ocean, the Maldives achieved independence in 1965 after 78 years as a British protectorate. A 1968 referendum ended the ad-Din sultanate's 815-year rule and established a republic.

The 1968 constitution vested broad executive powers in a president, who must be a male Sunni Muslim. The *Majlis* (parliament) has 40 directly elected members and eight presidential appointees who serve five-year terms. Every five years the Majlis chooses a sole presidential candidate whom citizens vote on in a yes-or-no referendum. A 1998 constitutional amendment permitted citizens to declare their candidacy for the presidential nomination. However, candidates cannot campaign for the nomination, and the Majlis still chooses the nominee.

President Maumoon Abdul Gayoom has ruled since 1978. The Maldives held its most recent presidential referendum on October 16, 1998, when Gayoom won a fifth term with the reported approval of 90.9 percent of participating voters. Under the recent constitutional amendment, four minor challengers had declared their candidacies for the presidential nomination. The most serious threat to Gayoom's survival came in 1988, when Indian commandos had to crush a coup attempt by a disgruntled business-man reportedly backed by Sri Lankan mercenaries. In the aftermath, the autocratic Gayoom strengthened the National Security Service and named several relatives to top government posts.

The London-based Amnesty International (AI) said in January 2000 that authori-ties had detained three politicians while they were campaigning for the November 19, 1999, parliamentary elections, and had reportedly tortured at least two of the men. Few details of the nonparty elections were available.

Political Rights and Civil Liberties:

Maldivians cannot change their government through elections, owing to the Gayoom administration's tight control over the electoral process, de facto ban on political parties, and use of restrictive laws to occasionally detain dissidents. Although a 1998 constitutional amend-ment brought some pluralism to the presidential nomination process, Amnesty Interna-tional reported in September 1998 that preparations for the upcoming presidential ref-erendum were "taking place in an atmosphere of fear and intimidation." In addition to arresting three candidates prior to the November 1999 parliamentary elections, authori-ties also restricted political gatherings during the campaign to small meetings on pri-vate premises. The government had detained five candidates prior to the 1994 Majlis elections. Nevertheless, in recent years the Majlis has rejected some government leg-islation and has become a forum for critical debate.

In its report for 1999, Amnesty International said the government continued to hold several possible prisoners of conscience. They included three men detained since 1996 in connection with a demonstration over electricity prices, and ten people from Faafu Magoodhoo Atoll whom authorities banished to a remote atoll in 1999 for seek-ing to organize a demonstration against the local atoll chief. Banishment is permitted as a punishment after a formal conviction on criminal charges. Authorities also continued to imprison Ismail Saadiq, a businessman and political dissident. Authorities placed Saadiq under house arrest for fraud in 1996, and in 1998 detained him and convicted him of fraud after he allegedly contacted a British Broadcasting Corporation reporter.

In a positive development, the government amended the 1990 Prevention of Ter-rorism Act (PTA) in 1998 to place limits on indefinite detention of individuals under investigation. However, if authorities have not begun legal proceedings after a period of roughly three weeks, judges can still authorize continued detention on a monthly basis.

While Gayoom rarely uses his powers to dismiss judges and overturn high court decisions, he reportedly influences judicial decisions. Trials fall short of international standards. Civil law is subordinate to *Sharia* (Islamic law), although civil law is gener-ally used in criminal and civil cases. Under Sharia, the testimony of two women is equal to that of one man in finance and inheritance matters.

The government has used several broadly drawn laws to restrict freedom of ex-pression. The penal code bans speech or actions that could "arouse people against the government." A 1968 law prohibits speech considered inimical to Islam, a threat to national security, or libelous. Under this law, the journalist Mohamed Nasheed spent nearly nine months in prison and under house arrest in 1996 and 1997 over a 1994 article criticizing election procedures. In addition, a court sentenced a Maldivian to six months in prison under this law in 1994 for making supposedly false statements about the government.

Authorities can shut newspapers and sanction journalists for articles allegedly containing unfounded criticism of the government, and regulations make editors responsible for the content of published material. In this climate, journalists practice self-censorship. Nevertheless, conditions for the media have improved somewhat since 1990, when authorities revoked the licenses of two outspoken publications and used the PTA to imprison several journalists, the last of whom was released in 1993. Today, some of the 60-odd private periodicals criticize government policies, though not the political system. The state-run Voice of the Maldives radio and a small state-run television service are the only broadcast media; both carry criticism of government performance, but not true opposition views. Foreign broadcasts are available.

In recent years, the government has sponsored programs to help make women aware of their rights. However, traditional norms continued to limit educational opportunities for girls and career choices for women. Under Sharia, men are favored in divorce and inheritance matters. Islam is the state religion, and the government requires all citizens to be Muslim. The law bans the practice of other religions.

There are no nongovernmental human rights groups. Workers lack the legal right to form trade unions, stage strikes, or bargain collectively. In practice there is no organized labor activity. Most workers are employed in nonformal jobs, though some work in the country's high-end tourism industry, which provides 40 percent of foreign exchange revenues. According to the United States State Department, employers often prevent foreign workers from leaving their worksites and meeting with Maldivians.

Mali

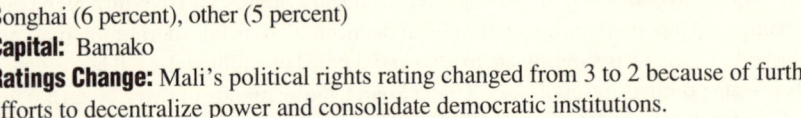

Polity: Presidential-parliamentary democracy
Economy: Mixed statist
Population: 11,200,000
PPP: $681
Life Expectancy: 54
Ethnic Groups: Mande (50 percent), Peul (17 percent), Voltaic (12 percent), Tuareg and Moor (10 percent), Songhai (6 percent), other (5 percent)
Capital: Bamako

Political Rights: 2*
Civil Liberties: 3
Status: Free

Ratings Change: Mali's political rights rating changed from 3 to 2 because of further efforts to decentralize power and consolidate democratic institutions.

Overview: The government of President Alpha Oumar Konaré continued to consolidate its democracy with new laws on party financing and the media in 2000. The media law included reduced penalties for libel, replacing jail terms with fines. In preparation for 2002 legislative and presidential elections, officials are revising logistical details for voter rolls and polling. A new government was formed in January, following the resignation of the prime minister. The media had persistently called for him to step down, saying his efforts to revitalize the economy were insufficient. Konaré, in January, quelled a mutiny by discontented soldiers who were demanding reportedly unpaid bonuses for peacekeeping duties in Sierra Leone and the Central African Republic.

After achieving independence from France in 1960, Mali was ruled by military or one-party dictators for more than 30 years. After soldiers killed more than 100 demonstrators demanding a multiparty system in 1991, President Moussa Traoré was overthrown by his own military. Traoré and his wife, Mariam, were sentenced to death in January 1999 for embezzlement. Traoré had received the death sentence in 1993 as well, for ordering troops to fire on demonstrators in 1991. All of the sentences have been commuted to life imprisonment. After the 1991 coup, a national conference organized open elections that most observers judged free and fair. Konaré and his Alliance for Democracy in Mali (ADEMA) won the presidency in April 1992.

Despite steady economic growth, Mali remains desperately poor with about 65 percent of its land area desert or semidesert. About 80 percent of the labor force is engaged in farming and fishing. Principal exports are cotton, livestock, and gold. Hundreds of thousands of Malians are economic migrants across Africa and Europe. Privatization of major state enterprises continues. An anticorruption commission published its fourth report in 2000, revealing embezzlement and mismanagement in several state-owned companies and public bodies.

Political Rights and Civil Liberties: Mali's people first chose their government freely and fairly in presidential and legislative elections in 1992. In 1997, little more than a quarter of registered voters participated as Konaré was overwhelmingly reelected against a weak candidate who alone broke an opposition boycott of the presidential contest. The first round of legislative elections in 1997 was voided by the constitutional court, although international observers saw incompetence rather than fraud as the principal problem. ADEMA holds 130 of 147 national assembly seats and allied parties hold 12. The opposition occupies 5.

ADEMA won 61.6 percent of the localities in local elections in 1999, while moderate opposition groups won most of the remainder. Radical opposition parties boycotted the polls, as they did in earlier presidential and parliamentary elections. One group, however, broke ranks and won ten localities. The central government in the capital, Bamako, stopped administering land use, schools, health centers, transport systems, and other services after the 1999 local elections.

Since the end of military rule, Mali's domestic political debate has been open and extensive. The government holds an annual Democracy and Human Rights Forum in December, in which citizens can air complaints in the presence of the media and international observers.

The judiciary is not independent of the executive, but has shown considerable autonomy in rendering anti-administration decisions, which President Konaré has in turn respected. Local chiefs, in consultation with elders, decide the majority of disputes in rural areas. Detainees are not always charged within the 48-hour period set by law. There are often lengthy delays in bringing people to trial.

Mali's human rights record is generally good, although there are reports of police brutality. Prisons are characterized by overcrowding, inadequate medical care, and limited food. The government permits visits by human rights monitors. Independent human rights groups, including the Malian Association for Human Rights and a local chapter of Amnesty International, operate openly and freely.

No ethnic group predominates in the government or the security forces, and political parties are not based on ethnicity. There are, however, longstanding tensions between the marginalized Moor and Tuareg pastoral groups and the more populous pastoral groups. A 1995 agreement ended the brutal multisided conflict among Tuareg guerrillas, black-ethnic militias, and government troops. Former guerrilla fighters have been integrated into the national army.

Mali's media are among Africa's most open. Approximately 40 independent newspapers operate freely, and at least 60 independent radio stations, including community stations broadcasting in regional languages, operate throughout the country. There is no locally produced independent television. The government controls one television station and many radio stations, but all present diverse views, including those critical of the government. Legislation in July 2000 provided for reduced penalties for libel, replacing jail terms with fines. The editor of the private newspaper *La Nation* was convicted of defaming Mali's armed forces minister in November 2000 and ordered to pay a fine.

Mali, predominantly Muslim, is a secular state, and minority and religious rights are protected by law. Religious associations must register with the government, but the law is not enforced.

Most formal legal advances in protection of women's rights have not been implemented, especially in rural areas. Societal discrimination against women persists, and social and cultural factors continue to limit their economic and educational opportunities. Women, however, hold some key portfolios in the cabinet, including the ministry of commerce and industry. Violence against women, including spousal abuse, is tolerated and common. Female genital mutilation remains legal, although the government has conducted educational campaigns against the practice. Numerous groups promote the rights of women and children.

Workers are guaranteed the right to join unions. Nearly all salaried employees are unionized. The right to strike is guaranteed, although there are some restrictions. Labor unions played a leading role in the pro-democracy movement and remain politically active. Although the constitution prohibits forced labor, Malian children have been sold into forced labor in Côte d'Ivoire by organized traffickers. The government is taking steps to halt the practice and repatriate the children. Hereditary servitude relationships link different ethnic groups, mainly in the north.

Malta

Polity: Parliamentary democracy
Economy: Mixed capitalist-statist
Population: 400,000
PPP: $16,447
Life Expectancy: 77
Ethnic Groups: Maltese (mixed Arab, Norman, Spanish, Italian, and English)
Capital: Valletta

Political Rights: 1
Civil Liberties: 1
Status: Free

Overview:

In 2000 Malta continued to make considerable progress in negotiations for membership in the European Union (EU). Prime Minister Eddie Fenech Adami of the Nationalist Party (PN) stated in February that as a member, Malta would strengthen the body's "Mediterranean dimension." The EU issued a report in November, which indicated that Malta is the best-equipped economically of the countries vying for EU membership. The prime minister promises to hold a national referendum on the issue of membership in 2002. The opposition, the Malta Labor Party (MLP), led by Alfred Sant, has pledged to disregard the outcome if the Labor party wins the next general elections.

Since it gained independence in 1964 within the Commonwealth and then became a republic in 1974, Malta has carefully maintained its neutrality, balancing its links with Europe to the north with ties to Arab nations to the south. The strategically located archipelago, of which Malta is the largest island, was occupied by a long succession of foreign powers. From independence in 1964 to 1971, Malta was governed by the PN, which pursued its policy of firm alignment with the West. In 1971, however, MLP came to power and implemented its policy on nonalignment and special friendship with leftist governments in Libya and Algeria. The PN returned to power in 1987 and filed an application for membership in the EU in 1991. But the MLP regained power in 1996 and suspended the application.

Alfred Sant, prime minister of the MLP, was ousted from his position in 1998 and the NP once again reclaimed power with Eddie Fenech Adami as prime minister. In 1999, the PN-dominated parliament installed Guido de Marco as president after he had served 22 years as deputy chairman of the party. The leading political parties, however, which have alternated in power with each other, have taken conflicting positions as to the direction in which Malta should lean: The currently ruling PN favors closer ties with Europe while the MLP formerly favored closer ties with Libya and Algeria, but now favors strict neutrality.

Political Rights and Civil Liberties:

Citizens of Malta can change their government democratically. Members of the house of representatives, the country's unicameral legislature, are elected on the basis of proportional representation every five years. Parliament elects the country's president to a five-year term. Although the post is largely ceremonial, the president is charged with formally appointing a prime minister and the cabinet of ministers.

The constitution provides for freedom of the press. Since 1992, the government has sponsored programs to diversify the media. In addition to several Maltese-language newspapers, a few English-language weeklies are published. Malta's two main political parties own television and radio stations, as well as newspapers, which promote their political views. Italian television and radio are also popular. Malta has one of the lowest rates of Internet usage in Europe, with only an estimated four percent of the population having access to the Internet.

Roman Catholicism is the state religion. The government grants subsidies only to Roman Catholic schools. Students in government schools may opt to decline instruction in Roman Catholicism. Freedom of worship by religious minorities is respected.

Workers have the right to associate freely and to strike. There are more than 35 independent trade unions that represent more than 50 percent of the population. All unions are independent of political parties; however, the largest, the General Workers' Union, is regarded to have informal ties with the MLP.

The judiciary is independent of the executive and legislative branches. The president, on the advice of the prime minister, appoints the chief justice and nine judges. The constitution requires a fair public trial, and defendants have the right to counsel of their choice. In 1999, Malta abolished the death penalty for all offenses, replacing it with life imprisonment.

A constitutional amendment banning gender discrimination took effect in 1993. While women constitute a growing portion of the workforce, they are underrepresented in management positions and political leadership. There are no women judges, and women make up only about nine percent of the members of parliament.

Marshall Islands

Polity: Parliamentary democracy and traditional chiefs
Political Rights: 1
Civil Liberties: 1
Status: Free

Economy: Capitalist-statist
Population: 100,000
PPP: na
Life Expectancy: 62
Ethnic Groups: Micronesian
Capital: Majuro

Overview:

President Kessai Note took office in January 2000. The country, along with several other Pacific Island countries, was implicated in allegations of money-laundering activities. The government contested this claim but introduced new measures to monitor the country's offshore banking activities. The U.S. government is also looking into the possibility that Asian criminal groups are using the Marshall Islands as a new transport point for entry into the United States.

The Marshall Islands, consisting of the Ralik and Ratak chains of coral atolls in the central Pacific Ocean, were purchased by Germany from Spain in 1899. Japan seized the islands in 1914, governing them under a League of Nations mandate until the U.S. Navy occupied them in 1945. In 1947, they became part of the U.S. Trust Territory of the Pacific Islands under United Nations trusteeship. The Marshall Islands district drafted a constitution. On May 1, 1979, it came into effect, and the parliament chose Amata Kabua as the country's first president. He was subsequently reelected to four successive four-year terms, the last beginning in January 1996.

In 1983, the Marshall Islands signed a Compact of Free Association with the United States and the agreement came into force in 1986. Under the Compact, the country is fully sovereign but allows the United States responsibility for defense. The Compact includes an economic assistance package, which supports as much as 55 percent of the national budget. Compact money rapidly expanded the service sector but many government institutions failed, spending surpassed receipts, and there was little economic development. All this left the country saddled with a large foreign debt.

The end of the cold war reduced the country's strategic importance to the United States. Thus, a new economic package under the Compact would likely be smaller than the current one. In anticipation of this change, the government is encouraging private-sector growth. The government also introduced an austerity program in 1995 that was designed by the Asian Development Bank to reduce the budget and the size of the civil service.

Amata Kabua's death in December 1996 left the country bereft of leadership. The president owed his political longevity to personal loyalties within parliament and a limited pool of viable alternative candidates. On January 14, 1997, parliament elected Imata Kabua, a long-time senator and a cousin of the late president, to finish the president's term, although the constitution mandates that the speaker of the senate should serve as acting president. In October 1998, Imata Kabua won a narrow victory in a no-confidence motion, the first in the country's history. The opposition charged that Kabua misused government funds and that his administration lacked accountability and transparency. The public also strongly criticized his administration's proposal to rent remote, uninhabited islands to foreign countries as nuclear waste dumps. In December 1999, voters ousted Kabua's government in a public poll and gave the opposition Democrats Party a majority in the parliament.

Negotiations for a new economic assistance package under the Compact began in Hawaii in October 1999. The Marshall Islands also petitioned the U.S. Congress to provide $27 million to meet the shortfall in the $45 million Compact Fund to settle 6,460 claims for injuries caused by nuclear tests in the region. Already, 40 percent of the claimants have died without receiving compensation, and new reports revealed that the fallout from nuclear weapons tests in the 1950s was at least 20 times greater than the U.S. estimate. Talks will likely end in 2001.

A public dispute between the supreme court chief justice and the designated head of the country's judicial service commission in October 1999 raised concern about the future of judicial appointments. At the swearing in of a new supreme court justice in May 2000, President Note reiterated his administration's support for judicial independence and commitment to keep political influence out of the judicial system.

Political Rights and Civil Liberties:

Citizens of the Marshall Islands can change their government democratically. The 1979 constitution provides for a bicameral parliament: the 33-seat house of representatives (*Nitijela*) is directly elected for a four-year term, and this lower house chooses a president, who holds executive powers as head of state and head of the government, from among its members. The Council of Chiefs, or upper Iroji, has 12 traditional leaders who offer advice on customary laws. Two ad hoc parties participated in the 1991 legislative elections, but they dissolved soon afterwards. Although no legal restrictions currently exist against the formation of political parties, no formal parties exist.

The government generally respects freedom of speech and of the press, but journalists occasionally practice self-censorship on sensitive political issues. A privately owned weekly newspaper publishes in both English and the Marshallese language. The government's *Marshall Islands Gazette*, a monthly, contains official news and avoids political coverage. There are two radio stations; one is state-owned, and both offer pluralistic views. A cable television company shows U.S. programs and occasionally covers local events. There are no restrictions on religious observance in this predominantly Christian country.

Freedom of assembly is respected in practice. The government broadly interprets constitutional guarantees of freedom of association, but no trade union has been formed. There is no formal right to strike or engage in collective bargaining, but no legal constraint exists in practice.

The judiciary is generally independent, and the rule of law is well established. In recent years, the parliament amended the Judiciary Act and passed a new legislative act to strengthen the judiciary in order to prevent government intervention. The government respects the right to a fair trial. Both the national and local police honor legal civil rights protections in performing their duties.

Freedom of internal movement is unrestricted, except on Kwajalein Atoll, the site of a major U.S. military installation. Although inheritance of property and traditional rank are matrilineal, and women hold a social status equal to men in most matters, most women working in the private sector hold low-wage jobs, and women are underrepresented in politics and government. Domestic violence has increased, but traditional culture dissuades many victims of domestic violence from reporting the crime or prosecuting spouses in the court system.

⬇ Mauritania

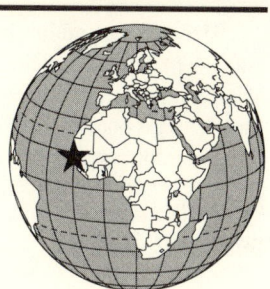

Polity: Dominant party (military-influenced)
Economy: Capitalist-statist
Population: 2,700,000
PPP: $1,563
Life Expectancy: 54
Ethnic Groups: Mixed Maur/black (40 percent), Maur (30 percent), black (30 percent)
Capital: Nouakchott

Political Rights: 6
Civil Liberties: 5
Status: Not Free

Trend Arrow: Mauritania received a downward trend arrow after the government banned the country's leading opposition party, closed its offices, and seized its property.

Overview:

The Islamic government of President Maaouya Ould Sid Ahmed Taya faced persistent demonstrations toward the end of the year. The dual nature of the protests posed one of the greatest threats to the government in recent years. Youths marched through the streets of the capital, Nouakchott, demanding that officials break diplomatic relations with Israel, following fighting in the Middle East. The demonstrators were also protesting the banning in late October of a popular opposition party, the Union of Democratic Forces-New Era (UFD-EN), led by former presidential candidate Ahmed Ould Daddah. He was detained briefly in April and again in December. The government said it banned Daddah's party for acting against the interests of the country and fomenting violence, namely by backing the anti-Israeli demonstrations. Mauritania established diplomatic ties with Israel in 1999.

After nearly six decades of French colonial rule, Mauritania's borders as an independent state were formalized in 1960. Its people include the dominant "white Maurs" of Arab extraction and the Arabic-speaking Muslim black Africans known as "black Maurs." Other, non-Muslim, black Africans inhabiting the country's southern frontiers along the Senegal River valley constitute approximately one-third of the population. For centuries, black Africans were subjugated and taken as slaves by both white and black Maurs. Slavery has been repeatedly outlawed, but remnants of servitude and credible allegations of chattel slavery persist.

A 1978 military coup ended a civilian one-party state. A 1984 internal purge installed Colonel Maaouya Ould Sid Ahmed Taya as junta chairman. In 1992, Taya won the country's first, and deeply flawed, multiparty election. His Social Democratic Republican Party (PRDS) ruled the country as a de facto one-party state after the main opposition parties boycotted national assembly elections in 1992. The incumbents maintained their grip on power through victories in the 1996 legislative and 1997 presidential elections.

Mauritania's basic political divisions are sharply defined along racial and ethnic lines. The country's narrowly based authoritarian regime has gradually become liberalized since 1992, but most power remains in the hands of the president and a very small elite around him.

Harassment and detention of opposition supporters and the media continued in 2000. There were reports that police had tortured and otherwise abused black Mauritanians after demonstrations in June over a land dispute in the southwest. Mauritania is one of the world's poorest countries and faces a virtually unpayable foreign debt. Its vast and mostly arid territory has few resources.

Political Rights and Civil Liberties: Mauritanians have never been permitted to choose their representatives or change their government in open, competitive elections. Electoral provisions in the country's 1991 French-style constitution have not been respected in practice. The absence of an independent election commission, state control of broadcasts, harassment of independent print media, and the incumbent's use of state resources to promote his candidacy devalued Taya's presidential victory. In deeply flawed 1996 legislative elections, the military-backed ruling PRDS won all but 7 of the 79 national assembly seats against a divided opposition. The umbrella Front of Opposition Parties dismissed the polls as fraudulent and boycotted the second round of the 1996 legislative polls and the 1997 presidential vote.

The government provided all candidates equal access to its two newspapers and electronic media for the January 1999 municipal elections. The vote, however, was boycotted by some of the opposition, and there was very low voter turnout. The government determined there were widespread abuses in some areas and held new elections in those communities. The ruling party scored an overwhelming majority.

Mauritania's judicial system is heavily influenced by the government. Many decisions are shaped by *Sharia* (Islamic law), especially in family and civil matters. The government is carrying out a program to improve judicial performance and independence. Legislation passed in 1999 created separate tribunals for specific types of disputes.

Numerous nongovernmental organizations operate, including human rights and antislavery groups. A handful of black-African activist groups and Islamist parties are banned. There are reports that black Africans are barred from holding meetings and are harassed when they attempt to do so without permission. The banned *El Hor* (Free Man) Movement promotes black rights, while widespread discrimination against blacks continues. As many as 100,000 blacks still live in conditions of servitude. In 1996, the U.S. Congress voted to suspend all nonhumanitarian aid to Mauritania until antislavery laws are properly enforced. Black-resistance movements continue to call for armed struggle against discrimination and enforced Arabization. The World Organization Against Torture said in August that it had received reports that police tortured and otherwise abused 83 black Mauritanians during and after demonstrations in June in the southwest. The demonstrators were protesting the actions of a regional governor who gave his brother a large concession of land allegedly belonging to *Haratines* (descendants of black slaves). Many black Mauritanians were expelled or fled during race-based attacks from 1990 to 1991. Upon their return, many had trouble regaining access to the land they had previously held.

Several demonstrators were detained briefly in November in anti-Israeli protests that were boosted by anger over the government's banning of the opposition UFD-EN. Prison conditions are harsh but improving. Authorities often ignore the requirements of a warrant to conduct home searches. Government surveillance of opposition figures reportedly continues.

Prepublication censorship, arrests of journalists, and seizures and bans of newspapers devalue constitutional guarantees of free expression. About 20 privately owned newspapers publish on a regular basis. All publications must be officially registered. The state owns the only two daily newspapers and monopolizes nearly all broadcast media. Independent publications openly criticize the government, but all publications must be submitted to the interior ministry prior to distribution. A community radio station focusing on women's issues was launched in July 1999.

Authorities seized at least seven independent weekly newspapers during 2000, according to Reporters Sans Frontiéres. It called on the government to repeal Article 11, under which the seizures were made. The article forbids dissemination of reports deemed to "attack the principles of Islam or the credibility of the state, harm the general interest, or disturb public order and security."

Mauritania is an Islamic state in which, by statute, all citizens are Sunni Muslims who may not possess other religious texts or enter non-Muslim households. The right to worship, however, is generally tolerated. Non-Mauritanian Shiite Muslims and Christians are permitted to worship privately, and some churches operate openly.

Societal discrimination against women is widespread but is improving. Under Sharia, a woman's testimony is given only half the weight of a man's. Legal protections regarding property and equality of pay are usually respected only in urban areas among the educated elite. At least one-quarter of women undergo female genital mutilation (FGM). The government has intensive media and education campaigns against this practice and against forced feeding of adolescent girls, known as *gavage*.

Approximately one-fourth of Mauritania's workers serve in the small formal sector. The government-allied Union of Mauritanian Workers is the dominant labor organization. The government has forcibly ended strikes and detained or banned union activists from the capital.

Mauritius

Polity: Parliamentary democracy
Economy: Capitalist
Population: 1,200,000
PPP: $8,312
Life Expectancy: 72
Ethnic Groups: Indo-Mauritian (68 percent), Creole (27 percent), Sino-Mauritian (3 percent), Franco-Mauritian (2 percent)
Capital: Port Louis

Political Rights: 1
Civil Liberties: 2
Status: Free

Overview:

In a surprise move, President Cassam Uteem dissolved the national assembly and called for early elections in August, in large part because of a series of corruption scandals that had led to the resignation of several cabinet ministers. In the elections, the opposition alliance, led by Anerood Jugnauth, won a resounding victory. Jugnauth, a former prime minister and leader of the Mauritian Socialist Movement, is allied with Paul Berenger, founder of the Mauritian Militant Movement (MMM). Jugnauth's party captured 54 parliamentary seats to only 6 for the former ruling party. Some 80 percent of eligible voters went to the polls.

Mauritius, which has no indigenous peoples, was seized and settled as a way station for European trade to the East Indies and India. Its ethnically mixed population is primarily descended from Indian subcontinental immigrants who were brought to the island as laborers during its 360 years of Dutch, French, and British colonial administration. Since gaining independence from Britain in 1968, Mauritius has maintained one of the developing world's most successful democracies. In1993, the island became a republic within the Commonwealth, with a largely ceremonial president as head of state.

Mauritius has achieved a stable democratic and constitutional order, and its focus on political competition rather than violent conflict demonstrates a level of political development enjoyed by few other African states. The political process is used to maintain ethnic balance and economic growth rather than dominance for any single group. In addition, political parties are not divided along the lines of the country's diverse ethnicities and religions.

The country's political stability is underpinned by steady economic growth and improvements in the island's infrastructure and standard of living. Unemployment and crime are rising, but the country's integrated, multinational population has provided a capable and reliable workforce that, along with preferential European and U.S. market access for sugar and garment exports, is attracting foreign investment. Economic development has been achieved, however, at the cost of the country's native forest and fauna, nearly all of which have been destroyed.

Political Rights and Civil Liberties: Citizens have the right to change their government democratically. The head of state is a president, elected by the national assembly for a five-year term. The present incumbent was first elected in June 1992. Executive power resides in the prime minister. The legislature is unicameral; its sole chamber, the national assembly, has 62 members directly elected by universal adult suffrage, and a maximum of 8 (currently 4) members appointed from unsuccessful parliamentary candidates who gained the largest number of votes. The members serve for five-year terms.

Since independence, Mauritius has regularly chosen its representatives in free, fair, and competitive elections. Decentralized structures govern the country's island dependencies. The largest of these is Rodrigues Island, which has its own government, local councils, and two seats in the national assembly.

The constitution guarantees freedom of expression and of the press, but all broadcast media are state owned and usually reflect government views. Several private daily and weekly publications, however, are often highly critical of both government and opposition politicians and their policies. Freedom of assembly and association is respected, although police occasionally refuse to issue permits for demonstrations. Numerous nongovernmental organizations operate.

The generally independent judiciary is headed by a supreme court. The legal system is an amalgam of French and British traditions. Civil rights are generally well respected, although cases of police brutality have been reported. Freedom of religion is respected. There are no known political prisoners or reports of political or extrajudicial killings.

Nine labor federations include 300 unions. Women constitute approximately 20 percent of the paid labor force and generally occupy a subordinate role in society. The law does not require equal pay for equal work or prohibit sexual harassment in the workplace. Women are underrepresented at the national university. The country is preparing a national gender-action plan with the long-term objective of greater equality. It addresses the integration of gender issues into the mainstream of government and private sector activities, and the enactment of a domestic violence act. Two women serve in the cabinet, and another two are parliamentarians.

Tensions between the Hindu majority and Muslim and Creole minorities persist, despite the general respect for constitutional prohibitions against discrimination, and constitute one of the country's few potential political flashpoints.

Mauritius was expected in 2000 to a register an eight percent economic growth while inflation is expected to run at around five percent. Just 2.5 percent of the country's labor force is unemployed. Per capita income in Mauritius is $ 3,710, one of the highest in Africa, while adult literacy is 83 percent.

Mexico

Polity: Presidential-parliamentarydemocracy
Economy: Capitalist-statist
Population: 99,600,000
PPP: $7,704
Life Expectancy: 72

Political Rights: 2*
Civil Liberties: 3*
Status: Free

Ethnic Groups: Mestizo (60 percent), Indian (30 percent), European (9 percent), other (1 percent)
Capital: Mexico City
Ratings Change: Mexico's political rights rating changed from 3 to 2, its civil liberties rating from 4 to 3, and its status from Partly Free to Free, due to an opposition party's victory in national elections for the first time in seven decades and to the government's decision to retire the military from internal security roles.

Overview:

In a come-from-behind victory that stunned the pollsters and delighted international financial markets, opposition party candidate Vicente Fox Quesada won Mexico's presidency on July 2, 2000, with 42.5 percent of the vote, ending more than seven decades of mostly overwhelming political hegemony of the Institutional Revolutionary Party (PRI). Fox, an innovative rancher and businessman, led his center-right National Action Party (PAN) to victory. Nearly becoming the largest party in the lower house of congress, PAN won enough state governorships to put the long-ruling PRI in danger of becoming a regional party.

The biggest immediate challenges facing Fox were tamping down the unrealistic expectations that his victory created and making strides against the pervasive corruption that fuels Mexico's major social problems of poverty and crime, and has allowed the country to become the headquarters of the world's drug cartels. In addition, a far greater respect for human rights and civil liberties, particularly in rural areas and in Native American communities, needs to be shown by Mexico's security agencies, whose record has improved somewhat in the last few years. One of Fox's first moves was to announce the withdrawal of the 180,000-strong army from its high-profile, U.S.-supported, internal security role. That role had help to corrupt the once-hermetic military even as it drew attention and energies away from badly needed police reform.

Mexico achieved independence from Spain in 1810 and established itself as a republic in 1822. Seven years after the Revolution of 1910, a new constitution was promulgated under which the United Mexican States became a federal republic consisting of 31 states and a federal district (Mexico City). Each state has elected governors and legislatures. The president is elected to a six-year term. A bicameral congress consists of a 128-member senate elected for six years, with at least one minority senator from each state, and a 500-member chamber of deputies elected for three years—300 directly and 200 through proportional representation.

Since its founding in 1929, the PRI has dominated the country by means of its corporatist, authoritarian structure maintained through co-optation, patronage, corruption, and repression. The formal business of government has taken place mostly in secret and with little legal foundation.

In 1988, PRI standard-bearer Carlos Salinas de Gortari, won the presidential election through massive and systematic fraud. Most Mexicans believe Salinas actually lost to Cuauhtemoc Cárdenas, who headed a coalition of leftist parties that later became the Party of the Democratic Revolution (PRD).

Under Salinas, the toast of both the George Bush and Bill Clinton administrations in the United States, corruption reached unparalleled proportions, and a top antidrug official complained that Mexico had become a "narco-democracy," before he fled to exile in the United States. Salinas conceded a few gubernatorial election victories to the PAN, which had supported his economic policies. In return, PAN dropped its demands for political reform and abandoned plans to establish a pro-democracy coalition with the PRD.

Until the outbreak of the Marxist-led Zapatista rebellion in the southern state of Chiapas on New Year's Day 1994, it was assumed that Salinas's handpicked successor, Luís Donaldo Colosio, would defeat Cárdenas and PAN congressman Diego Fernández de Cevallos in the 1994 presidential election. The Zapatistas' demands for democracy and clean elections resonated throughout Mexico. Colosio was assassinated on March 23, 1994. Salinas substituted Zedillo, a 42-year-old U.S.-trained economist with little political experience, as the PRI. Despite PRI hardliners' animosity toward the party's technocrats, they placed the government machinery—the enormous resources of the state as well as the broadcast media—firmly behind Zedillo.

On August 21, 1994, Zedillo won, with nearly 50 percent of the valid vote, and the PRI won overwhelming majorities in both houses of congress. Both PAN and the PRD disputed the election's legitimacy, and only PRI legislators in the chamber voted to affirm the results. The next month, the reform-minded PRI secretary-general was assassinated, his murder apparently the result of PRI infighting. (Salinas's brother, Raul, was convicted in 1999 for planning and ordering the assassination.)

Zedillo took office on December 1, 1994. Under Zedillo, a trend that had started with Salinas, or even before, accelerated, and Mexico became the leading supplier of illegal drugs to the United States, accounting for two-thirds of the cocaine and 20 to 30 percent of the heroin entering the country.

In 1996, opposition parties of the left and right won important municipal elections in three states. Postelectoral conflicts took place in several regions. In the southern states of Guerrero, Oaxaca, Tabasco, and Chiapas, where many of Mexico's indigenous people live, political violence continued to be a fact of life. But the elections left the PRI governing just two of Mexico's 12 largest cities.

In April 1996, the main political parties, with the exception of PAN, agreed on reforms aimed at bringing about fairer elections. The reforms introduced direct elections for the mayoralty of Mexico City and abolished government control of the federal electoral institute.

The climate in which Mexicans went to the polls several times in 1997 and 1998, which included increased public financing of political parties and guarantees of fairer access to television during elections, was substantially improved from that of past elections. For the first time, in 1997 voters chose the mayor of Mexico City—and elected PRD opposition leader Cárdenas—rather than having the municipal chief appointed by the president. That year an opposition coalition made up of the PRD, PAN, and two other parties took control of the lower house of congress following the July elections, and a consensus was reached whereby the presidencies of 61 house committees were allocated on an equitable basis. By year's end, PAN held six governorships.

Elections held in 1998 in several states for gubernatorial, legislative, and municipal posts showed an uneven ability of the opposition to build upon its successes in the state and federal elections. PRI candidates were able to win in contests that were not fixed, as the party won seven of ten gubernatorial contests. In 1999 the PRI nominated, in first-ever open-party competition, Francisco Labastida, hailed by some as the politician's return to the helm of a party ruled during the three previous administrations by technocrats. In September PAN nominated Fox, governor of Guanajuato state, while Cárdenas took leave of the Mexico City mayoralty and announced he would again lead the PRD's national ticket.

In 2000, the pragmatic Fox teamed up with the small Green Party to form the Alliance for Change; an effort to make common cause with the PRD was rebuffed by Cardenas, who before the election called Fox a "traitor" and a "loser." Despite election-eve polls suggesting Fox would lose, former Interior Minister Lambastida won 36 percent of the vote, and Cárdenas just 16.6 percent. The poor showing by Cárdenas suggested that support for the PRD, which had made electoral reform its standard, was collapsing as PRI hegemony disappeared. The PRD's congressional representation sank from a high of 116 to 52 following the June election; its consolation prize was winning the Mexico City mayoralty. However, the 2000 elections also appeared to herald an even more important role for the Mexican congress—less than a decade ago regarded as a PRI rubber stamp. As no party commands a majority, competition for votes in Congress will probably alter a balance of power previously in the executive branch's favor.

Following his election, Fox selected an eclectic cabinet whose new faces signaled an end to the revolving door of bureaucrats in top positions, and included leftist intellectuals, businessmen, and, as attorney general, a serving general—the latter choice bitterly opposed by human rights groups. Fox also announced plans to overhaul Mexico's notoriously corrupt and inefficient law enforcement agencies, breaking the political ties between the police and the presidency and removing the armed forces from the expanding internal security role assigned to them under Zedillo. In September two generals who have held important positions in the fight against insurgent groups and drug traffickers were arrested on drug charges, bringing to seven the number of generals prosecuted for their alleged involvement in the narcotics trade. Despite Mexico's booming economy, business leaders say soaring crime is costing them as much as ten percent of their profits. The collapse of the PRI was accompanied by the flight from justice of three senior party leaders, including a former governor accused of turning his state into a landing strip for the Colombian drug cartels; a former minister of tourism charged with embezzling $45 million; and the so-called She-Wolf of Chimalhuacan, whose supporters opened fire on political opponents in a postelection bloodbath that left ten dead.

Political Rights and Civil Liberties: Mexicans can choose their government democratically, although there were credible reports of ruling-party coercion through state-controlled enterprises and through somewhat unbalanced coverage of the election contests. The watershed June 2000 contest filled 500 congressional and 128 senate seats, numerous state and municipal posts, the mayoralty of Mexico City, and 11 state governorships. The newly independent Federal Election Institute strengthened the monitoring process, and Mexico spent an estimated $1.2 billion on efforts to minimize fraud and increase transparency. In addition, more than 800 foreign observers from 40 countries were on hand to monitor the balloting and counting processes. However, in a few states, such as Tabasco, old-style PRI tactics such as voter coercion, gift giving, and control of the media, were used in the 2000 elections.

Supreme court judges are appointed by the executive and approved by the senate. Throughout the latter years of PRI rule, the judicial system was weak, politicized, and riddled with the corruption infecting all official bodies. In most rural areas, respect for laws by official agencies is nearly nonexistent. Lower courts and law enforcement in general are undermined by widespread bribery. In May 1999, Adán Amezcua, who U.S. antidrug officials say is the world's biggest trafficker in synthetic drugs, was released by a Mexican court on the grounds of insufficient evidence. Mexico serves as a transit point for about half of the cocaine consumed in the United States, as well as a producer of a significant amount of heroin, marijuana and methampehtamines.

Constitutional guarantees regarding political and civic organizations are generally respected in the urban north and central parts of the country. However, political and civic expression is restricted throughout rural Mexico, in poor urban areas, and in poor southern states where the government frequently takes repressive measures against the left-wing PRD and peasant and indigenous groups. Civil society has grown in recent years: human rights, pro-democracy, women's, and environmental groups are active. However, government critics remain subject to forms of sophisticated intimidation that range from gentle warnings by government officials and anonymous death threats, to unwarranted detentions and jailings on dubious charges.

An official human rights commission was created in 1990. However, it is barred from examining political and labor rights violations, and cannot enforce its recommendations. Hundreds of arbitrary detentions, widespread torture, scores of extrajudicial executions, and a number of forced disappearances have been reported by nongovernmental organizations. According to Amnesty International there is "compelling evidence that extrajudicial executions are carried out" by the army, police, and paramilitary groups, as well as torture and ill-treatment.

Mexico's soaring crime rate and lack of effective law enforcement are serious barriers to economic development. Ten percent of all extortive kidnappings in Mexico, which ranks second only to Colombia in the number of attacks in Latin America, are believed to be carried out by former or serving police officers. Opinion polls suggest that between 80 and 90 percent of Mexicans do not think that the Mexican police are capable of dealing with the country's spiraling crime rate. Low standards of performance by Mexican law enforcement agencies can be traced, in part, to the fact that Mexican police officers frequently lack essential elements for their work, such as bulletproof vests, serviceable weapons, and adequate training. In recent years, dozens of law enforcement agents have died fighting the notorious Tijuana-based Arellano Felix drug cartel.

During the outbreak of the still-simmering Chiapas rebellion, the military was responsible for widespread human rights violations. Army counterinsurgency efforts continue to cause numerous rights violations in Chiapas and in Guerrero. The growing role of the military in internal security—ostensibly to combat domestic terrorism, drug trafficking, and street crime—has contributed to grave human rights problems, particularly in rural areas. The official human rights commission refuses to investigate some nearly 2,000 cases of reported human rights violations by the military. In late 1998, a small group of military officers staged a protest against the military court system and demanded the abolition of the exclusively military legal jurisdiction, which human rights groups say also exacerbates a widespread culture of impunity in rights prosecutions. In 1999, Amnesty International reported that "suspects have been detained, held in secret detention and subjected to torture—typically to extract confessions against suspected supporters of the armed opposition." Published reports offered continuing evidence of close links between drug traffickers and the armed forces, contradicting official versions that have sought to portray the military as less prone to corruption and drug cartel influence than is civilian law enforcement. In 2000, a Mexican army general, José Francisco Gallardo, who has been jailed since 1993 for proposing that the army establish an independent human rights ombudsman, was awarded an international freedom of speech award by the writers' group, PEN International. The choice of a highly respected military prosecutor as Fox's attorney general was criticized by human rights groups and members of the PRD as the foreshadowing of a continuation of miltary involvement in police affairs.

The media, while mostly private, depend on the government for advertising revenue. In 2000, Fox pledged to end the PRI practice of buying favorable stories and vowed to respect the media's independence. Mexico's newspaper industry has been considered one of Latin America's least independent and most openly corrupt. A handful of daily newspapers and weeklies are the exception. Until Fox's victory, the PRI dominated television, by far the country's most influential medium. Violent attacks against journalists are common, with reporters investigating police issues, narcotics trafficking, and public corruption at particular risk.

In 1992 the constitution was amended to restore the legal status of the Roman Catholic Church and other religious institutions. Priests and nuns were allowed to vote for the first time in nearly 80 years. Nonetheless, activist priests promoting the rights of Indians and the poor, particularly in southern states, remain subject to threats and intimidation by conservative landowners and local PRI bosses.

Officially recognized labor unions operate as political instruments of the PRI, and most are grouped under the Confederation of Mexican Workers, whose leadership in recent years has been increasingly challenged by trade union dissidents. The *maquiladora* regime of export-only production facilities has created substantial abuse of worker rights. Most maquiladora workers are young, uneducated women who accept lower pay more readily, with annual labor turnover averaging between 200 and 300 percent. They have no medical insurance, holidays, or profit sharing, and female employees are frequently the targets of sexual harassment and abuse. The companies also discriminate against pregnant women in order to avoid having to give them maternity leave. The government consistently fails to enforce child labor laws; some 4.5 million children under 14 years of age—12 percent of the child population-have jobs in Mexico. In September 2000 it was revealed that President-elect Fox's family illegally used child workers on their ranch and in their business.

Only 7 of Mexico's 31 states and the federal district have specific laws against domestic violence and sexual abuse, although some experts say that between five and seven of every ten Mexican women are the victims of abuse. In August 2000, a federal appeals court in San Francisco, California, granted a gay Mexican transvestite asylum in the United States, after saying he was a member of a particular "social group" persecuted in his homeland.

Independent unions and peasant organizations are subject to intimidation, blacklisting, and violent crackdowns. Dozens of labor and peasant leaders have been killed in recent years in ongoing land disputes, particularly in the southern states, where Indians constitute close to half the population. In December 2000, Fox backed down from a plan to relocate poor Indians in newly created towns after critics called it tantamount to the "ethnocide" perpetrated on indigenous peoples by Spanish settlers, who herded them into villages where they were more easily exploited and taxed.

Micronesia

Polity: Presidential-parliamentary democracy (federal)
Economy: Capitalist
Population: 100,000
PPP: na
Life Expectancy: 66
Ethnic Groups: Micronesian , Polynesian
Capital: Palikir

Political Rights: 1
Civil Liberties: 2
Status: Free

Overview: Like several other Pacific Island countries trying to develop an offshore banking industry, Micronesia has been linked to money-laundering activities and was blacklisted by the United States and West European countries.

The Federated States of Micronesia consists of 607 islands in the archipelago of the Caroline Islands located in the north Pacific Ocean. In 1899, Germany purchased the Carolines from Spain, and Japan seized the islands in 1915, ruling them from 1920 under a League of Nations mandate. During World War II, the United States occupied the islands, and they became a part of the U.S. Trust Territory of the Pacific in 1947.

In 1978, four districts of the Trust Territory (Yap, Chuuk, Pohnpei, and Kosrae) approved a constitution to create the Federated States of Micronesia. The United States granted the islands sovereignty in 1979, upon which the constitution took effect and the country elected its first president, Tosiwo Nakayama. In 1982, the territory concluded a Compact of Free Association with the United States, which came into force in 1986. Under the terms of the Compact, the country is fully sovereign, but the United States is responsible for defense until at least 2001. The United States obtains the right to maintain military installations on the islands and in exchange provides substantial financial assistance for development and other purposes. In 1990, the United Nations formally dissolved the trusteeship.

In 1991, the congress elected Bailey Olter of Pohnpei state, a former vice president under Nakayama, as the country's third president. Olter was elected to a second term in 1995 over Senator Jacob Nena of Kosrae state. After Olter suffered a stroke in July 1996, the congress installed Nena as acting president. In May 1999, Leo Falcam, the former vice president, replaced Nena as the new president.

Negotiations with the United States over the future of U.S. economic assistance under the Compact of Free Association continued. Micronesia seeks continued annual grant aid of approximately $84 million and access to many U.S. federal programs, including mail, education, and health services. Micronesia also proposed a $20 million trust fund. Talks will continue into 2001, and the U.S. funding level will probably be tied to improvements in health, education, infrastructure, capacity building, good governance, and private sector development.

As for aid from other countries, Micronesia met with the Consultative Group composed of development partners, international organizations, and donor countries. The group gave a positive review of the progress report prepared by the Micronesian government, particularly its emphasis on a participatory approach. Substantial public sector reform has already strengthened government finances and improved economic stability. The government recommended further reforms to strengthen capacity for accountability and transparency in social and economic management and in legal and regulatory systems, as well as the formulation of a long-term development strategy to make Micronesia more independent economically.

The economy is dependent on fishing, subsistence agriculture, tourism, and U.S. aid. In anticipation of the expiration of the current Compact in 2001, the government has been trying to bring in more foreign investment and expand the private sector. Keenly concerned about the effects of global climate change on the islands, Micronesia has ratified the Kyoto Protocol, which urges national and international actions to control and reduce greenhouse gas emissions. Micronesia is also one of two Pacific Island countries (the other is Papua New Guinea) to have signed the Basel Convention on the transboundary movement of hazardous waste. On another front, a cholera outbreak in Pohnpei state in May sent 80 people to the hospital and 160 additional cases were diagnosed. A state of emergency was declared.

Political Rights and Civil Liberties:

Citizens of the Federated States of Micronesia can change their government democratically. The constitution provides for a unicameral, 14-senator congress. One senator is elected at-large from each of the four states for a four-year term, with the remaining ten senators elected for two-year terms from single-member districts, based on population. The president and vice president are selected by congress from among its four at-large members. Although an informal rotation system for the top elected offices of the country is in practice, the perceived political dominance of Chuuk state, which holds nearly half of the population and a proportionate number of congressional seats, has created tensions with the three smaller states. Politics are based on state, clan, and individual loyalties. Political parties are permitted, but none has been formed.

Press freedom has increased in recent years. An independent weekly newspaper, *The Island Tribune*, launched in December 1997, explores controversial and politically sensitive issues. By contrast, also in 1997, the congress adopted a resolution calling for the deportation of the editor of the now-defunct *FSM News*, then the country's only independent newspaper. The editor, a Canadian citizen, said the action resulted from her exposures of alleged government corruption.

Each of the four state governments and a religious organization operate radio stations, and the residents of Pohnpei have access to satellite television. The federal government publishes a biweekly information bulletin, *The National Union*, and the state governments produce their own newsletters. Other papers, including the *Pohnpei Business News* and *Micronesia Weekly*, generally avoid sensitive topics. Religious freedom is respected in this predominantly Roman Catholic country.

Freedom of assembly and association are respected, but there are few nongovernmental organizations other than churches and student organizations. Workers have the right to form or join associations, but no unions have been formed because of the small size of the wage economy. Current laws do not guarantee collective bargaining.

The judiciary is independent. Trials are conducted fair and prison conditions meet minimum international standards. The local police are under the control of the civil authorities. In cases where the police were found guilty of mistreating citizens, the officers were subsequently dismissed from the force.

Domestic abuse is a growing problem. State and societal responses are inadequate, as it is commonly regarded as a private, family matter. The number of physical and sexual assault cases against women outside the family context has been increasing. Women are increasingly active in the private sector and in lower- and mid-level government positions, but they remain underrepresented at the highest levels of government.

Moldova

Polity: Parliamentary democracy
Economy: Mixed capitalist (transitional)
Population: 4,300,000
PPP: $1,947
Life Expectancy: 68
Ethnic Groups: Moldovan/Romanian (65 percent), Ukrainian (14 percent), Russian (13 percent), other (8 percent)
Capital: Chisinau

Political Rights:2
CivilLiberties:4
Status: Partly Free

Overview:
In the year 2000, Moldova ended direct elections of the president and became a parliamentary democracy. In doing so, it ended a constitutional crisis that had set parliament and President Petru Lucinschi against each other since the previous year. In late December, however, parliament failed to elect a president according to a revised electoral code, and President Lucinschi called for the body's dissolution. Early parliamentary elections are scheduled for February 2001. Lucinschi will perform his duties until a new parliament elects a new president. Despite ongoing diplomatic efforts in 2000, no progress was made in negotiating a settlement on the political status of the self-declared Dnestr Moldovan Republic (Transnistria).

In 1991, the Moldavian Soviet Socialist Republic declared independence and made Mircea Snegur, the chairman of the Communist supreme soviet, the first president of a democratic Republic of Moldova. In 1994, Snegur's centrist Agrarian Democratic Party (ADP) won a majority of seats in the country's first free and fair popular election. Petru Lucinschi, also a former Communist, defeated Snegur in 1996. The Communist Party won a plurality of votes in 1998 parliamentary elections, but three centrist parties united to form a new majority. Moldova has undertaken important economic reforms, replaced the Soviet-era constitution, and joined NATO's Partnership for Peace. The country's successes have been tempered, however, by an extremely low standard of living and by the situation in Transnistria.

When Moldova became a parliamentary democracy in 2000, President Lucinschi refused to participate in the December balloting by parliament. The Party of Moldovan Communists (PCM) nominated party leader Vladimir Voronin as its candidate, while a coalition of center-right parties and independent members of parliament nominated Pavel Barbalat, who heads Moldova's constitutional court. The constitutional court forced parliament to repeat its first vote when it found that Communist Party leaders had violated secret balloting rules and pressured party members to choose Voronin. Parliament voted two more times but still failed to elect a president in the first round.

When Barbalat's supporters boycotted a new round of voting on December 21, President Lucinschi moved to dissolve parliament. The constitutional court supported Lucinschi on the grounds that the boycott violated election law, which states that a new election must take place 15 days after the last vote. Lucinschi will officially dissolve parliament in January 2001, and early elections will take place in February.

Lucinschi, who urged centrist forces to form a bloc, will stay in power until a new parliament elects a new president.

Political Rights and Civil Liberties:

Moldova is a parliamentary democracy in which citizens age 18 and older can change their government under a system of universal, equal, and direct suffrage. Voters elect members of parliament by proportional representation to four-year terms in the unicameral parliament. Parliament, in turn, elects the prime minister. In 2000, Moldova ended direct elections of the president and increased the powers of the government and the prime minister. President Lucinschi vigorously opposed the plan but ultimately acquiesced. The year ended in crisis, though, when parliament failed to elect a president according to the new election rules.

Post-Soviet elections in Moldova have been free and fair. The self-declared government in Transnistria, however, severely limits the ability of voters in that region to participate in Moldovan elections. The last parliamentary elections took place in 1998. Fifteen parties competed in the election, but only four met the four percent threshold for representation. The PCM won a plurality of 40 seats in the 101-seat chamber. A coalition of the Democratic Convention of Moldova (CDM), the Party of Democratic Forces (PFD), and the Bloc for a Democratic and Prosperous Moldova (PMDP) formed a new majority with 26, 11, and 24 seats, respectively.

The constitution guarantees freedom of expression and access to public information. Organizations like Reporters Sans Frontiéres have reported some cases of intimidation and attacks on journalists who write about corruption or criticize public officials. In 2000, Moldovan courts issued two important rulings that affect the media. First, the constitutional court upheld a controversial civil code provision that imposes stiff fines and demands speedy retractions from journalists found guilty of libel. More than 800 libel suits have been filed in Moldova since 1991. Second, an appeals court upheld an order to revoke the licenses of eight radio and television stations that air considerable Russian-language programming. The court found the stations in violation of a legal requirement that 65 percent of their broadcasts be in Romanian. Amid sharp criticism of the court's decision, parliament amended the law so that it only applies to programs produced domestically. Also in 2000, parliament amended the electoral code so that foreign-owned media may not carry election advertisements.

Moldova's constitution guarantees religious freedom. By law, religious groups must register with the state, but the Bessarabian Orthodox Church, which broke with the Moldovan Orthodox Church in 1992, has been denied registration several times. In February 2000, the government again refused to register the church, and resolution of the conflict is pending before the European Court for Human Rights. Religious education became mandatory in primary schools in 2000, and instruction is scheduled to begin in 2001. In November, the Moldovan Orthodox Church threatened to excommunicate any member of parliament who supported a bill legalizing abortion.

Moldovan citizens may strike, petition the government, and participate freely in social organizations, political parties, and trade unions. Private organizations must register with the state, and demonstrations require permits from local authorities. Moldovan law allows collective bargaining but prohibits strikes by government employees and essential workers. In 2000, students in Chisinau boycotted classes when the city tried to end their public transportation benefits, farmers rallied in favor of lower taxes on their products, and retirees picketed to demand higher pensions. Also in 2000, parliament defined procedures for amending the constitution, including a provision for citizens to propose amendments.

Moldova's constitution calls for an independent judiciary. It also guarantees equality before the law and presumption of innocence. There is evidence that some prosecutors, judges, and law enforcement officials accept bribes. The investigation into the alleged illegal sale of material evidence by Nicolae Alexei, the head of the Interior Ministry's Department Against Organized Crime and Corruption, continued in 2000. The government has suspended Alexei, who claims the charges are politically motivated, until the case is resolved.

The constitution preserves a variety of personal freedoms and entitlements such as the rights to choose one's residence, move and travel freely, and have access to education. It also calls for a market economy rooted in "fair competition." In 2000, the government approved plans to privatize the wine and tobacco industries and completed the privatization of 1.5 million hectares of agricultural land. Despite accomplishments like these, Moldova remains one of the most impoverished countries in the region.

Monaco

Polity: Principality and parliamentary democracy
Economy: Capitalist-statist
Population: 30,000
PPP: na
Life Expectancy: na
Ethnic Groups: French (47 percent), Italian (16 percent), Monegasque (16 percent), other (21 percent)
Capital: Monaco

Political Rights: 2
Civil Liberties: 1
Status: Free

Overview: In 2000, the Principality of Monaco continued to face increasing criticism from France for not implementing its existing anti-laundering laws. The French government threatened to take legislative measures against Monaco unless it tightened control over the lax banking and tax regulations that have made Monaco an attractive place for money launderers and tax evaders. In response, Prince Rainier III defended Monaco's sovereignty, stating that it was time to renegotiate Monaco's ties with France.

For 51 years, Prince Rainier III has been responsible for Monaco's impressive economic growth. Under his direction, the economy has ended its exclusive dependence on gambling revenue. Its main sources of revenue are tourism, financial services, and banking.

The Principality of Monaco is an independent and sovereign state and a full member of the United Nations. It is closely associated with neighboring France, whose currency, the *franc*, is the legal tender in Monaco. In 1997, the royal Grimaldi family celebrated its 700th anniversary of rule over the principality. During the six centuries of Grimaldi rule, Monaco has been intermittently controlled by various European powers. It achieved independence from France in 1861. Under a treaty ratified in 1919, France pledged to protect the territorial integrity, sovereignty, and independence of the principality in return for a guarantee that Monegasque policy would conform to French interests.

Of 32,000 residents, Monaco is home to only 5,000 Monegasques. Only the Monegasques may participate in the election of the 18-member national council (legislature). The constitution also provides Monegasques with free education, financial assistance in case of unemployment or illness, and the right to hold elective office.

As head of state, Prince Rainier III holds executive authority, formally appoints the four-member cabinet, and proposes all legislation. Legislation proposed by the prince is drafted by the cabinet and voted upon by the national council. The prince holds veto power over the council. The prince also names the prime minister from a list of names proposed by the French government. In the elections that took place in February 1998, one party, the National and Democratic Union, won all the seats in the legislature.

Political Rights and Civil Liberties: Citizens of Monaco may change the national council and their municipal councils democratically. The council members are elected for five years by direct universal suffrage and a system of proportional representation. Under the 1962 constitution, the prince delegates judicial authority to the courts and tribunals, which adjudicate independently in his name. The judiciary includes a Supreme Tribunal, consisting of seven members appointed by the prince based on nominations by the national council; courts of cassation, appeal, and first instance; and a justice of the peace.

Freedom of expression is guaranteed by the constitution; however, denunciations of the Grimaldi family are prohibited by an official Monegasque penal code. Two monthly magazines and a weekly government journal are published in the principality, and French daily newspapers are widely available. Radio and television are government operated and sell time to commercial sponsors, and all French broadcasts are freely transmitted to the principality. France maintains a financial interest in Radio Monte Carlo, which broadcasts in several languages.

Roman Catholicism is the state religion in Monaco, but adherents of other faiths may practice freely. Workers are free to form unions, but fewer than ten percent of workers are unionized, and relatively few of these reside in the principality. Trade unions are independent of both the government and the Monegasque political parties. Anti-union discrimination is prohibited. Union members can be fired only with the agreement of a commission that includes two members from the employers' association and two from the labor movement.

The rights of women are respected, and women are fairly well represented in all professions. Of the 18 members of the national council, 4 are women. The law governing transmission of citizenship provides for equality of treatment between men and women who are Monegasque by birth. Only men, however, may transmit Monegasque citizenship acquired by naturalization to their children; women are denied this right.

Mongolia

Polity: Presidential-par-
liamentary democracy
Economy: Mixed
capitalist (transitional)
Population: 2,500,000
PPP: $1,541
Life Expectancy: 66

Political Rights: 2
Civil Liberties: 3
Status: Free

Ethnic Groups: Mongol (90 percent), Kazakh (4 percent),
Chinese (2 percent), Russian (2 percent), other (2 percent)
Capital: Ulaanbaatar

Overview: Promising to ease hardships stemming from the country's
wrenching transition to a market economy, Mongolia's former
Communist ruling party returned to power in a landslide vic-
tory in the July 2000 elections. Prime Minister Nambariin Enkhbayar took office pledging
more government assistance for disadvantaged groups, improvements in healthcare,
and a slower pace of privatization of roughly 17 large state companies.

China controlled this vast Central Asian region for two centuries, until 1911, and
again from 1919 until a Marxist revolt in 1921. The Soviet-backed Mongolian People's
Revolutionary Party (MPRP) formed a single-party Communist state in 1924. For the
next 65 years Mongolia was a virtual republic of the Soviet Union.

Following a series of pro-democracy hunger strikes, the government ended the
MPRP's status as the sole legal political party in May 1990. However, the MPRP easily defeated an unprepared opposition in Mongolia's first multiparty elections in July.
In September 1990, parliament named the MPRP's Punsalmaagiyn Orchirbat as president.

After the country adopted a new constitution that created a unicameral parliament, the MPRP easily won legislative elections in 1992. In 1993, party hardliners forced
Orchirbat off the MPRP ticket, but the president won reelection as the candidate of the
two main opposition parties, the National Democratic Party (NDP) and the Social
Democratic Party (SDP).

The economy returned to growth in 1994 after four years of contraction. However, the end of Soviet subsidies and the transition to a market economy continued to
cause severe social hardship. Promising better economic management, the opposition
won the June 1996 parliamentary elections to sweep the MPRP out of parliamentary
power after 72 years. The NDP, SDP, and two smaller parties ran as the Democratic
Union Coalition (DUC) and won 50 seats. Prime Minister Mendsaihan Enksaikhan, of
the SDP, introduced radical liberalization policies, including fiscal and monetary tightening, price decontrols, pension cuts, and tariff reductions. But the reforms coincided
with a sharp fall in world prices for two of Mongolia's biggest foreign revenue earners,
copper and cashmere, which contributed to huge budget and trade deficits.

With inflation and unemployment rising, the MPRP's Nachagyn Bagabandy, a
former parliamentary chairman, won the May 1997 presidential elections behind a
campaign stressing social issues. Bagabandy got 60.8 percent of the vote against

Orchirbat's 29.8 percent. Having lost the presidency, the fractious DUC also began to allow infighting to erode its performance and stability. Three DUC governments collapsed between April 1998 and July 1999.

The MPRP capitalized on the DUC's disarray to win 72 of the 76 seats in the July 2, 2000, parliamentary elections. Turnout was 75.8 percent. On July 26, parliament elected MPRP chairman Enkhbayar, 42, as prime minister. During the campaign, Enkhbayar had pledged to seek a "third way" between his party's still-powerful conservative wing and the government's rapid economic liberalization, which he said had increased social hardship. While the economy grew by 3.5 percent in 1999, poverty rates had doubled since 1991 and the state welfare system had largely collapsed. Moreover, the elections followed the worst winter in 30 years. Harsh weather conditions had killed 2.5 million livestock and caused thousands of nomadic families to lose their livelihood. Riven by infighting over the pace of reforms, the parties in the governing DUC contested the elections separately. The former Communists followed their national-level triumph with a landslide victory in local elections in October.

Political Rights and Civil Liberties: Mongolians can change their government through elections. In a report on the July 2000 elections, the Washington-based International Republican Institute (IRI) said its monitoring teams did not observe any systematic irregularities. However, the IRI recommended that the election law be reviewed to ensure more uniform election administration.

The 1992 constitution vested executive powers in a prime minister and created a directly elected, 76-seat *Great Hural* (parliament). The constitution also vested some governmental powers in a president, who is directly elected for a four-year term. The president must approve candidates for prime minister and can veto legislation, subject to a two-thirds parliamentary override. President Bagabandy's rejection of several parliamentary nominees for prime minister in 1998 created a still-unresolved constitutional question over the correct role of the president in approving prime ministers.

The judiciary is independent, but judges receive low salaries and corruption is reportedly a problem. Conditions in pretrial detention and prisons are life threatening. The United States State Department said in its annual human rights report for 1999 that 200 prisoners died in custody that year, mainly as the result of disease and poor prison management. Many inmates came into the prisons already suffering from illness or starvation because of the appalling conditions in police detention. Pretrial detention is often lengthy, which increases detainees' exposure to these conditions. New procedures have helped reduce the number of deaths per year, but implementation of the measures is limited in rural areas. Similarly, reforms have helped reduce incidences of police abuse of detainees and prisoners, although anecdotal evidence suggested that the reforms have had less impact in rural areas.

Mongolia has scores of private newspapers representing diverse viewpoints, although only about a dozen papers appear regularly. Radio is a key source of information in the countryside, and the one independent radio station reaches most areas. There are at least two private television services, each with limited reach. Foreign satellite and cable broadcasts are also available. A 1999 media law required the government to privatize all state-owned print media, and to transform the state television station and radio stations into a public broadcasting service headed by an independent board of governors. The actual privatization process has proceeded slowly. The law places the burden of proof on the defendants in slander and libel cases, which may have a chilling effect on the media.

Freedom of assembly and association continued to be respected. Women run many of the most effective nongovernmental organizations, including groups that organize voter-education programs and promote women's rights and child welfare. Women also make up a majority of university graduates, doctors, and lawyers, but they are underrepresented at the higher levels in government and the judiciary. Domestic violence continued to be a serious problem. Given Mongolia's dire economic problems, the government lacks the resources to deal adequately with the needs of children. School dropout rates are high, and there are several thousand street children in urban areas.

There is no official religion in this predominantly Buddhist country, and religious freedom is generally respected in practice. However, religious groups must register with the government. According to the U.S. State Department, in recent years the government has denied registration to some nonmainstream groups and forced them to close their offices and places of worship.

Trade unions are independent, although union membership continued to decline amid the privatization and restructuring of many large enterprises. Workers in sectors defined as essential cannot stage strikes. Although collective bargaining is legal, Mongolia's difficult economic situation often allows employers to unilaterally set wages and working conditions.

Petty corruption continued to be a problem, in part because government agencies operate with limited transparency. The country's first major corruption cases occurred in 1999, when a court sentenced three members of parliament from the then-ruling coalition to jail terms of up to five years for taking bribes related to a gambling license. Authorities have not identified any suspects in the 1998 murder of Sanjaasuren Zorig, the leader of the pro-democracy movement that ended single-party rule.

Morocco

Polity: Traditional monarchy and limited parliament
Economy: Capitalist-statist
Population: 28,800,000
PPP: $3,305
Life Expectancy: 67
Ethnic Groups: Arab and Berber (99 percent), other (1 percent)
Capital: Rabat

Political Rights: 5
Civil Liberties: 4
Status: Partly Free

Overview:

A year and a half after the accession of King Mohammad VI, Moroccans are still waiting for a better standard of living and institutional reforms to combat corruption and liberalize the political system. However, while economic initiatives to alleviate Morocco's high levels of unemployment, poverty, and illiteracy will require time to take effect, an increasingly confident Islamist opposition gains support among the poor. Moreover, the king's "new concept of authority," which has yet to materialize, gave way late in the year to renewed repression of human rights activists and journalists.

Morocco gained independence as a hereditary monarchy in 1956 after 44 years of French rule. Upon the death of his father, Mohammad V, in 1961, Hassan II assumed the throne and began a gradual and limited evolution of democratic institutions. Nevertheless, power remained highly centralized in the hands of the king, who appoints the prime minister and may dissolve the legislature at his discretion. Constitutional amendments passed in 1996 provide for a bicameral legislature with an upper house elected indirectly from various local government bodies and professional associations, and a 325-member, directly elected lower house, or house of representatives.

In March 1998, King Hassan responded to criticism of widespread fraud in the 1997 parliamentary elections by appointing a coalition government led by opposition socialist leader and former political prisoner Abderrahmane Youssoufi. Youssoufi leads a center-left government with broad support in the house of representatives. Pledging to transform Morocco's bleak human rights record, he has pursued a reformist program emphasizing social spending and respect for human rights. However, cabinet loyalists retained by the king restricted Youssoufi's ability to implement his agenda.

Upon Hassan's death in July 1999, Mohammad VI inherited a country with severe economic and social problems. Twenty percent of the population is unemployed, nearly half are illiterate, and a third live below the poverty line. The economy is heavily dependent on agriculture, and thus at the mercy of rainfall. A huge government debt threatens social spending, while some 50 percent of the budget pays for public sector salaries. Poverty has led to widespread grassroots support for Islamists, who traditionally step in with charity where the government fails to provide for its people. The king has attempted to co-opt this support by allocating funds for development projects in poverty-stricken areas and paying visits to rural communities to promote national reconciliation.

The government has sent mixed signals on economic and political reform, sparking speculation of disagreement among members of Morocco's power structure. With regard to the economy, the government has initiated the privatization of state-owned industries such as Royal Air Maroc and Maroc Telecom. A five-year economic plan covering 2000 to 2004 aims to improve infrastructure and create jobs, while a European Union association accord aims to achieve tariff-free trade with the EU by 2012. However, analysts and opposition figures stress the need to combat corruption and to streamline Morocco's bloated civil administration. Still, the government offered to create 17,000 new state jobs in May to avert a general strike.

The new king has also worked to promote civic freedom. Soon after taking power, he dismissed Driss Basri, the hardline interior minister apparently responsible for years of repression under Hassan. Thousands of prisoners have been freed, and exiled dissidents have returned. In April, Morocco inaugurated a center for human rights in Rabat to train prison wardens, judges, police officers, and teachers. A commission set up in 1999 to compensate victims of political repression began settling cases in April 2000. The government has also taken action against corruption; in August, 39 employees of Credit Agricole, which provides loans for agricultural projects, were arrested for mismanagement of public funds.

Yet political liberalization in Morocco has its limits. Labor, electoral, and press law reform, as well as constitutional reform that would clearly delineate executive authority, strengthen the legislature, and boost the independence of the judiciary, have not materialized. And the role of the king and the situation in Western Sahara continue to be subjects too sensitive for public debate. In late 2000, the government launched a crackdown on foreign and domestic independent media, closing newspapers and deporting several journalists. On UN Human Rights Day in December, as the king made a speech promising a constitutional democratic monarchy, riot police violently dispersed protesters, charging dozens of human rights activists with disturbing public order. This gap between government rhetoric and the reality on the streets has led to speculation that security forces are dictating policy, as they do in neighboring Algeria.

Political Rights and Civil Liberties: Moroccans' right to change their government democratically is limited. Although the house of representatives was elected in largely free balloting in 1997, its power is balanced by the 270-member upper house of parliament (Chamber of Advisors), and limited by the legal and de facto powers of the royal palace. Mohammad continues to rule under a constitution that grants him vast executive power. Constitutional changes must be approved by the king, who rules through his ministers, and no reform appears imminent. According to analysts, corruption and political interference pervade civil institutions, rendering them unfit to take on the responsibilities of governance. Provincial and local officials are appointed, while less powerful municipal councils are elected. Transparency and accountability are largely nonexistent.

Arbitrary arrest and detention occur, and prosecutors may extend administrative detention for up to a year. The king regularly pardons hundreds of prisoners during national and religious holidays. Human rights groups continue to call for independent investigations of torture, disappearances, and other abuses against opposition activists in the 1970s. A commission set up in 1999 to compensate victims of abuse and the families of disappeared opposition activists began settling cases in April. The commission has received almost 6,000 cases.

The judiciary is subject to corruption, bureaucracy, and governmental interference. Although judicial reform has been identified as a high priority of the government, very few steps have been taken to this end. Judges have been referred to disciplinary panels for punishment as a result of investigations into alleged corruption and misconduct. In an unprecedented display of independence, the supreme court in June overturned a military court decision to sentence an air force captain to prison for libeling the army. However, in another case, the king pardoned two journalists convicted of libeling the foreign minister, undercutting the judicial process before the journalists could appeal.

The press code allows confiscation and censorship of publications for libel, offensive reporting, or national security violations. The law also prohibits criticism of the monarchy, Islam, and Moroccan claims to Western Sahara. Broadcast media are mostly government controlled, and those that are not practice self-censorship. Foreign broadcasting is available via satellite. Violations against the press increased sharply in 2000. At least ten newspapers were banned or censored for coverage of Western Sahara and other controversial reporting. Three managers of 2M Television were sacked in April for broadcasting part of an interview with a Polisario official. In October, three France 3 journalists were placed under house arrest and reporters with Qatari Al-Jazeera television were banned from working. In November, authorities expelled the AFP bureau chief in Rabat. Three leading independent weeklies were closed in December for printing a letter allegedly implicating the prime minister in a plot to kill King Hassan. Although local and foreign media had their film confiscated while trying to cover clashes between police and human rights activists in December, Islamists posted video footage and photographs of the riots on the Internet. The government does not restrict Internet access, although the cost is prohibitive to most Moroccans.

The interior ministry requires permits for public gatherings, and quiet protests are usually tolerated. Protests in March for and against a draft law to grant women greater rights occurred without incident. However, police violently dispersed protesters in May demonstrating in support of a hunger-striking Tunisian journalist. About 30 people were arrested in Rabat following clashes between police and unemployed graduates protesting government policies in June, and the interior ministry banned demonstrations ahead of the 52nd anniversary of the Universal Declaration of Human Rights in December. Dozens of human rights activists were beaten and arrested as they defied the ban. Thirty-six members of the Moroccan Association of Human rights will be tried in February 2001 for organizing the illegal demonstrations. Hundreds of people were charged in connection with protests against the political ban on the Islamist Justice and Charity group. Under Mohammad, Islamists have assumed a more prominent role, circulating literature, opening unlicensed mosques, and staging demonstrations. Authorities released Justice and Charity leader Abdessalam Yassine from more than ten years of house arrest in May.

Although many women pursue careers in professions or in government, they face restrictions in advancement. Women's personal status is governed by the *moudouwana*, a code based on Islamic law that discriminates against women in divorce and inheritance matters. A 2000 government draft law to ban polygamy, raise the legal age of marriage, and grant women greater protection in divorce was shelved after massive demonstrations by conservative Islamists. Domestic violence is reportedly common, though much of it goes unreported. A victim's family may offer her rapist the opportunity to marry her to protect her honor, and the law is relatively lenient toward a man who kills his wife for adultery.

Islam is Morocco's official religion, and some 99 percent of Moroccans are Sunni Muslims. The government closely monitors mosque activities. Christianity and Judaism are tolerated and generally practiced freely. Proselytizing by Christians is prohibited; Bahais may not practice or participate in communal activities.

Some 60 percent of Moroccans claim Berber heritage. Increasing tolerance by the government has resulted in the establishment of numerous Berber cultural associations. Such groups criticize government policies emphasizing the use of Arabic in all aspects of life and prohibiting the teaching of the Berber language, Amazigh, in schools.

Morocco's heavily unionized formal labor sector includes 17 umbrella federations, some of which are aligned with political parties and all of which are subject to political pressure. Workers may bargain collectively and strike. Child labor is a serious problem, with up to half a million children working instead of attending school, according to government estimates. The U.S. State Department estimates that more than 10,000 children work as prostitutes in Casablanca alone. The government announced plans to fine parents if their children skip school, but most observers are skeptical about the authorities' ability to enforce the measure.

 Mozambique

Polity: Presidential-
parliamentary democracy
Economy: Mixed statist
Population: 19,100,000
PPP: $782
Life Expectancy: 44
Ethnic Groups: Indigenous tribal groups, including
Shangaan, Chokwe, Manyika, Sena, Makua (> 99 percent)
Capital: Maputo

Political Rights: 3
Civil Liberties: 4
Status: Partly Free

Trend Arrow: Mozambique received a downward trend arrow due to continuing political unrest in the wake of contested December 1999 national elections.

Overview:
Presidential and legislative elections took place in December 1999. President Joaquim Chissano and the ruling FRELIMO (Front for the Liberation of Mozambique) were re-elected, despite a strong showing by the opposition in both elections. The Carter Center, which observed the elections, determined that they showed signs of a maturing political system, although the opposition RENAMO (Mozambique National Resistance) party complained vociferously of fraud, and resultant political unrest continued throughout much of 2000. In addition, in 2000 a series of major floods seriously affected the Mozambican economy in 2000, killing 650 people and forcing 500,000 to flee their homes.

Portuguese traders and settlers arrived in the late fifteenth century. Full-scale colonization did not begin until the seventeenth century. In 1962 FRELIMO was established and launched a military campaign to drive out the Portuguese. In 1975 Mozambique gained independence. A one-party system was implemented, with FRELIMO as the sole legal party and the party leader, Samora Machel, as president of the republic. Independence was followed by 16 years of civil war against the rebels of RENAMO, a guerrilla movement supported first by Rhodesia (Zimbabwe) and later by South Africa.

In 1986 President Machel was killed in an airplane crash; Chissano became president. In 1989 FRELIMO formally abandoned Marxism-Leninism in favor of democratic socialism and a market economy. In 1992 a ceasefire was signed, followed by a full peace agreement. RENAMO recognized the government's legitimacy and agreed to begin operating as the opposition political party.

In 1994 the first multiparty elections were held. The elections attracted a 90 percent turnout and were judged a resounding success by Mozambicans and the international community, despite a last-minute pre-election boycott call by RENAMO, which accused FRELIMO of fraud. In large part due to pressure from its international sponsors, RENAMO decided to participate at the last minute. Its leader, Alfonso Dhaklama, captured 33.7 percent of the presidential vote as against 53.3 percent for the incumbent, Chissano. The parliamentary vote was much closer, although FRELIMO won a narrow, but workable, majority.

Only about 15 percent of registered voters participated in local elections in 1998. The campaign and voting were seen as largely free and fair, although FRELIMO's sweeping victory in all 33 contests was colored by a boycott by RENAMO and the Democratic Union, the only other party represented in the parliament.

Political divisions continue to characterize the country six years after negotiations ended 20 years of anticolonial and civil war. FRELIMO maintains its dominance of government institutions. RENAMO, its former guerrilla foe and now primary parliamentary opponent, complains bitterly of official manipulation of elections and the use of international aid to secure the ruling party's position. Both abuses by myriad security forces and banditry are endemic. While economic growth has continued with extensive foreign aid, widespread corruption has damaged the government's standing.

Political Rights and Civil Liberties: Mozambicans are able to select their president and parliament through competitive electoral processes, although this freedom is particularly constrained by the social, political, and economic ravages of years of civil war, in addition to a lack of familiarity with democratic practices. Democratic consolidation remains tenuous, but presidential and parliamentary elections of December 1999, together with Mozambique's previous elections, mark a step forward. The polls were marred by logistical and administrative difficulties, but were viewed by many Mozambicans and the international community as expressing the will of the people. These national elections were just the second since Mozambique adopted a pluralist multiparty system.

Continued claims by RENAMO of election fraud have resulted in a highly polarized political environment. In protest of alleged fraud, RENAMO deputies repeatedly walked out of parliament and otherwise interrupted its proceedings throughout 2000. At the peak of the boycott, RENAMO threatened to form a government of its own in the six northern and central provinces where it had won the most votes in the December elections. An anti-government demonstration in November resulted in the deaths of over 40 RENAMO supporters, and approximately 80 prisoners, mostly RENAMO backers, were suffocated under mysterious circumstances at about the some time. In December 2000, Chissano and Dhaklama held a meeting which raised hopes that the political impasse could be attenuated.

International assistance continues to play an important role in supporting Mozambique's democratization process. For example, more than 80 percent of those eligible registered to vote in the 1999 elections as part of a $40 million election process largely funded by the European Union and other donors. More controversially, some political campaigns were supported by foreign money. The National Elections Commission (NCE) was criticized by opposition parties and some independent observers for alleged pro-FRELIMO bias. Parliament is active and is an important player in the political process, although its power is overshadowed by that of the executive branch.

Mozambicans have a choice in terms of parties, although ideological differences between FRELIMO and RENAMO have narrowed since the end of the civil war. RENAMO had created a broader opposition umbrella with ten parties, although that has partially splintered. Both parties are criticized for lacking compelling messages for the country's seven million voters. RENAMO has been accused of maintaining groups of armed former guerillas. It has admitted that some former guerillas may still be active, but that they have yet to be incorporated into the new police force, as provided for under the 1994 peace agreement.

The independent media have enjoyed moderate growth, but publications in Maputo have little influence in the largely illiterate rural population. Criminal libel laws are another important deterrent to open expression. The constitution protects media freedom, but the state controls nearly all broadcast media and owns or influences all of the largest newspapers. There are more than a dozen licensed private radio and television stations, which also exercise some degree of self-censorship. The opposition receives inadequate coverage in government media, especially in national radio and television.

Nongovernmental organizations, including the Mozambican Human Rights League, are free to operate openly and issue critical reports. International human rights and humanitarian groups are also allowed to operate in the country. There is no reported interference with free religious practice.

Corruption within the legal sector remains a serious problem. A report by the Human Rights and Development Association (HRDA) in 1999 charged that rampant corruption within Mozambique's crumbling judicial system has robbed thousands of citizens of their right to a fair trial. The report suggested that Mozambique's constitution, which guarantees citizens the right to a speedy and fair trial with legal representation, was being undermined by the crisis. The HRDA report also criticized Mozambican jails as "massively overcrowded." The major Beira prison was built for only 120 inmates but currently holds between 600 and 700 prisoners.

Criminal suspects are usually detained for many months before appearing in court without any formal defense. Then they are tried only in the official language, Portuguese, which many Mozambicans speak very poorly. Mozambique has only 170 judges or magistrates and an estimated 200 defense lawyers for a population of 15 million. These problems are compounded by bureaucratic red tape. Bribery of judges by lawyers is alleged to be common practice. For example, judges regularly set bail so low on serious crimes that suspects simply fled justice.

During the period of one-party rule, FRELIMO tightly controlled Mozambique's labor movement. The Organization of Mozambican Workers, the country's major trade confederation, is now nominally independent. The Organization of Free and Independent Unions, a more independent group, was formed in 1994. All workers in nonessential services have the right to strike. The right to bargain collectively is legally protected.

Freedom of assembly is broadly guaranteed, but limited by notification and timing restrictions. Women suffer from both legal and societal discrimination. Domestic violence is reportedly common, despite initiatives by the government and civic groups to reduce it. Despite some economic gains, the country remains among the world's poorest and suffers from one of the world's highest infant mortality rates.

⬇ Namibia

Polity: Presidential-
parliamentary democracy
Economy: Capitalist-statist
Population: 1,800,000
PPP: $5,176
Life Expectancy: 50
Ethnic Groups: Ovambo (50 percent), Kavangos (9 percent),
Herero (7 percent), Damara (7 percent), Nama (5 percent), Caprivian (4 percent),
Bushmen (3 percent), Baster (2 percent), white (6 percent), mixed (7 percent)
Capital: Windhoek

Political Rights: 2
Civil Liberties: 3
Status: Free

Trend Arrow: Namibia received a downward trend arrow because of its involvement
in the war in neighboring Angola and abuses of civil liberties along the border region.

Overview: Tension in the Kavango region and the Caprivi Strip continued during 2000, and thousands of people were forced to flee their homes in those regions, both of which border Angola. There have been attacks against civilians, tourists, and humanitarian workers. Critics accused Namibia of abandoning its neutrality in the Angolan war after it granted Luanda the right to use its territory to launch attacks against strongholds of the National Union for the Total Independence of Angola (UNITA) under a December 1999 mutual defense pact. Amnesty International in March 2000 accused Angolan and Namibian government forces, as well as UNITA rebels, of rights abuses. It cited extrajudicial killings, tortures, arbitrary detentions, forcible deportations, and beatings. The government and the press have clashed over reporting on the border insecurity. Namibian opposition leaders have called for the unconditional withdrawal of all Namibian troops from the Democratic Republic of Congo, warning that the conflict could spill across the border.

Namibia was seized by German imperial forces in the late 1800s. Thousands of people were massacred by German troops in efforts to crush all resistance to colonial settlement and administration. The territory became a South African protectorate after German forces were expelled during World War I and was ruled under the apartheid system for 42 years after 1948. A United Nations-supervised democratic transition, with free and fair elections in which Sam Nujoma was elected president, followed 13 years of violent guerrilla war, and Namibia achieved independence in 1990.

The South West Africa People's Organization (SWAPO) scored a sweeping victory, and Nujoma was reelected president in the country's first postindependence elections in November 1994. Nujoma, the leader of the country's struggle against apartheid, has adopted an increasingly authoritarian governing style. He was easily returned to power with 77 percent of the vote for a third five-year term in the December 1999 elections that also saw SWAPO dominate national assembly polls. The party had succeeded in 1998 in passing a bitterly contested constitutional amendment to allow Nujoma to seek another term.

Capital-intensive extractive industries such as diamond and uranium mining have drawn significant foreign investment and are the centerpieces of Namibia's economic growth. Most Namibians, however, continue to live as subsistence farmers, and many lack basic services. Namibia's defense expenditure has soared by more than 100 percent since 1998, when it sent troops to the Democratic Republic of Congo. Continued insecurity in the northern Kavango region has taken its toll on the country's important tourism industry.

Political Rights and Civil Liberties:

Namibia's 1999 elections were judged as largely free and fair and allowed Namibians to exercise their constitutional right to choose their representatives for the third time. There were some instances of government harassment of the opposition, as well as unequal access to media coverage and campaign financing. SWAPO retained its two-thirds majority in the 72-member national assembly in 1999, increasing its number of seats from 53 to 55. The Congress of Democrats and the Turnhalle Alliance each got 7 seats. The United Democratic Front won 2, and the Monitor Action group got 1 seat.

In 1998, the electoral commission was removed from the prime minister's office and reorganized as an independent agency. While the president will still appoint commission members, he does so on the advice of a board that includes representatives of civil society. Political discussion is generally open and vigorous. The ruling party's main base is among the country's largest ethnic group, the Ovambo, whose prominence within SWAPO has evoked allegations of ethnic discrimination.

The constitution provides for an independent judiciary, and the government respects this. In rural areas, local chiefs use traditional courts that often ignore constitutional procedures. Freedom of religion is guaranteed and respected in practice. Freedom of assembly is guaranteed, except in situations of national emergency. Organizers of public meetings are required to obtain police approval, but the law is rarely enforced.

Respect for human rights in Namibia has been among the best in Africa, although allegations of abuses by security forces have emerged from the Caprivi Strip, the Kavango region, and the Democratic Republic of Congo. Amnesty International reported in March 2000 that Namibian security forces reportedly beat citizens and Angolan refugees during security operations in both Kavango and Caprivi that were the result of fighting between Angolan government troops and UNITA.

Fighting in Caprivi flared in October 1998 and in August 1999. There have been more than 100 claims against the government over alleged unlawful arrests following the security crackdown that followed the uprising by the Caprivi Liberation Army in August 1999. Claimants say they were unlawfully detained, and some said they were tortured. A Zambian human rights activist, who has lived in Namibia for 16 years, was expelled in June 2000, for alleged support of Caprivi secessionists. Caprivi, a finger of land poking eastwards out of northern Namibia along its borders with Angola and Botswana, differs geographically, politically, and in its ethnic makeup from the rest of Namibia. It was used by South Africa in that country's operations against SWAPO guerrillas. Caprivians accuse the government of neglect in the province, which is among the country's poorest. UNITA has been accused of supporting Caprivi insurgents.

The Herero and Damara peoples are among the minority ethnic groups demanding larger government allocations for development in their home areas. Former guerrilla fighters of the People's Liberation Army of Namibia continue to demand jobs, land, and other benefits that they had been promised.

Namibia's constitution guarantees the right to free speech and a free press, and those rights are usually respected in practice. Private radio stations and critical independent newspapers usually operate without official interference, but reporters for state-run media have been subjected to indirect and direct pressure to avoid reporting on controversial topics, such as the Caprivi issue. There are at least five private radio stations and one private television station. The state-run Namibia Broadcasting Corporation has regularly presented views critical of the government.

Despite constitutional guarantees, women continue to face serious discrimination in customary law and other traditional societal practices. Although violence against women is reportedly widespread, there is greater attention focused on the problems of rape and domestic violence. Women are increasingly involved in the political process, but remain seriously underrepresented in government and politics.

Constitutionally guaranteed union rights are respected. The two main union federations are the National Union of Namibian Workers and the Namibia Federation of Trade Unions. Collective bargaining is not practiced widely outside the mining and construction industries. Informal collective bargaining is increasingly common. Essential public sector workers do not have the right to strike. Domestic and farm laborers remain the country's most heavily exploited workers, in part because many are illiterate and do not know their rights.

Nauru

Polity: Presidential-parliamentary democracy
Economy: Mixed capitalist-statist
Population: 10,000
PPP: na
Life Expectancy: 61
Ethnic Groups: Nauruan (58 percent), other Pacific islander (26 percent), Chinese (8 percent), European (8 percent)
Capital: Yaren

Political Rights: 1
Civil Liberties: 3
Status: Free

Overview: Depletion of phosphates, the country's main foreign exchange earner for nearly a century, compels the government to develop alternative industries, one of which is to make Nauru into an offshore banking center. Lack of legal controls, however, has allegedly invited the inflow of money from questionable sources for money-laundering purposes. One estimate claims at least $70 million from Russia alone. At the end of 1999, the Group of 7, a grouping of the major industrialized countries, had decided to put Nauru and other Pacific Islands on a blacklist. The Nauruan government refused to answer to these accusations until four U.S. banks imposed a ban on U.S. dollar trade with the island in January 2000. In exchange for a lifting of the ban, the Nauruan government agreed to institute new banking laws and conduct closer monitoring of banking activities.

Nauru, an eight-square-mile island 1,600 miles northeast of New Zealand in the west-central Pacific, became a German protectorate in the 1880s. Following World War

I, Australia administered the island under a League of Nations mandate. The Japanese occupied Nauru during World War II, shipping 1,200 Nauru islanders to the island of Truk to work as forced laborers. In 1947, Nauru was made a United Nations Trust Territory under Australian administration. Greater autonomy was granted in 1966 with the election of a parliament, which was responsible for all matters except defense, foreign affairs, and the local phosphate industry. The country achieved full independence in 1968, and Hammer DeRoburt, who had been head chief of Nauru since 1956, became the first president in May 1968. Intense personal rivalries in the tiny, faction-ridden parliament have resulted in several changes of government in the last five years.

Nauru officially became a member of the United Nations in July 1999. China tried to block its entry because of Nauru's diplomatic relations with Taiwan, a major aid donor and investor in the island country. Nauru became a member country of the Commonwealth in May 1999, and was among the first to recognize the independence of West Papau, formerly Indonesia's Irian Jaya province.

In July 2000, Bernard Dowiyogo won back the presidency from Rene Harris in a close run in the 18-member parliament. Harris had held the presidency for only six days after beating Dowiyogo by a single vote in the April elections.

Phosphate mining gave Nauru a high per capita income but 90 years of phosphate mining has left 80 percent of the land uninhabitable. In 1989, Nauru sued Australia in the International Court of Justice for additional royalties for mining done during the trusteeship period. Nauru also claimed that Australia sold the phosphates domestically below world market prices, and sought compensation for physical devastation done to the island. Australia agreed to pay $70.4 million over 20 years in an out of court settlement reached in 1993.

Phosphate will likely become exhausted in the next 8 to 12 years. Future generations will draw income from the government's Nauru Phosphate Royalties Trust, but the trust lost millions of dollars through failed investments, speculation in the Tokyo stock market, and international financial scams. The government has carried out fiscal austerity programs, which have drastically reduced budgets, and is seeking ways to create new industries.

Political Rights and Civil Liberties: Citizens of Nauru can change their government democratically. The 1968 republican constitution provides for an 18-member parliament, representing 14 constituencies, directly elected for a three-year term. Parliament elects the president, who serves as head of state and head of government, from among its members. An elected Nauru Island Council serves as the local government and provides public services. All changes in government have occurred peacefully and in accordance with the constitution, and multiple candidates competed in recent parliamentary elections. There have been ad hoc political parties since independence, but politics is generally based on personal loyalties and occasionally on issue-based coalitions.

The government respects freedom of speech and the press. There is no regular independent news publication, but the government puts out information bulletins. The state owns Radio Nauru, which carries Radio Australia and BBC broadcasts, and the local Nauru TV.

Freedom of religion is respected in law and in practice. Freedom of assembly and association is respected. Workers have the constitutional right to form independent unions, but successive governments have generally discouraged labor organizing and no trade unions have formed. The private sector employs only one percent of all salaried workers. There is no legal basis for collective bargaining or holding strikes, and these activities rarely occur in practice.

The judiciary is independent and the right to public trial is upheld. Many cases are settled out of court through traditional mediation procedures. The police force has fewer than 100 members and is under civilian control. Some foreign workers have alleged that they receive inferior police protection compared to Nauruan citizens.

Citizens enjoy freedom of domestic and foreign travel. Foreign workers must apply to their employers for permission to leave the country during the period of their employment contracts. Those who leave without permission are likely to lose their jobs. A law requiring foreign workers who are fired to leave the country within 60 days has created serious hardship for many foreign workers. Women legally possess the same rights as men, but they continue to face discrimination in education and employment.

Nepal

Polity: Parliamentary democracy (insurgency)
Economy: Capitalist
Population: 23,900,000
PPP: $1,157
Life Expectancy: 58
Ethnic Groups: Newards, Indians, Tibetans, Gurungs, Sherpas, Magars, Tamangs, Bhotias, Rais, Limbus
Capital: Kathmandu

Political Rights: 3
Civil Liberties: 4
Status: Partly Free

Overview:
Despite winning a parliamentary majority in 1999, the ruling Nepali Congress (NC) party failed in 2000 to end the political instability that has plagued the country since its transition to democracy in the early 1990s. Consumed by infighting that threatened Prime Minister G. P. Koirala's job at year's end, the government also made little headway in tackling severe problems including corruption, poverty, and a Maoist insurgency that has killed some 1,500 people since 1996.

King Prithvi Narayan Shah unified this Himalayan land in 1769. Following two centuries of palace rule, the center-left NC won Nepal's first elections in 1959. King Mahendra abruptly dissolved parliament and banned political parties in 1960, and began ruling through a repressive *panchayat* (village council) system in 1962. Many of the parties worked underground until early 1990, when the NC and a coalition of Communist parties organized pro-democracy demonstrations that led King Birendra to legalize political parties in April. An interim government promulgated a constitution that vested executive power in the prime minister and cabinet. The constitution also created a bicameral parliament consisting of a 205-seat house of representatives that is directly elected for a five-year term, and an appointed, 60-member national council.

In Nepal's first multiparty elections in 32 years in 1991, Koirala, a veteran dissident, led the NC to a lower house majority. Splits within the NC forced the government to call midterm elections in November 1994. The Communist Party of Nepal (United Marxist-Leninist), or CPN-UML, won a narrow plurality with 88 seats.

With no party holding a parliamentary majority, the small, pro-monarchist National Democratic Party (RPP) used its swing votes to broker the rise and fall of successive governments. In an effort to end the instability, the NC and the CPN-UML formed a coalition government in December 1998—the country's sixth government in four years—and agreed to hold early elections in spring 1999.

Hopes for more stable government rose after the NC won a parliamentary majority in elections held on May 3 and May 17, 1999. The party formed a government under K. P. Bhattarai, who had led the NC to victory with 111 seats and had also headed the interim government during the democratic transition. The CPN-UML won 71 seats; RPP, 11; and four smaller parties, 12. The turnout was 66 percent. Key issues during the campaign included Nepal's stagnant economic development and rampant corruption; the continued presence of a decades-old Indian security post in Kalapani in far western Nepal; and an insurgency launched in February 1996 by the radical Communist Party of Nepal (Maoist), or CPN (Maoist), in the midwestern and western hills. The Maoists called for an end to the constitutional monarchy and of the feudal structure that persists in many parts of the country.

Trying to reduce subsidies that had contributed to a large budget deficit, the Bhattarai government raised prices of diesel, kerosene, electricity, and fertilizers by as much as 48 percent in October 1999. While leftist parties denounced the price increases, Bhattarai's rivals within the NC criticized the prime minister for failing to contain the Maoist insurgency, tackle corruption, reduce inflation, and initiate development projects.

By early 2000, Bhattarai's rivals within the party had gained the numbers to unseat him as NC leader and prime minister. Facing an intra-party no-confidence vote he seemed likely to lose, Bhattarai resigned on March 6. Koirala, 76, returned as Nepal's tenth prime minister in a decade on March 20. With the NC lacking strong internal discipline, aspiring party leaders continued trying to form majorities that would enable them to take power. In late December, Sher Bahadur Deuba, a former prime minister, collected the signatures of 56 MPs demanding Koirala's resignation and called for a no-confidence vote, which was scheduled for early 2001.

Political Rights and Civil Liberties:

Nepalese citizens can change their government through elections that are free though not entirely fair because of irregularities or violence in some districts. In the 1999 elections, interparty clashes led to several election-related deaths and caused postponements in dozens of constituencies. However, there was far less violence than during the 1997 local elections, when Maoist violence and threats forced the postponement of voting in parts of 15 of Nepal's 75 districts.

Under elected governments, Nepal's per capita gross domestic product, literacy rates, and health indicators have risen. However, wages have remained largely stagnant in real terms, rampant corruption and smuggling have undermined economic development, and criminal gangs have reportedly penetrated politics. The government has made few reforms to the civil service and ministries operate with limited transparency or accountability. In the absence of viable political institutions, parties frequently organize street demonstrations and general strikes that occasionally turn violent.

The supreme court is independent, but politicians reportedly manipulate lower courts, which are also reportedly rife with corruption. A 1999 report by the Kathmandu-based Institute for Legal Research and Resources alleged that corruption and the attitudes of officials largely prevent women from having recourse through the judiciary. The judicial system is heavily backlogged, and pretrial detention is often longer than the actual sentences that courts hand down to those convicted of crimes.

While human rights practices have improved considerably since the end of the absolute monarchy, the rule of law is weak and serious problems remain. Many of the most severe human rights abuses occur in the context of the CPN (Maoist) insurgency, which has directly affected 27 of Nepal's 75 districts. Amnesty International said in a February 2000 report that CPN (Maoist) guerrillas had killed 81 alleged police informants and other civilians between November 1998 and November 1999, and had committed a total of 200 such killings since launching the insurgency in 1996. Amnesty also said that of the 760 people killed by police since the insurgency began, more than half may have died in extrajudicial executions.

Many of the Maoists' victims, not only of killings but also of torture and kidnappings, have been suspected civilian informers, landowners, government officials, and members of mainstream political parties, particularly the NC and the CPN-UML. The insurgents have also set up "people's courts" in some parts of the country, which dispense summary justice. The guerrillas support their activities in part through extortion and looting. In addition to retaliating against alleged CPN (Maoist) members or supporters through extrajudicial executions, police have also been implicated in disappearances, arbitrary arrests and detentions, rapes, and torture in the context of the insurgency.

According to the United States State Department, authorities used the strict Public Security Act (PSA) to arrest 5,178 CPN (Maoist) members or sympathizers between the beginning of the insurgency and the end of 1999. Authorities charged 1,518 with crimes and released the remainder. The PSA allows authorities to detain suspects for up to 12 months without charge. In addition to using the PSA against the guerrillas, authorities have also occasionally detained peaceful protesters under this act and under the 1970 Public Offenses Act, which grants the 75 appointed chief district officers power to detain suspects for up to three months with a court order. In ordinary cases, police frequently use excessive force in routine situations, beat suspects to extract confessions, and hold detainees longer than permitted by courts and the law. The government established a National Human Rights Commission in 2000, but it lacked enforcement powers and was designed mainly to monitor human rights issues.

Conditions for journalists have worsened since the beginning of the Maoist insurgency. In recent years, authorities have detained several journalists on charges of having links to the guerrillas, or for reporting allegations of police abuses and corruption. Journalists are also constrained by the broadly drawn Press and Publications Act, which bans reporting that is disrespectful to the king, undermines national security or public order, or promotes animosity along religious or caste lines. While journalists practice some self-censorship, many of the hundreds of private newspapers and publications vigorously criticize government policies. With a national literacy rate of only 38 percent, many citizens depend on radio for their news. The government owns the influential Radio Nepal and the sole television station. News coverage on both services favors the ruling party. There are several private radio stations, and two private cable networks serve the Kathmandu Valley.

Successive governments have restricted demonstrations or other forms of public criticism of China's occupation of Tibet and Indian abuses in Kashmir. The government generally respects freedom of association, although it enforces a constitutional ban on political parties that are based on religious, caste, ethnic, tribal, or regional lines. Nongovernmental organizations (NGOs) operate freely. However, both police and CPN (Maoist) guerrillas occasionally threaten human rights activists to try to deter them from investigating rights violations.

Women rarely receive the same educational and employment opportunities as men and there are relatively few women in government and the civil service. Women also face discrimination under laws relating to property, divorce, and other areas. Studies and newspaper reports suggested that domestic violence and rape continued to be serious problems. The government has taken few measures to curb violence against women or assist victims. According to the International Labor Organization (ILO), organized gangs traffic some 5,000 to 7,000 girls to work in Indian brothels each year. Most victims are from the Tamang and other minority communities. Because the majority of prostitutes who return to Nepal are HIV-positive, nearly all returnees are shunned and are unable to obtain rehabilitation assistance. Advocates say authorities have only prosecuted 130 trafficking cases in recent years, according to a July Associated Press report. Moreover, local officials often facilitate trafficking.

Nepal's jails hold numerous women convicted of murder for having abortions or committing infanticide. Some of the women are rape victims who terminated their pregnancies. According to Unicef, in 40 percent of marriages the bride is under the age of 14.

Although the constitution describes Nepal as a Hindu kingdom, the actual percentage breakdown between Hindus and Buddhists is unknown. Members of the Hindu upper castes largely dominate parliament and the bureaucracy, and low-caste Hindus, ethnic minorities, and Christians face discrimination in the civil service, courts, and government institutions. The government banned the use of ethnic minority languages in government offices in 1999 in order to encourage the use of Nepali, the official language. Hindu militants and police occasionally harass Christians and Christian-based organizations.

Facing pressure from Beijing, the Nepalese government continued to return to China Tibetan refugees caught near the border, and introduced some cultural restrictions on the 20,000 Tibetans living in Nepal. Between 2,000 and 3,000 Tibetans escape into exile via Nepal each year, with most ending up in India. Nepal also hosts some 94,000 Bhutanese refugees.

While export-oriented carpet factories have reduced sharply their dependence on child labor, smaller carpet factories and other sectors continue to be dependent on child laborers. According to an ILO study, up to 40 percent of children work, although 60 percent of those who work also attend school. The U.S. State Department reported in its human rights country report for 1999 that an estimated 40,000 children are bonded laborers. Illegal bonded labor is prevalent in agriculture in the lowland Terai region, the western hills, and the Kathmandu Valley. In July, the government abolished the so-called Kamaiya system in the southern Terai that had kept an estimated 100,000 workers in bonded labor. However, news reports suggested that authorities failed to provide most freed laborers with land or housing, and many ended up as squatters on open fields.

Trade unions are independent, but are largely ineffective in organizing workers and bargaining collectively. By law, workers in certain "essential services," such as water supply, cannot stage strikes. In any case, more than 80 percent of the population is engaged in subsistence agriculture.

Netherlands

Polity: Parliamentary democracy
Economy: Mixed capitalist
Population: 15,900,000
PPP: $22,176
Life Expectancy: 78
Ethnic Groups: Dutch (91 percent), other (9 percent)
Capital: Amsterdam

Political Rights: 1
Civil Liberties: 1
Status: Free

Overview: Following a brief collapse in 1999 over a dispute about a proposed constitutional reform that would allow the public to amend and even veto laws already passed by the legislature, the Netherlands' center-left coalition government managed to restore its public support in 2000. The three-party coalition, which includes Prime Minister Wim Kok's Labor Party, the Liberal Party, and the Democracts-66 party has been in power since 1994. The "purple" coalition remains very popular because of favorable economic conditions and reforms made within the extensive social welfare system.

After the Dutch won independence from Spain in the sixteenth century, the House of Orange assumed sovereignty over the United Provinces of the Netherlands. A constitutional monarchy based on representative government emerged in the early 1800s. Queen Beatrix appoints the arbiters of executive authority (the council of ministers) and the governor of each province on the recommendation of the majority in parliament. The bicameral States General (parliament) consists of an indirectly elected First Chamber and a larger, more powerful, and directly elected Second Chamber.

From the end of World War II until December 1958, the Netherlands was governed by coalitions in which the Labor and Catholic parties predominated. From 1958 until 1994, governments were formed from center-right coalitions of Christian Democrats and Liberals, with the social-democratic-oriented Labor Party usually in opposition. Since 1994, the Labor Party has been a member of the governing center-left coalition.

Political Rights and Civil Liberties: The Dutch can change their government democratically. A series of amendments to the original constitution has provided for welfare and democratic reform. Local voting rights are accorded to foreigners after five years in residence. The Netherlands is the only country in the European Union without elected mayors. Mayors are currently appointed by the government from a list of candidates submitted by the municipal council.

The press is free and independent, although journalists practice self-censorship when reporting on the royal family. All Dutch newspapers cooperate in the administration of the independent Netherlands News Agency. Radio and television broadcasters operate autonomously under the supervision and regulation of the state and offer pluralistic views. Free speech is guaranteed, with the exception of promoting racism or incitement to racism. In September, the Dutch media protested over the prosecution of a journalist who had refused to reveal his sources, citing that the action was contrary to Article 10 of the European Treaty of Human Rights.

Freedom of religion is respected. Approximately 34 percent of the population is Roman Catholic; Protestants constitute 25 percent; and Muslims make up about 3 percent of the population. More than one-third of the population is unaffiliated with any religion. The government provides subsidies to church-affiliated schools based on the number of registered students.

A 24-member supreme court heads the country's independent judiciary, which also includes 5 courts of appeals, 19 district courts, and 62 lower courts. All judicial appointments are made by the crown on the basis of nominations by the parliament. Judges are nominally appointed for life, but retire at age 70. There is no jury system in Dutch courts.

Membership in labor unions is open to all workers, including military, police, and civil service employees. Workers are entitled to form or join unions of their own choosing without previous government authorization, and unions are free to affiliate with national trade union federations. Currently, about 28 percent of the workforce is unionized.

Immigrant groups face some de facto discrimination in housing and employment. Concentrated in larger cities, immigrants suffer from a high rate of unemployment. The government has been working for several years with employers' groups and unions to reduce minority unemployment levels to the national average. As a result of these efforts in recent years, the rate of job creation among ethnic minorities has been higher than among the general population. The Aliens Employment Act, which took effect in 2000, is expected to further increase the employment opportunities of minority groups and asylum seekers.

A new law to tighten criteria for acceptance of refugees was implemented in 1997; nevertheless, the country's asylum policies remain generous. Refugees whose applications for asylum are denied are allowed to remain temporarily.

Gender-based discrimination is prohibited. Women are well represented in the government, education, and other fields. Women constitute 36 percent of the membership in parliament. Legislation ending the 88-year-old ban on brothels, which had been approved in December 1999, went into effect in October. The lifting of the ban is intended to better regulate prostitution.

In 2000, the parliament voted to legalize same-sex marriages with the same pension, social security, and inheritance rights accorded to married heterosexual couples. A proposal to allow same-sex couples to adopt children was also approved. In November, by a vote of 104 to 40, the lower house of parliament approved a bill to legalize euthanasia and doctor-assisted suicide.

New Zealand

Polity: Parliamentary democracy
Economy: Capitalist
Population: 3,800,000
PPP: $17,288
Life Expectancy: 77
Ethnic Groups: New Zealand European (74.5 percent), Maori (10 percent), other European (4.5 percent), Pacific Islander (4 percent), Asian and other (7 percent)
Capital: Wellington

Political Rights: 1
Civil Liberties: 1
Status: Free

Overview:

Helen Clark, the Labor Party prime minister, upset her country's relations with neighbors around the region. Her endorsement of free trade within the region at the APEC summit in November, however, was a surprise, considering opposition from the Alliance Party, Labor's coalition partner, and its ally the Green Party. In domestic politics, personal attacks and verbal brawling worsened under the Clark government. Political scandals and controversies delayed the government's implementation of its "Closing the Gap" strategy to improve delivery of government services to the Maori minority. Sex education was finally made a part of the school curriculum, which critics consider long overdue. New Zealand's unplanned pregnancy rate is the second highest among developed countries and the country has a higher rate of sexually transmitted diseases than many other developed countries.

New Zealand achieved full self-government prior to World War II, and gained full independence from the United Kingdom in 1947. Since 1935, political power in this parliamentary democracy has alternated between the mildly conservative National Party and the center-left Labor Party, both of which helped to develop one of the world's most progressive welfare states.

In response to increasing global economic competition, the Labor government began restructuring the economy in 1984 by cutting farm subsidies, trimming tariffs, and privatizing many industries. The harsh effects of the economic reforms and a deep recession contributed to a National Party landslide at the 1990 parliamentary elections. However, Prime Minister Jim Bolger's National Party government pushed the reforms even further by slashing welfare payments, reworking the labor law to discourage collective bargaining, and ending universal free hospital care. An economic upswing helped the National Party to get re-elected in the 1993 elections and voters chose to replace the "first-past-the-post" electoral system with a mixed member proportional system (MMP) in a concurrent referendum. The MMP is designed to increase the representation of smaller parties by combining geographic constituencies with proportional representation balloting.

In the October 1996 elections for an expanded 120-seat parliament, the New Zealand First (NZF) Party entered into a coalition with the National Party. The strains of merging the National Party's fiscal conservatism with NZF's populism led to a policy drift. In October 1997, Transport Minister Jenny Shipley led an intraparty coup that forced Bolger to resign. As prime minister, Shipley announced a cabinet dominated by conservatives favoring further economic deregulation. Public criticisms of the fire service, electricity reform, and public sector accountability quickly eroded Shipley's popularity. The coalition collapsed in August 1998, when the NZF and the National Party clashed over plans to sell government-owned shares of Wellington International Airport, but Shipley managed to hold on to power with a narrow confidence vote a month later.

The Asian financial crisis sent New Zealand into a recession in 1998. Asia is the first destination for 40 percent of New Zealand's exports and the source of 30 percent of its tourists. Public discontent with the Shipley government helped the Labor and Alliance coalition government of Helen Clark to win the elections in November 1999.

Clark's outspoken style did not warm her to neighbors around the region. Tokyo was angered by her comments on Japanese whaling. Sultan Bolkiah of Brunei was insulted by her remarks about the kingdom's leadership of the Asia Pacific Economic Cooperation (APEC) organization this year. Tonga rebuked Clark for her proposal to aid Tongan democracy groups. Several Pacific Islands leaders did not warm to her remarks about how to bring peace and stability to the region. They also criticized New Zealand of not enforcing laws that would enable the prosecution of child-sex tourists from New Zealand. Relations with Australia soured because of her decision to hold steady defense spending and to terminate contracts for F-16 aircraft fighters made by the previous government.

On the domestic front in the year 2000, one cabinet member was dismissed for having an affair with a teenager, and allegations of financial impropriety and illicit sexual habits are made openly in the parliament. In August, the controversy that followed the murder of a journalist by a repeated sex offender compelled the government to introduce changes to the legal system, rewriting sentencing laws and mandating police checks for people who want to work with children.

Political Rights and Civil Liberties: New Zealanders can change their government democratically. New Zealand has no written constitution, but fundamental freedoms are respected in practice. The judiciary is independent. The private press is varied and vigorous. The broadcast media are both privately and publicly held and express pluralistic views. Civil society is advanced, and nongovernmental organizations, trade unions, and religion groups are outspoken. Religious freedom is respected. The authorities are responsive to complaints of rape and domestic violence, and a Domestic Violence Act came into effect in July 1997.

Trade unions are independent and engage in collective bargaining. The 1991 Employment Contracts Act (ECA) has weakened unions by banning compulsory membership and other practices that made trade unions the sole, mandatory negotiators on behalf of employees. Contracts are now generally drawn up at the factory, or even on an individual level; wages and union membership rolls have fallen. In 1994, the International Labor Organization (ILO) criticized a provision of the ECA prohibiting strikes designed to force an employer to sign on to a multicompany contract.

The Maori minority and the tiny Pacific Islander population face unofficial discrimination in employment and education. The 1983 Equal Employment Opportunities Policy, designed to bring more minorities into the public sector, has been only marginally successful. The Treaty of Waitangi, an agreement reached in the nineteenth century and codified in 1955, leases Maori land in perpetuity to the "settlers." Today, the rents received by the Maori on some 2,500 leases average far lower than those received by commercial landowners. Four parliamentary seats are reserved for Maori representatives. In the 1996 elections, 15 Maori politicians won seats, proportionate to the 13 percent Maori population. Maori activists say that the state-run television network's Maori-language programming is insufficient.

New Zealand has a long history of advancing women's rights. It was the first country in the world to give women the vote, in 1893. Women currently hold the positions of attorney general, chief justice, and governor-general (effectively, the head of state).

⬇ Nicaragua

Polity: Presidential-par-liamentary democracy
Economy: Capitalist-statist
Population: 5,100,000
PPP: $2,142
Life Expectancy: 68
Ethnic Groups: Mestizo (69 percent), European (17 percent), black (9 percent), Indian (5 percent)
Capital: Managua

Political Rights: 3
Civil Liberties: 3
Status: Partly Free

Trend Arrow: Nicaragua received a downward trend arrow due to increasing politicization of the electoral and judicial process, and the failure to protect the political and community rights of its indigenous peoples.

Overview:

Political reforms that denied a level playing field to smaller parties helped President Arnaldo Alemán and the opposition Sandinista party to maintain their grip on government power, in the midst of protests by other political factions excluded from access to electoral competition. The new rules, part of a package of 18 constitutional reforms signed into law by Alemán in January 2000, helped to disenfranchise Nicaragua's indigenous communities, and came as judicial independence continued under attack and high-level corruption, abetted and protected by the two largest parties' lock on power, continued unabated. In November 2000 municipal elections Sandinista candidates won the key mayoralty of Managua, the capital city, as well as 48 of 151 other top municipal posts up for grabs, including 11 of 17 state capitals. The strong showing bode well for the Sandinistas in the run-up to the November 2001 presidential elections.

The Republic of Nicaragua was established in 1838, 17 years after independence from Spain. Its history has been marked by internal strife and dictatorship. The authoritarian rule of the Somoza regime was overthrown in 1979 by the Sandinistas. Subsequently, the Sandinista National Liberation Front (FSLN) attempted to establish a Marxist government, which led to civil war and indirect U.S. intervention on behalf on the right-wing irregular army known as the Contras. The FSLN finally conceded in 1987 to a new constitution that provides for a president and a 96-member national assembly elected every six years. Shortly before the 1990 elections, hundreds of thousands of acres of farmland were turned over to peasant cooperatives under a land reform program, while Sandinista leaders confiscated the best luxury properties and businesses for themselves.

In 1990, the newspaper publisher Violeta Chamorro easily defeated the incumbent, President Daniel Ortega. Her 14-party National Opposition Union (UNO) won a legislative majority in the national assembly. Chamorro gave substantial authority to her son-in-law and presidency minister, Antonio Lacayo, who reached an agreement with Ortega's brother, Humberto, allowing Humberto to remain head of the military.

In 1994, the social democratic Sandinista Renewal Movement and the anti-Lacayo UNO factions proposed constitutional reforms to limit the powers of the president and end nepotism in presidential succession. Lacayo and Daniel Ortega opposed the measure. In February 1995, after passage of a law ensuring the military's autonomy, Humberto Ortega turned over command of the military to General Joaquin Cuadra. The army was reduced from 90,000 to 15,000 troops. Despite the apparent depoliticizing of the army, including the integration of former Contras, the leadership remained essentially the same. The armed forces continued to own a profitable network of businesses and property amassed under the Sandinistas.

Chamorro was forbidden by law to seek a second term. The 1996 elections were held under the auspices of the five-member Supreme Electoral Council, an independent branch of government. During the campaign, Daniel Ortega tried to portray himself as a moderate committed to national unity and reconciliation. Alemán ran on a platform that promised economic reforms, dismantling of the Sandinista-era bureaucracy, cleaning up of the army, and the return of property confiscated by the Sandinistas to its original owners. He defeated Ortega 51 to 38 percent, avoiding a runoff.

President Alemán's first priority was to reform the army and the police. Alemán named a civilian-led Defense Ministry, and a new military code was adopted. The size of the national police force was reduced from 16,000 to 6,800. Its leadership, however, is still composed largely of former Sandinista cadres.

In 1999, a governability pact was agreed to by Alemán's right-wing Liberal Constitutionalist Party government and the opposition, led by Daniel Ortega. Although the accord ended a 14-year congressional impasse, Nicaragua's smaller parties immediately protested that political power, including greater representation on both the supreme court and the Supreme Electoral Council, was being "carved up" between the two historic antagonists. The reforms guaranteed Alemán a seat in both the Nicaraguan and the Central American parliaments, thus assuring him immunity from prosecution. (Daniel Ortega's parliamentary immunity has frustrated attempts by his stepdaughter, Zoilamercia Narvaez, to bring a sexual abuse case against him.) After the percentage of votes needed to avoid a presidential runoff election was lowered, from 45 to 35 percent, Ortega's chances of winning back the presidency were greatly enhanced. The 1999 imprisonment of Comptroller-General Agustín Jarquín, whose office was probing suspicious land deals allegedly conducted by Alemán, was viewed as an important setback for judicial independence.

The November 2000 municipal elections proved to be the first test of the fairness of the deal struck by Alemán and the Sandinistas, which forced all parties to re-register, with their applications supported by 75,000 signatures. The Yátama party, led by long-time Indian activist Brooklyn Rivera, was initially denied a place on the ballot as a result of the deal, but won an initial court ruling with the support of a broad range of political, Roman Catholic Church, and nongovernmental organization representatives. Yátama's right to a place on the ballot, however, was overturned by the Nicaraguan supreme court, a highly politicized body with loyalties to the two major parties. At least one person died and 12 others were injured during demonstrations protesting the ruling.

Political Rights and Civil Liberties: Nicaraguans can change their government democratically. The military, which in nine years has shrunk from 90,000 to 14,000 members, remains a political force through substantial property and monetary holdings. Political parties are allowed to organize; however, changes in the political system in 1999 made it increasingly difficult for smaller parties to achieve electoral representation. Political and civic activities continue to be conditioned on occasional political violence, corruption, and drug-related crime. In March 1999, Comptroller-General Jarquín issued a report saying that Alemán's personal assets had increased 40-fold since he was elected mayor of Nicaragua in 1990. Reforms enacted by Alemán in 2000 gave the two major parties greater say in a restructured judiciary, elections authority, and the comptroller-general's office. Jarquín himself resigned in 2000 after his office was turned into a five-member collective body.

The judiciary is independent but continues to be susceptible to political influence and corruption. Large case backlogs, long delays in trials, and lengthy pretrial detentions have caused the supreme court and national assembly to initiate comprehensive structural reforms of the judicial system. The ministry of government oversees the National Police, which is formally charged with internal security; in practice, the police share this responsibility with the army in rural areas. In 1999, the army was called out to help police confront striking transportation workers. Reflecting enhanced civilian control, the conduct of security forces continues to improve, although abuses of human rights still occur. Abuses are particularly pronounced among members of the army carrying out rural law enforcement duties, as they occasionally kill criminal suspects instead of arresting them. Forced confessions to the police remain a problem, as do cases in which security forces arbitrarily arrest and detain citizens. Prison and police holding cell conditions are poor.

The print media are varied and partisan, representing hardline and moderate Sandinista, as well as pro- and anti-government, positions. Before leaving office, the Sandinistas privatized the national radio system, mostly to Sandinista loyalists. There are five television stations, three of which carry news programming with partisan political content. A September 1996 law established a professional journalists' guild requiring journalists in the Managua area to have a bachelor's degree in journalism or five years of journalistic experience; opposition forces claimed the law was a blow to freedom of expression. In 1999, journalists who were roughed up by Alemán's bodyguard were the objects of ridicule from the president himself. In late December, a Sandinista radio station controlled by a party dissident was forcibly shut down by riot police as authorities closed the station's installations and removed equipment under a judicial order.

Discrimination against women and indigenous people is a problem, although significant progress was recorded in 1998 in Native American rights. Violence against women, including rape and domestic abuse, remains a serious problem. Indigenous peoples, about six percent of the population, live in two autonomous regions—the Northern Autonomous Atlantic Region (RAAN) and the Southern Autonomous Atlantic Region (RAAS). These are primarily Miskito, Sumo, Rama, and Garifuna peoples. In 1998, Indian parties showed significant political strength in the March regional elections, in which 45 autonomous councils were chosen. Native American political rights were severely curtailed by legislation enacted in 2000 forcing parties to re-register with a nearly-impossible-to-achieve amount of signatures.

The Nicaraguan government has also failed to demarcate the ancestral lands of the Mayagna community of Awas Tingni, thus leaving the indigenous tribe without adequate means to secure their collective rights to ownership and enjoyment of their ancestral lands and the natural resources these contain. By granting logging concessions to a Korean timber company without the community's consent, the government has failed to provide adequate judicial protection for Awas Tingni property and related human rights. In late 2000, the case of the Awas Tingni was being considered by the Inter-American Court of Human Rights.

Labor rights are complicated by the Sandinistas' use of unions as violent instruments to influence government economic policy. By means of the public sector unions, the Sandinistas have managed to gain ownership of more than three dozen privatized state enterprises. The legal rights of non-Sandinista unions are not fully guaranteed. Citizens have no effective recourse when labor laws are violated either by the government or by violent Sandinista actions. Child labor is also a problem.

Niger

Polity: Presidential-parliamentary democracy
Economy: Capitalist
Population: 10,100,000
PPP: $739
Life Expectancy: 49

Political Rights: 4*
Civil Liberties: 4*
Status: Partly Free

Ethnic Groups: Hausa (56 percent), Djerma (22 percent), Fula (9 percent), Tuareg (8 percent), Beri Beri (4 percent), other (1 percent)
Capital: Niamey
Ratings Change: Niger's political rights and civil liberties ratings changed from 5 to 4 due to further consolidation of political reforms and a general easing of repression.

Overview:

The government of President Mamadou Tandja continued efforts to make political reforms and improve human rights, although a coalition of opposition parties complained of exclusion. Hundreds of supporters of the opposition Coordination of Democratic Forces protested in the capital, Niamey, in October 2000, accusing the government of denying its activists government jobs and access to state-run media. The Tandja administration, however, maintains good relations with the country's political opposition. Restrictions on the press have eased significantly under Tandja, but harsh penalties continued to be imposed at times.

After gaining independence from France in 1960, Niger was governed for 30 years by one-party and military regimes dominated by leaders of Hausa or Djerma ethnicity. After 13 years of direct military rule, Niger was transformed into a nominally civilian, one-party state in 1987 under General Ali Seibou. International pressure and pro-democracy demonstrations led by the umbrella organization Niger Union of Trade Union Workers forced Niger's rulers to accede to the Africa-wide trend towards democratization in 1990. An all-party national conference drafted a new constitution that was adopted in a national referendum in 1992.

Mahamane Ousmane, of the Alliance of Forces for Change, won a five-year term as the country's first democratically elected president in 1993 in elections deemed free and fair. General Ibrahim Baré Maïnassara overthrew Ousmane in 1996 and won fraudulent elections later that year. Maïnassara was assassinated in April 1999 by members of the presidential guard. Major Daouda Malam Wanke, the head of the guard, led a transitional government until elections were held the following November. A referendum on a new constitution was held in July 1999.

Niger is one of Africa's poorest countries and officials have warned of the threat of famine due to drought. The country has been struggling under a burdensome foreign debt, a portion of which international donors agreed to write off in December 2000.

Political Rights and Civil Liberties: The people of Niger have had two chances, in 1993 and 1999, to change their leaders democratically. The July 1996 presidential election that followed the January 1996 military coup was held under a revised constitution, and was not deemed free or fair by independent observers. Polls in 1999 were considered free and fair. A first round of presidential elections was held in October 1999. Tandja won the runoff in November with 60 percent of the vote.

Parliamentary elections in November 1996 were held in an atmosphere of intense intimidation and were boycotted by most opposition parties. In 1999, Tandja's party, the National Movement for the Development of Society, and its partner, the Democratic and Social Convention, achieved a two-thirds majority in the national assembly by winning 55 of the 83 seats. The other coalition, the Nigerien Party for Democracy and Socialism and the Rally for Democracy and Progress, won the other 28 seats.

The constitution provides for an independent judiciary, but courts are subject to executive interference and limited by scant training and resources. The supreme court has on occasion asserted its independence. The president is "politically unprosecutable," except in the case of treason, and may exercise exceptional powers in a crisis.

Respect for human rights has improved under the government of President Tandja. However, pretrial detention remains a problem, and detainees are often held for months or years. Prisons are characterized by overcrowding and poor health and sanitary conditions. The International Committee of the Red Cross and other humanitarian groups have unrestricted access to prisons and detention centers. Human rights and other nongovernmental organizations operate openly and freely in the country, and publish reports that are often highly critical of the government.

Constitutional guarantees of freedom of assembly and association are generally respected. Freedom of religion is respected, although, at times, Muslims have not been tolerant of the rights of minority religions to practice their faith. Political parties formed on religious, ethnic, or regional bases are barred. Islam is practiced by more than 90 percent of the population. Conservative Muslims in November violently demonstrated against a fashion show outside of Niamey that they called "satanic." The government banned eight Islamic associations following the violence. More than 200 protesters were detained briefly.

Discrimination against ethnic minorities persists, despite constitutional protections. The Hausa and Djerma ethnic groups dominate government and business. Tandja is the country's first president who is from neither group. Nomadic people, such as the Tuaregs and many Peul, continue to have less access to government services. The Maïnassara regime in 1999 forged a peace pact with the Democratic Revolutionary United Front, which is composed mostly of minority ethnic-Tobou people in southeastern Niger, ending the country's last serious insurgency.

Constitutional protections for free expression are guaranteed and are usually respected in practice. The National Communications Oversight Group was created in 1999 to provide for independence of the media and ethics in journalism. A government newspaper and at least a dozen private publications circulate; some of them are loosely affiliated with political parties. There are at least six private radio stations, some of which broadcast in local languages.

The founder and owner of the weekly *L'Enqueteur*, Sumana Maiga, was sentenced to eight months in prison and fined in November 2000, following publication of an article about the dispute between Benin and Niger concerning the island of Lete. The newspaper's managing editor and a journalist received six-month suspended sentences and were fined for "disturbing the public order" and "spreading false information." Reporters Sans Frontiéres said their trial was marked by irregularities, notably by the court's being unable to establish bad faith on the part of the journalists. *L'Enqueteur* ceased to appear as of October 25.

Women suffer extensive societal discrimination, especially in rural areas. Family law gives women inferior status in property, inheritance rights, and divorce. Islamic conservatives have squelched moves to amend portions of the legal code most discriminatory against women. Domestic violence against women is reportedly widespread. The government in August 1999 ratified the Convention for the Elimination of All Forms of Discrimination Against Women, angering some Islamic groups. Several women's rights organizations operate in the country.

Notice of intent must be given and negotiations attempted before a strike is legal, and workers can be required to provide essential services. Collective bargaining agreements are negotiated under the framework of a tripartite agreement among the government, employers, and unions.

Nigeria

Polity: Presidential-parliamentary democracy
Economy: Capitalist
Population: 123,300,000
PPP: $795
Life Expectancy: 50
Ethnic Groups: Hausa and Fulani (29 percent),
Yoruba (21 percent), Igbo (18 percent), other (32 percent)
Capital: Abuja

Political Rights: 4
Civil Liberties: 4*
Status: Partly Free

Ratings Change: Nigeria's civil liberties rating changed from 3 to 4 because of increasing interreligious and inter-ethnic clashes that left hundreds dead.

Overview:
A visit by U.S. President Bill Clinton in August served as symbolic approval for Nigeria's reentry onto the world stage after 15 years of corrupt military rule, and for steps taken by the elected government of President Olusegun Obasanjo to consolidate democracy, reduce corruption, and improve human rights. Although Clinton's visit brought a flood of aid to Nigeria, including $66 million in military aid, it did not lead to the government's hoped-for cancellation of the country's nearly $30 billion debt.

The military ruled Nigeria for all but ten years since independence from Britain in 1960. Its generals and their backers argued that they were the only ones who could keep a lid on simmering tensions between Muslims and Christians on the one hand and the 122 million people who constitute the country's 250 ethnic groups on the other hand. The Hausa-Fulani from northern Nigeria dominated the military and the government from independence until Obasanjo, who is from the north, was elected. The Yoruba and Igbo peoples and smaller groups in the south deeply resent northern domination, and what many see as exploitation of their far-richer lands. The north is largely Muslim while the south is mainly Christian.

Nigeria initially appeared to be emerging from several years of military rule under General Ibrahim Babangida in 1993, when presidential elections were held. Moshood Abiola, a Muslim Yoruba from the south, was widely considered the winner, but the military annulled the results. It continued to rule behind a puppet civilian administration until General Abacha, a principal architect of previous coups, took power himself in November 1993. A predominantly military Provisional Ruling Council (PRC) was appointed, and all democratic structures were dissolved and political parties banned. Abiola was arrested in June 1994 after declaring himself Nigeria's rightful president. He died in detention, after suffering from lack of proper medical care, just five weeks after Abacha himself died suddenly in June 1998.

The departure of the two most significant figures on Nigeria's political landscape opened possibilities for democratic change. General Abdulsalami Abubakar, the army chief of staff, emerged as the consensus choice of the military's PRC as the country's next leader and promised to oversee a transition to real civilian rule in 1999. Fraud and irregularities marred the polls, especially the presidential election, but most observers agreed that the election of Obasanjo reflected the will of the majority of voters. Obasanjo is a former general who led a military regime in Nigeria from 1976 to 1979, and spent three years in prison under Abacha.

Hostage-taking of oil workers and sabotage of petroleum installations in the southern Niger Delta region continued in 2000, and the government sent in the military to restore order, raising protests by human rights groups. Nine northern states have introduced *Sharia* (Islamic law), which allows amputation, flogging, and decapitation as penalties. Fighting between Christians and Muslims left hundreds dead during the year. Ethnic clashes and ethnic militancy are on the rise. A panel on human rights, modeled on South Africa's Truth and Reconciliation Commission, began hearing some 150 cases of alleged abuses spanning from the start of the Biafran war in 1966 through the regime of General Sani Abacha in the 1990s.

A priority of the Obasanjo government is to try to rid Nigeria of the corrupt practices of the past that have bled the country of billions of dollars in oil revenue. An anti-graft commission was set up in September 2000, and lawmakers in December passed an anti-corruption bill. The International Monetary Fund in August approved a $1 billion standby credit, and discussions were ongoing with the World Bank on a $3 billion concessionary loan. Most Nigerians are engaged in small-scale agriculture.

Political Rights and Civil Liberties: Nigerians had the right to change their government for the first time in 16 years in 1999. Although the voting was free, it was not fair in many areas in both the presidential and legislative polls. Irregularities occurred at each stage of the electoral process. During the presidential nominating convention, large sums of money were offered by both political camps to delegates to vote against political opponents. International observers witnessed serious irregularities during the presidential election, including the local purchase of false ballots and fraudulent tally sheets. The production of "ghost votes" in some states amounted to as much as 70 or 80 percent of the total reported votes. Obasanjo won the presidency, which carries a four-year term, with 63 percent of the vote compared with 37 percent for Samuel Oluyemi Falae of the Alliance for Democracy (AD). International observers confirmed the results and stated that, despite widespread fraud, Obasanjo's victory reflected the will of most voters.

Members of the bicameral national assembly are elected for four-year terms to 109 seats in the senate and 360 in the house of representatives. Obasanjo's People's Democratic Party won 59 senate seats and 206 house seats. The All People's Party won 24 seats in the senate and 74 in the house, while the AD won 20 senate seats and 68 house seats.

The Independent National Electoral Commission is working with several international electoral assistance organizations to help improve the process in 2003. No commission officials, however, have faced disciplinary action as result of their involvement in corrupt activities in the 1999 elections.

The judiciary is subject to political influence and is hampered by corruption and inefficiency. Lengthy pretrial detention remains a problem. The country's prisons are overcrowded, unhealthy, and life threatening. The government has allowed international nongovernmental organizations to visit detention facilities, and some improvements have been made.

Respect for human rights has improved considerably under Obasanjo. The Human Rights Violations Investigation Commission, which is modeled on South Africa's

Truth and Reconciliation Commission, began hearing about 150 cases during the year, or those deemed the most serious, of some 11,000 complaints that were filed. Despite these efforts, there are continuing reports of abuses. Members of the security forces, including the police, anticrime units, vigilante groups, and the armed forces committed serious violations. These included extrajudicial killings, arbitrary detentions, torture, and beatings. Human Rights Watch reported in December that security forces deployed to the oil-rich Niger Delta region carried out summary executions, assaults, and other abuses against civilians. The government has taken steps to curb the torture and beating of detainees and prisoners.

Freedom of speech and expression is guaranteed, and the Obasanjo government respected these rights far more than the previous military administrations. Several private radio and television stations broadcast, and numerous print publications operate largely unhindered. However, violations against press freedom continued during the year, according to the international Committee to Protect Journalists.

Armed members of the State Security Service raided the Abuja offices of the independent daily *This Day* in April and roughed up several employees. An editor who reportedly was targeted said the raid stemmed from reports about a state security advisor allegedly involved in graft under the Abacha regime. In January, more than 50 police, some heavily armed, stormed the International Press Center in Lagos with their guns drawn and arrested several people, including four journalists. The reporter Funmi Komolafe of the private daily *Vanguard* was beaten in July by a group of striking labor union workers before an interview with an official from the Nigeria Labor Union.

The freedoms of assembly and association are guaranteed and are usually respected in practice. The constitution prohibits ethnic discrimination and requires government offices to reflect the country's ethnic diversity. Obasanjo's government is both ethnically and religiously diverse, but societal discrimination is widely practiced and clashes frequently erupt among the country's 250 ethnic groups. A number of armed youth groups have emerged to defend their ethnic and economic interests, including the pro-Yoruba Oodua People's Congress (OPC), the pro-Hausa-Fulani Arewa People's Congress, and Ijaw militants of the Niger Delta. An OPC attack in October 2000 on Hausa-Fulanis living in Lagos claimed more than 100 lives. Ethnic minorities in the Delta region feel particularly discriminated against, mainly in terms of receiving a share of the country's oil wealth. A secessionist group, the Movement for the Actualization of the Sovereign State of Biafra, emerged during the year. Several people were killed in December when government troops were deployed against the group.

Religious freedom is guaranteed by the constitution, but officials often discriminate against those of a religion different from their own. Private businesses frequently practice religious discrimination. Religious violence has become increasingly common and often corresponds with regional and ethnic differences. Clashes between Christians and Muslims in the northern city of Kaduna in February and May 2000 left at least 200 people dead and forced thousands of people to flee their homes. An armed vigilante group has emerged in the northern state of Zamfara to enforce Sharia. Nine northern states have declared Islamic law since the return to democratic rule. Conflict between Shiite and Sunni Muslims occasionally flares.

Nigerian women face societal discrimination, although educational opportunities have eroded a number of barriers over the years. Women play a vital role in the country's informal economy. Marital rape is not considered a crime, and women of some ethnic groups are denied equal rights to inherit property. About 60 percent of Nigerian women are subjected to female genital mutilation. Trafficking in women for prostitution continued, particularly to Western European cities. Women's rights suffered serious setbacks in many northern states where Sharia law was declared during the year. Women were sentenced to be flogged for having premarital sex. Child labor, marriages, and trafficking remain common.

The transitional government of General Abubakar lifted decrees promulgated under Abacha that repressed labor rights, including the right to strike, and the country regained its position in the International Labor Organization. Workers, except members of the armed forces and those considered essential employees, may join trade unions. About ten percent of the workforce belong to unions. No laws prohibit retribution against strikers and strike leaders, but strikers who believe that they are victims of unfair retribution may submit their cases to the Industrial Arbitration Panel with prior approval of the Labor Ministry. The rights to organize and to bargain collectively are guaranteed.

Norway

Polity: Parliamentary democracy
Economy: Mixed capitalist
Population: 4,500,000
PPP: $26,342
Life Expectancy: 78
Ethnic Groups: Norwegian, Finnish, Lapp (Saami) minority
Capital: Oslo

Political Rights: 1
Civil Liberties: 1
Status: Free

Overview:

Prime Minister Kjell Magne Bondevik resigned in March after his coalition government lost a vote of no-confidence concerning a proposal to build gas power plants. Bondevik's minority government wanted to prevent any construction of gas power plants until new technology allowed for more environmentally friendly plants. After Bondevik submitted his resignation, King Harold V appointed Lens Stoltenberg of the opposition Labor Party to form a new government.

Since 1997, Norway has been ruled by a minority coalition of center-right parties led by the Christian People's Party. The alliance, which also includes the Liberal Party and the Center Party, holds 42 seats in the 165-seat *Storting* (parliament). The Labor Party, which has dominated Norway since the 1920s, holds 65 of the seats. Stoltenberg, a former finance minister, replaced Thorbjorn Jagland as the Labor Party's parliamentary leader, which subsequently bolstered the diminishing popularity of the Labor Party among the voters.

The Eisvold Convention, Norway's current constitution, was adopted during a period of de facto independence immediately prior to the acceptance of the Swedish monarch as king of Norway in 1814. After the peaceful dissolution of its relationship with the Swedish crown in 1905, Norway chose a sovereign from a Danish royal house and began to function as a constitutional monarchy with a multiparty parliamentary structure.

With the elections in 2001, the new government will most likely address the issue of membership in the European Union (EU) again. The Labor government negotiated membership in both 1972 and 1994; however, the Norwegian electorate rejected it each time by slim margins. Although Norway is not a member of the EU, it does enjoy nearly full access to the EU's single market through membership in the European Economic Area.

In October, the United Nations General Assembly elected Norway to a two-year term on the Security Council, beginning in January 2001.

Political Rights and Civil Liberties: Norwegians can change their government democratically. The Storting is directly elected for a four-year term by universal suffrage and proportional representation. It then selects one-quarter of its members to serve as the upper chamber (*Lagting*), while the remaining members make up the lower chamber (*Odelsting*). Neither body is subject to dissolution. A vote of no-confidence in the Storting results in the resignation of the cabinet, and the leader of the party that holds the most seats is then asked to form a new government.

Since 1989 the approximately 20,000-strong Lappic (Saamic) minority has elected an autonomous, 39-member assembly that functions as an advisory body on issues such as regional control of natural resources and preservation of Saami culture. In November, the government granted the Saami assembly its own parliament building in Karasjok. In 1999 the Center for Combating Ethnic Discrimination was established by the government to provide legal aid to persons exposed to discrimination on grounds of religion, race, or national or ethnic origin.

In recent years there have been some instances of xenophobic and nationalist sentiments. The leader of the far-rightist Progress Party, Carl Hagen, demanded that the number of immigrants granted asylum in Norway be reduced. Although 5.5 percent of Norway's population is of foreign origin, most foreigners come from northern Europe. Only about 10,000 asylum seekers enter the country each year.

Freedom of the press is constitutionally guaranteed, and many newspapers are subsidized by the state in order to promote political pluralism. The majority of newspapers are privately owned and openly partisan. Norway has one of the highest rates of Internet users per capita in the world.

The state finances the Evangelical Lutheran Church, in which 93 percent of the population holds nominal membership. The law requires that the monarch and at least half of the cabinet be Lutheran, and those professing the Lutheran Church are bound by law to bring up their children in that faith. Roman Catholics and other Protestants make up 4 percent of the population, and the other 3 percent have no religious affiliation. Other denominations do not have to register with the state unless they seek state support. Muslims, who constitute less than 1 percent, were granted by the government in March the right to broadcast calls to prayer in Oslo.

The constitution guarantees freedom of peaceful assembly and association and the right to strike. Sixty percent of the workforce belongs to the unions, which are free from government control. The Norwegian Federation of Trade Unions (LO), established 100 years ago, has about 850,000 members and is closely linked to the Labor Party. According to the International Labor Organization, Norwegian employees put in, on average, fewer hours at work than other Europeans. In May, 85,000 workers from various sectors, including public transportation and the newspaper and construction industries, went on strike, rejecting wage increases of three to four percent. This was the largest labor dispute in a decade.

The independent judiciary system is headed by a supreme court and operates at the local and national levels. The king, under advisement from the ministry of justice, appoints judges.

Women's rights are legally protected. In the Storting, women hold approximately 36 percent of the seats. Nevertheless, only 1 percent of the executives of Norway's 500 largest enterprises are women; in the public sector the figure is 11 percent.

Oman

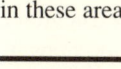

Polity: Traditional monarchy
Economy: Capitalist-statist
Population: 2,400,000
PPP: $9,960
Life Expectancy: 71
Ethnic Groups: Arab (74 percent), Indian (13 percent), other (13 percent)
Capital: Muscat

Political Rights: 6
Civil Liberties: 5*
Status: Not Free

Ratings Change: Oman's civil liberties rating changed from 6 to 5 because of improvements in property, business, and economic rights, and greater opportunities for women in these areas.

Overview:

On November 18, Omanis celebrated the 30th anniversary of the accession of Sultan Qabus ibn Sa'id al Sa'id. Held in high esteem by his citizens, the sultan has transformed Oman from an impoverished country to one with modern physical and financial infrastructure and social services, public utilities, health, and education on par with Western countries. Annual income per Omani is around $10,000, while women enjoy political rights and important positions in commerce, industry, and the professions.

The government revised election procedures for the *Majlis al-Shura*, or consultative council, prior to July 2000 elections in order to overcome unspecified "irregularities" in prior elections. Changes included direct registration of candidates with provincial governors rather than with tribal leaders, and an increase in the number of Omanis allowed to vote from 50,000 to 175,000. In addition, those elected would automatically take their seats; in the past, the electorate voted for twice the number of candidates as council seats, and the government chose the council from among those candidates. Voter registration was low, however, with only 115,000 eligible voters registered, and the number of candidates dropped to around 600, about 17 percent fewer than in 1997 polls. Electoral apathy was attributed to concerns over job security—nominees must leave their jobs if elected—tribal loyalty, and the council's lack of authority.

Great Britain played a protective role in Oman between 1798 and 1951, when it formally recognized the sultanate's independence. Sultan Qabus took power in 1970 by overthrowing his father in a palace coup. A five-year rebellion by left-wing guerrillas opposed to the sultan's regime was crushed in 1975 with military assistance from Saudi Arabia, Jordan, Iran, and Pakistan. Since a formal ceasefire in 1976, the sultan, who rules by decree on the advice of a council of ministers, has faced little opposition.

In 1991 Sultan Qabus established a 59-seat Majlis al-Shura, selecting members from lists of nominees proposed by the country's 59 provinces. Membership was expanded to 80 seats in 1994 and to 82 in 1997. The council may comment or make recommendations on proposed government legislation, and particularly economic policy, but it has no legislative power. In December 1997, the sultan appointed 41 members, including four women, to the new *Majlis al-Dawla*, or council of state. This council's functions and responsibilities are unclear. Together, the two bodies comprise the Majlis Oman, or council of Oman.

Oman continues to pursue a policy of economic liberalization designed to attract foreign investment and develop non-oil sectors of the economy. In August, the government announced that it would increase the legal maximum level of foreign ownership in local companies from 49 percent to 70 percent, effective January 1, 2001. There was speculation that this level would be raised to 100 percent in financial sector businesses by 2003. Tax laws have been amended to bring the tax liabilities of businesses with foreign ownership into line with those of locally owned firms. Natural gas, manufacturing, ports, and telecommunications have emerged as fledgling industries, but oil continues to account for 80 percent of export earnings and 40 percent of GDP. In October, Oman formalized its full membership in the World Trade Organization (WTO) as a developing nation. This classification extends the transition time for compliance with WTO rules.

Political Rights and Civil Liberties: Omanis cannot change their government democratically. The sultan has absolute power and rules by decree. The Majlis election in 2000 was somewhat fairer than past elections, although the government still chooses who among Omanis may vote. There are no political parties or other formal democratic institutions. Citizens may petition the government indirectly through their local governors to redress grievances, or may appeal directly to the sultan during his annual three-week tour of the country.

The Basic Law, Oman's first de facto written constitution, was promulgated by Sultan Qabus in 1996. In theory, it provides for an independent judiciary, due process, freedom of the press and of assembly, and prohibitions against discrimination on the basis of sex, ethnicity, race, religion, or social class. In reality, many of the laws and regulations required to implement these provisions have not been enacted.

The judiciary is subordinate to the sultan, who appoints all judges and has the final say on all rulings. Magistrate courts handle misdemeanors and criminal cases, and *Sharia* (Islamic law) courts handle personal status cases involving divorce and inheritance. A state security court handles matters of national security, and criminal cases as deemed necessary by the government. Security court defendants may not have counsel present and proceedings are not made public. The criminal code does not outline due process rights, though defendants are presumed innocent and do in fact enjoy some procedural safeguards. There are no jury trials; a single judge tries misdemeanors; a panel of three judges tries felonies and security offenses. Defendants in national security or serious felony trials may not appeal. Oman introduced the death penalty for drug smuggling and production in 1999.

Police are not required to obtain warrants prior to making arrests and do not always respect legal procedures for pretrial detention. Security forces reportedly abuse detainees, but the practice is not widespread.

Criticism of the sultan is prohibited, although authorities do tolerate criticism of government officials and policies. The 1984 Press and Publication Law provides for censorship of all domestic and imported publications. However, journalists generally censor themselves to avoid harassment. Radio and television are government controlled and offer only official views. Satellite dishes are widely available, giving citizens access to foreign broadcasts including Al-Jazeera, a popular Qatar-based television channel that provides lively political debate and uncensored interviews with regional opposition activists. Uncensored Internet access is available to citizens and foreigners; there were reportedly 50,000 Omanis online as of March 2000.

All public gatherings must be government approved, though this rule is not always strictly enforced. Omanis rarely stage protests, but in October some 200 university students demonstrated in solidarity with Palestinians during clashes between Israeli soldiers and Palestinians in the West Bank and Gaza. The demonstration ended peacefully. All associations must be registered with the government, and independent political groups and human rights organizations do not exist.

Islam is the state religion. Most Omanis are Ibadhi or Sunni Muslim, but there is a Shiite minority as well as small communities of Hindu and Christian citizens. Mosque sermons are monitored by the government for political content. Omani children must attend schools that provide instruction in Islam. Noncitizens, who are mainly immigrant workers from South Asia, are free to worship at churches and temples, some of which are built on land donated by the sultan. Non-Muslims may not proselytize Muslims, and non-Muslim groups may not publish religious material in the country. According to the U.S. State Department, relations between religious communities are amicable and religious discrimination is not a problem.

Despite noticeable gains in education and career opportunities, particularly for younger women, Omani women face discrimination in public and private life. According to the ministry of education, nearly 90 percent of girls eligible for elementary school enroll and roughly half the students at Sultan Qabus University are women. Women make up some 20 percent of civil servants and hold senior management posts in more than half of the top ten trading families in Oman. Women were allowed to vote and to stand in Shura council elections in 1994. However, traditional social pressures keep many women from taking part in public life. Sharia favors men in matters of family-related law such as inheritance, and a woman must have the permission of a male relative to travel abroad. Female genital mutilation is practiced in some rural areas.

There are no trade unions and no provisions for them under law. Employers of more than 50 workers must form a body of labor and management representatives to discuss working conditions. These committees may not negotiate wages. Strikes are illegal and do not occur. Foreign workers constitute at least 50 percent of the workforce and some 80 percent of the modern-sector workforce. Child labor is not widespread.

Pakistan

Polity: Military   **Political Rights:** 6*
Economy: Capitalist-statist **Civil Liberties:** 5
Population: 150,600,000   **Status:** Not Free
PPP: $1,715
Life Expectancy: 64
Ethnic Groups: Punjabi, Sindhi, Pashtun, Baloch
Capital: Islamabad
Ratings Change: Pakistan's political rights rating changed from 7 to 6 after the government held limited local elections in December 2000.

Overview:
Even as it pledged to return Pakistan to civilian rule in 2002 after cleaning up the country's finances and politics, Gen. Pervez Musharraf's military regime undermined the judiciary, cracked down on party activists, and backtracked on some social reforms in the face of pressure from Islamic fundamentalists. The government also carried out moderate economic reforms aimed at increasing state revenues.

Pakistan achieved independence in 1947 as a Muslim homeland with the partition of the former British India. Following a nine-month civil war, East Pakistan achieved independence in 1971 as the new state of Bangladesh. Deposing civilian governments at will, the army has ruled Pakistan for 26 of its 53 years of independence. As part of his efforts to consolidate power, the military dictator General Zia ul-Haq amended the constitution in 1985 to allow the president to dismiss elected governments. After Zia's death in 1988, successive presidents cited corruption and abuse of power in sacking elected governments headed by Benazir Bhutto of the Pakistan People's Party (PPP) in 1990, Nawaz Sharif of the Pakistan Muslim League (PML) in 1993, and Bhutto again in 1996.

With Bhutto having been discredited by corruption scandals during her last term, the PML and its allies won more than 160 seats in the February 1997 elections, although only 35 percent of eligible voters bothered to vote. Over the next 30 months Sharif largely ignored Pakistan's pressing economic and social problems while undermining every institution capable of challenging him. This included repealing the president's constitutional power to dismiss governments, forcing the resignations of the chief justice of the supreme court and of an army chief, and cracking down on the press and nongovernmental organizations (NGOs).

Sharif's downfall began in May and June 1999, when Indian troops bested Pakistani forces in skirmishes in Kashmir after Pakistani-backed Islamic militants seized strategic heights on the Indian side of the Line of Control. The fighting raised international concern because both countries had carried out underground nuclear tests in May 1998. Sharif ended the Kashmir crisis in July by ordering the militants to withdraw, but was blamed by the army for the debacle. On October 12, 1999, the army deposed Sharif in a bloodless coup after the prime minister tried to dismiss Musharraf, then army chief. Musharraf appointed himself "chief executive," declared a state of emergency, and issued the Provisional Constitution Order (PCO) suspending parliament, provincial assemblies, and the constitution, and prohibiting superior courts from making any decision against the chief executive or his subordinates.

Having justified his coup in part as a response to Pakistan's dire economic situation, Musharraf tried in 2000 to increase government revenues, which the World Bank says amount to only 15-16 percent of GDP. Musharraf had authorities begin documenting the black market economy and imposed a 15 percent retail tax in a country where less than one percent of the population pays taxes. The government also secured a standby loan from the International Monetary Fund in November. However, the Fund demanded further tax and other microeconomic liberalization measures in return for a long-term loan. The credibility provided by a long-term arrangement would help Islamabad to reschedule $38 billion in mostly government-held debt or to renew an existing debt moratorium that expired at year's end.

While making some progress on the economy, pressure from Islamic fundamentalist groups forced Musharraf to backtrack on pledges to crack down on public displays of weapons, to curb abuses of the blasphemy laws, and to bring under state control the *madrassahs* (religious schools) run by Islamists. The general also revived Islamic provisions in the now-suspended constitution in July, meaning that courts could potentially declare unconstitutional any secular laws thought to conflict with *Sharia* (Islamic law).

While many of Pakistan's political parties joined a coalition calling for the early restoration of democracy, Musharraf faced little real threat from these mostly secular groups. He also made it difficult for the PML to use Sharif as a rallying point by pardoning and then exiling the former prime minister to Saudi Arabia, for 10 years, in December. Courts had sentenced Sharif during the year to up to 25 years in prison for corruption, terrorism, and hijacking. The latter two charges were for ordering Karachi airport authorities to deny landing rights to a plane carrying Musharraf on the day of the coup.

Political Rights and Civil Liberties:

Pakistan continued to be ruled by a military government, headed by General Pervez Musharraf, that operated with limited transparency or accountability. Most of the government's key decision makers were reportedly officers, both serving and retired, of the hawkish Inter-Services Intelligence agency. While civilians still ran many agencies, the army set up monitoring teams to supervise civilian bureaucrats.

Musharraf pledged to honor a supreme court ruling in May calling for parliamentary elections by October 2002. The May decision also validated the 1999 coup and empowered the government to amend the constitution unilaterally. While he has vowed to foster a new class of ostensibly less corrupt politicians, Musharraf so far has made little use of his extensive powers to reform an electoral system that concentrated political power in perhaps 5,000 landowning families, which have long dominated both main parties and discouraged land and social reforms.

The 1973 constitution provides for a lower national assembly that is directly elected for a five-year term, and an 87-seat senate, whose members are appointed by the four provincial assemblies for six-year terms. The constitution also vests executive power in a prime minister, who must be Muslim, and authorizes an electoral college to choose the largely ceremonial president, who also must be Muslim, for a five-year term.

Pakistan has not formally annexed its Northern Areas—Hunza, Gilgit, and Baltistan—which form part of the disputed territory of Kashmir. Consequently, the roughly one million residents of the Northern Areas are not covered under the constitution and had no representation in the now-suspended federal parliament. Voting laws prevented several million bonded laborers throughout the country from voting because they lacked fixed addresses, and forced Christians and other minorities to vote on separate electoral rolls for at-large candidates. In the Federally Administered Tribal Areas (FATA) of the North-West Frontier Province (NWFP), tribal leaders prevented many women from voting in the 1997 elections.

In what it billed as the first step toward returning the country to democracy, the government held local elections in 18 out of Pakistan's 106 administrative districts on December 31. Capping a year in which it tried to weaken political parties, the government did not allow parties to compete in the local elections. The administration earlier had used laws governing sedition, public order, and terrorism to raid party offices and detain scores of party activists and leaders in Punjab and Sindh for criticizing the army in party meetings or attempting to hold demonstrations, according to an October report by the New York-based Human Rights Watch. Moreover, the regime amended the Political Parties Act in August to bar anyone with a court conviction from holding party office, and introduced a National Accountability Ordinance in 1999 that automatically prohibits persons convicted of corruption under the law from holding public office for 21 years. If applied, these laws could end the political careers of Bhutto and Sharif. Although Sharif may be able to sidestep the laws because he received a pardon, Bhutto remained in self-imposed exile after a court convicted her in absentia in 1999 on corruption charges and sentenced her to a five-year prison term.

The Musharraf regime undermined the supreme court's reputation for independence in January 2000, when it ordered all supreme and high court judges to swear under oath to uphold the state of emergency and the PCO. Authorities removed the chief justice of the supreme court and 14 other judges for refusing to take the oath. Sharif faced two trials in 2000, both of which were marred by procedural irregularities. Like Musharraf, Sharif and Bhutto had also tried while in office to manipulate the judiciary, which consists of civil and criminal courts and a special *Shariat* court for certain offenses under Islamic law. Lower courts remained plagued by corruption; intimidation by local officials, powerful individuals, and Islamic extremists; and heavy backlogs that led to lengthy pretrial detention.

The criminal courts include antiterrorism courts that operate with limited due process rights and that must conclude trials within seven days. The November 1999 National Accountability Ordinance vested broad powers of arrest and prosecution in a new National Accountability Bureau and established special courts to try corruption cases that operate with limited procedural safeguards. In late 1999 and 2000, authorities arrested dozens of politicians and businessmen on charges of corruption and of defaulting on their share of an estimated $2.75 billion in bad bank loans, although officials released some defaulters after they settled their accounts.

The Shariat court enforces the 1979 Hadood Ordinances, which criminalized nonmarital rape, extramarital sex, and several alcohol, gambling, and property offenses. The ordinances provided for both Koranic punishments, including death by stoning for adultery, as well as jail terms and fines. In part because of strict evidentiary standards, authorities have never carried out the Koranic punishments.

The FATA are under a separate legal system, the Frontier Crimes Regulation, which authorizes tribal elders and leaders to administer justice according to Sharia and tribal custom in proceedings that lack due process rights. Feudal landlords and tribal elders in rural Sindh province continued to adjudicate some disputes and impose punishment in unsanctioned courts called *jirgas*.

Anecdotal evidence suggests that police continue to routinely engage in crime; use excessive force in ordinary situations; arbitrarily arrest and detain citizens; extort money from prisoners and their families; accept money to register cases on false charges; rape female detainees and prisoners; commit extrajudicial killings; and torture detainees, often to extract confessions. However, some accounts suggested that in 1999 and 2000, incidences of torture may have declined somewhat from previous years. Prison conditions continued to be extremely poor. Some landlords in rural Sindh province and factions of the Karachi-based Muttahida Quami Movement (MQM) continued to operate private jails.

Violence among rival factions of the MQM, which represents Urdu-speaking migrants from India, and between the police and the MQM, killed several thousand people in Karachi in the 1990s, but appeared to abate somewhat in 2000. Sunni- and Shiite-based fundamentalist groups continued to engage in tit-for-tat killings, mainly in Punjab and Karachi. Shelling between Indian and Pakistani forces around the Line of Control in Kashmir continued to kill or displace numerous civilians.

The constitution and a series of colonial and postcolonial laws authorize the government to curb freedom of speech on subjects including the constitution, the armed forces, the judiciary, and religion. Governments have rarely used these provisions against the mainly private print media. However, under Sharif and Bhutto, authorities frequently detained, threatened, and assaulted journalists; attacked newspaper offices; and interfered with newspaper distribution. The Musharraf regime generally did not harass the press. However, Islamic fundamentalists and thugs hired by feudal landlords continued to harass journalists and occasionally attack newspaper offices. While journalists practiced some self-censorship, Pakistan continued to have some of the most outspoken newspapers in South Asia. Nearly all electronic media are state owned, and coverage favors the government.

After initially permitting some demonstrations, the military government banned in March all public political meetings, strikes, and rallies. Following the ban, authorities forcibly dispersed some protests and arrested activists to prevent other demonstrations. The military regime generally tolerated the work of NGOs. However, NGOs in Punjab province faced restrictions on registration following the provincial government's shutdown of nearly 2000 groups in 1999, according to a report in the Karachi-based *Dawn* newspaper. In recent years, Islamic fundamentalists have issued death threats against prominent human rights defenders.

While Pakistan is a secular country, there are numerous restrictions on religious freedom. Section 295-C of the penal code mandates the death sentence for defiling the name of the prophet Muhammad. Human rights groups say that Muslims occasionally bribe low-ranking police officials to file false blasphemy charges against Ahmadis, Christians, and Hindus. To date, appeals courts have overturned all blasphemy convictions, although suspects are forced to spend lengthy periods in prison and religious extremists have killed some persons accused of blasphemy. According to the United States State Department, authorities have charged nearly 200 Ahmadis under the law since its inception. Ahmadis consider themselves to be Muslims, but the constitution classifies them as a non-Muslim minority and the penal code prohibits Ahmadi religious practice. Ahmadis, Christians, and Hindus also face unofficial economic and societal discrimination and are occasionally subjected to violence and harassment.

A combination of traditional norms and weak law enforcement continued to contribute to rape, domestic violence, and other forms of abuse against women. Women faced difficulty in obtaining justice in rape cases because police and judges are reluctant to charge and punish offenders. Although less frequently than in the past, women are still charged under the Hudood Ordinances with adultery or other sexual misconduct arising from rape cases or alleged extramarital affairs. The threat of being charged with adultery may prevent some women from reporting rape. A parliamentary commission found that courts acquit 95 percent of women charged with adultery under the Hadood Ordinances, although those acquitted still face the stigma of having been accused of adultery and are often subjected to sexual abuse while detained. The nongovernmental Human Rights Commission of Pakistan said in a March report that more than 1,000 women died in Pakistan in 1999 as victims in honor killings. Generally committed by the husbands or brothers of the victims, honor killings punish women who supposedly brought dishonor to the family, often because of alleged adultery. The military government announced in April that honor killings would be treated as murder, although it is unclear to what extent this decision has been implemented. Traditionally, authorities generally have not severely punished these killings, either because they simply fail to enforce the law, or because they can excuse offenders or impose minor sentences under laws reducing punishment for actions supposedly caused by "grave and sudden provocation." In yet another problem, Pakistani women face unofficial discrimination in education and employment opportunities.

In recent years, criminal gangs have reportedly trafficked tens of thousands of Bangladeshi women to Pakistan for purposes of forced prostitution in Karachi or domestic labor, often with the complicity of corrupt local officials. Authorities detain annually some 2,000 trafficking victims on criminal charges under the Hadood Ordinances or for illegal entry. As a result of neighboring Afghanistan's continued civil conflict, Pakistan hosts more than 2 million Afghans in camps and cities throughout the country. However, it closed its borders in November, arguing that it lacks the resources to deal with more arrivals.

Pakistan's underfunded and corruption-plagued primary school system continued to offer limited educational opportunities for children, particularly girls. Despite some initiatives, enforcement of child labor laws continued to be inadequate. Children also continued to be subjected to prostitution, custodial abuse, and trafficking.

Despite 1992 legislation outlawing bonded labor and canceling enslaving debts, illegal bonded labor continued to be widespread. Trade unions are independent. The law restricts the right to strike, and workers in certain "essential" industries face restrictions on bargaining collectively and generally cannot hold strikes. Enforcement of labor laws continued to be limited.

Palau

Polity: Presidential
democracy and
traditional chiefs
Economy: Capitalist
Population: 20,000
PPP: na
Life Expectancy: 67
Ethnic Groups: Polynesian, Malayan, Melanesian
Capital: Koror

Political Rights: 1
Civil Liberties: 2
Status: Free

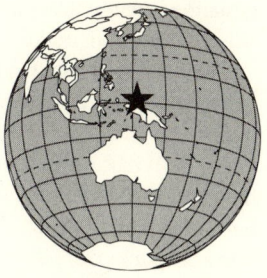

Overview:

Vice President Tommy Esang Remengesau was elected president in a narrow victory over Senator Peter Sugiyama in November. Esang will officially succeed President Kuniwo Nakamura in January 2001. Following the exchange of formal recognition in December 1999, the first Taiwan ambassador arrived in Palau in April 2000. During his visit to Taiwan to attend president-elect Chen Shui-bian's inauguration in May 2000, Nakamura asked for more Taiwanese investment in Palau.

The Republic of Palau is an archipelago of more than 300 islands and islets at the western end of the Caroline Islands in the Pacific Ocean. Purchased by Germany from Spain in 1889, Palau was seized in 1914 by Japan, which administered the islands under a League of Nations mandate from 1920. In 1944, the United States occupied the islands, which became part of the U.S. administered United Nations Trust Territory of the Pacific in 1947.

In 1979, Palau adopted a constitution requiring 75 percent approval at a referendum before nuclear-related activities could occur in its territory. In 1981, Palau became self-governing, though still under U.S. control as part of the Trust Territory. Haruo Remelik became the country's first president, and was reelected in November 1984 to a second four-year term. He was assassinated in 1985, and Alfonso Oiterong took over as acting president. In a special presidential election in August 1985, Oiterong was defeated by Lazarus Salii. In August 1988, President Salii was found dead in his office, an apparent suicide. Ngiratkel Etpison was elected his successor in November that year. Kuniwo Nakamura was elected president in 1992 and won his second four-year term in 1996. In October 1994, Palau gained full independence.

Between 1983 and 1990, Palau had seven plebiscites on the Compact of Free Association with the United States. None managed to cross the three-fourths majority required for approval. Several factors prevented the Compact's early adoption, including disagreements over the amount of U.S. aid commitment, concerns about the requisition of land for U.S. military purposes, and incompatibilities between provisions providing facilities for U.S. nuclear forces and Palau's nuclear-free constitution. In the presidential election in 1992, voters amended the constitution to require a simple majority for the passage of the Compact, which voters approved in 1993 with a 64 percent majority. Under the terms of the Compact, Palau has full sovereignty, but the United States takes responsibility for defense and obtains the right to maintain military facilities. In exchange, Palau is granted U.S. financial assistance over a 15-year period under an economic aid package. Palauans were concerned about the outcome of the negotiation because the country needs financial aid and wants continued access to some U.S. federal services.

Negotiations with the United States on the future of financial assistance under the Compact of Free Association began and will probably conclude in 2001. Palau, along with many other Pacific Island countries, was accused of involvement in money laundering activities by the United States and European countries. A national review committee reported in March that there was no credible evidence of illicit financial activities in the island country. The government said it would consider legal action against four U.S. banks that had put a ban on U.S. dollar trade with Palau, Vanuatu, and Nauru.

Political Rights and Civil Liberties: Citizens of Palau can change their government democratically. The constitution vests executive powers in the president, who is directly elected for a four-year term. The vice president is elected on a separate ticket. The bicameral parliament consists of a senate, whose 14 members are elected on a geographical basis, and a 16-seat house of representatives with one member elected from each of the 16 states. Elections are competitive and tend to revolve around personalities and issues rather than party affiliation. A 16-member Council of Chiefs advises the government on issues involving tribal laws and customs. The chiefs wield considerable traditional authority, and there are often tensions between the chiefs and political leaders.

The government respects freedom of speech and of the press. There are government and private newspapers, but the state-run radio and television broadcast services are the primary source of news and information. Two religious groups maintain independent radio stations. There is also a private cable television system with widespread coverage. Freedom of religion exists in this predominantly Roman Catholic country. Freedom of association is respected. There are currently no active employee organizations, and laws regarding the right to strike or to bargain collectively do not exist. The wage-earning sector is very small.

The judiciary is independent. There is also an independent special prosecutor and an independent public defender system. Local police are under direct civilian control, but foreign residents have reported that law enforcement officials are less thorough in their investigation of crimes against non-Palauan citizens.

Foreign nationals constitute nearly half the labor force and face discrimination in employment and education, as well as random violence. Employers occasionally coerce foreign workers, particularly domestic or unskilled laborers, into remaining at their jobs by withholding their passports. A controversial minimum-wage law, which took effect on January 1, 1999, applies only to Palauan citizens. Opponents of the law said that the new legislation would give foreign workers an advantage in the local labor market.

Inheritance of property and traditional rank is matrilineal, which gives women a high status in society. Nevertheless, domestic violence, often linked to alcohol or drug abuse, remains a problem, and many women are reluctant to report their spouses to law enforcement authorities. Limited opportunities and gender bias have also pushed many women from Palau to seek opportunities for education and a career through enlisting in the U.S. military. The government appointed its first female justice in August 2000; Kathleen M. Salii was named the new associate justice of the Palau supreme court.

Panama

Polity: Presidential-par-
liamentary democracy
Economy: Capitalist-
statist
Population: 2,900,000
PPP: $5,249
Life Expectancy: 74
Ethnic Groups: Mestizo (70 percent), West Indian
(14 percent), European (10 percent), Indian (6 percent)
Capital: Panama City

Political Rights: 1
Civil Liberties: 2
Status: Free

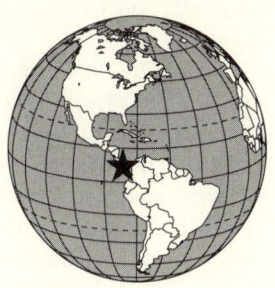

Overview:

The government of President Mireya Moscoso lost its razor-thin majority in congress at the end of her first year in office, after longtime opposition foes—the Revolutionary Democratic Party (PRD) and the Christian Democratic Party—signed a pact they said was designed to provide Panama with a strong congressional opposition. The newly invigorated opposition said that it was willing to cooperate with the government on economic reactivation, but that the government's lackluster performance proved the need to head off the emergence of leaders such as former Peruvian president Alberto Fujimori or Venezuela's Hugo Chavez by offering a viable alternative. In October 2000, the legislature strengthened laws against money laundering. In the year following the U.S. handover, the Panama Canal continued to operate smoothly, although the departure of the remaining U.S. troops and the closure of military bases has meant the loss to Panama of some $250 million in revenues.

Panama was part of Colombia until 1903, when a U.S.-supported revolt resulted in the proclamation of an independent Republic of Panama. A period of weak civilian rule ended with a 1968 military coup that brought General Omar Torrijos to power.

After the signing of the 1977 canal treaties with the United States, Torrijos promised democratization. The 1972 constitution was revised to provide for the direct election of a president and a legislative assembly for five year terms. After Torrijos's death in 1981, General Manuel Noriega emerged as Panamanian Defense Force (PDF) chief and rigged the 1984 election that brought to power the PRD, then the political arm of the PDF.

The Democratic Alliance of Civic Opposition (ADOC) won the 1989 election, but Noriega annulled the vote and declared himself head of state. He was removed during a U.S. military invasion, and ADOC's Guillermo Endara became president.

In 1994, the PRD capitalized on the Endara government's record of ineptness, and Ernesto Pérez Balladares, a 47-year-old millionaire and former banker, won the presidency with 33.3 percent of the vote. The PRD won 32 of 71 seats in the legislative assembly and, with the support of allied parties that won 6 seats, achieved an effective majority.

Pérez Balladares kept a campaign promise by choosing for his cabinet technocrats and politicians from across the ideological spectrum. But his orthodox free market economic policies led to widespread protests in 1995 by labor unions and students. The president's popularity declined when the government met protests with harsh crackdowns.

During the 1994 campaign, Pérez Balladares pledged to rid the country of drug influence. However, the PRD was accused of involvement in drug trafficking in the aftermath of the collapse of the Agro-Industrial and Commercial Bank of Panama (BANAICO) in January 1996. An investigation by the Banking Commission found accounts empty and $50 million unaccounted for, as well as evidence that the bank was a central money-laundering facility. BANAICO was named in several U.S. drug investigations, including one of José Castrillon Henao, a Colombian who was arrested in April 1996 as the reputed organizer of the Cali cartel's seagoing cocaine shipments to the United States. Alfredo Alemán, a board member of BANAICO, was a friend and top advisor to Pérez Balladares and was a major contributor to the party's 1994 campaign. Pérez Balladares himself was forced to admit that his campaign unknowingly accepted a contribution from Castrillon Henao, who was in May 1998 extradited to Florida to stand trial for money laundering. The Pérez Balladares administration further damaged its popularity when it restored government jobs and awarded a reported $35 million in back pay to former members of the Dignity Battalions, who had been Noriega's paramilitary enforcers.

In 1997, the son of a prominent PRD politician and two other Panamanians were found innocent of killing an unarmed U.S. soldier in 1992 in a trial plagued by political pressure and other irregularities. In August 1998, voters rejected by an almost two-to-one margin a referendum on a proposed constitutional amendment that would have enabled Pérez Balladares, whose government was mired in censorship, corruption, and an increasingly tenuous claim to fidelity to the rule of law, to stand for reelection.

In May 1999, Moscoso, the widow of three-time president Arnulfo Arias and herself an unsuccessful presidential candidate in 1994, won 44.8 percent of the votes, more than 7 percent above the amount garnered by her rival, Martín Torrijos, as the head of a PRD-led coalition. Moscoso's coalition, the Union for Panama, won just 24 congressional seats as compared to the PRD's 38. However, she was able to forge a deal with a group of small parties to give her coalition a working majority. The Moscoso government moved quickly to overturn an attempt by Pérez Balladares to pack the judiciary before he left office. It also sought to increase antinarcotics efforts with the United States, a joint partnership which had faltered under Pérez Balladares.

In 2000, repeated incursions into Panamanian territory by Colombian guerrillas continued to spark concerns in the region about the spillover effects of Colombia's civil war. Since being invaded by the United States in 1989, Panama has had no military. It relies on the police to provide both internal security and defense of its borders. The dozens of confrontations between armed Colombian groups and the Panamanian police, who suffered several injuries as a result of the fighting, have raised questions about whether the latter are up to the challenge provided by the seasoned Colombians. Three months after Panama was placed on a Group of 7 blacklist of "non-cooperative" banking havens, the congress approved a 21-point legislative amendment designed to combat hot-money transactions. At the end of 2000, Moscoso announced that she planned to create a truth commission to investigate the whereabouts of dozens of political dissidents who disappeared during the more than two decades of military rule.

Political Rights and Civil Liberties: Panama's citizens can change their government democratically. The 1999 national elections were considered free and fair by international observers. The constitution guarantees freedom of political and civic organization. In early 1999, Panama's largest political parties agreed to ban anonymous campaign contributions in an effort to stem the infiltration of drug money into the political process. Following the May 1999 elections, 5 of the 12 political parties that had taken part were dissolved after they failed to win the five percent minimum required by the electoral law.

The judicial system, headed by a supreme court, was revamped in 1990. It remains overworked, however, and its administration is inefficient, politicized, and prone to corruption. An unwieldy criminal code and a surge in cases, many against former soldiers and officials of the military period, complicate the judicial process. In February 1998 the supreme court declared unconstitutional the provisions that authorize the ombudsman's office to investigate the administration of justice, claiming that the watchdog agency's role violates the principle of judicial independence. In the final days of Pérez Balladares's presidency, a new three-person section of the supreme court was created. Pérez Balladares said the new branch was needed to speed up the judicial process; opponents accused him of trying to pack the court so as to shield himself from corruption investigations.

The PDF was dismantled after 1989, and the military was formally abolished in 1994. But the civilian-run Public Force (national police) that replaced the PDF is poorly disciplined and corrupt. Like the country's prison guards, officers frequently use "excessive force." It has been ineffectual against the drug trade, as Panama remains a major transshipment point for both cocaine and illicit arms—drug seizures rose 70 percent in 2000—as well as a money-laundering hub. Panama's banking sector is composed of 87 banks with a total of $37 billion in assets. The legislation approved in October 2000 extended money-laundering laws already on the books to cover revenues gained from arms trafficking, extortion, kidnapping, corruption, and auto theft. Prison sentences for money-laundering were increased to a maximum of 12 years. The legislation also tightened know-your-client requirements and placed stricter reporting requirements on deposits of more than $10,000 in banking and financial institutions.

The penal system is marked by violent disturbances in decrepit facilities packed with up to eight times their intended capacity. About two-thirds of prisoners face delays of about 18 months in having their cases heard. Panama also continues to be a major transshipment point for illegal aliens seeking to enter the United States, including large numbers from Ecuador.

Panama's media are a raucous assortment of radio and television stations, daily newspapers, and weekly publications. Restrictive media laws dating back to the Noriega regime remain on the books, however. The law permits officials to jail without trial anyone who defames the government. Legal codes establish government control of work permits for journalists, strict defamation and libel rules, and a clause that permits reporters to be punished for "damaging the nation's economy" or for national security reasons.

Labor unions are well organized. However, labor rights were diluted in 1995 when Pérez Balladares pushed labor code revisions through congress. When 49 unions initiated peaceful protests, the government cracked down in a series of violent clashes that resulted in four deaths and hundreds of arrests.

Since 1993, indigenous groups have protested the encroachment of illegal settlers on Indian lands and delays by the government in formally demarcating the boundaries of those lands. Indian communities do enjoy, however, a large degree of autonomy and self-government.

Papua New Guinea

Polity: Parliamentary democracy
Economy: Capitalist
Population: 4,800,000
PPP: $2,359
Life Expectancy: 58
Ethnic Groups: Papuan, Melanesian, Negrito, Micronesian, Polynesian
Capital: Port Moresby

Political Rights: 2
Civil Liberties: 3
Status: Free

Overview:

In the year marking the 25th anniversary of Papua New Guinea's independence, the government of this resource-rich country worked to end a longstanding separatist conflict and to revive an economy whose potential has been squandered by years of corruption and mismanagement.

This South Pacific country, consisting of the eastern part of New Guinea and some 600 smaller islands, achieved independence from Australia in 1975. While Papua New Guinea faces a host of challenges, including widespread poverty and rampant official corruption, its most destabilizing problem began in late 1988, when miners and landowners on Bougainville Island began guerrilla attacks against the Australian-owned Panguna copper mine which had provided 40 percent of the country's export revenue. The rebels demanded compensation and profit sharing. Situated 560 miles northeast of the capital, Bougainville is the largest island of the Solomons group, and its residents have cultural and linguistic ties to the population of the neighboring Solomon Islands. The rebels soon forced the mine to close, and in 1990 transformed their longstanding grievances into a low-grade secessionist struggle under the newly formed Bougainville Revolutionary Army (BRA).

Taking advantage of a ceasefire, Prime Minister Julius Chan swore in a Bougainville Transitional Government (BTG) on the island in 1995. In 1996, the ceasefire broke down and gunmen assassinated Theodore Miriung, the head of the BTG.

Having failed to achieve a peaceful solution to the conflict, Chan was ultimately forced to resign in March 1997 following a public outcry over a controversial $27 million contract with London-based Sandline International to provide mercenaries to aid the army on Bougainville. An anti-incumbent mood dominated the June 1997 elections, when voters swept Chan and 54 other members of parliament out of office. During the campaign, many citizens had complained that official corruption and rising crime were keeping the country impoverished despite its considerable mineral wealth. Bill Skate, a former opposition leader, formed a coalition government in July.

Like its predecessors, Skate's government faced widespread allegations of corruption, bribery, mismanagement, and nepotism. Facing a no-confidence vote, Skate resigned in July 1999. Parliament replaced him with Sir Mekere Morauta, the head of the People's Democratic Movement Party and a former governor of the reserve bank. Morauta formed a multiparty government and pledged to stabilize the *kina* and restore relations, which had collapsed in 1998, with the International Monetary Fund and the World Bank.

Following months of negotiations, the government and the leaders in Bougainville signed an accord on March 24, 2000 calling for elections for an autonomous government on the island, and for a vote on independence if the autonomy plan fails. The deal was facilitated by an improved security situation on Bouganiville following a ceasefire there brokered by Australia and New Zealand in 1998. While the latest accord set no timetable for the elections or a potential referendum, it marked a reversal from the government's earlier refusal to consider independence. On March 30, the governor-general swore in an appointed interim government in Bougainville pending local elections. However, the government and several rival Bougainville factions still faced outstanding issues including disarmament and the actual details of any autonomy plan.

During the year, the Morauta government continued to enact economic liberalization measures. In a move that angered state workers, the government said in February that it would privatize the airline and other major state-owned enterprises. Impressed with the reforms, bilateral and multilateral donors agreed in June to provide $300 million in loans and balance-of-payments support.

Political Rights and Civil Liberties: Citizens of Papua New Guinea can change their government through elections. The 1975 constitution vests executive power in a prime minister and a cabinet. Parliament has 89 at-large members and 20 members representing the 19 provinces and Port Moresby, all elected for five-year terms. A governor-general serves as head of state and represents the British monarchy.

Elections are generally marred by some irregularities and sporadic violence. Since independence, the parliamentary system has been characterized by unstable, shifting coalitions, and no prime minister has served a full term. Although most seats are chosen in single-member, simple plurality districts, Papua New Guinea has been an exception to the trend toward a two-party system that such electoral districts tend to produce elsewhere. In the 1997 elections, 13 parties won seats.

Since independence, politicians have faced the challenge of nation building in a country where roughly 700 tribes speak some 1,000 languages, and where extreme socioeconomic disparities exist between the cities and isolated highlands. Some 85 percent of the population lives in remote villages and engages in subsistence and small-scale agriculture.

While the judiciary is independent, the rule of law is weak. Police reportedly continued to occasionally use excessive force during arrests and to abuse detainees and prisoners. In the highlands, in recent years police have occasionally burned homes to punish communities suspected of harboring criminals or of participating in tribal warfare, or to punish crimes committed by individuals. Because of resource constraints on the police and judiciary, suspects frequently spend lengthy periods in detention.

The abuses by the police occur amid a crime problem that is among the most severe in the world, according to a 1998 Australian National University survey. While gang members known as "rascals" have long been responsible for a law-and-order crisis in urban areas, evidence suggested that crime is also becoming a serious problem in the rural areas. In May, the Chamber of Mines and Petroleum and the Australian high commissioner cited concerns about the deteriorating law-and-order situation in the Southern Highlands Province. The government's main response has been the 1993 Internal Security Act, which gave police expanded powers to conduct searches without warrants.

The army, army-backed paramilitary groups, and the BRA committed torture, disappearances, arbitrary detentions, and extrajudicial executions against civilians and combatants during the Bougainville conflict. By some estimates, during the war at least 20,000 combatants and civilians died, mostly as the result of malnutrition and disease.

The private press continued to report vigorously on allegations of official corruption and police abuse and other sensitive matters. Radio is both public and private and offers diverse views. The television service is privately owned. Citing public safety grounds, police frequently deny permits to hold demonstrations.

While some women have achieved prominence in business and the professions, women continued to be underrepresented in government and politics and faced significant, unofficial discrimination in education and employment opportunities. Rape and domestic violence continued to be serious problems. In rural areas, women are occasionally given as compensation to settle disputes between clans, although courts have ruled this practice illegal.

Reversing a long-standing policy, the government closed its border in December to refugees fleeing a decades-old separatist conflict in the neighboring Indonesian province of West Papua. Morauta said the government shut the border to signal respect for Indonesian sovereignty over the province, but that Papua New Guinea might provide refugee status to any West Papuans who managed to cross the border.

Though they have limited resources, nongovernmental organizations are active and outspoken. Unions are independent, and workers can and do bargain collectively and stage strikes. The International Labor Organization has criticized a law allowing the government to invalidate arbitration agreements or wage awards not considered to be in the national interest. A leader of the Teachers' Association alleged in March that many children under the age of 12 are employed as laborers on tea and coffee plantations in the highlands, although this could not be confirmed independently.

↑ Paraguay

Polity: Presidential-
parliamentary democracy
Economy: Capitalist-
statist
Population: 5,500,000
PPP: $4,288
Life Expectancy: 70

Political Rights: 4
Civil Liberties: 3
Status: Partly Free

Ethnic Groups: Mestizo (95 percent), Indian and European (5 percent)
Capital: Asuncion
Trend Arrow: Paraguay received an upward trend arrow due to a free and fair special election which resulted in the selection of a new vice-preisdent.

Overview:

Liberal party leader Julio Cesar Franco won the Paraguayan vice presidency in August 2000 in a special election designed to fill a post left vacant by a March 23,1999, hit-squad-style assassination that triggered the overthrow of the country's president. Franco's victory at the head of an opposition coalition was a blow to President Luis González Macchi, the former head of the senate, whose shaky grasp on power was already buffeted by internal divisions, labor unrest, and restlessness from within the ranks of the military anf the police. González Macchi assumed the presidency on March 28, 1999, after the forced resignation of Raul Cubas, who as chief executive was a stand-in for General Lino Oviedo—a former head of the army who led a 1996 coup attempt. Oviedo, who was detained in Brazil in 2000, was accused of masterminding the killing of his long-time rival, Vice President Luis María Argaña. The dead man's son, Felix Argaña, was the losing candidate in the race to replace his father in the 2000 election, a victim of González Macchi's inability to create a government of national unity and the first member of the Colorado Party to lose a presidential election in 60 years of uninter-rupted party rule.

In 1989 a coup ended the 35-year dictatorship of General Alfredo Stroessner. Oviedo himself stormed into the bunker of Latin America's oldest surviving dictator with a pistol in one hand and a grenade in the other and demanded that Stroessner surrender. General Andrés Rodriguez took over Stroessner's Colorado Party and engineered his own election to finish Stroessner's last presidential term. The Colorado Party won a majority in a vote for a constituent assembly, which produced the 1992 constitution. It provides for a president, a vice president, and a bicameral congress consisting of a 45-member senate and an 80-member chamber of deputies elected for five years. The president is elected by a simple majority, and reelection is prohibited. The constitution bans the active military from engaging in politics.

In the 1992 Colorado Party primary election, Luis María Argaña, an old-style machine-politician, apparently defeated the construction tycoon Juan Carlos Wasmosy. Rodriguez and Oviedo engineered a highly dubious recount that made Wasmosy the winner.

The 1993 candidates were Wasmosy, Domingo Laino of the center-left Authentic Radical Liberal Party (PLRA), and Guillermo Caballero Vargas, a wealthy business-man who founded the National Encounter Alliance. Wasmosy promised to modernize the economy. Laino played on his decades of resistance to Stroessner. Caballero Vargas campaigned as a centrist, free of the politics of the past.

Every poll showed Wasmosy trailing, until three weeks before the election, when Oviedo personally took over the direction of the campaign—in spite of the fact that he was an active military officer—and threatened a coup if the Colorado Party lost. Fear of a coup proved decisive, as Wasmosy won with 40.3 percent of the vote. Laino took 32 percent, and Caballero Vargas, 23.5.

Oviedo was then appointed army commander, and Wasmosy allowed him to eliminate rivals in the military through forced retirement. The partnership came to a bitter end when Wasmosy moved to reduce the influence of the drug-tainted military in government and it became increasingly obvious that Oviedo and a hardline Colorado Party faction planned to use Wasmosy as a stepping-stone for the general's own accession to the presidency. Wasmosy ordered Oviedo's resignation on April 22, 1996. The general in turn threatened a coup and mobilized the troops. Wasmosy took refuge in the U.S. embassy and prepared his resignation. International pressure and mass protests in Paraguay allowed Wasmosy to outmaneuver his rival, who then vowed to return as a presidential candidate in 1998.

Wasmosy's government was shaken by a number of corruption scandals. These included money laundering in the banking system by financial racketeers from neighboring countries and by drug traffickers, as well as two bank collapses provoked by the theft of assets by bank managers. In 1997, Oviedo won the Colorado Party presidential nomination by besting Argaña by 10,000 votes. Argaña's supporters claimed fraud, despite the fact that they controlled the party electoral tribunal, and demanded that 50,000 of the votes cast be reviewed.

Cubas, a civil engineer and originally Oviedo's vice presidential choice, was elected in May 1998, after Oviedo was jailed in March by a military tribunal for his 1996 attempted putsch and banned from standing for election. Despite the deep divisions within the Colorado Party, Cubas not only bested Laino 54 to 42 percent, but also led the party to majority status in both chambers of congress for the first time since 1989. One of Cubas's first acts was to free Oviedo, in a maneuver widely described as a "constitutional coup."

In early March 1999, an armed forces spokesman warned that the military would be obliged to defend Cubas if congress tried to remove him for failing to carry out a judicial order to send Oviedo back to jail. The murder of Argaña, a bitter Oviedo foe, and the killing of eight student protestors by rooftop snipers, ended the fiction of a truce in the long-ruling Colorado Party. After Cubas's impeachment by congress, González Macchi appointed a "national unity" government including members of the two main opposition parties—the PLRA and the National Encounter Party. More than 100 army officers, including several generals, believed to be Oviedo supporters were forced into retirement. Oviedo—who had received asylum from his long-time friend, Argentine president Carlos Menem, and who sought to surgically alter his appearance—fled to Brazil following the December 1999 change of government in Buenos Aires. In June he was jailed and awaiting possible extradition to Paraguay.

In May 2000, several dozen military and police officers were arrested following an unsuccessful effort by pro-Oviedo factions to oust González Macchi. In August Oviedo ordered his supporters, from his jail cell, to vote for Franco for vice president. At the same time two Brazilian congressmen sought to have him put on trial for drug- and money-laundering offenses. In October, a general who once headed the national antidrug effort was sentenced to seven years in prison for defrauding the government of several million dollars. Two men accused of assassinating Argaña were allowed to escape from the Argentine Federal Police headquarters in Buenos Aires, presumably with the help of high-ranking law enforcement officers there.

Political Rights and Civil Liberties:

The 1992 constitution provides for regular elections. The 2000 elections, although they were raucous, were considered free and fair by local standards. More than 80 percent of eligible voters participated in the 1998 elections. Although the presidential campaign was marred by the political proscriptions of Oviedo and threats against the national electoral tribunal, voter fraud was held to a minimum by the work of the tribunal, coverage by the media, and willingness of the military to stand firm in favor of the process.

The constitution guarantees free political and civic organization and religious expression. However, political rights and civil liberties are undermined by the government's tolerance of threats of intimidation and use of force, including imprisonment, by its supporters against those Oviedo followers who remain in the country. In the tense days following the August 2000 vice presidential balloting, the press was the target of intimidation, including physical attacks, by supporters of both candidates.

The judiciary, under the influence of the ruling party and the military, is susceptible to the corruption pervading all public and governmental institutions. Corruption cases languish for years in the courts, and most end up without resolution. The courts are generally unresponsive to human rights groups that present cases of rights violations committed either before or after the overthrow of Stroessner. Allegations include illegal detentions by police and torture during incarcerations, particularly in rural areas. Colombian drug traffickers continue to expand operations in Paraguay, and accusations of high official involvement in drug trafficking date back to the 1980s. In 1997, the commander of the national police was dismissed following a newspaper exposé about his force's involvement in car theft, corruption, and bribery. In November 1999, the congress began impeachment proceedings against Paraguay's top anticorruption official, who is accused of bribery and extortion. Transparency International ranks Paraguay 92 out of 99 nations rated for public corruption.

Overcrowding, unsanitary living conditions, and mistreatment are serious problems in Paraguayan prisons. More than 95 percent of the prisoners held are pending trial, many for months or years after arrest. The constitution permits detention without trial until the accused completes the minimum sentence for the alleged crime.

In Paraguay, there is only one state-owned medium, the Radio Nacional, which has a limited listenership. A number of private television and radio stations exist, as do a number of independent newspapers. However, journalists investigating corruption or covering strikes and protests are often the victims of intimidation and violent attacks by security forces. Free expression is also threatened by vague, potentially restrictive laws that mandate "responsible" behavior by journalists and media owners.

Peasant and Indian organizations demanding and illegally occupying land often meet with police crackdowns, death threats, detentions, and forced evictions by vigilante groups in the employ of landowners. Peasants have been killed in the ongoing disputes. Activist priests who support land reform are frequent targets of intimidation. The government's promise of land reform remains largely unfilled, as nearly 90 percent of agricultural land remains in the hands of foreign companies and a few hundred Paraguayan families. A program financed by the European Union to restore traditional lands to Native Americans in the eastern Chaco region has been riddled with fraud. According to official statistics, 39 percent of Paraguayans speak only Guarani, 49 percent are bilingual, and 12 percent speak only Spanish.

There are numerous trade unions and two major union federations. The 1992 constitution gives public sector workers the rights to organize, bargain collectively, and strike, and nearly all these workers belong to the ruling Colorado Party. A new labor code designed to protect worker rights was passed in October 1993.

Peru

Polity: Presidential (transitional)
Economy: Capitalist-statist
Population: 27,100,000
PPP: $4,282
Life Expectancy: 69
Ethnic Groups: Indian (45 percent), mestizo (37 percent), European (15 percent), other (3 percent)
Capital: Lima

Political Rights: 3*
Civil Liberties: 3*
Status: Partly Free

Ratings Change: Peru's political rights rating changed from 5 to 3 and its civil liberties rating changed from 4 to 3 due to the largely peaceful overthrow of autocratic president Alberto Fujimori and the installation of an opposition government committed to free and fair elections in 2001, as well as improvements in human rights and press freedom.

Overview:

In late November 2000, President Alberto Fujimori was removed from office; opposition forces assumed control of congress; and a highly respected opposition leader, Valentin Paniagua, was chosen as interim president of Peru. The beginning of the end for the autocratic Fujimori came during the May national elections; the major opposition candidate withdrew from competition rather than participate in a contest that international observers believed was neither free nor fair. Ironically, the final blow for a government that constantly wiretapped and videotaped its opponents came when a tape of Vladimiro Montesinos, Fujimori's political fixer and drug mafia mouthpiece known as the "Rasputin of the Andes," bribing an opposition congressman was released to the press. New elections were called for April 8, 2001, and a number of high-ranking military officers known for their loyalty to Fujimori and Montesinos were purged; the remaining general staff pledged its loyalty to the constitution and the civilian government. In early December 2000, Fujimori claimed that Montesinos was still wielding power from behind the scenes by blackmailing congressmen to force them to do his bidding after having videotaped them taking bribes.

Since independence in 1821, Peru has seen alternating periods of civilian and military rule. Civilian rule was restored in 1980 after 12 years of dictatorship. That same year, the Maoist Shining Path terrorist group launched a guerrilla war that killed 30,000 people over the next 13 years.

Fujimori, a university rector and engineer, defeated the novelist Mario Vargas Llosa in the 1990 election. In 1992 Fujimori, backed by the military, suspended the constitution and dissolved congress. The move was popular because of people's disdain for Peru's corrupt, elitist political establishment, and fear of the Shining Path.

Fujimori held a state-controlled election for an 80-member constituent assembly to replace the congress. The assembly drafted a constitution that established a unicameral congress more closely under presidential control. The constitution was approved in a state-controlled referendum following the capture of the Shining Path leader, Abimael Guzmán.

Fujimori's principal opponent in the 1995 election was former United Nations secretary-general Javier Perez de Cuellar, who vowed to end Fujimori's "dictatorship." Fujimori crushed his opponent with a massive public spending and propaganda campaign that utilized state resources. The National Intelligence Service, under de facto head Vladimiro Montesinos, a Fujimori ally and one-time legal counsel to drug kingpins, was employed to spy on and discredit Perez de Cuellar and other opposition candidates. On April 9, 1995, Fujimori won an easy victory, besting Perez de Cuellar by about three to one, while Fujimori's loose coalition of allies won a majority in the new 120-seat congress.

In August 1996 congress passed a law allowing Fujimori to run for a third term, despite a constitutional provision limiting the president to two terms. The law evaded this restriction by defining Fujimori's current term as his first under the 1993 constitution.

On April 22, 1997, the seizure of the Japanese ambassador's residence came to a violent end when a commando raid liberated all but one of the 72 hostages and killed all 14 of the insurgents. That May, the president of the seven-person Tribunal of Constitutional Guarantees—the body that assesses the constitutional legality of national legislation—resigned with the words "the rule of law has broken down in Peru." His action came after congress dismissed three other tribunal members who had ruled, at the end of 1996, that legislation designed to enable Fujimori to stand for reelection in the year 2000 was not applicable. In March 1998 the National Magistrates Council resigned en masse four months after Fujimori's congress altered the National Elections Commission so as to give the president increased influence. In late 1999, the U.S. Congress passed a resolution criticizing Fujimori for interfering with the judiciary, harassing the press, and manipulating Peruvian institutions in order to stay in power.

In the April 9, 2000, presidential elections. Fujimori beat Alejandro Toledo, a U.S.-educated economist who grew up in an Indian shantytown, by 49.9 percent to 40.2 percent. Fujimori, however, came in 20,000 votes short of an outright win, and a runoff election was slated for May 28. Toledo refused to participate in the second round, pointing out that, in addition to election-day voting irregularities, he had been routinely assaulted by Fujimori supporters in the earlier campaign, had suffered constant death threats and phone taps, was virtually blacked out from media coverage, and was the target of smear attacks in the press.

In late July, Fujimori sought to refurbish his democratic credentials by naming a former opposition presidential candidate as prime minister. U.S. efforts to take a strong line with Fujimori in support of reforms, however, were sandbagged in the Organization of American States (OAS), which had earlier refused to certify the elections as free and fair. However, U.S. pressure also flagged when the Clinton administration decided that isolating Fujimori internationally could cripple the regional war on drugs. In early September a videotape was released that showed Montesinos bribing an opposition congressman, at the same time that the spy chief was also being linked to an illegal shipment of arms to Colombian guerrillas. Coming after one of the most widely questioned elections the region had seen in decades, the ensuing scandal raised suspicions that Fujimori had secured a parliamentary majority—after having failed to win one outright in the April 9 general elections—by bribing opposition congressmen to change sides. On September 16th a weakened Fujimori agreed to call new elections for 2001 in which he would not run. During October, Montesinos and Fujimori engaged in a running battle to see who would control the military; when Montesinos lost, he hurriedly went into exile, only to return several weeks later and go into hiding, pursued unsuccessfully by a military manhunt led personally by his former boss.

Following Fujimori's overthrow, the new opposition-controlled congress began a process of renewal of the constitutional tribunal and reform of the constitution, so as to eliminate consecutive reelection and to forestall the rise of another Fujimori. The notorious National Intelligence Service, the key to Montesinos's sinister reach, was abolished. The attorney general, a Fujimori loyalist who had blocked investigations into corruption and abuses of power by high-government officials, was fired and replaced by a respected independent. An agreement was also reached to restart a judicial reform program aborted by Fujimori in 1999. At the end of 2000, Fujimori announced he was availing himself of his dual citizenship to remain in Japan. The government said it was opening a probe into allegations that Montesinos—a one-time Central Intelligence Agency asset who went into hiding after Fujimori was overthrown—had laundered more than $50 million through Swiss banks. In addition, the official in charge of organizing the 2001 general election raised the possibility that April 8 might be too soon to organize the voting.

Political Rights and Civil Liberties: Following Fujimori's overthrow, the new authorities began to prepare the conditions under which there would be sufficient time for opposition forces to organize themselves and for candidates to declare themselves. At the end of 2000, congress was reforming the constitution, replacing a single nationwide district for congressional elections with a system of multiple districts based on the departments (provinces) into which the country is divided for administrative purposes. The move is designed to provide fair representation for the almost 50 percent of the people who live outside of the four largest cities, and to guarantee them some attention from the state and from political parties, which traditionally have ignored them.

Under the December 1993 constitution, the president could rule virtually by decree; Fujimori was given the power to dissolve congress in the event of a "grave conflict" between the executive and legislature, as he did in 1992. The 1993 constitution also overturned Peru's tradition of no reelection.

On the eve of Fujimori's removal from office, reforms designed to guarantee judicial independence were re-initiated by the former opposition. These include abolishing executive personnel commissions, relocating the Council of the Magistracy as a politically autonomous entity, and regularizing the job tenure of the 70-odd percent of the judiciary with "provisional" status, a condition that allows them to be removed by executive fiat.

Public safety, particularly in Lima, is threatened by vicious warfare by opposing gangs—some of which use body armor and high-powered weapons—and violent crime. Police estimate that there are more than 1,000 criminal gangs in the capital alone. Torture was routine in police detention centers through most of 2000, and conditions remain deplorable in prisons for common criminals. On a positive note, in 2000 the national ombudsman released a report documenting the "disappearances" of more than 4,000 peasants during the 1980-1995 period of internal war against Shining Path terrorism. In addition to being the first official admission of such abuses, the report called for repeal of a blanket amnesty granted in 1995 for rights abuses committed by the security forces. Also, a number of defendants convicted of associations with terrorist movements by secret military courts were granted new trials in civilian courts, and their cases are being reinvestigated.

The press is largely privately owned. Radio and television are both privately and publicly owned. Since 1992, Peru has had one of the worst records of press freedom in the world. Many in the media, especially television and print journalists, were pressured into self-censorship or exile by a broad Fujimori government campaign of intimidation—abductions, death threats, libel suits, withholding of advertising, police harassment, arbitrary detention, physical mistreatment, and imprisonment on charges of "apology for terrorism." In September 1997, a government-controlled court stripped Baruch Ivcher, an Israeli émigré and the owner of the Channel 2 television station, of control of his media business and his Peruvian citizenship after the station aired reports linking the military to torture and corruption, as well as an exposé of a telephone espionage ring run by intelligence agents to spy on opposition politicians and journalists. By 2000, most newspapers and radio and television channels were controlled directly or indirectly by Montesinos. In August 2000 Ivcher had his citizenship restored, a move that allowed him to win the court battle over ownership of the station.

Racism against Peru's large Indian population is prevalent among the middle and upper classes, although the Fujimori government made some effort to combat it. On a positive note, Toledo, a peasant's son turned World Bank economist, embraced his indigenous heritage on the campaign trail, calling himself the "Rebel Indian." The provisions of the 1993 constitution and subsequent implementing legislation regarding the treatment of native lands are less explicit about the inalienability and unmarketability of these lands than were earlier constitutional and statutory protections.

In 1996 the International Labor Organization criticized the labor code for failing to protect workers from anti-union discrimination and for restricting collective bargaining rights. Forced labor, including child labor, is prevalent in the gold-mining region of the Amazon.

⬇ Philippines

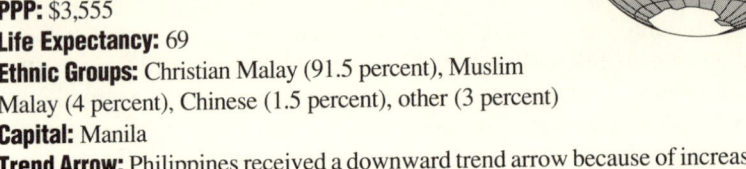

Polity: Presidential-parliamentary democracy (insurgencies)
Economy: Capitalist-statist
Population: 80,300,000
PPP: $3,555
Life Expectancy: 69
Ethnic Groups: Christian Malay (91.5 percent), Muslim Malay (4 percent), Chinese (1.5 percent), other (3 percent)
Capital: Manila

Political Rights: 2
Civil Liberties: 3
Status: Free

Trend Arrow: Philippines received a downward trend arrow because of increasing civil conflict in the southern Mindanao region and credible allegations of high-level official corruption.

Overview:

Following months of widespread allegations of cronyism and incompetence against President Joseph Estrada, at year's end the senate was conducting an impeachment trial over charges that Estrada received $11 million in kickbacks from tobacco taxes and illegal gambling rackets. Having publicly rebuked Estrada, Vice President Gloria Macapagal Arroyo was preparing to take power should the senate muster the two-thirds majority needed to convict the president.

The Philippines won independence in 1946 after 43 years under United States rule and occupation by the Japanese during World War II. The country slid into dictatorship in 1972, when the elected president, Ferdinand Marcos, declared martial law to circumvent a constitutional two-term limit. In February 1986, street protests and the defection of key military leaders and units, following a rigged election, ended Marcos's rule. His opponent in the election, Corazon Aquino, took office.

Aquino consolidated some democratic gains, but faced at least six coup attempts by reactionary army factions and other opponents. Under her successor, former army chief of staff Fidel Ramos, the government ended power shortages and weakened somewhat the considerable political and economic influence of large, family-owned monopolies. Ramos's economic liberalization policies helped increase the rate of gross domestic product (GDP) growth but widened income disparities.

With the popular Ramos ineligible to run for a second term, Vice President Joseph Estrada took 46.4 percent of the vote, defeating seven other candidates to win the May 11, 1998 presidential elections. While Estrada had campaigned on a pro-poor platform, his opponents denounced him as a hard-drinking philanderer with close ties to Marcos-era tycoons. Gloria Macapagal Arroyo, a senator and economist, won the separate vice presidential balloting. In concurrent house elections, Estrada's Struggle for a Democratic Philippines party won 110 seats and the LAKAS-National Union of Christian Democrats came in second with 50.

The new administration established several antipoverty programs targeted toward Estrada's lower-class constituency. However, by mid-1999, Estrada's approval ratings had dropped sharply amid a short-lived, controversial proposal to amend the constitution to further open the economy to foreign investment, criticism of the president's close ties with tycoons, whose business interests allegedly received preferential treatment from the administration, and allegations that Estrada set policy during late-night drinking sessions.

Although corruption allegations had dogged his administration ever since it took office, the first charge of actual criminal wrongdoing against Estrada himself came in October 2000, when a provincial governor alleged that the president had received tax and gambling kickbacks. The case went to the senate after the house of representatives impeached Estrada on November 13, on charges of bribery, graft, betrayal of public trust, and violation of the constitution. While the president denied the allegations, Vice President Arroyo and several other senior administration officials and congressional supporters called for Estrada to resign. Arroyo also formed a shadow cabinet and drafted an agenda for its first 100 days in office. While a broad coalition of middle class, business, and church interests also called for Estrada's resignation, polls suggested that he remained popular among poorer Filipinos.

The political maneuvering occurred as some of the worst fighting in the southern Mindanao region since the 1970s killed hundreds of soldiers and members of the Moro Islamic Liberation Front (MILF) and Abu Sayyaf, two leading Islamic-separatist groups in predominantly Muslim Mindanao. The fighting also displaced tens of thousands of civilians. Separately, the government made little progress in negotiations with leaders of the now-limited Communist insurgency that peaked in the 1970s.

Analysts said that the political and military developments and an expanding budget deficit undermined investor confidence in the country. GDP grew only 3.4 percent in the first half of the year. For the year, the stock market fell 30.2 percent and the *peso* slid 19.7 percent against the dollar.

Political Rights and Civil Liberties: Filipinos can change their government through elections. The 1987 constitution vests executive power in a president who is directly elected for a single six-year term. The congress consists of a senate with 24 directly elected members and a house of representatives with 201 directly elected members and up to 50 more appointed by the president.

While elections are generally free, some fraud and intimidation, and at least 47 election-related deaths, marred the 1998 national and local elections. Corruption, cronyism, and influence-peddling are widely considered to be rife in business and government. The World Bank reported in June that corruption had cost the Philippines an estimated $48 billion in the 20 years to 1997, and continued to cost the government $47 million per year, despite some progress. The Berlin-based Transparency International's 2000 Corruption Perceptions Index ranked the Philippines in a tie with India for 69th place out of 90 countries, with a score of 2.8 on a 0 to 10 scale. The least-corrupt country, Finland, received a 10. Many recent political and economic reforms have barely reached the countryside, where local clans and landowners hold considerable power.

While the country's overall human rights situation has improved considerably under elected governments, in recent years severe human rights violations have occurred in the context of the Islamic-based insurgencies in Mindanao. Police, soldiers, and local civilian militias continue to be accused of committing extrajudicial killings and disappearances during counterinsurgency operations. Civilians fleeing a government offensive on Jolo Island in September told local journalists that the army had carried out indiscriminate bombings as well as summary executions, arbitrary arrests, and "disappearances" of suspected Abu Sayyaf sympathizers, according to Amnesty International. Along with Communist insurgents elsewhere in the Philippines, the MILF and Abu Sayyaf continued to be implicated in cases of extrajudicial execution, torture, and arbitrary detention. Including killings by police of ordinary criminal suspects, the official Commission on Human Rights said it investigated a total of 185 extrajudicial killings in 1999 by security forces and insurgents.

At the height of fighting in May, roughly 600,000 out of Mindanao's population of 15 million people were displaced. Some 80,000 people fled their homes on Jolo Island during the army's September offensive, which freed some of the dozens of local and foreign hostages kidnapped for ransom during the year by Abu Sayyaf. While many villagers undoubtedly fled on their own accord, in recent years the MILF and Abu Sayyaf have forcibly evacuated civilians from their homes. Adding to the civilian misery, suspected Islamic-separatists killed dozens of people in bomb attacks on buses, marketplaces, and other civilian targets in Mindanao during the first half of the year.

The insurgencies in Mindanao occur in the context of complaints by the Moros, or Muslims, who live primarily in Mindanao, of economic and social discrimination by the country's Christian majority. A 1998 Asian Development Bank survey reported that Muslim-majority provinces in Mindanao lag behind other Mindanao provinces on most development indicators. Critics allege that a semiautonomous government, created under a 1996 peace accord that ended a 24-year insurgency by the Moro National Liberation Front, has few real powers and has made little progress in stimulating economic development in the four Mindanao provinces it nominally controls.

Despite some improvements in recent years, police continued to be accused of arbitrary detention and torture of ordinary criminal suspects. Taking advantage of the country's weak rule of law, security forces are reportedly often involved in extortion schemes, the drug trade, and illicit logging. While guarding private businesses in the countryside, civilian militias often violate the rights of local residents with near impunity.

While the judiciary is independent, courts continued to be understaffed, heavily backlogged, and rife with corruption. In practice, poor people often have little recourse under the law, while wealthy and powerful Filipinos frequently manipulate judges. Prison conditions are poor and dangerous.

The private press continued to be outspoken, although newspapers often resort to innuendo rather than doing any investigative reporting. In the countryside, illegal logging outfits, drug traffickers, and guerrillas occasionally harass and intimidate journalists. In the most serious incidents, gunmen have killed several journalists in recent years. Nongovernmental human rights organizations continued to be active, although in recent years local authorities have occasionally harassed activists.

Freedom of religion is respected in this predominantly Roman Catholic country. Muslims are underrepresented in senior government positions and politics. Constituting 18 percent of the population, indigenous people face occasional reprisal attacks during army counterinsurgency operations, societal discrimination, and displacement from ancestral lands by commercial projects. The government has been slow to implement a 1997 act designed to increase the amount of land held by the indigenous population. On several occasions, the Estrada administration forcibly displaced squatters from illegal urban settlements in order to clear the way for development projects, often without offering relocation as mandated by law.

Domestic violence, rape, violence against prostitutes, and trafficking of Filipino women abroad for the purpose of prostitution continued to be major problems. The government has made some efforts to curb trafficking by cracking down on illegal recruitment of women and discouraging employment migration. Women have made gains in educational opportunities, but still face private sector employment discrimination. The country has more than 100,000 street children and tens of thousands of child prostitutes. The Commission on Human Rights said in 1999 that the Communist New People's Army was increasingly recruiting child-soldiers.

Unions are independent but have brought relatively few workers into collective bargaining agreements. The International Labor Organization has criticized laws mandating arbitration for labor disputes in "essential" industries, authorizing penalties for strikes deemed illegal, and placing restrictions on the right of government workers to strike and bargain collectively. The law also places some restrictions on private sector workers' right to strike. Private sector employers often physically harass and intimidate union organizers, forcibly break strikes, and violate minimum wage standards. Many of these violations, along with sexual harassment, are reportedly most common in export-processing zones.

Poland

Polity: Presidential-parliamentary democracy
Economy: Mixed capitalist
Population: 38,600,000
PPP: $7,619
Life Expectancy: 73
Ethnic Groups: Polish (98 percent), German (1 percent), Ukrainian and Belarusian (1 percent)
Capital: Warsaw

Political Rights: 1
Civil Liberties: 2
Status: Free

Overview:

In the year 2000, Poland celebrated the 20th anniversary of Solidarity, the dynamic independent trade union movement that in the 1980s hastened communism's demise. Voters delivered a solid reelection victory in October 2000 to incumbent President Aleksander Kwasniewski, who pledged to make European Union (EU) membership his top priority. The collapse of Prime Minister Jerzy Buzek's parliamentary majority, the resolution of important cases before Poland's lustration court, and concern that Poland might not qualify for the first round of EU enlargement also marked the year.

From the fourteenth to the eighteenth centuries Poland and Lithuania maintained a powerful empire that Prussia, Austria, and Russia subsequently destroyed in three successive partitions. Poland enjoyed a window of independence from 1918 to 1939 but was forced into the Communist sphere at the end of World War II. Polish citizens endured a Soviet-style people's republic from 1952 to 1989, the year Lech Walesa and Solidarity forced the government to accept democratic reforms.

Voters elected Walesa president in 1990, and he presided over five years of economic and political transformation. Former Communist Aleksander Kwasniewski defeated Walesa in 1995 and remains in power today. Kwasniewski's Democratic Left Alliance (SLD) controlled the government from 1993 to 1997, when the opposition Solidarity Election Action (AWS) proved victorious in parliamentary elections. The smaller Freedom Union (UW) party joined the AWS in forming a majority government led by Prime Minister Buzek.

In June 2000, the UW withdrew its support from Buzek, whom it blamed for failing to rally support for important budget cuts and privatization programs. Five cabinet members resigned. Buzek now presides over an unpopular minority government that is expected to collapse before regular parliamentary elections in September 2001.

Poland's controversial 1998 lustration law requires candidates for political office to confess any cooperation with the Communist-era secret police. If a candidate denies cooperation and the lustration court determines he lied, the law bars him from public office for ten years. Prior to the 2000 presidential election, for example, independent candidate Andrzej Olechowski admitted collaborating with the secret police in the early 1970s. When Alexander Kwasniewski and Lech Walesa denied any spying, however, the State Protection Office (UOP) challenged them. The court ultimately cleared them of wrongdoing, but charges that the UOP's efforts were politically motivated cast doubt on the integrity and efficacy of the lustration process. In related news, parliament appointed a chair to the new National Memory Institute in 2000 and paved the way for Poles to open their Communist-era secret police files.

In October, voters reelected President Kwasniewski with 53.9 percent of the vote. His closest challenger, independent candidate Andrzej Olechowski, received only 17.3 percent. The remaining candidates performed as follows: Marian Krzaklewski, AWS, 15.57 percent; Jaroslaw Kalinowski, Polish Peasant Party, 5.95 percent; Andrzej Lepper, Self-Defense farmers' union, 3.05 percent. Seven candidates, including Lech Walesa, received less than 2 percent each. After his poor showing, Walesa retired from active political life.

The European Commission announced that Poland remains on course for EU membership sometime between 2003 and 2005 but needs to improve efficiency in the judiciary; intensify anticorruption efforts; jump-start agricultural reforms; and adhere to privatization plans in key industries like steel, defense, and energy. When the EU suggested that Poland might not qualify for the first round of enlargement, parliament accelerated its review of nearly 40 reform laws. In late December the government also created an inter-ministerial team to coordinate efforts against economic crime. Earlier in the month, Poles were shocked by the resignation of Silesian governor Marek Kempski, whose administration was known for its tough anticorruption stance. Kempski stepped down amid allegations that aides in his office were using their public posts to further private business deals.

Political Rights and Civil Liberties: Polish citizens who are age 18 or older can change their government democratically under a system of universal and equal suffrage by secret ballot. Voters elect the president and members of parliament. The president's appointment of the prime minister is subject to confirmation by the *Sejm*, parliament's lower house.

Elections in Poland are free and fair. The 1997 parliamentary election resulted in a change of government when the opposition AWS defeated the SLD. The AWS and the UW formed a coalition government led by Prime Minister Buzek. The next parliamentary elections are scheduled for 2001. In May 2000, in anticipation of the October election, parliament amended the Presidential Elections Act to comply with the 1997 constitution. Incumbent President Kwasniewski began his campaign with a strong lead in the polls. He easily defeated eleven opponents in the first round of voting.

The 1997 constitution guarantees freedom of expression and forbids censorship. Poland enjoys a wide diversity of media that comprises approximately 5,000 periodicals, 200 radio stations, and 9 television networks. This includes 4 public radio stations and 2 public television channels. Journalists object to a libel law that imposes strict penalties for slandering public officials. They also oppose the growing number of related lawsuits. President Kwasniewski won a legal suit in 2000 that forced the newspaper *Zycie* to issue a formal apology for claiming he had associated with a Russian spy back in 1997. The case sparked an important debate about journalists' burden of proof in reporting the news. During the 2000 presidential campaign, several candidates accused Polish Public Television (TVP) of favoring President Kwasniewski in its coverage. In response, Andrzej Kwiatkowski, the head of TVP's election coverage and a former Kwasniewski advisor, agreed to step down.

The state respects freedom of religion. More than 90 percent of Poles are Roman Catholic, and more than 60 percent worship regularly. In 2000, the state returned approximately $2 billion in communal property—synagogues, schools, cemeteries, etc.— to Polish Jews, and the first synagogue in Oswiecim (Auschwitz) opened since the end of World War II. The country's Roman Catholic bishops presented a letter in 2000 in which they asked for forgiveness "for those among us who show disdain for people of other denominations or tolerate anti-Semitism."

Polish citizens can petition the government, assemble freely, organize professional and other associations, and engage in collective bargaining. Public demonstrations require permits from local authorities. In 2000 members of the Self-Defense farmers' union protested government agricultural policies and demanded outstanding payments, while the National Trade Union Accord organized thousands of people to protest the country's high unemployment rate. Late in the year, the Union of Nurses and Midwives led thousands of nurses in a series of protests, hunger strikes, road blocks, and sit-ins to demand higher wages and better funding for the public health service. At year's end, the nurses and the government had not reached an agreement.

Poland has an independent judiciary, but courts are notorious for lengthy delays— up to 40 months in Warsaw—in processing cases. A January 2000 law seeks to relieve the burden by simplifying procedures and adding 400 court chambers for civil and criminal cases. Other reforms include strengthening the public prosecutor's office, adding more judges, and improving judicial training. Polish authorities also announced new measures aimed at combating corruption, including the creation a special police unit called the Central Anti-Corruption Office. In October parliament ratified a Council of Europe protocol to abolish the death penalty.

The constitution outlines a range of other personal rights and freedoms, including the right to privacy, the inviolability of the home, freedom of movement, and choice of residence. The constitution also specifies entitlements such as free education and health care.

At nearly 14 percent, unemployment in Poland is a serious problem. Even so, the country has a flourishing and competitive market economy in which the private sector makes up two-thirds of gross domestic product and 70 percent of total employment. The state respects property rights and encourages entrepreneurship, and it continues to privatize state enterprises. In 1999 the government signed a law on economic activity that widened the scope of entrepreneurship, gave equal status to domestic and foreign firms, and curbed state intervention in the economy. In 2000 parliament approved a five-day workweek but held the number of hours in the workweek at 42.

Portugal

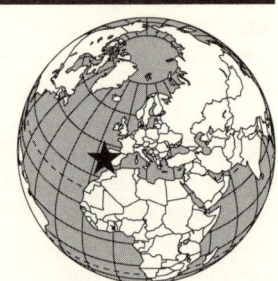

Polity: Presidential-parliamentary democracy
Economy: Mixed capitalist
Population: 10,000,000
PPP: $14,701
Life Expectancy: 75
Ethnic Groups: Portuguese, African minority
Capital: Lisbon

Political Rights: 1
Civil Liberties: 1
Status: Free

Overview:

Prime Minister Antonio Guterres's Socialist Party (PS) saw its parliamentary majority vanish in 2000, with the government and opposition sharing the same number of seats—115—at year's end. Amid warnings of an economic slowdown and threats by the opposition to veto the government's proposed 2001 budget, the prospect of early elections in the new year loomed large. Economic forecasts show Portugal lagging behind the European Union (EU) average, the first such prediction during five years of consecutive growth.

Formerly a great maritime and colonial empire, Portugal ended its monarchy in a bloodless revolution in 1910. The republic, plagued by chronic instability and violence, ended in a military revolt in 1926. A fascist dictatorship under Antonio Salazar lasted from 1932 to 1968. In 1968, the dying Salazar was replaced by his lieutenant, Marcello Caetano. During what is now termed the "Marcello spring," repression and censorship were relaxed somewhat and a liberal wing developed inside the one-party national assembly. In 1974, Caetano was overthrown in a bloodless coup by the Armed Forces Movement, which opposed the ongoing colonial wars in Mozambique and Angola. A transition to democracy then began with the election of a constitutional assembly that adopted a democratic constitution in 1976. The constitution was revised in 1982 to bring the military under civilian control, curb the president's powers, and abolish an unelected "Revolutionary Council." In 1989, a second revision of the constitution provided for further privatization of nationalized industries and state-owned media.

Prime Minister Guterres's Socialist government has ruled Portugal since 1995. Despite opposition from small left- and right-wing groups, the ruling Socialists and opposition Social Democrats both supported the country's entry into the European Monetary Union in 1999.

A reform- and market-minded Socialist, Prime Minister Guterres professed throughout 2000 to bring Portugal up to European-wide economic standards. Warning that defeat of his budget proposal would paralyze the country and plunge it into a political crisis, the prime minister still faced intense opposition criticism over his perceived lack of social security, education, judicial, and public administration reforms. Indeed, public opinion polls showed a majority of the public disappointed with his rule. It was against this backdrop that one prominent Portuguese economist predicted it would take Portugal 20 years to close the gap between its level of economic performance and that of the EU's average. Wages, pensions, and literacy levels also remained among the lowest in the EU. Despite full employment, there were widespread fears of the economy overheating and of an impending economic slowdown.

The election of the Socialist Party's Jorge Sampaio as president in 1996 marked the end of a conservative era in which Portugal benefited economically, but failed to satisfy its voters' eagerness for social change. While both President Sampaio and Prime Minister Guterres have vowed to continue economic reforms, issues such as education, health, housing, and the environment have assumed greater importance in the minds of constituents.

Political Rights and Civil Liberties:

The Portuguese can change their government democratically. In direct, competitive elections, voters, including a large number of Portuguese living abroad, select both the president and members of parliament. The president, who also commands the country's armed forces, is elected to a five-year term. The president receives advice from the Council of State, which includes six senior civilian officials, former presidents, five members chosen by the legislature, and five chosen by the president. The country's unicameral legislature includes up to 235 deputies. With the exception of fascist organizations, political association is unrestricted. Members of small, extreme-right groups, however, have run candidates for public office without interference. In 1997, the constitution was amended to allow immigrants to vote in presidential elections.

Full employment in Portugal led to a larger than normal influx of foreigners in 2000, mostly from the Maghreb, black Africa, and Eastern Europe. There are an estimated 200,000 foreigners in the country, representing 1.8 percent of the population. While anti-immigrant violence appears rare, a smoke bomb was thrown into a Lisbon disco in April. The toxic gas emitted from the canister left 7 dead and 65 injured. The disco is frequented mainly by African immigrants from Angola.

Portuguese courts are autonomous and operate only under the restraints of established law and the constitution. They include a constitutional court, a supreme court of justice, and judicial courts of the first and second instance. Separate administrative courts address administrative and tax disputes. They are generally noted for their adherence to traditional principles of independent jurisprudence, but inefficient bureaucratic organization has created an enormous backlog of cases in the system.

Freedoms of speech and assembly are respected with few exceptions. Although the law forbids insults directed at the government or the armed forces and statements intended to undermine the rule of law, the state has never prosecuted cases under this provision. Human rights organizations have repeatedly criticized Portugal for the occasional beating of prisoners and other detainees. In general, prison conditions are poor.

The print media, which are owned by political parties and private publishers, are free and competitive. Until 1990, all television and radio media, with the exception of the Roman Catholic radio station, were state owned. Although television broadcasting is dominated by the state-owned Radioteleivisao Portuguesa, two independent stations have operated in recent years.

Workers have the right to strike and are represented by competing Communist and non-Communist organizations. In recent years, the two principal labor federations, the General Union of Workers and the General Confederation of Portuguese Workers Intersindical, have charged "clandestine" companies with exploiting child labor in the impoverished north.

The status of women has improved with economic modernization. Concentrated in agricultural and domestic service, women workers constitute more than one-third of the official labor force. Despite a few prominent exceptions, female representation in government and politics averages less than ten percent. Sexual harassment is only illegal if committed by a superior in the workplace. According to the U.S. Department of State, Portugal's constitution provides for freedom of religion, and the government respects this right in practice.

Qatar

Polity: Traditional monarchy
Economy: Capitalist-statist
Population: 600,000
PPP: $20,987
Life Expectancy: 72

Political Rights: 6
Civil Liberties: 6
Status: Not Free

Ethnic Groups: Arab (40 percent), Pakistani (18 percent), Indian (18 percent), Iranian (10 percent), other (14 percent)
Capital: Doha

Overview:
Sheikh Hamad bin Khalifa al-Thani celebrated five years as Qatar's emir in 2000. In this short time, he has begun to improve political openness and transparency, relax press censorship, and initiate a strong policy of economic diversification and privatization. In foreign policy, he has taken a broadly pro-U.S., moderate-Arab position while continuing to maintain political stability at home.

Qatar became a British protectorate in 1919 and gained independence when Great Britain withdrew from the Persian Gulf in 1971. Under the 1970 Basic Law, an emir is chosen from among the adult males of the al-Thani family. The Basic Law also provides for a council of ministers and a partially-elected *Majlis al-Shura*, or advisory council. In practice, the 35-member Majlis is fully appointed.

In 1995, Sheikh Hamad, then crown prince and long recognized as the real power in the country, deposed his father in a palace coup while the emir vacationed in Switzerland. He has since taken steps toward gradual democratization. Press censorship was formally lifted with the dissolution of the information ministry in 1995, and in 1998 the emirate held direct elections to the board of the powerful chamber of commerce and industry.

In July 1999, Hamad appointed a committee to draw up a permanent constitution over three years with a provision for a directly elected parliament with legislative power.

Qatar's first election was held on March 8, 1999, for a 29-member advisory council on municipal affairs. Although the council is limited to issuing opinions on a narrow scope of issues, the election was regarded as a watershed in a region where rulers traditionally resist sharing power with their constituents. By allowing women to vote and to stand as candidates, Qatar became the first Persian Gulf state to hold a direct election on the basis of universal suffrage. Six women were among the 248 candidates, but none of them won seats.

Analysts note that Sheikh Hamad's commitment to democratic reform appears to outweigh that of his subjects. Unlike other countries in the region, Qatar has come under virtually no popular pressure to reform. Only 55 percent of eligible Qataris registered to vote in last year's municipal election. *The Economist* attributed the lack of enthusiasm to the strong conservative nature of Qatari society. Indeed, women candidates admitted to facing criticism of their decision to stand. And surprisingly, Qatar's leading families did not field candidates. Hamad's motives for promoting openness may include a belief that democratization promotes economic development, or that a boost to the legitimacy of his government may forestall the type of violent unrest plaguing other Arab states like neighboring Bahrain.

With only about 20 years left as a major oil exporter, Qatar has made a priority of diversifying and attracting foreign investment. It boasts the third-largest gas reserves in the world, and the government has adopted a strategy to lure foreign investment in gas in order to finance economic infrastructure, such as facilities for export-intensive industry, as well as physical infrastructure such as roads, airports, bridges, and power plants. Tax incentives and laws allowing increased foreign ownership in local firms are expected in the near future.

Under pressure from neighboring states, Qatar shut down the Israeli trade mission in Doha following renewed violence between Israelis and Palestinians in the fall. An ongoing dispute with Bahrain over two Gulf islands with potential oil reserves continues, with a ruling by the International Court of Justice at the Hague due by early 2001.

A Qatari high criminal court jailed 33 people, including a cousin of the emir, in February for "attempting to overthrow the head of state by force" in a failed 1996 coup. Eighty-five other defendants were acquitted, including 20 tried in absentia. The case reportedly went to an appeals court in September.

Political Rights and Civil Liberties: Qataris cannot change their government democratically. Political parties are illegal, and there are no organized opposition groups. The emir holds absolute power, though he consults with leading members of society on policy issues and works to achieve consensus with the appointed Majlis. Citizens have the right to appeal government decisions by petitioning the emir. March 1999 elections to the municipal advisory council were considered by international observers to be free and fair. Participation was surprisingly low: of 40,000 eligible voters, only 22,000 registered. But the vibrant campaign included televised debates, posters, and informal gatherings to discuss matters of municipal policy. The elected council reports to the minister of municipal affairs, who is not required to heed its advice and may dissolve it at will. In July 1999, the emir initiated work on a new constitution that is expected to provide for a directly elected parliament.

The civilian security force under the interior ministry includes the general police force; the investigatory police, or *mubahathat*, which handles sedition and espionage cases; the special state security investigative unit, or *mubahith*, which handles internal security and intelligence gathering; and the independent civilian intelligence service, or *mukhabarat*. Suspects in security cases may be detained indefinitely while under investigation and are generally denied access to counsel, though long-term detention occurs infrequently. Torture is reportedly not common.

The judiciary is not independent. Most judges are foreign nationals whose residence may be revoked at any time. However, courts have been known to summon senior officials and members of the ruling family as witnesses. Civil courts have jurisdiction in civil and commercial disputes, while *Sharia* (Islamic law) courts handle family, civil, and criminal cases. Sharia court trials are closed to the public, and lawyers are not permitted in the courtroom. While corporal punishment is practiced in accord with Sharia, amputation is prohibited.

Media in Qatar have been virtually free of government interference since the lifting of censorship in 1995, but self-censorship is still pervasive because of real or imagined social and political pressures. State-run television, radio, and newspapers generally avoid taboo subjects such as Islam and the royal family, but recently have criticized state funding of the royal family. The satellite television channel Al-Jazeera operates freely. Owned and operated by a member of the ruling family, the all-news channel presents interviews with dissidents and exiles throughout the region, lively debates that include opposition views, commentary on human rights issues, and discussions of the role of religion in Arab culture. The controversial coverage captivates Middle Eastern viewers while drawing furious protests from regional leaders. In 2000, the government announced plans to launch an "e-government" to make some public services available via the Internet within 18 months. Qatar reportedly has some 45,000 Internet users currently.

Freedom of association is limited to private social, sports, trade, professional, and cultural societies registered with the government. Political parties do not exist, and political demonstrations are prohibited.

Foreign nationals employed as domestic workers face sexual harassment and physical abuse. Although the authorities have investigated and punished several employers, most women apparently do not report abuse for fear of losing their residence permits. Some 25,000 Egyptian nationals live in Qatar, but hiring Egyptians was banned in 1996 when Qatari officials accused Egypt of involvement in the failed 1996 coup.

Women have made important gains in recent years. Although the number of women in the workforce is still very small, women have begun to find jobs in education, medicine, and the news media. According to one study, the number of Qatari women in government jobs increased by 61 percent between 1991 and 1997. Women participated as candidates and voters in municipal elections, making up 44 percent of registered voters. The government increasingly awards scholarships to women wishing to study abroad. Still, in this socially conservative country, society restricts women even where the law does not. Women may legally travel abroad alone, but most travel with male relatives. Legal discrimination still exists in family matters such as divorce and inheritance.

The Wahhabi order of Sunni Islam is the state religion. While public worship by non-Muslims is officially prohibited, services conducted privately with prior notification of authorities are tolerated, and a large foreign population practices discreetly. There is a small number of Shiite mosques. Public schools provide compulsory instruction in Islam. Since Sharia courts handle most civil claims, non-Muslims, who cannot bring suit in Sharia courts, are disadvantaged. The U.S. State Department notes an upward trend in religious freedom for Christians, including promised provision of land on which to build churches. In February 2000, the government identified a piece of land on which it will allow the construction of three churches: one Catholic, one Anglican, and one Orthodox.

Workers may not form unions or bargain collectively. They may belong to joint consultative committees of worker and management representatives that discuss such issues as working conditions and schedules, but not wages. The government's Labor Conciliation Board mediates disputes. Workers, except those in government or domestic employment, may strike if mediation fails. Employers sometimes exercise leverage over foreign workers by refusing to grant mandatory exit permits.

Romania

Polity: Presidential-parliamentary democracy
Economy: Mixed statist (transitional)
Population: 22,400,000
PPP: $5,648
Life Expectancy: 70
Ethnic Groups: Romanian (90 percent), Hungarian (7 percent), other, including German and Roma (3 percent)
Capital: Bucharest

Political Rights: 2
Civil Liberties: 2
Status: Free

Overview: Former President Ion Iliescu won a landslide victory in the December 10 presidential runoff against Vadim Corneliu Tudor of the Greater Romania Party (PRM). Iliescu, who was the first elected president, from 1990 to 1996, after the fall of Nicolae Ceausescu in 1989, defeated the far-right extremist leader with 66.83 percent of the vote.

Romanians' frustration with their economic position and increasing political instability had created a lack of confidence and support for the Democratic Convention of Romania (CDR), the coalition government of President Emil Constantinescu and Prime Minister Mugur Isarescu. Iliescu and his Party of Social Democracy (PDSR) won another chance at the presidency in late 2000 as a result of the CDR's failure to deliver on promises of reform, which included revamping the tax system, cutting public spending, and accelerating privatization.

In the November 2000 parliamentary elections, the PDSR won 65 of the 140 seats in the senate and 155 of the 327 seats in the chamber of deputies. The PRM gained 37 seats in the senate and 84 in the lower house; the National Liberal Party (PNL), 13 and 30; the Democratic Party (PD), 13 and 31; and the Democratic Alliance of Hungarians in Romania (UDMR), 12 and 27. The CDR, now the CDR 2000, did not gain the five percent that is required to hold seats in parliament. Adrian Nastase has been appointed prime minister.

Romania became independent following the 1878 Berlin Congress. It gained territory after World War I, but lost some to the Soviet Union and Bulgaria in 1940. When Soviet troops entered the country in 1944, King Michael dismissed the pro-German regime and backed the Allies. In 1945, he was forced to accept a Communist-led coalition government. The autarkic economics and repressive governance of Communist strongman Nicolae Ceausescu devastated Romania during his rule from 1965 to 1989.

On December 25, 1989, Ceausescu was tried and executed following a popular uprising and palace coup by disgruntled Communists. A provisional government was formed under Iliescu, a high-ranking Communist and the leader of the National Salvation Front (NSF). The 1992 parliamentary elections saw the NSF split between neo-Communist and more reformist members. In November 1996, the reformer Emil Constantinescu of the CDR defeated Iliescu in the presidential elections. Political bickering and lack of unification within the coalition resulted in the dismissal of Prime Minister Victor Ciorbea in 1998 and Prime Minister Radu Vasile in 1999.

The start of 2000 saw a new government, formed under Isarescu, focused on implementing reforms and improving the economic and social situation in the country. The intended reforms were overshadowed throughout the year by political squabbling, environmental disasters, and scandals, which included the collapse of the National Investment Fund (FNI), in which thousands of Romanians lost their life savings. Investors of FNI blamed the government for their losses, and as a result, many voted against the CDR in the parliamentary and presidential elections. President-elect Ion Iliescu was also implicated in two political scandals. In April he was accused of having developed a spy network with Russia during his last presidential term, and in May he was implicated in a money-laundering scandal with a French-Romanian businessman.

By December 2000, inflation was at 40 percent with unemployment reaching 11 percent. The World Bank issued a report which stated that 40 percent of Romanians live below the poverty line. Iliescu promises to continue negotiations with NATO and the European Union (EU) and push ahead with privatization and economic reforms while alleviating widespread poverty and eliminating corruption.

In March, Romania began accession talks with the EU and agreed on a medium-term development strategy. Romania has set 2007 as a possible date for EU membership. By the close of the year, the EU had not lifted the visa restrictions for Romania, as Romania has yet to strengthen its border controls or to issue passports that cannot be forged. Romania continues to rank last among the 12 countries vying for EU membership; however, under a reform deal reached in December, Romania will get 15 votes in the decision-making Council of Ministers when it does finally join the organization.

The new government plans to resume talks with the International Monetary Fund (IMF) in January 2001. The IMF withheld a third installment of a standby loan of $540 million as a result of Romania's failure to reduce the state budget arrears and privatize the banking sector. In 2001, Romania will chair the Organization for Security and Co-operation in Europe (OSCE).

Political Rights and Civil Liberties: Romanians can change their government democratically under a multiparty system enshrined in a 1991 post-Communist constitution. The OSCE found that the 2000 presidential and parliamentary elections were "further evidence that democratic elections are firmly entrenched in Romania." Voter turnout was at 57.5 percent, 20 percent lower than in the 1996 elections.

The 1991 constitution enshrines freedom of expression and the press, but it limits the boundaries of free expression by prohibiting "defamation of the country." Under Law No. 40 of the 1996 Romanian penal code, journalists face up to two years' imprisonment for libel and up to five years for disseminating false information that affects Romania's international relations or national security. In October, the Romanian Audiovisual Council, the regulatory body for broadcast media, lifted its ban on the use of Hungarian symbols and the use of languages other than Romanian in electronic media. Religious freedom is generally respected, although newer religious organizations are impeded from registering with the state secretary of religions. Lack of registration in turn denies adherents their right to freely exercise their religious beliefs and prevents them from building places of worship, cemeteries, and so on.

The constitution provides for freedom of assembly, and the government respects this right. Workers have the right to form unions and strike. Economic reforms and political turmoil have affected the Romanian population as several sectors, such as lawyers, teachers, and truckers, have gone on strike and demanded higher salaries, less taxation, better working conditions, and job security. In September, a trade union leader was murdered in the city of Iasi while trying to prevent large-scale job cuts at a privatized factory.

The Romanian justice system is divided into four courts: the courts of first instance, the tribunals, the courts of appeals, and the supreme court of justice. All are independent of other government branches but subject to influence by the executive branch. Under the law, judges are appointed, promoted, and transferred by the 15-member Higher Council of the Judiciary, which is elected for four-year terms by the two chambers of parliament. To diminish the politicization of the process, a 1997 revision of the law called for the members of the Higher Council to be appointed by the justice minister, not by parliament.

The chamber of deputies voted in June to decriminalize homosexuality, although people can still be jailed for "abnormal sexual practices" in public. The legislation to change Article 200 of the 1996 Penal Code, which punishes public displays of homosexuality, still needs senate approval.

Corruption is endemic in the government bureaucracy, civil service, and business. Property rights are secure, though the ability of citizens to start businesses continues to be encumbered by red tape, corruption, and organized crime.

There are no restrictions on travel within the country, and citizens who want to change their place of residence do not face any official barriers. Women have equal rights with men, though violence against women, including rape, continues to be a serious problem. Living conditions for children in state-run orphanages are in a terrible state according to an EU report. In order to be in line with EU standards, Romania established the National Agency for the Protection of Children's Rights, a short-term strategy to address the issues of child care institutions.

Russia

Polity: Presidential-par-
liamentary democracy
Economy: Mixed statist
(transitional)
Population: 145,200,000
PPP: $6,460
Life Expectancy: 67

Political Rights: 5*
Civil Liberties: 5
Status: Partly Free

Ethnic Groups: Russian (82 percent), Tatar (4 percent), Ukrainian (3 percent), other
(11 percent)
Capital: Moscow
Ratings Change: Russia's political rights rating changed from 4 to 5 due to reports of
serious irregularities in the March presidential elections and President Putin's increasing consolidation of central government authority.

Overview:

After securing a decisive victory in the March presidential
election, which was marred by widespread fraud, Vladimir
Putin moved quickly to consolidate his power by taking steps
to rein in the country's regional governors, wealthy business elite, and independent
media outlets. While Putin maintained that the efforts were necessary to eliminate
corruption and ensure economic and political stability, critics charged that his increasingly authoritarian tactics were stifling dissent and undermining the country's nascent
democratic institutions. Despite the ongoing war in Chechnya and a series of military
and security crises, the president continued to enjoy widespread popular support throughout the year.

With the collapse of the Soviet Union in December 1991, Russia reemerged as a
separate, independent state under the leadership of Boris Yeltsin, who had been elected
president in June of that year. Yeltsin was challenged by a hostile anti-reform legislature in 1992, as parliament replaced acting Prime Minister Yegor Gaidar, a principal
architect of reforms, with Viktor Chernomyrdin, a Soviet-era manager of the natural-
gas monopoly, Gazprom. The following year, Yeltsin put down an attempted coup by
hardliners in parliament, and a new constitution was approved creating a bicameral
national legislature, the Federal Assembly. The December 1995 parliamentary elections, in which 43 parties competed, saw the victory of Communists and nationalist
forces.

In the 1996 presidential elections, Yeltsin, who was openly supported by the
country's most influential media and business elites, easily defeated Communist Party
leader Gennady Zyuganov with 54 percent of the vote to 40 percent in a runoff in July.
The signing of a peace agreement in August with authorities in the republic of Chechnya
put an end to a nearly two-year war with the breakaway territory, in which Russia suffered a humiliating defeat and Chechnya's formal economy and infrastructure were
largely destroyed. However, a final decision on the region's status was officially deferred until 2001.

In March 1998, Yeltsin dismissed Prime Minister Chernomyrdin and his entire
government, citing the failure of economic reforms, and replaced him with the little-

known Energy Minister Sergei Kiriyenko. As the country's economic situation continued to worsen, the ruble collapsed in August, forcing a devaluation of the currency and precipitating the collapse of Russia's financial markets. In response, Yeltsin fired Kiriyenko, who was replaced by Foreign Minister Yevgeny Primakov in September. The new government, which did not include any well-known reformers, signaled a return to greater spending and state control.

An impending political crisis was averted in mid-1999, when Yeltsin survived an impeachment vote in parliament on May 15 over five charges, including starting the 1994-1996 war in Chechnya. Four days later, the legislature approved a longtime Yeltsin ally, Interior Minister Sergei Stepashin, as the new prime minister to replace Primakov, who had been dismissed by Yeltsin on May 12. However, Yeltsin abruptly removed Stepashin on August 9 and replaced him with Federal Security Service head Vladimir Putin. Yeltsin, whose term would expire in 2000 and who was ineligible to run for a third term, indicated that Putin was his preferred successor in the presidential elections scheduled for the following year.

The previous conflict with Chechnya was reignited in 1999 after an invasion by Chechen guerillas into the neighboring republic of Dagestan in early August, and a subsequent string of deadly bombings in several Russian cities that the Kremlin blamed on Chechen militants. The Kremlin responded by initiating an air and ground invasion of the breakaway republic that drove tens of thousands of civilians from their homes and led to accusations of human rights violations committed by both the Russian military and Chechen fighters. However, the campaign enjoyed broad popular support in Russia, fueled by the media's largely pro-government reporting. Putin's public approval rating rose dramatically as the result of his close association with the Chechen war, where guerilla-style fighting continued at year's end, and his reputation as a vigorous and disciplined leader in contrast to the ailing Yeltsin.

In the December 19 election for the 450-seat lower house of parliament (*Duma*), the Communist Party secured the largest number of votes, gaining 114 seats. The Unity bloc, a diverse grouping of political figures created by the Kremlin in September and endorsed by Putin, came in second with 73 seats. The seemingly powerful Fatherland-All Russia coalition, which united Moscow mayor Yuri Luzhkov's Fatherland group and the All Russia bloc of regional governors and was led by former Prime Minister Primakov, suffered a surprisingly poor showing with only 66 seats. Other parties that crossed the five percent threshold to enter parliament were the Union of Right Forces, led by former Deputy Prime Minister Boris Nemtsov and former Prime Minister Sergei Kiriyenko, with 29 seats; the reformist Yabloko, headed by Grigory Yavlinsky, with 20 seats; and the ultranationalist Zhirinovsky bloc, with 17 seats. The remaining seats were won by independent candidates or members of smaller parties.

While the Communists formed the single largest bloc, the results were widely regarded as an important victory for pro-government forces. The Unity bloc had appealed to voters on the basis of its image as a champion of the restoration of order and tough leadership, as embodied by Putin. In addition, Primakov saw his support decline in the face of both Putin's rise in popularity and the success of relentless media attacks by the pro-Kremlin ORT television network.

In a surprise end-of-the-year move, President Yeltsin announced his resignation on December 31, turning over the reins of power to Putin. Many observers maintained that his sudden departure was linked to Putin's signing of a guarantee of immunity from prosecution for Yeltsin, who recently had been at the center of several corruption scandals, as well as to his worsening health problems. His resignation served to move up the presidential poll by three months, from June to March 2000, dramatically shortening the election campaign period.

In a victory that had been widely anticipated, Putin secured 52.9 percent of the vote, more than the 50 percent required to avoid a second-round runoff. Communist Party leader Gennady Zyuganov received 29.2 percent, followed by Yabloko Party head Grigory Yavlinsky with 5.8 percent, Keremovo governor Aman Tuleev with 3 percent, and the leader of the Liberal Democratic Party of Russia (LDPR), Vladimir Zhirinovsky, with 2.7 percent. The remaining six candidates, including Samara governor Konstantin Titov and former Prosecutor General Yuri Skuratov, received less than 2 percent of the vote each. Overall voter turnout was 68.7 percent.

International election observers cited numerous and serious irregularities, including the use of some election commission staff to distribute campaign materials; ambiguities in legislation regarding financial disclosure requirements for candidates and their apparently arbitrary enforcement; the use of federal and regional government staff members to campaign for Putin; and biased media reporting of the campaign. According to a highly critical report by *The Moscow Times* that was compiled following a six-month investigation, Putin would have faced a second round runoff with Zyuganov if not for widespread fraud; the report did concede that Putin would most likely have won in the second round. The newspaper also pointed to instances of ballot box stuffing, the creation of "ghost" votes, and the burning of ballots supporting opposition candidates.

Among the various reasons cited for Putin's victory were the shortened campaign period, which benefited the already popular Putin over his opponents; the continuing popularity of the war in Chechnya; Putin's refusal to provide potentially controversial details of his political program; the earlier elimination from the race of former leading presidential hopefuls Yevgeny Primakov and Yuri Luzhkov; and positive portrayals of Putin by large media outlets controlled by the state and Kremlin supporters, particularly the ORT network. With Putin's victory becoming an increasingly foregone conclusion during the campaign period, most political figures, including opponents of the Kremlin administration, began to pledge their support to his candidacy. Two months after the election, parliament overwhelmingly approved Finance Minister Mikhail Kasyanov, who had served as Russia's chief foreign debt negotiator, as the new prime minister.

Shortly after taking office in March, Putin began challenging the long-standing political clout of the so-called oligarchs, members of the wealthy and powerful business elite, through a series of investigations and raids by tax officials. Among the targets were the auto giant AvtoVAZ, the energy company LUKOil, the electricity monopoly United Energy Systems, and the mining company Norilsk Nickel, as well as media magnates Vladimir Gusinsky and Boris Berezovsky. While Putin argued that his actions were part of a new anticorruption campaign, most analysts agreed that his efforts were an attempt to increase his own political power by limiting the influence of major business leaders over state policy.

In another bid to increase the central government's authority, Putin moved to rein in the country's often independent-minded 89 governors by pushing through legislation removing them from their positions in the upper house of parliament, allowing the president to suspend them for breaking federal laws, and adopting tax reforms that could reduce their economic power. He also created seven new "super regions" headed by Kremlin appointees, most of whom had backgrounds in the military or security services. Putin's policy was seen in sharp contrast to that of Boris Yelstin, who had accorded considerable autonomy to many of Russia's regions, which were often run as personal fiefdoms.

Despite early government promises of a rapid victory in Chechnya, the year 2000 ended with rebel forces engaging in various guerilla warfare tactics against Russian troops. Although Moscow captured the capital Grozny in February, the Russian military was unable to secure complete control over all of Chechnya's territory. Sniper attacks, car bombs, and suicide missions led to almost daily reports of casualties, while reports of serious human rights violations committed mostly by Russian soldiers continued at year's end.

Putin's popularity also managed to withstand several disasters, all of which occurred in August. The country's aging infrastructure and inadequate safety regulations were highlighted by a fire that destroyed Moscow's Ostankino television tower. A bomb attack in a crowded Moscow underpass, which left 13 people dead, was a frightening reminder of the deadly apartment bombings in 1999. The sinking of the nuclear submarine *Kursk* underscored the decay in the country's once-powerful navy and the urgent need for military reform. Putin's slow and confused response to the tragedy, which had resulted in the deaths of all 118 sailors on board, led to some of the harshest public criticisms of the president during the year.

Relations with the United States became further strained in 2000, particularly over Washington's plans to develop a new limited missile defense shield, which Moscow maintained would violate the 1972 Anti-Ballistic Missile Treaty. In early December, former naval officer Edmond Pope became the first American in 40 years convicted by Russia of espionage. After being sentenced to the maximum of 20 years in prison, he was pardoned by Putin two weeks later on humanitarian grounds. At the same time, Moscow's relations with former Soviet allies including Cuba and North Korea appeared to warm throughout the year.

The country's economy showed surprisingly strong signs of recovery, with growth estimated at some seven percent in 2000. Most of the increase was attributed to high world prices for one of Russia's primary export earners, oil, rather than to promised economic reform programs, which went largely unfulfilled. While parliament adopted a sweeping new tax code during the summer designed to increase government revenues, Putin ignored reforms in other areas, including an overhaul of the banking system and the protection of investor rights. With global oil prices beginning to decline by the end of the year, most analysts expressed concern over the sustainability of Russia's economic growth into 2001.

Political Rights and Civil Liberties:

While Russians can change their government democratically, the 2000 presidential vote was marred by serious examples of electoral fraud. The 1993 constitution established a strong president, who has the power to appoint, pending parliamentary confirmation, and to dismiss the prime minister. The bicameral legislature consists of a 450-member lower chamber (*Duma*), in which half of the members are elected in single-mandate constituencies and the other half by party lists, and an upper chamber (Federation Council), composed of 178 regional leaders. Despite various irregularities, the 1995 and 1999 parliamentary and 1996 presidential elections were deemed generally free and fair by international observers.

Although the constitution provides for freedom of speech and the press, the government increased its pressure on media outlets and journalists critical of the Kremlin. In a case that attracted international condemnation, Radio Free Europe/Radio Liberty reporter Andrei Babitsky was found guilty of violating Russian passport regulations while covering the war in Chechnya. Although he was fined several hundred dollars, the penalty was dropped under the terms of an amnesty program. Press freedom and human rights organizations protested his arrest and conviction, which they insisted was in retaliation for Babitsky's objective reporting of the war.

During the last several years, Russia's powerful businessmen acquired control of or funded many large media outlets, which in turn enjoyed connections to the Kremlin or other political figures. The country's leading independent media empire, Media-MOST, and its owner, Vladimir Gusinsky, became the target of tax raids and arrests on embezzlement charges in 2000 that President Putin claimed were part of his anticorruption campaign. While press freedom groups characterized the moves against Media-MOST as a politically motivated attempt to silence one of the few independent media groups critical of the Russian government and the war in Chechnya, the crackdown was also widely regarded as an effort to rein in one of the last oligarchs openly opposed to the current Kremlin.

Numerous journalists were harassed and assaulted during the year, including several who were killed, mostly for their reports exposing corruption. Igor Domnikov, a reporter with the newspaper *Novaya Gazeta*, was attacked in his apartment building in May and died after two months in a coma. Domnikov's colleagues maintain that the attack was an attempt to intimidate the staff of his paper, which specializes in investigative journalism. Other attacks against journalists with *Novaya Gazeta* included death threats made against reporter Oleg Sultanov, who had published articles on corruption in the country's oil industry, and the severe beating in December of journalist Oleg Lurye, who had written articles on high-level government corruption. In July, Sergei Novikov, the director of the independent radio station Vesna, was shot and killed in what his colleagues believe was retaliation for the station's numerous broadcasts on corruption in the Smolensk region. Vladivostok journalist Irina Grebneva was arrested and briefly imprisoned in July on politically motivated charges stemming from her exposés on local corruption.

Press freedom organizations expressed alarm at Press Minister Mikhail Lesin's June announcement that he intended to enforce a law requiring that all print media be licensed, and at the September adoption of a doctrine on information security providing restrictions on the free flow of certain information. The military continued to impose severe restrictions on journalists' access to the Chechen war zone, issuing accreditation primarily to those of proven loyalty to the government.

Freedom of religion is unevenly respected in this primarily Russian Orthodox country, with a controversial 1997 law on religion requiring churches to prove that they have existed for at least 15 years before being permitted to register. As registration is necessary for a religious group to conduct many of its activities, new, independent congregations are consequently restricted in their functions. Regional authorities often harass nontraditional groups, with Jehovah's Witnesses and Mormons among the frequent targets.

The government generally respects freedom of assembly, and numerous political rallies and other demonstrations occurred throughout the year. The Communist Party, which claims more than 500,000 members countrywide, remains the best organized political force. Most other parties lack strong organization, are centered around specific personalities rather than policy issues, and were formed by political and business elites rather than at the grassroots level. The first-ever conference for the nongovernmental organization (NGO) sector, which is still largely in its infancy, was held in October 2000 to provide ideas for increasing the role of NGOs in Russian society.

Although trade union rights are legally protected, in practice workers risk dismissal if they strike. The Federation of Independent Unions of Russia (FNPR), the successor to the Soviet-era organization, claims to represent 80 percent of all workers. As the dominant trade union movement enjoying often close affiliation with local political structures, the FNPR effectively places a constraint on the right to freedom of association. Approximately eight percent of union members belong to independent unions. In November 2000, more than 30,000 teachers in Far Eastern Russia went on strike over nearly $6 million in wage arrears. A government-proposed new labor code, which was under discussion at year's end, is opposed by labor leaders, who maintain that the law would diminish the power of trade unions and make it easier for employers to dismiss workers.

The judiciary is not fully independent and is subject to political interference, corruption, inadequate funding, and a lack of qualified personnel. In April, parliament dismissed Prosecutor-General Yuri Skuratov, who had investigated former President Yeltsin for corruption. The decision put an end to the more than one year political feud between Skuratov and Yeltsin, who had unsuccessfully attempted to fire Skuratov on three separate occasions the previous year. According to Human Rights Watch, police routinely use torture against detainees to extract confessions, but are rarely prosecuted for committing such abuses. Russia's prison system suffers from severe overcrowding, inadequate food and medical care, and widespread disease among inmates. Pretrial detention centers house more than 300,000 suspects, many of whom are held for several years in squalid conditions. A draft penal code passed two parliamentary readings by the end of 2000 and is expected to be adopted during its third and final reading in early 2001. The law would reduce overcrowding in Russia's prisons by limiting pretrial detentions to one year, implementing bail for minor crimes, and expanding the probation system.

In April 2000, the supreme court upheld a December 1999 St. Petersburg court acquittal of former navy captain Alexander Nikitin of espionage and disclosing state secrets. In September, the presidium of the supreme court dismissed the prosecution's appeal, effectively putting an end to the case. Nikitin had been arrested in 1996 after preparing a report for a Norwegian environmental group documenting radioactive pollution caused by Russia's nuclear submarines. In November 2000, the supreme court ordered a new trial for navy journalist Grigory Pasko, who had been acquitted of treason in 1999 for his reports on the navy's nuclear waste dumping practices; no trial date was set at year's end.

Corruption throughout the government and business world is pervasive, with members of the old Soviet Communist elite having used insider information and extrajudicial means to obtain control of key industrial and business sectors. Consequently, widespread corruption remains a serious obstacle to the creation of an effective market economy and an impediment to genuine equality of opportunity. More than two years after the case was first opened, prosecutors announced in December that lack of evidence had led them to close their investigation into allegations that a Swiss firm received kickbacks to renovate the Kremlin because of lack of evidence.

In accordance with an earlier constitutional court ruling that *propiskas*, or residence permits, violate the constitution, a Moscow city court ruled in December that several provisions of Moscow's propiska system were illegal, including limiting visitor registrations to six months, rejecting children from schools if their parents are not registered, and refusing registration to visitors living in an apartment with less than 12 square meters per person. According to human rights organizations, which welcomed the decision, the propiska rules had forced thousands of people to live illegally in Moscow and led to police harassment and problems finding employment.

Women are underrepresented in government and in management positions in the business world. Domestic violence remains a serious problem, with law enforcement authorities offering little protection or assistance.

Rwanda

Polity: Dominant party (military-dominated)
Economy: Mixed statist
Population: 7,200,000
PPP: $660
Life Expectancy: 41
Ethnic Groups: Hutu (80 percent), Tutsi (19 percent), Twa [Pygmy] (1 percent)
Capital: Kigali

Political Rights: 7
Civil Liberties: 6
Status: Not Free

Overview:

In 2000, the ruling Rwandan Patriotic Front (RPF) maintained its predominant role, although there were a number of important changes in the nation's senior leadership. President Pasteur Bizimungu resigned in March and was replaced by Vice President Paul Kagame, who had already been the de facto leader of the country. A new prime minister, Bernard Makuza, was appointed. The president of the national assembly fled into exile in the United States and was replaced. At year's end, preparations were underway for municipal elections which, although non-party in nature, are supposed to be held by secret ballot, unlike local elections in 1999. The security situation remained generally peaceful, with refugee reintegration continuing to take place.

Rwanda's ethnic divide is deeply rooted. National boundaries demarcated by Belgian colonists led to often violent competition for power within the fixed borders of a modern state. Traditional and Belgian-abetted Tutsi dominance ended with a Hutu rebellion in 1959 and independence in 1962. Hundreds of thousands of Tutsi were killed or fled the country in recurring violence during the next decades. In 1990, the RPF launched a guerrilla war to force the Hutu regime led by General Juvenal Habyarimana to accept power sharing and the return of Tutsi refugees. The Hutus' chauvinist solution to claims of land and power by Rwanda's Tutsi minority, which constituted approximately 15 percent of the pregenocide population, was to pursue their elimination as a people.

The 1994 genocide was launched after the suspicious deaths of President Habyarimana and Burundian president Cyprien Ntaryamira in a plane crash in Kigali. The ensuing massacres had been well plotted. Piles of imported machetes were distributed, and death lists were broadcast by radio. A small United Nations force in Rwanda fled as the killings spread and Tutsi rebels advanced. French troops intervened in late 1994, not to halt the genocide, but in a futile effort to preserve some territory for the crumbling genocidal regime that was so closely linked to the French government.

International relief efforts that eased the suffering among more than two million Hutu refugees along Rwanda's frontiers also allowed for the retraining and rearming of large numbers of former government troops. The UN, which had earlier ignored specific warnings of an impending genocide in 1994, failed to prevent such activities, and the Rwandan army took direct action, overrunning refugee camps in the Democratic Republic of the Congo. Nearly three million refugees subsequently returned to Rwanda between 1996 and 1998. Security has improved considerably since 1997, although isolated incidents of killings and "disappearances" continue.

The government, led by the Tutsi-dominated RPF, closely directs the country's political life. In 1999, it extended the transition period after which multiparty national elections could be held for an additional four years, arguing that the move was necessary because the poor security situation in the country did not permit elections to be held. Carefully controlled, nonparty local elections were held in 1999. The region continued to be highly unstable as Rwandans and Ugandans remained deeply implicated in the civil strife of the neighboring Democratic Republic of the Congo. This climate of unrest greatly complicates efforts to improve the exercise of human rights and fundamental freedoms.

Rwanda's economy is only now reaching pre-1990 production levels. The government's intervention in the Democratic Republic of the Congo conflict has also complicated economic development. Production of Rwanda's staple crop, coffee, suffered in 1998 and 1999, and with commodity prices low, export revenue dropped precipitously.

Political Rights and Civil Liberties:

Rwandans have never enjoyed their right to democratically choose their government. The government announced in 1999 that national multiparty elections would not take place until 2003 at the earliest. The current, self-appointed government is dominated by the RPF, but also includes several other political parties. The legislature is unicameral. Comprising 70 members, it was appointed in 1994 for a five-year term by the RPF-dominated government. Its mandate was extended by the government in June 1999 for a further four years. Municipal elections that had been scheduled for October 2000 were postponed to early 2001, because of legal and administrative delays.

Rwanda's basic governance charter is the Fundamental Law, an amalgam of the 1991 constitution, two agreements among various parties and groups, and the RPF's own 1994 declaration of governance. Political parties closely identified with the 1994 massacres are banned, and parties based on ethnicity or religion barred. Several other political parties operate and participate in government. There is some Hutu representation in the government, including Prime Minister Makuza, who is from the mainly Hutu Republican Democratic Movement (MDR) party.

Constitutional and legal safeguards regarding arrest procedures and detention are unevenly applied. The near destruction of Rwanda's legal system and the death or exile of most of the judiciary has dramatically impeded the government's ability to administer post-genocide justice. To help address this problem, the government has moved ahead with preparations to revive a traditional court system, the Gacaca, where elders will preside over community trials dealing with the less serious genocide offenses. By the end of 2000 this system, which requires the election of some 256,000 judges, had not yet become operational, and some observers expressed concern about its potential for partiality or the application of uneven or arbitrary standards.

There are two concurrent tribunals with jurisdiction over those accused of the 1994 genocide. The UN has set up the International Criminal Tribunal for Rwanda (ICTR) in Arusha, Tanzania. The tribunal, similar to that in The Hague dealing with those accused of crimes against humanity and genocide in the former Yugoslavia, is composed of international jurists. As the ICTR cannot impose the death penalty, many in Rwanda oppose it, and for the same reason, those accused of serious crimes attempt to have their cases heard there.

According to a report by the UN High Commission on Refugees (UNHCR) Special Representative, while the number of prisoners had decreased slightly since 1999, lack of resources and the drought of the past year have created serious difficulties. Some of those incarcerated for common law crimes went without eating for days, while overcrowding forced prisoners to be divided into shifts for sitting and sleeping.

Rwandan media are officially censored and constrained by fear of reprisals. Journalists accused of abetting or participating in genocide have been arrested. The state controls the broadcast media, and the few independent newspapers publishing in Kigali reportedly exercise considerable self-censorship. The role of the media in Rwanda has become a contentious test case for media freedom and responsibility. During the genocide, 50 journalists were murdered, while others broadcast incitements to the slaughter.

Local nongovernmental organizations such as the Collective Rwandan Leagues and Associations for the Defense of Human Rights operate openly. International human rights groups and relief organizations are also active. Numerous clerics were among both the victims and perpetrators of the genocide. Religious freedom is generally respected.

There is serious de facto discrimination against women despite legal protection for equal rights. Economic and social dislocation has forced women to take on many new roles, especially in the countryside. Constitutional provisions for labor rights include the right to form trade unions, engage in collective bargaining, and strike. The Central Union of Rwandan Workers, which was closely controlled by the previous regime, now has relatively greater independence.

St. Kitts-Nevis

Polity: Parliamentary democracy
Economy: Capitalist
Population: 40,000
PPP: $10,672
Life Expectancy: 70
Ethnic Groups: Black (95 percent), mulatto and white (5 percent)
Capital: Basseterre

Political Rights: 1
Civil Liberties: 2
Status: Free

Overview:
Prime Minister Denzil Douglas led his St. Kitts Labor Party (SKLP) to a stronger parliamentary majority in elections held on March 6, 2000, in the island-nation of St. Kitts-Nevis, winning all 8 seats on St. Kitts, out of 11 up for grabs for the 11-member national assembly. Opposition leader Kennedy Simmonds's People's Action Movement (PAM), which hoped to oust the SKLP, by winning 3 seats in St. Kitts and forming a coalition with the winners of seats in Nevis, instead lost its only seat on the island to the SKLP, which had previously held 7 seats. In February, gang leader Charles "Little Nut" Miller, a vicious representative of the Colombian drug cartel, who allegedly smuggled a ton of cocaine into the United States in 1994, was extradited to Miami after having fought for four years to stay in St. Kitts, where he had terrorized the population.

The national government comprises the prime minister, the cabinet, and the bicameral legislative assembly. Elected assembly members, eight from St. Kitts and three from Nevis, serve five-year terms. Senators, not to exceed two-thirds of the elected members, are appointed, one by the leader of the parliamentary opposition for every two by the prime minister. The British monarch is represented by a governor-general, who appoints as prime minister the leader of the party or coalition with at least a plurality of seats in the legislature. Nevis has a local assembly composed of five elected and three appointed members, and pays for all its own services except police and foreign relations. St. Kitts has no similar body. Nevis is accorded the constitutional right to secede if two-thirds of the elected legislators approve and two-thirds of voters endorse succession through a referendum.

The center-right PAM gained power in 1980 with the support of the Nevis Restoration Party (NRP). In 1983 the country achieved independence. The PAM-NRP coalition won majorities in the 1984 and 1989 elections.

In the 1993 elections the SKLP and the PAM each won four seats, though the former won the popular vote. The Concerned Citizens Movement (CCM) took two Nevis seats, and the NRP, one. The CCM opted not to join the coalition, leaving the PAM-NRP to rule with a five-seat plurality.

Douglas, the SKLP leader, protested the new government. Violence erupted, which led to a two-week state of emergency. The SKLP boycotted parliament in 1994. The PAM government was shaken by a drug-and-murder scandal that same year, and the weakened government agreed to hold early elections.

In the July 1995 elections the SKLP won seven of eight St. Kitts seats and 60 percent of the popular vote. The PAM took the eighth St. Kitts seat and 40 percent of the popular vote. On Nevis, the CCM retained its two seats and the NRP held on to the third. Following the vote, the PAM alleged that the SKLP dismissed or demoted PAM supporters and filled their positions with SKLP supporters.

In July 1996 Nevis premier Vance Armory, reacting to St. Kitts's unwelcome move to open a government office in Nevis, announced his intention to break the 100-year-old political link between the two islands. On October 13, 1997, Nevis's five-person parliament unanimously voted for secession. However, in a referendum on August 10, 1999, secessionists won only a simple majority of the vote, falling short of the two-thirds margin required by the constitution.

The amount of cocaine passing through the Caribbean en route to the United States has reportedly doubled in recent years. St. Kitts is one of more than ten Caribbean islands to sign drug-enforcement pacts with the United States. Nevis has more than 10,000 offshore businesses, operating under strict secrecy laws, and CCM secessionists argued these were the bedrock of island strength in a global economy. However, a principal argument used against secession was that Nevis alone could not withstand the wiles of drug traffickers and money launderers. Nevis has resisted central government efforts to impose stiffer regulations (companies set up on Nevis territory need submit "no annual return or accounts") on the crime-prone financial industry.

In going into the March 2000 elections, Douglas was able to tout his government's efforts at promoting resort construction in St. Kitts, combating crime and raising public employees' salaries. Although he increased the SKLP's numbers, in Nevis the CCM won two seats and the NRP held on to the other one. The SKLP's critics claimed that the country had accumulated $192 million in debt and had failed to reinvigorate the islands' sugar economy.

Political Rights and Civil Liberties:

Citizens are able to change their government democratically. The March 6 elections were free and fair. In the run-up to the secession referendum, Douglas promised to give Nevis a bigger role in federation affairs. Constitutional guarantees regarding free expression, the free exercise of religion, and the right to organize political parties, labor unions, and civic organizations are generally respected.

Drugs and money laundering have corrupted the political system. Apart from the 1995 drug-and-murder scandal, whose three hung juries suggest jury tampering and intimidation, there are also questions regarding business relations between SKLP leaders and the known drug trafficker Noel "Zambo" Heath.

The judiciary is generally independent. However, in March 1996 when the drug-and-murder scandal came to trial, the public prosecutions office failed to send a representative to present the case. The charges were dropped, raising suspicions of a government conspiracy. The highest court is the West Indies Supreme Court in St. Lucia, which includes a court of appeals and a high court. Under certain circumstances there is a right of appeal to the Privy Council in London.

The traditionally strong rule of law has been tested by the increase in drug-related crime and corruption. In 1995, it appeared that the police had become divided along political lines between the two main political parties. In June 1997, despite concerns of its cost to a country of 42,000 people, parliament passed a bill designed to create a 50-member Special Services Unit, which received some light infantry training, to wage war on heavily armed drug traffickers. The intimidation of witnesses and jurors is a problem. The national prison is overcrowded, and conditions are abysmal. In July 1998, the government hanged a convicted murderer, ending a 13-year hiatus in executions and defying pressure from Britain and human rights groups to end the death penalty.

A number of felons deported from the United States under the U.S. Illegal Immigration Reform and Immigrant Responsibility Act of 1996 have helped to make local law enforcement agencies in the region feel overwhelmed, as was the case in St. Kitts with Charles "Little Nut" Miller. The drug lord had in 1998 threatened to kill U.S. students at St. Kitts' Ross University if he was extradited, a magistrate had twice blocked Miller's extradition, but it was approved by the high court after police stopped and searched his car, finding two firearms, ammunition, and a small amount of marijuana.

Television and radio on St. Kitts are government owned, although managed by a Trinidadian company, and there are some government restrictions on opposition access to them. Prime Minister Douglas has pledged to privatize the St. Kitts media. Each major political party publishes a weekly or fortnightly newspaper. Opposition publications freely criticize the government, and international media are available.

The main labor union, the St. Kitts Trades and Labour Union, is associated with the ruling SKLP. The right to strike, while not specified by law, is recognized and generally respected in practice. Violence against women is a problem, and there is no domestic legislation prohibiting it. Reliable reports suggest that the country's economic citizenship program, which allows for the purchase of passports through investments ranging from $200,000 to $285,000, has facilitated the illegal immigration of persons from China and other countries into the United States and Canada.

St. Lucia

Polity: Parliamentary democracy
Economy: Capitalist
Population: 200,000
PPP: $5,183
Life Expectancy: 70
Ethnic Groups: Black (90 percent), mulatto (6 percent), East Indian (3 percent), white (1 percent)
Capital: Castries

Political Rights: 1
Civil Liberties: 2
Status: Free

Overview:　St. Lucians were stunned by a New Year's Eve, 2000, attack on worshippers gathering at a church service during which an Irish nun was killed. The outrage, in which men wielding torches and clubs stormed the Basilica of the Immaculate Conception Roman Catholic Church in Castries as the faithful filled the aisles for Holy Communion, fueled tensions between St. Lucia's mainly Christian population and members of the Rastafarian movement, to which the assailants reportedly belonged. Also in 2000, Prime Minister Kenny Anthony and the ruling St. Lucia Labour Party (SLP) gave their approval for regulated casino gambling, brushing aside objections from religious groups and the United Workers Party (UWP), to seemingly focus even more of their energies on revitalizing the country's tourism trade.

St. Lucia, a member of the Commonwealth, achieved independence in 1979. The British monarchy is represented by a governor-general. Under the 1979 constitution, a bicameral parliament consists of a 17-member house of assembly, elected for five years, and an 11-member senate. Six members of the upper body are appointed by the prime minister, three by the leader of the parliamentary opposition, and two by consultation with civic and religious organizations. The island is divided into eight regions, each with its own elected council and administrative services.

The UWP government was long headed by John Compton, whose decision to retire in March 1996 was apparently linked to a number of scandals that included an alleged affair with a teenager. He had also been accused of knowing about the misappropriation of United Nations funds. Soon after his retirement announcement, his deputy both as prime minister and party leader, 72-year-old George Mallet, announced his decision to retire, clearing the way for Compton's handpicked successor, a former director-general of the Organization of Eastern Caribbean States, Vaughan Lewis. Lewis had won Mallet's vacated seat in the February 1996 by-elections. Now holding a seat, Lewis was qualified to assume the party leadership. In April, since his party won the most seats, he automatically became the prime minister.

In June 1996, upon the retirement of Governor-General Sir Stanislaus James, Mallet was sworn in as the country's fourth governor-general over protests that the post be reserved for those outside the sphere of party politics.

Opposition leader Julian Hunte also stepped down after taking third place in the February 1996 by-elections. Anthony, a former education minister, replaced him as leader of the SLP. By the end of 1996 the SLP had merged with smaller opposition parties, and Anthony led the coalition to victory in the May 23, 1997, elections. In the biggest electoral landslide in the country's history, the SLP, out of power since 1982, won 16 of 17 seats in parliament and unseated Prime Minister Lewis with a 26-year-old political newcomer.

In 1998, Compton, prime minister for 29 years and a member of parliament for 40 years, returned to lead the UWP. Unemployment, estimated at 20 percent, remains a potential source of instability. Upon taking office, Anthony began to address concerns of an electorate weary of economic distress and reports of official corruption. In 1999, his government faced a series of issues concerning the hotel and airline industries, both vital for the tourism industry. The decision in early 2000 on casino gambling paved the way for a 300-room Hyatt hotel, which is due to open in March 2001, to be the first to win a gambling license. Police said the two men held in the church attack claimed that they were Rastafarians sent by God to fight corruption in the Catholic Church; Rasta leaders, however, denounced the attack, saying it contravened their belief in peaceful coexistence.

Political Rights and Civil Liberties:

Citizens are able to change their government through democratic elections. Constitutional guarantees regarding the right to organize political parties, labor unions, and civic groups are generally respected, as is the free exercise of religion.

The competition among political parties and allied civic organizations is heated, particularly during election campaigns when one side invariably accuses the other of occasional violence and harassment.

The judicial system is independent and includes a high court under the West Indies Supreme Court (based in St. Lucia), with ultimate appeal under certain circumstances to the Privy Council in London. The constitution requires public trials before an independent and impartial court. Traditionally, citizens have enjoyed a high degree of personal security, although there are episodic reports of police misuse of force. In recent years, an escalating crime wave, much of it drug related, violent clashes during banana farmers' strikes, and increased violence in schools sparked concern among citizens. The island's nineteenth-century prison, built to house a maximum of 101 inmates, in fact houses more than 350. In 2000 the government sought to finish construction of a new $17 million prison facility in the eastern part of the island.

The media carry a wide spectrum of views and are largely independent of the government. There are five privately owned newspapers, two privately held radio stations, and one partially government-funded radio station, as well as two privately owned television stations.

Civic groups are well organized and politically active, as are labor unions, which represent a majority of wage earners. Legislation passed in 1995 restricts the right to strike. The measure provides for a fine of about U.S.$2,000 or two years in prison for inciting any person to cease performing any lawful activity on his property or on the property of another person. The government said the measure was aimed at curtailing strikes in the banana industry, which employs more than 30 percent of the workforce. Nonetheless, in October 1996, a 14-day strike took place in which banana industry workers demanded a greater role in management decisions. The strike resulted in violence, and the police used tear gas and rubber bullets to disperse crowds, seriously injuring several people.

Though there are no official barriers to the participation of women in government, they are underrepresented. A growing awareness of the seriousness of violence against women has led the government and advocacy groups to take steps to offer better protection for victims of domestic violence.

St. Vincent and the Grenadines

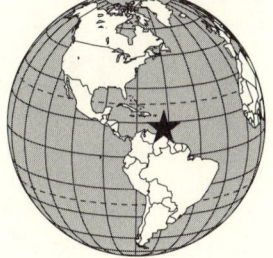

Polity: Parliamentary democracy
Economy: Capitalist
Population: 100,000
PPP: $4,692
Life Expectancy: 73
Ethnic Groups: Black (82 percent), other, including mulatto, East Indian, and white (18 percent)
Capital: Kingstown

Political Rights: 2
Civil Liberties: 1
Status: Free

Overview:

Ailing Prime Minister Sir James F. Mitchell, who had led this Windward Islands nation since 1986, relinquished the reins of government and leadership of the New Democratic Party (NDP) to Arnhim Eustace, his finance minister and chosen successor, in October 2000.

Mitchell was the second-longest-serving head of government in the Caribbean—after Fidel Castro—and had won all but one election in the ten times he stood for election. Earlier in the year a group of opposition political parties and social organizations formed the Organization for the Defense of Democracy (ODD) in response to what it called Mitchell's abuse of power and cronyism. The result was a Caricom-brokered agreement, the Grand Beach Accord, that called for new elections no later than March 2001, two years ahead of schedule, and helped to avoid further street demonstrations that Mitchell worried would damage his legacy as well as the country's record of stability.

St. Vincent and the Grenadines is a member of the Commonwealth, with the British monarchy represented by a governor-general. St. Vincent achieved independence in 1979, with jurisdiction over the northern Grenadine islets of Bequia, Canouan, Mayreau, Mustique, Prune Island, Petit St. Vincent, and Union Island.

The constitution provides for a 15-member unicameral house of assembly elected for five years. Six senators are appointed—four by the government and two by the opposition. The prime minister is the leader of the party or coalition commanding a majority in the house.

In 1994, Mitchell, the son of a seafarer who vanished in the Bermuda Triangle, won a third term as prime minister when his center-right NDP won 12 seats. The center-left alliance, comprising the St. Vincent Labour Party (SVLP), which had held power from 1979 to 1984, and the Movement for National Unity (MNU), won the remaining 3 seats. The opposition contested the results, charging that voter registration irregularities had occurred.

In 1995, Deputy Prime Minister Parnel Campbell faced charges of financial impropriety when, disregarding government regulations, he took a loan from an offshore bank. With the opposition parties, now united into the Unity Labour Party (ULP), pressing for a parliamentary vote of no-confidence, Campbell resigned. In 1998, Mitchell took advantage of internal divisions within the opposition to announce elections a year earlier than expected. Mitchell led the NDP to a narrow victory in the June 15, 1998, general elections, which were marked by opposition accusations of fraud, bribery, and intimidation. The ULP delayed its recognition of the NDP's fourth successive win and, in 1999, staged street demonstrations protesting the 1998 poll and demanding new elections.

In April 2000, passage of legislation raising the pensions of retired members of parliament set off a new round of street protests. In September, an offshore bank stripped of its government license demanded that Mitchell and six other officials return loans, gifts, and campaign contributions it alleges it gave them as payoffs, a charge Mitchell denied. A new political party, the People's Progressive Movement (PPM), was created by two former ULP members of parliament in preparation for the 2001 elections. Marijuana cultivation and narcotics smuggling remain major concerns.

Political Rights and Civil Liberties: Citizens can change their government through elections. Following the June 1998 elections, the government and the opposition began discussing constitutional reforms centering on electoral reform. The ULP claimed it would have won the contest, rather than see the NDP gallop to victory, if a proportional representation system—instead of the "first-past-the-post" framework copied from Britain—had been used. (The ULP won 7 of 15 parliamentary seats, but took 55 percent of the vote.)

The judicial system is independent. The highest court is the West Indies Supreme Court (based in St. Lucia), which includes a court of appeals and a high court. A right of ultimate appeal reports, under certain circumstances, to the Privy Council in London. Murder convictions carry a mandatory death sentence.

Penetration by the hemispheric drug trade is increasingly causing concern. There have been allegations of drug-related corruption within the government and the police force, and of money laundering in St. Vincent banks. The drug trade has also caused an increase in street crime. In 1995 the U.S. government described St. Vincent as becoming a drug-trafficking center and alleged that high-level government officials are involved in narcotics-related corruption. Since then, St. Vincent has taken steps to cooperate with U.S. antidrug trade efforts, such as signing an extradition treaty in 1996 with the United States. In December 1999, a marijuana eradication effort in St. Vincent's northern mountains stirred up controversy after U.S.-trained troops from the Regional Security System (RSS) were accused of brutality and indiscriminate crop destruction in what the Barbados-based RSS claimed was a highly successful exercise. One person, who police said was fleeing from a search scene armed with a shotgun, was killed.

Human rights are generally respected. In 1999 a local human rights organization accused police of using excessive force, illegal search and seizure, and of improperly informing detainees of their rights in order to extract confessions. The regional human rights organization, Caribbean Rights, estimates that 90 percent of convictions in St. Vincent are based on confessions.

The independent St. Vincent Human Rights Association has criticized long judicial delays and the large backlog of cases caused by personnel shortages in the local judiciary. It has also charged that the executive at times exerts inordinate influence over the courts. Prison conditions remain poor—one prison designed for 75 houses more than 400—and prisons are the target of allegations of mistreatment. Juvenile offenders are also housed in inadequate conditions.

The press is independent, with two privately owned independent weeklies—the *Vincentian* and the *News*—and several smaller, partisan papers. The opposition has charged the *Vincentian* with government favoritism. The only television station is privately owned and free from government interference. Satellite dishes and cable are available to those who can afford them. The radio station is government owned, and call-in programs are prohibited. Equal access to radio is mandated during electoral campaigns, but the ruling party takes inordinate advantage of state control over programming.

Constitutional guarantees regarding free expression, freedom of religion, and the right to organize political parties, labor unions, and civic organizations are generally respected. Violence against women, particularly domestic violence, is a major problem. Labor unions are active and permitted to strike.

Samoa

Polity: Parliamentary democracy and traditional chiefs
Economy: Capitalist
Population: 200,000
PPP: $3,832
Life Expectancy: 72
Ethnic Groups: Polynesian (93 percent), Euronesian [mixed] (7 percent)
Capital: Apia

Political Rights: 2
Civil Liberties: 2
Status: Free

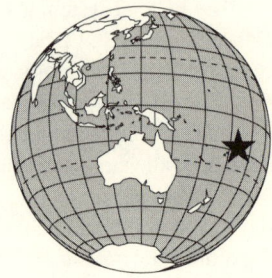

Overview: Unrest in the Solomon Islands and Fiji in the past 18 months has affected many economies in the Pacific Islands, which depend on air and shipping ports in these two countries for the international movement of goods and people. Many island leaders recognize that their own countries hold potential for conflicts rooted in ethnic rivalries, gaps in development and distribution of government services, and problems in governance. On October 30, Samoa hosted a meeting of the South Pacific Forum, a 16-member regional group, to find ways to address these issues. This was an important step forward, even if the Solomon Islands chose not to attend, since Pacific Island countries have generally been reluctant to openly discuss internal affairs.

The country consists of two volcanic islands and several minor islets located west of American Samoa in the south-central Pacific. In 1899, the United States annexed Eastern (American) Samoa, while the Western Samoan islands became a German protectorate. New Zealand occupied Western Samoa during World War II and acquired subsequent control of the territory first under a League of Nations and later a United Nations mandate. A new constitution was adopted in 1960, and on January 1, 1962, Western Samoa became the first Pacific Island state to gain independence.

The ruling Human Rights Protection Party (HRPP) has won a plurality in all five elections since 1982. At the first direct elections in 1991, Prime Minister Tofilau Eti Alesana won a third term after the HRPP secured 30 of the 47 parliamentary seats. In May 1996, the parliament reelected Tofilau for his fourth term. Under Tofilau's leadership, Samoa experienced an extended period of economic growth, and he expanded democracy by extending voting rights from only the *matai* (chiefs) to other citizens. However, corruption was widespread. In 1994, the country's chief auditor found half of the cabinet guilty of corrupt practices, but Tofilau only issued a public rebuke. Tofilau, ill with cancer, resigned in November 1998 after 16 years as prime minister. He was replaced by Tuilaepa, who had served as deputy prime minister and finance minister. In July 1998, Samoa formally changed its name from Western Samoa.

In July 1999, Luagalau Levaula Kamu, the public works minister, was assassinated at an event marking the 20th anniversary of the ruling party in the capital, Apia. This was the first political killing in Samoa since the islands gained independence from New Zealand in 1962. The murder was allegedly linked to Levaula's determination to stamp out corruption under the new administration of Prime Minister Tuilaepa. The prime minister stressed that the anticorruption drive would continue. Eletise Leafa Vitale, son of the minister for women's affairs, pleaded guilty to the killing and was given the death sentence. Toi Aukuso, former minister of communications, and women's affairs minister Leafa Vitale were also charged with conspiracy to commit murder. Although Samoa has retained the death penalty, it has never been carried out in this predominantly Christian country, and the Levaula family spoke out against the execution of Eletise. All this has sparked a debate on maintaining the death penalty. In an effort to curb violence, the government announced a gun amnesty in August 1999 to allow owners of illegal firearms one month to surrender them.

The government of Prime Minister Tuilaepa Sailele Malielegaoi continued in 2000 to combat corruption and had to answer to allegations of money-laundering activities in the islands. Public debate over the death sentence for the killer of the public works minister led Susuga Malietoa Tanumafili II, the head of state, to commute the sentence to life imprisonment. In October, the police allegedly forced 2,000 Christians out of their village. Police said they acted on court orders to evict the religious group.

Political Rights and Civil Liberties:

Samoans can change their government democratically. The 1960 constitution combines parliamentary democracy with traditional authority. However, until 1991, only the 25,000 matai, or chiefs of extended families, could sit in the unicameral parliament, *Fono Aoao Faitulafono*, and only two seats were reserved for citizens of non-Samoan descent. In a 1990 referendum, voters narrowly approved universal suffrage for parliament and increased the term from three to five years. The head of state is traditionally drawn from the four paramount chiefs and has the duty to appoint the prime minister and approve legislation. Susuga MalietoaTanumafili II is the head of state for life, but his successors will be elected by parliament for five-year terms. In rural areas, the government has limited influence, and the 360 village councils, or *fonos*, are the main authority. Several formal political parties exist, but the political process is defined more by individual personalities than strict party affiliation.

The state-owned broadcast media consist of the country's only television station and two radio stations. Both are heavily government controlled and restrict air time for opposition leaders. For example, National Development Party leader Tuiatua Tupua Tamasese Efi has been under a 15-year ban from appearing in government-owned media. In practice, however, the ban is not enforced. The government of Prime Minister Tofilau had also, on occasion, suppressed press freedom in the private media, which consist of two private radio stations, a satellite television company, several Samoan-language newspapers, and two English-language newspapers. In April 1998, Samoan journalists were ordered not to report on the proceedings of a Commission of Inquiry into the disappearance of a police file indicating that Tofilau was convicted in 1996 and fined on two counts of theft. A month later, high-ranking government officials received public funds to finance defamation suits. In this connection, *The Samoa Observer*, an independent newspaper, faced several lawsuits brought by government officials and business leaders over stories it published about public corruption and abuses of power. The government also withdrew all advertisements from the paper and Tofilau threatened to cancel the paper's business license. The paper's printing plant was burned down under suspicious circumstances and its editor assaulted by relatives of a government minister.

The matai often choose the religious denomination of their extended family in this predominantly Christian country, and there is strong societal pressure to support church leaders and projects financially. The government generally respects the right of assembly. There are two independent trade unions, plus the Public Service Association, which represents government workers. Strikes are legal, but infrequent. Collective bargaining is practiced mainly in the public sector.

The judiciary is independent, and defendants receive fair trials. However, many civil and criminal matters are handled by village fonos according to traditional law. The 1990 Village Fono Law provides some right of appeal in such cases to the Lands and Titles Courts and to the supreme court. Village fonos occasionally order houses burned, persons banned from villages, and other harsh punishments. In October 1998, five men reportedly were hog-tied, their homes were destroyed, and they were banished from the village for conducting a non-Methodist service in their village. The police force is under civilian control, but its impact is limited mostly to the capital city, while fonos generally enforce security measures in the rest of the country.

Domestic violence is a serious problem. Traditional norms discourage women from going to the police or the courts for protection, and pro-active government measures are insufficient. Women are discriminated against in employment and underrepresented in politics. The church is a powerful force in Samoan society. Some clerics have become more willing to speak out in the fight against AIDS, such as supporting the use of condoms. Although the numbers of HIV infections and AIDS cases are still low, AIDS and HIV are increasingly recognized by Samoans as a public health threat.

San Marino

Polity: Parliamentary democracy
Economy: Capitalist
Population: 30,000
PPP: na
Life Expectancy: 76
Ethnic Groups: Sanmarinese (83 percent), Italian (12 percent), other (5 percent)
Capital: San Marino

Political Rights: 1
Civil Liberties: 1
Status: Free

Overview: San Marino's current government, a centrist Christian Democratic-Socialist coalition, has ruled since 1993. The coalition returned to power after the May 1998 elections. San Marino has been governed by a long succession of coalition governments, which have dominated its modern multiparty democratic system. The three main political parties in San Marino are the Christian-Democratic Party (PDCS), the Socialist Party (PSS), and the Progressive Democratic Party (PPDS).

Founded in A.D.301, San Marino is the world's oldest and second-smallest republic. Although the Sanmarinese are ethnically and culturally Italian, they have succeeded in maintaining their independence since the fourth century. The papacy recognized San

Marino's independence in 1631. An 1862 customs union with Italy began an enduring relationship of political, economic, and security cooperation.

Despite substantial reliance on Italian assistance ranging from budget subsidies to news media, San Marino maintains its own political institutions and became a member of the United Nations in 1992. It is also a member of other major international organizations such as the Council of Europe, the World Trade Organization, the Organization for Security and Cooperation in Europe, the International Monetary Fund, and the International Labor Organization. Although San Marino has official relations with the European Union (EU), and participates in its security program, it is not a full member of the EU. In addition to agriculture, the country's vibrant, primarily private enterprise economy includes production of livestock, light manufacturing, and tourism, which constitutes 60 percent of government revenue.

San Marino's constitution, dating from the year 1600, vests legislative power in the Grand and General Council (parliament). Its 60 members are directly elected by proportional representation every five years. The secretary of state for foreign affairs has come to assume many of the prerogatives of a prime minister. Directly elected Auxiliary Councils serve as arbiters of local government in each of the country's nine municipalities. They are led by an elected captain and serve two-year terms. A ten-member Congress of State, or cabinet, is elected by the parliament for the duration of the term. Two members of the council are designated for six-month terms as executive captains-regent, one representing the city of San Marino and the other the countryside.

Political Rights and Civil Liberties:

San Marino's citizens can change their government democratically. The country has a long tradition of multiparty politics, with six parties represented in the current council. All citizens having reached the age of 18 have the right to vote. Women were permitted to stand as candidates for seats in the Grand and General Council for the first time in 1974.

San Marino has no formal asylum policy. However, it has allowed a small number of refugees to reside and work in the country. Immigrants and refugees are eligible for citizenship only after 30 years' residence. Those born in San Marino remain citizens and are able to vote no matter where they live.

The law provides for an independent judiciary, which is based on the Italian legal system. The judicial system delegates some of the authority to Italian magistrates, in both criminal and civil cases. A local conciliation judge handles cases of minor importance. Appeals go, in the first instance, to an Italian judge residing in Italy. The final court of review is San Marino's Council of Twelve, a group of judges chosen for six-year terms (four are replaced every two years) from among the members of the Grand and General Council.

There were no press freedom violations reported in San Marino in 2000. Newspapers are published by the government, some political parties, and trade unions. Italian newspapers and radio and television broadcasts are freely available. Radio Titano is the country's only privately owned radio station.

The law provides for freedom of religion, and the government respects this right in practice. Most Sanmarinese belong to the Roman Catholic Church; however, Catholicism is not the state religion. The Catholic Church does receive direct benefits from the State through income tax revenues if a taxpayer requests that 0.3 percent be allocated to the Church.

Workers are free to form and join unions under a 1961 law. Collective bargaining agreements carry the force of law. Unions may freely form domestic federations or join international labor federations. Union members constitute approximately one-half of the country's workforce. Trade unions are independent of the government and political parties; however, they have close informal ties with the parties, which exercise a strong influence on them. Freedom of association is respected. The right to strike is guaranteed, but no strikes have occurred in the last decade.

Women enjoy equal rights in the workplace and elsewhere. There have been no reports of discrimination towards women in salary or working conditions. All careers are open to women, including careers in the military and police as well as the highest public offices. Women constitute 13 percent of parliament.

São Tomé and Príncipe

Polity: Presidential-parliamentary democracy
Economy: Mixed statist (transitional)
Population: 200,000
PPP: $1,469
Life Expectancy: 64
Ethnic Groups: Mestico (Portuguese-African), African minority (Angola, Mozambique, immigrants)
Capital: São Tomé

Political Rights: 1
Civil Liberties: 2
Status: Free

Overview:	The year 2000 in São Tomé and Príncipe was marked by cabinet reshuffles and political maneuvering as officials began gearing up for presidential elections scheduled for July 2001. The leader of the ruling Movement for the Liberation of São Tomé and Príncipe-Social Democratic Party (MLSTP-PSD), Manuel Pinto da Costa, is likely to run against the incumbent, Miguel dos Anjos Trovoada. Pinto da Costa had served as president during the period of one-party rule. The winner of the election will inherit an economy dependent on foreign aid and battered by a fall in the world price of cocoa, its main export. A number of strikes disrupted the country during the year, including one by trade unions in March over the minimum wage that prompted the resignation of at least one government minister.

São Tomé and Príncipe comprises two islands approximately 125 miles off the coast of Gabon in the Gulf of Guinea. Seized by Portugal in 1522 and 1523, they became a Portuguese Overseas Province in 1951. Portugal granted local autonomy in 1973 and independence in 1975. Upon independence, the MLSTP-PSD, formed in 1960 as the Committee for the Liberation of São Tomé and Príncipe, took power, and functioned as the only legal party until a 1990 referendum established multiparty democracy. In 1991, Trovoada, an independent candidate backed by the opposition Democratic Convergence Party, became the first democratically elected president.

Parliamentary elections held in November 1998 gave the MLSTP-PSD an absolute majority. The balloting, which was conducted by an autonomous electoral commission, enabled the party to democratically regain the power that it had exercised for 16 years as the sole legal party before the country's democratic transition in 1992.

A group of demobilized army officers in 1998 threatened to take up arms against the government if promises of financial assistance and jobs for former soldiers were not met. The government then pledged to hasten restructuring of the armed forces and to seek greater assistance for the retired soldiers, many of whom had participated in an abortive and bloodless coup in 1995.

São Tomé and Príncipe is extremely poor, is struggling under a crushing debt, and has few local resources. Unemployment is endemic. The country has mostly relied on external assistance to develop its economy. Corruption is deeply entrenched. The International Monetary Fund in May 2000 approved about U.S.$8 million to support the government's 2000-2002 economic program. The government is trying to reduce its dependence on cocoa and diversify its economy. Efforts are underway to pursue offshore petroleum.

Political Rights and Civil Liberties:

The people of São Tomé and Príncipe have the right to change their government freely and fairly. Presidential and legislative elections in 1991 gave the country's citizens their first chance to elect their leader in an open, free, and fair contest. Legislative elections in 1994 were generally free and fair. The November 1998 contest, in which the MLSTP-PSD won 31 of the 55 seats in the unicameral national assembly, was apparently the country's most democratic election to date. The Independent Democratic Alliance Party, which supports President Trovoada, won 16 seats.

Trovoada had won a second five-year term in July 1996 after receiving 52.7 percent of the approximately 40,000 votes cast in a runoff election. Despite numerous allegations of vote buying and other irregularities, international observers declared the results free and fair.

An independent judiciary, including a supreme court with members designated by and responsible to the national assembly, was established by the August 1990 referendum on multiparty rule. It has ruled against both the government and the president. The court system is overburdened, understaffed, inadequately funded, and plagued by long delays in hearing cases. Prison conditions are reportedly harsh.

Constitutionally protected freedom of expression is respected in practice. One state-run and three independent newspapers are published. The state controls a local press agency and the only radio and television stations, but the national assembly, in November, approved a bill allowing for the creation of private broadcast outlets. Opposition parties receive free airtime on state-run stations, and newsletters and pamphlets criticizing the government circulate freely.

Freedom of assembly is respected. Citizens have the constitutional right to gather and demonstrate with advance notice of two days. They may also travel freely within the country and abroad. Freedom of religion is respected within this predominantly Roman Catholic country.

The constitution provides for equal rights for women, but they hold few leadership positions and encounter significant societal discrimination. Most occupy domestic roles and have less opportunity than men for education or formal sector employment. Domestic violence against women is reportedly common. Although legal recourse is available, many are either reluctant to bring legal action against their spouses or are ignorant of their rights. Women's groups, during the year, made demands through the press for greater rights.

The rights to organize, strike, and bargain collectively are guaranteed and respected. Because of its role as the main employer in the wage sector, the government remains the key interlocutor for labor on all matters, including wages. Working conditions on many of the state-owned plantations are harsh. A ten-day strike by health workers ended in November after government and union representatives reached agreement on the demands of the strikers. Education workers also staged strikes for better salaries and benefits.

Saudi Arabia

Polity: Traditional monarchy
Economy: Capitalist-statist
Population: 21,600,000
PPP: $10,158
Life Expectancy: 72
Ethnic Groups: Arab (90 percent), Afro-Asian (10 percent)
Capital: Riyadh

Political Rights: 7
Civil Liberties: 7
Status: Not Free

Overview:
Faced with its 18th straight year of budget deficits and an economy growing too slowly to sustain population growth, the Saudi ruling family introduced measures to promote foreign investment, privatize the state-dominated economy, and diversify away from dependence on oil revenue. However, declining living standards, increasing unemployment, official corruption, fiscal mismanagement, and the denial of basic political and civil rights continue to threaten social stability.

King Abd al-Aziz al-Saud consolidated the Nejd and Hejaz regions of the Arabian peninsula into the Kingdom of Saudi Arabia in 1932. His son, King Fahd Bin Abd al-Aziz al-Saud, ascended the throne in 1982 after a series of successions within the family. The king rules by decree and serves as prime minister as well as supreme religious leader. The overwhelming majority of Saudis belong to the Wahhabi sect of Sunni Islam. In 1992, King Fahd appointed a 60-member consultative council, or *Majlis al-Shura*. The Majlis plays only an advisory role and is not regarded as a significant political force. The king expanded it to 90 members, including three Shiite Muslims, in 1997.

King Fahd's poor health has raised concerns about succession. The system of fraternal succession adopted by Abd al-Aziz to prevent fratricide among his 44 sons presents the possibility that a series of aging, sickly potential rulers will leave Saudi Arabia with no direction at a time when waning prosperity requires strong leadership. Although Crown Prince Abdullah, 76, has effectively ruled since Fahd suffered a stroke in 1995, the succession after Abdullah is unclear. A 1994 decree gives the king the unilateral right to name his own successor, but philosophical and ideological rifts within the ruling family and varying degrees of power and spheres of influence among potential heirs will make any choice problematic. Of Abd al-Aziz's 25 living sons, many regard themselves as contenders, while others advocate passing power to the next generation.

Saudis have sacrificed civic freedom and political participation for material wealth, modernity, education, and a heavily subsidized welfare state in a social contract that has provided the main source of legitimacy for the government. However, economic mismanagement and lavish spending by members of the royal family, along with high population growth, pose an impending threat to this social contract. Unemployment is estimated at up to 35 percent and is expected to rise as a slow-growing job market contends with 100,000 people entering the workforce every year. Billions of dollars have disappeared in unbudgeted expenditures by royals as quality of life has declined for less affluent Saudis. While dissent has not surfaced as a threat to the regime since the early 1990s, there is concern over the decreased ability of the regime to placate citizens. A rare instance of unrest near the Yemeni border following a government crackdown on a Shiite religious minority group in April demonstrated discontent with abuses by Saudi Arabia's religious police.

The government enacted several measures this year aimed at promoting foreign investment and privatization, including tax reform and laws allowing full foreign ownership of enterprises and real estate. In April, Saudi officials began discussions with 12 international oil firms that proposed investment in projects worth up to $100 billion. A tourism authority was set up in hopes of stimulating a new industry, and a new law aimed at improving transparency bans cabinet ministers from holding top jobs in companies. However, a recent list of areas off limits to foreign investors includes insurance, media, military equipment, investment funds, and telecommunications, while many new measures designed to increase foreign investment require clarification. Moreover, despite decreases in security and defense spending, cutting subsidies to royals is seen as politically dangerous because of its potential to spark destabilizing feuds among branches of the royal family.

Three car bombs exploded in Riyadh in November and December, killing one British citizen and wounding five British and Irish nationals. No one claimed responsibility for the attacks, but many linked them to an enhanced climate of hostility toward Israel and its Western supporters resulting from the outbreak of violence between Israel and Palestinians late in the year. A Lebanese, a Belgian, and an American were reportedly held in connection with the bombings at year's end.

Political Rights and Civil Liberties: Saudis cannot change their government democratically. Political parties are illegal, the king rules by decree, and there are no elections at any level. Majlis membership is not representative of the population. A council of senior ruling family members was established in 2000 with Crown Prince Abdullah as chair. Membership includes a broad cross section of royals, including Prince Talal bin Abd al-Aziz, who has been a vocal proponent of liberalization. Noticeably absent is Interior Minister Nayef bin Abd al-Aziz, who is known for his ultra-conservative views. The apparent aim of the council is to facilitate decision making and to provide a wider power base for Abdullah in the interest of political stability.

In April, the government announced its intention to set up two human rights committees, whose responsibilities and activities are as yet unclear. Also, a United Nations investigator was invited to examine Saudi Arabia's justice system. Authorities denied that these moves came in response to criticism by international human rights monitors.

Judicial independence is undermined by the influence of the royal family and its associates. The king has broad powers to appoint or dismiss judges, and there is no standard penal or criminal code. Judges may define criminal offenses and set punishments at their discretion. The legal system is based on *Sharia* (Islamic law) and allows for corporal punishment such as flogging and amputation, which are widely practiced. Trials are routinely held in secret. Death by beheading is the prescribed punishment for rape, murder, armed robbery, adultery, apostasy, and drug trafficking. People sentenced to death are often unaware of the sentence and receive no advance notice of their execution. Some are never made aware of the charges against them. The law allows heirs of a victim to demand "blood money" in exchange for sparing the life of a murderer. At least 125 people were reportedly executed in 2000, compared with 98 in 1999 and 29 in 1998. Most of them were foreigners.

Arbitrary arrest and detention are widespread. Under a 1983 law, detainees may be held for 51 days without trial, but in practice they are often held longer. Detainees are rarely informed of their legal rights. Police routinely torture detainees, and signed confessions extracted under torture may be used, uncorroborated, as evidence. Detainees enjoy no due process safeguards or right to counsel. According to Human Rights Watch (HRW), about 400 inmates at the central prison in Al-Jawf rioted in August to protest poor prison conditions.

Freedom of expression is severely restricted by prohibitions on criticism of the government, Islam, and the ruling family. The government owns all domestic broadcast media and closely monitors privately owned but publicly subsidized print media. The information minister must approve and may remove all editors in chief. The entry of foreign journalists into the kingdom is tightly restricted, and foreign media are heavily censored where possible. The government outlawed the private ownership of satellite dishes in 1994. Internet access was made available in 1999 with filters to block information deemed pornographic, offensive to Islam, or a threat to state security. According to HRW, there are currently about 30 Internet service providers in Saudi Arabia, with some 100,000 subscribers. Authorities shut down a women-only Internet café in April for reasons of "public morality." In August, police blocked access to clubs hosted by the search engine Yahoo! because of pornographic and political content.

Political public demonstrations are prohibited, and public gatherings are segregated by sex. There are no publicly active human rights groups, and the government prohibits visits by international human rights groups and independent monitors.

Islam, particularly the Wahhabi branch of Sunni Islam, is the state religion, and all citizens must be Muslim. Shiite Muslims, who constitute about a third of the population, face systematic political and economic discrimination, such as arbitrary arrest on suspicion of subversion or pro-Iranian activities. Although accurate information is difficult to obtain, it appears that a member of the security forces was killed and several others wounded in clashes with demonstrators who protested the closure of a Shiite mosque in April. Apparently, hundreds of Shia from the Ismaili religious community took to the streets in Najran after Saudi religious police raided the mosque, seized books, and shut it down. Other accounts indicated that riots followed the arrest of a Shiite *imam* (prayer leader) and several of his followers. Scores of Shia were reportedly arrested in a crackdown following the riots. One tribal chief reported that 40 people had died in the unrest, but authorities denied the allegation. The government prohibits the practice of non-Muslim religions, but tolerates private worship.

Women are segregated in workplaces, schools, restaurants, and on public transportation, and they may not drive. They are required to wear the *abaya*, a black garment covering the head, most of the face, and the body. Officers of the Mutawwai'in, or Committee for the Promotion of Virtue and Prevention of Vice, harass women for violating conservative dress codes and for appearing in public with unrelated males. Women may not travel within or outside the kingdom without a male relative. Although they make up half the student population, women account for less than six percent of the workforce. They are not allowed to study engineering, law, or journalism. In the past two years, the issue of greater freedom for women has received wider attention. In 1999, women were issued identity cards for the first time, thus allowing them to be listed as citizens rather than as dependents on their families' cards. In 2000, a female member of the royal family was appointed assistant undersecretary at the ministry of education—the highest position ever held by a Saudi woman. In October, the government announced plans to allow women to join the police force. Businesswomen's associations are active throughout the country.

Government permission is required to form professional groups and associations, which must be nonpolitical. Trade unions, collective bargaining, and strikes are prohibited. Foreign workers are especially vulnerable to abuse, including beating and rape, and are often denied legitimate claims to wages, benefits, or compensation. They are not protected under labor law, and courts generally do not enforce the few legal protections provided to them. In a campaign to increase economic opportunities for Saudis, authorities offered an amnesty to illegal foreign workers, under which they could legalize their status or leave the country. Those remaining illegally after July 3 could be fined up to $27,000 and deported.

Senegal

Polity: Presidential-parliamentary democracy
Economy: Mixed capitalist
Population: 9,500,000
PPP: $1,307
Life Expectancy: 53
Ethnic Groups: Wolof (36 percent), Fulani (17 percent), Serer (17 percent), Diola (9 percent), Toucouleur (9 percent), Mandingo (9 percent), European and Lebanese (1 percent), other (2 percent)
Capital: Dakar

Political Rights: 3*
Civil Liberties: 4
Status: Partly Free

Ratings Change: Senegal's political rights raging changed from 4 to 3 following free and fair presidential elections that led to a peaceful transfer of power to an opposition candidate.

Overview:
Four decades of rule by the Socialist Party came to an end in Senegal when veteran opposition leader Abdoulaye Wade defeated Abdou Diouf in presidential elections in March 2000.

It was the fifth attempt by Wade, 74, of the Senegalese Democratic Party (PDS), to win the presidency. For the first time in the nation's history, the presidential poll went to a runoff. The result could influence democracy elsewhere in Africa, encouraging voters to change their perception that they are powerless against longtime leaders.

Wade promised to try to end the 18-year rebellion in the southern Casamance region, where fighting between the Movement of Democratic Forces of Casamance (MFDC) and government troops continued in 2000. Serious abuses by both sides have been reported. Wade dismissed previous negotiators in the Casamance crisis, including officials in neighboring Guinea-Bissau and The Gambia, after taking office in April, saying he would take personal charge. The government and MFDC began preliminary peace talks in December 2000.

Since independence from France in 1960, Senegal has escaped military or harshly authoritarian rule. President Léopold Senghor exercised de facto one-party rule under the Socialist Party for more than a decade after independence. Most political restrictions were lifted after 1981. Diouf succeeded Senghor in 1981 and won large victories in unfair elections in 1988 and 1993. The presidential poll in 2000 was judged free and fair by international observers.

Senegal's population is mostly engaged in subsistence agriculture. There has been steady growth in the industrial sector, but lack of open competition obstructs independent business development. Senegal, however, became the first West African country to receive a credit rating from Standard & Poor's, which placed Senegal at an equal level with Brazil and other countries in terms of economic stability in 2000.

Political Rights and Civil Liberties: The Senegalese have the right to choose their leaders freely. Voting regulations blatantly favored the former ruling party for the first three decades after independence. The party used state patronage and state media to protect its position. Changes to the 1992 Electoral Code lowered the voting age to 18, introduced secret balloting, and created a nominally fairer electoral framework. The National Observatory of Elections, which was created in 1997, performed credibly in overseeing the May 1998 legislative polls and the presidential elections in February and March 2000.

The presidential polls overturned four decades of rule by the Socialist Party. Diouf failed to win more than 50 percent of the vote in February and lost the runoff to Wade, who secured 58.5 percent of the vote, against 41.5 percent for Diouf. Eight candidates originally vied for the presidency, and opposition candidates that failed to gain enough votes in the first round of voting rallied behind Diouf.

A constitutional referendum is to be held in January 2001. If approved, the new constitution would create a semipresidential administration with greater powers for the prime minister. Legislative elections are scheduled for March 2001. The May 1998 polls returned the Socialist Party to a comfortable majority of seats in the national assembly, but also reflected a continuing slide in the party's share of the popular vote. Socialist Party candidates won 93 of 140 seats, while the PDS won 23 and Union for Democratic Renewal won 11. The election was judged by most observers to be fair, but the opposition complained of fraud, which has historically helped to ensure successive, robust, Socialist Party victories.

Poor pay and lack of tenure protections create conditions for external influence on a judiciary that is, by statute, independent. Uncharged detainees are incarcerated without legal counsel far beyond the lengthy periods already permitted by law. Muslims have the right to choose customary law or civil law for certain civil cases, such as those concerning inheritance and divorce.

In high-profile cases, there is often considerable interference from political and economic elites. International and local human rights groups criticized the Wade government in September 2000 after what appeared to be executive interference in efforts to prosecute exiled Chadian ruler Hissene Habre. A Senegalese court had indicted Habre in February on torture charges against Chadians during his eight-year rule, but the charges were later dismissed. Habre's attorney had been named as a special adviser to Wade.

Freedom of association and assembly is guaranteed, but authorities have sometimes limited this right in practice. There are credible reports that authorities often beat suspects during questioning and pretrial detention, despite constitutional protection against such treatment. Reports of disappearances in connection with the conflict in Casamance occur regularly. There are reports of extrajudicial killings by both government forces and MFDC rebels. The government rarely tries or punishes members of the armed forces for human rights abuses. Prison conditions are poor. Human rights groups, including the African Assembly for the Defense of Human Rights, working on local and regional issues, are among many nongovernmental organizations that operate freely.

Freedom of expression is generally respected, and members of the independent media are often highly critical of the government and political parties. There are at least five independent radio stations, some of which broadcast in rural areas. The government does not carry out formal censorship, but some self-censorship is practiced because of laws against "discrediting the state" and disseminating "false news."

Religious freedom in Senegal, which is 90 percent Muslim, is respected. Rivalries between Islamic groups have sometimes erupted in violence. One association, the Mourid, has often used its strong financial and political influence to back the former ruling party.

Constitutional rights afforded women are often not honored, especially in the countryside, and women have fewer chances than men for education and formal sector employment. Despite government campaigns, spousal abuse and other domestic violence against women are reportedly common. Many elements of Islamic and local customary law, particularly those regarding inheritance and marital relations, are discriminatory toward women. Although Senegal banned female genital mutilation in December 1999, it is still practiced among some ethnic groups.

Union rights to organize and strike are legally protected, but include notification requirements and can carry penalties. Nearly all of the country's small industrialized workforce is unionized, and workers are a potent political force. The National Confederation of Senegalese Workers is linked to, and provides an important political base for, the former ruling party. The National Union of Autonomous Labor Unions of Senegal, a smaller, rival confederation, is more independent.

Seychelles

Polity: Presidential-par-
liamentarydemocracy
Economy: Mixed statist
Population: 100,000
PPP: $10,600
Life Expectancy: 71
Ethnic Groups: Seychellois (mixture of Asian,
African and French)
Capital: Victoria

Political Rights: 3
Civil Liberties: 3
Status: Partly Free

Overview:
The year 2000 was a generally calm year for the Seychelles. President France Albert René and his ruling Seychelles People's Progressive Front (SPPF) party continued to exert nearly full control through a pervasive system of political patronage after being returned to power in the March 1998 elections. The government continued to implement its own homegrown form of economic liberalization.

The Seychelles, an archipelago of some 115 islands in the western Indian Ocean, was a French colony until 1810. It was then colonized by Britain until independence in 1976. The country functioned as a multiparty democracy for only one year until René, then prime minister, seized power by ousting President James Mancham. Mancham and other opposition leaders operated parties and human rights groups in exile after René made his SPPF the sole legal party. René and his party continue to control government jobs, contracts, and resources. René won one-party "show" elections in 1979, 1984, and 1989. By 1992, however, the SPPF had passed a constitutional amendment to legalize opposition parties, and many exiled leaders returned to participate in a constitutional commission and multiparty elections.

René won a legitimate electoral mandate in the country's first multiparty elections in 1993. The 1998 polls were accepted as generally legitimate by opposition parties, which had waged a vigorous campaign. The Seychelles National Party of the Reverend Wavel Ramkalawan emerged as the strongest opposition group by espousing economic liberalization, which René had resisted.

President René also heads the country's defense and interior ministries. Vice President James Michel, who also heads a number of ministries, has assumed a more prominent role in daily government affairs and has been viewed as René's likely successor. In a recent government reshuffle, however, Michel lost the portfolio of economic planning while conserving his other responsibilities as minister of finance, environment, land, and transport.

**Political Rights
and Civil Liberties:**
In presidential and legislative elections in March 1998, the Seychellois people were able to exercise their democratic right to choose their representatives. As in 1993, however, SPPF control over state resources and most media gave ruling-party candidates significant advantages in the polls. René won with 67 percent of the vote. The ruling SPPF won 30 national assembly seats. The Reverend Wavel Ramkalwan came in second in the presidential poll (19.5 percent), as did his party in the parliamentary election (3 seats).

The president and the national assembly are elected by universal adult suffrage for five-year terms. As amended in 1996, the 1993 constitution provides for a 34-member national assembly, with 25 members directly elected and 9 allocated on a proportional basis to parties with at least ten percent of the vote. Other amendments have strengthened presidential powers. Local governments composed of district councils were reconstituted in 1991 after their abolition two decades earlier.

The judiciary includes a supreme court, a constitutional court, a court of appeals, an industrial court, and magistrates' courts. Judges generally decide cases fairly, but still face interference in cases involving major economic or political actors.

Two private human rights-related organizations—Friends for a Democratic Society and the Center for Rights and Development—operate in the country along with other nongovernmental organizations. Churches in this predominantly Roman Catholic nation have also been strong voices for human rights and democratization, and generally function without government interference. Discrimination against foreign workers has been reported. Security forces have been accused of using excessive force, including torture and arbitrary detention, especially in attempting to curb crime.

Freedom of speech has improved since one-party rule ended in 1993, but self-censorship persists. There is one government daily newspaper, *The Nation*, and at least two other newspapers support or are published by the SPPF. Independent newspapers are sharply critical of the government, but government dominance and the threat of libel suits restrict media freedom. Opposition parties publish several newsletters and other publications. The opposition weekly *Regar* has been sued repeatedly for libel under broad constitutional restrictions on free expression. The government-controlled Seychelles Broadcasting Corporation, however, provided substantial coverage to opposition as well as government candidates during the last elections.

Women are less likely than men to be literate and they have fewer educational opportunities. While almost all adult females are classified as "economically active," most are engaged in subsistence agriculture. Domestic violence against women is reportedly widespread, but is rarely prosecuted and only lightly punished. Islanders of Creole extraction face de facto discrimination. Nearly all of the Seychelles' political and economic life is dominated by people of European and Asian origin. Approximately 34 percent of the total population is under 15 years of age.

The right to strike is formally protected by the 1993 Industrial Relations Act, but is limited by several regulations. The SPPF-associated National Workers' Union no longer monopolizes union activity. Two independent unions are now active. The government does not restrict domestic travel, but may deny passports for reasons of "national interest." Religious freedom is respected.

Seychelles has few natural resources and little industry. The government, however, has begun to diversify the economy and move it away from its heavy reliance on tourism, which contributed 70 per cent of foreign exchange earnings in 1998. Since the early 1990s, the government has implemented homegrown economic reforms with some progress. Government reforms include privatization of state farms, a reforestation project, and new marketing structures, as well as upgrading infrastructure and irrigation facilities for farms. The government is providing economic incentives to promote the production of bananas and mangoes and a dairy plant. Nearly all of the nation's hotels have been privatized, along with most of the tourist industry that the country relies on heavily for its foreign exchange. The fiscal deficit reached a record high of 24 percent of gross domestic product in 1998 and remained high at 17 percent in 1999. This deficit has been financed largely by domestic borrowing and drawdowns of reserves, which has resulted in a shortage of foreign exchange.

Sierra Leone

Polity: Presidential-parliamentary democracy (insurgencies)
Economy: Mixed capitalist
Population: 5,200,000
PPP: $458
Life Expectancy: 38
Ethnic Groups: Temne (30 percent), Mende (30 percent), other tribes (30 percent), Creole (10 percent)
Capital: Freetown

Political Rights: 4*
Civil Liberties: 5
Status: Partly Free

Ratings Change: Sierra Leone's political rights rating changed from 3 to 4 because those rights are barely exercised beyond the capital, with most of the countryside occupied by rebel forces.

Overview: Sierra Leone's tattered 1999 peace accord was resurrected in November 2000, which set the stage for the eventual deployment of United Nations peacekeepers throughout the countryside, including into sensitive diamond areas. However, deep mistrust of the rebel Revolutionary United Front (RUF) lingers. Its leader, Foday Sankoh, was captured by peacekeepers in May after more than 500 UN troops had been abducted and it appeared as if the country could go back to full-scale war. Sankoh reportedly has been replaced by another commander, but the RUF is divided and continues to carry out atrocities and buy weapons from neighboring Liberia, according to a UN report released in December. Sankoh could face war crimes charges now that the Special Court for Sierra Leone is being organized to address atrocities committed during the country's nearly decade-long war. Human rights abuses, including abduction, forced conscription, rape, mutilation, and summary execution continued throughout the countryside during the year.

Founded by Britain in 1787 as a haven for liberated slaves, Sierra Leone became independent in 1961. The RUF launched a guerrilla campaign from neighboring Liberia in 1991 to end 23 years of increasingly corrupt one-party rule by President Joseph Momoh. Power fell into the lap of Captain Valentine Strasser in 1992, when he and other junior officers attempted to confront Momoh about poor pay and working conditions at the front. Momoh fled the country. The Strasser regime hired South African soldiers from the security company Executive Outcomes to help win back key diamond areas. In January 1996, Brigadier Julius Maada-Bio quietly deposed Strasser. Elections proceeded despite military and rebel intimidation, and 60 percent of Sierra Leone's 1.6 million eligible voters cast ballots. In a second-round runoff vote in March 1996, Ahmed Tejan Kabbah, of the Sierra Leone People's Party, defeated John Karefa-Smart of the United National People's Party.

The following year, Major Johnny Paul Koroma toppled the Kabbah government, established the Armed Forces Revolutionary Council (AFRC), and invited the RUF to join the junta. Nigerian-led West African troops, backed by logistical and intelligence support from the British company Sandline, restored President Kabbah to power in February 1998, but the country continued to be wracked by war. Six months later, a peace agreement was signed between the government and the RUF.

The nearly 13,000-strong UN peacekeeping force, already the world's largest, has been beset by infighting and a limited mandate. The hostage crisis prompted the arrival of hundreds of British troops, who are not part of the peacekeeping force, to help train government forces and act as a deterrent to any possible attack on Freetown. In September, fighters from the rogue faction known as the West Side Boys held seven troops, including six British soldiers and one Sierra Leonean soldier, hostage. British troops stormed the camp and rescued the hostages, leading to the demise of the West Side Boys. In December, Britain announced that 300 Gurkha soldiers were to help train government troops.

Sierra Leone is potentially one of Africa's richest nations because of its vast diamond resources. However, smuggling and war have turned the country into one of the world's poorest. An international embargo imposed on uncertified Sierra Leonean diamonds has so far had little impact in bringing the war to an end. The country's economy relies heavily on foreign aid.

Political Rights and Civil Liberties: Presidential and legislative elections in February and March 1996 were imperfect, but the most legitimate since independence. President Kabbah's return to office after the AFRC's ouster reestablished representative government, although the legislative system, like most of the country's other institutions, is in disarray. Dozens of political parties have been formed, but most revolve around a personality and have little following. The RUF is now recognized as a legal political party, and its members will be allowed to contest elections.

The judiciary is active, but corruption and a lack of resources are impediments. Despite these obstacles, it has demonstrated independence, and a number of trials have been free and fair. There are often lengthy pretrial detentions in harsh conditions. Controversy surrounds the Special Court for Sierra Leone, which would try suspects under international and Sierra Leonean law. Many children have been abducted and forced to commit abuses during the war, and human rights groups are urging that fighters who had a leadership role be forced to take greater responsibility.

Human rights abuses, including abductions, maiming, rape, forced conscription, and extrajudicial killings, continue to be a widespread problem in the countryside. Human Rights Watch reported in November 2000 that the RUF and armed factions fighting on behalf of the government were responsible for ongoing atrocities against civilians. A number of national and international nongovernmental organizations operate openly in Freetown.

Freedom of speech and of the press is guaranteed, but the government at times restricts these rights. Reporters are intimidated not only by the security forces, but also by the country's various armed factions. Several government and private radio and television stations broadcast. The UN also began radio broadcasting during the year, disseminating information on humanitarian and peace issues. Dozens of newspapers are printed in Freetown, but most are of poor quality and often carry sensational or undocumented stories. Newspapers openly criticize the government and armed factions.

Fewer journalists were killed in Sierra Leone in 2000 than in 1999, when ten reporters were killed, but the country remained a dangerous place for reporters. Three journalists were killed in 2000, according to the Committee to Protect Journalists, an international media watchdog. Kurt Schork, with Reuters news agency, and Miguel Gil Moreno de Mora, of the Associated Press, were killed by rebels in an ambush outside Freetown in May. Two other Reuters journalists were wounded. Saoman Conteh, of the independent weekly *New Tablet*, was shot and killed by RUF fighters during a demonstration in May outside Foday Sankoh's home in Freetown.

Freedom of religion is guaranteed and respected in practice by the government. The rights of freedom of assembly and association are guaranteed, and these rights are generally respected in practice. A demonstration against Sankoh in May, however, was violently suppressed by RUF fighters. At least 19 people were killed.

Despite constitutionally guaranteed equal rights, women face extensive legal and de facto discrimination as well as limited access to education and formal sector jobs. Married women have fewer property rights than men, especially in rural areas, where customary law prevails. Female genital mutilation is widespread. Abuse of women, including rape, sexual assault, and sexual slavery, has escalated dramatically since the war began in 1991.

Workers have the right to join independent trade unions of their choice. About 60 percent of workers in urban areas, including government employees, are unionized. There is a legal framework for collective bargaining. No law prohibits retribution against strikers. Although the constitution prohibits forced labor, including that performed by children, rebel factions continued their practice of abducting civilians and forcing them to work as virtual slaves performing domestic duties or mining in diamond areas.

Singapore

Polity: Dominant party
Economy: Mixed capitalist
Population: 4,000,000
PPP: $24,210
Life Expectancy: 77
Ethnic Groups: Chinese (76 percent), Malay (15 percent), Indian (6 percent), other (3 percent)
Capital: Singapore

Political Rights: 5
Civil Liberties: 5
Status: Partly Free

Overview:
Saying it was time to make way for a new generation of politicians, Prime Minister Goh Chok Tong announced in April 2000 that he would step down following elections due by early 2002.

Singapore became a British colony in 1867. Occupied by the Japanese during World War II, the city-state became self-governing in 1959, entered the Malaysian Federation in 1963, and became fully independent in 1965 under Prime Minister Lee Kuan Yew. Under Lee, the ruling People's Action Party (PAP) built a welfare state and nurtured private enterprise while restricting individual freedoms. Before it lost a 1981 by-election, the PAP had won every seat in every election from 1968 to 1980. Lee resigned in 1990 in favor of his handpicked successor, Goh, now 58.

Goh has largely continued Lee's policies and maintained the PAP's dominance in parliament. With the opposition contesting only 36 of the 83 parliamentary seats in the January 2, 1997, elections, the PAP won 65 percent of the vote and 81 seats. The leftist Workers Party (WP) and the centrist Singapore People's Party each won 1 seat. However, the nine-day campaign featured a rare airing of diverse views on critical issues. Opposition calls for greater freedom of expression and criticism of rising costs of living appeared to resonate among young professionals. Goh responded by warning that neighborhoods voting against the PAP would be the lowest priority for upgrades of public housing estates, where some 85 percent of Singaporeans live. Following the election, Goh and ten other PAP leaders brought defamation charges over campaign statements made by two defeated WP candidates, party secretary-general J. B. Jeyaretnam and Tang Liang Hong. The courts ruled against both men, although the final judgments were for considerably less than the PAP leaders had sought.

Since expanding the president's powers in 1993, the government has used a strict vetting process to prevent any real competition for the office. After the Presidential Election Commission disqualified three other candidates on the grounds that they lacked the requisite competence or integrity, a PAP veteran and former ambassador, S. R. Nathan, 75, became president by default in August 1999.

While the PAP has not announced Goh's successor, an early favorite is one of Lee's two sons, Deputy Prime Minister Lee Hsien Loong. The younger Lee has taken a leading role in recent years on banking liberalization and other financial policy issues.

Political Rights and Civil Liberties:

Constitutionally, Singaporeans can change their government through elections. The 1959 constitution vested executive power in a prime minister and created a parliament that is directly elected for a five-year term. Two amendments authorize the government to appoint additional members of parliament to ensure that the opposition has at least three seats. Separately, a 1993 amendment provided for the president to be elected for a six-year term and vested the office with budget-oversight powers and some authority over civil service appointments and internal security matters.

The PAP runs an efficient, competent, and largely corruption-free administration and appears to enjoy considerable popular support. However, it limits dissent through its threats and actual use of defamation and security laws against political opponents; its control over the press; its restrictions on opposition political activities; and its use of patronage. Also limiting the opposition's success in elections is its difficulty in fielding viable slates for parliament's Group Representation Constituencies (GRC), which are multimember districts with up to six seats each. The party with a plurality in the district wins all the seats. The current parliament has 15 GRCs and only 9 single-member districts.

Notwithstanding the difficulty posed by the GRCs, the greatest constraint on Singapore's opposition is the government's use of the legal system against political foes. In recent years, courts have ruled consistently in favor of PAP members in defamation and libel suits, although they have acquitted defendants or reduced monetary damages in some cases. The pro-PAP rulings have chilled free speech, raised questions about judicial independence, and nearly bankrupted some opposition figures. Outside observers have criticized many of the rulings. For example, Amnesty International noted that a 1997 defamation conviction against WP leader Jeyaretnam was based on the alleged "innuendo" of his statement rather than on Jeyaretnam's actual words. In May 2000, the high court overturned a bankruptcy ruling against Jeyaretnam, 74, after he failed to maintain payments to an attorney on roughly $17,000 in libel damages stemming from a 1995 article. A bankruptcy ruling would have prevented Jeyaretnam from sitting in parliament.

It is difficult to determine whether the government pressures judges or whether it simply appoints judges who share its philosophy and who end up ruling in the PAP's favor. The president appoints supreme court judges on the recommendation of the prime minister with the advice of the chief justice, and appoints lower court judges on the recommendation of the chief justice. Chaired by the chief justice, the Legal Services Commission sets the terms of appointment for judges, many of whom have close ties to PAP leaders.

The government also uses the law to constrain the media and won several high-profile court cases against the press in the 1990s. A court fined two journalists and three economists in 1994 under the Official Secrets Act for publishing advance gross domestic product figures. Courts handed down contempt-of-court and libel rulings in 1995 against the *International Herald Tribune* and fined it $892,000. While foreign publications are available, authorities have temporarily restricted the circulation of *Time*, *Far Eastern Economic Review*, *The Economist*, and other publications in recent years following articles on Singapore that the government found offensive. The government took these measures under a 1986 amendment to the Newspaper and Printing Presses Act, which allows authorities to "gazette," or restrict circulation of, any foreign periodical for publishing articles allegedly interfering in domestic politics.

Moreover, most journalists work for media that are linked to the government. The privately held Singapore Press Holdings (SPH), which owns all general circulation newspapers, has close ties to the PAP. This is in part because by law, the government must approve the owners of key "management shares" in SPH. In addition, the government-affiliated Singapore International Media PTE, Ltd., operates all 4 free television stations and 10 of Singapore's 15 domestic radio stations. Four of the remaining 5 stations are operated by government-affiliated organizations. Given these constraints, journalists practice self-censorship regarding numerous political, social, and economic issues, and editorials and domestic news coverage strongly favor the PAP. Government-linked companies also provide the three Internet services and the cable television service. The government subjects movies, television, videos, music, and the Internet to censorship. However, in recent years authorities appear to have loosened their restrictions on the arts.

In this tightly controlled society, the government also prohibits discussion of sensitive racial issues and closely regulates public speech. Chee Soon Juan of the opposition Singapore Democratic Party served jail terms of 7 and 12 days in 1999 for violating the Public Entertainment Act by making a pair of speeches without licenses in December 1998 and January 1999. Chee opted to serve the sentences rather than pay fines, and alleged that on previous occasions authorities had denied or delayed granting licenses until it was too late to make arrangements to speak. In September 2000, the government inaugurated a "Speakers' Corner" in a downtown park, where Singaporeans can make public speeches without a license after registering with the police.

Under the 1966 Societies Act, the government has denied registration to groups it considers to be a threat to public order, although in 1999 it permitted opposition leaders Chee and Jeyaretnam to establish Singapore's first politically oriented nongovernmental organization, the nonpartisan Open Singapore Center. The act requires most organizations of more than ten people to be registered and restricts political activity to political parties. Despite this latter restriction, the PAP has close ties with ostensibly nonpolitical associations such as neighborhood groups, while authorities generally prevent opposition parties from forming similar groups. Freedom of assembly is restricted by regulations requiring police to approve any public assembly of more than five people.

While the government released its last political detainee held under the colonial-era Internal Security Act in 1989, it still uses the act to detain suspects in espionage and other cases. The act permits authorities to detain suspects without charge or trial for an unlimited number of two-year periods. The government also actively uses two other laws that permit detention without trial: one to detain people for alleged narcotics offenses or involvement in secret societies, the other to commit drug abusers to rehabilitation centers. A 1989 constitutional amendment prohibits judicial review of the substantive grounds of detentions under the ISA and antisubversion laws, and bars the judiciary from reviewing the constitutionality of such laws. ISA defendants also lack the right to a public trial.

While courts have jailed officers convicted of abusing detainees, police reportedly occasionally commit such abuses. Authorities use caning to punish approximately 30 offenses, including certain immigration violations.

The government generally respects freedom of religion, but continues to ban the Jehovah's Witnesses under the Societies Act on the grounds that its members refuse to perform military service. According to Amnesty International, at least 36 Jehovah's Witnesses were in prison in 1998 for conscientious objection to military service. The government also continued to bar meetings of Jehovah's Witnesses and of the Unification Church. Race riots between Malays and the majority Chinese killed scores of people in the 1960s, and the government takes measures to promote racial harmony and equity. However, Malays have not achieved the socioeconomic levels of the rest of the population and reportedly face unofficial discrimination in employment opportunities. The government has initiated programs to boost educational achievement among Malay students. Women are active in the professions but are underrepresented in government and politics.

Most unions are affiliated with the pro-government National Trade Unions Congress. The law prevents uniformed employees from unionizing. There have been no strikes since 1986, in part because labor shortages give employees considerable leverage. The labor shortages reflect the PAP's success in fostering Singapore's transformation from a low-wage economy to a regional high-technology and financial center.

Slovakia

Polity: Parliamentary democracy
Economy: Mixed capitalist
Population: 5,400,000
PPP: $9,699
Life Expectancy: 73
Ethnic Groups: Slovak (86 percent), Hungarian (11 percent), Roma (2 percent), Czech (1 percent)
Capital: Bratislava

Political Rights: 1
Civil Liberties: 2
Status: Free

Overview:

The Czech and Slovak Republics celebrated the end of their "velvet divorce" in 2000. Slovakia also began European Union (EU) accession talks, joined the Organization for Economic Cooperation and Development (OECD), intensified efforts to join NATO, and launched a national anticorruption program. The government of Prime Minister Mikulas Dzurinda survived two constitutional challenges to its power by Vladimir Meciar's Movement for a Democratic Slovakia (HZDS). President Rudolf Schuster survived life-threatening complications from surgery.

Communism in Czechoslovakia collapsed in 1989. The country held its first free elections in 1990 and began negotiations on separation into two independent states in 1991. In 1993, an independent Slovak constitution took effect and the Czechoslovak union was formally and peacefully dissolved.

Vladimir Meciar and the HZDS dominated Slovak politics until 1998. Meciar, who served three times as prime minister, battled with President Michal Kovac over executive and government powers, opposed direct presidential elections, resisted economic liberalization, and disregarded the rule of law and a free press. He is suspected of involvement in the 1995 kidnapping of Kovac's son. Under Meciar, Slovakia failed to meet the criteria for opening EU accession talks and to receive an invitation to join NATO.

In 1998, Meciar's HZDS received 27 percent of the vote and 43 seats in parliamentary elections. However, the opposition Slovak Democratic Coalition (SDK), which received 26.33 percent and 42 seats, managed to form a new government with the Democratic Left Party (SD), the Hungarian Coalition Party (SMK), and the Party of Civil Understanding (SOP). SDK leader Mikulas Dzurinda became prime minister.

Parliament failed five times in 1998 to elect a new president with a three-fifths majority. Finally, in January 1999, parliament amended the constitution and instituted popular presidential elections. Ten candidates participated in the May 1999 voting. Rudolph Schuster of the Party of Civic Understanding (SOP) defeated Meciar in the second round with 57 percent of the vote. Under Dzurinda and Schuster, Slovakia has improved judicial independence, intensified efforts to combat corruption, jump-started economic reforms, and become a candidate for membership in the EU.

In 2000, several events electrified Slovak politics but proved the constitution at work. In June, when President Schuster suffered life-threatening complications from surgery, his powers were transferred to Prime Minister Dzurinda and Parliamentary Chairman Jozef Migas. A month later, Schuster's powers were restored. The Dzurinda government survived two challenges from the HZDS—a failed no-confidence vote in April and an invalidated referendum in November on early parliamentary elections.

Corruption took the spotlight in 2000 when allegations of abuse of office touched the police, parliament, Meciar, and even Dzurinda. These accusations were balanced, in part, by the introduction of the National Program to Fight Corruption. Parliament approved laws on money laundering and freedom of access to information; the Justice Ministry launched a transparent privatization register on the Internet; and Bratislava police declared war on organized crime. By year's end, though, nongovernmental organizations had grown weary of bureaucratic delays in implementing the program.

Also in 2000, police closed their investigation into the 1995 abduction of former President Michal Kovac's son. Parliament lifted the immunity of 12 suspects, including former intelligence service chief Ivan Lexa, and prosecutors indicted them on charges of kidnapping and other crimes. In late December, though, parliament rejected legislation abolishing amnesties that Meciar granted in 1998 in connection with the case. It's unclear how this decision will affect the prosecution of Lexa and others.

Political Rights and Civil Liberties: Slovak citizens aged 18 and older can change their government democratically under a system of universal, equal, and direct suffrage. Voters elect the president and members of the unicameral National Council of the Slovak Republic (parliament).

Ten candidates competed in the 1999 presidential race. Public television channels gave equal airtime to candidates, and polling and vote counting were transparent and well organized. Rudolph Schuster, representing the SOP, defeated Meciar in the second round of voting. The Organization for Security and Cooperation in Europe (OSCE) gave the new presidential election law a positive evaluation.

Parliamentary elections in 1998 were also free and fair, but the OSCE criticized Meciar-inspired restrictions on private media and preelection coalitions. Sixteen parties participated, and six met the five percent threshold for securing seats. The HZDS lost its majority to a coalition of the SDK, the SD, the SMK, and the SOP. Parliament reversed the restrictions in 1999.

The constitution guarantees freedom of speech and bans censorship. The majority of media outlets are privately owned, and more than 80 percent of journalists belong to the Slovak Syndicate of Journalists. In June 2000, President Schuster signed a freedom-of-information law designed to increase government transparency and reduce corruption. The law takes effect in 2001. In December 2000, the controversial and pro-HZDS newspaper *Slovenska Republika* folded. After the HZDS defeat in 1998, the paper encountered difficulty attracting advertising revenue and ultimately could not overcome its debts.

The government respects religious freedom. Churches and religious organizations that register with the state receive government subsidies. In 2000, the government designated September 9th as Holocaust Victims Day of Commemoration, agreed to compensate the Jewish community for assets taken during World War II, and helped resolve a dispute between the Greek Catholic Church and the Orthodox Church over property seized from the former and transferred to the latter by the former Communist government. The government also completed a general treaty with the Vatican, but critics vowed to oppose future subtreaties that might affirm pro-Catholic views on divorce, abortion, homosexuality, and Catholic education in public schools. Approximately 60 percent of the population is Roman Catholic.

The government respects the right of persons to assemble peacefully, strike, petition state bodies, and associate in clubs, political parties, and trade unions. Judges, prosecutors, firefighters, and members of the armed forces may not strike. The Interior Ministry has identified more than 17,000 associations, foundations, and nonprofit organizations.

Minorities and ethnic groups have a constitutional right to help resolve issues that concern them. In 1999, parliament passed the Law on the Use of Minority Languages in Official Communications. In addition to Slovak, minority languages now may be used in locales where a minority group makes up 20 percent of the population. Roma continue to experience discrimination, but the Dzurinda government has taken positive steps to begin improving their situation. In 2000, 14 political parties and 29 nongovernmental organizations agreed to form a Roma coalition for the 2002 parliamentary election.

The constitution provides for an independent judiciary and a constitutional court. In 2000, nine new judges, including two ethnic Hungarians and one woman, joined the constitutional court. A United Nations envoy called the government's unsuccessful effort to fire supreme court chief Stefan Harabin "politically motivated," while the European Commission criticized some judges for perpetuating court delays, accepting bribes, and succumbing to political pressure. In July, parliament passed, in its first reading, extensive constitutional reforms designed, in part, to strengthen judicial independence, improve efficiency, and harmonize Slovak law with other Western legal systems. Final passage is expected in 2001.

Slovak citizens enjoy a range of personal rights and liberties. The government respects the inviolability of the home, the right to privacy, and the right to move and travel freely. The constitution provides protections for marriage, parenthood, and the family.

Slovakia has a market economy in which the private sector accounts for approximately 85 percent of gross domestic product (GDP). Small and medium-sized businesses alone account for 50 percent of GDP and approximately 70 percent of all enterprises. In 2000, the government sold the steelmaker VSZ, the nation's largest employer, to a U.S. concern and accelerated plans for privatization in the banking, energy, and telecommunications sectors. Despite progress in stabilizing the economy and accelerating reforms, unemployment topped 20 percent in 2000.

Slovenia

Polity: Parliamentary democracy
Economy: Mixed capitalist
Population: 2,000,000
PPP: $14,293
Life Expectancy: 75
Ethnic Groups: Slovene (91 percent), Croat (3 percent), Serb (2 percent), Muslim (1 percent), other (3 percent)
Capital: Ljubljana

Political Rights: 1
Civil Liberties: 2
Status: Free

Overview: In the year 2000—nine years after declaring independence—Slovenia established diplomatic relations with Yugoslavia and became the first transition economy in Central and Eastern Europe to graduate from the World Bank's financial and technical assistance programs. Privatization of large state enterprises and entry into the European Union (EU) and NATO remained central goals of the nation's political leaders. In April, the ruling coalition collapsed and Prime Minister Janez Drnovsek lost power following a no-confidence vote in parliament. He returned to office after his center-left Liberal Democracy of Slovenia (LDS) party proved victorious in October parliamentary elections.

Slovenia was part of the Hapsburg empire from 1335 to 1918, at which time it became part of the new Kingdom of Serbs, Croats, and Slovenes. It became a constituent republic of the Socialist Federal Republic of Yugoslavia after World War II and remained a part of Communist Yugoslavia until 1991. Since then, independent Slovenia has adopted a new constitution, held four free and fair direct elections, and undertaken important economic and political reforms.

In 1990, prior to independence, the Democratic United Opposition (DEMOS) secured victory in Slovenia's first multiparty parliamentary elections, and DEMOS leader Lojze Peterle became prime minister. Voters also elected former Communist leader Milan Kucan president. They elected Kucan the president of an independent Slovenia in 1992 and again in 1997.

After parliamentary elections in 1992 and 1996, Janez Drnovsek, the last president of the former Yugoslavia, formed center-left governments led by the LDS. In April 2000, however, Drnovsek's government collapsed when the Slovenian People's Party (SLS) withdrew and he lost a confidence vote in the national assembly. The SLS joined forces with the Slovenian Christian Democrats (SKD) and nominated Andrej Bajuk, an economist and an Argentine banker of Slovenian descent, to be prime minister. Parliament approved Bajuk after three rounds of voting.

An SLS+SKD coalition with the Social Democratic Party (SDS) proved short-lived, and Bajuk broke with the new party in August to form his own—the New Slovenian Party. He stayed in power until the October parliamentary elections, when Drnovsek's LDS won 36.21 percent of the vote and formed a coalition government with the SLS+SKD, the United List of Social Democrats (ZLSD), and the Slovenian Democratic Party of Pensioners (DeSUS). Official election results were LDS, 34 seats; SDS, 14; ZLSD, 11; SLS+SKD, 9; New Slovenian, 8; DeSUS, 4; Nationalist Party, 4; Youth Party, 4.

The European Commission (EC) announced in 2000 that Slovenia continues to make progress in meeting the requirements of EU membership. Still, the EC's annual progress report urged Slovenia to improve public administration, denationalize important sectors of the economy (including banks and utilities), and increase judicial efficiency. Slovenia hopes to join the EU in 2003 and NATO in 2002. In December, the accounting firm Pricewaterhouse Coopers named Slovenia the country most suited to join the EU based on four criteria: macroeconomic stability, productivity, infrastructure, and integration with Europe.

Political Rights and Civil Liberties: Slovenia is a parliamentary democracy with independent legislative, executive, and judicial branches of government. Voters can change their government under a system of universal, equal, and direct suffrage. They elect the president—largely a ceremonial post—and members of the 90-seat national assembly. Parliament chooses the prime minister. There is also a 40-seat national council, a largely advisory body that represents professional groups and local interests.

Elections in Slovenia are free and fair. Former Communist leader Milan Kucan has been the president since 1990. He is not eligible to run in the 2002 election. The LDS and Prime Minister Drnovsek have dominated Slovenia's post-Communist government for eight years. Drnovsek briefly lost power in 2000 to economist and center-right nominee Andrej Bajuk.

Parliament approved a new system of proportional representation in 2000. The new electoral code raises the threshold for securing seats from 3.2 percent to 4 percent and ends the use of preferential party lists for allocating seats to candidates who do not win direct mandates. This system guided parliamentary elections in October 2000, in which candidates from eight parties participated. When the LDS received a majority of the vote, it formed a new coalition government and returned Janez Drnovsek to the post of prime minister. The constitution entitles Italian and Hungarian ethnic communities to one deputy each in the national assembly.

The government respects the constitutional rights of freedom of speech, expression, and the press. Insulting public officials, however, is prohibited by law. The majority of print and electronic media are privately owned. State broadcaster Slovenia Radio-Television (RTV) has three radio stations and two television networks.

The constitution guarantees freedom of conscience and religion. In order to receive tax rebates, religious groups must register with the state. Approximately 70 percent of the population is Roman Catholic.

The government respects the right of individuals to assemble peacefully, form associations, participate in public affairs, and submit petitions. Military and police personnel may not join political parties. Workers enjoy the right to establish and join trade unions, to strike, and to bargain collectively.

Slovenia has an independent judiciary that consists of a supreme court, an administrative court, regional and district courts, and an appeals court. There is also a constitutional court. The constitution guarantees individuals due process, equality before the law, and a presumption of innocence until proven guilty. While the EU has criticized the judiciary for long court delays, it acknowledged efforts in 2000 to increase efficiency. These include the reorganization of courts, longer working hours, additions to personnel, financial incentives for increased productivity, the appointment of rotating judges to assist courts with high caseloads, and the introduction of minor offences that carry only warnings or fines.

Citizens of Slovenia enjoy many other personal rights and freedoms. These include the freedom to travel, move, and choose a place of residence; the right to privacy; the inviolability of the home; the right to health care and social security; and the freedom to work. The constitution provides special protection for marriage, the family, and children. It defines specific rights and obligations for parents.

Slovenia's gross domestic product (GDP) per capita is one of the highest in Central and Eastern Europe. The constitution guarantees—and the government respects—private property rights and free enterprise. Still, organizations like the World Bank, the European Commission, and the European Bank for Reconstruction and Development have urged Slovenia to move faster to divest itself of large state enterprises, to increase competition, and to improve the climate for foreign investment. The private sector accounts for approximately 55 percent of GDP. In January 2000, important legislation reforming the country's pay-as-you-go pension system took effect.

Solomon Islands

Polity: Parliamentary democracy
Economy: Capitalist
Population: 400,000
PPP: $1,940
Life Expectancy: 72

Political Rights: 4*
Civil Liberties: 4*
Status: Partly Free

Ethnic Groups: Melanesian (93 percent), Polynesian (4 percent), Micronesian (1.5 percent), other (1.5 percent)
Capital: Honiara
Ratings Change: The Solomon Islands' political rights rating changed from 1 to 4, its civil liberties rating from 2 to 4, and its status from Free to Partly Free, as a result of ethnic violence in the past 18 months which brought about a complete collapse of all government institutions.

Overview:
Ethnic violence between the Malaita Eagle Force (MEF) and the Istambu Freedom Movement (IFM) in the last 18 months brought about a practical collapse of all government institutions, killed more than 70 people, and ousted Prime Minister Bartholomew Ulufa'alu. New elections on June 28 elected Manassah Sogavare as the new prime minister.

In early August, Temotu, Western, and Choiseul provinces all declared themselves semiautonomous states in order to collect revenue to continue government services. A ceasefire agreement was reached later that month and signed on October 14. The conflict also crippled the island's economy and affected international commerce for other countries in the region. Guadacanal island has the country's only international airport and its two international seaports, which are region's transport hubs.

The Solomon Islands, a twin chain of islands stretching nearly 900 miles in the western Pacific, became a British protectorate in the late 1800s and an independent member of the Commonwealth in 1978.

Politics in this parliamentary system is characterized by frequently shifting partisan loyalties. In August 1997, Bartholomew Ulufa'alu, a former labor leader who headed the Alliance for Change and its dominant Solomon Islands Liberal Party, was elected the prime minister. Ulufa'alu pledged to implement public service and finance reforms to end government corruption and mismanagement. The restructuring program, which includes cutting more than 500 jobs from the oversized civil service, won his government critical support from foreign banks and aid donors. However, Ulufa'alu's government was shaken in mid-1998 by the defection of six parliamentarians. Ulufa'alu narrowly survived a vote of no-confidence in a special legislative session in September that year when the opposition was weakened by defection within its ranks.

Ethnic tensions between the Gwale people, who are natives of the island of Guadacanal, and those from the island of Malaita (60 miles away) worsened in January 1999, when Ezekiel Alebua, premier of Guadacanal, asked the government to pay his province for hosting the capital, Honiara, and suggested that people from outside the province should not be allowed to own land there. The Gwale majority has long complained that migrants from elsewhere in the Solomon Islands are taking local jobs and land. Fighting broke out in June 1999 when the IFM's lightly armed militants of the Gwale majority struck in the countryside and then moved to Honiara. The conflict caused at least six deaths and forced an estimated 25,000 Malaitans to flee from their homes or to return to Malaita. The government invited Commonwealth special envoy Sitiveni Rabuka, a former prime minister of Fiji, to mediate the conflict.

Business declined as much as 50 percent as a result of the violence. Tourism, a key source of revenue, was especially hard hit. The government declared state of emergency, and Alebua called for a media ban on statements about the ethnic unrest in his province. In July 1999, the conflict ended with the signing of the Honiara peace accord. Under the agreement, the militants agreed to disarm in return for an official review to ensure "even development" throughout the islands. On October 23, the Solomon Islands, Fiji, and New Zealand signed a peace agreement on the deployment of a multinational peacekeeping force. However, the peace process failed, and violence continued in the year 2000.

In June 2000, a coup led by MFF took over the capital, Honiara, and captured Ulufa'alu. Lawlessness ruled in the streets and militias shot at innocent people. To bring the MFF to the negotiation table, the new government of Sogavare paid $1.6 million in compensation for lost land and damaged property suffered by the Malaitans. The peace agreement includes provisions for laying down arms and establishing a ceasefire-monitoring group. Following this, a peace agreement was signed in Australia on October 14. Peace remains tenuous and the police are still unable to bring peace and order back to Honiara. To consolidate the peace process, a new Ministry of Rehabilitation, Reconstruction and Redirection will be created and premiers of the various provinces will meet to consider implementing a federal system.

Political instability has greatly reduced government revenue. Only $252 million in normal revenue is expected against a $471 million budget. Desperate for new funds, Sogavare sought additional assistance from Taiwan, even threatening to switch official diplomatic recognition to China. He also skipped the annual summit for South Pacific Island leaders in October to go instead on a fund-raising trip to East Asia.

Political Rights and Civil Liberties:

Citizens of the Solomon Islands can change their government democratically. Under the 1977 constitution, the 50-member unicameral parliament is directly elected for a four-year term. Executive power is vested in a prime minister and cabinet, and a governor-general serves as head of state. Traditional chiefs wield formal authority in local government. In July 1999, the Ulufa'alu government announced plans to amend the constitution to be more reflective of island traditions. Party affiliations are weak and based largely on personal loyalties.

The country's three private newspapers vigorously criticize government policies, but have limited circulation outside the towns. There is a private FM radio station; the radio service of the state-owned Solomon Islands Broadcasting Corporation is the most important source of information and generally offers diverse viewpoints. The government appointed a prominent local journalist to head the SIBC in 1998. In mid-1998, an Australian television channel began broadcasting to the Solomon Islands. Curbs on the media were imposed during the state of emergency in Guadacanal in 1999, and the government was slow in lifting them even after ending the emergency.

Religious freedom is respected in this predominantly Christian country. Freedom of assembly is also respected in practice. Although public assembly requires a government permit, none has been denied for political reasons. The law recognizes the right of workers to form and join unions and to strike. Approximately 10 to 15 percent of the population are employed in the wage economy, and about 60 to 70 percent of those are organized in trade unions. Disputes are usually referred to the independent Trade Disputes Panel for arbitration. Unions frequently exercise their right to bargain collectively. In July 1998, the Public Employees Union initiated a strike following the government's refusal to negotiate plans for downsizing the country's large public sector.

The judiciary is independent, and procedural safeguards are adequate, with a right of ultimate appeal in certain circumstances to the Privy Council in London. The constitution provides for an ombudsman's office to investigate claims of unfair treatment by the authorities, but its effectiveness is limited in practice by a lack of resources. There have been occasional reports of police abusing suspects. The government replaced the Police Field Force, a paramilitary unit, with regular police. In 1999, the Ulufa'alu government appointed a Maori from New Zealand as the new police commissioner to "delocalize" several senior government positions.

Citizens are free to travel domestically and overseas. Women face discrimination in education and employment opportunities. Critics have demanded greater government efforts to address domestic violence. Concern about AIDS has increased although the country has only one HIV-positive case reported and no AIDS cases.

Somalia

Polity: Presidential-par-
liamentary (transitional)
(insurgencies)
Economy: Mixed statist
Population: 7,300,000
PPP: na
Life Expectancy: 46

Political Rights: 6*
Civil Liberties: 7
Status: Not Free

Ethnic Groups: Somali (85 percent), other, including
Bantu and Arab (15 percent)
Capital: Mogadishu
Ratings Change: Somalia's political rights rating changed from 7 to 6 following the
election of a president and national assembly through peace talks held in Djibouti.

Overview:

A decade without a government in Somalia ended in August
2000, when representatives from civic and religious organizations, women's groups, and clans came together to elect a
president and parliament. The Inter-Governmental Authority for Development, as the
grassroots-inspired congress was called, voted for the 245 members of the Transitional
National Assembly, or parliament. Members of parliament then elected President
Abdiqassim Salad Hassan, 58, a former government minister and member of the Hawiye
clan, as the country's first president since the overthrow of General Mohammed Siad
Barre in 1991. The congress that elected Somalia's new government came out of peace
talks hosted by Djibouti.

Somalia, a Horn of Africa nation, has been wracked for more than a decade by
civil war, clan fighting, and natural disasters ranging from drought to flood to famine.
Extensive television coverage of famine and civil strife that took approximately 300,000
lives in 1991 and 1992 prompted a U.S.-led international intervention. The armed humanitarian mission in late 1992 quelled clan combat long enough to stop the famine,
but ended in urban guerrilla warfare against Somali militias. The last international forces
withdrew in March 1995 after the casualty count reached the thousands. Approximately
100 peacekeepers, including 18 U.S. soldiers, were killed. The $4 billion United Na-
tions intervention effort had little lasting impact.

Somalia gained independence in July 1960 with the union of British Somaliland
and territories to the south that had been an Italian colony. Other ethnic-Somali-inhab-
ited lands are now part of Djibouti, Ethiopia, and Kenya. General Siad Barre seized
power in 1969 and increasingly employed divisive clan politics to maintain power. Civil
war, starvation, banditry, and brutality have wracked Somalia since the struggle to topple
Barre began in the late 1980s. When Barre was deposed in January 1991, power was
claimed and contested by heavily armed guerilla movements and militias based on traditional ethnic and clan loyalties.

Although armed factions in Mogadishu still pose a threat, their power has diminished considerably because even their most ardent supporters seemed to realize they
had nothing to offer. This was clear when more than 120,000 people in the destroyed
capital, Mogadishu, turned out to welcome the new president. A government security

force was cobbled together from members of the former administration's military, the police, and militias to help deal with the threat of militia leaders. In November, a member of parliament was shot dead in front of his wife and children. The security situation, however, has improved considerably. No group controls more than a fraction of the country's territory. All of the country's warlords reject the government, but they are weaker than they have ever been. Banditry remains endemic.

Somalia's dollar economy hardly functions on a formal level. The private sector, however, is growing rapidly among those who are prepared to pay the high overhead costs associated with a country that lacks basic infrastructure, including running water and electricity.

Political Rights and Civil Liberties:

The elections in 2000 marked the first time Somalis have had an opportunity to choose their government on a somewhat national basis since 1969. Insecurity prevails in the countryside, preventing a popular vote from taking place. However, 3,000 representatives of civic and religious organizations, women's groups, and clans came together as the Inter-Governmental Authority for Development to elect a president and parliament in August. More than 20 candidates contested the first round of voting for the presidency. Four candidates began the second round, but one dropped out. In the third round, Abdiqassim Salad Hassan beat his closest rival, Abdullahi Ahmed Addow, by 145 votes to 92, easily getting more than the simple majority of 123 votes required. The Inter-Governmental Authority chose the lawyers who drafted the country's new charter.

The local administrations in Somaliland and Puntland, which rejected Somalia's peace process, have conducted some form of elections and installed apparently stable governments with functioning legislative arms and courts. In vast areas of the countryside, however, rival clan warlords still rule by force of arms.

Somalia's new charter provides for an independent judiciary, although a formal judicial system has ceased to exist. Islamic courts operating in Mogadishu have been effective in bringing a semblance of law and order to the city. Most of the courts are aligned with various subclans. Prison conditions are harsh in some areas, but improvements are under way.

Human rights abuses, including extrajudicial killings, torture, beatings, and arbitrary detention by Somalia's various armed factions, remain a problem, but security has improved markedly compared with previous years. Few politically motivated killings, disappearances, or incidents of torture were reported. Most violations are linked to banditry. Several international aid organizations, women's groups, and local human rights groups operate in the country.

Somalia's charter provides for press freedom. Independent radio and television stations have proliferated, including Horn Afrik, which provided live coverage of the Djibouti peace talks. Most of the independent newspapers or newsletters that circulate in Mogadishu are linked to one faction or another. Journalists face harassment; however, most receive the protection of the clan behind their publication.

The Republic of Somaliland has exercised de facto independence since May 1991. A clan conference led to a peace accord among its clan factions in 1997, establishing a presidency and bicameral parliament with proportional clan representation. Political parties are banned. Somaliland is far more cohesive than the rest of the country, although reports of some human rights abuses persist. Puntland was established as a regional government in 1998, with a presidency and a single-chamber quasi legislature known as the Council of Elders. Political parties are banned. The governor of the Hiiraan region in south-central Somalia announced in December that an autonomous regional government had been set up in Hiiraan. He said its structure would be similar to those of Somaliland and Puntland.

Although more than 80 percent of Somalis share a common ethnic heritage, religion, and nomadic-influenced culture, discrimination is widespread. Clans exclude one another from participation in social and political life. Minority clans are harassed, intimidated, and abused by armed gunmen. Clan rivalry often escalates into violence and has been responsible for the past decade of lawlessness.

Somalia is an Islamic state, and religious freedom is not guaranteed. The Sunni majority often view non-Sunni Muslims with suspicion. Members of the small Christian community face societal harassment if they proclaim their religion.

Women's groups were instrumental in galvanizing support for Somalia's peace process. As a result of their participation, women occupy at least 30 seats in parliament. The country's new charter prohibits sexual discrimination, but women experience such discrimination intensely under customary practices and variants of Koranic law. Polygyny is permitted, but polyandry is not. Those found guilty in the death of a woman must pay only half as much to the family as they would if the victim were a man. Infibulation, the most severe form of female genital mutilation, is routine. UN agencies and nongovernmental organizations are working to raise awareness about the health dangers of the practice. Various armed factions have recruited children into their militias.

The charter provides workers with the right to form unions, but civil war and factional fighting led to the dissolution of the single labor confederation, the government-controlled General Federation of Somali Trade Unions. Wages are established largely by ad hoc bartering and the influence of the clan affiliation.

South Africa

Polity: Presidential-parliamentary democracy
Economy: Capitalist-statist
Population: 43,400,000
PPP: $8,488
Life Expectancy: 53
Ethnic Groups: Black (75 percent), white (14 percent), mixed race (9 percent), Indian (2 percent)
Capital: Pretoria (administrative), Cape Town (legislative)

Political Rights: 1
Civil Liberties: 2
Status: Free

Overview: South Africa continues to be a powerful example of a positive democratic transition in an extremely diverse country. While its democratic political culture appears to be making progress, the country faces myriad and intractable problems of economic development and group relations. Tension has risen between the ruling African National Congress (ANC) and various groups, including the trade unions, elements of the press, traditional leaders and the white minority. President Thabo Mbeki has received increased criticism for his position on a number of issues, including his support for embattled President Robert Mugabe of Zimbabwe. Mbeki has also spent considerable political capital arguing that HIV does not necessarily cause AIDS.

Consolidation of South Africa's democratic transition continued under the new constitution that took effect in February 1997. The country's independent judiciary and other institutions that protect and promote basic rights continue to function, on balance, very well. The durability of these democratic structures, however, is uncertain in a country deeply divided by ethnicity and class, and plagued by rising crime, which has reached endemic proportions, and corruption.

The ANC leadership typically blames the former white-supremacist regime, which ruled the country from 1948 until the 1994 election, for many of the nation's ills, which also include serious economic hardship and a rocketing AIDS infection rate. This argument held particular currency in the first years after the regime change, but loses much of its potency as time passes.

South Africa's regional relations are highly sensitive and complicated. Angola continues to suffer from a civil war, and Zimbabwe has become increasingly unstable. Strife in the Great Lakes region, including the Democratic Republic of the Congo, also poses a threat to economic and political progress in the region. Former President Nelson Mandela has invested considerable time and effort into resolving Burundi's continuing civil strife.

Political Rights and Civil Liberties:

South Africans have the right, in theory and practice, to change their government. Two successful national elections have taken place since 1994. Elections for the 400-seat National Assembly and 90-seat National Council of Provinces are by proportional representation based on party lists. The National Assembly elects the president to serve concurrently with its five-year term. Local and municipal elections were held in 1995, 1996 and early December, 2000. The latter had been postponed due to continuing disagreements between the government and traditional chiefs, who fear losing power to the new authorities and the central government.

In general, the electoral process, including extensive civic and voter education, balanced state media coverage, and reliable balloting and vote counting, has worked properly. An exception is in KwaZulu/Natal, where political violence and credible allegations of vote rigging have devalued the process.

The South African constitution is one of the most liberal in the world. It includes a sweeping bill of rights. In early 2000 the parliament approved legislation outlawing discrimination on the basis of race, ethnicity, and sex. Parliament has passed more than 500 laws relating to the constitution, revamping the apartheid-era legal system.

In 2000, the cabinet endorsed a code of ethics that would require the president and national and provincial cabinet ministers to abide by standards of behavior dealing with potential and real conflicts of interest, and to disclose financial assets and gifts valued above a determined amount.

Despite its predominance, the ANC is not invulnerable. Other political parties are active and could conceivably challenge the ANC for power in future elections. The New National Party, for example, which ruled South Africa during the apartheid era, merged this year with the more liberal Democratic Party to form the Democratic Alliance.

The Truth and Reconciliation Commission has sought to heal divisions created by the apartheid regime through a series of open hearings. From 1996 to 1998, the commission received more than 20,000 submissions from victims and nearly 8,000 applications for amnesty from perpetrators. In 1998 the commission released a report on human rights abuses during the apartheid years that largely focused on atrocities by the white-minority government, but which also criticized the ANC.

More than two years after the official conclusion of the Truth and Reconciliation Commission's work on South Africa's past conflict, the commission continues to generate attention and controversy. Its amnesty committee has remained in existence to complete the task of assessing thousands of applications for amnesty from self-confessed perpetrators of human rights abuses.

The constitutionally mandated Human Rights Commission was appointed by parliament to "promote the observance of, respect for, and the protection of fundamental rights" and to "develop an awareness of fundamental rights among all people of the republic." A constitutional court has been created to enforce the rules of the new democracy. The 11-member court has functioned quite effectively and has demonstrated considerable independence. Lower courts generally respect legal provisions regarding arrest and detention, although courts remain understaffed. Efforts to end torture and other abuses by the national police force have been implemented.

Free expression in media and public discourse is generally respected. An array of newspapers and magazines publish reportage, analysis, and opinion sharply critical of the government, political parties, and other societal factors. Concerns about possible infringements on the freedom of the press, however, arose early in 2000, when the Human Rights Commission issued subpoenas to the editors of a number of leading publications to appear before an investigation into racism in the media. After receiving considerable criticism, the commission compromised, issuing "invitations" to the editors instead of legally binding subpoenas. Radio broadcasting has been dramatically liberalized, with scores of small community radio stations now operating. The state-owned South African Broadcasting Corporation is today far more independent than during apartheid, but still suffers from self-censorship.

Equal rights for women are guaranteed by the constitution and promoted by a constitutionally mandated Commission on Gender Equality. Legislation such as the Maintenance Act and the Domestic Violence Act are designed to protect women in financially inequitable and abusive relationships, and other areas of social inequity.

These laws, though a step in the right direction, nevertheless do not provide the infrastructure for their implementation. Discriminatory practices in customary law remain prevalent. In addition, the past several years have been marked by an increase in violence against women. It is estimated that every 26 seconds a woman is raped in South Africa. Violence against children is also reportedly widespread.

The breakdown of law and order is a serious problem. An estimated four million illegal firearms circulate in South Africa. Nationally police make arrests in only 45 percent of murder cases and 12 percent of robberies, compared to 70 percent and 30 percent respectively, in the U.S. In recent years South Africa has ranked first in the world in terms of the number of per capita rapes and armed robberies. Tension has also grown between elements of the nation's Muslim minority and the government. A number of self-styled vigilantes, some of them with links to criminals, have been charged with a string of violent actions, especially in the Cape Town area. In response, the government has considered constitutional changes that would limit suspects' civil rights. Racial tensions were also fanned by the airing of a videotape depicting white policemen beating suspected illegal immigrants

Rural and urban South Africans alike have fallen victim to crimes ranging from murder, rape, robbery, and assault, to racism, exploitation, theft, and corruption, which have clogged the country's judicial system. Prison conditions are characterized by overcrowding. In late 2000, the ministry of corrections was planning to release about 11,000 people charged with petty crimes who had been unable to make bail while awaiting trial. The prison system has a capacity of 100,000 but has been holding as many as 170,000.

Labor rights codified under the 1995 Labor Relations Act (LRA) are respected, and there are more than 250 trade unions. The right to strike can be exercised after reconciliation efforts. The LRA allows employers to hire replacement workers. The Congress of South African Trade Unions, the country's largest union federation, is formally linked to both the ANC and the South African Communist Party and was among the leaders of the anti-apartheid struggle. It maintained its ties to the government in 1998, despite growing unease with the ANC's economic direction. More radical unions are demanding quick redistribution of the national wealth. The ANC government has introduced several labor laws designed to protect the rights of workers, although it has taken other actions that weaken labor union positions in bargaining for job security, wages, and other benefits.

South Africa faces other serious problems, however. It has one of the fastest-growing AIDS infection rates in the world. The quality of schooling is extremely uneven. More than three-quarters of South Africa's people are black, but they share less than a third of the country's total income. The white minority retains most economic power. Corruption is a serious and growing problem. Unemployment stands at about 40 percent among blacks and 4 percent among whites; an estimated 500,000 private sector jobs have been lost since 1994. Half of the population of 41 million lives below the poverty line.

Spain

Polity: Parliamentary democracy
Economy: Mixed capitalist
Population: 39,500,000
PPP: $16,212
Life Expectancy: 78
Ethnic Groups: Spanish (72 percent), Catalan (16 percent), Galician (8 percent), Basque (2 percent), other (2 percent)
Capital: Madrid

Political Rights: 1
Civil Liberties: 2
Status: Free

Overview:

Spain suffered one of its worst years ever of separatist violence in 2000. After the Basque Fatherland and Liberty (ETA) separatist guerrilla movement ended an 18-month ceasefire in December 1999, the group stepped up its attacks in both frequency and lethality. Establishing a tough line against terrorism, center-right Prime Minister José Maria Aznar won reelection, capturing an absolute parliamentary majority. Aznar refused any resumption of negotiations with the leading Basque political group, the Basque Nationalist Party (PNV), until the PNV separated completely from the ETA. Despite the continuing violence, the government appeared to hold the allegiance of the street, with widespread peaceful civilian protests taking place during the year to condemn ETA attacks. Spain faced an immigration crisis in 2000, with tens of thousands of illegal immigrants arriving by boat from North Africa and violent clashes between Spaniards and foreign workers in the country's south. The sudden influx of immigrants was due in part to a surging economy and a lower-than-usual unemployment rate.

Spain's Basques were the first group known to have occupied the Iberian Peninsula. The country's current language and laws are based on those of the Romans, who arrived in the second century B.C. In the year 711, the Moors invaded from North Africa, ruling for 700 years.

The unification of present-day Spain dates to 1512. After a period of colonial influence and wealth, the country declined as a European power and was occupied by France in the early 1800s. Subsequent wars and revolts led to Spain's loss of its colonies in the Americas by that century's end. Francisco Franco began a long period of nationalist rule after the victory of his forces in the 1936-1939 civil war. In spite of the country's official neutrality, Franco followed Axis policies during World War II. Even with its closed economy, the country was transformed into a modern industrial nation in the postwar years. After a transitional period upon Franco's death in 1975, the country emerged as a parliamentary democracy. It joined the European Union (EU) in 1986.

In national elections held in March 2000, Prime Minister José Maria Aznar, leader of the centrist Popular Party (PP), won a resounding victory. The PP secured a parliamentary majority it had previously lacked, winning 183 out of 350 seats. The opposition Socialist Party posted its worst showing in 21 years, garnering just 34 percent of the vote and 125 seats. Surpassing all expectations at the polls, Aznar secured the firm victory with support from traditional Socialist voters. The creation of two million jobs during his first term, and other popular economic policies such as a privatization program, helped propel him to victory. By July, the opposition Socialists elected a new leader, appointing José Luis Rodriguez Zapatero, who, at 39 and espousing a "New Way" platform, is widely seen as a "Spanish Tony Blair" and the one best able to restructure the party after its devastating loss at the polls.

Terrorism dominated the political agenda in 2000. Basque separatists claimed responsibility for 23 murders during the year. The violence resumed with the ending of an 18-month-old ceasefire in December 1999 by the ETA, Europe's largest terrorist group. The Spanish government began negotiations with the ETA in 1998, with the aim of ending a conflict that has claimed approximately 800 lives since 1970. The two sides were emboldened to negotiate after witnessing the positive results of the signing of the Northern Ireland peace accords. But by November 1999, the ETA announced an end to the ceasefire, angered by what it perceived as slow progress in the talks.

Despite poll results showing only 30 percent of Basques aspiring to independence, the ETA staged some of its boldest attacks in recent memory. Politicians, judges, police officials, journalists, and moderate Basques were the targets of car bombings and execution-style murders. After the July slaying of Socialist politician Juan Maria Jauregui in Basque country, one of a dozen attacks that month, Prime Minister Aznar continued to insist on no talks with Basque separatists until the ETA declared a ceasefire. This followed widespread mass civil demonstrations denouncing the ETA and supporting the government. The political standoff appeared to widen in August, when the PNV, the leading Basque political party, refused to isolate the ETA by heeding Spanish government demands that it back out of the pact it had forged with the ETA's political wing, Euskal Herritarrok. The pact, signed in 1998, was designed to bring the ETA into the political mainstream. In September, the government carried out roundups of suspected ETA activists, including those involved with fund-raising and recruitment.

Political Rights and Civil Liberties:

Spanish citizens can change their government democratically. Spain has been governed democratically since 1977, after nearly 40 years of dictatorship under Franco and a brief transitional government under Adolfo Suarez. The country is divided into 17 autonomous regions with limited powers, including control over such areas as health, tourism, local police agencies, and instruction in regional languages. The bicameral federal legislature includes a territorially elected senate and a congress of deputies elected on the basis of proportional representation and universal suffrage. Although a law stipulates that women must occupy 25 percent of senior party posts and a feminist party has been officially registered since 1981, female participation in government remains minimal.

A Supreme Tribunal heads the judiciary, which includes territorial, provincial, regional, and municipal courts. The post-Franco constitution and 1996 parliamentary legislation established the right to trial by jury.

Freedom of speech and a free press are guaranteed. The press has been particularly influential in setting the political agenda in recent years, with national daily newspapers such as *El Mundo*, *ABC*, and *El Pais* covering corruption and other issues. A new conservative daily, *La Razon*, was launched in 1998. In addition to the state-controlled television station, which has been accused of pro-government bias, there are three independent commercial television stations. Members of the press were among ETA targets for assassination in 2000. A Spanish journalist for *El Mundo* was murdered outside his home in Basque country. Several letter bombs were also sent to journalists.

In April, five former Spanish security force members were each sentenced to more than 65 years in prison for their roles in the torture and murder of two suspected Basque separatists. They were alleged to have played a role in Spain's "Dirty War" of the 1980s, when government-funded death squads carried out numerous kidnappings and murders of suspected Basque separatists. The death squads are held responsible for 28 deaths between 1983 and 1987.

Spain lacks antidiscrimination laws, and ethnic minorities, particularly immigrants, continue to report bias and mistreatment. In particular, North African immigrants report physical abuse and discrimination by authorities and were the object of numerous attacks by Spanish civilians during the year.

Spain faced a huge influx of illegal immigrants in 2000, and a new problem on its southern Mediterranean shores. Scores of illegal immigrants, mostly North Africans, arrived by boat throughout the year, many not surviving the short, yet often treacherous, journey. Some estimates show 3,000 people drowned over the last five years while trying to reach Spain. By October, 10,000 people had tried to enter Spain illegally, double the 1999 figure for the same period. The Spanish interior ministry estimated during the year that 50,000 legal and illegal workers arrive each year, mostly from North Africa. There are approximately 150,000 undocumented people in the country. The increase in illegal immigration led to severe outbreaks of racial and anti-immigrant violence in 2000. While many immigrants do jobs most Spaniards turn down, animosity against immigrants remained high. In February Spaniards destroyed the homes of 500 North Africans working as farmers in the southern town of El Ejido.

The violence came on the heels of a late 1999 decision allowing 70,000 illegal immigrants to establish residency and to bring their dependents into the country. The law extends the same rights given to Spanish citizens in the areas of health, education, and legal services. However, in order to qualify, immigrants must prove that they have lived continuously in Spain since at least June 1, 1999.

The rights to freedom of association and collective bargaining are constitutionally guaranteed. The country has one of the lowest levels of trade union membership in the EU, and unions have failed to prevent passage of new labor laws facilitating dismissals and encouraging short-term contracting.

In 1978, the constitution disestablished Roman Catholicism as the state religion, but directed Spanish authorities to "keep in mind the religious beliefs of Spanish society." Freedom of worship and the separation of church and state are respected in practice. Spain is home to many cultural and linguistic groups, some—such as the Basques—with strong regional identities.

Sri Lanka

Polity: Presidential-
democracy
Economy: Mixed
capitalist-statist
Population: 19,200,000
PPP: $2,979
Life Expectancy: 73
Ethnic Groups: Sinhalese (74 percent), Tamil (18 percent), other (8 percent)
Capital: Colombo

Political Rights: 3
Civil Liberties: 4
Status: Partly Free

Overview:

Complicating her efforts to find a political solution to Sri Lanka's 17-year-old civil war, President Chandrika Kumaratunga's ruling coalition managed only a narrow victory in the October 2000 parliamentary elections. While still aiming to defeat the rebels on the battlefield, Kumaratunga had hoped that a strong election showing would allow her to pass constitutional amendments aimed at marginalizing the rebels by devolving power to minority Tamils.

Since independence from Great Britain in 1948, political power in this island-nation located in the Indian Ocean off southeastern India has alternated between the conservative United National Party (UNP) and the leftist Sri Lanka Freedom Party (SLFP). While the country has made impressive gains in literacy, basic health care, and other social needs, its economic development has been stunted and its social fabric tested by the civil war that began in 1983, which initially pitted several Tamil guerrilla groups against the government, which is dominated by the Sinhalese majority. The war came in the context of long-standing Tamil claims of discrimination in education and employment opportunities, the country's high unemployment rate, and a series of anti-Tamil riots pre-dating independence. By 1986, the Liberation Tigers of Tamil Eelam (LTTE), which called for an independent Tamil homeland in the Northern and Eastern Provinces, had eliminated most rival Tamil guerrilla groups and controlled much of the northern Jaffna Peninsula.

In a failed effort to disarm the LTTE, a UNP government brought in an Indian peacekeeping force between 1987 and 1990. By 1987, the government was also fighting an insurgency in the south by the Marxist, Sinhalese-based People's Liberation Front (JVP). The JVP insurgency, and the brutal methods used by the army and military-backed death squads to quell it in 1990, killed 60,000 people. A 1971 JVP insurgency had killed some 20,000 people.

As the civil war between the government and the LTTE continued, a suspected LTTE suicide bomber assassinated President Ranasinghe Premadasa in 1993. In 1994, Kumaratunga ended nearly two decades of UNP rule by leading an SLFP-dominated People's Alliance coalition to victory in parliamentary elections, and then won the presidential election against the widow of the UNP's original candidate, whom the LTTE had assassinated.

Early in her term, Kumaratunga tried unsuccessfully to negotiate a peace agreement with the LTTE. Since then, she has pursued a military solution while trying to pass constitutional amendments that would devolve power to eight semiautonomous regional councils, including one covering the contested north and east where Tamils would be in a majority. Yet Kumaratunga has been unable to enact the constitutional reforms because her coalition has neither the necessary two-thirds parliamentary majority nor enough support from opposition parties. The UNP, leftist parties, and the influential Buddhist clergy claim the proposals would lead to an independent Tamil state, while mainstream Tamil-based parties say the amendments do not offer Tamils enough autonomy. Meanwhile, the army recaptured the Jaffna Peninsula in 1996, but it suffered major losses in the northern Vanni jungle in 1998 and 1999 and lost much of Jaffna to the rebels in 2000.

Having made the amendments a centerpiece of her campaign, Kumaratunga won the early presidential elections on December 21, 1999. Under an estimated 73 percent turnout, the president took 51.12 percent of the vote against 42.71 percent for the UNP's Ranil Wickremasinghe, who had called for unconditional negotiations with the LTTE. Three days before the vote, separate bombings at PA and UNP rallies killed at least 38 people and slightly wounded Kumaratunga.

Although the PA won the most seats in the October 10, 2000, parliamentary elections, it failed to win a majority and will be able to pass the constitutional amendments only if it gains the UNP's support. Under a 70 percent turnout, the PA won 107 seats; the conservative UNP, 89; the JVP, 10; the Tamil United Liberation Front, 5; the Eelam People's Democratic party, 4; and the National Unity Alliance, 4.

Political Rights and Civil Liberties: Sri Lankans can change their government through elections. The 1978 constitution vested strong executive powers in a president who is directly elected for a six-year term and can dissolve parliament. The 225-member parliament is also directly elected for a six-year term, through a mix of single-seat, simple plurality districts and proportional representation.

While elections are generally free, they are marred by irregularities, violence, and intimidation. The independent Center for Monitoring Election Violence reported incidents of murder, bombing, or fraud at 365 polling centers in nearly half of the country's 168 electoral divisions during the October 10 parliamentary elections. The organization also recorded 71 election-related murders and over 1,000 assaults, threats, and other abuses in the weeks leading up to the vote. Given these developments, a European Union monitoring team said the campaign and voting took place "in an atmosphere of violence and intimidation." However, a Commonwealth monitoring team called the overall election process satisfactory, even though it reported bias in the state-media's coverage and misuse of state resources during the campaign. Following the December 1999 presidential elections, the UNP and some independent poll monitors had accused the governing People's Alliance of some electoral fraud and harassment of voters.

While the judiciary is independent, the rule of law is weak. This has allowed security forces to commit abuses with near impunity, often facilitated by sweeping security laws. Since the civil war began in 1983, successive governments have kept all or parts of Sri Lanka under a near continuous state of emergency. After the LTTE began a major spring offensive, Kumaratunga promulgated new, stricter emergency regulations and amendments in May and extended them islandwide. Previously, the emergency regulations had mainly been in force in the north and east and in Colombo. The new emergency regulations permitted authorities to restrict press freedom; temporarily banned public meetings and processions; and permitted officials to ban organizations considered to be a threat to national security, public order, or the provision of essential services. Like the measures they replaced, the new regulations allowed authorities to hold suspects in preventive detention for up to one year without charge, with a limited right to judicial review. In addition, they removed certain safeguards relating to detention and extended, to nine months, the maximum period that authorities can hold suspects without filing charges under nonpreventive detention procedures.

According to the United States State Department, authorities detained more than 1,970 people in 1999 under emergency regulations and the Prevention of Terrorism Act, which permits officials to detain suspects without charge for 18 months. Most were released after several days or within several months. Human rights groups allege that the security laws contain inadequate safeguards for detainees and facilitate long standing practices of torture and disappearances. Amnesty International said in 1999 that "torture continues to be reported almost (if not) daily" in the context of the civil war, while police officers "regularly torture" criminal suspects and people arrested over land disputes or other private matters.

While there has been little progress in reducing acts of torture, there has been a decline in the number of reported disappearances, notwithstanding several disappearances near Vavuniya in August that were reported by Amnesty International. Security forces were responsible for at least 761 extrajudicial killings or disappearances between April 1995, when the LTTE broke a ceasefire, and the end of 1999, according to the U.S. State Department. However, more than 600 of these disappearances occurred in 1996, when the army was consolidating its hold over the Jaffna Peninsula. Some observers attribute the subsequent drop in reported disappearances to the 1998 convictions of, and death sentences handed down against, five soldiers in the 1996 murders of a schoolgirl and three others in Jaffna.

Notwithstanding these convictions, the Kumaratunga government has generally not investigated disappearances that have occurred since it came to office in 1994. However, it has established commissions that investigated and reported on earlier disappearances that occurred in the context of the civil war with the LTTE or the JVP insurgency. The government said in 1997 that three commissions established in 1994 to inquire into disappearances between 1988 and 1994 had found evidence of 16,742 disappearances, mainly committed by security forces while suppressing the JVP. The government established a fourth commission in 1998 to investigate some 10,000 cases of disappearances that occurred in 1994 or earlier that the three commissions did not complete.

In addition to torture and disappearances, soldiers, police, and state-organized civilian militia, called home guards, have also committed extrajudicial executions and rapes of alleged LTTE supporters, as well as of Tamil civilians, in reprisal for LTTE attacks that killed soldiers or Sinhalese civilians. In response to urban terrorism attacks by the LTTE, authorities continued to detain and interrogate hundreds of Tamils, most of whom were released after a few days or hours. The estimated one million internally displaced persons as well as other Tamil civilians in the north and east faced arbitrary arrest, restrictions on their freedom of movement, and other abuses by soldiers and police.

The LTTE directly controls some territory in the northern Vanni jungle and maintains de facto control over many areas in the Eastern Province. The rebels continued to be responsible for summary executions of civilians who allegedly served as informers or otherwise cooperated with the army; disappearances; arbitrary abductions and detentions; torture; and forcible conscription of children. The group raises money through extortion, kidnapping, theft, and the seizure of Muslim homes, land, and businesses, and has used threats and attacks to close schools, courts, and government agencies in nominally government-held areas in its self-styled Tamil homeland. Malnutrition reportedly remained a problem in areas of the Vanni controlled by the LTTE, despite some government food and medicine shipments.

In an effort to silence rival Tamil views, the LTTE has in recent years killed several mainstream Tamil politicians and members of government-affiliated Tamil militias. The LTTE's urban terrorism attacks in Sinhalese-majority areas in recent years have killed hundreds of civilians, including several high-ranking government officials.

As part of its war against the LTTE, the military arms the People's Liberation Organization of Tamil Eelam (PLOTE) and several other anti-LTTE Tamil militia. PLOTE has committed extrajudicial killings, disappearances, torture, arbitrary detentions, and other abuses in the Eastern Province and northern Vavuniya town. During the year, errant shelling and artillery fire killed scores of civilians in northern and eastern Sri Lanka. Overall, the civil war has reportedly killed more than 60,000 people, including many civilians.

Much of the information from the war zones is fragmentary because the government has restricted press freedom in general and coverage of the war in particular. The new emergency regulations introduced by the government in May empowered authorities to arrest journalists, ban the sale and distribution of newspapers, shut down printing presses, and exercise prior censorship on all news coverage on broadly drawn "national security" grounds. The regulations superseded more limited censorship regulations imposed in 1998 that had only applied to war-related coverage. Using its new powers, the government censored war-related articles and shut down the sole Tamil-language newspaper in Jaffna City and a printing plant that had published the pro-opposition *Sunday Leader*. On June 30, the supreme court ruled on procedural grounds that the actions of the censor had no force in law. The next day, the government reimposed censorship in a way intended to correct the procedural problems. The government temporarily lifted much of the media censorship in advance of the October elections but continued to censor most war coverage. Authorities also continued to bar journalists from traveling to the war zone.

In addition to placing broad legal restrictions on the press, the Kumaratunga administration has filed criminal defamation charges against several editors, one of whom received a two-year suspended sentence in September over a 1995 article criticizing Kumaratunga's first year in office. In addition, security forces have occasionally harassed and assaulted journalists, particularly Tamils. While private newspapers, magazines, radio, and television stations criticize officials and government policies, journalists practice some self-censorship. The government controls the largest newspaper chain—Lake House Group—two major television stations, and a radio station. Political coverage in the state-owned media favors the ruling party. Unidentified gunmen killed three journalists in 1999 and a freelance reporter for the BBC in October 2000.

Women are underrepresented in politics and the civil service. Female employees in the private sector face some sexual harassment as well as discrimination in salary and promotion opportunities. Rape and domestic violence against women remain serious problems, and authorities weakly enforce existing laws.

Some of the worst communal violence in recent years occurred in late October, when Sinhalese mobs killed 26 suspected LTTE supporters and other Tamil detainees at a government-run rehabilitation center in central Banarawela town. Following Tamil protests against the massacre, clashes between Sinhalese and Tamils in several central hill districts killed up to four people.

While it is difficult to verify claims by some Tamils that they face discrimination in education and employment opportunities, some 75,000 of the estimated one million "hill Tamils" lack citizenship and face difficulty in accessing social services. Comprising just a part of the overall Tamil minority, the hill Tamils are descendants of workers whom the British brought to Sri Lanka from India in the nineteenth century to work on plantations.

Freedom of assembly is generally respected, although both main political parties occasionally disrupt each other's rallies and political events. Religious freedom is respected. Conditions in asylums and remand homes are often extremely poor.

Except in war-affected areas, human rights and social welfare nongovernmental organizations (NGOs) generally operate freely. Trade unions are independent and engage in collective bargaining. Except for civil servants, most workers can hold strikes. However, under the 1989 Essential Services Act, the president can declare a strike in any industry illegal. President Kumaratunga has used the act to end several strikes. Employers on tea plantations routinely violate the rights of the mainly hill Tamil workforce. Government surveys suggest more than 16,000 children between the ages of 10 and 14 work fulltime. A 1998 United Nations study estimated there are 30,000 child prostitutes in coastal resort areas, although the government and NGOs offer lower figures. In its annual report for 1999, the Central Bank said that gross domestic product grew by 4.3 percent in 1999, but would have grown an additional 2 to 3 percentage points without the war.

Sudan

Polity: Presidential-parliamentary (military-dominated)
Political Rights: 7
Civil Liberties: 7
Status: Not Free
Economy: Capitalist-statist
Population: 29,500,000
PPP: $1,394
Life Expectancy: 55
Ethnic Groups: Black (52 percent), Arab (39 percent), Beja (6 percent), other (3 percent)
Capital: Khartoum

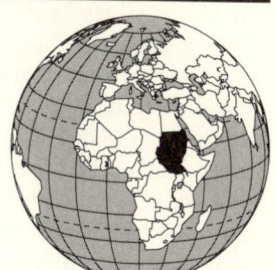

Overview:
Sudan's 18-year-old civil war continued in 2000 with no end in sight as African- and Arab-sponsored peace initiatives produced no substantial agreements. In a power struggle that

erupted in December 1999 with the dissolution of parliament and the imposition of a state of emergency, President Omar al-Bashir succeeded in sidelining the Islamist ideologue and head of the ruling National Congress (NC) party, Hassan al-Turabi. Al-Bashir spent most of 2000 consolidating his power and trying to mend diplomatic relations with neighboring states.

Africa's largest country has been embroiled in civil wars for 34 of its 44 years as an independent state. It achieved independence in 1956 after nearly 80 years of British rule. The Anyanya movement, representing mainly Christian and animist black Africans in southern Sudan, battled Arab Muslim government forces from 1956 to 1972. The south gained extensive autonomy under a 1972 accord, and for the next decade, an uneasy peace prevailed. In 1983, General Jafar Numeiri, who had toppled an elected government in 1969, restricted southern autonomy and imposed *Sharia* (Islamic law). Opposition led again to civil war, and Numeiri was overthrown in 1985. Civilian rule was restored in 1986 with an election that resulted in a government led by Sadiq al-Mahdi of the moderate Islamist Ummah party, but war continued. Lieutenant General Omar al-Bashir ousted al-Mahdi in a 1989 coup, and the latter spent seven years in prison or under house arrest before fleeing to Eritrea. Until 1999 al-Bashir ruled through a military-civilian regime backed by senior Muslim clerics including al-Turabi, who wielded considerable power as NC leader and speaker of the 400-member national assembly.

The current conflict broadly pits the country's Arab Muslim north against the black African animist and Christian south. Some pro-democracy northerners, however, have allied themselves with southern rebels, led by the Sudan People's Liberation Army (SPLA), to form the National Democratic Alliance (NDA), while northern rebels of the Sudan Allied Forces have staged attacks in northeastern Sudan. Some southern Sudanese groups have signed peace pacts with the government, and there is fighting among rival southern militias. A convoluted mix of historical, religious, ethnic, and cultural tensions makes peace elusive, while competition for economic resources fuels the conflict.

Despite a declared unilateral ceasefire, the government continued to bomb civilian and military targets, and to arm tribal militias as proxy fighting forces. Tens of thousands of people were displaced by fighting among various government and rebel factions, and international humanitarian efforts were hampered by ceasefire violations. Eleven major aid agencies, including Oxfam, CARE, and Save the Children, evacuated Sudan in March after refusing to sign an agreement with the SPLA that would have given the rebels significant control over their operations.

Peace talks hosted by Kenya under the auspices of the Intergovernmental Authority on Development (IGAD) between the government and the SPLA focused on the questions of southern self-determination, borders, and the application of Sharia in the south. Other initiatives included a joint Libyan-Egyptian plan, supported by the NDA, for a permanent ceasefire and a reconciliation process. However, neither initiative has produced significant results. In March, Ummah withdrew from the NDA, claiming that changes in the Sudanese political situation have permitted a reconciliation and a chance for Ummah to work within the political system. This move was seen as a boost for the government, as it leaves only one Muslim rebel group in the NDA. About 300 Ummah members returned to Khartoum from exile, including the party's leader, former prime minister Sadiq al-Mahdi. In September, al-Bashir traveled to Eritrea for an unprecedented meeting with exiled NDA leader Mohammad Osman al-Mirghani. They agreed to hold direct talks in the future.

The inauguration of a 950-mile oil pipeline from the Muglad basin to the Red Sea in May 1999 lent increased urgency to peace efforts. Built by a consortium of Chinese, Canadian, Malaysian, and Sudanese companies, the pipeline represents a threat to rebels, who regard it as increased government funding of the war against them. Rebels bombed the pipeline in September 1999, and fighting is reportedly more intense in oil-producing regions of the country.

Ongoing tensions between al-Turabi and al-Bashir escalated in December 1999. On the eve of a parliamentary vote on a plan by al-Turabi to curb al-Bashir's power, the president dissolved parliament, effectively neutralizing al-Turabi, and declared a three-month state of emergency. In subsequent moves to consolidate his power, al-Bashir replaced cabinet members with supporters, extended the state of emergency until the end of 2000, introduced a law allowing the formation of political parties, and called for presidential and parliamentary elections in December 2000. In May, he fired al-Turabi from his position as secretary-general of the NC, accusing him of undermining the party and harming Sudan's foreign relations. Al-Turabi and several of his deputies were barred from political activities, but al-Turabi formed his own party, the Popular National Congress, in June, and vowed to continue in politics.

Al-Turabi launched a campaign of public speeches against al-Bashir, calling the president's "coup" a detriment to democracy, accusing al-Bashir of betraying the Islamist movement, and accusing the government of rampant corruption. But al-Bashir has maintained the support of the military, opposition parties, his cabinet, the media, and regional leaders, who accuse al-Turabi of supporting radical Islamists in their own countries. Despite the fact that the Islamist nature of the government has not changed, al-Bashir was able to repair relations with several countries, including Eritrea, Saudi Arabia, Tunisia, Iran, and the United States, which resumed consular activities in Khartoum and lifted a ban on Sudanese imports of railway spare parts and foodstuffs. However, Sudan's alleged involvement in terrorism and its abominable human rights record cost it a revolving African seat on the UN Security Council in October. Members voted to grant Mauritius the seat instead.

As expected, al-Bashir and the NC won the overwhelming majority in December 2000 general elections. His challengers in the presidential race were former president Numeiri and three relative unknowns. Al-Bashir took 86 percent of the vote, while Numeiri took 9.6 percent. NC candidates stood uncontested for nearly a third of parliamentary seats, while over 100 seats are reserved for presidential appointees. Most opposition parties, including the NDA and Ummah, boycotted the polls, calling for a postponement until a political solution to the civil war is found and the constitution is reformed. Voting did not take place in some 17 rebel-held constituencies, and government claims of 66 percent voter turnout in some states were denounced as fictitious. The civil war, economic conditions, and the opposition boycott made the election irrelevant to most voters. A UN source predicted that given al-Bashir's reelection, "the situation in Sudan will remain exactly the same as it was before the election."

Political Rights and Civil Liberties: The Sudanese cannot change their government democratically. The December 2000 presidential and parliamentary elections cannot credibly be said to have reflected the will of the Sudanese people. The major opposition parties, which are believed to have the support of most Sudanese, boycotted in protest of what they called an attempt by a totalitarian regime to impart the appearance of fairness. The European Union declined an invitation to monitor the polls in order not to bestow legitimacy on the outcome. In March, Sudan adopted a law on political parties that permits any 100 eligible voters to form a political party. Parties may operate without being registered with the government, but must register in order to contest elections. Opposition groups rejected the law, saying that it maintains the government's authority to suspend party activity at will.

Serious human rights abuses by nearly every faction involved in the war have been reported. Secret police operate "ghost houses," or detention and torture centers, in several cities. As part of the government's war against Christians and African-traditional believers, armed forces routinely raid villages, burn homes, kill men, and abduct women and children to be used as slaves in the north. Though the government has not claimed responsibility for slavery in Sudan, in May 1999 it acknowledged the "problem of abduction and forced labor of women and children" and set up a committee to address it. The committee has not reported so far. Relief agencies have liberated thousands of slaves by purchasing them from captors in the north and returning them to the south. The government continued its deliberate bombing of civilian installations and relief sites, including two bombings in February and March that targeted hospitals and school children. Two CARE International relief workers were killed by rebels in an ambush in southern Sudan in January.

Although there has been no organized effort to compile casualty statistics in southern Sudan since 1994, the total number of people killed in the conflict is believed to exceed two million. According to the U.S. Committee for Refugees, some four million Sudanese were internally displaced at the end of 1999. The war's devastation has been compounded by famine and disease, much of which is man-made. Distribution of food and medical relief is hampered by fighting as well as by the government's deliberate blockage of aid shipments. A dispute between aid organizations and the SPLA resulted in the withdrawal of 11 major relief NGOs in March 2000.

The judiciary is not independent. The chief justice of the supreme court, who presides over the judiciary, is government appointed. Regular courts provide some due process safeguards, but special security and military courts are used to punish political opponents of the government. Criminal law is based on Sharia and provides for punishments that include flogging, amputation, crucifixion, and execution. Ten southern, predominantly non-Muslim states are exempt from parts of the criminal code. Security forces act with impunity, and arbitrary arrest, detention, and torture are widespread. Prison conditions do not meet international standards.

The government has gradually eased press restrictions since 1997, but journalists practice self-censorship to avoid harassment, arrest, and the closure of their publications. There are reportedly nine daily newspapers and a wide variety of Arabic- and English-language publications. All of these are subject to censorship. Penalties apply to journalists who allegedly harm the nation or economy or violate national security. A press law provision adopted in 1999 imposes penalties for "professional errors." Five journalists from the independent *As-Sahafa* daily were arrested in March for the publication of a series of articles by opponents of the regime. Editions of four dailies in Khartoum were seized for carrying statements by Hassan al-Turabi and his aides in

May. In August, one journalist was fined for defamation and one arrested for criticizing the government's handling of corruption cases. Independent journalist Mohammad Taha was apparently the victim of an assassination attempt in September after writing an article that allegedly defamed al-Turabi. The National Press Council prohibited the media from covering the attack. Broadcast media are government controlled and present only NC views. Despite restrictions on ownership of satellite dishes, citizens use them to access a variety of foreign media.

Emergency law severely restricts freedom of assembly and association. Four students were arrested following clashes with police at the University of Khartoum in April. The students were protesting a university decision to reorganize semesters. In June, one student was killed in clashes with authorities who blocked a seminar where an opposition human rights lawyer was scheduled to speak. Al-Turabi's Popular National Congress reported that dozens of its members had been arrested in various parts of the country after al-Bashir blamed the party for student protests in September that left at least three dead and many others injured.

The government treats Islam as the state religion, and the constitution claims Sharia as the source of its legislation. At least 75 percent of Sudanese are Muslim, though most southern Sudanese adhere to Christian or traditional indigenous beliefs. The overwhelming majority of those displaced or killed by war and famine in Sudan have been non-Muslims, and many starve because of a policy under which food is withheld pending conversion to Islam. Officials have used the word *jihad*, meaning a holy war against nonbelievers, to describe the government's campaign against the opposition, including forced conversion to Islam, and its policy of "depopulating" the Nuba mountains, a 30,000-square-mile area in the heart of Sudan and home to almost a million black Sudanese. Under the 1994 Societies Registration Act, religious groups must register in order to gather legally. Registration is reportedly difficult to obtain. The government denies the Roman Catholic Church permission to build churches while it destroys Christian schools, churches, and centers. Catholic priests face random detention and interrogation by police. Organizations associated with the banned Islamic Ummah and Democratic Unionist parties are regularly denied permission to hold public gatherings. Apostasy is a capital crime.

Women face discrimination in family matters such as marriage, divorce, and inheritance, which are governed by Sharia. Public-order police frequently harass women and monitor their dress for adherence to Islamic standards of modesty. Female genital mutilation occurs despite legal prohibition, and rape is reportedly routine in war zones. In September, the governor of Khartoum banned women from working in public places where they come into contact with men. The ban was suspended by the constitutional court pending a ruling on complaints from the Sudanese Women's Union and the Lawyers Union.

There are no independent trade unions. The Sudan Workers Trade Unions Federation is the main labor organization, with about 800,000 members. Local union elections in 1992 and 1997 were rigged to ensure the election of government-approved candidates. A lack of labor legislation limits the freedom of workers to organize and to bargain collectively.

Suriname

Polity: Presidential-parliamentary democracy
Economy: Capitalist-statist
Population: 400,000
PPP: $5,161
Life Expectancy: 70
Ethnic Groups: East Indian (37 percent), Creole (31 percent), Javanese (15 percent), other (17 percent)
Capital: Paramaribo

Political Rights: 1*
Civil Liberties: 2*
Status: Free

Ratings Change: Suriname's political rights rating changed from 3 to 1, its civil liberties rating from 3 to 2, and its status from Partly Free to Free, after the holding of free and fair parliamentary elections and the willingness of the government to call human rights violators into account for past crimes.

Overview:

On August 12, 2000, a former president, Ronald Venetiaan, returned to the presidency. After promising to fight corruption and speed economic development, he led his New Front for Democracy and Development coalition to a resounding victory in parliamentary elections on May 25. Venetiaan's center-right government replaced the troubled regime of Jules Wijdenbosch, who left behind a near empty treasury, 20 percent unemployment, 100 percent inflation, and a troubled legacy dating back to the days of former military strongman Desi Bourterse. The self-proclaimed "Jungle Man" Bourterse, who also stood for president, appeared to be closer to prosecution than to the presidency, after Suriname's highest court ruled that he must stand trial for his part in the 1982 massacre of some of Suriname's top political and academic leaders. The once all-powerful dictator also risked finally being brought to justice for drug trafficking, having been tried and convicted by a Dutch court in absentia on charges of having introduced more than two tons of cocaine into the Netherlands between 1989 and 1997. In late 2000, Bourterse denied reports that he was planning a coup attempt and training an army of Amerindians deep inside the country's interior.

The Republic of Suriname achieved independence from the Netherlands in 1975, which was 308 years after the Dutch acquired it from the English in exchange for the U.S. State of Delaware and the island of Manhattan. Five years after independence, a military coup, which brought Bourterse to power as the head of a regime that brutally suppressed civic and political opposition, initiated a decade of military intervention in politics. In 1987, Bourterse permitted elections under a constitution providing for a directly elected, 51-seat National Assembly, which serves a five-year term and selects the state president. If the National Assembly is unable to select a president with the required two-thirds vote, a People's Assembly, composed of parliament and regional and local officials, chooses the president. The New Front for Democracy and Development, a three-party coalition, handily won the 1987 elections. The military-organized National Democratic Party (NDP) won just three seats.

In 1990, the army ousted President Ramsewak Shankar, and Bourterse again took power. International pressure led to new elections in 1991. The New Front, a coalition of mainly East Indian, Creole, and Javanese parties, won a majority, although the NDP increased its share to 12. The National Assembly selected the Front's candidate, Venetiaan, as president.

Bourterse quit the army in 1992 in order to lead the NDP. The Venetiaan government took some constitutional steps to curb military influence and, in late 1995 and early 1996, purged several high-ranking pro-Bourterse military officials. The government's economic structural adjustment program led to social and labor unrest amidst an inflationary spiral and a collapse of the Surinamese currency.

During the campaign for the May 23, 1996, parliamentary elections, the NDP pledged to reverse many of the economic programs of the Venetiaan government. The four-party New Front lost seats, winning 24, and entered into a coalition with the smaller Central Bloc, consisting of two opposition groups. The alliance proved insufficient to gain the necessary two-thirds parliamentary majority needed to return Venetiaan to office.

Bourterse's NDP, with 16 seats, joined with the Javanese-based Party of National Unity and Solidarity and dissident members of the East Indian-based United Reform Party to press for the convening in September of the constitutionally mandated 869-member People's Assembly. The deadlock was broken when Wijdenbosch, a former deputy party leader under Bourterse, was elected president.

Protected by Wijdenbosch, Bourterse remained one step ahead of Dutch police as the Europeans sought his arrest. In late 1998, the government oversaw the takeover of Suriname's traditionally independent high court. In May 1999, massive antigovernment protests and a continuing economic crisis forced Wijdenbosch to sack his entire 15-person cabinet. Three weeks later he announced that elections would take place a year early.

In the 2000 national elections, Venetiaan's coalition won a majority of 51 National Assembly seats—three times as many as its closest rival. The new government promised to investigate all human rights violations that occurred in the past two decades, including the 1982 executions of 15 of the Bourterse regime's foremost opponents. Bourterse, who was army commander at the time of the killings, responded by saying that if he is brought up on charges he would release secrets—"all dirty"—about leaders of the new government that he apparently collected in the 1980s as the country's intelligence chief.

Political Rights and Civil Liberties: Citizens of Suriname can change their government democratically. Political parties mostly reflect the cleavages in Suriname's ethnically complex society, a factor contributing to parliamentary gridlock and, in the past, to Bourterse's popularity. A record 23 parties competed in the 2000 elections. Civic institutions remain weak.

The judiciary is weak, is susceptible to political influence, and suffers from ineffectiveness and a huge backlog of cases. The civilian police abuse detainees, particularly during arrests; guards mistreat prisoners; and the prisons are dangerously overcrowded.

In response to government plans to call Bourterse into account for the 1982 massacre—a long-standing demand of relatives of those murdered—Bourterse's allies released a letter from the former wife of the justice minister in which she tended to support claims that the minister was a bigamist, a spousal abuser, and a pedophile. In response, Bourterse, who says he has more derogatory information about other officials in his files, was sued for defamation.

The government generally respects freedom of expression. Radio is both public and private. A number of small commercial radio stations compete with the government-owned radio and television broadcasting system. State broadcast media generally offer pluralistic viewpoints.

Both indigenous and tribal peoples, the latter called Maroons—the descendants of escaped African slaves who formed autonomous communities in the rainforest in the seventeenth and eighteenth centuries—reside within Suriname's borders. Indigenous people number around 12,000 to 15,000 people (four percent of the population); Maroons number approximately 40,000 to 50,000. Their rights to their lands and resources, to cultural integrity, and to the autonomous administration of their affairs are not recognized under Surinamese law. Despite numerous attempts and agreements, all of which have been disregarded, between the state and the indigenous peoples and Maroons, this situation has not changed. A breakdown in the rule of law over the past five years, disputes between the executive and judiciary, and an absence of adequate domestic guarantees have forced the Maroons to seek protection of their rights through the Inter-American Commission on Human Rights.

Indigenous and Maroon land and resource rights are repeatedly violated: in particular, the state has granted large areas of land as concessions to logging and mining interests. These concessions were made without any form of consultation with affected village authorities and without any attempt to safeguard subsistence and other rights. Approximately 30,000 Brazilian small-scale gold miners, licensed by the state, and numerous local miners are working on indigenous and Maroon lands, causing severe environmental degradation, health epidemics (malaria and sexually transmitted diseases), and social problems. The state has made no attempt to mitigate the impact of local and multinational operators on the environment, and in general Suriname lacks environmental laws and monitoring capacity. Discrimination against indigenous peoples and Maroons is widespread in law and practice and is especially pronounced in the provision of education and health services.

Constitutional guarantees of gender equality are not enforced, and the Asian Marriage Act allows parents to arrange marriages. Human rights organizations function relatively freely. Several organizations specifically address violence against women, reports of the trafficking of Brazilian women for prostitution, and related issues.

Workers can join independent trade unions, and the labor movement is active in politics. Collective bargaining is legal and conducted fairly widely. Civil servants have no legal right to strike.

⬇ Swaziland

Polity: Traditional monarchy
Economy: Capitalist
Population: 1,000,000
PPP: $3,816
Life Expectancy: 61

Political Rights: 6
Civil Liberties: 5
Status: Not Free

Ethnic Groups: African (97 percent), European (3 percent)
Capital: Mbabane
Trend Arrow: Swaziland received a downward trend arrow because of increased repression of labor activists, students, and others who have been demanding political reform.

Overview: Swaziland was wracked by protests at the end of the year by labor groups, teachers, students, and others demanding political reforms in Africa's last remaining absolute monarchy. Authorities dispersed demonstrators with tear gas and rubber bullets, detained labor leaders, and temporarily closed the University of Swaziland. The government of King Mswati III also imposed a ban on labor union meetings in October after the Swaziland National Association of Teachers had allowed activists to discuss pro-democracy issues during a rally. The ban was lifted in December. Labor unions are at the forefront of Swaziland's democracy movement, which is gaining momentum, in part because of the backing of the powerful Congress of South African Trade Unions. It supported Swazi pro-democracy demonstrators who carried out a blockade of the country's borders in November. That month the government reintroduced a 60-day-detention-without-trial law. Harassment and muzzling of the press continued during the year.

Swaziland is the only southern African country without an elected government. King Mswati III is the latest monarch of the Dlamini dynasty, under which the Swazi kingdom expanded and contracted in conflicts with neighboring groups. Britain declared the kingdom a protectorate to prevent Boer expansion in the 1880s and assumed administrative power in 1903. In 1968, Swaziland regained its independence, and an elected parliament was added to the traditional kingship and chieftaincies. Sobhuza II, Mswati's predecessor, who died in 1983, ended the multiparty system in favor of the *tinkhundla* (local council) system in 1973.

The demonstrations in 2000 were sparked by a palace order to evict 200 villagers in eastern Swaziland who refused to recognize King Mswati III's brother as their chief. The government backed down on the eviction but refused to lift a 27-year ban on political parties as demanded by labor leaders and other activists. The Constitutional Review Commission, which was formed in 1996 and was to have completed its work in 1998, presented its report to the king in November. Political activists have little faith that it will lead to real reform because a majority of its members are traditional chiefs or members of the royal family. In addition, the media were banned from reporting on submissions to the commission.

Most Swazis remain engaged in subsistence agriculture. A drop in the world price of gold has hurt the economy, as many Swazi families depend on income from men working in South African mines.

Political Rights and Civil Liberties: Swazis are barred from exercising their right to elect their representatives or to change their government freely. All of Swaziland's citizens are subjects of an absolute monarch, King Mswati III. Royal decrees carry the full force of law. Voting in October 1998 legislative elections was marked by very low turnout and was neither open nor fair. It was based on the Swazi tinkhundla system of closely controlled nominations and voting that seeks to legitimatize the rule of King Mswati III and his Dlamini clan. Security forces arrested and briefly detained labor and other pro-democracy leaders before the elections and after a series of bomb blasts. The 55 elected members of the national assembly were government approved and were joined by 10 royal appointees. The king also appoints 20 members of the senate, with the remaining 10 selected by the national assembly.

The dual-system judiciary, which is based on Western and traditional law, is generally independent in most civil cases, although the royal family and the government can influence the courts. In 1998, the king issued an administrative order that strengthened the judicial powers of traditional chiefs appointed by the king. Prison conditions have improved slightly.

There are regular reports of police brutality, including torture and beatings. Security forces generally operate with impunity. Authorities detained trade union leader Jan Sithole in November and barred him from speaking to the media following a pro-democracy strike. Two other labor leaders were also detained. Domestic nongovernmental human rights groups operate openly.

Freedom of expression is seriously restricted, especially regarding political issues or matters regarding the royal family. Legislation bans publication of any criticism of the monarchy, and the constitutional commission has broad authority to prosecute people who "belittle" or "insult" it. Self-censorship is widespread. Broadcast and print media from South Africa are received in the country. The government in February closed the state-owned Swazi Observer media group, which includes the daily *Swazi Observer*, the *Weekend Observer*, and the weekly *Intsatseli* following a series of reports that criticized the police activities. Two South African journalists, of the South African daily *The Sowetan*, were expelled in November after trying to attend the court hearing of Mario Masuku, the leader of the banned People's United Democratic Movement.

Freedom of religion is respected, although there are no formal constitutional provisions protecting the practice. The government restricts freedom of assembly and association. A 1973 decree prohibits meetings of a political nature without police consent. More than 40 university students were charged with misconduct and vandalism in November after disrupting lectures during a nationwide pro-democracy strike.

The Legal Code provides some protection against sexual harassment, but in general Swazi women encounter discrimination in both formal and customary law. Employment regulations requiring equal pay for equal work are obeyed unevenly. Married women are considered minors, requiring spousal permission to enter into almost any form of economic activity, and they are allowed only limited inheritance rights. Violence against women is common, despite traditional strictures against it.

The Swaziland Federation of Trade Unions, the country's largest labor organization, has been a leader in demands for democratization. Unions are able to operate independently under the Industrial Relations Act, which allows workers in all elements of the economy, including the public sector, to join unions. Wage agreements are often reached by collective bargaining, and 80 percent of the private workforce is unionized. The United States had threatened to impose trade sanctions against Swaziland, but backed off in December after the government amended a controversial labor law that made workers liable for losses incurred as a result of industrial action.

Sweden

Polity: Parliamentary democracy
Economy: Mixed capitalist
Population: 8,900,000
PPP: $20,659
Life Expectancy: 79
Ethnic Groups: Swedish (89 percent), Finnish (2 percent), other, including Lapp [Saami] (9 percent)
Capital: Stockholm

Political Rights: 1
Civil Liberties: 1
Status: Free

Overview:

Since 1998, Prime Minister Goran Persson has led a left-of-center coalition including his Social Democratic Party (SDP), the former Communist Left Party, and the Green Party. In 2000 the minority government saw its support slip, partly over issues of tax cuts and welfare reform. With general elections scheduled for 2002, the prospect of an early election gained ground during the year.

In June, the International Monetary Fund urged Sweden to cut taxes, which amount to 52.9 percent of Gross Domestic Product, the highest in the Organization for Economic Cooperation and Development (OECD). Sweden administers one of the world's most extensive welfare systems. Criticism of the Persson government mounted during the year, with charges that high taxes make Sweden less competitive and encourage a "brain drain" of young, educated professionals.

Sweden is faced with the difficult decision of whether to join the European Monetary Union (EMU). A referendum on the issue may be held in 2001. While the country joined the European Union (EU) in 1995, it did so grudgingly. The SDP's two coalition partners oppose joining the EMU and are unenthusiastic about Sweden's having joined the EU. After Denmark's decision in September 2000 not to adopt the common European currency, Prime Minister Persson, a proponent of the euro, faced a greater task in convincing his countrymen of the currency's benefits.

Although it has been nonaligned and neutral since World War I, in November Prime Minister Persson announced his intention to end Sweden's policy of military neutrality, declaring the stance irrelevant in the post-cold-war era. The announcement raised some concern among political opponents that Sweden would necessarily have to initiate a process of forward planning in the event of having to form alliances in wartime, as well as identify potential enemies. While continuing to rule out NATO membership, Persson insisted that non-neutrality would place Sweden in a better position to address post-cold-war issues such as disarmament, nuclear nonproliferation, and European stability. Instability in the Balkans during the 1990s led to an increase of immigrants to Sweden from Yugoslavia, sparking intolerance and nationalist and extremist violence. Sweden is an active member of NATO's Partnership for Peace program.

Sweden is a constitutional monarchy and a multiparty parliamentary democracy. After monarchical alliances with Finland, Denmark, and Norway between the eleventh and nineteenth centuries, Sweden emerged as a modern democracy.

Political Rights and Civil Liberties: Swedes can change their government democratically. The 310-member, unicameral *Riksdag* (parliament) is elected every four years through universal suffrage. To ensure absolute proportionality for all parties that secure more than four percent of the vote, an additional 39 representatives are selected from a national pool of candidates. Single-party majority governments are rare.

Citizens abroad are entitled to vote by absentee ballot in national elections, and non-nationals in residence for three years may vote in local elections. The Saami (Lapp) community elects its own local parliament with significant powers over education and culture. The Saami parliament serves as an advisory body to the government. The role of King Carl Gustaf XVI, who was crowned in 1973, is ceremonial. The prime minister is appointed by the speaker of the house and confirmed by the Riksdag.

The media are independent. Most newspapers and periodicals are privately owned. The government subsidizes daily newspapers regardless of their political affiliation. The ethnic press is entitled to the same kind of subsidies as the Swedish press. The Swedish Broadcasting Corporation and the Swedish Television Company broadcast weekly radio and television programs in several immigrant languages. In recent years, new satellite- and ground-based commercial television channels and radio stations ended the government monopoly on broadcasting. Internet penetration rates in Sweden are among the highest in the world, with more than half the population online.

Citizens may freely express their ideas and criticize their government. The government is empowered to prevent publication of information related to national security. A quasi-government body censors extremely graphic violence from film, video, and television.

International human rights groups have criticized Sweden for its immigration policies, which have severely limited the number of refugees admitted annually. Nordic immigrants may become citizens after two years, while others must wait a minimum of five years. Critics charge that the country does not systematically provide asylum seekers with adequate legal counsel or access to an appeals process. The jobless rate among non-Nordic immigrants is close to 20 percent, whereas among the general population it is about 6 percent. Immigrants, half of whom are from other Nordic countries, make up about 12 percent of the Swedish population.

Dozens of violent incidents with anti-immigrant or racist overtones are reported annually, and the government supports volunteer groups that oppose racism. The Nationalsocialistick Front, the leading neo-Nazi group in Sweden, has an estimated 1,500 members and was recently permitted to register as a political party. Although the country's 17,000 Saami enjoy some political autonomy, Sweden was the last Nordic country to approve a parliament for its Lappic population.

Religious freedom is constitutionally guaranteed. Approximately 85 percent of the population is Lutheran. On January 1, 2000, Sweden officially disestablished the Church of Sweden from the state, following the norm in Western Europe of severing ties between the state and an official religion. The move effectively reduced the once substantial subsidies to the church and redirected them to other religious institutions, including those associated with Roman Catholics, Muslims, and Jews. The growing numbers of non-Lutherans in Sweden prompted the move. There are approximately 200,000 Muslims, 160,000 Roman Catholics, 100,000 Orthodox Christians, and 16,000 Jews in Sweden.

Freedom of assembly and association is guaranteed, as are the rights to strike and participate in unions. Strong and well-organized trade union federations represent 90 percent of the labor force. Despite historic ties with the SDP, the labor movement has become increasingly independent.

The country's independent judiciary includes 6 courts of appeal, 100 district courts, a supreme court, and a parallel system of administrative courts.

Women constitute approximately 45 percent of the labor force, but their wage levels lag behind those of men. Sweden has the highest proportion of female politicians in the world. More than 40 percent of the country's members of parliament are women, along with half the cabinet.

Switzerland

Polity: Parliamentary democracy (federal)
Economy: Capitalist
Population: 7,100,000
PPP: $25,512
Life Expectancy: 79
Ethnic Groups: German (65 percent), French (18 percent), Italian (10 percent), Romansch (1 percent), other (6 percent)
Capital: Berne

Political Rights: 1
Civil Liberties: 1
Status: Free

Overview:

After Switzerland's body politic lurched to the right in the 1999 national elections, the increasingly sensitive immigration issue dominated the country's political life in 2000. While voters roundly rejected a referendum on establishing a ceiling on immigration, all applications for citizenship submitted by former residents of the Balkans were rejected in a local vote. A poll revealed deep-rooted anti-Semitism in Switzerland today and more firms came forward admitting they used slave labor during World War II. President Adolf Ogi resigned in October.

With the exception of a brief period of centralized power under Napoleonic rule, Switzerland has remained a confederation of local communities as established in the Pact of 1291. Most responsibility for public affairs rests at the local and cantonal levels. The 1815 Congress of Vienna formalized the country's borders and recognized its perpetual neutrality. Switzerland is often cited as a rare example of peaceful coexistence in a multiethnic state. The republic is divided into 20 cantons and 6 half-cantons and includes German, French, Italian, and Romansch communities.

In October 1999, the right-wing Swiss People's Party, with its popular and combative member, Christoph Blocher, registered dramatic gains in national elections. Running on an anti-immigration and anti-European Union (EU) platform, the party went on to become the second largest in parliament, earning 44 seats against the 51 held by the ruling Social Democrats.

In October 2000, President Ogi, who was also defense minister, announced his resignation. Since Ogi is a member of the Swiss People's Party, which is highly radicalized by Blocher, his resignation touched off widespread speculation about a succession battle that would disturb the country's so-called magic formula, whereby four of Switzerland's main political parties share seven government posts.

In July, a U.S. court approved a $1.25 billion restitution deal between Swiss banks and relatives of Holocaust victims. The settlement offers restitution to the heirs of Holocaust victims who had opened some 50,000 bank accounts in Switzerland. The deal also compensates the relatives of those whose assets were plundered by the Nazis and transferred to Switzerland during the war.

After coming under intense international pressure during the year, Switzerland moved to make its notoriously opaque banking system less secretive. Investigations were initiated against key Russian business people suspected of money laundering. Public assets deposited into Swiss accounts by Nigeria, Pakistan, and other countries were also investigated.

Officially neutral and nonaligned, Switzerland is not a member of the United Nations or the European Union (EU). In a 1986 national referendum, voters rejected UN membership by a three to one margin. In a 1992 referendum, a narrow majority of voters rejected joining the European Economic Area, membership in which is seen as a step toward EU membership. Since then, the government has grown increasingly anxious to negotiate a pact with the EU to give Swiss industries and service sectors some benefits of access to the single European market. In May 2000, voters approved a referendum that would establish a bilateral arrangement with the EU to allow Union citizens to enter and leave Switzerland without visas, a development that many among the right feared would encourage a greater influx of foreigners into the country. In 1996, Switzerland joined NATO's Partnership for Peace program, through which it can participate in nonmilitary humanitarian and training missions.

Political Rights and Civil Liberties: The Swiss can change their government democratically. Free and fair elections are held at regular intervals. Initiatives and referenda give citizens an additional degree of involvement in the legislative process. The cantonal system allows considerable local autonomy, and localities' linguistic and cultural heritages are zealously preserved.

At the national level, both houses of the Federal Assembly have equal authority. After legislation has been passed both in the directly elected, 200-member National Council and in the Council of States, which includes two members from each canton, it cannot be vetoed by the executive or reviewed by the judiciary. The seven members of the Federal Council (*Bundesrat*) exercise executive authority. They are chosen from the Federal Assembly according to a "magic formula" that ensures representation of each party, region, and language group. Each year, one member serves as president.

The judicial system functions primarily at the cantonal level, with the exception of a federal supreme court that reviews cantonal court decisions involving federal law.

Switzerland's judiciary is independent. The government's postal ministry operates broadcasting services, and the broadcast media enjoy editorial autonomy. Foreign broadcast media are readily accessible. In addition, there are many private television and radio stations. Privately owned daily, weekly, and monthly publications are available in each of the most common languages and are free from government interference.

Freedoms of speech, assembly, association, and religion are observed. While no single state church exists, many cantons support one or several churches. Taxpayers may opt not to contribute to church funds, yet in many instances, companies cannot. Human rights monitors operate freely.

The country's antiracist law prohibits racist or anti-Semitic speech and actions, and is strictly enforced by the government. In November 1998, the Federal Commission against Racism, the country's official human rights watchdog, warned that "latent anti-Semitism is again being increasingly expressed by word and by deed." A March 2000 poll revealed deep-rooted anti-Semitism in Swiss society. Sixteen percent of respondents acknowledged holding fundamentally anti-Semitic views, while 60 percent admitted to holding anti-Semitic sympathies. At a time when the country is being held accountable to a greater degree than ever before for its treatment of Nazi victims, in particular for turning away Jewish refugees fleeing German persecution during the World War II, 45 percent of those polled believed the country owes no apology to the Jews for its wartime behavior.

During the Kosovo war of 1999, thousands of ethnic Albanian refugees expelled from the Serbian province flooded into Switzerland. As a result, Swiss voters approved tighter asylum laws in a June 1999 vote. The new rules made it harder for refugees to claim asylum based on persecution in their home countries. Voter approval was highest in the German-speaking region, whose citizens were the most vocal in denouncing the presence of Kosovar Albanians.

In 2000, citizenship became even harder to obtain for those hailing originally from the Balkans. In a local referendum held in March, residents of Emmen, in Lucerne canton, approved only 8 of 56 citizenship applications. The approvals were granted only to those of Italian origin. All those denied citizenship were of Balkan background. The vote was based on detailed personal information, including the salaries, tax status, and hobbies of the applicants. The far-right People's Party countenanced the vote. Some within the party advocated similar votes throughout the country. The referendum was put forward in part because Switzerland's population growth is due almost entirely to immigration. Voters were apparently mindful of the potential public relations and economic damage should the measure pass.

In a seeming rebuke of the March referendum, voters rejected a proposed limit on the number of foreigners to be admitted into Switzerland annually. Currently, foreigners constitute 19.3 percent of the country's population, while the proposed measure would have instituted an 18 percent ceiling.

In 1995, federal laws aimed at dissuading drug traffickers from entering Switzerland authorized pretrial detention of legal residents for as long as nine months. With 33,000 drug addicts in a population of seven million, the use of hard drugs has become one of the country's most pernicious social ailments. In June 1999, Swiss citizens voted to continue a state program that provides heroin, under medical supervision, to hardened addicts.

Although a law on gender equality took effect in 1996, women still face some barriers to political and social advancement. In March 2000 voters rejected minimum quotas for women in parliament. Only two women serve in the seven-member governing coalition, and women occupy only 22 percent of parliamentary seats. While legal parity formally exists between the sexes, some studies have estimated women's earnings to be 15 percent lower than men's for equal work. Women were not granted federal suffrage until 1971, and the half-canton Appenzell-Innerrhoden did not relinquish its status as the last bastion of all-male suffrage in Europe until 1990. Until the mid-1980s, women were prohibited from participating in the Bundesrat. In 1997, journalists revealed that hundreds of women had been forcibly sterilized under a cantonal law passed in 1928. In June 1999, Swiss voters rejected a government proposal to introduce paid maternity leave. Swiss law bans women from working for two months after giving birth, but without any guaranteed wages during that period.

Workers may organize and participate in unions and enjoy the right to strike and bargain collectively. Unions are independent of the government and political parties, and approximately one-third of the workforce holds union membership.

↑ Syria

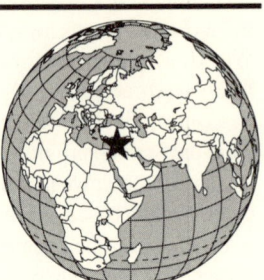

Polity: Dominant party (military-dominated)
Economy: Mixed statist
Population: 16,500,000
[Note: about 38,200 people live in the Israeli-occupied Golan Heights, including some 20,000 Israeli settlers]
PPP: $2,892
Life Expectancy: 69
Ethnic Groups: Arab (90 percent), other, including Kurd and Armenian (10 percent)
Capital: Damascus

Political Rights: 7
Civil Liberties: 7
Status: Not Free

Trend Arrow: Syria received an upward trend arrow due to a small relaxation of controls over freedom of assembly and freedom of expression.

Overview:

Syrian leader Hafez al-Assad died in June after 30 years of authoritarian rule, but not before overseeing a government changeover and cabinet reshuffle. His son, 34-year-old Bashar, whom the elder Assad had groomed as his eventual replacement, assumed power in a smooth succession immediately following his father's death. The new Western-educated and seemingly reform-minded Syrian leader relaxed his country's longtime repression of all forms of free expression and vowed to implement much needed economic reforms. He also granted amnesty to some 600 political prisoners during the year. However, Bashar's latitude for implementing sweeping change is curtailed by those grown accustomed to benefiting from the repressive status quo. Many analysts predict Bashar will be forced to walk a tightrope in the foreseeable future as he balances modernizing his country with placating his foes. Peace talks with Israel remained stalled during the year over disagreement on final border arrangements for the Israeli-occupied Golan Heights. Syria faced renewed and more extensive calls for withdrawal of its forces from Lebanon during the year, especially once Israel withdrew its troops from that country in May.

Following four centuries of rule under the Ottoman Empire, Syria came under French control after World War I and gained independence in 1941. A 1963 military coup brought the pan-Arab, Socialist Baath Party to power. As head of the Baath military wing, Hafez al-Assad took power in a 1970 coup and formally became president of the secular regime in 1971. Members of the Alawite Muslim minority, which constitutes 12 percent of the population, were installed in most key military and intelligence positions and continue to hold those positions today.

The 1973 constitution vests executive power in the president, who must be a Muslim and who is nominated by the Baath Party to be elected through popular referendum. The 250-member People's Assembly holds little independent legislative power. The minimum age for president was lowered in June from 40 to 34, when Bashar al-Assad, at age 34, assumed the presidency.

In the late 1970s, the fundamentalist Muslim Brotherhood, drawn from the Sunni majority, carried out antigovernment attacks in several northern and central towns. In 1982, the government sent the army into the northern town of Hama to crush a Muslim Brotherhood rebellion. As many as 20,000 militants and civilians died in the resulting bloodshed, which decisively ended active opposition to the regime to this day.

In February, Syria's new president continued with the anticorruption drive initiated by his father, when many officials perceived to be opponents of Bashar were purged from their posts. Those thought to pose a threat to lucrative trade routes controlled by the Assad family were also removed. A new cabinet was installed in March, ushering in younger leaders intent on fulfilling much needed social and economic reforms and determined to root out corruption. Government estimates put the cost of corruption at $50,000 per day. Former Prime Minister Mahmoud el-Zoubi was expelled from the Baath party and summoned to trial in May on embezzlement charges, but committed suicide upon receiving the court summons.

In June, after Bashar became president, the 90-member central committee of the governing Baath party was overhauled with the election of 62 new members, among them top army officials, indicating a concerted effort on the new president's part to ensure loyalty at the highest levels of government and to consolidate his rule.

Intensive peace negotiations with Israel broke down in January over disagreements on final borders around the Golan Heights. A March summit between U.S. president Bill Clinton and Hafez al-Assad, designed to sound out the Syrian leader on his peace terms and jump-start negotiations with Israel, failed to produce any forward momentum. The key sticking point centered on which country should control a strip of shoreline along the eastern edge of the Sea of Galilee, located below the western slopes of the Golan. The sea serves as Israel's primary fresh water source. Israel has agreed in principle to a return of all of the Golan in return for security guarantees. Prior to losing the Golan in 1967, Syria had used the territory to shell northern Israeli towns.

The specter of war between Syria and Israel appeared to grow late in the year. In October, at an Islamic nations conference called in the midst of raging violence in the Palestinian territories, Syria called for an end to the normalization of relations between Arab and Muslim states and Israel. Syria, which continues to maintain its 35,000-strong troop presence in Lebanon, appeared to authorize Hezbollah guerilla attacks against

Israeli forces – including kidnapping of soldiers –from southern Lebanon, ostensibly as a pressure tactic to force Israel to return the Golan Heights on Syrian terms. President Assad publicly praised Hezbollah for its attacks. In November, an Israeli Army intelligence assessment concluded that Syria would go to war should Israel retaliate for Hezbollah attacks by striking Syrian interests in Lebanon. Syria remains on the U.S. State Department list of states that support terrorism, and continues to support radical Palestinian terror groups opposed to the Israeli-Palestinian peace process.

Syria faced growing calls within Lebanon for the withdrawal of Syrian troops from that country. Israeli troops pulled out of their self-declared "security zone" in southern Lebanon in May, thus ostensibly removing Syria's justification for its troop presence, according to many analysts. Many felt more emboldened in criticizing the Syrian presence with Bashar in power; his father had dealt harshly with any dissent related to Syria's Lebanese occupation. Indeed, calls for independence from Syria cut across Lebanon's political spectrum and were loudest among the Maronite Christian community. In September, a previously unknown group called Citizens for a Free and Sovereign Lebanon carried out attacks against Syrian nationals in Lebanon. However, Lebanon's parliamentary elections in 2000 did demonstrate the country's fealty to Syria, with most members of parliament maintaining close ties with the Syrian regime.

Syria proceeded to cement its warming relations with Iraq during the year. In February the two countries formally reestablished diplomatic ties, which had been severed in 1980 at the outbreak of the Iran-Iraq war. Syria's upgrade in relations with Iraq were for largely geopolitical and economic reasons. Both countries rely on water from the Tigris and Euphrates Rivers, whose headwaters sit in Turkey, where dam construction on the rivers is underway. The Syrian move toward Iraq was also seen as a way to counter Iran's influence in Lebanon; Iran supports Hezbollah and would be uneasy about any Syrian efforts to rein in the guerilla group. Syria also reportedly held secret talks with the Iraqi leadership to ensure Iraq's backing in the event of a Syrian-Israeli war. In November, Syria and Iraq reopened a petroleum pipeline running between the two countries. As a result, Syria is technically in violation of United Nations (UN) sanctions against Iraq. The proceeds from the sale of oil will probably be used to finance President Assad's new job-creation plan. His stated goal is to create 440,000 much needed jobs for unemployed young people. Many analysts commented that Bashar's hold on power depended on the success of the jobs plan.

Syria's economy is characterized by antiquated infrastructure and an overbearing and corrupt bureaucracy. There are no industrial zones; nor is there a modern banking system. Agriculture accounts for roughly 50 percent of exchange earnings and exports, and farmers make up 30 percent of the Syrian workforce, a segment of the economy hit hard by a 1999 drought. Oil accounts for approximately half of the country's exports, but many predict Syria will have to import oil within ten years as fields dry up. With the population growing two times faster than the economy, Bashar al-Assad has stated his intention to combat corruption and attract foreign investment. In April he liberalized the rules against holding foreign currency and narrowed the powers of the economic security courts. Towards the end of the year, however, his drive to modernize the economy appeared to taper off, leading to speculation that he faces significant challenges from those used to benefiting from a closed, statist economy.

Syria is known to be a major transit point of processed opiates, including heroin, from Central Asia. It is estimated the country earns $1 billion a year on drug smuggling to the Middle East, Europe, and North Africa. Hafez al-Assad was known to use the lucrative drug income to pay off allies and opponents alike, a practice many predict Bashar will follow, especially in the short term while his hold on power remains more precarious.

Political Rights and Civil Liberties: Syrians cannot change their government democratically, though they ostensibly vote for the president and the People's Assembly. President Assad maintains absolute authority in the military-backed regime.

The Emergency Law, in effect almost continuously since 1963, allows authorities to carry out preventative arrests and to supersede due process safeguards in searches, detentions, and trials in the military-controlled state security courts, which handle political and security cases. Several independent security services operate independently of each other and without judicial oversight. Authorities monitor personal communications and conduct surveillance of suspected security threats.

The judiciary is subservient to the government. Defendants in ordinary civil criminal cases have some due process rights, though there are no jury trials. In state security courts, confessions obtained through torture are generally admitted as evidence. Nevertheless, acquittals have been granted in political cases.

While hundreds of political prisoners remain behind bars, President Assad authorized the amnesty of almost half of them—approximately 600—in November 2000. Previously, in July, he had ordered the release of members of the banned Muslim Brotherhood and Communists. The move, albeit a continuation of a process of gradual prisoner releases begun by his late father, was seen as consistent with Bashar's attempts to liberalize Syrian society.

While freedom of expression is sharply restricted, there were growing signs during the year that critical voices have earned greater tolerance under the new president. Writers, actors, lawyers, journalists, and artists put forward a petition calling for a free press, political reform, an end to martial law, the creation of independent political parties, and the release of political prisoners. Critiques of the Syrian economy also appeared in state-run newspapers after the death of Hafez al-Assad. Notably, no one was punished for speaking out on these issues. All media remain owned and operated by the government and the Baath Party. Satellite dishes are illegal, although they are increasingly tolerated.

Despite the apparent gains in press freedoms, Syrian journalist Nizar Nayyuf remained in a Damascus prison during the year. According to Reporters Sans Frontières, Nayyuf is in extremely grave condition and close to death. His jailers, who have demanded he declare as "false" his past statements regarding Syria's human rights record, have repeatedly tortured him.

Internet access in Syria remains inchoate and highly restricted. Government ministries, some businesses, universities, and hospitals are connected to the Internet, although on government-controlled servers. While private access is not sanctioned, some private homes are believed to be connected to the Internet via Lebanese service providers. The government reduced the monthly fees for Internet accounts by half in July, although most private citizens cannot afford them. Bashar al-Assad is leading the drive to connect Syria to the Internet, but the country's ruling structure and intelligence services remain steadfastly against widespread access.

Freedom of assembly is largely nonexistent. Technically, the interior ministry must grant citizens permission to hold meetings, and the government or Baath Party organizes most public demonstrations. However, with Bashar now in power, citizens feel more emboldened to meet and criticize the government. In October, Syrian intellectuals began meeting regularly to debate issues surrounding social, economic, and political reform. They have issued calls for the creation of civil institutions such as an independent press, trade unions and associations, and political parties. Freedom of association is restricted. Private associations must register with the government, which usually grants registration to groups that are nonpolitical.

The state prohibits Jehovah's Witnesses and Seventh-Day Adventists from worshiping as a community and from owning property. The security apparatus closely monitors the tiny Jewish community, and Jews are generally barred from government employment. They are also the only minority group required to have their religion noted on their passports and identity cards. Religious instruction is mandatory in schools, with government-approved teachers and curricula. Separate classes are provided for Christian and Muslim students.

Although the regime has supported Kurdish struggles abroad, the Kurdish minority in Syria faces cultural and linguistic restrictions, and suspected Kurdish activists are routinely dismissed from schools and jobs. Some 200,000 Kurdish Syrians are stateless and unable to obtain passports, identity cards, or birth certificates as a result of a policy some years ago under which Kurds were stripped of their Syrian nationality. The government never restored their nationality, though the policy ended after the 1960s. As a result, these Kurds are unable to own land, to gain government employment, or to vote.

Traditional norms place Syrian women at a disadvantage in marriage, divorce, and inheritance matters. Syrian law stipulates that an accused rapist can be acquitted if he marries his victim. Violence against women, including rape, is high in Syria. Women also face legal restrictions on passing citizenship on to children.

All unions must belong to the government-controlled General Federation of Trade Unions. By law, the government can nullify any private sector collective-bargaining agreement. Strikes are prohibited in the agricultural sector and rarely occur in other sectors owing to previous government crackdowns.

Taiwan (Rep. of China)

Polity: Presidential democracy
Economy: Mixed capitalist
Population: 22,300,000
PPP: na
Life Expectancy: 75
Ethnic Groups: Taiwanese (84 percent), mainland Chinese (14 percent), Aborigine (2 percent)
Capital: Taipei

Political Rights: 1*
Civil Liberties: 2
Status: Free

Ratings Change: Taiwan's political rights rating changed from 2 to 1 due to free and fair presidential elections, and the subsequent orderly transfer of power, in which the Nationalist Party was defeated after over half a century of rule.

Overview:

Democratic Progressive Party (DPP) candidate Chen Shui-bien defeated Nationalist Party candidate Vice President Lien Chen in the March 2000 presidential elections. Chen's victory ended 55 years of Nationalist Party, or Kuomintang (KMT), rule. This peaceful transition of power in May was soon followed by political storms and challenges to unseat Chen. In international diplomacy, Chen's government outlined a new approach which will depart from the statist approach to pursue cooperation between civil society groups in Taiwan and overseas. The new approach will also emphasize human rights and democracy, areas Taiwan believes it has a competitive edge over Beijing. But to ease Beijing's anxiety about his new government, Chen declared in his inauguration speech that his government would not declare independence if Taiwan were not attacked. On December 28, Beijing accepted Taiwan's proposal to open two offshore islands to goods and passengers from the mainland and to allow island residents to travel directly to the Chinese mainland.

Taiwan, located 100 miles off the southern coast of mainland China, became the home of a government-in-exile in 1949, when the Communist victory on the mainland forced KMT leader Chiang Kai-shek to retreat to the island and establish a Nationalist government there. Both Beijing and Taipei officially consider Taiwan a province of China, although Taipei has abandoned its long-standing claim to be the legitimate government of mainland China. Native Taiwanese constitute 84 percent of the population, while mainlanders and their descendants make up the rest, along with a tiny minority of aboriginal peoples.

After four decades of authoritarian KMT rule, Taiwan's democratic transition began with the lifting of martial law in 1987. Lee Teng-hui became the first native Taiwanese president in 1988. Under his leadership, he asserted native Taiwanese control of the KMT, marginalized its mainlander faction, and de-emphasized the party's commitment to eventual reunification with China. In 1993, Lien Chen was chosen as the first native Taiwanese premier. A viable opposition to the KMT emerged in the country's first multiparty elections in 1991. The Democratic People's Party, which officially favors formal independence from mainland China, won several seats in the national assembly. The widening political space and public dissatisfaction with the KMT's factionalism, corruption and alleged organized crime links had weakened electoral support for the ruling party. At the November 1997 local elections, the Democratic People's Party downplayed its independence platform and promised clean, responsive government to narrowly defeat the KMT, for the first time, in the number of administrative posts and in the popular vote, at 43 percent versus 42 percent.

Civil society has gained strength in Taiwan in recent years. Public criticisms and protests against government policies toward aboriginal peoples, the environment, nuclear power, corruption, and other public policy issues have become commonplace. The election of Chen of the DPP in the March 2000 presidential elections was a historic victory for democracy in Taiwan.

The DPP had long advocated independence from China. Chen, who took office in May, chose not to chair the government's National Unification Council, whose official purpose is to promote unification with China. But Chinese anxiety must be dealt with and Chen won only 39 percent of the vote. Thus, in addition to his inaugural pledge to refrain from declaring independence, Chen appointed Tang Fei of the KMT, a supporter of reunification with the Chinese mainland, as the prime minister. Beijing welcomed his gestures and softened its criticisms of Chen. Yet, Beijing worked to pressure Chen by inviting Taiwan legislators to visit China. By the end of October, more than a third of the 221 Taiwan legislators had traveled to the Chinese mainland.

Maintaining Taiwan's status as a national entity in the international community of nations has been a struggle for the government. Today, only 29 countries in Latin America, Africa, the Caribbean and the Pacific Islands have formal ties with Taiwan. Chen's government announced a new approach to international diplomacy, which will depart from a strict state-centered model. Although Taiwan will continue to apply for membership in the United Nations, the government will also cooperate with civil society organizations at home and overseas and emphasize human rights and democracy— areas in which Taiwan has a competitive edge over mainland China. In August, Chen took a six-country tour, which included an overnight stopover in the United States on his way to the Dominican Republic.

The auspicious start for Chen quickly turned into a battle to defend his presidency against the newly coalesced opposition. At the end of September, Tang resigned as prime minister as a result of differences with Chen over construction of the country's fourth nuclear power plant, which the DPP opposes. Relations with the KMT further soured when Chen appointed DPP member Chang Chun-hsiung to replace Tang. An ill-timed announcement on October 27 that the government would halt construction of the disputed nuclear power plant was the final breaking point. Just half an hour before the announcement, Chen and KMT Chairman Lien Chan had met to mend fences with Chen promising to consider the KMT position. The KMT also considered Chen's decision a challenge to the legislative process since the previous KMT-led government had approved the $6 billion project and work has already begun. A presidential recall motion was swiftly introduced. If the opposition captures a two-thirds majority in the legislature, or 147 of 220 votes, a national referendum will follow. The three opposition parties hold 141 votes, while the DPP has only 67 seats and the independents 12.

Chen's handling of this and other affairs also rocked public confidence in his government. The stock market lost 40 percent of its value in the second half of 2000. Only the crash of a Singapore Airliner on October 31 and a severe typhoon in early November allowed Chen's government a brief respite from the political battles. Critics say Chen needs to set clear priorities, better coordinate his administration, and approach the opposition with greater flexibility as he works to implement his campaign promises, including new bills to crack-down on financial and corporate corruption and bar those convicted of organized criminal activities from standing for elections.

Political Rights and Civil Liberties: The people of Taiwan can change their government democratically. The country's transition from an authoritarian to a democratic state was consolidated by the March 1996 presidential election. The constitution vests executive power in a president, who appoints the premier without parliamentary confirmation and can dissolve the legislature. The national assembly can amend the constitution and, until 1994, elected the president and vice president. The government has five specialized *yuan* (branches), including a legislature that, since 1992, is directly elected for a three-year term. For five decades as the ruling party, the KMT maintained a political advantage through its influence over much of the broadcast media and its considerable business interests in Taiwan's industrial sector. Democratization throughout the 1990s allowed opposition parties to compete in elections and have an impact on national policy.

Taiwan today enjoys one of the freest media environments in Asia, despite some continuing legal restrictions and political pressures. There are laws prohibiting advocacy of formal independence from China and communism, and police can censor or ban publications considered seditious or treasonous. These provisions, however, are not generally enforced in practice. Authorities have refused to register some nongovernmental organizations with the name "Taiwan" in their titles, but such groups operate freely. Courts occasionally convict journalists for criminal libel in cases brought by the government or politicians. Most media are privately owned and express a wide variety of viewpoints. The four major television networks are owned by or closely associated with the government, opposition political parties, or the military. The government respects constitutional provisions for freedom of religion.

The law allows only one labor federation. This has enabled the pro-KMT Chinese Federation of Labor to maintain a monopoly for decades. The right to strike and bargain collectively is limited by laws that allow the authorities to impose mandatory dispute mediation and other restrictions. About 31 percent of the country's labor force belong to more than 3,000 registered unions.

The judiciary is not fully independent. It remains susceptible to corruption, and was exposed to political influence under the KMT. A number of judges were indicted in 1998 for accepting bribes. Judges are now drawn increasingly from outside the ruling party. The Anti-Hoodlum Law allows police to detain alleged "hoodlums" on the basis of testimony by unidentified informants. In 1998, a new organization of prosecutors was established to promote ongoing political reform, including higher professional standards. There are still reports of police abusing suspects, conducting personal identity and vehicle checks with widespread discretion, and obtaining evidence illegally with few ramifications. Prisons are overcrowded, and conditions are harsh in detention camps for illegal immigrants, whose number has grown in recent years. A new law was adopted in May 1998 to ban companies connected with political parties from bidding for public contracts. Bid riggers could get the maximum sentence of life imprisonment.

In recent years, Taiwan has considerably relaxed travel restrictions on its citizens to the Chinese mainland, although many limits on mainland Chinese visitors remain in force. In 1999, the government launched an investigation into the background of more than 100,000 immigrants and visitors from China after intelligence agencies said that some of these people were involved in espionage and other illegal activities.

Women continue to face discrimination in employment. Rape and domestic violence are serious problems, particularly in a culture that discourages open discussion and the use of legal interventions. New legislation adopted in June 1998 requires all city and county governments to establish domestic violence prevention centers. The country's 357,000 aboriginal descendants of Malayo-Polynesians suffer from social and economic alienation and have restricted influence over policy decisions regarding their land and natural resources.

Tajikistan

Polity: Presidential
Economy: Statist
Population: 6,400,000
PPP: $1,041
Life Expectancy: 68
Ethnic Groups: Tajik (65 percent), Uzbek (25 percent), Russian (4 percent), other (6 percent)
Capital: Dushanbe

Political Rights: 6
Civil Liberties: 6
Status: Not Free

Overview:
While the February and March 2000 parliamentary elections represented the culmination of the 1997 peace agreement between the government and the United Tajik Opposition (UTO) that ended the country's five-year civil war, Tajikistan's future stability and prospects for national reconciliation remain uncertain. Despite the inclusion of former warring parties in the electoral process, the poll was marred by serious irregularities and failed to meet minimum democratic standards. Paramilitary forces and armed criminal gangs continued to compromise the security situation, with bombings, shootouts, and assassination attempts occurring throughout the year.

Conquered by Russia in the late 1800s, Tajikistan was made an autonomous region within Uzbekistan in 1924 and a separate socialist republic of the U.S.S.R. in 1929. However, the ancient cities of Samarkand and Bukhara, the two main centers of Tajik culture, remained part of Uzbekistan. Tajikistan declared independence from the U.S.S.R. in September 1991, and two months later, former Communist Party leader Rakhman Nabiyev was elected president.

Nabiyev's increasing consolidation of power of the old guard, many of whom were from the more prosperous northern province of Leninabad, at the expense of other regional factions, led to increasing opposition to his rule. In May 1992, supporters and opponents of Nabiyev clashed in the streets of Dushanbe, with the violence quickly spreading beyond the capital. Specifically, clans from the Garm and Kurgan-Tyube regions in the east and the Pamiris from the mountainous southern Gorno-Badakhshan area in the south sought to unseat the ruling northern Leninabadi and southern Kulyabis from power. These long-simmering clan-based tensions, combined with various anti-Communist and Islamist movements, soon plunged the country into a five-year civil war for central government control by rival regional-political groupings. In September, Communist hardliners forced the resignation of President Nabiyev, who was replaced in November by leading Communist Party member and ethnic-Kulyabi Emomali Rakhmonov. The following month, Rakhmonov launched attacks in the Garm and Gorno-Badakhshan regions, causing tens of thousands to flee into neighboring Afghanistan.

In November 1994, Rakhmonov won presidential elections with a reported 58 percent of the vote against Abdumalik Abdullajanov, a former premier from Leninabad. Most opposition candidates were prevented from competing by the country's election law, and the Islamic Renaissance Party (IRP) and Tajik Democratic Party (TDP) boycotted the poll. March 1995 parliamentary elections, in which the majority of seats were won by pro-government candidates, were boycotted by the UTO, a coalition of various secular and Islamic opposition groups including the IRP. Established in 1993, the UTO emerged as the main opposition force fighting against President Rakhmonov's government during the war.

Following a December 1996 ceasefire, President Rakhmonov and UTO leader Said Abdullo Nuri signed a formal peace agreement in Moscow on June 27, 1997, officially ending the civil war, which had claimed tens of thousands of lives and left several hundred thousand refugees. The accord called for opposition forces to be merged into the regular army, granted an amnesty for UTO members, provided for the UTO to be allotted 30 percent of senior government posts, and established a 26-member National Reconciliation Commission (NRC), with seats evenly divided between the government and the UTO. The NRC was charged with implementing the peace agreements, including preparing amendments for a referendum on constitutional changes that would lead to fair parliamentary elections. By the end of 1998, nearly all exiled UTO leaders and Tajik refugees from Afghanistan had returned, although the government had pushed back parliamentary elections scheduled for June of that year.

During 1999, the government and the UTO took steps towards implementing the peace accord. Parliament adopted a resolution in May granting a general amnesty applicable to more than 5,000 opposition fighters; several members of the UTO were appointed to government posts; and the UTO announced that it had disbanded all of its military formations. In a September nationwide referendum, voters overwhelmingly approved a series of constitutional amendments that considerably expanded the powers of the president. At the same time, the amendments also permitted the formation of religion-based political parties, opening the way for the legal operation of the Islamic opposition, including the IRP, which constitutes the backbone of the UTO; a May 1998 law on political parties had banned religious parties.

In the November presidential election, two of the three opposition candidates to President Rakhmonov were barred from participating less than one month before the poll, ostensibly for failure to collect the necessary number of signatures to be included on the ballot. A third candidate, Economics Minister and IRP member Davlat Usmon, withdrew from the race in protest. According to official election results, Rakhmonov received 97 percent of the vote, and Usmon, 2 percent. International election observers cited numerous irregularities, including widespread multiple voting and restrictions on opposition candidates' access to the media. The Organization for Security and Cooperation in Europe (OSCE) refused to send monitors because of serious flaws observed during the pre-election period.

As the final stage in the implementation of the 1997 peace accord, Tajikistan held parliamentary elections in February (for the 63-seat lower house) and March (for the 33-member upper house) 2000. In the February poll, the People's Democratic Party (PDP) of President Rakhmonov received nearly 65 percent of the vote, followed by the Communist Party with 20 percent and the IRP, which was plagued by internal divisions, with 7 percent. Election officials claimed that voter turnout exceeded 87 percent, a figure widely believed to be inflated. Although the participation of six parties and a number of independent candidates in the poll provided some political pluralism, international election observers, including a joint OSCE-United Nations mission, cited a number of serious problems, including evidence of proxy voting, the exclusion of certain opposition parties, biased state media coverage, and a lack of transparency in the tabulation of votes. In the March elections to the upper house of parliament, in which regional assemblies elected 25 members and President Rakhmonov appointed the remaining 8, the PDP obtained the overwhelming majority of seats.

With the conclusion of the 1997 peace agreement following the parliamentary elections, the NRC formally disbanded and the UN observer mission withdrew after about six years in Tajikistan. However, not all of the provisions of the peace accord were implemented, as demobilization of opposition factions remained incomplete and the government did not meet the 30 percent quota of senior government posts to be awarded to the UTO. The country's security situation remained precarious as outbreaks of violence linked to regional clan feuds, political rivalries, and competition for the lucrative drug trade continued throughout the country. Dushanbe's failure to crush Islamic guerillas on its territory, thought mostly to be members of the Islamic Movement of Uzbekistan (IMU), which is struggling to overthrow the Uzbekistan government and was blamed for armed incursions into the Kyrgyz Republic in 1999, has strained relations with the neighboring governments of Tashkent and Bishkek.

After years of economic devastation wrought by the civil war, Tajikistan remains the poorest nation in Central Asia. The country's worst drought in 70 years, which greatly reduced the annual harvest, resulted in urgent appeals for emergency aid to prevent mass famine. Recent Taliban victories in northern Afghanistan fueled fears of large numbers of Afghan refugees seeking safety in Tajikistan, which would overwhelm the already impoverished nation.

Political Rights and Civil Liberties: Citizens of Tajikistan cannot change their government democratically. The 1994 constitution provides for a strong, directly elected executive who enjoys broad authority to appoint and dismiss officials. Amendments to the constitution adopted in a 1999 referendum further increased the powers of the president by extending his term in office from five to seven years and creating a full-time, bicameral parliament whose members would be appointed directly by the president or elected by indirect vote through local parliaments led by presidential appointees. Neither the country's presidential polls in 1994 and 1999 nor the parliamentary elections of 1995 and 2000 were free and fair.

Despite formal guarantees for freedom of speech and the press, media freedoms remain severely curtailed by the government. Independent journalists continue to be threatened by removal of their accreditation, denial of access to state printing facilities, unprosecuted violence, and the closure of the media outlets with which they are affiliated. Consequently, self-censorship among journalists is widespread. In May 2000, the director of state radio and television was killed by gunmen with automatic rifles as he arrived home from work; there was speculation that his murder may have been linked to his professional activities. No independent radio stations have yet received operating licenses. In June, Tajikistan's first Internet café opened in Dushanbe.

Freedom of religion is generally respected in this predominantly Muslim country, although some restrictions exist. The state Committee on Religious Affairs registers religious communities, largely to ensure that they do not become overtly political. A constitutional referendum of September 1999 legalized the formation of religion-based political parties after an earlier ban in 1998. During 2000, hundreds of alleged members of the banned extremist Islamic organization, Hizb-ut-Tahrir, were arrested on various criminal charges, including distribution of anti-state literature. In August, seven were sentenced to several years in prison for membership in an illegal criminal group and for planning to overthrow the government. Reports from international and local sources indicated that the suspects had been physically mistreated and held incommunicado while in detention.

The state strictly controls freedom of assembly and association for organizations of a political nature. Nongovernmental organizations and political groups must obtain permits to hold public demonstrations, which at times the authorities have used excessive force to disrupt. Although a ban on religion-based parties was lifted in 1999, the government has stopped or limited the activities of certain other political parties. Despite legal rights to form and join trade unions, labor rights are largely ignored in practice, and all trade unions in Tajikistan are state controlled.

The judiciary enjoys little independence from the executive branch, on which most judges depend for their positions. Many judges are poorly trained and inexperienced, and bribery is reportedly widespread. Police routinely conduct arbitrary searches and seizures and beat detainees to obtain confessions. Prison conditions have been described as life-threatening because of overcrowding and unsanitary conditions. High levels of criminal and political violence and lawlessness continue to directly or indirectly affect the personal security of most citizens. Numerous bomb attacks and killings committed by members of the security forces, the UTO, or unaligned armed factions occurred throughout 2000. In the weeks preceding the parliamentary election, a series of bomb blasts in Dushanbe killed eight people, including a prominent pro-government candidate, and another ruling party member was shot dead in June.

The government generally respects the right of its citizens to choose a place of residence and to travel. However, checkpoints manned by interior ministry troops and customs officials have extorted money from drivers and passengers, limiting their freedom of movement. Corruption is reportedly pervasive throughout the government, civil service, and business sectors. Barriers to private enterprise, including the widespread practice of bribe payments, restrict equality of opportunity. Although women are employed throughout the government, academia, and the business world, they continue to face traditional societal discrimination. Domestic violence is reportedly common, and there are credible reports of the trafficking of the women for prostitution.

Tanzania

Polity: Dominant party
Economy: Mixed statist
Population: 35,300,000
PPP: $480
Life Expectancy: 48
Ethnic Groups: African (99 percent), other, including Asian, European, and Arab (1 percent)
Capital: Dar-es-Salaam

Political Rights: 4
Civil Liberties: 4
Status: Partly Free

Overview:
Tanzania held legislative and presidential elections in October 2000, the second since the reintroduction of multiparty politics. Incumbent President Benjamin Mkapa won reelection with about 70 percent of the vote, and the ruling Chama Cha Mapazindi (CCM) won an overwhelming victory in the 275-member legislature. The conduct of these elections represented a modest improvement over the preceding polls in 1995. They were marred, however, by fraudulent polls biased in favor of the ruling party in the federated semiautonomous isles of Zanzibar and Pemba. The status of these islands in relation to the mainland has long provoked tension. The opposition Civic United Front (CUF) and independent observers convincingly demonstrated that the ruling CCM had engaged in fraud to maintain its power.

After Tanzania gained independence from Britain in 1961, the CCM, under President Julius Nyerere, dominated the country's political life. The Zanzibar and Pemba Islands were merged with Tanganyika to become the Union of Tanzania, after Arab sultans who had long ruled the islands were deposed in a violent 1964 revolution. For much of his presidency, President Nyerere espoused a collectivist economic philosophy known in Swahili as *ujaama*. Although it may have been useful in promoting a sense of community and nationality, this policy resulted in significant economic dislocation and decline, the effects of which continue to be felt. During Nyerere's tenure, Tanzania also played an important role as a Front Line State in the international response to white-controlled regimes in southern Africa.

Nyerere retained strong influence after he officially retired in 1985. Although opposition parties were legalized in 1992, the CCM continues to dominate the country's political life. Progress towards democratic consolidation and strong economic growth remain inhibited by high levels of corruption and weak opposition parties.

Although Tanzania has avoided the civil strife that has wracked many of its neighbors, there are a number of serious issues which, if not addressed, could affect the country's longer-term stability. These include mainland Tanzania's long-term relationship with the Zanzibar archipelago; the presence in western Tanzania of 800,000 refugees from Burundi, the Democratic Republic of the Congo, and Rwanda; and the need for relief of the country's $8 billion debt.

Political Rights and Civil Liberties:
The ability of Tanzanians to freely choose their political leaders is not yet firmly entrenched in practice. Although the 2000 national elections avoided the massive logistical and admin-

istrative chaos of the preceding elections, the CCM continues to enjoy considerable advantages of incumbency that inhibit the realistic prospect of alternation of power. In addition, the 2000 elections in Zanzibar demonstrated that this progress was not uniform nationwide. Massive electoral irregularities prompted authorities to annul the vote in almost one-third of constituencies. Ballot papers arrived hours late in some areas and many people were unable to vote. A claim by the CUF leader that the CCM had manipulated the election to avoid defeat was bolstered by observers from the Commonwealth and the Organization of African Unity.

The previous legislative and presidential elections, in 1995, had been the most open on mainland Tanzania since independence, but the CCM's landslide legislative victory was, in particular, seriously tainted by fraud and administrative irregularities. In addition, extensive use of state broadcasting and other government resources during the campaign favored the ruling party. The CCM won 80 percent of the 232 directly elected seats in the national assembly. The voting in Zanzibar was plainly fraudulent, with the island's high court summarily rejecting opposition demands for fresh polls.

Thirteen opposition parties have formal status. Some of them are active, but they tend to be divided and ineffective. The CUF has sought to establish significant support on the Tanzanian mainland, and its presidential candidate received the second highest number of votes in the 2000 presidential elections. Another major opposition party, the National Convention for Constitution and Reform (NCCR-Mageuzi), whose candidate, Augustine Mrema, was runner-up to President Benjamin Mkapa in the 1995 presidential election, has split into two. Parties with parliamentary representation receive government subsidies, but they criticize the low level of funding and the formula by which it is allocated.

President Mkapa has at times demonstrated considerable irritability over actions of the political opposition. He has warned, for example, that the multiparty political system should not be used as a pretext to indulge in criminal political activities in the country.

Tanzania's judiciary has displayed signs of autonomy after decades of subservience to the one-party CCM regime, but it remains subject to considerable political influence. Constitutional protections for the right to free assembly are generally, but not always, respected. Laws allow rallies only by officially registered political parties, which may not be formed on religious, ethnic, or regional bases and cannot oppose the union of Zanzibar and the mainland. Freedom of religion is respected.

Print and electronic media are active, but media impact is largely limited to major urban areas. Private radio and television stations began receiving licenses at the beginning of 1994, but they are not allowed to cover more than 25 percent of the country's territory, according to the 1993 Broadcasting Act. The stated rationale for the limitation is to protect national interests. In Zanzibar the government controls the electronic media.

Arrest and pretrial detention laws are often ignored. Prison conditions are harsh, and police abuses are said to be common. According to government estimates there are approximately 45,000 inmates in the country's prisons although their collective capacity is only 21,537. Such overcrowding has caused widespread concern. Questions are being raised regarding the safety and health of prisoners, including minors and women, who have been subjected to sexual harassment and human rights abuses.

Many nongovernmental organizations are active, and some have been able to influence the public policy process. The broad distribution of Tanzania's population among many ethnic groups has largely diffused potential ethnic rivalries that have wracked neighboring countries. The refugee influx is currently a big burden for Tanzania, which alone hosts more than 800,000 refugees. It is also estimated that over 26,000 refugees have been naturalised since 1961.

Women's rights guaranteed by the constitution and other laws are not uniformly protected. Especially in rural areas and in Zanzibar, traditional or Islamic customs discriminatory toward women prevail in family law, and women have fewer educational and economic opportunities. Domestic violence against women is reportedly common and is rarely prosecuted. Human rights groups have sought laws to bar forced marriages, which are most common among Tanzania's coastal peoples. The employment of children as domestic servants is widespread.

Workers do not have the right to organize and join trade unions freely. Essential workers are barred from striking. Other workers' right to strike is restricted by complex notification and mediation requirements. Collective bargaining effectively exists only in the small private sector. Approximately 85 percent of Tanzania's people survive through subsistence agriculture. Economic decline in Zanzibar continues to dim the islands' prospects.

Corruption remains a serious problem, although the government has made some attempts to address it. In 1996, for example, President Mkapa dismissed the Dar es Salaam city council for alleged corruption. He created the Commission of Ethics, whose purpose is to assure greater openness and transparency in the government's financial dealings. Members of the government must submit written documents to the commission disclosing their personal finances.

In reality, however, the government has not succeeded in curbing corruption. Tanzania ranked 76th out of 90 countries in Transparency International's 2000 Corruption Perception Index. Corruption and mismanagement have hindered growth and reduced confidence in the current administration. Interpol has warned that Tanzania has become a major center for the transport of drugs from Asia to Europe.

Thailand

Polity: Parliamentary democracy
Economy: Capitalist-statist
Population: 62,000,000
PPP: $5,456
Life Expectancy: 69
Ethnic Groups: Thai (75 percent), Chinese (14 percent), other (11 percent)
Capital: Bangkok

Political Rights: 2
Civil Liberties: 3
Status: Free

Overview:

Despite being indicted in December 2000 for failing to properly disclose assets, the head of a populist party continued to be a strong favorite to become Thailand's next prime minister after elections scheduled for January 2001. A victory by Thaksin Shinawatra, a telecommunications tycoon turned conservative politician, could sideline the current government's ambitious but incomplete political and economic reforms.

Known as Siam until 1939, Thailand is the only Southeast Asian nation never colonized by a European country. Soldiers seized power in 1932 and established a constitutional monarchy. During the next six decades, the army overthrew or attempted to overthrow the government 16 more times and the country alternated between military and civilian rule. The last military intervention came in 1991, when the army deposed a hugely corrupt elected government. Following elections in April 1992, the new parliament appointed the coup leader, General Suchinda Kraprayoon, as prime minister. Bangkok's middle class organized demonstrations against Suchinda that climaxed in May, when soldiers shot dead more than 50 protesters. Following intervention by Thailand's revered monarch, King Bhumibol Alduyadej, Suchinda resigned, and Thailand returned to civilian rule.

Thailand's economy recorded the world's fastest growth between 1984 and 1995, but by 1997 it was weakened by slowing exports, $63 billion in private foreign debt, and a poorly supervised banking system burdened by bad property loans. After spending billions of dollars in a fruitless defense against speculators, the government floated the *baht* in July 1997, and in August agreed to a $17.2 billion loan package led by the International Monetary Fund (IMF) and conditioned on financial austerity. Middle-class street protests in Bangkok against corruption and economic mismanagement helped persuade parliament to approve a reformist constitution in September and to elect the Democratic Party's Chuan Leekpai, a former prime minister with a clean reputation, as the head of a new six-party coalition in November.

In 1998 and 1999, the Chuan government maintained high interest rates, shut down some financial institutions and bailed out others, and passed tough bankruptcy and foreclosure laws. The opposition said the tight monetary policy hurt farmers and other ordinary Thais by pushing the economy into recession. The economy contracted an estimated 7 to 8 percent in 1998, but grew 4.3 percent in 1999.

With poorer Thais still facing severe economic hardship in the aftermath of the financial crisis, Thaksin, a former deputy prime minister, emerged in spring 2000 as the leading contender to unseat Chuan as prime minister in the upcoming parliamentary elections. An old-style, patronage-oriented politician who could reverse recent political reforms and economic liberalization if elected, Thaksin promised a raft of new government programs to help poorer Thais and small and medium-sized businesses. A July World Bank study confirmed that despite Thailand's tentative economic recovery, its social crisis continued and the poorest workers were disproportionately affected through reduced wages and higher unemployment. Yet with the election nearing and polls showing Thaksin's party heading for victory, the National Counter Corruption Commission (NCC) concluded on December 26 that Thaksin had deliberately falsified statements disclosing his wealth both before and after he was a cabinet minister in 1998. Thaksin denied the charges. Snap opinion polls offered no consensus on how the scandal would affect either him or his party in the elections. If the constitutional court endorses the indictment, Thaksin will be barred from politics for five years.

While deflecting Thaksin's criticism that it had not done enough to help poorer Thais, the government campaigned on its record of shoring up the country's foreign currency reserves, returning the economy to growth, and stabilizing the baht, despite the currency's 13.5 percent drop against the dollar during the year. In what was viewed a key step toward resolving the banking system's $25 billion worth of nonperforming loans, a court approved in December a restructuring plan for the country's most indebted company, Thai Petrochemical Industries, despite strong opposition from the firm's management.

Political Rights and Civil Liberties: Thai citizens can change their government through elections that are marred by fraud and irregularities. The 1997 constitution created a house of representatives, whose 400 single-member constituencies and 100 party-list seats are directly elected for a four-year term, and a 200-seat senate that is directly elected for a six-year term. Following the first-ever direct senate election on March 4, 2000, the newly established Election Commission overturned the victories of 78 candidates on grounds of fraud and ordered new elections that took four rounds and five months to complete.

While the constitution contains numerous provisions for decentralizing power, the government has taken few steps to devolve power to the provinces. The issue of decentralization is particularly sensitive in Thailand, where the urban middle class has become increasingly empowered and the rural poor are still largely politically marginalized.

In the face of opposition from conservative politicians and bureaucrats, the Chuan government also has carried out few legal, judicial, and civil service reforms. Recent studies by the official Civil Service Commission, the Thai Chamber of Commerce, the World Bank, and the Berlin-based Transparency International suggested that official corruption and limited bureaucratic transparency continued to be serious problems. Nevertheless, the anticorruption institutions created by the 1997 constitution are having an impact. In addition to the NCCC's ruling against Thaksin and the Election Commission's tough stand against corruption in the senate vote, in August the constitutional court banned Sanan Kachornprasart, a former interior minister and one of Thailand's most powerful politicians, from holding office for five years after upholding an earlier corruption ruling by the NCCC.

Having ruled intermittently in the twentieth century, the army now appears to have relatively little influence in politics. However, the civilian government is not fully in control of the military, and in rural areas senior officers reportedly continued to run illicit business operations.

The judiciary is independent but continued to be hobbled by a lack of qualified judges, huge backlogs, and rampant corruption. In criminal cases, due process safeguards are generally adequate, but indigent defendants are not guaranteed an attorney. According to the United States State Department, the sole political prisoner is a Muslim cleric who was sentenced in 1994 to a 12-year term for leading a 1990 political protest.

The police force is highly corrupt and inadequately trained. Each year officers commit several extrajudicial executions of drug traffickers and other criminal suspects with virtual impunity while trying to deal with an increasingly violent narcotics trade. Police occasionally beat suspects to extract confessions and rape female detainees. Conditions in prisons and immigration detention centers are poor.

While the government rarely restricts free expression, laws remain in place against speech that defames the monarchy (*lese majesty*), incites public disturbances, threatens national security, or insults Buddhism. In addition, the constitution permits the government to restrict freedom of expression on national security, public order, and other grounds.

The press continued to criticize government policies and publicize corruption and human rights abuses, but journalists faced occasional intimidation and exercised some self-censorship regarding the military, the monarchy, the judiciary, and other sensitive issues. Under the 1941 Printing and Advertisement Act, police issue several warnings each year to publications for disturbing the peace, interfering with public safety, or offending public morals. The government or the military either directly or indirectly own or operate most radio and television stations. However, there is a private cable television network and a private television station, along with several private radio stations. The law requires radio stations to renew their licenses every year and to broadcast government-produced newscasts twice daily. Overall, the broadcast media generally offer diverse views.

While Bangkok's middle class and rural farmers frequently hold demonstrations without interference from authorities, police occasionally use excessive force against protesters. Nongovernmental organizations are active but face some police harassment and intimidation.

Prostitution is illegal but widespread. Many local officials, police, and soldiers are complicit in trafficking schemes, and the government barely enforces antitrafficking and antiprostitution laws. Many prostitutes, particularly women and girls from hill tribes and those trafficked from neighboring countries, are forcibly brought into the trade and are subjected to physical abuse and confinement. Girls sold into prostitution by their families become bonded laborers. Rape and domestic violence continued to be problems. The government has taken some steps to raise awareness about domestic violence and to assist victims, but police do not enforce vigorously relevant laws.

While women are increasingly entering the professions, they are underrepresented in politics and government and are concentrated in lower-paying jobs. Employers often give female salaried workers lower pay for equal work and deny female wage earners the minimum wage.

Religious freedom is respected in this predominantly Buddhist country. Muslim Malays make up ten percent of the population and face unofficial societal and employment discrimination. The 700,000 to 800,000 members of hill tribes also face societal discrimination. While the government took some steps in 2000 to make access to citizenship easier, roughly half of hill tribe members reportedly still lack documentation of citizenship or eligibility for citizenship. They cannot vote or own land, have difficulty in obtaining social services, and are not protected by labor laws.

Maintaining its long-standing policy of harboring refugees fleeing conflict in neighboring Southeast Asian countries, the government continued to provide temporary asylum in its border areas to some 120,000 refugees who fled fighting and gross human rights abuses in Burma. However, the Thai government began in late 1999 ordering Burmese refugees in Bangkok and other cities, most of whom are political dissidents, to move to border areas or risk deportation. In February, authorities deported to Burma five Burmese living in Bangkok. At the same time, newly arriving refugees from Burma had a harder time making asylum claims, according to the New York-based Human Rights Watch. The hardening of government attitudes followed two short-lived hostage crises, one at the Burmese embassy in Bangkok in October 1999 and the other at a provincial hospital in January 2000. Small militant Burmese groups were behind both incidents.

There are several independent trade unions, but employers reportedly continued to discriminate against workers who are union activists. While collective bargaining is legal, private sector employers maintain considerable leverage and generally set wages unilaterally. In February, parliament reinstated the right of state enterprise workers to form unions and bargain collectively. Enforcement of child labor and minimum wage laws continued to be lax. Working conditions in private factories are often poor and dangerous, and there are reportedly numerous forced labor sweatshops.

↑ Togo

Polity: Dominant party (military-influenced)
Economy: Mixed statist
Population: 5,000,000
PPP: $1,372
Life Expectancy: 49
Ethnic Groups: Ewe, Mina, Kabye, 34 other tribes (99 percent), European and Syrian-Lebanese (1 percent)
Capital: Lomé

Political Rights: 5
Civil Liberties: 5
Status: Partly Free

Trend Arrow: Togo received an upward trend arrow for a general easing of repression and for allowing an international investigation into allegations of state-sponsored killings following controversial 1998 presidential elections.

Overview: The government of President Gnasingbé Eyadéma made an uncharacteristic move toward openness in 2000 by allowing an international panel to investigate reports of hundreds of state-sponsored killings following the June 1998 presidential elections. Togo had called for the investigation after the rights group Amnesty International made the allegations in a May 1999 report that had initially prompted Togo to pursue legal action. The investigative team, made up of representatives from the United Nations and the Organization of African Unity, visited Togo in November. Further progress was made in 2000 in healing the rift over the 1998 elections. The government and opposition in July set up an independent electoral commission with an opposition lawyer as its chairman. The European Union (EU) hailed the move, noting that it could help lead to a resumption of aid, which was suspended in 1993 because of the government's resistance to democratic reform.

Togoland was a German colony for more than three decades until France seized it at the outset of World War I. It was held as French territory until its independence in 1960. After assuming direct power in 1967, Eyadéma suspended the constitution and extended his repressive rule through mock elections and a puppet political party. In 1991, free political parties were legalized, and multiparty elections were promised. The transition faltered, however, as soldiers and secret police harassed, attacked, or killed opposition supporters.

The government has been criticized for reported sanctions busting. In September, it announced a ban on uncertified diamonds from Angola following accusations by a UN panel that Togo had facilitated arms transfers to rebels in Angola in exchange for diamonds.

Eighty percent of Togolese are engaged in subsistence agriculture. Corruption, military spending, and large, inefficient state-owned companies impede economic growth.

Political Rights and Civil Liberties:

The Togolese people cannot choose their representatives freely. In the 1993 presidential election, which the opposition boycotted, Eyadéma claimed to have won 96 percent of the vote. His June 1998 reelection was blatantly fraudulent, with the government claiming he had won approximately 51 percent of the vote, thereby avoiding a runoff election against a single opposition candidate. Electoral rolls were suspect, and multiple voter cards were issued. The National Election Commission was not independent and was either incapable of, or unwilling to, provide adequate logistical support. Hundreds of domestic, EU-trained observers were denied accreditation. Eyadéma spent lavishly and used state resources for his campaign. State media coverage was heavily biased in his favor and virtually ignored Gilchrest Olympio, the main opposition candidate. Olympio, the leader of the Union of Forces for Change party, declared from exile that he was the real winner with 59 percent of the vote. He is the son of the country's founding president, who was murdered in 1963 as Eyadéma, then a demobilized sergeant who had served in France's colonial wars, led an army coup to topple the country's democratically elected government.

Violence and intimidation marred the 1994 legislative elections. Opposition parties won a majority in the national assembly, but splits and flawed 1996 by-elections allowed Eyadéma's Rally of the Togolese People party to regain control of the legislature. The opposition boycotted March 1999 legislative polls, which were marred by fraud and saw the ruling party win 79 out of 81 seats contested. The remaining 2 seats went to independent candidates.

The judiciary is still heavily influenced by the president. Traditional courts handle many minor matters. Courts are understaffed and inadequately funded. Pretrial detentions are lengthy, and prisons are severely overcrowded.

Killing, arbitrary arrest, and torture continue, although they have abated. Security forces commit abuses with impunity, and illegal detention is common. Human rights groups are closely monitored and sometimes harassed. Constitutionally protected religious freedom is generally respected. Freedom of assembly is allowed, but is often restricted among the government's political opponents. Demonstrations are often banned or violently halted. Ethnic discrimination is rife. Political and military power is narrowly held by members of a few ethnic groups from northern Togo, especially Eyadéma's Kabye ethnic group. Southerners dominate the country's commerce, and violence occasionally flares between the two groups.

A number of private newspapers publish in Lomé, but independent journalists are subject to harassment and the perpetual threat of various criminal charges. Private radio and television stations offer little independent local coverage. The government controls the broadcast media and allows little opposition access. The Press and Communication Code of 1998 declares in its first article that the media are free, but restricts press freedom in most of the 108 other articles. Libel is a criminal offense; it is a crime punishable by up to three months in prison to "offend the honor, dignity or esteem" of the president or other government leaders. The Togolese Media Observatory, which includes both government and private journalists, was established in November 1999 and is charged with protecting press freedom and improving the professionalism of journalists.

Despite constitutional guarantees of equality, women's opportunities for education and employment are limited. A husband may legally bar his wife from working or may receive her earnings. Customary law bars women's rights in divorce and inheritance rights to widows. Violence against women is common. Female genital mutilation is widely practiced by the country's northern ethnic groups. A 1998 law prohibiting the practice is not enforced. Several organizations promote the rights of women.

Togo's constitution includes the right to form and join unions, but essential workers are excluded. Health care workers may not strike. Only 20 percent of the labor force is unionized. Unions have the right to bargain collectively, but most labor agreements are brokered by the government in tripartite talks with unions and management. Several labor federations are politically aligned.

Tonga

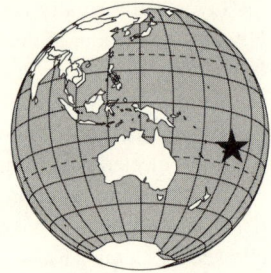

Polity: Traditional monarchy
Economy: Capitalist
Population: 100,000
PPP: na
Life Expectancy: na
Ethnic Groups: Polynesian
Capital: Nuku'alofa

Political Rights: 5
Civil Liberties: 3
Status: Partly Free

Overview: King Taufa'ahau Tupou IV appointed his youngest son, 41-year-old Prince 'Ulukalala Lavaka Ato, as prime minister in January 2000. This surprised observers who expected the king to appoint his eldest son, Crown Prince Pupouto'a, to the position. In July, Foreign Secretary Tu'a Taumoepeau Tupou was replaced by Mrs. Akosita Fineanganofo. Mr. Tupou heads Tonga's first mission to the United Nations. Tonga received military logistics aid worth nearly $170,000 from China after shifting diplomatic ties from Taiwan to China last year. In April, the Tonga police minister charged on several occasions that New Zealand was interfering in the kingdom's internal affairs by proposing to give aid to its pro-democracy movement.

Tonga is made up of 169 islands in the South Pacific, with a predominantly Polynesian population. It was unified as a kingdom under King George Tupou I in 1845. In 1970, Tonga became an independent member of the Commonwealth after 70 years of British influence. King Taufa'ahau Tupou has reigned since 1945. The country's longest-serving prime minister, Prince Fatafehi Tu'ipelehake, the king's brother, died in 1999. The prince was prime minister from 1965 to 1991, when illness compelled him to retire. Tonga gained full membership to the UN in 1999.

The 30-seat parliament serves a three-year term and consists of 12 ministers from the privy council, 9 nobles selected by and from Tonga's 33 noble families, and 9 People's Representatives (commoners) elected by universal suffrage. The government has not responded to the democratic opposition's call for holding direct elections for all 30 parliamentary seats and allowing the parliament, rather than the king, select to the privy council (cabinet). However, the government has allowed a democratic party to participate in elections and hold political rallies. In the 1990 legislative elections, pro-democracy candidates won five commoner seats. In August 1992, reform-oriented commoner representatives, led by Akilisi Pohiva, formed the pro-democracy movement (PDM). At the 1993 elections, pro-democracy candidates won six commoner seats. In 1994, the pro-democracy movement organized Tonga's first political party, the Tonga Democratic Party, which was subsequently renamed the People's Party. In the January 1996 elections, pro-democracy candidates took all nine commoner seats. The pro-democracy movement organized a convention to discuss a new, more democratic constitution (the current one has remained virtually unchanged since 1875) in January 1999. The government did not endorse the meeting but showed a more relaxed attitude by allowing non-Tongans to attend the meeting and government civil servants to participate in their personal capacity. However, in the March 1999 elections, democratic candidates won only 5 of the commoners' seats. Some observers questioned whether this signaled a decline in support for the pro-democracy movement.

The government has also been more receptive to the pro-democracy movement's call for greater transparency and accountability. In 1999, former Lands Minister Fakafanua stood trial for charges of bribery, misuse of public funds, abuse of power, and fraud. In 1988, after receiving a petition of more than 1,000 signatures, the king ordered a parliamentary investigation of Nobel Fusitu'a, speaker of the parliament, for charges of financial mismanagement and abuse of power.

The Tongan economy continued to struggle in 2000. Also, like many other Pacific Island-nations trying to develop alternative economic development options, Tonga was implicated in money laundering activities and was blacklisted by the United States and several European countries. The government also allegedly gave exclusive rights to an Australian company to conduct genetic research on the Tongan people. Tonga's small population makes it easier for researchers to trace lineage and genealogy as they seek to understand the function of specific human genes. Human rights groups said that the agreement was never publicly discussed. Television Tonga, a new public television station, was officially launched on July 4th.

Political Rights and Civil Liberties:

Tongans have limited democratic means to change their government. The 1875 constitution grants the king and hereditary nobles a perpetual majority in parliament with a total of 21 out of 30 seats. This allows legislation to be passed without the assent of the popularly elected People's Representatives, whose 9 seats represent roughly 95 percent of the population. Nevertheless, the commoner representatives have managed, on occasion, to reject legislation and the budget when joined by some noble representatives. The king has broad executive powers, appoints the prime minister, and appoints and heads the privy council. The king and the nobility also hold a preeminent position in society through substantial land holdings.

Criticisms against the king, his family, and the government are not well tolerated.

In 1985, Pohiva disclosed that assemblymen granted themselves pay raises. He has faced harassment since. In the early 1990s, he was fined for allegedly defaming the crown prince. In 1998, the supreme court acquitted Pohiva of criminal libel charges for a statement regarding the business dealings of the king's daughter, but he was found guilty of two defamation charges over comments about Police Minister Clive Edwards. The Tonga-based editor of the *Times of Tonga* was also found guilty of defaming Edwards and fined about $400. Michael Field, a correspondent for Agence France Presse, has been denied entry into Tonga since 1993, after writing about Tonga's pro-democracy movement and allegations of government financial mismanagement.

The government weekly *Tonga Chronicle* carries some opposition views. There are several private newspapers, including the *Times of Tonga*, *Kele'a*, and an outspoken Roman Catholic Church newsletter. Political coverage on the Tonga Broadcast Commission's Radio Tonga favors the government, and the state owns the country's two television stations.

Religious freedom is respected in this predominantly Christian society. There are no significant restrictions on freedom of assembly. The 1964 Trade Union Act recognizes the right of workers to form independent unions. None has formed because most Tongans engage in subsistence agriculture. The king appoints all judges, and the lower levels of the judiciary are not independent. The supreme court is independent and uses expatriate judges.

Citizens are free to travel domestically and abroad. Women generally occupy a subordinate role in this male-dominated society. Few women participate in the formal labor force, and they cannot own land or hold noble titles.

Trinidad and Tobago

Polity: Parliamentary democracy
Political Rights: 2*
Civil Liberties: 2
Economy: Capitalist-statist
Status: Free
Population: 1,300,000
PPP: $7,485
Life Expectancy: 74
Ethnic Groups: Black (43 percent), East Indian (40 percent), mixed (14 percent), other, including white and Chinese (3 percent)
Capital: Port-of-Spain
Ratings Change: Trinidad and Tobago's political rights rating changed from 1 to 2 due to the tone of the 2000 national campaign and credible, though still unproven, complaints of some electoral manipulation.

Overview:

Prime Minister Basdeo Panday's pro-business United National Congress (UNC) government swept to a bitterly fought and narrowly won victory in national elections held December 10, 2000, after a campaign marred by opposition claims of electoral corruption and worries about an upsurge of violent crime. During his first five-year term, the British-trained Panday, a lawyer and former trade unionist, presided over an economy that has become the powerhouse among the smaller nations of the Caribbean basin. However, his bid for reelection was clouded by worries about increasing drug crime and the country's growing reputation as a way station for Colombian cartels shipping cocaine northward to the United States. The hard-fought contest boosted electoral participation by 13 percent—76 percent of the nation's 947,447 eligible voters cast ballots—with a large number of young people turning out to vote. The intractable ethnic divide between the islands' East Indian and African communities also helped to keep the vote close. In the aftermath of the contest, the *Trinidad Express* editorialized that the election "certainly set some kind of record for just how tasteless and inconsiderate election campaigns can be."

Trinidad and Tobago, a member of the Commonwealth, achieved independence in 1962. The 1976 constitution established the two-island nation as a republic with a president, elected by a majority of both houses of parliament, replacing the former governor-general. Executive authority remains vested in the prime minister. The bicameral parliament consists of a 36-member house of representatives elected for five years and a 31-member senate, with 25 senators appointed by the prime minister and 6 by the opposition.

In the 1986 elections the National Alliance for Reconstruction (NAR), a coalition that bridges traditional political differences between black and East Indian communities, led by A. N. R. Robinson, soundly defeated the black-based People's National Movement (PNM), which had ruled for 30 years. The coalition unraveled when Basdeo Panday, the country's most prominent East Indian politician, was expelled; he then formed the East Indian-based UNC.

In July 1991 a radical black Muslim group briefly seized parliament. Tensions increased between black and East Indian communities, each roughly 40 percent of the population, as the latter edged towards numeric, and thus political, advantage. In December 1991 Patrick Manning led the PNM to victory by taking 21 of 36 parliamentary seats. Manning's government deregulated the economy and floated the currency, but the social costs of these economic reforms caused the PNM's popularity to decline. Manning called snap elections for November 6, 1995.

The election campaign focused on unemployment and the effects of the structural adjustment program. Voting ran largely along ethnic lines, with East Indians voting overwhelmingly for the UNC and blacks for the PNM. Each party won 17 seats on Trinidad. The NAR retained its two seats on Tobago. The NAR entered into a coalition with the UNC in exchange for a ministerial position for former Prime Minister Robinson and a promise of greater autonomy for Tobago. UNC leader Panday became Trinidad's first prime minister of East Indian descent.

In March 1996 Robinson was elected president. A series of incidents with Venezuela involving maritime rights—revolving around oil exploration and fishing rights, and Venezuelan drug-interdiction efforts—dominated the news. Internal divisions within the NAR, resulting from the strain of being the minority member of a governing coalition, threatened to cause the coalition to disappear. More recently, unemployment has fallen to its lowest level in a decade and a half.

In 1997 there were growing accusations about sweetheart contracts and patronage jobs, and Panday responded by assailing the "lies, half truths and innuendoes" of the opposition press. In 1998, Panday continued his campaign, as his government chose not to renew the work permit of Barbadian newsman Julian Rogers, in apparent reprisal for his having broadcast telephone calls from government critics. In April 1999, Information Minister Rupert Griffith reminded the media of the government's power to grant and revoke broadcast licenses and warned that local media operations were being examined "under a microscope."

In 1999, the Panday government brushed aside criticism from international human rights groups and allowed 10 of the more than 100 prisoners on death row to be hanged, in part out of concern over the islands' growing drug trade. The local appeal of the move was underscored when the government used the day that the first three men were executed to announce the holding of local elections the following month. Despite the move, the PNM, led by former Prime Minister Manning, made strong gains in the July 12 vote, in a contest marked by appeals along racial lines. On New Year's Eve, 1999, the chairman of a regional development corporation, who had criticized corruption in the government's unemployment program, was murdered after complaining to Panday that his local government minister had made threats against him.

In the December 2000 elections, Panday's UNC won 19 parliamentary seats to the PNM's 16, with the NAR winning 1 of the 2 on the island of Tobago. In the aftermath of his party's defeat, Manning said he was considering charges against two victorious UNC candidates who, he said, filed false nominating petitions as a result of holding dual citizenship. The PNM also claimed that the UNC had tried to pad voter rolls in highly competitive districts. Panday's swearing-in ceremony was delayed by nine days due to recounts in several constituencies and the threat of legal action by the PNM. On December 31, 2000, President Arthur Robinson refused to swear in six nominees to Panday's cabinet who had been defeated in the election, saying such appointments "undermine democracy."

Political Rights and Civil Liberties: Citizens of Trinidad and Tobago can change their government democratically. Despite preelection complaints about ruling-party padding of the voter rolls, and PNM charges that the UNC offered its members financial inducements to defect, a Commonwealth observer group has given the election high marks in a preliminary report.

The judiciary is independent, although subject to some political pressure, and the Privy Council in London serves as the recourse of ultimate appeal. As a result of rising crime rates, the court system is severely backlogged, in some cases for up to five years, with an estimated 20,000 criminal cases awaiting trial. Prisons are grossly overcrowded; the government does permit visits to them by human rights monitors, who in general operate freely. There are more than 100 prisoners on death row.

In May 1999, the government withdrew as a state party from the American Convention on Human Rights, which prohibits countries from extending the death penalty beyond those crimes for which it was in effect at the time the treaty was ratified. In June, three men, including the reputed drug lord Dole Chadee, were hanged for their role in the 1994 murder of a couple and their two children—the first executions in five years—and their executions were followed by seven more within a month. In June 2000, the country withdrew entirely from the International Covenant on Civil and Political Rights. Amnesty International, which has been at odds with the Panday government over the death penalty, charged that "as a consequence...international human rights experts will no longer be able to examine the claims of those aggrieved citizens who may have suffered violations of their most fundamental rights."

As the country is an important transshipment point for cocaine, an estimated 80 percent of all crimes are believed to involve narcotics. High levels of drug-related violence and common crime continue to undermine the protection of civil liberties. There have been more than two dozen drug-related killings in recent years, including the still-unsolved murder of former Attorney General Selwyn Richardson. Successive governments have also failed to enforce certain criminal laws. Corruption in the police force—often drug related—is endemic, and law enforcement inefficiency results in the dismissal of some criminal cases. In December 2000, Panday admitted that despite government efforts to finance reforms, something was "fundamentally wrong" with the police force.

The Panday government has won some points for its antidrug efforts and has been a principal proponent of a regional witness-protection program. It has also signed several antinarcotics accords with the United States.

The press is privately owned and vigorous and offers pluralistic views; however, in May 1997, the government floated a restrictive journalistic code of conduct that the Media Association of Trinidad and Tobago said led to instances in which reporters and other press workers were physically attacked. In 1998, Panday's refusal to allow the renewal of the work permit of a respected Barbadian broadcaster became a regional cause célèbre. He also reiterated his refusal to sign the Inter-American Press Association's Chapultepec Declaration on press freedom until it addressed instances of media dissemination of "lies, half-truths and innuendoes." The broadcast media are both private and public. Freedom of association and assembly is respected. In 2000, a high court judge ordered Panday to pay newspaper publisher Ken Gordon, an Afro-Trinidadian, $120,000 for defamation, after calling him a "pseudo-racist."

Domestic violence and other violence against women is extensive and remains a low priority for police and prosecutors. However, in a 1999 landmark ruling, the court of appeals overturned a death sentence and reduced the charge from murder to manslaughter in the case of a woman the court said suffered from battered-wife syndrome. Persons infected with HIV/AIDS are the focus of community ostracism and government neglect.

Labor unions are well organized, powerful, and politically active, although union membership has declined. Strikes are legal and occur frequently.

Tunisia

Polity: Presidential (dominant party)
Economy: Mixed capitalist
Population: 9,600,000
PPP: $5,404
Life Expectancy: 70
Ethnic Groups: Arab (98 percent), other (2 percent)
Capital: Tunis

Political Rights: 6
Civil Liberties: 5
Status: Not Free

Overview:

Outbursts of social unrest in 2000 reflected growing public dissatisfaction with government corruption, declining standards of living, and a lack of civic freedom. As a loss of confidence challenged President Zine el-Abidine Ben Ali's legitimacy at home, new attention to Tunisia's bleak human rights record brought criticism from abroad.

Following Tunisia's independence from France in 1956, President Habib Bourguiba pursued secular, pro-Western policies while moving toward social liberalization and modernization. In 1987, Prime Minister Ben Ali succeeded Bourguiba, who was deemed medically unfit to govern, and offered brief promise of an open political system. However, his rule became increasingly autocratic and repressive. Intolerant of public criticism, he has allowed almost no credible opposition to exist; opposition parties have been banned or crippled by arrests and harassment. The government has consistently targeted trade unionists, human rights activists, student leaders, and the media, but it treats Islamists most harshly, claiming the need to avoid the kind of unrest seen in neighboring Algeria. Ben Ali has escaped meaningful criticism from Western governments, in part because much of the worst abuse is aimed at Islamic fundamentalists, but also because Tunisia is an important trading partner for several European countries.

The 1959 constitution provides for a president with broad powers, including the right to select the prime minister and to rule by decree during legislative adjournments. Under Ben Ali, the role of prime minister was reduced from leader of the government to "coordinator" of ministerial activities. The unicameral legislature is elected to five-year terms by universal suffrage. The president appoints a governor to each of Tunisia's 23 provinces, and municipal councils are elected.

Presidential and legislative elections held in October 1999 were widely described as a farce. Despite the prior amendment of electoral laws to relax restrictions on presidential candidacy and to mandate a 20 percent allotment of legislative seats to opposition candidates, Ben Ali won 99.4 percent of the presidential vote and his party, the Constitutional Democratic Rally (RCD), won 80 percent of parliamentary seats. Elections in May 2000 for seats in Tunisia's 257 municipalities were equally suspect; the RCD won 94 percent of seats after running unopposed in nearly 75 percent of municipalities. In both elections, opposition candidates openly acknowledged that their role was largely symbolic.

Dissatisfaction with Ben Ali's government has increased since the October 1999 polls, the results of which were seen as insulting to the public's intelligence. In February 2000, taxi drivers went on strike to protest new government regulations that would leave them even more vulnerable to arbitrary abuse and extortion by police. Provoked by rumors of an impending increase in basic food prices, students and unemployed workers rioted for up to ten days in February throughout southern Tunisia against declining living standards, government corruption, and unemployment. Prisoners staged hunger strikes during the year to protest mistreatment and poor conditions.

Several cases drew international attention to Tunisia's human rights problems and highlighted decreasing official tolerance of dissent. Journalist Taoufik Ben Brik and his family suffered ongoing harassment and intimidation by authorities for his publication of articles in foreign newspapers detailing Tunisian human rights abuses. In July, leading activist Moncef Marzouki was fired from a university lectureship after President Ben Ali publicly denounced government critics as traitors. Marzouki, who criticized human rights abuses and corruption by authorities, was charged with defamation and disturbing public order, and sentenced in December to 12 months in prison. These cases and others, such as the refusal of Ben Ali to allow the live broadcast of Bourguiba's funeral in April, drew rare criticism from Western governments. Observers warned that given Ben Ali's waning popularity, opposition forces may prove politically destabilizing if not given room to participate openly in the political process.

Political Rights and Civil Liberties:

Tunisians cannot change their government democratically. The ruling RCD and its predecessor parties have controlled the political system since independence. No political party based on religion or region is permitted, and all parties must be licensed. Despite a slight relaxation of restrictions on opposition candidates in the 1999 presidential elections, the elections were neither open nor competitive. The two opposition leaders who met the stringent conditions placed on potential candidates were little-known figures who received almost no media attention.

The judiciary is subject to political interference by the president and the government. Despite 1999 legal reforms that broadened the state's definition of torture and reduced the length of incommunicado detention, illegal detention and torture continued in 2000. Four students testified in November about abuses they endured—including beatings, rapes, and burnings—at the hands of police after being arrested for taking part in protests. A June report by a Tunisian human rights group documented poor conditions, inadequate medical care, degrading treatment, and regular physical abuse in prisons. In December, President Ben Ali announced that the government would make compensation payments to anyone held in police custody without reasonable grounds, and to anyone imprisoned but later exonerated by the courts. At least four people died in custody during 2000 under suspicious circumstances. By year's end, no investigation into these cases had taken place.

Suspected Islamist sympathizers face severe repression. Actual or suspected members of the outlawed An-Nahdha movement constitute the majority of an estimated 1,000 to 2,000 political prisoners in Tunisia, according to Human Rights Watch. Many others are in exile. Former political prisoners and their families are often deprived of their passports, monitored and searched by police, and discriminated against with regard to employment.

The press code prohibits subversion and defamation, both broadly defined, under threat of fines and confiscation. The government uses newsprint subsidies and control over public advertising revenues to limit dissent and encourage self-censorship. Prepublication submission requirements allow authorities to seize publications at will. Foreign publications are censored. Domestic broadcasting is government controlled and presents only pro-government views. As two new ad hoc committees set up to suggest press law reforms began meeting in May, Ben Ali met with private newspaper publishers and told them to be more daring in their reporting: "Be critical as long as what you are saying is true." Authorities charged Taoufik Ben Brik in April with publishing false information and offending public institutions, and confiscated his passport. The journalist began a 42-day hunger strike in April in the offices of the Aloes publishing house. Authorities seized the publishing house and assaulted reporters and rights activists who went to Ben Brik's home to visit him. In May, the charges against him were dropped and he was allowed to travel, but his brother was jailed for abusing a security official. In November, the journalist was detained at the Tunis airport after arriving from Paris. Police seized dozens of books from him, calling them "illegal imports." Riad Ben Fadhel, a journalist who criticized the government's handling of Ben Brik's case, was the target of an assassination attempt in May. A French weekly faced repeated distribution delays over controversial articles.

Permission is required for public gatherings. Hundreds of demonstrators were arrested in February for protesting rumored increases in food prices. About 70 students were charged with damaging public property and spreading false information. Twenty-six were jailed, including nine who were later pardoned by Ben Ali. The government continued to deny legal status to domestic human rights organizations, and detained, harassed, and prosecuted activists for "belonging to an unauthorized association." A delegation of monitors from Amnesty International and the International Federation of Human Rights Leagues (FIDH) was prevented from entering Tunisia in July.

Islam is the state religion, and it is practiced under intense government scrutiny. The government controls and subsidizes mosques and pays the salaries of prayer leaders. Proselytizing by non-Muslims is prohibited. Other religions are generally tolerated, with the exception of Bahai, whose adherents may not practice publicly.

General equality for women has advanced more in Tunisia than elsewhere in the Arab world. Inheritance law is based on *Sharia* (Islamic law) and discriminates against women, although the government enacted legislation in 1998 to improve women's rights in matters of divorce and property ownership. Women are well represented in academia and the professions. Twenty-one seats in the national legislature went to women in October 1999 elections.

Tunisia's sole labor federation, the Tunisian General Federation of Labor, operates under severe government constraints. Workers may bargain collectively and strike.

Turkey

Polity: Presidential-parliamentary democracy (military-influenced) (insurgency)
Economy: Capitalist-statist
Population: 65,300,000
PPP: $6,422
Life Expectancy: 69
Ethnic Groups: Turk (80 percent), Kurd (20 percent)
Capital: Ankara

Political Rights: 4
Civil Liberties: 5
Status: Partly Free

Overview:

The debate over conditions for accession to the European Union (EU) began to dominate Turkey's political scene in 2000. While the coalition government of Prime Minister Bulent Ecevit demonstrated significant commitment to implementing the necessary economic measures, it has made very little progress on the political reforms required to guarantee democracy, the rule of law, and human rights. Turkey's reluctance to undertake these reforms reflects a struggle within the country between those who advocate membership as the route to modernity and prosperity, and the entrenched interests of those who champion the status quo under the pretext of protecting the Turkish founding principles of national unity and secularism.

Mustapha Kemal Ataturk, who launched a reform program under which Turkey abandoned much of its Ottoman and Islamic heritage, proclaimed Turkey a republic in 1923. His secular, nationalistic legacy has profoundly influenced Turkish politics ever since, most notably in the post-World War II period. The doctrine of "Kemalism" has been used by the military to justify three coups since 1960. Turkey returned to civilian rule in 1983.

In 1995, the Islamist *Refah* (Welfare) party took advantage of discontent over corruption, high inflation, and unemployment to win a majority in general elections. After the collapse of a center-right coalition, Refah and the center-right True Path (DYP) formed Turkey's first Islamist-led coalition government in June 1996. Refah Prime Minister Necmettin Erbakan almost immediately found himself at odds with the military, which regards itself as the guardian of Turkish secularism, over such government policies as allowing female civil servants to wear traditional headscarves. Erbakan resigned under intense military pressure in June 1997. Refah was outlawed in January 1998 for "conspiring against the secular order," and Erbakan and five other Refah leaders were banned from politics for five years. Most remaining Refah MPs launched the Virtue party in February 1998.

A ruling coalition of the center-right Motherland (ANAP), the social-democratic Democratic Left (DSP), and the conservative Democratic Turkey parties under ANAP's Mesut Yilmaz collapsed in November 1998 over corruption charges. The DSP's Ecevit headed an interim government until the April 1999 general elections. The DSP won 22 percent of the vote, the far-right National Action Party (MHP) 18 percent, and Virtue 16 percent. ANAP and DYP won 13 and 12 percent, respectively. The Kurdish People's Democracy Party (HADEP) did not win the 10 percent of the vote required to send members to parliament, but won control of 37 local administrations despite attempts by Turkey's chief prosecutor to ban it. Ecevit assembled an unlikely coalition of the DSP, MHP, and ANAP, and won a vote of confidence in June.

Despite several challenges to its cohesiveness, the governing coalition has proved remarkably stable. In February 2000, Ecevit initiated a campaign to amend the constitution to allow a second presidential term for Suleyman Demirel, whose term ended in May. His goal was apparently to prevent rivalry over Demirel's successor from destabilizing the coalition, which launched an ambitious IMF-backed economic reform program in January. Parliament rejected the amendments in April, leading many to predict serious infighting and perhaps dissolution of the government. However, party leaders unanimously approved the candidacy of Ahmet Necdet Sezer, the chief justice of the constitutional court and an outspoken advocate of democratic reforms. Sezer was elected president by parliament in May.

Sezer's election was welcomed by Western allies, particularly within the EU. The first Turkish president who is neither a politician nor a general, he has urged relaxation of antiterror laws and other legislation that restricts free speech, political parties, and the rights of Kurds. Although the president's role is largely ceremonial, it carries a degree of moral influence and he may serve as a power broker in times of crisis. Moreover, the president is far less vulnerable to military pressure than government ministers are, and so he may impart a sense of stability as well as advance his own agenda. Sezer demonstrated his commitment to the rule of law and political reform in August, when he twice vetoed a government decree that would facilitate the removal of public servants suspected of fundamentalist or separatist sympathies. Asserting that laws should be subject to parliamentary approval, Sezer clashed with military leaders who accused him of hindering the fight against radical Islam, and his poll ratings soared. In September, Sezer vetoed a decree on banking reform for the same reason. In October, the constitutional court annulled the law authorizing the government to issue decrees with the force of law.

Since being formally declared a candidate for EU membership in 1999, Turkey has outlined a set of economic and political goals that it must meet in order to fulfill the membership criteria. On the economic side, Turkey has made considerable progress, lifting obstacles to privatization, attracting foreign investment, lowering inflation, and tackling corruption. Further work needs to be done to expand growth and to close a significant income gap between Turkey and the EU; average median income in Turkey is about a third that of other Europeean countries. In November, a criminal investigation into ten banks taken under state administration because of corruption and mismanagement led to a loss of confidence in the banking system and a liquidity crisis. A financial collapse was averted in December when the IMF extended an emergency loan on the conditions that Turkey undertake major bank restructuring and increase the pace of privatization.

Political reform, including constitutional reforms and measures to improve human rights, train civil servants, curb the military's role in politics, and prevent terrorism while upholding freedom of expression and Kurdish cultural rights, presents a greater challenge. The army's insistence upon protecting Turkish society from the twin threats of political Islam and Kurdish separatism continues to impede political progress. Kurdish and Islamist political parties, organizations, and individuals faced severe harassment, arrest, and other restrictions on political and social freedom during 2000. The Virtue and HADEP parties faced a possible ban by the constitutional court, while HADEP members were arrested for allegedly supporting Kurdish terrorism. The Kurdistan Workers' Party (PKK), whose leader, Abdullah Ocalan, is currently on death row following his capture last year, announced the end of its insurgency in February. Ocalan himself renounced separatism and called for reconciliation. The government rejected his overtures, and although fighting between Kurd separatists and Turkish troops has declined dramatically, Turkey continues to deny Kurds many basic rights.

Political Rights and Civil Liberties: Turkish citizens can change their government democratically, though the military wields considerable influence in political matters, especially regarding defense and security. The 1982 constitution provides for a parliament, the Grand National Assembly (currently 550 seats), that is directly elected to five-year terms. The assembly elects the president to one seven-year term. Islamist and Kurdish political parties suffered intimidation in advance of parliamentary elections in April 1999. Some 500 HADEP members and supporters were arrested, party rallies were blocked, a small pro-Kurdish party was banned, and ballots cast for HADEP were destroyed. Security forces launched an all-out campaign against "antisecular propaganda," blocking female Muslim students wearing headscarves from attending classes, jailing a former Istanbul mayor for quoting from an allegedly antisecular poem, and arresting hundreds of Islamists.

The European Commission's 2000 report on Turkey's progress toward EU accession stated that in the last year, "the economic, social, and cultural rights situation has not improved, particularly when it comes to the enjoyment of cultural rights for all Turks irrespective of ethnic origin." However, it welcomed initiatives to encourage debate on these issues, including the publication by a parliamentary human rights commission of nine reports on police brutality and torture in Turkey; the work of the Supreme Board of Coordination for Human Rights, which includes members from all ministries and state organs and has identified key legislative priorities with regard to human rights; and the government's signing in August 2000 of the International Covenant on Civil and Political Rights and the International Covenant on Economic, Social, and Cultural Rights.

The 15-year-old conflict between the Turkish military and the PKK, which has claimed as many as 37,000 lives, continues only sporadically since the PKK announced the end of its insurrection in February. A few splinter Kurdish elements have vowed to continue fighting for a separate Kurdish state, however, and the Turkish military made several incursions into northern Iraq to attack PKK bases there during the year. Four southeastern provinces remain under emergency law. Civil governors throughout the region may authorize military operations, expel citizens suspected of Kurdish sympathies, ban demonstrations, and confiscate publications. During 2000, the government began a campaign of reconciliation in the impoverished region, sending the army to build roads and houses, teach literacy, set up youth clubs, and even to reportedly pay for weddings. Local governors reported that more than 2,000 people had returned to their homes in the southeast under a new "return to village" project. However, many of the hundreds of thousands of Kurds whose homes were razed or burned by the military have been placed in "central villages," which are heavily secured by soldiers in order to prevent villagers from organizing against the state. The army has forcibly depopulated more than half the 5,000 villages and hamlets in the region.

A crackdown on the radical Islamist Hizbollah beginning in January drew international attention to atrocities committed by the group against Kurds since the early 1990s. The organization reportedly tortured and killed some 2,000 Kurdish professionals, politicians, and businessmen between 1992 and 1996 with the tacit consent of Turkish authorities, whose struggle against Kurdish militants was in full swing. In February, new evidence arose that the government of Tansu Ciller in the mid-1990s actually supplied arms to Hizbollah. Observers speculate that having effectively disabled the PKK in late 1999, the government no longer needed Hizbollah's counterinsurgency efforts, and the crackdown ensued. The group's leader was killed in a clash with police in January. Raids that followed led to the arrests of some 1,600 suspected Islamist militants, and to the discovery of more than 100 bodies, mostly Kurds, by the end of 2000.

The judiciary is susceptible to government influence through the High Council of Judges and Prosecutors, which names judges and prosecutors to the high courts and controls appointments and promotions of those in lower courts. The council is appointed by the president, and its decisions are not subject to review. State security courts, which try terrorist offenses, limit procedural safeguards and the right to appeal.

Prison conditions are abysmal, characterized by widespread torture, sexual abuse, and denial of medical attention to inmates. The parliamentary human rights committee has published nine reports on torture in Turkey since May 2000, based on inspections of police stations and prisons between 1998 and 2000. However, little has been done to stop the practice, and the conviction and sentencing of offending officials is rare. Prison riots occur frequently because of overcrowding and anger over conditions. Five people were killed and more than 20 held hostage in two days of unrest sparked by gang rivalry in a western Turkish prison in November. In December, security forces stormed more than 20 prisons in an effort to end a hunger strike by inmates protesting plans to move them to maximum-security facilities. At least 31 people, including two soldiers, were killed in the unrest, which lasted four days in some areas. Parliament approved an amnesty law in December that resulted in the release of some 20,000 inmates by year's end.

Freedom of expression in Turkey is limited by the criminal code, which forbids insulting state officials and incitement to racial or ethnic hatred. The Anti-Terror Law prohibits separatist propaganda. The military, Kurds, and political Islam are highly sensitive subjects and frequently earn journalists criminal penalties. Following unrest in Turkish prisons in December, the Supreme Board of Radio and Television (RTUK) imposed restrictions on broadcast media, and a state security court ruled to ban the publication or broadcast of "statements from illegal organizations or information liable to incite hatred, hostility, or crimes." At least three newspapers faced charges or investigation under the measure by year's end. By June, at least 13 publications, most of them pro-Kurdish, were banned in the southeast. Reporters Sans Frontiéres reported that dozens of radio and television stations were suspended during 2000. Journalists and nonjournalists continued to face arrest and prosecution for expression; a university student was detained in May for handing out leaflets seen as insulting to former president Demirel. The books of Kurdish writer Mehmed Uzun were removed from bookshelves in April, and former prime minister Necmettin Erbakan was sentenced to a year in prison for an "antisecular" speech he gave in 1994. In a positive development, pressure from the EU led to a government announcement in December that it would consider allowing limited broadcasting in Kurdish.

Authorities may restrict freedom of association and assembly on the grounds of maintaining public order, and prior notice of gatherings is required. Scores of prisoners' relatives were arrested in 2000 for demonstrating against new "F-type" prisons, which consist of small cells rather than the traditional large wards. Pro-Kurdish political parties and NGOs face severe harassment and restrictions on their activities. Three Kurdish mayors, all HADEP members, were detained and removed from their posts in February for allegedly supporting terrorism. Scores of demonstrators protesting the arrests were beaten and detained in Diyarbakir. The mayors were later released and allowed to return to their posts after international protests. More than 150 Kurds were detained in March after authorities banned public celebrations of the Kurdish New Year in several cities. Pro-Kurdish human rights activist Akin Birdal was returned to prison in March for speeches in 1995 and 1996 that allegedly incited racial hatred. Birdal had been released temporarily in 1999 for medical reasons. Several HADEP members were arrested in raids on party offices throughout the year, and the party faced a possible ban by the constitutional court at year's end.

Islamists also faced official harassment. A Turkish court in February upheld a 1999 decision to strip Merve Kavakci, a Virtue MP, of her Turkish citizenship because she attempted to take her oath of office while wearing a traditional headscarf. University students were barred from classes and sometimes arrested for wearing the headscarf. Virtue, like the Kurdish HADEP, was under threat of closure by the constitutional court at the end of 2000. In October, a state security court began the trial in absentia of Fetullah Gulen, a prominent Islamic moderate resident in the United States, on charges of plotting to overthrow the secular government.

Roughly 99 percent of Turks are Sunni Muslim. Religious freedom is restricted by limits on worship to designated sites, constraints on building houses of worship for minority religions, and military-backed government crackdowns on political Islam. A 1998 law placed all mosques under government administration, requiring official authorization for the construction of mosques and forbidding the wearing of uniforms and masks (including headscarves) by demonstrators. In March, two Turkish Christians were detained for "insulting Islam" by distributing copies of the Bible. They were released in May pending trial. Several people were detained overnight in May following a police raid on an apartment where a group was holding Protestant services.

Women face discrimination in family matters such as inheritance, marriage, and divorce. Social norms make it difficult to prosecute rape cases, and the penalty for rape may be reduced if a woman was not a virgin prior to her attack. The justice ministry in 1999 banned the practice of subjecting women and girls to gynecological exams to determine virginity.

Workers may form unions, bargain collectively, and strike, with the exception of public servants and workers engaged in the protection of life and property. This category includes workers in the mining and petroleum industries, sanitation, defense, and education. According to the International Confederation of Free Trade Unions, Turkey does not adequately protect workers from anti-union discrimination. Thousands of workers held a one-day strike in December to protest government plans to adopt IMF-backed austerity measures.

Turkmenistan

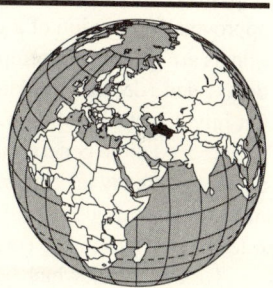

Polity: Presidential
Economy: Statist
Population: 5,200,000
PPP: $2,550
Life Expectancy: 66
Ethnic Groups: Turkmen (77 percent), Uzbek (9 percent), Russian (7 percent), Kazakh (2 percent), other (5 percent)
Capital: Ashgabat

Political Rights: 7
Civil Liberties: 7
Status: Not Free

Overview:

Turkmenistan's already isolated position in the international community was further reinforced in 2000, as the government banned Turkmen citizens from holding foreign bank accounts, ordered the monitoring of foreign nationals, and shut down the last independent Internet service providers. In this energy-rich country suffering from limited export routes, plans to construct a U.S.-backed gas pipeline project to Turkey showed little real progress throughout the year.

The southernmost republic of the former Soviet Union, Turkmenistan was conquered by the Mongols in the thirteenth century and seized by Russia in the late 1800s. Having been incorporated into the U.S.S.R. in 1924, Turkmenistan gained formal independence in 1991 with the dissolution of the Soviet Union.

Saparmurat Niyazov, the former head of the Turkmenistan Communist Party, ran unopposed in elections to the newly created post of president in October 1990. After the adoption of a new constitution in 1992, Niyazov was reelected as the sole candidate for a five-year term with a reported 99.5 percent of the vote. The main opposition group, Agzybirlik, which was formed in 1989 by leading intellectuals, was banned and its leaders harassed. Niyazov's tenure as president was extended for an additional five years, to the year 2002, by a 1994 referendum that exempted him from having to run again in 1997 as originally scheduled. In December 1994 parliamentary elections, only Niyazov's Democratic Party of Turkmenistan (DPT), the renamed Communist Party, was permitted to field candidates.

In December 12, 1999, elections to the National Assembly (*Mejlis*), 104 candidates competed for the legislature's 50 seats. Every candidate was selected by the government, and virtually all were members of President Niyazov's DPT. According to government claims, voter turnout was 98.9 percent. The Organization for Security and Cooperation in Europe (OSCE), which cited the lack of provisions for participation by nongovernmental parties and the executive branch's control of the nomination of candidates, refused to send even a limited assessment mission. Some diplomatic observers noted various irregularities, including empty polling stations.

In a further consolidation of President Niyazov's extensive powers, parliament unanimously voted in late December to make Niyazov president for life. With this decision, Turkmenistan became the first Commonwealth of Independent States (CIS) country to formally abandon presidential elections.

Already one of the most closed societies in the world, Turkmenistan took several steps in 2000 to further isolate itself from the international community. In June, Niyazov approved the creation of a government council to register and monitor all foreign nationals arriving into or temporarily residing in the country. The same month, the president issued a decree forbidding Turkmen citizens from holding accounts in foreign banks. On July 20, a new policy was announced in which potential university students would be screened three generations back to exclude all but the most "worthy" applicants. In a country already lacking most basic school supplies, Niyazov ordered the destruction in October of thousands of new history textbooks that he claimed had overstated the role of other nations in Turkmenistan's history.

Turkmenistan, which has the fourth-largest known natural gas reserves in the world, has struggled to bring its energy resources to foreign markets in the face of limited export routes and nonpaying customers. In 1999, a joint venture of Royal Dutch/Shell and PSG announced plans to build a 1,250-mile gas pipeline stretching from gas fields in Turkmenistan through Azerbaijan and Georgia to Turkey. The estimated $2.5 billion project, which would allow Turkmen gas to bypass Russian and Iranian routes, is supported by the United States as a way of reducing the influence of both Moscow and Tehran in Central Asia. However, a September 2000 agreement for Turkmenistan to sell increased amounts of gas to Russia, which would deprive the pipeline of much of its supply source, as well as disputes with rival supplier Azerbaijan over sharing pipeline space, have cast ongoing doubts on the project's future viability. Turkmenistan continued to pursue other energy development options throughout the year, including possible gas routes to China through Afghanistan.

Despite the country's wealth of natural resources, there have been few reforms of the Soviet command system, and the majority of citizens live in poverty. The economy suffers from low levels of gross domestic product (GDP) and record low harvests, and major industries remain state owned. In late 2000, Niyazov announced plans to build a 1,300-square-mile artificial lake in the Karakum Desert to increase the country's agricultural output. However, critics charge that the plan, which is estimated to eventually cost between $4 billion and $6 billion, is neither environmentally nor economically sound.

Political Rights and Civil Liberties: Citizens of Turkmenistan cannot change their government democratically. President Niyazov enjoys virtually absolute power over all branches and levels of the government. He has established an extensive cult of personality, including the erection of monuments to his leadership throughout the country. In 1994, he renamed himself Turkmenbashi, or leader of the Turkmen. The country has two national legislative bodies: the unicameral National Assembly (*Mejlis*), composed of 50 members elected in single-mandate constituencies for five-year terms, is the main legislature; and the People's Council (*Khalk Maslakhaty*), consisting of members of the Mejlis, 50 directly elected representatives, and various regional and other executive and judicial officials, meets infrequently to address certain major issues. Neither parliamentary body enjoys genuine independence from the executive. The 1994 and 1999 parliamentary elections were neither free nor fair.

Freedom of speech and the press is severely restricted by the government, which controls all radio and television broadcasts and print media. Reports of dissenting political views are banned, as are even mild forms of criticism of the president. Subscriptions to foreign newspapers, other than Russian ones, are severely restricted. Foreign journalists have limited opportunities to visit Turkmenistan and are often restricted to certain locations. Radio Liberty's Turkmen language service has been called the only source of nongovernmental information for most Turkmen citizens. The government revoked the licenses of all Internet service providers in May 2000, leaving only the state-owned Turkmentelekom to provide Internet access. In August, Niyazov launched a new television station, the "Epoch of Turkmenbashi," devoted to covering his supposed accomplishments and initiatives.

The government restricts freedom of religion through means including strict registration requirements. Only Sunni Muslims and Russian Orthodox Christians have been able to meet the criterion of having at least 500 members. Members of religious groups that are not legally registered by the government, including Baptists, Pentecostals, and Baha'is, are frequently harassed by security forces. A Seventh-Day Adventist Church was demolished by authorities in November 1999, with ten people reportedly in the building when destruction began. Since independence, Turkmenistan, which is overwhelmingly Sunni Muslim, has enjoyed a modest revival of Islam.

While the constitution guarantees peaceful assembly and association, these rights are restricted in practice. Only one political party, the Niyazov-led DPT, has been officially registered. Opposition parties have been banned, and virtually all of their leading members have either fled abroad or face harassment and detention in Turkmenistan. Social and cultural organizations are allowed to function, but often face difficulty registering. The government-controlled Colleagues Union is the only legal central trade union permitted. There are no legal guarantees for workers to form or join unions or to bargain collectively.

The judicial system is subservient to the president, who appoints and removes judges without legislative review. The authorities frequently deny rights of due process, including public trials and access to defense attorneys. There are no independent lawyers, with the exception of a few retired legal officials, to represent defendants in trials. Police abuse of suspects and prisoners, often to obtain confessions, is reportedly widespread, and prisons are overcrowded and unsanitary. In May 2000, parliament adopted a law prohibiting searches of private homes by the security services without the prior approval of a special commission composed of senior government, law enforcement, and public organization officials.

In February 2000, Nurbedi Nurmamedov, one of the founders of the unregistered opposition movement Agzybirlik, was convicted on charges of hooliganism and attempted murder and sentenced to eight years in prison. His arrest a month earlier followed his criticism of the 1999 parliamentary elections and the decision to extend indefinitely Niyazov's term as president. Unlike most opponents of the regime, Nurmamedov was one of the few who had chosen to remain in Turkmenistan, despite years of persecution by the authorities for his political activities. In late December, Nurmamedov was released from prison under a general presidential amnesty, although he had to repent on national television and swear an oath of loyalty to Niyazov.

Citizens are required to carry internal passports for identification. Although residence permits are not required, place of residence is registered in passports. Obtaining passports and exit visas for foreign travel is difficult for most nonofficial travelers and allegedly often requires payment of bribes to government officials. The security services regularly monitor the activities of those critical of the government. A continuing Soviet-style command economy and widespread corruption diminish equality of opportunity.

Traditional social-religious norms limit occupations for women to mostly those of homemaker and mother, and anecdotal reports suggest that domestic violence is common.

Tuvalu

Polity: Parliamentary
democracy
Economy: Capitalist
Population: 10,000
PPP: na
Life Expectancy: na
Ethnic Groups: Polynesian (96 percent), other (4 percent)
Capital: Funafuti

Political Rights: 1
Civil Liberties: 1
Status: Free

Overview:
On December 8, prime minister Ionatana Ionatana suffered a heart attack and died immediately after a speech at a public function. Deputy prime ministery Lagitupu Tuilimu assumed leadership of the country until a by-election is held in Ionatana's Funafuti constituency. The year 2000 also saw Tuvalu's admission to the United Nations as the 189th member. A dormitory fire killed 18 schoolgirls and their matron in March. The absence of elected officials at their memorial provoked strong public criticisms against the government. Ionatana's government closed a deal to lease the country's Internet domain name (.tv) to a Canadian firm for $50 million.

Tuvalu, formerly known as the Ellice Islands, is a small, predominantly Polynesian country, consisting of nine atolls stretching over 500,000 miles of the western Pacific Ocean. The islands were proclaimed a British protectorate with the Gilbert Islands (now independent Kiribati) in 1892 and were formally annexed by Britain in 1915-1916, when the Gilbert and Ellice Islands Colony was established. The Ellice and Gilbert Islands separated in October 1975, and the former was renamed Tuvalu. The country became an independent member of the Commonwealth in 1978. In Tuvalu's first post-independence general election in September 1971, Dr. Tomasi Puapua was elected prime minister. In April 1999, parliament elected Ionatana Ionatana, a former education minister, as the new prime minister.

The primarily subsistence economy consists mainly of coconuts, taro, and fishing. Much of the government's revenue comes from the sale of stamps and coins, sale of fishing licenses to foreign fishing companies, and remittances by some 1,500 Tuvalu citizens working overseas (mostly as merchant seamen or phosphate miners on Nauru and Kiribati). Interest from the Tuvalu Trust Fund, established in 1987 by major aid donors, covers one-fourth of the annual budget. In recent years, the country has leased unused telephone numbers to international providers of telephone sex lines. Although these contracts have been controversial in this conservative Christian country, they brought in necessary income, providing an estimated 10 percent of the government budget.

In 2000, the government found another novel way to bring in revenue. A contract to lease the country's Internet domain name to a foreign firm will bring the country $50 million over 10 years and give Tuvalu a 15-percent stake in the Canadian company. Political turmoil in Fiji and the Solomon Islands in 1999 and 2000 affected Tuvalu's economy, which relies on the international shipping ports in its two neighboring countries to bring in foodstuff, construction materials and other essentials.

As a low-lying island state, just 4.6 meters above the sea level, Tuvalu is highly concerned about the effects of global climate change. Tuvalu is one of 16 countries that have ratified the Kyoto Protocol, which urges national action and international cooperation to reduce emissions of greenhouse gases.

Political Rights and Civil Liberties:

Citizens of Tuvalu can change their government democratically. The 1978 constitution vests executive power in a prime minister and a cabinet of up to four ministers. The 12-member parliament, *Fale I Fono*, is directly elected for a four-year term. The prime minister appoints and can dismiss the governor-general, who is a Tuvalu citizen and represents the queen of England, who is head of state, for a four-year term. The governor-general appoints the cabinet members and can name a chief executive or dissolve parliament if its members cannot agree on a premier. Each of the country's 9 islands is administered by directly elected, six-person councils, which are influenced by village-based hereditary elders who wield considerable traditional authority. Political parties are legal, but no formal parties have been established. Most elections hinge on village-based allegiances rather than policy issues.

Freedom of speech and the press is respected. The government broadcasts over Radio Tuvalu and publishes the fortnightly newspaper *Tuvalu Echoes* in the Tuvalu language and English, and there is a monthly religious newsletter. Although most of the population belongs to the Protestant Church of Tuvalu, all religious faiths can practice freely.

The government respects freedom of assembly and association. Workers are free to join independent trade unions, bargain collectively, and stage strikes. Only the Tuvalu Seamen's Union, with about 600 members, has been organized and registered. No strikes have ever occurred, largely because most of the population is engaged outside the wage economy. Civil servants, teachers, and nurses, who total less than 1,000 employees, have formed associations, but these do not yet have union status.

The judiciary is independent. Citizens receive fair public trials with procedural safeguards based on English common law and have a right of ultimate appeal under certain circumstances to the Privy Council in London. The small police force is under civilian control.

Citizens are free to travel within the country and abroad. Traditional social restrictions limit employment opportunities for women, though many are securing jobs in education and health care and are becoming more politically active. Although gender discrimination exists, violence against women appears rare.

Uganda

Polity: Dominant party (military-influenced)
Economy: Capitalist-statist
Population: 23,300,000
PPP: $1,074
Life Expectancy: 41
Ethnic Groups: Baganda (17 percent), Karamojong (12 percent), Basogo (8 percent), Iteso (8 percent), Langi (6 percent), Rwanda (6 percent), other (43 percent)
Capital: Kampala

Political Rights: 6*
Civil Liberties: 5
Status: Partly Free

Ratings Change: Uganda's political rights rating changed from 5 to 6 due to the 2000 constitutional referendum which resulted in an extension of restrictions on political party activities.

Overview:

Uganda held a referendum in June 2000 on whether to remove a ban on political party activities. The results were mixed. Almost 90 percent of those voting supported continuation of the current de facto single-party system. Opposition parties had called for a boycott, however, and overall voter turnout was just over 50 percent. The regional situation remained tense, with Ugandan military forces remaining in the Democratic Republic of the Congo in response to rebel attacks in the eastern part of that country. Ugandan soldiers have been accused of profiteering, including dealing in diamonds, timber, and gold. Rwandan and Ugandan troops clashed in Kisangani, killing at least 600 people. A religious cult (Movement for the Restoration of Ten Commandments) mass suicide in rural Uganda resulted in more than 900 deaths.

Uganda has experienced considerable political instability since independence from Britain in 1962. An increasingly authoritarian president, Milton Obote, was overthrown by Idi Amin in 1971. Amin's brutality and buffoonery made world headlines as hundreds of thousands of people were killed. Amin's 1978 invasion of Tanzania finally led to his demise. Tanzanian forces and Ugandan exiles routed Amin's army and prepared for Obote's return to power in the fraudulent 1980 elections. Obote and his backers from northern Uganda savagely repressed his critics, who were primarily from southern Ugandan ethnic groups. Approximately 250,000 people were killed as political opponents were tortured and murdered and soldiers terrorized the countryside. Obote was ousted for a second time in a 1985 army coup. Conditions continued to worsen until Yoweri Museveni led his National Resistance Army into Kampala in January 1986.

President Museveni's National Resistance Movement (NRM) dominates the nation's political life. The press and civil society remain relatively free and active, despite some crackdowns. In addition, the parliament has become increasingly assertive, occasionally rejecting appointments or policy initiatives proposed by the executive branch.

Manipulation and exploitation of ethnic divisions pose a serious threat to peace in Uganda. Baganda people in the country's south continue to demand more recognition of their traditional kingdom. Northern ethnic groups complain of government neglect; that region, along with the western region, are subject to continuing guerilla activities.

Political Rights and Civil Liberties:

Ugandans do not have the right to select their government through democratic political competition. The country's only open multiparty elections were held in 1961 in preparation for the country's independence from Britain. Since 1986, political parties have been banned, and candidates stand as individuals in elections. President Museveni did not ban the old political parties; they were, however, prevented from operating. Arguing that first-past-the-post democracy exacerbates religious and ethnic tensions in Africa, Museveni substituted an allegedly nonpartisan, "Movement" system. Since 1996 when he was confirmed by an election as president, any distinction between Museveni's system and a single-party state appears to be academic. A 1999 report by Human Rights Watch concludes that "the NRM has consolidated its monopoly on political power through exclusive access to state funding and machinery, widespread and sometimes compulsory political education programs."

Presidential elections are due in 2001. In 1996, Ugandans voted for their president and parliamentarians in elections without open party competition. State media and other official resources were mobilized in support of Museveni's successful candidacy, and the ban on formal party activities further hindered the opposition. Most observers believe that Museveni would have won handily in a multiparty contest and described the balloting and counting as largely transparent. The opposition claimed that the elections were rigged and boycotted subsequent parliamentary polls. Supporters of the opposition parties were allowed to contest on an individual basis, and several were elected. Overall, the elections maintained the NRM's hold on the legislature, its comfortable majority buttressed by dozens of presidentially nominated special interest representatives.

Central political power rests firmly in the hands of the NRM. Important policy issues, such as the decision to intervene directly in the war in the Democratic Republic of the Congo, are taken without significant public or parliamentary debate or input. Nonetheless, some space is allowed for parliament and civil society to function. Parliament, for example, has occasionally censured government ministers accused of corruption and forced budgetary amendments. There is no state religion, and freedom of worship is constitutionally protected and respected. Various Christian sects and the country's Muslim minority practice their creeds freely.

With parliamentary approval, the president names a judicial commission that oversees judicial appointments. The judiciary is still influenced by the executive despite increasing autonomy. It is also constrained by inadequate resources and the army's occasional refusal to respect civilian courts. At times, the government liberally applies the charge of treason against nonviolent political dissidents. Local courts are subject to bribery and corruption. Prison conditions are difficult, especially in local jails. More than 500 prisoners die annually as a result of poor diet, lack of sanitation, and inadequate medical care. Serious human rights violations by rebel groups and the Uganda People's Defense Forces have been reported.

In a display of judicial independence, in August, 2000 Uganda's constitutional court voided one of two laws validating the June referendum on political party activities. The court ruled that the act had been passed without a quorum in parliament. A second, related law was also being challenged in the courts by the opposition Democratic Party late in 2000. Uganda's parliament, which has a huge pro-government majority, however, subsequently amended the constitution to effectively annul these legal challenges. There is some freedom of expression. The independent print media, which include more than two dozen daily and weekly newspapers, are often highly critical of the government and offer a range of opposition views. Buttressed by legislation limiting press freedoms, however, the government at times selectively arrests or harasses journalists. Several private radio stations and two private television stations report on local political developments. The largest newspapers and broadcasting facilities that reach rural areas remain state owned. Governmental corruption is reported. Opposition positions are also presented, but the coverage is often not balanced. Journalists have asked parliament to enact a freedom-of-information act so that the public is not denied information.

Women experience discrimination based on traditional law, particularly in rural areas, and are treated unequally under inheritance, divorce, and citizenship statutes. A woman cannot obtain a passport without her husband's permission. Domestic violence against women is widespread. Uganda has, by contrast, legislated quotas for women officials from all elected bodies from village councils to the national parliament. Presently, there are 17 women ministers, including the vice president, out of a 62-member cabinet. Almost 20 percent of Uganda's parliament is female. One-third of local council seats must, by law, go to women.

The National Organization of Trade Unions, the country's largest labor federation, is independent of the government and political parties. An array of essential workers is barred from forming unions. Strikes are permitted only after a lengthy reconciliation process.

Most Ugandans are subsistence farmers. Despite overall growth under President Museveni, Uganda's economy has recently slowed; 46 percent of the population lives below the poverty line. Foreign aid donors, who pay more than half of the government's running costs, are increasingly concerned. In March the International Monetary Fund delayed an $18 million loan to Uganda, largely because of increased defense spending. Aid donors calculate that corruption costs Uganda at least $200 million a year.

Ukraine

Polity: Presidential-parliamentary democracy
Economy: Mixed capitalist (transitional)
Population: 49,500,000
PPP: $3,194
Life Expectancy: 69
Ethnic Groups: Ukrainian (73 percent), Russian (22 percent), other (5 percent)
Capital: Kiev

Political Rights: 4*
Civil Liberties: 4
Status: Partly Free

Ratings Change: Ukraine's political rights rating changed from 3 to 4 due to the inability of the legislative and executive branches of government to represent voters' interests effectively and to increasing evidence that powerful oligarchs wield undue influence over public policies and institutions.

Overview:

For much of 2000, the legislative and executive branches of government in Ukraine were deadlocked. President Leonid Kuchma attempted to increase his powers unconstitutionally and threatened to dissolve parliament. When legislators formed a pro-government majority and tried to replace Oleksandr Tkachenko, Speaker of the Verkhovna Rada, his supporters physically resisted and forced the new majority to convene a rival session. Evidence mounted that powerful business interests exert undue influence over public institutions, while allegations that Kuchma is linked to the murder of journalist Hryhoriy Gongadze threatened to topple his presidency. Also in 2000, Ukraine abolished the death penalty and closed the Chernobyl nuclear power plant.

In December 1991, Ukraine ended more than 300 years of Russian ascendancy when voters ratified a declaration of independence and elected Leonid Kravchuk president. In 1994, Communists proved victorious in parliamentary elections, and Leonid Kuchma, a former Soviet director of military production, defeated Kravchuk. Since then, Kuchma has struggled against a Communist-led parliament to effect reforms.

In the 1999 presidential election, Kuchma defeated Communist Party leader Petro Symonenko in the second round of voting with 56.21 percent of the vote. Symonenko received only 37.5 percent. Kuchma appointed reformer Viktor Yushchenko, a former head of the Central Bank, to the post of prime minister. He also threatened to dissolve parliament if it refused to support economic reforms.

In January 2000, a pro-government majority formed by 241 deputies from 11 parties called for Oleksandr Tkachenko's resignation. When Tkachenko's supporters blocked a vote on his removal, the new majority convened a rival session and elected a pro-government parliamentary leadership. Regular legislative sessions resumed before the constitutional court could rule on the new leadership's legitimacy.

Kuchma issued controversial decrees on abolishing collective farms and streamlining the executive branch. He also set out with Prime Minister Yushchenko to recapture $2.6 billion in loans from the International Monetary Fund (IMF). By the end of 2000, they had largely met the IMF's conditions: the adoption of a balanced budget for

2001, passage of a banking law, and the submission to parliament of a list of state enterprises slated for privatization.

In January 2000, Kuchma called for a national referendum on constitutional amendments to increase his powers. He proposed six questions: (1) Should the president be able to dissolve parliament, if voters express no confidence in the body in a national referendum? (2) Should the president be able to dissolve parliament for failure to form a majority or to adopt a state budget? (3) Should the immunity of parliamentary deputies from arrest and criminal prosecution be limited? (4) Should the number of parliamentary deputies be reduced from 450 to 300? (5) Should parliament have two chambers? (6) Should Ukraine be able to adopt a constitution by national referendum?

The constitutional court threw out questions 1 and 6. Voters considered the rest in an April 16 referendum. Turnout reached nearly 80 percent, and the response to each question was, overwhelmingly, yes. Since then, parliament has stalled a vote to enact the amendments.

Corruption is a serious problem in Ukraine. In Transparency International's 2000 Corruption Perceptions Index, Ukraine ranked the third most corrupt country in the world. A survey by the World Bank and the European Bank for Reconstruction and Development of 247 Ukrainian businesses revealed that 32 percent were affected by illegal payments to influence public policy and public institutions. In November 2000, Deputy Prime Minister Yulia Tymoshenko promised to fight corruption in what she called Ukraine's "most corrupt" industry—coal mining.

In related news, Ukraine's decision to privatize key state industries has piqued the interest of Russia's powerful oligarchs. Already the government has sold large stakes in the Mykolayiv Alumina plant and Kyivinvestbank to Russian businesses. In 2000, a Swiss court convicted former Prime Minister Pavlo Lazarenko of money laundering, while public officials including President Kuchma, Oleksandr Tkachenko, and Yulia Tymoshenko denied allegations of involvement in bribery and embezzlement schemes. Parliament lifted the immunity of Viktor Zherdytskyy, a lawmaker accused of embezzling nearly $40 million in funds for Ukrainian victims of the Nazi regime.

In November 2000, journalists from the on-line magazine *Ukrainska Pravda* identified the decapitated body of their colleague Hryhoriy Gongadze. They suspected that Gongadze's disappearance and death were linked to his frequent criticisms of President Kuchma and the government. In a dramatic turn of events, opposition parliamentarian Oleksandr Moroz released an audio tape that, if authenticated, could link Kuchma and other senior officials to the murder. A parliamentary commission, promising a thorough investigation, has appealed to Western groups for assistance in analyzing the tape. An officer with the Ukrainian Security Service claimed responsibility for the recording.

Political Rights and Civil Liberties: Ukrainian voters can change their government democratically. Citizens aged 18 and older enjoy universal, equal, and direct suffrage. They elect the president and delegates to the Verkhovna Rada, the 450-seat unicameral parliament. The president appoints the prime minister and other cabinet members.

The 1997 parliamentary election law outlines a system of proportional-majoritarian representation. The Organization for Security and Cooperation in Europe (OSCE) concluded that elections to the Verkhovna Rada in 1998 were generally free and fair, but it noted serious irregularities. Twenty-one parties and nine coalitions registered for that election. Eight groups received a mandate.

The International Foundation for Election Systems (IFES) concluded that the 1999 presidential election law lends greater transparency and accountability to the process. Nevertheless, observers declared the November 1999 election unfair because of intimidation of independent media, biased coverage by state media, intimidation of candidates and their supporters, and illegal campaigning by state officials. Nineteen candidates successfully registered for the election.

The 1996 constitution guarantees freedom of speech and expression. The government frequently disregards these rights, particularly during election campaigns. There are 8,300 print publications registered with the state; 673 publications are state-owned. There are also 516 television and radio companies; the state owns 133 broadcasters. The OSCE has reported that editorial independence is difficult to maintain, because state-owned media depend on government support and private media are largely controlled by financial and political clans. Reporters Sans Frontieres reported at least twenty attacks and threats against journalists in 2000. The brutal murder of journalist Hryhoriy Gongadze particularly alarmed the country when evidence was presented that, if authenticated, could implicate President Kuchma and other senior government officials.

The constitution and the Law on Freedom of Conscience and Religion define religious rights in Ukraine. There are some restrictions on the activities of foreign religious organizations, and all religious groups must register with the state. Sixty-six percent of respondents to an August 2000 survey conducted by the Ukrainian Center for Economic and Political Studies said that there is "complete freedom of conscience and equality of faiths before the law" in Ukraine. More than 50 percent of respondents who described themselves as "believers" agreed that religion is "one of the elements of a democratic society."

Despite strict registration requirements, Ukraine has several thousand nongovernmental organizations. The constitution guarantees the right to peaceful assembly but requires advance notification to government authorities. In 2000, for example, 40,000 coal miners protested against delays in receiving back wages; 6,000 teachers rallied to demand wage increases; and more than 10,000 victims of Chernobyl who are eligible for government support marched in favor of better benefits.

The judiciary consists of a supreme court, regional courts, and district courts. There is also a constitutional court. The constitution guarantees equality before the law, although the president, members of parliament, and judges enjoy are immune from criminal prosecution unless parliament consents. The judiciary is inefficient and subject to corruption. The 1996 constitution requires parliament to reform the judiciary, but to date no law has been passed. The constitutional court is largely free of political interference.

The government generally respects personal autonomy and privacy. To receive social and medical benefits from the state, however, persons still must register at work and in their place of residence. The constitution also guarantees individuals the right to own property, to work, and to engage in entrepreneurial activity. Crime, corruption, and the slow pace of economic reform have effectively limited these rights.

United Arab Emirates

Polity: Federation of traditional monarchies
Economy: Capitalist-statist
Population: 2,800,000
PPP: $17,719
Life Expectancy: 75
Ethnic Groups: Arab, Iranian, South Asian
Capital: Abu Dhabi

Political Rights: 6
Civil Liberties: 5
Status: Not Free

Overview: The United Arab Emirates continued to promote itself as a regional commercial center during 2000, while also working to boost its influence in the Persian Gulf through major arms purchases and regional diplomacy.

The seven emirates that constitute the UAE formed a unified federation after gaining independence from Great Britain in 1971. Under the 1971 provisional constitution, the emirate rulers make up the Federal Supreme Council, the highest legislative and executive body. The council elects a state president and vice president from among its membership, and the president appoints the prime minister and cabinet. A 40-member Federal National Council, composed of delegates appointed by the seven rulers, serves as an advisory body with no legislative authority. While there are separate consultative councils in several emirates, there are no political parties or popular elections.

Sheikh Zayed bin Sultan al-Nahayan has served as president since independence and is considered largely responsible for the country's unification, development, and economic success. The 2000 United Nations Human Development Report placed the UAE among the world's top performers in terms of quality of life as measured by real income, life expectancy, and educational standards.

The UAE boasts a free market economy based on oil and gas production, trade, and services. The economy provides citizens with a high per capita income but is heavily dependent on foreign workers, who constitute some 80 percent of the population. The government has made strides in diversifying the economy. The Dubai Ports Authority has acquired a string of contracts at major port facilities in the Arab peninsula and the Red Sea, making the UAE a leader in regional shipping. The government has also established a number of free zones, offering low living costs, new infrastructure, long land leases, customs and tax exemptions, 100 percent foreign ownership, and repatriation guarantees to investors. One such zone, the Dubai Internet City, opened in November with some 200 e-commerce firms registered to operate.

The UAE has maintained a generally pro-Western foreign policy since the Persian Gulf War and continues to cooperate militarily with the United States, Britain, and France. Iran and the UAE have been locked in a dispute since 1992 over three islands, located near the Strait of Hormuz, which Iran controls in defiance of UAE claims to the territory. Improved relations between Iran and several Arab states have fueled anxiety in the UAE about the regional balance of power. In response, the UAE has increased its defense spending; recent purchases include 80 F-16s from the U.S. and an antiaircraft system from Russia. The UAE has also improved relations with neighbors. It reopened its embassy in Iraq in April for the first time since the Gulf War, came to an agreement with Oman over a section of their disputed border, and arranged with Bahrain to allow free movement of citizens. An agreement with Syria aims to establish a customs-free trade zone by 2003.

Political Rights and Civil Liberties:

Citizens of the UAE cannot change their government democratically. There are no elections at any level, political parties are illegal, and the Federal Supreme Council holds all executive and legislative authority. The seven emirate rulers, their extended families, and their allies wield political control in their respective emirates. Citizens may voice concerns to their leaders through open *majlises* (gatherings) held by the emirate rulers.

The judiciary is not independent; its decisions are subject to review by the political leadership. The judicial system comprises both *Sharia* (Islamic) law and secular courts. There are no jury trials, but due process protections exist in both religious and secular courts. Military courts try only military personnel, and there is no separate state security court system. Sharia allows for corporal punishment for such crimes as adultery, prostitution, and drug or alcohol abuse. Drug trafficking has been a capital offense since 1995, though executions are rarely reported. Police may enter homes without warrants or probable cause, but their actions are subject to review and disciplinary action.

Journalists routinely censor themselves when reporting on government policy, national security, and religion, and refrain from criticizing the ruling families. The print media are largely privately owned but receive government subsidies. Foreign publications are censored. Broadcast media are government-owned and present only government views. Satellite dishes are widely owned and provide foreign broadcasting without censorship. The UAE is the most Internet-connected country in the Arab world, with some 400,000 users by March 2000. In April, the government announced that civil servants must bring public services on-line within 18 months or risk losing their jobs.

The government limits freedom of assembly and association. Permits are required for organized public gatherings. Political discussion is generally confined to gatherings in private homes which are tolerated by officials. Private associations must be licensed, but enforcement is inconsistent.

Islam is the official religion of the UAE. About 85 percent of citizens are Sunni Muslim, and 15 percent Shiite. About 95 percent of Sunni mosques are government funded or subsidized. Shia are free to worship and to maintain mosques. The government ensures that religious sermons do not deviate frequently or significantly from approved topics. A limited number of Christians are granted legal recognition. Other non-Muslims may practice freely but may not proselytize or distribute religious literature.

Women are well represented in education, government, and the professions, but face discrimination in benefits and promotion. There are numerous NGOs that focus on women's issues such as domestic violence. Islamic law discriminates against women in family matters such as divorce and inheritance, and tradition keeps many women from working. A married woman must have her husband's consent to accept employment or to travel abroad. The first all-female shopping mall opened early in 2000 in Abu Dhabi. Its aim is to provide privacy to women who wish to shop without wearing the *abaya*, a head-to-toe covering required in the presence of men by strict Islamic dress codes.

Trade unions, strikes, and collective bargaining are illegal in the UAE and do not occur. Foreign nationals make up about 85 to 90 percent of the workforce, and sometimes fall prey to abuse by managers who take most of their earnings and force them to work long hours in extreme heat or under other dangerous conditions. Labor law offers some protection, but most abuse goes unreported.

↑ United Kingdom

Polity: Parliamentary democracy
Economy: Mixed capitalist
Population: 59,800,000
PPP: $20,336
Life Expectancy: 77
Ethnic Groups: English (82 percent), Scottish (10 percent), Irish (2 percent), Welsh (2 percent), other, including Indian and Pakistani (4 percent)
Capital: London

Political Rights: 1
Civil Liberties: 2
Status: Free

Trend Arrow: The United Kingdom received an upward trend arrow for its implementation of the Human Rights Act, the country's first codified charter of rights.

Overview:
Despite a series of setbacks including losses in local elections, disputes over pensions, and fuel tax protests, Tony Blair's governing Labour party regained its wide lead in opinion polls by the end of 2000. However, the government's success is widely seen to be the result of infighting within the opposition Conservative (Tory) party, which has split into hardline and liberal factions. It is widely believed that Blair will call elections for May 2001 and win another term, but he will face increasing pressure to deliver on promises to improve health and other public services, education, and criminal justice.

In a long-awaited boost to human rights, Britain formally enacted the Human Rights Act in October, charging British courts with protecting the rights of British citizens under the European Convention on Human Rights (ECHR). The law represents the closest thing to a written constitution to exist in British history, as well as a significant shift in power to the judiciary.

The United Kingdom of Great Britain and Northern Ireland encompasses the two formerly separate kingdoms of England and Scotland, the ancient principality of Wales, and the six counties of the Irish province of Ulster (see Northern Ireland under Related Territories). The British parliament has an elected House of Commons with 659 members chosen by plurality vote from single-member districts and a House of Lords with 478 hereditary and appointed members. Reforms to make the Lords more representative are ongoing; an initiative by the government in September 2000 allows all United Kingdom, Irish, and Commonwealth citizens over age 21 to nominate themselves for ten new seats. The candidates will be chosen by a six-member commission in the Lords based on an application procedure. By October, 191 people had submitted applications. A cabinet of ministers appointed from the majority party exercises executive power on behalf of the mainly ceremonial sovereign. Queen Elizabeth II nominates the party leader with the most support in the House of Commons to form a government.

Blair's "New Labour," so called because of its radical shift from its socialist past, adopted Conservative-style positions on a number of issues and swept the general elections in May 1997. The government continues to define itself as it goes along by blending traditional Labour and Tory policies. Since taking office, Labour has abandoned tax-and-spend policies, devolved monetary policy to the Bank of England, and maintained strict spending limits. However, it has also reintroduced the minimum wage and restored rights to trade unions.

Devolution of power to Scotland and Wales took place in May 1999, with each territory establishing its own legislature. The 129-member Scottish parliament and the 60-member Welsh assembly exercise control over transportation, health, education, and housing, while foreign, defense, and economic policies remain under British control. The Labour party dominated parliamentary elections in both territories. On December 1, 1999, Britain officially handed over power to a new 108-member Northern Ireland Assembly in Belfast. The shared-power arrangement between the Ulster Unionists and Sinn Fein, the political wing of the Irish Republican Army (IRA), arose from the Good Friday Agreement of April 1998. Central to the agreement was the IRA's promise to agree to a timetable for decommissioning its arms. Disagreements about decommissioning led to the suspension of the executive and assembly in February 2000. The institutions were reinstated in May, but internal feuding among loyalist paramilitary organizations and disputes over police reform, disarmament, and the British military presence continued to threaten the agreement.

During 2000, Labour achievements such as House of Lords reform; a stable economy; low unemployment; devolution of power to Scotland, Wales, Northern Ireland, and a new London city council; and improvements in primary education were overshadowed by criticism of the government's failure to deliver on its key promise to revive public services. After years of underinvestment, transport systems are in disrepair, secondary schools are substandard, and the National Health Service is ill-equipped to handle its workload. Pension spending as a proportion of GDP is significantly lower than in the rest of Europe, and by most accounts insufficient. In fact, the government's ability to honor its commitments was hampered by two-year spending limits imposed by the previous Conservative government. In July, Blair introduced a spending plan designed to win back disillusioned traditional Labour supporters. The plan called for spending increases to improve health, education, transport, and policing, and to develop poor areas.

Labour suffered a sweeping defeat in local elections in April, losing 15 local councils as Conservatives gained 16. Voter turnout was estimated at 30 percent. The most embarrassing loss occurred in London, where voters elected former Labourite Ken Livingstone the first mayor since former Prime Minister Margaret Thatcher abolished the Greater London Council in 1986. Livingstone, who headed the last local London government, was expelled from the Labour because he decided to run as an independent following the party's decision not to back him. The Labour candidate came in third.

Rising fuel prices led to widespread protest blockades of oil refineries and storage facilities by truckers in September. Demanding that the government cut fuel taxes, demonstrators all but halted gasoline deliveries, forcing the closure of gas stations;

cutbacks in ambulance, fire department, and hospital services; school shutdowns; and train cancellations throughout the country. Blair, refusing to accede to the demands, saw the government's approval ratings plummet. Two polls in mid-September showed Conservatives leading, by a slight margin, for the first time since 1992.

By December, the government had rebounded to lead 48 percent to 33 percent in polls. Many attributed this success to the Conservatives' inability to capitalize on the government's setbacks. The party is beset by infighting between hardliners, led by party leader William Hague, and liberals, led by shadow chancellor of the exchequer Michael Portillo. Liberals have sought to promote the Tories as modern, inclusive, and more tolerant, particularly regarding homosexuals. The feud has hurt the Conservatives' image and fueled speculation that Hague will lose the party leadership to Portillo if Labour wins a large majority in general elections expected in spring 2001.

Political Rights and Civil Liberties: Citizens of the United Kingdom can change their government democratically. Voters are registered by government survey and include both Irish and Commonwealth citizens resident in Britain. British subjects abroad retain voting rights for 20 years after emigration. Welsh and Scottish legislatures have authority over matters of regional importance such as education, health, and some economic matters. The Scottish parliament has limited power to collect taxes. In 1999, the government abolished hereditary peerage in the House of Lords and dismissed more than 600 hereditary peers. Critics expressed concern that the move would allow the government to pack the house with cronies; hereditary peers had constituted more than half the Lords' membership, while the balance were government appointees.

The Human Rights Act, effectively Britain's first written charter of rights, came into force in October. Under the law, British citizens who feel their rights have been violated may take their grievances to British courts rather than seek redress in the European Court of Human Rights. British Law Lords will declare whether specific British laws comply with the European Convention. The law represents a significant shift in power to the courts, because although judges will not have the right to strike down legislation, the government will face enormous political pressure to bring laws into line with European standards.

Legal attempts by the government to combat crime and corruption have been widely denounced as dangerous to basic freedoms. The Terrorism Act 2000, a permanent legislation to replace emergency laws concerning political violence, was passed in July and will become effective in 2001. Amnesty International released a briefing on the bill, outlining concerns about provisions such as arrest, entry, and search and seizure without warrant; denial of a detainee's access to counsel upon arrest and during interrogation; detention without trial for up to 12 days; and the shifting of the burden of proof from prosecution to defense.

A government report issued in 1999 found London's police force "riven with pernicious and institutionalized racism." The findings stem from complaints of police harassment of blacks and specifically, the case of Stephen Lawrence, an 18-year-old black student stabbed to death in 1993 by a group of white youths. No one has yet been convicted of the killing despite five arrests and eight separate investigation teams. Many allege that the investigation has been bungled because the victim was black. In 2000, the UN Committee on the Elimination of Racial Discrimination reported that criticism of police for their handling of the Lawrence case has provoked a police backlash against minorities. The report also noted that blacks make up a disproportionate number of those killed in police custody. Human rights campaigners asserted that black people are six times more likely to be stopped and searched by police, are overrepresented in prisons, and often receive longer sentences than whites or Asians.

Though uncensored and mostly private, the British press is subject to strict libel and obscenity laws. Print media are privately owned and independent, though many of the national daily newspapers are aligned with political parties. The BBC runs about half the electronic media in the country. It is funded by the government but is editorially independent. In October, the government announced its intention to strip the BBC governors of their regulatory authority after the governors decided to change the time of the main nightly news broadcast, prompting a dispute with the culture secretary. Under the current system, the BBC is regulated by its government-appointed governors, while commercial broadcasters are regulated by an independent commission. BBC regulation will reportedly be handled by a separate authority responsible for the entire broadcasting industry. The Human Rights Act provides a statutory right to free expression in Britain for the first time, although the European Convention makes exceptions in the interest of public safety, health, morals, and the reputations and rights of others. Parliament passed freedom-of-information legislation in 2000, granting access to a wide range of information previously denied, including police data. The law, which is expected to come into force in 2002, has been sharply criticized by rights groups for excluding information regarding national security, defense, international resolutions, individual and public safety, commercial interests, and law enforcement.

In October, new regulations gave employers the right to monitor staff phone calls, e-mail, and Internet activity without consent. In July, measures were introduced to allow authorities to intercept e-mail and other electronic communication without a warrant for reasons of national security, prevention of crime, and national "well-being."

Attacks on British refugee asylum policy continued in 2000. The Immigration and Asylum Act, enacted in April, seeks to deter asylum seekers by offering them vouchers redeemable for goods instead of cash welfare benefits. In addition, asylum seekers will be dispersed among 13 designated sites around Britain instead of being allowed to settle where they choose, and refugees whose applications for asylum are turned down will be allowed only one appeal. While Conservatives criticized the government's asylum policy as too soft, rights activists charged that the new law, which does not allow vendors to give change in cash for vouchers that exceed the value of goods purchased, would demean and reinforce prejudice against refugees. Britain has been unable to handle an increasing influx of refugees; currently some 103,000 people and their families await decisions on asylum applications. The process has taken up to five years in some cases.

British workers are free to form and join independent trade unions. Britain introduced a national minimum wage in 1999. Legislation introduced in mid-2000 requires employers to offer part-time workers the same benefits, wages, and conditions of employment, such as parental leave and sick pay, as those enjoyed by full-time workers doing the same type of work. With an estimated 44 percent of Britain's female workers in part-time employment, the new regulations help boost women's equality in the workplace.

United States of America

Polity: Presidential-
parliamentary democracy
(federal)
Economy: Capitalist
Population: 275,600,000
PPP: $29,605
Life Expectancy: 77

Political Rights: 1
Civil Liberties: 1
Status: Free

Ethnic Groups: White (73 percent), black (13 percent), Hispanic
(10 percent), Asian-Pacific (3 percent), native American (1 percent)
Capital: Washington, D.C.

Overview: George W. Bush was certified as the forty-third president of
the United States after one of the closest and most controversial elections in the country's history. Bush, the nominee of
the Republican Party and a son of former President George Bush, actually received
slightly fewer popular votes than his Democratic rival, Vice President Al Gore. Gore
received 50,996,064 votes, or 48.39 percent of the total, to Bush's 50,456,167 votes,
or 47.88 percent. A third candidate, Ralph Nader, representing the environmentally
oriented Green Party, received slightly less than 3 percent. In the end, however, Bush
was declared the winner because he won a majority of votes in the Electoral College,
an institution that is unique to the U. S. system of federalism. Bush prevailed in the
Electoral College by the razor-thin margin of 271 to 266.

Almost as important as the final result was the controversy over the election results in the state of Florida. Given the narrow margin of the national results, Florida's
electoral votes were essential to determining the contest's outcome. On election night,
it appeared that Bush had won the state by fewer than 1,000 votes. The Florida results,
however, were immediately challenged by the Gore campaign, which charged that the
ballots of thousands of likely Gore voters had not been counted. Gore demanded that
votes be recounted by hand in certain heavily Democratic counties; the Bush forces
argued that a selective recount was unfair. Ultimately, it took five weeks, marked by
numerous court challenges, until Bush was declared the winner, after the U.S. Supreme
Court had ruled by a five-to-four margin against a hand recount.

The U.S. federal government has three branches, executive, legislative, and judicial. In addition, the American federal system gives substantial powers to state and local
governments and the citizenry.

The president and vice president are elected by popular vote to four-year terms.
The technical device for the election of a president is the Electoral College. The voters
in each state and Washington, D.C., cast their ballots for a slate of electors pledged to
a specific candidate. The electors pledged to the candidate who received the most popular
votes go on to vote for their candidate in the Electoral College.

The U.S. Congress is bicameral. There are 435 members of the House of Representatives as well as nonvoting members from Washington, D.C., and several related territories. Each state is guaranteed at least one representative in the House. The rest are
apportioned on the basis of population. In the 2000 elections, Republicans continued

their domination of the House by winning 221 seats to 212 for the Democrats, with 2 independent. This result represented a net gain of 2 seats for the Democrats. The 100-member Senate has two members from each state, regardless of population. Each senator serves a six-year term. In the 2000 election, Republicans and Democrats each won 50 Senate seats. In such a situation, the Republicans will maintain effective control of the Senate, as the vice president, in this case Republican Dick Cheney, is empowered to cast a ballot to break tie votes.

Political Rights and Civil Liberties:

Americans can change their government democratically. Voter turnout has been relatively low in recent years; in the 2000 presidential elections, voter turnout stood at 51.2 percent of the voting-age population, an increase of more than two percent from the 1996 presidential contest, but considerably lower than that of 1960, when voter participation stood at more than 60 percent. Elections are competitive, but congressional incumbents win in a majority of cases. In recent years, the cost of political campaigns has risen substantially. Much of a candidate's time is consumed with fund-raising, and while Congress has periodically passed laws imposing limitations on political contributions, candidates have found ways to circumvent the spirit of the laws and court decisions have limited the laws' effectiveness. Some critics have argued that generous contributions by business, labor unions, and other "special interests" have made it practically impossible for candidates to dislodge incumbents. Recent elections, however, have tended to weaken the thrust of that argument. In the 1994 midterm election, Republican challengers ousted a substantial number of Democratic incumbents, and in the 1998 elections, Democratic challengers defeated a significant number of sitting Republicans.

The American political system is overwhelmingly dominated by the two major parties. Various insurgent parties of the Left and Right have issued periodic challenges through the years, with little success. In 2000, neither of the two principal small-party presidential candidates, Ralph Nader of the Green Party and Pat Buchanan of the Reform Party, fared well, though Nader's vote total contributed to Bush's triumph by siphoning support from Gore. In 1998, Jesse Ventura, a former professional wrestler, was elected governor of Minnesota on the Reform Party line.

The two major parties choose their presidential candidates through a lengthy and expensive process during the winter and spring of election years. Party members vote for their preferred candidates either in primary elections or in local meetings of party members, called caucuses. The nominating process has been criticized for its cost and length, and for the sometimes undue influence of unrepresentative minority factions. Defenders of the system claim that allowing rank-and-file party members to participate in the nominating process is more democratic than the system in countries where a small group of party leaders selects the nominee. In 2000, George Bush faced a strong challenge within the Republican Party from Senator John McCain, while Gore was forced to beat back an impressive challenge by former Senator Bill Bradley.

A recent trend has been the increased use of initiatives and referenda to determine issues of public policy. Some states, California most notably, permit public initiatives on almost any issue of public concern; in other states, strict limits are placed on the practice. In recent years, voters in various states have decided on such issues as the imposition of restrictions on illegal immigrants, the legality of assisted suicide, the use of marijuana for medicinal purposes, affirmative action for women and minorities, and casino gambling.

The American media are free and competitive. Some observers have expressed concern over the trend towards the ownership of the largest and most influential newspapers, magazines, and television networks by large corporate conglomerates. Another worrying trend is the enhanced role of television, where news is covered in a superficial and sensationalistic way, at the expense of newspapers. On the other hand, some point to the explosion of new, specialized journals as well as the Internet and public affairs programming on cable television in arguing that Americans have suffered no loss of alternative viewpoints or in-depth coverage of public issues.

Public and private discussion is very open in the United States. In recent years, concern has been expressed over the adoption by many universities of restrictive codes designed to prohibit speech that is deemed insulting to women, racial minorities, and homosexuals. Several of these codes have been struck down by the courts.

The U. S. court system has long been a subject of controversy. Some conservative critics accuse judges of being overly "activist" by issuing rulings on issues which, critics contend, should be resolved through the legislative process. Ironically, the Supreme Court's decision to halt the recount of the presidential vote in Florida was attacked by many liberals as an act of overzealous judicial activism. More recently, the courts have been at the center of controversial lawsuits that seek millions of dollars in damages from tobacco firms and handgun manufacturers. Some fear that such actions could establish a trend towards social regulation through lawsuits rather than by acts of Congress or state legislatures.

The past year has seen the continuation of a trend towards the decrease in crime throughout the country. Instances of violent crime are at their lowest level in years, especially in major cities like New York. The reason for the decrease is a source of debate, though some credit is given new strategies of zero-tolerance law enforcement adopted in a number of cities. These tactics, in turn, have elicited the criticism of civil liberties organizations, which claim that police abuse of civilians is on the increase. A controversy has recently arisen over what is called racial profiling, a policing tactic in which the members of racial minorities are singled out for questioning during investigations. The federal Justice Department has already launched investigations of racial profiling in several parts of the country, including the state of New Jersey, where officials have admitted that racial profiling was practiced.

The U. S. has freedom of association. Trade unions are free, but have been in decline for some years and today represent the lowest percentage of American workers in the postwar period.

The American economy enjoyed a relatively strong year in 2000, with an official unemployment rate under four percent and one of the world's lowest rates of inflation. More so than in most other countries, the U.S. economy is well integrated into the world economy. The Clinton administration strongly supported free trade and the further integration of the American economy into the world trading system. Recently, the United States has been the scene of several major protests directed at the key institutions of the global economy, including the World Trade Organization, the World Bank, and the International Monetary Fund.

There is religious freedom in America. In 2000, a milestone was established when a Jew, Joseph Lieberman, was nominated for vice president by the Democratic Party.

This was the first time that either of the major parties had nominated a Jewish candidate for either president or vice president. A persisting controversy involves the separation of church and state, in particular regarding whether federal money may be given to organizations or projects sponsored by religious groups. Although the courts have generally ruled in favor of strict separation of church and state, the Supreme Court in 1998 let stand a lower court decision which allowed students who attended church-sponsored schools in Milwaukee, Wisconsin, to receive government tuition assistance.

Race relations remained one of America's most serious problems. African-Americans remain disproportionately poor, less likely to complete high school or college, more likely to have out-of-wedlock births, and more likely to suffer major health problems than other groups. Although a substantial degree of integration has been achieved in a number of American institutions, residential segregation is still high as is the tendency of blacks and Hispanics to predominate in the public schools of major cities. Blacks did, however, benefit from the high growth and low unemployment that characterized the economy in the last several years.

One sign of racial division was the presidential election result, where blacks gave an estimated 92 percent of their votes to Democrat Al Gore. A number of prominent black leaders, most notably the Rev. Jesse Jackson, protested the decision of the Supreme Court to stop the hand counting of Florida ballots and asserted that thousands of black voters in Florida had been disenfranchised.

Affirmative action programs remained a source of friction. In recent years, affirmative action plans that give advantages to minority groups or women have suffered reversals through referenda and court decisions. As an alternative to traditional affirmative action plans, two states, Florida and Texas, have adopted schemes to give a specified percentage of top high school graduates automatic admission to state universities. Some predict that such plans may be expanded in the future in an attempt to replace policies based solely on race and gender.

America continued to permit high levels of legal immigration. At the same time, the U.S. has beefed up its patrols at the border with Mexico in an attempt to stem the flood of illegal immigrants. One result has been an increased number of clashes between the border patrol and illegal immigrants. The U.S. has also adopted stricter criteria for the approval of political asylum, and some have raised concerns over the incarceration of some asylum seekers in prisons with regular criminals.

American women have made significant gains in recent years, and have benefited from affirmative action laws, antidiscrimination measures, and judicial decisions that have penalized corporations millions of dollars in discrimination cases.

American Indians continued to suffer disproportionately from poverty and social problems such as alcoholism. In recent years, some Indian reservations have experienced some economic progress through the development of gambling casinos on Indian property. However, many have expressed doubts that casino gambling will lead to broad economic development for the majority of impoverished Indians.

Uruguay

Polity: Presidential-parliamentary democracy
Economy: Capitalist-statist
Population: 3,300,000
PPP: $8,623
Life Expectancy: 74
Ethnic Groups: White (88 percent), mestizo (8 percent), black (4 percent)
Capital: Montevideo

Political Rights: 1
Civil Liberties: 1*
Status: Free

Ratings Change: Uruguay's civil liberties rating changed from 2 to 1 due to the Batlle government's willingness to seek reconciliation based on truth about what happened during a period of military dictatorship.

Overview:
President Jorge Batlle, who took office on March 1, 2000, immediately sought an honest accounting of the human rights situation under a former military regime whose reputation for viciousness had turned Uruguay's reputation as the "Switzerland of Latin America" on its head. Within days of his inauguration, Batlle personally helped the Argentine poet Juan Gelman to track down a granddaughter born in captivity and adopted by a Uruguayan military family. However, Batlle faced a delicate balancing act at national reconciliation, with the armed forces and former leftist guerrillas saying that they had nothing to apologize for, and members of his own party deeply offended that Batlle was stirring up the past.

After gaining independence from Spain, the Oriental Republic of Uruguay was established in 1830. The Colorado Party dominated a relatively democratic political system throughout the 1960s. The 1967 constitution established a bicameral congress consisting of a 99-member chamber of deputies and a 31-member senate, with every member serving a five-year term. The president is also directly elected for a five-year term.

An economic crisis, social unrest, and the activities of the Tupamaro urban guerrilla movement led to a right-wing military takeover in 1973, even though the Tupamaros had been largely crushed a year earlier. During the period of military rule, Uruguay had the largest number of political prisoners per capita in the world and was known as "the torture chamber of Latin America." Civilian rule was restored through negotiations between the regime and civilian politicians. Julio Sanguinetti won the presidential elections in 1984 with military support. In 1989 Luis Alberto Lacalle was elected president as the candidate of the centrist National Party, Uruguay's other traditional political grouping. His popularity plummeted, however, as he attempted to liberalize one of Latin America's most statist economies.

In the 1994 campaign, Sanguinetti ran as a social democrat. The two other main contenders were the leftist Broad Front's Tabaré Vasquez, a moderate socialist medical doctor, and the National Party's Alberto Volante. The 1994 election was the closest ever. The Colorado Party won 31.4 percent of the vote; the National Party, 30.2 percent; and the Broad Front, 30 percent.

Sanguinetti took office in March 1995 and enjoyed considerable congressional support, in part as a result of the inclusion of numerous National Party members in his cabinet. He won legislative support for an austerity package that partially dismantled the country's welfare state. A series of labor stoppages and a sharp decline in Sanguinetti's popularity followed.

In 1998, the National Party was wracked by mutual accusations of corruption, mostly dating from the time of the Lacalle government. In 1999, public safety and an 11 percent unemployment rate continued to be primary concerns. On October 31, Vazquez, a popular mayor of Montevideo, won 39 percent of the vote against Batlle's 31.7, in the first round of the presidential contest. By establishing itself as the single largest political force in the country—winning 40 of 99 seats in the lower house and 12 of 31 in the senate—the election appeared to constitute a serious challenge by the Uruguayan left to the country's traditional, but ailing, two-party system. Just three weeks before the final round of voting, the chief of the Uruguayan army, General Fernán Amado, warned that human rights violations committed during the previous dictatorship were "a closed chapter."

In the second round the National Party backed Batlle, a 72-year-old senator and five-time presidential candidate whose father and great-uncle had been respected Colorado Party presidents. Faced with dismal economic prospects and a choice between presidential candidates representing the moderate right and an eclectic left, in 1999 Uruguayans gave Batlle 52 percent of the vote. Upon taking office, the new president incorporated several National Party members into his cabinet. In the May 23, 2000, local elections, the Broad Front coalition lost significant ground, with the Blancos re-emerging to win in 13 of Uruguay's 19 departments.

Batlle's help to Gelman, a one time Montonero guerrilla whose son and daughter-in-law were killed by the Argentine military, was seen as an affront to Batlle's long-time rival Sanguinetti, who had accepted throughout his two terms the Uruguayan military's apparent inability to locate the poet's granddaughter. Sanguinetti's supporters claimed that Batlle's actions were designed to embarrass the former president. In August, the Uruguayan government appointed a peace commission of leading citizens and human rights activists to look into the fate of 164 Uruguayans who disappeared in Uruguay and neighboring Argentina during the 1973-1984 dictatorship. Both Sanguinetti and Lacalle condemned the action, saying it was ruled out by a 1986 amnesty that was ratified by a referendum three years later. At the same time, Batlle's honeymoon with the left, based largely on his willingness to seek answers about what happened during the military regime, was severely tested by the president's equally firm determination to reduce spending and taxes and to privatize previously sacrosanct state monopolies. Of particular concern to both Batlle and the opposition are the country's 12 percent unemployment rate, a crisis-ridden rural sector, and violent crime.

Political Rights and Civil Liberties: Citizens of Uruguay can change their government democratically. In 1999, for the first time, Uruguayan parties selected a single presidential candidate in open primary elections. Previously, the parties had fielded a number of candidates, and the candidates with the most votes had then accumulated the votes cast for the others. Constitutional guarantees regarding free expression, freedom of religion, and the right to form political parties, labor unions, and civic organizations are generally respected. The former Tupamaro guerrillas now participate in the system as part of the Broad Front. Uruguayans of all political tendencies pride themselves on their refusal to make a public issue of the private lives of public officials.

The judiciary is relatively independent, but has become increasingly inefficient in the face of escalating crime, particularly street violence and organized crime, which continued to be a major issue in 2000. The court system is severely backlogged, and suspects under arrest often spend more time in jail than they would were they to be convicted and serve the maximum sentence for their alleged crime. Allegations of police mistreatment, particularly of youthful offenders, have increased; however, prosecutions of such acts are also occurring more frequently. Prison conditions do not meet international standards.

In 1991, a decision by the Inter-American Commission on Human Rights of the Organization of American States ruled that the 1985 law that granted the military amnesty from rights violations during the years of dictatorship violated key provisions of the American Convention on Human Rights. (During Sanguinetti's first government, from 1985 to 1990, a military commission he appointed cleared the armed forces of responsibility for hundreds of brutal detentions and the "disappearances" of more than 150 Uruguayans at home or in neighboring countries.) Sanguinetti has remained steadfast in refusing to accede to further investigations of the issue, a policy that was reversed by Batlle.

The press is privately owned, and broadcasting is both commercial and public. Numerous daily newspapers publish, many associated with political parties; there are also a number of weeklies. In 1996 a number of publications ceased production because of a government suspension of tax exemptions on the import of newsprint. In addition, a June 1996 decree requires government authorization in order to import newsprint.

Civic organizations have proliferated since the return of civilian rule. Numerous women's rights groups focus on violence against women, societal discrimination and other problems. The small black minority continues to face discrimination. Uruguay's continuing economic crisis has forced thousands of formerly middle-class citizens to join rural migrants in the shantytowns ringing Montevideo.

Workers exercise their right to join unions, bargain collectively, and hold strikes. Unions are well organized and politically powerful. Strikes are sometimes marked by violent clashes and sabotage.

Uzbekistan

Polity: Presidential (dominant party)
Economy: Statist
Population: 24,800,000
PPP: $2,053
Life Expectancy: 68
Ethnic Groups: Uzbek (80 percent), Russian (6 percent), Tajik (5 percent), Kazakh (3 percent), other (6 percent)
Capital: Tashkent

Political Rights: 7
Civil Liberties: 6
Status: Not Free

Overview:
Amid renewed attacks by the radical Islamic Movement of Uzbekistan (IMU) in August 2000, the government continued to use the threat of armed Islamic extremists to justify its repression of independent Muslim groups and political opponents of the regime. Some analysts speculated that the ongoing crackdown on moderate religious Muslims and dissidents, combined with widespread poverty and unemployment, might lead to growing public support for the IMU, which controls valuable narcotics routes throughout Central Asia. In a vote strongly criticized by international observers and opposition leaders in exile for virtually guaranteeing a victory for the incumbent, Islam Karimov was overwhelmingly reelected in the country's January presidential poll.

Located along the ancient trade route of the famous Silk Road, Uzbekistan was conquered by Genghis Khan in the thirteenth and Timur (Tamerlane) in the fourteenth century. By the late 1800s, the territory had been incorporated into the Russian empire. The Uzbekistan Soviet Socialist Republic was established in 1924, and its eastern region was detached and made a separate Tajik Soviet republic five years later.

On December 29, 1991, the country's independence was endorsed in a popular referendum by more than 98 percent of the electorate. In a parallel vote, Islam Karimov, former Communist Party leader and chairman of the People's Democratic Party (PDP), the successor to the Communist Party, was elected president with a reported 88 percent of the vote. His rival, a prominent poet and the chairman of the *Erk* (Freedom) Party, Mohammed Solih, officially received 12 percent. However, Erk members charged election fraud, claiming that Solih actually had received more than 50 percent. The largest opposition group, *Birlik* (Unity), was barred from contesting the election and later refused legal registration as a political party. The Islamic Renaissance Party (IRP) and other religion-based groups were banned entirely.

Only pro-government parties were allowed to compete in elections to the first post-Soviet legislature in December 1994 and January 1995. A February 1995 national referendum to extend Karimov's first five-year term in office until the year 2000 was allegedly approved by 99 percent of the country's voters. In 1997, the government moved to eliminate religion as a potential source of political opposition after the murder of several police officers in the Fergana Valley, an area regarded as a center of militant Islam. The authorities arrested hundreds of alleged suspects, many solely for their supposed affiliation with unofficial Muslim groups.

The Uzbek government used a series of deadly car bombings in Tashkent in February 1999, which it labeled assassination attempts on President Karimov by Islamic militants, as a pretext to intensify mass arrests and trials both targeting religious Muslims and members of political opposition groups. Hundreds of defendants were eventually convicted and imprisoned for their alleged involvement, including some who were given the death penalty. As a result of the crackdowns, many Uzbeks, including members of the IMU, a radical group seeking to overthrow Uzbekistan's secular government and replace it with an Islamic state, fled to neighboring countries. In August, two groups of militants, most of whom appeared to be IMU members, attempted to enter Uzbekistan by crossing from Tajikistan into neighboring Kyrgyzstan, where they took several villages hostage. Uzbekistan agreed to a request by the Kyrgyz government for assistance in fighting the rebels, who released the last of their hostages in early October.

Of the five parties that competed in December's parliamentary election, all supported the president and differed little in their political platforms. International monitors, including the Organization for Security and Cooperation in Europe (OSCE), noted numerous irregularities, including the interference of local governors in the nomination of candidates and the conduct of the elections, and the suspiciously high voter-turnout figure of more than 90 percent.

The January 9, 2000, presidential elections resulted in an expected victory for incumbent Islam Karimov, who defeated his only opponent, Marxist-history professor Abdulhasiz Dzhalalov, with 92 percent of the vote. Voter turnout was a reported 93 percent. Karimov's former party, the PDP, from which he resigned in 1996, nominated its first secretary Dzhalalov with Karimov's consent, while Karimov ran as a candidate of the recently established Fidokorlar party. Uzbekistan's government refused to register genuinely independent opposition parties, and it did not permit members of those parties to stand as candidates. Dzhalalov, a public supporter of Karimov's policies, was quoted during the campaign as stating that he himself intended to vote for Karimov. The OSCE, which had refused to send observers, stated that the election could not be considered competitive, as voters had no genuine choice.

In August, IMU militants engaged in armed clashes with government troops in southeastern Uzbekistan. While Tashkent alleged that the guerillas had entered Uzbek territory from bases in neighboring Tajikistan, Dushanbe denied the charge. Uzbekistan also accused Afghanistan's ruling Taliban of harboring many IMU members. The following month, the U.S. government placed the IMU on its list of international terrorist organizations for its reported links to the Saudi financier Osama bin Laden, whom the U.S. has accused of masterminding several terrorist attacks around the world.

In what Human Rights Watch termed a political show trial, Uzbekistan's supreme court in November found 12 men guilty of involvement with the IMU and of treason and terrorist attacks, including the February 1999 Tashkent bombings. Two of the defendants, prominent IMU leaders Juma Namangani and Tokhir Yuldash, were sentenced to death, while the other 10 suspects, including exiled Erk leader Mohammed Solih, were given between 12 and 20 years in prison. Nine of the 12 accused, including Namangani, Yuldash, and Solih, were not present during the proceedings. According to Human Rights Watch, the trial violated international law forbidding trials in absentia, the prosecution failed to provide concrete evidence of the defendants' guilt, and the peaceful opposition was condemned along with militants.

Political Rights and Civil Liberties: Citizens of Uzbekistan cannot change their government democratically. President Karimov and the executive branch dominate the legislature and judiciary, and the government severely represses all political opposition. The primary purpose of the 250-member rubber-stamp national legislature is to confirm decisions made by the executive branch. The 1994-1995 and 1999 parliamentary elections, and the 2000 presidential poll, in which only pro-government candidates could participate, were neither free nor fair.

The state severely restricts freedom of speech and the press, allowing virtually no criticism of the authorities, particularly President Karimov. Consequently, self-censorship among print and broadcast journalists is widespread. The country's few private broadcast and print media outlets avoid political issues, are generally local or regional in scope, and suffer from administrative and financial constraints.

Under the pretext of fighting armed Islamic extremists, the government continued its harsh campaign against religious organizations, particularly Muslim groups, not sanctioned by the state. Over the last several years, thousands of pious Muslims have been arrested and imprisoned on trumped-up charges of anti-constitutional activities, while their family members are frequently harassed and persecuted. Authorities have targeted members of the banned and highly secretive *Hizb-ut-Tahrir* (Party of Liberation) Islamic group for engaging in unregistered religious activity, which is a crime in Uzbekistan. The 1998 Law on Freedom of Conscience and Religious Organizations imposes strict registration criteria and severely restricts proselytizing, the teaching of religious subjects without official permission, and the wearing of religious garments in public. Revisions to the criminal code in May 1998 and May 1999 increased penalties for violating the law and other statutes on religious activities. Officially approved Muslim and Jewish communities, the Russian Orthodox Church, and some other Christian denominations face few serious restrictions on their activities.

Permits for public demonstrations, which must be approved by the government, are not routinely granted. No genuine political opposition groups function legally or participate in the government. A 1997 law prohibits parties based on ethnic or religious lines and those advocating war or subversion of the constitutional order. Members of unregistered opposition groups, including Birlik and Erk, are subject to harassment and discrimination, and some have gone into voluntary exile abroad. The country's two leading human rights groups, the Human Rights Society of Uzbekistan (HRSU) and the Independent Human Rights Organization of Uzbekistan (NOPCHU), have been denied registration repeatedly and have faced ongoing harassment by the authorities. In 1999, two of the country's most prominent human rights advocates, Mahbuba Kasymova and Ismail Adylov of NOPCHU, were sentenced to five and six years, respectively, in prison on politically motivated charges. On December 22, 2000, Kasymova was suddenly released from prison, apparently as a result of pressure from international human rights groups and the U.S. government, although Adylov remained incarcerated at year's end.

Although a 1992 trade union law guarantees the right of workers to form and join unions, it does not mention the right to strike. The Council of the Federation of Trade Unions (CFTU), which is the successor to the Soviet-era confederation, is the country's sole trade union group and remains dependent on the state.

The judiciary is subservient to the president, who appoints all judges and can remove them from office at any time. Police routinely physically abuse suspects to extract confessions, which are routinely admitted by judges, and arbitrary arrest and detention are common. Law enforcement authorities reportedly often plant narcotics, weapons, and banned religious leaflets on suspected members of Islamic groups or political opponents to justify their arrest. Prisons suffer from severe overcrowding and shortages of food and medicine. The Jaslik labor camp in the northwestern region of Karakalpakistan houses thousands of prisoners, convicted for their political and religious beliefs, in appalling conditions.

Widespread corruption, bureaucratic regulations, and the government's continued tight control over the economy limit most citizens' equality of opportunity. Women's educational and professional prospects are restricted by traditional cultural and religious norms and by ongoing economic difficulties throughout the country. According to Human Rights Watch, police discourage women from filing complaints of domestic abuse and fail to conduct investigations when reports are made, while judges are generally lenient in the prosecution of domestic violence cases.

Vanuatu

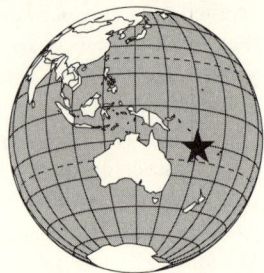

Polity: Parliamentary democracy
Economy: Capitalist-statist
Population: 200,000
PPP: $3,120
Life Expectancy: 68
Ethnic Groups: Melanesian (94 percent), French (4 percent), other (2 percent)
Capital: Port Vila

Political Rights: 1
Civil Liberties: 3
Status: Free

Overview:
Vanuatu celebrated 20 years of independence in June 2000. Public sector reforms and economic and governance reforms, which started in the mid-1990s are continuing, but citizen's groups complained that the gap between rich and poor is worsening. Ethnic violence in the Solomon Islands prompted the government of Prime Minister Barak Tame Sope to stress priority in addressing gaps in distributing government services.

Located in the southwestern Pacific, this predominantly Melanesian archipelago, formerly the New Hebrides, was an Anglo-French condominium until it became independent in 1980. The condominium agreement divided the islands into English- and French-speaking communities, creating rifts that continue today. In 1999, Prime Minister Donald Kalpokas called on all government ministries to use both English and French, the country's two official languages, in their work.

Politics in the islands is also divided between the English- and French-speaking communities, and factional rivalries contributed to frequent changes of government. The first postindependence government, led by Prime Minister Father Walter Lini's anglophone Vanua'aku Pati (VP) party, largely excluded francophones from key posts. In 1991, a divided VP ousted Lini, who left to form the National United Party (NUP). This split the anglophone vote and allowed the francophone Union of Moderate Parties

(UMP) to win a plurality in the December 1991 elections and form a government under Maxime Carlot. Several coalition governments, which lasted from several months to two years, followed. In the past five years, the country has had eight changes of government. In November 1999, Barak Tame Sope of the Melanesian Progressive Party was chosen prime minister after winning 28 votes in the 52-seat parliament. The new government promised to reduce the power of department heads, to review the recruitment of foreign advisers, and to reconsider the value-added tax.

The government introduced the Comprehensive Reform Program after the exposure of alleged corruption and abuses by senior government officials, including reports that several high-ranking politicians were involved in selling passports to foreign nationals. A report by ombudsman Patterson in January 1998 found that the Vanuatu National Provident Fund, a national retirement scheme for workers, had improperly given loans to leading politicians. The disclosure sparked immediate public protests in the capital and attempts by investors to withdraw their savings, which escalated into widespread rioting and looting. A four-week nationwide state of emergency was declared, during which time the police questioned and arrested more than 500 people.

The Comprehensive Reform Program includes an overhaul of state administration and increased private sector development. The government would also reduce the country's public service sector by about ten percent and enact a strict leadership code of conduct. To rebuild public confidence, the government established a special unit to recover and manage more than $25 million in debt for the Vanuatu National Provident Fund, as well as the Development Bank of Vanuatu, and the National Bank of Vanuatu, which were all plagued by bad loans and political interference.

To reduce reliance on overseas aid, the country has been working to develop alternative income sources. The sale of fishing licenses to foreign fishing companies is now an important source of income for the government. In June 2000, the 300-member National Fishermen Cooperative criticized a fishing agreement with a Taiwan-owned fishing company. The union faulted the Taiwanese company for dangerous work conditions (29 Vanuatu fishermen have died) and a poor record in paying salaries. Vanuatu was also accused of involvement in money-laundering activities in its bid to set up an offshore banking industry. It joined seven other Pacific Islands to sign the "Pacific Islands Prudential Regulation and Supervision Initiative" to end illicit financial operations in the region.

Observers said that the government continued to try to expand its power. Ombudsman Harrington Alatoa expressed concern in February over the government's attempt to gag the *Trading Post* from carrying further news on the sinking of the MV Latua in August 1999, in which 27 lives were lost, as well as the government's delay in releasing the official Commission of Enquiry reports on this incident. Also, a bill was introduced in April to allow the prime minister and his cabinet to hire and fire civil servants. Opposition leader Edward Natapei said the bill was unconstitutional. He charged that, under the constitution, civil servants are independent of the government because they are hired by the Public Service Commission.

Political Rights and Civil Liberties: Citizens of Vanuatu can change their government democratically. The constitution vests executive power in a prime minister. The unicameral, 52-member parliament is directly elected for a four-year term. A largely ceremonial president is elected for a five-year term by an electoral college consisting of the 49 members of parliament and the 6 provincial council presidents. Although the 1998 national elections were regarded as generally free and fair, there were allegations of voting irregularities.

In this multiparty state, there is considerable freedom for the media. There are independent newspapers as well as political party newsletters. In November 1998, state-owned Television Blong Vanuatu announced that it would screen more locally produced program materials. In April 1999, the Vanuatu Broadcasting and Television Corporation decided to allow pay television to commence service. In June 2000, enactment of the Freedom Telecommunications Law ended the two-decade long monopoly of Telecommunications Vanuatu Limited and a new bilingual paper, the *Port Vila Press*, was launched in November. Nonetheless, the government owns most of the country's media, including a television station serving the capital, two radio stations, and the *Vanuatu Weekly* newspaper, so that its voice is the most prominent.

Religious freedom is respected in this predominantly Christian country. Freedom of assembly and association is upheld. There are five active, independent trade unions operating under the umbrella of the Vanuatu Council of Trade Unions although more than 80 percent of the population relies on subsistence agriculture and fishing. Unions can exercise their right to organize and bargain collectively.

Although the judicial system is generally independent, the government has, at times, attempted to pressure the largely expatriate judiciary in politically sensitive cases. After the arrest of some 500 suspected rioters in January 1998, there were credible reports that police assaulted or otherwise poorly treated prisoners. Subsequently, 18 police and military officers were charged with intentional assault. In 1999, the Ombudsman's Office reported that the country's jails fail to meet the minimum international standards and the constitutional rights of inmates are often violated.

The country's small ethnic-minority communities are discriminated against in land ownership. Women have limited opportunities in education and politics, and recent high-profile court cases involving violence against women strengthened the call for more public education on the issue and for an increase in the number of women in the judicial system. In February 2000, Marie Noelle Patterson, National Council of Women chairperson and a former ombudsman, called for more education on violence against women and increase in the number of women in the judiciary system. This followed a supreme court decision to suspend a jail sentence for a man who had murdered his wife and a 10-week jail term for a man charged with molesting his two stepdaughters. Women's groups also demanded stricter sentences for sex offenders.

Venezuela

Polity: Presidential-parliamentary democracy
Political Rights: 3*
Civil Liberties: 5*
Economy: Capitalist-statist
Status: Partly Free
Population: 24,200,000
PPP: $5,808
Life Expectancy: 73
Ethnic Groups: Mestizo (67 percent), European (21 percent), black (10 percent), Indian (2 percent)
Capital: Caracas

Ratings Change: Venezuela's political rights rating changed from 4 to 3 due to improvements in the political climate and elections process surrounding the national vote held in July. However, its civil liberties rating changed from 4 to 5 due to President Hugo Chavez expanding his attempt to centralize control from the state sector to civil society, including a naked power grab aimed at the country's independent trade unions.

Overview:

President Hugo Chávez, Venezuela's would-be savior and former military plotter, appeared to be riding the tiger of a sputtering revolution at the end of 2000, as Venezuelans showed increasing weariness with his controversial overhaul of their country's democratic institutions. Chávez, who won nearly 60 percent of the vote in a July 2000 presidential election, found little popular enthusiasm in a national referendum conducted in December that approved his attempt to curb the power of the country's labor bosses. Organized labor and the media continued throughout 2000 to be favorite whipping boys for the demagogic former army paratrooper, whose international forays included highly visible embraces of Cuba's Fidel Castro and Iraq's Saddam Hussein. In 1999, capital flight from Venezuela was estimated to be some $8 billion as the economy contracted by 7.2 percent, and many upper-class *venezolanos*, mindful of Chávez's boast that his government is "doing away with the tyranny of the elite," have packed themselves and their businesses off to Miami. In September 2000 Transparency International ranked Venezuela as one of the most corrupt countries in the world.

The Republic of Venezuela was established in 1830, nine years after independence from Spain. Long periods of instability and military rule ended with the establishment in 1961 of civilian rule. Under the 1961 constitution, the president and a bicameral congress are elected for five years. The senate has at least two members from each of the 21 states and the federal district of Caracas. The chamber of deputies has 189 seats.

Until 1993, the social-democratic Democratic Action (AD) Party and the Social Christian Party (COPEI) dominated politics. Former President Carlos Andres Pérez (1989-93) of the AD was nearly overthrown by Chávez and other nationalist military officers in two 1992 coup attempts in which dozens were killed. In 1993 Pérez was charged with corruption and removed from office by congress.

Rafael Caldera, a former president (1969-1974) of COPEI and a populist, was elected president in late 1993 at the head of the 16-party National Convergence, which included Communists, other leftists, and right-wing groups. Caldera's term was marked by a national banking collapse (in 1994), the suspension of a number of civil liberties, mounting violent crime, social unrest, and rumors of a military coup. In 1995, Caldera's reputation for honesty was tarnished by allegations of corruption among his inner circle. With crime soaring, oil wealth drying up, and the country in the worst economic crisis in 50 years, popular disillusionment with politics deepened.

At the beginning of 1998, the early presidential favorite was a former beauty queen whose appeal stemmed largely from her own roots outside the corrupt political establishment famous for its interlocking system of privilege and graft. Chávez's antiestablishment, anticorruption populism also played well in a country whose elites considered politics their private preserve. As his victory appeared more likely, Chávez moved toward the center, abandoning rhetoric in which he criticized the free market and promised to "fry" opposition leaders. Last-minute efforts to find a consensus candidate against Chávez were largely unsuccessful, and the Yale-educated businessman Henrique Salas, the other leading presidential contender, steered away from association with the old political order. Salas, a respected two-term former state governor, won just 40 percent of the vote, to Chávez's 57 percent. Chávez took power of the world's number three oil-exporting country in February 1999.

Upon taking office, Chávez promptly dismantled Venezuela's political system of checks and balances, ostensibly to destroy a discredited two-party system that for four decades presided over several oil booms but has left four out of five Venezuelans impoverished. He gutted the power of the opposition-controlled congress and placed the judiciary under executive branch tutelage.

Critics charged Chávez with militarizing politics and politicizing the military, with Chávez's army colleagues given a far bigger say in the day-to-day running of the country. Tens of thousands of soldiers were dispatched to build public works, 34 senior military officers were promoted without congressional approval, and regional army commands were given oversight powers of local elected officials. Generals were appointed to senior posts such as presidential chief of staff, head of the secret police, and head of the internal revenue service.

A constituent assembly dominated by Chávez followers drafted a new constitution that would make censorship of the press easier, allow a newly strengthened chief executive the right to dissolve congress, and make it possible for Chávez to retain power until 2013. Congress and the supreme court were dismissed after Venezuelans approved the new constitution in a national referendum December 15. In a positive move, the assembly offered the nation's 500,000 Indians constitutional guarantees to conserve their cultures and languages.

Despite Chávez's 21-point lead in the presidential contest, the July 2000 election marked a resurgence of a political opposition that had been hamstrung in its efforts to contest his stripping of congress, and the judiciary of their independence and power. His ruling coalition, the Patriotic Pole, fell short of the two-thirds majority it needed in congress to rubber-stamp presidential appointments and spending decisions. Opposition parties won most of the country's governorships, about half the mayoralties, and a significant share of power in the new congress. In addition, Chávez found a number of key civilian and military allies deserting him throughout the year, many of whom joined forces with the opposition, including his erstwhile friend and colleague Lt. Col. Francisco Arias Cardenas, who had run second in the presidential race. In response, in November, Chávez's congressional allies granted him special fast-track powers that allowed him to decree a wide range of laws without parliamentary debate. Chávez's foreign policy forays also won him significant suspicion among Venezuela's traditional allies, particularly after suspected ties to Ecuador's unsuccessful military coup leaders were revealed.

Political Rights and Civil Liberties:

Citizens can change their government democratically, although Chávez supporters appear at times on the verge of mob rule, particularly as constitutional checks and balances have been removed. The July 2000 elections were considered by international observers to be free and fair. However, government critics claim that democratic rule has been damaged significantly as independent institutions have lost their autonomy and the concentration of political power has put Chávez at the top of a pyramid of executive-branch power unprecedented in modern times.

Until Chávez took power, the judicial system was headed by a nominally independent supreme court, although the court was highly politicized, was undermined by the chronic corruption (including the growing influence of narcotics traffickers) that permeates the entire political system, and was unresponsive to charges of rights abuses. Chávez, by sacking scores of judges, has successfully subordinated the legal system to his presidency. In August, 1999, supreme court president Cecilia Sosa resigned in protest after the court backed the assembly as it moved to give itself the power to dismiss judges and overhaul the country's judicial system. "The court simply committed suicide to avoid being assassinated," Sosa said. "But the result is the same—it is dead." In August 2000, a senior official who led the effort to replace corrupt or negligent judges resigned, complaining that cronyism prevailing in a Chávez-dominated judicial-reform commission led to the removal of controversial judges, who were replaced with Chávez's own political allies. In November, opposition legislators slammed as unconstitutional a nomination process to select the country's supreme court and other public offices, saying that the selection committee was packed with pro-Chávez legislators rather than made up of civil society representatives, as stipulated. An unwieldy new judicial code has hampered some law enforcement efforts.

Citizen security in general remains threatened by a narcotics-fueled crime wave that has resulted in hundreds of killings monthly in major cities and vigilante mob killings of alleged criminals. In 2000 the murder rate reached 21 per day, double what it was two years ago; during the Christmas weekend alone, 144 homicides were logged, with 60 percent of the killings reportedly score-settling with criminal gangs or in shootouts with the police. A recent study ranked Venezuela as second of the ten most violent nations in the Americas and Europe.

Widespread arbitrary detention and torture of suspects, as well as dozens of extra-judicial killings by military security forces and the police, have increased as crime continues to soar. By mid-2000, an estimated 500 people had been killed by the police, a sign that, some observers say, is evidence of a growing vigilante mentality among law enforcement personnel. Since the 1992 coup attempts, weakened civilian governments have had less authority over the military and the police, and rights abuses overall are committed with impunity. A separate system of armed forces courts retains jurisdiction over members of the military accused of rights violations and common criminal crimes, and decisions by these cannot be appealed in civilian court. Chávez's decision to preside over all military promotions and transfers has concentrated enormous patronage within the armed forces in his own hands. His meddling in all aspects of military affairs caused something of a backlash in 2000, as 42 of 93 retiring officers who were to receive one of the armed forces' highest honors preferred to stay away from the July ceremony rather than receive the recognition from Chávez's hands. In a disturbing trend, in October 2000, Chávez named two serving generals to head the world's second-largest state oil company and its U.S. refining and market branch.

Venezuela's 32 prisons, the most violent in the world, hold some 23,000 inmates—of whom fewer than one-third have been convicted of a crime—even though they were designed to hold no more than 14,000. Deadly prison riots are common, and inmate gangs have a striking degree of control over the penal system.

The press is mostly privately owned, although the practice of journalism is supervised by an association of broadcasters under government control. Since 1994, the media in general have faced a pattern of intimidation. International media monitors have condemned a constitutional article approved by the constituent assembly that would require journalists to publish or broadcast "truthful information," a move that they say opens the door to government censorship.

Few Indians hold title to their land, and indigenous communities trying to defend their legal land rights are subject to abuse, including killing, by gold miners and corrupt rural police. In 1999, the constituent assembly voted to include a chapter in the new constitution that sets forth the legal rights of indigenous peoples and communities in accordance with standards set by the International Labor Organization. Chapter VII would guarantee "the right to exist as indigenous peoples and communities with their own social and economic organization, their cultures and traditions, and their language and religion." In the July 2000 national elections, three indigenous candidates were elected to the national assembly, eight to regional legislative congresses, and four Indians won mayoralties.

Labor unions are well organized, but highly politicized and prone to corruption. Chávez supporters have sought to break what they term a "stranglehold" of corrupt labor leaders on the job market, a move labor activists say tramples on the rights of private organizations. The referendum approved in December 2000 allows Chávez to dissolve the Venezuelan Worker's Confederation and to organize new state-supervised elections of union representatives, a move that opposition and labor leaders say is the first step towards establishing a government-controlled labor union. Security forces frequently break up strikes and arrest trade unionists.

Vietnam

Polity: One party
Economy: Statist
Population: 78,700,000
PPP: $1,689
Life Expectancy: 68

Political Rights: 7
Civil Liberties: 6*
Status: Not Free

Ethnic Groups: Vietnamese (85-90 percent), Chinese (3 percent), other, including Muong, Tai, Meo, Khmer, Man, Cham (7-12 percentz)
Capital: Hanoi
Ratings Change: Vietnam's civil liberties rating changed from 7 to 6 due to a broadening of access to the Internet and Western media in the larger cities and improvement in the government's overall human rights record.

Overview:

The year 2000 marked the 25th anniversary of the end of the Vietnam War, but celebrations were largely limited to government-organized events. The Vietnamese economy continued to struggle to recover from the effects of the Asian financial crisis. The country's first stock exchange opened in Ho Chi Minh City in August.

In November, U.S. President Bill Clinton made a historic three-day visit to the country to further reconciliation between the two nations and promote new trade, education, and science and technology exchanges. A landmark bilateral trade was signed in July to put economic and trade affairs at the center of U.S.-Vietnam bilateral relations. The agreement will increase Vietnam's exports to the United States from $455 million in 1999 to around $770 annually in the next few years.

In April, a two-year campaign to criticize and clean up the Vietnamese Communist Party (VCP) ended. Although the government continues to crack down on corruption and abuses, which are major sources of public grievance, few people believe significant changes have been made. On the other hand, the government showed greater tolerance of public criticisms. From June to October 2000, almost 100 peasants camped in front of the prime minister's office to protest corruption and abuse by provincial officials. Unlike in the past, security forces did not arrest the protesters. The government also showed increased tolerance of criticisms by intellectuals. This year the government gave amnesty to 12,000 prisoners, who human rights groups believe were held for political or religious reasons. Hanoi's inability to respond, however, could worsen public frustration and discontent with the regime.

Vietnam was colonized by France in the nineteenth century and was occupied by Japan during World War II. It gained independence in 1954 and was divided into the Republic of South Vietnam and the Communist-ruled Democratic Republic of Vietnam in the north. After years of fighting, North Vietnam crushed the U.S.-backed South in 1975 and reunited the country under a Communist government in 1976.

In 1986, the government began decentralizing economic decision making, encouraging small-scale private enterprise, and dismantling collectivized agriculture. Economic reforms accelerated as Soviet aid dwindled after 1990, and Vietnam looked increasingly to Asia and the West. The 1992 constitution codified many economic reforms, but the VCP remains the sole legal party. A president, who is nominally elected, replaced the collective state council. In practice, the VCP makes all key decisions and the government maintains a firm hand over society. The unrest and financial turmoil that swept other Southeast Asian countries in 1997 strengthened the position of hardliners and military figures, anxious about economic reform.

In its effort to reform the economy and recover from the Asian financial crisis that began in 1997, the government began to shed itself of money-losing state-owned enterprises by removing caps on private ownership. The Enterprise Law was passed in 1999 to simplify the establishment of local private enterprises and progress was made on establishing legal ownership and transfer of property rights. Yet, the government maintains the use of licenses and regulations to bring in revenue and maintain control. In 1999, all locally owned trading and tourism firms were required to register their branches or representative offices. In 2000, the government decreed that all singers, musicians and dancers must hold special permits to hold live performances. Sending workers overseas is another way the government deals with high unemployment.

The government launched campaigns to crack-down on corruption and abuse of power and even expanded the penal code to cover economic crimes and introduced stiffer sentences. But critics say that these actions only serve to appease public discontent and divert blame for its own economic mismanagement. Punishment is especially light for VCP members, who are often the most egregious offenders. Those found guilty are usually given a reprimand, while expulsion from the party is the norm in severe cases. The next party congress, held once every five years, is scheduled for March 2001. Observers believe that a major party decision on the term "bac lot," or exploit, to describe relations between bosses and workers is necessary to encourage private business growth and create employment. Bac lot also affects party members who want to enter business. Critics charge that ambiguities have encouraged abuses of power in some cases and stifled ambition in others. In the long term, the party could risk losing its membership base if people find business more attractive than membership in the Vietnamese Communist Party.

Many social problems have worsened in recent years as a result of severe government spending cuts to social services. Many children have lost access to public education and health services. The number of HIV cases is rising. Public health experts fear that the merger of the Steering Committee for Social Evils with two other government committees focused, respectively, on drug abuse and HIV/AIDS, may indicate a law-and-order approach, rather than a more sympathetic public health approach, to deal with this disease. More than 1,800 Vietnamese have died from AIDS, and more than 20,000 HIV cases have been reported. Estimates of total infection range up to 150,000. Drug use and youth crimes are also increasing. The government has launched nationwide antidrug campaigns and concluded treaties with neighboring countries to stem the flow of drugs.

Political Rights and Civil Liberties: The Vietnamese cannot change their government democratically. The VCP maintains tight control of all political, economic, religious, and social affairs. The Politburo and its five-member Standing Committee decide important policy and leadership issues. The Fatherland Front, a VCP mass organization, controls candidate selection for the national assembly. New membership in the VCP has been falling in recent years. Today about 2.3 million are members out of a population of 79 million.

The judiciary is not independent. The president appoints judges, and the VCP instructs them on rulings. Though somewhat less aggressively than in past years, authorities continue to monitor the population through mandatory household registrations, block wardens, and surveillance of communications, informants, and official peasant associations. A new draft of the criminal code subjects fewer offenses to the death sentence, and the government may switch from shooting to using lethal injections and electrocution as "more civilized ways" of execution. Several thousand prisoners, including political and religious dissidents, were released in 1998 in two mass amnesties, but no official reasons were given.

The media are state-owned. The government has shut down newspapers for violating the narrow limits on permissible reporting and has restricted the entry of many Western and regional newspapers that are critical of the regime. In one case, a prominent newspaper editor was detained for more than a year for reporting on high-level corruption. Internet access is growing at 30 percent annually and foreign language media, such as newspapers, magazines and CNN broadcasts, are obtainable in the cities. There are currently no government controls on Internet access. The government has announced plans to regulate local Internet use, but will probably have limited impact, as shown by experience in other countries.

Assemblies require a permit and are limited to occasional small demonstrations over nonpolitical issues. The Vietnamese have some latitude to criticize government corruption and inefficiency, but it is illegal to advocate political reform. Foreign aid money has helped to launch several nongovernmental organizations (NGOs) in Vietnam. Although they are government controlled or licensed, NGOs offer another avenue for assistance to better reach the grassroots communities. There are now around 300 government-approved NGOs.

All clergy must belong to government-organized religious organizations and must obtain permission to hold meetings or training seminars, operate religious schools, appoint clergy, and repair places of worship. A number of Protestant and Catholic leaders remain in prison, although several were released from detention in 1999. The government has tried to justify its control by alleging collusion between Christians and Vietnam's enemies, but it recognizes that government persecutions are often counterproductive. Since 1975 the number of Protestants has grown from 150,000 to 800,000 people and many belong to the highland minority groups.

All unions must belong to the state-controlled Vietnam General Confederation of Labor, and all union leaders are VCP members. The 1994 Labor Code recognizes only a limited right to strike and allows the prime minister or the court to terminate strikes for the national good.

Although local authorities impose internal travel, education, and employment restrictions on ethnic minorities, people can more freely travel within the country. Over a decade of economic reform has expanded individual freedom for Vietnamese citizens. But women continue to face social and employment discrimination. Prostitution of women and children and international trafficking for that purpose are reportedly increasing.

Yemen

Polity: Dominant party (military-influenced) (traditional chiefs)
Economy: Capitalist-statist
Population: 17,000,000
PPP: $719
Life Expectancy: 59
Ethnic Groups: Predominantly Arab, some Afro-Arab, South Asian
Capital: Sanaa

Political Rights: 5
Civil Liberties: 6
Status: Not Free

Overview:
President Ali Abdullah Saleh identified national reconciliation as Yemen's major priority during celebrations in May to commemorate ten years of unification. However, bitterness prevails among many southerners who continue to see unity as northern domination. Despite an economic reform plan launched in 1995, the south remains largely undeveloped and poor after decades of Communist rule. Southern Yemenis are also dissatisfied with official corruption, cronyism, and restrictions on political and civic participation. Saleh's General People's Congress (GPC) party dominates the government and parliament, limiting or barring representation by the main opposition Yemeni Socialist Party (YSP) of former South Yemen. Presidential elections in 1999, in which parliament blocked the only credible opposition nominee from standing, were widely seen as an insult, or as one YSP official said, "poor stage management." Observers agree that Saleh's greatest challenge is the need for comprehensive political and economic reform to combat Yemen's vast social problems and the mistrust between north and south.

After hundreds of years of rule by autocratic religious leaders, the northern Yemen Arab Republic came under military control in 1962. Field Marshall Saleh was elected president by a constituent assembly in 1978. The British controlled the southern People's Republic of Yemen from 1839 to 1967. Hardline Marxist nationals seized power in the southern capital of Aden following the British withdrawal. North and south were unified into the Republic of Yemen in 1990, with the GPC's Saleh as president and southern YSP leader Ali Salim al-Biedh as vice president.

In April 1993 parliamentary elections, Saleh and the GPC won the most seats and formed a coalition with the Islamic Islah party and the YSP. Parliament formally elected Saleh and al-Biedh president and vice president, respectively. However, al-Biedh boycotted the new government and called for demilitarization of the former north-south border, decentralization of authority, and investigation into dozens of preelection killings of YSP activists. The south attempted to secede in April 1994, sparking a 70-day civil war. Northern troops prevailed, and al-Biedh and other secessionist leaders fled the country.

Constitutional amendments in 1994 gave the chief executive broad powers and provided for direct presidential elections in 1999. Islah and the GPC formed a governing coalition in October 1994, and 13 opposition groups, led by the YSP, formed the Democratic Opposition Coalition in 1995. April 1997 elections to the 301-seat parliament were generally free and fair, though opposition members denounced the results as a government attempt to legitimize the "unfair" outcome of the civil war.

With the help of the World Bank and the IMF, Saleh has pursued an economic restructuring plan since 1995. A minor oil producer, Yemen is one of the Arab world's poorest nations. Unemployment is estimated at around 35 percent, while some 30 percent of Yemenis live in poverty. Yemen has made progress on reducing inflation and budget expenditures, but still needs to reform the civil service, eliminate corruption, and encourage private investment.

One barrier to foreign investment is Yemen's precarious security situation. The central government's influence is limited; in governorates outside the larger cities, tribal leaders hold sway. Violence is a problem, as illicit guns outnumber Yemenis by three to one, and Kalashnikov rifles are carried openly. In September, two soldiers were killed and others wounded as armed southern villagers confronted government troops seeking to arrest a suspected separatist. No accurate figures were available on the number of villagers killed in the gun battle, which reportedly lasted ten hours. Disgruntled tribesmen frequently take foreign tourists or oil workers as hostages in order to press the government to grant development projects or release imprisoned fellow tribesmen. These hostages are generally released unharmed and report having been well treated by their captors. Islamic militancy surfaces occasionally, as the ill-fated kidnapping of 16 Western tourists in December 1998 illustrates, and Yemen is rapidly gaining a reputation as a conduit for terrorism. The country has been identified as a source and transit point for terrorists, weapons, and funding for Osama Bin Laden's *Al-Qaida* organization. An apparent suicide bombing on October 12 aimed at the U.S. naval destroyer *Cole* killed 17 American soldiers and wounded dozens. One key suspect in the attack is believed to be linked with Bin Laden.

Political Rights and Civil Liberties:

The right of citizens to change their government is limited by the concentration of political power in the hands of a few leaders, particularly the president. The parliament is not an effective lawmaking body; it does little more than debate issues, and its power is limited by the president's authority to rule by decree. Presidential elections in 1999 were seen more as a referendum than an election, as the major opposition candidate was barred by parliament from running. Saleh's only opponent was a little-known GPC member whose campaign was financed by the government in an attempt to impart the appearance of credibility. The YSP led a coalition of opposition groups urging Yemenis to boycott the polls.

In November, parliament approved constitutional amendments that would extend the president's term from five to seven years, and that of parliament members from four to six years. The amendments would also create a second chamber of parliament, a 111-seat consultative council appointed by the president to assist in making laws. Opposition leaders denounced the amendments, calling them an attempt by Saleh to further consolidate his power and entrench the status quo. The amendments must be approved by a popular referendum, which is scheduled for February 2001.

The judiciary is not independent. Judges are susceptible to bribery and government influence, and many are poorly trained. Judicial independence is further hampered by the government's frequent reluctance to carry out sentences. Authorities set up a special court in 1999 to handle cases of kidnapping, which was made a capital offense after the kidnapping of 16 Western tourists by Islamic militants in late 1998. All courts are governed by *Sharia* (Islamic law), and there are no jury trials. The law lists 13 capital offenses, including some cases of adultery. Since 1999, the government has dismissed several judges accused of corruption or incompetence, and has allowed the World Bank to implement programs to help train judges. These reforms will require time to produce results. Local tribal leaders adjudicate land disputes and criminal cases in areas under their authority.

Various branches of the security forces carry out arbitrary arrest and detention on political grounds, and regularly flout due process rights. Amnesty International reported in March that torture, disappearance, and arbitrary detention persist in Yemen, and that legal safeguards concerning arrest, detention, and fair trial are routinely violated. The government has also failed to investigate hundreds of disappearances since the late 1960s in both north and south Yemen. Prisons are overcrowded and their sanitary conditions poor. Mistreatment occurs in private prisons as well as in official facilities. In April, three people died from suffocation as a result of being detained, allegedly by tribal leaders, in a container in Dhamar governorate.

A press law requires that newspapers reapply annually for licenses and that they show continuing evidence of about $5,000 in operating capital. The press is allowed a certain degree of freedom to criticize government officials and policies, yet the government restricts this freedom through legal harassment, detention, and prosecution. In February, a Sanaa court ordered the 30-day suspension of the opposition weekly *Al-Wahdawi* and placed a permanent ban on one of its contributors after the publication of an article seen as detrimental to Yemeni-Saudi relations. The editor of *Al-Ayyam* was charged with publishing false information and "insulting public institutions" in an interview with a Muslim cleric. Saif Haderi, editor of *Al-Choumou*, was suspended from the profession for ten months and fined in August for allegedly slandering the education minister. The weekly *Al-Rai al-Aam* was the target of a bombing in February. Broadcast media are government owned and present only government views—a significant limitation on access to information, given Yemen's 60 percent illiteracy rate.

Permits are required for public gatherings, which are monitored by government informers. Associations must register with the government. The independent Yemeni Human Rights Organization operates openly, and international human rights observers are allowed broad access. Members of the YSP face harassment and detention by authorities. In April, a YSP office in Abyan governorate was closed and up to 100 party members and supporters arrested under suspicion of planning a rally to commemorate the victims of two 1998 police killings. Five YSP members were detained in August for meeting without a permit. According to Human Rights Watch, YSP members report that up to $18 million in party funds remain frozen by the government. In September, police opened fire on Palestinians protesting plans to evict them from their camp in Sanaa.

Islam is the state religion; about 75 percent of Yemenis belong to the Shafai order of Sunni Islam, and 25 percent to the Zaydi order of Shia Islam. Followers of other religions may worship freely, but the government forbids proselytizing by non-Muslims, conversions, and the construction of new places of worship without permits. Yemeni Jews, who number about 500, face traditional restrictions on places of residence and employment.

Women face tremendous legal and traditional discrimination, and approximately

80 percent of Yemeni women are illiterate, compared with 35 percent of men. Women convicted of "moral offenses" are arbitrarily detained for indefinite periods under the penal code. In 1999, authorities reduced the minimum marriage age (15) for women, replacing it with the onset of puberty (age nine, according to conservatives). "Honor killings" occur in Yemen, although the number of such killings is difficult to determine because of failure to report or investigate them.

Workers may form unions, but the government regularly places its own personnel in influential positions inside unions and syndicates. Foreign, agricultural, and domestic workers receive limited protection under labor laws. The Yemeni Confederation of Labor Unions is the sole labor federation. The right to bargain collectively and to strike is limited; collective agreements may be invalidated if judged to "damage the economic interests of the country," and permission to strike must be obtained from the union federation.

Yugoslavia (Serbia & Montenegro)

Polity: Parliamentary democracy
Economy: Mixed statist (transitional)
Population: 10,700,000
PPP: na
Life Expectancy: 72
Ethnic Groups: Serbian (63 percent), Albanian (14 percent), Montenegrin (6 percent), Hungarian (4 percent), other (13 percent)
Capital: Belgrade

Political Rights: 4*
Civil Liberties: 4*
Status: Partly Free

Ratings Change: Yugoslavia's political rights and civil liberties ratings changed from 5 to 4 due to the overthrow of the Milosevic regime in October which swept to power a coalition of democratic forces that began instituting a wide variety of reforms, including freedom of the press, the organization of elections, and the rule of law.

Overview:

On October 5, 2000, the last of the great East European revolutions against communism took place in Belgrade, as a massive show of "people power" led to the overthrow of the Milosevic regime. With the Serbian opposition's victory, the political and social atmosphere in the Federal Republic of Yugoslavia (FRY) was transformed. The overthrow of the Milosevic regime also had important effects on regional stability, as the new leadership in Belgrade, led by FRY president Vojislav Kostunica, quickly began to normalize relations with the country's neighbors.

The FRY was proclaimed by two republics of the former Socialist Federal Republic of Yugoslavia (SFRY) in April 1992, after the latter disintegrated in 1991. Although formally the FRY had had a multiparty system, Milosevic's Socialist Party of Serbia (SPS) had an unfair advantage over the democratic opposition as a result of its control over the country's security forces, financial and monetary institutions, and the state-owned media. During the 1990s, however, Milosevic's control over the country slowly withered. The Serbian opposition's victory in municipal elections in the fall of 1996 resulted in the SPS losing control of the main urban areas in the country. In 1997, Milosevic's key ally in Montenegro lost control over that republic to an independence-oriented coalition of parties. In 1999, NATO occupied one of the FRY's two autonomous provinces, Kosovo, after a 78-day bombing campaign devastated much of the FRY's industrial and transportational infrastructure.

Throughout the 1990s, FRY citizens watched as economic mismanagement, war, and international sanctions reduced their living standard by more than a third. An added burden on the economy was the presence of 750,000 Serb refugees from Bosnia, Croatia, and Kosovo in the FRY—proportionally, the largest refugee population in Europe.

The beginning of the end for the Milosevic regime came in January 2000, when the long-bickering members of the Serbian opposition ended their internal squabbling and joined forces in their efforts to remove Milosevic from power. Their cause was greatly aided by Milosevic himself in July, when he unilaterally decided to rewrite the FRY constitution. The new constitutional changes significantly reduced Montenegro's role in the federal government and introduced new provisions calling for the federal president to be henceforth elected by direct popular vote. The latter move proved to be the greatest miscalculation of Milosevic's political career.

In August, 18 different opposition parties united under the banner of the Democratic Opposition of Serbia (DOS). DOS nominated Vojislav Kostunica, a 56-year-old constitutional lawyer and the leader of the Democratic Party of Serbia (DSS) as its candidate to oppose Milosevic in the presidential elections scheduled for September 24. Despite an electoral campaign in which the regime had numerous unfair advantages over the opposition, Kostunica managed to score a first-round victory against Milosevic, winning just over 50 percent of the popular vote to Milosevic's 37 percent. Milosevic nevertheless refused to admit defeat and scheduled a second-round runoff election for October. On October 4, the Federal Election Commission declared the entire election invalid and called for new elections, which would have kept Milosevic in power for an undetermined length of time. On October 5, however, approximately 1 million people from throughout Serbia converged on Belgrade to protest the regime's attempts to steal the election. Faced with this massive show of popular support for Kostunica, Milosevic's hitherto loyal security forces abandoned him, and on October 6 Milosevic publicly conceded to Kostunica.

The disintegration of the Milosevic regime was confirmed on December 23, when elections to the Serbian parliament resulted in a significant victory for the DOS; official results showed that the DOS had won approximately 64 percent of the votes cast, as opposed to 13 percent for Milosevic's SPS. The scale of the DOS's victory will allow the coalition to rewrite the Serbian constitution and eliminate many of its more authoritarian features. The DOS coalition itself, however, is likely to disintegrate at some point in 2001, which could lead to a period of political instability in the country and stymie further reform efforts.

Kostunica and the DOS coalition quickly set about developing new policies on both the domestic and international fronts. Kostunica has announced that his priorities as FRY president will be to resolve the constitutional crisis between Serbia and Montenegro, promote economic reform, and improve the FRY's external relations.

Political Rights and Civil Liberties:

Throughout the 1990s, the Milosevic regime used a variety of means to manipulate and falsify election results. The opposition's victory in the 1996 municipal elections was recognized only after three months of nightly demonstrations throughout the country. For most of the 1990s, opposition parties were routinely denied access to the main electronic media in the country, and the tabulation of votes was extremely suspect. Since the DOS has come to power, new documents have been released showing that Milosevic had in fact lost the December 1992 elections for the Serbian presidency to his challenger, the Serbian-American businessman Milan Panic. Despite these manipulations, however, opposition parties in the FRY were very active throughout the 1990s.

The DOS victory has considerably changed the situation in the FRY with regard to the electoral system. Foreign and domestic observers have claimed that Serbia's December parliamentary elections were the freest and fairest the country has ever had. Nevertheless, the media in the country did show a significant bias in favor of the DOS during the election campaign. Electoral reform is a top priority of the new authorities.

Cultural and ethnic minorities have their own political parties, media in their mother tongue, and other types of associations. After the DOS victory, a prominent Muslim politician from the Sandzak region, Dr. Rasim Ljajic, was named the federal government's minister for ethnic minorities. An important item on the new authorities' reform agenda is enacting constitutional and political reforms decentralizing power in Serbia and Montenegro to allow for more autonomy in places like the Sandzak, Vojvodina, and Kosovo.

According to the FRY constitution, all citizens enjoy freedom of religious belief and association. Ethnic and religious identities are closely intertwined in the region, however; consequently, increases in interethnic tensions often take on the appearance of religious intolerance. Restitution of church property nationalized by the Communists remains a point of dispute between church and state. The main religious organization in the country, the Serbian Orthodox Church, is leading a campaign to reinstate religion classes in elementary schools. In Montenegro, a significant point of contention is the sometimes violent controversy between the Serbian Orthodox Church and the so-called Montenegrin Orthodox Church, which is not recognized by other Orthodox churches.

FRY citizens enjoy freedom of association and assembly. In practice, however, these rights have often been circumscribed over the past decade. Opposition parties, independent trade unions, and nongovernmental organizations were persecuted and/or harassed in a variety of ways under the Milosevic regime. Upon coming to power in October, the democratic opposition quickly began drafting new laws and adopting new policies to protect the rights of these organizations.

Under the Milosevic regime, the FRY judiciary lost much of its independence. Nevertheless, many justices refused to bow to political pressure. In July 2000 more than a dozen judges who were known opposition sympathizers were removed from their positions. In late November, Nebojsa Simeunovic, a judge who had refused to issue warrants for the arrest of two opposition leaders on October 3, went missing; his body was found in the Danube several weeks later. The FRY judiciary has been criticized for especially harsh rulings against ethnic minorities, especially ethnic Albanians involved in violent opposition to FRY authorities or other types of nationalist activism. After the DOS came to power, the Kostunica government ordered the release of hundreds of

Albanians under arrest, including Dr. Flora Brovina, a well-known Albanian human rights activist.

Political terror, particularly in the form of assassination and kidnapping, was a major problem in the FRY in 2000. In January, the Serb paramilitary leader and organized-crime boss, Zeljko Raznjatovic-Arkan, was gunned down in a Belgrade hotel. In February, the federal defense minister, Pavle Bulatovic, was assassinated in a Belgrade restaurant. In June, a prominent opposition leader, Vuk Draskovic, was nearly assassinated on the Montenegrin coast. In August, Milosevic's one time sponsor and subsequent political opponent, Ivan Stambolic, was kidnapped in Belgrade. A host of lesser figures in the Yugoslav underworld have also been killed. In most cases, the perpetrators of these crimes have never been found.

There are no legal restrictions on the participation of women in politics; however, they are, in general, vastly underrepresented in higher levels of government. Although women are legally entitled to equal pay for equal work, traditional patriarchal attitudes prevalent throughout the Balkans often limit women's roles in the economy. Domestic violence remains a serious problem.

Zambia

Polity: Dominant party **Political Rights:** 5
Economy: Mixed statist **Civil Liberties:** 4
Population: 9,600,000 **Status:** Partly Free
PPP: $719
Life Expectancy: 41
Ethnic Groups: African (99 percent), European (1 percent)
Capital: Lusaka

Overview: Zambia's political environment in 2000 focused increasingly on presidential elections due in 2001. President Frederick Chiluba, who plans to step down at the end of his second term, has made it clear that he wants to play a central role in determining his successor. The ruling Movement for Multiparty Democracy (MMD) expelled Ben Mwila, the minister of Environment and Natural Resources, charging him with launching a premature campaign for the presidency. In May, former President Kenneth Kaunda relinquished the leadership of the United National Independence Party (UNIP) to the former governor of the Central Bank, Francis Nkhoma. Nkhoma won the hotly contested leadership contest against eight other candidates.

Zambia was ruled by President Kaunda and UNIP from independence from Britain in 1964 until the transition to a multiparty system in 1991. Kaunda's regime grew increasingly repressive and corrupt as it faced security and economic difficulties during the long guerrilla wars against white rule in neighboring Rhodesia (now Zimbabwe) and Portuguese-controlled Mozambique. UNIP's socialist policies, combined with a crash in the price of copper, Zambia's main export, precipitated an economic decline unchecked for two decades.

Kaunda permitted free elections in 1991 in the face of domestic unrest and international pressure. Former labor leader Chiluba and his MMD won convincingly. By contrast, the next national elections, in 1996, lacked legitimacy because of a series of repressive measures instituted by the government.

Economic liberalization and privatization have earned Zambia substantial external aid, but rampant corruption has distorted the economy and blocked sustainable growth. The country is among those suffering most from the AIDS pandemic; it is estimated Zambia will need to care for well over 600,000 AIDS orphans within a few years. President Chiluba stated in 2000 that the HIV infection rate among adults in this southern African nation was about 20 percent.

Political Rights and Civil Liberties:

The ability of Zambians to change their government democratically is not yet consolidated. Zambia's president and parliament are elected to serve concurrent five-year terms by universal adult suffrage. Zambians' constitutional right to change their government freely was honored in 1991 elections. The November 1996 presidential and parliamentary polls, however, were neither free nor fair. State resources and state media were mobilized extensively to support Chiluba and the ruling MMD. Serious irregularities plagued election preparations. Voters' lists were incomplete or otherwise suspect; independent monitors estimated that more than two million people were effectively disenfranchised. Candidate eligibility requirements were changed, which resulted in the exclusion of Kaunda, the most credible opposition candidate.

Most opposition parties boycotted the 1996 polls, in which the MMD renewed its parliamentary dominance. International observer groups that did monitor the polls, along with independent domestic monitors and opposition parties, declared the process and the results to be fraudulent. In response, Zambia's main opposition parties are pressing the government to agree to electoral law changes before next year's general election. They seek reforms to prevent ballot fraud and bribery

Some of Zambia's jurists retain a stubborn independence while others are subservient to Chiluba and the MMD. The court system is severely overburdened. Pretrial detainees are sometimes held for years under harsh conditions before their cases reach trial. The Magistrates and Judges Association identified congestion in prisons and delayed trials as extremely serious problems. Malnourishment and poor health care in Zambia's prisons cause many deaths. Many civil matters are decided by customary courts of variable quality and consistency whose decisions often conflict with both national law and constitutional protections.

In September 2000, parliament passed the State Proceedings Act, which would remove judicial checks on the decisions and actions of the government. If this legislation comes into force, the only legal redress for citizens who believe they have been wronged would be to sue the state. Many observers believe that the real reason for the amendments is political, in order to firm up Chiluba's political control of the country in the run-up to the 2001 elections. By late 2000 President Chiluba had yet to sign the bill into law.

Two prisoners on death row began the first-ever attempt to challenge the death penalty before a court of law. They petitioned the high court to overrule their sentences, arguing that capital punishment should be abolished from the statute books. If the petition succeeds, Zambia will become the second country in Africa, after South Africa, to abolish capital punishment.

Wiretapping, both legal and illegal, is reportedly routine. The government dominates broadcasting, and the few independent radio stations offer little political reporting. The Preservation of Public Security Act of 1960 is among many statutes used to harass and intimidate journalists. Security forces maintain surveillance of independent media and frequently arrest journalists. In one case, 12 journalists were charged with espionage after writing about Zambia's lack of military preparedness. Most were released, but *The Post's* editor in chief Fred M'membe remained accused of breaching the State Security Act. Finally, in late December, M'membe was acquitted by a high court judge. Other tools of harassment include criminal libel suits and defamation suits brought by MMD leaders in response to stories on corruption. The Zambia Independent Media Association launched public appeals on several cases of the government attempting to intimidate the press.

In early 2000 the minister of Information and Broadcasting Services, Newstead Zimba, alleged that the independent media in Zambia exercises "abuse of press freedom and other fundamental freedoms." Zimba said that government was considering recently submitted proposals for media-law reform and indicated that some of the reform proposals would be approved. He also stated that his ministry intended to establish an "autonomous" Independent Broadcasting Authority, (IBA), which would regulate all radio and television broadcasting in Zambia.

Constitutionally protected religious freedom has been respected in practice. Nongovernmental organizations (NGOs) engaged in human rights promotion, such as the Zambian Independent Monitoring Team, the Zambian Civic Education Association, and the Law Association of Zambia, operate openly. In 1999, however, the government drafted a policy that would closely regulate NGOs. The government human rights commission investigated frequent complaints about police brutality and denounced the torture of coup suspects, but had no power to bring charges against alleged perpetrators.

Societal discrimination remains a serious obstacle to women's rights. A 1998 regional human development report noted that Zambia was one of the lowest-performing countries in southern Africa in terms of women's empowerment. Women are denied full economic participation and are discriminated against in rural lands allocation. A married woman must have her husband's permission to obtain contraceptives. Discrimination against women is especially prevalent in traditional tribunals that are courts of first instance in most rural areas. Spousal abuse and other violence against women are reportedly common. A new political party, the Social Democratic Party, was founded in 2000 by Gwendoline Konie, a former diplomat, to focus on children's and women's issues.

Zambia's trade unions remain among Africa's strongest, and union rights are constitutionally guaranteed. The Zambia Congress of Trade Unions, an umbrella for Zambia's 19 largest unions, operates democratically without government interference. Collective bargaining rights are protected by the 1993 Industrial and Labor Relations Act, and unions negotiate directly with employers. About two-thirds of the country's 300,000 formal sector employees are union members.

Development is burdened by high levels of corruption and inflation. In early 2000 the Zambian Catholic Church criticized corruption and suppression of dissent. The official Anti-Corruption Commission showed few results, and a public-sector reform program also had little effect. Privatization of state enterprises continued slowly. There was limited progress on the sale of immense state-owned copper mines. New business formation is slowed by the country's weak financial structures.

↓ Zimbabwe

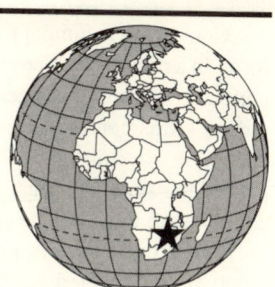

Polity: Dominant party
Economy: Capitalist-statist
Population: 11,300,000
PPP: $2,669
Life Expectancy: 44

Political Rights: 6
Civil Liberties: 5
Status: Partly Free

Ethnic Groups: Shona (71 percent), Ndebele (16 percent), other African (11 percent), white (1 percent), mixed and Asian (1 percent)
Capital: Harare
Trend Arrow: Zimbabwe received a downward trend arrow due to government-sponsored violence and manipulation designed to ensure the maintenance in power of the ruling party.

Overview:

Zimbabwe experienced a tumultuous year in 2000. Economic decline, especially rising food costs, fueled growing opposition to President Robert Mugabe's rule. War veterans and government supporters illegally occupied mainly white-owned landholdings, with the overt or complicit backing of the government, in defiance of judicial rulings. Parliamentary elections resulted in a major influx of opposition members from the Movement for Democratic Change (MDC). The MDC did not win a majority, however, because of intimidation and manipulation in the pre-electoral process and a constitutional provision empowering President Mugabe and allied traditional leaders to appoint one-fifth of parliament's members. Zimbabwean armed forces remained engaged in an open-ended, expensive and unpopular war in the Democratic Republic of the Congo, which nonetheless provides commercial and economic benefits for Mugabe's cronies.

Zimbabwe gained independence in 1980 after a violent guerrilla war against a white-minority regime that had declared unilateral independence from Britain in 1965 in what was then Northern Rhodesia. For a number of years Zimbabwe was relatively stable, although from 1983 to 1987, the government suppressed resistance on the part of the country's largest minority group, the Ndebele, to dominance by Mugabe's majority ethnic Shona group. Severe human rights abuses accompanied the struggle, which ended with an accord that brought Ndebele leaders into the government.

In recent years Mugabe has turned against student groups, labor unions, homosexuals and white landowners. Zimbabwe is now facing its worse crisis since achieving independence in 1980. The country is in the twilight of Mugabe's long rule and political dominance, although he may attempt to run again for president again in 2002. The grip of the ruling Zimbabwe African National Union–Patriotic Front (ZANU-PF) party's grip on parliament has been weakened, but it remains the predominant power through its control over the security forces and much of the economy. The party has dominated Zimbabwe since independence, enacting numerous laws and constitutional amendments to strengthen its hold on power. Yet Mugabe can no longer exercise unfettered power. The MDC has experienced rapid growth under its leader, Morgan Tsvangirai. The judiciary remains largely independent, and trade unions powerful. A small group of independent media promotes transparency.

Corruption is rampant, and living standards are dropping. A key issue is land reform. In a rupture with previous policy allowing the country's white minority to maintain some control of key economic sectors, government-backed occupations of white-owned farms continued throughout 2000. Several farmers were killed; others were beaten. In November about 300 war veterans and government supporters took over part of the supreme court. The court had determined that land resettlement did not comply with the law. The government announced, however, that it would neither stop nor reverse the takeovers. President Mugabe's "fast-track" program has identified about 3,000 of an estimated 4,500 farms for takeover.

Political Rights and Civil Liberties:

Zimbabweans do not yet have the right to change their government democratically. Since 1987, there have been 15 amendments to the constitution by ZANU-PF, which have made the constitution less democratic and given the government, and particularly members of the executive, more power. These include the scrapping of the post of prime minister in favor of an executive president in 1987 and the abolishment of the upper chamber of parliament, the senate. Perhaps most controversial is the provision that gives the president and traditional chiefs the right to nominate 30 members of parliament.

The 2000 parliamentary elections, in which 57 members of the opposition MDC were elected out of a total of 150 seats, were deemed by observers to be fundamentally flawed prior to balloting, because of violence and intimidation against opposition candidates and their supporters. Mugabe issued a pardon in October for thousands of people, most from ZANU-PF, for crimes committed during the election campaign. This included individuals guilty of assault, arson, kidnapping, torture and attempted murder. According to the Human Rights Forum, more than 18,000 people had their rights violated, and more than 90 percent of the perpetrators were ZANU-PF supporters or government officials. Voter registration and identification procedures and tabulation of results were judged by independent observers in some constituencies to have been highly irregular. The heavily state-controlled or state-influenced media offered limited coverage of opposition viewpoints, and ZANU-PF used state resources heavily in its campaigning.

The government has continued harassment of opposition figures in the post-election period. For example, Morgan Tsvangarai was briefly detained and three members of parliament from the MDC were arrested on charges of fomenting violence in October.

The government created a constitutional commission, which reported its findings to President Mugabe late in 1999. The official commission faced a counterpart organization, the National Constitutional Assembly, which was formed by a coalition of nongovernmental organizations (NGOs). The process of providing Zimbabwe with a new national constitution became a farce, however, when the head of the government-organized commission abruptly declared a draft version approved and presented it to President Mugabe. In effect, the government gave the country two choices: to endorse a government-sponsored but largely flawed draft constitution or face the continuation of the present, deeply unpopular national constitution. At times President Mugabe has invoked the Presidential Powers Act, which enables him to bypass normal governmental review and oversight procedures.

The judiciary remains largely independent and has repeatedly struck down or disputed government actions, most notably regarding the illegal occupation of farms. The Public Order and Security Bill, however, restricts rights, limiting public assembly and allowing police to impose arbitrary curfews. Intelligence agencies are included among law enforcement agencies empowered to disperse "illegal" assemblies and to arrest participants. Security forces, particularly the Central Intelligence Organization, often ignore basic rights regarding detention, search, and seizure. Judicial rulings are at times ignored by the government. In addition, the right of free assembly is constitutionally guaranteed but selectively respected.

There is an active NGO sector. Several groups, including the Catholic Commission for Justice and Peace, the Zimbabwe Human Rights Organization (Zimrights), and the Legal Relief Fund, focus on human rights. A 1997 report detailed the officially sanctioned brutality of the repression of Ndebele rebels in the mid-1980s, in which thousands of people were murdered by government forces, but perpetrators of the violence still enjoy impunity. Mugabe has continued his verbal attacks on homosexuals.

Prison conditions are harsh. Amnesty International reported in 1997 that Zimbabwean prisoners on death row sleep shackled and naked. The report argued that the dreadful conditions and psychological torment endured by death row inmates violated the right to be free from cruel, inhuman, or degrading punishment.

The government directly controls all broadcasting and several newspapers, including all dailies; it indirectly controls most others. A small independent press is overshadowed by state-run media. The Parliamentary Privileges and Immunities Act has been used to force journalists to reveal their sources regarding reports on corruption before the courts and parliament. In October the high court overturned a long-standing government ban on private radio stations. The police raided the new Capitol Radio station and shut it down. The government has appointed a seven-member Broadcasting Authority of Zimbabwe (BAZ), which will be responsible for planning and administering the broadcasting spectrum of Zimbabwe as well as defining and demarcating global license area plans for the country. The authority will, among others, also be in charge of inviting, selecting, and recommending prospective licenses to the minister of Information.

Women enjoy extensive legal protection, but de facto societal discrimination persists. Women have few legal rights outside formal marriage. The supreme court issued a ruling relegating African women to the status of "junior males" within the family, declaring that African women who marry under customary law leave their original families behind and therefore cannot inherit property. Married women still cannot hold property jointly with their husbands. Especially in rural areas, access to education and employment for women is difficult. Domestic violence against women is common; a 1997 survey by a women's organization found that more than 80 percent of women had been subjected to some form of physical abuse. Zimbabwe has signed international human rights treaties, such as the Women's Convention.

Zimbabwe's once lively economy continues its precipitous free fall. In October the World Bank announced that it would halt its lending to Zimbabwe because of the government's failure to meet its debt service provisions. Gross domestic product (GDP) is set to fall by at least six percent in 2000. Inflation is more than 60 percent, and the budget deficit is more than 27 percent of GDP. The government salary bill accounts for another 55 percent, resulting in a budget deficit even before other expenditures are taken into account. A 30 percent increase in the price of bread, and other food price increases have stoked popular unrest.

Armenia/Azerbaijan
Nagorno-Karabakh

Polity: Presidential
Economy: Mixed statist
Population: 150,000

Political Rights: 5
Civil Liberties: 6
Status: Not Free

Ethnic Groups: Armenian (95 percent), others, including
Assyrian, Greek (5 percent)

Overview:
The continuing efforts to find a peaceful settlement to the Nagorno-Karabakh conflict were temporarily overshadowed by a failed assassination attempt against President Arkady Ghukasian on March 22. Former Defense Minister Samvel Babayan, with whom Ghukasian had become embroiled in a growing confrontation, was charged with masterminding the crime. The incident apparently did little to disrupt the enclave's June parliamentary elections, in which the ruling Democratic Artsakh party enjoyed a slim victory. Internationally mediated attempts to solve the protracted Nagorno-Karabakh dispute, which is a primary impediment to the region's economic viability, showed few signs of long-term progress.

The region of Nagorno-Karabakh, whose population was overwhelmingly ethnic Armenian, was transferred from Armenian to Azerbaijani jurisdiction in 1923, and the Nagorno-Karabakh Autonomous Region was subsequently created. In 1930, Moscow permitted Azerbaijan to establish and resettle the border areas between Nagorno-Karabakh and Armenia.

In 1988, Nagorno-Karabakh's Supreme Soviet adopted a resolution calling for union with Armenia. The announcement, as well as February demonstrations in Yerevan over Nagorno-Karabakh's status, triggered violent attacks against Armenians in the Azerbaijan city of Sumgait shortly thereafter and in Baku in January 1990. During the late 1980s, skirmishes broke out along the Armenia-Azerbaijan border and around the Nagorno-Karabakh region.

Following multiparty elections for a new legislature, Nagorno-Karabakh's parliament adopted a declaration of independence at its inaugural session in January 1992. From 1991 to 1992, Azerbaijan besieged Stepanakert and occupied most of Nagorno-Karabakh. A series of counter offensives in 1993 and 1994 by Karabakh Armenians, assisted by Armenia, resulted in the capture of essentially the entire territory, as well as six Azerbaijan districts surrounding the enclave. By the time a Russian-brokered ceasefire was finally signed in May 1994, the war had resulted in thousands of casualties and nearly one million refugees.

In December 1994, the head of the state defense committee, Robert Kocharian, was selected by parliament for the newly established post of president. Parliament member Leonard Petrossian was subsequently chosen by Kocharian as prime minister. Generally fair elections to the 33-member parliament were held in April and May 1995. In November 1996, Kocharian defeated two other candidates in a popular vote for president.

In September 1997, Foreign Minister Arkady Ghukasian was elected president with

89 percent of the vote to replace Kocharian, who had been named prime minister of Armenia in March of that year. The poll was deemed generally free and fair by international observers, although the election was considered invalid by the international community, which did not recognize Nagorno-Karabakh's independence. Ghukasian reshuffled the government in June 1998, replacing Prime Minister Petrossian with Deputy Prime Minister Zhirayr Pogosian, reportedly over disagreements on economic policy.

In June 1999, Ghukasian dismissed Pogosian amid allegations that a surveillance device discovered in the president's office had been planted by Pogosian, possibly on the order of the powerful Defense Minister, Samvel Babayan. Some analysts speculated that Pogosian's dismissal indirectly targeted Babayan, with whom Ghukasian had become increasingly involved in a power struggle. Babayan was removed as defense minister the same month and dismissed as armed forces commander in December. Anushavan Danielian, a former deputy parliamentary speaker in Ukraine's Autonomous Republic of Crimea, was named the new prime minister.

On March 22, 2000, Ghukasian was seriously wounded by two gunmen during a failed assassination attempt. Police quickly arrested dozens of suspects, including Babayan and a number of his inner circle. Along with 14 other defendants, Babayan, who was charged with organizing the attack in order to seize power in the republic, was put on trial in mid-September in Stepanakert; the trial was ongoing at year's end. Nagorno-Karabakh authorities had denied his request for a transfer to an Armenian court, where he maintained he would receive a more fair trial. While some welcomed the detention of Babayan, who has been accused of corruption and reportedly wields considerable political and economic power in the territory, his supporters charged that the arrest was politically motivated.

In the territory's June 18 parliamentary vote, 123 candidates representing five parties competed in single-mandate constituencies for the National Assembly's 33 seats. Although no one party captured an absolute majority of seats, the ruling Democratic Artsakh party, which supports Ghukasian, enjoyed a slim victory, winning 13 seats. The Armenian Revolutionary Federation-Dashnaktsutiun won 9 seats, the center-right Armenakan Party captured 1 seat, and formally independent candidates, most of whom support Ghukasian, won 10. Approximately 50 election monitors from several countries observed the poll, including representatives from the British Helsinki Human Rights Group. International observers described the electoral campaign and voting process as calm and largely transparent, although problems were noted with the accuracy of some voter lists.

Although Azerbaijan's President Heydar Aliyev and Armenia's President Robert Kocharian conducted several high-level meetings during the year regarding Nagorno-Karabakh's status, the discussions failed to make any substantial progress in resolving the long-standing dispute. While Yerevan and Stepanakert have largely supported a peace proposal of the Organization for Security and Cooperation in Europe (OSCE) Minsk Group, which calls for a vaguely defined "common state" between Azerbaijan and Nagorno-Karabakh along loose horizontal lines, Baku has rejected the plan for not sufficiently restoring Azerbaijan's sovereignty over the disputed enclave. President Kocharian has maintained that Baku should conduct direct talks with Stepanakert, but Azerbaijan has refused to negotiate with Ghukasian, who has demanded direct representation in the peace process. The October 1999 murder of Armenia's Prime Minister

Vazgen Sarkisian and other top officials hampered the negotiating process well into the year 2000, as Armenia's government struggled to address the subsequent domestic political crisis.

Political Rights and Civil Liberties: Residents of Nagorno-Karabakh have the technical means to change their government democratically. Parliamentary elections in 1995 and 2000 were regarded as generally free and fair, as were the 1996 and 1997 presidential votes. A self-declared republic, Nagorno-Karabakh has enjoyed de facto independence from Azerbaijan since 1994 while retaining close political, economic, and military ties with Armenia. Nagorno-Karabakh's electoral law, which was revised in March 2000, calls for a single-mandate system to be used in parliamentary elections; lawmakers rejected the opposition's demands for the inclusion of party-based lists.

The government controls many of the broadcast media outlets, and most journalists practice self-censorship, particularly on subjects dealing with policies related to Azerbaijan and the peace process. Some observers maintain that the government used the attempted murder of President Ghukasian as a pretext to intensify attacks against its critics. According to one report, the telephones of several opposition journalists were cut two days after the shootings. On March 28, Vahram Aghajanian, a journalist who was well known for his criticism of the republic's leadership, was arrested in the wake of a police investigation into the failed assassination. Although not immediately charged with a crime, Aghajanian was eventually sentenced on April 12 to one year in prison for libeling Prime Minister Danielian. The charge stemmed from an article by Aghajanian that had appeared in December 1999 in *Tasnerod Nahang* (Tenth Province), a newspaper reportedly financed by Samvel Babayan. Aghajanian was released on April 27, and his sentence was suspended for two years on the condition that he not commit further crimes during this period. On April 15, *Tasnerod Nahang* announced that it was suspending publication for what it claims was ongoing harassment by the government.

With Christian Armenians constituting more than 95 percent of the territory's population, the Armenian Apostolic Church is the predominant religion. Years of conflict have constrained the religious rights of the few Muslims remaining in the region. Freedom of assembly and association is limited, although political parties and unions are allowed to organize. Seven parties are officially registered in the territory.

The judiciary, which is not independent in practice, is influenced by the executive branch and powerful political and clan forces. Babayan alleged that he had been physically assaulted during his interrogation and detention as a suspect in the failed assassination attempt against President Ghukasian. Prisoner-of-war exchanges between Armenia and Azerbaijan continued during the year.

The majority of those who fled the war continue to live in squalid conditions in refugee camps in Azerbaijan. No permanent peace agreement has been signed, and one-fifth of Azerbaijan's territory captured during the war remains occupied by Armenia.

The territory's fragile six-year peace has failed to bring significant improvement to the economy. Industrial capacity remains limited, with high unemployment forcing many residents to leave for neighboring countries in search of work. Widespread corruption, a lack of substantive economic reforms, and the control of most economic activity by powerful elites limit equality of opportunity for most residents.

China
Hong Kong

Polity: Appointed governor and partly-elected legislature
Economy: Capitalist
Population: 7,000,000
Ethnic Groups: Chinese (95 percent), other (5 percent)

Political Rights: 5
Civil Liberties: 3
Status: Partly Free

Overview:

Three years after Hong Kong reverted to Chinese rule amid fears that Beijing would undermine the territory's autonomy, ordinary residents continued in 2000 to shift their concerns toward day-to-day issues, including the economy and a growing gap in both wealth and political influence between themselves and a politically connected conservative elite.

Hong Kong consists of Hong Kong Island and Kowloon Peninsula, both ceded in perpetuity by China to Britain in the mid-1800s, and the mainland New Territories, which Britain "leased" for 99 years in 1898. The British ruled the colony through an appointed governor. The Legislative council (Legco) consisted of gubernatorial appointees, senior civil servants, and members chosen by limited-franchise "functional constituencies" representing business, the professions, and labor.

Under the 1984 Joint Declaration, Britain agreed to transfer sovereignty over Hong Kong to China in 1997, and Beijing pledged to maintain the territory's political, legal, and economic autonomy for 50 years. London and Beijing agreed in 1990 to hold the first-ever direct elections for 18 Legco seats in 1991, followed by elections for 20 seats in 1995, 24 in 1999, and 30 in 2003. China incorporated these plans into a post-1997 constitution for Hong Kong called the Basic Law.

The last colonial governor, Christopher Patten, introduced several reforms for the 1995 Legco elections, where pro-democracy candidates won 16 of the 20 directly elected seats. The changes included holding indirect elections for 10 previously appointed seats, and granting nearly 2.7 million workers a second vote for the 30 functional constituency seats. China claimed the reforms violated the Basic Law and pledged to dissolve all elected bodies after the handover.

A Beijing-organized selection committee chose shipping tycoon Tung Chee-hwa, China's preferred candidate, as the post-handover chief executive in December 1996. Immediately after the June 1997 handover, China replaced Legco with an appointed provisional legislature. In the May 1998 elections for a new Legco, pro-democracy candidates again won 16 of the 20 directly elected seats, though only 20 of 60 seats overall.

After two years of recession stemming from the Asian financial crisis that began in 1997, the economy grew by 11 percent in the second quarter of 2000. Yet many middle-class residents continued to be concerned with falling housing prices and job security. Moreover, perceptions of collusion between government and the few tycoons who dominate the economy were reinforced in June after a son of Li Ka-shing, Hong Kong's richest businessman, won a government contract to develop an industrial park without the routine bidding process. A mid-July government survey showed 60 percent of residents dissatisfied with the overall performance of Tung and his cabinet. In a society widely viewed as apathetic about politics, thousands of demonstrators held protests over the summer on issues ranging from falling housing values to pollution.

However, the opposition failed to capitalize on the public's mood at the September 10 elections for the 60-seat Legco. Under a relatively low 43.6 percent turnout, pro-democracy parties won only 15 of the 24 directly elected seats and 19 overall, 1 fewer than in the 1998 elections. Of these seats, the top opposition Democratic Party, led by Martin Lee, won 9 directly elected seats and 12 overall. Observers noted that the party continued to focus on rule-of-law issues even as voters became more concerned with economic and social matters. Meanwhile, the conservative Democratic Alliance won 11 seats, up from 10 in 1998.

Political Rights and Civil Liberties: Residents of Hong Kong cannot change their government through elections. Chief Executive Tung Chee-hwa was appointed by a 400-member selection committee, itself appointed by Beijing. In the current Legislative Council (Legco), only 24 of the 60 seats are directly elected. Thirty seats are chosen by functional constituencies representing business, professional, labor, and other groups, and 6 by an electoral committee. The Tung administration sharply restricted the franchise for the functional constituency seats from more than 2 million voters under the former colonial governor, Christopher Patten, to just 177,000 people out of Hong Kong's 3.1 million registered voters. In addition to voting in the Legco elections, the functional constituencies also chose 482 out of the electoral committee's 800 seats in a July 9 election. Of the committee's remaining seats, 182 candidates ran opposed and 136 seats went to officials and religious leaders. In a further setback to representative government, the Tung administration has abolished the mid-tier municipal councils and made nearly one-quarter of the local district council seats appointed rather than elected.

In addition to limiting the number of directly elected Legco seats, the Basic Law also limits the ability of legislators to initiate legislation. It also requires separate majorities from among the members elected from the geographical and functional constituencies to approve individual member's bills. Given these constraints, Legco has relatively little independent power. The Basic Law does permit direct elections for all Legco seats and for the chief executive after 2007. However, China's rubber-stamp National People's Congress (NPC), Hong Kong's chief executive, and Legco would have to approve these arrangements, the latter by a two-thirds majority at a time when only half of its members would be directly elected. Contributing to the public's cynicism over alleged collusion between the government and major companies, an October European Parliament report noted that, "a number of tycoons have an undue and dominant influence in certain sectors of Hong Kong's economy."

Citing several judicial and executive decisions, human rights activists say the rule of law has been undermined since the handover in 1997. The most contentious rulings involved the rights of mainland-born Chinese and their children to gain Hong Kong residency. Hong Kong's Court of Final Appeal issued a ruling in January 1999 that interpreted liberally the Basic Law's provisions on residency rights and stated that the court had the power of judicial review over both the Basic Law and NPC decisions involving the Basic Law. Concerned with a potentially large influx of mainlanders, the government asked China's NPC for its interpretation of the Basic Law's provisions on the right of abode. The NPC handed down a restrictive interpretation in June 1999 that effectively overturned the Court of Final Appeal's ruling.

Critics charged that the government's appeal to the NPC, and the NPC's ruling, raised doubts over whether any Court of Final Appeal decision is truly final. However, Article 158 of the Basic Law requires Hong Kong's courts to seek from the NPC an interpretation of the Basic Law on issues that are either Beijing's responsibility or that concern the relationship between Beijing and Hong Kong.

The debate over the Court of Final Appeal followed controversy over the judiciary in 1998, when human rights activists criticized authorities for not bringing charges in two sensitive cases. In separate decisions, the government declined to prosecute the China-run Xinhua news agency, for allegedly missing a deadline to respond to a freedom-of-information request, and the politically connected owner of the *Hong Kong Standard* accused of fraud. Despite these concerns, the judiciary is generally considered to be independent. An independent commission nominates judges, who have tenure until retirement age. Police abuse of suspects is not systemic but nonetheless is a continuing problem.

In order to comply with the Basic Law's Article 23, which requires the territory to have laws on treason, secession, sedition, and subversion, the Tung administration is drafting comprehensive legislation covering all four areas. The pre-handover Legco had maintained, though liberalized, existing laws on sedition and treason to comply with Basic Law requirements while preempting harsher post-handover legislation. The Tung administration has used clauses in the sedition and treason laws to delay enacting them until the comprehensive legislation is developed.

While Hong Kong residents generally continued to enjoy the same basic freedoms they had enjoyed before the handover, the legal basis for these rights is less clear. Immediately after the handover, the provisional legislature weakened Hong Kong's 1991 Bill of Rights; amended the Societies Ordinance to permit authorities to deny registration to, or to de-register, existing nongovernmental organizations on broad national security or public safety grounds; and amended the Public Order Ordinance to reintroduce licensing for demonstrations, which officials can deny on national security grounds.

In one of its few policies that overtly restrict basic rights, the government often confines demonstrators to "designated areas" in locations that sometimes reduce the visibility of the protest. Nevertheless, in 1999 there was an average of four demonstrations per day, slightly higher than the pre-handover rate, and police denied only one application, for an environmental group that planned to block traffic, according to the United States State Department.

Hong Kong's dozens of domestic newspapers and magazines practice some self-censorship regarding Chinese politics and local business. The state-run Radio Television Hong Kong is editorially independent, and there are several private television and radio stations. In a statement that raised some concerns over press freedom, Beijing's deputy representative in Hong Kong asked the territory's media in April to not "disseminate" Taiwan-independence views. This reversed Beijing's earlier position accepting factual reporting of advocacy of Taiwanese independence. While academic freedom is respected, a professor charged in July that a Tung aide had tried to pressure Hong Kong University into stopping polls that measured Tung's approval ratings.

Women have equal educational opportunities and are well represented in the government and civil service, but they face private sector discrimination. Although the government funds programs to reduce domestic violence and enforces relevant laws, sentences are generally lenient.

Unions are independent, but laws restrict some labor rights. The Trade Union Ordinance limits organizing and allows authorities to monitor union administration. In 1997, the provisional legislature repealed or tightened laws on collective bargaining, anti-union discrimination, the right to conduct union activity on company time, and the right to associate internationally without first notifying the government. The body also passed a new law that removed the legal right of collective bargaining, banned the use of union funds for political purposes, and placed restrictions on union executive appointments. The International Labor Organization said the new law breached several ILO conventions.

In a dramatic act to highlight their frustration with the government's restrictions on residency rights, a group of Chinese migrants set off a fire in the immigration office in August that killed an immigration officer and one of the migrants. Separately, the government shut down the last Vietnamese refugee camp in June after offering the remaining 2,000 refugees Hong Kong residency.

Macao

Polity: Appointed governor and partially elected legislature
Economy: Capitalist-statist
Population: 450,000
Ethnic Groups: Chinese, Macanese [mixed Portuguese and Asian ancestry], Portuguese

Political Rights: 6
Civil Liberties: 4
Status: Partly Free

Overview: Macao's economy rebounded after a four-year slump, and crime dropped in the territory's first year under Chinese sovereignty following 443 years of Portuguese rule. Despite some pre-handover fears that China would breach its commitment to respect the territory's autonomy, there were few signs in 2000 that Beijing was interfering with Macao's politics or economic affairs.

Under the Portuguese, Macao became the first European outpost in the Far East in 1557, the leading entrepot for European trade with China until the 1770s, and more recently a bawdy city of casinos and prostitution. The 1976 Organic Statute, or local constitution, vested executive power in a Lisbon-appointed governor and granted legislative power to both the Portuguese government (acting through the governor) and Macao's legislative assembly. The 23-member assembly has 8 directly elected members. Businesses and other interest groups name 8 members, and the governor (and now the chief executive) appointed 7.

Under the 1987 Sino-Portuguese Joint Declaration, the two sides agreed that China would assume sovereignty over Macao in 1999 and that the enclave would maintain its legal system and capitalist economy for 50 years. Beijing later announced that the legislature elected in 1996 would serve through the handover. At the 1996 elections, pro-China businessmen defeated leftist union and neighborhood association candidates to win 7 of the directly elected seats, with democratic activist Ng Kuok-cheong winning the eighth.

The 1996 elections had been held amid an economic recession that began in 1995 and a growing wave of gangland violence as Macao "triads," or criminal gangs, started waging violent battles for control of the VIP rooms in the territory's casinos. A series of gang-related murders and car bombings contributed to a drop in tourism, which accounts for 40 percent of gross domestic product (GDP). The drop in tourism, combined with the regional financial crisis that began in 1997, prolonged the recession.

Amid continuing public concerns over the economy and gangland violence, Portugal ceded sovereignty over the territory to China on December 20, 1999. Edmund Ho, a Canadian-educated banker, took office as chief executive to replace the colonial governor. A 199-member, Beijing-appointed selection committee had appointed Ho to the new office in May 1999.

In its first full year in office in 2000, the new administration presided over several positive developments. There was only one gang-related murder, following 18 in 1999, the London-based *Financial Times* reported in December. Observers said the Chinese government had helped Macao crack down on the triads, although the outgoing Portuguese also contributed significantly by jailing a major crime boss in November 1999. Moreover, economists estimated late in the year that Macao's GDP would post four percent growth for 2000.

In a closely watched decision, Ho is expected to open the territory's $3 billion legal gambling industry to competition after 2001, when the gaming monopoly held by tycoon Stanley Ho (no relation) since 1962 expires. The industry provides 60 percent of the government's revenues.

Political Rights and Civil Liberties:

Citizens of Macao lack the democratic means to change their government and had no input in the 1987 Joint Declaration ceding sovereignty to China or in the drafting of the Basic Law, Macao's postcolonial constitution, which China's rubber-stamp parliament promulgated in 1993. Amnesty International noted in 1999 that the Basic Law is "riddled with ambiguities," fails to guarantee several basic rights, and grants Beijing vaguely defined emergency powers. The organization also observed that Macao's legal system contains weak safeguards for the rights and freedoms ostensibly protected by the Basic Law. Beijing appeared to undermine the Basic Law in June 1999, when it passed a law permitting a Chinese army garrison in Macao after the handover and giving the troops police powers when requested by the chief executive. The Basic Law contains no provision for a garrison. Officials on both sides of the border insisted that the troops would have no responsibility for internal security.

As was the case with the colonial governor, the chief executive is appointed and holds broad executive powers with few institutional checks. This is in part because Portugal never developed the legislature into an effective body. Moreover, the Basic Law limits the types of bills that members can table. In a move that was legal but went against the spirit of having continuity in the post-handover legislature, Ho reappointed only 1 of the governor's 7 appointees to the body.

The Basic Law does provide for the number of directly elected seats to increase in the 2001 and 2005 elections. Moreover, after 2009 the legislature will be able to change its composition under a two-thirds voting rule, subject to the chief executive's approval. Political parties are legal, but no true parties exist.

The judiciary is independent and is based on Portuguese metropolitan law. The Basic Law requires the chief executive to appoint judges on the recommendation of an "independent commission composed of local judges, lawyers and eminent persons." The chief executive himself appoints the commission. There is a shortage of local bilingual lawyers and locally trained lawyers. The transition from Portuguese to Chinese sovereignty was marred by delays in translating legal documents into Chinese, as well as in replacing Portuguese expatriates in the 17,000 member civil service with ethnic Chinese. Corruption is reportedly rife in the police force and civil service.

The government owns controlling interests in the television and radio stations, which present relatively diverse viewpoints. The press is private but is not outspoken. Print journalists practice self-censorship about Beijing, and about Macao's triads, which have sent intimidating letters to newspapers. In addition, most newspapers offer limited coverage of people, groups, or activities that challenge the conservative political and business establishment or advocate greater democracy. Further limiting the range of views provided in the press, the pro-Beijing *Macao Daily* newspaper has a nearly 90 percent market share, the Associated Press reported in 1999.

Authorities restricted freedom of expression in December by temporarily detaining more than 30 members of the Falun Gong movement and breaking up small Falun Gong protests to mark the visit of Chinese president Jiang Zemin. The Falun Gong is banned in mainland China but is legal in Macao.

Women increasingly hold senior government posts but are underrepresented in politics and the civil service. The United Nations has raised concern over the trafficking of women from China, often by criminal gangs, into Macao for prostitution.

While Macao has several independent human rights groups, civil society is underdeveloped and Beijing controls many ostensibly nongovernmental groups. Nearly all private sector workers belong to the pro-Beijing General Association of Workers, a confederation that is more of a political organization than a labor advocate. Several small private sector unions and two of the four public sector unions are independent. Legislation protecting striking workers from dismissal is inadequate, and government enforcement of labor laws is lax. Foreign workers often work for less than half the wages of Macao citizens, live in controlled dormitories, and owe substantial money to proxies for the purchase of their jobs.

Tibet

Polity: One party   **Political Rights:** 7
Economy: Statist   **Civil Liberties:** 7
Population: 4,590,000*   **Status:** Not Free
Ethnic Groups: Tibetan, Han Chinese
*This figure from China's 1990 census includes 2.096 million Tibetans living in the Tibet Autonomous Region (TAR) and 2.494 million Tibetans living in areas of Eastern Tibet which, beginning in 1950, were incorporated into four Chinese provinces. Independent observers estimate that there are at least 6 million Tibetans under Chinese rule.

Overview:

While continuing their long-standing efforts to control day-to-day affairs in Tibetan monastaries, Chinese authorities also intensified restrictions on religious observance among government workers and party cadres and introduced new bans on religious practice among students and pensioners, before slightly easing the repression late in 2000.

With Tibet possessing a distinct national history dating back more than 2,000 years, Beijing's modern-day claim to the region is based solely on Mongol and Manchu imperial influence over Tibet in the thirteenth and eighteenth centuries, respectively. China invaded Tibet in late 1949 and in 1951 formally annexed the country. In an apparent effort to marginalize Tibetan national identity, China incorporated roughly half of Tibet into four southwestern Chinese provinces beginning in 1950. As a result, when China created in 1965 the Tibet Autonomous Region (TAR), which is autonomous only in name, it encompassed only half the territory of pre-invasion Tibet.

In what is perhaps the defining event of Beijing's occupation of Tibet, Chinese troops suppressed a local uprising in 1959 by killing an estimated 87,000 Tibetans in the Lhasa region alone. The massacre forced the Tibetan spiritual and temporal leader, the fourteenth Dalai Lama, Tenzin Gyatso, to flee to Dharamsala, India, with 80,000 supporters. The International Commission of Jurists called the Chinese occupation genocidal in 1960 and ruled that between 1911 and 1949, the year China invaded, Tibet had possessed all the attributes of statehood as defined under international law. During the Cultural Revolution, China imprisoned thousands of monks and nuns, destroyed nearly all of Tibet's 6,200 monasteries, and burned numerous sacred texts. By the late 1970s, an estimated 1.2 million Tibetans had died as a result of the occupation.

As resistance to Beijing's rule continued, Chinese soldiers forcibly broke up peaceful demonstrations throughout Tibet between 1987 and 1990. Beijing imposed martial law on Lhasa and surrounding areas in March 1989 following three days of anti-Chinese riots during which police killed at least 50 Tibetans. Authorities lifted martial law in May 1990.

Following a series of Chinese ideological campaigns in the 1990s aimed at gaining control over monastic affairs and undermining the exiled Dalai Lama's authority, there was a slight easing of repression late in 2000, according to some observers. The London-based Tibet Information Network (TIN) reported in December that over the previous four months authorities had slightly relaxed bans on religious activities in Lhasa, and were conducting fewer raids on the houses of government workers in search of religious objects. The changes came after authorities had in midyear intensified the raids; banned schoolchildren from visiting monasteries and temples during the summer break; warned government workers and party cadres against participating in religious practices and ordered them to withdraw their children from religious institutions; and tried to restrict public observance of a June Buddhist festival.

The lifting of some restrictions late in the year coincided with Beijing's decision to replace the architect of the recent crackdowns, Chen Kuiyan, with a more moderate figure as the region's Communist Party secretary. Yet the new senior leader, Guo Jinlong, 53, pledged to continue Chen's policies, and at year's end it was not clear how long the minor respite would last.

It is not clear why Beijing replaced Chen with Guo, who has served on several party committees in Sichuan Province and the TAR. One contributing factor may have been the escape into exile in late 1999 of the 15-year-old boy recognized by the Dalai Lama and accepted by Beijing as the seventeenth Karmapa, a leading religious figure. Beijing had interfered in the Karmapa's selection and education as part of its efforts to influence the next generation of Tibetan religious leaders. The most flagrant case of interference occurred in 1995, when Chinese authorities rejected and detained the Dalai Lama's selection of six-year-old Gedhun Choekyi Nyima as the eleventh reincarnation of the Panchen Lama, Tibetan Buddhism's second highest religious figure, and orchestrated the selection of another six-year-old boy as the Panchen Lama. Since the Panchen Lama identifies the reincarnated Dalai Lama, Beijing can potentially control the identification of the fifteenth Dalai Lama.

Political Rights and Civil Liberties: Tibetans lack the right of self-determination and cannot change their government through elections. The Chinese Communist Party (CCP) rules the Tibet Autonomous Region (TAR) through compliant government officials whose ranks include some Tibetans in largely ceremonial posts. While ethnic Tibetans have served as the TAR governor, none has ever held the peak post of TAR Party Secretary. In addition to maintaining tens of thousands of troops in Tibet, China's People's Liberation Army plays a significant administrative role. Most of China's policies affecting Tibetans apply both to those living in the TAR and to Tibetans living in parts of pre-invasion Tibet that Beijing has incorporated into China's Gansu, Qinghai, Sichuan, and Yunnan Provinces.

Authorities deny Tibetans nearly all basic rights including freedom of expression, assembly, association, and religion. Some of the worst abuses are against political dissidents. Security forces routinely resort to arbitrary arrest, imprisonment, and torture in response to nonviolent protest, including displaying Tibetan flags or other symbols of cultural identity, holding peaceful demonstrations, possessing a photograph of the Dalai Lama, forming prisoner lists, putting up posters, and distributing leaflets. The Dharamsala-based Tibetan Centre for Human Rights and Democracy (TCHRD) said in its annual report for 2000 that during the year it documented 26 arrests linked to political activities.

The CCP controls the judiciary, which has handed down lengthy prison terms to Tibetans convicted on political grounds. Monks and nuns make up approximately 73 percent of the 451 known political prisoners in Tibet, according to the TCHRD's annual report. In addition to using the judiciary to stifle dissent, authorities also frequently use administrative regulations to detain political prisoners without charge or trial for up to four years.

Throughout Tibet, security forces routinely torture detainees and inmates at police holding centers, prisons, and labor camps. In one of the most serious cases of abuse in recent years, authorities responded to protests at Lhasa's Drapchi prison in May 1998 with torture and beatings that led to the deaths of at least nine prisoners, including five nuns and three monks. There have also been reports of officials sexually abusing female prisoners and subjecting prisoners to forced labor.

While authorities permit some religious practices, they have strengthened their control over monastic affairs since 1996 under a "patriotic education campaign" that is aimed largely at undermining the Dalai Lama's influence as a religious and political leader. Under the campaign, government-run "work teams" have conducted political indoctrination sessions in hundreds of monasteries, aimed at coercing monks and nuns into opposing Tibetan independence, recognizing the Beijing-appointed Panchen Lama as the true Panchen Lama, and denouncing the Dalai Lama. Authorities have arrested dozens of monks and nuns for refusing to renounce their beliefs and expelled hundreds more from their religious institutions. Authorities expelled 862 monks and nuns from their monasteries and nunneries in 2000, bringing the total number of monastic expulsions under the campaign to 12,271, according to the TCHRD's annual report. As part of the campaign, Beijing banned all photographs of the Dalai Lama from monasteries in 1996. Evidence from the London-based Tibet Information Network (TIN) in 2000 suggested that authorities are increasingly extending the patriotic education campaign to Tibetan areas outside the TAR.

In addition to trying to coerce changes in political and religious ideology through the patriotic education campaign, the government continued to oversee day-to-day affairs in major monasteries and nunneries through state-organized "democratic management committees" that run each establishment. The government has also placed strict limits on the number of monks and nuns permitted in major monasteries, although these restrictions are not always enforced, and has interfered with the choice of monastic leaders. The boy the Dalai Lama identified as the reincarnation of the Panchen Lama is believed to be under house arrest in Beijing, along with his family. Moreover, authorities have tried to limit the building of new monasteries and nunneries, closed numerous religious institutions, and demolished several others.

While hundreds of religious figures hold nominal positions in local "people's congresses," authorities have banned Tibetan members of the Communist Party or government workers from religious practice. Reporting on what appeared to be a new effort to enforce these restrictions, the TIN said in August that authorities had recently ordered party cadres and government workers to withdraw their children from monasteries and nunneries in Lhasa, and had warned them that if they participated in religious practices, they faced fines and their children could be expelled from school. The London-based organization also reported that authorities had began carrying out searches for religious shrines and pictures of the Dalai Lama at the homes of party members in Lhasa and some outlying areas. Authorities have banned the sale of the Dalai Lama's photograph and displays of his photograph in state offices since 1994.

The TIN also reported that authorities imposed several additional restrictions on lay religious activity in 2000 that targeted not only party cadres and government workers but also students and pensioners. In June, the TAR government threatened civil servants with dismissal, schoolchildren with expulsion, and retired workers with loss of pensions if they publicly marked the Buddhist Sagadawa festival in Lhasa. Authorities also warned school students in Lhasa in July that they faced expulsion if they visited monasteries and temples during the summer holidays.

As one of China's 55 recognized ethnic minority groups, Tibetans receive some preferential treatment in university admissions and government employment. However, Tibetans need to learn Mandarin in order to take advantage of these preferences. In any case, Chinese officials announced in 1997 that they would begin teaching Chinese to Tibetan children starting in the first grade and in recent years have downgraded the use of Tibetan as a language of instruction in education, according to the U. S. State Department. The changes ostensibly are designed to give Tibetan youths more educational and employment opportunities. Beyond the issues of education and government employment, urban Tibetans face discrimination in private sector employment and housing. As in the rest of China, authorities reportedly subject farmers and herders to arbitrary taxes.

Beijing's draconian family planning policy is nominally more lenient towards Tibetans and other minorities. Urban Tibetans are permitted to have two children, while farmers and herders can have three or four children. However, authorities frequently enforce the nationwide one-child rule in Tibet for government workers and Communist Party members and in some cases reportedly use the threat of fines to coerce women into undergoing abortions and sterilizations. Moreover, the TIN reported in February that unofficial reports suggested that officials were for the first time applying a two-child limit to farmers and nomads in several counties.

Seeking to escape religious and political persecution, some 3,000 Tibetans flee to Nepal as refugees each year, according to the United Nations High Commissioner for Refugees. In yet another indication of Beijing's tight control over the region, a report on press freedom in Tibet released in May by the Paris-based Reporters Sans Frontiéres noted that Chinese authorities control all print and broadcast media in Tibet, except for about 20 or so clandestine publications that appear sporadically.

While government development policies have raised the living standards of ordinary Tibetans, the U. S. State Department noted in its human rights report for 1999 that Han Chinese are the primary beneficiaries of many development policies and programs. Moreover, Beijing has encouraged and facilitated the resettlement of Han Chinese into traditional Tibetan areas by providing economic incentives and by building roads and other infrastructure. The resettlement and rapid modernization have altered the demographic composition of the region, displaced Tibetan businesses, reduced employment opportunities for Tibetans, and further marginalized Tibetan cultural identity. Possibly reflecting these rapid social and economic changes and dislocations, prostitution is reportedly becoming a serious concern in Lhasa.

Ending a controversy that had raised questions about the World Bank's compliance with its own lending guidelines, China withdrew in July its request to the bank for a $40 million loan to help resettle some 58,000 mainly ethnic-Chinese farmers into an area of Qinghai province traditionally occupied by Tibetans and Mongolians. In deciding to carry out on its own the Qinghai component of the China Poverty Reduction Project, Beijing rejected the bank's request for project changes that would have led to a 15-month delay. The bank had proposed the changes after its own inspection team criticized the initial project design and appraisal for violating bank guidelines regarding projects affecting indigenous people, the environment, and other concerns.

Georgia
Abkhazia

Polity: Presidential
Economy: Mixed statist
Population: 520,000 (1992 est.);
280,000 (2000 est.)
Ethnic Groups: 1992 est.—Georgian (45 percent),
Abkhaz (17 percent), Russian (16 percent),
other (22 percent). Since 1993, most ethnic
Georgians have fled or been expelled from the territory.

Political Rights: 6
Civil Liberties: 5
Status: Not Free

Overview:

Six years after Abkhazia won de facto independence from Georgia in the early 1990s, the June 2000 signing of a stabilization protocol by the two sides sparked hopes over movement toward a lasting peace agreement. However, a final settlement to the protracted conflict remained elusive throughout the year, as Tbilisi and Sukhumi continued to disagree on the fundamental issue of the territory's political status.

Annexed by Russia in 1864, Abkhazia became an autonomous republic of Soviet Georgia in 1930. Following the collapse of the Soviet Union in 1991, Abkhazia declared its independence from Tbilisi the following year, igniting a war between Abkhaz secessionists and Georgian troops that lasted nearly 14 months. In September 1993, Abkhaz forces, with covert assistance from Russia, seized control of the city of Sukhumi, ultimately defeating the Georgian army and winning de facto independence for the territory. As a result of the conflict, more than 200,000 residents, mostly ethnic Georgians, fled Abkhazia, while casualty figures were estimated in the thousands. An internationally brokered ceasefire was signed in Moscow in 1994, although a final decision on the territory's status remains unresolved.

In June 1999, the Georgian leadership unsuccessfully lobbied for international condemnation of alleged ethnic cleansing in Abkhazia as a result of the 1992-1993 war, effectively ending Georgian hopes that the United Nations would sanction the use of force against the breakaway territory. In the October 1999 elections for president of Abkhazia, the incumbent, Vladislav Ardzinba, was the only candidate running for office; his inauguration ceremony was held in the capital Sukhumi in December. The Organization for Security and Cooperation in Europe (OSCE) and other international organizations refused to recognize the vote as legitimate. In a concurrent referendum on independence, the results of which were not recognized by any state, a reported 98 percent of voters supported independence for Abkhazia. Georgia denounced the polls as illegal and as an attempt to sabotage peace talks.

The unarmed, 102-member UN Observer Mission in Georgia (UNOMIG) remains stationed in the country to monitor the ceasefire and attempt to resolve violations, and some 1,500 Russian peacekeepers patrol the region under the auspices of the Commonwealth of Independent States. In June 2000, Georgian President Eduard Shevardnadze agreed to an extension of the mandate of the Russian peacekeepers past a June 30 deadline.

Georgia and Abkhazia signed a stabilization protocol on July 11, 2000, in which both sides agreed to deploy no more than 600 troops and police on each side of the conflict zone and to not resort to force in attempting to resolve disputes connected with the conflict. However, most analysts cautioned that hopes for a permanent settlement of the dispute are premature and that the protocol must be followed by more substantive talks.

Peace negotiations, which thus far have enjoyed only marginal success, have not found solutions acceptable to both parties on the main issues of the return of displaced persons and the region's final political status. While Tbilisi claims to be defending Georgia's territorial integrity, Sukhumi continues to insist on independence for Abkhazia, a status that has not been recognized by the international community. The 1994 ceasefire has been tenuous, with sporadic conflicts continuing along the Abkhazian border.

During a November 1999 OSCE meeting in Istanbul, Moscow agreed to close two of its four military bases in Georgia by mid-2001. While Russia began its withdrawal from the Vaziani base near Tbilisi in August 2000, the closure of its Gudauta base in Abkhazia has proven to be more problematic. The plan is opposed by many in the territory's leadership, including President Ardzinba, who regard Russia as an important ally against Georgian claims over the breakaway republic.

Political Rights and Civil Liberties: Residents of Abkhazia can elect government officials, but some 200,000 displaced Georgians could not vote in the 1999 presidential elections or in parliamentary and local elections in previous years. Although the November 1994 constitution established a presidential-parliamentary system of government, the president exercises almost complete control of the region. The ethnic-Georgian Abkhazian Supreme Council has been a government in exile in Tbilisi since being expelled from Abkhazia in 1993.

While several independent newspapers are published, the Abkhaz press generally publish mostly negative information on or superficial analysis of events in Georgia. Electronic media are controlled by the state and generally reflect government positions.

Freedom of religion is respected for Muslims, but Christian Georgians and Armenians face harassment and persecution. President Ardzinba issued a decree in 1995 banning Jehovah's Witnesses, and in April 1999, authorities reportedly detained several members of the group for violating the decree. In early May, they were released after their attorney argued that their detention violated a freedom of speech clause in the Abkhaz constitution.

An estimated two dozen nongovernmental organizations operate in Abkhazia, although most rely on funding from outside of the territory. Trade unions are former affiliates of the Georgian Confederation of Trade Unions. Freedom of assembly is restricted. According to Abkhaz media sources, some 500 opponents of Vladislav Ardzinba demonstrated in support of Ardzinba's resignation on April 27.

The constitution formally established an independent judiciary, but the system continues many Soviet-era practices. Most judges are nominated by the president and appointed with parliamentary approval.

Personal security remains a concern, and there are restrictions on travel in the conflict zone. On June 1, two UN observers, two employees of the Halo Trust anti-landmine organization, and an Abkhaz interpreter were kidnapped in a remote mountain gorge in the Kodori Valley, a conflict zone dividing Abkhazia and Georgia proper. Although the Georgian media reported that the abductors had demanded $300,000 for the hostages' release, all five were released safely by June 5 without any ransom having been paid. In August, a consultant with the OSCE Human Rights office in Sukhumi was murdered by unidentified gunmen. In December, two UN military observers were kidnapped in the republic's Kodor Gorge, although they were released unharmed three days later.

Close to 200,000 displaced persons who fled Abkhazia during the early 1990s are living in western Georgia, most in the Zugdidi district bordering Abkhazia. Gali, which is the last Georgian enclave in Abkhazia, is home to some 2,000 ethnic Georgians.

Agriculture, including the cultivation of tobacco, tea, and fruit, constitutes the main economic activity in the region. Large segments of the economy, much of which has been devastated by the war, are controlled by criminal organizations, and corruption is widespread.

India
Kashmir

Polity: Indian-administered

Economy: Capitalist-statist

Population: 8,500,000

Ethnic Groups: Muslim majority, Hindu minority

Political Rights: 6

Civil Liberties: 6

Status: Not Free

Overview:
Faced with a continuing insurgency in Kashmir that has killed some 30,000 civilians, soldiers, and guerrillas since 1989, India entered into short-lived talks in August 2000 with the largest of a dozen separatist groups fighting for independence from New Delhi and began a unilateral ceasefire late in the year. Having pulled out of the August talks, the militants also rejected the ceasefire and continued to attack Indian forces in Srinagar and elsewhere in Kashmir.

After centuries of rule in Kashmir by Afghan, Sikh, and local strongmen, the British seized control of the Himalayan land in 1846 and sold it to the Hindu maharajah of the neighboring principality of Jammu. The maharajah later incorporated Ladakh and other surrounding areas into what became the new princely state of Jammu and Kashmir. At the partition of British India in 1947, Maharajah Hari Singh attempted to preserve Jammu and Kashmir's independence. But after Pakistani tribesmen invaded, the maharajah agreed to Jammu and Kashmir's accession to India in return for promises of autonomy and eventual self-determination.

Within months of gaining their independence, India and Pakistan went to war in

Kashmir. A United Nations-brokered ceasefire in January 1949 established the present-day boundaries, which a UN Military Observer Group monitors. The boundaries gave Pakistan control of roughly one-third of Jammu and Kashmir, including the far northern and western areas. India retained most of the Kashmir Valley along with predominantly Hindu Jammu and Buddhist-majority Ladakh.

Under Article 370 of India's 1950 constitution and a 1952 accord, the territory received substantial autonomy. However, New Delhi began annulling the autonomy guarantees in 1953, and in 1957 formally annexed the two-thirds of Jammu and Kashmir under its control. Seeking strategic roads and passes, China seized a portion of Jammu and Kashmir in 1959. India and Pakistan fought a second, inconclusive war over the territory in 1965. Under the 1972 Simla accord, New Delhi and Islamabad agreed to respect the Line of Control and to resolve Kashmir's status through negotiation.

The insurgency began in 1989, two years after the pro-India National Conference party won state elections that were marred by widespread fraud and authorities began arresting members of a new, Muslim-based opposition party. Muslim-based militant groups assassinated several National Conference politicians and attacked government targets in the Kashmir Valley. The militant groups included the Jammu and Kashmir Liberation Front (JKLF) and other pro-independence groups consisting largely of indigenous Kashmiris, as well as Pakistani-backed Islamist groups that want to bring Kashmir under Islamabad's control. Muslims make up two-thirds of the state's population but are concentrated in the Kashmir Valley, which is barely one-fifth of the state's area.

As the violence escalated, New Delhi placed Jammu and Kashmir under federal rule in January 1990. By the mid-1990s, the Indian army had greatly weakened the JKLF and other indigenous groups and had secured most large Kashmir Valley towns and villages. The JKLF abandoned its armed struggle in 1994. The insurgency has since been controlled by the Pakistani-backed fundamentalist groups, which include in their ranks many non-Kashmiri, Islamic mercenaries. While militants have continued to carry out assassinations and bombings in Srinagar and other Kashmir Valley towns, much of the heavy fighting has shifted to Doda and other southern districts.

The October 1996 state elections returned Jammu and Kashmir to local rule for the first time since 1990. The National Conference, the only Kashmir-based party to contest the elections, won 57 of the 87 assembly seats and formed a government under party leader Farooq Abdullah. His administration is widely believed to be corrupt and incompetent.

In a sign of the difficulty in finding a peaceful solution to the conflict, talks between India and the largest armed group in Kashmir, Hizbul Mujahideen, broke down just days after they began in August 2000. In holding the meeting, New Delhi had dropped its long-standing precondition for talks, that the militants accept Indian sovereignty over its only Muslim-majority state. However, the initiative foundered when the Hizbul Mujahideen called off a unilateral ceasefire, which had enabled the talks to take place, after India refused to include Pakistan in the dialogue.

In late November, New Delhi announced that for the first time it would suspend counterinsurgency operations against Kashmiri militant groups during the Islamic holy month of Ramadan. Although Pakistan responded by saying it would exercise "maximum restraint" along the 450-mile Line of Control separating the Indian- and Pakistani-held parts of Kashmir, most militant groups rejected the ceasefire and continued to attack security forces. Nevertheless, India extended the ceasefire in late December for another month.

India's insistence that Pakistan be excluded from talks had hardened after the two countries fought weeks of border battles in Kashmir beginning in May 1999, when India began air and ground attacks to dislodge hundreds of Pakistani troops and Pakistani-backed mercenaries who had seized strategic heights in the Kargil-Dras region on the Indian side of the Line of Control. Pakistan withdrew the militants in early July 1999, but separatist violence later escalated.

Political Rights and Civil Liberties:

India has never held a referendum on Kashmiri self-determination as called for in a 1948 UN resolution. The state's residents can nominally change the local administration through elections. However, the 1996 state election was marred by violence and irregularities. Militants enforced boycotts, threatened election officials and candidates, and killed at least 20 people prior to and during the balloting. Soldiers and state-backed militias coerced some Kashmiris into voting. Violence and intimidation also severely disrupted voting in Kashmir during the 1999 Indian national elections, when militant groups again threatened to kill voters, assassinated at least three politicians, and carried out bombings and other attacks. The All Parties Hurriyat (Freedom) Conference (APHC), an umbrella group of 23 legal pro-independence and pro-Pakistan parties, urged voters to boycott the 1996 state elections and the national elections.

Facing heavy pressure from both the government and militants, the judiciary barely functions. The government frequently disregards judicial orders quashing detentions, while militants routinely threaten judges, witnesses, and the families of defendants.

In a continuing cycle of violence, Indian soldiers, federal paramilitary troops, and the police carried out arbitrary arrests and detentions, torture, "disappearances," and summary killings of suspected militants and alleged civilian sympathizers. After a decline over the past three years, there appeared to be an increase in the number of disappearances, with dozens being reported in the press in the first half of the year, Amnesty International said in August. Many disappearances apparently came in reprisal for militant killings of soldiers or police. Amnesty said that since 1990, up to 1,000 people have disappeared after being arrested by police or armed paramilitary forces.

In response to increased militant attacks on security forces following the 1999 Kargil conflict, army cordon-and-search operations had resumed in the Kashmir Valley and increased in the southern border districts, the New York-based Human Rights Watch said in March. During these operations, the army detained young men, assaulted other family members, and summarily executed suspected militants. Previously, Human Rights Watch had reported in 1999 that as Indian security forces had consolidated their hold over the Kashmir Valley in the mid-1990s, they had largely ended the cordon-and-search operations and reprisals against civilians that were common there in the early 1990s.

Many abuses by Indian forces are faciliated by the 1978 Public Safety Act (PSA) and other broadly drawn preventive detention laws, which authorities have used to "stifle and punish dissent" in Kashmir, according to a May report by Amnesty International. The PSA allows authorities to detain persons for up to two years without charge or trial. The organization said that "hundreds" of people are thought to be held in preventive detention or on a range of criminal charges despite court orders for their release, including some people who have been held without charge or trial since the early 1990s. Although detentions under the security laws are nonrenewable, authorities frequently re-arrest suspects on new charges and impose a new two-year detention. The report also said that torture is widely used in police stations and interrogation centers, leading each year to dozens of reported deaths in custody.

Further contributing to the army's ability to act with near impunity are two other broadly written laws, the Armed Forces Special Powers Act and the 1990 Disturbed Areas Act. The laws allow Indian forces to search homes and arrest suspects without a warrant, shoot suspects on sight, and destroy homes or buildings believed to house militants or arms. Moreover, the Special Powers Act requires New Delhi to approve any prosecution of Indian forces. While a state human rights commission has been investigating some human rights complaints since 1998, it cannot directly investigate abuses by the army or other federal security forces.

Nevertheless, there were two separate and rare efforts to bring soldiers to justice for rights violations in the fall, when a court-martial jailed an officer for seven years for raping a teenage girl during a February anti-insurgency operation, and seven police officers were indicted for the April shooting deaths of seven people. The shootings occurred during a protest held in response to the killings of five men by the security forces. The security forces claimed the five had been involved in the March massacre of 35 Sikhs at Chittisinghpora. The protesters claimed that the five men had been framed by the security forces.

Seeking support during security operations, the army has recruited former servicemen for Village Defense Committees whose members have committed extrajudicial executions, assaults, and other abuses. Since the mid-1990s, the army has also organized and armed militias composed of former militants that have reportedly carried out extrajudicial executions, disappearances, torture, and other abuses against pro-Pakistani militants as well as journalists and other civilians.

Armed with increasingly sophisticated and powerful weapons, militant groups continued to kill politicians, party workers, public employees, suspected informers, members of rival factions, soldiers, and Hindu civilians. Militants are suspected in the killings of least 100 mainly Hindu civilians in separate incidents on August 1 and 2, although soldiers reportedly also killed some civilians during these incidents. The attacks are the latest in a series of violent incidents against Kashmiri Hindus since 1990 that have forced tens of thousands of them to flee the Kashmir Valley for camps in Jammu and Delhi. Separatists have also kidnapped numerous government officials, politicians, and businessmen, and are accused of using rape to deter women from acting as informants.

Kashmir's journalists have been pressured by both the government and militants to suppress information about human rights abuses or that otherwise would be damaging to their side. In recent years, militant groups have kidnapped, tortured, killed, or otherwise harassed and threatened numerous journalists, and occasionally coerced newspapers into suspending publication. The Paris-based Reporters Sans Frontiéres said in April that nine journalists had been killed in the state since 1989. Authorities occasionally beat, detain, and harass journalists. Though generally not used, under India's 1971 Newspaper Incitements to Offenses Act (in effect only in Jammu and Kashmir), district magistrates can censor publications in certain circumstances. Given these constraints, journalists generally practice self-censorship, though they do report on some abuses by security forces.

Several human rights activists have been killed since 1989, and only a few individuals and groups continue to do human rights work. In recent years, authorities have briefly arrested APHC leaders either before or during peaceful protests and have broken up numerous pro-independence or anti-government demonstrations. Along the Line of Control separating the two adversaries, shelling by Indian and Pakistani troops each year kills numerous civilians, displaces many more, and disrupts schools and the local economy.

Indonesia

West Papua (Irian Jaya)

Polity: Dominant party (military-dominated)
Economy: Capitalist-statist
Population: 1,800,000
Ethnic Groups: Papuan

Political Rights: 5*
Civil Liberties: 5
Status: Partly Free

Ratings Change: West Papua's political rights rating changed from 6 to 5 because civil society groups and community leaders are increasingly able to advocate political views and take part in talks with Indonesian authorities.

Overview:

Following months of inconclusive talks between authorities and pro-independence leaders in West Papua, police detained or arrested dozens of Papuan leaders or alleged supporters of independence in late 2000 and enforced a ban on the flying of the Papuans' highly symbolic Morning Star flag. The arrests coincided with a wave of political violence in the territory that killed at least 17 people. While authorities released most of those detained, prosecutors charged five pro-independence figures with treason despite calls for their release from Indonesian president Abdurrahman Wahid.

After setting up the first European outpost in New Guinea in 1828, the Dutch agreed with Britain in 1848 to divide the island into western and eastern sections. Britain and Germany colonized the eastern part, which today is the independent state of Papua New Guinea. The Japanese occupied the Dutch-controlled western part during World War II. The Netherlands ceded administrative responsibility for the territory to Indonesia in 1963 under a 1962 United Nations agreement calling for a referendum on self-determination be held by 1969.

Seeking an independent homeland, a group of tribesmen called the Free Papua Movement (OPM) began waging a low-grade insurgency in the mid-1960s. As the insurgency continued, Jakarta organized in the summer of 1969 a tightly controlled "Act of Free Choice," in which some 1,025 traditional leaders voted unanimously for Indonesia to annex the territory. In 1973 Indonesia renamed the land, known locally as West Papua, "Irian Jaya."

As the OPM escalated its hit-and-run attacks against Indonesian troops, the army launched a counteroffensive in 1984 that drove hundreds of villagers into neighboring Papua New Guinea. That year, Indonesian forces also murdered the prominent anthropologist Arnold Ap. The army conducted more large-scale anti-OPM offensives in 1989.

While the OPM has continued to carry out some guerrilla attacks, Indonesia's democratic transition that began with President Suharto's ouster in 1998 has provided an opening for civil society groups to press Jakarta for independence. Suharto's successor, B. J. Habibie, began a "national dialogue" with West Papuan community leaders in 1999 but ended it after the West Papuans asked for independence. Habibie's successor, President Wahid, has also rejected independence for West Papua but has pledged to grant the territory autonomy. Nevertheless, the Papua Presidium Council, a West Papuan group that advocates independence, dialogue, and nonviolent protest, organized a week-long congress beginning on May 29, 2000 that called for Jakarta to recognize a 1961 West Papuan declaration of independence under Dutch rule that was never recognized internationally.

Despite these differences, Indonesian authorities and West Papuan leaders continued to hold intermittent talks until the crackdown late in the year. Agence France-Presse (AFP) reported on December 12 that authorities had arrested 155 independence supporters or students in the past two weeks in the provincial capital of Jayapura, of whom 12 were still being held. AFP also said that since the beginning of the month, political violence had killed at least 11 students or independence supporters, 4 non-native settlers, and 2 police officers.

Among those arrested were Theys Eluay and 4 other Presidium Council leaders. Eluay had helped negotiate a compromise under which West Papuans across the territory would limit the flying of the Morning Star flag, beginning at midnight on December 1. Jakarta had banned flag raisings in mid-October after Papuans in the highland town of Wamena killed at least 28 non-Papuans in retaliation for the police killings of two Papuans who were trying to raise the Morning Star.

Political Rights and Civil Liberties: West Papuans lack the right to self-determination. They were not permitted to participate in the 1962 "New York Agreement" between the Netherlands and the UN that transferred their land from Dutch to Indonesian sovereignty in 1963. Moreover, the 1969 referendum that ratified Indonesian rule was neither free nor fair. While the 1962 agreement did not specify a procedure for the referendum, it did call for a popular consultation to be held "in accordance with international practice," a standard that Jakarta seemingly ignored. The Indonesian military reportedly coerced the traditional leaders into approving Jakarta's rule, and the UN special observer reported that, "the administration exercised at all times a tight political control over the population." Nevertheless, the UN accepted the referendum.

As residents of Indonesia's 26th province, West Papuans can participate in Indonesian elections. In practice, they have limited means to hold either the local or central governments accountable. Papuans say authorities have expropriated their ancestral lands and granted mining, logging, and energy contracts in the resource-rich territory without adequate consultation or compensation, while investing little in local development projects. Papuans have also largely been excluded from employment in local government agencies and private mining operations in favor of immigrants from other parts of the archipelago. Indonesian rule has brought considerable economic development to the territory, but the benefits have gone disproportionately to foreign investors, immigrants, and the military.

Respect for basic rights in West Papua has improved markedly since President

Wahid took office in October 1999, despite the setbacks in late 2000. Signaling his tolerance for pro-independence advocacy, Wahid released 61 West Papuan political prisoners convicted for separatist activities and legalized the flying of the Morning Star flag in December 1999. While authorities had questioned West Papuan leaders following pro-independence demonstrations and flag-raising ceremonies, they had generally tolerated these activities up until late 2000.

Under former President Suharto, authorities had routinely jailed Papuans on subversion and other charges for peaceful pro-independence activities, and restricted expression, assembly, and association. In 1995, Indonesia's official National Commission on Human Rights accused the military of extrajudicial killings, torture, arbitrary arrest and detention, "disappearances," widespread surveillance of the local population, and destruction of property in the territory. Many abuses took place in Timika and other central highlands towns near the giant Grasberg copper and gold mine owned by Freeport Indonesia, the local subsidiary of the U.S.-based Freeport McMoRan Copper and Gold company. The level of human rights abuses began declining under Suharto's successor, President B. J. Habibie, who loosened some restrictions but generally did not tolerate pro-independence advocacy.

After decades of tight censorship, local newspapers reported fairly openly on political developments. Though most nongovernmental organizations have limited funds, the territory's civil society is active and growing.

Most West Papuans follow either indigenous beliefs or Christianity, and freedom of religion is generally respected. In part because of societal norms, women face unofficial discrimination in educational and employment opportunities.

The October massacre in Wamena was the worst of several incidents during the year where Papuans violently attacked or otherwise harassed non-Papuans. Some 170,000 non-Papuans came to West Papua under a largely defunct "transmigration" program that began in the 1970s. Critics say the presence of large numbers of non-Papuans in the territory jeopardizes local employment opportunities and threatens to marginalize the indigenous Melanesian culture. Along with traders who have moved into West Papua on their own, the transmigrants dominate the local economy and reportedly discriminate against the indigenous Papuans.

Iraq
Kurdistan

Polity: Dual leadership
Economy: Capitalist-statist
Population: 4,000,000
Ethnic Groups: Kurdish majority, Assyrian

Political Rights: 6
Civil Liberties: 6
Status: Not Free

Overview: Despite international efforts at mediation and numerous meetings between leaders of the Kurdistan Democratic Party (KDP) and the Patriotic Union of Kurdistan (PUK), the 1998 Washington Agreement on power sharing remains unimplemented. The agreement called for the establishment of an elected government after a transitional period of power sharing, arrangements for the equitable distribution of revenues from cross-border trade with Turkey, and the elimination of checkpoints to allow for freedom of movement throughout the region. The primary issue impeding cooperation appears to be the division of revenues, but other obstacles remain, including disputes over the composition of a joint regional government. The intermittent military conflict between the two sides has subsided, and the KDP in September announced its intention to withdraw armed militias from large areas under its control.

In April 1991, the United States, Britain, France, and Turkey established a secure region with a U.S.-enforced no-fly zone north of the 36th parallel in Iraq. Following the collapse of an autonomy agreement with the Iraqi government, the 105-member Iraqi Kurdistan National Assembly was created in 1991. After a 1992 vote produced no clear winner, the KDP and the PUK agreed to fill 50 seats each. The remaining 5 seats were reserved for Christian Assyrians. Disputes over power and revenue sharing erupted into civil war in 1994, precluding operation of the government and any further elections. Frequent clashes occurred up until the Washington Agreement in 1998.

Currently, Kurdistan is split into two parts, with the KDP controlling the western regions, and the PUK controlling the region of Suleimaniyah toward the southeast. Each party maintains its own administrative, legislative, and executive structures, and despite the institutions created in Irbil under power-sharing arrangements, the PUK has established its own courts and other bodies. On February 3, municipal elections took place in PUK-held areas without the participation of the KDP. As expected, the PUK dominated, winning 53 of 58 councils. The Movement of Islamic Unity won 4 seats, and the Party of Islamic Union won 1. Following the polls, opposition parties issued a joint statement endorsing the election and its results. Independent observers called the election generally fair despite minor irregularities. Most agreed that PUK leader Jalal Talabani gained renewed legitimacy through the party's victory. However, KDP leader Massoud Barzani denounced such elections and institution-building by the PUK as divisive. What they mean for the future of the peace efforts remains to be seen.

A report by UNICEF in the spring of 2000 concluded that children's health is improving in Iraqi Kurdistan while child mortality rates are rising in areas under Baghdad's control. In fact, studies have shown that indices of human welfare are generally improving in the north while they deteriorate in the south, leading international analysts and both major Kurdish parties to claim that the United Nations-sponsored oil-for-food program, which allows Iraq to sell oil for humanitarian assistance, works when administered by the UN and not by local officials. Two chief UN relief officials in Iraq resigned in 2000 in protest over the humanitarian situation in that country and blamed Iraqi, U.S., and British officials for hampering the administration of aid. Thanks to that program, as well as huge profits from illicit oil trade with Turkey and the proliferation of international aid organizations, Iraqi Kurds have seen remarkable improvements in housing, literacy, health care, employment, and education.

Political Rights and Civil Liberties:

Iraqi Kurds cannot change their government democratically, as factional strife has precluded parliamentary activity since 1995. However, the KDP and the PUK have separate administrations and cabinets for the territories under their control, and the PUK led generally free and fair municipal elections in February 2000. In December 1999, the KDP declared that it had formed a new government led by Najervan Barzani, nephew of the KDP leader. Reportedly, Barham Salih leads the administration under PUK control.

Although the KDP and the PUK maintain separate judicial systems in areas under their control, reliable information about judicial independence is difficult to obtain. Reportedly, hearings are conducted, adjudicated, and enforced by local officials of the two parties. The two groups also run separate prisons and detention facilities where human rights violations, including denial of due process and torture, have occurred. However, both sides regularly grant access to their prisons to delegations from the International Committee of the Red Cross, which noted improvements in conditions. According to Human Rights Watch, one prisoner exchange took place in March.

Political chaos has allowed the Turkish rebel Kurdistan Workers' Party (PKK) to use Iraqi Kurdistan as a base for its military insurgency against Turkey. Turkey repeatedly sent troops into northern Iraq in pursuit of PKK fighters during 2000. Fighting also broke out between PKK and KDP forces for several days in July, and between PKK and PUK forces for nearly two weeks in September. Dozens of casualties were reported in these battles. There are some 900,000 internally displaced persons throughout Kurdistan, with dozens of new arrivals every day from the Iraqi town of Kirkuk, where Iraqi officials continue to carry out a policy of "Arabization."

Observers report a generally open climate for discussion of political issues. Many independent newspapers and opposition television and radio broadcasts are widely available. The absence of a governing authority has allowed free expression to flourish, although many journalists have ties to political organizations. Kurdnet, a Kurdish satellite network, began broadcasting for three hours a day on January 1, 2000, from Suleimaniyah. In April, Voice of Islam, the radio station of the Islamic Unity Movement, was seized by security forces in Dohuk (near Irbil). Numerous political parties, social organizations, and cultural associations operate freely. However, PUK forces arrested members and supporters of the opposition Iraqi Workers' Communist Party (IWCP) during the summer following demonstrations that ensued when authorities cut water and power to IWCP bases. Two organizations affiliated with the IWCP were raided in late July.

Kurds are overwhelmingly Sunni Muslim. Ethnic and religious minorities face discrimination and harassment at the hands of Kurds in northern Iraq. According to the

Assyrian International News Agency, the KDP in particular has pursued policies of land expropriation, assassination, abduction, rape, and torture against Assyrians, all with impunity. Teaching of the Assyrian language is restricted. The 1999 murder of an Assyrian woman who was employed as a housekeeper by a KDP bureaucrat has not yet been resolved, and it was reported that the victim's brothers were abducted and beaten in March and April 2000 in order to quiet demands for an investigation into the case. The Turkoman ethnic minority faces similar discrimination, and has complained of a policy of "ethnic cleansing" against them by Kurdish authorities. In June, the Turkoman Students' Union building was attacked and occupied by KDP police. KDP forces raided Iraqi Turkoman Front headquarters in Irbil on July 12, killing two Turkoman security guards and injuring others. In August, the KDP attacked a Turkoman sports club.

Israel
Israeli-Administered Territories[a]
& Palestinian Authority-Administered Territories [b]

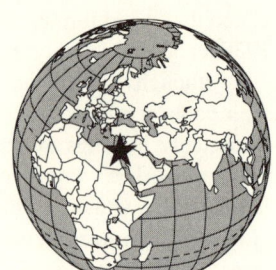

Polity: Military and PLO administered
Economy: Capitalist
Population: 3,152,631 (1,132,063: Gaza; 2,020,298: West Bank). In addition, there are some 171,000 Israeli settlers in the West Bank and about 172,000 in East Jerusalem. Some 6,500 Israeli settlers live in the Gaza Strip.

Political Rights: 6 [a]
Civil Liberties: 6 [a]*
Status: Not Free

Political Rights: 5 [b]
Civil Liberties: 6 [b]
Status: Not Free

Ethnic Groups: Palestinian, Jewish, Bedouin
Ratings Change: The Israeli-administered territories civil liberties rating changed from 5 to 6 because of deteriorating conditions as a result of the continual violence in the second half of 2000.

Overview: An all-out effort to reach a comprehensive peace between Israel and the Palestinians failed at Camp David, Maryland in July 2000. By the end of September, a full-fledged Palestinian *intifada* (uprising) erupted, destroying much of what was left of the Oslo peace process. By year's end, more than 300 Palestinians had been killed in clashes, many of them young people encouraged to confront Israeli forces. More than 50 Israeli troops and civilians were killed. The West Bank and Gaza Strip were effectively shut down, with Israel tightly restricting the movement of Palestinians both within and outside Palestinian-administered areas and those still under Israeli control. The Palestinian economy, already underdeveloped, suffered severe strains. The new intifada featured battles unprecedented in both scale and duration between armed Palestinian militias and security forces, and Israeli troops. Israel faced intense international criticism for its handling of the uprising, as did the Palestinian National Authority (PNA). Palestinian leader Yassir Arafat appeared undermined as factions of his Fatah organization and other groups took the lead — at times without his consultation or against his orders – in perpetuating the intifada. The Palestinian Authority continued to face accusations of autocratic leadership, mismanagement, and political corruption. Several Palestinians suspected of collaborating with Israel were sentenced to death after summary trials. Most types of sentences are usually handed down within hours of the passage of convictions.

The West Bank, Gaza, and East Jerusalem came under the British Mandate in 1920. After Palestinian rejection of a United Nations partition plan in 1947, Israel declared its independence on the portion of land allotted for Jewish settlement. The fledgling state was jointly attacked by neighboring Arab states in the 1948 War of Independence. While Israel maintained its sovereignty, Jordan seized East Jerusalem and the West Bank, while Egypt took control of Gaza. In the 1967 Six-Day War, Israel came to occupy the West Bank, Gaza, East Jerusalem, and the Golan Heights, which had been used by Syria to shell towns in northern Israel. Israel annexed East Jerusalem in 1967 and the Golan Heights in 1981.

Palestinians living in the West Bank and Gaza began attacking mainly military targets in 1987 to protest Israeli rule in what became known as the intifada. A series of secret negotiations between Israel and Arafat's Palestine Liberation Organization (PLO) conducted in Oslo, Norway, produced an agreement in August 1993. The Declaration of Principles provided for three Israeli troop withdrawals and gradual Palestinian autonomy in the West Bank and Gaza. U.S.-sponsored negotiations on the final status of East Jerusalem and the fate of refugees took place at Camp David in July 2000, but the Palestinians rejected what were widely considered significant compromise proposals by the Israelis on these issues.

Elections for the first Palestinian legislative council and head of the council's executive authority were held in January 1996 and were considered to be generally free and fair. Independents won 35 of the 88 council seats, while Arafat's Fatah movement won the remainder. Arafat won the chairmanship of the executive authority with 88 percent of the vote.

Most of Gaza and the West Bank town of Jericho were turned over to the PNA in May 1994. In late 1995, Israel began redeploying its forces in the West Bank. The election of Labor Party leader Ehud Barak as Israeli prime minister in May 1999 reinvigorated the Oslo peace process. Under the provisions of Oslo implemented so far, the Palestinians have full or partial control of 43 percent of the West Bank, or 60 percent of the territory's Palestinian population.

In September 1999, under U.S. and Egyptian auspices, the Palestinians and Israelis recommitted themselves to the Wye River interim agreement, crafted initially in October 1998 at Wye River Plantation, Maryland. The original agreement called for Israeli redeployment from 13.1 percent of the West Bank and provided for the transfer of 14.2 percent of jointly controlled land to Palestinian control in exchange for Palestinian security guarantees. Implementation of the accords stalled during Benjamin Netanyahu's term. Following the re-signing, Israel transferred 7 percent more of the West Bank to Palestinian civilian control, released 350 Palestinian prisoners from Israeli jails, allowed the opening of an airport in Gaza, and established a safe passage route, allowing Palestinians freer movement between autonomous zones.

In July 2000, Israeli and Palestinian negotiators, led respectively by Prime Minister Barak and Chairman Arafat, held two weeks of talks at Camp David under U.S. auspices. The talks culminated in the most far-reaching negotiations ever between the two sides. For the first time, Israel offered compromise proposals on Jerusalem, agreeing to some form of Palestinian control and quasi-sovereignty over East Jerusalem, which contains Islamic holy sites. Israel also offered 95 percent of the West Bank to the Palestinians and expressed some willingness to recompense and resettle a limited number of Palestinian refugees. The Palestinians rejected the Israeli offers, insisting on full sovereignty over East Jerusalem, 100 percent of the West Bank, and an Israeli commitment to a "right of return" of Palestinian refugees. No agreement was reached. Arafat left the talks committed to a unilateral declaration of independence in 2000, but was dissuaded by Arab allies who felt peace talks needed another chance.

At the end of September, perhaps in protest to the government's expressed willingness to compromise on Jerusalem, right-wing Likud leader Ariel Sharon visited the Temple Mount in Jerusalem's Old City, the site of the Al Aqsa Mosque. A widespread Palestinian uprising erupted, ultimately taking on a life of its own and lasting through the end of year. Despite attempts to reach ceasefires and restart the peace talks, violence confined largely to the West Bank and Gaza Strip persisted, claiming more than 300 Palestinian lives. Palestinian militias, including the Tanzim faction of Fatah and those associated with radical Islamic groups, carried out several ambush attacks and bombings against Israeli soldiers and settlers in Gaza and the West Bank. The use of roadside bombs by the Palestinians marked the introduction of new and more sophisticated tactical methods, ostensibly inspired by Hezbollah, the radical Shiite group that employed such tactics during its campaign against Israeli forces in southern Lebanon. Israel withdrew its troops from the area in June 2000.

In October, a Palestinian mob lynched two Israeli soldiers inside a police station in the West Bank city of Ramallah. Mobs also torched a synagogue in Jericho and destroyed Joseph's Tomb, a Jewish holy site in the West Bank.

Nearly 50 Israeli soldiers and civilians were killed by December 31. Israel blamed much of the violence on Palestinian radio and television broadcasts designed to incite attacks. Religious sermons calling for the death of all Jews and false reports of Israeli atrocities and impending attacks were routinely broadcast during the uprising. Israeli helicopter gunships attacked Palestinian transmitters in an effort to cease the inflammatory broadcasts.

In response to armed Palestinian attacks, including sustained shooting at homes in Gilo, a Jewish suburb of Jerusalem considered by Palestinians to be occupied land, Israel responded with heavy weapons, including helicopter-gunship and tank attacks on select Palestinian targets. Yassir Arafat's compound in Gaza was also hit by Israeli fire. While many attacks were preceded by warnings from the Israeli army to evacuate targeted areas, the Israeli Defense Forces adopted more offensive tactics as the uprising wore on; several top Palestinian military and militia figures suspected of orchestrating attacks against Israeli civilians and troops were killed in preemptive strikes, either by helicopter-gunships or commando units. Palestinians condemned Israel for the killings, regarding them as assassinations and war crimes.

The continuing violence underscored Palestinian leader Yassir Arafat's apparent loss of authority. After Arafat signed a cease-fire agreement with Israel in Sharm el-Sheik, Egypt, in October, Fatah leader Marwan Barghouti defied the Palestinian leader by declaring that the intifada would continue. Arafat's drop in popularity reflected increased factionalism; opinion polls indicated just 40 percent support for the Palestinian leader. Faced with rising criticism from the more radical Islamic camp, the PNA released from prison several members of Hamas and Islamic Jihad, including some who prepared bombs to explode civilian buses in Israel.

Government corruption and popular disaffection with the peace process have benefited Hamas, an Islamic group whose military wing is largely responsible for terrorist attacks against Israel. Vocal opposition to Israel and to Oslo has turned Hamas into a political alternative to Arafat's Fatah party.

Allegations of corruption and abuse of power have been increasingly problematic for Arafat's government. His autocratic tendencies have put him at odds with the legislative council. He frequently scuttles the legislative process or refuses to sign council rules into law.

Political Rights and Civil Liberties:

Palestinian residents of the West Bank, Gaza, and Jerusalem chose their first popularly elected government in 1996. Despite some irregularities, international observers regarded the vote as reasonably reflective of the will of the voters. The legislative council has complained of being marginalized by executive authority; though it has debated hundreds of draft laws, few have been signed into law. The Palestinian government indefinitely postponed local elections in May 1998, citing the threat of Israeli interference. However, most believe that democratic municipal elections would reflect widespread Palestinian disillusionment both with Oslo and with Arafat's leadership.

Although the Council passed a Basic Law in 1997, Arafat has yet to approve it. Such a law would outline the separation between legislative and executive authority and presumably curtail Arafat's own authority.

The PNA judiciary, consisting of criminal, civil, and state security courts, is not independent. According to a 2000 Human Rights Watch report, "the judiciary suffered from a severe lack of resources and executive branch interference, and trials fell far short of international fair trial standards." Zuheir Sourani was appointed attorney general in June 1999. The post had been vacant for 13 months after Fayez Abu Rahma resigned in April 1998 because of what he called continuous intervention by the minister of justice and the security services in judicial matters. In June 1999, LAW (Palestinian Society for the Protection of Human Rights) published a study charging interference of the executive branch into the Palestinian judiciary, citing the dismissal of judges critical of the executive branch.

Palestinian judges lack proper training and experience. Israeli demands for a Palestinian crackdown on terrorism have given rise to state security courts, which lack almost all due process rights. Suspected Islamic militants are rounded up en masse and often held without charge or trial. There are reportedly hundreds of administrative detainees currently in Palestinian jails and detention centers. The same courts are also used to try those suspected of collaborating with Israel or of drug trafficking. Defendants are not granted the right to appeal sentences and are often summarily tried and sentenced to death. Executions often take place immediately after sentencing.

Palestinian security forces routinely abuse, and sometimes torture, detainees. This practice is not prohibited under Palestinian law.

Palestinians accused by Israel of security offenses in Israeli-controlled areas are tried in Israeli military courts. Security offenses are broadly defined. Some due process protections exist in these courts, though there are limits on the right to counsel, bail, and the right to appeal. Administrative detention is widely used. Most convictions in Israeli military courts are based on confessions, which are often obtained through torture. Confessions are usually spoken in Arabic and translated into Hebrew for official records. Palestinian detainees seldom read Hebrew and thus sign confessions that they cannot read.

In September 1999, the Israeli supreme court outlawed the routine use of torture by the Israeli General Security Services (GSS) during the interrogation of suspected terrorists.

Israel continued to expand existing Jewish settlements in the West Bank and Gaza Strip in 2000. Some Palestinian structures built without permits were destroyed. Building permits are difficult for West Bank Palestinians to obtain. During the Palestinian uprising, Israeli forces destroyed several homes and olive groves providing cover for Palestinian gunmen.

Israel faced intense international criticism for its handling of the Palestinian uprising. Amnesty International, Human Rights Watch, and the United Nations condemned Israel for employing excessive lethal force against Palestinian demonstrators, pointing out that many demonstrators, especially stone-throwing youths, were shot in the upper body with live ammunition. Israel claimed it was pursuing a policy of restraint, pointing out that it provided prior warning before striking certain Palestinian targets in order to clear civilians from target areas. It also defended its policy of ambushing those thought to be planning terror attacks on the grounds that the strikes were precise and deliberately designed to avoid civilian casualties. Amnesty International criticized the PNA for not restraining children from participating in the demonstrations. Palestinian security forces were also criticized for not reining in militias whose armed attacks against Israelis further endangered Palestinian civilians. Palestinian militias carried out several ambush-style executions of fellow Palestinians suspected of collaborating with Israel.

Closures of the West Bank and Gaza Strip prevented more than 100,000 Palestinian day laborers from reaching their jobs in Israel. Restriction of movement between and among Palestinian towns and cities were denounced as collective punishment.

In September, Amnesty International criticized the PNA over the routine arrest and torture of critics. Over the last six years, dozens of journalists, religious figures, and academics have been arrested for publicly criticizing the PNA. Earlier, in April, a group of Palestinian academics, legislators, and politicians condemned the detention of Arafat critic Abdel-Sattar Qassim, arrested in November 1999 for signing a statement denouncing Arafat's tolerance of corruption in the PNA. Eventually released, Qassim was subsequently detained again in February 2000.

Under a 1995 Palestinian press law, journalists may be fined and jailed and newspapers closed for publishing "secret information" on Palestinian security forces or news that might harm national unity or incite violence. However, another press law, also signed in 1995, stipulates that Palestinian intelligence services do not reserve the right to interrogate, detain, or arrest journalists on the basis of their work. Still, several small media outlets are pressured by authorities to provide favorable coverage of Arafat and the PNA. Arbitrary arrests, threats, and physical abuse of journalists critical of the PNA are routine. Official Palestinian radio and television are government mouthpieces.

Chairman Arafat has yet to ratify a 1996 law passed by the Palestinian legislative council, that guarantees freedom of expression.

In October 2000, Reporters Sans Frontiéres (RSF) protested threats issued by Palestinian intelligence agents against Khaled Amayreh, editor in chief of *Akhbar el-Kihalil* newspaper. Amayreh was questioned after publishing an editorial critical of the Palestinian leadership. According to RSF, since 1995, more than 50 Palestinian journalists have been arrested and more than 20 assaulted by Palestinian security forces. In a special report released in November by the Committee to Protect Journalists (CPJ), Palestinian security forces were accused of harassing journalists and suppressing coverage critical of Chairman Arafat. In the same report, CPJ documented several cases in which journalists covering the uprising in the West Bank and Gaza were shot by Israeli and/or Palestinian forces.

Newspapers are subject to Israeli censorship on security matters, though such control has eased since 1993. Israeli authorities prohibit expressions of support for Hamas and other groups that call for the destruction of Israel.

The Israeli government limits freedom of assembly; military orders ban public gatherings of ten or more persons without a permit, though they are generally only enforced with regard to Palestinians. The PNA requires permits for rallies and demonstrations and prohibits violence and racist sloganeering. Private Palestinian organizations must register with Israeli authorities. In the PNA, Palestinian and pro-Islamic organizations that oppose Arafat's government have been harassed and detained. In March, Palestinian police banned unlicensed public marches and meetings after stone-throwing students in the West Bank attacked visiting French premier Lionel Jospin.

Despite the creation in October 1999 of a safe passage route allowing Palestinians to travel more freely between the West Bank and Gaza, their movements were severely curtailed as a result of the renewed intifada. Israel controls the route, and Palestinians must have valid permits to travel along it.

All West Bank and Gaza residents must have identification cards in order to obtain entry permits into Israel and Jerusalem. Israel often denies permits to applicants with no explanation. Even senior Palestinian officials are subject to long delays and searches at Israeli West Bank checkpoints. Israel frequently seals off the West Bank and Gaza in response to terrorist attacks, preventing tens of thousands of Palestinians from traveling to their jobs in Israel.

The border closings imposed throughout most of the uprising exacted a serious toll on the Palestinian economy. According to the UN, the Palestinian economy lost $8.6 million per day during closures. Approximately 38 percent of the workforce was unemployed, up from only 11 percent before the uprising began. The persistent violence caused a 50 percent increase in the poverty rate, to 32 percent of the population.

Palestinian women are underrepresented in most professions and encounter discrimination in employment. Under *Sharia* (Islamic law), women are disadvantaged in marriage, divorce, and inheritance matters. Rape, domestic abuse, and "honor killings," in which unmarried women thought not to be virgins are murdered by male relatives, continue. Since societal pressures prevent reporting of such incidents, the exact frequency of attacks is unknown.

Labor affairs in the West Bank and Gaza are governed by a combination of Jordanian law and PNA decisions pending the enactment of new Palestinian labor codes. Workers may establish and join unions without government authorization. Palestinian workers seeking to strike must submit to arbitration by the PNA Ministry of Labor. There are no laws in the PNA-ruled areas to protect the rights of striking workers. Palestinian workers in Jerusalem are subject to Israeli labor law.

The PNA generally respects freedom of religion, though no law exists protecting religious expression. Some Palestinian Christians have experienced intimidation and harassment by radical Islamic groups and PNA officials. On several occasions during the renewed intifada, Israel restricted the right of Muslim men under the age of 40 from praying on the Temple Mount compound in Jerusalem's Old City, for fear of violent confrontations.

Moldova
Transnistria

Polity: Presidential **Political Rights:** 6
Economy: Statist (transitional) **Civil Liberties:** 6
Population: 700,000 **Status:** Not Free
Ethnic Groups: Russian and Ukrainian (53 percent),
Moldovan-Romanian (40 percent), other (7 percent)

Overview: In the year 2000, the Dnestr Moldovan Republic (DMR), a breakaway region in the eastern part of Moldova, celebrated its tenth anniversary of self-declared independence. (In Moldovan, the region is called Transnistria.) Despite continued negotiations among high-level officials from Moldova, Ukraine, Russia, the DMR, and the Organization for Security and Cooperation in Europe (OSCE), the region's political status remained unresolved at year's end. In fact, DMR president Igor Smirnov strengthened his resolve in 2000 that the region should be a "sovereign and independent state." The DMR held elections for the entire 43-seat Supreme Soviet in December.

When the Moldovian Soviet Socialist Republic declared independence from the Soviet Union in 1991, pro-Russian separatists in Transnistria feared that Moldova would join with Romania. They reacted by declaring independence, establishing the DMR, and setting up an authoritarian presidential system. With weapons and other assistance from Russia's Fourteenth Army, the DMR leadership also fought a military conflict with Chisinau that ended with a 1992 ceasefire.

Representatives of the OSCE, Russia, and Ukraine have been acting as mediators in the negotiations between Moldova and the DMR. They also participate in the Joint Control Commission that monitors compliance with the ceasefire. Despite multiple agreements and memorandums of understanding since 1992, the question of DMR's political status remains unsettled.

In 1999, the two sides agreed to build relations based on common borders and shared economic, legal, defense, and social domains. In 2000, the OSCE stepped up its efforts to resolve the situation in Transnistria and sponsored several high-level meetings. Moldova and Russia formed special state committees to coordinate DMR-related policies. And former Russian foreign minister Yevgeny Primakov, who heads Russia's new committee, proposed the creation of a "common state" in which Moldova and the DMR would maintain separate constitutions, branches of government, armies, flags, and national anthems. The common state would share responsibility for foreign policy and border guards. Despite Moldova's willingness to negotiate Primakov's plan, the DMR leadership refused to attend several meetings. Ultimately, long-standing differences over DMR autonomy forestalled progress in 2000, although officials from both sides agreed in December to resume negotiations.

The failure of Russia to withdraw its Fourteenth Army has delayed resolution of the region's status. In 1994, Russia and Moldova agreed to a three-year timetable for removing all troops and arms, but Russia failed to meet the goal. In 1999, Russia agreed to complete the army's withdrawal by 2002. With more than two thousand troops and approximately 40,000 tons of weapons still in the region, Russia finally resumed its withdrawal in November 2000. Russian president Vladimir Putin surprised the DMR leadership earlier in the year when he stated publicly that Moscow views Transnistria as part of Moldova.

The year 2000 was also marked by President Smirnov's efforts to increase his power. In the summer, for example, he dismissed the government and appointed a new cabinet that will act as a consultative body rather than share joint leadership. The Supreme Soviet was transformed into a unicameral body with 43 members in 2000. In the December elections, supporters of Smirnov—including 7 candidates from the *Obnovleniye* (Renewal) bloc and 25 independent candidates—proved victorious. Two opposition groups, the *Edinstvo* (Unity) bloc and the *Vlast Narodu* (Power to the People) bloc, won 9 seats and 1 seat, respectively. Russian legislators and officials from disputed republics in Georgia and Armenia served as observers. Despite their differences, members of the new body unanimously support Transnistrian independence and the presence of Russia's military.

Political Rights and Civil Liberties:

Residents of Transnistria cannot elect their leaders democratically. They are also unable to participate freely in Moldovan elections. Parliamentary elections in December 2000 resulted in a victory for President Smirnov's supporters and the reelection of Grigori Marakusa as chairman of the unicameral Supreme Soviet. Marakusa has held this position continuously since 1990. Two opposition parties received a mandate. In the region's 1996 presidential election, incumbent Smirnov defeated challenger Vladimir Malakhov with 72 percent of the vote. While the DMR maintains its own legislative, executive and judicial branches of government, no country recognizes its sovereignty.

DMR authorities control most print and electronic media in Transnistria and restrict freedom of speech. While independent newspapers and television stations do exist, they frequently experience harassment for criticizing the DMR government. Authorities have also confiscated copies of independent newspapers without court orders.

The government restricts most political rights and civil liberties including freedom of association and assembly. Trade unions are holdovers from the Soviet-era, and the United Council of Labor Collectives works closely with the government. Authorities have denied registration to some religious groups and prevented them from distributing literature or leading public meetings.

DMR authorities discriminate again ethnic Moldovans, who make up 41 percent of the region's population. For example, the government has forced schools to teach Romanian using the Cyrillic rather than the Latin alphabet. In 1999, though, the first Romanian-language school opened in Tiraspol.

The local judiciary is not independent. Politically motivated killings and police harassment have been reported, and political prisoners are frequently denied access to lawyers. Police can detain suspects for up to 30 days. In 2000, the DMR introduced a moratorium on capital punishment which effectively stayed the execution of Ilie Illascu, a member of the "Tiraspol Six" opposition group that was convicted in 1993 for the killings of two separatist leaders. The OSCE and other international observers have charged that the trials did not meet international standards. Still in prison, Illascu gave up his Moldovan parliamentary seat in 2000 and accepted one in the Romanian parliament. He accused Moldovan authorities of deliberately dragging their feet in talks with the DMR.

Morocco
Western Sahara

Polity: Appointed governors
Economy: Capitalist
Population: 240,000
Ethnic Groups: Arab, Berber

Political Rights: 7
Civil Liberties: 6
Status: Not Free

Overview:
United Nations-sponsored talks between Moroccan officials and the Popular Front for the Liberation of Saguia el-Hamra and Rio de Oro (Polisario) failed to bring a referendum on the status of Western Sahara closer to fruition. UN Secretary-General Kofi Annan and his envoy for Western Sahara, former U.S. Secretary of State James Baker, were deeply pessimistic about the chances of the referendum being held at all, and Annan even questioned the wisdom of a poll whose results might go unrecognized by one party and might prove unenforceable. As the mediator of talks, Baker raised the possibility of limited autonomy for Western Sahara under Moroccan sovereignty. The Polisario rejected that option, and the deadlock continued.

Morocco and Mauritania partitioned Western Sahara in 1976 under a tripartite agreement with Spain, which had ruled the territory as a colony for 92 years. The Algerian-based Polisario opposed the partition with guerrilla units recruited largely from nomadic tribes indigenous to the region. The weaker of the two occupying forces, Mauritania signed a peace agreement with the Polisario in 1979, prompting Morocco to seize Mauritania's section of the territory.

The Polisario continued its guerrilla war against Morocco until 1991, when the UN Mission for a Referendum in Western Sahara (MINURSO) was established to oversee the details of an independence referendum. Since then, progress on voter identification and registration has been hindered by disputes over the composition of electoral lists. Morocco has been accused of padding voter lists with its own citizens in order to influence the referendum result. The UN voter-identification commission completed a list of 86,381 eligible voters in December 1999, but began hearing appeals from rejected pro-Morocco applicants, who number around 100,000, in January 2000. The appeals process is expected to take at least two years.

With the referendum at least two years away and refugee and security issues still unsettled, Annan sent Baker to mediate talks between Polisario and Moroccan officials throughout the year. Baker's suggestion of limited self-rule within Morocco met with disapproval from both sides, even though Morocco has always opposed a referendum. Meanwhile, international pressure for a solution increased. Algerian president Abdelaziz Bouteflika and King Mohammad of Morocco both realize that the dispute hampers investment, foreign aid, and bilateral relations. The U.S. Congress has threatened to end funding to MINURSO, which has cost nearly $500 million over nine years. In November, Annan announced his intention to go ahead with the referendum if Morocco fails to propose an alternative political solution.

Political Rights and Civil Liberties: Sahrawis have never been allowed to elect their own government. The four provinces of Western Sahara have held local elections organized and controlled by the Moroccan government, and pro-Moroccan Sahrawis fill the seats reserved for Western Sahara in the Moroccan legislature. About 165,000 civilian Sahrawi refugees and Polisario rebels live in four refugee camps in the desert outside Tindouf, Algeria. Called the Sahrawi Arab Democratic Republic (SADR), the territory has its own constitution, army, police force, national anthem, flag, and embassies in several countries.

Sahrawis are subject to Moroccan law. Since inheriting the Moroccan throne in July 1999, King Mohammad has tried to win the support of Sahrawis. He established an advisory council on the territory and set up a fund to finance projects in Western Sahara aimed at easing unemployment and other social problems. He also fired his interior minister, a long-time loyalist of former King Hassan who was responsible for the brutal administration of Western Sahara. Human rights groups report greater freedom from repression, but arbitrary arrests, unfair trials, and torture by Moroccan security forces continue. The legal maximum limit of 72 hours for incommunicado detention is not always respected. Amnesty International cites numerous cases of political prisoners detained for years following unfair trials, including that of Mohamed Daddach, a Sahrawi who has been in prison since 1979 for attempting to desert the Moroccan security forces, into which he had reportedly been forcibly enlisted.

More than 900 people "disappeared" at the hands of Moroccan security forces between the mid-1960s and the early 1990s. Though the government has released hundreds of Sahrawis after keeping them for years in secret detention centers, some 450 more remain unaccounted for. Another 70 are known by international human rights groups to have died in detention, but their deaths have not been acknowledged by the government. According to Amnesty International, many of those formerly disappeared are denied compensation or means of redress for their treatment by the government and are often intimidated or re-arrested by security forces.

Freedoms of assembly, expression, and association are severely restricted in Western Sahara, where criticism of the government and opposition activities are not tolerated. Political parties, nongovernmental organizations, and private media are virtually nonexistent, and suspected pro-independence activists and opponents of the government, including former political prisoners, are subject to surveillance and harassment. Beatings and ill-treatment of demonstrators have been reported. Violent confrontations in two towns between Moroccan security forces and Sahrawi student demonstrators were reported in March. The Western Sahara Referendum Support Association, based in Spain, reported that at least 56 Sahrawis were injured in the unrest.

Torture and other abuses by Polisario forces, including arbitrary killings, have been reported. However, verification of these reports is difficult because of scant access to areas under Polisario control. According to the International Committee of the Red Cross, the Polisario holds more than 1,900 Moroccan prisoners of war, most of whom have been held for more than 20 years. The group has released around 800 prisoners since the 1991 ceasefire, including 200 in December, as a gesture of goodwill.

Russia
Chechnya

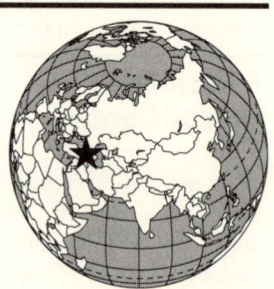

Polity: Presidential
Economy: Mixed statist
Population: 500,000 (est.)
Ethnic Groups: Chechen majority, small Russian minority

Political Rights: 7
Civil Liberties: 7
Status: Not Free

Overview:

Despite early pronouncements by Moscow of a quick victory over the breakaway territory, Russian troops exercised only nominal control over most of Chechnya by the end of 2000. Following the Russian capture of Grozny in February and the flight of most Chechen separatists to southern mountain strongholds, the conflict turned into a protracted guerilla-style war, with almost daily reports of rebel attacks against Russian soldiers. The increasingly demoralized and ill-equipped Russian army continued to commit serious human rights violations against the republic's civilian population, while plans to begin reconstruction of the devastated republic and repatriate tens of thousands of refugees displaced by the fighting remained unfulfilled at year's end.

A small Northern Caucasus republic covered by flat plains in the north-central portion and by high mountains in the south, Chechnya has been at war with Russia almost continuously since the late 1700s. After the Russian Revolution in 1917, Chechnya engaged in a succession of anti-Soviet uprisings. In February 1944, the Chechens were deported en masse to Kazakhstan under the pretext of their having collaborated with Germany during World War II. Although rehabilitated by Nikita Khrushchev in 1957 and allowed to return to their homeland, they continued to be politically suspect and were excluded from the region's administration.

In his first decree as head of state after his election as Chechnya's president in October 1991, former Soviet Air Force Commander Dzhokhar Dudayev proclaimed Chechnya's independence on November 1. Moscow responded by instituting an economic blockade of the republic and engaging in political intimidation of the territory's leadership.

Following clashes with parliament in June 1992, to which elections had been held in October 1991, Dudayev announced the introduction of direct presidential rule. Parliament was dissolved in June 1993, sparking a battle between parliamentary supporters and Dudayev's national guard. Although the legislature was eventually restored, power remained largely in the hands of Dudayev, whose rule was marked by corruption and the rise of powerful clans and criminal gangs.

In 1994, Russia began overtly to assist Chechen figures opposed to Dudayev with the aim of overthrowing the territory's president. Low-intensity conflicts developed in July, and fighting escalated in September. Citing the need to protect Moscow's national security and important economic interests, such as railways and energy pipelines connecting Russia and Azerbaijan through Chechnya, Yeltsin sent 40,000 Russian troops into Chechnya by mid-December 1994 and attacked the capital city on New Year's Eve.

As Chechen resistance grew, Russian forces intensified the shelling of Grozny and other population centers throughout 1995, with civilians becoming frequent targets. Chechen forces regrouped, making significant gains against ill-trained, undisciplined, and demoralized Russian troops. Russian public opposition to the war increased, fueled by criticism from much of the country's media. An agreement calling for an immediate cease-fire and demilitarization of the republic was signed by Russia and Chechnya in July, although the shaky truce failed to hold as clashes continued. In April 1996, President Dudayev reportedly was killed by a Russian missile.

With mounting Russian casualties, successful Chechen raids into Russia proper, and no imminent victory for Moscow, a peace deal was signed in August 1996. While calling for the withdrawal of most Russian forces from the breakaway territory, the document postponed a final settlement on the republic's status until 2001. Russia had suffered a humiliating defeat against the much smaller Chechen forces, while Chechnya's formal economy and infrastructure were virtually destroyed. The war had been marked by serious human rights violations committed by Russian government forces, as well as reported abuses by armed Chechen opposition groups.

On January 27, 1997, moderate Chechen Chief of Staff Aslan Maskhadov was elected president over 12 other candidates, including his principal rival, field commander Shamil Basayev. Concurrent national legislative elections ushered in the fifth parliament since 1990, as none of the previous ones had lasted their full term. Maskhadov, who subsequently named Basayev acting prime minister, sought to maintain Chechen sovereignty while pressing Moscow to help rebuild the republic. On May 12, Yeltsin and Maskhadov signed an accord that included a reference to Moscow's recognition of Maskhadov as Chechnya's legitimate president.

Throughout 1998, Basayev and other former field commanders formed an unruly opposition of often competing warlords, removing large areas of Chechnya from Maskhadov's control. Maskhadov's weakness was illustrated by a series of kidnappings and hostage-takings of foreign nationals, some of which were conducted by criminal gangs and others by militia groups attempting to discredit Chechnya's president.

In early August 1999, a group of more than 1,000 Chechen guerillas crossed into the neighboring republic of Dagestan, seizing several towns and declaring their intention to unite Chechnya and Dagestan as an independent Islamic state. Russian troops soon recaptured the villages and claimed to have driven the guerillas back into bases in Chechnya by late September. A few weeks later, a string of deadly bombings in Moscow and two other Russian cities killed nearly 300 people. Although the Kremlin blamed the attacks on Chechen militants, both the Chechen government and rebel groups denied any involvement.

In what was described by Moscow as an operation to destroy the Chechen guerillas, the Kremlin ordered air strikes on key Chechen military installations and economic targets in late September, and the subsequent deployment of ground troops in Chechnya. Although Russian troops advanced rapidly over the largely flat terrain in the northern third of the republic, their progress slowed considerably as they neared the heavily defended city of Grozny, which they entered in mid-December but had failed to capture by year's end. In a notable policy shift, then Russian Prime Minister Vladimir Putin in early October effectively withdrew Moscow's long-standing recognition of President Maskhadov as the republic's main legitimate authority.

Russia's increasingly deliberate and indiscriminate bomb attacks on civilian targets caused more than 200,000 people to flee Chechnya, most to the tiny neighboring republic of Ingushetia. In Grozny, tens of thousands of mostly elderly and infirm residents remained trapped in basements during the deadly air and artillery strikes. While Western governments and international organizations expressed growing condemnation of the attacks, the campaign enjoyed broad popular support in Russia, fueled by the media's one-sided reporting favoring the official government position.

In what Moscow declared to be a major turning point in the war, Russian troops finally captured the largely destroyed city of Grozny in early February 2000. As thousands of Chechen separatists fled the capital, the Russian military turned its offensive against the remaining rebel strongholds in the southern mountain region. Only days after the capture of the separatist-controlled town of Shatoi in early March had prompted Moscow to declare victory in Chechnya, rebels ambushed and killed a group of soldiers near Grozny. While Russian troops conducted air and artillery raids against towns suspected of harboring large numbers of Chechen fighters, frequently followed by often indiscriminate "mopping up" operations to check for remaining rebels, they became subject to almost daily guerilla bomb and sniper attacks by rebel forces. Chechen separatists also targeted and sometimes killed local Muslim officials who supported the pro-Moscow Chechen administration, including conducting a December assault on the office of the pro-Moscow mayor of Grozny, Bislan Gantamirov.

The international community continued to issue periodic condemnations of Moscow's operation in Chechnya. In April, the Council of Europe's Parliamentary Assembly voted to suspend Russia's voting rights in the organization, while the United Nations Human Rights Commission censured Russia for having committed "gross, widespread, and flagrant violations" of human rights in the breakaway republic.

In August, Aslanbek Aslakhanov, a retired police general, was elected with a reported 30 percent of the vote over 12 other candidates to represent Chechnya in Russia's parliament. Intense fighting had prevented voting from taking place in the breakaway territory during the nationwide legislative vote in December 1999. Human rights groups criticized the August election, which was run by the Russian military and during which no outside election observers were present, for being held while the war continued.

Following growing complaints that millions of rubles earmarked for reconstruction of the devastated republic had disappeared, Moscow appointed a special minister in late November to oversee Chechnya's socioeconomic development. However, most observers agree that a lasting solution will not be found as long as the current conflict continues.

Political Rights and Civil Liberties: With the resumption of war in Chechnya in 1999, residents of the republic currently do not have the means to change their government democratically. The 1997 presidential elections were characterized by international observers to have been reasonably free and fair. President Aslan Maskhadov fled the capital city in December 1999, and the parliament elected in 1997 ceased to function. Russia placed Moscow loyalists or Chechens opposed to Maskhadov's central government in various administrative posts throughout the republic. In June 2000, Putin enacted a decree establishing direct presidential rule over Chechnya, appointing Akhmed Kadyrov, a Muslim cleric and Chechnya's spiritual leader, to head the republic's administration. However, Kadyrov was denounced by Maskhadov and separatist Chechens as a traitor, while pro-Moscow Chechens objected to his support during the first Chechen war for the republic's independence.

The Russian military continued to impose severe restrictions on journalists' access to the Chechen war zone, issuing accreditation primarily to those of proven loyalty to the Russian government. In March 2000, Russia's information ministry issued a warning that journalists who interview Chechen leaders would be in violation of Russia's anti-terrorism laws. Few foreign reporters are allowed into the breakaway republic. The disruptive effects of the war, including limited electricity and other vital services and the displacement of large numbers of people, severely hinder news production and the flow of information to the general public. In late September 1999, Grozny's television station was damaged by Russian bomb attacks.

In February 2000, Russian agents announced that they had destroyed a television transmitter used by the rebel Kavkaz station; since then, Kavkaz bulletins have been distributed by hand on videotape. In May 2000, Russian security forces arrested Vakha Dadulagov, the editor of an underground Chechen newspaper *Ichkeria*, and charged him with inciting racial hatred. The following month, the paper's printing press was discovered by authorities and destroyed. In early June 2000, journalist Taisa Isaeva of the Chechen-Press news agency, which has been based in neighboring Georgia since March 2000, was arrested by Russian authorities, who claim that she was involved in several kidnapping incidents during the past several years.

Muslims enjoy freedom of worship, although the Wahhabi sect, a group with roots in Saudi Arabia and characterized by a strict observance of Islam, has been banned. Most religious Chechens practice Sufiism, a mystical form of Islam characterized by the veneration of local saints and by groups practicing their own rituals.

Since the resumption of war, the rule of law has become virtually nonexistent. Civilians have been subject to harassment and violence, including extrajudicial executions, at the hands of Russian soldiers. Human rights groups have charged that Russian soldiers have arbitrarily detained hundreds of men and that civilians have been tortured, beaten, and raped at Russian "filtration camps." Refugees who have returned to their homes have reported widespread looting by Russian troops and confiscation of their personal belongings, while Russian military authorities have shown general disregard for these abuses.

Travel both within and outside of the republic is severely restricted. Moscow officially closed the territory's borders following the resumption of war. The Russian military consistently failed to provide safe exit routes for many civilians out of the conflict zones. Refugees often faced long waits at border checkpoints or were forced to pay bribes to cross. Many Chechens, including those in Russian-occupied areas, fear to travel even short distances because of land mines and reports of Russian pilots shooting randomly at passing civilians. In January 2000, Russia's military commander in Chechnya issued an order proclaiming that only girls, women, and males under the age of 10 or over 60 would be considered refugees. Males between the ages of 10 and 60 would be forbidden from entering or leaving the republic and would have to undergo rigorous checks in detention centers for any guerilla affiliations. By the end of 2000, most of the refugees who had fled to Ingushetia had not returned to Chechnya because of lack of work and basic social services and fears for their personal safety.

Widespread corruption and the economic devastation caused by the war severely limit equality of opportunity. Ransoms obtained from kidnapping, counterfeiting, and the production of low-quality fuel out of oil stolen from pipelines provide money for guerillas and criminal elements. Residents of Russian-occupied areas report that many basic social and other services still have not been restored, as promised by Moscow. In November 2000, teachers in Chechen secondary schools began a strike to protest wage arrears of six months.

While women continue to face discrimination in a traditional male-dominated culture, the war has resulted in many women becoming the primary breadwinners for their families. According to Human Rights Watch, Russian soldiers rape Chechen women in areas controlled by the Russian military.

Turkey
Cyprus (T)

Polity: Presidential parliamentary democracy (Turkish-occupied)
Economy: Mixed capitalist
Population: 180,000
Ethnic Groups: Turkish Cypriot, Turkish, Greek Cypriot, Maronite

Political Rights: 2*
Civil Liberties: 2
Status: Free

Ratings Change: Turkish Cyprus' political rights rating changed from 4 to 2, and its status from Partly Free to Free, partially as a technical adjustment. However, the new score also reflects the increased activism of opposition parties, nongovernmental groups, and trade unions on the political stage, as well as a slight relaxation of travel restrictions.

Note: See Cyprus (Greek) under country reports

Overview: United Nations-sponsored proximity talks between Greek Cypriot leader Glafcos Clerides and Turkish Cypriot leader Rauf Denktash continued in 2000 but produced no new agreements. Denktash narrowly won reelection in April when his closest challenger, Turkish Cypriot prime minister Dervis Eroglu, withdrew from the race before a runoff vote. Denktash had won nearly 44 percent of the vote in the first round, short of the majority needed to win the election outright. The president faced an increasingly vocal opposition during the year, as massive demonstrations illustrated rising resentment of the Turkish army's role in the territory.

Annexed to Britain in 1914, Cyprus gained independence in 1960 after a ten-year guerrilla campaign demanding union with Greece. In July 1974, Greek Cypriot national guard members, backed by the military junta in power in Greece, staged an unsuccessful coup aimed at unification. Turkey invaded five days later, seized 37 percent of the island, and expelled 200,000 Greek Cypriots from the north. The Turkish Republic of Northern Cyprus (TRNC) declared its independence in 1982, but so far has been recognized only by Turkey, which maintains more than 35,000 troops in the territory and provides an estimated $200 million in annual assistance. The Green Line, a buffer zone controlled by a 1,200-strong UN peacekeeping force, has partitioned Cyprus since 1974. The capital, Lefkosa (Nicosia), remains the world's only divided capital city. Tensions and intermittent violence between the two populations have plagued the island since independence.

Negotiations on the future of the island have stalled over issues of security, territory, property and compensation, and the distribution of power on the island. The Greek Cypriots favor a federation with local autonomy, free movement, and a strong central government. Turkish Cypriots favor a confederation of two independent states, with shared bodies holding very limited powers. Instead of a central assembly, Turkish Cypriots propose a consultative council and joint overseas representation. Denktash refuses to meet directly with Clerides until Turkish Cyprus is internationally recognized as a state. Proximity talks broke down in 1997 when the European Union (EU) announced its decision to open accession negotiations with Greek Cyprus. Having been overlooked as a possible candidate for EU membership, Turkey strongly opposed this move. By the end of 1999, however, goodwill between Greece and Turkey in the aftermath of devastating earthquakes in both countries, and EU acceptance of Turkey as an official candidate for membership, brought the two sides back to the negotiating table.

The north is far less prosperous than the south. An embargo by the Greek Cypriots significantly hampers the northern economy. Turkish Cypriots' standard of living is roughly a third that of Greek Cypriots, and the north is almost totally reliant on the Cypriot Republic for a free but insufficient power supply that suffers frequent outages from 12 to 14 hours per day. However, a vibrant black market economy provides for a great deal of unaccounted for wealth.

The debate over the role of the Turkish army in the territory escalated during 2000 when Deputy Prime Minister Mustafa Akinci called for a constitutional amendment to make local police and firefighters accountable to the interior minister rather than the Turkish Cypriot armed forces, which are led by a Turkish general. The general responded by accusing Akinci of treason. A small left-wing newspaper, *Avrupa*, slammed the general and criticized the Turkish military presence in Cyprus. *Avrupa*'s editor, three journalists, and two others were then arrested on charges of espionage. On July 18, some 8,000 members of liberal political parties, trade unions, and NGOs took to the streets to protest the arrests, shouting anti-Denktash slogans and demanding the replacement of the army general. In September, another mass of protesters denounced Denktash's "intransigence" over the division of Cyprus, and in October, several thousand demonstrators rallied against a government spending package in a show of anger over economic dependence on Turkey. Turkish Cypriots' increasing disapproval of their leader weakens his position in negotiations for a settlement on the divided island.

Political Rights and Civil Liberties: Turkish Cypriots can change their government democratically. The TRNC's presidential-legislative system of government calls for the election of a leader and a national assembly every five years or less. Presidential elections have been considered generally free and fair by observers. The National Unity Party (UBP) took the most seats in the 50-member national assembly following December 1998 general elections. At least six other parties participated in those elections, four of them winning seats. Some 1,000 Greek and Maronite residents in the north are disenfranchised in Turkish Cypriot elections, but many vote in Cypriot Republic elections.

The judiciary is independent, and trials generally meet international standards of fairness. Civilians suspected of violating military zones are tried in military courts, which respect due process but have been accused of pro-military bias. Turkish Cypriot police sometimes flout due process rights and abuse and intimidate detainees. Detainees are ordinarily held no longer than 24 hours without charge.

Private newspapers and periodicals offer a wide range of views, while at least eight new private radio and three private television stations broadcast alongside government stations. International broadcasts are available without interference. The newspaper *Avrupa* has faced judicial harassment unprecedented in the TRNC for its criticism of Denktash, his policy on the division of the island, and the Turkish military presence in the territory. On May 26, 2000, hearings began before a criminal court on 75 lawsuits against the paper for "instigating hatred against the TRNC and the Turkish army." Four journalists from the paper were arrested in July for "espionage," and in November, *Avrupa*'s printing house was the target of an arson attack.

Advocates for Greek Cypriots living in the northern city of Karpassia claim that these individuals are denied freedom of movement, free speech, property ownership, and access to Greek media. Outstanding property claims arising from the 1974 division and population exchange remain an obstacle to a final peace and demilitarization settlement on the island. Approximately 85 percent of the land in the north is claimed by its original Greek Cypriot owners. In 1996, the European Court for Human Rights held Turkey responsible for denying a Greek Cypriot refugee access to her property since 1974. In 1998, the court ordered Turkey to pay her approximately $574,000 in compensation. Turkey has not yet complied.

Turkish Cypriot authorities generally respect freedom of assembly and association, and there are numerous political parties, trade unions, and nongovernmental organizations. About 99 percent of Turkish Cypriots are Sunni Muslim. There is a small Bahai community, and there are some 650 Greek Orthodox and Maronite residents in the north. All reportedly worship freely. Turkish Cypriots have difficulty traveling to other countries because travel documents issued by the TRNC are recognized only by Turkey. Some restrictions exist on travel to and from the south, but in May 2000 the Turkish Cypriot authorities eliminated the system of fees for crossing the buffer zone. Cypriots from both sides may freely visit religious sites in each other's territory.

A 1998 law grants Turkish Cypriot women who marry non-Muslim men a fair distribution of assets in case of divorce. Legal provisions that require equal pay for equal work are not respected in all sectors.

Workers may form independent trade unions, bargain collectively, and strike.

United Kingdom
Northern Ireland

Polity: Parliamentary democracy (Protestant/ Catholic power-sharing assembly)

Political Rights: 2*
Civil Liberties: 2*
Status: Free

Economy: Mixed capitalist
Population: 1,700,000
Ethnic Groups: Protestant [mostly Scottish and English descent], (57 percent), Irish Catholic (43 percent)
Ratings Change: Northern Ireland's political rights and civil liberties ratings changed from 3 to 2, and its status from Partly Free to Free, because of reduced sectarian violence, the functioning of the devolved Northern Ireland Assembly, a reduction of British troops in the territory, and efforts to reform policing.

Overview:

The peace process and the devolved government set out by the 1998 Good Friday Agreement were on shaky ground throughout most of 2000, as disputes over the decommissioning of weapons continued. The Irish Republican Army (IRA) refused to begin turning in its arms despite the admission of leaders of its political wing, Sinn Fein, to ministerial posts in the new government. The failure of the IRA to move on disarmament led to increasing unionist opposition to the power-sharing arrangement, even within the Ulster Unionist Party (UUP) of First Minister David Trimble. Trimble struggled throughout the year to salvage the peace process and maintain UUP support even as calls within his party to abandon the new government grew louder. By year's end, he had narrowly succeeded.

Northern Ireland comprises six of the nine counties of the Irish province of Ulster. At the insistence of the locally dominant Protestants, these counties remained part of the United Kingdom after the other 26 predominantly Catholic Irish counties gained independence in 1921. Catholics now constitute a majority in four of the six counties. The demographic trends have aroused anxiety among Protestants, who are largely descended from seventeenth-century Scottish and English settlers. Britain's 1920 Government of Ireland Act set up the Northern Irish parliament, which functioned until the British imposed direct rule in 1972.

Disorder resulting from a nonviolent Catholic civil rights movement in the 1960s prompted the deployment of British troops that remain in the territory today. Amid sectarian violence beginning in the 1970s, division grew within both the primarily Protestant unionist and Catholic nationalist communities. In addition to numerous political factions including the conservative UUP, the hardline Democratic Unionist Party (DUP), the interdenominational unionist Alliance Party, the moderate pro-nationalist Social Democratic and Labour Party (SDLP), and the nationalist Sinn Fein, paramilitary groups on both sides have engaged in terrorism.

Negotiations for a peace settlement began in June 1996, with Sinn Fein banned by Prime Minister John Major of Britain, pending a cessation and renunciation of violence by the IRA. British general elections in May 1997 brought significant gains for republicans and a new Labour government with a mandate to bolster the peace process. Sinn Fein took 17 percent of the Northern Ireland vote, while Tony Blair's Labour party won an overwhelming majority in the House of Commons. Blair immediately began to undertake confidence-building measures, such as reinstating official contacts between his government and Sinn Fein and repatriating republican prisoners from Northern Irish to Irish prisons. His efforts helped secure an IRA ceasefire, and Sinn Fein's participation in talks, in July 1997.

Intense determination by Blair and Irish prime minister Bertie Ahern kept negotiations on track despite a continuation of violence by paramilitary groups that had not declared ceasefires. U.S. president Bill Clinton sent his own envoy, former Senator George Mitchell, to chair negotiations. In April 1998, Mitchell presented a compromise plan that became the Good Friday Agreement. The agreement calls for a 108-member, directly elected Northern Ireland Assembly with full executive and legislative authority; a north-south council of Irish and Northern Irish officials to develop consultation, cooperation, and action on matters of mutual interest; and a council of British, Irish, Northern Irish, Scottish, and Welsh representatives to discuss particular policy issues. Perhaps most significantly, the Good Friday Agreement recognizes the "principle of consent," that is, that a united Ireland will not come about without the consent of a majority of people in both jurisdictions.

Elections to the new assembly took place in June 1998. Of almost 300 candidates representing 12 political parties, pro-agreement moderates and nationalists were the big winners. The UUP took 28 seats, while the Progressive Unionists (PUP), aligned with the UUP, took 2. The SDLP took 24, and Sinn Fein 18. Anti-agreement parties took 28 seats. The Alliance Party won 6 seats. Women candidates won just 12 seats. At the first session of the new legislature on July 1, David Trimble of the UUP and Seamus Mallon of the SDLP were elected first minister and deputy first minister, respectively. Britain officially handed power to the assembly in December 1999.

Disputes over the decommissioning of IRA weapons has stalled progress on peace and cooperation since negotiations began. Under the Good Friday Agreement, Sinn Fein led other participants to believe that steps toward disarmament would occur by February 2000. Not only did the IRA fail to take those steps, but, as many unionists pointed out, the IRA still had not explicitly and permanently renounced violence. The dispute led Britain to shut down the assembly and reassert control on February 11, 2000. In May, the IRA offered to open its arms dumps to independent inspection. Later that month, the IRA publicly stated its intention to put its arms "completely and verifiably beyond use." Although the statement included no actual concession, it was notable as the first time that the IRA had engaged in negotiations on its own behalf. Home rule was restored on May 29 under a British-Irish agreement that extended the IRA's disarmament deadline to 2001. Two DUP ministers boycotted their posts in protest of Sinn Fein's participation.

Increasing anti-agreement sentiment within the UUP created significant problems for David Trimble. During 2000, he faced five challenges to his leadership of the party, surviving as its leader by a narrow margin each time. The sentiment only intensified when the UUP suffered a disastrous defeat in a by-election in a South Antrim district that was traditionally a UUP stronghold. The seat went to the hardline, anti-agreement DUP. The issue of police reform created a political firestorm as unionists railed against proposed changes in the name and insignia of Northern Ireland's police force. Unionist demands that the British union flag fly over Belfast's official buildings on holidays sparked another protracted battle, as republicans demanded that the union flag be accompanied by the Irish tricolor. Each political fight left Trimble in a more precarious position. In October, he banned Sinn Fein from participating in the north-south ministerial council meetings pending IRA movement on disarmament. Despite this show of strength, the UUP plans to meet again in January 2001 to review progress on decommissioning. That meeting is likely to produce another challenge to Trimble and another opportunity for crisis in the Good Friday Agreement.

Despite the fragility of the Good Friday Agreement, there seems to be very little fear of a return to the scale of violence seen just a few years ago. Commentators speak of a sense of normalcy, and political leaders celebrate the beginning of "real politics." Indeed, competition among ministers for some six million pounds in funding from the British government delayed publication of the first government program of specific goals for the coming year. When finally published in October, the program was decidedly ordinary. It called for improvements in health care, education, and training; free public transportation for the elderly; economic competition; and the building of a north-south gas pipeline. However, perhaps the most striking evidence of transformation in Northern Ireland was pointed out by *The Economist* in November. Referring to Sinn Fein's decision to file a legal complaint against its ban from the north-south ministerial council, the magazine said, "When people who fairly recently threatened bloodshed, threaten instead to consult their lawyers, it is clear that Northern Ireland has come a long way."

Political Rights and Civil Liberties:

The people of Northern Ireland elected a 108-member legislature in free and fair elections in June 1998. The assembly has full executive and legislative power, though Britain maintains responsibility for defense and security.

The Good Friday Agreement specifically addresses a number of human rights issues. It requires the incorporation of the European Convention on Human Rights (ECHR) into Northern Irish law, so that aggrieved parties may take alleged violations of the convention to Northern Irish courts. It also requires Britain to promote equality in employment, to preserve and promote the Irish language, to reduce British troop deployments to peacetime levels, to establish an independent commission on police reform, and to appoint a body to review the criminal justice system. These reforms proceeded, but according to rights monitors, did not go far enough.

The British parliament passed the Police (Northern Ireland) Bill in November. Based on a report by an independent commission on police reform led by former Hong Kong governor Chris Patten, the law's most controversial provisions include changing the working title of the police force from the Royal Ulster Constabulary (RUC) to the more neutral Police Service of Northern Ireland, and changing the symbols used on police badges and uniforms. In addition, the law aims to create an equal ratio of Catholic and Protestant police officers, and to establish a policing board of 19 members, of which 10 would be nominated by the Northern Ireland assembly and 9 by the British Northern Ireland secretary. Human Rights Watch, along with nationalists, criticized the law for failing to incorporate several key provisions of the Patten report, including strong police accountability and protections for human rights.

Human Rights Watch also expressed concern over the failure of the Criminal Justice Review in its March report to address the effect of emergency law on the criminal justice system, to consider new judicial arrangements, to address issues arising from the passage of the Human Rights Act in 1998, and to include a provision for independent implementation of its report.

The Terrorism Act 2000 became law in July and will come into effect in 2001. The law replaces emergency laws throughout the United Kingdom and extends, for up to five years, most of the emergency provisions already in force in Northern Ireland, including nonjury Diplock courts for terrorist offenses; a lower standard of admissibility of confessions than in criminal courts; the interpretation of a suspect's silence as an admission of guilt; the imprisonment of suspected terrorists on the word of a senior police officer; and army and police powers of arrest, entry, search, and seizure without a warrant.

Sectarian violence has largely abated in Northern Ireland, although several attacks by loyalist and republican paramilitaries opposed to the Good Friday Agreement occurred. A feud between loyalist groups erupted in August in the lower Shankill Road area of Belfast. Before the paramilitary leaders called a truce in December, seven men had been killed, an 11-year-old girl shot, numerous people beaten, and homes attacked. Some 200 families were reportedly forced from their homes. Clashes also broke out during the annual summer marching season, when Protestant parades celebrate historic military victories over Catholics. The rerouting of one particular parade, away from a predominantly Catholic neighborhood in Portadown, County Armagh, by an independent parades commission led to massive riots and attacks on police by Protestants in July. Nobody was killed in the disturbances, but several police officers were injured.

Britain has shut down 32 military posts in Northern Ireland and has withdrawn nearly 4,000 soldiers. Current troop levels are comparable to those of the late 1960s, when organized sectarian violence began.

A new inquiry into the killings by British soldiers of 14 unarmed civil rights marchers in Londonderry on January 30, 1972, (Bloody Sunday) opened in March 2000. A previous tribunal was discredited after finding the army not liable for any of the killings. Also, the investigation continues into the August 1998 bombing in Omagh that killed 29 people and injured hundreds. The attack was allegedly carried out by the Real IRA, a republican splinter group. No prosecutions have taken place.

Anti-terror legislation may restrict the right of assembly, association, or freedom of expression, but it is not generally used to do so, and Northern Ireland enjoys a vibrant civil society. Women are well represented in the workplace and the professions, although domestic violence is considered to be a problem. The findings of a comprehensive study into racial prejudice in Northern Ireland were released in April. The study determined that racism is now twice as common as sectarianism, and that hostility is mainly directed at the traditional Irish nomadic Traveller community. In a University of Ulster survey of parents and children from racial minorities in schools, 66 percent of those interviewed reported racist name-calling and 13 percent reported physical harassment. A rising number of attacks on homosexuals led the RUC to announce in July the implementation of a monitoring system for homophobic incidents. Workers may bargain collectively and strike, and there are at least 33 trade unions in the territory.

United States
Puerto Rico

Polity: Parliamentary with elected governor
Economy: Capitalist
Population: 3,900,000
Ethnic Groups: Hispanic

Political Rights: 1
Civil Liberties: 2
Status: Free

Overview:

The year 2000 saw the election of a new governor whose platform was committed to the retention of Puerto Rico's status as a commonwealth of the United States as opposed to a change in status that would grant the island statehood. At the same time, the controversy over the use of the island of Vieques as a bombing target range by the U.S. Navy intensified.

Puerto Rico acquired the status of a commonwealth of the United States following approval by plebiscite in 1952. Under its terms, Puerto Rico exercises approximately the same control over its internal affairs as do the 50 U.S. states. Though U.S. citizens, residents cannot vote in presidential elections and are represented in the U.S. Congress by a delegate to the House of Representatives who can vote in committee but not on the floor. The commonwealth constitution, modeled after that of the U.S., provides for a governor and a bicameral legislature, consisting of a 28-member senate and a 54-member house of representatives, elected for four years. A supreme court heads an independent judiciary and the legal system is based on U.S. law.

Sila Maria Calderon of the pro-commonwealth Popular Democratic Party was elected governor, winning 48.5 percent of the vote against 45.7 percent for her main rival, Carlos Pesquera of the pro-statehood New Progressive Party (NPP). Calderon will succeed Pedro Rosello of the NPP, who had served two terms as governor. Calderon based her campaign on a pledge to end what she said was widespread corruption under the previous administration and to end a long-standing agreement that allowed the U.S. Navy to use the island of Vieques as a training ground and firing range.

The controversy over Vieques was triggered in 1999, when a Puerto Rican civilian was killed accidentally during a bombing exercise. The incident ignited protests by Puerto Ricans and stimulated a debate over American policy towards Puerto Rico. Protests continued during 1999 and into 2000. Eventually, Governor Rosello reached an agreement with the U.S. Navy that calls for the Navy to conduct a referendum that asks residents of Vieques whether they want the Navy to leave or whether they would allow service personnel to remain indefinitely in exchange for $50 million in economic aid. The referendum is scheduled for November 2001. Calderon, however, has vowed to hold a referendum before that date that would allow Vieques to eject the Navy immediately.

The island's relationship with the U.S. remains a fundamental issue. In a nonbinding 1993 referendum, voters narrowly opted to retain commonwealth status. Commonwealth status received 48.4 percent of the vote, statehood 46.3 percent, and independence 4.4 percent. The vote indicated significant gains for statehood, which in the last referendum, in 1967, received only 39 percent of the vote. Voters also opted for the status quo in a 1998 referendum. Although many more voters chose statehood over independence, the percentage who voted for no change in the island's status was greater than it had been in the 1993 referendum. In one of his last acts as president, Bill Clinton created a task force to study whether Puerto Rico should retain its current status, or become a state or an independent country.

Any vote to change the island's status would have to be approved by the U.S. Congress. As Washington seeks to cut the federal deficit, the benefits the island receives under Section 936 of the Internal Revenue Code will be phased out over the next ten years. This fundamental change in U.S.-Puerto Rican economic relations would mean the eventual end to a system in which subsidiaries of U.S. companies operating on the island receive income tax and wage credits. The tax-free status of interest earned on income would also be eliminated.

In 1999, Clinton provoked a controversy when he released eleven Puerto Rican nationalists who had been sentenced to long prison terms for their involvement in terrorist activities. The decision was made despite the strong objections of the Federal Bureau of Investigation. Although Puerto Ricans generally supported the clemency move, the release of the prisoners did not spark renewed interest in national independence on the island.

Political Rights and Civil Liberties: As U.S. citizens, Puerto Ricans are guaranteed all civil liberties granted in the U.S. The press and broadcast media are well developed, highly varied, and critical. In recent years, the Puerto Rican Journalists' Association has charged successive governments with denying complete access to official information. During 1998, a major controversy broke out between the Rosello administration and the island's largest newspaper, *El Nuevo Dia*. In March, the Inter-American Press Association urged the government to end an "ugly campaign of harassment" against the newspaper. The controversy was resolved when the government agreed to end the practice of using advertising to influence news coverage. Labor unions are well organized and have the right to strike.

The greatest cause for concern is the steep rise in criminal violence in recent years, much of which is drug related. Puerto Rico is now the Caribbean's main drug-transshipment point. Since mid-1993, about 80 public housing projects, or about two-fifths of the total, have been under the control of the National Guard, the first time U.S. military units have been routinely deployed to fight crime.

Yugoslavia
Kosovo

Polity: Internationally protectorate
Economy: Mixed-statist (transitional)
Population: 2,100,000 (est.)

Political Rights: 6
Civil Liberties: 6
Status: Not Free

Ethnic Groups: Albanians (over 90 percent), Serbs and Montenegrins (5 percent), others, including Roma, Bosniacs, Turks, Gorani (5 percent)
Capital: Pristina
Trend Arrow: Kosovo received a downward trend arrow because of violent persecution of ethnic minorities and attacks on the political opposition to the armed guerrillas involved in last year's conflict over Kosovo.

Overview:

Despite a large international presence in the disputed Yugoslav province, including a NATO-led international peacekeeping force of more than 40,000 troops, the position of ethnic minorities in Kosovo showed no improvement during the course of 2000. Similarly, politicians and political parties opposed to the armed guerrillas constituting the former Kosovo Liberation Army continued to be the targets of persistent attacks. Although municipal elections were held in the province on October 28, a systematic campaign of assassinations, kidnappings, and other forms of intimidation both before and after the elections overshadowed the victory of moderate forces in the elections.

Control over the Yugoslav province of Kosovo has been a source of conflict between Albanians and Serbs in the Balkans for most of the twentieth century. The latest round of tensions erupted in the early 1980s, soon after the death of the former Communist dictator of Yugoslavia, Josip Broz Tito. In 1981, Albanians in Kosovo began a series of demonstrations, in some cases asking that Kosovo be granted the status of an equal republic within the former Yugoslav federation, and in some cases demanding outright independence. In the late 1980s, Slobodan Milosevic rose to power promising to restore order in the province and to improve the position of the Serbs living there. In 1989 and 1990, a series of legislative and constitutional acts eliminated Kosovo's autonomy within the Yugoslav federation. Under the leadership of a pacifist literature scholar from Pristina, Ibrahim Rugova, the Kosovo Albanian population responded by withdrawing from the social and political life of the former Yugoslav federation and setting up an entire parallel society, replete with quasi-governmental institutions, hospitals, and school systems.

For much of the 1990s, an uneasy but generally nonviolent status quo was maintained. In late 1997, a shadowy guerrilla movement called the Kosovo Liberation Army (KLA) began a series of attacks on Serbian police forces, government officials, and Serb refugees in the province. The violence in the province continued to escalate, and in March 1999, NATO launched a 78-day air campaign against Yugoslavia to force it to accede to a settlement drafted by the international community. During the war, some 800,000 Kosovo Albanians fled the province, some forcibly expelled by Yugoslav security forces, others fleeing the NATO bombing itself. Under the terms of United Nations Security Council Resolution (UNSCR) 1244 of June 1999, Yugoslav forces withdrew from the province, and a NATO-led peacekeeping force assumed responsibility for security in Kosovo. UNSCR 1244 turned Kosovo into a protectorate of the international community, while officially maintaining Yugoslav sovereignty over the province.

Since international forces moved into Kosovo in mid-1999, a campaign of reverse ethnic cleansing has been taking place. More than 250,000 Serbs, Roma (Gypsies), Bosniacs, Croats, Turks, and Jews have been forced to flee the province, while the NATO-led peacekeeping force on the ground in Kosovo, the Kosovo Force (KFOR), has failed to improve the security situation for ethnic minorities in the province. Most of the non-Albanian population that remains in Kosovo live in small clusters of villages or in urban ghettoes under round-the-clock KFOR protection. The largest Serb population left in Kosovo is concentrated in a triangular-shaped piece of territory north of the Ibar River.

A similarly troubling problem has been the widespread and systematic terror campaign waged against political opponents of the officially disbanded KLA, aimed primarily at Rugova's Democratic League of Kosovo (LDK), as well as against individuals working against the business and criminal interests of former KLA members. In September, Rexhep Luci, Pristina's planning director, was assassinated after beginning a campaign to demolish illegally constructed buildings in Pristina. Despite these attacks, the LDK scored a significant victory in the municipal elections, winning approximately 60 percent of the votes cast. It remains unclear, however, whether the LDK can wrest effective control from more extreme elements within the province.

The overall failure of the international community to create a secure environment in the province has made Kosovo a European hub for Albanian organized-crime syndicates trafficking in narcotics, illegal aliens, stolen cars, and prostitutes.

Political Rights and Civil Liberties: According to UNSCR 1244, ultimate authority within the provinces resides with the UN Special Representative in the province, who is appointed by the UN secretary-general. The UN Mission in Kosovo (UNMIK) is responsible for implementing civilian aspects of the agreement ending the war. Under UNMIK's authority, municipal elections were held in October 2000, in which more than 50 parties competed. The elections were marred, however, by considerable violence, including numerous attacks against officials of Rugova's LDK party both before and after the vote. The Serbs, the largest ethnic minority in the province, estimated to number 100,000 to 150,000, boycotted the elections, citing concerns over freedom of movement to and from voting sites. The instability in the province has reduced the willingness of the international community to hold provincial elections for a local assembly, which were originally envisioned for 2001.

Freedom of expression is limited because of the overall lack of security in the province. In April, a newspaper linked to members of the former KLA printed the name, workplace, and photograph of a local Serb it had branded a "war criminal." Within two weeks, the individual in question had been stabbed to death. UNMIK responded by shutting down the paper for a few days, but the paper resumed operation soon thereafter and international authorities proved unable to stop it.

The Albanian population in Kosovo on the whole enjoys freedom of belief and religious association. Throughout the year, however, there were frequent attacks on

Orthodox churches and other holy sites associated with the Serb population. Officially, freedom of association exists, but throughout 2000, extremists frequently disrupted gatherings of political opponents.

Kosovo lacks a functioning criminal justice system. By mid-2000, a year after NATO occupied the province, more than 500 murders had taken place in Kosovo, but there had not been a single conviction. Witnesses are frequently intimidated or killed, and judges are afraid to rule against local extremists. UNMIK plans to bring international judges into the province and to call up more international police, but the response has been poor. Several leading members of the formally disbanded KLA are under investigation for war crimes by the International Tribunal for the Former Yugoslavia (ICTY) for actions committed before, during, and after the NATO intervention.

During last year's war, Yugoslav forces often intentionally destroyed many land registries and personal documents belonging to the Albanian population. In postwar Kosovo it has been difficult to prove legal ownership of various forms of property. Expropriations from individuals (generally ethnic minorities) of their apartments or houses are commonplace. Racketeers connected to local authorities extort bribes from local businesspeople, as well as from members of the international community working in the province.

Gender equality continues to be a serious problem in Kosovo Albanian society. Patriarchal societal attitudes often limit a woman's ability to gain an education or to choose the marriage partner of her choice.

Survey Methodology— 2000-2001

Since its inception in the 1970s, Freedom House's *Freedom in the World* survey has provided an annual evaluation of political rights and civil liberties throughout the world. The survey attempts to judge all countries and territories by a single standard and to emphasize the importance of democracy and freedom. At a minimum, a democracy is a political system in which the people choose their authoritative leaders freely from among competing groups and individuals who were not designated by the government. Freedom represents the opportunity to act spontaneously in a variety of fields outside the control of the government and other centers of potential domination.

The survey rates countries and territories based on real world situations caused by state and nongovernmental factors, rather than on governmental intentions or legislation alone. Freedom House does not rate governments per se, but rather the rights and freedoms enjoyed by individuals in each country or territory. The survey does not base its judgment solely on the political conditions in a country or territory (i.e., war, terrorism), but by the effect which these conditions have on freedom.

Freedom House does not maintain a culture-bound view of democracy. The survey demonstrates that, in addition to countries in Europe and the Americas, there are free states with varying forms of democracy functioning among people of all races and religions in Africa, the Pacific, and Asia. In some Pacific islands, free countries can have political systems based on competing family groups and personalities rather than on European- or American-style political parties. In recent years, there has been a proliferation of democracies in developing countries, and the survey reflects their growing numbers. To reach its conclusions, the survey team employs a broad range of sources of information, including foreign and domestic news reports, nongovernmental organization publications, think tank and academic analyses, and individual professional contacts.

DEFINITIONS AND CATEGORIES OF THE SURVEY

The survey's concept of freedom encompasses two general sets of characteristics grouped under political rights and civil liberties. Political rights enable people to participate freely in the political process, which is the system by which the polity chooses authoritative policy makers and attempts to make binding decisions affecting the national, regional, or local community. In a free society, this represents the right of all adults to vote and compete for public office, and for elected representatives to have a decisive vote on public policies. Civil liberties include the freedoms to develop views, institutions, and personal autonomy apart from the state.

The survey assigns each country or territory under consideration two numerical ratings, one for political rights and one for civil liberties. These two ratings are then averaged to determine an overall status of "Free," "Partly Free," or "Not Free." (See the following section, "Rating System for Political Rights and Civil Liberties," for a detailed description of the survey's methodology.)

Freedom House rates both independent countries and select territories. For the purposes of the survey, countries are defined as internationally recognized independent states whose governments reside within their officially claimed borders. In the case of Cyprus, two sets of ratings are provided, as there are two governments on that divided island. This does not imply that Freedom House endorses Cypriot division. We note only that neither the predominantly Greek Republic of Cyprus, nor the Turkish-occupied, predominantly Turkish territory of the Republic of Northern Cyprus, is the *de facto* government for the entire island.

Freedom House divides territories into two categories: related territories and disputed territories. Related territories consist mostly of colonies, protectorates, and island dependencies of sovereign states which are in some relation of dependency to that state and whose relationship is not currently in serious legal or political dispute. Puerto Rico and Hong Kong are examples of related territories. Disputed territories represent areas within internationally recognized sovereign states which often are dominated by a minority ethnic group and whose status is in serious political or violent dispute. This group also includes territories whose incorporation into nation-states is not universally recognized. In some cases, the issue of dispute is the desire of the majority of the population of that territory to secede from the sovereign state and either form an independent country or become part of a neighboring state. Tibet, Kashmir, and Abkhazia are examples of disputed territories. Beginning with the 2000-2001 survey, only those 17 territories about which reports have been written were assigned ratings or a status designation.

The survey assigns the designation of "electoral democracy" to those countries which have met minimum standards for free and fair elections as judged by various international election observers. Among the basic criteria are that voters should have access to information about candidates and their platforms, that they should be able to vote without undue pressure from the authorities, and that candidates should be able to campaign free from intimidation. The presence of certain irregularities during the electoral process does not automatically disqualify a country from being designated an electoral democracy. All "Free" countries in the survey would qualify as electoral democracies, as would some "Partly Free" countries.

RATING SYSTEM FOR POLITICAL RIGHTS AND CIVIL LIBERTIES

The survey rates political rights and civil liberties separately on a scale of 1 to 7, with 1 representing the most free and 7 the least free. A country or territory is assigned to a particular rating based on the individual survey authors' responses to a series of checklist questions and the judgments of the survey team at Freedom House. The authors assign initial ratings to countries or territories by awarding from 0 to 4 raw points per checklist item, depending on the comparative rights or liberties present. (In the surveys completed from 1989-90 through 1992-93, the methodology allowed for a less nuanced range of 0 to 2 raw points per question.) The only exception to the addition of 0 to 4 raw points per checklist item is additional discretionary question B in the political rights checklist, for which 1 to 4 raw points are subtracted depending on the severity of the situation. The highest possible score for political rights is 32 points, based on up to 4 points for each of eight questions. The highest possible score for civil liberties is 56 points, based on up to 4 points for each of fourteen questions. After the countries and territories have been assigned political rights and civil liberties ratings based on the total number of raw points in each of the two categories, the survey team makes minor adjustments to account for factors such as extreme violence, the intensity of which may not be reflected in answering the checklist questions.

Almost without exception, countries and territories have ratings in political rights and civil liberties that are within two ratings numbers of each other. Without a well-developed civil society, it is difficult, if not impossible, to have an atmosphere supportive of democracy. A society that does not enjoy free individual and group expressions in nonpolitical matters is not likely to make an exception for political ones. Consequently, there is no country in the survey with a rating of 6 or 7 for civil liberties and, at the same time, a rating of 1 or 2 for political rights.

A change in a country's political rights or civil liberties situation since the previous survey may be indicated by a political rights or civil liberties ratings change (depending on the total raw points), and possibly a status change. Freedom House also assigns upward or downward trend arrows to countries and territories to indicate general positive or negative trends since the previous survey which are not necessarily reflected in the raw points and do not warrant a ratings change. A country cannot receive both a numerical ratings change and a trend arrow in the same year, nor can it receive trend arrows in the same direction in two successive years.

Political Rights

Category Number	Raw Points
1	28-32
2	23-27
3	19-22
4	14-18
5	10-13
6	5-9
7	0-4

Civi Liberties

Category Number	Raw Points
1	50-56
2	42-49
3	34-41
4	26-33
5	17-25
6	9-16
7	0-8

POLITICAL RIGHTS CHECKLIST

1. Is the head of state and/or head of government or other chief authority elected through free and fair elections?

2. Are the legislative representatives elected through free and fair elections?

3. Are there fair electoral laws, equal campaigning opportunities, fair polling, and honest tabulation of ballots?

4. Are the voters able to endow their freely elected representatives with real power?

5. Do the people have the right to organize in different political parties or other competitive political groupings of their choice, and is the system open to the rise and fall of these competing parties or groupings?

6. Is there a significant opposition vote, de facto opposition power, and a realistic possibility for the opposition to increase its support or gain power through elections?

7. Are the people free from domination by the military, foreign powers, totalitarian parties, religious hierarchies, economic oligarchies, or any other powerful group?

8. Do cultural, ethnic, religious, and other minority groups have reasonable self-determination, self-government, autonomy, or participation through informal consensus in the decision-making process?

Additional discretionary Political Rights questions:

A. For traditional monarchies that have no parties or electoral process, does the system provide for consultation with the people, encourage discussion of policy, and allow the right to petition the ruler?

B.   Is the government or occupying power deliberately changing the ethnic composition of a country or territory so as to destroy a culture or tip the political balance in favor of another group?

To answer the political rights questions, Freedom House considers the extent to which the system offers voters the opportunity to choose freely from among candidates, and to what extent the candidates are chosen independently of the state. However, formal electoral procedures are not the only factors that determine the real distribution of power. In many countries, the military retains a significant political role, while in others, the king maintains considerable power over the elected politicians. The more that people suffer under such domination by unelected forces, the less chance the country has of receiving credit for self-determination in the survey.

CIVIL LIBERTIES CHECKLIST

A.   Freedom of Expression and Belief

1.   Are there free and independent media and other forms of cultural expression? (Note: in cases where the media are state-controlled but offer pluralistic points of view, the Survey gives the system credit.)

2.   Are there free religious institutions and is there free private and public religious expression?

B.   Association and Organizational Rights

1.   Is there freedom of assembly, demonstration, and open public discussion?

2.   Is there freedom of political or quasi-political organization? (Note: this includes political parties, civic organizations, ad hoc issue groups, etc.)

3.   Are there free trade unions and peasant organizations or equivalents, and is there effective collective bargaining? Are there free professional and other private organizations?

C.   Rule of Law and Human Rights

1.   Is there an independent judiciary?

2.   Does the rule of law prevail in civil and criminal matters? Is the population treated equally under the law? Are police under direct civilian control?

3.   Is there protection from political terror, unjustified imprisonment, exile, or torture, whether by groups that support or oppose the system? Is there freedom from war and insurgencies? (Note: freedom from war and insurgencies enhances the liberties in a free society, but the absence of wars and insurgencies does not in and of itself make a not free society free.)

4. Is there freedom from extreme government indifference and corruption?

D.   Personal Autonomy and Economic Rights

1.   Is there open and free private discussion?

2.   Is there personal autonomy? Does the state control travel, choice of residence, or choice of employment? Is there freedom from indoctrination and excessive dependency on the state?

3.   Are property rights secure? Do citizens have the right to establish private businesses?

Is private business activity unduly influenced by government officials, the security forces, or organized crime?

4. Are there personal social freedoms, including gender equality, choice of marriage partners, and size of family?

5. Is there equality of opportunity, including freedom from exploitation by or dependency on landlords, employers, union leaders, bureaucrats, or other types of obstacles to a share of legitimate economic gains?

When analyzing the civil liberties checklist, Freedom House does not mistake constitutional guarantees of human rights for those rights in practice. For states and territories with small populations, particularly tiny island nations, the absence of trade unions and other forms of association is not necessarily viewed as a negative situation unless the government or other centers of domination are deliberately blocking their establishment or operation. In some cases, the small size of these countries and territories may result in a lack of sufficient institutional complexity to allow for full comparison with larger countries. The question of equality of opportunity implies a free choice of employment and education. Extreme inequality of opportunity prevents disadvantaged individuals from enjoying full exercise of civil liberties. Typically, very poor countries and territories lack both opportunities for economic advancement and other liberties included on this checklist. The question on extreme government indifference and corruption highlights the fact that the human rights of a country's residents suffer when governments ignore the social and economic welfare of large sectors of the population. Government corruption can pervert the political process and hamper the development of a free economy.

EXPLANATION OF POLITICAL RIGHTS AND CIVIL LIBERTIES RATINGS
Political Rights

Countries and territories which receive a rating of 1 for political rights come closest to the ideals suggested by the checklist questions, beginning with free and fair elections. Those who are elected rule, there are competitive parties or other political groupings, and the opposition plays an important role and has actual power. Citizens enjoy self-determination or an extremely high degree of autonomy (in the case of territories), and minority groups have reasonable self-government or can participate in the government through informal consensus. With the exception of such entities as tiny island states, these countries and territories have decentralized political power and free sub-national elections.

Countries and territories rated 2 in political rights are less free than those rated 1. Such factors as gross political corruption, violence, political discrimination against minorities, and foreign or military influence on politics may be present and weaken the quality of democracy.

The same conditions which undermine freedom in countries and territories with a rating of 2 may also weaken political rights in those with a rating of 3, 4, and 5. Other damaging elements can include civil war, heavy military involvement in politics, lingering royal power, unfair elections, and one-party dominance. However, states and territories in these categories may still enjoy some elements of political rights, including the freedom to organize quasi-political groups, reasonably free referenda, or other significant means of popular influence on government.

Countries and territories with political rights rated 6 have systems ruled by military juntas, one-party dictatorships, religious hierarchies, or autocrats. These regimes may allow only a minimal manifestation of political rights, such as competitive local elections or some degree of representation or autonomy for minorities. Some countries and territories rated 6 are in the early or aborted stages of democratic transition. A few states are traditional monarchies that mitigate their relative lack of political rights through the use of consultation with their subjects, toleration of political discussion, and acceptance of public petitions.

For countries and territories with a rating of 7, political rights are absent or virtually nonexistent due to the extremely oppressive nature of the regime or severe oppression in combination with civil war. States and territories in this group may also be marked by extreme violence or warlord rule which dominates political power in the absence of an authoritative, functioning central government.

Civil Liberties

Countries and territories which receive a rating of 1 come closest to the ideals expressed in the civil liberties checklist, including freedom of expression, assembly, association, and religion. They are distinguished by an established and generally equitable system of rule of law and are comparatively free of extreme government indifference and corruption. Countries and territories with this rating enjoy free economic activity and tend to strive for equality of opportunity.

States and territories with a rating of 2 have deficiencies in three or four aspects of civil liberties, but are still relatively free.

Countries and territories which have received a rating of 3, 4, and 5 range from those that are in at least partial compliance with virtually all checklist standards to those with a combination of high or medium scores for some questions and low or very low scores on other questions. The level of oppression increases at each successive rating level, particularly in the areas of censorship, political terror, and the prevention of free association. There are also many cases in which groups opposed to the state engage in political terror that undermines other freedoms. Therefore, a poor rating for a country is not necessarily a comment on the intentions of the government, but may reflect real restrictions on liberty caused by nongovernmental terror.

Countries and territories rated 6 are characterized by a few partial rights, such as some religious and social freedoms, some highly restricted private business activity, and relatively free private discussion. In general, people in these states and territories experience severely restricted expression and association, and there are almost always political prisoners and other manifestations of political terror.

States and territories with a rating of 7 have virtually no freedom. An overwhelming and justified fear of repression characterizes these societies.

EXPLANATION OF FREE, PARTLY FREE, NOT FREE

The survey assigns each country and territory the status of "Free," "Partly Free," or "Not Free" by averaging their political rights and civil liberties ratings. Those whose ratings average 1-2.5 are generally considered "Free," 3-5.5 "Partly Free," and 5.5-7 "Not Free." The dividing line between "Partly Free" and "Not Free" usually falls within the group whose ratings numbers average 5.5. For example, countries that receive a rating of 6 for political rights and 5 for civil liberties, or a 5 for political rights and a 6 for civil liberties, could be either "Partly Free" or "Not Free." The total number of raw points is the definitive factor which determines the final status. Countries and territories with combined raw scores of 0-30 points are "Not Free," 31-59 points are "Partly Free," and 60-88 are "Free." Based on raw points, this year there is one unusual case: Mali's ratings average 3.0, but it is "Free."

It should be emphasized that the "Free," "Partly Free," and "Not Free" labels are highly simplified terms that each cover a broad third of the available raw points. Therefore, countries and territories within each category, especially those at either end of each category, can have quite different human rights situations. In order to see the distinctions within each category, one should examine a country or territory's political rights and civil liberties ratings.

The differences in raw points between countries in the three broad categories represent distinctions in the real world. There are obstacles which "Partly Free" countries must overcome before they can be called "Free," just as there are impediments which prevent "Not Free" countries from being called "Partly Free." Countries at the lowest rung of the "Free" category (2 in political rights and 3 in civil liberties, or 3 in political rights and 2 in civil liberties) differ from those at the upper end of the "Partly Free" group (e.g., 3 for both political rights and civil liberties). Typically, there is more violence and/or military influence on politics at 3, 3 than at 2, 3.

The distinction between the least repressive "Not Free" countries and the worst "Partly Free" may be less obvious than the gap between "Partly Free" and "Free," but at "Partly Free," there is at least one additional factor that keeps a country from being assigned to the "Not Free" category. For example, Lebanon, which was rated 6, 5 "Partly Free" in 1994, was rated 6, 5, but "Not Free," in 1995 after its legislature unilaterally extended the incumbent president's term indefinitely. Though not sufficient to drop the country's political rights rating to 7, there was enough of a drop in raw points to change its category.

Freedom House does not view democracy as a static concept, and the survey recognizes that a democratic country does not necessarily belong in our category of "Free" states. A democracy can lose freedom and become merely "Partly Free." Sri Lanka and Colombia are recent examples of such "Partly Free" democracies. In other cases, countries that replaced military regimes with elected governments can have less than complete transitions to liberal democracy. Guatemala fits the description of this kind of "Partly Free" democracy. Some scholars use the term "semi-democracy" or "formal democracy," instead of "Partly Free" democracy, to refer to countries that are democratic in form but less than free in substance.

The designation "Free" does not mean that a country enjoys perfect freedom or lacks serious problems. As an institution which advocates human rights, Freedom House remains concerned about a variety of social problems and civil liberties questions in the U.S. and other countries that the survey places in the "Free" category. An improvement in a country's rating does not mean that human rights campaigns should cease. On the contrary, the findings of the survey should be regarded as a means to encourage improvements in the political rights and civil liberties conditions in all countries.

Tables and Ratings

Table of Independent Countries

Country	PR	CL	Freedom Rating	Country	PR	CL	Freedom Rating
Afghanistan	7	7	Not Free	Dominica	1	1	Free
⬆ Albania	4	5	Partly Free	Dominican	2	2▲	Free
Algeria	6	5	Not Free	Republic			
Andorra	1	1	Free	East Timor	6	3▲	Partly Free
⬆ Angola	6	6	Not Free	Ecuador	3▼	3	Partly Free
Antigua and	4	2▲	Partly Free	Egypt	6	5	Not Free
Barbuda				El Salvador	2	3	Free
Argentina	1▲	2▲	Free	Equatorial Guinea	7	7	Not Free
Armenia	4	4	Partly Free	Eritrea	7	5	Not Free
Australia	1	1	Free	Estonia	1	2	Free
Austria	1	1	Free	Ethiopia	5	5	Partly Free
Azerbaijan	6	5▼	Partly Free	Fiji	6▼	3	Partly Free
Bahamas	1	1	Free	Finland	1	1	Free
Bahrain	7	6	Not Free	⬆ France	1	2	Free
Bangladesh	3	4	Partly Free	Gabon	5	4	Partly Free
Barbados	1	1	Free	The Gambia	7	5	Not Free
Belarus	6	6	Not Free	Georgia	4▼	4	Partly Free
Belgium	1	2	Free	Germany	1	2	Free
Belize	1	1	Free	Ghana	2▲	3	Free
Benin	2	2▲	Free	Greece	1	3	Free
Bhutan	7	6	Not Free	Grenada	1	2	Free
Bolivia	1	3	Free	⬇ Guatemala	3	4	Partly Free
Bosnia-Herzegovina	5	4▲	Partly Free	⬇ Guinea	6	5	Not Free
Botswana	2	2	Free	Guinea-Bissau	4▼	5	Partly Free
Brazil	3	3▲	Partly Free	Guyana	2	2	Free
Brunei	7	5	Not Free	Haiti	6▼	5	Not Free
Bulgaria	2	3	Free	Honduras	3	3	Free
⬆ Burkina Faso	4	4	Partly Free	Hungary	1	2	Free
Burma	7	7	Not Free	Iceland	1	1	Free
Burundi	6	6	Not Free	India	2	3	Free
Cambodia	6	6	Not Free	Indonesia	3▼	4	Partly Free
Cameroon	7	6	Not Free	⬇ Iran	6	6	Not Free
Canada	1	1	Free	Iraq	7	7	Not Free
Cape Verde	1	2	Free	Ireland	1	1	Free
Central African	3	4	Partly Free	Israel	1	3▼	Free
Republic				Italy	1	2	Free
Chad	6	5	Not Free	⬇ Jamaica	2	2	Free
Chile	2	2	Free	Japan	1	2	Free
China (P.R.C.)	7	6	Not Free	Jordan	4	4	Partly Free
Colombia	4	4	Partly Free	⬇ Kazakhstan	6	5	Not Free
⬇ Comoros	6	4	Partly Free	⬇ Kenya	6	5	Not Free
Congo (Brazzaville)	6	4▲	Partly Free	Kiribati	1	1	Free
Congo (Kinshasa)	7	6	Not Free	Korea, North	7	7	Not Free
Costa Rica	1	2	Free	Korea, South	2	2	Free
Côte d'Ivoire	6	5▼	Partly Free	Kuwait	4	5	Partly Free
Croatia	2▲	3▲	Free	Kyrgyz Republic	6▼	5	Not Free
Cuba	7	7	Not Free	⬇ Laos	7	6	Not Free
Cyprus (G)	1	1	Free	Latvia	1	2	Free
Czech Republic	1	2	Free	Lebanon	6	5	Not Free
Denmark	1	1	Free	⬇ Lesotho	4	4	Partly Free
Djibouti	4	5▲	Partly Free	Liberia	5▼	6▼	Partly Free

Country	PR	CL	Freedom Rating
Libya	7	7	Not Free
Liechtenstein	1	1	Free
Lithuania	1	2	Free
Luxembourg	1	1	Free
Macedonia	4▼	3	Partly Free
Madagascar	2	4	Partly Free
Malawi	3	3	Partly Free
Malaysia	5	5	Partly Free
Maldives	6	5	Not Free
Mali	2▲	3	Free
Malta	1	1	Free
Marshall Islands	1	1	Free
⬇ Mauritania	6▼	5	Not Free
Mauritius	1	2	Free
Mexico	2▲	3▲	Free
Micronesia	1	2	Free
Moldova	2	4	Partly Free
Monaco	2	1	Free
Mongolia	2	3	Free
Morocco	5	4	Partly Free
⬇ Mozambique	3	4	Partly Free
⬇ Namibia	2	3	Free
Nauru	1	3	Free
Nepal	3	4	Partly Free
Netherlands	1	1	Free
New Zealand	1	1	Free
⬇ Nicaragua	3	3	Partly Free
Niger	4▲	4▲	Partly Free
Nigeria	4	4▼	Partly Free
Norway	1	1	Free
Oman	6	5▲	Not Free
Pakistan	6▲	5	Not Free
Palau	1	2	Free
Panama	1	2	Free
Papua New Guinea	2	3	Free
⬆ Paraguay	4	3	Partly Free
Peru	3▲	4▲	Partly Free
⬇ Philippines	2	3	Free
Poland	1	2	Free
Portugal	1	1	Free
Qatar	6	6	Not Free
Romania	2	2	Free
Russia	5▼	5	Partly Free
Rwanda	7	6	Not Free
St. Kitts and Nevis	1	2	Free
St. Lucia	1	2	Free
St. Vincent and the Grenadines	2	1	Free
Samoa	2	2	Free
San Marino	1	1	Free
Sao Tome and Príncipe	1	2	Free
Saudi Arabia	7	7	Not Free
Senegal	3▲	4	Partly Free

Country	PR	CL	Freedom Rating
Seychelles	3	3	Partly Free
Sierra Leone	4▼	5	Partly Free
Singapore	5	5	Partly Free
Slovakia	1	2	Free
Slovenia	1	2	Free
Solomon Islands	4▼	4▼	Partly Free
Somalia	6▲	7	Not Free
South Africa	1	2	Free
Spain	1	2	Free
Sri Lanka	3	4	Partly Free
Sudan	7	7	Not Free
Suriname	1▲	2▲	Free
⬇ Swaziland	6	5	Not Free
Sweden	1	1	Free
Switzerland	1	1	Free
⬆ Syria	7	7	Not Free
Taiwan (Rep. of China)	1▲	2	Free
Tajikistan	6	6	Not Free
Tanzania	4	4	Partly Free
Thailand	2	3	Free
⬆ Togo	5	5	Partly Free
Tonga	5	3	Partly Free
Trinidad and Tobago	2▼	2	Free
Tunisia	6	5	Not Free
Turkey	4	5	Partly Free
Turkmenistan	7	7	Not Free
Tuvalu	1	1	Free
Uganda	6▼	5	Partly Free
Ukraine	4▼	4	Partly Free
United Arab Emirates	6	5	Not Free
⬆ United Kingdom*	1	2	Free
United States	1	1	Free
Uruguay	1	1▲	Free
Uzbekistan	7	6	Not Free
Vanuatu	1	3	Free
Venezuela	3▲	5▼	Partly Free
Vietnam	7	6▲	Not Free
Yemen	5	6	Not Free
Yugoslavia (Serbia and Montenegro)	4▲	4▲	Partly Free
Zambia	5	4	Partly Free
⬇ Zimbabwe	6	5	Partly Free

PR and CL stand for Political Rights and Civil Liberties.
1 represents the most free and 7 the least free category.

⬆⬇ up or down indicates a general trend in freedom.

▲▼ up or down indicates a change in Political Rights or Civil Liberties since the last *Survey*.

The Freedom Rating is an overall judgment based on *Survey* results. See the essay on Survey methodology for more details.

* Excluding Northern Ireland.

Table of Disputed Territories

Country	PR	CL	Freedom Rating
Armenia/Azerbaijan Nagorno-Karabakh	5	6	Not Free
China Tibet	7	7	Not Free
Georgia Abkhazia	6	5	Not Free
India Kashmir	6	6	Not Free
Indonesia West Papua	5▲	5	Partly Free
Irqaq Kurdistan	6	6	Not Free
Israel Israeli-Administered territories	6	6▼	Not Free
Palestinian Authority-Administered territories	5	6	Not Free
Moldova Transdniester	6	6	Not Free
Morocco Western Sahara	7	6	Not Free
Russia Chechnya	7	7	Not Free
Turkey Cyprus (T)	2▲	2	Partly Free
⬇ Yugoslavia Kosovo	6	6	Not Free

Table of Related Territories

Country	PR	CL	Freedom Rating
China Hong Kong	5	3	Partly Free
Macao	6	4	Partly Free
United Kingdom Northern Ireland	2▲	2▲	Free
United States of America Puerto Rico	1	2	Free

Table of Social and Economic Indicators

Country	Real GDP Per Capita (PPP$)	Life Expectancy	Country	Real GDP Per Capita (PPP$)	Life Expectancy
Afghanistan	na	46	East Timor	na	46
Albania	2,804	73	Ecuador	3,003	70
Algeria	4,792	69	Egypt	3,041	67
Andorra	na	na	El Salvador	4,036	69
Angola	1,821	47	Equatorial Guinea	1,817	50
Antigua and Barbuda	9,277	76	Eritrea	833	51
Argentina	12,013	73	Estonia	7,682	69
Armenia	2,072	71	Ethiopia	574	43
Australia	22,452	78	Fiji	4,231	73
Austria	23,166	77	Finland	20,847	77
Azerbaijan	2,175	70	France	21,175	78
Bahamas	14,614	74	Gabon	6,353	52
Bahrain	13,111	73	The Gambia	1,453	47
Bangladesh	1,361	59	Georgia	3,353	73
Barbados	12,001	77	Germany	22,169	77
Belarus	6,319	68	Ghana	1,735	60
Belgium	23,223	77	Greece	13,943	78
Belize	4,566	75	Grenada	5,838	72
Benin	867	54	Guatemala	3,505	64
Bhutan	1,536	61	Guinea	1,782	47
Bolivia	2,269	62	Guinea-Bissau	616	45
Bosnia-Herzegovina	na	73	Guyana	3,403	65
Botswana	6,103	46	Haiti	1,383	54
Brazil	6,625	67	Honduras	2,433	70
Brunei	16,765	76	Hungary	10,232	71
Bulgaria	4,809	71	Iceland	25,110	79
Burkina Faso	870	45	India	2,077	63
Burma	1,199	61	Indonesia	2,651	66
Burundi	570	43	Iran	5,121	70
Cambodia	1,257	54	Iraq	3,197	64
Cameroon	1,474	55	Ireland	21,482	77
Canada	23,582	79	Israel	17,301	78
Cape Verde	3,233	69	Italy	20,585	78
Central African Republic	1,118	45	Jamaica	3,389	75
Chad	856	48	Japan	23,257	80
Chile	8,787	75	Jordan	3,347	70
China	3,105	70	Kazakhstan	4,378	68
Colombia	6,006	71	Kenya	980	51
Comoros	1,398	59	Kiribati	na	62
Congo (Brazzaville)	995	49	Korea, North	na	70
Congo (Kinshasa)	822	51	Korea, South	13,478	73
Costa Rica	5,987	76	Kuwait	25,314	76
Cote d'Ivoire	1,598	47	Kyrgyz Republic	2,317	68
Croatia	6,749	73	Laos	1,734	54
Cuba	3,967	76	Latvia	5,728	69
Cyprus (Greek)	17,482	78	Lebanon	4,326	70
Czech Republic	12,362	74	Lesotho	1,626	55
Denmark	24,218	76	Liberia	na	50
Djibouti	1,266	51	Libya	6,697	70
Dominica	5,102	76	Liechtenstein	na	72
Dominican Republic	4,598	71	Lithuania	6,436	70

Table of Social and Economic Indicators

Country	Real GDP Per Capita (PPP$)	Life Expectancy	Country	Real GDP Per Capita (PPP$)	Life Expectancy
Luxembourg	33,505	77	Slovenia	14,293	75
Macedonia	4,254	73	Solomon Islands	1,940	72
Madagascar	756	58	Somalia	na	46
Malawi	523	40	South Africa	8,488	53
Malaysia	8,137	72	Spain	16,212	78
Maldives	4,083	65	Sri Lanka	2,979	73
Mali	681	54	Sudan	1,394	55
Malta	16,447	77	Suriname	5,161	70
Marshall Islands	na	65	Swaziland	3,816	61
Mauritania	1,563	54	Sweden	20,659	79
Mauritius	8,312	72	Switzerland	25,512	79
Mexico	7,704	72	Syria	2,892	69
Micronesia	na	66	Taiwan (Rep. of China)	na	75
Moldova	1,947	68	Tajikistan	1,041	68
Monaco	na	na	Tanzania	480	48
Mongolia	1,541	66	Thailand	5,456	69
Morocco	3,305	67	Togo	1,372	49
Mozambique	782	44	Tonga	na	na
Namibia	5,176	50	Trinidad and Tobago	7,485	74
Nauru	na	61	Tunisia	5,404	70
Nepal	1,157	58	Turkey	6,422	69
Netherlands	22,176	78	Turkmenistan	2,550	66
New Zealand	17,288	77	Tuvalu	na	na
Nicaragua	2,142	68	Uganda	1,074	41
Niger	739	49	Ukraine	3,194	69
Nigeria	795	50	United Arab Emirates	17,719	75
Norway	26,342	78	United Kingdom	20,336	77
Oman	9,960	71	United States	29,605	77
Pakistan	1,715	64	Uruguay	8,623	74
Palau	na	67	Uzbekistan	2,053	68
Panama	5,249	74	Vanuatu	3,120	68
Papua New Guinea	2,359	58	Venezuela	5,808	73
Paraguay	4,288	70	Vietnam	1,689	68
Peru	4,282	69	Yemen	719	59
Philippines	3,555	69	Yugoslavia		
Poland	7,619	73	(Serbia and Montenegro)	na	72
Portugal	14,701	76	Zambia	719	41
Qatar	20,987	72	Zimbabwe	2,669	44
Romania	5,648	70			
Russia	6,460	67			
Rwanda	660	41			
St. Kitts and Nevis	10,672	70			
St. Lucia	5,183	70			
St. Vincent and Grenadines	4,692	73			
Samoa	3,832	72			
San Marino	na	80			
Sao Tome and Principe	1,469	64			
Saudi Arabia	10,158	72			
Senegal	1,307	53			
Seychelles	10,600	71			
Sierra Leone	458	38			
Singapore	24,210	77			
Slovakia	9,699	73			

Combined Average Ratings: Independent Countries

FREE	Sao Tome and Principe	Central African Republic	NOT FREE
1.0	Slovakia	Guatemala	**5.5**
Andorra	Slovenia	Indonesia	Algeria
Australia	South Africa	Macedonia	Chad
Austria	Spain	Mozambique	Egypt
Bahamas	Suriname	Nepal	Guinea
Barbados	Taiwan	Paraguay	Haiti
Belize	United Kingdom	Senegal	Kazakhstan
Canada		Sri Lanka	Kenya
Cyprus (G)	**2.0**		Kyrgyz Republic
Denmark	Benin	**4.0**	Lebanon
Dominica	Bolivia	Armenia	Maldives
Finland	Botswana	Burkina Faso	Mauritania
Grenada	Chile	Colombia	Oman
Iceland	Dominican Republic	Georgia	Pakistan
Ireland	Greece	Jordan	Swaziland
Kiribati	Guyana	Lesotho	Tunisia
Liechtenstein	Israel	Niger	United Arab Emirates
Luxembourg	Jamaica	Nigeria	Yemen
Malta	Korea, South	Solomon Islands	
Marshall Islands	Nauru	Tanzania	**6.0**
Netherlands	Romania	Tonga	Angola
New Zealand	Samoa	Venezuela	Belarus
Norway	Trinidad and Tobago	Yugoslavia	Brunei
Portugal	Vanuatu		Burundi
San Marino		**4.5**	Cambodia
Sweden	**2.5**	Albania	Eritrea
Switzerland	Bulgaria	Bosnia-Herzegovina	The Gambia
Tuvalu	Croatia	Djibouti	Iran
United States	El Salvador	East Timor	Qatar
Uruguay	Ghana	Fiji	Tajikistan
	India	Gabon	
1.5	Mali	Guinea-Bissau	**6.5**
Argentina	Mexico	Kuwait	Bahrain
Belgium	Mongolia	Morocco	Bhutan
Cape Verde	Namibia	Sierra Leone	Cameroon
Costa Rica	Papua New Guinea	Turkey	China (PRC)
Czech Republic	Philippines	Ukraine	Congo (Kinshasa)
Estonia	Thailand	Zambia	Laos
France			Rwanda
Germany	**PARTLY FREE**	**5.0**	Somalia
Hungary		Comoros	Uzbekistan
Italy	**3.0**	Congo (Brazzaville)	Vietnam
Japan	Antigua and Barbuda	Ethiopia	
Latvia	Brazil	Malaysia	**7.0**
Lithuania	Ecuador	Russia	Afghanistan
Mauritius	Honduras	Singapore	Burma
Micronesia	Madagascar	Togo	Cuba
Monaco	Malawi		Equatorial Guinea
Palau	Moldova	**5.5**	Iraq
Panama	Nicaragua	Azerbaijan	Korea, North
Poland	Peru	Cote d'Ivoire	Libya
St. Kitts and Nevis	Seychelles	Liberia	Saudi Arabia
St. Lucia		Uganda	Sudan
St. Vincent and Grenadines	**3.5**	Zimbabwe	Syria
	Bangladesh		Turkmenistan

Combined Average Ratings: Related Territories

FREE
1.5
Puerto Rico (US)

2.0
Northern Ireland (UK)

PARTLY FREE
4.0
Hong Kong (China)

5.0
Macao (China)

Combined Average Ratings: Disputed Territories

FREE	Nagorno-Karabakh	Kurdistan (Iraq)
2.0	(Armenia)	Transnistria (Moldova)
Cyprus (Turkey)	Palestinian Authority-	
	Administered Territories	**6.5**
PARTLY FREE	(Israel)	Western Sahara
5.0		(Morocco)
West Papua (Indonesia)	**6.0**	
	Israeli-Administered	**7.0**
NOT FREE	Territories (Israel)	Chechnya (Russia)
5.5	Kashmir (India)	Tibet (China)
Abkhazia (Georgia)	Kosovo (Yugoslavia)	

Electoral Democracies (120)

Albania Presidential-parliamentary democracy	**El Salvador** Presidential-parliamentary democracy
Andorra Parliamentary democracy	**Estonia** Parliamentary democracy
Argentina Presidential-parliamentary democracy (federal)	**Finland** Parliamentary democracy
Armenia Presidential-parliamentary democracy	**France** Presidential-parliamentary democracy
Australia Parliamentary democracy (federal)	**Georgia** Presidential-parliamentary democracy
Austria Parliamentary democracy (federal)	**Germany** Parliamentary democracy (federal)
Bahamas Parliamentary democracy	**Ghana** Presidential-parliamentary democracy
Bangladesh Parliamentary democracy	**Greece** Parliamentary democracy
Barbados Parliamentary democracy	**Grenada** Parliamentary democracy
Belgium Parliamentary democracy (federal)	**Guatemala** Presidential-parliamentary democracy
Belize Parliamentary democracy	**Guinea-Bissau** Presidential-parliamentary democracy
Benin Presidential-parliamentary democracy	**Guyana** Parliamentary democracy
Bolivia Presidential-parliamentary democracy	**Honduras** Presidential-parliamentary democracy
Botswana Parliamentary democracy and traditional chiefs	**Hungary** Parliamentary democracy
Brazil Presidential-parliamentary democracy (federal)	**Iceland** Parliamentary democracy
Bulgaria Parliamentary democracy	**India** Parliamentary democracy
Canada Parliamentary democracy (federal)	**Indonesia** Presidential-parliamentary democracy (military-influenced)
Cape Verde Presidential-parliamentary democracy	**Ireland** Parliamentary democracy
Central African Republic Presidential-parliamentary democracy	**Israel** Parliamentary democracy
Chile Presidential-parliamentary democracy	**Italy** Parliamentary democracy
Colombia Presidential-parliamentary democracy (insurgencies)	**Jamaica** Parliamentary democracy
Costa Rica Presidential-parliamentary democracy	**Japan** Parliamentary democracy
Croatia Parliamentary democracy	**Kiribati** Presidential-parliamentary democracy
Cyprus Presidential-parliamentary democracy	**Korea, South** Presidential-parliamentary democracy
Czech Republic Parliamentary democracy	**Latvia** Parliamentary democracy
Denmark Parliamentary democracy	**Liberia** Presidential-parliamentary democracy
Djibouti Presidential-parliamentary democracy (dominant party)	**Liechtenstein** Principality and parliamentary democracy
Dominica Parliamentary democracy	**Lithuania** Parliamentary democracy
Dominican Republic Presidential-parliamentary democracy	**Luxembourg** Parliamentary democracy
Ecuador Presidential-parliamentary democracy	

Macedonia
Parliamentary democracy
Madagascar
Presidential-parliamentary democracy
Malawi
Presidential-parliamentary democracy
Mali
Presidential-parliamentary democracy
Malta
Parliamentary democracy
Marshall Islands
Parliamentary democracy and traditional chiefs
Mauritius
Parliamentary democracy
Mexico
Presidential-parliamentary democracy
Micronesia
Presidential-parliamentary democracy (federal)
Moldova
Parliamentary democracy
Monaco
Principality and parliamentary democracy
Mongolia
Presidential-parliamentary democracy
Mozambique
Presidential-parliamentary democracy
Namibia
Presidential-parliamentary democracy
Nauru
Presidential-parliamentary democracy
Nepal
Parliamentary democracy (insurgency)
Netherlands
Parliamentary democracy
New Zealand
Parliamentary democracy
Nicaragua
Presidential-parliamentary democracy
Niger
Presidential-parliamentary democracy
Nigeria
Presidential-parliamentary democracy
Norway
Parliamentary democracy
Palau
Presidential democracy and traditional chiefs
Panama
Presidential-parliamentary democracy
Papua New Guinea
Parliamentary democracy
Paraguay
Presidential-parliamentary democracy
Philippines
Presidential-parliamentary democracy (insurgencies)
Poland
Presidential-parliamentary democracy
Portugal
Presidential-parliamentary democracy
Romania
Presidential-parliamentary democracy
Russia
Presidential-parliamentary democracy

St. Kitts and Nevis
Parliamentary democracy
St. Lucia
Parliamentary democracy
St. Vincent and the Grenadines
Parliamentary democracy
Samoa
Parliamentary democracy and traditional chiefs
San Marino
Parliamentary democracy
Sao Tome and Principe
Presidential-parliamentary democracy
Senegal
Presidential-parliamentary democracy
Seychelles
Presidential-parliamentary democracy
Sierra Leone
Presidential-parliamentary democracy (insurgencies)
Slovakia
Parliamentary democracy
Slovenia
Parliamentary democracy
Solomon Islands
Parliamentary democracy
South Africa
Presidential-parliamentary democracy
Spain
Parliamentary democracy
Sri Lanka
Presidential democracy
Suriname
Presidential-parliamentary democracy
Sweden
Parliamentary democracy
Switzerland
Parliamentary democracy (federal)
Taiwan
Presidential democracy
Thailand
Parliamentary democracy
Trinidad and Tobago
Parliamentary democracy
Turkey
Presidential-parliamentary democracy (military-influenced) (insurgency)
Tuvalu
Parliamentary democracy
Ukraine
Presidential-parliamentary democracy
United Kingdom
Parliamentary democracy
United States of America
Presidential-parliamentary democracy (federal)
Uruguay
Presidential-parliamentary democracy
Vanuatu
Parliamentary democracy
Venezuela
Presidential-parliamentary democracy
Yugoslavia
Parliamentary democracy

Sources

Publications

Africa Confidential
Africa Online
Africa Recovery Magazine
Agence France-Presse
Al-Ahram [Egypt]
AllAfrica.com
Arabic News
Armenian Information Service
Asia Week
Asian Bulletin
Asian Survey
Asian Wall Street Journal
Associated Press
Assyrian International News Agency
The Atlantic Monthly
Balkan Medja [Bulgaria]
The Baltic Times
The Bangkok Times
British Broadcasting Corporation (BBC)
Business Eastern Europe
Cable News Network (CNN)
Caretas [Peru]
Carib News
Caribbean Insight
Caribbean Review
Catholic Standard [Guyana]
Central America Report
Central Europe Review
The Chechen Times
China Daily
Christian Science Monitor
CIA World Factbook
Clarin [Argentina]
Columbia Journalism Review
Communications Law in Transition
Constitution Finder, University of Richmond
Il Corriere della Sera [Italy]
Covcas Bulletin [France]
Czech News Agency
The Daily Star [Lebanon]
Dani [Bosnia-Herzegovina]
Dawn News Bulletin (All Burma Students
    Democratic Front)
Deutsche Presse Agenteur
East European Constitutional Review
The Economist
The Economist Intelligence Unit reports
eCountries.com
Editor & Publisher
Eesti Paevaleht [Estonia]
EFE Spanish News Agency
EPOCA [Mexico]
Ethiopian Review
Evenimentul Zilei [Romania]
Far Eastern Economic Review
The Financial Times
El Financiero [Mexico]
Fedworld.gov [United States]
Free Labour World
The Free Press [Ghana]
The Georgian Times
The Globe & Mail [Canada]
The Guardian

Gulf News [United Arab Emirates]
Gulf Times [Qatar]
Ha'aretz [Israel]
Hemisphere
Hong Kong Digest
Hornet Online
HuriNet
The Independent [United Kingdom]
Index of Economic Freedom (Heritage Foundation)
Index on Censorship
Indian Ocean Newsletter
International Crisis Group South Balkans
Project Reports
InterPress News Service
The Irish Times
Islamic Republic News Agency [Iran]
ITAR-TASS
Jerusalem Post
Jordan Times
La Jornada [Mexico]
Journal of Commerce
Journal of Democracy
Kathmandu Post
Keesings Record of World Events
Kiev Post
Klipsan Press Election Notes
Lettre du Continent
Lexis-Nexis
Los Angeles Times
Mail & Guardian Weekly [South Africa]
Miami Herald
The Middle East
Middle East International
Middle East Quarterly
The Middle East Times
Miist [Ukraine]
Monitor [Uganda]
Monitorul [Romania]
Morocco Press
The Moscow Times
La Nacion [Argentina]
The Nation
New African
The New Republic
New Vision [Uganda]
New York Newsday
The New York Times
The New Yorker
The New Zealand Herald
Nezavisne Novine [Bosnia-Herzegovina]
North-South Magazine
El Nuevo Herald [Florida]
The Observer [United Kingdom]
Oman Daily Observer
The Other Side of Mexico
Pacific Islands News Agency
Pan African News Agency
Political Handbook of the World
The Post [Zambia]
Postimees [Estonia]
Proceso [Mexico]
Radio Australia reports
Radio Free Europe-Radio Liberty reports
Reforma [Mexico]
Reporter [Bosnia-Herzegovina]
La Repubblica
Reuters
The Saigon Times Daily
Slobodna Bosna [Bosnia-Herzegovina]

Le Soleil [Senegal]
South China Morning Post [Hong Kong]
Sposterihach [Ukraine]
The Standard [Kenya]
The Statesman [India]
The Straits Times [Singapore]
Swiss Press Review
Tehran Times
The Tico Times [Costa Rica]
The Times of Central Asia
The Times of London
Transcaucasus: A Chronology
Transitions Online
Ukrainian Press Agency
Ukrainian Weekly
Uncaptive Minds (Institute for Democracy
    in Eastern Europe)
United Nations Development Program Human
    Development Report 2000
U.S. News and World Report
U.S. State Department Country Reports on
    Human Rights, 2000
Voice of America Online
Voice of Bahrain
Vreme [Yugoslavia]
Vuelta [Mexico]
The Wall Street Journal
The Washington Post
The Washington Times
The Week in Germany
West Africa
World Population Data Sheet 2000
    (Population Reference Bureau)
Xinhua News Agency
Yemen Times

Organizations

AFL-CIO
Africa Policy Information Center
Africa Rights [United Kingdom]
American Anti-Slavery Group
American Institute for Free Labor Development
American Kurdish Information Network
Amnesty International
Andean Commission of Jurists
Anti-Slavery International
Article 19 [United Kingdom]
Association Pour La Fondation Mohsen Hachtroudi
Azerbaijan National Democracy Foundation
Bahrain Freedom Movement
Baltic Media Centre
Bangladesh National Women Lawyers Association
British Helsinki Human Rights Group
B'tzelem [Israel]
Caribbean Institute for the Promotion of Human Rights
Caribbean Rights
The Carter Center
Center for Free Speech [Nigeria]
Center for Strategic and International Studies
Chadian Association for the Protection of Human Rights
Child Workers in Nepal
Chilean Human Rights Commission
Civic Alliance [Mexico]
Civil Society Development Foundation
Committee of Churches for Emergency Help [Paraguay]
Committee to Protect Journalists
Constitutional Rights Project [Nigeria]
Council for Democracy [Mexico]

Council of Europe
Croatian Democracy Project
Cuban Committee for Human Rights
Democratic Initiatives [Ukraine]
East-West Institute
Elections Canada
Emerging Europe Research Group
Equal Access Committee [Ukraine]
Estonian Institute for Human Rights
Ethnic Federation of Romani [Romania]
European Bank for Reconstruction and Development
European Commission
European Institute for the Media
Fray Bartocome de Las Casas Center for
    Human Rights [Mexico]
Free Africa Foundation
Free and Democratic Bulgaria Foundation
Free Trade Union Institute
Group for Mutual Support [Guatemala]
Guyana Human Rights Group
Haitian Center for Human Rights
Helsinki Committee for Human Rights in Serbia
Honduran Committee for the Defense of Human Rights
Hong Kong Human Rights Monitor
Human Rights Commission [El Salvador]
Human Rights Commission of Pakistan
Human Rights Organization of Bhutan
Human Rights Organization of Nepal
Human Rights Watch
Immigration and Refugee Board of Canada
Indian Law Resource Center
Inform [Sri Lanka]
Institute for Legal Research and Resources [Nepal]
Institute for the Study of Conflict, Ideology and Policy
Institute for War and Peace Reporting [United Kingdom]
Inter-American Commission on Human Rights
Inter-American Dialogue
Inter-American Press Association
International Campaign for Tibet
International Commission of Jurists
International Confederation of Free Trade Unions
International Federation of Journalists
International Foundation for Electoral Systems
International Freedom of Expression Exchange
International Helsinki Federation for Human Rights
International Human Rights Law Group
International League for Human Rights
International Press Institute
International Republican Institute
International Research and Exchange Board
Iraqi National Congress
Jaan Tonisson Institute [Estonia]
Jamaica Council for Human Rights
Jamestown Foundation
Kuwait Online
Latin American Association for Human Rights
Latin American Ombudsmen Institute
Latvian Center for Human Rights and Ethnic Studies
Latvian Human Rights Institute
Lawyers Committee for Human Rights
Lawyers for Human Rights and Legal Aid [Pakistan]
Lithuanian Free Market Institute
Media Institute of South Africa
Mexican Human Rights Academy
National Coalition for Haitian Refugees
National Coordinating Office for Human Rights [Peru]
National Democratic Institute for International Affairs
National Endowment for Democracy
Network for the Defense of Independent Media in Africa

North-South Center [Florida]
Open Society Institute
Operation Lifeline Sudan
Organization for Security and Cooperation in Europe
Organization of American States
Pacific Island Development Program [Hawaii]
Panamanian Committee for Human Rights
Peoples Forum for Human Rights, Bhutan
Permanent Commission on Human Rights [Nicaragua]
Physicians for Human Rights
Reporters Sans Frontieres
Royal Institute of International Affairs
Runejel Junam Council of Ethnic Communities [Guatemala]
Stratfor
Support for Improvement in Governance and Management in Central and Eastern European Countries (SIGMA)
Tibet Information Network
Tibetan Center for Human Rights and Democracy

Transparency International
Tutela Legal [El Salvador]
Ukrainian Center for Independent Political Research
UNICEF
Union of Councils for Soviet Jews
U.N. Integrated Regional Information Networks
U.S. Committee for Refugees
Venezuelan Human Rights Education Action Program
Vicaria de la Solidaridad [Chile]
Vietnam Committee on Human Rights
Voice of Bahrain
Washington Office on Africa
Washington Office on Latin America
West Africa Journalists Association
Women Acting Together for Change [Nepal]
Women's Commission for Refugee Women and Children
World Algerian Action Coalition
The World Bank
World Press Freedom Committee
Zambia Independent Monitoring Association